Financial Accounting

SIXTH EDITION

J. DAVID SPICELAND
University of Memphis

WAYNE THOMAS
University of Oklahoma

DON HERRMANN
Oklahoma State University

FINANCIAL ACCOUNTING, SIXTH EDITION

Published by McGraw Hill LLC, 1325 Avenue of the Americas, New York, NY 10121. Copyright © 2022 by McGraw Hill LLC. All rights reserved. Printed in the United States of America. Previous editions © 2019, 2016, 2014. No part of this publication may be reproduced or distributed in any form or by any means, or stored in a database or retrieval system, without the prior written consent of McGraw Hill LLC, including, but not limited to, in any network or other electronic storage or transmission, or broadcast for distance learning.

Some ancillaries, including electronic and print components, may not be available to customers outside the United States.

This book is printed on acid-free paper.

1 2 3 4 5 6 7 8 9 LWI 26 25 24 23 22 21

ISBN 978-1-260-78652-1 (bound edition)
MHID 1-260-78652-8 (bound edition)
ISBN 978-1-264-14031-2 (loose-leaf edition)
MHID 1-264-14031-2 (loose-leaf edition)

Director: *Rebecca Olson*
Senior Portfolio Manager: *Noelle Bathurst*
Product Developers: *Christina Sanders and Danielle McLimore*
Executive Marketing Manager: *Lauren Schur*
Content Project Managers: *Pat Frederickson and Angela Norris*
Buyer: *Laura Fuller*
Designer: *Matt Diamond and Laurie Entringer*
Content Licensing Specialist: *Traci Vaske*
Cover Image: *Daniel Dempster Photography/Alamy Stock Photo*
Compositor: *SPi Global*

All credits appearing on page or at the end of the book are considered to be an extension of the copyright page.

Library of Congress Cataloging-in-Publication Data

Names: Spiceland, J. David, 1949- author. | Thomas, Wayne, 1969- author. |
   Herrmann, Don, author.
Title: Financial accounting / J. David Spiceland, University of Memphis,
   Wayne Thomas, University of Oklahoma, Don Herrmann, Oklahoma State
   University.
Description: Sixth edition. | New York, NY : McGraw Hill LLC, [2022] |
   Includes index. | Audience: Ages 18+
Identifiers: LCCN 2021013236 (print) | LCCN 2021013237 (ebook) | ISBN
   9781260786521 (paperback) | ISBN 9781264140305 (ebook other)
Subjects: LCSH: Accounting.
Classification: LCC HF5636 .S77 2022 (print) | LCC HF5636 (ebook) | DDC
   657—dc23
LC record available at https://lccn.loc.gov/2021013236
LC ebook record available at https://lccn.loc.gov/2021013237sw

The Internet addresses listed in the text were accurate at the time of publication. The inclusion of a website does not indicate an endorsement by the authors or McGraw Hill LLC, and McGraw Hill LLC does not guarantee the accuracy of the information presented at these sites.

mheducation.com/highered

Dedicated to

David's wife Charlene, daughters Denise and Jessica, and three sons Mike, Michael, and David

Wayne's wife Julee, daughter Olivia and her husband Corbin, son Jake and his wife Bekah, and other sons Eli and Luke.

Don's wife Mary, daughter Rachel, and three sons David, Nathan, and Micah

In addition, David and Wayne would like to dedicate the sixth edition of Financial Accounting *to Don Herrmann, who lost his battle with brain cancer on May 8, 2018. Don was a true friend, and his lasting impact on us will never be forgotten.*

About the Authors

DAVID SPICELAND

Courtesy of David Spiceland

David Spiceland is Accounting Professor Emeritus at the University of Memphis. He received his BS degree in finance from the University of Tennessee, his MBA from Southern Illinois University, and his PhD in accounting from the University of Arkansas.

Professor Spiceland's primary research interests are in earnings management and educational research. He has published articles in a variety of journals, including *The Accounting Review, Accounting and Business Research, Journal of Financial Research, Advances in Quantitative Analysis of Finance and Accounting,* and most accounting education journals: *Issues in Accounting Education, Journal of Accounting Education, Advances in Accounting Education, The Accounting Educators' Journal, Accounting Education, The Journal of Asynchronous Learning Networks,* and *Journal of Business Education.* David has received university and college awards and recognition for his teaching, research, and technological innovations in the classroom. David is a co-author on McGraw Hill's best-selling *Intermediate Accounting* text, with Mark Nelson, and Wayne Thomas.

David enjoys playing basketball, is a former all-state linebacker, and an avid fisherman. Cooking is a passion for David, who served as sous chef for Paula Deen at a Mid-South Fair cooking demonstration.

WAYNE THOMAS

Shevaun Williams & Associates

Wayne Thomas is the Senior Associate Dean for Faculty and Research Innovation, and the David C. Steed Chair of Accounting at the University of Oklahoma, where he teaches introductory financial accounting, intermediate accounting, and MBAs. He received his bachelor's degree in accounting from Southwestern Oklahoma State University, and his master's and PhD in accounting from Oklahoma State University.

Wayne has won teaching awards at the university, college, and departmental levels, and has received the Outstanding Educator Award from the Oklahoma Society of CPAs. In addition to *Financial Accounting,* he also co-authors McGraw Hill's best-selling *Intermediate Accounting,* with David Spiceland, Mark Nelson, and Jennifer Winchel. He also co-authors McGraw Hill's *Financial Accounting for Managers* with Michael Drake, Jake Thornock, and David Spiceland.

His primary research interests include accounting information in capital markets, techniques used by managers to manipulate earnings, the importance of financial disclosures, and financial statement analysis. He previously served as an editor of *The Accounting Review* and has published articles in a variety of journals, including *The Accounting Review, Journal of Accounting and Economics, Journal of Accounting Research, Review of Accounting Studies,* and *Contemporary Accounting Research.* He has won several research awards, including the American Accounting Association's Competitive Manuscript Award and the University of Oklahoma's highest research award, being named a George Lynn Cross Research Professor.

Wayne is married to Julee and they have four kids, Olivia, Jake, Eli, and Luke. He enjoys sports (basketball, tennis, golf, biking and ping pong), crossword puzzles, the outdoors, and spending time with his family.

DON HERRMANN

Courtesy of Don Herrmann

Don Herrmann passed away on May 8, 2018, after a 14-month battle with brain cancer. He was the Deloitte Professor of Accounting at Oklahoma State University, where he had been on the faculty since 2005. Don won several teaching awards and enjoyed teaching financial accounting, intermediate accounting, and doctoral students. He received his bachelor's degree in business from John Brown University, his master's degree in accounting from Kansas State University, and his PhD in accounting from Oklahoma State University. He was active in the AAA and served as president of the International Accounting Section.

Don was best known for his warm and welcoming personality. He enjoyed serving in his local community and church, as well as hosting families and students in his home. His outgoing nature wasn't the type that filled a room with his presence, but it was the type that filled a one-on-one conversation with purpose.

Above all else, family was first to Don. Some of his favorite family activities included camping, going to amusement parks, and coaching little league sports. He is survived by his wonderful wife Mary and four amazing children Rachel, David, Nathan, and Micah. As he battled through the different stages of cancer, he often reflected on his family. He was so proud of them and talked about them with a humble thankfulness.

Those of us who knew Don were fortunate to share our lives with him. He lived with a sense of purpose and a solid foundation. That foundation continues through his family and the people he's touched. He will be missed by many.

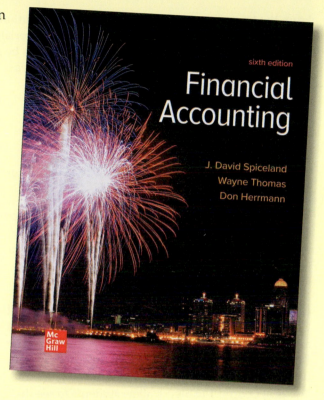

Don't you love those moments in your course when students are fully engaged? When the "Aha!" revelations are bursting like fireworks? David Spiceland, Wayne Thomas, and Don Herrmann have developed a unique set of materials based directly on their collective years in the classroom. They've brought together best practices by (1) building a Framework for Financial Accounting; (2) reinforcing the Framework in each chapter's text and end-of-chapter assignments; and (3) enriching that Framework using real-world companies, Excel assignments, General Ledger problems, data analytics tools, and a variety of auto-graded ethics, earnings management, and real-world cases. The material is communicated in a student-friendly conversational writing style. After the proven success of the first five editions of *Financial Accounting,* we are confident that the sixth edition will not only motivate, engage, and challenge students—it will illuminate the financial accounting course like never before.

Spiceland's Accounting Series

The Spiceland Accounting series includes:

- *Financial Accounting 6e*
- *Intermediate Accounting 11e*
- *Financial Accounting for Managers, 1e*

Financial Accounting and Intermediate Accounting have proven records of market-leading success by engaging a broad range of students, offering a wide array of resources necessary for building accounting concepts, and giving instructors the variety of tools they need to structure their unique courses.

The authors are proud to introduce a new book in the series, Financial Accounting for Managers, for which they are joined by authors Michael Drake and Jake Thornock. Financial Accounting for Managers brings the proven Spiceland approach to today's students, featuring modern companies, robust analysis sections, auto-graded cases, and a focus on helping students think critically about how accounting information fuels business decisions.

The Spiceland Accounting Series is fully integrated with McGraw Hill's Connect, an educational platform that seamlessly joins Spiceland's superior content with enhanced digital tools to deliver precisely what a student needs, when and how they need it.

CREATING FUTURE BUSINESS LEADERS

From the first edition of *Financial Accounting,* the authors have been talking with standard setters, auditors, and business leaders across the country to ensure their materials are consistent with what's being practiced in the business world and presented in such a way to help students be ready for business success. In keeping with this feedback, the authors have focused their approach on five key areas:

- Developing an organized learning framework
- Fostering decision-making and analysis skills
- Helping students become better problem solvers
- Developing real-world perspectives & career-ready students
- Using technology to enhance learning

The result? Better-prepared students who have greater potential to take on leadership roles when they graduate and enter the business world.

Developing an Organized Learning Framework

The first step in student engagement is helping them see the "big picture." The authors introduce an overall framework for financial accounting in Chapter 1 and then apply this framework to specific topics throughout the text and in a summary **Chapter Framework** illustration in each chapter. Within each chapter, students will see this framework on display with mini-financial statements presented in the margin for each journal entry.

Fostering Decision-Making and Analysis Skills

Companies today cite decision-making and analysis skills as top desired skills among recent graduates. Students are given opportunities to see real business decision-making practices in each chapter's—**Decision Maker's Perspectives** and **Decision Points**. Instructors can help students build their Excel, Tableau, and data visualization skills using a wide variety of **Data Analytics** and **Excel** assignments that are auto-gradable in Connect. Finally, **General Ledger Problems** allow students to see the big picture of how information flows through the accounting cycle—letting them solve problems as businesspeople would, by analyzing the effect of transactions on the financial statements.

Helping Students Become Better Problem Solvers

Students check their understanding along the way by using **Key Points** within each Learning Objective and in-chapter **Let's Review** problems of the chapter's primary topics. These items prepare students to successfully complete the assigned end-of-chapter materials. Let's Review problems are complemented by videos. The **Common Mistakes** feature is a student favorite, helping them avoid mistakes that regularly trip up both learners and professionals.

Developing Real-World Perspectives & Career-Ready Students

The authors know that students are most engaged when they see real-world examples that are applicable to their lives and future careers. As the chapter's topics are being presented, references to real companies in the chapter opening **Feature Story** and other related companies help keep topics relevant. Instructors can assign **Real-World Perspective** cases including Great Adventures Continuing Problem, Financial Analysis, Comparative Analysis, EDGAR Research, Ethics, and Earnings Management. Each of these cases is auto-gradable in Connect, allowing additional decision-making practice for students and ease of grading for instructors.

Using Technology to Enhance Learning

Today's students live online and seek out videos to aid their learning. Spiceland *Financial Accounting* reinforces students' conceptual understanding with videos such as **Let's Review**, **Interactive Illustrations**, **Concept Overview**, **Chapter Framework** and **Applying Excel**. End-of-chapter exercises are supplemented with **Hints/Guided Example videos**, and additional online resources like adaptive-learning **SmartBook**.

DEVELOPING AN ORGANIZED LEARNING FRAMEWORK

An Organized Learning Framework: The Big Picture

With a wide variety of students enrolled in financial accounting courses, getting them interested in the content and making it enjoyable to learn can be challenging. Spiceland's *Financial Accounting* achieves this by helping students see the "big picture." The authors introduce a simple overall framework for financial accounting—measure, communicate, make decisions—and then revisit and apply this framework throughout the text. This **organized learning framework** naturally fosters engagement by continually reminding students that accounting helps millions of people make informed business decisions.

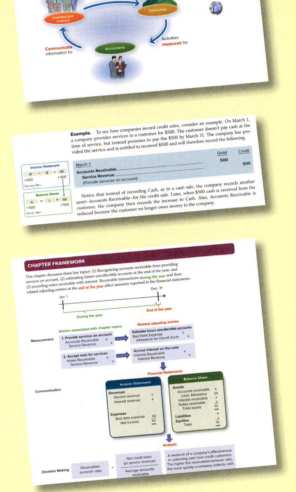

An Organized Learning Framework: In Each Chapter

The framework of financial accounting is further reinforced within each chapter:

- New to the sixth edition, the authors include mini-financial statements with each journal entry. These figures continually remind students that every business activity that is *measured* is also *communicated* in the financial statements.
- New Chapter Framework illustrations have been added to the end of each chapter, providing students a flowchart visual through which they can see how the chapter's primary topics fit into the *measurement/ communication/decision-making* framework of financial accounting. Each Chapter Framework includes five multiple-choice questions, with ten total questions assignable in Connect.
- A wide range of end-of-chapter assignments reinforce the *measurement* and *communication* functions of financial accounting.

> "Overall the chapters are very well organized so that **students would be able to build their foundation effectively**."
>
> —Jin Dong Park, *Towson University*

An Organized Learning Framework: Tying It All Together

To complete the *measurement/communication/decision-making* framework, Analysis sections are offered at the end of topical chapters (4-11). Using two real-world companies in each chapter, these sections are meant to highlight how the chapter's previous discussion of measurement and communication can be analyzed and used by decision-makers to understand a company's financial condition and performance. The Financial Statement Analysis chapter allows students to take a deep dive into these concepts by analyzing the financial statements of Nike and VF corporation.

Finally, the book's chapter layout provides an overall framework to the topics of the course. After an overview of the framework of financial accounting in Chapter 1, the **accounting cycle chapters** clearly distinguish activities During the Period (Chapter 2) from End of the Period (Chapter 3). Chapters 4 -10 cover specific topics in **balance sheet order**, followed by Chapter 11 cash flows and Chapter 12 financial statement analysis.

FOSTERING DECISION-MAKING & ANALYSIS SKILLS

In today's environment, business graduates are being asked more than ever to be equipped in analyzing data and making decisions. To address this need, each chapter includes **Decision Maker's Perspective** sections, which offer insights into how the information discussed in the chapters affects decisions made by investors, creditors, managers, and others. Each chapter also contains **Decision Points** highlighting specific decisions in the chapter that can be made using financial accounting information.

New! Data Analytics assignments are provided with each chapter. Instructors can visit Connect to find a variety of auto-graded Data Analytics questions that introduce students to seeing data presented in the types of visual formats they'll see in today's business environments. These exercises have been thoughtfully developed and scaffolded to build data analytics exposure and skills. Assignable, auto-gradable materials include:

- Data Visualizations - Familiarize students with data visualizations. Students interpret data in a static visual to answer accounting questions.
- Tableau Dashboard Activities - Easily introduce students to Tableau. Students learn to gather the information they need from a live embedded Tableau dashboard - no prior knowledge of Tableau needed.
- Applying Tableau cases - Build student's data analytics skills. Students download an Excel file and build a Tableau dashboard with video tutorial guidance. Once they've completed their dashboard, they'll use it to answer auto-graded questions in Connect.

Decision Maker's Perspective

Investors Understand One-Time Gains

Investors typically take a close look at the components of a company's profits. For example, Ford Motor Company announced that it had earned a net income for the fourth quarter (the final three months of the year) of $13.6 billion. Analysts had expected Ford to earn only $1.7 to $2.0 billion for that period. The day that Ford announced this earnings news, its stock price *fell* about 4.5%.

Why would Ford's stock price fall on a day when the company reported these seemingly high profits? A closer inspection of Ford's income statement shows that it included a one-time gain of $12.4 billion for the fourth quarter. After subtracting this one-time gain, Ford actually earned only about $1.2 billion from normal operations, easily missing analysts' expectations. This disappointing earnings performance is the reason the company's stock price fell.

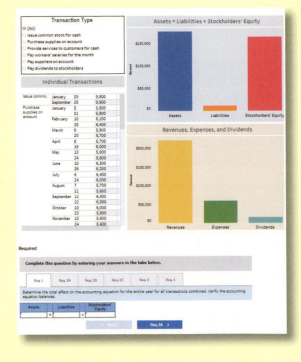

HELPING STUDENTS BECOME BETTER PROBLEM SOLVERS

Building Better Problem Solvers In honing analytical skills and becoming good problem solvers, it's crucial that students have the right tools and guidance to help them along the way—especially when learning the accounting cycle. The **accounting cycle chapters** clearly distinguish activities During the Period (Chapter 2) from End of the Period (Chapter 3). Chapters 4–10 cover specific topics in **balance sheet order.** Throughout the chapters, several features keep students on the right track as they learn the accounting process.

General Ledger Problems Expanded general ledger problems provide a much-improved student experience when working with accounting cycle questions with improved navigation and less scrolling. Students can audit their mistakes by easily linking back to their original entries and are able to see how the numbers flow through the various financial statements. Many general ledger problems include an analysis tab that allows students to demonstrate their critical thinking skills and a deeper understanding of accounting concepts.

The Great Adventures Continuing Problem progresses from chapter to chapter, encompassing the accounting issues of each new chapter as the story unfolds. These problems allow students to see how each chapter's topics can be integrated into the operations of a single company. Great Adventures problems are also available in McGraw Hill Connect's General Ledger format.

Let's Review sections within each chapter test students' comprehension of key concepts. These short review exercises, with solutions, are intended to reinforce understanding of specific chapter material and allow students to apply concepts and procedures learned in the chapter prior to attempting their homework assignment. Each Let's Review exercise also contains **Suggested Homework,** which enables instructors to easily assign corresponding homework. For the sixth edition, 22 **Let's Review Videos** show students how to solve the exercise and model that approach for related homework.

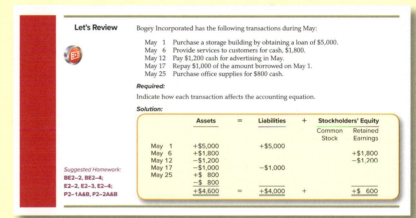

Common Mistakes made by students and professionals are highlighted throughout each of the chapters. With greater awareness of the potential pitfalls, students can avoid making the same mistakes and gain a deeper understanding of the chapter material.

COMMON MISTAKE

When recording the interest payable on a borrowed amount, students sometimes mistakenly credit the liability associated with the principal amount (Notes Payable). We record interest payable in a *separate account* (Interest Payable) to keep the balance owed for principal separate from the balance owed for interest.

The **Flip Side** feature demonstrates how various transactions are viewed by each side. Including the "flip side" of a transaction—in context—enhances students' understanding of both the initial and the related transaction. Selected homework materials also include the Flip Side transactions, to reinforce student understanding.

Interest Receivable. We can see an example of accrued revenues if we review the flip side of transaction (2), which we discussed in the previous section as interest expense. The bank lends Eagle Soccer Academy $100,000 and charges Eagle annual interest of 12% (or 1% per month) on the borrowed amount. Interest for the month of December is $1,000 (= $100,000 × 12% × 1/12). *At the end of December,* the bank needs an adjusting entry to record an asset for the amount expected to be received (Interest Receivable) from Eagle and to recognize revenue (Interest Revenue).

Flip Side

The bank's end-of-period adjusting entry is presented below.

Key Points provide quick synopses of the critical pieces of information presented throughout each chapter.

KEY POINT

Adjusting entries are a necessary part of accrual-basis accounting. They are used to record changes in assets and liabilities (and their related revenues and expenses) that have occurred during the period but have not yet been recorded by the end of the period.

DEVELOPING REAL-WORLD PERSPECTIVES & CAREER-READY STUDENTS

Students retain more information when they see how concepts are applied in the real world. Each chapter begins with a Feature Story that involves real companies and offers business insights related to the material in the chapter. As the chapter's topics are being presented, references to the companies in the Feature Story and other related companies help keep topics relevant. The authors understand that students are best engaged when the discussion involves companies that students find interesting and whose products are services are familiar, such as Apple, American Eagle Outfitters, Best Buy, Six Flags, Disney, and Zoom. In Chapter 12, full financial statement analysis is provided for Nike versus VF Corporation. The authors carry these real-world companies into the end-of-chapter material, asking students to analyze real-world situations.

The **Real-World Perspectives** section of each chapter offers cases and activities that ask students to apply the knowledge and skills they've learned to real, realistic, or provocative situations. Students are placed in the role of decision maker, presented with a set of information, and asked to draw conclusions that test their understanding of the issues discussed in the chapters. Each chapter offers an engaging mix of activities and opportunities to perform real-world financial accounting analysis, conduct EDGAR research, understand earnings management, address ethical dilemmas, and practice written communication. Ethics, Earnings Management, EDGAR and Financial Analysis cases are auto-gradable in Connect.

Financial Analysis: American Eagle Outfitters, Inc. & The Buckle, Inc. ask students to gather information from the annual report of American Eagle located in Appendix A and Buckle in Appendix B. **Comparative Analysis**—In addition to separately analyzing the financial information of American Eagle and Buckle, students are asked to compare financial information between the two companies. These questions are auto-gradable in Connect!

Excel activities and exercises help foster career readiness by offering students hands-on training in multiple ways:

- **New! Integrated Excel** assignments pair the power of Microsoft Excel with the power of Connect. A seamless integration of Excel within Connect, Integrated Excel questions allow students to work in live, auto-graded Excel spreadsheets -- no additional logins, no need to upload or download files. Instructors can choose to grade by formula or solution value, and students receive instant cell-level feedback via integrated Check My Work functionality.
- **Applying Excel** features in each chapter help build students' Excel skills, showing them how Excel can be used to make efficient calculations and analysis. Applying Excel video solutions housed in Connect complement the feature, allowing students to view the power of Excel to analyze business scenarios.

Connect and Spiceland's *Financial Accounting* are tightly integrated to continue honing students' conceptual understanding, problem-solving, decision-making & analysis skills.

All end-of-chapter items in the textbook that can be built into Connect have been included with feedback and explanations and many with **Hints/Guided Example Videos** to help students work through their homework in an effective manner.

ASSESSMENT & PRACTICE: END-OF-CHAPTER AND TEST BANK

Algorithmic Content & End-of-Chapter assignments

New algorithmic problems have been added, allowing students more practice and you more opportunities for students to demonstrate their understanding.

Extensive end-of-chapter assignments are available in the text and Connect:
- Self-Study Questions
- Data Analytics & Excel
- Review Questions
- Brief Exercises
- Exercises (set Set B in the test bank)
- Problems Set A & B (with Set C in the test bank)
- Real-World Perspectives
  - Great Adventures continuing case
  - Financial analysis cases
  - Ethics case
  - EDGAR Research case
  - Written Communication case
  - Earnings Management case

Concept Overview Videos

Concept Overview Videos provide engaging narratives of all chapter learning objectives in an assignable, interactive online format. These videos follow the structure of the text and match specific learning objectives within each chapter of *Financial Accounting.* Concept Overview Videos provide additional explanation and enhancement of material from the text chapter, allowing students to learn, study, and practice at their own pace. Assignable assessment questions paired with the videos help students test their knowledge, ensuring that they are retaining concepts.

Hints/Guided Example Videos

Hint/Guided Example videos are narrated, animated, and step-by-step walkthroughs of algorithmic versions of assigned exercises in Connect. Presented to the student as hints, Guided Examples provide just-in-time remediation—and help—students get immediate feedback, focused on the areas where they need the most guidance.

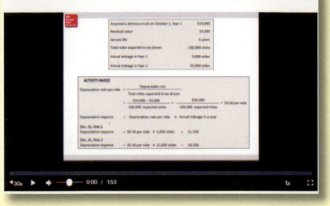

Interactive Illustration Videos

Interactive Illustrations provide video-based explanations of key illustrations in the chapter. These videos transform a static illustration in the text into a dynamic, step-by-step walk through of the illustration, deepening students' understanding of the concepts or the calculations shown.

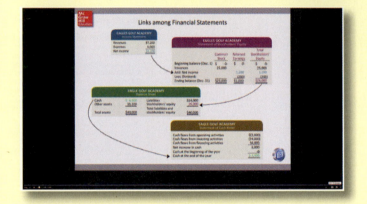

Let's Review Videos

Let's Review videos relate to the Let's Review sections in the text, showing students how to solve certain exercises. In walking students through a particular scenario or question, these videos model how students can approach problem solving.

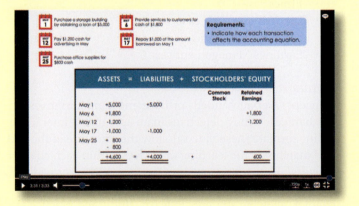

Test Builder in Connect

Available within Connect, Test Builder is a cloud-based tool that enables instructors to format tests that can be printed or administered within a LMS. Test Builder offers a modern, streamlined interface for easy content configuration that matches course needs, without requiring a download.

Test Builder allows you to:
- access all test bank content from a particular title.
- easily pinpoint the most relevant content through robust filtering options.
- manipulate the order of questions or scramble questions and/or answers.
- pin questions to a specific location within a test.
- determine your preferred treatment of algorithmic questions.
- choose the layout and spacing.
- add instructions and configure default settings.

Test Builder provides a secure interface for better protection of content and allows for just-in-time updates to flow directly into assessments.

Remote Proctoring & Browser-Locking Capabilities

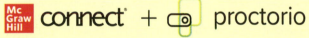 New remote proctoring and browser-locking capabilities, hosted by Proctorio within Connect, provide control of the assessment environment by enabling security options and verifying the identity of the student.

Seamlessly integrated within Connect, these services allow instructors to control students' assessment experience by restricting browser activity, recording students' activity, and verifying students are doing their own work.

Instant and detailed reporting gives instructors an at-a-glance view of potential academic integrity concerns, thereby avoiding personal bias and supporting evidence-based claims.

NEW IN THE SIXTH EDITION

We've incorporated an enormous amount of feedback from over 700 reviewers, focus group, and symposium participants over the last five editions. The list of changes and improvements on the next few pages is testament to the many hours that reviewers spent thinking about and analyzing our earlier editions, helping us to make *Financial Accounting* the **best book of its kind.**

Overall Updates in the Sixth Edition:

- **Text was reduced** in many places to simplify and clarify discussion.
- **Feature stories, real-world examples, and ratio analyses** in each chapter were updated to the most recent year.
- **Financial statement effects** were highlighted in the margin of all journal entries.
- **Chapter Framework** illustrations at the end of each chapter were modified to include Analysis in most chapters.
- **Five self-study multiple-choice questions** were added to the Chapter Framework illustration in each chapter. **Five additional questions** are available online.
- **Great Adventures Continuing Case** adds content from each successive chapter to build a comprehensive set of financial statements.
- **Financial Analysis Cases** using American Eagle Outfitter (Appendix A) and Buckle (Appendix B) were updated for each chapter.
- **An auto-gradable EDGAR Research Case** was added to each chapter.
- **Ethics Cases** and **Earnings Management Cases** are now algorithmic and auto-gradable.
- **Written Communication Cases** were added to Connect to allow instructors the option of manual grading.
- **Integrated Excel, Applying Excel, Data Visualizations, Tableau Dashboard Activities, and Applying Tableau** are available online in Connect.
- **Revised illustrations** throughout the text to continue to offer clear and visual learning tools for students.
- **Usage data** from SmartBook and Connect were used in developing changes to the 6th edition.

CHAPTER 1:

- Revised the explanation of stockholders' equity in LO1–2 to focus on how those claims arise.
- Changed discussion of the statement of stockholders' equity in LO1–3 and the calculation of retained earnings.
- Revised Illustrations 1–6, 1–7, and 1–8 to make clearer the link between financial statements.
- The Great Adventure Continuing Case was modified to be auto-graded in Connect.

CHAPTER 2:

- Revised discussion of Illustration 2–6 to make clear the effects of debits and credits in the expanded accounting equation.
- Revised discussion to make clear the meaning of the balance of retained earnings in an unadjusted trial balance.

CHAPTER 3:

- Revised and reduced discussion in LO3–1 and LO3–2 to explain timing differences caused by accrual-basis accounting.
- Modified Illustrations 3–2 and 3–3 to differentiate revenue and expense recognition under accrual-basis versus cash-basis accounting.
- Modified adjusting entry illustrations to include related entries made during the year.
- Included a T-account in the margin beside each of the adjusting entries to

emphasize the effect on asset and liability balances.
- Expanded E3–7 to include transactions during the year.
- Revised and clarified the timing of accrual accounting in E3–8, E3–10, E3–12, E3–13, P3–1A&B, P3–3A&B, and P3–4A&B.
- Added BE3–21, BE3–22, BE3–23, BE3–24, and BE3–25 to include the financial statement effects of adjusting entries.
- Revised BE3–14, BE–18, E3–13, P3–3A, and P3–5B to exclude depreciation (several other assignments include depreciation).

CHAPTER 4:

- Changed the feature story to focus on Live Nation Entertainment.
- Expanded discussion of types of payments received from customer to more modern forms.
- Revised discussion of bank reconciliation to include more modern transactions and revised several related end-of-chapter assignments in a similar way.
- Expanded discussion of the reasons to explain cash holdings in the Analysis section.

CHAPTER 5:

- Revised the Feature Story to provide additional discussion of net revenues reported.
- Revised Part A in several places to emphasize revenue being reported for

the amount the company is entitled to receive from customers.
- Added BE5–2 for sales discounts and BE5–18 for notes receivable and interest.
- Added BE5–22, BE5–23, BE5–24, BE5–25, and BE5–26 to determine financial statement effects of transactions.

CHAPTER 6:

- Modified Illustrations 6–6 and 6–7 to make clear the calculation of ending inventory and cost of goods sold.
- Modified Illustration 6–9 to improve clarity.
- Added discussion in Part B to clarify how inventory transactions are recorded and reported in practice under FIFO and LIFO.
- Added BE6-15 to record adjusting entry for lower of cost or net realizable value.
- Added BE6–24, BE6–25, BE6–26, BE6–27, and BE6–28 to determine financial statement effects of transactions.

CHAPTER 7:

- Modified discussion of capitalizing versus expensing an expenditure in LO7–1.
- Modified discussion of purchased versus internally developed intangible assets in LO7–2.
- Created new Illustration 7–6 to demonstrate the difference in treatment between purchased and internally-developed patent.
- Created new Illustration 7–13 to demonstrate partial-year depreciation.

- Changed companies used in the Analysis section to Disney and Netflix.
- Added BE7–11 and BE7–17 to record depreciation.
- Added BE7–23, BE7–24, BE7–25, BE7–26, and BE7–27 to determine financial statement effects of transactions.
- Changed E7–4 to include various expenditures related to intangibles.

CHAPTER 8:
- Revised discussion of notes payable and associated interest (Learning Objective 8–2).
- Added discussion and journal entry for reclassifying current portion of long-term debt.
- Added BE8–9 to reclassify current portion of long-term debt.
- Added BE8–19, BE8–20, BE8–21, and BE8–22 to determine financial statement effects of transactions.
- Added E8–12 for recording long-term notes payable and reclassifying current portion.

CHAPTER 9:
- Revised Part A to include a simple overview of installment notes, leases, and bonds issued at face amount.
- Revised discussion of reclassification of current portion of long-term installment notes.

- Provided additional clarification of the meaning of discounts and premiums on bonds.
- Added carrying value to Glossary.
- Added BE9–4, BE9–5, E9–4, and E9–5 on installment notes.
- Added P3–9A and P3–9B on leases.
- Added E9–9 for comparison of installment note and lease.
- Added BE9–24, BE9–25, and BE9–26 to determine financial statement effects of transactions.
- Revised E9–1 to include a comparison of interest payments and dividend payments.

CHAPTER 10:
- Changed the feature story to Zoom.
- Modified Illustrations 10–3, 10–4, and 10–5.
- Added Key Point for retained earnings.
- Added discussion of Apple's recent 4-for-1 stock split.
- Changed Illustration 10–18 to include analysis of Citigroup's equity section of the balance sheet.
- Modified text to include a bullet list of items reported in the statement of stockholders' equity in Illustration 10–20.
- Changed the Analysis section to include Zoom versus Microsoft.
- Added BE10–10 and BE10–11.

- Added BE10–18, BE10–19, BE10–20, BE10–21, and BE10–22 to determine financial statement effects of transactions.
- Added E10–4, E10–9, and E10–10.
- Revised E10–2.

CHAPTER 11:
- Revised Illustration 11–8 and its related discussion.
- Clarified the discussion of the indirect method in LO 11–3 to tie directly to income statement adjustments and balance sheet adjustments.
- Added new E11–10 and E11–11 for investing and financing cash flows.

CHAPTER 12:
- Changed Feature Story to VF Corporation.
- Changed comparison to Nike versus VF Corporation throughout the chapter.

APPENDIX C:
- Added new Illustration C–11 to demonstrate effect of interest rates on present value and future value relationship.
- Added new EC–3, EC–4, EC–7, EC–8, EC–12, EC–13, EC–15, and EC–16.

APPENDIX D:
- Simplified the discussion of debt investments to include purchase of bonds at face amount as the primary example.
- Added new ED–10 for purchase of debt investment at face amount.

Instructors: Student Success Starts with You

Tools to enhance your unique voice

Want to build your own course? No problem. Prefer to use an OLC-aligned, prebuilt course? Easy. Want to make changes throughout the semester? Sure. And you'll save time with Connect's auto-grading too.

65%
Less Time Grading

Study made personal

Incorporate adaptive study resources like SmartBook® 2.0 into your course and help your students be better prepared in less time. Learn more about the powerful personalized learning experience available in SmartBook 2.0 at **www.mheducation.com/highered/connect/smartbook**

Laptop: McGraw Hill; Woman/dog: George Doyle/Getty Images

Affordable solutions, added value

Make technology work for you with LMS integration for single sign-on access, mobile access to the digital textbook, and reports to quickly show you how each of your students is doing. And with our Inclusive Access program you can provide all these tools at a discount to your students. Ask your McGraw Hill representative for more information.

Padlock: Jobalou/Getty Images

Solutions for your challenges

A product isn't a solution. Real solutions are affordable, reliable, and come with training and ongoing support when you need it and how you want it. Visit **www.supportateverystep.com** for videos and resources both you and your students can use throughout the semester.

Checkmark: Jobalou/Getty Images

Students: Get Learning that Fits You

Effective tools for efficient studying

Connect is designed to help you be more productive with simple, flexible, intuitive tools that maximize your study time and meet your individual learning needs. Get learning that works for you with Connect.

Study anytime, anywhere

Download the free ReadAnywhere app and access your online eBook, SmartBook 2.0, or Adaptive Learning Assignments when it's convenient, even if you're offline. And since the app automatically syncs with your Connect account, all of your work is available every time you open it. Find out more at **www.mheducation.com/readanywhere**

> *"I really liked this app—it made it easy to study when you don't have your text-book in front of you."*
>
> - Jordan Cunningham, Eastern Washington University

Calendar: owattaphotos/Getty Images

Everything you need in one place

Your Connect course has everything you need—whether reading on your digital eBook or completing assignments for class, Connect makes it easy to get your work done.

Learning for everyone

McGraw Hill works directly with Accessibility Services Departments and faculty to meet the learning needs of all students. Please contact your Accessibility Services Office and ask them to email accessibility@mheducation.com, or visit **www.mheducation.com/about/accessibility** for more information.

Top: Jenner Images/Getty Images, Left: Hero Images/Getty Images, Right: Hero Images/Getty Images

The version of *Financial Accounting* you are reading would not be the same book without the valuable suggestions, keen insights, and constructive criticisms of the list of reviewers below. Each professor listed here contributed in substantive ways to the organization of chapters, coverage of topics, and selective use of pedagogy. We are grateful to them for taking the time to read each chapter and offer their insights.

We also acknowledge those reviewers who helped in the genesis of this text with the first second and third edition reviews—we appreciate your efforts to this day!

BOARD OF ADVISER MEMBERS

Margaret Atkinson, *Stark State College*
Gina Bello, *Nassau Community College*
Darlene Booth-Bell, *Coastal Carolina University*
Amy Bourne, *Oregon State University*
Elizabeth Cannata, *Johnson and Wales University*
Elizabeth Capener, *San Jose State University*
Maryann Capone, *Nassau Community College*
Tom Collins, *University of Wisconsin, Platteville*
Patricia Conn Ryan, *Johnson and Wales University*
Edward Conrad, *U. of Akron*
Caroline Falconetti, *Nassau Community College*
Kelly Gamble, *Valdosta State University*
Deb Jones, *Wayne State University*
Gregory Krivacek, *Robert Morris University of Pennsylvania*
Rose Layton, *University of Southern California*
Azita Mohaved, *East Carolina University*
Jin Park, *Towson University*
Jonathan Pemick, *Palm Beach State*
Karen Schuele, *John Carroll University*
Veena Srinivasan, *Arizona State University*
Joel Strong, *St. Cloud State University*
Rob Stussie, *University of Arizona*
Julie Suh, *University of Southern California*
Joseph Trainor, *Saint Johns University*
Lauren Wade, *San Diego Mesa College*
Valerie Williams, *Duquesne University*
Mindy Wolfe, *Arizona State University*
Jan Workman, *East Carolina University*
Michael Yu, *University of West Georgia*

FIFTH EDITION REVIEWERS

Philip Babin, *University of Memphis*
Stacy Bibelhauser, *Western Kentucky University*
Jeffrey Brennan, *Austin Community College*
Lisa Busto, *William Rainey Harper College*
Casey Colson, *Valdosta State University*
Sandra Copa, *North Hennepin Community College*
David DeBoskey, *San Diego State University*
Ming Deng, *Baruch College*
Vicky Dominquez, *College of Southern Nevada*
Steven Hegemann, *University of Nebraska–Lincoln*
Shirley Hunter, *University of North Carolina–Charlotte*
John Ivanauskas, *Anoka Ramsey Community College*
Sudha Krishnan, *California State University Long Beach*
Tal Kroll, *Ozarks Technical Community College*
Dawn Mason, *Western Michigan University*
Nate Nguyen, *Colorado State University*
Jeff Reinking, *University of Central Florida*
Noema Santos, *State College of Florida*
Randy Serrett, *University of Houston Downtown*
Kevin Smith, *Utah Valley University*
Gloria Stuart, *Georgia Southern University*
Stephen Bradley Wilson, *Santa Ana College*
Wanda Wong, *Chabot College*
Thomas Zeller, *Loyola University of Chicago*

FOURTH EDITION REVIEWERS

Stephanie Bacik, *Wake Technical Community College*
Stacy Bibelhauser, *Western Kentucky University*
Elizabeth Cannata, *Johnson & Wales University*
Jacqueline Conrecode, *Florida Gulf Coast University*
Cheryl Corke, *Genesee Community College*
Ming Deng, *The Bernard M. Baruch College, CUNY*
Jerrilyn Eisenhauer, *Tulsa Community College*
Caroline Falconetti, *Nassau Community College*
Lisa Gillespie, *Loyola University Chicago*
Michelle Grant, *Bossier Parish Community College*
Steven Hegemann, *University of Nebraska*
Kenneth Horowitz, *Mercer County Community College*
Maureen McBeth, *College of DuPage*
Staci Mizell, *Lone Star College System*
Jeff Paterson, *Florida State University*
Michael Paz, *Cornell University*
Matthew Reidenbach, *Pace University*
Jeff Reinking, *University of Central Florida*
Gregory Ritter, *University of Memphis*
Brian Schmoldt, *Madison College*
Dean Steria, *SUNY Plattsburgh*
Joel Strong, *St. Cloud State University*
Gloria Stuart, *Georgia Southern University*
Robert Stussie, *University of Arizona*
Mark Ulrich, *St. John's University*
Candace Witherspoon, *Valdosta State University*
Mindy Wolfe, *Arizona State University*

... WHO SHAPED THIS BOOK

We also would like to acknowledge the many talented people who contributed to the creation of this sixth edition and thank them for their valuable contributions. Teressa Farough did a wonderful job accuracy checking our manuscript. Mark McCarthy of East Carolina University contributed a helpful accuracy check of the page proofs; we thank him for his speedy and insightful comments. We also appreciate the willingness of The Buckle, Inc., and American Eagle Outfitters, Inc., to allow us to use their companies' annual reports.

Thanks to Rachel Cox of Oklahoma State University for reviewing the Test Bank, and to Jeannie Folk of Northwestern University for revising the test bank and the PowerPoint. Helen Roybark of Radford University for accuracy checking the PowerPoint. Beth Kobylarz did an outstanding job as Lead Subject Matter Expert for the revisions to Connect; Mark Sears and Ashley Newton of the University of Oklahoma and all of the staff at AnsrSource contributed their invaluable expertise as Connect reviewers. Ashley Newton of the University of Oklahoma also did a wonderful job with the Concept Overview Videos and Applying Excel video resources.

We also appreciate the expert attention given to this project by the staff at McGraw Hill Education, especially Tim Vertovec, Vice President BEC Portfolio, Rebecca Olson, Executive Director; Noelle Bathurst, Senior Portfolio Manager; Lauren Schur, Marketing Manager; Christina Sanders, Lead Product Developer; Danielle McLimore, Assessment Product Developer; Kevin Moran, Director of Digital Content; Pat Frederickson, Lead Content Project Manager; Angela Norris, Senior Content Project Manager; Matt Diamond, Senior Designer; Traci Vaske, Senior Content Licensing Specialist; and Laura Fuller, Buyer.

SUPPLEMENTS WITH THE SAME VOICE

Last but not least, we thank the authors of *Financial Accounting,* who write all of the major **supplements,** including the Solutions Manual, Instructor's Manual, all end-of-chapter material, additional online Exercises and Problems. The test bank includes over 3,000 questions, including more than 1,900 multiple-choice questions and more than 1,125 other types of questions and problems. The authors actively engage in the development of ALL technology-related supplements, such as SmartBook, Interactive Illustrations, Let's Review videos, Chapter Framework videos, Applying Excel videos, Auto-Graded Integrated Excel, Auto-Graded Excel Simulations, and PowerPoints.

Contents in Brief

Contents

11 CHAPTER
Statement of Cash Flows 540

12 CHAPTER
Financial Statement Analysis 600

Fireworks Images Credits: Holly Hildreth/McGraw Hill and Daniel Dempster Photography/Alamy Stock Photo.

1

A Framework for Financial Accounting

Learning Objectives

PART A: ACCOUNTING AS A MEASUREMENT/COMMUNICATION PROCESS

- ■ **LO1–1** Describe the two primary functions of financial accounting.
- ■ **LO1–2** Understand the business activities that financial accounting measures.
- ■ **LO1–3** Determine how financial accounting information is communicated through financial statements.
- ■ **LO1–4** Describe the role that financial accounting plays in the decision-making process.

PART B: FINANCIAL ACCOUNTING INFORMATION

- ■ **LO1–5** Explain the term generally accepted accounting principles (GAAP) and describe the role of GAAP in financial accounting.

PART C: CAREERS IN ACCOUNTING

- ■ **LO1–6** Identify career opportunities in accounting.

APPENDIX: CONCEPTUAL FRAMEWORK

- ■ **LO1–7** Explain the nature of the conceptual framework used to develop generally accepted accounting principles.

SELF-STUDY MATERIALS

- ■ Let's Review—Measuring business activities (p. 8).
- ■ Let's Review—Communicating through financial statements (p. 17).
- ■ Chapter Framework with questions and answers available (p. 31).
- ■ Key Points by Learning Objective (p. 32).
- ■ Glossary of Key Terms (p. 33).
- ■ Self-Study Questions with answers available (p. 34).
- ■ Videos including Concept Overview, Applying Excel, Let's Review, and Interactive Illustrations to demonstrate key topics (in Connect).

WHY STUDY ACCOUNTING? BECAUSE IT'S THE LANGUAGE OF BUSINESS

Some of you are reading this book because you are majoring in accounting, and it's obvious why you need to get a good understanding of this material. Others of you are not majoring in accounting. Perhaps you're planning a major in finance, management information systems, marketing, supply chain, or a major outside of business or just reading this book to learn more about accounting. You may be wondering if the material in this book will be important for you. To help you make that decision, consider the following.

Feature Story

Managers, investors, lenders, suppliers, customers, and many others make important decisions every day about a company. They make decisions related to how a company finances its operations, manages its operating costs, minimizes its risks, utilizes its resources, maintains its supply chain, and generates profits for its owners, to name just a few. To make good decisions, these individuals need timely and reliable information.

This is where accounting plays an important role in our society. The primary functions of accounting are to measure the activities of a company and communicate those measurements to help individuals make good decisions. The better the information they have, the better the decisions they'll make. Understanding accounting means understanding the *language of business*. When you speak that language, you'll be able to better communicate with others, make better decisions, help others make better decisions, and play a role in creating a more prosperous society.

You'll see in this book how accounting information helps tell a company's financial story. Telling this story involves critical thinking and professional judgment. These skills require a dynamic profession filled with individuals who are well-equipped to make business decisions and be part of any management team. Given the importance of business decisions in our society, there should be no surprise that demand for accounting information and for accountants remains strong. No matter what you choose as a major, if your goals are to make better business decisions, accounting will help you get there.

Rawpixel.com/Shutterstock

PART A

ACCOUNTING AS A MEASUREMENT/ COMMUNICATION PROCESS

Welcome to accounting. A common misconception about this course is that it is a math class, much like college algebra, calculus, or business statistics. You will soon see that this is *not* a math class. Don't say to yourself, "I'm not good at math, so I probably won't be good at accounting." Though it's true that we use numbers heavily throughout each chapter, accounting is far more than adding, subtracting, and solving for unknown variables. So, what exactly is accounting? We'll take a close look at this next.

Defining Accounting

■ **LO1–1**

Describe the two primary functions of financial accounting.

Accounting is "the language of business." It's the language companies use to tell their financial story. More precisely, accounting is a system of maintaining records of a company's operations and communicating that information to decision makers. The earliest use of such systematic recordkeeping dates back thousands of years to when records were kept of delivered agricultural products. Using accounting to maintain a record of multiple transactions allowed for better exchange among individuals and aided in the development of more complex societies.[1] In this book, you'll learn how to read, interpret, and communicate a company's financial story using the language of business.

Millions of people every day must make informed decisions about companies. Illustration 1–1 identifies some of those people and examples of decisions they make about the companies.

ILLUSTRATION 1–1

Decisions People Make About Companies

Make decisions about: People → Companies

1. **Investors** decide whether to invest in stock.
2. **Creditors** decide whether to lend money.
3. **Customers** decide whether to purchase products.
4. **Suppliers** decide the customer's ability to pay for supplies.
5. **Managers** decide production and expansion.
6. **Employees** decide employment opportunities.
7. **Competitors** decide market share and profitability.
8. **Regulators** decide on social welfare.
9. **Tax authorities** decide on taxation policies.
10. **Local communities** decide on environmental issues.

To make the decisions outlined in Illustration 1–1, these people need information. This is where accounting plays a key role. As Illustration 1–2 shows, accountants **measure the activities of the company and communicate those measurements to others.**

Accounting information that is provided for *internal* users (managers) is referred to as **managerial accounting;** that provided to *external* users is referred to as **financial accounting.** In this book, we focus on financial accounting. Formally defined, the two functions of financial accounting are to measure business activities of a company and then to communicate those measurements to *external* parties for decision-making purposes.

As you study the business activities discussed in this book, it is important for you to keep in mind this "framework" for financial accounting. For each activity, ask yourself

1. How is the business activity being measured?
2. How is the business activity being communicated?

---

[1]S. Basu and G. Waymire. 2006. Recordkeeping and Human Evolution. *Accounting Horizons* 20 (3): 201–229.

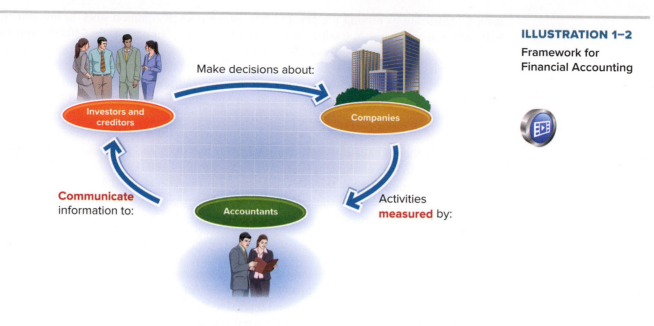

ILLUSTRATION 1–2
Framework for
Financial Accounting

These are the two functions of financial accounting. You'll better understand *why* this process exists by thinking about *how* the measurements being communicated help people make better decisions.

For example, **investors** want to make good decisions related to buying and selling their shares of the company's stock: Will the company's stock increase or decrease in value? The value of a stock is tied directly to the company's ability to make a profit, so what activities reflect the company's profitability? How should those activities be measured, and how should they be communicated in formal accounting reports?

As another example, **creditors** make decisions related to lending money to the company: Will the company be able to repay its debt and interest when they come due? How can debt activity be measured and how can it be communicated so that creditors better understand the ability of the company to have sufficient cash to repay debt and interest in the short term and the long term?

KEY POINT

The two primary functions of financial accounting are to measure business activities of a company and to communicate information about those activities to investors and creditors and other outside users for decision-making purposes.

User's Guide For learning objectives throughout this book, you will see boxed sections, like this one, titled *Key Point*. These boxed items will highlight the central focus of the learning objectives.

Measuring Business Activities

Let's first look at the typical activities of a start-up business. We'll do this with a simple example. Suppose you want to start a soccer academy. The "goal" of the academy is to provide lessons to develop junior players for top university programs and perhaps even one day to play in a professional league. Let's look at some initial activities of your new company, which you've decided to name **Eagle Soccer Academy.**

Let's assume you need about $300,000 to get the business up and running. You don't have that amount of money to start the business, so you begin by looking for investors. With their money, **investors** buy ownership in the company and have the right to share in the company's profits. Each share of ownership is typically referred to as a share of common stock. You develop a business proposal, explaining your target customers, funds needed, expected profits, and benefits your company will bring to the community. You pitch your idea to

■ **LO1–2**
Understand the business activities that financial accounting measures.

several organizations around the city and sell 7,000 shares of common stock to investors for $140,000 ($20 per share). You sell 2,000 additional shares to your parents for $40,000. You also purchase 1,000 of your own shares for $20,000, giving you 10% ownership (1,000 shares/10,000 total shares issued). Your company has now received $200,000 from investors.

To raise the remaining cash needed, you turn to **creditors.** Creditors lend money to a company, expecting to be paid back the loan amount plus interest. Impressed by your business proposal and ability to raise funding from investors, a local bank lends you $100,000 with 12% annual interest, which you agree to repay within three years.

Now, with the $300,000 of cash obtained from investors and creditors, your company buys equipment. This equipment costs $120,000, leaving $180,000 cash for future use. At this point, your company has the following resources that can be used for operations.

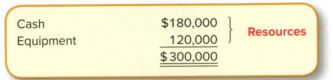

Cash	$180,000	}	**Resources**
Equipment	120,000		
	$300,000		

Who has the claims to the company's resources? Answer: The investors and creditors. Creditors have claims equal to the amount loaned to the company, $100,000. In other words, $100,000 of the company's resources are promised to the local bank. Investors have claims to all remaining resources, $200,000.

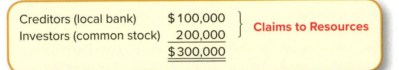

Creditors (local bank)	$100,000	}	**Claims to Resources**
Investors (common stock)	200,000		
	$300,000		

We'll continue the example of Eagle Soccer Academy in more detail in a moment. For now, we can see that the company has engaged in financing and investing activities, and it will soon begin operating activities.

- **Financing activities** include transactions the company has with investors and creditors, such as issuing stock ($200,000) and borrowing money from a local bank ($100,000).
- **Investing activities** include transactions involving the purchase and sale of resources that are expected to benefit the company for several years, such as the purchase of equipment for $120,000. With the necessary resources in place, the company is ready to begin operations.
- **Operating activities** will include transactions that relate to the primary operations of the company, such as providing products and services to customers and the associated costs of doing so, like rent, salaries, utilities, taxes, and advertising.

Types of Business Organizations   Notice that you are both the manager and an investor of Eagle Soccer Academy. You manage the resources of the company on behalf of the owners (stockholders, in this case), while you are also an investor helping to align your interests with the other investors in the company. This is common in many start-up businesses. Mark Cuban, the owner of the Dallas Mavericks and a tech-savvy entrepreneur, refers to a manager who also owns shares in the company as having "skin in the game." Companies that issue shares of stock often form as corporations.

A corporation is a company that is legally separate from its owners. The advantage of being legally separate is that the stockholders have limited liability. **Limited liability** prevents stockholders from being held personally responsible for the financial obligations of the corporation. Stockholders of Eagle Soccer Academy can lose their investment of $200,000 if the company fails, but they cannot lose any of their personal assets (such as homes, cars, computers, and furniture).

A sole proprietorship is a business owned by one person; a partnership is a business owned by two or more persons. If you had decided to start Eagle Soccer Academy without outside investors, you could have formed a sole proprietorship, or you and a friend could have formed a partnership. However, because you did not have the necessary resources to start the business, being a sole proprietorship (or even one member of a partnership) was not a viable option. Thus, a disadvantage of selecting the sole proprietorship or partnership form of business is that owners must have sufficient personal funds to finance the business in addition to the ability to borrow money. Another disadvantage of being a sole proprietorship or partnership is that neither offers limited liability. Owners (and partners) are held personally responsible for the activities of the business.

A potential disadvantage of a corporation is *double taxation:* (1) the company first pays corporate income taxes on income it earns and (2) stockholders then pay personal income taxes when the company distributes that income as dividends to them. There are many complexities in tax laws, and these laws are subject to change. For certain types of corporations and in certain instances, corporations may pay a higher or lower overall tax rate compared to partnerships and sole proprietorships.

Because most of the largest companies in the United States are corporations, in this book we focus primarily on accounting from a corporation's perspective. Focusing on corporations also highlights the importance of financial accounting—to measure and communicate activities of a company for investors (stockholders) and creditors (lenders, such as a local bank). (A more detailed discussion of the advantages and disadvantages of a corporation is provided in Chapter 10.)

ASSETS, LIABILITIES, AND STOCKHOLDERS' EQUITY

What information would Eagle's investors and creditors be interested in knowing to determine whether their investment in the company was a good decision? **Ultimately, investors and creditors want to know about the company's resources and their claims to those resources.** Accounting uses some conventional names to describe such resources and claims.

Assets are the total resources of a company. At this point, Eagle Soccer Academy has two assets—cash of $180,000 and equipment of $120,000—equaling total resources of $300,000. Of course, there are many other possible resources that a company can have, such as supplies, inventory for sale to customers, buildings, land, and investments. You'll learn about these and many other assets throughout this book.

Liabilities are amounts owed to creditors. Eagle Soccer Academy has a liability of $100,000 to the local bank. Other examples of liabilities would be amounts owed to suppliers, employees, utility companies, and the government (in the form of taxes). Liabilities typically include claims that must be paid by a specified date.

Stockholders' equity represents the owners' claims to resources. These claims arise from two primary sources: (1) contributions by the owners themselves and (2) net resources generated by company operations. To this point, Eagle Soccer Academy has contributions from owners of $200,000.

The accounting equation in Illustration 1-3 shows the relationship among the three measurement categories. The equation shows that a company's assets equal its liabilities plus stockholders' equity. Alternatively, a company's resources equal creditors' and owners' claims to those resources.

Assets	=	Liabilities	+	Stockholders' Equity
		(creditors' claims)		(owners' claims)
Resources		Claims to Resources		

ILLUSTRATION 1–3

The Accounting Equation

The accounting equation for Eagle Soccer Academy would be

Assets	=	Liabilities	+	Stockholders' Equity
(resources)		(creditors' claims)		(owners' claims)
$300,000	=	$100,000	+	$200,000

The accounting equation illustrates a fundamental model of business valuation. The value of a company to its owners equals total resources of the company minus amounts owed to creditors. Creditors expect to receive only resources equal to the amount owed them. Stockholders, on the other hand, can claim all of the company's resources in excess of the amount owed to creditors.

REVENUES, EXPENSES, AND DIVIDENDS

Of course, all owners hope their claims to the company's resources increase over time. This increase occurs when the company makes a profit. Stockholders claim all resources in excess of amounts owed to creditors; thus, profits of the company are claimed solely by stockholders. We calculate a company's profits by comparing its revenues and expenses.

Revenues are the amounts recognized when the company sells products or provides services to customers. For example, when you or one of your employees provides soccer training to a customer, the company recognizes revenue. However, as you've probably heard, "It takes money to make money." To operate the academy, you'll encounter many costs.

Expenses are the costs of providing products and services and other business activities during the current period. For example, to operate the soccer academy, you'll have costs related to salaries, rent, supplies, and utilities. These are typical expenses of most companies.

Common Terms
Other common names for net income include earnings or profit.

Net income is the difference between revenues and expenses. All businesses want revenues to be greater than expenses, producing a positive net income and adding to stockholders' equity in the business. However, if expenses exceed revenues, as happens from time to time, the difference between them is a negative amount—a **net loss.**

You'll notice the use of the term *net* to describe a company's profitability. In business, the term *net* is used often to describe the difference between two amounts. Here, we measure revenues *net* of (or minus) expenses, to calculate the net income or net loss. If we assume that by the end of the first month of operations Eagle Soccer Academy has total revenues of $72,000 and total expenses of $58,000, then we would say that the company has *net income* of $14,000 for the month.

Dividends are cash payments to stockholders. We just saw that the first month of operations of Eagle Soccer Academy generated net income of $14,000. From these profits, let's suppose the company decides to make a cash payment of $4,000 to stockholders. The remaining $10,000 of profits are retained in the company to help grow future operations. Thus, when Eagle has net income of $14,000, stockholders receive a total benefit of $14,000, equal to $4,000 of dividends received and $10,000 retained in the company they own.

Dividends Are Not an Expense.   Recall earlier we defined expenses as the costs necessary to run the business to produce revenues. Dividends, on the other hand, are not costs related to providing products and services to *customers;* dividends are distributions (most often cash) to the *owners* of the company—the stockholders.

Let's Review

User's Guide Let's Review exercises test your comprehension of key concepts covered in the chapter text.

Suggested Homework:
BE1–4;
E1–2, E1–3;
P1–2A&B

Match the term with the appropriate definition.

1. _____ Assets
2. _____ Liabilities
3. _____ Stockholders' Equity
4. _____ Dividends
5. _____ Revenues
6. _____ Expenses

a. Costs of selling products or services.
b. Sales of products or services to customers.
c. Amounts owed.
d. Distributions to stockholders.
e. Owners' claims to resources.
f. Resources of a company.

Solution:

1. f; 2. c; 3. e; 4. d; 5. b; 6. a

In summary, the measurement role of accounting is to create a record of the activities of a company. To make this possible, a company must maintain an accurate record of its assets, liabilities, stockholders' equity, revenues, expenses, and dividends. Be sure you understand the meaning of these items. We will refer to them throughout this book. Illustration 1–4 summarizes the business activities and the categories that measure them.

Activities Related to:	Measurement Category	Relationship
• Resources of the company • Amounts owed • Stockholders' investment	• Assets • Liabilities • Stockholders' equity	**Accounting Equation** **(A = L + SE)**
• Distributions to stockholders	• Dividends	
• Sales of products or services • Costs of providing sales	• Revenues • Expenses	**Net Income** **(R − E = NI)**

ILLUSTRATION 1–4

Business Activities and Their Measurement

KEY POINT

The measurement role of accounting is to create a record of the activities of a company. To make this possible, a company must maintain an accurate record of its assets, liabilities, stockholders' equity, revenues, expenses, and dividends.

As you learn to measure business activities, you will often find it helpful to consider both sides of the transaction: When someone pays cash, someone else receives cash; when someone borrows money, another lends money. Likewise, an expense for one company can be a revenue for another company; one company's asset can be another company's liability. Throughout this book, you will find discussions of the "flip side" of certain transactions, indicated by the icon you see here. In addition, certain homework problems, also marked by the icon, will ask you specifically to address the "flip side" in your computations. (See Exercise 1–2 and its flip side in Exercise 1-3 for the first such example.)

Flip Side

Communicating through Financial Statements

We've discussed that different business activities produce assets, liabilities, stockholders' equity, dividends, revenues, and expenses, and that the first important role of financial accounting is to *measure* the relevant transactions of a company. Its second vital role is to *communicate* these business activities to those outside the company. The primary means of communicating business activities is through financial statements.

Financial statements are periodic reports published by the company for the purpose of providing information to external users. There are four primary financial statements:

1. Income statement
2. Statement of stockholders' equity
3. Balance sheet
4. Statement of cash flows

■ **LO1–3**

Determine how financial accounting information is communicated through financial statements.

These financial statements give investors and creditors the key information they need when making decisions about a company: Should I buy the company's stock? Should I lend money to the company? Is management efficiently operating the company? **Without these financial statements, it would be difficult for those outside the company to see what's going on inside.**

Let's go through a simple set of financial statements to see what they look like. We'll continue with our example of Eagle Soccer Academy. Actual companies' financial statements often report items you haven't yet encountered. However, because actual companies' financial information will be useful in helping you understand certain accounting topics, we'll sample them often throughout this book.

INCOME STATEMENT

The **income statement** is a financial statement that reports the company's revenues and expenses over an interval of time. It shows whether the company was able to generate enough revenue to cover the expenses of running the business. If revenues exceed expenses, then the company reports *net income:*

Revenues − Expenses = Net Income

Common Terms
Other common names for the income statement include *statement of operations, statement of income, and profit and loss statement.*

If expenses exceed revenues, then the company reports a *net loss.*

On December 1, 2024 Eagle Soccer Academy began operations by offering lessons to junior players. At the end of the first month of operations, Eagle Soccer Academy reports its income statement as shown in Illustration 1–5.

ILLUSTRATION 1–5

Income Statement for Eagle Soccer Academy

EAGLE SOCCER ACADEMY	
Income Statement	
For the month ended December 31, 2024	
Revenues	
Service revenue	**$72,000**
Expenses	
Rent expense	5,000
Supplies expense	10,000
Salaries expense	31,000
Utilities expense	9,000
Interest expense	1,000
Other expenses	2,000
Total expenses	58,000
Net income	**$14,000**

Here are some specifics about Eagle's income statement:

- **Heading**—The heading includes the company's name, the title of the financial statement, and the time period covered by the financial statement. Because Eagle began operations on December 1, this income statement shows activity occurring *from* December 1 *to* December 31, 2024.
- **Revenues**—Eagle provides soccer lessons and bills customers a total of **$72,000** during the month of December.
- **Expenses**—Eagle has costs for business activities of **$58,000** during the month of December. These are typical costs that we might expect of any company, such as rent, supplies, salaries, utilities, interest, and other items. Each of these costs is reported in a separate account. An **account** maintains a record of the business activities related to a particular item.
- **Net income**—Revenues *exceed* expenses ($72,000 is greater than $58,000), and thus the company has generated a profit for its owners of **$14,000**.
- **Underlines**—In a financial statement, a single underline generally represents a subtotal (in this case, total revenues or total expenses), while a double underline indicates a final total (in this case, net income).

The fact that Eagle reports a positive net income is, in some sense, a signal of the company's success. The company is able to charge its customers a price higher than the costs of running the business. Do you assume most companies sell their products and services for a profit? It's not as easy as you might think. In recent years, companies such as **Tesla**, **eBay**, **Uber**, **Boeing**, **General Electric**, **Wayfair**, **Fitbit**, and thousands of others have reported net losses.

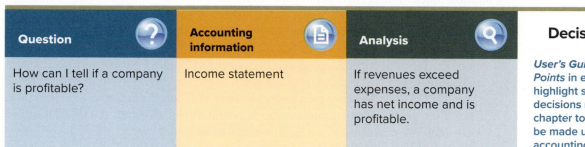

KEY POINT

The income statement compares revenues and expenses for the current period to assess the company's ability to generate a profit from running its operations.

Question	Accounting information	Analysis
How can I tell if a company is profitable?	Income statement	If revenues exceed expenses, a company has net income and is profitable.

Decision Point

User's Guide Decision Points in each chapter highlight specific decisions related to chapter topics that can be made using financial accounting information.

STATEMENT OF STOCKHOLDERS' EQUITY

The **statement of stockholders' equity** is a financial statement that summarizes the changes in stockholders' equity over an interval of time. Stockholders' equity arises from two primary sources—common stock and retained earnings.

$$\text{Stockholders' Equity} = \text{Common Stock} + \text{Retained Earnings}$$

1. **Common stock** (*external* source of equity) represents amounts invested by stockholders (owners) when they purchase shares of stock. The change in common stock over the period is shown as:

$$\text{Beginning Common Stock} + \text{New Issuances} = \text{Ending Common Stock}$$

2. **Retained earnings** (*internal* source of equity) represent *all net income minus all dividends over the life of the company*. The change in retained earnings over the period is shown as:

$$\text{Beginning Retained Earnings} + \text{Net Income} - \text{Dividends} = \text{Ending Retained Earnings}$$

Think of retained earnings this way. A company that has net income has generated resources for owners through its operations. Those resources can either be returned to owners for their personal use (dividend payments) or retained in the business for future use. From the company's perspective, we need to account for the total net income retained in the business. That's the balance of retained earnings. In each period, the beginning balance of retained earnings is updated for the current period's net income minus dividends to calculate ending retained earnings. This same calculation repeats each period.

Illustration 1–6 shows the statement of stockholders' equity for Eagle Soccer Academy.

EAGLE SOCCER ACADEMY Statement of Stockholders' Equity For the month ended December 31, 2024			
	Common Stock	Retained Earnings	Total Stockholders' Equity
Beginning balance (Dec. 1)*	$ -0-	$ -0-	$ -0-
Issuance of common stock	200,000		200,000
Add: **Net income for the period**		14,000	14,000
Less: Dividends		(4,000)	(4,000)
Ending balance (Dec. 31)	**$200,000**	**$10,000**	**$210,000**

ILLUSTRATION 1–6
Statement of Stockholders' Equity for Eagle Soccer Academy

From the income statement

Accounting convention uses parentheses to signify an amount to be subtracted (such as dividends here).

*Beginning balances are zero only because this is the first month of operations for Eagle. Normally, beginning balances for Common Stock and Retained Earnings equal ending balances from the previous period.

Here are some specifics about Eagle's statement of stockholders' equity:

- **Heading**—The statement of stockholders' equity reports the activity for common stock and retained earnings over an *interval of time.* Similar to the income statement, the period of time in this example is December 1 to December 31, 2024.
- **Common Stock**—When Eagle begins operations on December 1, the balance of common stock is $0. This would be true of any company beginning operations. During December, Eagle issues 10,000 shares of common stock for $20 per share, so the balance of common stock increases by **$200,000**.
- **Retained Earnings**—Retained Earnings also begins the first month of operations with a balance of $0. For the month of December, retained earnings increase by net income of **$14,000** and decrease by $4,000 for dividends paid to stockholders. We show the amount of net income in blue here to emphasize that it came from the income statement (Illustration 1–5). The ending balance of **$10,000** represents all net income minus all dividends over the life of the company, which is only one month to this point in our example.
- **Total Stockholders' Equity**—The third column shows that the two components—common stock and retained earnings—add to equal total stockholders' equity of **$210,000**.

User's Guide
Throughout each chapter, you will see sections titled Common Mistake. Information in these boxes will help you avoid common mistakes on exams, quizzes, and homework.

COMMON MISTAKE

Dividends represent the payment of cash but are not considered an expense in running the business. Students sometimes mistakenly include the amount of dividends as an expense in the income statement, rather than as a distribution of net income in the statement of stockholders' equity.

KEY POINT

The statement of stockholders' equity reports information related to changes in common stock and retained earnings each period. The change in retained earnings equals net income less dividends for the period.

Statement of Retained Earnings.   Notice the middle column of the statement of stockholders' equity in Illustration 1–6. This column sometimes is referred to as the *statement of retained earnings.* In practice, companies don't report retained earnings in a separate statement from common stock, so that's why we demonstrate the statement of stockholders' equity. Nevertheless, it's useful to see that this column highlights how net income (revenues minus expenses) from the income statement links to total stockholders' equity by adding to the balance of retained earnings.

Decision Point

Question	Accounting information	Analysis
Was the change in stockholders' equity the result of external or internal sources?	Statement of stockholders' equity	When a company sells common stock, equity increases due to external sources. When a company has profits during the year in excess of dividends paid, equity increases due to internal sources.

BALANCE SHEET

The balance sheet is a financial statement that presents the financial position of the company on a particular date. The financial position of a company is summarized by the accounting equation (see Illustration 1–3):

$$\text{Assets} = \text{Liabilities} + \text{Stockholders' Equity}$$

As discussed earlier, this equation provides a fundamental model of business valuation. Assets are the resources of the company, and liabilities are amounts owed to creditors. Stockholders have equity in the company to the extent that assets exceed liabilities. Creditors also need to understand the balance sheet; it's the company's assets that will be used to pay liabilities as they become due. Illustration 1–7 shows the balance sheet of Eagle Soccer Academy.

EAGLE SOCCER ACADEMY
Balance Sheet
December 31, 2024

Assets		Liabilities	
Cash	$ 137,000	Accounts payable	$ 23,000
Accounts receivable	27,000	Salaries payable	3,000
Supplies	13,000	Utilities payable	9,000
Equipment, net	118,000	Interest payable	1,000
Other assets	55,000	Notes payable	100,000
		Other liabilities	4,000
		Total liabilities	**140,000**
		Stockholders' Equity	
		Common stock	200,000
		Retained earnings	10,000
		Total stockholders' equity	**210,000**
		Total liabilities and	
Total assets	**$350,000**	**stockholders' equity**	**$350,000**

ILLUSTRATION 1–7

Balance Sheet for Eagle Soccer Academy

Common Terms
Another name for the balance sheet is the *statement of financial position.*

From the statement of stockholders' equity

Here are some specifics about Eagle's balance sheet:

- **Heading**—The balance sheet reports assets, liabilities, and stockholders' equity at a *point in time,* in contrast to the income statement, which shows revenue and expense activities over an *interval of time.* For example, Eagle's income statement shows revenue and expense activity occurring *from* December 1 *to* December 31, 2024; its balance sheet shows assets, liabilities, and stockholders' equity of the company *on* December 31, 2024.
- **Assets**—These are the resources of a company. Eagle has total assets of $350,000. *Cash* is a resource because it can be used to make purchases. *Accounts receivable* is a resource because they represent the right to receive cash from customers that have already been provided products or services. *Supplies* include resources used to run the soccer academy, such as paper, cleaning supplies, and soccer balls. *Equipment* is a resource that can be used to provide services to customers.
- **Liabilities**—These are the amounts owed by a company. Eagle has total liabilities of $140,000. These include amounts owed to regular vendors (accounts payable), as well as amounts owed for other items such as employee salaries, utilities, interest, and bank borrowing (notes payable). Many liabilities are referred to as "payables," to signify amounts the company will "pay" in the future.
- **Stockholders' equity**—The difference between total assets and total liabilities of $210,000 represents stockholders' equity. Total stockholders' equity includes the amount of common stock plus the amount of retained earnings from the statement of stockholders' equity. We show the stockholders' equity items in purple here, to indicate they came from the statement of stockholders' equity (Illustration 1–6).
- **Accounting Equation**—Notice that the amounts listed in the "balance sheet" show that the accounting equation "balances."

The income statement is like a video (shows events over time), whereas a balance sheet is like a photograph (shows events at a point in time).

Total assets must equal total liabilities and stockholders' equity.

Assets	=	Liabilities	+	Stockholders' Equity
(resources)		(creditors' claims)		(owners' claims)
$350,000	=	$140,000	+	$210,000

 KEY POINT

The balance sheet demonstrates that the company's resources (assets) equal creditors' claims (liabilities) plus owners' claims (stockholders' equity) to those resources on a particular date.

Decision Point

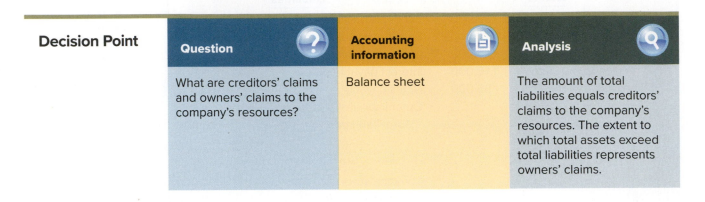

Question	Accounting information	Analysis
What are creditors' claims and owners' claims to the company's resources?	Balance sheet	The amount of total liabilities equals creditors' claims to the company's resources. The extent to which total assets exceed total liabilities represents owners' claims.

STATEMENT OF CASH FLOWS

The **statement of cash flows** is a financial statement that measures activities involving cash receipts and cash payments over an interval of time. We can classify all cash transactions into three categories that correspond to the three fundamental business activities—operating, investing, and financing.

- **Operating cash flows** include cash receipts and cash payments for transactions involving revenue and expense activities during the period. In other words, operating activities include the cash effects of the same activities that are reported in the income statement to calculate net income. Suppose Eagle received $49,000 from customers, paid $28,000 for salaries, and paid $60,000 for rent.
- **Investing cash flows** generally include cash transactions for the purchase and sale of investments and long-term assets. Long-term assets are resources owned by a company that are thought to provide benefits for more than one year. Eagle had only one investing cash flow—purchase of equipment for $120,000.
- **Financing cash flows** include cash transactions with lenders, such as borrowing money and repaying debt, and with stockholders, such as issuing stock and paying dividends. Eagle issued stock for $200,000, borrowed $100,000 from the bank, and paid dividends of $4,000 to stockholders.

Illustration 1–8 provides the statement of cash flows for Eagle Soccer Academy. Inflows are shown as positive amounts; outflows are shown in parentheses to indicate negative cash flows. The final line in each section shows, in the right-most column, the difference between inflows and outflows as *net cash flow* for that type of activity.

 KEY POINT

The statement of cash flows reports cash transactions from operating, investing, and financing activities for the period.

EAGLE SOCCER ACADEMY
Statement of Cash Flows
For the month ended December 31, 2024

Cash Flows from Operating Activities

Cash inflows:		
From customers	$ 49,000	
Cash outflows:		
For salaries	(28,000)	
For rent	(60,000)	
Net cash flows from operating activities		$ (39,000)

Cash Flows from Investing Activities

Purchase equipment	(120,000)	
Net cash flows from investing activities		(120,000)

Cash Flows from Financing Activities

Issue common stock	200,000	
Borrow from bank	100,000	
Pay dividends	(4,000)	
Net cash flows from financing activities		296,000
Net increase in cash		137,000
Cash at the beginning of the period		-0-
Cash at the end of the period		$137,000

The total of the net cash flows from operating, investing, and financing activities equals the *net change in cash* during the period.

$$\text{Change in cash} = \text{Operating cash flows} + \text{Investing cash flows} + \text{Financing cash flows}$$

For Eagle, that net change in cash for December was an increase of $137,000. That amount equals the sum of its operating cash flows of −$39,000, investing cash flows of −$120,000, and financing cash flows of $296,000. We next add the beginning balance of cash. Because this is the first month of operations for Eagle, cash at the beginning of the period is zero. The ending balance of cash is the same as that reported in the balance sheet in Illustration 1–7. This reconciliation of the beginning and ending cash balances emphasizes that the statement of cash flows explains *why* the cash reported in the balance sheet changed from one period to the next.

Decision Maker's Perspective

The statement of cash flows can be an important source of information to investors and creditors. For example, investors use the relationship between net income (revenues minus expenses) and operating cash flows (cash flows from revenue and expense activities) to forecast a company's future profitability. Creditors compare operating cash flows and investing cash flows to assess a company's ability to repay debt. Financing activities provide information to investors and creditors about the mix of external financing of the company.

User's Guide Decision Maker's Perspective sections discuss the usefulness of accounting information to decision makers such as investors, creditors, and company managers.

THE LINKS AMONG FINANCIAL STATEMENTS

The four financial statements are linked, because events that are reported in one financial statement often affect amounts reported in another. Many times, a single business transaction, such as receiving cash from a customer when providing services, will affect more than one of the financial statements. Providing services to a customer, for example, results in

revenues recorded in the income statement, which are used to calculate net income. Net income, in turn, is reported in the calculation of retained earnings in the statement of stockholders' equity. Then, the ending balance of retained earnings is reported in the balance sheet. **Thus, any transaction that affects the income statement ultimately affects the balance sheet through the balance of retained earnings.** The cash received from customers will be reported as part of the ending cash balance in the balance sheet and as part of operating cash flows in the statement of cash flows.

Illustration 1–9 shows the links among the financial statements of Eagle Soccer Academy in Illustrations 1–5, 1–6, 1–7, and 1–8.

- Link [1] shows that net income from the income statement is reported in the statement of stockholders' equity as part of the calculation of retained earnings.
- Link [2] shows that after calculating the balance of retained earnings, the amount of total stockholders' equity can be reported in the balance sheet. Finally,
- Link [3] demonstrates that the balance of cash in the balance sheet equals the amount of cash reported in the statement of cash flows.

ILLUSTRATION 1–9

Links among Financial Statements

[1] Notice that the amount of net income in the income statement reappears in the statement of stockholders' equity.

[2] Notice that the ending balance in the statement of stockholders' equity reappears in the balance sheet.

[3] Notice that the amount of cash in the balance sheet reappears as the ending cash balance in the statement of cash flows.

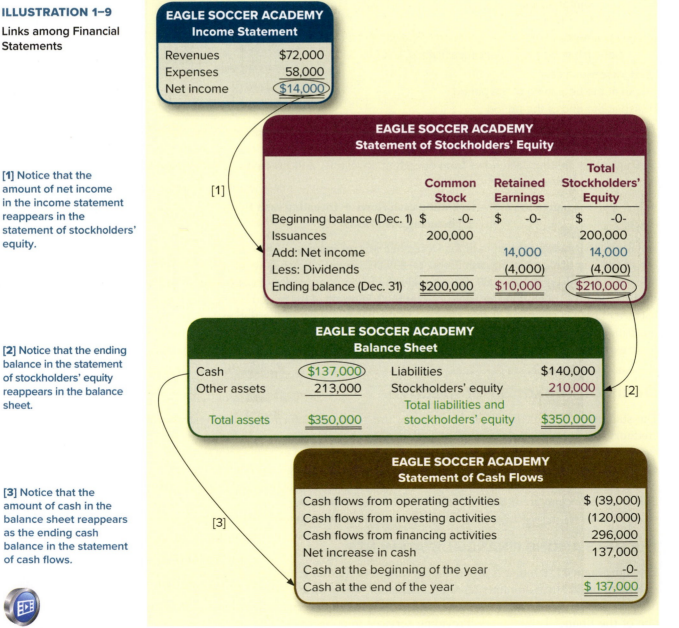

EAGLE SOCCER ACADEMY
Income Statement

Revenues	$72,000
Expenses	58,000
Net income	$14,000

EAGLE SOCCER ACADEMY
Statement of Stockholders' Equity

	Common Stock	Retained Earnings	Total Stockholders' Equity
Beginning balance (Dec. 1)	$ -0-	$ -0-	$ -0-
Issuances	200,000		200,000
Add: Net income		14,000	14,000
Less: Dividends		(4,000)	(4,000)
Ending balance (Dec. 31)	$200,000	$10,000	$210,000

EAGLE SOCCER ACADEMY
Balance Sheet

Cash	$137,000	Liabilities	$140,000
Other assets	213,000	Stockholders' equity	210,000
		Total liabilities and	
Total assets	$350,000	stockholders' equity	$350,000

EAGLE SOCCER ACADEMY
Statement of Cash Flows

Cash flows from operating activities	$ (39,000)
Cash flows from investing activities	(120,000)
Cash flows from financing activities	296,000
Net increase in cash	137,000
Cash at the beginning of the year	-0-
Cash at the end of the year	$ 137,000

Let's Review

Test your understanding of what you've read so far. The Computer Shop repairs laptops, desktops, and mainframe computers. On December 31, 2024, the company reports the following year-end amounts:

Assets:	Cash	$10,000	Revenues:	Service	$65,000
	Supplies	8,000			
	Equipment, net	26,000			
			Expenses:	Rent	6,000
Liabilities:	Accounts payable	4,000		Supplies	14,000
	Notes payable	10,000		Salaries	40,000

Additional information:

a. The balance of retained earnings at the beginning of the year is $7,000.

b. The company pays dividends of $1,000 on December 31, 2024.

c. Common stock is $15,000 at the beginning of the year, and additional shares are issued for $4,000 during 2024.

Required:

Prepare the (1) income statement, (2) statement of stockholders' equity, and (3) balance sheet.

Solution:

Suggested Homework:
BE1–7, BE1–8;
E1–6, E1–7, E1–8;
P1–3A&B, P1–5A&B

1. Income statement:

THE COMPUTER SHOP
Income Statement
Year ended Dec. 31, 2024

Revenues:	
Service revenue	$65,000
Expenses:	
Rent expense	6,000
Supplies expense	14,000
Salaries expense	40,000
Net income	$ 5,000

2. Statement of stockholders' equity:

THE COMPUTER SHOP
Statement of Stockholders' Equity
Year ended Dec. 31, 2024

	Common Stock	Retained Earnings	Total Stockholders' Equity
Beginning balance (Jan. 1)	$15,000	$ 7,000	$22,000
Issuance of common stock	4,000		4,000
Add: Net income		5,000	5,000
Less: Dividends		(1,000)	(1,000)
Ending balance (Dec. 31)	$19,000	$11,000	$30,000

3. Balance sheet:

THE COMPUTER SHOP
Balance Sheet
December 31, 2024

Assets		Liabilities	
Cash	$10,000	Accounts payable	$ 4,000
Supplies	8,000	Notes payable	10,000
Equipment	26,000	**Stockholders' Equity**	
		Common stock	19,000
		Retained earnings	11,000
Total assets	$44,000	Total liabilities and stockholders' equity	$44,000

KEY POINT

All transactions that affect revenues or expenses reported in the income statement ultimately affect the balance sheet through the balance in retained earnings.

OTHER INFORMATION REPORTED TO OUTSIDERS

The financial statements are a key component of a company's *annual report*, the term most often used to describe the formal document detailing a company's activities and financial performance. As the name suggests, annual reports are provided by companies each year. Two other important components of the annual report are (1) management's discussion and analysis and (2) note disclosures to the financial statements.

The **management discussion and analysis** (MD&A) section typically includes management's views on significant events, trends, and uncertainties pertaining to the company's operations and resources. **Note disclosures** offer additional information either to explain the information presented in the financial statements or to provide information not included in the financial statements. For example, companies are required to report total revenues in the income statement, but they also often report revenues itemized by geographic region in a note disclosure. We'll discuss these items throughout this book. For now, if you'd like to see an abbreviated version of an actual company's annual report with financial statements, see Appendix A (**American Eagle Outfitters**) or Appendix B (**Buckle**) near the end of this book.

Making Decisions with Accounting Information

■ LO1–4

Describe the role that financial accounting plays in the decision-making process.

To this point, you've had a simple, first look at how companies measure and communicate financial information to external users. Subsequent chapters will provide an even more detailed view of this measurement/communication process. However, before proceeding, it's important first to consider why we are studying financial accounting. Does it matter? In other words, does the use of financial accounting information result in better business decisions?

One of the rewarding things about studying financial accounting is that it does matter! The concepts in this course have an impact on everyday business decisions as well as wide-ranging economic consequences. We'll see an example of this next and then more examples throughout the rest of this book.

Most prospering economies in the world today are structured around free markets. In free markets, firms are allowed to compete and customers are free to choose from a variety of products and services. From which company do you prefer to buy a laptop computer—**Dell**, **Hewlett-Packard**, or **Apple**? Competition among these companies helps determine the prices they charge customers and the amounts they spend on computer components, salaries, manufacturing and distribution facilities, warranties, research and development, and other business-related activities. Can these companies offer you the laptop computer you want for a price above their costs? If they can, they'll earn a profit and stay in business. If they cannot, they'll eventually go out of business. Because companies know they are directly competing with each other, they work harder and more efficiently to please you, the customer.

Successful companies use their resources efficiently to sell products and services for a profit. When a company is able to make a profit, investors and creditors are willing to transfer their resources to it, and the company will expand its profitable operations even further.

Unsuccessful companies either offer lower-quality products and services or do not efficiently keep their costs low. In either case, they are not profitable. When a company is unprofitable, investors will neither invest in nor lend to the firm. Without these sources of financing, eventually the company will fail. Clearly, you don't want to invest in an unsuccessful company and then watch your investment shrink as the company loses your money.

But how do investors and creditors know the successful companies from the unsuccessful companies? How do they get the information necessary to make good investment decisions that help develop a prosperous society? Here's where financial accounting enters the picture. **Investors and creditors rely heavily on financial accounting information in making investment and lending decisions.**

This idea has been visualized by the Pathways Commission of the American Accounting Association (**pathwayscommission.org**) in Illustration 1–10. Accounting serves an important role in a prosperous society by measuring economic activity and communicating useful information to help investors and creditors make good decisions. Throughout this book, you'll practice the judgment and skills necessary to produce accounting information, and you'll begin to see how this information is helpful in making good decisions.

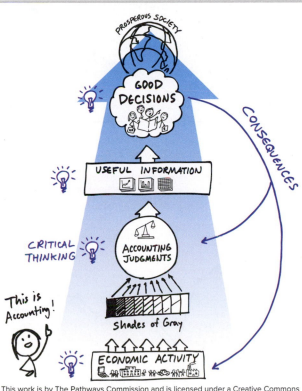

This work is by The Pathways Commission and is licensed under a Creative Commons Attribution-NoDerivs 3.0 Unported License.

ILLUSTRATION 1–10

Pathways Commission Visualization: "THIS is Accounting!"

Reprinted with permission from the American Accounting Association.

KEY POINT

Financial accounting serves an important role by providing information useful in investment and lending decisions.

To demonstrate the importance of financial accounting information to investment decisions, we can look at the relationship between changes in stock prices and changes in net income over 20 years. As an investor, you will make money from an increase in the stock price of a company in which you invest (you can sell the stock for more than you bought it). So as an investor, you are looking for companies whose stock price is likely to increase. Is there a way to find such companies? Interestingly, there is: **No other single piece of company information better explains companies' stock price performance than does financial accounting net income,** the bottom line in the income statement.

What if you were able to accurately predict the direction of companies' changes in net income over the next year—that is, whether it would increase or decrease—and then you invested $1,000 in companies that were going to have an *increase?* In contrast, what if instead you invested in companies that would have a *decrease* in net income? Illustration 1–11 shows what would happen to your $1,000 investment over 20 years for each scenario.

ILLUSTRATION 1–11

Relationship between
Changes in Stock
Prices and Changes
in Net Income over a
20-Year Period

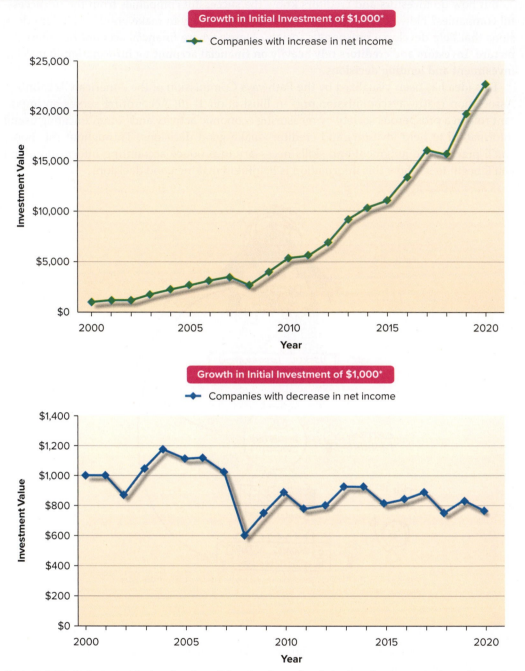

You can see that if you had invested $1,000 in companies with an increase in net income, your investment would have increased to $22,729 over the 20-year period. If instead you had invested $1,000 in companies with a decrease in net income, your $1,000 investment would have shrunk to $771 over this same period. This dramatic difference in the value of the investment demonstrates the importance of financial accounting information to investors. This book will provide you a thorough understanding of how net income is calculated and presented in financial statements. As you can see from the charts above, if you are able to predict the change in financial accounting's measure of profitability—net income—then you can predict the change in stock prices as well.

Investors and creditors also use information reported in the balance sheet. Consider a company's total liabilities, often referred to as *total debt.* Expanding debt levels limit management's ability to respond quickly and effectively to business situations. The "overhanging" debt, which involves legal obligation of repayment, restricts management's ability to engage in new profit-generating activities. Increased debt levels also increase interest payment burdens on the company. Failure to pay interest or to repay debt can result in creditors forcing the company to declare bankruptcy and go out of business. Understandably, then, investors and creditors keep a close eye on the company's debt level and its ability to repay.

 KEY POINT

> No single piece of company information better explains companies' stock price performance than does financial accounting net income. A company's debt level is an important indicator of management's ability to respond to business situations and the possibility of bankruptcy.

FINANCIAL ACCOUNTING INFORMATION

PART B

Recall that accounting serves two main functions: It (1) measures business activities and (2) communicates those measurements to investors and creditors so they can make decisions. Although this process might seem straightforward, some issues have been heavily debated, and the answers have changed over time. How do we measure assets? When do we record revenues? What do we classify as an expense? How should we present financial statements? Next, we'll take a look at factors that shape the measurement and communication processes of financial accounting.

Financial Accounting Standards

Because financial accounting information is so vital to investors and creditors, formal standards have been established. The rules of financial accounting are called **generally accepted accounting principles**, often abbreviated as **GAAP** (pronounced *gap*). The fact that all companies use these same rules is critical to financial statement users. It helps investors to accurately *compare* financial information among companies when they are making decisions about where to invest or lend their resources.

■ **LO1–5**
Explain the term generally accepted accounting principles (GAAP) and describe the role of GAAP in financial accounting.

STANDARD SETTING TODAY

Financial accounting and reporting standards in the United States are established primarily by the **Financial Accounting Standards Board (FASB)** (pronounced either by the letters themselves or as *faz-be*). The FASB is an independent, private-sector body with full-time voting members and a very large support staff. Members include representatives from the accounting profession, large corporations, financial analysts, accounting educators, and government agencies.

Not all countries follow the same accounting and reporting standards. For example, accounting practices differ between the United States, the United Kingdom, and Japan. In recent years, the accounting profession has undertaken a project whose goal is to eliminate differences in accounting standards around the world. The standard-setting body responsible for this convergence effort is the **International Accounting Standards Board (IASB)**, as detailed in the box titled "What is the IASB?".

More than 120 countries have chosen to forgo their own country-specific standards and either require or allow International Financial Reporting Standards (IFRS) as their national standards. That movement, coupled with the convergence of U.S. GAAP and IFRS, caused many to predict that both sets of rules, or perhaps only IFRS, would be acceptable for financial reporting in the United States. Currently, however, that seems unlikely.

For information about the activities of the Financial Accounting Standards Board, see its website, *www.fasb.org*.

INTERNATIONAL FINANCIAL REPORTING STANDARDS (IFRS)

WHAT IS THE IASB?

The global counterpart to the FASB is the International Accounting Standards Board (IASB). In many ways, this organization functions like the FASB. The IASB's objectives are (1) to develop a single set of high-quality, understandable global accounting standards, (2) to promote the use of those standards, and (3) to bring about the convergence of national accounting standards and international accounting standards around the world. In 2002, the FASB and IASB signed the Norwalk Agreement, formalizing their commitment to convergence of U.S. and international accounting standards. The standards being developed and promoted by the IASB are called **International Financial Reporting Standards (IFRS)**. The FASB and IASB have made several efforts to converge U.S. GAAP and IFRS, although important differences remain. (*For more discussion, see Appendix E.*)

For information about the activities of the International Accounting Standards Board, see its website, *www.iasb.org*.

 KEY POINT

The rules of financial accounting are called generally accepted accounting principles (GAAP). The Financial Accounting Standards Board (FASB) is an independent, private body that has primary responsibility for the establishment of GAAP in the United States.

STANDARD SETTING IN THE PAST CENTURY

Pressures on the accounting profession to establish uniform accounting standards began to surface after the stock market crash of 1929. The Dow Jones Industrial Average, a major stock market index in the United States, fell 40% over the period September 3 to October 29 that year. The Dow bottomed out in July 1932, after losing 89% of its value.

Many blamed financial accounting for the stock market crash and the ensuing Great Depression of the 1930s. At the time of the crash, accounting practices and reporting procedures were not well established, providing the opportunity for companies to engage in inaccurate financial reporting to enhance their reported performance. This led to many stocks being valued too highly. As investors began to recognize this, their confidence in the stock market fell. They panicked and sold stocks in a frenzy. The Dow did not reach pre-crash levels again until 1954.

The 1933 Securities Act and the Securities Exchange Act of 1934 were designed to restore investor confidence in financial accounting. The 1933 act sets forth accounting and disclosure requirements for initial offerings of securities (stocks and bonds). The 1934 act created a government agency, the **Securities and Exchange Commission (SEC).** The 1934 act gives the SEC the power to require companies that publicly trade their stock to prepare periodic financial statements for distribution to investors and creditors.

While Congress has given the SEC both the power and the responsibility for setting accounting and reporting standards for publicly traded companies, the SEC has delegated the primary responsibility for setting accounting standards to the private sector, currently the FASB. Note that the SEC delegated only the responsibility, not the authority, to set these standards. The power still lies with the SEC. If the SEC does not agree with a particular standard issued by the FASB, it can force a change in the standard. In fact, it has done so in the past.

THE IMPORTANCE OF AUDITORS

For many businesses, there is a natural separation between those who run the business (managers) and those who own the business or finance operations (investors and creditors). This separation creates the need to ensure honest financial reporting. While it is the responsibility of management to apply GAAP when communicating with investors and creditors through financial statements, sometimes those in charge of preparing financial statements do not always follow the rules. Instead, some purposely provide misleading financial accounting information, commonly referred to as "cooking the books." The phrase implies that the accounting records ("books") have been presented in an altered form ("cooked"). Managers may cook the books for several reasons, such as to hide the poor operating performance of the company or to increase their personal wealth at stockholders' expense.

To help ensure that management has, in fact, appropriately applied GAAP, the SEC requires independent outside verification of the financial statements of publicly traded companies. Such independent examination is done by **auditors**, who are *not* employees of the company, but who are hired by the company as an independent party to express a professional opinion of the extent to which financial statements are prepared in compliance with GAAP and are free of material misstatement. If auditors find mistakes or fraudulent reporting behavior, they require the company to correct all significant information before issuing financial statements. **Auditors play a major role in investors' and creditors' decisions by adding credibility to a company's financial statements.**

Common Terms
The auditor's report is also commonly referred to as the *auditor's opinion.*

Illustration 1–12 presents an excerpt from the auditor's report for **Dick's Sporting Goods, Inc**. The auditor's report indicates that the financial statements for the period mentioned have been prepared in conformity with GAAP.

ILLUSTRATION 1–12

Excerpts from the Independent Auditor's Report of **Dick's Sporting Goods, Inc.**

Dick's Sporting Goods, Inc.
Report of Independent Auditors

To the Board of Directors and Stockholders of
Dick's Sporting Goods, Inc.
Pittsburgh, Pennsylvania

We have audited the accompanying consolidated balance sheets of DICK'S Sporting Goods, Inc. and subsidiaries (the "Company") as of February 1, 2020, and February 2, 2019, the related consolidated statements of income, comprehensive income, changes in stockholders' equity, and cash flows, for each of the three years in the period ended February 1, 2020, and the related notes (collectively referred to as the "financial statements").

In our opinion, the financial statements present fairly, in all material respects, the financial position of the Company as of February 1, 2020, and February 2, 2019, and the results of its operations and its cash flows for each of the three years in the period ended February 1, 2020, in conformity with accounting principles generally accepted in the United States of America.

To further enhance the credibility of financial reporting, Congress established in 2002 the **Public Company Accounting Oversight Board (PCAOB).** The role of the PCAOB is to ensure that auditors follow a strict set of guidelines when conducting their audits of public companies' financial statements. The PCAOB is a government entity that, simply stated, "audits the auditors."

OBJECTIVES OF FINANCIAL ACCOUNTING

After measuring business activities and communicating those measurements to investors and creditors, what do financial accountants hope to have achieved? What benefit will their services have brought to users of financial statements? The FASB has explicitly stated the specific objectives of financial accounting. These objectives are presented in Illustration 1–13.

The first objective is specific to investors and creditors. In addition to those users, though, financial accounting information is likely to have general usefulness to other

ILLUSTRATION 1–13

Objectives of Financial
Accounting

Financial accounting should provide information that:

1. Is useful to investors and creditors in making decisions.
2. Helps to predict cash flows.
3. Tells about economic resources, claims to resources, and changes in resources and claims.

groups of external users, who are interested in essentially the same financial aspects of a business as are investors and creditors. Some of these other groups were discussed in Illustration 1–1.

The second objective refers to the specific cash flow information needs of investors and creditors. The third objective emphasizes the need for information about economic resources (assets) and claims to those resources (liabilities and stockholders' equity) and their changes over time.

KEY POINT

The primary objective of financial accounting is to provide useful information to investors and creditors in making decisions.

Underlying these three key objectives is a conceptual framework that is the foundation upon which financial accounting is built. We discuss the FASB's conceptual framework in detail in the appendix to this chapter.

An Ethical Foundation

Like all structures, accounting requires a strong foundation. For accounting, part of that foundation is the ethical behavior of those who practice its rules. You have probably encountered the topic of ethics in other business courses. **Ethics** refers to a code or moral system that provides criteria for evaluating right and wrong behavior. Investors, creditors, government, and the general public rely on general ethical behavior among those who record and report the financial activities of businesses. A lack of public trust in financial reporting can undermine business and the economy.

Public outrage over accounting scandals at high-profile companies increased the pressure on lawmakers to pass measures that would restore credibility and investor confidence in the financial reporting process. These pressures resulted in the issuance of what is commonly referred to as the **Sarbanes-Oxley Act (SOX)**, named for the two congressmen who sponsored the bill. The Sarbanes-Oxley Act provides for the regulation of auditors and the types of services they furnish to clients, increases accountability of corporate executives, addresses conflicts of interest for securities analysts, and provides for stiff criminal penalties for violators. These increased requirements have dramatically increased the need for good accounting and, at the same time, highlighted the value of accounting information to investors and creditors. We discuss the specific provisions of SOX in more detail in Chapter 4.

Important as such legislation is in supporting the ethical foundation of accounting, it is equally important that accountants themselves have their own personal standards for ethical conduct. You cannot, though, just go out and suddenly obtain ethics when you need them. ("I'd like a pound of ethics, please.") Rather, accountants need to *develop* their ability to identify ethical situations and know the difference between right and wrong in the context of the accounting topics you will learn in this course. One of the keys to ethical decision making is having an appreciation for how your actions affect others.

When you face ethical dilemmas in your professional life (and indeed in your personal life), you can apply the following simple four-step framework as you think through what to do:

1. Understand the ethical decision you face.
2. Specify the options for alternative courses of action.
3. Identify the impact of each option on the stakeholders.
4. Make a decision.

For accountants, ethical decisions most often involve understanding how their actions affect amounts reported in the financial statements. Throughout the book, we will discuss some ethical decisions related to accounting and will make clear their financial reporting impact. These discussions will give you opportunities to practice some ethical decision making in a classroom setting. You can also practice applying the four-step framework to Ethical Dilemma (like the one below) or in Ethics cases located at the end of each chapter.

ETHICAL DILEMMA

Blend Images/Hill Street Studios/ Gifford Sun/Getty Images

You have been the manager of a local restaurant for the past five years. Because of increased competition, you notice you're getting fewer customers. Despite all your attempts to attract new customers and cut costs, the restaurant's profitability continues to decline. The restaurant owner tells you that if this year's profit is lower than last year's, you'll lose your job.

When preparing financial statements at the end of the year, you notice that this year's profit *is* lower. You know that by purposely understating certain expenses, you can falsely report higher profits to the owner for this year. That will allow you to keep your job for at least one more year and look for a new job in the meantime.

What should you do? What if you really believe the lower profitability is caused by factors outside your control? Would this make the false reporting acceptable?

User's Guide
Throughout the book, you will see boxed discussions of *Ethical Dilemmas.* These dilemmas are designed to raise your awareness of accounting issues that have ethical ramifications.

CAREERS IN ACCOUNTING

PART C

Whether you plan to major in accounting or not, this section is important for you. Accounting majors need to realize the many different options available upon graduation. Those who do not plan to major in accounting need a solid understanding of the many different business decisions involving accounting information.

After completing the first course in accounting, you will have some idea whether you enjoy accounting and might like to major in it. You will also find out through exams, quizzes, and homework whether you have the aptitude to be good at it. Realize, however, that besides being good at the technical side of accounting, you will need interpersonal skills such as working well in teams, making presentations to clients, and leading co-workers in complex projects. If you do major in accounting, the job prospects are numerous.

Demand for Accounting

One of the greatest benefits of an accounting degree is the wide variety of job opportunities it opens to you. With an accounting degree, you can apply for almost any position available

CAREER CORNER

Over 20,000 employees join public accounting firms in entry-level jobs each year, and thousands more go into other areas of accounting. While financial accountants learn how to measure business transactions and prepare financial reports, they also learn a great deal about the business itself. Because of this widespread business knowledge, accountants often play a key role on the management team. In fact, it should come as no surprise to learn that most chief financial officers (CFOs) started their careers as accountants.

Accounting, because of its dynamic and professional nature, offers an attractive career option. You can learn more about a career in accounting by visiting the website of the American Institute of Certified Public Accountants (**www.aicpa.org**). There, you can look under the *Career* link to find current information about job opportunities, salaries, work life for women, how to write a resume, how to interview, and other general career advice. You can also visit (**www.thiswaytocpa.com**). For salary and other job-related information, consult the website of the U.S. Bureau of Labor Statistics (**www.bls.gov**). There are a wide variety of jobs in accounting and, therefore a wide variety of starting salaries, typically ranging from $50,000 to $70,000. The demand for accounting positions is expected to grow 6% per year for the next ten years.

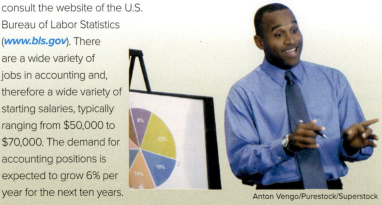

Anton Vengo/Purestock/Superstock

to finance majors. However, it doesn't work the other way: Finance majors often lack the accounting background necessary to apply for accounting positions.

For the past several years, accounting has ranked as one of the top majors on university campuses. Because of their importance in our society, accountants are in high demand. And because of this high demand, accounting salaries are on the rise. Starting salaries are among the highest of all majors across the university.

Career Options in Accounting

The first big decision a student makes as an accounting major is the choice between a career in public accounting and a career in private accounting.

PUBLIC ACCOUNTING

Public accounting firms are professional service firms that traditionally have focused on three areas: auditing, tax preparation/planning, and business consulting. We already have discussed the role of *auditors* in attesting to the conformity of companies' financial statements with GAAP. *Tax preparation/planning* is an increasingly important activity in the United States, as the complexity of tax laws related to personal and corporate taxes continues to increase. *Business consulting* is perhaps the most lucrative activity of accountants. Managers who want to better understand their companies' financial strengths and weaknesses often turn to public accountants for guidance. Who knows the business activities better than the one measuring and communicating them?

If you choose a career in public accounting, the next big decision is whether to work for one of the "Big 4" public accounting firms (**Deloitte**, **Ernst & Young**, **PricewaterhouseCoopers**, and **KPMG**) or one of the thousands of medium or smaller-sized firms. The Big 4 firms are huge, each having annual revenues in the billions. They audit almost all the Fortune 500 companies in the United States and most of the largest companies around the world, and they hire thousands of accounting majors each year. The thousands of smaller international, regional, and local accounting firms also hire thousands of accounting majors right out of college.

Most public accountants become *Certified Public Accountants (CPAs)*. You become a CPA by passing the four parts of the CPA exam and meeting minimum work experience requirements (in some states). Most states require that you have 150 semester hours (225 quarter hours) of college credit to take the exam. Becoming a CPA can provide a big boost in salary and long-term job opportunities.

PRIVATE ACCOUNTING

A career in **private accounting** means providing accounting services to the company that employs you. Every major company in the world needs employees with training and

■ **LO1–6**
Identify career opportunities in accounting.

User's Guide
Throughout the book, you will see sections titled *Career Corner*. These sections highlight a link between a particular topic and a business career, and thus are intended for both accounting majors and nonmajors.

experience in financial accounting, management accounting, taxation, internal auditing, and accounting information systems. Whereas working as a public accountant provides the advantage of experience working with a number of different clients, private accountants sometimes earn higher starting salaries. In fact, many accounting students begin their careers in public accounting, gaining experience across a wide array of companies and industries, and then eventually switch over to one of their favorite clients as private accountants. Other students take positions directly in private accounting right out of college.

Because of their special training and valuable knowledge base, both public and private accountants are expanding their roles to include the following: financial planning, information technology development, financial analysis, forensic accounting, information risk management, investment banking, environmental accounting, tax law, FBI work, management consulting, and much, much more. Illustration 1–14 outlines just a few of the many career options in public and private accounting. In addition, there are career opportunities in government accounting and education.

	Public Accounting (Big 4 and Non-Big 4)	Private Accounting
Who are the clients?	Corporations Governments Nonprofit organizations Individuals	Your particular employer
What are the traditional career opportunities?	Auditors Tax preparers/planners Business consultants	Financial accountants Managerial accountants Internal auditors Tax preparers Payroll managers
What other career opportunities are available?	Financial planners Information technology developers Financial analysts Forensic accountants Information risk managers Investment bankers Environmental accountants Financial advisors Tax lawyers	Information managers Management advisors Tax planners Acquisition specialists FBI agents Sports agents

ILLUSTRATION 1–14

Some of the Career Options in Accounting

KEY POINT

Because of the high demand for accounting graduates, wide range of job opportunities, and increasing salaries, this is a great time to obtain a degree in accounting.

CONCEPTUAL FRAMEWORK

APPENDIX

■ **LO1–7**

Explain the nature of the conceptual framework used to develop generally accepted accounting principles.

The FASB establishes financial accounting standards based on a **conceptual framework**, which you can think of as the "theory" of accounting. In much the same way that our nation's Constitution provides the underlying principles that guide the "correctness" of all laws, the FASB's conceptual framework prescribes the correctness of financial accounting rules. Having a conceptual framework provides standard setters with a benchmark for creating a consistent set of financial reporting rules now and in the future. It also provides others with a *written* framework so that everyone understands the underlying concepts that accountants are to consider in preparing and interpreting financial accounting information.

 **KEY POINT**

The conceptual framework provides an underlying foundation for the development of accounting standards and interpretation of accounting information.

In the chapter, we discussed the three objectives of financial accounting as outlined in the FASB's conceptual framework. Financial accounting should provide information that:

1. Is useful to investors and creditors in making decisions.
2. Helps to predict cash flows.
3. Tells about economic resources, claims to resources, and changes in resources and claims.

To satisfy these stated objectives, financial reporting of accounting information should possess certain characteristics to be useful. What are the desired characteristics? Illustration 1–15 provides a graphical depiction of the qualitative characteristics of useful financial information.

ILLUSTRATION 1–15   Qualitative Characteristics of Useful Financial Information

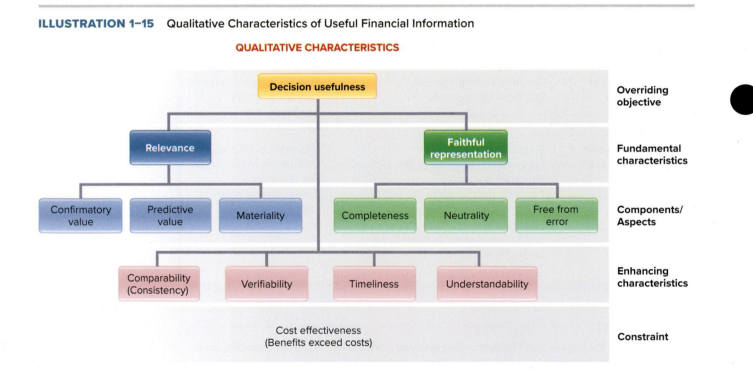

Notice that at the top of the figure is **decision usefulness**—the ability of the information to be useful in decision making. Accounting information should help investors, lenders, and other creditors make important decisions about providing funds to a company.

FUNDAMENTAL QUALITATIVE CHARACTERISTICS

The two fundamental decision-specific qualitative characteristics that make accounting information useful are *relevance* and *faithful representation.* Both are critical. No matter how representative, if information is not relevant to the decision at hand, it is useless. Conversely, relevant information is of little value if it does not faithfully represent the underlying activity.

Relevance.   To have *relevance*, accounting information should possess *confirmatory value* and/or *predictive value*. Generally, useful information will possess both of these components. For example, the ability of **Nike** to report a positive net income confirms that its management is effectively and efficiently using the company's resources to sell quality products. In this case, net income has *confirmatory value*. At the same time, reporting a positive and growing net income for several consecutive years should provide information that has *predictive value* for the company's future cash-generating ability.

Materiality reflects the impact of financial accounting information on investors' and creditors' decisions. Unless an item is material in amount or nature—that is, sufficient in amount or nature to affect a decision—it need not be reported in accordance with GAAP. Based on the concept of materiality, Nike probably does not record all its assets as assets. Most companies record assets such as wastebaskets and staplers as *expenses*, even though these items will benefit the company for a long period. Recording a $6 wastebasket as a current expense instead of a long-term asset for a multibillion-dollar company like Nike has no impact on investors' decisions. Thus, materiality is an aspect of the relevance characteristic with regard to values users deem significant in their decision-making process.

Faithful Representation.   To be a *faithful representation* of business activities, accounting information should be complete, neutral, and free from error. *Completeness* means including all information necessary for faithful representation of the business activity the firm is reporting. For example, when Nike reports inventory in its balance sheet, investors understand it to represent *all* items (and only those items) that are intended for sale to customers in the ordinary course of business. If the amount reported for inventory includes only some of the items to be sold, then it lacks completeness. Adequate note disclosure is another important component of completeness. Nike must disclose in the notes to the financial statements the method it used to calculate inventory reported on its balance sheet. (We discuss alternative inventory methods in Chapter 6.)

Neutrality means to be unbiased, and this characteristic is highly related to the establishment of accounting standards. Because of the topic and the nature of the business, sometimes a new accounting standard may affect one group of companies over others. In such cases, the FASB must convince the financial community that this was a *consequence* of the standard, and not an *objective* used to set the standard. For example, the FASB requires that all research and development (R&D) costs be reported as an expense in the income statement, reducing the current year's net income. The FASB's objective in adopting this approach was not to weaken the financial appearance of those companies in R&D-intensive industries, such as telecommunications, pharmaceuticals, and software, even though that may have been an effect.

Free from error indicates that reported amounts reflect the best available information. As you'll come to find out in this course, some amounts reported in the financial statements are based on estimates, and the accuracy of those estimates is subject to uncertainty. Because of this, financial statements are not expected to be completely free of error, but they are expected to reflect management's unbiased judgments and due diligence in reflecting appropriate accounting principles.

 KEY POINT

To be useful for decision making, accounting information should have relevance and faithful representation.

ENHANCING QUALITATIVE CHARACTERISTICS

Four enhancing qualitative characteristics are comparability, verifiability, timeliness, and understandability. **Comparability** refers to the ability of users to see similarities and differences between two different business activities. For example, how does **Nike**'s net income compare with net income for other sports apparel companies such as **Under Armour**? Comparability also refers to the ability of users to see similarities and differences in the same company over time. How does Nike's net income this year compare to last year's? Closely related to the notion of comparability is consistency. **Consistency** refers to the use of similar accounting procedures either over time for the same company or across companies at the same point in time. Comparability of financial information is the overriding goal, while consistency of accounting procedures is a means of achieving that goal.

Verifiability implies a consensus among different measurers. For instance, different graders will arrive at the same exam score for multiple-choice tests, but they are more likely to differ in scoring essay exams. Multiple-choice tests are highly verifiable. The same idea holds in the business world. For example, the price Nike pays to purchase a trademark of another company is usually verifiable because there is an exchange of cash at a certain point in time. In contrast, the value of a patent for a new product or design that Nike develops internally over an extended period is more subjective and less verifiable.

Firms must also disclose information related to net income that is *timely*. **Timeliness** refers to information being available to users early enough to allow them to use it in the decision process. Large companies like Nike are required to report information related to net income within 40 days after the end of the quarter and within 60 days after the end of the year.

Understandability means that users must be able to understand the information within the context of the decision they are making. This is a user-specific quality because users will differ in their ability to comprehend any set of information.

 KEY POINT

Four characteristics of financial reporting enhance its usefulness. These characteristics include comparability, verifiability, timeliness, and understandability.

COST CONSTRAINT

Sometimes, certain information involves more time and effort than the information is worth. For example, if a friend asks what you did today, she probably wants to know the general outline of your day, but does not want to hear a recital of every move you made. Similarly, there may be a cost constraint (limit) to reporting financial information.

The **cost constraint** suggests that financial accounting information is provided only when the benefits of doing so exceed the costs. For example, knowing the profit margin earned by Nike in each country provides decision-useful information to investors and creditors. However, this information is also helpful to the company's current and potential competitors, such as Under Armour, as it makes its own expansion plans. The competitive costs of providing this information may outweigh the benefits.

UNDERLYING ASSUMPTIONS

For the qualitative characteristics described above to be applied to accounting information, four basic assumptions must be made to support the existence of GAAP. As pictured in Illustration 1–16, they are (1) the economic entity assumption, (2) the monetary unit assumption, (3) the periodicity assumption, and (4) the going concern assumption.

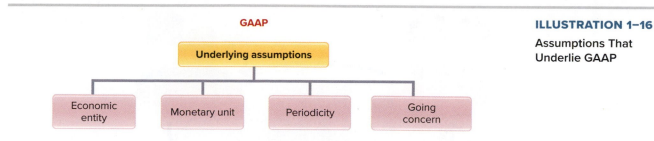

ILLUSTRATION 1–16

Assumptions That Underlie GAAP

Economic Entity Assumption. The economic entity assumption states that we can identify all economic events with a particular economic entity. In other words, only business transactions involving Nike should be reported as part of Nike's financial accounting information. Another key aspect of this assumption is the distinction between the economic activities of owners and those of the company. For example, Nike co-founder and chairman Phil Knight's personal residence is not an asset of Nike, Inc.

Monetary Unit Assumption. Information would be difficult to use if, for example, we listed assets as "three machines, two trucks, and a building." According to the monetary unit assumption, in order to *measure* financial statement elements, we need a unit or scale of measurement. The dollar in the United States is the most appropriate common denominator to express information about financial statement elements and changes in those elements. In Europe, the common denominator is the euro. Nike has operations throughout the world, so it must translate all its financial information to U.S. dollars under the monetary unit assumption.

Periodicity Assumption. The periodicity assumption relates to the qualitative characteristic of *timeliness.* External users need *periodic* information to make decisions. The periodicity assumption divides the economic life of an enterprise (presumed to be indefinite) into artificial time periods for periodic financial reporting. Corporations like Nike, whose securities are publicly traded, are required to provide financial information to the SEC on a quarterly *and* an annual basis. Quarterly reports are more timely, while annual reports allow the full application of GAAP.

Going Concern Assumption. The going concern assumption states that in the absence of information to the contrary, a business entity will continue to operate indefinitely. This assumption is critical to many broad and specific accounting principles. It provides justification for measuring many assets based on their original costs (a practice known as the *historical cost principle*). If we knew an enterprise was going to cease operations in the near future, we would measure assets and liabilities not at their original costs but at their current liquidation values.

CHAPTER FRAMEWORK

A Framework for Financial Accounting

Measurement and Communication. Two primary functions of financial accounting are to *measure* activities of a company and *communicate* those measurements to investors and other people for making decisions. The measurement process involves recording transactions into accounts. The balances of these accounts are used to communicate information in the four primary financial statements. For more detailed illustrations of financial statements, see the corresponding illustrations in the chapter. A comprehensive list of accounts used to measure activities is provided at the end of this book.

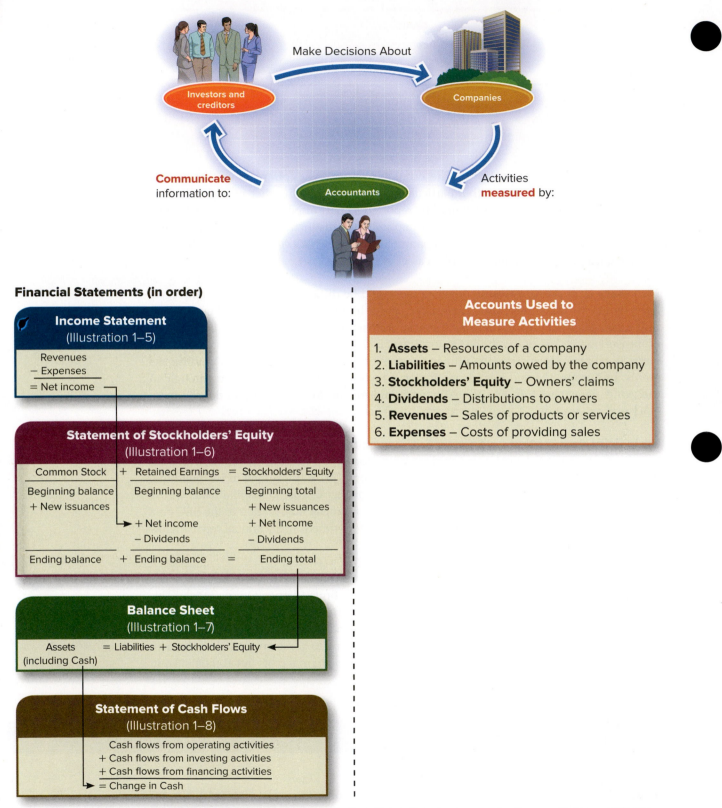

Financial Statements (in order)

Income Statement
(Illustration 1–5)

| Revenues |
| − Expenses |
| = Net income |

Statement of Stockholders' Equity
(Illustration 1–6)

Common Stock	+	Retained Earnings	=	Stockholders' Equity
Beginning balance		Beginning balance		Beginning total
+ New issuances				+ New issuances
		+ Net income		+ Net income
		− Dividends		− Dividends
Ending balance	+	Ending balance	=	Ending total

Balance Sheet
(Illustration 1–7)

| Assets (including Cash) | = Liabilities + Stockholders' Equity |

Statement of Cash Flows
(Illustration 1–8)

| Cash flows from operating activities |
| + Cash flows from investing activities |
| + Cash flows from financing activities |
| = Change in Cash |

Accounts Used to Measure Activities

1. **Assets** – Resources of a company
2. **Liabilities** – Amounts owed by the company
3. **Stockholders' Equity** – Owners' claims
4. **Dividends** – Distributions to owners
5. **Revenues** – Sales of products or services
6. **Expenses** – Costs of providing sales

Decision Making.   The procedures that dictate how to measure business activities and how to communicate those measurements through financial statements to decision makers are known as generally accepted accounting principles (GAAP). In the United States, GAAP is established primarily by the Financial Accounting Standards Board (FASB). The objectives of financial accounting are to provide information that:

1. Is useful to investors and creditors in making decisions.
2. Helps to predict cash flows.
3. Tells about the economic resources, claims to resources, and changes in resources.

Chapter Framework Questions

1. **Measurement:** The resources of a company are referred to as
   a. Stockholders' equity.
   b. Dividends.
   c. Liabilities.
   d. Assets.

2. **Measurement:** Revenues refer to
   a. Resources of the company.
   b. Sales of products or services.
   c. Amounts owed by the company.
   d. Amounts owed to the company.

3. **Communication (income statement):** Information reported in the income statement includes
   a. Cash flows from operating, investing, and financing equal the change in cash.
   b. Assets equal liabilities plus stockholders' equity.
   c. Revenues minus expenses equal net income.
   d. The change in common stock and change in retained earnings equal the change in total stockholders' equity.

4. **Communication (balance sheet):** Information reported in the balance sheet includes
   a. Cash flows from operating, investing, and financing activities equal the change in cash.
   b. Assets equal liabilities plus stockholders' equity.
   c. Revenues minus expenses equal net income.
   d. The change in common stock and change in retained earnings equal the change in total stockholders' equity.

5. **Decision making:** The objective(s) of financial accounting is (are) to provide information that
   a. Is useful to investors and creditors in making decisions.
   b. Helps to predict cash flows.
   c. Tells about the economic resources, claims to resources, and changes in resources.
   d. All of the above are objectives of financial accounting.

Note: For answers, see the last page of the chapter.

KEY POINTS BY LEARNING OBJECTIVE

LO1–1   Describe the two primary functions of financial accounting.

The two primary functions of financial accounting are to measure business activities of a company and to communicate information about those activities to investors and creditors and other outside users for decision-making purposes.

LO1–2   Understand the business activities that financial accounting measures.

The measurement role of accounting is to create a record of the activities of a company. To make this possible, a company must maintain an accurate record of its assets, liabilities, stockholders' equity, revenues, expenses, and dividends.

LO1–3   Determine how financial accounting information is communicated through financial statements.

The income statement compares revenues and expenses for the current period to assess the company's ability to generate a profit from running its operations.

The statement of stockholders' equity reports information related to changes in common stock and retained earnings each period. The change in retained earnings equals net income less dividends for the period.

The balance sheet demonstrates that the company's resources (assets) equal creditors' claims (liabilities) plus owners' claims (stockholders' equity) to those resources on a particular date.

The statement of cash flows reports cash transactions from operating, investing, and financing activities for the period.

All transactions that affect revenues or expenses reported in the income statement ultimately affect the balance sheet through the balance in retained earnings.

LO1–4 **Describe the role that financial accounting plays in the decision-making process.**

Financial accounting serves an important role by providing information useful in investment and lending decisions.

No single piece of company information better explains companies' stock price performance than does financial accounting net income. A company's debt level is an important indicator of management's ability to respond to business situations and the possibility of bankruptcy.

LO1–5 **Explain the term generally accepted accounting principles (GAAP) and describe the role of GAAP in financial accounting.**

The rules of financial accounting are called generally accepted accounting principles (GAAP). The Financial Accounting Standards Board (FASB) is an independent, private body that has primary responsibility for the establishment of GAAP in the United States.

The primary objective of financial accounting is to provide useful information to investors and creditors in making decisions.

LO1–6 **Identify career opportunities in accounting.**

Because of the high demand for accounting graduates, the wide range of job opportunities, and increasing salaries, this is a great time to obtain a degree in accounting.

Appendix

LO1–7 **Explain the nature of the conceptual framework used to develop generally accepted accounting principles.**

The conceptual framework provides an underlying foundation for the development of accounting standards and interpretation of accounting information.

To be useful for decision making, accounting information should have relevance (confirmatory value, predictive value, and materiality) and faithful representation (completeness, neutrality, and free from error).

Four characteristics of financial reporting enhance its usefulness. These characteristics include comparability, verifiability, timeliness, and understandability.

GLOSSARY

Account: A record of the business activities related to a particular item. **p. 10**

Accounting: A system of maintaining records of a company's operations and communicating that information to decision makers. **p. 4**

Accounting equation: Equation that shows a company's resources (assets) equal creditors' and owners' claims to those resources (liabilities and stockholders' equity). **p. 7**

Assets: Resources of a company. **p. 7**

Auditors: Trained individuals hired by a company as an independent party to express a professional opinion of the conformity of that company's financial statements with GAAP. **p. 23**

Balance sheet: A financial statement that presents the financial position of the company on a particular date. **p. 12**

Common stock: Amounts invested by stockholders when they purchase shares of stock; external source of equity. **p. 11**

Comparability: The ability of users to see similarities and differences between two different business activities. **p. 29**

Consistency: The use of similar accounting procedures either over time for the same company, or across companies at the same point in time. **p. 30**

Corporation: An entity that is legally separate from its owners. **p. 6**

Cost constraint: Financial accounting information is provided only when the benefits of doing so exceed the costs. **p. 30**

Creditors: Lend money to a company, expecting to be paid back the loan amount plus interest. **p. 6**

Decision usefulness: The ability of the information to be useful in decision making. **p. 28**

Dividends: Distributions to stockholders, typically in the form of cash. **p. 8**

Economic entity assumption: All economic events with a particular economic entity can be identified. **p. 31**

Ethics: A code or moral system that provides criteria for evaluating right and wrong behavior. **p. 24**

Expenses: Costs of providing products and services and other business activities during the current period. **p. 8**

Faithful representation: Accounting information that is complete, neutral, and free from error. **p. 29**

Financial accounting: Measurement of business activities of a company and communication of those measurements to external parties for decision-making purposes. **p. 4**

Financial Accounting Standards Board (FASB): An independent, private body that has primary responsibility for the establishment of GAAP in the United States. **p. 21**

Financial statements: Periodic reports published by the company for the purpose of providing information to external users. **p. 9**

Generally accepted accounting principles (GAAP): The rules of financial accounting. **p. 21**

Going concern assumption: In the absence of information to the contrary, a business entity will continue to operate indefinitely. **p. 31**

Income statement: A financial statement that reports the company's revenues and expenses over an interval of time. **p. 10**

International Accounting Standards Board (IASB): An international accounting standard-setting body responsible for the convergence of accounting standards worldwide. **p. 21**

International Financial Reporting Standards (IFRS): The standards being developed and promoted by the International Accounting Standards Board. **p. 22**

Liabilities: Amounts owed to creditors. **p. 7**

Monetary unit assumption: A unit or scale of measurement can be used to measure financial statement elements. **p. 31**

Net income: Difference between revenues and expenses. **p. 8**

Partnership: Business owned by two or more persons. **p. 6**

Periodicity assumption: The economic life of an enterprise (presumed to be indefinite) can be divided into artificial time periods for financial reporting. **p. 31**

Relevance: Accounting information that possesses confirmatory value and/or predictive value, and that is material. **p. 29**

Retained earnings: All net income minus all dividends over the life of the company; internal source of equity. **p. 11**

Revenues: Amounts recognized when the company sells products or services to customers. **p. 8**

Sarbanes-Oxley Act (SOX): Formally titled the Public Company Accounting Reform and Investor Protection Act of 2002, this act provides regulation of auditors and the types of services they furnish to clients, increases accountability of corporate executives, addresses conflicts of interest for securities analysts, and provides for stiff criminal penalties for violators. **p. 24**

Sole proprietorship: A business owned by one person. **p. 6**

Statement of cash flows: A financial statement that measures activities involving cash receipts and cash payments over an interval of time. **p. 14**

Statement of stockholders' equity: A financial statement that summarizes the changes in stockholders' equity over an interval of time. **p. 11**

Stockholders' equity: Owners' claims to resources, which arise primarily from contributions by the owners and company operations. **p. 7**

Timeliness: Information being available to users early enough to allow them to use it in the decision process. **p. 30**

Understandability: Users must understand the information within the context of the decision they are making. **p. 30**

Verifiability: A consensus among different measurers. **p. 30**

SELF-STUDY QUESTIONS

1. Based on the introductory section of this chapter, which course is most like financial accounting? **(LO1–1)**
   a. College algebra.
   b. Foreign language.
   c. Molecular biology.
   d. Physical education.

2. Based on the introductory section of this chapter, financial accounting also can be described as a way to **(LO1–1)**
   a. Tell the financial story of a company.
   b. Calculate the amount of taxes owed to the government.
   c. Determine employee satisfaction with their work environment.
   d. Measure the personal net worth of stockholders.

3. Financial accounting serves which primary function(s)? **(LO1–1)**
   a. Measures business activities.
   b. Communicates business activities to interested parties.
   c. Makes business decisions on behalf of interested parties.
   d. Both *a.* and *b.* are functions of financial accounting.

4. Resources of a company are referred to as **(LO1–2)**
   a. Liabilities.
   b. Stockholders' equity.
   c. Dividends.
   d. Assets.

5. Sales of products or services are referred to as **(LO1–2)**
   a. Assets.
   b. Revenues.
   c. Liabilities.
   d. Expenses.

6. Amounts owed by the company are referred to as **(LO1–2)**
   a. Expenses.
   b. Dividends.
   c. Liabilities.
   d. Assets.

7. Which financial statement conveys a company's ability to generate profits in the current period? **(LO1–3)**
   a. Income statement.
   b. Statement of cash flows.
   c. Balance sheet.
   d. Statement of stockholders' equity.

8. Which financial statement shows that a company's resources equal claims to those resources? **(LO1–3)**
   a. Income statement.
   b. Statement of stockholders' equity.
   c. Balance sheet.
   d. Statement of cash flows.

9. A company reports the following in its income statement: Total revenues of $500,000 and total expenses of $300,000. Which of the following is true? **(LO1–3)**
   a. Net income equals $200,000.
   b. Total dividends equal $200,000.
   c. Total assets equal $200,000.
   d. Total stockholders' equity equals $200,000.

10. A company reports the following in its balance sheet: Total assets of $800,000 and total liabilities of $700,000. Which of the following is true? **(LO1–3)**
    a. Net income equals $100,000.
    b. Total expenses equal $1,500,000.
    c. Total revenues equal $1,500,000.
    d. Total stockholders' equity equals $100,000.

11. Why does financial accounting have a positive impact on our society? **(LO1–4)**

   a. It entails a detailed transaction record necessary for filing taxes with the Internal Revenue Service (IRS).

   b. It allows investors and creditors to redirect their resources to successful companies and away from unsuccessful companies.

   c. It prevents competitors from being able to steal the company's customers.

   d. It provides a system of useful internal reports for management decision making.

12. The body of rules and procedures that guide the measurement and communication of financial accounting information is known as **(LO1–5)**

   a. Standards of professional compliance (SPC).

   b. Code of ethical decisions (COED).

   c. Rules of financial reporting (RFP).

   d. Generally accepted accounting principles (GAAP).

13. Financial accounting and reporting standards in the United States are established primarily by the **(LO1–5)**

   a. Securities and Exchange Commission (SEC).

   b. Financial Accounting Standards Board (FASB).

   c. International Accounting Standards Board (IASB).

   d. The U.S. Congress.

14. What is a benefit to a career in accounting? **(LO1–6)**

   a. High salaries.

   b. Wide range of job opportunities.

   c. High demand for accounting graduates.

   d. All of these answer choices are correct.

15. What are the two fundamental qualitative characteristics identified by the Financial Accounting Standards Board's (FASB) conceptual framework? **(LO1–7)**

   a. Relevance and faithful representation.

   b. Materiality and efficiency.

   c. Comparability and consistency.

   d. Costs and benefits.

Note: For answers, see the last page of the chapter.

DATA ANALYTICS & EXCEL

Visit Connect to find a variety of Data Analytics questions that help build Excel, Tableau, and data visualization skills. Assignable materials include Integrated Excel, Applying Excel, Data Visualizations, Tableau Dashboard Activities, and Applying Tableau Cases.

REVIEW QUESTIONS

■ **LO1–1**   1. Explain what it means to say that an accounting class is not the same as a math class.

■ **LO1–1**   2. Identify some of the people interested in making decisions about a company.

■ **LO1–1**   3. What is the basic difference between financial accounting and managerial accounting?

■ **LO1–1**   4. What are the two primary functions of financial accounting?

■ **LO1–2**   5. What are the three basic business activities that financial accounting seeks to measure and communicate to external parties? Define each.

■ **LO1–2**   6. What are a few of the typical financing activities for a company like **United Parcel Service, Inc. (UPS)**, the world's largest package delivery company and a leading global provider of specialized transportation and logistics services?

■ **LO1–2**   7. What are a few of the typical investing activities for a company like **Caesars Entertainment**, developer and operator of high-end hotels and casinos?

■ **LO1–2**   8. What are a few of the typical operating activities for a company like **Oracle Corporation**, one of the world's leading suppliers of software for information management?

■ **LO1–2**   9. What are the three major legal forms of business organizations? Which one is chosen by most of the largest companies in the United States?

■ **LO1–2**   10. Provide the basic definition for each of the account types: assets, liabilities, stockholders' equity, dividends, revenues, and expenses.

■ **LO1–2**   11. What are the major advantages and disadvantages of each of the legal forms of business organizations?

■ **LO1–3**   12. What are the four primary financial statements? What basic information is shown on each?

13. What does it mean to say that the income statement, statement of stockholders' equity, and statement of cash flows measure activity over an *interval of time,* but the balance sheet measures activity at a *point in time?*   ■ LO1–3

14. Give some examples of the basic revenues and expenses for a company like **The Walt Disney Company**.   ■ LO1–3

15. What is the accounting equation? Which financial statement reports the accounting equation?   ■ LO1–3

16. Give some examples of the basic assets and liabilities of a company like **Walmart**.   ■ LO1–3

17. "The retained earnings account is a link between the income statement and the balance sheet." Explain what this means.   ■ LO1–3

18. What are the three types of cash flows reported in the statement of cash flows? Give an example of each type of activity for a company like **Oakley, Inc.**, a designer, manufacturer, and distributor of high-performance eyewear, footwear, watches, and athletic equipment.   ■ LO1–3

19. In addition to financial statements, what are some other ways to disclose financial information to external users?   ■ LO1–3

20. How does financial accounting have an impact on society?   ■ LO1–4

21. What is meant by GAAP? Why should companies follow GAAP in reporting to external users?   ■ LO1–5

22. Which body is primarily responsible for the establishment of GAAP in the United States? What body serves this function on an international basis?   ■ LO1–5

23. In general terms, explain the terms U.S. GAAP and IFRS.   ■ LO1–5

24. What was the primary reason for the establishment of the 1933 Securities Act and the 1934 Securities Exchange Act? What power does the Securities and Exchange Commission (SEC) have?   ■ LO1–5

25. What is the role of the auditor in the financial reporting process?   ■ LO1–5

26. According to FASB, what are the three primary objectives of financial reporting?   ■ LO1–5

27. What are some of the benefits to obtaining a degree in accounting? What is the difference between a career in public accounting and private accounting? What are some of the traditional careers of accounting graduates? What new areas are accountants expanding into?   ■ LO1–6

28. Discuss the terms *relevance* and *faithful representation* as they relate to financial accounting information.   ■ LO1–7

29. What are the three components/aspects of relevance? What are the three components/aspects of faithful representation?   ■ LO1–7

30. What is meant by the term *cost effectiveness* in financial reporting?   ■ LO1–7

31. Define the four basic assumptions underlying GAAP.   ■ LO1–7

BRIEF EXERCISES

BE1–1 Indicate whether the definition provided is true or false.

Define accounting **(LO1–1)**

(True/False) Accounting can be defined as:

1. _____ The language of business.
2. _____ A measurement/communication process.
3. _____ A mathematics course.

BE1–2 Match each business activity with its description.

Identify the different types of business activities **(LO1–2)**

Business Activities	Descriptions
1. _____ Financing	a. Transactions related to revenues and expenses.
2. _____ Investing	b. Transactions with lenders and owners.
3. _____ Operating	c. Transactions involving the purchase and sale of productive assets.

BE1–3 Match each form of business organization with its description.

Business Organizations	Descriptions
1. _____ Sole proprietorship	a. Business owned by two or more persons.
2. _____ Partnership	b. Entity legally separate from its owners.
3. _____ Corporation	c. Business owned by a single person.

BE1–4 Match each account type with its description.

Account Classifications	Descriptions
1. _____ Assets	a. Sales of products or services.
2. _____ Liabilities	b. Owners' claims to resources.
3. _____ Stockholders' equity	c. Distributions to stockholders.
4. _____ Dividends	d. Costs of selling products or services.
5. _____ Revenues	e. Resources of a company.
6. _____ Expenses	f. Amounts owed.

BE1–5 For each transaction, indicate whether each account would be classified in the balance sheet as (a) an asset, (b) a liability, or (c) stockholders' equity; in the income statement as (d) a revenue or (e) an expense; or in the statement of stockholders' equity as (f) a dividend.

Account Classifications	Accounts	Related Transactions
1. _____	Rent expense	Cost of rent.
2. _____	Interest revenue	Interest earned on savings account.
3. _____	Dividends	Cash payments to stockholders.
4. _____	Land	Land used for operations.
5. _____	Accounts payable	Amounts owed to suppliers.

BE1–6 For each transaction, indicate whether each account would be classified in the balance sheet as (a) an asset, (b) a liability, or (c) stockholders' equity; in the income statement as (d) a revenue or (e) an expense; or in the statement of stockholders' equity as (f) a dividend.

Account Classifications	Accounts	Related Transactions
1. _____	Utilities payable	Amounts owed for utilities.
2. _____	Cash	Cash available for use.
3. _____	Salaries expense	Cost of salaries.
4. _____	Common stock	Shares of ownership sold to investors.
5. _____	Service revenue	Sale of services to customers.

BE1–7 Match each financial statement with its description.

Financial Statements	Related Transactions
1. _____ Income statement	a. Change in owners' claims to resources.
2. _____ Statement of stockholders' equity	b. Profitability of the company.
3. _____ Balance sheet	c. Change in cash as a result of operating, investing, and financing activities.
4. _____ Statement of cash flows	d. Resources equal creditors' and owners' claims to those resources.

BE1–8 Determine on which financial statement you find the following items.

Financial Statements	Items
1. _____ Income statement	a. The change in retained earnings due to net income and dividends.
2. _____ Statement of stockholders' equity	b. Amount of cash received from borrowing money from a local bank.
3. _____ Balance sheet	c. Revenue from sales to customers during the year.
4. _____ Statement of cash flows	d. Total amounts owed to workers at the end of the year.

BE1–9 Each of these parties plays a role in the quality of financial reporting. Match each group with its function.

Identify different groups engaged in providing high-quality financial reporting (LO1–5)

Groups	Functions
1. _____ Financial Accounting Standards Board	a. Group that has been given power by Congress to enforce the proper application of financial reporting rules for companies whose securities are publicly traded.
2. _____ International Accounting Standards Board	b. Independent, private-sector group that is primarily responsible for setting financial reporting standards in the United States.
3. _____ Securities and Exchange Commission	c. Independent intermediaries that help to ensure that management appropriately applies financial reporting rules in preparing the company's financial statements.
4. _____ Auditors	d. Body that is attempting to develop a single set of high-quality, understandable global accounting standards.

BE1–10 Indicate which of the following are objectives of financial accounting.

Identify the objectives of financial accounting (LO1–5)

(Yes/No)	Objectives
1. _____	Provide information that is useful to investors and creditors.
2. _____	Guarantee that businesses will not go bankrupt.
3. _____	Provide information about resources and claims to resources.
4. _____	Prevent competitors from offering lower-priced products.
5. _____	Provide information to help users in predicting future cash flows.
6. _____	Maximize tax revenue to the federal government.

BE1–11 Below are possible career opportunities for those earning a degree in accounting. Indicate whether the statement related to each career is true or false.

Identify careers for accounting majors (LO1–6)

(True/False)	Someone earning a degree in accounting could pursue the following career:
1. _____	Auditor
2. _____	Tax preparer
3. _____	Business consultant
4. _____	Financial planner
5. _____	Forensic investigator
6. _____	Tax planner
7. _____	Financial analyst
8. _____	Information technology developer
9. _____	Investment banker
10. _____	Tax lawyer
11. _____	FBI agent
12. _____	Information risk manager

Identify the
components/aspects of
relevance **(LO1–7)**

BE1–12 Match each of the components of relevance with its definition.

Relevance	Definitions
1 ._____ Confirmatory value	a. Information is useful in helping to forecast future outcomes.
2 ._____ Predictive value	
3 ._____ Materiality	b. Information provides feedback on past activities.
	c. The nature or amount of an item has the ability to affect decisions.

Identify the components/
aspects of faithful
representation **(LO1–7)**

BE1–13 Match each of the components of faithful representation with its definition.

Faithful Representation	Definition
1 ._____ Free from error	a. All information necessary to describe an item is reported.
2 ._____ Neutrality	
3 ._____ Completeness	b. Information that does not bias the decision maker.
	c. Reported amounts reflect the best available information.

EXERCISES

Identify the different
types of business
activities **(LO1–2)**

E1–1 The following provides a list of transactions and a list of business activities.

Transactions	Business Activities
1. _____ Borrow from the bank.	a. Financing
2. _____ Provide services to customers.	b. Investing
3. _____ Issue common stock to investors.	c. Operating
4. _____ Purchase land.	
5. _____ Pay rent for the current period.	
6. _____ Pay dividends to stockholders.	
7. _____ Purchase building.	

Required:

Match the transaction with the business activity by indicating the letter that corresponds to the appropriate business activity.

Identify account
classifications and
business activities **(LO1–2)**

Flip Side of E1–3

E1–2 Falcon Incorporated has the following transactions with Wildcat Corporation.

Transactions	Falcon's Related Account
1. Falcon purchases common stock of Wildcat.	Investment
2. Falcon borrows from Wildcat by signing a note.	Notes payable
3. Falcon provides services to Wildcat.	Service revenue
4. Falcon pays interest to Wildcat on borrowing.	Interest expense

Required:

1. For each transaction, indicate whether Falcon would report the related account in the balance sheet or income statement.
2. For accounts in the balance sheet, indicate whether it would be classified as an asset, liability, or stockholders' equity. For accounts in the income statement, indicate whether it would be classified as a revenue or an expense.
3. Indicate whether each transaction is classified as operating, investing, or financing activity.

Identify account
classifications and
business activities **(LO1–2)**

Flip Side of E1–2

E1–3 The transactions in this problem are identical to those in E1–2, but now with a focus on Wildcat.

Transactions	Wildcat's Related Account
1. Wildcat issues common stock to Falcon.	Common stock
2. Wildcat lends to Falcon by accepting a note.	Notes receivable
3. Wildcat receives services from Falcon.	Service fee expense
4. Wildcat receives interest from Falcon on lending.	Interest revenue

Required:
1. For each transaction, indicate whether Wildcat would report the related account in the balance sheet or income statement.
2. For accounts in the balance sheet, indicate whether it would be classified as an asset, liability, or stockholders' equity. For accounts in the income statement, indicate whether it would be classified as a revenue or an expense.
3. Indicate whether each transaction is classified as operating, investing, or financing activity.

E1–4 Eagle Corp. operates magnetic resonance imaging (MRI) clinics throughout the Northeast. At the end of the current period, the company reports the following amounts: Assets = $50,000; Liabilities = $27,000; Dividends = $3,000; Revenues = $14,000; Expenses = $9,000.

Calculate net income and stockholders' equity (LO1–2)

Required:
1. Calculate net income.
2. Calculate stockholders' equity at the end of the period.

E1–5 Cougar's Accounting Services provides low-cost tax advice and preparation to those with financial need. At the end of the current period, the company reports the following amounts: Assets = $19,000; Liabilities = $15,000; Revenues = $28,000; Expenses = $33,000.

Calculate net loss and stockholders' equity (LO1–2)

Required:
1. Calculate net loss.
2. Calculate stockholders' equity at the end of the period.

E1–6 Below are the account balances for Cowboy Law Firm at the end of December.

Prepare an income statement (LO1–3)

Accounts	Balances
Cash	$ 5,400
Salaries expense	2,200
Accounts payable	3,400
Retained earnings	3,900
Utilities expense	1,200
Supplies	13,800
Service revenue	9,300
Common stock	6,000

Required:
Use only the appropriate accounts to prepare an income statement.

E1–7 At the beginning of the year (January 1), Buffalo Drilling has $11,000 of common stock outstanding and retained earnings of $8,200. During the year, Buffalo reports net income of $8,500 and pays dividends of $3,200. In addition, Buffalo issues additional common stock for $8,000.

Prepare a statement of stockholders' equity (LO1–3)

Required:
Prepare the statement of stockholders' equity at the end of the year (December 31).

E1–8 Wolfpack Construction has the following account balances at the end of the year.

Prepare a balance sheet (LO1–3)

Accounts	Balances
Equipment	$26,000
Accounts payable	3,000
Salaries expense	33,000
Common stock	11,000
Land	18,000
Notes payable	20,000
Service revenue	39,000
Cash	6,000
Retained earnings	?

Required:
Use only the appropriate accounts to prepare a balance sheet.

Prepare a statement of cash flows (LO1–3)

E1–9 Tiger Trade has the following cash transactions for the period.

Accounts	Amounts
Cash received from sale of products to customers	$ 40,000
Cash received from the bank for long-term loan	45,000
Cash paid to purchase factory equipment	(50,000)
Cash paid to merchandise suppliers	(12,000)
Cash received from the sale of an unused warehouse	13,000
Cash paid to workers	(24,000)
Cash paid for advertisement	(4,000)
Cash received for sale of services to customers	30,000
Cash paid for dividends to stockholders	(6,000)

Required:
1. Calculate the ending balance of cash, assuming the balance of cash at the beginning of the period is $5,000.
2. Prepare a statement of cash flows.

Link the income statement to the statement of stockholders' equity (LO1–3)

E1–10 On December 31, 2024, Fighting Okra Cooking Services reports the following revenues and expenses.

Service revenue	$75,000	Rent expense	$10,600
Postage expense	1,500	Salaries expense	24,000
Legal fees expense	2,400	Supplies expense	14,500

In addition, the balance of common stock at the beginning of the year was $200,000, and the balance of retained earnings was $32,000. During the year, the company issued additional shares of common stock for $25,000 and paid dividends of $10,000.

Required:
1. Prepare an income statement.
2. Prepare a statement of stockholders' equity.

Link the statement of stockholders' equity to the balance sheet (LO1–3)

E1–11 At the beginning of 2024, Artichoke Academy reported a balance in common stock of $150,000 and a balance in retained earnings of $50,000. During the year, the company issued additional shares of stock for $40,000, earned net income of $30,000, and paid dividends of $10,000. In addition, the company reported balances for the following assets and liabilities on December 31.

Assets		Liabilities	
Cash	$ 52,600	Accounts payable	$ 9,100
Supplies	13,400	Utilities payable	2,400
Prepaid rent	24,000	Salaries payable	3,500
Land	200,000	Notes payable	15,000

Required:
1. Prepare a statement of stockholders' equity.
2. Prepare a balance sheet.

E1–12 Squirrel Tree Services reports the following amounts on December 31, 2024.

Link the balance sheet
to the statement of cash
flows **(LO1–3)**

Assets		Liabilities and Stockholders' Equity	
Cash	$ 7,700	Accounts payable	$ 9,700
Supplies	1,800	Salaries payable	3,500
Prepaid insurance	3,500	Notes payable	20,000
Building	72,000	Common stock	40,000
		Retained earnings	11,800

In addition, the company reported the following cash flows.

Cash Inflows		Cash Outflows	
Customers	$60,000	Employee salaries	$22,000
Borrow from the bank (note)	20,000	Supplies	4,000
Sale of investments	10,000	Dividends	6,500
		Purchase building	62,000

Required:
1. Prepare a balance sheet.
2. Prepare a statement of cash flows.

E1–13 Each of the following independent situations represents amounts shown on the four basic financial statements.

Compute missing
amounts from financial
statements **(LO1–3)**

1. Revenues = $27,000; Expenses = $18,000; Net income = _____.
2. Increase in stockholders' equity = $17,000; Issuance of common stock = $11,000; Net income = $12,000; Dividends = _____.
3. Assets = $24,000; Stockholders' equity = $15,000; Liabilities = _____.
4. Total change in cash = $26,000; Net operating cash flows = $34,000; Net investing cash flows = ($17,000); Net financing cash flows = _____.

Required:
Fill in the missing blanks using your knowledge of amounts that appear on the financial statements.

E1–14 During its first five years of operations, Red Raider Consulting reports net income and pays dividends as follows.

Calculate the balance of
retained earnings **(LO1–3)**

Year	Net Income	Dividends	Retained Earnings
1	$1,700	$ 600	_____
2	2,200	600	_____
3	3,100	1,500	_____
4	4,200	1,500	_____
5	5,400	1,500	_____

Required:
Calculate the balance of retained earnings at the end of each year. Note that retained earnings will always equal $0 at the beginning of year 1.

E1–15 Below are approximate amounts related to retained earnings reported by five companies in previous years.

Calculate amounts related
to the balance of retained
earnings **(LO1–3)**

1. **Coca-Cola** reports an increase in retained earnings of $3.2 billion and net income of $6.9 billion. What is the amount of dividends?
2. **PepsiCo** reports an increase in retained earnings of $3.4 billion and dividends of $2.6 billion. What is the amount of net income?
3. **Alphabet** reports an increase in retained earnings of $1.6 billion and net income of $1.6 billion. What is the amount of dividends?

4. **Sirius XM Satellite Radio** reports beginning retained earnings of −$1.6 billion, net loss of $1.0 billion, and $0 dividends. What is the amount of ending retained earnings?
5. **Abercrombie & Fitch** reports ending retained earnings of $1.56 billion, net income of $0.43 billion, and dividends of $0.06 billion. What is the amount of beginning retained earnings?

Required:
Calculate the answer to each.

Use the accounting equation to calculate amounts related to the balance sheet (LO1–3)

E1–16 Below are approximate amounts related to balance sheet information reported by five companies in previous years.
1. **ExxonMobil** reports total assets of $228 billion and total liabilities of $107 billion. What is the amount of stockholders' equity?
2. **Citigroup** reports total liabilities of $1,500 billion and stockholders' equity of $110 billion. What is the amount of total assets?
3. **Amazon.com** reports total assets of $4.7 billion and total stockholders' equity of $0.3 billion. What is the amount of total liabilities?
4. **Nike** reports an increase in assets of $1.2 billion and an increase in liabilities of $0.3 billion. What is the amount of the change in stockholders' equity?
5. **Kellogg's** reports a decrease in liabilities of $0.34 billion and an increase in stockholders' equity of $0.02 billion. What is the amount of the change in total assets?

Required:
Calculate the answer to each.

Calculate missing amounts related to the statement of cash flows (LO1–3)

E1–17 Below are approximate amounts related to cash flow information reported by five companies in previous years.
1. **KraftHeinz** reports operating cash flows of $3.6 billion, investing cash flows of $0.6 billion, and financing cash flows of −$4.2 billion. What is the amount of the change in total cash?
2. **Hillshire Brands** reports operating cash flows of $1.4 billion, investing cash flows of −$0.3 billion, and financing cash flows of −$1.4 billion. If the beginning cash amount is $0.7 billion, what is the ending cash amount?
3. **Performance Food Group** reports operating cash flows of $0.07 billion, investing cash flows of $0.63 billion, and a change in total cash of $0.04 billion. What is the amount of cash flows from financing activities?
4. **Smithfield Foods** reports operating cash flows of $0.60 billion, financing cash flows of $0.42 billion, and a change in total cash of $0.02 billion. What is the amount of cash flows from investing activities?
5. **Tyson Foods** reports investing cash flows of −$1.42 billion, financing cash flows of $1.03 billion, and a change in total cash of $0.02 billion. What is the amount of cash flows from operating activities?

Required:
Calculate the answer to each.

Understand the role of the auditor (LO1–5)

E1–18 Below are concepts associated with the role of the auditor in financial reporting.

Concept	Description
1. _____ Securities and Exchange Commission	a. Phrase meaning to present the accounting records in an altered format.
2. _____ Need for auditing	b. Auditors are not employees of the company they audit.
3. _____ Cooking the books	c. Responsible for applying generally accepted accounting principles (GAAP).
4. _____ Management	d. Regulatory body that requires audits of all publicly traded companies.
5. _____ Auditor	
6. _____ Independent	e. Separation of management from those who own the business or finance operations.
7. _____ Opinion	f. Party that reports on whether a company's financial statements are in accordance with GAAP.
	g. View expressed by an auditor as to the accuracy of a company's financial statements.

Required:

Match each concept with its description.

E1–19 The qualitative characteristics outlined in the FASB's conceptual framework include:

Identify the purpose
of qualitative
characteristics **(LO1–7)**

Fundamental Characteristics		Enhancing Characteristics
Relevance	**Faithful Representation**	g. Comparability
a. Confirmatory value	d. Completeness	h. Verifiability
b. Predictive value	e. Neutrality	i. Timeliness
c. Materiality	f. Free from error	j. Understandability

Consider the following independent situations.

1. In deciding whether to invest in **Southwest Airlines** or **American Airlines**, investors evaluate the companies' income statements. _____
2. To provide the most reliable information about future sales, **Walmart**'s management uses an appropriate process to estimate the decline in inventory value each year. _____
3. In deciding whether to loan money, **Wells Fargo** uses balance sheet information to forecast the probability of bankruptcy. _____
4. **IBM** is required to issue public financial statements within 60 days of its year-end. _____
5. Employees of **Starbucks** can use the company's financial statements to analyze the efficiency with which management has conducted operations over the past year. _____
6. When first requiring firms to prepare a statement of cash flows, the FASB's intent was not to discourage or promote investment in the automobile industry. _____
7. When **Harley-Davidson** reports revenue for the year, the amount includes sales not only in the United States but also those outside the United States. _____
8. The amount of total assets reported by **General Mills** can be substantiated by its auditors. _____
9. The **Cheesecake Factory** prepares its balance sheet in a clear format using basic accounting terminology to allow users to easily comprehend the company's assets, liabilities, and stockholders' equity. _____
10. **Target** prepays $600 to rent a post office box for the next six months and decides to record the entire payment to Rent expense (instead of Prepaid rent) in the current month. _____

Required:

Determine which qualitative characteristic best applies to each situation. Note: Each of the 10 characteristics is used once and only once.

E1–20 Below are the four underlying assumptions of generally accepted accounting principles.

Identify business
assumptions underlying
GAAP **(LO1–7)**

Assumptions	Descriptions
1. _____ Economic entity	a. A common denominator is needed to measure all business activities.
2. _____ Going concern	b. Economic events can be identified with a particular economic body.
3. _____ Periodicity	c. In the absence of information to the contrary, it is anticipated that a business entity will continue to operate indefinitely.
4. _____ Monetary unit	d. The economic life of a company can be divided into artificial time intervals for financial reporting.

Required:

Match each business assumption with its description.

PROBLEMS: SET A

Classify business activities (LO1–2)

P1–1A Below are typical transactions for **Hewlett-Packard**.

Type of Business Activity	Transactions
1. _____	Pay amount owed to the bank for previous borrowing.
2. _____	Pay utility costs.
3. _____	Purchase equipment to be used in operations.
4. _____	Provide services to customers.
5. _____	Purchase office supplies.
6. _____	Purchase a building.
7. _____	Pay workers' salaries.
8. _____	Pay for research and development costs.
9. _____	Pay taxes to the IRS.
10. _____	Sell common stock to investors.

Required:

Indicate whether each transaction is classified as a financing, investing, or operating activity.

Assign account classifications (LO1–2)

P1–2A Account classifications include assets, liabilities, stockholders' equity, dividends, revenues, and expenses.

Account Classifications	Accounts	Related Transactions
1. _____	Common stock	Sale of common stock to investors.
2. _____	Equipment	Equipment used for operations.
3. _____	Salaries payable	Amounts owed to employees.
4. _____	Service revenue	Sales of services to customers.
5. _____	Utilities expense	Cost of utilities.
6. _____	Supplies	Purchase of office supplies.
7. _____	Research and development expense	Cost of research and development.
8. _____	Land	Property used for operations.
9. _____	Income tax payable	Amounts owed to the IRS for taxes.
10. _____	Interest payable	Amount of interest owed on borrowing.

Required:

For each transaction, indicate whether the related account would be classified in the balance sheet as (a) an asset, (b) a liability, or (c) stockholders' equity; in the income statement as (d) a revenue or (e) an expense; or in the statement of stockholders' equity as (f) a dividend.

Prepare financial statements (LO1–3)

P1–3A Longhorn Corporation provides low-cost food delivery services to senior citizens. At the end of the year on December 31, 2024, the company reports the following amounts:

Cash	$ 1,200	Service revenue	$67,700
Equipment	29,000	Salaries expense	53,400
Accounts payable	4,400	Buildings	40,000
Delivery expense	2,600	Supplies	3,400
Rent expense	5,500	Salaries payable	800

In addition, the company had common stock of $40,000 at the beginning of the year and issued an additional $4,000 during the year. The company also had retained earnings of $18,200 at the beginning of the year.

Required:
Prepare the income statement, statement of stockholders' equity, and balance sheet for Long-horn Corporation.

P1–4A Below are incomplete financial statements for Bulldog, Inc.

Understand the format of financial statements and the links among them **(LO1–3)**

BULLDOG, INC.
Income Statement
Year ended Dec. 31, 2024

Revenues	$39,000
Expenses:	
Salaries	(a)
Advertising	6,000
Utilities	4,000
Net income	(b)

BULLDOG, INC.
Statement of Stockholders' Equity
Year ended Dec. 31, 2024

	Common Stock	Retained Earnings	Total Stk. Equity
Beginning balance	$10,000	$ 7,000	$17,000
Issuances	1,100		1,100
Add: Net income		(c)	(c)
Less: Dividends		(3,000)	(3,000)
Ending balance	$11,100	$10,000	$21,100

BULLDOG, INC.
Balance Sheet
Dec. 31, 2024

Assets		**Liabilities**	
Cash	$ 4,000	Accounts payable	(d)
Accounts receivable	3,000	**Stockholders' Equity**	
Supplies	9,000	Common stock	(e)
Equipment	10,000	Retained earnings	(f)
		Total liabilities and	
Total assets	$26,000	stockholders' equity	(g)

Required:
Calculate the missing amounts.

P1–5A Cornhusker Company provides the following information at the end of 2024.

Prepare financial statements **(LO1–3)**

Cash remaining	$ 4,800
Rent expense for the year	7,000
Land that has been purchased	21,000
Retained earnings	12,400
Utility expense for the year	4,900
Accounts receivable from customers	7,200
Service revenue recognized during the year	37,000
Salary expense for the year	13,300
Accounts payable to suppliers	2,200
Dividends paid to shareholders during the year	3,200
Common stock that has been issued prior to 2024	16,000
Salaries owed at the end of the year	2,400
Insurance expense for the year	3,500
Retained earnings at the beginning of the year	7,300

Required:
Prepare the income statement, statement of stockholders' equity, and balance sheet for Cornhusker Company on December 31, 2024. No common stock is issued during 2024.

Identify underlying
assumptions of
GAAP (LO1–7)

P1–6A The four underlying assumptions of generally accepted accounting principles are economic entity, monetary unit, periodicity, and going concern. Consider the four independent situations below.

1. Jumbo's is a local restaurant. Due to a bad shipment of potatoes, several of the company's customers become ill, and the company receives considerable bad publicity. Revenues are way down, several of its bills are past due, and the company is making plans to close the restaurant at the end of the month. The company continues to report its assets in the balance sheet at historical (original) cost.

2. Gorloks Tax Services is owned and operated by Sam Martin. The company has the usual business assets: land, building, cash, equipment, and supplies. In addition, Sam decides to buy a boat for him and his family to enjoy on the weekends. Sam includes the boat as an asset in the balance sheet of Gorloks Tax Services.

3. Claim Jumpers International, a U.S.-based company, has operations in the United States and in Europe. For the current year, the company purchased two trucks in the United States for $10,000 and three trucks in Europe for €20,000 (euros). Because of the differences in currencies, the company reported "Five Trucks" with no corresponding amount in the balance sheet.

4. Cobbers Etc. sells specialty music equipment ranging from African bongo drums to grand pianos. Because of the fluctuating nature of the business, management decides to publish financial statements only when a substantial amount of activity has taken place. Its last set of financial statements covered a period of 14 months, and the set of financial statements before that covered a period of 18 months.

Required:
For each situation, indicate which of the underlying assumptions of GAAP is violated.

Understand the
components of the
FASB's conceptual
framework (LO1–7)

P1–7A Listed below are nine terms and definitions associated with the FASB's conceptual framework.

Terms	Definitions
1._____ Completeness	a. Requires the consideration of the costs and value of information.
2._____ Comparability	b. Ability to make comparisons between firms.
3._____ Neutrality	c. Comprehending the meaning of accounting information.
4._____ Understandability	d. Including all information necessary to report the business activity.
5._____ Cost effectiveness	e. The business will last indefinitely unless there is evidence otherwise.
6._____ Verifiability	f. Recording transactions only for the company.
7._____ Decision usefulness	g. Implies consensus among different measures.
8._____ Economic entity assumption	h. Accounting should be useful in making decisions.
9._____ Going concern assumption	i. Accounting information should not favor a particular group.

Required:
Pair each term with its related definition.

PROBLEMS: SET B

P1–1B Below are typical transactions for **Caterpillar Inc.**

Classify business activities (LO1–2)

Type of Business Activity	Transactions
1. _____	Pay for advertising.
2. _____	Pay dividends to stockholders.
3. _____	Collect cash from customer for previous sale.
4. _____	Purchase a building to be used for operations.
5. _____	Purchase equipment.
6. _____	Sell land.
7. _____	Receive a loan from the bank by signing a note.
8. _____	Pay suppliers for purchase of supplies.
9. _____	Provide services to customers.
10. _____	Invest in securities of another company.

Required:
Indicate whether each transaction is classified as a financing, investing, or operating activity.

P1–2B Account classifications include assets, liabilities, stockholders' equity, dividends, revenues, and expenses.

Assign account classifications (LO1–2)

Account Classifications	Accounts	Related Transactions
1. _____	Cash	Receive cash from customers.
2. _____	Service revenue	Provide services to customers.
3. _____	Supplies	Purchase supplies.
4. _____	Buildings	Purchase factory for operations.
5. _____	Advertising expense	Pay for cost of advertising.
6. _____	Equipment	Purchase equipment for operations.
7. _____	Interest expense	Pay for cost of interest.
8. _____	Accounts payable	Purchase supplies on credit.
9. _____	Dividends	Distribute cash to stockholders.
10. _____	Notes payable	Borrow from the bank.

Required:
For each transaction, indicate whether the related account would be classified in the balance sheet as (a) an asset, (b) a liability, or (c) stockholders' equity; in the income statement as (d) a revenue or (e) an expense; or in the statement of stockholders' equity as (f) a dividend.

P1–3B Gator Investments provides financial services related to investment selections, retirement planning, and general insurance needs. At the end of the year on December 31, 2024, the company reports the following amounts:

Prepare financial statements (LO1–3)

Advertising expense	$ 33,500	Service revenue	$127,600
Buildings	150,000	Interest expense	3,500
Salaries expense	65,100	Utilities expense	15,500
Accounts payable	6,400	Equipment	27,000
Cash	5,500	Notes payable	30,000

In addition, the company had common stock of $100,000 at the beginning of the year and issued an additional $11,000 during the year. The company also had retained earnings of $30,300 at the beginning of the year and paid dividends of $5,200.

Required:
Prepare the income statement, statement of stockholders' equity, and balance sheet for Gator Investments.

Understand the format of financial statements and the link among them (LO1–3)

P1–4B Below are incomplete financial statements for Cyclone, Inc.

CYCLONE, INC. Income Statement Year ended Dec. 31, 2024	
Revenues	(a)
Expenses:	
Salaries	$13,000
Rent	7,000
Advertising	5,000
Net income	(b)

CYCLONE, INC.
Statement of Stockholders' Equity
Year ended Dec. 31, 2024

	Common Stock	Retained Earnings	Total Stk. Equity
Beginning balance	$14,000	$7,000	$21,000
Issuances of stock	(c)		(c)
Add: Net income		5,000	5,000
Less: Dividends		(d)	(d)
Ending balance	$17,000	$8,000	$25,000

CYCLONE, INC.
Balance Sheet
Dec. 31, 2024

Assets		Liabilities	
Cash	$ 1,100	Accounts payable	$4,000
Supplies	(e)	**Stockholders' Equity**	
Land	6,000	Common stock	(g)
Building	16,000	Retained earnings	(h)
		Total liabilities and	
Total assets	(f)	stockholders' equity	(i)

Required:
Calculate the missing amounts.

Prepare financial statements (LO1–3)

P1–5B Tar Heel Corporation provides the following information at the end of 2024.

Salaries payable to workers at the end of the year	$ 3,300
Advertising expense for the year	10,400
Building that has been purchased	80,000
Supplies at the end of the year	4,600
Retained earnings	40,000
Utilities expense for the year	6,000
Note payable to the bank	25,000
Service revenue performed during the year	69,400
Salary expense for the year	26,700
Accounts payable to suppliers	7,700
Dividends paid to shareholders during the year	(?)
Common stock that has been issued, including $6,000 that was issued this year	27,000
Cash remaining	5,200
Interest expense for the year	2,100
Accounts receivable from customers	13,200
Retained earnings at the beginning of the year	26,800

Required:
Prepare the income statement, statement of stockholders' equity, and balance sheet for Tar Heel Corporation on December 31, 2024.

P1–6B The four underlying assumptions of generally accepted accounting principles are economic entity, monetary unit, periodicity, and going concern. Consider the following four independent situations.

Identify underlying assumptions of GAAP (LO1–7)

1. Mound Builders Groceries has over 1,000 grocery stores throughout the Northwest. Approximately 200,000 customers visit its stores each day. Because of the continual nature of grocery sales, the company does not publish an income statement. The company feels that it has an indefinite life, and a periodic report would mislead investors.
2. Trolls Shipping provides delivery of packages between the United States and Japan. During the current year, the company delivered 3,000 packages for its U.S. customers totaling $25,000 in revenue. For its Japanese customers, the company delivered 1,000 packages totaling ¥1,000,000 (yen). The company's income statement indicates that total revenue equals 4,000 packages delivered with no corresponding amount in the income statement.
3. Slugs Typewriter has provided some of the finest typewriters in town for the past 50 years. Because of the advance of electronic word processors and computers, customer demand has dwindled over the years to almost nothing in the current year, and the company can no longer pay its debts. For the most recent year, the company reports its assets in the balance sheet at historical (original) cost.
4. Blue Hose Carpet specializes in the installation of carpet and wood flooring. The company has the usual business expenses: salaries, supplies, utilities, advertising, and taxes. John Brewer, the company's owner, took his wife and two daughters to Disney World. John reported the airfare and hotel expenses in the income statement of Blue Hose Carpet.

Required:
For each situation, indicate which of the underlying assumptions of GAAP is violated.

P1–7B Listed below are several terms and definitions associated with the FASB's conceptual framework.

Understand the components of the FASB's conceptual framework (LO1–7)

Terms	Definitions
1. _____ Predictive value	a. Decreases in equity resulting from transfers to owners.
2. _____ Relevance	
3. _____ Timeliness	b. Business transactions are measured using a common denominator.
4. _____ Dividends	
5. _____ Confirmatory value	c. The indefinite life of a company can be broken into definite periods.
6. _____ Faithful representation	
7. _____ Materiality	d. Information helps in understanding prior activities.
8. _____ Monetary unit assumption	
9. _____ Periodicity assumption	e. Agreement between a measure and the phenomenon it represents.
	f. Information arrives prior to the decision.
	g. Information is related to the decision at hand.
	h. Information is useful in predicting the future.
	i. Concerns the relative size of an item and its effect on decisions.

Required:
Pair each term with its related definition.

REAL-WORLD PERSPECTIVES

Data Analytics & Excel

Visit Connect to find a variety of Data Analytics questions that help build Excel, Tableau, and data visualization skills. Assignable materials include Integrated Excel, Applying Excel, Data Visualizations, Tableau Dashboard Activities, and Applying Tableau Cases.

Great Adventures

(The Great Adventures problem continues in each chapter.)

RWP1–1 Tony Matheson plans to graduate from college in May 2024 after spending four years earning a degree in sports and recreation management. Since beginning T-ball at age five, he's been actively involved in sports and enjoys the outdoors. Each summer growing up, he and his father would spend two weeks at a father/son outdoor camp. These fond memories are part of the reason he chose his major. He wants to remain involved in these outdoor activities and provide others with the same adventures he was able to share with his dad. He decides to start an outdoor adventure company. However, he's not sure he has the business background necessary to do this.

This is where Suzie Ramos can help. Suzie also plans to graduate in May 2024 with a major in business. Suzie and Tony first met their sophomore year and have been friends ever since, as they share a strong interest in sports and outdoor activities.

They decide to name their company Great Adventures. They will provide clinics for a variety of outdoor activities such as kayaking, mountain biking, rock climbing, wilderness survival techniques, orienteering, backpacking, and other adventure sports.

Required:

1. Tony and Suzie are concerned about personal liability from customers who are injured during outdoor adventure activities. Which of the three basic forms of business organization do you recommend for Great Adventures (sole proprietorship, partnership, or corporation)?
2. Great Adventures plans to maintain records of transactions in accounts such as Cash, Common Stock, Service Revenue, Salaries Expense, Accounts Payable, Equipment, Advertising Expense, Supplies, Salaries Payable, and Insurance Expense. (a) For each of these accounts, indicate whether the account would be reported in the balance sheet or income statement. (b) For accounts in the balance sheet, indicate whether it would be classified as an asset, liability, or stockholders' equity. (c) For accounts in the income statement, indicate whether it would be classified as a revenue or an expense.

American Eagle Outfitters, Inc.

RWP1–2 Financial information for **American Eagle** is presented in **Appendix A** at the end of the book.

Required:

1. Determine the amounts American Eagle reports for total assets, total liabilities, and total stockholders' equity in the balance sheet for the most recent year. Verify that the basic accounting equation balances.
2. American Eagle refers to its income statement using another name. What is it?
3. Determine the amounts American Eagle reports for net sales and net income in its income statement for the most recent year.
4. For investing activities, what is the item having the largest inflow and the item having the largest outflow for the most recent year reported in the statement of cash flows? For financing activities, what is the item having the largest inflow and the item having the largest outflow?
5. Who is the company's auditor? (See the Report of Independent Registered Public Accounting Firm.) What does the report indicate about the amounts reported in the company's financial statements?

The Buckle, Inc.

RWP1–3 Financial information for **Buckle** is presented in **Appendix B** at the end of the book.

Required:

1. Determine the amounts Buckle reports for total assets, total liabilities, and total stockholders' equity in the balance sheet for the most recent year. Verify that the basic accounting equation balances.
2. Buckle refers to its income statement using another name. What is it?

3. Determine the amounts Buckle reports for net sales and net income in its income statement for the most recent year.
4. For investing activities, what is the item having the largest inflow and the item having the largest outflow for the most recent year reported in the statement of cash flows? For financing activities, what is the item having the largest inflow and the item having the largest outflow?
5. Who is the company's auditor? (See the Report of Independent Registered Public Accounting Firm.) What does the report indicate about the amounts reported in the company's financial statements?

American Eagle Outfitters, Inc. vs. The Buckle, Inc.

Comparative Analysis
Continuing Case

RWP1–4 Financial information for **American Eagle** is presented in **Appendix A** at the end of the book, and financial information for **Buckle** is presented in **Appendix B** at the end of the book.

Required:
1. Which company reports higher total assets?
2. Which company reports higher total liabilities? Does this always mean this company has a higher chance of not being able to repay its debt and declare bankruptcy? Explain.
3. What relevant information do total assets and total liabilities provide to creditors deciding whether to lend money to American Eagle versus Buckle?
4. Which company reports higher net income? Does this always mean this company's operations are more profitable? Explain.
5. What relevant information does net income provide to investors who are deciding whether to invest in American Eagle versus Buckle?

EDGAR Research

RWP1–5 Using EDGAR (Electronic Data Gathering, Analysis, and Retrieval system), find the annual report (10-K) for **Facebook** for the year ended **December 31, 2019**. Locate the "Consolidated Statements of Income" and "Consolidated Balance Sheets" and answer the following questions. You may also find the annual report at the company's website.

Required:
1. What did the company report for "Revenue" in the most recent year?
2. What did the company report for "Research and development" expenses in the most recent year?
3. Did net income increase or decrease in the most recent year compared to the previous year and by how much?
4. What did the company report for total assets in the most recent year?
5. What did the company report for total liabilities in the most recent year?
6. Do assets equal liabilities plus stockholders' equity?

Ethics

RWP1–6 Suppose an auditor has been paid $1,000,000 each year for the past several years by a company to perform the audit of its annual financial statements. This company is the auditor's largest client. In the current year, the auditor notices that the preliminary income statement excludes certain expenses that typically are shown. When asked, management tells the auditor that these expenses do not reflect the company's true performance, so they will not be shown in this year's income statement. Plus, management informs the auditor that it will be paying $1,200,000 for this year's audit, and management commits to using the auditor for at least five more years.

Required:
1. Understand the reporting effect: Does the audit arrangement described above have the potential to jeopardize the auditor's opinion of management's decision not to report certain expenses?
2. Specify the options: Are auditors employees of the company who must accept requests of management?

3. Identify the impact: Do investors, creditors, and others rely on the fair presentation of financial statements?
4. Make a decision: Should the auditor accept management's decision not to report the expenses this year?

Written Communication

RWP1–7 Maria comes to you for investment advice. She asks, "Which company's stock should I buy? There are so many companies to choose from and I don't know anything about any of them."

Required:

Respond to Maria by explaining the two functions of financial accounting. Specifically address the four financial statements reported by companies and the information contained in each. Also explain the role of the auditor in the preparation of financial statements.

Answers to Chapter Framework Questions

1. d   2. b   3. c   4. b   5. d

Answers to Self-Study Questions

1. b   2. a   3. d   4. d   5. b   6. c   7. a   8. c   9. a   10. d   11. b   12. d   13. b   14. d   15. a

2

The Accounting Cycle: During the Period

Learning Objectives

PART A: MEASURING BUSINESS ACTIVITIES

- **LO2–1** Identify the basic steps in measuring external transactions.
- **LO2–2** Analyze the impact of external transactions on the accounting equation.

PART B: DEBITS AND CREDITS

- **LO2–3** Assess whether the impact of external transactions results in a debit or credit to an account balance.
- **LO2–4** Record transactions in a journal using debits and credits.
- **LO2–5** Post transactions to the general ledger.
- **LO2–6** Prepare a trial balance.

SELF-STUDY MATERIALS

- Let's Review—Effects of transactions on the accounting equation (p. 70).
- Let's Review—Effects of debits and credit on account balances (p. 73).
- Let's Review—Recording transactions in a journal (p. 82).
- Chapter Framework with questions and answers available (p. 85).
- Key Points by Learning Objective (p. 87).
- Glossary of Key Terms (p. 87).
- Self-Study Questions with answers available (p. 88).
- Videos including Concept Overview, Applying Excel, Let's Review, and Interactive Illustrations to demonstrate key topics (in Connect)

WALMART: SHELVES OF BUSINESS TRANSACTIONS

Walmart opened its first store in Rogers, Arkansas, in 1962. By 1967, the company had increased to 24 stores totaling $12,600,000 in sales, and the following year it expanded operations to Missouri and Oklahoma. Today, Wal-Mart Stores, Inc. (the parent company) is the world's largest retailer with over $500,000,000,000 in sales. (That's $500 billion!) With more than 2.3 million employees worldwide, it's the largest private employer in the United States and Mexico and one of the largest in Canada. Each year Walmart purchases from over 100,000 vendors, merchandise totaling nearly $400 billion. More than 265 million customers visit Walmart stores each week.

Feature Story

With billions of transactions with customers, suppliers, employees, and government agencies, how does Walmart's management keep track of the company's financial position? How do investors know whether the company is profitable and whether management is efficiently running the company? How do creditors know whether they should lend money to the company and whether the company will be able to pay its financial obligations as they become due?

To answer these questions, a system must be in place that can measure billions of transactions of Walmart, summarize those measurements in an efficient way, and then communicate them to management and other decision makers. These are the roles of financial accounting.

In this chapter, we review the measurement process financial accountants use to identify, analyze, record, and summarize transactions. We'll see that financial accounting involves assessing the impact that business transactions have on the company's financial position. These effects are then recorded in accounts. For example, all of Walmart's cash transactions (increases and decreases) are recorded in the Cash account. We then summarize all of the increases and decreases in an account over the accounting period to calculate the account's balance. A list of all account balances provides a summary picture of the company's current financial position and performance during the year.

Without the measurement process of financial accounting, it would be nearly impossible to analyze a company's operations. Having a firm grasp of this measurement process is key to understanding financial accounting.

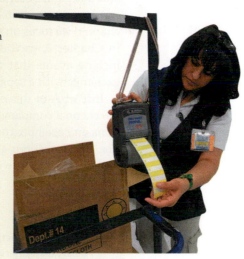

ZUMA Press Inc/Alamy Stock Photo

MEASURING BUSINESS ACTIVITIES

Recall from Chapter 1 that the two functions of financial accounting are to (1) measure business activities of the company and (2) communicate those measurements to external parties for decision-making purposes. The full set of procedures used to accomplish this two-step measurement/communication process is referred to as the accounting cycle. In this chapter, we'll focus on the procedures related to *measuring* business activities *during the accounting period.* In Chapter 3, we'll complete the accounting cycle by examining the remaining procedures that occur at the *end of the accounting period.* Although nearly every company accomplishes the accounting cycle using a computerized accounting system, this chapter shows a manual system to help you better understand the basic model underlying computerized programs.

External Transactions

■ LO2–1

Identify the basic steps in measuring external transactions.

A company has business transactions with many different individuals and other companies. Examples are selling products to a customer, purchasing supplies from a vendor, paying salaries to an employee, and borrowing money from a bank. These transactions are often referred to as external transactions because they are conducted between the company and a separate economic entity. We need to measure these business transactions, so they can be communicated to investors, creditors, and other financial statement users. In this chapter, we focus on the measurement of external transactions occurring during the period. In Chapter 3, we'll discuss *internal transactions* measured at the end of the period. These include events that affect the financial position of the company, but do not include an exchange with a separate company or individual.

In Part A of this chapter, we'll cover 10 basic business transactions to understand their effects on a company's financial position. Then, in Part B we'll cover those same 10 transactions and see how companies formally record those transactions in the accounting records. The 10 transactions are clearly labeled in Part A and Part B so you can compare the analysis of the transactions with the recording of the transactions.

 KEY POINT

External transactions are transactions between the company and a separate company or individual. Internal transactions do not include an exchange with a separate economic entity.

Measuring external transactions is a six-step process, as outlined in Illustration 2–1. **These steps are the foundation for the remaining chapters in this book.** Make sure you understand them before you proceed.

ILLUSTRATION 2–1

Six Steps in Measuring External Transactions

Step 1 Use source documents to identify **accounts** affected by an external transaction.
Step 2 Analyze the impact of the transaction on the **accounting equation.**
Step 3 Assess whether the transaction results in a **debit** or **credit** to account balances.
Step 4 Record the transaction in a **journal** using debits and credits.
Step 5 Post the transaction to the **general ledger.**
Step 6 Prepare a **trial balance.**

The first step in the measurement process involves gathering information about a transaction. Source documents such as sales invoices, bills from suppliers, and signed contracts provide information related to external transactions. These source documents usually identify the date and nature of each transaction, the participating parties, and the monetary terms. For example, a sales invoice might identify the date of sale, the customer, the specific items sold, the dollar amount of the sale, and the payment terms.

Steps 2–6 involve conventions used by accountants to capture the effects of transactions in accounts. An **account** provides a record of the business activities related to a particular item. For instance, *asset accounts* include Cash, Supplies, and Equipment. All transactions affecting cash are recorded in the Cash account. When a company receives cash, an increase is recorded in the Cash account. When the company pays cash, a decrease is recorded in the Cash account. The balance of the account equals all increases minus all decreases. This is the way that all accounts work.

Examples of *liability accounts* include Accounts Payable, Salaries Payable, Utilities Payable, and Taxes Payable. Each of these accounts keeps a record of amounts owed as a result of the related transactions. *Stockholders' equity accounts* include Common Stock and Retained Earnings. A list of all account names used to record transactions of a company is referred to as the **chart of accounts**. (Later in the chapter, we'll see a preliminary chart of accounts. **A representative chart of accounts can be found at the end of the book.** Keep it handy for reference throughout the course.)

In this chapter and throughout the remainder of the book, you'll learn how to compute the balance of each account and eventually use these account balances to prepare the financial statements introduced in Chapter 1. But first, let's work through steps 2–6 of the measurement process to see how external business transactions are summarized in account balances.

KEY POINT

The six-step measurement process (Illustration 2–1) is the foundation of financial accounting. To understand this process, it is important to realize in Step 2 that we analyze the effects of business transactions on the accounting equation (Part A of this chapter). Then, in Step 3 we begin the process of translating those effects into the accounting records (Part B of this chapter).

Effects of Transactions on the Basic Accounting Equation

The activities we want to record are those that affect the financial position of the company. That means they affect the accounting equation you learned about in Chapter 1. Remember, the basic accounting equation shows that assets equal liabilities plus stockholders' equity. In other words, resources of the company equal claims to those resources by creditors and owners.

■ **LO2–2**
Analyze the impact of external transactions on the accounting equation.

Assets	=	**Liabilities**	+	**Stockholders' Equity**
		(creditors' claims)		(owners' claims)
Resources		**Claims to Resources**		

The basic accounting equation

When **Walmart** borrows cash from a bank, its financial position is affected because assets (cash) increase and liabilities (the loan payable to the bank) increase. So, Walmart records that event in its accounting records. On the other hand, when Walmart hires Ralph as a front-door greeter, that action doesn't change the company's assets, liabilities, or stockholders' equity; Walmart's financial position is unaffected the day Ralph is hired, and until he begins work. Yes, Walmart hopes that hiring Ralph will favorably affect its financial position in the future, but the hiring itself does not.

The basic accounting equation must always remain in balance: The left side (assets) equals the right side (liabilities plus stockholders' equity). **Each transaction will have a dual effect.** If one side of the equation increases, then the other side of the equation increases by the same amount. That's what happens, for example, when Walmart borrows cash.

Sometimes, though, a transaction will not affect the *total* of either side. Let's say **Chick-fil-A** buys new cash registers for its restaurants, paying cash. One asset (equipment) goes up; another asset (cash) goes down by the same amount. There's no change to assets *as a whole*. The accounting equation remains in balance. You can tell whether a transaction affects the accounting equation by considering its impact on the company's total resources—its total assets.

As the balance in an account changes, we record the increase or decrease in that specific account. Let's say we have $50,000 in cash. That's the *balance* in the Cash account. If we then collect $1,000 cash from a customer, the balance in the Cash account is now $51,000.

To see the effect of each transaction, ask yourself these questions:

1. **"What is one account in the accounting equation affected by the transaction? Does that account increase or decrease?"**
2. **"What is a second account in the accounting equation affected by the transaction? Does that account increase or decrease?"**

After noting the effects of the transaction on the accounting equation, ask yourself this:

3. **"Do assets equal liabilities plus stockholders' equity?"**

The answer to the third question must be "yes."

Most business transactions affect only two accounts. However, there are some transactions that affect more than two accounts, and we'll cover those in later chapters. They are known as *compound transactions*.

Example.   The best way to understand the impact of a transaction on the accounting equation is to see it demonstrated by a few examples. Let's return to Eagle Soccer Academy from Chapter 1. Illustration 2–2 summarizes the external transactions for Eagle during December, the first month of operations. (You may also want to refer back to the financial statements in Illustrations 1–5, 1–6, 1–7, and 1–8 to remind yourself how the transactions will eventually be reported.) We discuss the impact of these 10 transactions on the accounting equation later in this chapter.

ILLUSTRATION 2–2

External Transactions of Eagle Soccer Academy

Transaction	Date	Description
(1)	Dec. 1	Sell shares of common stock for $200,000 to obtain the funds necessary to start the business.
(2)	Dec. 1	Borrow $100,000 from the local bank and sign a note promising to repay the full amount of the debt in three years.
(3)	Dec. 1	Purchase equipment necessary for giving soccer training, $120,000 cash.
(4)	Dec. 1	Pay one year of rent in advance, $60,000 ($5,000 per month).
(5)	Dec. 6	Purchase supplies on account, $23,000.
(6)	Dec. 12	Provide soccer training to customers for cash, $43,000.
(7)	Dec. 17	Provide soccer training to customers on account, $20,000.
(8)	Dec. 23	Receive cash in advance for soccer training sessions to be given in the future, $6,000.
(9)	Dec. 28	Pay salaries to employees, $28,000.
(10)	Dec. 30	Pay cash dividends of $4,000 to shareholders.

TRANSACTION (1): ISSUE COMMON STOCK

To begin operations, Eagle Soccer Academy needs cash. To generate cash from external sources, Eagle sells shares of common stock to investors for $200,000. In other words, the company receives cash of $200,000 from investors, who in turn become owners of the company by receiving shares of common stock.

Eagle Soccer Academy

Stock Certificate

Investors

It's time to ask the three questions we asked earlier:

1. **"What is one account in the accounting equation affected by the transaction? Does that account increase or decrease?"**

   Answer: **Cash.** Cash is a resource owned by the company, which makes it an asset. The company receives cash from investors, so cash and total assets **increase** by $200,000.

2. **"What is a second account in the accounting equation affected by the transaction? Does that account increase or decrease?"**

   Answer: **Common Stock.** Common Stock is a stockholders' equity account. Issuing common stock to investors in exchange for $200,000 cash increases the amount of common stock owned by the company's stockholders, so common stock and total stockholders' equity **increase.**

   Issuing common stock for cash increases both sides of the accounting equation:

Assets	=	Liabilities	+	Stockholders' Equity
Cash				Common Stock
(1) +$200,000	=			+$200,000

TRANSACTION (1)

Initial investment of $200,000 by stockholders

3. **"Do assets equal liabilities plus stockholders' equity?"**

   Answer: **Yes.**

Note that the accounting equation balances. If one side of the equation increases, so does the other side. We can use this same series of questions to understand the effect of *any* business transaction.

 COMMON MISTAKE

It's sometimes tempting to *decrease* cash as a way of recording an investor's initial investment. However, we account for transactions *from the company's perspective,* and the company *received* cash from the stockholder—an increase in cash.

TRANSACTION (2): BORROW CASH FROM THE BANK

Seeking cash from another external source, Eagle borrows $100,000 from the bank and signs a note promising to repay the loan amount in three years.[1]

---

[1]Some banks and other lending institutions might require companies to have a history of profitable operations, rising cash balances, or other evidence of ability to repay prior to lending. Here, we'll assume Eagle's $200,000 cash generated from investments by stockholders gives the bank confidence in Eagle's ability to repay the debt.

Eagle Soccer Academy   Bank

IOU

1. **"What is one account in the accounting equation affected by the transaction? Does that account increase or decrease?"**

   Answer: **Cash.** Cash is a resource owned by the company, which makes it an asset. The company receives cash, so cash and total assets **increase.**

2. **"What is a second account in the accounting equation affected by the transaction? Does that account increase or decrease?"**

   Answer: **Notes Payable.** Notes payable represent amounts owed to creditors (the bank in this case), which makes them a liability. The company incurs debt when signing the note, so notes payable and total liabilities **increase.**

   Borrowing by signing a note causes both assets and liabilities to increase:

TRANSACTION (2)

Borrow $100,000 from the bank and sign a three-year note

	Assets	=	Liabilities	+	Stockholders' Equity
	Cash		Notes Payable		Common Stock
Bal.	$ 200,000				$200,000
(2)	+**$100,000**		+**$100,000**		
Bal.	$ 300,000		$ 100,000		$200,000
	$ 300,000	=		$300,000	

3. **"Do assets equal liabilities plus stockholders' equity?"**

   Answer: **Yes.**

   After these two transactions, the accounting equation remains in balance. Notice that the $100,000 cash collected on the note adds to the $200,000 cash received from stockholders. The total resources of the company equal $300,000. Creditors' claims to those resources total $100,000, and the remaining $200,000 in resources were provided by stockholders.

   Regardless of the number of transactions occurring during the period, the accounting equation always must remain in balance. For brevity, we do not address the three-question process for Eagle's remaining eight transactions, but you should ask yourself those questions until you feel comfortable with the process.

 KEY POINT

After each transaction, the accounting equation must always remain in balance. In other words, assets must always equal liabilities plus stockholders' equity.

TRANSACTION (3): PURCHASE EQUIPMENT

Once Eagle obtains financing by issuing common stock and borrowing from the bank, the company can invest in long-term assets necessary to operate the business.

Eagle Soccer Academy

Supplier

Buying equipment from a supplier causes one asset (equipment) to increase and another asset (cash) to decrease:

TRANSACTION (3)

Purchase equipment with cash, $120,000

	Assets		=	Liabilities	+	Stockholders' Equity
	Cash	Equipment		Notes Payable		Common Stock
Bal.	$ 300,000			$100,000		$200,000
(3)	−$120,000	+$120,000				
Bal.	$ 180,000	$ 120,000		$100,000		$200,000
	$300,000		=		$300,000	

Because purchasing one asset (equipment) with another asset (cash) has no effect on total assets, the accounting equation remains in balance.

TRANSACTION (4): PAY FOR RENT IN ADVANCE

On December 1, Eagle signs an agreement with a local soccer club to rent its indoor facilities and practice fields to provide soccer training to its customers. At the time the agreement is signed, Eagle pays one year of rent in advance, $60,000 ($5,000/month). Because the rent paid is for occupying space in the future, we record it as an asset representing a resource of the company. We call the asset *prepaid rent.* Other common examples of prepaid assets include prepaid insurance, prepaid advertising, and other prepaid services. These items often are purchased prior to their use.

Rental Space

LEASE

Eagle Soccer Academy

Landlord

Paying rent in advance causes one asset (prepaid rent) to increase and one asset (cash) to decrease:

TRANSACTION (4)

Pay one year of rent in advance, $60,000

	Assets			=	Liabilities	+	Stockholders' Equity
	Cash	Prepaid Rent	Equipment		Notes Payable		Common Stock
Bal.	$180,000		$120,000		$100,000		$200,000
(4)	−$ 60,000	+$60,000					
Bal.	$120,000	$60,000	$120,000		$100,000		$200,000
		$300,000		=		$300,000	

TRANSACTION (5): PURCHASE SUPPLIES ON ACCOUNT

On December 6, Eagle purchases $23,000 of supplies on account. The phrase *on account* indicates that the company does not pay cash immediately, but promises to pay cash in the future. While supplies represent a resource of the company (an asset), the promise to pay the supplier (vendor) later is an obligation. We refer to a liability of this type, in which we purchase something on account, as an *account payable*. The term *payable* means "to be paid in the future." Thus, the Accounts Payable account is a record of specific people and companies to whom we expect to pay cash in the future.[2]

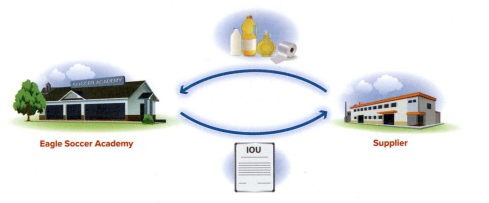

Eagle Soccer Academy   IOU   **Supplier**

Purchasing supplies with the promise to pay cash in the future causes an asset (supplies) to increase and also causes a liability (accounts payable) to increase:

TRANSACTION (5)

Purchase supplies on account, $23,000

	Assets				=	Liabilities		+	Stockholders' Equity
	Cash	Supplies	Prepaid Rent	Equipment		Accounts Payable	Notes Payable		Common Stock
Bal.	$120,000		$60,000	$120,000			$100,000		$200,000
(5)		+$23,000				+$23,000			
Bal.	$120,000	$23,000	$60,000	$120,000		$ 23,000	$100,000		$200,000
		$323,000			=		$323,000		

Later, when the company pays cash to those suppliers, an asset decreases (cash) and a liability decreases (accounts payable). Accounts payable decrease because those amounts are no longer owed to suppliers once the cash has been paid.

Effects of Transactions on the Expanded Accounting Equation

As discussed in Chapter 1, we can divide stockholders' equity into its two components—common stock and retained earnings. Common stock represents investments by

[2]Companies often purchase their supplies on account, usually being required to pay the invoice within 30 to 60 days. In some cases, new companies may be required to establish a relationship with the supplier or provide evidence of ability to repay before the supplier will provide supplies on account.

stockholders. Retained earnings represents net income reported over the life of the company that has *not* been distributed to stockholders as dividends. Both common stock and retained earnings represent stockholders' claims to the company's resources. Next, we can split retained earnings into its three components—revenues, expenses, and dividends—where revenues and expenses will ultimately be represented as net income. Illustration 2–3 presents the expanded accounting equation, which shows these components.

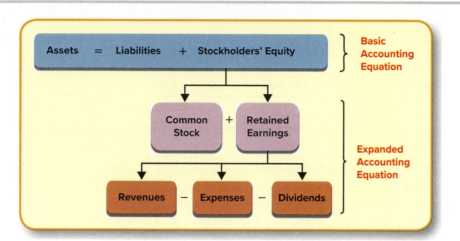

ILLUSTRATION 2–3

Expanded Accounting Equation

Be sure to notice the effects of revenues, expenses, and dividends on retained earnings (and therefore on total stockholders' equity) in the expanded accounting equation:

1. We *add* revenues to calculate retained earnings. That's because revenues increase net income, and net income increases stockholders' claims to resources. **Therefore, an *increase* in revenues has the effect of increasing stockholders' equity in the basic accounting equation.**

2. We *subtract* expenses and dividends to calculate retained earnings. Expenses reduce net income, and dividends represent a distribution of net income to stockholders. Both expenses and dividends reduce stockholders' claims to the company's resources. **Therefore, an *increase* in expenses or dividends has the effect of *decreasing* stockholders' equity in the basic accounting equation.**

 KEY POINT

The expanded accounting equation demonstrates that revenues increase retained earnings while expenses and dividends decrease retained earnings. Retained earnings is a component of stockholders' equity.

TRANSACTION (6): PROVIDE SERVICES FOR CASH

To see an example of how revenue affects the expanded accounting equation, let's first consider the **revenue recognition principle**, which states that companies recognize revenue *at the time they provide goods and services to customers.* The amount of revenue to recognize equals the amount the company is *entitled to receive* from customers. In transaction (6), Eagle provides soccer training to customers who pay cash at the time of the service, $43,000. Because Eagle has provided services, it is entitled to the cash of $43,000 and has revenues for that amount.

Eagle Soccer Academy   Training   Customers

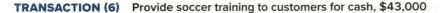

Providing services to customers for cash causes an asset (cash) and stockholders' equity (service revenue) to increase:

TRANSACTION (6)   Provide soccer training to customers for cash, $43,000

	Assets			=	Liabilities		+	Stockholders' Equity		
Cash	Supplies	Prepaid Rent	Equipment		Accounts Payable	Notes Payable		Common Stock	Retained Earnings	**Raise account**
Bal. $120,000	$23,000	$60,000	$120,000		$23,000	$100,000		$200,000		**title**
(6) +$ 43,000									+$43,000	
Bal. $163,000	$23,000	$60,000	$120,000		$23,000	$100,000		$200,000	$ 43,000	**Revenue**
$366,000				=				$366,000		

Notice that an increase in Service Revenue increases stockholders' equity by increasing the Retained Earnings account (+$43,000). Therefore, the basic accounting equation remains in balance (Assets = Liabilities + Stockholders' Equity).

As shown previously in Illustration 2–3, revenues are a component of retained earnings. When a company recognizes revenue, the amount of retained earnings (or net income) in the business increases. We can increase retained earnings by increasing its revenue component. Stated another way, an increase in revenues increases net income, which increases retained earnings, which increases total stockholders' equity:

TRANSACTION (7): PROVIDE SERVICES ON ACCOUNT

In transaction (7), other customers receive soccer training but do not pay cash at the time of the service. Instead, these customers promise to pay $20,000 cash at some time in the future. Does failure to receive cash at the time of the service prevent Eagle from recognizing revenue? No. According to the revenue recognition principle discussed previously in transaction (6), Eagle has provided those services to customers and, therefore has revenue for the amount it is entitled to receive. In addition, the *right* to receive cash from a customer is something of value the company owns, and therefore represents an asset. When a customer does not immediately pay for services with cash, we traditionally say the services are performed "on account," and we recognize an asset called *accounts receivable*. The term *receivable* means "to be received in the future." Thus, the Accounts Receivable account is a record of specific people and companies from whom we expect to receive cash in the future.

Providing services to customers on account causes an asset (accounts receivable) and stockholders' equity (service revenue) to increase:

TRANSACTION (7)   Provide soccer training to customers on account, $20,000

	Assets				=	Liabilities		+	Stockholders' Equity	
Cash	Accounts Receivable	Supplies	Prepaid Rent	Equipment		Accounts Payable	Notes Payable		Common Stock	Retained Earnings
Bal. $163,000		$23,000	$60,000	$120,000		$23,000	$100,000		$200,000	$43,000
(7)	+$20,000									+$20,000 Service
Bal. $163,000	$20,000	$23,000	$60,000	$120,000		$23,000	$100,000		$200,000	$63,000 Revenue
	$386,000				=			$386,000		

Later, when the company receives cash from those customers, one asset increases (cash) and another asset decreases (accounts receivable). Accounts receivable decrease because those amounts are no longer receivable from customers once the cash has been collected.

TRANSACTION (8): RECEIVE CASH IN ADVANCE FROM CUSTOMERS

Rather than providing services before receiving cash as in transaction (7), companies sometimes receive cash in advance from customers. In transaction (8), Eagle receives $6,000 from customers for soccer training to be provided later. In this case, Eagle cannot report revenue from training at the time it receives this cash because it has yet to provide services to those customers. Recall that the *revenue recognition principle* states that revenue is recognized when goods and services are provided to customers. In the case of transaction (8), receiving cash in advance from customers creates an obligation for the company to perform services in the future. This future obligation is a liability (or debt), most commonly referred to as *deferred revenue*.[3]

Eagle Soccer Academy   IOU   Customers

Training

Receiving cash in advance causes an asset (cash) and a liability (deferred revenue) to increase:

TRANSACTION (8)   Receive cash in advance from customers, $6,000

	Assets				=	Liabilities			+	Stockholders' Equity	
Cash	Accounts Receivable	Supplies	Prepaid Rent	Equipment		Accounts Payable	Deferred Revenue	Notes Payable		Common Stock	Retained Earnings
Bal. $163,000	$20,000	$23,000	$60,000	$120,000		$23,000		$100,000		$200,000	$63,000
(8) +$ 6,000							+$6,000				
Bal. $169,000	$20,000	$23,000	$60,000	$120,000		$23,000	$6,000	$100,000		$200,000	$63,000
	$392,000				=			$392,000			

---

[3] Deferred revenue is sometimes referred to as unearned revenue. The use of the term *deferred revenue* is increasingly popular in practice and is more consistent with the FASB's 2014 update of the revenue recognition principle (ASU No. 2014-09), which eliminates the "earnings" process in defining revenue. The term *deferred revenue* is also helpful in emphasizing that revenue is initially deferred but will be recognized eventually when the service is provided.

COMMON MISTAKE

Don't let the account name fool you. Even though the term *revenue* appears in the account title for *deferred revenue,* this is not a revenue account. *Deferred* indicates that the company has yet to provide services even though it has collected the customer's cash. The company owes the customer a service, which creates a liability.

TRANSACTION (9): PAY SALARIES TO EMPLOYEES

Companies incur a variety of costs in running the business. In transaction (9), Eagle pays salaries to employees for work in the current month. Because these salaries represent a cost of operations during the current period, Eagle records them in the current month as salaries expense of $28,000.

Labor

Eagle Soccer Academy

Employee

Paying salaries for the current period causes an asset (cash) to decrease and stockholders' equity to decrease (and salaries expense to increase):

TRANSACTION (9)   Pay salaries to employees, $28,000

		Assets				=	Liabilities			+	Stockholders' Equity	
	Cash	Accounts Receivable	Supplies	Prepaid Rent	Equipment		Accounts Payable	Deferred Revenue	Notes Payable		Common Stock	Retained Earnings
Bal.	$169,000	$20,000	$23,000	$60,000	$120,000		$23,000	$6,000	$100,000		$200,000	$63,000
(9)	−$28,000											−$28,000 Salaries Expense
Bal.	$141,000	$20,000	$23,000	$60,000	$120,000		$23,000	$6,000	$100,000		$200,000	$35,000
		$364,000				=			$364,000			

Notice that an *increase* in Salaries Expense results in a *decrease* in Retained Earnings (−$28,000). As a result, the accounting equation remains in balance, with both sides decreasing by $28,000. The concept of expenses flowing into retained earnings is the same concept that we see in transactions (6) and (7) where revenues also flow into retained earnings, but in the opposite direction.

Expenses *reduce* net income and therefore *reduce* the amount of retained earnings, a stockholders' equity account. Stated another way, an increase in expenses decreases net income, which decreases retained earnings, which decreases total stockholders' equity:

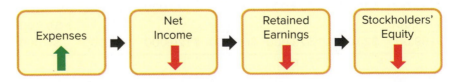

Expenses → Net Income → Retained Earnings → Stockholders' Equity

Beyond salaries expense, companies have a number of other expenses. Most expense accounts are labeled with the word *expense* in the title. For instance, common expense accounts include Supplies Expense, Utilities Expense, Rent Expense, Advertising Expense, Interest Expense, and Insurance Expense.

When a company has a cost that benefits future periods, then we typically record an asset rather than an expense. For example, in transaction (3) we had the cost of equipment, in transaction (4) we had the cost of rent, and in transaction (5) we had the cost of supplies. In each of these transactions, the cost represented the purchase of a resource that will provide a benefit to the company beyond the date of the transaction, so we recorded each of these as assets.

TRANSACTION (10): PAY CASH DIVIDENDS

The final transaction of Eagle Soccer Academy for the month is the payment of a $4,000 cash dividend to stockholders. Recall from the previous chapter that a dividend represents a distribution to the owners (stockholders) of the company.[4]

TRANSACTION (10)   Pay dividends to stockholders, $4,000

		Assets				=	Liabilities			+	Stockholders' Equity	
	Cash	Accounts Receivable	Supplies	Prepaid Rent	Equipment		Accounts Payable	Deferred Revenue	Notes Payable		Common Stock	Retained Earnings
Bal.	$141,100	$20,000	$23,000	$60,000	$120,000		$23,000	$6,000	$100,000		$200,000	$35,000
(10)	−$ 4,000											−$4,000 Dividends
Bal.	$137,000	$20,000	$23,000	$60,000	$120,000		$23,000	$6,000	$100,000		$200,000	$31,000
		$360,000				=		$360,000				

Paying dividends causes an asset (cash) to decrease and stockholders' equity to decrease (and dividends to increase):

Like expenses, dividends reduce retained earnings, but dividends are *not* expenses. Instead, dividends are distributions of part of the company's net income to the owners, reducing the amount of earnings that have been retained in the business. Therefore, an *increase* in Dividends results in a *decrease* in Retained Earnings (−$4,000). The accounting equation remains in balance, with both sides decreasing by $4,000. Because Retained Earnings is a stockholders' equity account, when retained earnings decreases, so does stockholders' equity:

---

[4] Normally a company wouldn't pay dividends after only a month in business, but we make this assumption here for purposes of illustration.

COMMON MISTAKE

Students often believe a payment of dividends to owners increases stockholders' equity. Remember, you are accounting for the resources *of the company*. While stockholders have more personal cash after dividends have been paid, the company in which they own stock has *fewer* resources (less cash).

Illustration 2–4 summarizes all 10 of the month's transactions we just analyzed for Eagle Soccer Academy. Notice that the accounting equation remains in balance.

ILLUSTRATION 2–4   Summary of All 10 External Transactions of Eagle Soccer Academy

	Assets					=	Liabilities			+	Stockholders' Equity	
	Cash	Accounts Receivable	Supplies	Prepaid Rent	Equipment		Accounts Payable	Deferred Revenue	Notes Payable		Common Stock	Retained Earnings
Dec. 1	$0	$0	$0	$0	$0		$0	$0	$0		$0	$0
(1)	+200,000										+200,000	
(2)	+100,000								+100,000			
(3)	−120,000				+120,000							
(4)	−60,000			+60,000								
(5)			+23,000				+23,000					
(6)	+43,000											+43,000 Service Revenue
(7)		+20,000										+20,000 Service Revenue
(8)	+6,000							+6,000				
(9)	−28,000											−28,000 Salaries Expense
(10)	−4,000											−4,000 Dividends
Dec. 31	$137,000	$20,000	$23,000	$60,000	$120,000		$23,000	$6,000	$100,000		$200,000	$31,000
	$360,000					=					$360,000	

Let's Review

Bogey Incorporated has the following transactions during May:

May 1   Purchase a storage building by obtaining a loan of $5,000.
May 6   Provide services to customers for cash, $1,800.
May 12 Pay $1,200 cash for advertising in May.
May 17 Repay $1,000 of the amount borrowed on May 1.
May 25 Purchase office supplies for $800 cash.

Required:

Indicate how each transaction affects the accounting equation.

Solution:

	Assets	=	Liabilities	+	Stockholders' Equity	
					Common Stock	Retained Earnings
May 1	+$5,000		+$5,000			
May 6	+$1,800					+$1,800
May 12	−$1,200					−$1,200
May 17	−$1,000		−$1,000			
May 25	+$ 800					
	−$ 800					
	+$4,600	=	+$4,000	+		+$ 600

Suggested Homework:
BE2–2, BE2–4;
E2–2, E2–3, E2–4;
P2–1A&B, P2–2A&B

DEBITS AND CREDITS

As we saw in the previous section, transactions have the effect of increasing or decreasing account balances. While the terms *increase* and *decrease* are well understood, accountants more often use the terms *debit* and *credit* to indicate whether an account balance has increased or decreased. Here, we introduce those terms, discuss their effect on account balances, and show how we record transactions using debits and credits.

Effects on Account Balances in the Basic Accounting Equation

You will need to learn how to increase and decrease account balances using the terms debit and credit because that's the language of accounting. Although debit and credit are derived from Latin terms, today, **debit** simply means "left," and **credit** means "right." Their use dates back to 1494 and a Franciscan monk by the name of Luca Pacioli.

> **■ LO2–3**
> Assess whether the impact of external transactions results in a debit or credit to an account balance.

   Look at the accounting equation in Illustration 2–5. Like every equation, there is a left-hand side and a right-hand side. Assets are on the left-hand side of the equal sign, while liabilities and stockholders' equity are on the right-hand side. In accounting terminology, **we refer to increases in assets (left-hand side accounts) as debits, and we refer to decreases in assets as credits.** For example, if a company receives cash (an asset), the balance of the Cash account increases, so we refer to the increase as a "debit to cash." We would refer to a decrease in cash as a "credit to cash."

ILLUSTRATION 2–5

Debit and Credit Effects on Accounts in the Basic Accounting Equation

   Just the opposite is true for liabilities and stockholders' equity. These accounts are on the right-hand side of the accounting equation. **We refer to increases in liabilities and stockholders' equity (right-hand side accounts) as credits, and decreases in those accounts as debits.**

COMMON MISTAKE

Some students think the term "debit" *always* means increase, and "credit" *always* means decrease. While this is true for assets, it is *not* true for liabilities and stockholders' equity. Liabilities and stockholders' equity increase with a credit and decrease with a debit.

KEY POINT

For the basic accounting equation (Assets = Liabilities + Stockholders' Equity), assets (left side) increase with *debits*. Liabilities and stockholders' equity (right side) increase with *credits*. The opposite is true to decrease any of these accounts.

Effects on Account Balances in the Expanded Accounting Equation

As we discussed previously in Illustration 2–3, we can expand the basic accounting equation to include the components of stockholders' equity (common stock and retained earnings)

and the components of retained earnings (revenues, expenses, and dividends). Because common stock and retained earnings are part of stockholders' equity (right-hand side), it follows directly that we increase both with a credit, and decrease both with a debit. For the components of retained earnings:

- **Revenues** increase retained earnings ("there's more to keep"). Retained Earnings is a credit account, so we increase revenues with a credit.
- **Expenses**, on the other hand, decrease retained earnings ("there's less to keep"). Thus, we do the opposite of what we do with revenues; we increase expenses with a debit.
- **Dividends**, similar to expenses, decrease retained earnings, so we increase dividends with a debit.
- For each of these components, **we do the opposite to decrease the balance**.

Illustration 2-6 summarizes the effects of debits and credits on the expanded accounting equation.

ILLUSTRATION 2–6

Debit and Credit Effects on Accounts in the Expanded Accounting Equation

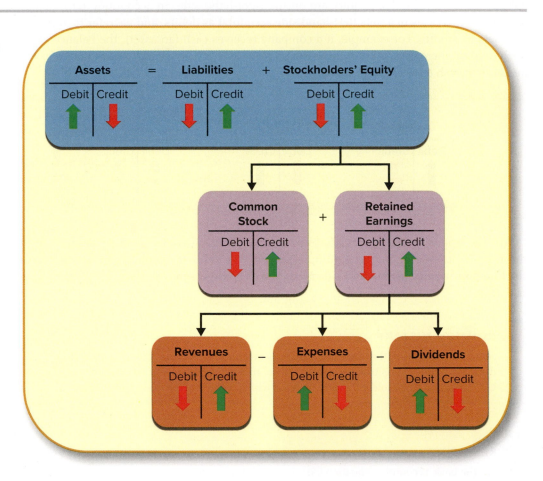

 KEY POINT

The Retained Earnings account is a stockholders' equity account that normally has a credit balance. The Retained Earnings account has three components—revenues, expenses, and dividends. The difference between revenues (increased by credits) and expenses (increased by debits) equals net income. Net income increases the balance of Retained Earnings. Dividends (increased by debits) decrease the balance of Retained Earnings.

Decision Point

Question	Accounting information	Analysis
How much profit has a company generated over its lifetime for its owners and retained for use in the business?	Retained earnings	The balance of retained earnings provides a representation of annual net income (revenue minus expenses) accumulated over the life of the company, less the total dividends distributed over the life of the company.

Illustration 2–7 provides a simple memory aid that can help you remember debits and credits. Remember the acronym **DEALOR** and you'll be able to recall the effect that debits and credits have on account balances.

ILLUSTRATION 2–7

Effects of Debit and Credit on Each Account Type

In accounting terminology, debit means left, and credit means right. Let's split **DEALOR** into its left and right side. The three accounts on the left, or debit, side of **DEALOR**—**D**ividends, **E**xpenses, and **A**ssets—increase with a debit and decrease with a credit. In contrast, the three accounts on the right, or credit, side—**L**iabilities, **O**wners' (stockholders') equity, and **R**evenues—increase with a credit and decrease with a debit.

Common Terms Another name for stockholders' equity is *owners' equity*, since stockholders are the owners of a company.

Let's Review

Bogey Incorporated has the following transactions during May:

May 1 Purchase a storage building by obtaining a loan of $5,000.
May 6 Provide services to customers for cash, $1,800.
May 12 Pay $1,200 cash for advertising in May.
May 17 Repay $1,000 of the amount borrowed on May 1.
May 25 Purchase office supplies for $800 cash.

Required:

For each transaction, (1) identify the two accounts involved, (2) the type of account, (3) whether the transaction increases or decreases the account balance, and (4) whether the increase or decrease would be recorded with a debit or credit.

Solution:

Date	(1) Accounts Involved	(2) Account Type	(3) Increase or Decrease	(4) Debit or Credit
May 1	Buildings	Asset	Increase	Debit
	Notes Payable	Liability	Increase	Credit
May 6	Cash	Asset	Increase	Debit
	Service Revenue	Revenue	Increase	Credit

(continued)

(concluded)

Date	(1) Accounts Involved	(2) Account Type	(3) Increase or Decrease	(4) Debit or Credit
May 12	Advertising Expense	Expense	Increase	Debit
	Cash	Asset	Decrease	Credit
May 17	Notes Payable	Liability	Decrease	Debit
	Cash	Asset	Decrease	Credit
May 25	Supplies	Asset	Increase	Debit
	Cash	Asset	Decrease	Credit

Suggested Homework:
BE2–5, BE2–6;
E2–6, E2–7;
P2–3A&B

Recording Transactions in a Journal

■ **LO2–4**

Record transactions in a journal using debits and credits.

We have just discussed whether the impact of an external transaction results in a debit or credit to an account balance. Next, we'll learn how to formally record transactions using those same debits and credits in a journal. A **journal** provides a chronological record of all transactions affecting a firm. Prior to the widespread use of computers, companies recorded their transactions in paper-based journals. Thus, the term **journal entry** was used to describe the format for recording a transaction. Today, nearly all companies have easy access to computers, and paper-based journals have become obsolete, but journal entries continue to be made in a computerized accounting information system. Illustration 2–8 shows the format we'll use throughout the book to record a company's transactions.

ILLUSTRATION 2–8

Format for Recording a Business Transaction, or Journal Entry

Date	Debit	Credit
Account Name	Amount	
Account Name		Amount
(Description of transaction)		

The entry that records a transaction has a place for the date of the transaction, the relevant account names, debit amounts, credit amounts, and a description of the transaction. We first list the account to be debited; below that, and indented to the right, we list the account to be credited. The entry has two amount columns—one for debits, one for credits. Because the amounts always represent dollar amounts (not number of units, for example), the dollar sign ($) is not used. As you might expect, the left-hand column is for debits, and the right-hand column is for credits. A brief description of the transaction is customarily included at the bottom to leave an information trail for later reference if necessary.

Illustration 2–8 displays only one debit and one credit. However, it's certainly possible to have more than one debit or more than one credit in a journal entry as the result of a business transaction. These are known as *compound entries.* The important point is: **for each journal entry, total debits must equal total credits.** This means the sum of all amounts that are debited must equal the sum of all amounts that are credited.

 COMMON MISTAKE

Many students forget to indent the credit account names. For the account credited, be sure to indent both the account name and the amount.

Think of recording a transaction as if you're writing a sentence form of the "accounting language." For example, recall in transaction (1) that "On December 1, Eagle Soccer Academy sells shares of common stock to investors for cash of $200,000." Here is this same sentence about transaction (1) written in the language of accounting:

December 1	Debit	Credit
Cash *(+A)*	200,000	
Common Stock *(+SE)*		200,000
(Issue common stock for cash)		

TRANSACTION (1)
Initial investment of $200,000 by stockholders

Just as every English sentence uses at least one noun and one verb, every accounting sentence includes at least one debit and one credit. While not a formal part of recording transactions, we'll use a notation in parentheses beside the account name in Chapters 2 and 3 to help you get more familiar with the effect of debits and credits on the account balance. Thus, the entry shows that transaction (1) causes total assets to increase (+A) and total stockholders' equity to increase (+SE). Increases to assets are recorded with a debit, and increases to stockholders' equity are recorded with a credit. **You will need to learn to read and write in the language of accounting, as this is the language used throughout the business world.**

KEY POINT

For each transaction, total debits must equal total credits.

COMMON MISTAKE

Students sometimes hear the phrase "assets are the debit accounts" and believe it indicates that assets can only be debited. This is incorrect! Assets, or any account, can be *either* debited or credited. Rather, this phrase indicates that debiting the asset account will increase the balance and that an asset account normally will have a debit balance. Similarly, the phrase "liabilities and stockholders' equity are the credit accounts" does *not* mean that these accounts cannot be debited. They will be debited when their balances decrease. Rather, the phrase means that crediting the liabilities and stockholders' equity accounts increases their balances, and they normally will have a credit balance.

The formal account names used to record transactions in the journal are listed in the *chart of accounts.* Illustration 2–9 provides the chart of accounts for Eagle Soccer Academy based on the 10 transactions covered to this point. Later, we'll introduce other transactions and accounts for Eagle. **At the back of the book, you'll see a chart of accounts that includes all accounts used throughout the book.**

ILLUSTRATION 2–9
Preliminary Chart of Accounts for Eagle Soccer Academy

EAGLE SOCCER ACADEMY
Chart of Accounts (preliminary)

Assets	Liabilities	Stockholders' Equity
Cash	Accounts Payable	Common Stock
Accounts Receivable	Deferred Revenue	Retained Earnings
Supplies	Notes Payable	**Dividends:**
Prepaid Rent		Dividends
Equipment		**Revenues:**
		Service Revenue
		Expenses:
		Salaries Expense

Posting to the General Ledger

As discussed in the previous section, a journal provides in a single location a chronological listing of every transaction affecting a company. As such, it serves as a handy way to review specific transactions and to locate any accounting errors at their original source. But it's not a convenient format for calculating account balances to use in preparing financial statements. You don't need to stretch your imagination too far to see that even for a very small

■ **LO2–5**
Post transactions to the general ledger.

company with few transactions, calculating account balances from a list of journal entries would very soon become unmanageable. Just imagine how lengthy the journal would be for **Walmart**. If each sales transaction with a customer took about one inch of space, the journal would be over 150,000 miles long by the end of the year.

To make the calculation of account balances more efficient, we need to collect all transactions, per account, in one location. We do this through a process called *posting*. Formally, **posting** is the process of transferring the debit and credit information from the journal to individual accounts in the general ledger. The **general ledger** provides, in a single collection, each account with its individual transactions and resulting account balance.

A general ledger account includes an account title, transaction date, transaction description, and columns for debits, credits, and the cumulative account balance. Illustration 2–10 presents the basic format used for general ledger accounts.

ILLUSTRATION 2–10

General Ledger Account

Account: Title					
Date	Description	Debit	Credit	Balance

After all individual transactions for the period are posted to a general ledger account, we **aggregate** these individual amounts to compute a single ending account balance. It is this process of measuring each transaction and then aggregating those measurements that allows efficient communication of accounting information to financial statements users.

Of course, computerized systems automatically and instantly post information from the journal to the general ledger accounts and calculate account balances. Here, we will see the formal process of recording transactions in a journal and then posting them to the general ledger by working through the 10 transactions of Eagle Soccer Academy listed in Illustration 2–2.

TRANSACTION (1): ISSUE COMMON STOCK

In transaction (1), Eagle issues common stock for $200,000 cash. As demonstrated in the previous section, Eagle records a debit to Cash and a credit to Common Stock in the journal. We debit Cash because it's an asset account, and asset balances increase with a debit. We credit Common Stock because it's a stockholders' equity account, and these balances increase with a credit.

Now, let's record the transaction in the journal and then post the debit and credit to the general ledger accounts.

TRANSACTION (1)

Initial investment of $200,000 by stockholders

December 1	Debit	Credit
Cash (+A)	200,000	
Common Stock (+SE)		200,000
(Issue common stock for cash)		

Account: Cash					
Date	Description	Debit	Credit	Balance
Dec. 1	Beginning balance			0
Dec. 1	Issue common stock for cash	200,000		200,000

Account: Common Stock					
Date	Description	Debit	Credit	Balance
Dec. 1	Beginning balance			0
Dec. 1	Issue common stock for cash		200,000	200,000

Notice that posting involves simply moving the debit to Cash from the journal entry to a debit (or left side) in the Cash general ledger account, increasing its balance by $200,000. The credit to Common Stock from the journal entry becomes a credit (or right side) in the Common Stock general ledger account, increasing its balance by $200,000.

The first row of the general ledger account is the balance at the beginning of the period. In this case, the balance is $0 for both accounts because Eagle is just beginning operations.

TRANSACTION (2): BORROW CASH FROM THE BANK

In transaction (2), Eagle borrows $100,000 cash from a bank. The company has an increase in cash (an asset) and an increase in the amount owed (a liability). Assets increase with a debit, so we debit Cash for $100,000. Liabilities increase with a credit, so we credit Notes Payable for $100,000. Let's record the transaction in the journal and then post the debit and credit to the general ledger accounts.

December 1	Debit	Credit
Cash *(+A)*...	**100,000**	
Notes Payable *(+L)*		**100,000**
(Borrow cash by signing three-year note)		

TRANSACTION (2)
Borrow $100,000 from the bank and sign a three-year note

Account: Cash				
Date	Description	Debit	Credit	Balance
Dec. 1	Beginning balance			0
Dec. 1	Issue common stock for cash	200,000		200,000
Dec. 1	Borrow cash by signing note	**100,000**		300,000

Account: Notes Payable				
Date	Description	Debit	Credit	Balance
Dec. 1	Beginning balance			0
Dec. 1	Borrow cash by signing note		**100,000**	100,000

We see that the balance in both accounts increases by $100,000. The balance of the Cash account is now $300,000, which includes $200,000 cash received from stockholders in transaction (1) plus $100,000 cash received from the bank in transaction (2). The balance of the Notes Payable account increases from $0 to $100,000.

As we go through transactions (3)–(10) next, **notice how each individual transaction is recorded in the journal but then adds to or subtracts from the account's total balance in the general ledger.**

In addition, from this point forward we'll use a simplified version of the general ledger account, commonly referred to as a **T-account**. A T-account includes the account title at the top, one side for recording debits, and one side for recording credits. Consistent with our previous discussion of debits and credits, the left side of the T-account is the debit column, and the right side is the credit column. **You can see that the name *T-account* comes from the natural T shape formed in the general ledger by the debit and credit columns.** Shown next are the T-accounts for Cash and Notes Payable after posting transaction (2).

Cash		Notes Payable	
(1) 200,000			(2) **100,000**
(2) **100,000**			
Bal. 300,000			Bal. 100,000

TRANSACTION (3): PURCHASE EQUIPMENT

In transaction (3), Eagle purchases equipment with $120,000 cash. The company has an increase in equipment (an asset) and a decrease in cash (an asset). Assets increase with a debit, so we debit Equipment for $120,000. Assets decrease with a credit, so we credit Cash for $120,000.

TRANSACTION (3)

Purchase equipment with cash, $120,000

December 1	Debit	Credit
Equipment (+A)...	120,000	
Cash (−A)		120,000
(Purchase equipment with cash)		

Equipment				Cash			
(3)	120,000			(1)	200,000	(3)	120,000
				(2)	100,000		
Bal.	120,000			Bal.	180,000		

For Cash (a *debit* account), notice that the $120,000 *credit* decreases the balance from $300,000 to $180,000.

TRANSACTION (4): PAY FOR RENT IN ADVANCE

In transaction (4), Eagle pays $60,000 cash for one year of rent. The company has an increase in prepaid rent (an asset) and a decrease in cash (an asset). Assets increase with a debit, so we debit Prepaid Rent for $60,000. Assets decrease with a credit, so we credit Cash for $60,000.

TRANSACTION (4)

Pay for one year of rent in advance, $60,000

December 1	Debit	Credit
Prepaid Rent (+A)..	60,000	
Cash (−A)		60,000
(Prepay one year of rent with cash)		

Prepaid Rent				Cash			
(4)	60,000			(1)	200,000	(3)	120,000
				(2)	100,000	(4)	60,000
Bal.	60,000			Bal.	120,000		

TRANSACTION (5): PURCHASE SUPPLIES ON ACCOUNT

In transaction (5), Eagle purchases supplies on account for $23,000. The company has an increase in supplies (an asset) and an increase in amounts owed to suppliers (a liability). Assets increase with a debit, so we debit Supplies for $23,000. Liabilities increase with a credit, so we credit Accounts Payable for $23,000.

TRANSACTION (5)

Purchase supplies on account, $23,000

December 6	Debit	Credit
Supplies (+A)...	23,000	
Accounts Payable (+L)...		23,000
(Purchase supplies on account)		

Supplies			Accounts Payable		
(5)	23,000			(5)	23,000
Bal.	23,000			Bal.	23,000

Later, when the company pays cash to those suppliers, accounts payable (a liability) decrease so we would debit Accounts Payable, and cash (an asset) decreases so we credit Cash.

TRANSACTION (6): PROVIDE SERVICES FOR CASH

In transaction (6), Eagle provides soccer training to customers for $43,000 cash. The company has an increase in cash (an asset) and an increase in service revenue (a revenue). Assets increase with a debit, so we debit Cash for $43,000. Revenues increase with a credit, so we credit Service Revenue for $43,000.

December 12	Debit	Credit
Cash (+A)..	43,000	
Service Revenue (+R, +SE)...		43,000
(Provide training to customers for cash)		

TRANSACTION (6)
Provide soccer training to customers for cash, $43,000

Cash				Service Revenue	
(1)	200,000	(3) 120,000		(6)	43,000
(2)	100,000	(4) 60,000			
(6)	**43,000**				
Bal.	163,000			Bal.	43,000

Notice that the increase to revenue also increases stockholders' equity. Recall from Illustration 2-6 that revenue is a component of retained earnings (an equity account).

TRANSACTION (7): PROVIDE SERVICES ON ACCOUNT

In transaction (7), Eagle provides soccer training to customers on account for $20,000. The company has an increase in amounts expected to be received from customers (an asset) and an increase in service revenue (a revenue). Assets increase with a debit, so we debit Accounts Receivable for $20,000. Revenues increase with a credit, so we credit Service Revenue for $20,000.

December 17	Debit	Credit
Accounts Receivable (+A)..	20,000	
Service Revenue (+R, +SE)...		20,000
(Provide training to customers on account)		

TRANSACTION (7)
Provide soccer training to customers on account, $20,000

Accounts Receivable			Service Revenue	
(7)	**20,000**		(6)	43,000
			(7)	**20,000**
Bal.	20,000		Bal.	63,000

Later, when the company receives cash from those customers on account, cash (an asset) increases so we debit Cash, and accounts receivable (an asset) decrease so we credit Accounts Receivable.

TRANSACTION (8): RECEIVE CASH IN ADVANCE FROM CUSTOMERS

In transaction (8), Eagle receives $6,000 cash in advance from customers for soccer training to be provided in the future. The company has an increase in cash (an asset) and an increase in obligations to provide future services (a liability). Assets increase with a debit, so we debit Cash for $6,000. Liabilities increase with a credit, so we credit Deferred Revenue for $6,000.

TRANSACTION (8)

Receive cash in advance from customers, $6,000

December 23	Debit	Credit
Cash (+A)..	6,000	
Deferred Revenue (+L)...		6,000
(Receive cash in advance from customers)		

Cash				Deferred Revenue	
(1) 200,000	(3) 120,000				(8) 6,000
(2) 100,000	(4) 60,000				
(6) 43,000					
(8) 6,000					
Bal. 169,000					Bal. 6,000

TRANSACTION (9): PAY SALARIES TO EMPLOYEES

In transaction (9), Eagle pays $28,000 cash for employee salaries during the month. The company has an increase in employee costs for work in the current period (an expense) and a decrease in cash (an asset). Expenses increase with a debit, so we debit Salaries Expense for $28,000. Assets decrease with a credit, so we credit Cash for $28,000.

TRANSACTION (9)

Pay salaries to employees, $28,000

December 28	Debit	Credit
Salaries Expense (+E, −SE)	28,000	
Cash (−A)...		28,000
(Pay salaries to employees)		

Salaries Expense		Cash	
(9) 28,000		(1) 200,000	(3) 120,000
		(2) 100,000	(4) 60,000
		(6) 43,000	(9) 28,000
		(8) 6,000	
Bal. 28,000		Bal. 141,000	

Notice that the increase to expense also decreases stockholders' equity. Recall from Illustration 2-6 that expense is a component of retained earnings (an equity account).

TRANSACTION (10): PAY CASH DIVIDENDS

In transaction (10), Eagle pays $4,000 in cash dividends to stockholders. The company has an increase in the Dividends account and a decrease in cash (an asset). Dividends increase with a debit, so we debit Dividends for $4,000. Assets decrease with a credit, so we credit Cash for $4,000.

TRANSACTION (10)

Pay cash dividends to stockholders, $4,000

December 30	Debit	Credit
Dividends (+D, −SE)...	4,000	
Cash (−A)		4,000
(Pay cash dividends)		

Dividends		Cash	
(10) 4,000		(1) 200,000	(3) 120,000
		(2) 100,000	(4) 60,000
		(6) 43,000	(9) 28,000
		(8) 6,000	(10) 4,000
Bal. 4,000		Bal. 137,000	

Notice that the increase to dividends also decreases stockholders' equity. Again, recall Illustration 2-6 to see that dividends ultimately reduce retained earnings and stockholders' equity.

 KEY POINT

Posting is the process of transferring the debit and credit information from transactions recorded in the journal to individual accounts in the general ledger.

A summary of the external transactions that have been recorded in a journal for Eagle Soccer Academy is provided in Illustration 2–11.

		Debit	Credit
(1)	**December 1**		
	Cash (+A)	200,000	
	Common Stock (+SE)		200,000
	(Issue common stock for cash)		
(2)	**December 1**		
	Cash (+A)	100,000	
	Notes Payable (+L)		100,000
	(Borrow cash by signing three-year note)		
(3)	**December 1**		
	Equipment (+A)	120,000	
	Cash (−A)		120,000
	(Purchase equipment for cash)		
(4)	**December 1**		
	Prepaid Rent (+A)	60,000	
	Cash (−A)		60,000
	(Prepay one year of rent with cash)		
(5)	**December 6**		
	Supplies (+A)	23,000	
	Accounts Payable (+L)		23,000
	(Purchase supplies on account)		
(6)	**December 12**		
	Cash (+A)	43,000	
	Service Revenue (+R, +SE)		43,000
	(Provide training to customers for cash)		
(7)	**December 17**		
	Accounts Receivable (+A)	20,000	
	Service Revenue (+R, +SE)		20,000
	(Provide training to customers on account)		
(8)	**December 23**		
	Cash (+A)	6,000	
	Deferred Revenue (+L)		6,000
	(Receive cash in advance from customers)		
(9)	**December 28**		
	Salaries Expense (+E, −SE)	28,000	
	Cash (−A)		28,000
	(Pay salaries to employees)		
(10)	**December 30**		
	Dividends (+D, −SE)	4,000	
	Cash (−A)		4,000
	(Pay cash dividends)		

ILLUSTRATION 2–11

Summary of Journal Entries Recorded for Transactions of Eagle Soccer Academy

Illustration 2–12 provides the general ledger accounts after posting the journal entries summarized in Illustration 2–11. Account balances are in bold, and transaction numbers are shown in parentheses.

ILLUSTRATION 2–12   Posting of External Transactions of Eagle Soccer Academy from Journal Entries to General Ledger Accounts

Assets	=	Liabilities	+	Stockholders' Equity

Cash

(1)	200,000	(3)	120,000
(2)	100,000	(4)	60,000
(6)	43,000	(9)	28,000
(8)	6,000	(10)	4,000
Bal.137,000			

Accounts Receivable

| (7) | 20,000 |
| **Bal. 20,000** | |

Accounts Payable

| | (5) | 23,000 |
| | **Bal. 23,000** | |

Common Stock

| | (1) | 200,000 |
| | **Bal. 200,000** | |

Retained Earnings

| | 0 |
| | 0 |

Supplies

| (5) | 23,000 |
| **Bal. 23,000** | |

Prepaid Rent

| (4) | 60,000 |
| **Bal. 60,000** | |

Deferred Revenue

| | (8) | 6,000 |
| | **Bal. 6,000** | |

Service Revenue

	(6)	43,000
	(7)	20,000
	Bal. 63,000	

Salaries Expense

| (9) | 28,000 |
| **Bal. 28,000** | |

Equipment

| (3) | 120,000 |
| **Bal. 120,000** | |

Notes Payable

| | (2) | 100,000 |
| | **Bal. 100,000** | |

Dividends

| (10) 4,000 |
| **Bal. 4,000** |

Transaction numbers are shown in parentheses. Account balances are in bold.

Let's Review

Bogey Incorporated has the following transactions during May:

May 1   Purchase a storage building by obtaining a loan of $5,000.
May 6   Provide services to customers for cash, $1,800.
May 12   Pay $1,200 cash for advertising in May.
May 17   Repay $1,000 of the amount borrowed on May 1.
May 25   Purchase office supplies for $800 cash.

Required:

1. Record each transaction.

2. Post the transactions to the Cash T-account, assuming a beginning cash balance of $2,500 on May 1.

Solution:

1. Record each transaction.

May 1	Debit	Credit
Buildings *(+A)*	**5,000**	
Notes Payable *(+L)*		**5,000**
(Purchase building with note payable)		

May 6	Debit	Credit
Cash *(+A)*	**1,800**	
Service Revenue *(+R, +SE)*		**1,800**
(Provide services for cash)		

May 12	Debit	Credit
Advertising Expense *(+E, −SE)*	1,200	
Cash *(−A)*..		1,200
(Pay for advertising)		

May 17	Debit	Credit
Notes Payable *(−L)*	1,000	
Cash *(−A)*..		1,000
(Repay portion of note)		

May 25	Debit	Credit
Supplies *(+A)*	800	
Cash *(−A)*..		800
(Purchase supplies for cash)		

2. Post the transactions to the Cash T-account, assuming a beginning cash balance of $2,500 on May 1.

	Cash			
Beginning balance	2,500			
May 6	1,800			
		1,200	May 12	
		1,000	May 17	
		800	May 25	
Ending balance	1,300			

Suggested Homework:
BE2–7, BE2–8;
E2–8, E2–10, E2–11;
P2–4A&B, P2–5A&B

Trial Balance

After we've posted journal entries to the general ledger accounts, **the sum of the accounts with debit balances should equal the sum of the accounts with credit balances.** This is expected because debits were equal to credits for every journal entry posted to those ledger accounts. To prove this and to check for any errors in posting, we prepare a trial balance. A **trial balance** is a list of all accounts and their balances at a particular date, showing that total debits equal total credits. Another purpose of the trial balance is to assist us in preparing adjusting entries (for *internal* transactions). We discuss adjusting entries in Chapter 3.

Using the account balances calculated in Illustration 2–12, we can now prepare the trial balance of Eagle Soccer Academy. The trial balance appears in Illustration 2–13. Notice that accounts are listed with the debit balances in one column and the credit balances in another column. Asset, expense, and dividend accounts normally have debit balances. Liability, stockholders' equity, and revenue accounts normally have credit balances. (Remember the acronym DEALOR from Illustration 2–7.) As expected, total debits ($392,000) equal total credits ($392,000).

■ **LO2–6**
Prepare a trial balance.

⊗ COMMON MISTAKE

Just because the debits and credits are equal in a trial balance does not necessarily mean that all balances are correct. A trial balance could contain offsetting errors. For example, if we overstate cash and revenue each by $1,000, both accounts will be in error, but the trial balance will still balance, since the overstatement to cash increases debits by $1,000 and the overstatement to revenue increases credits by $1,000.

ILLUSTRATION 2–13

Trial Balance of Eagle
Soccer Academy

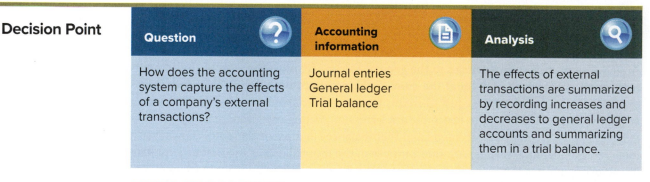

EAGLE SOCCER ACADEMY
Trial Balance
December 31, 2024

Accounts	Debit	Credit
Cash	$137,000	
Accounts Receivable	20,000	
Supplies	23,000	
Prepaid Rent	60,000	
Equipment	120,000	
Accounts Payable		$ 23,000
Deferred Revenue		6,000
Notes Payable		100,000
Common Stock		200,000
Retained Earnings		0
Dividends	4,000	
Service Revenue		63,000
Salaries Expense	28,000	
Totals	$392,000	$392,000

Total debits equal total
credits.

Retained Earnings.   Notice the balance of Retained Earnings in the trial balance is $0. As we explained earlier, retained earnings is a composite of three other types of accounts—revenues, expenses, and dividends. Those three accounts have balances at this point, but those balances haven't yet been transferred to the Retained Earnings account. This transfer is known as the *closing process,* and we will discuss it in Chapter 3. Since this is the first period of the company's operations, retained earnings will start at $0. As time goes by, retained earnings will accumulate a balance that is carried forward each period.

Decision Point

Question ❓	Accounting information 📄	Analysis 🔍
How does the accounting system capture the effects of a company's external transactions?	Journal entries General ledger Trial balance	The effects of external transactions are summarized by recording increases and decreases to general ledger accounts and summarizing them in a trial balance.

ORDER OF ACCOUNTS

The trial balance is used *for internal purposes only* and provides a check on the equality of the debits and credits. Because the trial balance is not a published financial statement to be used by external parties, there is no required order for listing accounts in the trial balance. However, most companies list accounts in the following order: assets, liabilities, stockholders' equity, dividends, revenues, and expenses. As we'll see in Chapter 3, the trial balance simplifies preparation of the published financial statements. Asset, liability, and stockholders' equity accounts are reported in the balance sheet. Dividends are reported in the statement of stockholders' equity. Revenue and expense accounts are reported in the income statement. Having the accounts listed in order of those classifications in the trial balance makes it easier to prepare the financial statements.

 KEY POINT

A trial balance is a list of all accounts and their balances at a particular date. Debits must equal credits, but that doesn't necessarily mean that all account balances are correct.

CAREER CORNER

The accuracy of account balances is essential for providing useful information to decision makers, such as investors and creditors. That's why the Securities and Exchange Commission (SEC) requires all companies with publicly traded stock to have their reported account balances verified by an independent audit firm. Auditors use their understanding of accounting principles and business practices to provide an opinion of reasonable assurance that account balances are free from material misstatements resulting from errors and fraud. Tens of thousands of audits are performed each year. Because of the huge demand for auditors and the valuable work experience it provides, many accounting majors begin their career as auditors.

CHAPTER FRAMEWORK

This chapter discusses two key topics related to the measurement function of financial accounting: (1) analyzing the impact of transactions on the accounting equation and (2) recording these transactions in a journal using debits and credits. These topics are best understood by first knowing the basic accounting equation and seeing how the stockholders' equity component expands to other accounts.

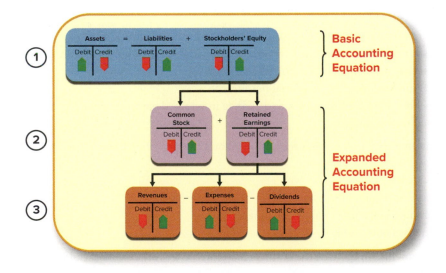

Measurement.

① The basic accounting equation shows assets equal liabilities plus stockholders' equity.
   1. **Assets**—Resources of the company (Examples: Cash, accounts receivable, supplies, prepaid rent, equipment, and land).
   2. **Liabilities**—Creditors' claims to resources (Examples: Accounts payable, salaries payable, utilities payable, deferred revenue, and notes payable).
   3. **Stockholders' Equity**—Owners' claims to resources (Examples: Common stock and retained earnings).

② Owners have claims equal to common stock plus retained earnings.
   1. **Common Stock**—Investments by owners in the company.
   2. **Retained Earnings**—Net income (revenues minus expenses) accumulated over the life of the company, less total dividends distributed over the life of the company.

③ There are three components of retained earnings.
  1. **Revenues**—Resources generated by the company in selling products and services to customers (Examples: Service revenue and interest revenue).
  2. **Expenses**—Resources used by the company in providing products and services to customers (Examples: Salaries expense, supplies expense, utilities expense, rent expense, and interest expense).
  3. **Dividends**—Distributions to owners.

To record increases and decreases in account balances caused by business transactions, accountants use the terms **debit** and **credit**. To help learn this measurement system, remember the acronym **DEALOR** and the rule "debits on the left; credits on the right."

- The *left-side accounts*—**D**ividends, **E**xpenses, and **A**ssets—increase with *debits*.
- The *right-side accounts*—**L**iabilities, **O**wners' (stockholders') equity, and **R**evenues—increase with *credits*.

To decrease balances in any of these accounts, you use the opposite.

The format used for recording debits and credits is known as a journal entry and is shown below. For each transaction, total debits must equal total credits.

Journal Entry.

Date	Debit	Credit
Account Name	Amount	
Account Name		Amount
(Description of transaction)		

Chapter Framework Questions

1. **Measurement:** The basic accounting equation shows
   a. Cash flows from operating, investing, and financing equal the change in cash.
   b. Assets equal liabilities plus stockholders' equity.
   c. Revenues minus expenses equal net income.
   d. The change in common stock and change in retained earnings equal the change in total stockholders' equity.

2. **Measurement:** The expanded accounting shows the two primary components of stockholders' equity are
   a. Dividends and liabilities.
   b. Assets and liabilities.
   c. Common stock and retained earnings.
   d. Expenses and assets.

3. **Measurement:** An increase in revenues has which effect on total stockholders' equity?
   a. Increase.
   b. Decrease.
   c. No effect.

4. **Measurement:** To record an increase in the balance of an asset account, a journal entry would include a _____ to the asset account.
   a. Debit.
   b. Credit.

5. **Measurement:** To record a decrease in the balance of an asset account, a journal entry would include a _____ to the asset account.
   a. Debit.
   b. Credit.

Note: For answers, see the last page of the chapter.

KEY POINTS BY LEARNING OBJECTIVE

LO2–1   Identify the basic steps in measuring external transactions.

External transactions are transactions between the company and a separate company or individual. Internal transactions do not include an exchange with a separate economic entity.

The six-step measurement process (Illustration 2–1) is the foundation of financial accounting. To understand this process, it is important to realize in step 2 that we analyze the effects of business transactions on the accounting equation (Part A of this chapter). Then, in step 3 we begin the process of translating those effects into the accounting records (Part B of this chapter).

LO2–2   Analyze the impact of external transactions on the accounting equation.

After each transaction, the accounting equation must always remain in balance. In other words, assets always must equal liabilities plus stockholders' equity.

The expanded accounting equation demonstrates that revenues increase retained earnings while expenses and dividends decrease retained earnings. Retained earnings is a component of stockholders' equity.

LO2–3   Assess whether the impact of external transactions results in a debit or credit to an account balance.

For the basic accounting equation (Assets = Liabilities + Stockholders' Equity), assets (left side) increase with *debits*. Liabilities and stockholders' equity (right side) increase with *credits*. The opposite is true to decrease any of these accounts.

The Retained Earnings account is a stockholders' equity account that normally has a credit balance. The Retained Earnings account has three components—revenues, expenses, and dividends. The difference between revenues (increased by credits) and expenses (increased by debits) equals net income. Net income increases the balance of Retained Earnings. Dividends (increased by debits) decrease the balance of Retained Earnings.

LO2–4   Record transactions in a journal using debits and credits.

For each transaction, total debits must equal total credits.

LO2–5   Post transactions to the general ledger.

Posting is the process of transferring the debit and credit information from transactions recorded in the journal to individual accounts in the general ledger.

LO2–6   Prepare a trial balance.

A trial balance is a list of all accounts and their balances at a particular date. Debits must equal credits, but that doesn't necessarily mean that all account balances are correct.

GLOSSARY

Account: A record of the business activities related to a particular item. **p. 59**

Accounting cycle: Full set of procedures used to accomplish the measurement/communication process of financial accounting. **p. 58**

Chart of accounts: A list of all account names used to record transactions of a company. **p. 59**

Credit: Right side of an account. Indicates a decrease to asset, expense, or dividend accounts, and an increase to liability, stockholders' equity, or revenue accounts. **p. 71**

Debit: Left side of an account. Indicates an increase to asset, expense, or dividend accounts, and a decrease to liability, stockholders' equity, or revenue accounts. **p. 71**

External transactions: Transactions the firm conducts with a separate economic entity. **p. 58**

General ledger: A collection of each account with its individual transactions and resulting account balance. **p. 76**

Journal: A chronological record of all transactions affecting a firm. **p. 74**

Journal entry: The format used for recording business transactions. **p. 74**

Posting: The process of transferring the debit and credit information from the journal to individual accounts in the general ledger. **p. 76**

Revenue recognition principle: Record revenue in the period in which we provide goods and services to customers for the amount the company is entitled to receive. **p. 65**

T-account: A simplified form of a general ledger account with space at the top for the account title, one side for recording debits, and one side for recording credits. **p. 77**

Trial balance: A list of all accounts and their balances at a particular date, showing that total debits equal total credits. **p. 83**

SELF-STUDY QUESTIONS

1. Which of the following represents an external transaction? **(LO2–1)**
   a. Lapse of insurance due to passage of time.
   b. Use of office supplies by employees over time.
   c. Payment of utility bill.
   d. Salaries earned by employees but not yet paid.

2. Which of the following is *not* a step in the process of measuring external transactions? **(LO2–1)**
   a. Analyze the impact of the transaction on the accounting equation.
   b. Record the transaction using debits and credits.
   c. Post the transaction to the T-account in the general ledger.
   d. All of the above are steps in the measurement process of external transactions.

3. Which of the following transactions causes an increase in total assets? **(LO2–2)**
   a. Pay employee salaries for the current month.
   b. Pay dividends to stockholders.
   c. Issue common stock in exchange for cash.
   d. Purchase office equipment for cash.

4. Which of the following transactions causes an increase in stockholders' equity? **(LO2–2)**
   a. Pay dividends to stockholders.
   b. Obtain cash by borrowing from a local bank.
   c. Provide services to customers on account.
   d. Purchase advertising on a local radio station.

5. If a company has an increase in total expenses of $10,000, which of the following is possible? **(LO2–2)**
   a. Total liabilities decrease by $10,000.
   b. Total assets increase by $10,000.
   c. Total stockholders' equity increases by $10,000.
   d. Total assets decrease by $10,000.

6. If a company has an increase in total revenues of $10,000, which of the following is possible? **(LO2–2)**
   a. Total assets increase by $10,000.
   b. Total liabilities increase by $10,000.
   c. Total stockholders' equity decreases by $10,000.
   d. Either *b.* or *c.* is correct.

7. Which of the following causes the accounting equation *not* to balance? **(LO2–2)**
   a. Increase assets; increase liabilities.
   b. Decrease assets; increase expenses.
   c. Increase assets; increase dividends.
   d. Decrease liabilities; increase revenues.

8. In the language of accounting, the term "debit" always means **(LO2–3)**
   a. Increase.
   b. Decrease.

   c. Left-hand side.
   d. Right-hand side.

9. A debit is used to increase which of the following accounts? **(LO2–3)**
   a. Utilities Expense.
   b. Accounts Payable.
   c. Service Revenue.
   d. Common Stock.

10. A credit is used to increase which of the following accounts? **(LO2–3)**
    a. Dividends.
    b. Insurance Expense.
    c. Cash.
    d. Service Revenue.

11. The purchase of supplies with cash would be recorded as **(LO2–4)**
    a. Debit Cash; Credit Supplies Expense.
    b. Debit Supplies; Credit Cash.
    c. Debit Cash; Credit Supplies.
    d. Debit Supplies Expense; Credit Cash.

12. The payment for utilities of the current month would be recorded as **(LO2–4)**
    a. Debit Cash; Credit Utilities Payable.
    b. Debit Utilities Expense; Credit Utilities Payable.
    c. Debit Utilities Expense; Credit Cash.
    d. Debit Utilities Payable; Credit Cash.

13. Providing services to customers on account for $100 is recorded as **(LO2–4)**

	Debit	Credit
a. Accounts Receivable	100	
Service Revenue		100
b. Cash	100	
Accounts Receivable		100
c. Service Revenue	100	
Accounts Receivable		100
d. Service Expense	100	
Accounts Payable		100

14. Posting is the process of **(LO2–5)**
    a. Analyzing the impact of the transaction on the accounting equation.
    b. Obtaining information about external transactions from source documents.
    c. Transferring the debit and credit information from the journal to individual accounts in the general ledger.
    d. Listing all accounts and their balances at a particular date and showing the equality of total debits and total credits.

15. A trial balance can best be explained as a list of **(LO2–6)**
    a. The income statement accounts used to calculate net income.
    b. Revenue, expense, and dividend accounts used to show the balances of the components of retained earnings.
    c. The balance sheet accounts used to show the equality of the accounting equation.
    d. All accounts and their balances at a particular date.

Note: For answers, see the last page of the chapter.

DATA ANALYTICS & EXCEL

Visit Connect to find a variety of Data Analytics questions that help build Excel, Tableau, and data visualization skills. Assignable materials include **Integrated Excel**, **Applying Excel**, **Data Visualizations**, **Tableau Dashboard Activities**, and **Applying Tableau Cases**.

REVIEW QUESTIONS

1. Explain the difference between external transactions and internal transactions. If a company purchases supplies from a local vendor, would this be classified as an external or internal transaction? ■ **LO2–1**

2. List the steps we use to measure external transactions. ■ **LO2–1**

3. Each external transaction will have a dual effect on the accounting equation. Explain what this means. ■ **LO2–2**

4. Describe the impact of each of these external transactions on the basic accounting equation. ■ **LO2–2**
    a. Receive a loan from the bank.
    b. Pay employee salaries for the current period.
    c. Receive cash from customers for services provided in the current period.
    d. Purchase equipment by paying cash.

5. Jerry believes that "dual effect" indicates that, for all transactions, one account will increase and one account will decrease. Is Jerry correct? Explain. ■ **LO2–2**

6. What is the normal balance (debit or credit) of assets, liabilities, stockholders' equity, revenues, and expenses? ■ **LO2–3**

7. Jenny has learned that assets have debit balances, while liabilities have credit balances. Based on this, she believes that asset accounts can only be debited and liabilities can only be credited. Is Jenny correct? When would we credit an asset and when would we debit a liability? ■ **LO2–3**

8. For each of the following accounts, indicate whether we use a debit or a credit to *increase* the balance of the account. ■ **LO2–3**
    a. Cash.
    b. Salaries Payable.
    c. Utilities Expense.
    d. Service Revenue.

9. For each of the following accounts, indicate whether we use a debit or a credit to *decrease* the balance of the account. (Compare your answers to those for *Question 8*.) ■ **LO2–3**
    a. Cash.
    b. Salaries Payable.
    c. Utilities Expense.
    d. Service Revenue.

10. Suzanne knows that an increase to an expense reduces retained earnings (a stockholders' equity account). However, she also knows that expense accounts have a *debit* balance, while retained earnings normally has a *credit* balance. Are these two pieces of information consistent? Explain. ■ **LO2–3**

■ LO2–4   11. What is a journal? What is a journal entry?

■ LO2–4   12. Provide the proper format for recording a transaction.

■ LO2–4   13. Explain the phrase "debits equal credits" with regard to journal entries.

■ LO2–4   14. Record each of the following external transactions using debits and credits.
      a. Receive cash of $1,200 for providing services to a customer.
      b. Pay rent of $500 for the current month.
      c. Purchase a building for $10,000 by signing a note with the bank.

■ LO2–4   15. Describe the events that correspond to the following transactions.

	Debit	Credit
a. Supplies...	20,000	
Cash..		20,000
b. Accounts Receivable...................................	30,000	
Service Revenue		30,000
c. Accounts Payable..	10,000	
Cash..		10,000

■ LO2–5   16. What does a T-account represent? What is the left side of the T-account called? What is the right side called?

■ LO2–5   17. Describe what we mean by posting. Post the transactions in *Question* 15 to appropriate T-accounts.

■ LO2–5   18. What is a general ledger? How does it relate to the chart of accounts?

■ LO2–6   19. What is a trial balance? To what does the term "balance" refer?

■ LO2–6   20. If total debits equal total credits in the trial balance, does this indicate that all transactions have been properly accounted for? Explain.

BRIEF EXERCISES

Mc Graw Hill **connect**

List steps in the measurement process (LO2–1)

BE2–1 Below are the steps in the measurement process of external transactions. Arrange them from first (1) to last (6).

_____ a. Post the transaction to the T-accounts in the general ledger.

_____ b. Assess whether the impact of the transaction results in a debit or credit to account balances.

_____ c. Use source documents to identify accounts affected by an external transaction.

_____ d. Analyze the impact of the transaction on the accounting equation.

_____ e. Prepare a trial balance.

_____ f. Record the transaction using debits and credits.

Balance the accounting equation (LO2–2)

BE2–2 Using the notion that the accounting equation (Assets = Liabilities + Stockholders' Equity) must remain in balance, indicate whether each of the following transactions is possible.
a. Cash increases; Accounts Payable decreases.
b. Service Revenue increases; Salaries Payable increases.
c. Advertising Expense increases; Cash decreases.

BE2–3 Suppose a local company has the following balance sheet accounts:

Balance the accounting equation (LO2–2)

Accounts	Balances
Land	$ 9,000
Equipment	?
Salaries Payable	4,300
Notes Payable	?
Supplies	2,100
Cash	7,200
Stockholders' Equity	13,500
Accounts Payable	1,700
Prepaid Rent	3,200

Calculate the missing amounts assuming the business has total assets of $37,500.

BE2–4 The following transactions occur for Badger Biking Company during the month of June:

a. Provide services to customers on account for $50,000.
b. Purchase bike equipment by signing a note with the bank for $35,000.
c. Repay $10,000 of the note in (b) above.
d. Pay utilities of $5,000 for the current month.

Analyze the impact of transactions on the accounting equation (LO2–2)

Analyze each transaction and indicate the amount of increases and decreases in the accounting equation.

	Assets	=	Liabilities	+	Stockholders' Equity
(a)	_____		_____		_____
(b)	_____		_____		_____
(c)	_____		_____		_____
(d)	_____		_____		_____

BE2–5 For each of the following accounts, indicate whether a debit or credit is used to increase (+) or decrease (−) the balance of the account. The solution for the first one is provided as an example.

Understand the effect of debits and credits on accounts (LO2–3)

Account	Debit	Credit
Asset	+	−
Liability	_____	_____
Common Stock	_____	_____
Retained Earnings	_____	_____
Dividends	_____	_____
Revenue	_____	_____
Expense	_____	_____

BE2–6 Fill in the blanks below with the word "debit" or "credit."

Understand the effect of debits and credits on accounts (LO2–3)

a. The balance of an *asset* account increases with a _____ and decreases with a _____.
b. The balance of a *liability* account increases with a _____ and decreases with a _____.
c. The balance of a *stockholders' equity* account increases with a _____ and decreases with _____.
d. The balance of a *revenue* account increases with a _____ and decreases with a _____.
e. The balance of an *expense* account increases with a _____ and decreases with a _____.

BE2–7 The following transactions occur for the Panther Detective Agency during the month of July:

Record transactions (LO2–4)

1. Purchase a truck and sign a note payable, $15,000.
2. Purchase office supplies for cash, $600.
3. Pay $800 in rent for the current month.

Record the transactions. The company uses the following accounts: Cash, Supplies, Equipment (for the truck), Notes Payable, and Rent Expense.

BE2–8 The following transactions occur for Cardinal Music Academy during the month of October:

1. Provide music lessons to students for $17,000 cash.
2. Purchase prepaid insurance to protect musical equipment over the next year for $4,200 cash.
3. Purchase musical equipment for $20,000 cash.
4. Obtain a loan from a bank by signing a note for $30,000.

Record the transactions. The company uses the following accounts: Cash, Prepaid Insurance, Equipment, Notes Payable, and Service Revenue.

BE2–9 Consider the following T-account for cash.

Cash	
13,000	8,200
4,400	1,900
3,500	5,500

1. Compute the balance of the Cash account.
2. Give some examples of transactions that would have resulted in the $4,400 posting to the account.
3. Give some examples of transactions that would have resulted in the $1,900 posting to the account.

BE2–10 The following transactions occur for the Wolfpack Shoe Company during the month of June:

a. Provide services to customers for $30,000 and receive cash.
b. Purchase office supplies on account for $20,000.
c. Pay $7,000 in salaries to employees for work performed during the month.

1. Analyze each transaction. For each transaction, indicate by how much each category in the accounting equation increases or decreases.

	Assets	=	Liabilities	+	Stockholders' Equity
(a)	_____		_____		_____
(b)	_____		_____		_____
(c)	_____		_____		_____

2. Record the transactions. The company uses the following accounts: Cash, Supplies, Accounts Payable, Salaries Expense, and Service Revenue.
3. Post the transactions to T-accounts. Assume the opening balance in each of the accounts is zero.

BE2–11 Using the following information, prepare a trial balance. Assume all asset, dividend, and expense accounts have debit balances and all liability, stockholders' equity, and revenue accounts have credit balances. List the accounts in the following order: assets, liabilities, stockholders' equity, dividends, revenues, and expenses.

Cash	$6,100	Dividends	$ 500
Salaries Payable	700	Rent Expense	2,000
Prepaid Rent	900	Accounts Receivable	4,400
Accounts Payable	2,000	Common Stock	6,200
Retained Earnings	2,000	Service Revenue	7,100
Salaries Expense	3,000	Advertising Expense	1,100

Record transactions (LO2–4)

Analyze T-accounts (LO2–5)

Analyze the impact of transactions on the accounting equation, record transactions, and post (LO2–2, 2–3, 2–4, 2–5)

Prepare a trial balance (LO2–6)

BE2–12 Your study partner is having trouble getting total debits to equal total credits in the trial balance. Prepare a corrected trial balance by placing each account balance in the correct debit or credit column.

Correct a trial balance (LO2–6)

Trial Balance

Accounts	Debit	Credit
Cash	$ 7,300	
Accounts Receivable		$ 2,100
Equipment	10,400	
Accounts Payable	3,900	
Deferred Revenue		1,100
Common Stock	11,000	
Retained Earnings		3,900
Dividends	600	
Service Revenue		4,500
Salaries Expense	3,200	
Utilities Expense		800
Total	$36,400	$12,400

EXERCISES

E2–1 Listed below are several terms and phrases associated with the measurement process for external transactions.

Identify terms associated with the measurement process (LO2–1)

List A	List B
_____ 1. Account	a. Record of all transactions affecting a company.
_____ 2. Analyze transactions	b. Determine the dual effect of business events on the accounting equation.
_____ 3. Journal	c. List of accounts and their balances.
_____ 4. Post	d. Summary of the effects of all transactions related to a particular item over a period of time.
_____ 5. Trial balance	e. Transfer balances from the journal to the general ledger.

Required:

Pair each item from List A with the item from List B to which it is most appropriately associated.

E2–2 Below are the external transactions for Shockers Incorporated.

1. Issue common stock in exchange for cash.
2. Purchase equipment by signing a note payable.
3. Provide services to customers on account.
4. Pay rent for the current month.
5. Pay insurance for the current month.
6. Collect cash from customers on account.

Analyze the impact of transactions on the accounting equation (LO2–2)

	Assets	=	Liabilities	+	Stockholders' Equity
1.	Increase	=	No effect	+	Increase
2.	_____		_____		_____
3.	_____		_____		_____
4.	_____		_____		_____
5.	_____		_____		_____
6.	_____		_____		_____

Required:

Analyze each transaction. Under each category in the accounting equation, indicate whether the transaction increases, decreases, or has no effect. The first item is provided as an example.

Analyze the impact of transactions on the accounting equation (LO2–2)

E2–3 Green Wave Company plans to own and operate a storage rental facility. For the first month of operations, the company had the following transactions.

1. Issue 10,000 shares of common stock in exchange for $32,000 in cash.
2. Purchase land for $19,000. A note payable is signed for the full amount.
3. Purchase storage container equipment for $8,000 cash.
4. Hire three employees for $2,000 per month.
5. Receive cash of $12,000 in rental fees for the current month.
6. Purchase office supplies for $2,000 on account.
7. Pay employees $6,000 for the first month's salaries.

Required:

For each transaction, describe the dual effect on the accounting equation. For example, in the first transaction, (1) assets increase and (2) stockholders' equity increases.

Analyze the impact of transactions on the accounting equation (LO2–2)

E2–4 Boilermaker House Painting Company incurs the following transactions for September.

1. Paint houses in the current month for $15,000 on account.
2. Purchase painting equipment for $16,000 cash.
3. Purchase office supplies on account for $2,500.
4. Pay employee salaries of $3,200 for the current month.
5. Purchase advertising to appear in the current month, $1,200.
6. Pay office rent of $4,400 for the current month.
7. Receive $10,000 from customers in (1) above.
8. Receive cash of $5,000 in advance from a customer who plans to have his house painted in the following month.

Required:

For each transaction, describe the dual effect on the accounting equation. For example, for the first transaction, (1) assets increase and (2) stockholders' equity increases.

Understand the components of retained earnings (LO2–2)

E2–5 At the beginning of April, Owl Corporation has a balance of $13,000 in the Retained Earnings account. During the month of April, Owl had the following external transactions.

1. Issue common stock for cash, $11,000.
2. Provide services to customers on account, $8,500.
3. Provide services to customers in exchange for cash, $3,200.
4. Purchase equipment and pay cash, $7,600.
5. Pay rent for April, $1,100.
6. Pay employee salaries for April, $3,500.
7. Pay dividends to stockholders, $2,000.

Required:

Using the external transactions above, compute the balance of Retained Earnings at April 30.

Indicate the debit or credit balance of accounts (LO2–3)

E2–6 Below is a list of common accounts.

Accounts	Debit or Credit
Cash	1. _____
Service Revenue	2. _____
Salaries Expense	3. _____
Accounts Payable	4. _____
Equipment	5. _____
Retained Earnings	6. _____
Utilities Expense	7. _____
Accounts Receivable	8. _____

(continued)

(concluded)

Accounts	Debit or Credit
Dividends	9. _____
Common Stock	10. _____

Required:

Indicate whether the normal balance of each account is a debit or a credit.

E2–7 Below are several external transactions for Hokies Company.

Associate debits and credits with external transactions (LO2–3)

	Account Debited	Account Credited
Example: Purchase equipment in exchange for cash.	*Equipment*	*Cash*
1. Pay a cash dividend.	_____	_____
2. Pay rent in advance for the next three months.	_____	_____
3. Provide services to customers on account.	_____	_____
4. Purchase office supplies on account.	_____	_____
5. Pay salaries for the current month.	_____	_____
6. Issue common stock in exchange for cash.	_____	_____
7. Collect cash from customers for services provided in (3) above.	_____	_____
8. Borrow cash from the bank and sign a note.	_____	_____
9. Pay for the current month's utilities.	_____	_____
10. Pay for office supplies purchased in (4) above.	_____	_____

Hokies uses the following accounts:

Accounts Payable	Equipment	Accounts Receivable
Cash	Supplies	Utilities Expense
Prepaid Rent	Rent Expense	Service Revenue
Common Stock	Notes Payable	Retained Earnings
Salaries Payable	Salaries Expense	Dividends

Required:

Indicate which accounts should be debited and which should be credited.

E2–8 Terrapin Company engages in the following external transactions for November.
1. Purchase equipment in exchange for cash of $23,400.
2. Provide services to customers and receive cash of $6,800.
3. Pay the current month's rent of $1,300.
4. Purchase office supplies on account for $1,000.
5. Pay employee salaries of $2,100 for the current month.

Record transactions (LO2–4)

Required:

Record the transactions. Terrapin uses the following accounts: Cash, Supplies, Equipment, Accounts Payable, Service Revenue, Rent Expense, and Salaries Expense.

E2–9 Below are recorded transactions of Yellow Jacket Corporation for August.

Identify transactions (LO2–4)

	Debit	Credit
1. Equipment	8,800	
Cash		8,800
2. Accounts Receivable	3,200	
Service Revenue		3,200
3. Salaries Expense	1,900	
Cash		1,900
4. Cash	1,500	
Deferred Revenue		1,500
5. Dividends	900	
Cash		900

Required:

Provide an explanation for each transaction.

E2–10 Sun Devil Hair Design has the following transactions during the month of February.

February 2	Pay $700 for radio advertising for February.
February 7	Purchase beauty supplies of $1,300 on account.
February 14	Provide beauty services of $2,900 to customers and receive cash.
February 15	Pay employee salaries for the current month of $900.
February 25	Provide beauty services of $1,000 to customers on account.
February 28	Pay utility bill for the current month of $300.

Required:

Record each transaction. Sun Devil uses the following accounts: Cash, Accounts Receivable, Supplies, Accounts Payable, Service Revenue, Advertising Expense, Salaries Expense, and Utilities Expense.

E2–11 Bearcat Construction begins operations in March and has the following transactions.

March 1	Issue common stock for $21,000.
March 5	Obtain $9,000 loan from the bank by signing a note.
March 10	Purchase construction equipment for $25,000 cash.
March 15	Purchase advertising for the current month for $1,100 cash.
March 22	Provide construction services for $18,000 on account.
March 27	Receive $13,000 cash on account from March 22 services.
March 28	Pay salaries for the current month of $6,000.

Required:

Record each transaction. Bearcat uses the following accounts: Cash, Accounts Receivable, Equipment, Notes Payable, Common Stock, Service Revenue, Advertising Expense, and Salaries Expense.

E2–12 Below are several transactions for Scarlet Knight Corporation. A junior accountant, recently employed by the company, proposes to record the following transactions.

External Transaction	Accounts	Debit	Credit
1. Owners invest $15,000 in the company and receive common stock.	Common Stock Cash	15,000	15,000
2. Receive cash of $4,000 for services provided in the current period.	Cash Service Revenue	4,000	4,000
3. Purchase office supplies on account, $300.	Supplies Cash	300	300
4. Pay $600 for next month's rent.	Rent Expense Cash	600	600
5. Purchase office equipment with cash of $2,200.	Cash Equipment	2,200	2,200

Required:

Assess whether the junior accountant correctly proposes how to record each transaction. If incorrect, provide the correction.

E2–13 Below are several transactions for Crimson Tide Corporation. A junior accountant, recently employed by the company, proposes to record the following transactions.

External Transaction	Accounts	Debit	Credit
1. Pay cash dividends of $800 to stockholders.	Cash Dividends	800	800
2. Provide services on account for customers, $3,400.	Cash Service Revenue	3,400	3,400

(continued)

(concluded)

External Transaction	Accounts	Debit	Credit
3. Pay a $500 utilities bill for the current period.	Utilities Expense Cash	500	 500
4. Receive cash of $400 from previously billed customers.	Cash Service Revenue	400	 400
5. Pay for supplies previously purchased on account, $1,200.	Supplies Expense Cash	1,200	 1,200

Required:

Assess whether the junior accountant correctly proposes how to record each transaction. If incorrect, provide the correction.

E2–14 Consider the following transactions.

1. Receive cash from customers, $15,000.
2. Pay cash for employee salaries, $9,000.
3. Pay cash for rent, $3,000.
4. Receive cash from sale of equipment, $8,000.
5. Pay cash for utilities, $1,000.
6. Receive cash from a bank loan, $4,000.
7. Pay cash for advertising, $7,000.
8. Purchase supplies on account, $3,000.

Post transactions to Cash T-account **(LO2–5)**

Required:

Post transactions to the Cash T-account and calculate the ending balance. The beginning balance in the Cash T-account is $5,000.

E2–15 Consider the recorded transactions below.

Post transactions to T-accounts **(LO2–5)**

	Debit	Credit
1. Accounts Receivable	8,400	
Service Revenue		8,400
2. Supplies	2,300	
Accounts Payable		2,300
3. Cash	10,200	
Accounts Receivable		10,200
4. Advertising Expense	1,000	
Cash		1,000
5. Accounts Payable	3,700	
Cash		3,700
6. Cash	1,100	
Deferred Revenue		1,100

Required:

Post each transaction to T-accounts and compute the ending balance of each account. The beginning balance of each account before the transactions is: Cash, $3,400; Accounts Receivable, $4,200; Supplies, $400; Accounts Payable, $3,500; Deferred Revenue, $300. Service Revenue and Advertising Expense each have a beginning balance of zero.

E2–16 Below are T-accounts. The first row in each is the beginning balance, and the numbers in parentheses are transaction numbers.

Identify transactions **(LO2–5)**

Cash					Accounts Receivable					Supplies	
8,000					2,000					1,000	
(1) 20,000	14,000	(5)	(2)		5,000	4,000	(3)	(4)		6,000	
(3) 4,000	7,000	(6)									
11,000					3,000					7,000	

Accounts Payable			Service Revenue			Salaries Expense		
		2,000			0			0
(6)	7,000	6,000 (4)			20,000 (1)	(5)	14,000	
					5,000 (2)			
		1,000			25,000			14,000

Required:

Provide an explanation for each transaction.

Prepare a trial balance (LO2–6)

E2–17 Below is the complete list of accounts of Sooner Company and the related balance at the end of April. All accounts have their normal debit or credit balance. Cash, $3,900; Prepaid Rent, $7,400; Accounts Payable $4,300; Common Stock, $40,000; Service Revenue, $25,400; Salaries Expense, $8,200; Accounts Receivable, $6,100; Land, $60,000; Deferred Revenue, $2,300; Retained Earnings, $23,000; Supplies Expense, $9,400.

Required:

Prepare a trial balance with the list of accounts in the following order: assets, liabilities, stockholders' equity, revenues, and expenses.

Prepare a trial balance (LO2–6)

E2–18 Below is the complete list of accounts of Cobras Incorporated and the related balance at the end of March. All accounts have their normal debit or credit balance. Supplies, $1,000; Buildings, $55,000; Salaries Payable, $500; Common Stock, $35,000; Accounts Payable, $2,200; Utilities Expense, $3,700; Prepaid Insurance, $1,200; Service Revenue, $19,500; Accounts Receivable, $4,200; Cash, $3,500; Salaries Expense, $6,400; Retained Earnings, $17,800.

Required:

Prepare a trial balance with the list of accounts in the following order: assets, liabilities, stockholders' equity, revenues, and expenses.

Record transactions, post to T-accounts, and prepare a trial balance (LO2–4, 2–5, 2–6)

E2–19 Green Wave Company plans to own and operate a storage rental facility. For the first month of operations, the company has the following transactions.

1. January 1   Issue 10,000 shares of common stock in exchange for $42,000 in cash.
2. January 5   Purchase land for $24,000. A note payable is signed for the full amount.
3. January 9   Purchase storage container equipment for $9,000 cash.
4. January 12 Hire three employees for $3,000 per month.
5. January 18 Receive cash of $13,000 in rental fees for the current month.
6. January 23 Purchase office supplies for $3,000 on account.
7. January 31 Pay employees $9,000 for the first month's salaries.

Required:

1. Record each transaction. Green Wave uses the following accounts: Cash, Supplies, Land, Equipment, Common Stock, Accounts Payable, Notes Payable, Service Revenue, and Salaries Expense.
2. Post each transaction to T-accounts and compute the ending balance of each account. Since this is the first month of operations, all T-accounts have a beginning balance of zero.
3. After calculating the ending balance of each account, prepare a trial balance.

Record transactions, post to T-accounts, and prepare a trial balance (LO2–4, 2–5, 2–6)

E2–20 Boilermaker House Painting Company incurs the following transactions for September.

1. September 3   Paint houses in the current month for $20,000 on account.
2. September 8   Purchase painting equipment for $21,000 cash.
3. September 12 Purchase office supplies on account for $3,500.

4.   September 15   Pay employee salaries of $4,200 for the current month.
5.   September 19   Purchase advertising to appear in the current month for $1,000 cash.
6.   September 22   Pay office rent of $5,400 for the current month.
7.   September 26   Receive $15,000 from customers in (1) above.
8.   September 30   Receive cash of $6,000 in advance from a customer who plans to have his
                     house painted in the following month.

Required:

1. Record each transaction. Boilermaker uses the following accounts: Cash, Accounts
    Receivable, Supplies, Equipment, Accounts Payable, Deferred Revenue, Common Stock,
    Retained Earnings, Service Revenue, Salaries Expense, Advertising Expense, and Rent
    Expense.
2. Post each transaction to T-accounts and compute the ending balance of each account. At the
    beginning of September, the company had the following account balances: Cash, $46,100;
    Accounts Receivable, $1,700; Supplies, $500; Equipment, $7,400; Accounts Payable, $1,200;
    Common Stock, $25,000; Retained Earnings, $29,500. All other accounts had a beginning
    balance of zero.
3. After calculating the ending balance of each account, prepare a trial balance.

PROBLEMS: SET A

Mc Graw Hill connect®

P2–1A Below is a list of activities for Jayhawk Corporation.

Analyze the impact
of transactions on
the accounting
equation **(LO2–2)**

Transaction	Assets	=	Liabilities	+	Stockholders' Equity
1. *Issue common stock in exchange for cash.*	*Increase*	=	*No effect*	+	*Increase*
2. Purchase business supplies on account.	_____		_____		_____
3. Pay for legal services for the current month.	_____		_____		_____
4. Provide services to customers on account.	_____		_____		_____
5. Pay employee salaries for the current month.	_____		_____		_____
6. Provide services to customers for cash.	_____		_____		_____
7. Pay for advertising for the current month.	_____		_____		_____
8. Repay loan from the bank.	_____		_____		_____
9. Pay dividends to stockholders.	_____		_____		_____
10. Receive cash from customers in (4) above.	_____		_____		_____
11. Pay for supplies purchased in (2) above.	_____		_____		_____

Required:

For each activity, indicate whether the transaction increases, decreases, or has no effect on
assets, liabilities, and stockholders' equity.

Analyze the impact
of transactions on
the accounting
equation (LO2–2)

P2–2A Below is a list of activities for Purple Cow Incorporated.

Transaction	Assets	=	Liabilities	+	Stockholders' Equity
1. *Provide services to customers on account, $1,600.*	+$1,600	=	$0	+	+$1,600
2. Pay $400 for current month's rent.	_____		_____		_____
3. Hire a new employee, who will be paid $500 at the end of each month.	_____		_____		_____
4. Pay $100 for advertising aired in the current period.	_____		_____		_____
5. Purchase office supplies for $400 cash.	_____		_____		_____
6. Receive cash of $1,000 from customers in (1) above.	_____		_____		_____
7. Obtain a loan from the bank for $7,000.	_____		_____		_____
8. Receive a bill of $200 for utility costs in the current period.	_____		_____		_____
9. Issue common stock for $10,000 cash.	_____		_____		_____
10. Pay $500 to employee in (3) above.	_____		_____		_____
Totals	_____	=	_____	+	_____

Required:

For each activity, indicate the impact on the accounting equation. After doing so for all transactions, ensure that the accounting equation remains in balance.

Identify the type
of account and its
normal debit or credit
balance (LO2–3)

P2–3A Below is a list of typical accounts.

Accounts	Type of Account	Normal Balance (Debit or Credit)
1. Salaries Payable	_____	_____
2. Common Stock	_____	_____
3. Prepaid Rent	_____	_____
4. Buildings	_____	_____
5. Utilities Expense	_____	_____
6. Equipment	_____	_____
7. Rent Expense	_____	_____
8. Notes Payable	_____	_____
9. Salaries Expense	_____	_____
10. Insurance Expense	_____	_____
11. Cash	_____	_____
12. Service Revenue	_____	_____

Required:

For each account, indicate (1) the type of account and (2) whether the normal account balance is a debit or credit. For the type of account, choose from asset, liability, stockholders' equity, dividend, revenue, or expense.

Record
transactions (LO2–4)

Flip Side of P2–5A

P2–4A Jake owns a lawn maintenance company, and Luke owns a machine repair shop. For the month of July, the following transactions occurred.

July 3   Jake provides lawn services to Luke's repair shop on account, $500.
July 6   One of Jake's mowers malfunctions. Luke provides repair services to Jake on account, $450.

July	9	Luke pays $500 to Jake for lawn services provided on July 3.
July	14	Luke borrows $600 from Jake by signing a note.
July	18	Jake purchases advertising in a local newspaper for the remainder of July and pays cash, $110.
July	20	Jake pays $450 to Luke for services provided on July 6.
July	27	Luke performs repair services for other customers for cash, $800.
July	30	Luke pays employee salaries for the month, $300.
July	31	Luke pays $600 to Jake for money borrowed on July 14.

Required:

Record the transactions for Jake's Lawn Maintenance Company. Keep in mind that Jake may not need to record all transactions.

P2–5A Refer to the transactions described in P2–4A.

Analyze the impact of transactions on the accounting equation and record transactions (LO2–2, 2–4)

Flip Side of P2–4A

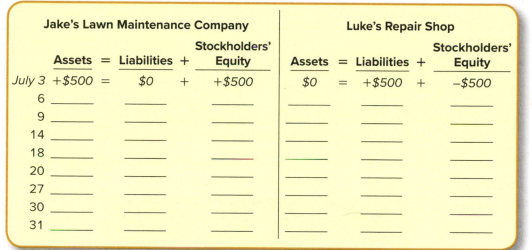

Jake's Lawn Maintenance Company

	Assets	=	Liabilities	+	Stockholders' Equity
July 3	+$500	=	$0	+	+$500
6					
9					
14					
18					
20					
27					
30					
31					

Luke's Repair Shop

Assets	=	Liabilities	+	Stockholders' Equity
$0	=	+$500	+	–$500

Required:

1. Record each transaction for Luke's Repair Shop. Keep in mind that Luke may not need to record all transactions.
2. Using the format shown above, indicate the impact of each transaction on the accounting equation for each company.

P2–6A Below are the account balances of Bruins Company at the end of November.

Prepare a trial balance (LO2–6)

Accounts	Balances	Accounts	Balances
Cash	$40,000	Common Stock	$50,000
Accounts Receivable	50,000	Retained Earnings	35,000
Supplies	1,100	Dividends	1,100
Prepaid Rent	3,000	Service Revenue	65,000
Equipment	?	Salaries Expense	30,000
Accounts Payable	17,000	Rent Expense	12,000
Salaries Payable	5,000	Interest Expense	3,000
Interest Payable	3,000	Supplies Expense	7,000
Deferred Revenue	9,000	Utilities Expense	6,000
Notes Payable	30,000		

Required:

Prepare a trial balance by placing amounts in the appropriate debit or credit column and determining the balance of the Equipment account.

Complete the steps in the measurement of external transactions (LO2–4, 2–5, 2–6)

GL

P2–7A Below are the transactions for Ute Sewing Shop for March, the first month of operations.

March 1   Issue common stock in exchange for cash of $3,000.
March 3   Purchase sewing equipment by signing a note with the local bank, $2,700.
March 5   Pay rent of $600 for March.
March 7   Martha, a customer, places an order for alterations to several dresses. Ute estimates that the alterations will cost Martha $800. Martha is not required to pay for the alterations until the work is complete.
March 12   Purchase sewing supplies for $130 on account. This material will be used to provide services to customers.
March 15   Ute delivers altered dresses to Martha and receives $800.
March 19   Ute agrees to alter 10 business suits for Bob, who has lost a significant amount of weight recently. Ute receives $700 from Bob and promises the suits to be completed by March 25.
March 25   Ute delivers 10 altered business suits to Bob.
March 30   Pay utilities of $95 for the current period.
March 31   Pay dividends of $150 to stockholders.

Required:
1. Record each transaction.
2. Post each transaction to the appropriate T-accounts.
3. Calculate the balance of each account at March 31.
4. Prepare a trial balance as of March 31.
Ute uses the following accounts: Cash, Supplies, Equipment, Accounts Payable, Deferred Revenue, Notes Payable, Common Stock, Dividends, Service Revenue, Rent Expense, and Utilities Expense.

Complete the steps in the measurement of external transactions (LO2–4, 2–5, 2–6)

GL

P2–8A Pirates Incorporated had the following balances at the beginning of September.

PIRATES INCORPORATED Trial Balance September 1		
Accounts	**Debits**	**Credits**
Cash	$ 6,500	
Accounts Receivable	2,500	
Supplies	7,600	
Land	11,200	
Accounts Payable		$ 7,500
Notes Payable		3,000
Common Stock		9,000
Retained Earnings		8,300
Total	$27,800	$27,800

The following transactions occur in September.

September 1   Provide services to customers for cash, $4,700.
September 2   Purchase land with a long-term note for $6,400 from Crimson Company.
September 4   Receive an invoice for $500 from the local newspaper for an advertisement that appeared on September 2.
September 8   Provide services to customers on account for $6,000.
September 10   Purchase supplies on account for $1,100.
September 13   Pay $4,000 to Crimson Company for a long-term note.
September 18   Receive $5,000 from customers on account.
September 20   Pay $900 for September's rent.
September 30   Pay September's utility bill of $2,000.
September 30   Pay employees $4,000 for salaries for the month of September.
September 30   Pay a cash dividend of $1,100 to shareholders.

Required:
1. Record each transaction.
2. Post each transaction to the appropriate T-accounts.
3. Calculate the balance of each account at September 30. (*Hint:* Be sure to include the balance at the beginning of September in each T-account.)
4. Prepare a trial balance as of September 30.

P2–9A RiverHawk Expeditions provides guided tours in scenic mountainous areas. After the first 11 months of operations in 2024, RiverHawk has the following account balances.

Complete the steps in the measurement of external transactions
(LO2–4, 2–5, 2–6)

RIVERHAWK EXPEDITIONS
Trial Balance
November 30, 2024

Accounts	Debits	Credits
Cash	$ 9,200	
Accounts Receivable	4,500	
Prepaid Insurance	400	
Equipment	24,100	
Land	170,000	
Accounts Payable		$ 3,300
Notes Payable		50,000
Common Stock		120,000
Retained Earnings		14,100
Dividends	5,000	
Service Revenue		75,000
Advertising Expense	11,000	
Salaries Expense	28,300	
Rent Expense	9,900	
Totals	$262,400	$262,400

The following transactions occur during December 2024:

December 1	Pay rent for mountain lodges for the month of December, $900.
December 5	Provide guided tour to customers in Grand Teton National Park for cash, $2,800.
December 8	Borrow from a local bank by signing a note payable, $10,000. The note is due in one year with a 6% interest rate.
December 12	Receive cash from customers as payment for a guided tour that occurred on November 28, $3,500.
December 13	Issue additional shares of common stock for cash, $20,000.
December 15	Pay employee salaries for the first half of the month, $1,200.
December 17	Purchase advertising on several local radio stations to be aired during the following two weeks, $1,000.
December 22	Provide guided tour to customers in Yellowstone National Park on account, $3,200.
December 23	One of the customers from the December 22 tour claims to have seen the legendary creature Bigfoot. The company believes this exciting news will create additional revenue of $20,000 next year.
December 26	Purchase several pieces of hiking equipment to give customers a more enjoyable adventure, such as night-vision goggles, GPS, long-range binoculars, and video cameras, for cash, $28,500.
December 28	Pay cash on accounts payable, $1,500.
December 31	Pay dividends to stockholders, $2,000.

Required:
1. Record each transaction.
2. Post each transaction to the appropriate T-accounts.

3. Calculate the balance of each account at December 31, 2024. (*Hint:* Be sure to include the balance at the beginning of December in each T-account.)
4. Prepare a trial balance as of December 31, 2024.

PROBLEMS: SET B

Mc Graw Hill connect®

Analyze the impact of transactions on the accounting equation (LO2–2)

P2–1B Below is a list of activities for Tigers Corporation.

Transaction	Assets	=	Liabilities	+	Stockholders' Equity
1. *Obtain a loan at the bank.*	*Increase*	=	*Increase*	+	*No effect*
2. Purchase a machine to use in operations for cash.	_____		_____		_____
3. Provide services to customers for cash.	_____		_____		_____
4. Pay employee salaries for the current month.	_____		_____		_____
5. Repay loan from the bank in (1) above.	_____		_____		_____
6. Customers pay cash in advance of services.	_____		_____		_____
7. Pay for maintenance costs in the current month.	_____		_____		_____
8. Pay for advertising in the current month.	_____		_____		_____
9. Purchase office supplies on account.	_____		_____		_____
10. Provide services to customers on account.	_____		_____		_____
11. Pay dividends to stockholders.	_____		_____		_____

Required:

For each activity, indicate whether the transaction increases, decreases, or has no effect on assets, liabilities, and stockholders' equity.

Analyze the impact of transactions on the accounting equation (LO2–2)

P2–2B Below is a list of activities for Vikings Incorporated.

Transaction	Assets	=	Liabilities	+	Stockholders' Equity
1. *Issue common stock in exchange for cash, $15,000.*	*+ $15,000*	=	*$0*	+	*+$15,000*
2. Obtain a loan from the bank for $9,000.	_____		_____		_____
3. Receive cash of $1,200 in advance from customers.	_____		_____		_____
4. Purchase supplies on account, $2,400.	_____		_____		_____
5. Pay one year of rent in advance, $12,000.	_____		_____		_____
6. Provide services to customers on account, $3,000.	_____		_____		_____
7. Repay $4,000 of the loan in (2) above.	_____		_____		_____
8. Pay the full amount for supplies purchased in (4) above.	_____		_____		_____
9. Provide services to customers in (3) above.	_____		_____		_____
10. Pay cash dividends of $1,000 to stockholders.	_____		_____		_____
Totals	_____	=	_____	+	_____

Required:

For each activity, indicate the impact on the accounting equation. After doing all the transactions, ensure that the accounting equation remains in balance.

P2–3B Below is a list of typical accounts.

Identify the type of account and its normal debit or credit balance **(LO2–3)**

Accounts	Type of Account	Normal Balance (Debit or Credit)
1. Supplies	_____	_____
2. Advertising Expense	_____	_____
3. Prepaid Insurance	_____	_____
4. Supplies Expense	_____	_____
5. Accounts Payable	_____	_____
6. Equipment	_____	_____
7. Dividends	_____	_____
8. Accounts Receivable	_____	_____
9. Retained Earnings	_____	_____
10. Deferred Revenue	_____	_____
11. Service Revenue	_____	_____
12. Utilities Payable	_____	_____

Required:

For each account, indicate (1) the type of account and (2) whether the normal account balance is a debit or credit. For type of account, choose from asset, liability, stockholders' equity, dividend, revenue, or expense.

P2–4B Eli owns an insurance office, while Olivia operates a maintenance service that provides basic custodial duties. For the month of May, the following transactions occurred.

Record transactions **(LO2–4)**

Flip Side of P2–5B

May 2	Olivia decides that she will need insurance for a one-day special event at the end of the month and pays Eli $300 in advance.
May 5	Olivia provides maintenance services to Eli's insurance offices on account, $425.
May 7	Eli borrows $500 from Olivia by signing a note.
May 14	Olivia purchases maintenance supplies from Spot Corporation, paying cash of $200.
May 19	Eli pays $425 to Olivia for maintenance services provided on May 5.
May 25	Eli pays the utility bill for the month of May, $135.
May 28	Olivia receives insurance services from Eli equaling the amount paid on May 2.
May 31	Eli pays $500 to Olivia for money borrowed on May 7.

Required:

Record each transaction for Eli's Insurance Services. Keep in mind that Eli may not need to record each transaction.

P2–5B Refer to the transactions described in P2–4B.

Analyze the impact of transactions on the accounting equation and record transactions **(LO2–2, 2–4)**

Flip Side of P2–4B

	Eli's Insurance Services				Olivia's Maintenance Services		
	Assets	= Liabilities +	Stockholders' Equity		Assets	= Liabilities +	Stockholders' Equity
May 2	+$300	= +$300 +	$0		+$300	= $0 +	$0
					−$300		
5	_____	_____	_____		_____	_____	_____
7	_____	_____	_____		_____	_____	_____

	Eli's Insurance Services			Olivia's Maintenance Services		
	Assets	= Liabilities +	Stockholders' Equity	Assets	= Liabilities +	Stockholders' Equity
14	———	———	———	———	———	———
19	———	———	———	———	———	———
25	———	———	———	———	———	———
28	———	———	———	———	———	———
31	———	———	———	———	———	———

Required:

1. Record transactions for Olivia's Maintenance Services. Keep in mind that Olivia may not need to record each transaction.
2. Using the format shown, indicate the impact of each transaction on the accounting equation for each company.

Prepare a trial balance (LO2–6)

P2–6B Below are account balances of Ducks Company at the end of September.

Accounts	Balances	Accounts	Balances
Cash	$25,000	Retained Earnings	$13,000
Accounts Receivable	14,000	Dividends	4,000
Supplies	7,000	Service Revenue	?
Prepaid Insurance	5,000	Salaries Expense	9,000
Equipment	28,000	Insurance Expense	8,000
Accounts Payable	7,000	Advertising Expense	1,100
Salaries Payable	4,000	Supplies Expense	10,000
Utilities Payable	1,100	Entertainment Expense	6,000
Deferred Revenue	9,000	Utilities Expense	1,100
Common Stock	29,000		

Required:

Prepare a trial balance by placing amounts in the appropriate debit or credit column and determining the balance of the Service Revenue account.

Complete the steps in the measurement of external transactions (LO2–4, 2–5, 2–6)

P2–7B Below are the transactions for Salukis Car Cleaning for June, the first month of operations.

June 1	Obtain a loan of $70,000 from the bank by signing a note.
June 2	Issue common stock in exchange for cash of $40,000.
June 7	Purchase car wash equipment for $75,000 cash.
June 10	Purchase cleaning supplies of $8,000 on account.
June 12	Wash 500 cars for $10 each. All customers pay cash.
June 16	Pay employees $900 for work performed.
June 19	Pay for advertising in a local newspaper, costing $500.
June 23	Wash 600 cars for $10 each on account.
June 29	Pay employees $950 for work performed.
June 30	A utility bill of $1,400 for the current month is paid.
June 30	Pay dividends of $600 to stockholders.

Required:

1. Record each transaction.
2. Post each transaction to the appropriate T-accounts.
3. Calculate the balance of each account.
4. Prepare a trial balance for June.

Salukis uses the following accounts: Cash, Accounts Receivable, Supplies, Equipment, Accounts Payable, Notes Payable, Common Stock, Dividends, Service Revenue, Salaries Expense, Advertising Expense, and Utilities Expense.

P2–8B Buckeye Incorporated had the following balances at the beginning of November.

Complete the steps in the measurement of external transactions (LO2–4, 2–5, 2–6)

BUCKEYE INCORPORATED
Trial Balance
November 1

Accounts	Debits	Credits
Cash	$ 3,200	
Accounts Receivable	600	
Supplies	700	
Equipment	9,400	
Accounts Payable		$ 2,000
Notes Payable		4,000
Common Stock		7,000
Retained Earnings		900
Totals	$13,900	$13,900

The following transactions occur in November.

November 1	Issue common stock in exchange for $13,000 cash.
November 2	Purchase equipment with a long-term note for $3,500 from Spartan Corporation.
November 4	Purchase supplies for $1,000 on account.
November 10	Provide services to customers on account for $9,000.
November 15	Pay creditors on account, $1,100.
November 20	Pay employees $3,000 for the first half of the month.
November 22	Provide services to customers for $11,000 cash.
November 24	Pay $1,400 on the note from Spartan Corporation.
November 26	Collect $7,000 on account from customers.
November 28	Pay $1,100 to the local utility company for November gas and electricity.
November 30	Pay $5,000 rent for November.

Required:

1. Record each transaction.
2. Post each transaction to the appropriate T-accounts.
3. Calculate the balance of each account at November 30. (*Hint:* Be sure to include the balance at the beginning of November in each T-account.)
4. Prepare a trial balance as of November 30.

P2–9B Thunder Cat Services specializes in training and veterinary services to household pets, such as dogs, birds, lizards, fish, horses, and of course, cats. After the first 11 months of operations in 2024, Thunder Cat has the following account balances:

Complete the steps in the measurement of external transactions (LO2–4, 2–5, 2–6)

THUNDER CAT SERVICES
Trial Balance
November 30, 2024

Accounts	Debits	Credits
Cash	$ 19,400	
Supplies	1,500	
Prepaid Rent	7,200	
Equipment	83,700	
Buildings	240,000	
Accounts Payable		$ 9,800
Deferred Revenue		2,000
Common Stock		125,000
Retained Earnings		75,500
Dividends	9,000	
Service Revenue		264,000
Salaries Expense	65,000	
Advertising Expense	18,200	
Utilities Expense	32,300	
Totals	$476,300	$476,300

The following transactions occur during December 2024:

December	4	Purchase pet supplies on account, $2,900.
December	8	Pay for fliers to be distributed to local residences to advertise the company's services, $3,200.
December	9	Pay for supplies purchased on December 4.
December	11	Thunder Cat provides services to customers for cash, $27,400.
December	12	Issue additional shares of common stock for cash, $5,000.
December	16	Pay cash on accounts payable, $6,300.
December	19	Purchase equipment with cash, $7,700.
December	22	Pay utilities for December, $4,500.
December	24	Receive cash from customers for services to be provided next January, $2,300.
December	27	One of Thunder Cat's trainers takes a part-time job at the zoo and earns a salary of $1,200. The zoo and Thunder Cat Services are separate companies.
December	30	Pay employee salaries for the current month, $7,000.
December	31	Pay dividends to stockholders, $3,000.

Required:

1. Record each transaction.
2. Post each transaction to the appropriate T-accounts.
3. Calculate the balance of each account at December 31, 2024. (*Hint:* Be sure to include the balance at the beginning of December in each T-account.)
4. Prepare a trial balance as of December 31, 2024.

REAL-WORLD PERSPECTIVES

Data Analytics & Excel

Visit Connect to find a variety of Data Analytics questions that help build Excel, Tableau, and data visualization skills. Assignable materials include Integrated Excel, Applying Excel, Data Visualizations, Tableau Dashboard Activities, and Applying Tableau Cases.

General Ledger Continuing Case

Great Adventures

(This is a continuation of the Great Adventures problem from Chapter 1.)

RWP2–1 Tony and Suzie graduate from college in May 2024 and begin developing their new business. They begin by offering clinics for basic outdoor activities such as mountain biking or kayaking. Upon developing a customer base, they'll hold their first adventure races. These races will involve four-person teams that race from one checkpoint to the next using a combination of kayaking, mountain biking, orienteering, and trail running. In the long run, they plan to sell outdoor gear and develop a ropes course for outdoor enthusiasts.

On July 1, 2024, Tony and Suzie organize their new company as a corporation, Great Adventures Inc. The articles of incorporation state that the corporation will sell 20,000 shares of common stock for $1 each. Each share of stock represents a unit of ownership. Tony and Suzie will act as co-presidents of the company. The following business activities occur during July for Great Adventures.

July 1	Sell $10,000 of common stock to Suzie.
July 1	Sell $10,000 of common stock to Tony.
July 1	Purchase a one-year insurance policy for $4,800 ($400 per month) to cover injuries to participants during outdoor clinics.
July 2	Pay legal fees of $1,500 associated with incorporation.
July 4	Purchase office supplies of $1,800 on account.
July 7	Pay $300 to a local newspaper for advertising to appear immediately for an upcoming mountain biking clinic to be held on July 15. Attendees will be charged $50 the day of the clinic.
July 8	Purchase 10 mountain bikes, paying $12,000 cash.
July 15	On the day of the clinic, Great Adventures receives cash of $2,000 from 40 bikers. Tony conducts the mountain biking clinic.
July 22	Because of the success of the first mountain biking clinic, Tony holds another mountain biking clinic and the company receives $2,300.

July 24   Pay $700 to a local radio station for advertising to appear immediately. A kayaking clinic will
            be held on August 10, and attendees can pay $100 in advance or $150 on the day of the clinic.

July 30   Great Adventures receives cash of $4,000 in advance from 40 kayakers for the
            upcoming kayak clinic.

Required:

1. Record each transaction in July for Great Adventures. [Note: These same transactions can be
   assigned as part of a more complete accounting cycle in Chapter 3's RWP3–1.]
2. Post each transaction to T-accounts.
3. Prepare a trial balance.

American Eagle Outfitters, Inc.

**Financial Analysis
Continuing Case**

RWP2–2 Financial information for **American Eagle** is presented in **Appendix A** at the end of the book.

Required:

1. Calculate American Eagle's percentage change in total assets and percentage change in net
   sales for the most recent year.
2. Calculate American Eagle's percentage change in net income for the most recent year.
3. Did American Eagle issue any common stock in the most recent year?
4. Do you see the term *debit* or *credit* listed in the balance sheet? Which account types in the
   balance sheet increase with a debit and which ones increase with a credit?
5. Do you see the term *debit* or *credit* listed in the income statement? Which account types in
   the income statement increase with a debit? Which increase with a credit?

The Buckle, Inc.

**Financial Analysis
Continuing Case**

RWP2–3 Financial information for **Buckle** is presented in **Appendix B** at the end of the book.

Required:

1. Calculate Buckle's percentage change in total assets and percentage change in net sales for
   the most recent year.
2. Calculate Buckle's percentage change in net income for the most recent year.
3. Did Buckle issue any common stock in the most recent year?
4. Do you see the term *debit* or *credit* listed in the balance sheet? Which account types in the
   balance sheet increase with a debit and which ones increase with a credit?
5. Do you see the term *debit* or *credit* listed in the income statement? Which account types in
   the income statement increase with a debit? Which increase with a credit?

American Eagle Outfitters, Inc. vs. The Buckle, Inc.

**Comparative Analysis
Continuing Case**

RWP2–4 Financial information for **American Eagle** is presented in **Appendix A** at the end of the
book, and financial information for **Buckle** is presented in **Appendix B** at the end of the book.

Required:

Determine which company's growth rate in total assets, net sales, and net income is greater.
Why do you think this might be the case?

EDGAR Research

RWP2–5 Using EDGAR (Electronic Data Gathering, Analysis, and Retrieval system),
find the annual report (10-K) for **Apple** for the year ended **September 28, 2019**. Locate the
"Consolidated Statements of Operations" (income statement) and "Consolidated Balance
Sheets." You also may find the annual report at the company's website.

Required:

Determine the following from the company's financial statements:

1. What amount does the company report for accounts receivable? What does this amount represent?
2. What amount does the company report for accounts payable? What does this amount represent?

3. The company reports a single amount for "Other current liabilities" in the liability section of the balance sheet. What are some possible liabilities included in this amount?
4. What amount does the company report for common stock (including additional paid-in capital)? What does this amount represent?
5. Determine whether the company's total assets equal total liabilities plus total stockholders' (or shareholders') equity.
6. What amount does the company report for net sales? When a sale is made, does the company debit or credit the Sales Revenue account?
7. Do the company's total revenues exceed total expenses? By how much?

Ethics

RWP2–6 Larry has been the chief financial officer (CFO) of Maxima Auto Service for the past 10 years. The company has reported profits each year it's been in business. However, this year has been a tough one. Increased competition and the rising costs of labor have reduced the company's profits. On December 30, Larry informs Robert, the company's president and Larry's closest friend for the past 10 years, that it looks like the company will report a net loss (total expenses will be greater than total revenues) of about $50,000 this year.

The next day, December 31, while Larry is preparing the year-end reports, Robert stops by Larry's office to tell him that an additional $75,000 of revenues needs to be reported and that the company can now report a profit. When Larry asks about the source of the $75,000, Robert tells him, "Earlier in the month some customers paid for auto services with cash, and with this cash I bought additional assets for the company. That's why the $75,000 never showed up in the bank statement. I just forgot to tell you about this earlier." When Larry asks for more specifics about these transactions, Robert mumbles, "I can't recall where I placed the customer sales invoices or the purchase receipts for the assets, but don't worry; I know they're here somewhere. We've been friends for a lot of years and you can trust me. Now, let's hurry and finish those reports and I'll treat you to dinner tonight at the restaurant of your choice."

Required:
1. Understand the reporting effect: What effect does reporting additional revenue have on reported profit?
2. Specify the options: If the additional revenue is not reported, do both Robert and Larry potentially lose benefits?
3. Identify the impact: Does reporting the additional revenue strengthen the company's financial appearance to those outside the company?
4. Make a decision: Should Larry report the additional revenue without source documents?

Written Communication

RWP2–7 Barth Interior provides decorating advice to its clients. Three recent transactions of the company include
a. Providing decorating services of $500 on account to one of its clients.
b. Paying $1,200 for an employee's salary in the current period.
c. Purchasing office equipment for $2,700 by paying cash.

Required:
Write a memo to your instructor describing the first five steps of the six-step measurement process presented in Illustration 2–1 for each of the three transactions. Separately explain step six for all transactions combined.

Answers to Chapter Framework Questions
1. b   2. c   3. a   4. a   5. b

Answers to Self-Study Questions
1. c   2. d   3. c   4. c   5. d   6. a   7. c   8. c   9. a   10. d   11. b   12. c   13. a   14. c   15. d

3

The Accounting Cycle: End of the Period

Learning Objectives

PART A: THE MEASUREMENT PROCESS

- **LO3–1** Understand when assets, liabilities, revenues, and expenses are recorded.
- **LO3–2** Distinguish between accrual-basis and cash-basis accounting.
- **LO3–3** Demonstrate the purposes and recording of adjusting entries.
- **LO3–4** Post adjusting entries and prepare an adjusted trial balance.

PART B: THE REPORTING PROCESS: FINANCIAL STATEMENTS

- **LO3–5** Prepare financial statements using the adjusted trial balance.

PART C: THE CLOSING PROCESS

- **LO3–6** Demonstrate the purposes and recording of closing entries.
- **LO3–7** Post closing entries and prepare a post-closing trial balance.

SELF-STUDY MATERIALS

- Let's Review—Accrual-basis compared with cash-basis (p. 118).
- Let's Review—Adjusting entries (p. 128).
- Let's Review—Closing entries (p. 142).
- Chapter Framework with questions and answers available (p. 143).
- Key Points by Learning Objective (p. 145).
- Glossary of Key Terms (p. 146).
- Self-Study Questions with answers available (p. 146).
- Videos including Concept Overview, Applying Excel, Let's Review, and Interactive Illustrations to demonstrate key topics (in Connect)

FEDERAL EXPRESS: DELIVERING PROFITS TO INVESTORS

Wouldn't it be great to put $1,000 into the stock market and watch your investment really grow? Which stock should you buy? Where should you buy it? There are thousands of stocks listed on stock exchanges in the United States and thousands of others listed throughout the world. With so many choices, how do you tell the winning stocks from the losing stocks? The single piece of information that best distinguishes them is *net income*.

To see an example of the power of net income in explaining movements in stock prices, consider the following information for **FedEx Corporation** (**FedEx**). Over the 20-year period from 2001–2020, FedEx's net income increased in 14 of 20 years. For the other six years, net income decreased. What happened to FedEx's stock price in each of these years? In the years that net income increased, FedEx's stock price *rose* an average of 18.3%. In contrast, in the years that net income decreased, FedEx's stock price *fell* an average of 8.6%. The goal is clear: Predict the direction of the change in net income and you'll predict the change in stock prices.

Why does the change in net income provide a good indicator for the change in stock prices each year? Answer: Because it reliably measures the ability of a company to generate profits (or resources) for its investors, the stockholders.

An increase in net income typically signals the company has increased its ability to generate resources for its investors. As that ability increases, investors are willing to pay a higher price to own the stock. The opposite is true for activities that decrease the company's ability to generate resources. These activities will cause net income to decrease.

In this chapter, we'll discuss how a company reports its profits and available resources in financial statements. Important in this reporting process is making sure that amounts in these financial statements are updated at the end of the period to reflect the activities of a company.

Dennis MacDonald/Alamy Stock Photo

PART A

THE MEASUREMENT PROCESS

In Chapter 2, we started the accounting cycle process by recording and posting transactions that occurred *during the period.* In this chapter, we'll complete the accounting cycle process at the *end of the period.* As summarized in Illustration 3–1, on the last day of the period we need to

1. Record and post **adjusting entries** (complete the measurement process).
2. Prepare **financial statements** (the reporting process).
3. Record and post **closing entries** (the closing process).

ILLUSTRATION 3–1

The Accounting Cycle

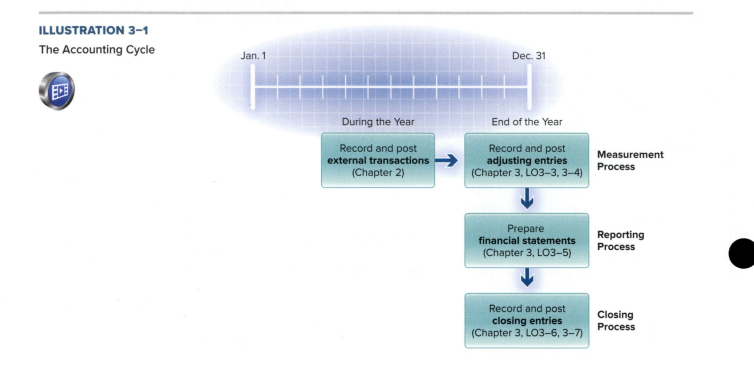

LO3–1

Understand when assets, liabilities, revenues, and expenses are recorded.

Accrual-Basis Accounting

Before discussing adjusting entries, let's first look back at the measurement process we started in Chapter 2. In Chapter 2, we used **accrual-basis accounting** to record transactions. In simple terms, accrual-basis accounting means we record.

Assets—at the time those resources are obtained.
Liabilities—at the time those obligations occur.
Revenues—at the time goods and services are provided to customers.
Expenses—at the time costs are used in running the company.

Under accrual-basis accounting, an attempt is made to record economic events as they occur. The intent is to provide accurate and timely information to financial statement users to make better decisions.

For example, when **FedEx** delivers a package, **American Eagle** sells a shirt, or **GEICO** provides insurance coverage, the company records revenue at that time. If a company sells goods or services to a customer in 2024, the company should report the revenue in its 2024 income statement. If the company sells goods or services to a customer in 2025, it should report the revenue in the 2025 income statement. This is the **revenue recognition principle** we discussed in Chapter 2.[1]

Similarly, costs used in business operations to help generate revenues are reported as expenses in those periods. When FedEx delivers packages in 2024, the company will have costs of fuel for delivery trucks, salaries for delivery people, and supplies used in making deliveries. These costs will be reported as expenses in the 2024 income statement, along with the revenues they help to produce. Some costs (known as period costs) are more difficult to relate directly to a particular revenue activity, so we report those based on the period they occur (such as rent, advertising, or administrative salaries).

 KEY POINT

Under accrual-basis accounting, economic events that affect assets, liabilities, revenues, and expenses are recorded as they occur.

Accrual-Basis Compared with Cash-Basis Accounting

One way to better understand accrual-basis accounting is to compare it to an alternative measurement method—cash-basis accounting. Under **cash-basis accounting**, we record transactions **only at the time** *cash* **is received or paid.** If cash is not received or paid, no transaction is recorded.

■ **LO3–2**
Distinguish between accrual-basis and cash-basis accounting.

REVENUE-RELATED TRANSACTIONS

To demonstrate the timing difference between accrual-basis accounting versus cash-basis accounting, let's refer back to the transactions of Eagle Soccer Academy. Illustration 3–2 lists three revenue-related transactions and summarizes revenue recognition under each method.

ILLUSTRATION 3–2   Accrual-Basis versus Cash-Basis for Revenue-Related Transactions

Transaction	Description	Accrual-Basis		Cash-Basis	
		Service Provided?	Revenue Recorded	Cash Received?	Revenue Recorded
(6) Dec. 12	Provide soccer training to customers for cash, $43,000.	Yes →	$43,000	Yes →	$43,000
(7) Dec. 17	Provide soccer training to customers on account, $20,000.	Yes →	$20,000	No	$0 Not recorded until cash received
(8) Dec. 23	Receive cash in advance for soccer training sessions to be given in the future, $6,000.	No	$0 Record as Deferred Revenue (liability) until services provided.	Yes →	$6,000

---

[1]The revenue recognition principle was revised by Accounting Standards Update No. 2014-09, "Revenues from Contracts with Customers," effective for public companies for annual periods beginning after December 15, 2017. Prior to this update, revenue recognition relied on the concepts of "revenue being earned" and "cash being collected or collectible." Our discussion of revenue recognition is based on the new standard.

For accrual-basis accounting, we need to ask ourselves, "Was a service provided to customers at the time of the transaction?" The answer is "Yes" for transactions (6) and (7). Therefore, we recognize revenue on those dates for the amount the company is entitled to receive [cash in transaction (6) and accounts receivable in transaction (7)].

For transaction (8), no service has been provided to those customers, so no revenue is recognized at that time. Instead, we initially record Deferred Revenue (a liability account) for the cash received. Revenue is not recorded until those services are provided.

For cash-basis accounting, we simply ask ourselves, "Was *cash received* from customers?" The answer is "Yes" for transactions (6) and (8). Under cash-basis accounting, we recognize revenue on those dates for the amount of cash received. We record nothing on December 17 because no cash was received.

EXPENSE-RELATED TRANSACTIONS

Illustration 3–3 lists three of the expense-related transactions of Eagle Soccer Academy and summarizes accrual-basis accounting versus cash-basis accounting.

ILLUSTRATION 3–3   Accrual-Basis Expense versus Cash-Basis Expense

		Accrual-Basis		Cash-Basis	
Transaction	Description	Cost Used?	Expense Recorded	Cash Paid?	Expense Recorded
(4) Dec. 1	Pay one year of rent in advance, $60,000 ($5,000 per month).	No	$0 Record as Prepaid Rent (asset) until rent expires ($5,000/month)	Yes →	$60,000
(5) Dec. 6	Purchase supplies on account, $23,000.	No	$0 Record as Supplies (asset) until supplies used	No	$0 Not recorded until cash paid
(9) Dec. 28	Pay salaries to employees, $28,000.	Yes →	$28,000	Yes →	$28,000

For accrual-basis accounting, we need to ask ourselves, Was a *cost used* at the time of the transaction?" The answer is "Yes" for transaction (9), so we recognize an expense on that date equal to the cost of salaries in December. For transactions (4) and (5), no costs were used at the time of the transaction, so no expense would be recorded. Instead, for transaction (4) we record Prepaid Rent (an asset). The cost of rent will be expensed as the rent expires. For transaction (5), we record Supplies (an asset). The cost of these supplies will be expensed once they are used.

For cash-basis accounting, we simply ask ourselves, "Was *cash paid* for activities related to business operations?" The answer is "Yes" for transactions (4) and (9). Under cash-basis accounting, we recognize expenses on those dates for the amount of cash paid. No entry is made for transaction (5) on December 6 because no cash was paid.

TIMING DIFFERENCES

Under both accrual-basis and cash-basis accounting, all revenues and expenses are eventually recorded for the same *amount*. For example, the $6,000 received from customers in advance on December 23 eventually will be recognized as revenue under both accounting methods because the services will be provided at some point (accrual-basis) and cash has been received (cash-basis).

Similarly for expenses, the $60,000 of rent purchased on December 1 will be expensed fully after one year under both accounting methods because the rental space will have been used (accrual-basis) and cash has been paid (cash-basis). The $23,000 of supplies purchased on December 6 will be expensed fully once those supplies are used (accrual-basis) and cash has been paid (cash-basis). **The difference between accrual-basis accounting and cash-basis accounting is in the *timing* of when we record those revenues and expenses.**

COMMON MISTAKE

It's easy at first to think that revenue should be recorded only when cash is received. However, under accrual-basis accounting, we record revenues when goods and services are provided to customers, regardless of when cash is received from those customers. Similarly, you might think that expenses can be recorded only when cash is paid, but we record expenses when costs are presumed to have been used, regardless of when cash is paid.

No Timing Differences.   Sometimes cash flows occur *at the same time* as the related revenue and expense activity. For example, look at transaction (4) where Eagle received $43,000 cash from customers at the time it provided services on December 12. Here, there is no timing difference between revenue recognition under accrual-basis and cash-basis accounting. The inflow of cash occurs in the same period that the services are provided.

Similarly, in transaction (9) Eagle paid salaries of $28,000 for work done by employees in December. There is no timing difference between expense recognition under accrual-basis and cash-basis accounting. The outflow of cash occurs in the same period as the cost used for providing services.

Generally Accepted Accounting Principles.   Cash-basis accounting may seem appealing because it is essentially how we think about the inflow and outflow of cash from our bank accounts. However, **cash-basis accounting is not part of generally accepted accounting principles (GAAP).** All major companies use accrual-basis accounting to properly record revenues when goods and services are provided and to properly record expenses in the period those costs have been used in company operations. Accrual-basis accounting is focused on the *timing* of transactions and events in the accounting cycle.

Cash-basis accounting is not part of generally accepted accounting principles (GAAP).

KEY POINT

The difference between accrual-basis accounting and cash-basis accounting is timing. Under accrual-basis accounting, we record revenues when we provide goods and services to customers, and we record expenses when costs are used in company operations. Under cash-basis accounting, we record revenues when we receive cash, and we record expenses when we pay cash. Cash-basis accounting is not allowed for financial reporting purposes for most major companies.

Cavalier Company experienced the following set of events:

Let's Review

May: *Receives cash* from customers for services to be provided in June.
June: *Provides services* to customers who prepaid in May.
May: *Pays cash* for supplies but does not use them.
June: *Uses supplies* purchased in May.

Required:

1. Indicate in which month Cavalier records revenues under
   a. Accrual-basis accounting.
   b. Cash-basis accounting.
2. Indicate in which month Cavalier records expenses under
   a. Accrual-basis accounting.
   b. Cash-basis accounting.

Suggested Homework:
BE3–4, BE3–5;
E3–3, E3–4;
P3–1A & B; P3–2A & B

Solution:

1a. June   1b. May   2a. June   2b. May

Adjusting Entries

■ **LO3–3**
Demonstrate the purposes
and recording of adjusting
entries.

As we discussed earlier in this chapter, accrual-basis accounting creates timing differences between cash inflows and their related revenues, and between cash outflows and their related expenses. **These timing differences are recorded as assets and liabilities under accrual-basis accounting**.

By the end of the year, we need to make sure all assets and liabilities are stated at their proper amounts. We do this with adjusting entries. We'll use adjusting entries to update balances of assets and liabilities (and their related revenues and expenses). These updates are needed because transactions have occurred during the period but have not yet been recorded.

Let's first examine why adjusting entries are needed in the case of **cash flows occurring *before* the revenues and expenses are recognized**. This concept is demonstrated in Illustration 3–4A.

Prepaid expenses occur when a company pays cash to purchase an asset in advance of using that asset. For example, when cash is paid for rent in advance of the rental period, we record Prepaid Rent (an asset). That rent expires every day, but we don't need to decrease the balance of Prepaid Rent every day. Instead, we'll wait until the end of the reporting period, determine the total amount of rent expired during the period, and do a single adjusting entry to decrease the balance of Prepaid Rent to its remaining amount. We'll also recognize Rent Expense for the cost of rent expired during the period.

Deferred revenues occur when cash is received from customers in advance of the services to be provided. This creates a liability to the company, recorded in the Deferred Revenue account. The company might provide those services every day, but we don't need to record a decrease to the balance of Deferred Revenue every day. Instead, we'll wait until the end of the reporting period, determine the total amount of services provided, and do a single adjusting entry to decrease the balance of Deferred Revenue to its remaining amount. We'll also recognize Service Revenue for the services provided during the period.

Adjusting entries are also needed in the case of **cash flows occurring *after* the revenues and expenses are recognized**. This concept is demonstrated in Illustration 3–4B.

Accrued expenses occur when a company incurs costs, such as salaries, by the end of the current period but will not pay those salaries until the following period. An adjusting entry is needed in the current period to record salaries payable (a liability) for the amount to be paid and to recognize salaries expense.

Accrued revenues occur when a company provides goods and services and therefore generates the right to receive cash from a customer. An adjusting entry is needed in the current period to record the amount receivable (an asset) and to recognize revenue, even though that cash won't be received until a future period.

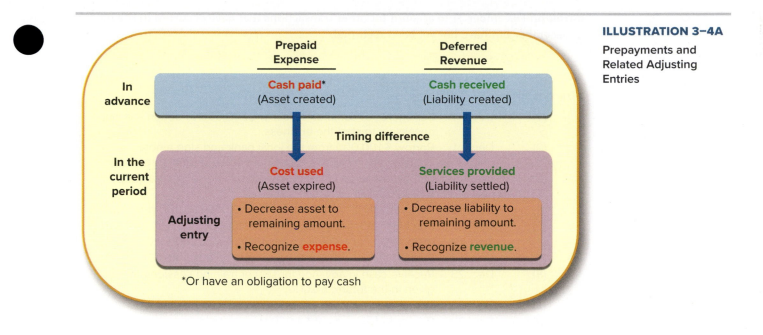

ILLUSTRATION 3–4A

Prepayments and Related Adjusting Entries

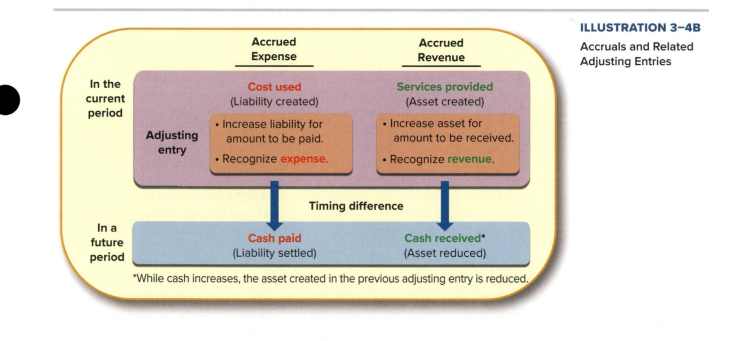

ILLUSTRATION 3–4B

Accruals and Related Adjusting Entries

KEY POINT

Adjusting entries are a necessary part of accrual-basis accounting. They are used to record changes in assets and liabilities (and their related revenues and expenses) that have occurred during the period but have not yet been recorded by the end of the period.

In the four sections to follow, we'll discuss each type of adjusting entry and work through several examples for Eagle Soccer Academy. It will help if we first look back to the external transactions of Eagle Soccer Academy from Chapter 2. For easy reference, we've restated these transactions in Illustration 3–5. These transactions have already been recorded in the month of December. In the next four sections, we'll prepare all adjusting entries on December 31 to account for other transactions that have occurred in the month of December but have not yet been recorded.

ILLUSTRATION 3–5

External Transactions of Eagle Soccer Academy

Transaction	Date	Description
(1)	Dec. 1	Sell shares of common stock for $200,000 to obtain the funds necessary to start the business.
(2)	Dec. 1	Borrow $100,000 from the local bank and sign a note promising to repay the full amount of the debt in three years.
(3)	Dec. 1	Purchase equipment necessary for giving soccer training, $120,000 cash.
(4)	Dec. 1	Pay one year of rent in advance, $60,000 ($5,000 per month).
(5)	Dec. 6	Purchase supplies on account, $23,000.
(6)	Dec. 12	Provide soccer training to customers for cash, $43,000.
(7)	Dec. 17	Provide soccer training to customers on account, $20,000.
(8)	Dec. 23	Receive cash in advance for soccer training sessions to be given in the future, $6,000.
(9)	Dec. 28	Pay salaries to employees, $28,000.
(10)	Dec. 30	Pay cash dividends of $4,000 to shareholders.

PREPAID EXPENSES

Prepaid expenses arise when a company pays cash (or has an obligation to pay cash) to acquire an asset that is not used until a later period. There is a timing difference—cash is paid now, and then later, the expense is recognized (refer back to Illustration 3–4A). Common examples include the purchase of buildings, equipment, or supplies or the payment of rent in advance. These payments are recorded as assets at the time of purchase. **In the period these assets are used, an adjusting entry is needed to (1) decrease the asset's balance to its remaining (unused) amount and (2) recognize an expense for the cost of asset used.**

Eagle Soccer Academy had three prepaid expenses during December: It purchased equipment on December 1, rent on December 1, and supplies on December 6. Each of these items will be used in the future and was recorded as an asset at the time of purchase. *By the end of December,* the company has used a portion of each asset, and the accounting records need to reflect this change in assets and expenses. Let's now look at the adjusting entry needed for each of these prepaid expenses.

Prepaid Rent.   On December 1, Eagle Soccer Academy purchased one year of rent in advance for $60,000 ($5,000 per month). The agreement allows Eagle to have rental space for one year, so we recorded the $60,000 cash payment on December 1 as an asset—Prepaid Rent. Eagle's ability to use the rented space, however, will expire over time. By December 31, one month of rent has expired. An adjusting entry is needed to reduce the balance of Prepaid Rent to its remaining amount and to recognize an expense (Rent Expense) for the cost of rent for the month of December.

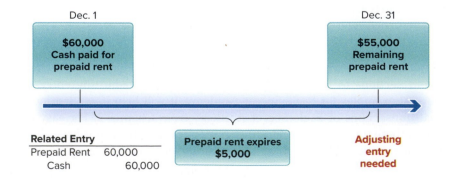

The end-of-period **adjusting entry** for expiration of prepaid rent is below.

December 31	Debit	Credit
Rent Expense *(+E, −SE)*...	**5,000**	
Prepaid Rent *(−A)*..		**5,000**
(Reduce prepaid rent due to the passage of time)		

Prepaid Rent		
60,000		12/1
	5,000 **Adj.**	12/31
55,000		

Notice that this adjusting entry includes a $5,000 expense (+E), which reduces net income and stockholders' equity (−SE). The entry also also reduces the balance in the asset account, Prepaid Rent (−A), by $5,000. The Prepaid Rent account will now have a balance of $55,000 (= $60,000 − $5,000 adjustment), which equals the remaining amount of prepaid rent for the next 11 months. We adjust any other assets that expire over time (such as prepaid insurance) in a similar manner.

COMMON MISTAKE

When a cash prepayment has occurred, students sometimes confuse the initial cash entry (the prepayment) with the adjusting entry that follows. The cash flow is not the adjusting entry. The adjusting entry is to recognize the expense that has occurred after the cash flow.

Supplies. On December 6, Eagle purchased supplies for $23,000 on account. Those supplies were expected to be used at a later time and were recorded as an asset—Supplies. Assume that *at the end of December* a count of supplies reveals that only $13,000 of supplies remains. What happened to the other $10,000 of supplies? Apparently, this is the amount of supplies used throughout the month. Since it's not cost-efficient to record the consumption of supplies every day, the Supplies account has not been updated each day. On December 31, an adjusting entry is needed to reduce the Supplies account to the remaining amount and to recognize the expense (Supplies Expense) for the cost of supplies used in December.

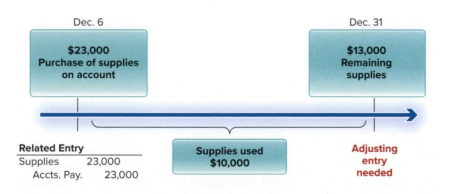

The end-of-period **adjusting entry** for supplies is below.

December 31	Debit	Credit
Supplies Expense *(+E, −SE)*..	**10,000**	
Supplies *(−A)*..		**10,000**
(Consume supplies during the current period)		

Supplies		
23,000		12/6
	10,000 **Adj.**	12/31
13,000		

This adjusting entry includes a $10,000 expense, which reduces net income and stockholders' equity. The entry also reduces the balance in the asset account, Supplies, by $10,000. The Supplies account will now have a balance of $13,000 (= $23,000 − $10,000 adjustment), which equals the remaining amount of supplies.

Depreciable Assets.   On December 1, Eagle purchased equipment for $120,000 cash. Let's assume that Eagle estimates the equipment will be used for the next five years (60 months), so the purchase was recorded as an asset—Equipment. As each month passes, the equipment will be used and its benefits will expire. Therefore, by December 31, one month of the equipment's use has expired. An adjusting entry is needed to reduce the asset to the remaining amount to be used in the future and to recognize an expense for the cost of equipment used in December. The cost of the equipment for one month's use is $2,000 (= $120,000 × 1/60).

Unlike prepayments for rent and supplies that typically expire within one year, equipment is an asset that typically expires in more than one year. We record the reduction in the cost of assets that have longer lives using a concept called *depreciation*. **Depreciation** is the process of allocating the cost of an asset, such as equipment, to expense over the asset's useful life. We discuss this in detail in Chapter 7; here we will cover just the basics.

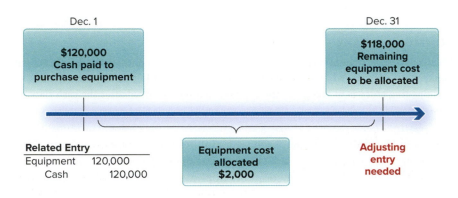

The end-of-period **adjusting entry** to record one month of depreciation for equipment is below.

Equipment, net				December 31	Debit	Credit

Equipment, net
12/1 120,000
12/31   2,000 **Adj.**
     118,000

December 31	Debit	Credit
Depreciation Expense (+E, −SE)...	**2,000**	
Accumulated Depreciation (−A)...		**2,000**
(Depreciation expense = $120,000 ÷ 60 months = $2,000 per month)		

This adjusting entry includes a $2,000 expense, which reduces net income and stockholders' equity. The entry also reduces assets by $2,000. Notice, however, that we didn't reduce Equipment directly, by crediting the asset account itself. Instead, we reduce the asset *indirectly* by crediting an account called *Accumulated Depreciation*. The Accumulated Depreciation account is called a *contra account*. A **contra account** is an account with a balance that is opposite, or "contra," to that of its related accounts.

Common Terms Another common name for *book value* is *carrying value* because this is the amount the asset is "carried" in the books.

The normal balance in the Accumulated Depreciation contra asset account is a *credit*, which is opposite to the normal *debit* balance in an asset account. The reason we use a contra account is to keep the original balance of the asset intact while reducing its current balance indirectly. In the balance sheet, we report equipment at its current **book value**, which equals its original cost "net of" accumulated depreciation.

Illustration 3–6 shows how **Federal Express** records its property and equipment at original cost and then subtracts accumulated depreciation. As you will see in Chapter 7, depreciation is an *estimate* based on expected useful life and is an attempt to *allocate the cost of the asset over its useful life*. Depreciation is a calculation internal to the company, and the cost of the asset less accumulated depreciation does not necessarily represent market value (what the asset could be sold for in the market).

FEDERAL EXPRESS Balance Sheet (partial) ($ in millions)	
Property and Equipment, at Cost	
Aircraft and related equipment	$24,518
Package handling and ground support equipment	11,382
Information technology	6,884
Vehicles and trailers	9,101
Facilities and other	13,139
	65,024
Less accumulated depreciation	(31,416)
Net property and equipment	**$33,608**

ILLUSTRATION 3–6

Reporting Depreciation of Property and Equipment for Federal Express

ETHICAL DILEMMA

LightField Studios/Shutterstock

You have recently been employed by a large clothing retailer. One of your tasks is to help prepare financial statements for external distribution. The company's lender, National Savings & Loan, requires that financial statements be prepared according to generally accepted accounting principles (GAAP). During the months of November and December 2024, the company spent $1 million on a major TV advertising campaign. The $1 million included the costs of producing the commercials as well as the broadcast time purchased to run them. Because the advertising will be aired in 2024 only, you charge all the costs to advertising expense in 2024, in accordance with requirements of GAAP.

The company's chief financial officer (CFO), who hired you, asks you for a favor. Instead of charging the costs to advertising expense, he asks you to set up an asset called prepaid advertising and to wait until 2025 to record advertising expense. The CFO explains, "This ad campaign has produced significant sales in 2024; but I think it will continue to bring in customers throughout 2025. By recording the ad costs as an asset, we can match the cost of the advertising with the additional sales in 2025. Besides, if we expense the advertising in 2024, we will show an operating loss in our income statement. The bank requires that we continue to show profits in order to maintain our loan in good standing. Failure to remain in good standing could mean we'd have to lay off some of our recent hires." As a staff accountant, should you knowingly record advertising costs incorrectly if asked to do so by your superior? Does your answer change if you believe that misreporting will save employee jobs?

DEFERRED REVENUES

Deferred revenues arise when a company receives cash in advance from customers, but products and services won't be provided until a later period. This creates a timing difference between when the cash is received and when related revenue is recognized (refer back to Illustration 3–4A). Examples include receiving cash in advance from customers for subscriptions, memberships, and gift cards. When a company receives cash before providing services to customers, it *owes* the customer a service in return. This creates a liability. **In the period those services are provided, the liability is settled, and an adjusting entry is needed to (1) decrease the liability to its remaining amount owed and (2) recognize revenue.**

Eagle Soccer Academy had deferred revenue during December. On December 23, Eagle received $6,000 from customers who were to be given soccer lessons in the future. At the time these payments were received from customers, Eagle became obligated to provide lessons, so we recorded this transaction as a liability—Deferred Revenue.

Assume that *by the end of December,* Eagle has provided lessons worth $2,000. On December 31, an adjusting entry is needed to reduce the Deferred Revenue account to the remaining amount owed and to recognize the revenue (Service Revenue) for the services provided in December.

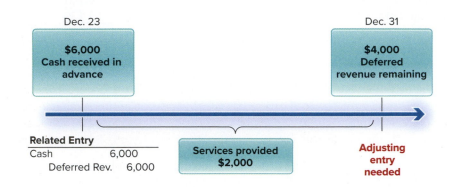

The end-of-period **adjusting entry** to account for the services provided is below.

Deferred Revenue	
12/23	6,000
12/31 **Adj.** 2,000	
	4,000

December 31	Debit	Credit
Deferred Revenue (−L)..	**2,000**	
Service Revenue (+R, +SE)		**2,000**
(Provide services to customers who paid in advance)		

This adjusting entry includes a $2,000 revenue, which increases net income and stockholders' equity. The entry also reduces the balance in the liability account, Deferred Revenue, by $2,000. The Deferred Revenue account will now have a balance of $4,000 (= $6,000 − $2,000 adjustment), which equals the remaining amount of services owed to customers.

Illustration 3–7 shows an example of deferred revenue for **Lowe's Companies, Inc.**

ILLUSTRATION 3–7

Reporting Deferred Revenues and Other Current Liabilities for Lowe's Companies, Inc.

LOWE'S COMPANIES, INC. Balance Sheet (partial) ($ in millions)	
Current liabilities:	
Short-term borrowings	$ 1,941
Current maturities of long-term debt	597
Current operating lease liabilities	501
Accounts payable	7,659
Accrued compensation and employee benefits	684
Deferred revenue	**1,219**
Other current liabilities	2,581
Total current liabilities	$15,182

In its annual report, Lowe's discusses that deferred revenues consist of "amounts received for which customers have not yet taken possession of merchandise or for which installation has not yet been completed." Deferred revenues also include "stored-value cards, which include gift cards and returned merchandise credits." The deferred liability will be settled as merchandise and services are provided to those customers.[2]

Now that we've discussed prepaid expenses and deferred revenues, let's look at the two other categories of adjusting entries—accrued expenses and accrued revenues. Accruals are the opposite of prepayments. **With accruals, the cash flow occurs *after* either the expense or the revenue is recorded.** Walking through some examples using Eagle Soccer Academy will demonstrate both types of accruals.

ACCRUED EXPENSES

Accrued expenses occur when a company has used costs in the current period, but the company hasn't yet paid cash for those costs. This creates a timing differences between when an expense is recognized and when the related cash is paid (refer back to Illustration 3–4B). Common examples include the current cost of employee salaries, utilities, interest, and taxes that won't be paid until the following period. **Because the company has used these costs to operate the company in the current period and is obligated to pay them, an adjusting entry is needed to (1) record the liability to be paid and (2) recognize the cost as an expense.**

Eagle Soccer Academy has three accrued expenses *by the end of December:* employee salaries, utilities, and interest. Each of these items represents costs used to operate the company during the month of December, and the company is obligated to pay for these costs in the future. Let's now look at the adjusting entry needed for each of these accrued expenses.

Accrued Salaries.   On December 28, Eagle paid salaries of $28,000. These salaries were a cost used to operate the company during December, and therefore the company recorded the cash payment as an expense in December—Salaries Expense.

By the end of December, employees have earned $3,000 in additional salaries. But what if Eagle doesn't plan to pay the employees until the end of the week, January 4? Eagle still needs to record the obligation that exists as of December 31. Those salaries represent costs that have been used in December. On December 31, an adjusting entry is needed to record the liability (Salaries Payable) for the amount owed and to recognize the additional expense (Salaries Expense). In January, four more days of salaries expense ($4,000) will be recorded, and then workers will be paid for the entire week.

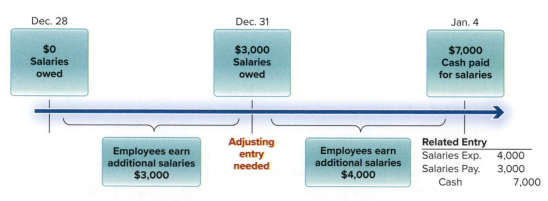

The end-of-period **adjusting entry** for accrued salaries is below.

December 31	Debit	Credit
Salaries Expense *(+E, −SE)*	**3,000**	
Salaries Payable *(+L)*..		**3,000**
(Salaries incurred, but not paid, in the current period)		

Salaries Payable	
	0 12/28
	3,000 **Adj.** 12/31
	3,000

---

[2]The Deferred Revenue account is sometimes referred to as the Unearned Revenue account. The use of the term *Deferred Revenue* is increasingly popular in practice and is more consistent with the FASB's 2014 update of the revenue recognition principle (ASU No. 2014-09), which eliminates the "earnings" process in defining revenue. The term *Deferred Revenue* is also helpful in emphasizing that revenue is initially deferred but will be recorded eventually when the service is provided.

This adjusting entry increases liabilities to the amount owed as of December 31. The entry also increases expenses, which decreases net income and stockholders' equity. The Salaries Expense account will now have a balance of $31,000 (= $28,000 + $3,000 adjustment), which equals the cost of all salaries in December.

Accrued Utility Costs.   Assume that *at the end of December*, Eagle receives a utility bill for $9,000 associated with operations in December. Eagle plans to pay the bill on January 6. Even though Eagle won't pay the cash until January, those costs were used in December. On December 31, an adjusting entry is needed to record the liability (Utilities Payable) for the amount owed and to recognize the expense (Utilities Expense) for the cost of utilities used in December.

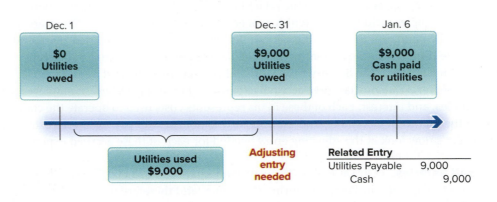

The end-of-period **adjusting entry** is below.

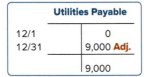

December 31	Debit	Credit
Utilities Expense *(+E, −SE)*...	**9,000**	
Utilities Payable *(+L)*		**9,000**
(Utilities used, but not paid, in the current period)		

Accrued Interest.   In transaction (2) of Illustration 3–5, Eagle borrowed $100,000 from the bank to begin operations. Assume the bank charges Eagle annual interest of 12% (or 1% per month) on the borrowed amount. Interest is due in one year, but repayment of the $100,000 borrowed is not due for three years. By the end of the first month, the loan has accrued interest of $1,000 calculated as follows:

$$\begin{array}{ccccccc} \text{Amount of} & & \text{Annual} & & \text{Fraction} & & \\ \text{note payable} & \times & \text{interest rate} & \times & \text{of the year} & = & \text{Interest} \\ \$100,000 & \times & 12\% & \times & 1/12 & = & \$1,000 \end{array}$$

Notice that we multiplied by 1/12 to calculate the interest for one month. If we had calculated interest for a two-month period, we would have multiplied by 2/12; for three months we would have multiplied by 3/12; and so on.

Although Eagle won't pay the interest until later, $1,000 is the cost of using the borrowed funds *by the end of December* and needs to be recorded. Eagle didn't record the interest each day, because it is impractical to record interest on a daily basis. So, on December 31, an adjusting entry is needed to record this liability (Interest Payable) for the amount owed and to recognize the expense (Interest Expense) for the month of December. Additional interest expense of $11,000 will be recorded over the next 11 months, and then the full year's interest will be paid.

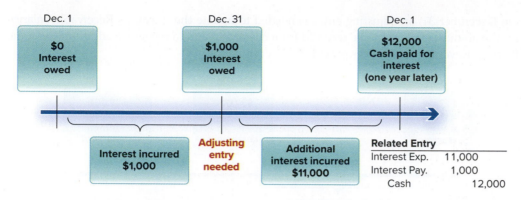

Dec. 1	Dec. 31	Dec. 1
$0 Interest owed	$1,000 Interest owed	$12,000 Cash paid for interest (one year later)

| Interest incurred $1,000 | **Adjusting entry needed** | Additional interest incurred $11,000 |

Related Entry

Interest Exp.	11,000	
Interest Pay.	1,000	
Cash		12,000

The end-of-period **adjusting entry** for interest payable is below.

December 31	Debit	Credit
Interest Expense *(+E, −SE)*..	**1,000**	
Interest Payable *(+L)*		**1,000**
(Interest incurred, but not paid, in the current period)		

Interest Payable

	0	12/1
	1,000 **Adj.**	12/31
1,000		

COMMON MISTAKE

When recording the interest payable on a borrowed amount, students sometimes mistakenly credit the liability associated with the principal amount (Notes Payable). We record interest payable in a *separate account* (Interest Payable) to keep the balance owed for principal separate from the balance owed for interest.

ACCRUED REVENUES

Accrued revenues occur when a company provides products or services but hasn't yet received cash. This creates a timing difference between when revenue is recognized and when the related cash is received (refer back to Illustration 3–4B). Examples include selling products and services to customers on account or being owed interest on amounts lent to others. **Because the company has provided products and services in the current period and has the right to receive payment, an adjusting entry is needed to (1) record an asset for the amount expected to be received and (2) recognize revenue.**

Interest Receivable. We can see an example of accrued revenues if we review the flip side of transaction (2), which we discussed in the previous section as interest expense. The bank lends Eagle Soccer Academy $100,000 and charges Eagle annual interest of 12% (or 1% per month) on the borrowed amount. Interest for the month of December is $1,000 (= $100,000 × 12% × 1/12). *At the end of December,* the bank needs an adjusting entry to record an asset for the amount expected to be received (Interest Receivable) from Eagle and to recognize revenue (Interest Revenue).

Flip Side

The bank's end-of-period adjusting entry is presented below.

December 31	Debit	Credit
Interest Receivable *(+A)*	**1,000**	
Interest Revenue *(+R, +SE)*...		**1,000**
(Interest earned, but not received, in the current period)		

Interest Receivable

	0	12/1
Adj. 1,000		12/31
1,000		

Accounts Receivable. Eagle Soccer Academy has previously recorded Accounts Receivable of $20,000 for services provided to customers on account on December 17. Assume that *by the end of December,* Eagle provides $7,000 of additional soccer training to customers from December 17 to December 31. The company has not yet collected cash or billed those customers. Eagle expects to receive all $27,000 from customers in the future (January 8–14).

On December 31, an adjusting entry is needed to update the Accounts Receivable balance for the amount expected to be received from customers and to recognize additional revenue (Service Revenue) for services provided in December.

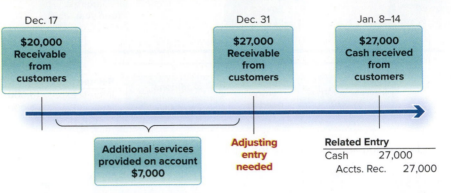

The end-of-period **adjusting entry** is below.

Accounts Receivable		
12/17	20,000	
12/31	**Adj.** 7,000	
	27,000	

December 31	Debit	Credit
Accounts Receivable *(+A)*	**7,000**	
Service Revenue *(+R, +SE)*		**7,000**
(Bill customers for services provided during the current period)		

🔑 **KEY POINT**

> Adjusting entries are needed when cash flows or obligations occur *before* the revenue- or expense-related activity (prepayment) or when cash flows occur *after* the revenue- or expense-related activity (accrual).

NO ADJUSTMENT NECESSARY

Notice that we didn't make any adjusting entries associated with transaction (1) or (10) for Eagle Soccer Academy in Illustration 3–5. Transaction (1) is the sale of common stock, and transaction (10) is the payment of dividends to common stockholders. **These are transactions with *owners* and, therefore, do not involve the recognition of revenues or expenses.**

Similarly, transactions (6) and (9) did not require adjustment because there are *no timing differences.* **Transactions in which we receive cash at the same time we record revenue or in which we pay cash at the same time we record an expense do *not* require adjusting entries.** For example, when Eagle provides soccer training to customers for cash on December 12 [transaction (6)], the company records Service Revenue at the same time it records the cash received, and no corresponding period-end adjusting entry is needed. Similarly, when Eagle pays salaries to employees on December 28 [transaction (9)], the company records Salaries Expense at the same time it records cash paid, and no corresponding period-end adjusting entry is needed.

🔑 **KEY POINT**

> Adjusting entries are *unnecessary* in two cases: (1) for transactions that do not involve revenue or expense activities and (2) for transactions that result in revenues or expenses being recorded at the same time as the cash flow.

Let's Review

Below are four scenarios for a local **Midas Muffler** shop for the month of December.

Scenario 1: On December 1, the balance of maintenance supplies totals $400. On December 15, the shop purchases an additional $200 of maintenance supplies with cash. By the end of December, only $100 of maintenance supplies remain.

Scenario 2: On December 4, Midas receives $6,000 cash from a local moving company in an agreement to provide truck maintenance of $1,000 each month for the next six months, beginning in December.

Scenario 3: Mechanics have worked the final four days in December, earning $600, but have not yet been paid. Midas plans to pay its mechanics on January 2.

Scenario 4: Customers receiving $250 of maintenance services from Midas on December 29 have not been billed as of the end of the month. These customers will be billed on January 3 and are expected to pay the full amount owed on January 6.

Required:

For each of the scenarios:
1. Indicate the type of adjusting entry needed.
2. Record the related entry transaction and the December 31 adjusting entry.

Solution:

Scenario 1: Adjusting entry type: Prepaid expense.

December 15 (related entry)	Debit	Credit
Supplies *(+A)*..	200	
Cash *(−A)*..		200
(Purchase maintenance supplies with cash)		

December 31 (adjusting entry)	Debit	Credit
Supplies Expense *(+E, −SE)*..	500	
Supplies *(−A)*...		500
(Consume supplies)		
($400 + $200 − $100 = $500)		

Scenario 2: Adjusting entry type: Deferred revenue.

December 4 (related entry)	Debit	Credit
Cash *(+A)*..	6,000	
Deferred Revenue *(+L)*..		6,000
(Receive cash in advance from customers)		

December 31 (adjusting entry)	Debit	Credit
Deferred Revenue *(−L)*..	1,000	
Service Revenue *(+R, +SE)*		1,000
(Provide first of six months of services)		

Scenario 3: Adjusting entry type: Accrued expense.

December 31 (adjusting entry)	Debit	Credit
Salaries Expense *(+E, −SE)*..	600	
Salaries Payable *(+L)*..		600
(Owe for salaries earned by employees in the current period)		

January 2 (related entry)	Debit	Credit
Salaries Payable *(−L)*..	600	
Cash *(−A)*..		600
(Pay salaries owed)		

Scenario 4: Adjusting entry type: Accrued revenue.

December 31 (adjusting entry)	Debit	Credit
Accounts Receivable (+A)...	250	
Service Revenue (+R, +SE)		250
(Provide maintenance service on account)		

January 6 (related entry)	Debit	Credit
Cash (+A)...	250	
Accounts Receivable (−A)...		250
(Collect cash from customers previously billed)		

Suggested Homework:
BE3–6, BE3–10;
E3–7, E3–8;
P3–3A & B, P3–4A & B

Adjusted Trial Balance

■ **LO3–4**

Post adjusting entries and prepare an adjusted trial balance.

To complete the measurement process, we need to update the balances of the assets, liabilities, revenues, and expenses for changes created by adjusting entries. In Illustration 3–8, we summarize the eight adjusting entries of Eagle Soccer Academy recorded in the previous section. (Note the adjusting entry for interest revenue is excluded because this entry is recorded by the bank, not Eagle Soccer Academy.) To update balances, we post the adjusting entries to the appropriate accounts in the general ledger, as demonstrated in Illustration 3–9.

ILLUSTRATION 3–8

Summary of Adjusting Entries for Eagle Soccer Academy

December 31	Debit	Credit
(a) **Rent Expense** (+E, −SE)...	5,000	
Prepaid Rent (−A)		5,000
(Reduce prepaid rent due to the passage of time)		
(b) **Supplies Expense** (+E, −SE)..	10,000	
Supplies (−A)...		10,000
(Consume supplies during the current period)		
(c) **Depreciation Expense** (+E, −SE)...	2,000	
Accumulated Depreciation (−A)...		2,000
(Depreciate equipment)		
(d) **Deferred Revenue** (−L)...	2,000	
Service Revenue (+R, +SE)...		2,000
(Provide services to customers who paid in advance)		
(e) **Salaries Expense** (+E, −SE)..	3,000	
Salaries Payable (+L)...		3,000
(Salaries incurred, but not paid, in the current period)		
(f) **Utilities Expense** (+E, −SE)	9,000	
Utilities Payable (+L)...		9,000
(Utilities used, but not paid, in the current period)		
(g) **Interest Expense** (+E, −SE)..	1,000	
Interest Payable (+L)..		1,000
(Interest incurred, but not paid, in the current period)		
(h) **Accounts Receivable** (+A)	7,000	
Service Revenue (+R, +SE)...		7,000
(Bill customers for services provided during the current period)		

ILLUSTRATION 3–9 Posting the Adjusting Entries (in **red**) of Eagle Soccer Academy to General Ledger Accounts

	Assets	=	Liabilities	+	Stockholders' Equity	

Cash

(1)	200,000	(3)	120,000
(2)	100,000	(4)	60,000
(6)	43,000	(9)	28,000
(8)	6,000	(10)	4,000
Bal. 137,000			

Accounts Payable

		(5)	23,000
		Bal.	23,000

Common Stock

		(1)	200,000
		Bal. 200,000	

Retained Earnings

			0
		Bal.	0

Accounts Receivable

(7)	20,000
(h)	7,000
Bal.	27,000

Deferred Revenue

		(8)	6,000
(d) 2,000			
		Bal.	4,000

Dividends

(10)	4,000
Bal.	4,000

Service Revenue

		(6)	43,000
		(7)	20,000
		(d)	2,000
		(h)	7,000
		Bal.	72,000

Supplies

(5)	23,000		
		(b)	10,000
Bal.	13,000		

Salaries Payable

		(e)	3,000
		Bal.	3,000

Rent Expense

(a)	5,000
Bal.	5,000

Supplies Expense

(b)	10,000
Bal.	10,000

Prepaid Rent

(4)	60,000		
		(a)	5,000
Bal.	55,000		

Utilities Payable

		(f)	9,000
		Bal.	9,000

Depreciation Expense

(c)	2,000
Bal.	2,000

Salaries Expense

(9)	28,000
(e)	3,000
Bal.	31,000

Equipment

(3)	120,000
Bal. 120,000	

Interest Payable

		(g)	1,000
		Bal.	1,000

Utilities Expense

(f)	9,000
Bal.	9,000

Interest Expense

(g)	1,000
Bal.	1,000

Accumulated Depreciation

		(c)	2,000
		Bal.	2,000

Notes Payable

		(2)	100,000
		Bal. 100,000	

- Amounts in black represent external transactions during the month of December. Numbers in parentheses refer to transaction numbers in Illustration 3–5.
- Amounts in red represent adjusting entries at the end of December. Letters in parentheses refer to adjusting entries in Illustration 3–8.
- Amounts in **bold** represent ending balances.

COMMON MISTAKE

Students sometimes mistakenly include the Cash account in an adjusting entry. Typical adjusting entries will never include the Cash account. Note that every adjusting entry includes both an income statement account and a balance sheet account.

KEY POINT

We post adjusting entries to the general ledger to update the account balances.

After we've posted the adjusting entries to the general ledger accounts, we're ready to prepare an *adjusted* trial balance. An **adjusted trial balance** is a list of all accounts and their balances *after we have updated account balances for adjusting entries.* Illustration 3–10 shows the adjusted trial balance. The adjusted trial balance includes the adjusted balances of all general ledger accounts shown in Illustration 3–9. Note that total debits equal total credits.

ILLUSTRATION 3–10

Adjusted Trial Balance for Eagle Soccer Academy

EAGLE SOCCER ACADEMY Adjusted Trial Balance December 31, 2024		
Accounts	**Debit**	**Credit**
Cash	$137,000	
Accounts Receivable	27,000	
Supplies	13,000	
Prepaid Rent	55,000	
Equipment	120,000	
Accumulated Depreciation		$ 2,000
Accounts Payable		23,000
Deferred Revenue		4,000
Salaries Payable		3,000
Utilities Payable		9,000
Interest Payable		1,000
Notes Payable		100,000
Common Stock		200,000
Retained Earnings		0
Dividends	4,000	
Service Revenue		72,000
Rent Expense	5,000	
Supplies Expense	10,000	
Depreciation Expense	2,000	
Salaries Expense	31,000	
Utilities Expense	9,000	
Interest Expense	1,000	
Totals	$414,000	$ 414,000

KEY POINT

An adjusted trial balance is a list of all accounts and their balances at a particular date, after we have updated account balances for adjusting entries.

PART B

THE REPORTING PROCESS: FINANCIAL STATEMENTS

■ **LO3–5**

Prepare financial statements using the adjusted trial balance.

Once the adjusted trial balance is complete, we prepare financial statements. Illustration 3–11 describes the relationship between the adjusted trial balance and the financial statements. Notice the color coding of the accounts, to indicate their relationships to the financial statements.

Revenue and expense accounts are reported in the income statement. The difference between total revenues and total expenses equals net income. All asset, liability, and stockholders' equity accounts are reported in the balance sheet. The balance sheet confirms the equality of the basic accounting equation.

ILLUSTRATION 3–11   Relationship between Adjusted Trial Balance and Financial Statements

EAGLE SOCCER ACADEMY
Adjusted Trial Balance
December 2024

Accounts	Debits	Credits
Cash	$ 137,000	
Accounts Receivable	27,000	
Supplies	13,000	
Prepaid Rent	55,000	
Equipment	120,000	
Accumulated Depreciation		$ 2,000
Accounts Payable		23,000
Salaries Payable		4,000
Utilities Payable		3,000
Deferred Revenue		9,000
Interest Payable		1,000
Notes Payable		100,000
Common Stock		200,000
Retained Earnings		0
Dividends	4,000	
Service Revenue		72,000
Rent Expense	5,000	
Supplies Expense	10,000	
Depreciation Expense	2,000	
Salaries Expense	31,000	
Utilities Expense	9,000	
Interest Expense	1,000	
Totals	$ 414,000	$ 414,000

EAGLE SOCCER ACADEMY
Income Statement
For the period ended December 2024

Revenues	
Service Revenue	$72,000
Expense	
Rent Expense	5,000
Supplies Expense	10,000
Depreciation Expense	2,000
Salaries Expense	31,000
Utilities Expense	9,000
Interest Expense	1,000
Total Expenses	58,000
Net Income	$14,000

EAGLE SOCCER ACADEMY
Statement of Stockholders' Equity
For the period ended December 2024

	Common Stock	Retained Earnings
Beginning balance (Dec. 1)	$ -0-	$ -0-
Issuance of common stock	200,000	
Add: Net income for the period		14,000
Less: Dividends		(4,000)
Ending balance (Dec. 31)	$ 200,000	$ 10,000

EAGLE SOCCER ACADEMY
Balance Sheet
December 2024

Assets		Liabilities	
Current assets:		Current liabilities:	
Cash	$ 137,000	Accounts Payable	$ 23,000
Accounts Receivable	27,000	Deferred Revenue	4,000
Supplies	13,000	Salaries Payable	3,000
Prepaid Rent	55,000	Utilities Payable	9,000
Total current assets	232,000	Interest Payable	1,000
		Total current liabilities	40,000
Long-term assets:			
Equipment	120,000	Long-term liabilities:	
Less: Accum. Depr.	(2,000)	Notes Payable	100,000
		Total liabilities	140,000
		Stockholders' Equity	
		Common Stock	200,000
		Retained Earnings	10,000
		Total stockholders' equity	210,000
		Total liabilities and	
Total assets	$ 350,000	stockholders' equity	$ 350,000

Income Statement

Illustration 3–12 shows the income statement of Eagle Soccer Academy for the period ended December 31, 2024. The account names and amounts are those shown at the bottom of the adjusted trial balance in Illustration 3–11.

There are four items to note about the income statement.

1. **Total revenues** include products and services provided to customers during the reporting period.

EAGLE SOCCER ACADEMY
Income Statement
For the period ended December 31, 2024

Revenues	
Service revenue	**$72,000**
Expenses	
Rent expense	5,000
Supplies expense	10,000
Depreciation expense	2,000
Salaries expense	31,000
Utilities expense	9,000
Interest expense	1,000
Total expenses	58,000
Net income	**$14,000**

2. **Total expenses** include costs used to operate the business during the reporting period.

3. **Net income** equals total revenues minus total expenses.

4. The income statement reports revenues and expenses **over an interval of time.** In this example, Eagle started operations on December 1, 2024, so the revenues and expenses reported in the income statement are those occurring from December 1 through December 31, 2024.

The income statement of Eagle Soccer Academy shows the company had revenues of $72,000 from providing services to customers in December. The costs used for operating the business in December are reported as expenses of $58,000. Revenues minus expenses equal net income of $14,000. This amount represents profit generated by the company for its owners and provides some indication of management's success in operating the company.

Statement of Stockholders' Equity

The statement of stockholders' equity summarizes the changes in each stockholders' equity account. Illustration 3–13 shows the statement of stockholders' equity for Eagle Soccer Academy.

EAGLE SOCCER ACADEMY
Statement of Stockholders' Equity
For the period ended December 31, 2024

	Common Stock	Retained Earnings	Total Stockholders' Equity
Beginning balance (Dec. 1)	$ -0-	$ -0-	$ -0-
Issuance of common stock	200,000		200,000
Add: Net income for the period		**14,000**	**14,000**
Less: Dividends		(4,000)	(4,000)
Ending balance (Dec. 31)	**$200,000**	**$10,000**	**$210,000**

From the income statement →

Total stockholders' equity increases from $0 at the beginning of December to $210,000 by the end of December. The increase occurs as a result of a $200,000 investment by the owners (stockholders) when they bought common stock plus an increase of **$10,000** when the company generated a profit of **$14,000** for its stockholders and distributed $4,000 of dividends.

You've seen that retained earnings has three components: revenues, expenses, and dividends. In the adjusted trial balance, the balance of the Retained Earnings account is its balance at the beginning of the accounting period—the balance *before* all revenue, expense, and dividend transactions. For Eagle Soccer Academy, the beginning balance of Retained Earnings equals $0 since this is the first month of operations. Ending Retained Earnings equals its beginning balance of $0 plus the effects of all revenue and expense transactions (net income of **$14,000**) less dividends of **$4,000** paid to stockholders. Since dividends represent the payment of company resources (typically cash) to owners, they will have a negative effect on the stockholders' equity (retained earnings) of the company.

Balance Sheet

The balance sheet you saw in Chapter 1 contained the key asset, liability, and stockholders' equity accounts, presented as a rather simple list. Here, we introduce a slightly more complex form, called the classified balance sheet. A **classified balance sheet** groups a company's asset and liability accounts into current and long-term categories. We'll use the numbers from the adjusted trial balance to present the classified balance sheet for Eagle Soccer Academy in Illustration 3–14.

ILLUSTRATION 3–14

Classified Balance Sheet for Eagle Soccer Academy

EAGLE SOCCER ACADEMY
Balance Sheet
December 31, 2024

Assets		Liabilities	
Current assets:		Current liabilities:	
Cash	$ 137,000	Accounts payable	$ 23,000
Accounts receivable	27,000	Deferred revenue	4,000
Supplies	13,000	Salaries payable	3,000
Prepaid rent	55,000	Utilities payable	9,000
Total current assets	**232,000**	Interest payable	1,000
		Total current liabilities	**40,000**
Long-term assets:			
Equipment	120,000	Long-term liabilities:	
Less: Accum. depr.	(2,000)	Notes payable	100,000
		Total liabilities	**140,000**
		Stockholders' Equity	
		Common stock	**200,000**
		Retained earnings	**10,000**
		Total stockholders' equity	**210,000**
Total assets	**$350,000**	Total liabilities and stockholders' equity	**$350,000**

From the statement of stockholders' equity

There are five items to note about the classified balance sheet.

1. **Total assets** are separated into current and long-term assets.
2. **Total liabilities** are separated into current and long-term liabilities.
3. **Total stockholders' equity** includes common stock and retained earnings from the statement of stockholders' equity.
4. Total assets must equal total liabilities plus stockholders' equity.
5. The balance sheet reports assets, liabilities, and stockholders' equity at a **point in time.**

We discuss each one of these items next.

Assets.   The classified balance sheet separates assets into two major categories:
- *Current assets*—those that provide a benefit *within the next year.*
- *Long-term assets*—those that provide a benefit for *more than one year.*

Current assets are typically listed in *order of liquidity.* The liquidity of an asset refers to how quickly it can be converted to cash. Recall that Eagle has borrowed $100,000 from a local bank. This bank wants to know the likelihood that Eagle will have enough cash to repay the borrowed amount plus the interest as they become due.

Cash is the most liquid of all assets, so it's listed first. *Accounts receivable* are amounts owed by customers to the company. They are generally collected within one month, so they are highly liquid assets and typically listed after cash. Next, we list prepaid expenses, such as *supplies* and *prepaid rent.* While these assets will not be converted to cash, they are expected to be consumed (or used up) within the next year, so they are included as current assets.

In a few rare cases, companies that have *operating cycles* longer than one year will extend the definition of current assets to those that provide a benefit within the next operating cycle. For a service company (like Eagle Soccer Academy), an **operating cycle** is the average time it takes to provide a service to a customer and then collect that customer's cash. For a company that sells products, an operating cycle would include the time it typically takes to purchase or manufacture those products to the time the company collects cash from selling those products to customers.

Long-term assets are expected to be converted to cash after one year or to be consumed for longer than one year. Long-term assets consist of the following types of assets:

- *Long-term investments*—investments in another company's debt or stock. We discuss long-term investments in debt and equity securities in Appendix D at the end of the book.
- *Property, plant, and equipment*—long-term productive assets used in the normal course of business, such as land, buildings, equipment, and machinery. Eagle's purchase of equipment is an example of a purchase of property, plant, and equipment. We discuss property, plant, and equipment in Chapter 7.
- *Intangible assets*—assets that lack physical substance but have long-term value to a company, such as patents, copyrights, trademarks, and franchises. We discuss intangible assets in Chapter 7.

After listing all of the assets, we see that total assets equal **$350,000**. This means that *in accounting terms* Eagle has resources of $350,000 that will provide benefits to the company in the future.

Liabilities.   After assets, liabilities are listed next. They too are divided into two major categories:

- *Current liabilities*—those that are due *within one year of the balance sheet date.*
- *Long-term liabilities*—those that are due in *more than one year.*

Investors and creditors of Eagle want to know whether the cash being generated by the assets will be enough to meet the company's obligations in the near future (current liabilities) as well as the longer term (long-term liabilities). For example, the ratio of current assets to current liabilities (referred to as the *current ratio*) would be helpful for understanding if a company is likely to have enough current resources to meet current obligations.

Current liabilities are typically required to be paid within one year. Eagle has many.

Accounts payable are amounts owed for previous purchases of supplies on account.

Deferred revenue represents amounts received in advance from customers for services to be provided in the future. Therefore, though the company does not expect to pay cash within the next year, it does expect to provide those services within one year. By providing services, the company fulfills its current obligation to its customers.

Salaries payable are amounts owed to employees; *utilities payable* are amounts owed to the utility company. These obligations are expected to be paid within one year.

Interest payable is the final current liability listed. As of December 31, the company owes one month of interest on the borrowing, but the bank will not require the interest to be paid until 11 months from now (next December 1). Nevertheless, for accounting purposes, this is an amount that is due within one year as of December 31, so it is listed as a current liability.

Long-term liabilities are amounts that are due in more than one year. Eagle only has one—bank borrowing of $100,000 that occurred on December 1. The borrowing was for three years, so as of December 31, the borrowing is due in two years and 11 months. Because the due date is more than one year from the balance sheet date, the amount is listed as a long-term liability. Eagle's total liabilities include $40,000 of current liabilities plus $100,000 of long-term liabilities, for a total of $140,000.

Decision Maker's Perspective

Is the Balance Sheet Like a Photo or an MRI?

In Chapter 1, we mentioned that a balance sheet is like a photograph since it shows events at a point in time, whereas an income statement is like a video since it shows events over time. This is a common comparison used in describing the two primary financial statements.

However, rather than a photograph, maybe a better description of the balance sheet is an MRI (magnetic resonance imaging). MRIs are commonly used by physicians to diagnose and treat medical conditions. Whereas a photo conveys a clear image recognized by everyone, an MRI is a little more hazy and needs specialized medical training to utilize the full benefits of the image.

In the same way, items reported in the balance sheet are also a little hazy. As we will learn later, accounting numbers are subject to interpretation and companies have some leeway in reporting the numbers. Likewise, to utilize the full benefits of the balance sheet (and the other financial statements as well), users need specialized training in accounting and finance, beginning with the basic fundamentals obtained in this first accounting course.

Stockholders' Equity. The final section of the classified balance sheet is the stockholders' equity section. The amounts for the two stockholders' equity accounts—Common Stock and Retained Earnings—can be obtained directly from the statement of stockholders' equity. The balance of *Common Stock* is the total amount issued. The balance of *Retained Earnings* is the total net income over the life of the company (just the first month of operations in this example) less dividends.

It's also the case that the amount of total stockholders' equity confirms that total assets (**$350,000**) equal total liabilities plus stockholders' equity (**$350,000**). We achieve this equality only by including the correct balance of **$10,000** for Retained Earnings from the statement of stockholders' equity, not the balance of $0 from the adjusted trial balance.

Finally, note that the balance sheet reports amounts for assets, liabilities, and stockholders' equity at a *point in time.* For Eagle, these are the balances of these accounts as of a single day—December 31. These balances may have been different the day before or the day after, but as of December 31, these are the balances.

 KEY POINT

We prepare the income statement, statement of stockholders' equity, and balance sheet from the adjusted trial balance. The income statement provides a measure of net income (profitability), calculated as revenues minus expenses. The balance sheet demonstrates that assets equal liabilities plus stockholders' equity (the basic accounting equation).

Statement of Cash Flows

The final financial statement we need to prepare is the statement of cash flows. As discussed in Chapter 1, the statement of cash flows measures activities involving cash receipts and cash payments, reflecting a company's operating, investing, and financing activities. We'll take another brief look at the statement of cash flows in Chapter 4 and then discuss it in detail in Chapter 11.

PART C

THE CLOSING PROCESS

■ **LO3–6**
Demonstrate the purposes and recording of closing entries.

All accounts that appear in the balance sheet, including Retained Earnings, are **permanent accounts**. This means we carry forward their balances from one period to the next. For example, if Cash (an asset) or Accounts Payable (a liability) has a balance of $1,000 at the end of the year, then that's also the balance at the beginning of next year. However, that's not the case with **temporary accounts**—revenues, expenses, and dividends. For these accounts, we transfer each balance at the end of the year to one account—Retained Earnings—and then all revenue, expense, and dividend accounts start with a $0 balance at the beginning of next year. We accomplish the transfer of balances from temporary accounts to Retained Earnings with closing entries.

Closing Entries

Closing entries transfer the balances of all temporary accounts (revenues, expenses, and dividends) to the balance of the Retained Earnings account. To demonstrate closing entries, refer back to Eagle Soccer Academy. We can transfer the balances of all revenue and expense accounts, and the dividend account, to the balance of the Retained Earnings account with the closing entries shown in Illustration 3–15.

ILLUSTRATION 3–15

Closing Entries for Eagle Soccer Academy

December 31	Debit	Credit
(a) Service Revenue..	**72,000**	
Retained Earnings..		**72,000**
(Close revenues to retained earnings)		
(b) Retained Earnings...	**58,000**	
Rent Expense..		**5,000**
Supplies Expense...		**10,000**
Depreciation Expense..		**2,000**
Salaries Expense..		**31,000**
Utilities Expense..		**9,000**
Interest Expense..		**1,000**
(Close expenses to retained earnings)		
(c) Retained Earnings...	**4,000**	
Dividends...		**4,000**
(Close dividends to retained earnings)		

- **Revenues**—All revenue accounts have credit balances. To transfer these balances to the Retained Earnings account, we debit each of these revenue accounts for its balance and credit Retained Earnings for the total. The revenues included in closing entries are the same as those in Eagle's income statement (Illustration 3–12).
- **Expenses**—All expense accounts have debit balances. To transfer these balances to the Retained Earnings account, we credit each of these accounts for its balance and debit Retained Earnings for the total. The expenses included in closing entries are the same as those in Eagle's income statement (Illustration 3–12).

- **Dividends**—The Dividends account has a debit balance. To transfer this balance to the Retained Earnings account, we credit Dividends for its balance and debit Retained Earnings for the same amount. Dividends are reported in Eagle's statement of stockholders' equity[3] (Illustration 3–13).

Now ask yourself these two questions:

1. *What is the balance of each individual revenue, expense, and dividend account* ***after*** *closing entries?* Answer: Zero. We have "closed" these accounts to a balance of $0, so we can start from scratch in measuring revenues, expenses, and dividends of the next period.

2. *What is the ending balance of Retained Earnings* ***after*** *closing entries?* Answer: The beginning balance of Retained Earnings plus net income (revenues minus expenses) less dividends for the period. In this example, the beginning balance is $0 because this is Eagle's first month of operations (there was no net income or dividends before this month). After closing entries, the balance is updated to reflect all transactions related to revenues, expenses, and dividends during the period. This can be seen in the T-account below.

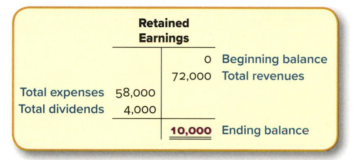

The ending balance of Retained Earnings on December 31, 2024, will be its beginning balance in the following period beginning January 1, 2025. Then we'll close revenues, expenses, and dividends in that period to Retained Earnings, and this cycle will continue each period.

KEY POINT

Closing entries serve two purposes: (1) to transfer the balances of temporary accounts (revenues, expenses, and dividends) to the Retained Earnings account and (2) to reduce the balances of these temporary accounts to zero to prepare them for measuring activity in the next period. Closing entries increase retained earnings by the amount of revenues for the period and decrease retained earnings by the amount of expenses and dividends for the period.

Closing entries *do not affect the balances of permanent accounts* (assets, liabilities, and permanent stockholders' equity accounts) *other than retained earnings.* Permanent accounts carry a cumulative balance throughout the life of the company.

COMMON MISTAKE

Students sometimes believe that closing entries are meant to reduce the balance of Retained Earnings to zero. Retained Earnings is a *permanent account,* representing the accumulation of all revenues, expenses, and dividends over the life of the company.

---

[3]Sometimes companies prepare closing entries by closing revenues and expenses to a temporary account called Income Summary. The Income Summary account is then closed to Retained Earnings. This alternative set of closing entries provides the same effect of closing revenues and expenses to the Retained Earnings account, as we show in Illustration 3–15. A computerized accounting system performs the closing process automatically without the Income Summary account.

Post-Closing Trial Balance

■ LO3–7
Post closing entries and prepare a post-closing trial balance.

After we have prepared closing entries, we post amounts to the accounts in the general ledger. Illustration 3–16 demonstrates the process of posting the closing entries. The current balance of each account reflects transactions during the period (in black), adjusting entries (in **red**), and closing entries (in **blue**).

ILLUSTRATION 3–16 Posting the Closing Entries to Adjusted Balances of Ledger Accounts

Assets = Liabilities + Stockholders' Equity

Cash
(1)	200,000	(3)	120,000
(2)	100,000	(4)	60,000
(6)	43,000	(9)	28,000
(8)	6,000	(10)	4,000
Bal. 137,000			

Accounts Receivable
(7)	20,000	
(h)	7,000	
Bal. 27,000		

Supplies
(5)	23,000		
		(b)	10,000
Bal. 13,000			

Prepaid Rent
(4)	60,000		
		(a)	5,000
Bal. 55,000			

Equipment
(3)	120,000	
Bal. 120,000		

Accumulated Depreciation
	(c)	2,000
	Bal.	**2,000**

Accounts Payable
	(5)	23,000
	Bal.	**23,000**

Deferred Revenue
		(8)	6,000
(d)	2,000		
		Bal.	**4,000**

Salaries Payable
	(e)	3,000
	Bal.	**3,000**

Utilities Payable
	(f)	9,000
	Bal.	**9,000**

Interest Payable
	(g)	1,000
	Bal.	**1,000**

Notes Payable
	(2)	100,000
	Bal. 100,000	

Common Stock
	(1)	200,000
	Bal. 200,000	

Dividends
(10)	4,000	
	(c)	4,000
Bal. 4,000		

Rent Expense
(a)	5,000		
		(b)	5,000
Bal.	**0**		

Depreciation Expense
(c)	2,000		
		(b)	2,000
Bal.	**0**		

Utilities Expense
(f)	9,000		
		(b)	9,000
Bal.	**0**		

Retained Earnings
			0
		(a)	72,000
		(b) 580,000	
		(c) 40,000	
		Bal. 10,000	

Service Revenue
		(6)	43,000
		(7)	20,000
		(d)	2,000
		(h)	7,000
(a)	7,200		
		Bal.	**0**

Supplies Expense
(b)	10,000		
		(b)	10,000
Bal.	**0**		

Salaries Expense
(9)	28,000		
(e)	3,000		
		(b)	31,000
Bal.	**0**		

Interest Expense
(g)	1,000		
		(b)	1,000
Bal.	**0**		

- Amounts in black represent external transactions during the month of December. Numbers in parentheses refer to transaction numbers in Illustration 3–5.
- Amounts in red represent adjusting entries at the end of December. Letters in parentheses refer to adjusting entries in Illustration 3–8.
- Amounts in blue represent closing entries at the end of December. Letters in parentheses refer to closing entries in Illustration 3–15.
- Amounts in **bold** represent ending balances.

KEY POINT

After we post the closing entries to the general ledger, the balance of Retained Earnings equals the amount shown in the balance sheet. The balances of all revenue, expense, and dividend accounts are zero at that point.

After we post the closing entries, the **$10,000** balance of Retained Earnings now equals the amount shown in the balance sheet. In addition, the ending balances of all revenue, expense, and dividend accounts are now zero and ready to begin the next period.

We are now ready to prepare a post-closing trial balance. The **post-closing trial balance** is a list of all accounts and their balances at a particular date *after we have updated account balances for closing entries.* The post-closing trial balance helps to verify that we prepared and posted closing entries correctly and that the accounts are now ready for the next period's transactions.

Illustration 3–17 shows the post-closing trial balance for Eagle Soccer Academy as of December 31.

Notice that the post-closing trial balance does not include any revenues, expenses, or dividends, because these accounts all have zero balances after closing entries. The balance of Retained Earnings has been updated from the adjusted trial balance to include all revenues, expenses, and dividends for the period.

ILLUSTRATION 3–17

Post-Closing Trial Balance for Eagle Soccer Academy

EAGLE SOCCER ACADEMY
Post-Closing Trial Balance
December 31, 2024

Accounts	Debit	Credit
Cash	$137,000	
Accounts Receivable	27,000	
Supplies	13,000	
Prepaid Rent	55,000	
Equipment	120,000	
Accumulated Depreciation		$ 2,000
Accounts Payable		23,000
Deferred Revenue		4,000
Salaries Payable		3,000
Utilities Payable		9,000
Interest Payable		1,000
Notes Payable		100,000
Common Stock		200,000
Retained Earnings		10,000
Totals	$352,000	$352,000

CAREER CORNER

In practice, accountants do not prepare closing entries. Virtually all companies have accounting software packages that automatically update the Retained Earnings account and move the temporary accounts at the end of the year. Of course, accounting information systems go far beyond automatic closing entries. In today's competitive global environment, businesses demand information systems that can eliminate redundant tasks and quickly gather, process, and disseminate information to decision makers. Ordinary business processes—such as selling goods to customers, purchasing supplies, managing employees, and managing inventory—can be handled more efficiently with customized information systems. Employers recognize that individuals with strong information technology skills mixed with accounting knowledge add value to the company.

Decision Point

Question	Accounting information	Analysis
The amounts reported for revenues and expenses represent activity over what period of time?	Income statement	Revenue and expense accounts measure activity only for the current reporting period (usually a month, quarter, or year). At the end of each period, they are closed and begin the next period at zero.

Let's Review

Below is the adjusted trial balance of Beckham Soccer Academy for December 31, 2024.

BECKHAM SOCCER ACADEMY
Adjusted Trial Balance
December 31, 2024

Accounts	Debit	Credit
Cash	$ 2,600	
Supplies	3,900	
Accounts Payable		$ 1,000
Salaries Payable		300
Common Stock		3,000
Retained Earnings		1,700
Dividends	200	
Service Revenue		4,300
Salaries Expense	2,400	
Supplies Expense	700	
Rent Expense	500	
Totals	$10,300	$10,300

Required:

1. Prepare closing entries.
2. Post the closing entries to the Retained Earnings T-account.
3. Prepare a post-closing trial balance.

Solution:

1. Closing entries.

December 31	Debit	Credit
Service Revenue	4,300	
Retained Earnings		4,300
(Close revenues to retained earnings)		
Retained Earnings	3,600	
Salaries Expense		2,400
Supplies Expense		700
Rent Expense		500
(Close expenses to retained earnings)		
Retained Earnings	200	
Dividends		200
(Close dividends to retained earnings)		

2. Retained Earnings T-account with closing entries posted.

Retained Earnings		
	1,700	Beginning balance
	4,300	Total revenues
Total expenses 3,600		
Total dividends 200		
	2,200	Ending balance

3. Post-closing trial balance.

BECKHAM SOCCER ACADEMY
Post-Closing Trial Balance
December 31, 2024

Accounts	Debit	Credit
Cash	$2,600	
Supplies	3,900	
Accounts Payable		$1,000
Salaries Payable		300
Common Stock		3,000
Retained Earnings		2,200
Totals	$6,500	$6,500

Suggested Homework:
BE3–19, BE3–20;
E3–17, E3–18;
P3–7A & B; P3–8A & B

CHAPTER FRAMEWORK

This chapter discusses the steps in the accounting cycle at the **end of the year**:

(1) **Prepare adjusting entries**—Adjusting entries are used to record changes in assets and liabilities (and their related revenues and expenses) that have occurred **during the year** but have not yet been recorded.

(2) **Prepare financial statements**—The income statement reports revenues minus expenses to equal net income. A classified balance sheet reports assets and liabilities as current or long-term and reports stockholders' equity.

(3) **Prepare closing entries**—After the financial statements are prepared, all revenue, expense, and dividend accounts are closed (reduced to zero) by transferring their balances to the Retained Earnings account.

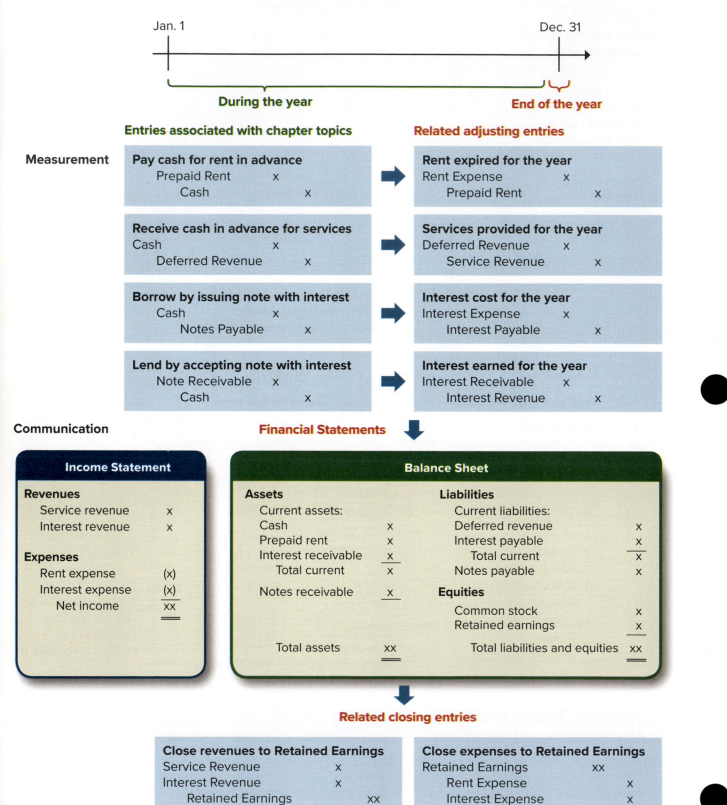

As an example, using the first transaction at the top of the illustration, a company pays cash during the year for rent in advance. Prepaid Rent (an asset) is recorded, and the Cash account is reduced. By the end of the year, a portion of the prepaid rent has expired, so an adjusting entry is recorded to reduce Prepaid Rent and increase Rent Expense for the amount of rent expired. Rent Expense is reported in the income statement for the amount of rent expired during the year, and Prepaid Rent is reported in the balance sheet for the remaining amount of rent not expired during the year. In a closing entry at the end of the year, Rent Expense is closed to Retained Earnings, reducing the balance of Rent Expense to zero and reducing the balance of Retained Earnings by the amount of Rent Expense.

Chapter Framework Questions

1. **Measurement (during the year):** During the year, a company pays cash for rent in advance of the rental period. This transaction is recorded with an increase to
   - a. Prepaid Rent (an asset).
   - b. Rent Expense (an expense).
   - c. Rent Payable (a liability).
   - d. Rent Revenue (a revenue).

2. **Measurement (end of the year):** At the end of the year, the adjusting entry needed to record the amount of Prepaid Rent expired for the year includes
   - a. Debit Prepaid Rent; credit Cash.
   - b. Debit Prepaid Rent; credit Rent Expense.
   - c. Debit Rent Expense; credit Prepaid Rent.
   - d. Debit Cash; credit Prepaid Rent.

3. **Communication (income statement):** When a company prepays rent during the year, which of the following best explains the amount to report for Rent Expense in the income statement at the end of the year?
   - a. Total cash paid for rent.
   - b. The amount of rent expired during the year.
   - c. The amount of rent not expired by the end of the year.

4. **Communication (balance sheet):** When a company prepays rent during the year, which of the following best explains the amount to report for Prepaid Rent in the balance sheet at the end of the year?
   - a. Total cash paid for rent.
   - b. The amount of rent expired during the year.
   - c. The amount of rent not expired at the end of the year.

5. At end of the year, a company prepares closing entries, which include(s)
   - a. Reducing the balances of all revenue accounts and expense accounts to zero.
   - b. Increasing the balance of Retained Earnings by the amount of total revenues.
   - c. Decreasing the balance of Retained Earnings by the amount of total expenses.
   - d. Closing entries include all of the above.

Note: For answers, see the last page of the chapter.

KEY POINTS BY LEARNING OBJECTIVE

LO3–1 Understand when assets, liabilities, revenues, and expenses are recorded.

Under accrual-basis accounting, economic events that affect assets, liabilities, revenues, and expenses are recorded as they occur.

LO3–2 Distinguish between accrual-basis and cash-basis accounting.

The difference between accrual-basis accounting and cash-basis accounting is *timing*. Under accrual-basis accounting, we record revenues when we provide goods and services to customers, and we record expenses when costs are used in company operations. Under cash-basis accounting, we record revenues when we receive cash, and we record expenses when we pay cash. Cash-basis accounting is not allowed for financial reporting purposes for most major companies.

LO3–3 Demonstrate the purposes and recording of adjusting entries.

Adjusting entries are a necessary part of accrual-basis accounting. They are used to record changes in assets and liabilities (and their related revenues and expenses) that have occurred during the period but have not yet been recorded by the end of the period.

Adjusting entries are needed when cash flows or obligations occur *before* the revenue- or expense-related activity (prepayment) or when cash flows occur *after* the revenue- or expense-related activity (accrual).

Adjusting entries are *unnecessary* in two cases: (1) for transactions that do not involve revenue or expense activities and (2) for transactions that result in revenues or expenses being recorded at the same time as the cash flow.

LO3–4 Post adjusting entries and prepare an adjusted trial balance.

We post adjusting entries to the general ledger to update the account balances.

An adjusted trial balance is a list of all accounts and their balances at a particular date, after we have updated account balances for adjusting entries.

LO3–5 Prepare financial statements using the adjusted trial balance.

We prepare the income statement, statement of stockholders' equity, and balance sheet from the adjusted trial balance. The income statement provides a measure of net income (profitability), calculated as revenues minus expenses. The balance sheet demonstrates that assets equal liabilities plus stockholders' equity (the basic accounting equation).

LO3–6 Demonstrate the purposes and recording of closing entries.

Closing entries serve two purposes: (1) to transfer the balances of temporary accounts (revenues, expenses, and dividends) to the Retained Earnings account and (2) to reduce the balances of these temporary accounts to zero to prepare them for measuring activity in the next period.

Closing entries increase retained earnings by the amount of revenues for the period and decrease retained earnings by the amount of expenses and dividends for the period.

LO3–7 Post closing entries and prepare a post-closing trial balance.

After we post the closing entries to the general ledger, the balance of Retained Earnings equals the amount shown in the balance sheet. The balances of all revenue, expense, and dividend accounts are zero at that point.

GLOSSARY

Accrual-basis accounting: Record revenues when goods and services are provided to customers, and record expenses for the costs used to provide those goods and services to customers. **p. 114**

Accrued expenses: Occur when a company has used costs in the current period, but the company hasn't yet paid cash for those costs. **p. 125**

Accrued revenues: Occur when a company provides products or services but hasn't yet received cash. **p. 127**

Adjusted trial balance: A list of all accounts and their balances after we have updated account balances for adjusting entries. **p. 132**

Adjusting entries: Entries at the end of the period used to update balances of revenues and expenses (and changes in their related assets and liabilities) that have occurred during the period but that we have not yet recorded. **p. 118**

Book value: An asset's original cost less accumulated depreciation. **p. 122**

Cash-basis accounting: Record revenues at the time cash is received and expenses at the time cash is paid. **p. 115**

Classified balance sheet: Balance sheet that groups a company's assets into current assets and long-term assets and that separates liabilities into current liabilities and long-term liabilities. **p. 135**

Closing entries: Entries that transfer the balances of all temporary accounts (revenues, expenses, and dividends) to the balance of the Retained Earnings account. **p. 138**

Contra account: An account with a balance that is opposite, or "contra," to that of its related accounts. **p. 122**

Deferred revenues: Arise when a company receives cash in advance from customers, but goods and services won't be provided until a later period. **p. 123**

Depreciation: The process of allocating the cost of a long-term asset to expense over its useful life. **p. 122**

Permanent accounts: All accounts that appear in the balance sheet; account balances are carried forward from period to period. **p. 138**

Post-closing trial balance: A list of all accounts and their balances at a particular date after we have updated account balances for closing entries. **p. 141**

Prepaid expenses: Arise when a company pays cash (or has an obligation to pay cash) to acquire an asset that is not used until a later period. **p. 120**

Revenue recognition principle: Record revenue in the period in which we provide goods and services to customers. **p. 115**

Temporary accounts: All revenue, expense, and dividend accounts; account balances are maintained for a single period and then closed (or zeroed out) and transferred to the balance of the Retained Earnings account at the end of the period. **p. 138**

SELF-STUDY QUESTIONS

1. On May 5, Johnson Plumbing receives a phone call from a customer needing a new water heater and schedules a service visit for May 7. On May 7, Johnson installs the new water heater. The customer pays for services on May 10. According to the *revenue recognition principle,* on which date should Johnson record service revenue? **(LO3–1)**

   a. May 5 (date of phone call).
   b. May 7 (date of service).
   c. May 10 (date of cash receipt).
   d. Evenly over the three dates.

2. On January 17, Papa's Pizza signs a contract with Bug Zappers for exterminating services related to a recent

sighting of cockroaches in the restaurant. Papa's pays for the extermination service on January 29, and Bug Zappers sprays for bugs on February 7. On which date should Papa's Pizza record the extermination expense using accrual-basis accounting? **(LO3–1)**

a. January 17 (date of the contract).

b. January 29 (date of cash payment).

c. February 7 (date of extermination service).

d. Evenly over the three dates.

3. Refer to the information in *Self-Study Question* 1. Using *cash-basis accounting,* on which date should Johnson record service revenue? **(LO3–2)**

a. May 5 (date of phone call).

b. May 7 (date of service).

c. May 10 (date of cash receipt).

d. Evenly over the three dates.

4. Refer to the information in *Self-Study Question* 2. Using *cash-basis accounting,* on which date should Papa's Pizza record the extermination expense? **(LO3–2)**

a. January 17 (date of the contract).

b. January 29 (date of cash payment).

c. February 7 (date of extermination service).

d. Evenly over the three dates.

5. Which of the following is *not* a characteristic of adjusting entries? **(LO3–3)**

a. Reduce the balances of revenue, expense, and dividend accounts to zero.

b. Allow for proper recognition of revenues and expenses.

c. Are part of accrual-basis accounting.

d. Are recorded at the end of the accounting period.

6. On November 1, 2024, a company receives cash of $6,000 from a customer for services to be provided evenly over the next six months. Deferred revenue is recorded at that time. Which of the following adjusting entries is needed on December 31, 2024? **(LO3–3)**

a. Debit Deferred Revenue for $2,000; Credit Cash for $2,000.

b. Debit Deferred Revenue for $2,000; Credit Service Revenue for $2,000.

c. Debit Deferred Revenue for $6,000; Credit Service Revenue for $6,000.

d. Debit Service Revenue for $2,000; Credit Deferred Revenue for $4,000.

7. A company owes employee salaries of $5,000 on December 31 for work completed in the current year, but the company doesn't plan to pay those salaries until the following year. What adjusting entry, if any, is needed on December 31? **(LO3–3)**

a. Debit Salaries Payable for $5,000; Credit Salaries Expense for $5,000.

b. Debit Salaries Payable for $5,000; Credit Cash for $5,000.

c. Debit Salaries Expense for $5,000; Credit Salaries Payable for $5,000.

d. No adjusting entry is needed.

8. Ambassador Hotels purchases one year of fire insurance coverage on December 1 for $24,000 ($2,000 per month), debiting Prepaid Insurance. On December 31, Ambassador would record the following year-end adjusting entry: **(LO3–3)**

	Debit	Credit
a. Insurance Expense.............	24,000	
Prepaid Insurance		24,000
b. Insurance Expense.............	2,000	
Prepaid Insurance		2,000
c. Insurance Expense.............	22,000	
Prepaid Insurance		22,000
d. No entry is required on December 31 because full cash payment was made on December 1 and the insurance does not expire until the following November 30.		

9. An adjusted trial balance **(LO3–4)**

a. Lists all accounts and their balances at a particular date after updating account balances for adjusting entries.

b. Is used to prepare the financial statements.

c. Includes balances for revenues, expenses, and dividends.

d. All the above.

10. Which of the following describes the information reported in the income statement? **(LO3–5)**

a. Net income for the period calculated as revenues minus expenses.

b. Total assets equal total liabilities plus stockholders' equity.

c. Change in stockholders' equity through changes in common stock and retained earnings.

d. Net cash flows from operating, investing, and financing activities.

11. Which of the following describes the information reported in the statement of stockholders' equity? **(LO3–5)**

a. Net income for the period calculated as revenues minus expenses.

b. Total assets equal total liabilities plus stockholders' equity.

c. Change in stockholders' equity through changes in common stock and retained earnings.

d. Net cash flows from operating, investing, and financing activities.

12. In a classified balance sheet, liabilities are separated into two categories based on **(LO3–5)**

a. The amount of the obligation to be satisfied—large versus small.

b. To whom the obligation is owed—those inside versus those outside of the company.

c. The nature of the obligation—determinable amount versus estimated amount.

d. The length of time until the obligation is expected to be satisfied—less than one year versus more than one year.

13. In a classified balance sheet, long-term assets used in the normal course of business are known as **(LO3–5)**

a. Investments.

b. Property, plant, and equipment.

c. Intangible assets.

d. Total assets.

14. Which of the following describes the purpose(s) of closing entries? **(LO3–6)**

a. Adjust the balances of asset and liability accounts for unrecorded activity during the period.

b. Transfer the balances of temporary accounts (revenues, expenses, and dividends) to Retained Earnings.

c. Reduce the balances of the temporary accounts to zero to prepare them for measuring activity in the next period.

d. Both *b.* and *c.*

15. Which of the following accounts is *not* listed in a post-closing trial balance? **(LO3–7)**

a. Prepaid Rent.

b. Accounts Payable.

c. Salaries Expense.

d. Retained Earnings.

Note: For answers, see the last page of the chapter.

DATA ANALYTICS & EXCEL

Visit Connect to find a variety of Data Analytics questions that help build Excel, Tableau, and data visualization skills. Assignable materials include Integrated Excel, Applying Excel, Data Visualizations, Tableau Dashboard Activities, **and** Applying Tableau **cases.**

REVIEW QUESTIONS

■ **LO3–1**

1. Discuss the major principle that describes recording revenues.

■ **LO3–1**

2. Discuss the major principle that describes recording expenses.

■ **LO3–1**

3. Samantha is a first-year accounting student. She doesn't think it matters that expenses are reported in the same period's income statement with the related revenues. She feels that "as long as revenues and expenses are recorded in any period, that's good enough." Help her understand why reporting expenses with the revenues they help to generate is important.

■ **LO3–2**

4. Describe when revenues and expenses are recognized using cash-basis accounting. How does this differ from accrual-basis accounting?

■ **LO3–2**

Flip Side of Question 7

5. Executive Lawn provides $100 of landscape maintenance to Peterson Law on April 10. Consider three scenarios:

a. Peterson pays for the lawn service in advance on March 28.

b. Peterson pays for the lawn service on April 10, the day of service.

c. Peterson pays for the lawn service the following month on May 2.

If Executive Lawn uses accrual-basis accounting, on which date would Executive Lawn record the $100 revenue for each scenario?

■ **LO3–2**

Flip Side of Question 8

6. Consider the information in *Question* 5. Using cash-basis accounting, on which date would Executive Lawn record the $100 revenue for each scenario?

7. Peterson Law asks Executive Lawn to provide $100 of landscape maintenance. Executive Lawn provides the service on April 10. Consider three scenarios:

a. Peterson pays for the lawn service in advance on March 28.

■ **LO3–2**

Flip Side of Question 5

b. Peterson pays for the lawn service on April 10, the day of service.

c. Peterson pays for the lawn service the following month on May 2.

If Peterson Law uses accrual-basis accounting, on which date would Peterson Law record the $100 expense for each scenario?

8. Consider the information in *Question 7*. Using cash-basis accounting, on which date would Peterson Law record the $100 expense for each scenario?

    ■ **LO3–2**

    Flip Side of Question 6

9. Why are adjusting entries necessary under accrual-basis accounting?

    ■ **LO3–3**

10. There are two basic types of adjusting entries—prepayments and accruals. Describe each in terms of the timing of revenue and expense recognition versus the flow of cash.

    ■ **LO3–3**

11. Provide an example of a prepaid expense. Describe the adjusting entry associated with a prepaid expense.

    ■ **LO3–3**

12. Provide an example of a deferred revenue. Describe the adjusting entry associated with a deferred revenue.

    ■ **LO3–3**

13. Provide an example of an accrued expense. Describe the adjusting entry associated with an accrued expense.

    ■ **LO3–3**

14. Provide an example of an accrued revenue. Describe the adjusting entry associated with an accrued revenue.

    ■ **LO3–3**

15. Sequoya Printing purchases office supplies for $75 on October 2. The staff uses the office supplies continually on a daily basis throughout the month. By the end of the month, office supplies of $25 remain. Record the month-end adjusting entry for office supplies (assuming the balance of Office Supplies at the beginning of October was $0).

    ■ **LO3–3**

16. Jackson Rental receives its September utility bill of $320 on September 30 but does not pay the bill until October 10. Jackson's accountant records the utility expense of $320 on October 10 at the time of payment. Will this cause any of Jackson's accounts to be misstated at the end of September? If so, indicate which ones and the direction of the misstatement.

    ■ **LO3–3**

17. Global Printing publishes several types of magazines. Customers are required to pay for magazines in advance. On November 5, Global receives cash of $120,000 for prepaid subscriptions. By the end of November, Global has distributed $20,000 of magazines to customers. Record the month-end adjusting entry.

    ■ **LO3–3**

18. At the end of May, Robertson Corporation has provided services to customers, but it has not yet billed these customers nor have any of them paid for those services. If Robertson makes no adjusting entry associated with these unpaid services provided, will any accounts be misstated? If so, indicate which ones and the direction of the misstatement.

    ■ **LO3–3**

19. Fill in the blank associated with each adjusting entry:
    a. *Prepaid expense:* Debit Supplies Expense; credit _____.
    b. *Deferred revenue:* Debit _____; credit Service Revenue.
    c. *Accrued expense:* Debit _____; credit Salaries Payable.
    d. *Accrued revenue:* Debit Accounts Receivable; credit _____.

    ■ **LO3–3**

20. What is the purpose of the adjusted trial balance? How do the adjusted trial balance and the (unadjusted) trial balance differ?

    ■ **LO3–4**

21. Explain what is meant by the term *classified* when referring to a balance sheet.

    ■ **LO3–5**

22. At the end of the period, Sanders Company reports the following amounts: Assets = $12,000; Liabilities = $8,000; Revenues = $5,000; Expenses = $3,000. Calculate stockholders' equity.

    ■ **LO3–5**

23. What are the two purposes of preparing closing entries?

    ■ **LO3–6**

24. What does it mean to close temporary accounts? Which of the following account types are closed: assets, liabilities, dividends, revenues, and expenses?

    ■ **LO3–6**

25. Describe the debits and credits for the three closing entries required at the end of a reporting period.

    ■ **LO3–6**

■ **LO3–6**   26. In its first four years of operations, Chance Communications reports net income of $300, $900, $1,500, and $2,400, respectively, and pays dividends of $200 per year. What would be the balance of Retained Earnings at the end of the fourth year?

■ **LO3–6**   27. Matt has been told by his instructor that dividends reduce retained earnings (and therefore stockholders' equity). However, since he knows that stockholders are receiving the dividends, Matt doesn't understand how paying dividends would *decrease* stockholders' equity. Explain this to Matt.

■ **LO3–7**   28. How do the adjusted trial balance and the post-closing trial balance differ? Which accounts are shown in the adjusted trial balance but not in the post-closing trial balance? Which account is shown in both trial balances but with a different balance on each?

BRIEF EXERCISES

Determine effects of revenue-related transactions (LO3–1)

BE3–1 Below are transactions for Lobos, Inc., during the month of December. Determine whether each transaction increases, decreases, or has no effect on assets, liabilities, and revenues in December.
a. Receive $1,200 cash from customers for services to be provided next month.
b. Perform $900 of services during the month and bill customers. Customers are expected to pay next month.
c. Perform $2,300 of services during the month and receive full cash payment from customers at the time of service.

Determine effects of expense-related transactions (LO3–1)

BE3–2 Below are transactions for Bronco Corporation during the month of June. Determine whether each transaction increases, decreases, or has no effect on assets, liabilities, and expenses in June.
a. Pay $600 cash to employees for work performed during June.
b. Receive a $200 telephone bill for the month of June, but Bronco does not plan to pay the bill until early next month.
c. Pay $500 on account for supplies purchased last month. All supplies were used last month.

Calculate net income (LO3–1)

BE3–3 Hoya Corporation reports the following amounts: Assets = $18,000; Liabilities = $3,000; Stockholders' equity = $15,000; Dividends = $3,000; Revenues = $17,000; and Expenses = $12,000. What amount is reported for net income?

Analyze the impact of transactions on the balance of cash, cash-basis net income, and accrual-basis net income (LO3–1, 3–2)

BE3–4 Consider the following set of transactions occurring during the month of May for Bison Consulting Company. For each transaction, indicate the impact on (1) the balance of cash, (2) cash-basis net income, and (3) accrual-basis net income for May. The first answer is provided as an example.

In the month of May	Cash Balance	Cash-Basis Net Income	Accrual-Basis Net Income
(a) *Receive $1,500 from customers who were billed for services in April.*	*+$1,500*	*+$1,500*	*$0*
(b) Provide $3,200 of consulting services to a local business. Payment is not expected until June.	_____	_____	_____
(c) Purchase office supplies for $400 on account. All supplies are used by the end of May.	_____	_____	_____
(d) Pay $600 to workers. $400 is for work in May and $200 is for work in April.	_____	_____	_____
(e) Pay $200 to advertise in a local newspaper in May.	_____	_____	_____
Totals	_____	_____	_____

BE3–5 Rebel Technology maintains its records using cash-basis accounting. Consider the following:
- During the year, the company received cash from customers, $50,000, and paid cash for salaries, $21,900.
- At the beginning of the year, customers owe Rebel $1,100. By the end of the year, customers owe $8,000.
- At the beginning of the year, Rebel owes salaries of $7,000. At the end of the year, Rebel owes salaries of $4,000.

Determine cash-basis net income and accrual-basis net income for the year.

Determine accrual-basis and cash-basis net income (LO3–1, 3–2)

BE3–6 At the beginning of the year, Golden Gopher Company reports a balance in Supplies of $500. During the year, Golden Gopher purchases an additional $3,300 of supplies for cash. By the end of the year, only $300 of supplies remains. (1) Record the purchase of supplies during the year. (2) Record the adjusting entry at the end of the year. (3) Calculate the year-end adjusted balances of Supplies and Supplies Expense.

Record the adjusting entry for supplies (LO3–3)

BE3–7 Suppose Hoosiers, a specialty clothing store, rents space at a local mall for one year, paying $25,200 ($2,100/month) in advance on October 1. (1) Record the payment of rent in advance on October 1. (2) Record the adjusting entry on December 31. (3) Calculate the year-end adjusted balances of Prepaid Rent and Rent Expense (assuming the balance of Prepaid Rent at the beginning of the year is $0).

Record the adjusting entry for prepaid rent (LO3–3)

BE3–8 Mountaineer Excavation operates in a low-lying area that is subject to heavy rains and flooding. Because of this, Mountaineer purchases one year of flood insurance in advance on March 1, paying $36,000 ($3,000/month). (1) Record the purchase of insurance in advance on March 1. (2) Record the adjusting entry on December 31. (3) Calculate the year-end adjusted balances of Prepaid Insurance and Insurance Expense (assuming the balance of Prepaid Insurance at the beginning of the year is $0).

Record the adjusting entry for prepaid insurance (LO3–3)

BE3–9 Beaver Construction purchases new equipment for $50,400 cash on April 1, 2024. At the time of purchase, the equipment is expected to be used in operations for seven years (84 months) and have no resale or scrap value at the end. Beaver depreciates equipment evenly over the 84 months ($600/month). (1) Record the purchase of equipment on April 1. (2) Record the adjusting entry for depreciation on December 31, 2024. (3) Calculate the year-end adjusted balances of Accumulated Depreciation and Depreciation Expense (assuming the balance of Accumulated Depreciation at the beginning of 2024 is $0).

Record the adjusting entry for depreciation (LO3–3)

BE3–10 Suppose a customer rents a vehicle for three months from Commodores Rental on November 1, paying $6,000 ($2,000/month). (1) Record the rental for Commodores on November 1. (2) Record the adjusting entry on December 31. (3) Calculate the year-end adjusted balances of Deferred Revenue and Service Revenue (assuming the balance of Deferred Revenue at the beginning of the year is $0).

Record the adjusting entry for deferred revenue (LO3–3)

BE3–11 Fighting Irish Incorporated pays its employees $5,600 every two weeks ($400/day). The current two-week pay period ends on December 28, 2024, and employees are paid $5,600. The next two-week pay period ends on January 11, 2025, and employees are paid $5,600. (1) Record the adjusting entry on December 31, 2024. (2) Calculate the 2024 year-end adjusted balance of Salaries Payable (assuming the balance of Salaries Payable before adjustment in 2024 is $0).

Record the adjusting entry for salaries payable (LO3–3)

BE3–12 Midshipmen Company borrows $15,000 from Falcon Company on July 1, 2024. Midshipmen repays the amount borrowed and pays interest of 12% (1%/month) on June 30, 2025. (1) Record the borrowing for Midshipmen on July 1, 2024. (2) Record the adjusting entry for Midshipmen on December 31, 2024. (3) Calculate the 2024 year-end adjusted balances of Interest Payable and Interest Expense (assuming the balance of Interest Payable at the beginning of the year is $0).

Record the adjusting entry for interest payable (LO3–3)
Flip Side of BE3–13

BE3–13 Refer to the information in BE3–12. (1) Record the lending for Falcon on July 1, 2024. (2) Record the adjusting entry for Falcon on December 31, 2024. (3) Calculate the 2024 year-end adjusted balances of Interest Receivable and Interest Revenue (assuming the balance of Interest Receivable at the beginning of the year is $0).

Record the adjusting entry for interest receivable (LO3–3)
Flip Side of BE3–12

Assign accounts to financial statements (LO3–5)

BE3–14 For each of the following accounts, indicate whether the account is shown in the income statement or the balance sheet:

Accounts	Financial Statement
1. Accounts Receivable	_____
2. Deferred Revenue	_____
3. Supplies Expense	_____
4. Salaries Payable	_____
5. Rent Expense	_____
6. Service Revenue	_____

Understand the purpose of financial statements (LO3–5)

BE3–15 Below are the four primary financial statements. Match each financial statement with its primary purpose to investors.

Financial Statements

1. _____ Income statement
2. _____ Statement of stockholders' equity
3. _____ Balance sheet
4. _____ Statement of cash flows

Purposes

a. Provides measures of resources and claims to those resources at the end of the year.
b. Provides an indication of the company's ability to make a profit during the current year.
c. Provides a measure of net increases and decreases in cash for the current year.
d. Shows changes in owners' claims to resources for the current year.

Prepare an income statement (LO3–5)

BE3–16 The following account balances appear in the 2024 adjusted trial balance of Beavers Corporation: Service Revenue, $275,000; Salaries Expense, $110,000; Supplies Expense, $20,000; Rent Expense, $26,000; Advertising Expense Expense, $44,000; and Delivery Expense, $18,000. Prepare an income statement for the year ended December 31, 2024.

Prepare a statement of stockholders' equity (LO3–5)

BE3–17 The following account balances appear in the 2024 adjusted trial balance of Spiders Corporation: Common Stock, $30,000; Retained Earnings, $8,000; Dividends, $1,000; Service Revenue, $28,000; Salaries Expense, $16,000; and Rent Expense, $9,000. No common stock was issued during the year. Prepare the statement of stockholders' equity for the year ended December 31, 2024.

Prepare a classified balance sheet (LO3–5)

BE3–18 The following account balances appear in the 2024 adjusted trial balance of Blue Devils Corporation: Cash, $5,000; Accounts Receivable, $9,000; Supplies, $19,000; Land, $75,000; Accounts Payable, $26,000; Salaries Payable, $16,000; Common Stock, $60,000; and Retained Earnings, _____. Prepare the December 31, 2024, classified balance sheet including the correct balance for retained earnings.

Record closing entries (LO3–6)

BE3–19 The year-end adjusted trial balance of Aggies Corporation included the following account balances: Retained Earnings, $230,000; Service Revenue, $900,000; Salaries Expense, $390,000; Rent Expense, $150,000; Interest Expense, $85,000; and Dividends, $60,000. Record the necessary closing entries.

Prepare a post-closing trial balance (LO3–7)

BE3–20 The year-end adjusted trial balance of Hilltoppers Corporation included the following account balances: Cash, $5,000; Equipment, $17,000; Accounts Payable, $3,000; Common Stock, $11,000; Retained Earnings, $8,100; Dividends, $1,100; Service Revenue, $16,000; Salaries Expense, $11,000; and Utilities Expense, $4,000. Prepare the post-closing trial balance.

Determine financial statement effects of supplies used (LO3–3)

BE3–21 Refer to the information in BE3–6. Determine the financial statement effects for (1) the purchase of supplies during the year and (2) the adjusting entry for supplies used by the end of the year.

BE3–22 Refer to the information in BE3–7. Determine the financial statement effects for (1) the payment of rent in advance on October 1 and (b) the adjusting entry for rent expired by December 31.

Determine financial statement effects of prepaid rent expired **(LO3–3)**

BE3–23 Refer to the information in BE3–10. Determine the financial statement effects for (1) the cash received in advance on November 1 and (2) the adjusting entry for services provided by December 31.

Determine financial statement effects of deferred revenue being satisfied **(LO3–3)**

BE3–24 Refer to the information in BE3–11. Determine the financial statement effects of the adjusting entry for salaries owed on December 31, 2024.

Determine financial statement effects of salaries owed **(LO3–3)**

BE3–25 Refer to the information in BE3–13. Determine the financial statement effects for (1) the borrowing on July 1, 2024, and (2) the adjusting entry for interest owed on December 31, 2024.

Determine financial statement effects of interest earned **(LO3–3)**

EXERCISES

E3–1 Consider the following situations:
1. **American Airlines** collects cash on June 12 from the sale of a ticket to a customer. The flight occurs on August 16.
2. A customer purchases sunglasses from **Eddie Bauer** on January 27 on account. Eddie Bauer receives payment from the customer on February 2.
3. On March 30, a customer preorders 10 supreme pizzas (without onions) from **Pizza Hut** for a birthday party. The pizzas are prepared and delivered on April 2. The company receives cash at the time of delivery.
4. A customer pays in advance for a three-month subscription to **Sports Illustrated** on July 1. Issues are scheduled for delivery each week from July 1 through September 30.

Determine the timing of revenue recognition **(LO3–1)**

Required:
For each situation, determine the date for which the company recognizes the revenue under accrual-basis accounting.

E3–2 Consider the following situations:
1. **American Airlines** operates a flight from Dallas to Los Angeles on August 16. The pilots' salaries associated with the flight are paid on September 2.
2. **Eddie Bauer** pays cash on January 6 to purchase sunglasses from a wholesale distributor. The sunglasses are sold to customers on January 27.
3. On January 1, **Pizza Hut** pays for a one-year property insurance policy with coverage starting immediately.
4. **Sports Illustrated** signs an agreement with CBS on January 12 to provide television advertisements during the Super Bowl. Payment is due within 3 weeks after February 4, the day of the Super Bowl. Sports Illustrated makes the payment on February 23.

Determine the timing of expense recognition **(LO3–1)**

Required:
For each situation, determine the date for which the company recognizes the expense under accrual-basis accounting.

E3–3 Refer to the situations discussed in E3–1.

Differentiate cash-basis revenues from accrual-basis revenues **(LO3–2)**

Required:
For each situation, determine the date for which the company recognizes revenue using cash-basis accounting.

Differentiate cash-basis expenses from accrual-basis expenses (LO3–2)

E3–4 Refer to the situation discussed in E3–2.

Required:
For each situation, determine the date for which the company recognizes the expense using cash-basis accounting.

Determine the amount of net income (LO3–1)

E3–5 During the course of your examination of the financial statements of Trojan Corporation for the year ended December 31, 2024, you come across several items needing further consideration. Currently, net income is $100,000.

1. An insurance policy covering 12 months was purchased on October 1, 2024, for $24,000. The entire amount was debited to Prepaid Insurance and no adjusting entry was made for this item in 2024.
2. During 2024, the company received a $4,000 cash advance from a customer for services to be performed in 2025. The $4,000 was incorrectly credited to Service Revenue.
3. Purchases of supplies during the year were incorrectly recorded to Supplies Expense. You discover that supplies costing $2,750 were on hand at December 31, 2024.
4. Trojan borrowed $70,000 from a local bank on September 1, 2024. Principal and interest at 9% will be paid on August 31, 2025. No accrual was made for interest in 2024.

Required:
Using the information in 1 through 4 above, determine the proper amount of net income as of December 31, 2024.

Organize the steps in the accounting cycle (LO3–3, 3–4, 3–5, 3–6, 3–7)

E3–6 Listed below are all the steps in the accounting cycle.

(a) Record and post adjusting entries.
(b) Post the transaction to the T-account in the general ledger.
(c) Record the transaction.
(d) Prepare financial statements (income statement, statement of stockholders' equity, balance sheet, and statement of cash flows).
(e) Record and post closing entries.
(f) Prepare a trial balance.
(g) Analyze the impact of the transaction on the accounting equation.
(h) Assess whether the transaction results in a debit or a credit to the account balance.
(i) Use source documents to identify accounts affected by external transactions.

Required:
List the steps in proper order.

Record year-end adjusting entries (LO3–3)

E3–7 Golden Eagle Company has the following balances at the end of November:

	November 30	
	Debit	**Credit**
Supplies	$2,000	
Prepaid Insurance	8,000	
Salaries Payable		$11,000
Deferred Revenue		0

The following information is known for the month of December:
1. Purchases of supplies for cash during December were $4,500. Supplies on hand at the end of December equal $3,500.
2. No insurance payments are made in December. Insurance expired in December is $2,000.

3. November salaries payable of $11,000 were paid to employees in December. Additional salaries for December owed at the end of the year are $16,000.
4. On December 1, Golden Eagle received $4,500 from a customer for rent for the period December through February. By the end of December, one month of rent has been provided.

Required:

For each item, (a) record any transaction during the month of December, and (b) prepare the related December 31 year-end adjusting entry.

E3–8 Consider the following transactions for Huskies Insurance Company:
1. Income taxes for the year total $42,000 but won't be paid until next April 15.
2. On June 30, the company lent its chief financial officer $50,000; principal and interest at 7% are due in one year.
3. On October 1, the company received $16,000 from a customer for a one-year property insurance policy. Deferred Revenue was credited on October 1.

Required:

For each item, record the necessary adjusting entry for Huskies Insurance at its year-end of December 31. No adjusting entries were made during the year.

Record year-end adjusting entries (LO3–3)

E3–9 Refer to the information in E3–8.

Required:

For each of the adjusting entries in E3–8, indicate by how much net income in the income statement is higher or lower if the adjusting entry is not recorded.

Calculate the effects on net income of not recording adjusting entries (LO3–3)

E3–10 Consider the following situations for Shocker:
1. On November 28, 2024, Shocker received a $4,500 payment from a customer for services to be rendered evenly over the next three months. Deferred Revenue was credited on November 28.
2. On December 1, 2024, the company paid a local radio station $2,700 for 30 radio ads that were to be aired, 10 per month, throughout December, January, and February. Prepaid Advertising was debited on December 1.
3. Employee salaries for the month of December totaling $8,000 will be paid on January 7, 2025.
4. On August 31, 2024, Shocker borrowed $70,000 from a local bank. A note was signed with principal and 9% interest to be paid on August 31, 2025.

Record year-end adjusting entries (LO3–3)

Required:

Record the necessary adjusting entries for Shocker at December 31, 2024. No adjusting entries were made during the year.

E3–11 Refer to the information in E3–10.

Required:

For each of the adjusting entries recorded in E3–10, indicate by how much the assets, liabilities, and stockholders' equity in the December 31, 2024, balance sheet is higher or lower if the adjusting entry is not recorded.

Calculate the effects on the accounting equation of not recording adjusting entries (LO3–3, 3–4)

E3–12 Below are transactions for Wolverine Company during 2024.
1. On December 1, 2024, Wolverine received $4,000 cash from a company that rents office space from Wolverine. The payment, representing rent for December and January, was credited to Deferred Revenue on December 1.
2. Wolverine purchased a one-year property insurance policy on July 1, 2024, for $13,200. The payment was debited to Prepaid Insurance for the entire amount on July 1.
3. Employee salaries of $3,000 for the month of December will be paid in early January 2025.
4. On November 1, 2024, the company borrowed $15,000 from a bank. The loan requires principal and interest at 10% to be paid on October 30, 2025.
5. Office supplies at the beginning of 2024 totaled $1,000. On August 15, Wolverine purchased an additional $3,400 of office supplies, debiting the Supplies account. By the end of the year, $500 of office supplies remains.

Record year-end adjusting entries (LO3–3)

Required:

Record the necessary adjusting entries at December 31, 2024, for Wolverine Company. You do not need to record transactions made during the year. Assume that no financial statements were prepared during the year and no adjusting entries were recorded.

Record year-end adjusting entries (LO3–3)

E3–13 Below are transactions for Hurricane Company during 2024.

1. On October 1, 2024, Hurricane lent $9,000 to another company. The other company signed a note indicating principal and 12% interest will be paid to Hurricane on September 30, 2025.
2. On November 1, 2024, Hurricane paid its landlord $4,500 representing rent for the months of November through January. The payment was debited to Prepaid Rent for the entire amount on November 1.
3. On August 1, 2024, Hurricane collected $13,200 in advance from another company that is renting a portion of Hurricane's factory. The $13,200 represents one year's rent and the entire amount was credited to Deferred Revenue.
4. Utilities owed at the end of the year are $5,500.
5. Salaries for the year earned by employees but not paid to them or recorded are $5,000.
6. Hurricane began the year with $1,500 in supplies. During the year, the company purchased $5,500 in supplies and debited that amount to Supplies. At year-end, supplies costing $3,500 remain on hand.

Required:

Record the necessary adjusting entries at December 31, 2024, for Hurricane Company for each of the situations. Assume that no financial statements were prepared during the year and no adjusting entries were recorded.

Prepare an adjusted trial balance (LO3–3, 3–4)

E3–14 The December 31, 2024, unadjusted trial balance for Demon Deacons Corporation is presented below.

Accounts	Debit	Credit
Cash	$10,000	
Accounts Receivable	15,000	
Prepaid Rent	7,200	
Supplies	4,000	
Deferred Revenue		$ 3,000
Common Stock		11,000
Retained Earnings		6,000
Service Revenue		51,200
Salaries Expense	35,000	
	$71,200	$71,200

At year-end, the following additional information is available:

1. The balance of Prepaid Rent, $7,200, represents payment on October 31, 2024, for rent from November 1, 2024, to April 30, 2025.
2. The balance of Deferred Revenue, $3,000, represents payment in advance from a customer. By the end of the year, $750 of the services have been provided.
3. An additional $700 in salaries is owed to employees at the end of the year but will not be paid until January 4, 2025.
4. The balance of Supplies, $4,000, represents the amount of office supplies on hand at the beginning of the year of $1,700 plus an additional $2,300 purchased throughout 2024. By the end of 2024, only $800 of supplies remains.

Required:

1. Update account balances for the year-end information by recording any necessary adjusting entries. No prior adjustments have been made in 2024.
2. Prepare an adjusted trial balance as of December 31, 2024.

E3–15 Below are the restated amounts of net income and retained earnings for Volunteers Inc. and Raiders Inc. for the period 2015–2024. Volunteers began operations in 2016, while Raiders began several years earlier.

Calculate the balance of retained earnings **(LO3–5)**

	VOLUNTEERS INC. ($ in millions)		RAIDERS INC. ($ in millions)	
Year	Net Income (Loss)	Retained Earnings	Net Income (Loss)	Retained Earnings
2015	—	$0	$ 35	$11
2016	$ 30	_____	(43)	_____
2017	(7)	_____	63	_____
2018	41	_____	63	_____
2019	135	_____	102	_____
2020	30	_____	135	_____
2021	(131)	_____	(42)	_____
2022	577	_____	74	_____
2023	359	_____	110	_____
2024	360	_____	162	_____

Required:

Calculate the balance of retained earnings each year for each company. Neither company paid dividends during this time.

E3–16 The December 31, 2024, adjusted trial balance for Fightin' Blue Hens Corporation is presented below.

Prepare financial statements from an adjusted trial balance **(LO3–5)**

Accounts	Debit	Credit
Cash	$ 12,000	
Accounts Receivable	150,000	
Prepaid Rent	6,000	
Supplies	30,000	
Land	265,000	
Accounts Payable		$ 12,000
Salaries Payable		11,000
Interest Payable		5,000
Notes Payable (due in two years)		40,000
Common Stock		300,000
Retained Earnings		60,000
Service Revenue		500,000
Salaries Expense	400,000	
Rent Expense	20,000	
Utilities Expense	40,000	
Interest Expense	5,000	
Totals	$928,000	$928,000

Required:

1. Prepare an income statement for the year ended December 31, 2024.
2. Prepare a statement of stockholders' equity for the year ended December 31, 2024, assuming no common stock was issued during 2024.
3. Prepare a classified balance sheet as of December 31, 2024.

Record closing
entries (LO3–6)

E3–17 Seminoles Corporation's fiscal year-end is December 31, 2024. The following is a partial adjusted trial balance as of December 31.

Accounts	Debit	Credit
Retained Earnings		$30,000
Dividends	$ 3,000	
Service Revenue		50,000
Interest Revenue		6,000
Salaries Expense	15,000	
Rent Expense	6,000	
Advertising Expense	3,000	
Insurance Expense	11,000	
Interest Expense	5,000	

Required:
1. Prepare the necessary closing entries.
2. Calculate the ending balance of Retained Earnings.

Record closing entries and
prepare a post-closing
trial balance (LO3–6, 3–7)

E3–18 Laker Incorporated's fiscal year-end is December 31, 2024. The following is an adjusted trial balance as of December 31.

Accounts	Debit	Credit
Cash	$ 12,000	
Supplies	39,000	
Prepaid Rent	30,000	
Accounts Payable		$ 3,000
Notes Payable		30,000
Common Stock		40,000
Retained Earnings		9,000
Dividends	4,000	
Service Revenue		54,000
Salaries Expense	20,000	
Advertising Expense	13,000	
Rent Expense	10,000	
Utilities Expense	8,000	
Totals	$136,000	$136,000

Required:
1. Prepare the necessary closing entries.
2. Calculate the ending balance of Retained Earnings.
3. Prepare a post-closing trial balance.

Record closing entries and
prepare a post-closing
trial balance (LO3–6, 3–7)

E3–19 Refer to the adjusted trial balance in E3–16.

Required:
1. Record the necessary closing entries at December 31, 2024.
2. Prepare a post-closing trial balance.

E3–20 On January 1, 2024, Red Flash Photography had the following balances: Cash, $12,000; Supplies, $8,000; Land, $60,000; Deferred Revenue, $5,000; Common Stock $50,000; and Retained Earnings, $25,000. During 2024, the company had the following transactions:

Record transactions and prepare adjusting entries, adjusted trial balance, financial statements, and closing entries (LO3–3, 3–4, 3–5, 3–6, 3–7)

1. February   15   Issue additional shares of common stock, $20,000.
2. May   20   Provide services to customers for cash, $35,000, and on account, $30,000.
3. August   31   Pay salaries to employees for work in 2024, $23,000.
4. October   1   Purchase rental space for one year, $12,000.
5. November 17   Purchase supplies on account, $22,000.
6. December 30   Pay dividends, $2,000.

The following information is available on December 31, 2024:
1. Employees are owed an additional $4,000 in salaries.
2. Three months of the rental space have expired.
3. Supplies of $5,000 remain on hand. All other supplies have been used.
4. All of the services associated with the beginning deferred revenue have been performed.

Required:
1. Record the transactions that occurred during the year.
2. Record the adjusting entries at the end of the year.
3. Prepare an adjusted trial balance.
4. Prepare an income statement, statement of stockholders' equity, and classified balance sheet.
5. Prepare closing entries.

E3–21 On January 1, 2024, the general ledger of Dynamite Fireworks includes the following account balances:

Complete the accounting cycle LO3–3, 3–4, 3–5, 3–6

Accounts	Debit	Credit
Cash	$23,800	
Accounts Receivable	5,200	
Supplies	3,100	
Land	50,000	
Accounts Payable		$ 3,200
Common Stock		65,000
Retained Earnings		13,900
Totals	$82,100	$82,100

During January 2024, the following transactions occur:

January 2   Purchase rental space for one year in advance, $6,000 ($500/month).
January 9   Purchase additional supplies on account, $3,500
January 13   Provide services to customers on account, $25,500.
January 17   Receive cash in advance from customers for services to be provided in the future, $3,700.
January 20   Pay cash for salaries, $11,500.
January 22   Receive cash on accounts receivable, $24,100.
January 29   Pay cash on accounts payable, $4,000.

Required:
1. Record each of the transactions listed above.
2. Record adjusting entries on January 31.
   a. Rent for the month of January has expired.
   b. Supplies remaining at the end of January total $2,800. All other supplies have been used.
   c. By the end of January, $3,200 of services has been provided to customers who paid in advance on January 17.
   d. Unpaid salaries at the end of January are $5,800.
3. Prepare an adjusted trial balance as of January 31, 2024, after updating beginning balances (above) for transactions during January (Requirement 1) and adjusting entries at the end of January (Requirement 2).

4. Prepare an income statement for the period ended January 31, 2024.
5. Prepare a classified balance sheet as of January 31, 2024.
6. Record closing entries.
7. Analyze the following features of Dynamite Fireworks' financial condition:
    a. What is the amount of profit reported for the month of January?
    b. Calculate the ratio of current assets to current liabilities (current ratio) at the end of January.
    c. Based on Dynamite Fireworks' profit and ratio of current assets to current liabilities, indicate whether Dynamite Fireworks appears to be in good or bad financial condition.

PROBLEMS: SET A

Determine accrual-basis and cash-basis revenues and expenses (LO3–1, 3–2)

P3–1A Consider the following transactions.

Transaction	Accrual-basis		Cash-basis	
	Revenue	Expense	Revenue	Expense
1. Receive cash from customers in advance of services to be provided, $600.	_____	_____	_____	_____
2. Pay utilities bill for the previous period, $150.	_____	_____	_____	_____
3. Pay for insurance in advance of the period to be covered, $2,000.	_____	_____	_____	_____
4. Pay workers' salaries for the current period, $800.	_____	_____	_____	_____
5. Incur costs for employee salaries in the current period but do not pay, $1,000.	_____	_____	_____	_____
6. Receive cash from customers at the time of service, $1,700.	_____	_____	_____	_____
7. Purchase office supplies on account, $330.	_____	_____	_____	_____
8. Borrow cash from the bank, $4,000.	_____	_____	_____	_____
9. Receive cash from customers for services performed in the previous period, $750.	_____	_____	_____	_____
10. Pay for advertising to appear in the current period, $450.	_____	_____	_____	_____

Required:
For each transaction, determine the amount of revenue or expense, if any, that is recorded under accrual-basis accounting and under cash-basis accounting in the current period.

Convert cash-basis accounting to accrual-basis accounting (LO3–1, 3–2)

P3–2A Minutemen Law Services maintains its books using cash-basis accounting. However, the company decides to borrow $100,000 from a local bank, and the bank requires Minutemen to provide annual financial statements prepared using accrual-basis accounting as part of the creditworthiness verification. During 2024, the company records the following cash flows:

Cash collected from customers		$70,000
Cash paid for:		
Salaries	$36,000	
Supplies	4,000	
Rent	5,000	
Insurance	7,000	
Utilities	3,000	55,000
Net cash flows		$15,000

You are able to determine the following information:

	January 1, 2024	December 31, 2024
Accounts Receivable	$21,000	$24,000
Prepaid Insurance	-0-	3,700
Supplies	5,000	2,000
Salaries Payable	2,700	4,400

Required:

Prepare an accrual-basis income statement for the year ended December 31, 2024, by calculating accrual-basis revenues and expenses.

P3–3A The information necessary for preparing the 2024 year-end adjusting entries for Gamecock Advertising Agency appears below. Gamecock's fiscal year-end is December 31.

Record adjusting entries (LO3–3)

1. On July 1, 2024, Gamecock received $6,000 from a customer for advertising services to be given evenly over the next 10 months. Gamecock credited Deferred Revenue on July 1.
2. At the end of the year, income taxes owed are $7,000.
3. On May 1, 2024, the company paid $4,800 for a two-year fire and liability insurance policy. The company debited Prepaid Insurance on May 1.
4. On September 1, 2024, the company borrowed $20,000 from a local bank and signed a note. Principal and interest at 12% will be paid on August 31, 2025.
5. At year-end there is a $2,700 debit balance in the Supplies (asset) account. Only $1,000 of supplies remains on hand at the end of the year.

Required:

Record the necessary adjusting entries on December 31, 2024. No prior adjustments have been made during 2024.

P3–4A Buzzard Bicycle specializes in custom painting and design of bicycles. December 31 is the company's fiscal year-end. Information necessary to prepare the year-end adjusting entries appears below.

Record adjusting entries (LO3–3)

1. A three-year fire insurance policy was purchased on July 1, 2024, for $18,000. The company debited Prepaid Insurance for the entire amount on July 1.
2. Employee salaries of $25,000 for the month of December will be paid in early January.
3. On November 1, 2024, the company received $6,000 in cash from a customer requesting a custom design for six identical bikes ($1,000 each). Deferred Revenue was credited for the entire amount on November 1. By the end of the year, four of the bikes have been completed.
4. Supplies at the beginning of the year totaled $2,000. During 2024, additional supplies of $18,000 were purchased, and the entire amount was debited to Supplies at the time of purchase. Supplies remaining at the end of the year total $4,000.
5. Buzzard paid a local radio station $12,000 for four months of advertising on December 1, 2024. The advertising will appear evenly over the four-month period. The company debited Prepaid Advertising for the entire amount on December 1.
6. Buzzard borrowed $36,000 on March 1, 2024. The principal is due to be paid in five years. Interest is payable each March 1 at an annual rate of 10%.

Required:

Record the necessary adjusting entries on December 31, 2024.

P3–5A Boilermaker Unlimited specializes in building new homes and remodeling existing homes. Remodeling projects include adding game rooms, changing kitchen cabinets and countertops, and updating bathrooms. Below is the year-end adjusted trial balance of Boilermaker Unlimited.

Prepare financial statements from an adjusted trial balance when net income is positive (LO3–5)

BOILERMAKER UNLIMITED
Adjusted Trial Balance
December 31, 2024

Accounts	Debits	Credits
Cash	$ 16,000	
Accounts Receivable	25,000	
Supplies	32,000	
Prepaid Insurance	7,000	
Investments (long-term)	425,000	
Accounts Payable		$ 31,000
Salaries Payable		28,000
Utilities Payable		5,000
Notes Payable (due in 5 years)		150,000
Common Stock		200,000
Retained Earnings		31,000
Dividends	26,000	
Service Revenue—new construction		450,000
Service Revenue—remodeling		280,000
Salaries Expense	160,000	
Supplies Expense	285,000	
Rent Expense	50,000	
Insurance Expense	25,000	
Utilities Expense	42,000	
Interest Expense	9,000	
Service Fee Expense	73,000	
Totals	$1,175,000	$1,175,000

Required:

Prepare an income statement, statement of stockholders' equity, and classified balance sheet. In preparing the statement of stockholders' equity, note that during the year the company issued additional common stock for $30,000. This amount is included in the amount for Common Stock in the adjusted trial balance.

Record closing entries and prepare a post-closing trial balance (LO3–6, 3–7)

P3–6A The year-end financial statements of Rattlers Tax Services are provided below.

RATTLERS TAX SERVICES
Income Statement

Service revenue		$77,500
Expenses:		
Salaries	$46,000	
Utilities	8,200	
Insurance	5,800	
Supplies	2,100	62,100
Net income		$15,400

RATTLERS TAX SERVICES
Statement of Stockholders' Equity

	Common Stock	Retained Earnings	Total S. Equity
Beg. bal., Jan. 1	$60,000	$24,500	$ 84,500
Issue stock	30,000		30,000
Net income		15,400	15,400
Dividends		(6,000)	(6,000)
Ending bal., Dec. 31	$90,000	$33,900	$123,900

RATTLERS TAX SERVICES
Balance Sheet

Assets		Liabilities	
Cash	$ 4,700	Accounts payable	$ 3,000
Accounts receivable	7,200	**Stockholders' Equity**	
Land	115,000	Common stock	$90,000	
		Retained earnings	33,900	123,900
Total assets	$126,900	Total liabs. and equities	$126,900

Required:
1. Record year-end closing entries.
2. Prepare a post-closing trial balance. (*Hint:* The balance of Retained Earnings will be the amount shown in the balance sheet.)

P3–7A Crimson Tide Music Academy offers lessons in playing a wide range of musical instruments. The *unadjusted* trial balance as of December 31, 2024, appears below. December 31 is the company's fiscal year-end.

Complete the accounting cycle after adjusting entries (LO3–4, 3–5, 3–6, 3–7)

Accounts	Debit	Credit
Cash	$ 10,300	
Accounts Receivable	9,500	
Interest Receivable	-0-	
Supplies	2,000	
Prepaid Rent	7,200	
Land	78,000	
Notes Receivable	20,000	
Accounts Payable		$ 7,700
Salaries Payable		-0-
Deferred Revenue		5,300
Utilities Payable		-0-
Common Stock		79,000
Retained Earnings		19,700
Service Revenue		42,200
Interest Revenue		-0-
Salaries Expense	24,500	
Rent Expense	-0-	
Supplies Expense	-0-	
Utilities Expense	2,400	
Totals	$153,900	$153,900

In addition, the company had the following year-end adjusting entries.

	Debit	Credit
a. Salaries Expense	2,100	
Salaries Payable		2,100
b. Interest Receivable	800	
Interest Revenue		800
c. Supplies Expense	1,300	
Supplies		1,300
d. Deferred Revenue	3,300	
Service Revenue		3,300
e. Rent Expense	5,400	
Prepaid Rent		5,400
f. Utilities Expense	200	
Utilities Payable		200

Required:

Complete the following steps:

1. Enter the unadjusted balances from the trial balance into T-accounts.
2. Post the adjusting entries to the accounts.
3. Prepare an adjusted trial balance.
4. Prepare an income statement and a statement of shareholders' equity for the year ended December 31, 2024, and a classified balance sheet as of December 31, 2024. Assume that no common stock is issued during the year.
5. Record closing entries.
6. Post closing entries to the accounts.
7. Prepare a post-closing trial balance.

Complete the full accounting cycle (LO3–3, 3–4, 3–5, 3–6, 3–7)

P3–8A The general ledger of Red Storm Cleaners at January 1, 2024, includes the following account balances:

Accounts	Debits	Credits
Cash	$20,000	
Accounts Receivable	8,000	
Supplies	4,000	
Equipment	15,000	
Accumulated Depreciation		$ 5,000
Salaries Payable		7,500
Common Stock		25,000
Retained Earnings		9,500
Totals	$47,000	$47,000

The following is a summary of the transactions for the year:

1.	March	12	Provide services to customers, $60,000, of which $21,000 is on account.
2.	May	2	Collect on accounts receivable, $18,000.
3.	June	30	Issue shares of common stock in exchange for $6,000 cash.
4.	August	1	Pay salaries of $7,500 from 2023 (prior year).
5.	September	25	Pay repairs and maintenance expenses, $13,000.
6.	October	19	Purchase equipment for $8,000 cash.
7.	December	30	Pay $1,100 cash dividends to stockholders.

Required:

1. Set up the necessary T-accounts and enter the beginning balances from the trial balance. In addition to the accounts shown, the company also has accounts for Dividends, Service Revenue, Salaries Expense, Repairs and Maintenance Expense, Depreciation Expense, and Supplies Expense.
2. Record each of the summary transactions listed above.
3. Post the transactions to the accounts.
4. Prepare an unadjusted trial balance.
5. Record adjusting entries. Accrued salaries at year-end amounted to $19,600. Depreciation for the year on the equipment is $5,000. Office supplies remaining on hand at the end of the year equal $1,200.
6. Post adjusting entries.
7. Prepare an adjusted trial balance.
8. Prepare an income statement for 2024 and a classified balance sheet as of December 31, 2024.
9. Record closing entries.
10. Post closing entries.
11. Prepare a post-closing trial balance.

P3–9A The general ledger of Zips Storage at January 1, 2024, includes the following account balances:

Complete the full accounting cycle (LO3–3, 3–4, 3–5, 3–6, 3–7)

Accounts	Debits	Credits
Cash	$ 24,600	
Accounts Receivable	15,400	
Prepaid Insurance	12,000	
Land	148,000	
Accounts Payable		$ 6,700
Deferred Revenue		5,800
Common Stock		143,000
Retained Earnings		44,500
Totals	$200,000	$200,000

The following is a summary of the transactions for the year:

1. January 9 — Provide storage services for cash, $134,100, and on account, $52,200.
2. February 12 — Collect on accounts receivable, $51,500.
3. April 25 — Receive cash in advance from customers, $12,900.
4. May 6 — Purchase supplies on account, $9,200.
5. July 15 — Pay property taxes, $8,500.
6. September 10 — Pay on accounts payable, $11,400.
7. October 31 — Pay salaries, $123,600.
8. November 20 — Issue shares of common stock in exchange for $27,000 cash.
9. December 30 — Pay $2,800 cash dividends to stockholders.

Required:

1. Set up the necessary T-accounts and enter the beginning balances from the trial balance. In addition to the accounts shown, the company has accounts for Supplies, Dividends, Service Revenue, Salaries Expense, Property Tax Expense, Supplies Expense, and Insurance Expense.
2. Record each of the summary transactions listed above.
3. Post the transactions to the accounts.
4. Prepare an unadjusted trial balance.
5. Record adjusting entries. Insurance expired during the year is $7,000. Supplies remaining on hand at the end of the year equal $2,900. Provide services of $11,800 related to cash paid in advance by customers.
6. Post adjusting entries.
7. Prepare an adjusted trial balance.
8. Prepare an income statement for 2024 and a classified balance sheet as of December 31, 2024.
9. Record closing entries.
10. Post closing entries
11. Prepare a post-closing trial balance.

PROBLEMS: SET B

P3–1B Consider the following transactions.

Determine accrual-basis and cash-basis revenues and expenses (LO3–1, 3–2)

	Accrual-Basis		Cash-Basis	
Transaction	Revenue	Expense	Revenue	Expense
1. Receive cash from customers at the time of service, $3,700.	_____	_____	_____	_____
2. Issue common stock for cash, $6,000.	_____	_____	_____	_____

3. Receive cash from customers who were billed in the previous period, $1,700. _____ _____ _____ _____
4. Incur utilities cost in the current period but do not pay, $600. _____ _____ _____ _____
5. Pay workers' salaries for the current period, $700. _____ _____ _____ _____
6. Pay for rent in advance of the period to be covered, $3,600. _____ _____ _____ _____
7. Repay a long-term note to the bank, $3,000. _____ _____ _____ _____
8. Pay workers' salaries for the previous period, $850. _____ _____ _____ _____
9. Pay dividends to stockholders, $500. _____ _____ _____ _____
10. Purchase office supplies for cash, $540. _____ _____ _____ _____

Required:

For each transaction, determine the amount of revenue or expense, if any, that is recorded under accrual-basis accounting and under cash-basis accounting.

Convert cash-basis accounting to accrual-basis accounting (LO3–1, 3–2)

P3–2B Horned Frogs Fine Cooking maintains its books using cash-basis accounting. However, the company recently borrowed $50,000 from a local bank, and the bank requires the company to provide annual financial statements prepared using accrual-basis accounting as part of the creditworthiness verification. During 2024, the company records the following cash flows:

Cash collected from customers		$65,000
Cash paid for:		
Salaries	$23,000	
Supplies	9,000	
Repairs and maintenance	8,000	
Insurance	4,000	
Advertising	6,000	50,000
Net cash flows		$15,000

You are able to determine the following information:

	January 1, 2024	December 31, 2024
Accounts Receivable	$18,000	$13,000
Prepaid Insurance	1,700	4,200
Supplies	-0-	2,000
Salaries Payable	4,200	2,800

Required:

Prepare an accrual-basis income statement for December 31, 2024, by calculating accrual-basis revenues and expenses.

Record adjusting entries (LO3–3)

P3–3B The information necessary for preparing the 2024 year-end adjusting entries for Bearcat Personal Training Academy appears below. Bearcat's fiscal year-end is December 31.

1. At the end of the year, Bearcat calculated that it owed $24,000 in income taxes. Those taxes won't be paid until next April 15.
2. Salaries owed (but not paid) to employees for work from December 16 through December 31, 2024, are $4,000.
3. On March 1, 2024, Bearcat lent an employee $20,000. The employee signed a note requiring principal and interest at 9% to be paid on February 28, 2025.
4. On April 1, 2024, Bearcat paid an insurance company $13,200 for a two-year fire insurance policy. The entire $13,200 was debited to Prepaid Insurance on April 1 at the time of the purchase.
5. Bearcat used $1,700 of supplies in 2024. The Supplies account was debited at the time of purchases.

6. Bearcat received $2,700 from a customer on October 31, 2024, for three months of personal training that began November 1, 2024. Bearcat credited Deferred Revenue on October 31 at the time of cash receipt.
7. On December 1, 2024, Bearcat paid $6,000 rent to the owner of the building. The payment represents rent for December 2024 through February 2025, at $2,000 per month. Prepaid Rent was debited on December 1 at the time of the payment.

Required:
Record the necessary adjusting entries at December 31, 2024. No prior adjustments have been made during 2024.

P3–4B Grasshopper Lawn Service provides general lawn maintenance to customers. The company's fiscal year-end is December 31. Information necessary to prepare the year-end adjusting entries appears below.

Record adjusting entries (LO3–3)

1. On October 1, 2024, Grasshopper lent $60,000 to another company. A note was accepted with principal and 8% interest to be recieved on September 30, 2025.
2. On November 1, 2024, the company paid its landlord $7,500 representing rent for the months of November through January. Prepaid Rent was debited for the entire amount on November 1.
3. On August 1, 2024, Grasshopper collected $12,000 in advance rent from another company that is renting a portion of Grasshopper's building. The $12,000 represents one year's rent, and the entire amount was credited to Deferred Revenue on August 1.
4. Depreciation for the year is $18,000.
5. Vacation pay for the year that had been earned by employees but not paid to them or recorded is $8,000. The company records vacation pay as Salaries Expense.
6. Grasshopper began the year with $17,000 in its Supplies account. During the year $62,000 in supplies were purchased and debited to the Supplies account at the time of purchase. At year-end, supplies costing $22,000 remain on hand.

Required:
Prepare the necessary adjusting entries on December 31, 2024.

P3–5B Orange Designs provides consulting services related to home decoration. Orange Designs provides customers with recommendations for a full range of home décor, including window treatments, carpet and wood flooring, paint colors, furniture, and much more. Below is the year-end adjusted trial balance of Orange Designs.

Prepare financial statements from an adjusted trial balance (LO3–5)

ORANGE DESIGNS Adjusted Trial Balance December 31, 2024		
Accounts	**Debits**	**Credits**
Cash	$ 6,000	
Accounts Receivable	5,000	
Supplies	3,000	
Prepaid Rent	7,000	
Buildings	120,000	
Accumulated Depreciation		$ 22,000
Accounts Payable		4,000
Salaries Payable		5,000
Utilities Payable		1,000
Notes Payable (due in four years)		30,000
Common Stock		60,000
Retained Earnings		16,000
Service Revenues		112,000
Salaries Expense	43,000	
Rent Expense	19,000	
Depreciation Expense	8,000	
Supplies Expense	9,000	
Advertising Expense	14,000	
Utilities Expense	13,000	
Interest Expense	3,000	
Totals	$250,000	$250,000

Required:

Prepare an income statement, statement of stockholders' equity, and classified balance sheet. In preparing the statement of stockholders' equity, note that during the year the company issued additional common stock of $11,000. This amount is included in the amount for Common Stock in the adjusted trial balance.

Record closing entries and prepare a post-closing trial balance (LO3–6, 3–7)

P3–6B The year-end financial statements of Fighting Illini Financial Services are provided below.

FIGHTING ILLINI
Income Statement

Service revenue		$89,700
Expenses:		
Salaries	$50,000	
Supplies	10,100	
Rent	8,500	
Delivery	4,700	73,300
Net income		$16,400

FIGHTING ILLINI
Statement of Stockholders' Equity

	Common Stock	Retained Earnings	Total S. Equity
Beg. bal., Jan. 1	$70,000	$33,300	$103,300
Issue stock	20,000		20,000
Net income		16,400	16,400
Dividends		(7,000)	(7,000)
Ending bal., Dec. 31	$90,000	$42,700	$132,700

FIGHTING ILLINI
Balance Sheet

Assets			Liabilities		
Cash	$ 7,600		Accounts payable		$ 5,100
Accounts receivable	10,200		**Stockholders' Equity**		
Land	120,000		Common stock	$90,000	
			Retained earnings	42,700	132,700
Total assets	$137,800		Total liabs. and equities		$ 137,800

Required:

1. Record year-end closing entries.
2. Prepare a post-closing trial balance. (*Hint:* The balance of retained earnings will be the amount shown in the balance sheet.)

Complete the accounting cycle after adjusting entries (LO3–4, 3–5, 3–6, 3–7)

P3–7B Jaguar Auto Company provides general car maintenance to customers. The company's fiscal year-end is December 31. The December 31, 2024, trial balance (before any adjusting entries) appears below.

Accounts	Debits	Credits
Cash	$ 76,000	
Accounts Receivable	15,000	
Supplies	27,000	
Prepaid Insurance	24,000	
Equipment	95,000	
Accumulated Depreciation		$ 37,000
Accounts Payable		12,000
Salaries Payable		-0-
Deferred Revenue		60,000
Interest Payable		-0-
Notes Payable		35,000
Common Stock		35,000
Retained Earnings		10,000

(continued)

(concluded)

Accounts	Debits	Credits
Dividends	3,000	
Service Revenue		227,000
Salaries Expense	164,000	
Depreciation Expense	-0-	
Insurance Expense	-0-	
Supplies Expense	-0-	
Utilities Expense	12,000	
Interest Expense	-0-	
Totals	$416,000	$416,000

In addition, the company had the following year-end adjusting entries.

	Debit	Credit
a. Depreciation Expense	10,000	
Accumulated Depreciation		10,000
b. Salaries Expense	4,000	
Salaries Payable		4,000
c. Interest Expense	1,000	
Interest Payable		1,000
d. Insurance Expense	20,000	
Prepaid Insurance		20,000
e. Supplies Expense	22,000	
Supplies		22,000
f. Deferred Revenue	15,000	
Service Revenue		15,000

Required:

Complete the following steps:

1. Enter the unadjusted balances from the trial balance into T-accounts.
2. Post the adjusting entries to the accounts.
3. Prepare an adjusted trial balance.
4. Prepare an income statement and a statement of shareholders' equity for the year ended December 31, 2024, and a classified balance sheet as of December 31, 2024. Assume that no common stock is issued during the year.
5. Record closing entries.
6. Post closing entries to the accounts.
7. Prepare a post-closing trial balance.

P3–8B The general ledger of Pipers Plumbing at January 1, 2024, includes the following account balances:

Complete the full accounting cycle (LO3–3, 3–4, 3–5, 3–6, 3–7)

Accounts	Debits	Credits
Cash	$ 4,500	
Accounts Receivable	9,500	
Supplies	3,500	
Equipment	36,000	
Accumulated Depreciation		$ 8,000
Accounts Payable		6,000
Utilities Payable		7,000
Deferred Revenue		-0-
Common Stock		23,000
Retained Earnings		9,500
Totals	$53,500	$53,500

The following is a summary of the transactions for the year:

1. January   24   Provide plumbing services for cash, $20,000, and on account, $65,000.
2. March   13   Collect on accounts receivable, $53,000.
3. May   6   Issue shares of common stock in exchange for $11,000 cash.
4. June   30   Pay salaries for the current year, $33,000.
5. September   15   Pay utilities of $7,000 from 2023 (prior year).
6. November   24   Receive cash in advance from customers, $10,000.
7. December   30   Pay $3,000 cash dividends to stockholders.

Required:

1. Set up the necessary T-accounts and enter the beginning balances from the trial balance. In addition to the accounts shown, the company has accounts for Dividends, Service Revenue, Salaries Expense, Utilities Expense, Supplies Expense, and Depreciation Expense.
2. Record each of the summary transactions listed above.
3. Post the transactions to the accounts.
4. Prepare an unadjusted trial balance.
5. Record adjusting entries. Depreciation for the year on the machinery is $8,000. Plumbing supplies remaining on hand at the end of the year equal $1,100. Of the $10,000 paid in advance by customers, $7,000 of the work has been completed by the end of the year. Accrued utilities at year-end amounted to $6,000.
6. Post adjusting entries.
7. Prepare an adjusted trial balance.
8. Prepare an income statement for 2024 and a classified balance sheet as of December 31, 2024.
9. Record closing entries.
10. Post closing entries
11. Prepare a post-closing trial balance.

Complete the full accounting cycle (LO3–3, 3–4, 3–5, 3–6, 3–7)

P3–9B The general ledger of Jackrabbit Rentals at January 1, 2024, includes the following account balances:

Accounts	Debits	Credits
Cash	$ 41,500	
Accounts Receivable	25,700	
Land	110,800	
Accounts Payable		$ 15,300
Notes Payable (due in 2 years)		30,000
Common Stock		100,000
Retained Earnings		32,700
Totals	$178,000	$178,000

The following is a summary of the transactions for the year:

1. January   12   Provide services to customers on account, $62,400.
2. February   25   Provide services to customers for cash, $75,300.
3 March   19   Collect on accounts receivable, $45,700.
4. April   30   Issue shares of common stock in exchange for $30,000 cash.
5. June   16   Purchase supplies on account, $12,100.
6. July   7   Pay on accounts payable, $11,300.
7. September   30   Pay salaries for employee work in the current year, $64,200.
8. November   22   Pay advertising for the current year, $22,500.
9. December   30   Pay $2,900 cash dividends to stockholders.

Required:

1. Set up the necessary T-accounts and enter the beginning balances from the trial balance. In addition to the accounts shown, the company also has accounts for Supplies, Salaries Payable, Interest Payable, Dividends, Service Revenue, Salaries Expense, Advertising Expense, Interest Expense, and Supplies Expense.

2. Record each of the summary transactions listed above.
3. Post the transactions to the accounts.
4. Prepare an unadjusted trial balance.
5. Record adjusting entries. Accrued interest on the notes payable at year-end amounted to $2,500 and will be paid January 1, 2025. Accrued salaries at year-end amounted to $1,500 and will be paid on January 5, 2025. Supplies remaining on hand at the end of the year equal $2,300.
6. Post adjusting entries.
7. Prepare an adjusted trial balance.
8. Prepare an income statement for 2024 and a classified balance sheet as of December 31, 2024.
9. Record closing entries.
10. Post closing entries.
11. Prepare a post-closing trial balance.

REAL-WORLD PERSPECTIVES

Data Analytics & Excel

Visit Connect to find a variety of Data Analytics questions that help build Excel, Tableau, and data visualization skills. Assignable materials include Integrated Excel, Applying Excel, Data Visualizations, Tableau Dashboard Activities, and Applying Tableau cases.

Great Adventures

(This is a continuation of the Great Adventures problem from earlier chapters.)

General Ledger
Continuing Case

RWP3–1 You may refer to the opening story of Tony and Suzie and their decision to start Great Adventures in RWP 1–1. More of their story and the first set of transactions for the company in July are presented in RWP 2–1 and repeated here.

July 1	Sell $10,000 of common stock to Suzie.
1	Sell $10,000 of common stock to Tony.
1	Purchase a one-year insurance policy for $4,800 ($400 per month) to cover injuries to participants during outdoor clinics.
2	Pay legal fees of $1,500 associated with incorporation.
4	Purchase office supplies of $1,800 on account.
7	Pay $300 to a local newspaper for advertising to appear immediately for an upcoming mountain biking clinic to be held on July 15. Attendees will be charged $50 the day of the clinic.
8	Purchase 10 mountain bikes, paying $12,000 cash.
15	On the day of the clinic, Great Adventures receives cash of $2,000 from 40 bikers. Tony and Suzie conduct the mountain biking clinic.
22	Because of the success of the first mountain biking clinic, Tony and Suzie hold another mountain biking clinic, and the company receives $2,300.
24	Pay $700 to a local radio station for advertising to appear immediately. A kayaking clinic will be held on August 10, and attendees can pay $100 in advance or $150 on the day of the clinic.
30	Great Adventures receives cash of $4,000 in advance from 40 kayakers for the upcoming kayak clinic.

The following transactions occur over the remainder of 2024.

Aug. 1	Great Adventures obtains a $30,000 low-interest loan for the company from the city council, which has recently passed an initiative encouraging business development related to outdoor activities. The loan is due in three years, and 6% annual interest is due each year on July 31.
Aug. 4	The company purchases 14 kayaks, paying $28,000 cash.
Aug. 10	Tony and Suzie conduct the first kayak clinic. In addition to the $4,000 that was received in advance from kayakers on July 30, the company receives additional cash of $3,000 from 20 new kayakers on the day of the clinic.
Aug. 17	Tony and Suzie conduct a second kayak clinic, and the company receives $10,500 cash.
Aug. 24	Office supplies of $1,800 purchased on July 4 are paid in full.

(continued)

Sep. 1	To provide better storage of mountain bikes and kayaks when not in use, the company rents a storage shed for one year, paying $2,400 ($200 per month) in advance.
Sep. 21	Tony and Suzie conduct a rock-climbing clinic. The company receives $13,200 cash.
Oct. 17	Tony and Suzie conduct an orienteering clinic. Participants practice how to understand a topographical map, read an altimeter, use a compass, and orient through heavily wooded areas. The company receives $17,900 cash.
Dec. 1	Tony and Suzie decide to hold the company's first adventure race on December 15. Four-person teams will race from checkpoint to checkpoint using a combination of mountain biking, kayaking, orienteering, trail running, and rock-climbing skills. The first team in each category to complete all checkpoints in order wins. The entry fee for each team is $500.
Dec. 5	To help organize and promote the race, Tony hires his college roommate, Victor. Victor will be paid $50 in salary for each team that competes in the race. His salary will be paid after the race.
Dec. 8	The company pays $1,200 to purchase a permit from a state park where the race will be held. The amount is recorded as a miscellaneous expense.
Dec. 12	The company purchases racing supplies for $2,800 on account due in 30 days. Supplies include trophies for the top-finishing teams in each category, promotional shirts, snack foods and drinks for participants, and field markers to prepare the racecourse.
Dec. 15	The company receives $20,000 cash from a total of forty teams, and the race is held.
Dec. 16	The company pays Victor's salary of $2,000.
Dec. 31	The company pays a dividend of $4,000 ($2,000 to Tony and $2,000 to Suzie).
Dec. 31	Using his personal money, Tony purchases a diamond ring for $4,500. Tony surprises Suzie by proposing that they get married. Suzie accepts and they get married!

The following information relates to year-end adjusting entries as of December 31, 2024.

a. Depreciation of the mountain bikes purchased on July 8 and kayaks purchased on August 4 totals $8,000.

b. Six months' of the one-year insurance policy purchased on July 1 has expired.

c. Four months of the one-year rental agreement purchased on September 1 has expired.

d. Of the $1,800 of office supplies purchased on July 4, $300 remains.

e. Interest expense on the $30,000 loan obtained from the city council on August 1 should be recorded.

f. Of the $2,800 of racing supplies purchased on December 12, $200 remains.

g. Suzie calculates that the company owes $14,000 in income taxes.

Required:

1. Record transactions from July 1 through December 31.
2. Record adjusting entries as of December 31, 2024.
3. Post transactions from July 1 through December 31 and adjusting entries on December 31 to T-accounts.
4. Prepare an adjusted trial balance as of December 31, 2024.
5. For the period July 1 to December 31, 2024, prepare an income statement and statement of stockholders' equity. Prepare a classified balance sheet as of December 31, 2024.
6. Record closing entries as of December 31, 2024.
7. Post closing entries to T-accounts.
8. Prepare a post-closing trial balance as of December 31, 2024.

Financial Analysis Continuing Case

American Eagle Outfitters, Inc.

RWP3–2 Financial information for **American Eagle** is presented in **Appendix A** at the end of the book.

Required:

1. For the most recent year, what amount does American Eagle report for current assets? What is the ratio of current assets to total assets?

2. For the most recent year, what amount does American Eagle report for current liabilities? What is the ratio of current liabilities to total liabilities?
3. What is the change in retained earnings reported in the balance sheet?
4. For the most recent year, what is the amount of net income reported in the income statement?

The Buckle, Inc.

Financial Analysis
Continuing Case

RWP3–3 Financial information for **Buckle** is presented in **Appendix B** at the end of the book.

Required:
1. For the most recent year, what amount does Buckle report for current assets? What is the ratio of current assets to total assets?
2. For the most recent year, what amount does Buckle report for current liabilities? What is the ratio of current liabilities to total liabilities?
3. For the most recent year, what is the change in retained earnings reported in the balance sheet?
4. For the most recent year, what is the amount of net income reported in the income statement?
5. Using your answers in 3 and 4 above, calculate the amount of dividends paid during the year. Verify your answer by looking at the retained earnings column in the statement of stockholders' equity.

American Eagle Outfitters, Inc. vs. The Buckle, Inc.

Comparative Analysis
Continuing Case

RWP3–4 Financial information for **American Eagle** is presented in **Appendix A** at the end of the book, and financial information for **Buckle** is presented in **Appendix B** at the end of the book.

Required:
1. Determine which company maintains a higher ratio of current assets to total assets. How might this be an advantage for the company?
2. Determine which company maintains a higher ratio of current liabilities to total liabilities. How might this be a disadvantage for the company?
3. The dividend payout ratio equals dividends paid during the year divided by net income. Determine which company has a higher dividend payout ratio. Why might this be the case?

EDGAR Research

RWP3–5 Using EDGAR (Electronic Data Gathering, Analysis, and Retrieval system), find the annual report (10-K) for **McDonald's** for the year ended **December 31, 2019.** Locate the "Consolidated Statement of Income" (income statement) and "Consolidated Balance Sheets." You may also find the annual report at the company's website.

Required:
Determine the following from the company's financial statements:
1. Do the company's revenues exceed expenses? What is the amount of net income?
2. Did net income increase in the most recent year compared to the previous year?
3. What amounts are reported for current assets and total assets?
4. What amount is reported for current liabilities? Does the company have any long-term liabilities?
5. By how much did retained earnings increase/decrease in the most recent year compared to the previous year?
6. What is the amount of dividends paid to common stockholders? This information can be found in the statement of shareholders' equity or the statement of cash flows.
7. Does the change in retained earnings equal net income minus dividends?

Ethics

RWP3–6 You have recently been hired as the assistant controller for Stanton Temperton Corporation, which rents building space in major metropolitan areas. Customers are required to pay six months of rent in advance. At the end of 2024, the company's president, Jim Temperton, notices that net income has fallen compared to last year. In 2023, the company reported pretax profit of $330,000, but in 2024 the pretax profit is only $280,000. This concerns Jim for two reasons. First, his year-end bonus is tied directly to pretax profits. Second, shareholders may see a decline in profitability as a weakness in the company and begin to sell their stock. With the sell-off of stock, Jim's personal investment in the company's stock, as well as his company-operated retirement plan, will be in jeopardy of severe losses.

After close inspection of the financial statements, Jim notices that the balance of the Deferred Revenue account is $120,000. This amount represents payments in advance from long-term customers ($80,000) and from relatively new customers ($40,000). Jim comes to you, the company's accountant, and suggests that the company should recognize as revenue in 2024 the $80,000 received in advance from long-term customers. He offers the following explanation: "First, we have received these customers' cash by the end of 2024, so there is no question about their ability to pay. Second, we have a long-term history of fulfilling our obligation to these customers. We have always stood by our commitments to our customers and we always will. We earned that money when we got them to sign the six-month contract."

Required:
1. Understand the reporting effect: What are the effects on pretax profits of reporting the $80,000 as service revenue?
2. Specify the options: Instead of reporting the $80,000 as revenue, how else might you report this amount?
3. Identify the impact: Are investors and creditors potentially affected by Jim's suggestion?
4. Make a decision: As a staff employee, should you follow Jim's suggestion?

Written Communication

RWP3–7 You are a tutor for introductory financial accounting. You tell the students, "Recording adjusting entries is a critical step in the accounting cycle, and the two major classifications of adjusting entries are prepayments and accruals." Chris, one of the students in the class, says, "I don't understand."

Required:
Respond to Chris.
1. When do prepayments occur? When do accruals occur?
2. Describe the appropriate adjusting entry for prepaid expenses and for deferred revenues. What is the effect on net income, assets, liabilities, and stockholders' equity of not recording a required adjusting entry for prepayments?
3. Describe the required adjusting entry for accrued expenses and for accrued revenues. What is the effect on net income, assets, liabilities, and shareholders' equity of not recording a required adjusting entry for accruals?

Answers to Chapter Framework Questions
1. a   2. c   3. b   4. c   5. d

Answers to Self-Study Questions
1. b   2. c   3. c   4. b   5. a   6. b   7. c   8. b   9. d   10. a   11. c   12. d   13. b   14. d   15. c

Cash and Internal Controls

Learning Objectives

PART A: INTERNAL CONTROLS

- **LO4–1** Discuss the impact of accounting scandals and the passage of the Sarbanes-Oxley Act.
- **LO4–2** Identify the components, responsibilities, and limitations of internal control.

PART B: CASH

- **LO4–3** Define cash and cash equivalents.
- **LO4–4** Understand controls over cash receipts and cash disbursements.
- **LO4–5** Reconcile a bank statement.
- **LO4–6** Account for employee purchases.

PART C: STATEMENT OF CASH FLOWS

- **LO4–7** Identify the major inflows and outflows of cash.

ANALYSIS: CASH ANALYSIS

- **LO4–8** Demonstrate the link between cash reported in the balance sheet and cash reported in the statement of cash flows.

SELF-STUDY MATERIALS

- Let's Review—Bank reconciliation (p. 195).
- Let's Review—Types of cash flow (p. 200).
- Chapter Framework with questions and answers available (p. 203).
- Key Points by Learning Objective (p. 204).
- Glossary of Key Terms (p. 204).
- Self-Study Questions with answers available (p. 205).
- Videos including Concept Overview, Applying Excel, Let's Review, and Interactive Illustrations demonstrate key topics (Connect).

LIVE NATION ENTERTAINMENT: INTERNAL CONTROLS ARE A HIT

Feature Story

According to research conducted by the Association of Certified Fraud Examiners (ACFE, **www.acfe.com**), U.S. organizations lose an estimated $1 *trillion* (or about 5% of their total revenue) to fraud each year. This occurs despite increased corporate emphasis on antifraud controls and recent legislation to combat fraud. While some employees steal office supplies, inventory, and equipment, the asset most often targeted is cash. Cash fraud includes skimming cash receipts before they are recorded; stealing cash that has already been recorded; and falsely disbursing cash through fraudulent billing, expense reimbursement, or payroll. Companies also lose cash to fraud when customers illegally utilize the products and services of a company without paying. This would include customer theft and illegal access to venues and online service.

Companies that rely heavily on a large number of transactions with customers and vendors, have dispersed operations, and employ many individuals are especially susceptible to fraud. **Live Nation Entertainment** is one of the world's largest live entertainment companies. The company hosts approximately 40,000 events and sells 500,000,000 tickets each year. The company also has more than 10,000 employees, with offices in over 40 countries. With such large and dispersed activities, Live Nation Entertainment faces the considerable challenges of ensuring tickets are sold to all who attend their events, collecting all cash from operators at its broad distribution of venues, and preventing employee theft and misreporting of hours worked.

Momcilog/iStock/Getty Images

The revenue streams generated by admissions and concessions are fully supported by information systems to monitor cash flow and to detect fraud and inventory theft. Simpler approaches to internal control include *separation of duties*. For example, one person sells tickets, another collects the tickets, and another accounts for cash received. This prevents the ticket seller from pocketing a customer's cash and then allowing admission without a ticket being produced. For each event, the number of tickets sold should exactly match the number people attending and the cash collected.

In this chapter, we discuss much more about fraud and ways to prevent it. We will also examine specific internal controls related to cash. At the end of the chapter, we'll analyze the cash balances of Live Nation Entertainment versus **AMC Networks**.

PART A

INTERNAL CONTROLS

As you saw in Chapters 1 through 3, the key roles of financial accounting are to measure business activities and to communicate those activities to external decision makers. It is important to the usefulness of this measurement/communication process that the numbers provided by financial accountants are *correct.* The decisions of investors and creditors rely on financial statements and other disclosed accounting information to *accurately* portray the activities of the company.

You might be surprised, though, to learn that some companies' published financial statements are *incorrect.* A study published by Audit Analytics (*2019 Financial Restatements Review*) reports 484 restatements in 2019. How could this happen? What can be done to help prevent it?

Companies issue incorrect financial statements for two reasons—errors and fraud. First, companies sometimes make accidental errors in recording (or failing to record) transactions or in applying accounting rules. When these errors are later discovered, companies often have to restate the financial statements affected. Even though these errors may be unintentional, they nevertheless can create confusion and weaken investors' and creditors' confidence in the important information role that accounting serves.

The second reason for incorrect financial accounting information relates to fraud. *Fraud* occurs when a person intentionally deceives another person for personal gain or to damage that person. Specifically related to business activities, the Association of Certified Fraud Examiners (ACFE) defines **occupational fraud** as the use of one's occupation for personal enrichment through the deliberate misuse or misapplication of the employer's resources.

The first source of occupational fraud is misuse of company resources. As discussed in the chapter-opening Feature Story, occupational fraud is a big business, with companies expecting to lose, on average, 5% of their total revenues to fraud each year. For a company like **Live Nation Entertainment**, 5% of total revenues would equal nearly $600 million lost to fraud in a single year. Cash is the asset most commonly involved with fraudulent activity. A significant portion of this chapter discusses the procedures businesses use to maintain control over cash receipts and cash disbursements.

The second source of occupational fraud involves financial statement manipulation. Here, those in charge of communicating financial accounting information falsify reports. You may have heard the phrase "cooking the books." The phrase implies that the accounting records ("books") have been presented in an altered form ("cooked"). Some managers are willing to cook the books for personal gain. Motives for such deception might be maximizing their compensation, increasing the company's stock price, and preserving their jobs.

The three elements necessary for every fraud are commonly referred to as the **fraud triangle** and are shown below in Illustration 4–1.

What can be done to help minimize fraud? At least one of the three elements of the fraud triangle must be eliminated. Of the three elements, companies have the greatest ability to eliminate *opportunity.* To eliminate opportunity, companies implement formal procedures known as **internal controls**. These represent a company's plan to (1) safeguard the company's assets and (2) improve the accuracy and reliability of accounting information. In this

Tero Vesalainen/Shutterstock

ILLUSTRATION 4–1

Fraud Triangle

Opportunity – the situation allows the fraud to occur.

Motivation – someone feels the need to commit fraud, such as the need for money.

Rationalization – justification for the deceptive act by the one committing the fraud.

chapter, we'll discuss the basic principles and procedures of companies' internal controls (with a deeper look at cash controls). The quality of internal controls directly affects the quality of financial accounting.

Accounting Scandals and Response by Congress

Managers are entrusted with the resources of both the company's lenders (liabilities) and its owners (stockholders' equity). In this sense, managers of the company act as stewards or caretakers of the company's assets. However, in recent years some managers shirked their ethical responsibilities and misused or misreported the company's funds. In many cases, top executives misreported accounting information to cover up their company's poor operating performance. Such fraudulent activity is costly: The ACFE reports that the median loss caused by fraudulent financial statement schemes, for example, is $975,000 per instance. As you become more familiar with specific accounting topics throughout the remainder of this book, you'll begin to understand how amounts reported in the financial statements can be manipulated by managers.

■ LO4–1
Discuss the impact of accounting scandals and the passage of the Sarbanes-Oxley Act.

Two of the highest-profile cases of accounting fraud in U.S. history are the collapses of **Enron** and **WorldCom**. Enron used questionable accounting practices to avoid reporting billions in debt and losses in its financial statements. WorldCom misclassified certain expenditures to overstate assets and profitability by $11 billion. Both companies hoped to fool investors into overvaluing the company's stock. Other common types of financial statement fraud include creating fictitious revenues, improperly valuing assets, hiding liabilities, and mismatching revenues and expenses.

As the Enron and WorldCom frauds (as well as several others) were being uncovered in 2001 and 2002, the stock prices of these companies plummeted. Investors lost nearly $200 billion as a result. Employees of these companies also suffered. Both firms declared bankruptcy, resulting in employee termination; reduced salaries and increased workloads for those who were left; and loss of employee retirement funds, stock options, and health benefits.

SARBANES-OXLEY ACT OF 2002

In response to these corporate accounting scandals and public outrage over seemingly widespread unethical behavior of top executives, Congress passed the **Sarbanes-Oxley Act**, also known as the *Public Company Accounting Reform and Investor Protection Act of 2002* and commonly referred to as *SOX*. SOX applies to all companies that are required to file financial statements with the SEC and represents one of the greatest reforms in business practices in U.S. history. The act established a variety of guidelines related to auditor–client relations and internal control procedures. Illustration 4–2 provides an overview of the major provisions of SOX, including the creation of the Public Company Accounting Oversight Board (PCAOB) to oversee audits of public companies.

The last provision listed in Illustration 4–2, internal controls under Section 404, requires company management and auditors to document and assess the effectiveness of a company's internal controls—processes that could affect financial reporting. PCAOB chairman William McDonough explained the significance of this part of the law: "In the past, internal controls were merely considered by auditors; now they will have to be tested and examined in detail" (**PCAOBUS.org**, June 18, 2004). Whether you are an investor, an employee, a manager, or an auditor, understanding a company's internal controls is important.

 KEY POINT

The accounting scandals in the early 2000s prompted passage of the Sarbanes-Oxley Act (SOX). Among other stipulations, SOX sets forth a variety of guidelines related to auditor–client relations and additional internal controls. Section 404, in particular, requires company management and auditors to document and assess the effectiveness of a company's internal controls.

ILLUSTRATION 4–2

Major Provisions of the Sarbanes-Oxley Act of 2002

Oversight board	The Public Company Accounting Oversight Board (PCAOB) has the authority to establish standards dealing with auditing, quality control, ethics, independence, and other activities relating to the preparation of audited financial reports. The board consists of five members who are appointed by the Securities and Exchange Commission.
Corporate executive accountability	Corporate executives must personally certify the company's financial statements and financial disclosures. Severe financial penalties and the possibility of imprisonment are consequences of fraudulent misstatement.
Nonaudit services	It's unlawful for the auditors of public companies to also perform certain nonaudit services, such as investment advising, for their clients.
Retention of work papers	Auditors of public companies must retain all work papers for seven years or face a prison term for willful violation.
Auditor rotation	The lead auditor in charge of auditing a particular company (referred to as the *audit partner*) must rotate off that company within five years and allow a new audit partner to take the lead.
Conflicts of interest	Audit firms are not allowed to audit public companies whose chief executives worked for the audit firm and participated in that company's audit during the preceding year.
Hiring of auditor	Audit firms are hired by the audit committee of the board of directors of the company, not by company management.
Internal control	Section 404 of the act requires (a) that company management document and assess the effectiveness of all internal control processes that could affect financial reporting and (b) that company auditors express an opinion on whether management's assessment of the effectiveness of internal control is fairly stated. Smaller companies are exempt from requirement (b).

Framework for Internal Control

■ **LO4–2**

Identify the components, responsibilities, and limitations of internal control.

As noted earlier, internal control is a company's plan to (1) safeguard the company's assets and (2) improve the accuracy and reliability of accounting information. Effective internal control builds a wall to prevent misuse of company funds by employees and fraudulent or errant financial reporting. Strong internal control systems allow greater reliance by investors on reported financial statements.

COMPONENTS OF INTERNAL CONTROL

A framework for designing an internal control system was provided by the *Committee of Sponsoring Organizations (COSO)* of the Treadway Commission. COSO (**www.coso.org**) is dedicated to improving the quality of financial reporting through, among other things, effective internal controls. COSO suggests that internal control consists of five components, displayed in Illustration 4–3.

Internal control components are built on the foundation of the ethical tone set by top management in its control environment. From there, management assesses risks, implements specific control activities, and continuously monitors all systems. Running throughout this structure is the need for timely information and communication. Employees at all levels must understand the importance of high-quality information. Lower-level employees must report information accurately and in a timely manner to those higher in the organization. Top executives of a company then must effectively communicate this information to external parties such as investors and creditors through financial statements.

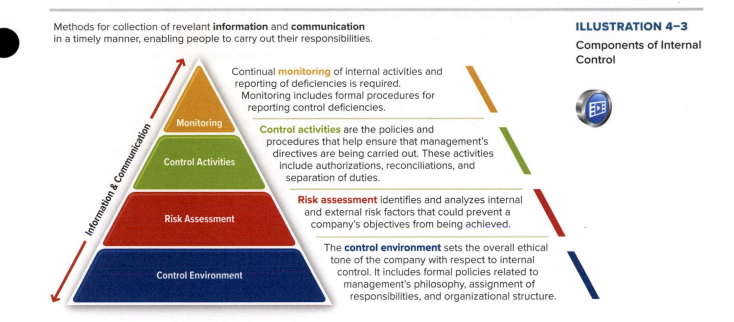

Methods for collection of revelant **information** and **communication** in a timely manner, enabling people to carry out their responsibilities.

Information & Communication

Monitoring — Continual **monitoring** of internal activities and reporting of deficiencies is required. Monitoring includes formal procedures for reporting control deficiencies.

Control Activities — **Control activities** are the policies and procedures that help ensure that management's directives are being carried out. These activities include authorizations, reconciliations, and separation of duties.

Risk Assessment — **Risk assessment** identifies and analyzes internal and external risk factors that could prevent a company's objectives from being achieved.

Control Environment — The **control environment** sets the overall ethical tone of the company with respect to internal control. It includes formal policies related to management's philosophy, assignment of responsibilities, and organizational structure.

ILLUSTRATION 4–3

Components of Internal Control

To see an example of how internal controls are linked to the information provided in financial statements, let's look at the description given by Live Nation Entertainment in its annual report (see Illustration 4–4).

LIVE NATION ENTERTAINMENT
Notes to the Financial Statements (excerpt)

Our management, including our Chief Executive Officer and Chief Financial Officer, does not expect that our disclosure controls and procedures or internal controls will prevent all possible errors and fraud. Our disclosure controls and procedures are, however, designed to provide reasonable assurance of achieving their objectives, and our Chief Executive Officer and Chief Financial Officer have concluded that our disclosure controls and procedures are effective at that reasonable assurance level.

ILLUSTRATION 4–4

Live Nation Entertainment's Discussion of Internal Controls over Financial Reporting

Movie Theatre Example. Let's look at how the five components of internal control apply in actual practice. Here, we apply them to operating a movie theatre.

The overall attitudes and actions of management greatly affect the *control environment*. If employees notice unethical behavior or comments by management, they are more likely to behave in a similar manner, wasting the company's resources. Wouldn't you be more comfortable investing in or lending to a movie theatre if it were run by a highly ethical person, rather than someone of questionable character?

Risk assessment includes careful consideration of internal and external risk factors. Internal risks include issues such as unsafe lighting, faulty video projectors, unsanitary bathrooms, and employee incompetence with regard to food preparation. Common examples of external risks include a vendor supplying low-quality popcorn, moviegoers' security in the parking lot, or perhaps the decline in customer demand due to uncontrollable factors such as the COVID-19 outbreak or external competition from on-demand services at home. These internal and external risk factors put the company's objectives in jeopardy.

Control activities include a variety of policies and procedures used to protect a company's assets. There are two general types of control activities: preventive and detective. *Preventive controls* are designed to keep errors or fraud from occurring in the first place. *Detective controls* are designed to detect errors or fraud that already have occurred.

Examples of preventive controls include:

1. **Separation of duties.** A set of procedures intended to separate employees' duties for authorizing transactions, recording transactions, and controlling related assets is referred to as **separation of duties**. As shown in Illustration 4–5, when a customer comes into the theatre to watch a movie, the employee selling the movie ticket should not also be the employee in charge of collecting the tickets. The employee recording the cash sale should not also have direct access to company cash by filling in as a ticket cashier or being responsible for the daily cash deposits.

   Fraud is prevented by not allowing the same person to be responsible for both controlling the asset and accounting for the asset. This applies not only to cash but other assets as well. For example, employees who have physical control of theatre inventory (candy bars, T-shirts, and so on) should not also be in charge of accounting for that inventory.

2. **Physical controls** over assets and accounting records. Each night, money from ticket sales should be placed in the theatre's safe or deposited at the bank. Important documents should be kept in fireproof files, and electronic records should be backed up daily and require user-ID and password for access. Concession supplies should be kept in a locked room with access allowed only to authorized personnel.

3. **Proper authorization** to prevent improper use of the company's resources. The theatre should establish formal guidelines on how to handle cash receipts and make purchases. For example, only management should be authorized to make purchases over a certain amount.

4. **Employee management.** The company should provide employees with appropriate guidance to ensure they have the knowledge necessary to carry out their job duties. Employees should be made fully aware of the company's internal control procedures, ethical responsibilities, and channels for reporting irregular activities.

5. **E-commerce controls.** E-commerce refers to the wide range of electronic activities of a company, such as buying and selling over the Internet, digital information processing, and electronic communication. Given the tremendous growth of e-commerce activities in recent years, internal controls over these activities are becoming increasingly important. For example, only authorized personnel should have passwords to conduct electronic business transactions. The company should maintain and systematically check the firewall settings to prevent unauthorized

ILLUSTRATION 4–5   Separation of Duties

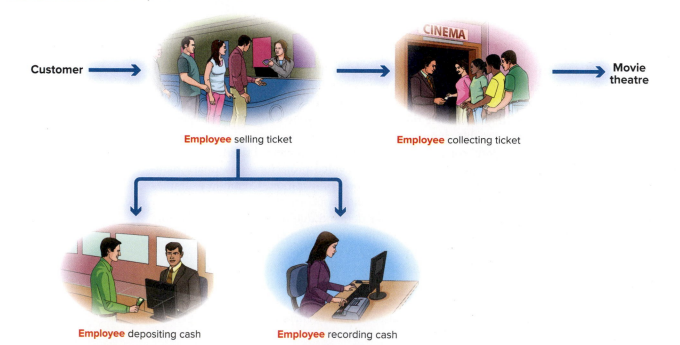

Customer → Employee selling ticket → Employee collecting ticket → Movie theatre

Employee depositing cash

Employee recording cash

access to accounts and credit card numbers. All employees should update the system's antivirus software periodically.

Examples of detective controls include:

1. **Reconciliations.** Management should periodically determine whether the amount of physical assets of the company (cash, supplies, inventory, and other property) agree with the accounting records. For example, accounting personnel should routinely reconcile the company's cash records with those of its bank, and any discrepancy should be investigated. Later in this chapter we'll see an example of how to prepare a bank reconciliation for Starlight Productions.

2. **Performance reviews.** The actual performance of individuals or processes should be checked against their expected performance. For example, the amount of concessions sold should be compared to the number of tickets sold over a period of time. If concession sales are lower than expected for a given number of tickets, employees could be wasting food, stealing snacks, or giving it to their friends for free. Alternatively, vendors may be supplying lower-quality food, driving down sales. Management may also wish to evaluate the overall performance of the theatre by comparing ticket sales for the current year with ticket sales for the previous year.

3. **Audits.** Many companies, such as those companies listed on a stock exchange, are required to have an independent auditor attest to the adequacy of their internal control procedures. Other companies can voluntarily choose each year to have an auditor assess their internal control procedures to detect any deficiencies or fraudulent behavior of employees.

Monitoring of internal controls needs to occur on an ongoing basis. The theatre manager needs to actively review daily operations to ensure that control procedures work effectively. For instance, the manager should compare daily cash from ticket sales with the number of tickets issued, compare concession sales with units purchased, and make sure employees are paid only for actual hours worked.

Information and communication depend on the reliability of the accounting information system itself. If the accountant's office has papers scattered everywhere, and you learn the company still does all its accounting by hand without a computer, wouldn't you, as an investor or lender, be a bit worried? A system should be in place to ensure that current transactions of the company are reflected in current reports. Employees also should be aware of procedures in place to deal with any perceived internal control failures. For example, an anonymous tip hotline should be in place to encourage communication about unethical activities, such as an employee giving concession items for free to her friends. Historically, employee tips have been the most common means of detecting employee fraud.

RESPONSIBILITIES FOR INTERNAL CONTROL

Everyone in a company has an impact on the operation and effectiveness of internal controls, but **the top executives are the ones who must take final responsibility for their establishment and success.** The CEO and CFO sign a report each year assessing whether the internal controls are adequate. Section 404 of SOX requires not only that companies document their internal controls and assess their adequacy, but that the company's auditors provide an opinion on management's assessment. A recent survey by Financial Executives International reports that the average total cost to a public company in complying with Section 404 is nearly $4 million.

The Public Company Accounting Oversight Board (PCAOB) further requires the auditor to express its own opinion on whether the company has maintained effective internal control over financial reporting. Illustration 4–6 provides an excerpt from Live Nation Entertainment's auditor's report.

LIMITATIONS OF INTERNAL CONTROL

Unfortunately, even with the best internal control systems, financial misstatements can occur. While better internal control systems will more likely detect operating and reporting errors, no internal control system can turn a bad employee into a good one. No internal control system is perfect.

ILLUSTRATION 4–6
Excerpt from Live Nation Entertainment's Auditor's Report Related to Effectiveness of Internal Controls

> **LIVE NATION ENTERTAINMENT**
> **Auditor's Report (excerpt)**
>
> We have audited Live Nation Entertainment, Inc.'s internal control over financial reporting as of December 31, 2019, based on criteria established in the Internal Control—Integrated Framework issued by the Committee of Sponsoring Organizations of the Treadway Commission (2013 framework) (the COSO criteria). In our opinion, Live Nation Entertainment, Inc. (the Company) maintained, in all material respects, effective internal control over financial reporting as of December 31, 2019, based on the COSO criteria.

Internal control systems are especially susceptible to collusion. **Collusion** occurs when two or more people act in coordination to circumvent internal controls. Going back to our movie theatre example, if the ticket cashier and the ticket taker, or the ticket cashier and the accountant, decide to work together to steal cash, theft will be much more difficult to detect. Fraud cases that involve collusion are typically several times more severe than are fraud cases involving one person. This suggests that collusion is effective in circumventing control procedures.

Top-level employees who have the ability to override internal control features also have opportunity to commit fraud. For example, managers may be required to obtain approval from the chief financial officer (CFO) for all large purchases. However, if the CFO uses the company's funds to purchase a boat for personal use at a lake home, fewer controls are in place to detect this misappropriation. Even if lower-level employees suspect wrongdoing, they may be unwilling to confront their boss about the issue.

Finally, because there are natural risks to running any business, **effective internal controls and ethical employees alone cannot ensure a company's success, or even survival.** Most companies recognize the limitations of internal controls and provide an explicit discussion of these issues in their annual report.

KEY POINT

Internal control refers to a company's plan to improve the accuracy and reliability of accounting information and safeguard the company's assets. Five key components to an internal control system are (1) control environment, (2) risk assessment, (3) control activities, (4) monitoring, and (5) information and communication. Control activities include those designed to prevent or detect fraudulent or erroneous behavior.

Decision Point

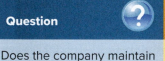

Question	Accounting information	Analysis
Does the company maintain adequate internal controls?	Management's discussion, auditor's opinion	If management or the auditor notes any deficiencies in internal controls, financial accounting information may be unreliable.

PART B

CASH

Among all of the company's assets, cash is the one most susceptible to employee fraud. The obvious way employees steal cash is by physically removing it from the company, such as pulling it out of the cash register and walking out the door. However, there are other, less obvious ways to commit fraud with a company's cash. An employee could falsify documents, causing the company to overpay the employee for certain expenses, issue an inflated paycheck, or make payment to a fictitious company. Because of these possibilities, companies develop strict procedures to maintain control of cash. Before discussing some of these controls, let's first understand what "cash" includes.

Cash and Cash Equivalents

The amount of **cash** held by a company is reported in its balance sheet. This amount includes currency, coins, and balances in savings and checking accounts, as well as items acceptable for deposit in these accounts, such as checks received from customers.

In addition, when a company sells products or services to customers who use *credit cards* or *debit cards,* the cash to be collected from those sales is nearly always included in the total cash balance immediately. The reason is that cash from those transactions typically will be deposited electronically into the company's bank account within a few days.

The balance of cash also includes **cash equivalents**, which are defined as short-term investments that have a maturity date no longer than three months *from the date of purchase.* Common examples of such investments are money market funds, Treasury bills, and certificates of deposit.

The important point to understand is that all forms of cash and cash equivalents usually are combined and reported as a single asset in the balance sheet of most companies. Illustration 4–7 demonstrates the components that make up the total cash balance. This balance is usually referred to as "cash" or "cash and cash equivalents."

■ **LO4–3**
Define cash and cash equivalents.

Decision Maker's Perspective

How Much Cash Is Enough?

Investors and creditors closely monitor the amount of cash a company holds. The company needs enough cash, or enough other assets that can quickly be converted to cash, to pay obligations as they become due. Available cash also helps a company respond quickly to new, profitable opportunities before competitors do.

On the other hand, having too much cash leads to inefficient use of funds and could signal that a company's management does not see additional opportunities for profitable expansion. In recent years, cash holdings of U.S. companies have increased enormously. This is partly due to the financial crisis of 2008. As uncertainty in the business environment increases, companies hold more cash to prevent bankruptcy caused by short-term negative shocks in the business cycle.

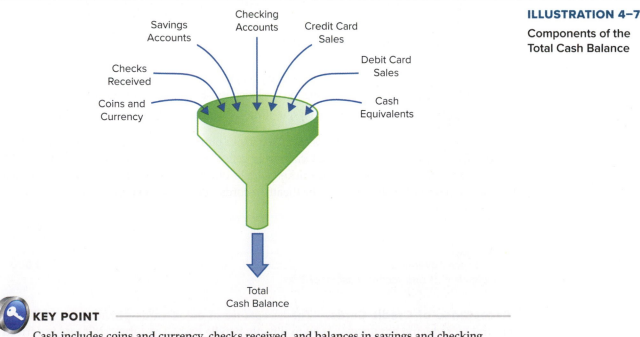

ILLUSTRATION 4–7

Components of the Total Cash Balance

KEY POINT

Cash includes coins and currency, checks received, and balances in savings and checking accounts. The cash balance also includes credit card and debit card sales, as well as cash equivalents, defined as investments that mature within three months from the date of purchase (such as money market funds, Treasury bills, and certificates of deposit).

Cash Controls

Management must safeguard all assets against possible misuse. Again, because cash is especially susceptible to theft, internal control of cash is a key issue.

CONTROLS OVER CASH RECEIPTS

Companies collect payments from customers in a variety of ways.

- **Cash and checks ("paper").** Both forms of payment were once very common but are on the decline, especially with younger customers.
- **Credit cards and debit cards ("plastic").** Credit cards offer the advantage of allowing customers to purchase on credit, while debit cards withdraw funds immediately from the customer's bank account.
- **Mobile payments.** Customers can electronically store credit cards and debit cards on their mobile device, eliminating the need to carry a physical wallet.
- **Electronic funds transfers (EFTs).** Customers often transfer funds directly from their bank account to the company's bank. This form of payment is especially useful for recurring costs, such as monthly rent and utilities. The automation saves time, helps to prevent late payment, and avoids the need to handle cash.
- **Prepaid cards.** Often referred to as gift cards, customers use these much like debit cards, except that expenditures are applied to the card's balance (not a bank account balance). The ease of transferring funds from one individual to the next is why these are easy gifts.
- **Cryptocurrencies.** Cryptocurrencies represent digital money that allows peer-to-peer transactions without the need for a third-party bank or credit card company. While relatively few businesses currently accept cryptocurrencies, these types of payment seem more likely in the future, as blockchain technology is expected to help prevent fraud.

Acceptance of Cash and Checks.   While it might surprise you, many companies still receive cash and checks. These forms of payment are more susceptible to theft, fraud, and being lost or destroyed. For this reason, companies have established specific controls over their receipt:

1. Open mail each day, and make a list of cash and checks received, including the amount and payer's name.
2. Designate an employee to deposit cash and checks into the company's bank account each day, different from the person who receives cash and checks.
3. Have another employee record cash receipts in the accounting records as soon as possible. Verify cash receipts by comparing the bank deposit slip with the accounting records.
4. Accept credit cards or debit cards, to limit the amount of cash employees handle.

Whether a customer uses cash or a check to make a purchase, the company records the transaction as a cash sale. Let's assume a local theatre sells tickets for the entire day totaling $3,000. Some customers pay cash for those tickets, while others use a check. Regardless of which method of payment customers use, the theatre records all of those ticket sales as cash sales.

	Debit	Credit
Cash	3,000	
Service Revenue...		3,000
(Sell tickets and receive cash or check)		

Acceptance of Credit Cards.   The acceptance of credit cards provides an additional control by reducing employees' need to directly handle cash. The term *credit card* is derived from the fact that the issuer, such as **Visa**® or **MasterCard**®, extends credit (lends money) to the cardholder each time the cardholder uses the card. Meanwhile, the credit card company deposits cash in the company's bank for the amount of the sale, less service fees.

Credit card companies earn revenues primarily in two ways. First, the cardholder has a specified grace period before he or she has to pay the credit card balance in full. If the balance is not paid by the end of the grace period, the issuing company will charge a fee (interest). Second, credit card companies charge the *retailer*, not the customer, for the use of the credit card. This charge generally ranges from 2% to 4% of the amount of the sale.

For example, suppose a movie theatre accepts MasterCard as payment for $2,000 worth of movie tickets, and MasterCard charges the movie theatre a service fee of 3% (or $60 on sales of $2,000). Moviegoers don't pay cash to the theatre at the time of sale, but Master-Card deposits cash, less the service fee expense, into the theatre's account, usually within 1–3 days. Therefore, the theatre records the $2,000 credit card transaction as $1,940 cash received and $60 service fee expense.

	Debit	Credit
Cash..	1,940	
Service Fee Expense...	60	
Service Revenue...		2,000
(Sell tickets with credit card and 3% service fee)		

From the seller's perspective, the only difference between a cash sale and a credit card sale is that the seller must pay a fee to the credit card company for allowing the customer to use a credit card.

Decision Point

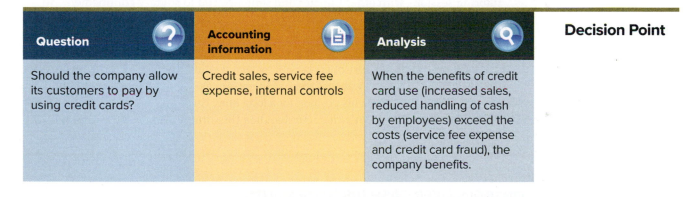

Question	Accounting information	Analysis
Should the company allow its customers to pay by using credit cards?	Credit sales, service fee expense, internal controls	When the benefits of credit card use (increased sales, reduced handling of cash by employees) exceed the costs (service fee expense and credit card fraud), the company benefits.

Acceptance of Debit Cards.   *Debit cards* also provide an additional control for cash receipts. Like credit cards, debit cards offer customers a way to purchase goods and services without a physical exchange of cash. They differ, however, in that most debit cards (sometimes referred to as *check cards*) work just like a check and withdraw funds directly from the cardholder's bank account at the time of use. (Recall that credit cards don't remove cash from the cardholder's account after each transaction.)

Similar to credit cards, the use of debit cards by customers results in a fee being charged to the retailer. However, the fees charged for debit cards are typically much lower than those charged for credit cards. Debit card transactions are recorded similar to credit card transactions.

Mobile payments and electronic funds transfers are also recorded as cash receipts, similar to the discussion above, and often include service fees. The way companies account for prepaid cards (gift cards) differs somewhat because the company receives cash ahead of providing the good or service. We'll discuss these transactions in Chapter 8.

COMMON MISTAKE

The term *debit card* can cause some confusion for someone in the first accounting course. Throughout this course, we refer to an increase in cash as a *debit* to cash. However, using your debit card will result in a decrease in your cash account. The term *debit card* refers to the bank's liability to the company being decreased (debited) when the company uses a debit card. Don't let this confuse you.

ETHICAL DILEMMA

Digital Vision LTD./Superstock

Suppose that you were sent to prison for a crime you did not commit. While in prison, the warden learns that you have taken financial accounting and are really good at "keeping the books." In fact, you are so good at accounting that you offer to teach other inmates basic financial skills that they'll use someday after being released.

However, the warden plans to use his position of authority at the prison to steal money. He uses prisoners as low-cost labor to do projects around town. Because other legitimate companies cannot compete with these low costs, they bribe the warden *not* to bid on jobs. The warden asks you to use your accounting skills to participate in a financial scam by falsifying documents and creating a false set of accounting records that will allow the warden's bribes to go undetected by state prison authorities. In other words, he wants you to "cook the books."

When you object to helping with this scam, the warden threatens to end your tutoring sessions with other inmates and sentence you to solitary confinement. To further sway your decision, he promises that if you'll help, he'll make your prison life easy by giving you special meals and other favors.

What would you do in this situation? If you help the warden steal money, you benefit personally, and the other prisoners benefit by your continued tutoring sessions. However, the warden physically abuses some of the prisoners, and helping him steal money means that he'll remain in his position for a long time, continuing his abusive behavior.

To see how Tim Robbin's character handled this situation, check out the movie *The Shawshank Redemption*.

CONTROLS OVER CASH DISBURSEMENTS

Managers should design proper controls for cash disbursements to prevent any unauthorized payments and ensure proper recording. Consistent with our discussion of cash receipts, cash disbursements include not only disbursing physical cash, but also writing checks and using credit cards and debit cards to make payments. All these forms of payment constitute cash disbursement and require formal internal control procedures. Common controls over cash disbursements include the following:

1. Make all disbursements, other than very small ones, by check, debit card, or credit card. This provides a permanent record of all disbursements.

2. Authorize all expenditures before purchase and verify the accuracy of the purchase itself. The employee who authorizes payment should not also be the employee who prepares the check.

3. Make sure checks are serially numbered and signed only by authorized employees. Require two signatures for larger checks.

4. Periodically compare amounts shown in the debit card and credit card statements with purchase receipts. The employee verifying the accuracy of the debit card and credit card statements should not also be the employee responsible for actual purchases.

5. Set maximum purchase limits on debit cards and credit cards. Give approval to purchase above these amounts only to upper-level employees.

6. Employees responsible for making cash disbursements should not also be in charge of cash receipts.

When the movie theatre pays $1,000 to advertise its show times, it records the following transaction, regardless of whether it pays with cash, a check, or a debit card.

	Debit	Credit
Advertising Expense...	**1,000**	
Cash		**1,000**
(Purchase advertising with cash, check, or debit card)		

Because credit cards allow the purchaser to delay payment for several weeks or even months, if the theatre uses a credit card to pay for the $1,000 worth of advertising, it would record the purchase as follows.

	Debit	Credit
Advertising Expense...	**1,000**	
Accounts Payable...		**1,000**
(Purchase advertising with credit card)		

Smaller companies often use credit cards to make purchases, whereas larger companies buy on account (or on credit). Both result in payment by the company being somewhat delayed, and therefore both types of purchases result in Accounts Payable being recorded. In addition, in practice when we record Accounts Payable, we would also indicate the specific credit card or specific vendor that is owed.

 KEY POINT

> Because cash is the asset of a company most susceptible to employee fraud, controls over cash receipts and cash disbursements are an important part of a company's overall internal control system. Important controls over cash receipts include separation of duties for those who handle cash and independent verification of cash receipts. Important controls over cash disbursements include payment by check, credit card, or debit card, separation of duties, and various authorization and documentation procedures.

Bank Reconciliation

Another important control used by nearly all companies to help maintain control of cash is a bank reconciliation. A **bank reconciliation** matches the balance of cash in the bank account with the balance of cash in the company's own records. Differences in these two balances can occur because of either timing differences or errors.

Timing differences **in cash occur when the company records transactions either before or after the bank records the same transactions.** For example, when a company receives cash for selling products and services, the company records an increase to cash immediately. The bank, however, doesn't record an increase until the cash is later deposited.

Other times, it's the bank that is the first to record a transaction. For example, banks may charge service fees for a variety of items. These fees immediately reduce the bank's record of the company's balance for cash. However, the company may not be immediately aware of these fees.

Errors **can be made either by the company or its bank and may be accidental or intentional.** An *accidental* error might occur if the company mistakenly were to record a payment for $117 as $171 in its records, or if the bank improperly processed a deposit of $1,100 as a $1,010 deposit. An *intentional* error is the result of theft. If the company records a daily deposit of $5,000 but an employee deposits only $500 into the bank account and pockets the rest, the bank reconciliation will reveal the missing $4,500. It is the *possibility* of these errors, or even outright fraudulent activities, that makes the bank reconciliation a useful cash control tool. That's why bank reconciliations are prepared frequently by most companies.

■ **LO4–5**
Reconcile a bank statement.

Starlight Productions Example.   To see how a bank reconciliation is prepared, we will use the monthly record of the company's activity from the bank, called a *bank statement,* and we will use the monthly activity from the company, called *cash receipts* and *cash disbursements.* Let's start by examining those particular records of Starlight Productions for the month of March.

At the end of March, Starlight's own record of cash activity reveals a cash balance of **$34,600** (see Illustration 4–8). Starlight's monthly bank statement, however, shows the bank's cash balance at the end of March is **$26,400** (see Illustration 4–9). Why do these balances differ? To ensure that all cash transactions have been properly recorded, we need to reconcile these two balances by identifying (1) timing differences created by cash activity reported by either First Bank or Starlight but not recorded by the other and (2) any errors.

ILLUSTRATION 4–8

Company Records of Cash Activities

STARLIGHT PRODUCTIONS
Cash Account Records
March 1, 2024, to March 31, 2024

Cash Receipts			Cash Disbursements			
Date	**Description**	**Amount**	**Date**	**Description**	**Memo**	**Amount**
3/5	Sales	$ 3,600	3/1	EFT	Salaries	$ 7,200
3/12	Sales	5,900	3/5	EFT	Rent	4,500
3/16	Sales	4,200	3/10	DC	Advertising	3,000
3/20	Sales	7,400	3/17	CHK 294	Supplies	2,700
3/24	Sales	6,300	3/23	DC	Repairs	2,100
3/30	Sales	8,500	3/28	CHK 295	Insurance	5,400
		$35,900				$24,900

SUMMARY OF TRANSACTIONS

Beginning Cash Balance March 1, 2024	+	Cash Receipts	−	Cash Disbursements	=	Ending Cash Balance March 31, 2024
$23,600		$35,900		$24,900		**$34,600**

ILLUSTRATION 4–9

Bank Statement

P.O. Box 26788
Odessa, TX 79760
(432) 799-BANK

First Bank
A Name You Can Trust

Member FDIC

Account Holder:	Starlight Productions 221B Baker Street Odessa, TX 79760	Account Number:	4061009619
		Statement Date:	March 31, 2024

Account Summary

Beginning Balance March 1, 2024	Deposits and Credits		Withdrawals and Debits		Ending Balance March 31, 2024
	No.	Total	No.	Total	
$23,600	4	$29,600	8	$26,800	**$26,400**

Account Details

Deposits and Credits			Withdrawals and Debits		
Date	Amount	Description	Date	Amount	Description
3/8	$3,600	DEP	3/1	$ 7,200	EFT
3/14	5,900	DEP	3/5	4,500	EFT
3/19	4,200	DEP	3/10	3,300	DC
3/22	7,400	DEP	3/21	2,700	CHK 294
3/26	6,300	DEP	3/23	2,100	DC

ILLUSTRATION 4–9

Continued

Account Details					
Deposits and Credits			**Withdrawals and Debits**		
Date	Amount	Description	Date	Amount	Description
3/29	2,000	NOTE	3/27	4,100	NSF
3/29	200	INT	3/31	2,800	SF
			3/31	100	
	$29,600			$26,800	

Desc.	**DEP** Customer deposit	**INT** Interest earned	**SF** Service fees
	NOTE Note collected	**CHK** Customer check	**NSF** Nonsufficient funds
	EFT Electronic funds transfer	**DC** Debit card	

COMMON MISTAKE

Notice that bank statements refer to an increase (or deposit) in the cash balance as a *credit* and a decrease (or withdrawal) as a *debit*. This terminology is the opposite of that used in financial accounting, where *debit* refers to an increase in cash and *credit* refers to a decrease in cash. The reason for the difference in terminology is a difference in perspective. When a company makes a deposit, it views this as an increase to cash, so it records a debit to the Cash account. However, the bank views this same deposit as an increase in the amount owed to the company, or a liability, which is recorded as a credit. Similarly, a withdrawal of cash from the bank is viewed by the company as a decrease to its Cash account, so it is recorded with a credit, but the bank views this withdrawal as a decrease to the amount owed to the company, so it debits its liability.

Reconciling the bank account involves the following three steps:

1. Reconcile the **bank's** cash balance.
2. Reconcile the **company's** cash balance.
3. Update the company's Cash account by recording items identified in step 2.

STEP 1: RECONCILE THE BANK'S CASH BALANCE

Illustration 4–10 highlights the *differences* in cash collections reported in the company records and those reported in the bank statement. The differences are circled in red. When preparing the bank reconciliation, we need to focus only on those items. The amounts *not circled* have been recorded by both the company and the bank, so these items are already reconciled and therefore do not need further attention.

In step 1, we reconcile the *bank's* cash balance by determining which cash transactions have been recorded by the company but not yet recorded by the bank. As shown on the left

ILLUSTRATION 4–10

Differences in Cash Collections

Company Records			Bank Statement		
Cash Receipts			**Deposits and Credits**		
Date	Description	Amount	Date	Amount	Desc.
3/5	Sales	$3,600	3/8	$3,600	DEP
3/12	Sales	5,900	3/14	5,900	DEP
3/16	Sales	4,200	3/19	4,200	DEP
3/20	Sales	7,400	3/22	7,400	DEP
3/24	Sales	6,300	3/26	6,300	DEP
3/30	Sales	8,500	3/29	2,000	NOTE
			3/29	200	INT

Deposit Outstanding
not in bank statement

Cash increases
not in company records

Amounts circled in red are used to prepare the bank reconciliation.

side of Illustration 4–10, Starlight's records reveal that cash of $8,500 has been received by the company but is not yet reflected as an increase in the bank's cash balance by the end of March. These are known as **deposits outstanding**. Deposits outstanding cause the bank's balance to be less than the company's balance of cash. [Note: We'll address the items circled in the bank statement in step 2 below.]

Now let's compare Starlight's cash disbursements to the bank statement's list of withdrawals and debits in Illustration 4–11.

ILLUSTRATION 4–11

Differences in Cash Payments

Amounts circled in red are used to prepare the bank reconciliation.

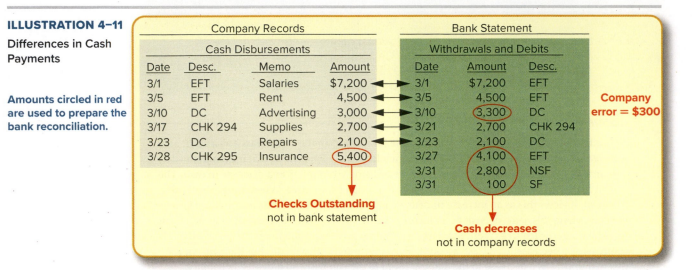

The company records show that the company has written two checks during the month of March, but only check #294 is shown in the bank statement. This means check #295 (for $5,400) remains outstanding and has not yet been subtracted from the bank's balance. This is an example of **checks outstanding**. Checks outstanding cause the bank's balance to be more than the company's balance of cash. (Notice also that a debit card (DC) transaction was incorrectly recorded by the company for $3,000 instead of $3,300. We'll address this $300 company error and other items circled in the bank statement in step 2.)

Starlight's bank reconciliation is shown in Illustration 4–12. For now, look only at the left side. **We adjust the bank's cash balance per bank statement by adding deposits outstanding**

ILLUSTRATION 4–12   Bank Reconciliation

STARLIGHT Productions
Bank Reconciliation
March 31, 2024

Bank's Cash Balance		Company's Cash Balance		
Per bank statement	$26,400	Per general ledger	$34,600	
Deposits outstanding	8,500	Note received	2,000	
		Interest received	200	Step 3: Update company records
Checks outstanding	(5,400)	EFT for utilities	(4,100)	
		NSF check from customer	(2,800)	
		Service fee	(100)	
		Corrected advertising expense	(300)	
Bank balance per reconciliation	$29,500	Company balance per reconciliation	$29,500	

Step 1   Step 2

———— Reconciled ————

and subtracting checks outstanding. The bank balance per reconciliation of $29,500 is what the bank's balance of cash would be if no deposits or checks were outstanding. We would also need to look for and correct any bank errors, but there are none here. Next, we'll look at step 2 to determine the amounts shown on the right side of Illustration 4–12.

STEP 2: RECONCILE THE COMPANY'S CASH BALANCE

In step 2, we reconcile the *company's* cash balance per general ledger by determining which cash transactions have been recorded by the bank but not yet recorded by the company. Let's first compare the bank statement's list of deposits and credits to the company's record of cash receipts. To see these, look back at Illustration 4–10 for the items circled in the bank statement.

Notes received and interest earned.   First Bank received $2,200 cash from a note owed to Starlight ($2,000 principal plus $200 related interest). These two items increase the company's cash balance, but the company didn't know about them until it examined the bank statement. Direct deposits by others into the company's bank account have become increasingly popular in recent years because of the ease of electronic banking. Common situations include recurring payments from customers, real estate transactions, collection agencies, and note collections.

Now let's compare the bank statement's list of withdrawals and debits to the company's record of cash disbursements. To see these, look back at Illustration 4–11 for the items circled in the bank statement. The bank statement reveals four amounts: three that are not yet recorded in Starlight's cash records, and one item recorded incorrectly by Starlight. These four items include the following:

1. **Unrecorded payments.** An electronic funds transfer (EFT) for utilities ($4,100) was made, but Starlight's accountant forgot to record this transaction. EFTs are automatic transfers from one bank account to another (sometimes referred to as electronic checks or e-checks). Companies are more frequently using EFTs to handle routine expenditures such as monthly rent payments, salaries, or utility bills.

2. **NSF checks.** Starlight received and deposited a check from a customer for $2,800. The bank later determines this customer's account has "nonsufficient funds" to pay the check. This is an **NSF check**. Starlight previously recorded cash received from this customer, and now First Bank is notifying Starlight that its cash balance is being decreased because the customer did not pay with a valid check.

3. **Bank service fees.** First Bank charges service fees of $100 to Starlight. Banks charge fees for various activities related to monthly maintenance, overdraft penalties, ATM use, wire transfers, foreign currency exchanges, automatic payments, collections of notes, and other account services. These fees may not be known by the company until examination of the bank statement.

4. **Company errors.** The final item relates to a company error in recording a debit card transaction. A debit card was used for $3,300 of advertising, but Starlight's accountant recorded the transaction incorrectly for $3,000. First Bank processed the debit card for the correct amount of $3,300. This means Starlight needs to reduce its cash balance by an additional $300 for advertising expense. In addition, the company may want to review its internal control procedures to identify the source of the error.

These four items decrease the company's cash balance, but the company didn't know about them until it examined the bank statement.

The company balance per reconciliation is calculated on the right side of Illustration 4–12. The company's reconciled balance is $29,500 and matches the bank's reconciled balance, providing some indication that cash is not being mishandled by employees.

COMMON MISTAKE

Students sometimes mistake an NSF check from a customer as a bad check written *by* the company instead of one written *to* the company. When an NSF check occurs, the company has deposited a customer's check but the customer did not have enough funds to cover the check. The company must adjust its balance of cash downward to reverse the increase in cash it recorded at the time of deposit. The effect of this bounced customer check creates an account receivable for the company until the customer honors the funds it owes.

STEP 3: UPDATE THE COMPANY'S CASH ACCOUNT

As a final step in the reconciliation process, a company must update the balance in its Cash account to adjust for the items used to reconcile the *company's* cash balance (right side of Illustration 4–12). Remember, these are amounts the company didn't know until it examined the bank statement.

For reconciliation items that increase the company's balance of cash, we debit Cash. We credit Notes Receivable because the company has collected cash from the note, decreasing that asset account (−$2,000). We also credit Interest Revenue for interest earned from the note ($200).

March 31, 2024	Debit	Credit
Cash	**2,200**	
Notes Receivable..		**2,000**
Interest Revenue		**200**
(Record note collected and interest earned)		

For reconciliation items that decrease the company's balance of cash, we credit Cash.

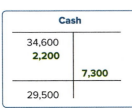

Cash	
34,600	
2,200	
	7,300
29,500	

March 31, 2024	Debit	Credit
Utilities Expense	**4,100**	
Accounts Receivable	**2,800**	
Service Fee Expense	**100**	
Advertising Expense	**300**	
Cash		**7,300**
(Record utilities payment, NSF check, bank service fee, and correction for advertising)		

Accounts Receivable is debited to increase that asset account (+$2,800), to show that the customer who paid with an NSF check still owes the company money. The other debits are needed to record the items related to cash outflows.

 COMMON MISTAKE

Some students try to update the Cash account for deposits outstanding, checks outstanding, or a bank error. The company does *not* need to adjust for these items related to reconciling the bank's balance because they are already properly recorded in the company's accounting records.

In the uncommon event that the two balances at the end of the bank reconciliation schedule are not equal, management investigates the discrepancy to check for wrongdoing or errors by company employees or the bank. If the company cannot resolve the discrepancy, it records the difference to either Miscellaneous Expense or Miscellaneous Revenue, depending on whether it has a debit or credit balance. For example, suppose a company is unable to account for $100 of missing cash. In this event, the company records the following transaction, increasing Miscellaneous Expense and decreasing Cash.

	Debit	Credit
Miscellaneous Expense	100	
Cash		100
(Record loss of $100 cash)		

Illustration 4–13 summarizes the basic items included in a bank reconciliation. **For the reconciliation to be complete, the reconciled bank balance must equal the reconciled company balance.**

ILLUSTRATION 4–13

Summary of Items Included in the Bank Reconciliation

	Bank's Cash Balance	Company's Cash Balance
	Per bank statement	Per general ledger
Timing Differences	+ Deposits outstanding − Checks outstanding	+ Notes received by bank + Interest received − Unrecorded payments − NSF checks from customers − Bank service fees
Errors	± Bank errors	± Company errors
	= **Bank balance per reconciliation**	= **Company balance per reconciliation**

KEY POINT

In a bank reconciliation we reconcile the *bank's* cash balance for (1) cash transactions already recorded by the company but not yet recorded by the bank and (2) bank errors. Similarly, we reconcile the *company's* cash balance for (1) cash transactions already recorded by the bank but not yet recorded by the company and (2) company errors. After we complete the reconciliations, the amounts for the bank balance and the company balance should be equal. Any adjustments to the company's balance need to be recorded.

Let's Review

At the end of April 2024, Showtime Theatre's accounting records show a cash balance of $4,800. The April bank statement reports a cash balance of $3,700. The following information is gathered from the bank statement and company records:

Checks outstanding	$1,900	Customer's NSF check	$1,300
Deposits outstanding	1,600	Service fee	200
Interest earned	70		

In addition, Showtime discovered it correctly paid for advertising with a check for $220 but incorrectly recorded the check in the company's records for $250. The bank correctly processed the check for $220.

Required:

1. Prepare a bank reconciliation for the month of April 2024.
2. Prepare entries to update the balance of cash in the company's records.

Solution:

1. Bank reconciliation:

SHOWTIME THEATRE
Bank Reconciliation
April 30, 2024

Bank's Cash Balance		_Company's Cash Balance_	
Per bank statement	$3,700	Per general ledger	$4,800
Deposits outstanding	+1,600	Interest earned	+70
		Company error	+30
Checks outstanding	−1,900	Service fee	−200
		NSF check received	−1,300
Bank balance per reconciliation	$3,400	Company balance per reconciliation	$3,400

2. Entries to update the company's balance of cash:

April 30, 2024	Debit	Credit
Cash	100	
Interest Revenue		70
Advertising Expense		30
(Record interest earned and error correction)		
Service Fee Expense	200	
Accounts Receivable	1,300	
Cash		1,500
(Record service fee and NSF check of customer)		

Suggested Homework:
BE4–8, BE4–12;
E4–9, E4–10;
P4–2A&B, P4–3A&B

Employee Purchases

■ LO4–6
Account for employee purchases.

You probably pay for many of your purchases with a debit card, credit card, or check. For example, when you go out to eat with your friends at a local restaurant, you might use your debit card. You could also use your credit card for an online purchase, or maybe a check for a mail-in donation to your favorite charity. However, it's also nice to have a little cash in your wallet for quick expenditures. For example, you might decide to buy a soda from a machine or a hot dog at the game.

The same way you have multiple methods to make purchases, so do many employees on behalf of their company. For example, a traveling salesperson might be on the road and need to take a client to dinner, put gas in the car, or stay in a hotel that night. To do so, the salesperson can use a company-issued debit card or credit card (often referred to as **purchase cards**).

Similarly, an office manager might decide to have a lunch meeting for the staff and needs actual cash available to pay for pizza delivery. Cash on hand to pay for these minor purchases is referred to as a **petty cash fund**, and the employee responsible for the fund is often referred to as the _petty cash custodian_.

Employee purchases should be included in the accounting records by the end of the reporting period. Employee purchases made with debit cards and checks will be captured in the accounting records at the time the bank reconciliation is prepared, like we saw in the previous section. In this section, we discuss how to account for employee purchases using credit cards and the petty cash fund. Those expenditures typically are not immediately recorded in the accounting records, yet they are legitimate business transactions during the period.

Let's work through an example of Starlight Productions. In May, Starlight withdraws cash of $200 from the bank to have on hand in the petty cash fund. Starlight also issues credit cards to its purchasing manager and marketing manager. At the time these cards are issued, nothing is recorded because no expenditures have been made. However, for the petty cash fund, cash has been withdrawn from the bank, so we record the following entry that formally shows the transfer of cash from the bank to cash on hand in the petty cash fund:

May 1	Debit	Credit
Petty Cash (on hand)	**200**	
Cash (checking account)		**200**
(Establish the petty cash fund)		

A	=	L	+	SE
+200				
−200				

During May, the petty cash custodian provides cash to employees for an office lunch and package delivery and places vouchers documenting the purposes of those expenditures in the petty cash fund. In addition, the purchasing manager and the marketing manager used their credit cards for expenditures related to their positions. Suppose the following items and amounts occur:

Petty Cash Fund (Cash)		Purchasing Manager (Credit Card)		Marketing Manager (Credit Card)	
Item	Amount	Item	Amount	Item	Amount
Lunch	$60	Supplies	$800	Advertising	$1,500
Delivery	$90	Supplies	$600	Postage	$1,200

At the end of May, the company's accountant collects vouchers from the petty cash fund and credit card receipts from the purchasing manager and marketing manager.

Let's first record expenditures made with credit cards. These expenditures typically are not paid immediately, so they are recorded as Accounts Payable until paid. If the company's accountant decides to pay the credit card balance at the time of reconciliation, then the $4,100 credit would be to Cash.

May 31	Debit	Credit
Supplies ($800 + $600)	**1,400**	
Advertising Expense	**1,500**	
Postage Expense	**1,200**	
Accounts Payable		**4,100**
(Recognize employee expenditures with credit cards)		

A	=	L	+	SE
+1,400				
				−1,500 Exp▲
				−1,200 Exp▲
		+4,100		

Now let's record expenditures from the petty cash fund.

May 31	Debit	Credit
Entertainment Expense	**60**	
Delivery Expense	**90**	
Cash		**150**
(Recognize employee expenditures from the petty cash fund)		

A	=	L	+	SE
				−60 Exp▲
				−90 Exp▲
−150				

Also at the end of the period, the $200 petty cash fund needs to be replenished. Cash of $150 has been disbursed during May ($60 for lunch and $90 for delivery). The fund has only $50 remaining, so management withdraws an additional $150 from the bank to place in the fund. The fund's physical balance will once again be $200.

What if only $30 physically remains in the petty cash fund at the end of May, when there should be $50? It could be that $20 was stolen from the fund, or the fund could be missing a receipt for $20 to show where it was spent. If the question is not resolved, the firm will likely charge the $20 to Miscellaneous Expense.

KEY POINT

To make purchases on behalf of the company, some employees are allowed to use debit cards and credit cards (purchase cards), write checks, and spend available cash on hand (petty cash fund). At the end of the period, all employee purchases are recorded, and the petty cash fund is replenished.

In addition to accounting for employee purchases, a system of internal control needs to be in place to ensure that all expenditures are legitimate and that company resources are not being wasted or stolen. Those controls include items such as the following:

- Employees should be required to provide receipts and justification for those receipts on a timely basis.
- A separate employee reviews receipts and supporting documents to ensure all expenditures are made appropriately.
- Credit card receipts are reconciled to credit card statements, just like we reconciled checks and debit card transactions to the bank statement.
- Spending limits are placed on employees who are authorized to use a company credit card or have access to company cash. Major expenditures require pre-approval through formal purchasing procedures.
- Only those employees that need to make timely business expenditures should receive authorization.

PART C

■ **LO4–7**
Identify the major inflows and outflows of cash.

STATEMENT OF CASH FLOWS

To this point, we've considered several internal controls related to cash. Here, we discuss how companies report cash activities to external parties. Companies report cash in two financial statements—in the balance sheet and in the statement of cash flows. As we discussed in Chapter 3, companies report cash as an asset in the balance sheet. The amount is typically reported as a current asset and represents cash *available* for spending at the end of the reporting period.

In addition, some companies separately report **restricted cash.** Restricted cash represents cash that is *not available* for current operations. Examples of restricted cash include cash set aside by the company for specific purposes such as repaying debt, purchasing equipment, or making investments in the future.

The balance sheet provides only the final balance for cash. It does not provide any details regarding cash receipts and cash payments. Companies report information about cash receipts and payments during the period in a statement of cash flows. **From the statement of cash flows, investors know a company's cash inflows and cash outflows related to (1) operating activities, (2) investing activities, and (3) financing activities.** We'll provide a complete discussion of the statement of cash flows in Chapter 11. Here, we briefly introduce the basics of the statement to help you understand that its purpose is to report activity related to the key topic of this chapter—cash.

Recall from Chapter 1 the three fundamental types of business activities relating to cash:

- *Operating activities* include cash transactions involving revenue and expense events during the period. In other words, operating activities include the cash effect of the same activities that are reported in the income statement to calculate net income.
- *Investing activities,* as the name implies, include cash investments in long-term assets and investment securities. When the firm later sells those assets, we consider those transactions investing activities also. So, investing activities tend to involve long-term assets.
- *Financing activities* include transactions designed to raise cash or finance the business. There are two ways to do this: borrow cash from lenders or raise cash from stockholders. We also consider cash outflows to repay debt and cash dividends to stockholders to be financing activities. So, financing activities involve liabilities and stockholders' equity.

It's easiest to understand cash flow information by looking at the underlying transactions. To do this, we'll refer back to the external transactions of Eagle Soccer Academy introduced in Chapters 1 through 3. For convenience, Illustration 4–14 lists those transactions and analyzes their effects on the company's cash.

Which transactions involve the exchange of cash? All transactions except (5) and (7) involve either the receipt (inflow) or payment (outflow) of cash. **Only transactions involving** *cash* **affect a company's** *cash* **flows.**

ILLUSTRATION 4–14

External Transactions of
Eagle Soccer Academy

Transaction	External Transactions in December	Type of Activity	Is Cash Involved?	Inflow or Outflow?
(1)	Sell shares of common stock for $200,000 to obtain the funds necessary to start the business.	Financing	**YES**	Inflow
(2)	Borrow $100,000 from the local bank and sign a note promising to repay the full amount of the debt in three years.	Financing	**YES**	Inflow
(3)	Purchase equipment necessary for giving soccer training, $120,000 cash.	Investing	**YES**	Outflow
(4)	Pay one year of rent in advance, $60,000 ($5,000 per month).	Operating	**YES**	Outflow
(5)	Purchase supplies on account, $23,000.	Operating	NO	—
(6)	Provide soccer training to customers for cash, $43,000.	Operating	**YES**	Inflow
(7)	Provide soccer training to customers on account, $20,000.	Operating	NO	—
(8)	Receive cash in advance for soccer training sessions to be given in the future, $6,000.	Operating	**YES**	Inflow
(9)	Pay salaries to employees, $28,000.	Operating	**YES**	Outflow
(10)	Pay cash dividends of $4,000 to shareholders.	Financing	**YES**	Outflow

Illustration 4–15 presents the statement of cash flows for Eagle Soccer Academy using what's called the *direct method* of reporting operating activities. Corresponding transaction numbers are in brackets. (In Chapter 11 we'll discuss the *indirect method*.)

From the statement of cash flows, investors and creditors can see that the major source of cash inflow for Eagle is the issuance of common stock, a financing activity. Eagle has also

ILLUSTRATION 4–15

Statement of Cash
Flows for Eagle Soccer
Academy

EAGLE SOCCER ACADEMY
Statement of Cash Flows
For the period ended December 31, 2024

Cash Flows from Operating Activities

Cash inflows:		
From customers [6 and 8]	$ 49,000	
Cash outflows:		
For salaries [9]	(28,000)	
For rent [4]	(60,000)	
Net cash flows from operating activities		$ (39,000)

Cash Flows from Investing Activities

Purchase equipment [3]	(120,000)	
Net cash flows from investing activities		(120,000)

Cash Flows from Financing Activities

Issue common stock [1]	200,000	
Borrow from bank [2]	100,000	
Pay dividends [10]	(4,000)	
Net cash flows from financing activities		296,000
Net increase in cash		137,000
Cash at the beginning of the period		-0-
Cash at the end of the period		**$137,000**

Numbers in brackets
correspond to the
external transaction
numbers of Eagle
Soccer Academy in
Illustration 4–14.

received cash from bank borrowing, which must be repaid. The company is also investing in its future by purchasing equipment. Eagle reports this amount as an investing outflow.

With regard to the three types of business activities, the cash flow that's related most directly to the company's profitability is net cash flows from operating activities. For Eagle Soccer Academy, net cash flows from operating activities are −$39,000. This means that cash *outflows* related to operating activities exceed inflows. Stated another way, cash outflows related to expense activities exceed cash inflows related to revenue activities. While Eagle reports net income of $14,000 in its income statement (see Illustration 3–12 in Chapter 3), these same activities are not able to generate positive cash flows for the company. Ultimately, companies must be able to generate positive operating cash flows to maintain long-term success.

The final amount reported in the statement of cash flows, **$137,000**, is the same amount of cash reported in the balance sheet. You can verify this is the case for Eagle Soccer Academy by referring back to the balance sheet reported in Illustration 3–14 in Chapter 3.

 **KEY POINT**

The statement of cash flows reports all cash activities for the period. *Operating activities* include those transactions involving revenue and expense activities. *Investing activities* include cash investments in long-term assets and investment securities. *Financing activities* include transactions designed to finance the business through borrowing and owner investment.

Decision Point

Question	Accounting information	Analysis
Is the company able to generate enough cash from internal sources to maintain operations?	Statement of cash flows	Cash flows generated from internal sources include operating and investing activities. For established companies, the sum of these amounts should be positive. Otherwise, the company will need to rely on external funding (lenders and stockholders), which is not sustainable in the long term.

Let's Review

A company reports in its current year each of the transactions listed below.

Required:

Indicate whether each transaction should be reported as an operating, investing, or financing cash flow in the company's statement of cash flows, and whether each is a cash inflow or outflow.

Transaction	Type of Cash Flow	Inflow or Outflow
1. Pay employees' salaries.	_____	_____
2. Obtain a loan at the bank.	_____	_____
3. Purchase a building with cash.	_____	_____
4. Purchase equipment by issuing note payable to seller.	_____	_____

Suggested Homework:
BE4–14, BE4–15;
E4–14, E4–15;
P4–4A&B, P4–5A&B

Solution:

1. Operating—outflow.
2. Financing—inflow.
3. Investing—outflow.
4. Not reported as a cash flow because no cash is involved in the transaction.

CASH ANALYSIS
Live Nation Entertainment vs. AMC Networks

ANALYSIS

■ **LO4–8**
Demonstrate the link between cash reported in the balance sheet and cash reported in the statement of cash flows.

The amount of cash reported by a company is important to investors and creditors for many reasons. Cash is needed to pay debt when it comes due. Cash also gives the company the financial flexibility to respond to its changing business environment, such as purchasing additional assets, hiring more employees, and engaging in strategic acquisitions.

However, having too much cash represents excess resources that are idle and not being used to produce revenues. Investors may also view excess cash as a signal that management does not see additional opportunities for profitable expansion. Some managers have been shown to spend excess cash inefficiently on less profitable projects.

Let's examine the cash holdings of two large entertainment companies, **Live Nation Entertainment** and **AMC Networks**.

CASH REPORTING

The balance sheet reports a company's total cash balance at the end of the year. The cash balance at the end of the previous year is the beginning balance of cash in the current year. We can use consecutive balance sheets to determine the change in cash for the year.

The statement of cash flows reports the net cash flows during the year by type of activity. Notice that the sum of the three activities in the statement of cash flows equals the change in total cash from one period to the next in the balance sheet. This demonstrates the link between the cash reported in consecutive balance sheets and net cash flows reported in the statement of cash flows.

($ in millions) Balance Sheet:	Live Nation Entertainment	AMC Networks
Cash and cash equivalents (ending)	$2,474.2	$ 816.2
Cash and cash equivalents (beginning)	2,378.2	554.9
Change in cash for the year	**$ 96.0**	**$ 261.3**
Statement of Cash Flows:		
Operating cash flows	$ 469.8	$ 483.7
Investing cash flows	(691.0)	(89.7)
Financing cash flows	328.9	(131.1)
Foreign currency effects	(11.7)	(1.6)
Net cash flows for the year	**$ 96.0**	**$ 261.3**

Both companies had an increase in cash for the year. We can analyze the statement of cash flows to see why cash increased by this amount. Both companies generated about the same amount of operating cash flows. However, Live Nation Entertainment used a large debt issuance (financing cash flows) for purchases of property and equipment and for acquisition of venue management and concert promotion businesses located in Canada, Belgium, and the United States (investing cash flows). AMC Networks had limited investing and financing activities.

CASH HOLDINGS

Live Nation Entertainment's ratio of cash to noncash assets is 29.1%. This same ratio for AMC Networks is 17.1%.

($ in millions)	Live Nation Entertainment	AMC Networks
Cash and cash equivalents	$2,474.2	$ 816.2
Noncash assets	$8,501.4	$4,780.5
Ratio	29.1%	17.1%

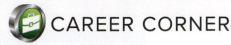
Financial analysts offer investment advice to their clients—banks, insurance companies, mutual funds, securities firms, and individual investors. This advice usually comes in the form of a formal recommendation (buy, hold, or sell). Before giving an opinion, analysts develop a detailed understanding of a company's operations through discussions with management, analysis of competitors, and projections of industry trends. They also develop a detailed understanding of a company's financial statements, including its cash holdings.

Understanding a company's cash balance involves knowing the trade-offs between having too much or too little cash. With too little cash, a company may not be able to pay its debts as they become due or may not be able to take advantage of profitable opportunities. Having too much cash can draw criticisms from analysts because management is not efficiently using stockholders' resources (idle cash). In that case, analysts often call for managers to return idle cash to stockholders by paying additional dividends. The importance of understanding these trade-offs is why many finance majors and MBA students, pursuing careers as financial analysts, take additional accounting-related courses when earning their degrees and even after graduation.

anekoho/Shutterstock

Below are some factors that possibly explain why one company holds more cash than another.

- **Profitability.** Companies that generate higher profits may naturally have more cash available.
- **Growth.** Growth companies tend to have less cash available because of their higher capital spending on new opportunities.
- **Reserves.** Companies sometimes hold larger amounts of cash in anticipation of major acquisitions or for payment of upcoming large debt payments.
- **Volatility of operations.** Companies with more volatile operations tend to hold more cash. Short-term negative shocks in the business cycle can cause a company to default on its debt and enter bankruptcy. These companies tend to keep more cash in reserve.
- **Foreign operations.** Historically, companies in the United States had to pay additional income taxes on foreign profits once those profits were returned as cash to the United States. To avoid these additional taxes, companies with major international operations (such as **Apple**, **Microsoft**, and **Google**) often kept the cash from foreign profits in those foreign countries, causing them to have higher overall cash balances.
- **Dividend policy.** Companies that pay greater dividends tend to have less cash available. Some companies choose to return a higher portion of their earnings to stockholders in the form of cash dividends.

Can these factors help to explain why Live Nation Entertainment holds more cash than AMC Networks? Possibly. Live Nation Entertainment is a larger company engaged in more acquisitions of other companies and with more international operations. Live Nation Entertainment generates approximately 34% of its revenues outside of the U.S., while AMC Network generates only about 23%. In addition, AMC Networks uses a portion of its cash to buy its own stock (treasury shares), while Live Nation Entertainment has limited activity of this type.

 KEY POINT

A company's cash balance should be high enough to ensure that it can pay debts as they become due, but not so high that cash is idle and not being used effectively.

CHAPTER FRAMEWORK

All company transactions should pass through the filter of a company's internal controls. Internal controls include activities meant to detect errors or fraud that have occurred, as well as prevent errors or fraud in the first place. Cash is perhaps the asset most susceptible to error and fraud. For this reason, most companies develop specific procedures to maintain control of cash.

Two cash control activities are (1) reconciling a company's balance of cash with its bank's balance of cash and (2) regularly accounting for and verifying employee purchases in the petty cash fund and with company-issued debit and credit cards. These internal control procedures help to safeguard cash and ensure its accuracy in the balance sheet and statement of cash flows.

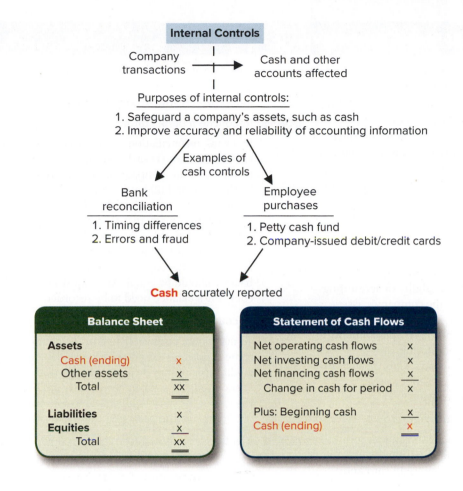

Chapter Framework Questions

1. The primary purpose(s) of a company's internal controls is (are) to
   a. Safeguard a company's assets.
   b. Improve accuracy and reliability of accounting information.
   c. Both *a.* and *b.* are purposes of internal controls.
2. An example of internal controls over cash includes
   a. A bank reconciliation.
   b. A balance sheet provided to investor at the end of the year.
   c. Disclosures by management related to planned operations.
3. A bank reconciliation reconciles the difference between the bank's balance of cash and the company's balance of cash related to
   a. Timing differences.
   b. Errors and fraud.
   c. Both *a.* and *b.* represent differences that should be reconciled.
4. A primary benefit of performing a bank reconciliation is
   a. Accuracy of revenues reported in the income statement.
   b. Accuracy of cash reported in the balance sheet.
   c. Accuracy of liabilities reported in the balance sheet.
5. A primary benefit of internal controls over cash is to improve
   a. Management's ability to assess which of its company's products is most profitable.
   b. Creditors understanding of a company's total obligations.
   c. The amounts reported in the statement of cash flows.

Note: For answers, see the last page of the chapter.

KEY POINTS BY LEARNING OBJECTIVE

LO4–1 Discuss the impact of accounting scandals and the passage of the Sarbanes-Oxley Act.

The accounting scandals in the early 2000s prompted passage of the Sarbanes-Oxley Act (SOX). Among other stipulations, SOX sets forth a variety of guidelines related to auditor–client relations and additional internal controls. Section 404, in particular, requires company management and auditors to document and assess the effectiveness of a company's internal controls.

LO4–2 Identify the components, responsibilities, and limitations of internal control.

Internal control refers to a company's plan to improve the accuracy and reliability of accounting information and safeguard the company's assets. Five key components to an internal control system are (1) control environment, (2) risk assessment, (3) control activities, (4) monitoring, and (5) information and communication. Control activities include those designed to prevent or detect fraudulent or erroneous behavior.

LO4–3 Define cash and cash equivalents.

Cash includes coins and currency, checks received, and balances in savings and checking accounts. The cash balance also includes credit card and debit card sales, as well as cash equivalents, defined as investments that mature within three months from the date of purchase (such as money market funds, Treasury bills, and certificates of deposit).

LO4–4 Understand controls over cash receipts and cash disbursements.

Because cash is the asset of a company most susceptible to employee fraud, controls over cash receipts and cash disbursements are an important part of a company's overall internal control system. Important controls over cash receipts include segregation of duties for those who handle cash and independent verification of cash receipts. Important controls over cash disbursements include payment by check, credit card, or debit card, separation of duties, and various authorization and documentation procedures.

LO4–5 Reconcile a bank statement.

In a bank reconciliation we reconcile the *bank's* cash balance for (1) cash transactions already recorded by the company but not yet recorded by the bank and (2) bank errors. Similarly, we reconcile the *company's* cash balance for (1) cash transactions already recorded by the bank but not yet recorded by the company and (2) company errors. After we complete the reconciliations, the amounts for the bank balance and the company balance should be equal. Any adjustments to the company's balance need to be recorded.

LO4–6 Account for employee purchases.

To make purchases on behalf of the company, some employees are allowed to use debit cards and credit cards (purchase cards), write checks, and spend available cash on hand (petty cash fund). At the end of the period, all employee purchases are recorded, and the petty cash fund is replenished.

LO4–7 Identify the major inflows and outflows of cash.

The statement of cash flows reports all cash activities for the period. *Operating activities* include those transactions involving revenues and expenses. *Investing activities* include cash investments in long-term assets and investment securities. *Financing activities* include transactions designed to finance the business through borrowing and owner investment.

Analysis

LO4–8 Demonstrate the link between cash reported in the balance sheet and cash reported in the statement of cash flows.

A company's cash balance should be high enough to ensure that it can pay debts as they become due, but not so high that cash is idle and not being used effectively.

GLOSSARY

Bank reconciliation: Matching the balance of cash in the bank account with the balance of cash in the company's own records. **p. 189**

Cash: Currency, coins, balances in savings and checking accounts, items acceptable for deposit in these accounts (such as checks received from customers), credit card and debit card sales, and cash equivalents. **p. 185**

Cash equivalents: Short-term investments that have a maturity date no longer than three months from the date of purchase. **p. 185**

Checks outstanding: Checks the company has written that have not been subtracted from the bank's record of the company's balance. **p. 192**

Collusion: Two or more people acting in coordination to circumvent internal controls. **p. 184**

Deposits outstanding: Cash receipts of the company that have not been added to the bank's record of the company's balance. **p. 192**

Fraud triangle: The three elements present for every fraud—motivation, rationalization, and opportunity. **p. 178**

Internal controls: A company's plans to (1) safeguard the company's assets and (2) improve the accuracy and reliability of accounting information. **p. 178**

NSF check: A check received and deposited by a company that is later determined by the bank to have nonsufficient funds. Also known as a "bad" check from a customer. **p. 193**

Occupational fraud: The use of one's occupation for personal enrichment through the deliberate misuse or misapplication of the employer's resources. **p. 178**

Petty cash fund: Small amount of cash kept on hand to pay for minor purchases. **p. 196**

Purchase cards: Company-issued debit cards or credit cards that allow authorized employees to make purchases on behalf of the company. **p. 196**

Sarbanes-Oxley Act: Known as the *Public Company Accounting Reform and Investor Protection Act of 2002* and commonly referred to as *SOX;* the act established a variety of guidelines related to auditor–client relations and internal control procedures. **p. 179**

Separation of duties: Authorizing transactions, recording transactions, and controlling related assets should be separated among employees. **p. 182**

SELF-STUDY QUESTIONS

1. Fraudulent reporting by management could include **(LO4–1)**
   a. Fictitious revenues from a fake customer.
   b. Improper asset valuation.
   c. Mismatching revenues and expenses.
   d. All of the above.

2. The Sarbanes-Oxley Act (SOX) mandates which of the following? **(LO4–1)**
   a. Increased regulations related to auditor–client relations.
   b. Increased regulations related to internal control.
   c. Increased regulations related to corporate executive accountability.
   d. All of the above.

3. What is the concept behind *separation of duties* in establishing internal control? **(LO4–2)**
   a. Employee fraud is less likely to occur when access to assets and access to accounting records are separated.
   b. The company's financial accountant should not share information with the company's tax accountant.
   c. Duties of middle-level managers of the company should be clearly separated from those of top executives.
   d. The external auditors of the company should have no contact with managers while the audit is taking place.

4. Which of the following is an example of detective controls? **(LO4–2)**
   a. The company should establish formal guidelines to handle cash receipts and make purchases.
   b. Important documents should be kept in a safe place, and electronic files should be backed up regularly.
   c. Employees should be made aware of the company's internal control policies.
   d. Management periodically determines whether the amount of physical assets agree with the accounting records.

5. Which of the following is considered cash for financial reporting purposes? **(LO4–3)**
   a. Accounts receivable from customers who are expected to pay.
   b. Investments with maturity dates less than three months from the date of purchase.
   c. Credit cards used by the company to purchase office supplies.
   d. Accounts payable to local vendors used on a regular basis.

6. Which of the following generally would be considered good internal control of cash disbursements? **(LO4–4)**
   a. Make all cash disbursements using cash rather than debit cards or credit cards.
   b. Set maximum purchase limits on debit cards and credit cards.
   c. The employee responsible for making cash disbursements should be in charge of cash receipts.
   d. The employee who authorizes payments should also prepare the check.

7. Which of the following generally would *not* be considered good internal control of cash receipts? **(LO4–4)**
   a. Allowing customers to pay with a debit card.
   b. Requiring the employee receiving the cash from the customer to also deposit the cash into the company's bank account.
   c. Recording cash receipts as soon as they are received.
   d. Allowing customers to pay with a credit card.

8. Which of the following adjusts the bank's balance of cash in a bank reconciliation? **(LO4–5)**
   a. NSF checks from customers.
   b. Service fees.
   c. An error by the company.
   d. Checks outstanding.

9. Which of the following adjusts the company's balance of cash in a bank reconciliation? **(LO4–5)**
   a. Notes collected by the bank.
   b. Checks outstanding.
   c. Deposits outstanding.
   d. An error by the bank.

10. Employee purchases of supplies with a company-issued credit card is typically recorded with a credit to **(LO4–6)**
    a. Accounts Payable.
    b. Supplies.
    c. Cash.
    d. Supplies Expense.

11. The purpose of a petty cash fund is to **(LO4–6)**
    a. Provide a convenient form of payment for the company's customers.
    b. Pay employee salaries at the end of each period.
    c. Provide cash on hand for minor expenditures.
    d. Allow the company to save cash for major future purchases.

12. Operating cash flows would include which of the following? **(LO4–7)**
    a. Repayment of borrowed money.
    b. Payment for employee salaries.
    c. Services provided to customers on account.
    d. Payment for a new operating equipment.

13. Investing cash flows would include which of the following? **(LO4–7)**
    a. Payment for advertising.
    b. Payment of dividends to stockholders.
    c. Cash sales to customers.
    d. Payment for land.

14. At the end of the previous year, a company's balance sheet reports cash of $30,000. For the current year, the company's statement of cash flows reports operating cash inflows of $90,000; investing outflows of $110,000; and financing inflows of $40,000. What amount of cash will be reported in the current year's balance sheet? **(LO4–8)**
    a. $90,000.
    b. $20,000.
    c. $50,000.
    d. $120,000.

15. Which of the following could cause a company to have a high ratio of cash to noncash assets? **(LO4–8)**
    a. Highly volatile operations.
    b. Low dividend payments.
    c. Significant foreign operations.
    d. All of these factors could contribute to a high ratio of cash to noncash assets.

Note: For answers, see the last page of the chapter.

DATA ANALYTICS & EXCEL

Visit Connect to find a variety of Data Analytics questions that help build Excel, Tableau, and data visualization skills. Assignable materials include Integrated Excel, Applying Excel, Data Visualizations, Tableau Dashboard Activities, **and** Applying Tableau cases.

REVIEW QUESTIONS

■ **LO4–1**   1. Define occupational fraud. Describe two common means of occupational fraud.

■ **LO4–1**   2. What is internal control? Why should a company establish an internal control system?

■ **LO4–1**   3. "Managers are stewards of the company's assets." Discuss what this means.

■ **LO4–1**   4. Why are some managers motivated to manipulate amounts reported in the financial statements?

■ **LO4–1**   5. What is meant by the fraud triangle, and what can companies do to help prevent fraud?

■ **LO4–1**   6. What are some of the major provisions of the Sarbanes-Oxley Act?

■ **LO4–2**   7. Briefly describe the five components of internal control outlined by the Committee of Sponsoring Organizations (COSO).

■ **LO4–2**   8. Describe the difference between preventive controls and detective controls. What are examples of each?

■ **LO4–2**   9. What is meant by separation of duties?

■ **LO4–2**   10. Who has responsibility for internal control in an organization? According to guidelines set forth in Section 404 of the Sarbanes-Oxley Act, what role does the auditor play in internal control?

11. What are some limitations of internal control?   ■ **LO4–2**

12. To what does collusion refer?   ■ **LO4–2**

13. Is fraud more likely to occur when it is being committed by top-level employees? Explain.   ■ **LO4–2**

14. Define cash and cash equivalents.   ■ **LO4–3**

15. Describe how the purchase of items with a check is recorded.   ■ **LO4–3**

16. Discuss basic controls for cash receipts.   ■ **LO4–4**

17. What is a credit card? How are credit card sales reported?   ■ **LO4–4**

18. What is a debit card? How are debit card sales reported?   ■ **LO4–4**

19. Discuss basic controls for cash disbursements.   ■ **LO4–4**

20. How are credit card purchases reported?   ■ **LO4–4**

21. What is a bank reconciliation? How can it help in determining whether proper control of cash has been maintained?   ■ **LO4–5**

22. What are two primary reasons that the company's balance of cash will differ between its own records and those of the bank?   ■ **LO4–5**

23. Give some examples of timing differences in cash transactions that firms need to account for in a bank reconciliation.   ■ **LO4–5**

24. After preparing a bank reconciliation, what adjustments does the company need to make to its records?   ■ **LO4–5**

25. What are purchase cards and a petty cash fund?   ■ **LO4–6**

26. Describe how management maintains control over employee purchases with credit cards and the petty cash fund.   ■ **LO4–6**

27. The change in cash for the year can be calculated by comparing the balance of cash reported in this year's and last year's balance sheet. Why is the statement of cash flows needed?   ■ **LO4–7**

28. Describe the operating, investing, and financing sections of the statement of cash flows.   ■ **LO4–7**

29. Why is an analysis of the company's cash balance important?   ■ **LO4–8**

30. We compared **Live Nation Entertainment** and **AMC Networks** at the end of this chapter. What reasons were given for the differences of amounts held in their Cash accounts?   ■ **LO4–8**

BRIEF EXERCISES

BE4–1 Match each of the following provisions of the Sarbanes-Oxley Act (SOX) with its description.

Identify terms associated with the Sarbanes-Oxley Act **(LO4–1)**

Major Provisions of the Sarbanes-Oxley Act

_____ 1. Oversight board
_____ 2. Corporate executive accountability
_____ 3. Auditor rotation
_____ 4. Nonaudit services
_____ 5. Internal control

Descriptions

a. Executives must personally certify the company's financial statements.

b. Audit firm cannot provide a variety of other services to its client, such as investment advising.

c. PCAOB establishes standards related to the preparation of audited financial reports.

d. Lead audit partners are required to change every five years.

e. Management must document the effectiveness of procedures that could affect financial reporting.

Identify terms associated with components of internal control (LO4–2)

BE4–2 Match each of the following components of internal control with its description.

Components of Internal Control	Descriptions
_____ 1. Control environment	a. Procedures for maintaining separation of duties.
_____ 2. Risk assessment	b. Routine activities that are meant to continually observe internal control activities.
_____ 3. Control activities	c. Transfer of data from lower managers to top executives for accurate financial reporting.
_____ 4. Information and communication	d. Formal policies to evaluate internal and external threats to achieving company objectives.
_____ 5. Monitoring	e. Overall attitude of the company with respect to internal controls.

Define control activities associated with internal control (LO4–2)

BE4–3 Match each of the following control activities with its definition.

Control Activities	Definitions
_____ 1. Separation of duties	a. The company should maintain security over assets and accounting records.
_____ 2. Physical controls	b. Management should periodically determine whether the amounts of physical assets of the company match the accounting records.
_____ 3. Proper authorization	c. The company should provide employees with appropriate guidance to ensure they have the knowledge necessary to carry out their job duties.
_____ 4. Employee management	d. The actual performance of individuals or processes should be checked against their expected performance.
_____ 5. Reconciliations	e. Authorizing transactions, recording transactions, and maintaining control of the related assets should be separated among employees.
_____ 6. Performance reviews	f. To prevent improper use of the company's resources, only certain employees are allowed to carry out certain business activities.

Identify cash and cash equivalents (LO4–3)

BE4–4 Determine whether the firm reports each of the following items as part of cash and cash equivalents in the balance sheet.

Item	Cash or Cash Equivalent? (yes/no)
1. Currency	_____
2. Inventory for sale to customers	_____
3. Balance in savings account	_____
4. Checks	_____
5. Accounts receivable	_____
6. Investments purchased with maturities of less than three months	_____

Determine cash sales (LO4–4)

BE4–5 During the year, the following sales transactions occur. There is a charge of 3% on all credit card transactions and a 1% charge on all debit card transactions. Calculate the amount recorded as cash receipts from these transactions.

1. Total cash sales = $500,000
2. Total check sales = $350,000
3. Total credit card sales = $600,000
4. Total debit card sales = $200,000

Record cash expenditures (LO4–4)

BE4–6 Record the following transactions.

1. Pay employee salaries of $600 by issuing checks.

2. Purchase computer equipment of $1,000 using a credit card.
3. Pay for maintenance of $400 for a company vehicle using a debit card.

BE4–7 Match each term associated with a bank reconciliation with its description.

Identify terms associated with a bank reconciliation **(LO4–5)**

Terms	Descriptions
_____ 1. Checks outstanding	a. Cash receipts received by the company but not yet recorded by the bank.
_____ 2. NSF checks from customers	b. Fees imposed by the bank to the company for providing routine services.
_____ 3. Company error	c. Checks written to the company that are returned by the bank as not having adequate funds.
_____ 4. Note collected	d. Checks written by the company but not yet recorded by the bank.
_____ 5. Deposits outstanding	e. Amount collected by the bank on behalf of the company in a lending arrangement.
_____ 6. Bank service fees	f. The company recorded a deposit twice.

BE4–8 Indicate whether the firm should add or subtract each item below from its balance of cash or the bank's balance of cash in preparing a bank reconciliation. The first answer is provided as an example. If an item is not a reconciling item, state "No entry."

Prepare a bank reconciliation **(LO4–5)**

Reconciliation Items	Bank Balance	Company Balance
1. Checks outstanding	Subtract	No entry
2. NSF checks from customers	_____	_____
3. Deposit recorded twice by company	_____	_____
4. EFT to pay rent not recorded by the company.	_____	_____
5. Deposits outstanding	_____	_____
6. Bank service fees	_____	_____

BE4–9 Damon Company receives its monthly bank statement, which reports a balance of $2,000. After comparing this to the company's cash records, Damon's accountants determine that deposits outstanding total $4,200 and checks outstanding total $4,450.

Reconcile timing differences in the bank's balance **(LO4–5)**

Required:
Calculate the reconciled bank balance for cash.

BE4–10 Bourne Incorporated reports a cash balance at the end of the month of $2,620. A comparison of the company's cash records with the monthly bank statement reveals several additional cash transactions: bank service fees ($85), an NSF check from a customer ($350), a debit card used for the purchase of supplies ($100), and a customer's note receivable collected by the bank ($1,000) plus interest earned ($35).

Reconcile timing differences in the company's balance **(LO4–5)**

Required:
Calculate the reconciled company balance for cash.

BE4–11 Refer to the information in BE4–10.

Record adjustments to the company's cash balance **(LO4–5)**

Required:
Record the necessary entries to adjust the balance of cash.

BE4–12 Brangelina Adoption Agency's general ledger shows a cash balance of $11,663. The balance of cash in the March-end bank statement is $7,345. A review of the bank statement reveals the following additional information: deposits outstanding of $2,803, bank service fees of $85, and unrecorded electronic funds transfer for utilities of $1,430. Calculate the correct balance of cash at the end of March.

Prepare a bank reconciliation **(LO4–5)**

Record employee purchases (LO4–6)

BE4–13 Clooney Corp. establishes a petty cash fund for $225 and issues a credit card to its office manager. By the end of the month, employees made one expenditure from the petty cash fund (entertainment, $25) and three expenditures with the credit card (postage, $60; delivery, $85; supplies expense, $50). Separately record employee credit card expenditures and employee petty cash expenditures. The credit card balance will be paid later.

Match types of cash flows with their definitions (LO4–7)

BE4–14 Match each type of cash flow to its definition.

Types of Cash Flows	Definitions
_____ 1. Operating cash flows	a. Cash flows related to long-term assets and investment securities.
_____ 2. Investing cash flows	b. Cash flows related to long-term liabilities and stockholders' equity.
_____ 3. Financing cash flows	c. Cash flows related to revenues and expenses.

Determine operating cash flows (LO4–7)

BE4–15 Eastwood Enterprises offers horseback riding lessons. During the month of June, the company provides lessons on account totaling $5,100. By the end of the month, the company received on account $4,500 of this amount. In addition, Eastwood received $500 on account from customers who were provided lessons in May. Determine the amount of operating cash flows Eastwood will report as received from customers in June.

Determine investing cash flows (LO4–7)

BE4–16 On January 12, Ferrell Incorporated obtains a permit to start a comedy club, which will operate only on Saturday nights. To prepare the club for the grand opening, Ferrell purchases tables and chairs for $13,000 cash on January 16. Ferrell also purchases cleaning supplies on account for an additional $3,000. Determine the amount of investing cash flows Ferrell would report in January.

Determine financing cash flows (LO4–7)

BE4–17 Smith Law Firm specializes in the preparation of wills for estate planning. On October 1, 2024, the company begins operations by issuing stock for $11,000 and obtaining a loan from a local bank for $35,000. By the end of 2024, the company provides will preparation services of $42,000 cash and pays employee salaries of $33,000. In addition, Smith pays $3,000 in cash dividends to stockholders on December 31, 2024. Determine the amount of financing cash flows Smith would report in 2024.

Calculate the ratio of cash to noncash assets (LO4–8)

BE4–18 For each company, calculate the ratio of cash to noncash assets.

	Cash	Total Assets	Total Liabilities
Tuohy Incorporated	$4,200	$23,400	$3,600
Oher Corporation	$3,500	$25,700	$6,200

EXERCISES

Answer true-or-false questions about occupational fraud (LO4–1)

E4–1 Below are several statements about occupational fraud.
1. For most large companies, occupational fraud is minimal and internal control procedures are unnecessary.
2. Managers have a variety of reasons for manipulating the numbers in financial statements, such as maximizing their compensation, increasing the company's stock price, and preserving their jobs.
3. Internal control procedures include formal policies and procedures related to (a) safeguarding the company's assets and (b) improving the accuracy and reliability of accounting information.
4. "Cooking the books" is a phrase used by accountants to indicate the preparation of financial statements that are free of manipulation.
5. Most occupational fraud cases involve misuse of the company's resources.
6. Common types of financial statement fraud include creating fictitious revenues from a fake customer, improperly valuing assets, hiding liabilities, and mismatching revenues and expenses.

Required:

State whether the answer to each of the statements is true or false.

E4–2 Below are several statements about the Sarbanes-Oxley Act (SOX).

1. SOX represents legislation passed in response to several accounting scandals in the early 2000s.
2. The requirements outlined in SOX apply only to those companies expected to have weak internal controls or to have manipulated financial statements in the past.
3. Section 404 of SOX requires both company management and auditors to document and assess the effectiveness of a company's internal control processes that could affect financial reporting.
4. Severe financial penalties and the possibility of imprisonment are consequences of fraudulent misstatement.
5. With the establishment of SOX, management now has primary responsibility for hiring an external audit firm.
6. The lead auditor in charge of auditing a particular company must rotate off that company only when occupational fraud is suspected.

Answer true-or-false questions about the Sarbanes-Oxley Act (LO4–1)

Required:

State whether the answer to each of the statements is true or false.

E4–3 Below are several statements about internal controls.

1. The components of internal control are built on the foundation of the ethical tone set by top management.
2. Once every three months, managers need to review operations to ensure that control procedures work effectively.
3. Collusion refers to the act of a single individual circumventing internal control procedures.
4. Detective control procedures are designed to detect errors or fraud that have already occurred, while preventive control procedures are designed to keep errors or fraud from occurring in the first place.
5. Fraud committed by top-level employees is more difficult to detect because those employees more often have the ability to override internal control features.
6. A good example of separation of duties would be having one person collect cash from customers and account for it, while having another person order inventory and maintain control over it.
7. Employee tips historically have been the most common means of detecting employee fraud.
8. Detective controls include reconciling the physical assets of the company with the accounting records and comparing actual performance of individuals or processes against their expected performance.
9. Effective internal controls and ethical employees ensure a company's success.

Answer true-or-false questions about internal controls (LO4–2)

Required:

State whether the answer to each of the statements is true or false.

E4–4 Below are several scenarios related to control activities of a company.

1. A manufacturing company compares total sales in the current year to those in the previous year but does not compare the cost of production.
2. So that employees can have easy access to office supplies, a company keeps supplies in unlocked cabinets in multiple locations.
3. At the end of each day, a single employee collects all cash received from customers, records the total, and makes the deposit at the bank.
4. At the end of the year only, the company compares its cash records to the bank's records of cash deposited and withdrawn during the year.
5. A company encourages employees to call an anonymous hotline if they believe other employees are circumventing internal control features.
6. All employees have the authority to refund a customer's money.

Determine control activity violations (LO4–2)

Required:

For each scenario, determine which control activity is violated. Control activities include separation of duties, physical controls, proper authorization, employee management, reconciliations, and performance reviews. If no control activity is violated, state "none."

Calculate the amount of cash to report (LO4–3)

E4–5 Below are several amounts reported at the end of the year.

Currency located at the company	$1,050
Supplies	3,200
Short-term investments that mature within three months	1,950
Accounts receivable	3,500
Balance in savings account	8,500
Checks received from customers but not yet deposited	650
Prepaid rent	1,450
Coins located at the company	110
Equipment	9,400
Balance in checking account	6,200

Required:

Calculate the amount of cash to report in the balance sheet.

Discuss internal control procedures related to cash receipts (LO4–4)

E4–6 Douglas and Son, Inc., uses the following process for its cash receipts: The company typically receives cash and check sales each day and places them in a single drawer. Each Friday, the cash clerk records the amount of cash received and deposits the money in the bank account. Each quarter, the controller requests information from the bank necessary to prepare a bank reconciliation.

Required:

Discuss Douglas and Son's internal control procedures related to cash receipts, noting both weaknesses and strengths.

Discuss internal control procedures related to cash disbursements (LO4–4)

E4–7 Goldie and Kate operate a small clothing store that has annual revenues of about $100,000. The company has established the following procedures related to cash disbursements: The petty cash fund consists of $10,000. Employees place a receipt in the fund when making expenditures from it and obtain the necessary cash. For any expenditure not made with the petty cash fund, the employee writes a check. Employees are not required to obtain permission to write a check but are asked to use good judgment. Any check written for more than $5,000 can be signed only by Goldie or Kate.

Required:

Discuss Goldie and Kate's internal control procedures related to cash disbursements, noting both weaknesses and strengths.

Discuss internal control procedures related to cash receipts (LO4–4)

E4–8 Janice Dodds opens the mail for Ajax Plumbing Company. She lists all customer checks on a spreadsheet that includes the name of the customer and the check amount. The checks, along with the spreadsheet, are then sent to Jim Seymour in the accounting department, who records the checks and deposits them daily in the company's checking account.

Required:

Describe how the company could improve its internal control procedure for the handling of its cash receipts.

Calculate the balance of cash using a bank reconciliation (LO4–5)

E4–9 Spielberg Company's general ledger shows a cash account balance of $23,220 on July 31, 2024. Cash sales of $1,885 for the last three days of the month have not yet been deposited. The bank statement dated July 31 shows bank service fees of $55 and an NSF check from a customer of $250. The bank processes all checks written by the company by July 31 and lists them on the bank statement, except for one check totaling $1,460. The bank statement shows a balance of $22,490 on July 31.

Required:
1. Prepare a bank reconciliation to calculate the correct balance of cash on July 31, 2024.
2. Record the necessary entry(ies) to adjust the balance for cash.

E4–10 On August 31, 2024, the general ledger of the Dean Acting Academy shows a balance for cash of $7,944. Cash receipts yet to be deposited into the checking account total $3,338. The company's balance of cash does not reflect a debit card payment for the purchase of postage expense ($75) or an electronic funds transfer for rent expense ($1,500). The bank statement also revealed the company recorded a debit card transaction for supplies of $400, but the actual amount was $500. These amounts are included in the balance of cash of $2,931 reported by the bank as of the end of August.

Calculate the balance of cash using a bank reconciliation (LO4–5)

Required:
1. Prepare a bank reconciliation to calculate the correct ending balance of cash on August 31, 2024.
2. Record the necessary entry(ies) to adjust the balance for cash.

E4–11 On October 31, 2024, Damon Company's general ledger shows a cash account balance of $8,397. The company's cash receipts for the month total $74,320, of which $71,295 has been deposited in the bank. In addition, the company has written checks for $3,467, of which $1,982 has been processed by the bank.

Calculate the balance of cash using a bank reconciliation (LO4–5)

   The bank statement reveals an ending balance of $11,727 and includes the following items not yet recorded by Damon: bank service fees of $150, note receivable collected by the bank of $5,000, and interest earned on the note of $320. After closer inspection, Damon realizes that the bank incorrectly charged the company's account $300 for an automatic withdrawal that should have been charged to another customer's account. The bank agrees to the error.

Required:
1. Prepare a bank reconciliation to calculate the correct ending balance of cash on October 31, 2024.
2. Record the necessary entries to adjust the balance for cash.

E4–12 Halle's Berry Farm establishes a $200 petty cash fund on September 4 to pay for minor cash expenditures. The fund is replenished at the end of each month. At the end of September, the fund contains $30 in cash. The company has also issued a credit card and authorized its office manager to make purchases. Expenditures for the month include the following items:

Record transactions for employee purchases (LO4–6)

Entertainment for office party (petty cash)	$170
Repairs and maintenance (credit card)	420
Postage (credit card)	575
Delivery cost (credit card)	285

Required:
1. Record the establishment of the petty cash fund on September 4.
2. Record credit card expenditures during the month. The credit card balance is not yet paid.
3. Record petty cash expenditures during the month.

E4–13 T. L. Jones Trucking Services establishes a petty cash fund on April 3 for $200. By the end of April, the fund has a cash balance of $97. The company has also issued a credit card and authorized its office manager to make purchases. Expenditures for the month include the following items:

Record transactions for employee purchases (LO4–6)

Utilities (credit card)	$435
Entertainment (petty cash)	44
Postage (petty cash)	59
Repairs and maintenance (credit card)	630

Required:
1. Record the establishment of the petty cash fund on April 3.
2. Record credit card expenditures during the month. The credit card balance is paid in full on April 30.
3. Record petty cash expenditures during the month.

Classify cash flows (LO4–7)

E4–14 Below are several transactions for Witherspoon Incorporated, a small manufacturer of decorative glass designs.

Transaction	Cash Involved? (yes or no)	Operating, Investing, or Financing? (if cash involved)	Inflow or Outflow?
a. Borrow cash from the bank.			
b. Purchase supplies on account.			
c. Purchase equipment with cash.			
d. Provide services on account.			
e. Pay cash on account for *b.* above.			
f. Sell for cash a warehouse no longer in use.			
g. Receive cash on account for *d.* above.			
h. Pay cash to workers for salaries.			

Required:
For each transaction, indicate (1) whether cash is involved (yes or no), and, if cash is involved, (2) whether Witherspoon should classify it as operating, investing, or financing in a statement of cash flows, and (3) whether the cash is an inflow or outflow. Enter N/A if the question is not applicable to the statement.

Calculate net cash flows (LO4–7)

E4–15 Below are several transactions for Meyers Corporation for 2024.

Transaction	Cash Flows	Operating, Investing, or Financing?
a. Issue common stock for cash, $60,000.		
b. Purchase building and land with cash, $45,000.		
c. Provide services to customers on account, $8,000.		
d. Pay utilities on building, $1,500.		
e. Collect $6,000 on account from customers.		
f. Pay employee salaries, $10,000.		
g. Pay dividends to stockholders, $5,000.		
Net cash flows for the year		

Required:
1. For each transaction, determine the amount of cash flows (indicate inflows with a "+" and outflows with a "−"). If cash is involved in the transaction, indicate whether Meyers should classify it as operating, investing, or financing in a statement of cash flows. Enter N/A if the question is not applicable to the statement.
2. Calculate net cash flows for the year.
3. Assuming the balance of cash on January 1, 2024, equals $5,400, calculate the balance of cash on December 31, 2024.

Calculate operating cash flows (LO4–7)

E4–16 Following are cash transactions for Goldman Incorporated, which provides consulting services related to mining of precious metals.

a. Cash used for purchase of office supplies, $2,400.
b. Cash provided from consulting to customers, $50,600.
c. Cash used for purchase of mining equipment, $83,000.
d. Cash provided from long-term borrowing, $70,000.
e. Cash used for payment of employee salaries, $25,000.
f. Cash used for payment of office rent, $13,000.
g. Cash provided from sale of equipment purchased in c. above, $23,500.
h. Cash used to repay a portion of the long-term borrowing in d. above, $45,000.
i. Cash used to pay office utilities, $5,300.
j. Purchase of company vehicle, paying $11,000 cash.

Required:
Calculate cash flows from operating activities.

E4–17 Refer to the information in E4–16.

Calculate investing cash flows **(LO4–7)**

Required:
Calculate cash flows from investing activities.

E4–18 Refer to the information in E4–16.

Calculate financing cash flows **(LO4–7)**

Required:
Calculate cash flows from financing activities.

E4–19 Consider the following information:
1. Service Revenue for the year = $80,000. Of this amount, $70,000 is collected during the year and $10,000 is expected to be collected next year.
2. Salaries Expense for the year = $40,000. Of this amount, $35,000 is paid during the year and $5,000 is expected to be paid next year.
3. Advertising Expense for the year = $10,000. All of this amount is paid during the year.
4. Supplies Expense for the year = $4,000. No supplies were purchased during the year.
5. Utilities Expense for the year = $12,000. Of this amount, $11,000 is paid during the year and $1,000 is expected to be paid next year.
6. Cash collected in advance from customers for services to be provided next year (Unearned Revenue) = $2,000.

Compare operating cash flows to net income **(LO4–7)**

Required:
1. Calculate operating cash flows.
2. Calculate net income.
3. Explain why these two amounts differ.

E4–20 Below are amounts (in millions) for Glasco Company and Sullivan Company.

Analyze the ratio of cash to noncash assets **(LO4–8)**

	GLASCO COMPANY		SULLIVAN COMPANY	
Year	Operating Cash Flows	Foreign Revenues	Operating Cash Flows	Foreign Revenues
1	$450	$700	$280	$0
2	$130	$750	$300	$0
3	$320	$800	$320	$0

Both companies have total revenues of $2,500, $3,000, and $3,500 in each year.

Required:
Make a prediction as to which firm will have the higher ratio of cash to noncash assets at the end of year 3.

PROBLEMS: SET A

McGraw Hill connect

Discuss control
procedures for cash
receipts (LO4–4)

P4–1A The Carmike 8 Cinema is a modern theatre located close to a college campus. The cashier, located in a box office at the theatre entrance, receives cash from customers and operates a machine that ejects serially numbered tickets for each film. Customers then enter the theatre lobby where they can purchase refreshments at the concession stand. To gain admission to the movie, a customer hands the ticket to a ticket taker stationed some 50 feet from the box office at the theatre lobby entrance. The ticket taker tears the ticket in half, returns the stub to the customer, and allows the customer to enter the theatre hallway through a turnstile, which has an automatic counter of people entering. The ticket taker drops the other half of the ticket stub into a locked box.

Required:

1. What internal controls are present in the handling of cash receipts?
2. What steps should the theatre manager take regularly to give maximum effectiveness to these controls?
3. Assume the cashier and the ticket taker decide to work together in an effort to steal from the movie theatre. What action(s) might they take?
4. For each idea proposed in number 3 above, what additional control features could Carmike 8 Cinema add to catch the thieves and reduce the risk of future thefts?

Prepare the bank
reconciliation and record
cash adjustments (LO4–5)

P4–2A Oscar's Red Carpet Store maintains a checking account with Academy Bank. Oscar's sells carpet each day but makes bank deposits only once per week. The following provides information from the company's cash ledger for the month ending February 28, 2024.

	Date	Amount		NO.	Date	Amount
Deposits:	2/4	$ 2,700	Checks:	323	2/12	$ 2,500
	2/11	2,300		324	2/19	2,200
	2/18	3,200		325	2/27	200
	2/25	4,100		326	2/28	700
Cash receipts:	2/26–2/28	1,600		327	2/28	1,900
		$ 13,900				$ 7,500

Balance on February 1	$ 6,800
Receipts	13,900
Disbursements	(7,500)
Balance on February 28	$ 13,200

Information from February's bank statement and company records reveals the following additional information:

a. The ending cash balance recorded in the bank statement is $13,145.
b. Cash receipts of $1,600 from 2/26–2/28 are outstanding.
c. Checks 325 and 327 are outstanding.
d. The deposit on 2/11 includes a customer's check for $200 that did not clear the bank (NSF check).
e. Check 323 was written for $2,800 for advertising in February. The bank properly recorded the check for this amount.
f. An EFT withdrawal for Oscar's February rent was made on February 4 for $1,100.
g. Debit card transactions include $4,700 for legal fees expense and $400 for entertainment expense.
h. In January, one of Oscar's suppliers, Titanic Fabrics, borrowed $6,000 from Oscar. On February 24, Titanic paid $6,270 ($6,000 borrowed amount plus $270 interest) directly to Academy Bank in payment for January's borrowing.
i. Academy Bank charged service fees of $125 to Oscar's for the month.

Required:

1. Prepare a bank reconciliation for Oscar's checking account on February 28, 2024.
2. Record the necessary cash adjustments.

P4–3A The cash records and bank statement for the month of May for Diaz Entertainment are shown below.

Prepare the bank reconciliation and record cash adjustments **(LO4–5)**

DIAZ ENTERTAINMENT
Cash Account Records
May 1, 2024, to May 31, 2024

Cash Balance May 1, 2024		Cash Receipts		Cash Disbursements		Cash Balance May 31, 2024
$5,280	+	$12,040	−	$12,220	=	$5,100

	Cash Receipts			Cash Disbursements		
Date	Desc.	Amount	Date	Desc.	Memo	Amount
5/3	Sales	$ 1,460	5/7	DC	Legal fees	$ 1,300
5/10	Sales	1,890	5/12	DC	Property tax	1,670
5/17	Sales	2,520	5/15	DC	Salaries	3,600
5/24	Sales	2,990	5/22	DC	Advertising	1,500
5/31	Sales	3,180	5/30	CHK #471	Supplies	550
			5/31	CHK #472	Salaries	3,600
		$12,040				$12,220

P.O. Box 162647
Bowlegs, OK 74830
(405) 369-CASH

Midwest Bank
Looking Out For You

Member FDIC

Account Holder:	Diaz Entertainment 124 Saddle Blvd. Bowlegs, OK 74830	Account Number:	7772854360
		Statement Date:	May 31, 2024

Account Summary

Beginning Balance May 1, 2024	Deposits and Credits		Withdrawals and Debits		Ending Balance May 31, 2024
	No.	Total	No.	Total	
$6,260	7	$10,050	9	$10,100	$6,210

Account Details

Deposits and Credits			Withdrawals and Debits				Daily Balance	
Date	Amount	Desc.	Date	No.	Amount	Desc.	Date	Amount
5/4	$ 1,460	DEP	5/1	469	$ 550	CHK	5/1	$5,710
5/11	1,890	DEP	5/2	470	430	CHK	5/2	5,280
5/18	2,520	DEP	5/7		1,300	DC	5/4	6,740
5/20	1,100	NOTE	5/11		400	NSF	5/9	5,440
5/20	60	INT	5/12		1,670	DC	5/11	6,930
5/25	2,990	DEP	5/15		3,600	DC	5/12	5,260
5/31	30	INT	5/20		600	EFT	5/18	4,180
			5/22		1,500	DC	5/20	4,740
			5/31		50	SF	5/25	6,230
	$10,050				$10,100		5/31	$6,210

Desc.	**DEP** Customer deposit	**INT** Interest earned	**SF** Service fees
	NOTE Note collected	**CHK** Customer check	**NSF** Nonsufficient funds
	EFT Electronic funds transfer	**DC** Debit card	

Additional information:

a. The difference in the beginning balances in the company's records and the bank statement relates to checks #469 and #470, which are outstanding as of April 30, 2024 (prior month).

b. The bank made the EFT on May 20 in error. The bank accidentally charged Diaz for payment that should have been made on another account.

Required:

1. Prepare a bank reconciliation for Diaz's checking account on May 31, 2024.
2. Record the necessary cash adjustments.

Prepare the statement of cash flows (LO4–7)

P4–4A Below is a summary of all transactions of Pixar Toy Manufacturing for the month of August 2024.

Cash Transactions	
Cash collections from:	
Customers	$ 93,500
Sale of unused warehouse	36,000
Bank borrowing	26,000
Cash payments for:	
Employee salaries	(65,300)
Office rent	(19,000)
Manufacturing equipment	(46,000)
Office utilities	(11,800)
Dividends to stockholders	(6,700)
Materials to make toys	(27,700)
Noncash Transactions	
Sales to customers on account	16,400
Purchase of materials on account	13,900
Purchase equipment with promissory note to pay later	18,500

Required:

Prepare a statement of cash flows for the month of August 2024, properly classifying each of the transactions into operating, investing, and financing activities. The cash balance at the beginning of August is $25,500.

Record transactions, post to the Cash T-account, and prepare the statement of cash flows (LO4–7)

P4–5A Rocky owns and operates Balboa's Gym located in Philadelphia. The following transactions occur for the month of October:

1.	October 2	Receive membership dues for the month of October totaling $8,500.
2.	October 5	Issue common stock in exchange for cash, $12,000.
3.	October 9	Purchase additional boxing equipment for $9,600, paying one-half of the amount in cash and issuing a note payable to the seller for the other one-half due by the end of the year.
4.	October 12	Pay $1,500 for advertising regarding a special membership rate available during the month of October.
5.	October 19	Pay dividends to stockholders, $4,400.
6.	October 22	Pay liability insurance to cover accidents to members for the next six months, starting November 1, $6,900.
7.	October 25	Receive cash in advance for November memberships, $5,600.
8.	October 30	Receive, but do not pay, utilities bill for the month, $5,200.
9.	October 31	Pay employees' salaries for the month, $7,300.

Required:

1. Record each transaction.
2. Identify the transactions involving cash.

3. Assuming the balance of cash at the beginning of October is $16,600, post each cash transaction to the Cash T-account and compute the ending cash balance.
4. Prepare a statement of cash flows for the month of October, properly classifying each of the cash transactions into operating, investing, and financing activities.
5. Verify that the net cash flows reported in the statement of cash flows equal the change in the cash balance for the month.

PROBLEMS: SET B

P4–1B At the end of February, Howard Productions' accounting records reveal a balance for cash equal to $19,225. However, the balance of cash in the bank at the end of February is only $735. Howard is concerned and asks the company's accountant to reconcile the two balances. Examination of the bank statement and company records at the end of February reveals the following information:

| NSF checks from customers | $5,278 | Service fees | $159 |
| Deposits outstanding | 7,692 | Checks outstanding | 489 |

Prepare a bank reconciliation and discuss cash procedures (LO4–4, 4–5)

In addition, during February the company's accountant wrote a check to one of its suppliers for $150. The check was recorded correctly in the company's records for $150 but processed incorrectly by the bank for $1,500. Howard has contacted the bank, which has agreed to fix the error. Finally, a petty cash fund of $4,500 was established during February. This amount was withdrawn from the checking account but not recorded.

Required:
1. Calculate the correct ending balance of cash at the end of February.
2. Discuss any problems you see with the company's cash procedures.

P4–2B On October 31, 2024, the bank statement for the cash account of Blockwood Video shows a balance of $12,751, while the company's records show a cash balance of $12,381. Information that might be useful in preparing a bank reconciliation is as follows:

Prepare the bank reconciliation and record cash adjustments (LO4–5)

a. Outstanding checks are $1,280.
b. The October 31 cash receipts of $835 are not deposited in the bank until November 2.
c. The EFT payment for utilities of $147 is correctly recorded by the bank but is recorded by Blockwood as a disbursement of $174.
d. In accordance with prior authorization, the bank withdraws $560 directly from the account as payment on a note payable. The interest portion of that payment is $60 and the principal portion is $500. Blockwood has not recorded the direct withdrawal.
e. Bank service fees of $34 are listed on the bank statement.
f. A deposit of $577 is recorded by the bank on October 13, but it did not belong to Blockwood. The deposit should have been made to the account of Hollybuster Video, a separate company.
g. The bank statement includes a charge of $85 for an NSF check from a customer. The check is returned with the bank statement, and the company will seek payment from the customer.

Required:
1. Prepare a bank reconciliation for the Blockwood checking account on October 31, 2024.
2. Record the necessary cash adjustments.

P4–3B The cash records and bank statement for the month of July for Glover Incorporated are shown next.

Prepare the bank reconciliation and record cash adjustments (LO4–5)

GLOVER INCORPORATED
Cash Account Records
July 1, 2024, to July 31, 2024

Cash Balance July 1, 2024		Cash Receipts		Cash Disbursements		Cash Balance July 31, 2024
$7,510	+	$8,720	−	$10,560	=	$5,670

Cash Receipts			Cash Disbursements			
Date	Desc.	Amount	Date	Desc.	Memo	Amount
7/9	Sales	$2,660	7/7	EFT	Rent	$ 1,600
7/21	Sales	3,240	7/12	EFT	Salaries	2,060
7/31	Sales	2,820	7/19	DC	Equipment	4,500
			7/22	CHK #531	Utilities	1,000
			7/30	CHK #532	Advertising	1,400
		$8,720				$10,560

P.O. Box 123878
Gotebo, OK 73041
(580) 377-OKIE

Fidelity Union
You Can Bank On Us

Member FDIC

Account Holder:	Glover Incorporated 519 Main Street Gotebo, OK 73041	Account Number:	2252790471
		Statement Date:	July 31, 2024

Beginning Balance July 1, 2024	Deposits and Credits		Withdrawals and Debits		Ending Balance July 31, 2024
	No.	Total	No.	Total	
$8,200	3	$5,960	7	$10,410	$3,750

Deposits and Credits			Withdrawals and Debits				Daily Balance	
Date	Amount	Desc.	Date	No.	Amount	Desc.	Date	Amount
7/10	$2,660	DEP	7/2	530	$ 690	CHK	7/2	$7,510
7/22	3,240	DEP	7/7		1,600	EFT	7/10	8,570
7/31	60	INT	7/12		2,060	EFT	7/14	6,510
			7/18		500	NSF	7/18	6,010
			7/19		4,900	DC	7/22	4,350
			7/26		600	EFT	7/26	3,750
			7/30		60	SF	7/30	3,690
	$5,960				$10,410		7/31	$3,750

Desc.
DEP Customer deposit **INT** Interest earned **SF** Service fees
NOTE Note collected **CHK** Customer check **NSF** Nonsufficient funds
EFT Electronic funds transfer **DC** Debit card

Additional information:

a. The difference in the beginning balances in the company's records and the bank statement relates to check #530, which is outstanding as of June 30, 2024.

b. The debit card transaction for the purchase of equipment on 7/19 is correctly processed by the bank.

c. The EFT on July 26 in the bank statement relates to the purchase of office supplies.

Required:

1. Prepare a bank reconciliation for Glover's checking account on July 31, 2024.
2. Record the necessary cash adjustments.

Prepare the statement of cash flows (LO4–7)

P4–4B Following is a summary of all transactions of Dreamworks Bedding Supplies for the month of August 2024.

Cash Transactions

Cash collections from:

Customers	$ 80,400
Sale of unused land	15,700
Issuance of common stock	30,000
Interest earned on savings account	300

Cash payments for:

Employee salaries	(47,100)
Delivery truck	(34,500)
Advertising expense	(5,900)
Office supplies	(3,800)
Repayment of borrowing	(9,000)
Bedding material	(13,000)

Noncash Transactions

Sales to customers on account	12,300
Purchase of materials on account	8,400
Purchase equipment with promissory note to pay later	92,000

Required:

Prepare a statement of cash flows for the month of August, properly classifying each of the transactions into operating, investing, and financing activities. The cash balance at the beginning of August is $8,300.

P4–5B Peter loves dogs and cats. For the past several years, he has owned and operated Homeward Bound, which temporarily houses pets while their owners go on vacation. For the month of June, the company has the following transactions:

Record transactions, post to the Cash T-account, and prepare the statement of cash flows (LO4–7)

1.	June 2	Obtain cash by borrowing $19,000 from the bank by signing a note.
2.	June 3	Pay rent for the current month, $1,200.
3.	June 7	Provide services to customers, $5,200 for cash and $3,500 on account.
4.	June 11	Purchase cages and equipment necessary to maintain the animals, $8,400 cash.
5.	June 17	Pay employees' salaries for the first half of the month, $6,500.
6.	June 22	Pay dividends to stockholders, $1,550.
7.	June 25	Receive cash in advance from a customer who wants to house his two dogs (Chance and Shadow) and cat (Sassy) while he goes on vacation the month of July, $2,100.
8.	June 28	Pay utilities for the month, $3,300.
9.	June 30	Record salaries earned by employees for the second half of the month, $6,500. Payment will be made on July 2.

Required:

1. Record each transaction.
2. Identify the transactions involving cash.
3. Assuming the balance of cash at the beginning of June is $14,700, post each cash transaction to the Cash T-account and compute the ending cash balance.
4. Prepare a statement of cash flows for the month of June, properly classifying each of the cash transactions into operating, investing, and financing activities.
5. Verify that the net cash flows reported in the statement of cash flows equal the change in the cash balance for the month.

Data Analytics & Excel

Visit Connect to find a variety of Data Analytics questions that help build Excel, Tableau, and data visualization skills. Assignable materials include **Integrated Excel**, **Applying Excel**, **Data Visualizations**, **Tableau Dashboard Activities**, and **Applying Tableau cases**.

General Ledger Continuing Case

Great Adventures

(This is a continuation of the Great Adventures problem from earlier chapters.)

RWP–1 An examination of the cash activities during the year shows the following.

GREAT ADVENTURES
Cash Account Records
July 1, 2024, to December 31, 2024

Cash Receipts			Cash Disbursements			
Date	Desc.	Amount	Date	Check#	Desc.	Amount
7/1	Stock sale	$ 20,000	7/1	101	Insurance	$ 4,800
7/15	Clinic receipts	2,000	7/2	102	Legal fees	1,500
7/22	Clinic receipts	2,300	7/7	DC	Advertising	300
7/30	Clinic receipts	4,000	7/8	103	Bikes	12,000
8/1	Borrowing	30,000	7/24	DC	Advertising	700
8/10	Clinic receipts	3,000	8/4	104	Kayaks	28,000
8/17	Clinic receipts	10,500	8/24	DC	Office supplies	1,800
9/21	Clinic receipts	13,200	9/1	105	Rent	2,400
10/17	Clinic receipts	17,900	12/8	106	Race permit	1,200
12/15	Race receipts	20,000	12/16	107	Salary	2,000
			12/31	108	Dividend	2,000
			12/31	109	Dividend	2,000
		$122,900				$58,700

SUMMARY OF TRANSACTIONS

Beginning Cash Balance July 1, 2024		Cash Receipts		Cash Disbursements		Ending Cash Balance December 31, 2024
$0	+	$122,900	−	$58,700	=	$64,200

Suzie has not reconciled the company's cash balance with that of the bank since the company was started. She asks Summit Bank to provide her with a six-month bank statement. To save time, Suzie makes deposits at the bank only on the first day of each month.

After comparing the two balances, Suzie has some concern because the bank's balance of $50,500 is substantially less than the company's balance of $64,200.

Required:

1. Discuss any problems you see with Great Adventures' internal control procedures related to cash.
2. Prepare Great Adventures' bank reconciliation for the six-month period ended December 31, 2024, and any necessary entries to adjust cash.
3. How did failure to reconcile the bank statement affect the reported amounts for assets, liabilities, stockholders' equity, revenues, and expenses?

Summit Bank
Leading You to the Top

Member FDIC

Account Holder:	Great Adventures, Inc.		Account Number:	1124537774
			Statement Date:	Dec. 31, 2024

Account Summary

Beginning Balance July 1, 2024	Deposits and Credits		Withdrawals and Debits		Ending Balance December 31, 2024
	No.	Total	No.	Total	
$0	8	$103,400	11	$52,900	$50,500

Account Details

Deposits and Credits			Withdrawals and Debits				Daily Balance	
Date	Amount	Desc.	Date	No.	Amount	Desc.	Date	Amount
7/1	$ 20,000	DEP	7/1	101	$ 4,800	CHK	7/1	$15,200
8/1	8,300	DEP	7/7	102	1,500	CHK	7/7	13,400
8/1	30,000	DEP	7/7		300	DC	7/14	1,400
9/1	13,500	DEP	7/14	103	12,000	CHK	7/24	700
9/30	200	INT	7/24		700	DC	8/1	39,000
10/1	13,200	DEP	8/9	104	28,000	CHK	8/9	11,000
11/1	17,900	DEP	8/24		1,800	DC	8/24	9,200
12/31	300	INT	9/2	105	2,400	CHK	9/1	22,700
			9/30		100	SF	9/2	20,300
			12/10	106	1,200	CHK	9/30	20,400
			12/31		100	SF	10/1	33,600
							11/1	51,500
							12/10	50,300
	$103,400				$52,900		12/31	$50,500

Desc.	**DEP** Customer deposit	**INT** Interest earned	**SF** Service fees
	CHK Customer check	**DC** Debit card	

American Eagle Outfitters, Inc.

Financial Analysis
Continuing Case

RWP4–2 Financial information for **American Eagle** is presented in **Appendix A** at the end of the book.

Required:

1. What does the Report of Independent Registered Public Accounting Firm indicate about American Eagle's internal controls?
2. In the summary of significant accounting policies, how does American Eagle define cash equivalents?
3. What is the amount of cash reported in the two most recent years? By how much has cash increased/decreased?
4. Determine the amounts American Eagle reports for net cash flows from operating activities, investing activities, and financing activities in its statement of cash flows for the most recent year. What are total cash flows for the year for continuing operations?
5. Compare your answers in *Question* 4 to the increase/decrease you calculated in *Question* 3. (Note: Include any effect of exchange rates on cash as an additional cash flow in *Question* 4.)
6. What is American Eagle's ratio of cash to noncash assets?

Financial Analysis Continuing Case

The Buckle, Inc.

RWP4–3 Financial information for **Buckle** is presented in **Appendix B** at the end of the book.

Required:
1. What does the Report of Independent Registered Public Accounting Firm indicate about Buckle's internal controls?
2. In the summary of significant accounting policies, how does Buckle define cash equivalents?
3. What is the amount of cash reported in the two most recent years? By how much has cash increased/decreased?
4. Determine the amounts Buckle reports for net cash flows from operating activities, investing activities, and financing activities in its statement of cash flows for the most recent year. What are total cash flows for the year?
5. Compare your answers in *Question* 4 to the increase/decrease you calculated in *Question* 3. (Note: Include any effect of exchange rates on cash as an additional cash flow in *Question* 4.)
6. What is Buckle's ratio of cash to noncash assets?

Comparative Analysis Continuing Case

American Eagle Outfitters, Inc., vs. The Buckle, Inc.

RWP4–4 Financial information for **American Eagle** is presented in **Appendix A** at the end of the book, and financial information for **Buckle** is presented in **Appendix B** at the end of the book.

Required:
1. Which company has a higher ratio of cash to noncash assets? What might this mean about the two companies' operations?
2. Which company has a higher ratio of cash to current liabilities? What might this mean about the two companies' ability to pay debt?

EDGAR Research

RWP4–5 Using EDGAR (Electronic Data Gathering, Analysis, and Retrieval system), find the annual report (10-K) for **The Kroger Company** for the year ended **February 1, 2020.** Locate the "Consolidated Balance Sheets" and "Consolidated Statements of Cash Flows." You may also find the annual report at the company's website. Financial accounting information can often be found at financial websites. These websites are useful for collecting information about a company's stock price, analysts' forecasts, dividend history, historical financial accounting information, and much more. One such site is Yahoo! Finance (**finance.yahoo.com**).

Required:
1. Determine Kroger's cash flows from (a) operating activities, (b) investing activities, and (c) financing activities for the most recent year.
2. From the balance sheet, determine the change in cash for the most recent year.
3. Does the company's total cash flows equal the change in the balance of cash shown on the first line of the balance sheet this year versus last year?
4. Does the company's auditor state that the company has maintained "effective internal control over financial reporting" in the Report of Independent Registered Public Accounting Firm?

Ethics

RWP4–6 Between his freshman and sophomore years of college, Jack takes a job as ticket collector at a local movie theatre. Moviegoers purchase a ticket from a separate employee outside the theatre and then enter through a single set of doors. Jack takes half their ticket, and they proceed to the movie of their choice.

Besides trying to earn enough money for college the next year, Jack loves to watch movies. One of the perks of working for the movie theatre is that all employees are allowed to watch one free movie per day. However, the employee handbook states that friends and family of employees are not allowed to watch free movies. In addition, employees must pay full price for all concession items.

Soon after starting work at the theatre, Jack notices that most other employees regularly bring their friends and family to the movie without purchasing a ticket. When Jack stops them at the door to ask for their ticket, they say, "Jack, no one really follows that policy. Just be cool and let us in. You can do the same." Jack even notices that upper management does not follow the policy of no family and friends watching free movies. Furthermore, employees commonly bring their own cups to get free soft drinks and their own containers to eat free popcorn.

Jack considers whether he should also start bringing friends and family and enjoying the free popcorn and beverages. He reasons, "Why should I be the only one following the rules? If everyone else is doing it, including upper management, what harm would it be for me to do it too? After all, when you watch a movie, you aren't really stealing anything, and popcorn and drinks cost hardly anything. Plus, I really need to save for college."

Required:

1. Understand the effect: Does allowing free entrance and free concessions violate company policy?
2. Specify the options: Can Jack choose to follow the company's written policies?
3. Identify the impact: Does upper management's violation of the policy likely impact other employees?
4. Make a decision: Should Jack follow the company's policies?

Written Communication

RWP4–7 Consider the following independent situations:

1. John Smith is the petty-cash custodian. John approves all requests for payment out of the $200 fund, which is replenished at the end of each month. At the end of each month, John submits a list of all accounts and amounts to be charged, and a check is written to him for the total amount. John is the only person ever to tally the fund.
2. All of the company's cash disbursements are made by check. Each check must be supported by an approved voucher, which is, in turn, supported by the appropriate invoice and, for purchases, a receiving document. The vouchers are approved by Dean Leiser, the chief accountant, after reviewing the supporting documentation. Betty Hanson prepares the checks for Leiser's signature. Leiser also maintains the company's check register (the cash disbursements journal) and reconciles the bank account at the end of each month.
3. Fran Jones opens the company's mail and lists all checks and cash received from customers. A copy of the list is sent to Jerry McDonald, who maintains the general ledger accounts. Fran prepares and makes the daily deposit at the bank. Fran also maintains the subsidiary ledger for accounts receivable, which is used to generate monthly statements to customers.

Required:

Write a memo to your instructor indicating the apparent internal control weaknesses and suggest alternative procedures to eliminate the weaknesses.

Answers to Chapter Framework Questions

1. c   2. a   3. c   4. b   5. c

Answers to Self-Study Questions

1. d   2. d   3. a   4. d   5. b   6. b   7. b   8. d   9. a   10. a   11. c   12. b   13. d   14. c   15. d

Receivables
and Sales

TENET HEALTHCARE: BAD DEBTS CAUSE PAIN TO INVESTORS

Tenet Healthcare Corporation is one of the largest hospital chains in the United States. The company operates 65 hospitals and 500 other healthcare facilities, employs over 110,000 people, and sees millions of patients each year. Everything seems fine, right?

Wrong. Over the period 2017–2019, Tenet reported net losses of $825 million. One of the key reasons for Tenet's poor operating performance was "uncompensated care." Uncompensated care occurs when patients receive services but are either unable or unwilling to pay. Though hospitals try to minimize these costs, federal law requires that patients not be denied emergency treatment due to inability to pay.

Companies, like Tenet, can report revenue only for the amount they are *entitled* to receive. In the case of Tenet, the company must reduce its reported amount of revenue for discounted services provided to uninsured and underinsured patients. Estimates of this uncompensated care over the 2017–2019 period may have been as much as $5 billion, easily enough to have turned the company's losses into large profits.

In addition, Tenet provides some services to customers without receiving immediate payments but for which it is unconditionally entitled to receive payment. Tenet bills these customers, hoping to receive cash in the future. These amounts to be received are reported as accounts receivable. Most customers end up paying, but some customers don't ever pay. At the end of each year, Tenet is required to *estimate* the amount of receivables not expected to be collected (bad debts), further reducing the company's reported profitability and total assets.

As you can see from this discussion, health care providers face enormous challenges in providing individuals with necessary health care while maintaining profitability. At the end of the chapter, we'll analyze how well management of **Tenet Healthcare Corporation** collects cash from customers and compare the results with **CVS Health.** Generally, the better a company is at collecting cash from customers, the more efficiently managers can run the business and the more profitable the company will be.

Comstock Images/SuperStock

PART A

RECOGNIZING ACCOUNTS RECEIVABLE

As we learned in Chapter 2, companies sometimes provide goods or services to customers, not for cash, but on account. These transactions are known as *credit sales* (or sometimes *sales on account* or *services on account*).

Credit sales typically include an informal credit agreement supported by an invoice. An **invoice** is a source document that identifies the date of sale, the customer, the specific items sold, the dollar amount of the sale, and the payment terms. Payment terms typically require the customer to pay within 30 to 60 days after the sale.

Credit Sales and Accounts Receivable

■ LO5–1

Recognize accounts receivable at the time of credit sales.

Credit sales transfer goods or services to a customer today while bearing the risk of collecting payment from that customer in the future. At the time of a credit sale, a company will record:

- **Accounts receivable.** **Accounts receivable** represent amounts owed to a company by its customers from the sale of goods or services on account. The legal right to receive cash is valuable and represents an asset of the company.
- **Revenue.** Even though no cash is received at the time of the credit sale, the seller records revenue immediately once goods or services are provided to the customer, and future collection from the customer is probable. The amount of revenue to record is the amount the company is *entitled* to receive.

Example. To see how companies record credit sales, consider an example. On March 1, a company provides services to a customer for $500. The customer doesn't pay cash at the time of service, but instead promises to pay the $500 by March 31. The company has provided the service and is entitled to received $500 and will therefore record the following.

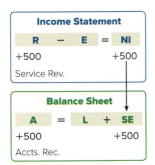

March 1	Debit	Credit
Accounts Receivable..	500	
Service Revenue		500
(Provide services on account)		

Notice that instead of recording Cash, as in a cash sale, the company records another asset—Accounts Receivable—for the credit sale. Later, when $500 cash is received from the customer, the company then records the increase to Cash. Also, Accounts Receivable is reduced because the customer no longer owes money to the company.

March 31	Debit	Credit
Cash..	500	
Accounts Receivable		500
(Receive cash on account)		

KEY POINT

Companies record an asset (accounts receivable) and revenue when they sell goods or services to their customers on account, expecting collection in the future. Once the receivable is collected, the balance of accounts receivable is reduced.

Benefits and Cost of Extending Credit. Credit sales are common for many business transactions. Often, buyers find it more convenient to make multiple purchases using credit and then make a single payment to the seller at the end of the month. In other situations, buyers may not have sufficient cash available at the time of the purchase, or the transaction amount exceeds typical credit card limits. In such cases, the seller must be willing to allow a credit sale in order for the transaction to occur.

The **benefit of extending credit** is that the seller makes it more convenient for the buyer to purchase goods and services. In the long term, credit sales should benefit the seller by increasing profitability of the company.

The **cost of extending credit** is the delay in collecting cash from customers, and as already discussed, some customers may end up not paying at all. These disadvantages reduce the operating efficiency of the company and lead to lower profitability.

As you study receivables, realize that one company's right to *collect* cash corresponds to another company's (or individual's) obligation to *pay* cash. One company's account receivable is the flip side of another company's account payable. In Chapter 6, we discuss accounts payable in the context of inventory purchases on account. In Chapter 8, we again discuss accounts payable, but in the context of current liabilities.

Flip Side

OTHER TYPES OF RECEIVABLES

Other types of receivables are less common than accounts receivable. *Nontrade receivables* are receivables that originate from sources other than customers. They include tax refund claims, interest receivable, and loans by the company to other entities, including stockholders and employees. When receivables are accompanied by formal credit arrangements made with written debt instruments (or notes), we refer to them as *notes receivable*. We'll consider notes receivable later in this chapter.

Net Revenues

When a company sells goods or services to its customers, it often offers a variety of discounts and guarantees that can reduce the amount of cash the company is *entitled to receive* from those customers. For many companies, these are large amounts that significantly reduce the reported amount of revenue. In this section, we'll discuss four of these transactions:

■ **LO5–2**
Calculate net revenues using returns, allowances, and discounts.

1. Trade discounts
2. Sales returns
3. Sales allowances
4. Sales discounts

After accounting for each of these reductions, a company will calculate its **net revenues** as total revenues less any amounts for returns, allowances, and discounts.

Common Terms Net revenues are also referred to as *net sales*.

TRADE DISCOUNTS

Trade discounts represent a reduction in the listed price of a good or service. Companies typically use trade discounts to provide incentives to larger customers or consumer groups to purchase from the company. Trade discounts also can be a way to change prices without publishing a new price list or to disguise real prices from competitors. Because sellers are entitled to receive only the discounted amount, they record the sales transaction at this lower amount.

As an example, assume F.Y.Eye typically provides laser eye surgery for $3,000. To help generate new business, the company offers laser eye surgery in the month of March for only $2,400, which represents a trade discount of 20% ($3,000 × 20% = $600 trade discount). F.Y.Eye provides this discounted service on account to a customer on March 1.

March 1	Debit	Credit
Accounts Receivable..	2,400	
Service Revenue		2,400
(Provide services of $3,000 on account for the trade discount price of $2,400)		

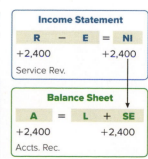

Income Statement

R	–	E	=	NI
+2,400				+2,400
Service Rev.				

Balance Sheet

A	=	L	+	SE
+2,400				+2,400
Accts. Rec.				

Notice the following two points:

1. Even though F.Y.Eye normally charges $3,000 for this service, the company can record revenue for only $2,400, because that's the amount the company is entitled to receive from this customer.

2. The trade discount of $600 is recorded *indirectly* by simply recording revenue equal to the discounted price. We don't keep track in a separate account of trade discounts given to customers. As you'll see next, that's not the case with sales returns, sales allowances, and sales discounts.

SALES RETURNS AND SALES ALLOWANCES

If a customer returns goods previously purchased, we call that a **sales return**. If the customer doesn't return goods but the seller instead reduces the customer's balance owed for goods or services provided, we call that a **sales allowance**. Let's look at an example of each.

Sales Returns.   On March 2, F.Y.Eye sells sunglasses to one of its customers for $200 on account. The sale would be recorded as

Income Statement		
R	− E =	NI
+200		+200
Sales Rev.		

Balance Sheet		
A	= L +	SE
+200		+200
Accts. Rec.		

March 2	Debit	Credit
Accounts Receivable...	200	
Sales Revenue		200
(Sell goods on account)		

Companies often use the "Sales Revenue" account to refer to the sale of goods (inventory). The "Service Revenue" account typically refers to the sale of services. In Chapter 6, we'll cover many transactions involving the buying and selling of inventory.

Suppose on March 4 the customer decides she doesn't want the sunglasses and returns the pair. F.Y.Eye needs to record the return by reducing accounts receivable and reducing the revenue recorded on March 2.

Income Statement		
R	− E =	NI
−200		−200
Sales Ret.↑		

Balance Sheet		
A	= L +	SE
−200		−200
Accts. Rec.		

March 4	Debit	Credit
Sales Returns..	200	
Accounts Receivable		200
(Customer return on account)		

The decrease to Accounts Receivable on March 4 reduces total assets, offsetting the increase to Accounts Receivable on March 2. Since the customer has returned the sunglasses, F.Y.Eye no longer has this receivable of $200. [If the sale on March 2 was for cash, F.Y.Eye would issue a cash refund and credit the Cash account instead.]

Also, because F.Y.Eye is no longer entitled to receive payment from the customer, the sales revenue of $200 previously recognized on March 2 needs to be reduced. **We reduce revenue for sales returns using a contra revenue account—Sales Returns.**

A **contra revenue account** is an account with a balance that is opposite, or "contra," to that of its related revenue account. **The reason we use a contra revenue account is to keep a record of the total revenue recognized separate from the reduction due to subsequent sales returns.** Managers want to keep a record of not only how much their companies are selling, but also how much is being returned. A high proportion of returns could be an indication of inventory problems, so it's important to keep track of both Sales Revenue and Sales Returns.

Sales Allowances.   Sales allowances occur when the seller reduces the customer's balance owed or provides at least a partial refund because of some deficiency in the company's good or service. For example, suppose the customer having laser eye surgery on March 1

for $2,400 is not completely satisfied with the outcome of the surgery. F.Y.Eye may allow a $400 reduction in the amount owed by the customer. In this case, the amount the company is entitled to receive has been reduced to $2,000, and the $2,400 of revenue previously recognized needs to be reduced by the amount of the sales allowance. **We record the sales allowance in a contra revenue account—Sales Allowances.**

March 5	Debit	Credit
Sales Allowances	400	
Accounts Receivable		400
(Provide sales allowance for previous credit sale)		

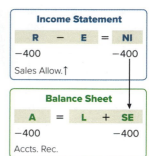

The effect of this transaction is to reduce the Accounts Receivable account and reduce net revenues.

Companies sometimes combine their sales returns and sales allowances in a single Sales Returns and Allowances account, or more simply a single Sales Returns account. For homework, use separate Sales Returns and Sales Allowances accounts.

 COMMON MISTAKE

Students sometimes misclassify contra revenue accounts—sales returns and sales allowances—as expenses. Like expenses, contra revenues have normal debit balances and reduce the reported amount of net income. However, contra revenues represent *reductions* of revenues, whereas expenses represent the separate costs of generating revenues.

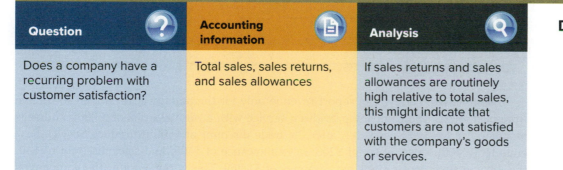

Decision Point

Question ❓	Accounting information 📄	Analysis 🔍
Does a company have a recurring problem with customer satisfaction?	Total sales, sales returns, and sales allowances	If sales returns and sales allowances are routinely high relative to total sales, this might indicate that customers are not satisfied with the company's goods or services.

SALES DISCOUNTS

Unlike a trade discount, a **sales discount** represents a reduction, not in the selling price of a good or service, but in the amount to be received from a credit customer if collection occurs within a specified period of time. **A sales discount is intended to provide incentive to the customer for quick payment.**

Discount terms, such as 2/10, n/30, are a shorthand way to communicate the amount of the discount and the time period within which it's available. The term "2/10," pronounced "two ten," for example, indicates the customer will receive a 2% discount if the amount owed is paid within 10 days. The term "n/30," pronounced "net thirty," means that if the customer does *not* take the discount, full payment net of any returns or allowances is due within 30 days.

Continuing our example above, assume F.Y.Eye wants its customer to pay quickly and therefore offers terms of 2/10, n/30. This means that if cash is collected from the customer within 10 days, the amount due will be reduced by 2%. The customer owes $2,000 after the $600 trade discount and the $400 sales allowance. So, if the customer pays within 10 days, she will receive a sales discount of $40 (= $2,000 × 2%).

Collection During the Discount Period.   First, let's see what happens when cash is collected from the customer on March 10, which is within the 10-day discount period. F.Y.Eye records the following entry:

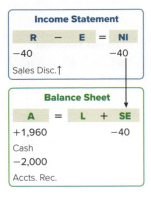

Income Statement		
R	− E =	NI
−40		−40
Sales Disc.↑		

Balance Sheet		
A	= L +	SE
+1,960		−40
Cash		
−2,000		
Accts. Rec.		

March 10	Debit	Credit
Cash...	1,960	
Sales Discounts	40	
Accounts Receivable		2,000
(Collect cash on account with a 2% sales discount)		

Notice that F.Y.Eye receives only $1,960 cash, the $2,000 amount owed less the $40 sales discount. Similar to sales returns and sales allowances, **we record sales discounts in a contra revenue account—Sales Discounts.** The reason we use a contra revenue account is to be able to keep the total revenue separate from the reduction in that revenue due to quick payment. The effect of this transaction is to reduce assets and net revenues of the company by $40.

It's easier to see the relationship between total revenues and related contra accounts by looking at the partial income statement of F.Y.Eye in Illustration 5–1.

ILLUSTRATION 5–1

Income Statement Reporting Revenues Net of Sales Returns, Allowances, and Discounts

F.Y.Eye	
Income Statement (partial)	
Service revenue	$2,400
Sales revenue	200
Less: Sales returns	(200)
Less: Sales allowances	(400)
Less: Sales discounts	(40)
Net revenues	**$1,960**

To summarize, F.Y.Eye can report revenue only for the amount it is entitled to receive from customers. The company provides a service with a normal price of $3,000 and sells merchandise for $200. However, after the trade discount of $600 (to reduce Service Revenue to $2,400), sales return of $200, sales allowance of $400, and sales discount of $40, the income statement reports net revenues of **$1,960**. This is the amount the company is entitled to receive from customers from providing goods or services.

Also at the time of cash collection on March 10, F.Y.Eye credits Accounts Receivable for the full $2,000, even though it receives cash of only $1,960. The reason is that the $2,000 balance in Accounts Receivable is "received in full" by the combination of the $1,960 cash collection and the $40 sales discount. The balance of Accounts Receivable now equals $0, as demonstrated in Illustration 5–2.

ILLUSTRATION 5–2

Balance of Accounts Receivable after Credit Sales, Sales Return, Sales Allowance, and Collection on Account after Sales Discount

	Accounts Receivable		
Credit sale of $2,400 after $600 trade discount	Mar. 1 2,400		
Credit sale of $200	Mar. 2 200		
		Mar. 4 200	Sales return of $200
		Mar. 5 400	Sales allowance of $400
		Mar. 10 2,000	Cash collection of $1,960 with $40 sales discount
Ending balance	Bal. 0		

Collection After the Discount Period. Now let's consider our second scenario. Assume that cash is not collected from the customer until March 31, which is *not* within the 10-day discount period. F.Y.Eye records the following transaction at the time it collects cash.

March 31	Debit	Credit
Cash...	2,000	
Accounts Receivable		2,000
(Collect cash on account)		

Income Statement

R	–	E	=	NI
		No effect		

Balance Sheet

A	=	L	+	SE
+2,000				
Cash				
−2,000				
Accts. Rec.				

Notice that there is no indication in recording the transaction that the customer does not take the sales discount. This is the typical way to record a cash collection on account when no sales discounts are involved. Accounts Receivable is credited for $2,000 to reduce its balance to $0.

 KEY POINT

Revenues are reported for the amount the company is entitled to receive. This amount equals total revenues minus trade discounts, sales returns, sales allowances, and sales discounts. Trade discounts reduce revenue directly, while sales returns, sales allowances, and sales discounts are recorded in separate contra revenue accounts and subtracted when calculating net revenues.

Snap-Crackle-Pop (SCP) Chiropractic normally charges $120 for a full spinal adjustment. Currently, the company is offering a $20 discount to senior citizens. In addition, SCP offers terms 2/10, n/30 to all customers receiving services on account. The following events occur.

Let's Review

June 18	David, age 72, calls to set up an appointment.
June 20	David visits SCP and receives a spinal adjustment for the discounted price.
June 29	David pays for his office visit.

Required:

1. On what date should SCP record patient revenue?
2. Record patient revenue for SCP.
3. Record the cash collection for SCP assuming SCP receives David's payment in full on June 29 (within the discount period).
4. Calculate the balance of Accounts Receivable after the collection of cash using a T-account format, and then calculate the balance of net revenues as shown in the income statement.

Solution:

1. SCP should record patient revenue on June 20—the date the service is provided.
2. Record patient revenue:

June 20	Debit	Credit
Accounts Receivable..	100	
Service Revenue		100
(Provide services on account)		
(Revenue = $120 less $20 trade discount)		

3. Record the cash collection from David within the discount period:

June 29	Debit	Credit
Cash...	98	
Sales Discounts	2	
Accounts Receivable		100
(Collect cash on account with a 2% sales discount)		
(Sales discount = $100 × 2%)		

4. Balance of Accounts Receivable and calculation of net revenues:

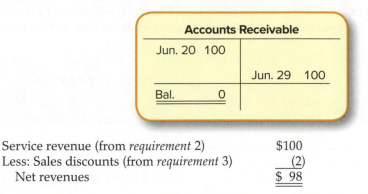

Suggested Homework:

BE5–1, BE5–2;

E5–2, E5–3;

P5–2A&B

Service revenue (from *requirement* 2)	$100
Less: Sales discounts (from *requirement* 3)	(2)
Net revenues	$ 98

END-OF-PERIOD ADJUSTMENT FOR CONTRA REVENUES

The discussion above deals with how companies record contra revenues—sales returns, sales allowances, and sales discounts—*during the year.* However, companies also must adjust for these amounts at the *end of the year* using adjusting entries. The revenue recognition standard (ASU No. 2014-09, effective for annual periods beginning after December 15, 2017) requires a company to report revenues equal to the amount of cash the company "expects to be entitled to receive." Those expectations could change as new information becomes available.[1]

We can see how this works with a simple example. Suppose General Health sells medical parts and consultation services of $400,000 on account during 2024. Also during 2024, some customers return unused parts of $10,000, while others receive allowances of $14,000 and sales discounts of $6,000 for quick payment. These contra revenue transactions reduce the amount of cash to be received from customers, so at the time they occur we need to reduce revenues. To reduce revenues, we record (debit) Sales Returns for $10,000, Sales Allowances for $14,000, and Sales Discounts for $6,000. The procedures for recording these amounts were discussed earlier.

In addition, at the end of 2024 the company must *estimate* any additional returns, allowances, and discounts that will occur in 2025 *as a result of sales transactions in 2024.* The reason is that some activities associated with sales transactions in 2024 will not occur until 2025 but will affect the final amount of cash received from customers. Continuing our example, suppose the company estimates an additional $2,000 in sales returns, $3,000 in sales allowances, and $1,000 in sales discounts in 2025 associated with sales in 2024. These estimates represent a reduction in the cash the company is entitled to receive, so according to the revenue recognition standard, we need to reduce revenue in 2024 for their amounts as well.

As shown in Illustration 5–3, the amounts reported for contra revenues in the 2024 income statement include (1) *actual* returns, allowances, and discounts during 2024 plus

ILLUSTRATION 5–3

Income Statement Reporting Revenues Net of Sales Returns, Allowances, and Discounts with End-of-Period Estimates

GENERAL HEALTH Income Statement (partial) For the year ended 2024	
Sales and service revenue	$ 400,000
Less: Sales returns ($10,000 actual + $2,000 estimate)	(12,000)
Less: Sales allowances ($14,000 actual + $3,000 estimate)	(17,000)
Less: Sales discounts ($6,000 actual + $1,000 estimate)	(7,000)
Net revenues	**$364,000**

[1]The adjustment to revenues for expected cash to be received does not include the expectation that some customers will fail to pay amounts owed (bad debts). These amounts are reported as a separate expense (Bad Debt Expense), as we'll discuss in Part B of this chapter.

(2) *estimates* of returns, allowances, and discounts expected to occur in 2025 that relate to transactions in 2024. The result is net revenues for 2024 of **$364,000**.[2]

The adjusting entries to record these estimated contra revenues at the end of the year can be somewhat complicated, so we leave them to a more advanced accounting course. For now, the important points to understand are:

1. Revenues are reported for the amount of cash a company expects to be entitled to receive from customers for providing goods and services.
2. Total revenues are reduced by sales returns, sales allowances, and sales discounts that occur during the year.
3. Total revenues are further reduced by an adjusting entry at the end of the year for the estimate of additional sales returns, sales allowances, and sales discounts expected to occur in the future but that relate to the current year.

ESTIMATING UNCOLLECTIBLE ACCOUNTS

PART B

Rather than accept only cash payment at the time of sale, should companies extend credit to their customers by selling to them on account? **The *upside* of extending credit to customers is that it boosts sales by allowing customers the ability to purchase on account and pay cash later.** Just think of how many times you wanted to buy food, clothes, electronics, or other items, but you didn't have cash with you. You're not alone. Many customers may not have cash readily available to make a purchase or, for other reasons, simply prefer to buy on credit.

The *downside* of extending credit to customers is that not all customers will pay fully on their accounts. Even the most well-meaning customers may find themselves in difficult financial circumstances beyond their control, limiting their ability to repay. Customers' accounts receivable we no longer expect to collect are referred to as **uncollectible accounts**, or *bad debts*.

KEY POINT

Customers' accounts receivable we no longer expect to collect are referred to as *uncollectible accounts*, or *bad debts*.

Allowance Method (GAAP)

Generally accepted accounting principles (GAAP) require that we account for uncollectible accounts using what's called the **allowance method**. **Under the allowance method, a company reports its accounts receivable for the net amount *expected* to be collected.** To do this, the company must estimate the amount of *current* accounts receivable that will prove uncollectible in the *future* and report this estimate as a contra asset to its accounts receivable.[3]

■ **LO5–3**
Establish an allowance for uncollectible accounts.

Accounts receivable we do not expect to collect have no benefit to the company. Thus, to avoid overstating the assets of the company, we need to reduce accounts receivable in the balance sheet by an estimate of the amount expected not to be collected.

Estimated uncollectible accounts reduce assets.

It's important to understand the following key point. Using the allowance method, we account for events (customers' bad debts) that have *not yet* occurred but that are likely to occur. This is different from other transactions you've learned about up to this point. Those earlier transactions involved recording events that have already occurred, such as

---

[2]Alternatively, a company could record estimates of total sales returns, allowances, and discounts at the time of the sale, and then revise that estimate downward at the end of the year based on actual amounts that have occurred. This alternate approach results in the same amount of net revenues being reported in the income statement. In practice, companies likely will find it easier to record sales returns, allowances, and discounts as they actually occur and then have a year-end adjusting entry for expected future amounts, as discussed in the text.
[3]Later in the chapter, we'll look at a second method—the direct write-off method. The direct write-off method is used for tax purposes but is generally not permitted for financial reporting.

purchasing supplies, paying employees, and providing services to customers. **Under the allowance method, companies are required to estimate** *future* **uncollectible accounts and report those estimates in the** *current* **year.**

KEY POINT

Under the allowance method, accounts receivable are reported for the net amount expected to be collected. At the end of the current year, estimated future uncollectible accounts are reported in a contra asset account, reducing net accounts receivable.

To understand how to apply the allowance method, we'll consider the following three stages in the process:

1. At the end of the initial year, establish an allowance by estimating future uncollectible accounts (LO5–3).
2. During the subsequent year, write off actual bad debts as uncollectible (LO5–4). Note that *actual* write-offs may differ from the previous year's *estimate*.
3. At the end of the subsequent year, once again estimate future uncollectible accounts (LO5–5).

ESTABLISHING AN ALLOWANCE FOR UNCOLLECTIBLE ACCOUNTS

Consider the following example. In 2024, its first year of operations, Kimzey Medical Clinic bills customers $50 million for emergency care services provided. By the end of the year, $20 million remains due from customers. Those receivables are assets of the company. However, because Kimzey cannot always verify patients' ability to pay before administering care, it does *not* expect to receive the full $20 million. **The receivables not expected to be collected should not be counted in assets of the company.**

Because this is Kimzey's first year of operations, it hasn't established a record of customer bad debts. Kimzey's credit manager relies on industry data and decides that 30% of the total year-end accounts receivable of $20 million is a reasonable estimate of amounts that won't be collected. To establish an allowance for future uncollectible accounts of $6 million (= $20 million × 30%), Kimzey records the following:

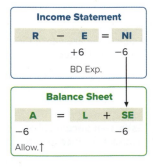

December 31, 2024 ($ in millions)	Debit	Credit
Bad Debt Expense	6	
Allowance for Uncollectible Accounts...		6
(Establish an allowance for future bad debts)		
($20 million × 30% = $6 million)		

The entry to establish an allowance for uncollectible accounts affects the reported financial position of the company by reducing assets and increasing expenses.

Because the nature of the accounts in this adjusting entry differs somewhat from those in other year-end adjusting entries we covered in Chapter 3, let's take a closer look at each of the accounts involved.

Common Terms The allowance for uncollectible accounts is sometimes referred to as the *allowance for doubtful accounts.*

Allowance for Uncollectible Accounts. Companies report their estimate of future bad debts using an **allowance for uncollectible accounts**. Allowance for Uncollectible Accounts is a contra asset account that represents the amount of accounts receivable not expected to be collected. The allowance account provides a way to *reduce accounts receivable* indirectly, rather than decreasing the accounts receivable balance itself.

We report the allowance for uncollectible accounts in the asset section of the balance sheet, but it represents a reduction in the balance of accounts receivable. The difference between total accounts receivable and the allowance for uncollectible accounts equals

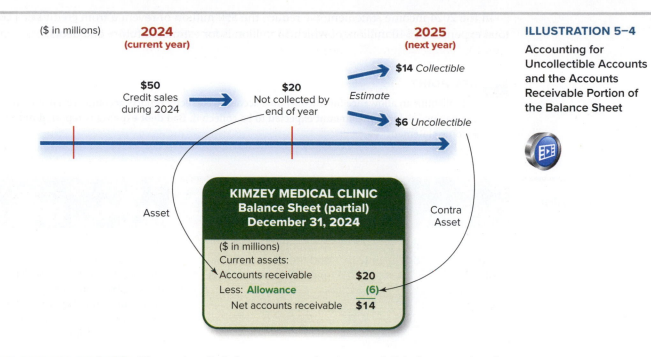

ILLUSTRATION 5–4

Accounting for
Uncollectible Accounts
and the Accounts
Receivable Portion of
the Balance Sheet

net accounts receivable. Illustration 5–4 demonstrates the concept behind accounting for future uncollectible accounts and how the accounts receivable portion of Kimzey's year-end balance sheet appears.

After we estimate uncollectible accounts to be **$6** million, we reduce the $20 million balance of accounts receivable and report them at their estimated collectible amount of $14 million. But is this estimate correct? Only time will tell. Kimzey's prediction of $6 million for uncollectible accounts might be too high, or it might be too low. In either case, it's generally more informative than making no estimate at all. [Later in the chapter, we'll find out how close the estimate is.]

COMMON MISTAKE

Because Allowance for Uncollectible Accounts has a normal credit balance, students sometimes misclassify this account as a liability, which also has a normal credit balance. Instead, a contra asset represents a reduction in a related asset.

Bad Debt Expense.   The adjusting entry to establish the allowance account also includes **bad debt expense.** Bad debt expense represents the cost of estimated future bad debts that is reported as an expense in the current year's income statement, along with other expenses. Illustration 5–5 shows the income statement for Kimzey Medical Clinic after estimating bad debt expense.

Common Terms Bad
debt expense sometimes
is referred to as *uncollectible accounts
expense* or *provision for
doubtful accounts.*

ILLUSTRATION 5–5

Income Statement
Showing Bad Debt
Expense

KIMZEY MEDICAL CLINIC
Income Statement
For the year ended 2024

($ in millions)		
Revenue from credit sales		**$50**
Expenses:		
Bad debt expense	$ 6	
Other operating expenses	34	40
Net income		$10

In the 2024 income statement, we reduce the $50 million of revenue from credit sales by total expenses of $40 million, of which **$6** million is for estimated future bad debts.

KEY POINT

Establishing an allowance for uncollectible accounts correctly reports accounts receivable in the balance sheet at the amount expected to be collected. Bad debt expense is reported in the income statement.

Decision Point

Question	Accounting information	Analysis
Are the company's credit sales policies too lenient?	Accounts receivable and the allowance for uncollectible accounts	A high ratio of the allowance for uncollectible accounts to total accounts receivable could be an indication that the company extends too much credit to high-risk customers.

WRITING OFF ACCOUNTS RECEIVABLE

■ **LO5–4**
Write off accounts receivable as uncollectible.

To continue with our example of Kimzey Medical Clinic, let's suppose that on February 23, 2025 (the following year), Kimzey receives notice that one of its former patients, Bruce Easley, has filed for bankruptcy protection against all creditors. Based on this information, Kimzey believes it is unlikely Bruce will pay his account of $4,000. Remember, Kimzey previously allowed for the likelihood that *some* of its customers would not pay, though it didn't know which ones. Now that it *knows* a specific customer will not pay, it can adjust the allowance and reduce the accounts receivable balance itself. Upon receiving news of this *actual* bad debt, Kimzey records the following.

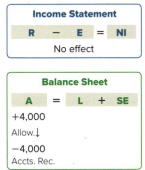

Income Statement			
R	− E	=	NI
No effect			

Balance Sheet			
A	=	L	+ SE
+4,000			
Allow.↓			
−4,000			
Accts. Rec.			

February 23, 2025	Debit	Credit
Allowance for Uncollectible Accounts	4,000	
Accounts Receivable		4,000
(Write off a customer's account)		

Overall, the write-off of the account receivable has no effect on total amounts reported in the balance sheet or in the income statement. There is no decrease in total assets and no decrease in net income with the write-off. Here's why: **We have already recorded the negative effects of the bad news.** Kimzey recorded those effects when it *estimated* future bad debts at the end of 2024 by recording bad debt expense and the allowance account. So, when Bruce declares bankruptcy in the following year, 2025, we had already allowed for this bad debt. The write-off on February 23, 2025, reduces both an asset account (Accounts Receivable) and its contra asset account (Allowance for Uncollectible Accounts), leaving the *net* receivable unaffected. Thus, the entry to record the actual write-off results in no change to total assets and no change to net income.

COMMON MISTAKE

Students often mistakenly record bad debt expense when they write off an uncollectible account. The bad debt expense was recorded in a prior year at the time of estimating uncollectible accounts.

KEY POINT

Writing off a customer's account as uncollectible reduces the balance of accounts receivable but also reduces the contra asset—allowance for uncollectible accounts. The net effect is that there is no change in the *net* receivable (accounts receivable less the allowance) or in total assets.

COLLECTING ON ACCOUNTS PREVIOUSLY WRITTEN OFF

Later in 2025, on September 8, Bruce's bankruptcy proceedings are complete. Kimzey had expected to receive none of the $4,000 Bruce owed. However, after liquidating all assets, Bruce is able to pay each of his creditors 25% of the amount due them. So, when Kimzey receives payment of $1,000 (= $4,000 × 25%), it makes the following two entries.

The first entry simply reverses a portion of the previous entry that Kimzey made on February 23 to write off the account. The second entry records the collection of the account receivable. Notice that in both entries the amounts have offsetting effects on total assets. **Therefore, collecting cash on an account previously written off also has no effect on total assets and no effect on net income.**

September 8, 2025	Debit	Credit
Accounts Receivable...	**1,000**	
Allowance for Uncollectible Accounts...		**1,000**
(Reestablish portion of account previously written off)		
Cash..	**1,000**	
Accounts Receivable		**1,000**
(Collect cash on account)		

Income Statement

R	–	E	=	NI
		No effect		

Balance Sheet

A	=	L	+	SE
+1,000				
Accts. Rec.				
–1,000				
Allow.↑				
+1,000				
Cash				
–1,000				
Accts. Rec.				

Of course, the two entries above could have been recorded as a single entry by debiting Cash and crediting Allowance for Uncollectible Accounts. The debit to Accounts Receivable in the first entry and the credit to Accounts Receivable in the second entry exactly offset one another. Two entries are used here to help emphasize (1) the reversal of the prior write-off and (2) the cash collection on account.

ADJUSTING THE ALLOWANCE IN SUBSEQUENT YEARS

At the end of 2025 (the clinic's second year of operations), Kimzey Medical Clinic must once again prepare financial statements, and this means once again making a year-end adjusting entry to estimate uncollectible accounts. Suppose that Kimzey has credit sales of $80 million in 2025 and has year-end accounts receivable of $30 million. What portion of the $30 million in accounts receivable does Kimzey not expect to collect? Kimzey is required to report that estimate in Allowance for Uncollectible Accounts in its year-end balance sheet as a contra asset to accounts receivable.

In our example for Kimzey, we previously established an allowance for uncollectible accounts in 2024 by applying a *single* estimated percentage (30%) to total accounts receivable. This is known as the **percentage-of-receivables method**. This method sometimes is referred to as a *balance sheet method* because we base the estimate of bad debts on a balance sheet account—accounts receivable.[4] For this method, the percentage may be estimated using current economic conditions, company history, and industry guidelines.

At the end of 2025, we could once again multiply total accounts receivable by a single percentage to get an estimate of future uncollectible accounts. However, a more accurate method is to consider the various *ages* of individual accounts receivable, using a higher

■ LO5–5
Adjust the allowance for uncollectible accounts in subsequent years.

---

[4]In the appendix to this chapter, we'll consider an income statement method—percentage-of-credit-sales method. In practice, companies are required to use a balance sheet method for financial reporting purposes, so that will be our focus here.

percentage of uncollectible for "old" accounts than for "new" accounts. This is known as the **aging method**. For instance, accounts that are 120 days past due are older than accounts that are 60 days past due. **The older the account, the less likely it is to be collected.** The aging method is a more detailed application of the percentage-of-receivables method, so it also is a balance sheet method.

Illustration 5–6 lists eight of Kimzey's individual patients' accounts, including the amount owed by each patient and the number of days past due by the end of 2025. For simplicity, all remaining patients' accounts are summarized in the "Others" row. Shirley Akin owes $12,000, and this amount is not yet due; Cara Lott owes $4,000, and this amount is more than 120 days past due; and so on.

ILLUSTRATION 5–6

Kimzey's Accounts Receivable Aging Schedule

The estimated percent uncollectible increases with age.

Patients	Not Yet Due	Days Past Due		More than 120	Total
		1–60	61–120		
Shirley Akin	$ 12,000				$ 12,000
Cara Lott				$ 4,000	4,000
Ben Greene		$ 5,000			5,000
Anita Hand			$ 7,000		7,000
Ima Hertz	9,000				9,000
Noah Luck		8,000			8,000
Phil Sikley	6,000				6,000
Justin Payne				10,000	10,000
Others	15,973,000	8,987,000	3,993,000	986,000	29,939,000
Total Accounts Receivable	$16,000,000	$ 9,000,000	$ 4,000,000	$1,000,000	$30,000,000
Estimated Percent Uncollectible	10%	30%	50%	70%	
Estimated Amount Uncollectible	$ 1,600,000	$2,700,000	$2,000,000	$ 700,000	$ 7,000,000

Notice that each age group has its own estimate of the percent uncollectible, and this percentage increases with the age of the account. The "Not Yet Due" column has an estimated 10% percent uncollectible. The "1–60" days past due column has an estimated 30% uncollectible, since these accounts are older and less likely to be collected. The estimated percentage uncollectible continues to increase as the account becomes more past due. Summing the estimated amount uncollectible for each age group results in a total estimate of $7,000,000.

KEY POINT

Using the aging method to estimate uncollectible accounts is more accurate than applying a single percentage to all accounts receivable. The aging method recognizes that the longer accounts are past due, the less likely they are to be collected.

So, if the estimated amount uncollectible is $7 million, then Allowance for Uncollectible Accounts needs to have an ending balance of $7 million. We need to (1) know the current balance of Allowance for Uncollectible Accounts and then (2) determine the adjusting entry needed so that the ending balance will be $7 million. To determine these, it might help to visualize the T-account of Allowance for Uncollectible Accounts, as shown in Illustration 5–7.

At the end of 2024 (previous year) Kimzey estimated future bad debts to be **$6 million**. This is the beginning balance of Allowance for Uncollectible Accounts in 2025. Let's assume, however, that only **$4 million** of accounts were actually written off in 2025. This means the balance of the allowance account at the end of 2025, prior to any year-end adjusting entry, has a leftover amount of **$2 million.** If we want the ending balance to be $7 million, by how much does the $2 million current balance need to be adjusted?

Kimzey needs to record an adjusting entry for $5 million to increase the current balance of $2 million credit to the estimated ending balance of $7 million credit.

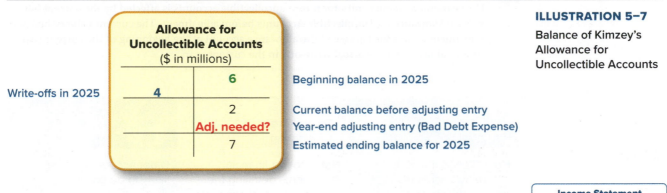

ILLUSTRATION 5–7

Balance of Kimzey's Allowance for Uncollectible Accounts

December 31, 2025 ($ in millions)	Debit	Credit
Bad Debt Expense	5	
Allowance for Uncollectible Accounts		5
(Adjust allowance using the aging method)		

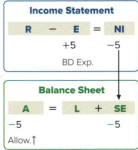

After the adjusting entry, the allowance account will have a balance of **$7** million, and Kimzey can report this amount in its balance sheet. This is shown in Illustration 5–8.

ILLUSTRATION 5–8

Accounts Receivable Portion of the Balance Sheet

KIMZEY MEDICAL CLINIC
Balance Sheet (partial)
December 31, 2025

Assets

($ in millions)
Current assets:

Accounts receivable	$30	
Less: **Allowance for uncollectible accounts**	(7)	
Net accounts receivable		$23

In its 2025 income statement, Kimzey will report bad debt expense of only **$5** million (not **$7** million). This is the amount recorded for bad debt expense in the year-end adjusting entry. The income statement is shown in Illustration 5–9, along with credit sales of $80 million and other operating expenses of $50 million.

ILLUSTRATION 5–9

Bad Debt Expense in the Income Statement

KIMZEY MEDICAL CLINIC
Income Statement
For the year ended 2025

($ in millions)

Revenue from credit sales		$80
Expenses:		
Bad debt expense	$ 5	
Other operating expenses	50	55
Net income		$25

The process of estimating an allowance for uncollectible accounts, writing off bad debts in the following period, and then reestimating the allowance at the end of the period is one that occurs throughout the company's life.

KEY POINT

The year-end adjusting entry for future uncollectible accounts is affected by the current balance of Allowance for Uncollectible Accounts before adjustment. The current balance before adjustment equals the balance of the allowance account at the beginning of the current year (or end of last year) less actual write-offs in the current year.

Decision Point

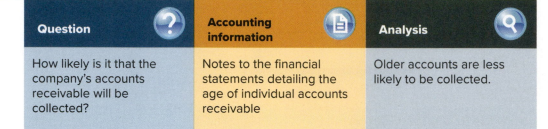

Question	Accounting information	Analysis
How likely is it that the company's accounts receivable will be collected?	Notes to the financial statements detailing the age of individual accounts receivable	Older accounts are less likely to be collected.

Understanding the Balance of Allowance for Uncollectible Accounts. Notice in our example that the balance of Allowance for Uncollectible Accounts in 2025 before the year-end adjusting entry is a $2 million *credit*. That $2 million credit is the result of estimating bad debts at the end of 2024 to be $6 million but actual bad debts in 2025 being only $4 million. Therefore, **a *credit* balance before adjustment indicates that the balance of the allowance account at the beginning of the year (or end of last year) may have been too high.** However, it's possible that some of the estimated uncollectible accounts have not proven bad yet.

A *debit* **balance before adjustment indicates that the balance of the allowance account at the beginning of the year was too low.** In the case of a debit balance, we've written off more bad debts in the current year than we had estimated. We'll discuss an example that involves a debit balance in the Let's Review problem at the end of this section. **The year-end adjusting entry is affected by the extent to which the previous year's ending balance of Allowance for Uncollectible Accounts differs from the current year's actual amount of uncollectible accounts.**

Users of financial statements must realize that some of the amounts reported in financial statements are estimates, and estimating the future almost always results in some inaccuracy. Illustration 5–10 provides an excerpt from the annual report of Tenet Healthcare Corporation.

ILLUSTRATION 5–10

Excerpt from Tenet Healthcare Corporation's Annual Report

TENET HEALTHCARE CORPORATION
Notes to the Financial Statements (excerpt)

The preparation of financial statements, in conformity with accounting principles generally accepted in the United States of America ("GAAP"), requires us to make estimates and assumptions that affect the amounts reported in our Consolidated Financial Statements and these accompanying notes. We regularly evaluate the accounting policies and estimates we use. In general, we base the estimates on historical experience and on assumptions that we believe to be reasonable given the particular circumstances in which we operate. Although we believe all adjustments considered necessary for a fair presentation have been included, actual results may vary from those estimates.

ILLUSTRATION 5–11

Excerpt from
Tenet Healthcare
Corporation's Annual
Report

TENET HEALTHCARE CORPORATION
Notes to the Financial Statements (excerpt)

The following tables present the approximate aging by payer of our net accounts receivable from the continuing operations:

Age	Medicare	Medicaid	Managed Care	Indemnity, Self-Pay, and Other	Total
0–60 days	$172	$34	$ 906	$126	$1,238
61–120 days	9	14	259	84	366
121–180 days	4	7	162	60	233
Over 180 days	4	14	291	330	639
Total	$189	$69	$1,618	$600	$2,476

Illustration 5–11 presents Tenet Healthcare's policy of estimating uncollectible accounts using the aging method.

Subsidiary Ledgers.   Using the aging method requires a company to maintain records for individual customer accounts to help in tracking amounts expected to be received and the portion of those amounts estimated to be uncollectible. This idea was demonstrated in Illustration 5–6. A subsidiary ledger contains a group of individual accounts associated with a particular general ledger control account. For example, the subsidiary ledger for accounts receivable keeps track of all increases and decreases to individual customers' accounts. The balances of all individual accounts then sum to the balance of total accounts receivable in the general ledger and reported in the balance sheet. Subsidiary ledgers are also used for accounts payable, property and equipment, investments, and other accounts.

Community Medical is an outpatient health facility that provides minor surgical and other health-related services to the local community. Many of the patients do not have medical insurance. These customers are required to pay for services within 30 days of receiving treatment. At the beginning of 2024, Community Medical's allowance for uncollectible accounts was a $100,000 credit.

Let's Review

Required:

1. Record the write-off of $120,000 of actual accounts receivable that became uncollectible during 2024.
2. Estimate the allowance for future uncollectible accounts using the following age groups, amount of accounts receivable within each age group, and estimated percent uncollectible at the end of 2024:

Age Group	Amount Receivable	Estimated Percent Uncollectible	Estimated Amount Uncollectible
Not yet due	$600,000	10%	
1–45 days past due	200,000	20%	
More than 45 days past due	50,000	60%	
Total	$850,000		

3. Use a T-account to determine the year-end adjustment needed for the allowance account.

4. Record the year-end adjusting entry for uncollectible accounts.

5. Prepare a partial balance sheet showing accounts receivable and the allowance for uncollectible accounts.

Solution:

1. Write-off of actual accounts receivable during 2024:

	Debit	Credit
Allowance for Uncollectible Accounts.................................	120,000	
Accounts Receivable..		120,000

2. Estimate of the allowance for future uncollectible accounts:

Age Group	Amount Receivable	Estimated Percent Uncollectible	Estimated Amount Uncollectible
Not yet due	$600,000	10%	$ 60,000
1–45 days past due	200,000	20%	40,000
More than 45 days past due	50,000	60%	30,000
Total	$850,000		$130,000

3. Year-end adjusting entry to the allowance account:

Allowance for Uncollectible Accounts

		100,000 — Beginning balance
Write-offs	120,000	
Balance before adj. entry	20,000	
		Adj. needed? — Year-end adjusting entry
		130,000 — Estimated ending balance

4. Year-end adjusting entry for uncollectible accounts:

December 31, 2024	Debit	Credit
Bad Debt Expense	150,000	
Allowance for Uncollectible Accounts................................		150,000*

*Notice from the T-account in *requirement* 3 that the balance of the allowance account before adjustment is a $20,000 *debit*. Based on the estimated allowance of a $130,000 *credit*, we need a credit adjustment of $150,000. Of this adjustment, $20,000 is needed to get the allowance account to a zero balance, and the remaining $130,000 credit adjusts the account to the estimated ending balance.

COMMUNITY MEDICAL
Balance Sheet (partial)
December 31, 2024

Assets

Current assets:		
Accounts receivable	$850,000	
Less: Allowance for uncollectible accounts	(130,000)	
Net accounts receivable		$720,000

Suggested Homework:
BE5–5, BE5–12;
E5–10, E5–11;
P5–4A&B, P5–6A&B

■ **LO5–6**
Contrast the allowance method and direct write-off method when accounting for uncollectible accounts.

Direct Write-Off Method (Not GAAP)

We've just seen how the *allowance method* for uncollectible accounts works. This is the method required for financial reporting by generally accepted accounting principles (GAAP).

However, for tax reporting, companies use an alternative method commonly referred to as the *direct write-off method.* Under the **direct write-off method**, we write off bad debts only at the time they actually become uncollectible, unlike the allowance method which requires estimation of uncollectible accounts before they even occur.

It is important to emphasize that the direct write-off method is generally not allowed for financial reporting under GAAP. It is only used in financial reporting if uncollectible accounts are not anticipated or are expected to be very small. **The direct write-off method is primarily used for tax reporting.** Companies do not report a tax deduction for bad debts until those bad debts are actually uncollectible.

To see how the direct write-off method works, suppose a company provides services on account for $100,000 in 2024, but makes no allowance for uncollectible accounts at the end of the year. Then, in the following year on September 17, 2025, an account of $2,000 becomes uncollectible. The company records the actual write-off as follows.

September 17, 2025	Debit	Credit
Bad Debt Expense	**2,000**	
Accounts Receivable		**2,000**
(Write off uncollectible account directly)		

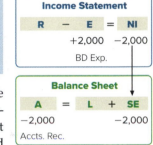

Notice that bad debt expense is recorded in the year of the write-off (2025) instead of the year of the service revenue (2024). Total assets are also reduced by crediting Accounts Receivable at the time of the actual write-off (2025). Compared to the allowance method, the direct write-off method causes assets to be overstated and operating expenses to be understated in 2024. **This is why the direct write-off method of accounting for uncollectible accounts is generally not permitted for financial reporting purposes except in limited circumstances.**

Illustration 5–12 highlights the timing difference between the allowance method and the direct write-off method for our example. For simplicity, assume that our *estimate* of uncollectible accounts of $2,000 at the end of 2024 turns out to be correct, and *actual* bad debts in 2025 are $2,000.

ILLUSTRATION 5–12 Comparing the Allowance Method and the Direct Write-off Method for Recording Uncollectible Accounts

2024	Allowance Method			Direct Write-off Method	
Year-end Adj. Entry (Estimate = $2,000)	**Bad Debt Expense**	2,000		No adjusting entry	
	Allowance for Uncollectible Accts.		2,000		
2025					
Actual Write-offs (Actual = $2,000)	Allowance for Uncollectible Accts.	2,000		**Bad Debt Expense**	2,000
	Accounts Receivable		2,000	Accounts Receivable	2,000

Under the allowance method, future bad debts are *estimated* and recorded as an expense and a reduction in assets in 2024. Bad debt expense is recorded in the same period (2024) as the revenue it helps to create (also in 2024). Under the direct write-off method, though, we make no attempt to estimate future bad debts. We record bad debt expense in the period the account proves uncollectible. In this case, we report the bad debt expense and reduction in assets in 2025. The direct write-off method violates GAAP, because accounts receivable are reported in the current period (2024) for an amount greater than the cash that is expected to be collected in the following period (2025).

 COMMON MISTAKE

Some students erroneously think firms should reduce total assets and record bad debt expense at the time the bad debt actually occurs. However, companies *anticipate* future bad debts and establish an allowance for those estimates.

Notice that, either way, the ultimate effect is a $2,000 debit to Bad Debt Expense and a $2,000 credit to Accounts Receivable. The balance of Allowance for Uncollectible Accounts cancels out; it initially increases with a credit for the estimate of bad debts and then decreases with a debit for actual bad debts. **The difference between the two methods is in the timing.** The direct write-off method is less timely in recognizing uncollectible accounts.

KEY POINT

The direct write-off method waits to reduce accounts receivable and record bad debt expense until accounts receivable prove uncollectible in the future. This leads to accounts receivable being overstated in the current year. The direct write-off method generally is not acceptable for financial reporting.

Decision Maker's Perspective

Managing Bad Debt Estimates

While the allowance method is conceptually superior to the direct write-off method and more accurately reports assets, it does have one disadvantage. This disadvantage arises from the fact that reported amounts under the allowance method represent management estimates. If so inclined, management could use these estimates to manipulate reported earnings. For example, if management wants to boost earnings in the current year, it can intentionally *underestimate* future uncollectible accounts. Similarly, if a company is having an especially good year and management wants to "reserve" earnings for the future, it can intentionally *overestimate* future uncollectible accounts. Having a large expense in the current year means there is less of a charge to bad debt expense in a future year, increasing future earnings. Other expenses, such as rent expense, are much more difficult to manipulate because their reported amounts don't rely on management estimates. These expenses are evidenced by past transactions, and their amounts are verifiable to the penny using a receipt or an invoice.

HealthSouth Corporation appears to have used estimates of uncollectible accounts to manipulate earnings. In the early 1990s, HealthSouth reported large amounts of bad debt expense, building large reserves in the allowance account. Then in the mid-1990s, as additional earnings were needed to meet analysts' expectations, HealthSouth was able to report low amounts for bad debt expense because of the previously inflated allowance account. In 1999, when it became apparent that HealthSouth's earnings were falling dramatically, the company took a "big bath" by reporting a very large charge to bad debt expense. Some companies feel that if they are going to have a bad year, they might as well release all the bad news at once. This makes it possible to report better news in future years.

ETHICAL DILEMMA

Glow Images/Getty Images

Philip Stanton, the executive manager of Thomson Pharmaceutical, receives a bonus if the company's net income in the current year exceeds net income in the past year. By the end of 2024, it appears that net income for 2024 will easily exceed net income for 2023. Philip has asked Mary Beth Williams, the company's controller, to try to reduce this year's income and "bank" some of the profits for future years. Mary Beth suggests that the company's bad debt expense as a percentage of accounts receivable for 2024 be increased from 10% to 15%. She believes 10% is the more accurate estimate but knows that both the corporation's internal and external auditors allow some flexibility in estimates. What is the effect of increasing the estimate of bad debts from 10% to 15% of accounts receivable? How does this "bank" income for future years? Why does Mary Beth's proposal present an ethical dilemma?

NOTES RECEIVABLE AND INTEREST

Notes receivable are similar to accounts receivable but are more formal credit arrangements evidenced by a written debt instrument, or *note.* Notes receivable typically arise from loans to other entities (including affiliated companies); loans to stockholders and employees; and occasionally the sale of merchandise, other assets, or services.

Accounting for Notes Receivable

Like accounts receivable, notes receivable are assets. We classify notes receivable as either *current* or *noncurrent,* depending on the expected collection date. If the time to maturity is longer than one year, the note receivable is a long-term asset.

■ **LO5–7**
Account for notes receivable and interest revenue.

Example.   On February 1, 2024, Kimzey Medical Clinic provides services of $10,000 to a patient, Justin Payne, who is not able to pay immediately. In place of payment, Justin offers Kimzey a six-month, 12% promissory note. Because of the large amount of the receivable, Kimzey agrees to accept the promissory note as a way to increase the likelihood of eventually receiving payment. In addition, because of the delay in payment, Kimzey would like to charge interest on the outstanding balance. A formal promissory note provides an explicit statement of the interest charges. Illustration 5–13 shows an example of a typical note receivable.

ILLUSTRATION 5–13
Note Receivable

Face value ⟶ $ 10,000	Date February 1, 2024
Due date ⟶ Six months after date I promise to pay to the	
order of Kimzey Medical Clinic	
Payee Ten thousand and no/100 dollars	
for value received with interest at the rate of ⟶ 12% .	
Interest rate	
Maker ⟶ *Justin Payne*	

Kimzey records the note receivable as follows.

February 1, 2024	Debit	Credit
Notes Receivable	**10,000**	
Service Revenue		**10,000**
(Accept a six-month, 12% note receivable for services provided)		

Income Statement

R	−	E	=	NI
+10,000				+10,000
Service Rev.				

Balance Sheet

A	=	L	+	SE
+10,000				+10,000
Notes Rec.				

Another example of the use of notes receivable is to replace existing accounts receivable. For example, suppose that Justin received $10,000 of services on account, but Kimzey originally recorded the amount due as Accounts Receivable. Over time, it became apparent that Justin would not be able to pay quickly, so Kimzey required Justin to sign a six-month, 12% promissory note on February 1, 2024. When Justin signs the note, Kimzey records the following transaction to reclassify the existing account receivable as a note receivable.

Income Statement

R	−	E	=	NI
		No effect		

February 1, 2024	Debit	Credit
Notes Receivable	**10,000**	
Accounts Receivable		**10,000**
(Reclassify accounts receivable as notes receivable)		

Balance Sheet

A	=	L	+	SE
+10,000				
Notes Rec.				
−10,000				
Accts. Rec.				

Flip Side

Recognize that the transaction has no impact on the accounting equation; it is simply a matter of reclassifying assets. One asset (notes receivable) increases, while another asset (accounts receivable) decreases.

How would the patient, Justin Payne, record the previous transaction? By signing the note, Justin has an account payable that becomes reclassified as a note payable. He records the issuance of the note payable on February 1 as follows.

Income Statement

R	−	E	=	NI

No effect

Balance Sheet

A	=	L	+	SE

+10,000
Notes Pay.
−10,000
Accts. Pay.

February 1, 2024	Debit	Credit
Accounts Payable	10,000	
Notes Payable..		10,000
(Reclassify accounts payable as notes payable)		

Just as one company's account payable is another company's account receivable, there is also a note payable for every note receivable. We address notes payable in Chapter 8, but if you have a good understanding of notes receivable, then you have a head start with its flip side—notes payable.

 KEY POINT

Notes receivable are similar to accounts receivable except that notes receivable are formal credit arrangements made with a written debt instrument, or *note.*

INTEREST CALCULATION

Many of the same issues we discussed concerning accounts receivable, such as allowing for uncollectible accounts, also apply to notes receivable. The one issue that usually applies to notes receivable but not to accounts receivable is interest. You're probably familiar with the concept of interest. You may be earning interest on money in a savings account, and you might be paying interest on student loans, a car loan, or a credit card.

In the previous example, Kimzey accepted a six-month, 12% promissory note. The "12%" indicates the *annual* interest rate charged by the payee. The terms of the six-month note mean that Kimzey will charge Justin Payne one-half year of interest, or 6%, on the face value. Interest on Kimzey's note receivable is calculated as follows.

Interest calculation

Interest	=	Face value	×	Annual interest rate	×	Fraction of the year
$600	=	$10,000	×	12%	×	6/12

 KEY POINT

We calculate interest as the face value of the note multiplied by the stated annual interest rate multiplied by the appropriate fraction of the year that the note is outstanding.

COLLECTION OF NOTES RECEIVABLE

We record the collection of notes receivable the same way as collection of accounts receivable, except that we also record interest earned as interest revenue in the income statement.

Continuing the previous example, suppose that on August 1, 2024, the maturity date, Justin repays the note and interest in full as promised. Kimzey will record the following.

August 1, 2024	Debit	Credit
Cash...	10,600	
Notes Receivable...		10,000
Interest Revenue..		600
(Collect note receivable and interest)		
(Interest revenue = $10,000 × 12% × 6/12)		

Income Statement

R	–	E	=	NI
+600				+600
Int. Rev.				

Balance Sheet

A	=	L	+	SE
+10,600				+600
Cash				
−10,000				
Notes Rec.				

Over the six-month period, Kimzey earns interest revenue of $600. The credit to Notes Receivable reduces the balance in that account to $0, which is the amount Justin owes after payment to Kimzey.

ACCRUED INTEREST

It frequently happens that a note is issued in one year and the maturity date occurs in the following year. For example, what if Justin Payne issued the previous six-month note to Kimzey on November 1, 2024, instead of February 1, 2024? In that case, the $10,000 face value (principal) and $600 interest on the six-month note are not due until May 1, 2025. The length of the note (six months) and interest rate (12%) remain the same, and so the total interest of $600 charged to Justin remains the same. However, Kimzey will earn interest revenue in two separate accounting periods (assuming Kimzey uses a calendar year): for two months of the six-month note in 2024 (November and December), and for four months in the next year (January through April). Illustration 5–14 demonstrates the calculation of interest revenue over time. Interest receivable from Kimzey's six-month, $10,000, 12% note is $100 per month (= $10,000 × 12% × 1/12).

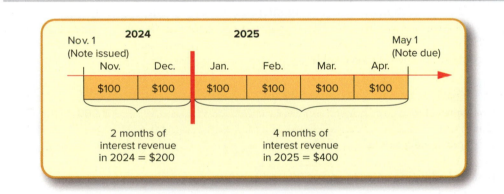

ILLUSTRATION 5–14

Calculating Interest Revenue over Time for Kimzey Medical Clinic

Because Kimzey earns two months of interest in 2024, it must accrue that interest of **$200** on December 31, 2024 (even though no cash has been collected). The adjusting entry to accrue interest revenue follows.

December 31, 2024	Debit	Credit
Interest Receivable..	200	
Interest Revenue..		200
(Accrue interest revenue)		
(Interest revenue = $10,000 × 12% × 2/12)		

Income Statement

R	–	E	=	NI
+200				+200
Int. Rev.				

Balance Sheet

A	=	L	+	SE
+200				+200
Int. Rec.				

On May 1, 2025, the maturity date, Kimzey records the collection of the note receivable of $10,000 plus interest of $600. Notice that the cash collected for interest includes **$200** receivable from 2024, as well as $400 of additional interest revenue related to four months in 2025.

Income Statement

R	−	E	=	NI
+400				+400
Int. Rev.				

Balance Sheet

A	=	L	+	SE
+10,600				+400
Cash				
−10,000				
Notes Rec.				
−200				
Int. Rec.				

May 1, 2025	Debit	Credit
Cash..	10,600	
Notes Receivable		10,000
Interest Receivable (from 2024)...		200
Interest Revenue (from 2025)		400
(Collect note receivable and interest)		
(Interest revenue = $10,000 × 12% × 4/12)		

The entry on May 1, 2025, eliminates the balances of the note receivable and interest receivable recorded in 2024.

KEY POINT

We record interest earned on notes receivable but not yet collected by the end of the year as interest receivable and interest revenue.

Let's Review

General Hospital has a policy of lending any employee up to $3,000 for a period of 12 months at a fixed interest rate of 9%. Chevy Chase has worked for General Hospital for more than 10 years and wishes to take his family on a summer vacation. On May 1, 2024, he borrows $3,000 from General Hospital to be repaid in 12 months.

Required:

1. Record the loan of cash and acceptance of the note receivable by General Hospital.
2. Record General Hospital's year-end adjusting entry to accrue interest revenue.
3. Record the collection of the note with interest from Chevy Chase on May 1, 2025.

Solution:

1. Acceptance of the note receivable:

May 1, 2024	Debit	Credit
Notes Receivable	3,000	
Cash		3,000
(Accept note receivable)		

2. Year-end adjusting entry to accrue interest revenue:

December 31, 2024	Debit	Credit
Interest Receivable..	180	
Interest Revenue (8 months' interest)		180
(Accrue interest revenue)		
(Interest revenue = $3,000 × 9% × 8/12)		

3. Collection of the note with interest:

May 1, 2025	Debit	Credit
Cash...	3,270	
Notes Receivable		3,000
Interest Receivable..		180
Interest Revenue (4 months' interest)		90
(Collect note receivable and interest)		
(Interest revenue = $3,000 × 9% × 4/12)		

Suggested Homework:
BE5–14, BE5–15;
E5–15, E5–17;
P5–8A&B

RECEIVABLES ANALYSIS
Tenet vs. CVS Health

The amount of a company's accounts receivable is influenced by a variety of factors, including the level of sales, the nature of the product or service sold, and credit and collection policies. These factors are, of course, related. For example, a change in credit policies could affect sales. More liberal credit policies—allowing customers a longer time to pay or offering cash discounts for early payment—often are initiated with the specific objective of increasing sales volume.

Management's choice of credit and collection policies results in trade-offs. For example, when a company attempts to boost sales by allowing customers more time to pay, that policy also creates an increase in the required investment in receivables and may increase bad debts because older accounts are less likely to be collected. Offering discounts for early payment may increase sales volume, accelerate customer payment, and reduce bad debts, but at the same time it reduces the amount of cash collected from customers who take advantage of the discounts.

Investors, creditors, and financial analysts can gain important insights by monitoring a company's investment in receivables. Two important ratios that help in understanding the company's effectiveness in managing receivables are the *receivables turnover ratio* and the *average collection period*. We discuss those measures and then compare them for **Tenet Healthcare Corporation** and **CVS Health**.

RECEIVABLES TURNOVER RATIO

The balance of a company's accounts receivable is affected by several factors, such as the level of credit sales, the nature of products or services sold, and the company's credit and collection policies. Because collection of cash is vital to the company's operations, management closely monitors their ability to collect cash from customers. The more quickly a company is able to collect cash, the more quickly that cash can be used for company operations and the less likely the customer is to default on payment.

The receivables turnover ratio provides a measure of a company's ability to collect cash from customers. The ratio shows the *number of times* during a year that the average accounts receivable balance is collected (or "turns over"). We calculate it as follows:

■ **LO5–8**
Calculate key ratios investors use to monitor a company's effectiveness in managing receivables.

$$\text{Receivables turnover ratio} = \frac{\text{Net credit sales}}{\text{Average accounts receivable}}$$

The "net" in net credit sales refers to total credit sales net of discounts, returns, and allowances (similar to net revenues calculated earlier in the chapter). The amount for net credit sales is obtained from the current period's income statement. Average accounts receivable equals the average of accounts receivable reported in this period's and last period's balance sheets. Last period's ending accounts receivable are this period's beginning accounts receivable. **The more frequently a business is able to "turn over" its average accounts receivable, the more effective a company is at granting credit to and collecting cash from its customers.**

AVERAGE COLLECTION PERIOD

The average collection period is another way to express the same efficiency measure. This ratio shows the approximate *number of days* the average accounts receivable balance is outstanding. It is calculated as 365 days divided by the receivables turnover ratio.

$$\text{Average collection period} = \frac{356 \text{ days}}{\text{Receivables turnover ratio}}$$

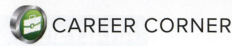

CAREER CORNER

Companies that make large amounts of credit sales often employ credit analysts. These analysts are responsible for deciding whether to extend credit to potential customers. To make this decision, credit analysts focus on the customer's credit history (such as delinquency in paying bills) and information about current financial position, generally found using amounts in the financial statements. When the credit risk is too high, the analyst will advise management to reject the customer's request for goods and services, or perhaps limit the amount of credit extended. Management must then face a difficult trade-off: the potential gains from additional customer revenues versus the risk of an eventual uncollectible account. Credit analysts are most commonly employed by financial institutions ranging from banks to credit rating agencies and investment companies.

Brand X/Jupiterimages/Getty Images

Companies typically strive for a high receivables turnover ratio and a correspondingly low average collection period. As a company's sales increase, receivables also likely will increase. If the percentage increase in receivables is greater than the percentage increase in sales, the receivables turnover ratio will decline (and the average collection period will increase). A declining turnover ratio could indicate that customers are dissatisfied with the product, the company is selling to high-risk customers, or the company's payment terms for attracting new customers are too generous, all of which could increase sales returns and bad debts.

Of course, what's "high" and what's "low" for these ratios depends on the situation. Companies may wish to evaluate these ratios relative to the prior year's ratios, ratios of other firms in the same industry, or specific targets set by management.

As a practical matter, companies often do not separately report net credit sales versus net cash sales. They report only net sales as a total. Because of this, the receivables turnover ratio is most commonly calculated as net sales divided by average accounts receivable. This ratio can be interpreted as how well management collects cash from all sales to customers.

Let's compare **Tenet Healthcare Corporation** to **CVS Health**. Below are relevant amounts for each company.

($ in millions)	Net Sales	Beginning Accounts Receivable	Ending Accounts Receivable
Tenet Healthcare	$ 18,479	$ 2,743	$ 2,595
CVS Health	256,776	17,631	19,617

To compute the receivables turnover ratio, we need the average accounts receivable, which is the beginning amount plus the ending amount, divided by 2.

Tenet Healthcare	Average accounts receivable = ($2,743 + $2,595) ÷ 2 = **$2,669**
CVS Health	Average accounts receivable = ($17,631 + $19,617) ÷ 2 = **$18,624**

As shown in Illustration 5–15, we can divide net sales by average accounts receivable to compute the receivables turnover ratio. Then, we divide 365 days by the receivables turnover ratio to compute the average collection period.

ILLUSTRATION 5–15

Comparison of Receivables Ratios between Tenet Healthcare Corporation and CVS Health

	Receivables Turnover Ratio	Average Collection Period
Tenet Healthcare	$18,479 ÷ **$2,669** = 6.9	365 ÷ 6.9 = 52.9
CVS Health	$256,776 ÷ **$18,624** = 13.8	365 ÷ 13.8 = 26.4

From Illustration 5–15, we see that CVS Health has a higher receivables turnover and a shorter collection period, indicating that the company more efficiently collects cash from patients than does Tenet. This difference is not surprising. Tenet provides health care directly to patients, many of whom are uninsured or underinsured. It's not surprising that Tenet's collection period is relatively long. In contrast, CVS Health obtains most of its revenue through its pharmacies and retail clinics. Thus, it does not face many of the patient health care challenges that Tenet does.

Having enough cash is important to running any business. The more quickly a company can collect its receivables, the more quickly it can use that cash to generate even more cash by reinvesting in the business and generating additional sales.

KEY POINT

The receivables turnover ratio and average collection period can provide an indication of management's ability to collect cash from customers in a timely manner.

Decision Point

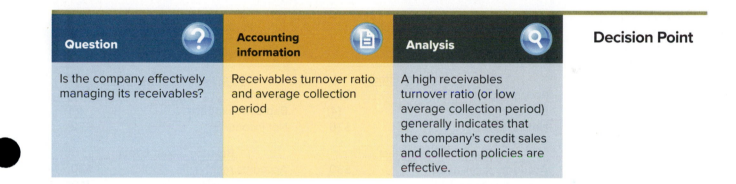

Question	Accounting information	Analysis
Is the company effectively managing its receivables?	Receivables turnover ratio and average collection period	A high receivables turnover ratio (or low average collection period) generally indicates that the company's credit sales and collection policies are effective.

PERCENTAGE-OF-CREDIT-SALES METHOD

APPENDIX

■ **LO5–9**
Estimate uncollectible accounts using the percentage-of-credit-sales method.

In the chapter, we estimated uncollectible accounts based on a percentage of total accounts receivable (*percentage-of-receivables method*) or based on the age of individual accounts receivable (*aging method*). We refer to both of these as a *balance sheet method,* because we base the estimate of bad debts on a balance sheet account—accounts receivable.

As an alternative, we can estimate uncollectible accounts using an income statement account—credit sales. Estimating uncollectible accounts using a percentage of credit sales is aptly referred to as the *percentage-of-credit-sales method* or the *income statement method*. In this appendix, we consider the percentage-of-credit-sales method.

Assume Kimzey bills customers $80 million for services, with $30 million in accounts receivable remaining at the end of 2025. Also assume the balance of the allowance account, before adjustment, is a $2 million credit. Consider the following estimates of uncollectible accounts:

1. Percentage-of-receivables approach = 20% of total accounts receivable.
2. Percentage-of-credit-sales approach = 10% of credit sales.

Illustration 5–16 demonstrates the differences in the two methods when adjusting for estimates of uncollectible accounts. **Notice that the two methods for estimating uncollectible accounts result in different adjustments.**

Because the amounts of the adjustments differ, the effects on the financial statements differ. Recall that the balance of the allowance account before adjustment is a $2 million credit. After adjustment, the balance of the allowance account will differ between the two methods, as will the amount of bad debt expense. Illustration 5–17 summarizes the differences in financial statement effects.

ILLUSTRATION 5–16

Adjusting for Estimates of Uncollectible Accounts

Percentage-of-Receivables Method		Percentage-of-Credit-Sales Method	
Estimate of Uncollectible Accounts		**Estimate of Uncollectible Accounts**	
• 20% of accounts receivable at the end of 2025 will not be collected.		• 10% of credit sales in 2025 will not be collected.	
• 20% of $30 million = $6 million.		• 10% of $80 million = $8 million.	
• Adjust Allowance account from $2 million existing balance to estimate of $6 million.		• Ignore $2 million existing balance of Allowance account and add $8 million.	
Adjusting Entry ($ in millions)		**Adjusting Entry ($ in millions)**	
Bad Debt Expense	4	Bad Debt Expense	8
Allowance for Uncoll. Accts.	4	Allowance for Uncoll. Accts.	8

ILLUSTRATION 5–17

Financial Statement Effects of Estimating Uncollectible Accounts

Percentage-of-Receivables Method ($ in millions)		Percentage-of-Credit-Sales Method ($ in millions)	
Income Statement Effect		**Income Statement Effect**	
Revenues	$80	Revenues	$80
Bad debt expense	(4)	Bad debt expense	(8)
Net income	$76	Net income	$72
Balance Sheet Effect		**Balance Sheet Effect**	
Accounts receivable	$30	Accounts receivable	$30
Less: Allowance	(6)*	Less: Allowance	(10)*
Net accounts receivable	$24	Net accounts receivable	$20
*$6 = $2 + $4 (adjustment)		*$10 = $2 + $8 (adjustment)	

From an income statement perspective, some argue that the percentage-of-credit-sales method provides a better method for estimating bad debts because expenses (bad debts) are better matched with revenues (credit sales). A better matching of expenses and revenues results in a more accurate measure of net income for the period. From a balance sheet perspective, though, the percentage-of-receivables method is preferable because assets (net accounts receivable) are reported closer to the amount expected to be collected.

The current emphasis on better measurement of assets (balance sheet focus) outweighs the emphasis on better measurement of net income (income statement focus). **This is why the percentage-of-receivables method (balance sheet method) is the preferable method, while the percentage-of-credit-sales method (income statement method) is allowed only if amounts do not differ significantly from estimates using the percentage-of-receivables method.**

KEY POINT

When applying the percentage-of-credit-sales method, we adjust the allowance for uncollectible accounts for the current year's credit sales that we don't expect to collect (rather than adjusting at the end of the year for the percentage of accounts receivable we don't expect to collect).

CHAPTER FRAMEWORK

This chapter discusses three key topics: (1) Recognizing accounts receivable from providing services on account, (2) estimating future uncollectible accounts at the end of the year, and (3) recording notes receivable with interest. Receivable transactions **during the year** and their related adjusting entries at the **end of the year** affect amounts reported in the financial statements.

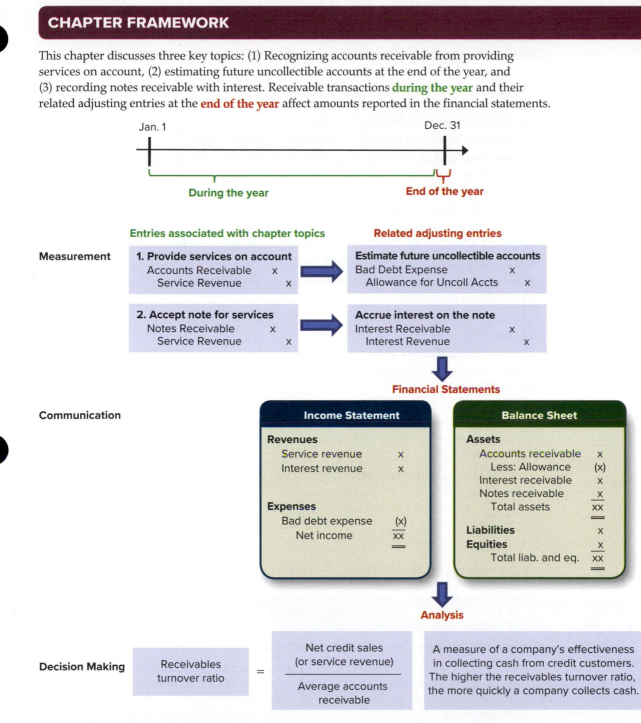

1. **Provide services on account.** During the year, a company provides services to customers on account and expects to receive payment in the future. The right to receive cash from customers is an asset. The amount of revenue to record is the amount the company is *entitled* to receive (which can be further reduced by discounts, returns, and allowances). At the end of the year, an adjusting entry is made to **estimate future uncollectible accounts.** These are customer accounts not expected to be collected. Allowance for Uncollectible Accounts is reported as a contra (or negative) asset account in the balance sheet.

2. **Accept note for services.** During the year, a company provides services and accepts a written promise (or note) from a customer for future payment. The note specifies when the customer's payment is due and the interest that will be earned over that time. At the end of the year, an adjusting entry is made to **accrue interest on the note** for the current year. The amount of accrued interest is the interest earned in the current year.

Chapter Framework Questions

1. **Measurement (during the year):** During the year, a company provides services to customers on account and expects to receive cash in the future. The company records these services on account to which of the following accounts?
   a. Cash.
   b. Accounts Receivable.
   c. Allowance for Uncollectible Accounts.
   d. Services on account are not recorded until the cash is collected.

2. **Measurement (end of the year):** At the end of the year, an adjusting entry is recorded to estimate future uncollectible accounts. The adjusting entry involves:
   a. Debit Bad Debt Expense; credit Allowance for Uncollectible Accounts.
   b. Debit Bad Debt Expense; credit Accounts Receivable.
   c. Debit Service Revenue; credit Accounts Receivable.
   d. Debit Allowance for Uncollectible Accounts; credit Accounts Receivable.

3. **Communication (income statement):** The balance of Bad Debt Expense from estimating *future* uncollectible accounts has what effect on the income statement in the *current* year?
   a Increases net income.
   b. Decreases net income.
   c. No effect.

4. **Communication (balance sheet):** Which of the following is reported in the balance sheet as a contra (or negative) asset account equal to the amount of estimated future uncollectible accounts?
   a. Bad Debt Expense.
   b. Accounts Receivable.
   c. Allowance for Uncollectible Accounts.
   d. Service Revenue.

5. **Decision Making (ratio analysis):** A company that provides credit sales or services to customers and then more effectively collects cash from those credit customers would report a _____ receivables turnover ratio.
   a. Higher.
   b. Lower.

Note: For answers, see the last page of the chapter.

KEY POINTS BY LEARNING OBJECTIVE

LO5–1 Recognize accounts receivable at the time of credit sales.

Companies record an asset (accounts receivable) and revenue when they sell goods or services to their customers on account, expecting collection in the future. Once the receivable is collected, the balance of accounts receivable is reduced.

LO5–2 Calculate net revenues using returns, allowances, and discounts.

Revenues are reported for the amount the company is entitled to receive. This amount equals total revenues minus trade discounts, sales returns, sales allowances, and sales discounts. Trade discounts reduce revenue directly, while sales returns, sales allowances, and sales discounts are recorded in separate contra revenue accounts and subtracted when calculating net revenues.

LO5–3 Establish an allowance for uncollectible accounts.

Customers' accounts receivable we no longer expect to collect are referred to as *uncollectible accounts*, or *bad debts*.

Under the allowance method, accounts receivable are reported for the net amount expected to be collected. At the end of the current year, estimated future uncollectible accounts are reported in a contra asset account, reducing net accounts receivable.

Establishing an allowance for uncollectible accounts correctly reports accounts receivable in the balance sheet at the amount expected to be collected. Bad debt expense is reported in the income statement.

LO5–4 Write off accounts receivable as uncollectible.

Writing off a customer's account as uncollectible reduces the balance of accounts receivable but also reduces the contra asset—allowance for uncollectible accounts. The net effect is that there is no change in the *net* receivable (accounts receivable less the allowance) or in total assets.

LO5–5 Adjust the allowance for uncollectible accounts in subsequent years.

Using the aging method to estimate uncollectible accounts is more accurate than applying a single percentage to all accounts receivable. The aging method recognizes that the longer accounts are past due, the less likely they are to be collected.

The year-end adjusting entry for future uncollectible accounts is affected by the current balance of Allowance for Uncollectible Accounts before adjustment. The current balance before adjustment equals the balance of the allowance account at the beginning of the current year (or end of last year) less actual write-offs in the current year.

LO5–6 Contrast the allowance method and direct write-off method when accounting for uncollectible accounts.

The direct write-off method waits to reduce accounts receivable and record bad debt expense until accounts receivable prove uncollectible. This leads to accounts receivable being overstated in the current year. The direct write-off method generally is not acceptable for financial reporting.

LO5–7 Account for notes receivable and interest revenue.

Notes receivable are similar to accounts receivable except that notes receivable are formal credit arrangements made with a written debt instrument, or *note*.

We calculate interest as the face value of the note multiplied by the stated annual interest rate multiplied by the appropriate fraction of the year that the note is outstanding.

We record interest earned on notes receivable but not yet collected by the end of the year as interest receivable and interest revenue.

LO5–8 Calculate key ratios investors use to monitor a company's effectiveness in managing receivables.

The receivables turnover ratio and average collection period can provide an indication of management's ability to collect cash from customers in a timely manner.

Appendix

LO5–9 Estimate uncollectible accounts using the percentage-of-credit-sales method.

When applying the percentage-of-credit-sales method, we adjust the allowance for uncollectible accounts for the current year's credit sales that we don't expect to collect (rather than adjusting at the end of the year for the percentage of accounts receivable we don't expect to collect).

GLOSSARY

Accounts receivable: The amounts owed to the company by its customers from the sale of goods or services on account. p. 228

Aging method: Basing the estimate of future bad debts on the various ages of individual accounts receivable, using a higher percentage for "old" accounts than for "new" accounts. p. 240

Allowance for uncollectible accounts: Contra asset account representing the amount of accounts receivable not expected to be collected. p. 236

Allowance method: Method of reporting accounts receivable for the net amount expected to be collected. p. 235

Average collection period: Approximate number of days the average accounts receivable balance is outstanding. It equals 365 divided by the receivables turnover ratio. p. 251

Bad debt expense: The cost of estimated future bad debts that is reported as an expense in the current year's income statement. p. 237

Contra revenue account: An account with a balance that is opposite, or "contra," to that of its related revenue account. p. 230

Credit sales: Transfer of goods or services to a customer today while bearing the risk of collecting payment from that customer in the future. Also known as *sales on account* or *services on account*. p. 228

Direct write-off method: Recording bad debt expense at the time we know the account is actually uncollectible. p. 245

Invoice: A source document that identifies the date of sale, the customer, the specific items sold, the dollar amount of the sale, and the payment terms. p. 228

Net accounts receivable: The difference between total accounts receivable and the allowance for uncollectible accounts. p. 237

Net revenues: A company's total revenues less any discounts, returns, and allowances. p. 229

Notes receivable: Formal credit arrangements evidenced by a written debt instrument, or *note*. p. 247

Percentage-of-receivables method: Method of estimating uncollectible accounts based on the percentage of accounts receivable expected not to be collected. p. 239

Receivables turnover ratio: Number of times during a year that the average accounts receivable balance is collected (or "turns over"). It equals net credit sales divided by average accounts receivable. p. 251

Sales allowance: Seller reduces the customer's balance owed or provides at least a partial refund because of some deficiency in the company's good or service. p. 230

Sales discount: Reduction in the amount to be received from a credit customer if collection on account occurs within a specified period of time. p. 231

Sales return: Customer returns a product. **p. 230**

Subsidiary ledger: A group of individual accounts associated with a particular general ledger control account. **p. 243**

Trade discount: Reduction in the listed price of a good or service. **p. 229**

Uncollectible accounts: Customers' accounts that no longer are considered collectible. **p. 235**

SELF-STUDY QUESTIONS

1. Accounts receivable are best described as **(LO5–1)**
   a. Liabilities of the company that represent the amount owed to suppliers.
   b. Amounts that have previously been received from customers.
   c. Assets of the company representing the amount owed by customers.
   d. Amounts that have previously been paid to suppliers.

2. On March 17, Fox Lumber sells materials to Whitney Construction for $12,000, terms 2/10, n/30. Whitney pays for the materials on March 23. What amount would Fox record as revenue on March 17? **(LO5–2)**
   a. $12,400.
   b. $11,760.
   c. $12,000.
   d. $12,240.

3. Refer to the information in the previous question. What is the amount of net revenues (sales minus sales discounts) as of March 23? **(LO5–2)**
   a. $0.
   b. $11,760.
   c. $12,000.
   d. $12,240.

4. The allowance method for uncollectible accounts **(LO5–3)**
   a. Is required by generally accepted accounting principles.
   b. Allows for the possibility that some accounts will not be collected.
   c. Reports net accounts receivable for the amount of cash expected to be collected.
   d. All of the above are correct.

5. At the end of its first year of operations, a company estimates future uncollectible accounts to be $4,500. The company's year-end adjusting entry would include **(LO5–3)**
   a. A credit to Accounts Receivable for $4,500.
   b. A credit to Allowance for Uncollectible Accounts for $4,500.
   c. A debit to Allowance for Uncollectible Accounts for $4,500.
   d. No adjusting entry is necessary because the accounts are not yet actual bad debts.

6. Using the allowance method, the entry to record a write-off of accounts receivable will include **(LO5–4)**
   a. A debit to Bad Debt Expense.
   b. A debit to Allowance for Uncollectible Accounts.
   c. No entry because an allowance for uncollectible accounts was established in an earlier period.
   d. A debit to Service Revenue.

7. Using the allowance method, the effect on the current year's financial statements of writing off an account receivable generally is to **(LO5–4)**
   a. Decrease total assets.
   b. Decrease net income.
   c. Both *a*. and *b*.
   d. Neither *a*. nor *b*.

8. A company has the following account balances at the end of the year:
   - Credit Sales = $400,000
   - Accounts receivable = $80,000
   - Allowance for Uncollectible Accounts = $400 *credit*

   The company estimates future uncollectible accounts to be 4% of accounts receivable. At what amount would Bad Debt Expense be reported in the current year's income statement? **(LO5–5)**
   a. $400.
   b. $2,800.
   c. $3,200.
   d. $3,600.

9. A company has the following account balances at the end of the year:
   - Credit Sales = $400,000
   - Accounts receivable = $80,000
   - Allowance for Uncollectible Accounts = $400 *debit*

   The company estimates future uncollectible accounts to be 4% of accounts receivable. At what amount would Bad Debt Expense be reported in the current year's income statement? **(LO5–5)**
   a. $400.
   b. $2,800.
   c. $3,200.
   d. $3,600.

10. Kidz Incorporated reports the following aging schedule of its accounts receivable with the estimated percent uncollectible.

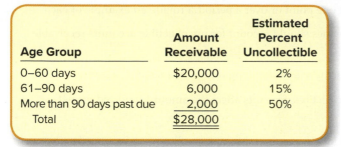

Age Group	Amount Receivable	Estimated Percent Uncollectible
0–60 days	$20,000	2%
61–90 days	6,000	15%
More than 90 days past due	2,000	50%
Total	$28,000	

At what amount would Allowance for Uncollectible Accounts be reported in the current year's balance sheet? **(LO5–5)**

a. $1,150.
b. $1,900.
c. $2,300.
d. $5,900.

11. The direct write-off method is generally not permitted for financial reporting purposes because **(LO5–6)**

a. Compared to the allowance method, it would allow greater flexibility to managers in manipulating reported net income.
b. This method is primarily used for tax purposes.
c. It is too difficult to accurately estimate future bad debts.
d. Accounts receivable are not stated for the amount of cash expected to be collected.

12. On January 1, 2024, Nees Manufacturing lends $10,000 to Roberson Supply using a 9% note due in eight months. Calculate the amount of interest revenue Nees will record on September 1, 2024, the date that the note is due. **(LO5–7)**

a. $300.
b. $600.
c. $900.
d. $1,000.

13. On May 1, 2024, Nees Manufacturing lends $10,000 to Roberson Supply using a 9% note due in 12 months. Nees has a December 31 year-end. Calculate the amount of interest revenue Nees will report in its 2024 and 2025 income statements. **(LO5–7)**

a. 2024 = $300; 2025 = $600.
b. 2024 = $600; 2025 = $300.
c. 2024 = $900; 2025 = $0.
d. 2024 = $0; 2025 = $900.

14. At the beginning of 2024, Clay Ventures has total accounts receivable of $100,000. By the end of 2024, Clay reports net credit sales of $900,000 and total accounts receivable of $200,000. What is the receivables turnover ratio for Clay Ventures? **(LO5–8)**

a. 2.0.
b. 4.5.
c. 6.0.
d. 9.0.

15. A company has the following account balances at the end of the year:

• Credit Sales = $400,000
• Accounts receivable = $80,000
• Allowance for Uncollectible Accounts = $400 *credit*

The company estimates 1% of credit sales will be uncollectible. At what amount would Allowance for Uncollectible Accounts be reported in the current year's balance sheet? **(LO5–9)**

a. $4,000.
b. $4,400.
c. $3,600.
d. $800.

Note: For answers, see the last page of the chapter.

DATA ANALYTICS & EXCEL

Visit Connect to find a variety of Data Analytics questions that help build Excel, Tableau, and data visualization skills. Assignable materials include Integrated Excel, Applying Excel, Data Visualizations, Tableau Dashboard Activities, and Applying Tableau Cases.

REVIEW QUESTIONS

1. When recording a credit sale, what account do we debit? Describe where this account is reported in the financial statements. ■ **LO5–1**

2. What is the difference between a trade receivable and a nontrade receivable? ■ **LO5–1**

3. Explain the difference between a trade discount and a sales discount. Where are sales discounts reported in the income statement? ■ **LO5–2**

4. Briefly explain the accounting treatment for sales returns and allowances. Where are these accounts reported in the income statement? ■ **LO5–2**

■ LO5–2   5. Revenue can be recognized at one point or over a period. Provide an example of each.

■ LO5–3   6. Explain the correct way companies should account for uncollectible accounts receivable (bad debts).

■ LO5–3   7. What two purposes do firms achieve by estimating future uncollectible accounts?

■ LO5–3   8. How does accounting for uncollectible accounts affect the amount reported for net accounts receivable?

■ LO5–3   9. What are the financial statement effects of establishing an allowance for uncollectible accounts?

■ LO5–3   10. We report accounts receivable in the balance sheet at the amount expected to be collected. Explain what this term means.

■ LO5–4   11. When we have established an allowance for uncollectible accounts, how do we write off an account receivable as uncollectible? What effect does this write-off have on the reported amount of total assets and net income at the time of the write-off?

■ LO5–4   12. Allowance for Uncollectible Accounts is a contra asset account, which means that its normal balance is a credit. However, it is possible for the account to have a debit balance before year-end adjusting entries are recorded. Explain how this could happen.

■ LO5–4   13. If at the end of the year Allowance for Uncollectible Accounts has a credit balance before any adjusting entries, what might that tell us about last year's ending balance of the account?

■ LO5–5   14. What does the *age* of accounts receivable refer to? How can we use an aging method to estimate uncollectible accounts receivable?

■ LO5–5   15. Describe the year-end adjusting entries to the allowance for uncollectible accounts in the year subsequent to establishing it.

■ LO5–6   16. Discuss the differences between the allowance method and the direct write-off method for recording uncollectible accounts. Which of the two is acceptable under financial accounting rules?

■ LO5–7   17. Notes receivable differ from accounts receivable in that notes receivable represent *written* debt instruments. What is one other common difference between notes receivable and accounts receivable?

■ LO5–7   18. With respect to notes receivable, explain what each of these represent: (a) face value, (b) annual interest rate, and (c) fraction of the year.

■ LO5–7   19. What will be the total interest earned on a 6%, $2,000 note receivable that is due in nine months?

■ LO5–7   20. Interest on a note receivable typically is due along with the face value at the note's maturity date. If the end of the accounting period occurs before the maturity date, how do we record interest earned but not yet collected?

■ LO5–8   21. How is the receivables turnover ratio measured? What does this ratio indicate? Is a higher or lower receivables turnover preferable?

■ LO5–8   22. How is the average collection period of receivables measured? What does this ratio indicate? Is a higher or lower average collection period preferable?

■ LO5–8   23. How can effectively managing receivables benefit a company?

■ LO5–9   24. Which method, the percentage-of-receivables method or the percentage-of-credit-sales method, is typically used in practice? Why?

■ LO5–9   25. Explain why the percentage-of-receivables method is referred to as the *balance sheet method* and the percentage-of-credit-sales method is referred to as the *income statement method*.

BRIEF EXERCISES

BE5–1 The Giles Agency offers a 12% trade discount when providing advertising services of $1,000 or more to its customers. Audrey's Antiques decides to purchase advertising services of $3,500 (not including the trade discount), while Michael's Motors purchases only $700 of advertising. Both services are provided on account. Record both transactions for The Giles Agency, accounting for any trade discounts.

Record accounts receivable and trade discount (LO5–2)

BE5–2 On February 3, a company provides services on account for $25,000, terms 2/10, n/30. On February 9, the company receives payment from the customer for those services on February 3. Record the service on account on February 3 and the collection of cash on February 9.

Record credit sale and cash collection with a sales discount (LO5–1, 5–2)

BE5–3 Kelly's Jewelry has the following transactions during the year: total jewelry sales = $750,000; sales discounts = $20,000; sales returns = $50,000; sales allowances = $30,000. In addition, at the end of the year the company estimates the following transactions associated with jewelry sales in the current year will occur next year: sales discounts = $2,000; sales returns = $6,000; sales allowances = $4,000. Compute net sales.

Calculate net sales (LO5–2)

BE5–4 At the end of the first year of operations, Mayberry Advertising had accounts receivable of $20,000. Management of the company estimates that 10% of the accounts will not be collected. What adjusting entry would Mayberry Advertising record to establish Allowance for Uncollectible Accounts?

Establish an allowance for uncollectible accounts (LO5–3)

BE5–5 At the beginning of the year, Mitchum Enterprises allows for estimated uncollectible accounts of $15,000. By the end of the year, actual bad debts total $17,000. Record the write-off to uncollectible accounts. Following the write-off, what is the balance of Allowance for Uncollectible Accounts?

Record the write-off of uncollectible accounts (LO5–4)

BE5–6 Barnes Books allows for possible bad debts. On May 7, Barnes writes off a customer account of $7,000. On September 9, the customer unexpectedly pays the $7,000 balance. Record the cash collection on September 9.

Record collection of account previously written off (LO5–4)

BE5–7 At the end of the year, Mercy Cosmetics' balance of Allowance for Uncollectible Accounts is $600 (*credit*) before adjustment. The balance of Accounts Receivable is $25,000. The company estimates that 12% of accounts will not be collected over the next year. What adjusting entry would Mercy Cosmetics record for Allowance for Uncollectible Accounts?

Record the adjusting entry for uncollectible accounts (LO5–5)

BE5–8 Refer to the information in BE5–7, but now assume that the balance of Allowance for Uncollectible Accounts before adjustment is $600 (*debit*). The company still estimates future uncollectible accounts to be 12% of Accounts Receivable. What is the adjusting entry Mercy Cosmetics would record for Allowance for Uncollectible Accounts? Does the amount of the adjustment differ from BE5–7? If so, why?

Record the adjusting entry for uncollectible accounts (LO5–5)

BE5–9 At the end of the year, Dahir Incorporated's balance of Allowance for Uncollectible Accounts is $3,000 (*credit*) before adjustment. The company estimates future uncollectible accounts to be $15,000. What adjusting entry would Dahir record for Allowance for Uncollectible Accounts?

Record the adjusting entry for uncollectible accounts (LO5–5)

BE5–10 Refer to the information in BE5–9, but now assume that the balance of Allowance for Uncollectible Accounts before adjustment is $3,000 (*debit*). The company still estimates future uncollectible accounts to be $15,000. What is the adjusting entry Dahir would record for Allowance for Uncollectible Accounts? Does the amount of the adjustment differ from BE5–9? If so, why?

Record the adjusting entry for uncollectible accounts (LO5–5)

Calculate uncollectible accounts using the aging method (LO5–5)

BE5–11 Williamson Distributors separates its accounts receivable into three age groups for purposes of estimating the percentage of uncollectible accounts.

1. Accounts not yet due = $40,000; estimated uncollectible = 5%.
2. Accounts 1–30 days past due = $11,000; estimated uncollectible = 20%.
3. Accounts more than 30 days past due = $5,000; estimated uncollectible = 30%.

Compute the total estimated uncollectible accounts.

Calculate uncollectible accounts using the aging method (LO5–5)

BE5–12 Spade Agency separates its accounts receivable into three age groups for purposes of estimating the percentage of uncollectible accounts.

1. Accounts not yet due = $25,000; estimated uncollectible = 4%.
2. Accounts 1–60 days past due = $10,000; estimated uncollectible = 25%.
3. Accounts more than 60 days past due = $5,000; estimated uncollectible = 50%.

In addition, the balance of Allowance for Uncollectible Accounts before adjustment is $1,000 (*credit*). Compute the total estimated uncollectible accounts and record the year-end adjusting entry.

Use the direct write-off method to account for uncollectible accounts (LO5–6)

BE5–13 At the end of 2024, Worthy Co.'s balance for Accounts Receivable is $20,000, while the company's total assets equal $1,500,000. In addition, the company expects to collect all of its receivables in 2025. In 2025, however, one customer owing $2,000 becomes a bad debt on March 14. Record the write off of this customer's account in 2025 using the direct write-off method.

Use the direct write-off method to account for uncollectible accounts (LO5–6)

BE5–14 Sanders Inc. is a small brick manufacturer that uses the direct write-off method to account for uncollectible accounts. At the end of 2024, its balance for Accounts Receivable is $35,000. The company estimates that of this amount, $4,000 is not likely to be collected in 2025. In 2025, the actual amount of bad debts is $3,000. Record, if necessary, an adjusting entry for estimated uncollectible accounts at the end of 2024 and the actual bad debts in 2025.

Use the direct write-off method to account for uncollectible accounts (LO5–6)

BE5–15 Brady is hired in 2024 to be the accountant for Anderson Manufacturing, a private company. At the end of 2024, the balance of Accounts Receivable is $29,000. In the past, Anderson has used only the direct write-off method to account for bad debts. Based on a detailed analysis of amounts owed, Brady believes the best estimate of future bad debts is $9,000. If Anderson continues to use the direct write-off method to account for uncollectible accounts, what adjusting entry, if any, would Brady record at the end of 2024? What adjusting entry, if any, would Brady record if Anderson instead uses the allowance method to account for uncollectible accounts?

Calculate amounts related to interest (LO5–7)

BE5–16 Calculate the missing amount for each of the following notes receivable.

Face Value	Annual Interest Rate	Fraction of the Year	Interest
$11,000	6%	4 months	(a)
$30,000	5%	(b)	$1,500
$35,000	(c)	6 months	$1,225
(d)	8%	6 months	$ 700

Calculate interest revenue on notes receivable (LO5–7)

BE5–17 On October 1, 2024, Ogneva Corporation loans one of its employees $40,000 and accepts a 12-month, 9% note receivable. Calculate the amount of interest revenue Ogneva will recognize in 2024 and 2025.

Record notes receivable and interest (LO5–7)

BE5–18 Refer to the information in BE5–17. Record (a) lending of $40,000 cash to an employee on October 1, 2024, (b) the adjusting entry for interest on December 31, 2024, and (c) collection of cash for the note and interest on October 1, 2025.

BE5–19 At the end of the year, Brinkley Incorporated's balance of Allowance for Uncollectible Accounts is $4,000 (*credit*) before adjustment. The company estimates future uncollectible accounts to be 3% of credit sales for the year. Credit sales for the year total $135,000. What is the adjusting entry Brinkley would record for Allowance for Uncollectible Accounts using the percentage-of-credit-sales method?

Use the percentage-of-credit-sales method to adjust for uncollectible accounts (LO5–9)

BE5–20 Refer to the information in BE5–19, but now assume that the balance of Allowance for Uncollectible Accounts before adjustment is $4,000 (*debit*). The company still estimates future uncollectible accounts to be 3% of credit sales for the year. What adjusting entry would Brinkley record for Allowance for Uncollectible Accounts using the percentage-of-credit-sales method?

Use the percentage-of-credit-sales method to adjust for uncollectible accounts (LO5–9)

BE5–21 Match each of the following terms with its definition.

Define terms related to receivables (LO5–1, 5–2, 5–3, 5–4, 5–5, 5–6, 5–7)

Terms	Definitions
_____ 1. Accounts receivable	a. Reductions in amount owed by customers because of deficiency in products or services.
_____ 2. Credit sales	
_____ 3. Sales allowances	b. Formal credit arrangements evidenced by a written debt instrument.
_____ 4. Allowance method	
_____ 5. Notes receivable	c. Amount of cash owed to the company by customers from the sale of products or services on account.
_____ 6. Direct write-off method	
_____ 7. Net revenues	d. Recording bad debt expense at the time the account is known to be uncollectible.
_____ 8. Sales discounts	
_____ 9. Aging method	e. Sales on account to customers.
	f. Reductions in amount owed by customers if payment on account is made within a specified period of time.
	g. Total revenues less returns, allowances, and discounts.
	h. Recording an adjusting entry at the end of each period for the estimate of future uncollectible accounts.
	i. Estimated percentage of uncollectible accounts is greater for "old" accounts than for "new" accounts.

BE5–22 Refer to the information in BE5–2. Determine the financial statement effects when the company provides services on account on February 3 and collects cash from the customer on February 9.

Determine financial statement effects of credit sale with sales discount (LO5–1, 5–2)

BE5–23 Refer to the information in BE5–4. Determine the financial statement effects of the adjusting entry to allow for uncollectible accounts.

Determine financial statement effects of allowing for uncollectible accounts (LO5–3)

BE5–24 Refer to the information in BE5–5. Determine the financial statement effects of writing off an uncollectible account.

Determine financial statement effects of writing off uncollectible accounts (LO5–4)

BE5–25 Refer to the information in BE5–6. Determine the financial statement effects of collecting cash from an account previously written off as uncollectible.

Determine financial statement effects of collecting previous write-off (LO5–4)

BE5–26 Refer to the information in BE5–18. Determine the financial statement effects of (a) lending $40,000 cash to an employee, (b) interest on the note as of December 31, 2024, and (c) collecting cash for the note and interest on October 1, 2025.

Determine financial statement effects of notes receivable and interest (LO5–7)

EXERCISES

Record credit sale (LO5–1)

E5–1 On May 7, Juanita Construction provides services on account to Michael Wolfe for $4,000. Michael pays for those services on May 13.

Required:

For Juanita Construction, record the service on account on May 7 and the collection of cash on May 13.

Record cash sales with a trade discount (LO5–2)

E5–2 Merry Maidens Cleaning generally charges $300 for a detailed cleaning of a normal-size home. However, to generate additional business, Merry Maidens is offering a new-customer discount of 10%. On May 1, Ms. E. Pearson has Merry Maidens clean her house and pays cash equal to the discounted price.

Required:

Record the revenue recognized by Merry Maidens Cleaning on May 1.

Record credit sale and cash collection with a sales discount (LO5–1, 5–2)

E5–3 On March 12, Medical Waste Services provides services on account to Grace Hospital for $11,000, terms 2/10, n/30. Grace pays for those services on March 20.

Required:

For Medical Waste Services, record the service on account on March 12 and the collection of cash on March 20.

Record credit sale and cash collection (LO5–1, 5–2)

Flip Side of E5–5

E5–4 Refer to the information in E5–3, but now assume that Grace does not pay for services until March 31, missing the 2% sales discount.

Required:

For Medical Waste Services, record the service on account on March 12 and the collection of cash on March 31.

Record credit purchase and cash payment (LO5–1, 5–2)

Flip Side of E5–4

E5–5 Refer to the information in E5–4.

Required:

For Grace Hospital, record the purchase of services on account on March 12 and the payment of cash on March 31.

E5–6 On April 25, Foreman Electric installs wiring in a new home for $3,500 on account. However, on April 27, Foreman's electrical work does not pass inspection, and Foreman grants the customer an allowance of $600 because of the problem. On April 30, the customer makes full payment of the balance owed.

Record credit sales with a sales allowance (LO5–1, 5–2)

Required:
1. Record the credit sale on April 25.
2. Record the sales allowance on April 27.
3. Record the cash collection on April 30.
4. Calculate net sales reported in the income statement.

Establish an allowance for uncollectible accounts and write off accounts receivable (LO5–3, 5–4)

E5–7 During 2024, its first year of operations, Pave Construction provides services on account of $160,000. By the end of 2024, cash collections on these accounts total $110,000. Pave estimates that 25% of the uncollected accounts will be uncollectible. In 2025, the company writes off uncollectible accounts of $10,000.

Required:
1. Record the adjusting entry for uncollectible accounts on December 31, 2024.
2. Record the write-off of accounts receivable in 2025 and calculate the balance of Allowance for Uncollectible Accounts at the end of 2025 (before adjustment in 2025).
3. Assume the same facts as above but assume actual write-offs in 2025 were $15,000. Record the write-off of accounts receivable in 2025 and calculate the balance of Allowance for Uncollectible Accounts at the end of 2025 (before adjustment in 2025).

E5–8 Physicians' Hospital has the following balances on December 31, 2024, before any adjustment: Accounts Receivable = $60,000; Allowance for Uncollectible Accounts = $1,100 *(credit)*. On December 31, 2024, Physicians' estimates uncollectible accounts to be 15% of accounts receivable.

Record the adjusting entry for uncollectible accounts and calculate net accounts receivable **(LO5–5)**

Required:
1. Record the adjusting entry for uncollectible accounts on December 31, 2024.
2. Determine the amount at which bad debt expense is reported in the income statement and the allowance for uncollectible accounts is reported in the balance sheet.
3. Calculate net accounts receivable reported in the balance sheet.

E5–9 Southwest Pediatrics has the following balances on December 31, 2024, before any adjustment: Accounts Receivable = $130,000; Allowance for Uncollectible Accounts = $2,100 *(debit)*. On December 31, 2024, Southwest estimates uncollectible accounts to be 20% of accounts receivable.

Record the adjusting entry for uncollectible accounts and calculate net accounts receivable **(LO5–5)**

Required:
1. Record the adjusting entry for uncollectible accounts on December 31, 2024.
2. Determine the amount at which bad debt expense is reported in the income statement and the allowance for uncollectible accounts is reported in the balance sheet.
3. Calculate net accounts receivable reported in the balance sheet.

E5–10 Mercy Hospital has the following balances on December 31, 2024, before any adjustment: Accounts Receivable = $70,000; Allowance for Uncollectible Accounts = $1,400 *(credit)*. Mercy estimates uncollectible accounts based on an aging of accounts receivable as shown below.

Record the adjusting entry for uncollectible accounts using the aging method **(LO5–5)**

Age Group	Amount Receivable	Estimated Percent Uncollectible
Not yet due	$50,000	15%
0–30 days past due	11,000	20%
31–90 days past due	8,000	45%
More than 90 days past due	1,000	85%
Total	$70,000	

Required:
1. Estimate the amount of uncollectible receivables.
2. Record the adjusting entry for uncollectible accounts on December 31, 2024.
3. Calculate net accounts receivable reported in the balance sheet.

E5–11 The Physical Therapy Center specializes in helping patients regain motor skills after serious accidents. The center has the following balances on December 31, 2024, before any adjustment: Accounts Receivable = $110,000; Allowance for Uncollectible Accounts = $4,000 *(debit)*. The center estimates uncollectible accounts based on an aging of accounts receivable as shown below.

Record the adjusting entry for uncollectible accounts using the aging method **(LO5–5)**

Age Group	Amount Receivable	Estimated Percent Uncollectible
Not yet due	$ 60,000	4%
0–60 days past due	26,000	20%
61–120 days past due	16,000	30%
More than 120 days past due	8,000	85%
Total	$110,000	

Required:
1. Estimate the amount of uncollectible receivables.
2. Record the adjusting entry for uncollectible accounts on December 31, 2024.
3. Calculate net accounts receivable reported in the balance sheet.

Identify the financial
statement effects of
transactions related to
accounts receivable and
allowance for uncollectible
accounts (LO5–3, 5–4,
5–5)

E5–12 Consider the following transactions associated with accounts receivable and the allowance for uncollectible accounts.

Credit Sales Transaction Cycle	Assets	Liabilities	Stockholders' Equity	Revenues	Expenses
1. Provide services on account					
2. Estimate uncollectible accounts					
3. Write off accounts as uncollectible					
4. Collect on account previously written off					

Required:

For each transaction, indicate whether it would increase (I), decrease (D), or have no effect (NE) on the account totals. (*Hint:* Make sure the accounting equation, Assets = Liabilities + Stockholders' Equity, remains in balance after each transaction.)

Compare the allowance
method and the direct
write-off method (LO5–6)

E5–13 At the beginning of 2024, Best Heating & Air (BHA) has a balance of $26,000 in accounts receivable. Because BHA is a privately owned company, the company has used only the direct write-off method to account for uncollectible accounts. However, at the end of 2024, BHA wishes to obtain a loan at the local bank, which requires the preparation of proper financial statements. This means that BHA now will need to use the allowance method. The following transactions occur during 2024 and 2025.

1. During 2024, install air conditioning systems on account, $190,000.
2. During 2024, collect $185,000 from customers on account.
3. At the end of 2024, estimate that uncollectible accounts total 15% of ending accounts receivable.
4. In 2025, customers' accounts totaling $3,000 are written off as uncollectible.

Required:

1. Record each transaction using the allowance method.
2. Record each transaction using the direct write-off method.
3. Calculate bad debt expense for 2024 and 2025 under the allowance method and under the direct write-off method, prior to any adjusting entries in 2025.

Record notes
receivable (LO5–7)

E5–14 During 2024, LeBron Corporation accepts the following notes receivable.

1. On April 1, LeBron provides services to a customer on account. The customer signs a four-month, 9% note for $7,000.
2. On June 1, LeBron lends cash to one of the company's vendors by accepting a six-month, 10% note for $11,000.
3. On November 1, LeBron allows a customer to convert a past-due account receivable to a three-month, 8% note receivable for $6,000.

Required:

Record the acceptance of each of the notes receivable.

Record notes
receivable and interest
revenue (LO5–7)

Flip Side of E5–16

E5–15 On March 1, Terrell & Associates provides legal services to Whole Grain Bakery regarding some recent food poisoning complaints. Legal services total $11,000. In payment for the services, Whole Grain Bakery signs a 9% note requiring the payment of the face amount and interest to Terrell & Associates on September 1.

Required:

For Terrell & Associates, record the acceptance of the note receivable on March 1 and the cash collection on September 1.

E5–16 Refer to the information in E5–15.

Record notes payable and interest expense **(LO5–7)**

Flip Side of E5–15

Required:

For Whole Grain Bakery, record the issuance of the note payable on March 1 and the cash payment on September 1.

Record notes receivable and interest revenue **(LO5–7)**

E5–17 On April 1, 2024, Shoemaker Corporation realizes that one of its main suppliers is having difficulty meeting delivery schedules, which is hurting Shoemaker's business. The supplier explains that it has a temporary lack of funds that is slowing its production cycle. Shoemaker agrees to lend $600,000 to its supplier using a 12-month, 11% note.

Required:

Record the following transactions for Shoemaker Corporation.
1. The loan of $600,000 and acceptance of the note receivable on April 1, 2024.
2. The adjusting entry for accrued interest on December 31, 2024.
3. Cash collection of the note and interest on April 1, 2025.

E5–18 Below are amounts (in millions) from three companies' annual reports.

Calculate receivables ratios **(LO5–8)**

	Beginning Accounts Receivable	Ending Accounts Receivable	Net Sales
WalCo	$1,815	$2,762	$322,427
TarMart	6,166	6,694	67,878
CostGet	629	665	68,963

Required:

For each company, calculate the receivables turnover ratio and the average collection period (rounded to one decimal place). Which company appears most efficient in collecting cash from sales?

E5–19 Suzuki Supply reports the following amounts at the end of 2024 (before adjustment).

Compare the percentage-of-receivables method and the percentage-of-credit-sales method **(LO5–9)**

Credit Sales for 2024	$260,000	
Accounts Receivable, December 31, 2024	55,000	
Allowance for Uncollectible Accounts, December 31, 2024	1,100	*(credit)*

Required:

1. Record the adjusting entry for uncollectible accounts using the percentage-of-receivables method. Suzuki estimates 12% of receivables will not be collected.
2. Record the adjusting entry for uncollectible accounts using the percentage-of-credit-sales method. Suzuki estimates 3% of credit sales will not be collected.
3. Calculate the effect on net income (before taxes) and total assets in 2024 for each method.

E5–20 Refer to the information in E5–19, but now assume that the balance of the Allowance for Uncollectible Accounts on December 31, 2024, is $1,100 *(debit)* (before adjustment).

Compare the percentage-of-receivables method and the percentage-of-credit-sales method **(LO5–9)**

Required:

1. Record the adjusting entry for uncollectible accounts using the percentage-of-receivables method. Suzuki estimates 12% of receivables will not be collected.
2. Record the adjusting entry for uncollectible accounts using the percentage-of-credit-sales method. Suzuki estimates 3% of credit sales will not be collected.
3. Calculate the effect on net income (before taxes) and total assets in 2024 for each method.

Complete the accounting
cycle using receivable
transactions **(LO5–1, 5–4,
5–5, 5–7, 5–8)**

E5–21 On January 1, 2024, the general ledger of 3D Family Fireworks includes the following
account balances:

Accounts	Debit	Credit
Cash	$ 23,900	
Accounts Receivable	13,600	
Allowance for Uncollectible Accounts		$ 1,400
Supplies	2,500	
Notes Receivable (6%, due in 2 years)	20,000	
Land	77,000	
Accounts Payable		7,200
Common Stock		96,000
Retained Earnings		32,400
Totals	$137,000	$137,000

During January 2024, the following transactions occur:

January 2	Provide services to customers for cash, $35,100.
January 6	Provide services to customers on account, $72,400.
January 15	Write off accounts receivable as uncollectible, $1,000. (Assume the company uses the allowance method)
January 20	Pay cash for salaries, $31,400.
January 22	Receive cash on accounts receivable, $70,000.
January 25	Pay cash on accounts payable, $5,500.
January 30	Pay cash for utilities during January, $13,700.

Required:
1. Record each of the transactions listed above.
2. Record adjusting entries on January 31.
   a. The company estimates future uncollectible accounts. The company determines $5,000 of accounts receivable on January 31 are past due, and 20% of these accounts are estimated to be uncollectible. The *remaining* accounts receivable on January 31 are not past due, and 5% of these accounts are estimated to be uncollectible. (*Hint:* Use the January 31 accounts receivable balance calculated in the general ledger to split total accounts receivable into the $5,000 past due and the remaining amount not past due.)
   b. Supplies at the end of January total $700. All other supplies have been used.
   c. Accrued interest revenue on notes receivable for January. Interest is expected to be received each December 31.
   d. Unpaid salaries at the end of January are $33,500.
3. Prepare an adjusted trial balance as of January 31, 2024, after updating beginning balances (above) for transactions during January (*requirement* 1) and adjusting entries at the end of January (*requirement* 2).
4. Prepare an income statement for the period ended January 31, 2024.
5. Prepare a classified balance sheet as of January 31, 2024.
6. Record closing entries.
7. Analyze how well 3D Family Fireworks manages its receivables:
   a. Calculate the receivables turnover ratio for the month of January. (*Hint:* For the numerator, use total services provided to customers on account.) If the industry average of the receivables turnover ratios for the month of January is 4.2 times, is the company collecting cash from customers *more* or *less* efficiently than other companies in the same industry?
   b. Calculate the ratio of Allowance for Uncollectible Accounts to Accounts Receivable at the end of January. Based on a comparison of this ratio to the same ratio at the beginning of January, does the company expect an *improvement* or *worsening* in cash collections from customers on credit sales?

E5–22 The general ledger of Pop's Fireworks includes the following account balances in 2024:

Complete the accounting cycle using receivable transactions **(LO5–1, 5–2, 5–4, 5–5, 5–7)**

Accounts	Debit	Credit
Cash	$ 21,200	
Accounts Receivable	41,500	
Allowance for Uncollectible Accounts		$ 2,200
Supplies	6,700	
Notes Receivable (8%, due in 2 years)	10,000	
Land	85,000	
Accounts Payable		12,300
Common Stock		106,000
Retained Earnings		29,900
Service Revenue		124,800
Salaries Expense	70,900	
Utilities Expense	24,200	
Supplies Expense	15,700	
Totals	$275,200	$275,200

In addition, the following transactions occurred during 2024 and are not yet reflected in the account balances above:

1. Provide additional services on account for $7,000. All services on account include terms 2/10, n/30.
2. Receive cash from customers within 10 days of the services being provided on account. The customers were originally charged $5,000.
3. Write off customer accounts of $1,500 as uncollectible.

Required:
1. Record each of the transactions listed above.
2. Record the following adjusting entries on December 31.
   a. Estimate that 10% of the balance of accounts receivable (after transactions in *requirement* 1) will not be collected. (*Hint:* Use the January 31 accounts receivable balance calculated in the general ledger to determine the total estimate of uncollectible accounts.)
   b. Accrue interest on the note receivable of $10,000, which was accepted on October 1, 2024. Interest is due each September 30.
3. Prepare an adjusted trial balance as of December 31, 2024, after updating account balances for transactions during the year (*requirement* 1) and adjusting entries at the end of the year (*requirement* 2).
4. Prepare an income statement for the period ended December 31, 2024.
5. Prepare a classified balance sheet as of December 31, 2024.
6. Record closing entries.
7. Analyze the following information:
   a. By how much does the year-end estimate of future uncollectible accounts reduce net income in 2024?
   b. What is the ending balance of Allowance for Uncollectible Accounts?
   c. What amount of cash is expected to be collected from accounts receivable?

PROBLEMS: SET A

P5–1A Assume the following scenarios.

Calculate the amount of revenue to recognize **(LO5–1)**

Scenario 1:   During 2024, **IBM** provides consulting services on its mainframe computer for $11,000 on account. The customer does not pay for those services until 2025.

Scenario 2:   On January 1, 2024, **Gold's Gym** sells a one-year membership for $1,200 cash. Normally, this type of membership would cost $1,600, but the company is offering a 25% "New Year's Resolution" discount.

Scenario 3:   During 2024, **The Manitowoc Company** provides shipbuilding services to the U.S. Navy for $450,000. The U.S. Navy will pay $150,000 at the end of each year for the next three years, beginning in 2024.

Scenario 4:   During 2024, **Goodyear** sells tires to customers on account for $35,000. By the end of the year, collections total $30,000. At the end of 2025, it becomes apparent that the remaining $5,000 will never be collected from customers.

Required:

For each scenario, calculate the amount of revenue to be recognized in 2024.

Record transactions related to credit sales and contra revenues (LO5–1, 5–2)

P5–2A Outdoor Expo provides guided fishing tours. The company charges $300 per person but offers a 20% discount to parties of four or more. Consider the following transactions during the month of May.

May 2   Charlene books a fishing tour with Outdoor Expo for herself and four friends at the group discount price ($1,200 = $240 × 5). The tour is scheduled for May 7.
May 7   The fishing tour occurs. Outdoor Expo asks that payment be made within 30 days of the tour and offers a 6% discount for payment within 15 days.
May 9   Charlene is upset that no one caught a single fish and asks management for a discount. Outdoor Expo has a strict policy of no discounts related to number of fish caught.
May 15   Upon deeper investigation, management of Outdoor Expo discovers that Charlene's tour was led by a new guide who did not take the group to some of the better fishing spots. In concession, management offers a sales allowance of 30% of the amount due.
May 20   Outdoor Expo receives the amount owed by Charlene.

Required:

1. Record the necessary transaction(s) for Outdoor Expo on each date.
2. Show how Outdoor Expo would present net revenues in its income statement.

Record transactions related to accounts receivable (LO5–3, 5–4, 5–5)

P5–3A The following events occur for The Underwood Corporation during 2024 and 2025, its first two years of operations.

June 12, 2024   Provide services to customers on account for $41,000.
September 17, 2024   Receive $25,000 from customers on account.
December 31, 2024   Estimate that 45% of accounts receivable at the end of the year will not be received.
March 4, 2025   Provide services to customers on account for $56,000.
May 20, 2025   Receive $10,000 from customers for services provided in 2024.
July 2, 2025   Write off the remaining amounts owed from services provided in 2024.
October 19, 2025   Receive $45,000 from customers for services provided in 2025.
December 31, 2025   Estimate that 45% of accounts receivable at the end of the year will not be received.

Required:

1. Record transactions for each date.
2. Post transactions to the following accounts: Cash, Accounts Receivable, and Allowance for Uncollectible Accounts.
3. Calculate net accounts receivable reported in the balance sheet at the end of 2024 and 2025.

Record transactions related to uncollectible accounts (LO5–4, 5–5)

P5–4A Pearl E. White Orthodontist specializes in correcting misaligned teeth. During 2024, Pearl provides services on account of $590,000. Of this amount, $80,000 remains receivable at the end of the year. An aging schedule as of December 31, 2024, is provided below.

Age Group	Amount Receivable	Estimated Percent Uncollectible
Not yet due	$40,000	4%
0–90 days past due	16,000	20%
91–180 days past due	11,000	25%
More than 180 days past due	13,000	80%
Total	$80,000	

Required:
1. Calculate the allowance for uncollectible accounts.
2. Record the December 31, 2024, adjusting entry, assuming the balance of Allowance for Uncollectible Accounts before adjustment is $5,000 (*credit*).
3. On July 19, 2025, a customer's account balance of $8,000 is written off as uncollectible. Record the write-off.
4. On September 30, 2025, the customer whose account was written off in *requirement* 3 unexpectedly pays the full amount. Record the cash collection.

P5–5A In an effort to boost sales in the current year, Roy's Gym has implemented a new program where members do not have to pay for their annual membership until the end of the year. The program seems to have substantially increased membership and revenues. Below are year-end amounts.

Compare the direct write-off method to the allowance method **(LO5–3, 5–6)**

	Membership Revenues	Accounts Receivable
Last year	$150,000	$ 6,000
Current year	450,000	170,000

Arnold, the owner, realizes that many members have not paid their annual membership fees by the end of the year. However, Arnold believes that no allowance for uncollectible accounts should be reported in the current year because none of the nonpaying members' accounts have proven uncollectible. Arnold wants to use the direct write-off method to record bad debts, waiting until the end of next year before writing off any accounts.

Required:
1. Do you agree with Arnold's reasoning for not reporting any allowance for future uncollectible accounts? Explain.
2. Suppose that similar programs in the past have resulted in uncollectible accounts of approximately 70%. If Arnold uses the allowance method, what should be the balance of Allowance for Uncollectible Accounts at the end of the current year?
3. Based on your answer in *requirement* 2, for what amount will total assets and expenses be misstated in the current year if Arnold uses the direct write-off method? Ignore tax effects.

P5–6A Willie Cheetum is the CEO of Happy Foods, a distributor of produce to grocery store chains throughout the Midwest. At the end of the year, the company's accounting manager provides Willie with the following information, before any adjustment.

Using estimates of uncollectible accounts to overstate income **(5–5)**

Accounts receivable	$1,100,000
Estimated percentage uncollectible	9%
Allowance for uncollectible accounts	$40,000 (*credit*)
Operating income	$260,000

Willie's compensation contract states that if the company generates operating income of at least $210,000, he will get a salary bonus early next year.

Required:
1. Record the adjusting entry for uncollectible accounts using the accountant's estimate of 9% of accounts receivable.
2. After the adjusting entry is recorded in *requirement* 1, what is the revised amount of operating income? Will Willie get his salary bonus?
3. Willie instructs the accountant to record the adjusting entry for uncollectible accounts using 6% rather than 9% of accounts receivable. Now will Willie get his salary bonus? Explain.
4. By how much would total assets and operating income be misstated using the 6% amount?

P5–7A Humanity International sells medical and food supplies to those in need in underdeveloped countries. Customers in these countries are often very poor and must purchase items on account. At the end of 2024, total accounts receivable equal $1,300,000. The company understands that it's dealing with high credit risk clients. These countries are often in the

Overestimating future uncollectible accounts **(LO5–3, 5–4)**

middle of a financial crisis, civil war, severe drought, or some other difficult circumstance. Because of this, Humanity International typically estimates the percentage of uncollectible accounts to be 35% (= $455,000). Actual write-offs in 2025 total only $300,000, which means that the company significantly overestimated uncollectible accounts in 2024. It appears that efforts by the International Monetary Fund (IMF) and the United Nations (UN), and a mild winter mixed with adequate spring rains, have provided for more stable economic conditions than were expected, helping customers to pay on their accounts.

Required:
1. Record the adjusting entry for uncollectible accounts at the end of 2024, assuming there is no balance in Allowance for Uncollectible Accounts at the end of 2024 before any adjustment.
2. By the end of 2025, Humanity International has the benefit of hindsight to know that estimates of uncollectible accounts in 2024 were too high. How did this overestimation affect the reported amounts of total assets and expenses at the end of 2024? Ignore tax effects.
3. Should Humanity International prepare new financial statements for 2024 to show the correct amount of uncollectible accounts? Explain.

Record long-term notes receivable and interest revenue (LO5–7)

P5–8A On December 1, 2024, Liang Chemical provides services to a customer for $90,000. In payment for the services, the customer signs a three-year, 10% note. The face amount is due at the end of the third year, while annual interest is due each December 1.

Required:
1. Record the acceptance of the note on December 1, 2024.
2. Record the adjusting entry for interest revenue on December 31 for 2024, 2025, and 2026, and the collection of annual interest on December 1, 2025 and 2026.
3. Record the cash collection on December 1, 2027.

Calculate and analyze ratios (LO5–8)

P5–9A Assume selected financial data for **Walmart** and **Target**, two close competitors in the retail industry, are as follows:

($ in millions)	Net Sales	Beginning Accounts Receivable	Ending Accounts Receivable
Walmart	$443,854	$5,089	$5,937
Target	68,466	6,153	5,927

Required:
1. Calculate the receivables turnover ratio and average collection period for Walmart and Target. Round your answers to one decimal place. Which company has more favorable ratios? Compare your calculations with those for **Tenet Healthcare** and **CVS Health** reported in the chapter text. Which industry maintains a higher receivables turnover?
2. Because most companies do not separately report cash sales and credit sales, the calculations used here and in the chapter text use companies' reported amount of net sales, which is a combination of cash sales and credit sales. How would including cash sales affect the receivables turnover ratio? How does this help to explain your answer in *requirement* 1 above?

PROBLEMS: SET B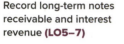

Calculate the amount of revenue to recognize (LO5–1)

P5–1B Assume the following scenarios.

Scenario 1:   During 2024, **The Hubbard Group** provides services of $900,000 for repair of a state highway. The company receives an initial payment of $300,000 with the balance to be received the following year.

Scenario 2:   **Rolling Stone** magazine typically charges $80 for a one-year subscription. On January 1, 2024, Herman, age 72, purchases a one-year subscription to the magazine and receives a 15% senior citizen discount.

Scenario 3:   During 2024, **Waste Management** provides services on account for $30,000. The customer pays for those services in 2025.

Scenario 4:   During 2024, **Sysco Corporation** sells grocery items to one of its customers for $260,000 on account. Cash collections on those sales are $180,000 in 2024 and $60,000 in 2025. The remaining $20,000 is written off as uncollectible in 2025.

Required:

For each scenario, calculate the amount of revenue to be recognized in 2024.

P5–2B Data Recovery Services (DRS) specializes in data recovery from crashed hard drives. The price charged varies based on the extent of damage and the amount of data being recovered. DRS offers a 10% discount to students and faculty at educational institutions. Consider the following transactions during the month of June.

*Record transactions related to credit sales and contra revenues **(LO5–1, 5–2)***

June 10	Rashid's hard drive crashes and he sends it to DRS.
June 12	After initial evaluation, DRS e-mails Rashid to let him know that full data recovery will cost $3,000.
June 13	Rashid informs DRS that he would like them to recover the data and that he is a student at UCLA, qualifying him for a 10% educational discount and reducing the cost by $300 (= $3,000 × 10%).
June 16	DRS performs the work and claims to be successful in recovering all data. DRS asks Rashid to pay within 30 days of today's date, offering a 2% discount for payment within 10 days.
June 19	When Rashid receives the hard drive, he notices that DRS did not successfully recover all data. Approximately 30% of the data has not been recovered and he informs DRS.
June 20	DRS reduces the amount Rashid owes by 30%.
June 30	DRS receives the amount owed by Rashid.

Required:

1. Record the necessary transaction(s) for Data Recovery Services on each date.
2. Show how net revenues would be presented in the income statement.
3. Calculate net revenues if Rashid had paid his bill on June 25.

P5–3B The following events occur for Municipal Engineering during 2024 and 2025, its first two years of operations.

*Record transactions related to accounts receivable **(LO5–3, 5–4, 5–5)***

February 2, 2024	Provide services to customers on account for $38,000.
July 23, 2024	Receive $27,000 from customers on account.
December 31, 2024	Estimate that 25% of uncollected accounts will not be received.
April 12, 2025	Provide services to customers on account for $51,000.
June 28, 2025	Receive $6,000 from customers for services provided in 2024.
September 13, 2025	Write off the remaining amounts owed from services provided in 2024.
October 5, 2025	Receive $45,000 from customers for services provided in 2025.
December 31, 2025	Estimate that 25% of uncollected accounts will not be received.

Required:

1. Record transactions for each date.
2. Post transactions to the following accounts: Cash, Accounts Receivable, and Allowance for Uncollectible Accounts.
3. Calculate net accounts receivable reported in the balance sheet at the end of 2024 and 2025.

P5–4B Facial Cosmetics provides plastic surgery primarily to hide the appearance of unwanted scars and other blemishes. During 2024, the company provides services of $410,000 on account. Of this amount, $60,000 remains uncollected at the end of the year. An aging schedule as of December 31, 2024, follows.

*Record transactions related to uncollectible accounts **(LO5–4, 5–5)***

Age Group	Amount Receivable	Estimated Percent Uncollectible
Not yet due	$40,000	3%
0–30 days past due	11,000	4%
31–60 days past due	8,000	11%
More than 60 days past due	1,000	25%
Total	$60,000	

Required:
1. Calculate the allowance for uncollectible accounts.
2. Record the December 31, 2024, adjusting entry, assuming the balance of Allowance for Uncollectible Accounts before adjustment is $400 (*debit*).
3. On April 3, 2025, a customer's account balance of $500 is written off as uncollectible. Record the write-off.
4. On July 17, 2025, the customer whose account was written off in *requirement* 3 unexpectedly pays $100 of the amount but does not expect to pay any additional amounts. Record the cash collection.

Compare the direct write-off method to the allowance method (LO5–3, 5–6)

P5–5B Letni Corporation engages in the manufacture and sale of semiconductor chips for the computing and communications industries. During the past year, operating revenues remained relatively flat compared to the prior year but management notices a big increase in accounts receivable. The increase in receivables is largely due to the recent economic slowdown in the computing and telecommunications industries. Many of the company's customers are having financial difficulty, lengthening the period of time it takes to collect on accounts. Below are year-end amounts.

Age Group	Operating Revenue	Accounts Receivable	Average Age	Accounts Written Off
Two years ago	$1,300,000	$150,000	5 days	$ 0
Last year	1,600,000	160,000	7 days	1,000
Current year	1,700,000	330,000	40 days	0

Paul, the CEO of Letni, notices that accounts written off over the past three years have been minimal and, therefore, suggests that no allowance for uncollectible accounts be established in the current year. Any account proving uncollectible can be charged to next year's financial statements (the direct write-off method).

Required:
1. Do you agree with Paul's reasoning? Explain.
2. Suppose that other companies in these industries have had similar increasing trends in accounts receivable aging. These companies also had very successful collections in the past but now estimate uncollectible accounts to be 25% because of the significant downturn in the industries. If Letni uses the allowance method estimated at 25% of accounts receivable, what should be the balance of Allowance for Uncollectible Accounts at the end of the current year?
3. Based on your answer in *requirement* 2, for what amount will total assets and expenses be misstated in the current year if Letni uses the direct write-off method? Ignore tax effects.

Using estimates of uncollectible accounts to understate income (5–5)

P5–6B Wanda B. Rich is the CEO of Outlet Flooring, a discount provider of carpet, tile, wood, and laminate flooring. At the end of the year, the company's accountant provides Wanda with the following information, before any adjustment.

Accounts receivable	$11,000,000
Estimated percentage uncollectible	4%
Allowance for uncollectible accounts	$110,000 (*credit*)
Operating income	$2,900,000

Wanda has significant stock ownership in the company and, therefore, would like to keep the stock price high. Analysts on Wall Street expect the company to have operating income of $2,200,000. The fact that actual operating income is well above this amount will make investors happy and help maintain a high stock price. Meeting analysts' expectations will also help Wanda keep her job.

Required:
1. Record the adjusting entry for uncollectible accounts using the accountant's estimate of 4% of accounts receivable.
2. After the adjusting entry is recorded in *requirement* 1, what is the revised amount of operating income? Will Outlet Flooring still meet analysts' expectations?
3. Wanda instructs the accountant to instead record $700,000 as bad debt expense so that operating income will exactly meet analysts' expectations. By how much would total assets and operating income be misstated if the accountant records this amount?
4. Why would Wanda be motivated to manage operating income in this way?

P5–7B By the end of its first year of operations, Previts Corporation has credit sales of $750,000 and accounts receivable of $350,000. Given it's the first year of operations, Previts' management is unsure how much allowance for uncollectible accounts it should establish. One of the company's competitors, which has been in the same industry for an extended period, estimates uncollectible accounts to be 2% of ending accounts receivable, so Previts decides to use that same amount. However, actual write-offs in the following year were 25% of the $350,000 (= $87,500). Previts' inexperience in the industry led to making sales to high credit risk customers.

Underestimating future uncollectible accounts (LO5–3, 5–4)

Required:
1. Record the adjusting entry for uncollectible accounts at the end of the first year of operations using the 2% estimate of accounts receivable.
2. By the end of the second year, Previts has the benefit of hindsight to know that estimates of uncollectible accounts in the first year were too low. By how much did Previts underestimate uncollectible accounts in the first year? How did this underestimation affect the reported amounts of total assets and expenses at the end of the first year? Ignore tax effects.
3. Should Previts prepare new financial statements for the first year of operations to show the correct amount of uncollectible accounts? Explain.

P5–8B On April 15, 2024, Sampson Consulting provides services to a customer for $110,000. To pay for the services, the customer signs a three-year, 12% note. The face amount is due at the end of the third year, while annual interest is due each April 15. (*Hint:* Because the note is accepted during the middle of the month, Sampson plans to recognize one-half month of interest revenue in April 2024, and one-half month of interest revenue in April 2027.)

Record long-term notes receivable and interest revenue (LO5–7)

Required:
1. Record the acceptance of the note on April 15, 2024.
2. Record the adjusting entry for interest revenue on December 31 for 2024, 2025, and 2026, and the collection of annual interest on April 15, 2025 and 2026.
3. Record the cash collection on April 15, 2027.

P5–9B Assume selected financial data for **Sun Health Group** and **Select Medical Corporation**, two companies in the health-care industry, are as follows:

Calculate and analyze ratios (LO5–8)

($ in millions)	Net Sales	Beginning Accounts Receivable	Ending Accounts Receivable
Sun Health	$1,930	$215	$202
Select Medical	2,240	414	353

Required:
1. Calculate the receivables turnover ratio and average collection period for Sun Health and Select Medical. Round your answers to one decimal place. Compare your calculations with

those for **Tenet Healthcare** and **CVS Health** reported in the chapter text. Which of the four companies has the most favorable receivables turnover?

2. How does the receivables turnover ratio reflect the efficiency of management? Discuss factors that affect the receivables turnover ratio.

REAL-WORLD PERSPECTIVES

Data Analytics & Excel

Visit Connect to find a variety of Data Analytics questions that help build Excel, Tableau, and data visualization skills. Assignable materials include Integrated Excel, Applying Excel, Data Visualizations, Tableau Dashboard Activities, and Applying Tableau Cases.

General Ledger Continuing Case

Great Adventures

(This is a continuation of the Great Adventures problem from earlier chapters.)

RWP5–1 Tony and Suzie are ready to expand Great Adventures even further in 2025. Tony believes that many groups in the community (for example, Boys and Girls Clubs, church groups, civic groups, and local businesses) would like to hold one-day outings for their members. Groups would engage in outdoor activities such as rock climbing, fishing, capture the flag, paintball, treasure hunts, scavenger hunts, nature hikes, and so on. The purpose of these one-day events would be for each member of the group to learn the importance of TEAM (Together Everyone Achieves More).

Tony knows that most people are not familiar with these types of activities, so to encourage business he allows groups to participate in the event before paying. He offers a 5% quick-payment discount to those that pay within 10 days after the event. He also guarantees that at least eight hours of outdoor activities will be provided or the customer will receive a 20% discount. For the first six months of the year, the following activities occur for TEAM operations.

Jan.	24	Great Adventures purchases outdoor gear such as ropes, helmets, harnesses, compasses, and other miscellaneous equipment for $5,000 cash.
Feb.	25	Kendall's Boys and Girls Club participates in a one-day TEAM adventure. Normally, Tony would charge a group of this size $3,500, but he wants to encourage kids to exercise more and enjoy the outdoors so he charges the group only $3,000. Great Adventures provides these services on account.
Feb.	28	Great Adventures receives payment from the Boys and Girls Club for the full amount owed, less the 5% quick-payment discount.
Mar.	19	Reynold's Management has its employees participate in a one-day TEAM adventure. Great Adventures provides services on account for $4,000, and Reynold's agrees to pay within 30 days.
Mar.	27	Great Adventures receives payment from Reynolds for the full amount owed, less the 5% quick-payment discount.
Apr.	7	Several men from the Elks Lodge decide to participate in a TEAM adventure. Great Adventures receives $7,500 immediately and the event is scheduled for the following week.
Apr.	14	The TEAM adventure is held for members of the Elks Lodge.
Apr.	30	Myers Manufacturing participates in a TEAM adventure. Great Adventures provides services on account for $6,000, and Myers agrees to pay within 30 days.
May	31	Myers Manufacturing fails to pay the amount owed within the specified period and agrees to sign a three-month, 8% note receivable to replace the existing account receivable.
Jun.	15	Several MBA groups participate in TEAM adventures. Great Adventures provides services on account for $24,000 to these groups, with payment due in July.

Required:
1. Record TEAM adventure transactions occurring during the first six months of 2025.
2. Consider the following information as of June 30, 2025.
   a. Suzie estimates uncollectible accounts to be 10% of accounts receivable from the MBA groups on June 15. Record the adjusting entry for uncollectible accounts.
   b. Accrue one month of interest on the note receivable from Myers Manufacturing.
   c. Prepare a partial balance sheet showing the net accounts receivable section.

The Great Adventures continuing problem also can be assigned using the General Ledger software in Connect. Students will be given an existing trial balance and asked to prepare (1) the journal entries above, (2) financial statements, and (3) closing entries.

American Eagle Outfitters, Inc.

Financial Analysis
Continuing Case

RWP5–2 Financial information for **American Eagle** is presented in **Appendix A** at the end of the book.

Required:
1. Determine whether the trend in net sales has been increasing or decreasing for the past three years.
2. In which financial statement is the balance of accounts receivable reported? Explain why using net sales to calculate the receivables turnover ratio might not be a good indicator of a company's ability to efficiently manage receivables for a retail company like American Eagle, which typically sells clothing for cash.
3. Does American Eagle indicate in the balance sheet that the company likely has an allowance for uncollectible accounts?

The Buckle, Inc.

Financial Analysis
Continuing Case

RWP5–3 Financial information for **Buckle** is presented in **Appendix B** at the end of the book.

Required:
1. Determine whether the trend in net sales has been increasing or decreasing for the past three years.
2. In which financial statement is the balance of accounts receivable reported? Explain why using net sales to calculate the receivables turnover ratio might not be a good indicator of a company's ability to efficiently manage receivables for a retail company like Buckle, which typically sells clothing for cash.
3. Does Buckle indicate in the balance sheet that the company likely has an allowance for uncollectible accounts?

American Eagle Outfitters, Inc. vs. The Buckle, Inc.

Comparative Analysis
Continuing Case

RWP5–4 Financial information for **American Eagle** is presented in **Appendix A** at the end of the book, and financial information for **Buckle** is presented in **Appendix B** at the end of the book.

Required:
Try to estimate each company's ratio of total current receivables to total current assets. Do you see problems with either company's management of receivables?

EDGAR Research

RWP5–5 Using EDGAR (Electronic Data Gathering, Analysis, and Retrieval system), find the annual report (10-K) for **Avon Products** for the year ended **December 31, 2019.** Locate the "Consolidated Statement of Operations" (income statement) and "Consolidated Balance Sheets." You may also find the annual report at the company's website.

Required:

Answer the following questions related to the company's accounts receivable and bad debts:

1. What is the amount of net accounts receivable at the end of the year? What is the amount of total accounts receivable?
2. What is the amount of bad debt expense for the year? (*Hint:* Check the statement of cash flows.)
3. Determine the amount of actual bad debt write-offs made during the year. Assume that all bad debts relate only to trade accounts receivable. Did the company underestimate or overestimate bad debts?
4. Calculate the receivables turnover ratio and average collection period for the most recent year. Round your answers to one decimal place and use net accounts receivable in the calculation. Assuming the industry averages for the receivables turnover ratio and average collection period are 10.5 times and 34.8 days, respectively, what do you conclude about the receivables of Avon?

Ethics

RWP5–6 You have recently been hired as the assistant controller for Stanton Industries. Your immediate superior is the controller who, in turn, reports to the vice president of finance.

The controller has assigned you the task of preparing the year-end adjusting entries. For receivables, you have prepared an aging of accounts receivable and have applied historical percentages to the balances of each of the age categories. The analysis indicates that an appropriate balance for Allowance for Uncollectible Accounts is $180,000. The existing balance in the allowance account prior to any adjustment is a $20,000 credit balance.

After showing your analysis to the controller, he tells you to change the aging category of a large account from over 120 days to current status and to prepare a new invoice to the customer with a revised date that agrees with the new aging category. This will change the required allowance for uncollectible accounts from $180,000 to $135,000. Tactfully, you ask the controller for an explanation for the change and he tells you, "We need the extra income; the bottom line is too low."

Required:

1. Understand the reporting effect: What is the effect on income before taxes of lowering the allowance estimate from $180,000 to $135,000, as requested by the controller?
2. Specify the options: If you do not make the change, how would the additional $45,000 of Allowance for Uncollectible Accounts affect total assets?
3. Identify the impact: Are investors and creditors potentially harmed by the controller's suggestion?
4. Make a decision: Should you follow the controller's suggestion?

Written Communication

RWP5–7 You have been hired as a consultant by a parts manufacturing firm to provide advice as to the proper accounting methods the company should use in some key areas. In the area of receivables, the company president does not understand your recommendation to use the allowance method for uncollectible accounts. She stated, "Financial statements should be based on objective data rather than the guesswork required for the allowance method. Besides, since my uncollectibles are fairly constant from period to period, with significant variations occurring infrequently, the direct write-off method is just as good as the allowance method."

Required:

Draft a one-page response in the form of a memo to the president in support of your recommendation for the company to use the allowance method.

Earnings Management

RWP5–8 Ernie Upshaw is the supervising manager of Sleep Tight Bedding. At the end of the year, the company's accounting manager provides Ernie with the following information, before any adjustment.

Accounts receivable	$500,000
Estimated percent uncollectible	9%
Allowance for uncollectible accounts	$20,000 (*debit*)
Operating income	$320,000

In the previous year, Sleep Tight Bedding reported operating income (after adjustment) of $275,000. Ernie knows that it's important to report an upward trend in earnings. This is important not only for Ernie's compensation and employment, but also for the company's stock price. If investors see a decline in earnings, the stock price could drop significantly, and Ernie owns a large amount of the company's stock. This has caused Ernie many sleepless nights.

Required:

1. Record the adjusting entry for uncollectible accounts using the accounting manager's estimate of 9% of accounts receivable.
2. After the adjusting entry is recorded in *requirement* 1, what is the revised amount of operating income? Does operating income increase or decrease compared to the previous year?
3. Ernie instructs the accounting manager to record the adjusting entry for uncollectible accounts using 4% rather than 9% of accounts receivable. After this adjustment, does operating income increase or decrease compared to the previous year?
4. By how much would total assets and expenses be misstated using the 4% amount?

Answers to Chapter Framework Questions

1. b   2. a   3. b   4. c   5. a

Answers to Self-Study Questions

1. c   2. c   3. b   4. d   5. b   6. b   7. d   8. b   9. d   10. c   11. d   12. b   13. b   14. c   15. b

Inventory and Cost of Goods Sold

Learning Objectives

PART A: REPORTING INVENTORY AND COST OF GOODS SOLD

- **LO6–1** Understand that inventory flows from manufacturing companies to merchandising companies and is reported as an asset in the balance sheet.
- **LO6–2** Understand how cost of goods sold is reported in a multiple-step income statement.
- **LO6–3** Determine the cost of goods sold and ending inventory using different inventory cost methods.
- **LO6–4** Explain the financial statement effects and tax effects of inventory cost methods.

PART B: RECORDING INVENTORY TRANSACTIONS

- **LO6–5** Record inventory transactions using a perpetual inventory system.

PART C: LOWER OF COST AND NET REALIZABLE VALUE

- **LO6–6** Apply the lower of cost and net realizable value rule for inventories.

ANALYSIS: INVENTORY ANALYSIS

- **LO6–7** Analyze management of inventory using the inventory turnover ratio and gross profit ratio.

APPENDICES A AND B

- **LO6–8** Record inventory transactions using a periodic inventory system.
- **LO6–9** Determine the financial statement effects of inventory errors.

SELF-STUDY MATERIALS

- Let's Review—Inventory cost methods (p. 292).
- Let's Review—Recording transactions using a perpetual inventory system (p. 303).
- Let's Review—Lower of cost and net realizable value (p. 307).
- Chapter Framework (p. 317).
- Key Points by Learning Objective (p. 319).
- Glossary of Key Terms (p. 320).
- Self-Study Questions with answers available (p. 320).
- Videos including Concept Overview, Applying Excel, Let's Review, and Interactive Illustrations demonstrate key topics (Connect).

BEST BUY: TAKING INVENTORY OF ELECTRONICS SOLD

Best Buy Co., Inc., is the largest consumer electronics retailer in the United States. You are probably familiar with most of the products offered by Best Buy—computers, computer software, TVs, video games, music, mobile phones, digital and video cameras, home appliances (washing machines, dryers, and refrigerators), and other related merchandise.

Merchandise inventory for sale to customers is the single largest asset owned by Best Buy, as it is for many retail companies. At any given time, Best Buy holds about $5 billion in inventory, or about 35% of the company's total assets. Proper management of inventory is key to the company's success.

Management of Best Buy knows there is a fine line between having too little and too much inventory. Having too little inventory reduces the selection of products available to customers, ultimately reducing sales revenue. On the other hand, in a technology-based industry where changes occur rapidly, having too much inventory can leave the store holding outdated inventory. Just think of what happens to the value of computers when the next generation becomes available. Managers don't want to get stuck with old inventory that is decreasing in value. Besides obsolescence, other costs associated with holding large inventories are storage, insurance, and shrinkage (theft). Holding less inventory also provides access to money that can be invested elsewhere within the company.

For now, Best Buy seems to be taking the right steps with its inventory. Look below at the company's revenues from sales of inventory compared to the cost of the inventory sold. These amounts are reported in the company's income statement ($ in millions). The difference between net sales (a revenue) and cost of goods sold (an expense) is called *gross profit*, and it has averaged nearly $10 billion over the period 2018–2020.

Fiscal Years Ended	2020	2019	2018
Net sales	$43,638	$42,879	$42,151
Cost of goods sold	33,590	32,918	32,275
Gross profit	$10,048	$ 9,961	$ 9,876

In this chapter, we explore how to account for the purchase and sale of inventory items. We'll see how inventory (an asset in the balance sheet) turns into cost of goods sold (an expense in the income statement) once it is sold, and how these amounts can affect business decisions. At the end of the chapter, we'll analyze inventory transactions of **Best Buy** versus **Tiffany**.

A katz/Shutterstock

REPORTING INVENTORY AND COST OF GOODS SOLD

In preceding chapters, we dealt with companies that provide a service. **Service companies** such as **FedEx**, **Zoom**, **AT&T**, and **Marriott Hotels** generate revenues by providing services to their customers. FedEx delivers packages, Zoom provides video conferencing, AT&T provides media and telecommunications services, and Marriott offers you a place to stay the night. Many companies, though, generate revenues by selling inventory rather than a service.

Part A of this chapter introduces the concept of inventory and demonstrates the different methods used to calculate the cost of inventory for external reporting. Once you understand this, then you're ready to see, in Part B and Part C, how companies actually maintain their own (internal) records of inventory transactions and the adjustments that are sometimes needed to prepare financial statements.

Types of Inventory

■ **LO6–1**
Understand that inventory flows from manufacturing companies to merchandising companies and is reported as an asset in the balance sheet.

Inventory is a current asset.

Inventory includes items a company intends for sale to customers in the ordinary course of business. You already are familiar with several types of inventory—clothes at **Lululemon**, shoes at **Famous Footwear**, grocery items at **Publix Super Markets**, digital equipment at **Best Buy**, building supplies at **The Home Depot**, and so on. We typically report inventory as a current asset in the balance sheet—an *asset* because it represents a valuable resource to the company, and *current* because the company expects to convert it to cash in the near term.

MANUFACTURING COMPANIES

Manufacturing companies produce the inventories they sell, rather than buying them in finished form from suppliers. **Apple Inc.**, **Coca-Cola**, **Harley-Davidson**, **ExxonMobil**, **Ford**, **Sony**, and **Intel** are manufacturers. Manufacturing companies buy the inputs for the products they manufacture. Thus, we classify inventory for a manufacturer into three categories: (1) raw materials, (2) work in process, and (3) finished goods:

- *Raw materials* inventory includes the cost of components that will become part of the finished product but have not yet been used in production.
- *Work-in-process* inventory refers to the products that have been started in the production process but are not yet complete at the end of the period. The total costs include raw materials, direct labor, and indirect manufacturing costs called *overhead*.
- *Finished goods* inventory is the cost of fully assembled but unshipped inventory at the end of the reporting period.

Intel manufactures the components that are used to build computers. At any given time, Intel's inventory includes the cost of materials that will be used to build computer components (raw materials), partially manufactured components (work-in-process), and fully assembled but unsold components (finished goods). These separate inventory accounts are added together and reported by Intel as total inventories.

MERCHANDISING COMPANIES

Common Terms
Inventory is sometimes referred to as *merchandise inventory.*

Merchandising companies, such as **Best Buy**, don't manufacture computers or their components. Instead, Best Buy purchases finished computers from manufacturers, and then these computers are sold to customers like you. Merchandising companies may assemble, sort, repackage, redistribute, store, refrigerate, deliver, or install the inventory, but they do not manufacture it. They simply serve as intermediaries in the process of moving inventory from the manufacturer to the end user. Illustration 6–1 shows the different inventory

ILLUSTRATION 6–1

Inventory Amounts
for a Manufacturing
Company (Intel) Versus
a Merchandising
Company (Best Buy)

INVENTORY (from balance sheets)		
Inventory accounts ($ in millions)	**Intel**	**Best Buy**
Raw materials	$ 840	
Work in process	6,225	
Finished goods	1,679	
Merchandise inventories		$5,174
Total inventories	$8,744	$5,174

accounts for Intel (a manufacturing company) and Best Buy (a merchandising company), as
reported in their balance sheets.

Wholesalers and Retailers.   Merchandising companies can further be classified as
wholesalers or retailers. *Wholesalers* resell inventory to retail companies or to professional
users. For example, a wholesale food service company like **Sysco Corporation** supplies food
to restaurants, schools, and sporting events but generally does not sell food directly to the
public. Also, Sysco does not transform the food prior to sale; it just stores the food, repack-
ages it as necessary, and delivers it.

Retailers purchase inventory from manufacturers or wholesalers and then sell this inventory to end users. You probably are more familiar with retail companies because these are
the companies from which you buy products. **Amazon**, **Best Buy**, **Target**, **Lowe's**, **Macy's**,
Gap, **Costco**, and **McDonald's** are retailers. Merchandising companies typically hold their
inventories in a single category simply called *inventory*.

 KEY POINT

Service companies record revenues when providing services to customers. Merchandising and
manufacturing companies record revenues when selling inventory to customers.

FLOW OF INVENTORY COSTS

Illustration 6–2 summarizes the flow of inventory costs for manufacturing and merchandising companies, as well as the sale of services by service companies.

Inventory's journey begins when manufacturing companies purchase raw materials, hire
workers, and incur manufacturing overhead during production. Once the products are finished, manufacturers normally pass finished goods inventory to merchandising companies,
whether wholesalers or retailers. Merchandising companies then sell finished goods to you,
the end user. In some cases, manufacturers may sell directly to end users.

Some companies sell goods and also provide services to customers. For example,
IBM generates about half its revenues from selling its inventories of hardware and software and the other half from providing services like consulting, systems maintenance, and
financing.

In this chapter, we focus on merchandising companies, both wholesalers and retailers.
Still, most of the accounting principles and procedures discussed here also apply to manufacturing companies. We do not attempt to address all the unique problems of accumulating
the direct costs of raw materials and labor and allocating manufacturing overhead. We leave
those details for managerial and cost accounting courses. In this course, we focus on the
financial reporting implications of inventory cost flows.

ILLUSTRATION 6–2

Types of Companies
and Flow of Inventory
Costs

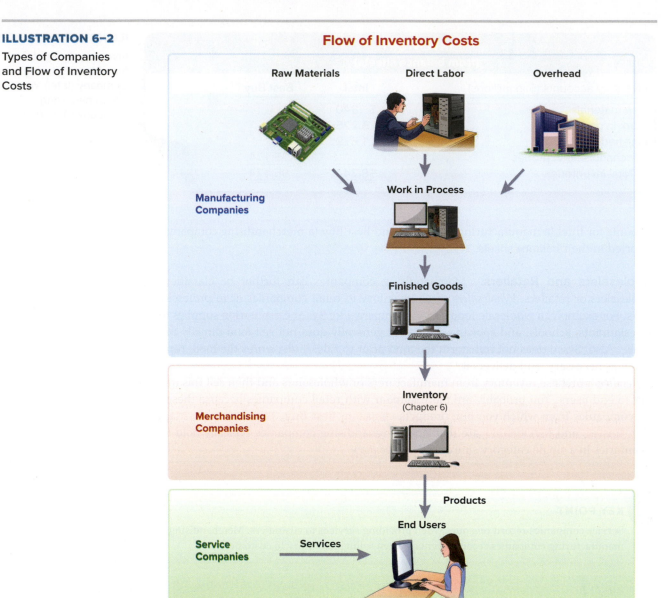

Multiple-Step Income Statement

■ **LO6–2**

Understand how cost of
goods sold is reported in
a multiple-step income
statement.

We've discussed that inventory is reported as an asset in the balance sheet. The amount reported is the cost of inventory *not yet sold* at the end of the year. Now let's discuss how we report **cost of goods sold**, an expense in the income statement, for the cost of the inventory *sold* during the year.

Assume a local **Best Buy** begins the year with $20,000 of inventory of the latest Bose noise canceling headphones. That amount represents how much Best Buy spent to purchase the inventory of these headphones on hand at the beginning of the year. During the year, the company purchases additional headphones for $90,000. The total cost of inventory (headphones) available for sale is $110,000 (= $20,000 + $90,000), as depicted in Illustration 6–3.

Now, here's where we'll see the direct relationship between ending inventory and cost of goods sold. Of the $110,000 in inventory available for sale, assume that by the end of the year the purchase cost of the remaining headphones *not sold* equals $30,000. This is the amount reported for ending inventory in the balance sheet. What is the amount reported for cost of goods *sold*? If $30,000 of the inventory available for sale was not sold, then the remaining portion of $80,000 (= $110,000 − $30,000) was sold. This is the amount reported for cost of goods sold as an expense in the income statement.

ILLUSTRATION 6–3

Relationship between Inventory and Cost of Goods Sold

 KEY POINT

Inventory is a current asset reported in the balance sheet and represents the cost of inventory *not yet sold* at the end of the period. Cost of goods sold is an expense reported in the income statement and represents the cost of inventory *sold.*

To see how **Best Buy** actually reports its cost of goods sold as an expense, as well as its other income statement items, let's look at Illustration 6–4.

The format of Best Buy's income statement is called the **multiple-step income statement**, referring to the fact that the income statement reports *multiple* levels of income (or profit).

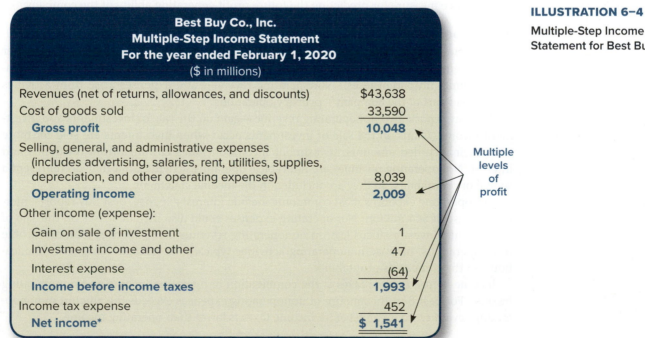

ILLUSTRATION 6–4

Multiple-Step Income Statement for Best Buy

*Amounts include those from Best Buy's actual income statement excluding small adjustments for discontinued operations and noncontrolling interest.

Most companies choose to report their income statement similar to the one shown for Best Buy. The reason why companies choose the multiple-step format is to show the revenues and expenses that arise from different types of activities. By separating revenues and expenses into their different types, investors and creditors are better able to determine the source of a company's profitability. Understanding the source of current profitability often enables a better prediction of future profitability. Let's review each level of profitability.

LEVELS OF PROFITABILITY

Gross Profit.   Inventory transactions are typically the most important activities of a merchandising company. For this reason, companies report the revenues and expenses directly associated with these transactions in the top section of a multiple-step income statement.

Revenues include the sale of products and services to customers. Inventory sales are commonly referred to as *sales revenue*, while providing services is referred to as *service revenue*. Best Buy reports its revenues after subtracting customer returns, allowances, and discounts, as discussed in Chapter 5, although the company does not list these amounts separately in the income statement. The net amount of revenues is commonly referred to as **net sales.**

Cost of goods sold is the cost of inventory sold during the year. Best Buy's cost of goods sold includes not only the cost of the physical merchandise purchased from suppliers, but also costs related to getting inventory ready for sale, such as shipping and other costs for its distribution network.

Gross profit equals net revenues (or net sales) minus cost of goods. Best Buy's gross profit of more than $10 billion shows the company can easily sell its inventory for more than its cost.

Operating Income.   After gross profit, the next items reported are *Selling, general, and administrative expenses,* often referred to as **operating expenses.** We discussed several types of operating expenses in earlier chapters—advertising, salaries, rent, utilities, supplies, and depreciation. These costs are normal for operating most companies. Best Buy has total operating expenses of $8,039 million, and like most companies, does not list individual operating expense amounts in the income statement.

Operating income (or sometimes referred to as income from operations) equals gross profit minus operating expenses. It measures profitability from *primary* operations, a key performance measure for predicting the future profit-generating ability of the company.

Income before Income Taxes.   After operating income, a company reports *nonoperating* revenues and expenses. Best Buy refers to these items as *Other income (expense).* Other income items are shown as positive amounts, and other expense items are shown as negative amounts (in parentheses). Nonoperating revenues and expenses arise from activities that are *not* part of the company's primary operations.

Best Buy reports two nonoperating revenues—gain on the sale of investments and investment income. Gains on the sale of investments occur when investments are sold for more than their recorded amounts. Investment income includes earnings from dividends and interest. Nonoperating revenues are not typical operating activities, but they do represent a source of profitability, so they are included in the income statement.

Nonoperating expenses most commonly include interest expense. Best Buy reports interest expense of $64 million. Nonoperating expenses could also include losses on the sale of investments. Investors focus less on nonoperating revenues and expenses than on income from operations, because nonoperating activities typically do not have long-term implications on the company's profitability.

Income before income taxes is the combination of operating income and nonoperating income. For Best Buy, the amount of nonoperating expenses exceeds the amount of nonoperating revenues, so income before income taxes is lower than operating income.

Net Income.   Next, a company subtracts *income tax expense* to find its bottom-line **net income.** Income tax expense is reported separately because it represents a significant expense. It's also the case that most major corporations (formally referred to as C corporations) are tax-paying entities, while income taxes of sole proprietorships and partnerships are paid at the individual owner level. By separately reporting income tax expense, the income statement clearly labels the difference in profitability associated with the income taxes of a corporation.

Best Buy's income tax expense equals 22.7% of income before taxes (= $452 ÷ $1,993). The actual corporate tax rate for Best Buy in 2020 was 21% for federal taxes plus approximately 3% for state taxes. Companies sometimes pay a lower rate if they operate in foreign jurisdictions with lower tax rates. The percentage of taxes can also vary because tax rules differ from financial reporting rules. Differences in reporting rules can result in financial income differing from taxable income in any particular year.

 KEY POINT

A multiple-step income statement reports multiple levels of profitability. **Gross profit** equals net revenues (or net sales) minus cost of goods sold. **Operating income** equals gross profit minus operating expenses. **Income before income taxes** equals operating income plus nonoperating revenues and minus nonoperating expenses. **Net income** equals all revenues minus all expenses.

Decision Maker's Perspective

Investors Understand One-Time Gains

Investors typically take a close look at the components of a company's profits. For example, Ford Motor Company announced that it had earned a net income for the fourth quarter (the final three months of the year) of $13.6 billion. Analysts had expected Ford to earn only $1.7 to $2.0 billion for that period. The day that Ford announced this earnings news, its stock price *fell* about 4.5%.

Why would Ford's stock price fall on a day when the company reported these seemingly high profits? A closer inspection of Ford's income statement shows that it included a one-time gain of $12.4 billion for the fourth quarter. After subtracting this one-time gain, Ford actually earned only about $1.2 billion from normal operations, easily missing analysts' expectations. This disappointing earnings performance is the reason the company's stock price fell.

Inventory Cost Methods

To this point, we've discussed the cost of inventory without considering how we determine that cost. We do that now by considering four methods for inventory costing:

1. Specific identification
2. First-in, first-out (FIFO)
3. Last-in, first-out (LIFO)
4. Weighted-average cost

We'll examine the inventory transactions for Mario's Game Shop in Illustration 6–5. There are 100 units of inventory at the beginning of the year and then two purchases are made during the year—one on April 25 and one on October 19. (Note the different unit costs at the time of each purchase.) There are **1,000** units available for sale.

During the year, the company sells **800** units of inventory for $15 each. While most companies sell their products continuously throughout the year, for simplicity we'll assume 300 units are sold on July 17, and 500 units are sold on December 15.

■ **LO6–3**
Determine the cost of goods sold and ending inventory using different inventory cost methods.

ILLUSTRATION 6–5

Inventory Transactions
for Mario's Game Shop

Date	Transaction	Number of Units	Unit Cost	Total Cost
Jan. 1	Beginning inventory	100	$ 7	$ 700
Apr. 25	Purchase	300	9	2,700
Oct. 19	Purchase	600	11	6,600
	Total available for sale	**1,000**		**$10,000**
Jul. 17	Sale (for $15 each)	300		
Dec. 15	Sale (for $15 each)	500		
	Total units sold	**800**		
Dec. 31	Ending inventory	**200**		

There are **200** units remaining in ending inventory at the end of the year (1,000 available − 800 sold). But which 200? Do they include some of the $7 units from beginning inventory? Are they 200 of the $9 units from the April 25 purchase? Or, do they include some $11 units from the October 19 purchase? **The answer depends on which of the four inventory methods is used.**

SPECIFIC IDENTIFICATION

The **specific identification method** is the method you might think of as the most logical. It matches—or *identifies*—each unit of inventory with its actual cost. For example, an automobile has a unique serial number that we can match to an invoice identifying the actual purchase price. Fine jewelry and pieces of art are other possibilities. Specific identification works well in such cases.

The specific identification method records *actual* units sold.

In our example for Mario's Game Shop, we might have been able to track each of the 800 units sold. Suppose the *actual* units sold include 100 units of beginning inventory, 200 units of the April 25 purchase, and 500 units of the October 19 purchase. The cost of those units would be reported as cost of goods sold. The cost of the 200 units remaining (consisting of 100 from the April 25 purchase and 100 from the October 19 purchase) would be reported as ending inventory.

However, keeping track of each unit of inventory typically is not practicable for most companies. Consider the inventory at **The Home Depot** or **Macy's**: large stores and numerous items, many of which are relatively inexpensive. Specific identification would be very difficult for such merchandisers. Although bar codes and RFID tags now make it possible to instantly track purchases and sales of specific types of inventory, it may be too costly to know the specific unit cost for each individual sale. **For that reason, the specific identification method is used primarily by companies with unique, expensive products with low sales volume.**

FIFO, LIFO, and weighted-average *assume* which units are sold.

Most companies instead use one of the three inventory cost flow assumptions—FIFO, LIFO, or weighted-average cost. Note the use of the word *assumptions*. FIFO, LIFO, and weighted-average cost *assume* a particular pattern of inventory cost flows. However, the *actual* flow of inventory does not need to match the *assumed* cost flow in order for the company to use a particular method. This is a crucial point. **Companies are allowed to report inventory costs by *assuming* which units of inventory are sold and not sold, even if this does not match the *actual* flow.** This is another example of using estimates in financial accounting.

FIRST-IN, FIRST-OUT

Using the **first-in, first-out (FIFO) method**, we assume that the first units purchased (the first in) are the first ones sold (the first out). We assume that beginning inventory sells first, followed by the inventory from the first purchase during the year, followed by the inventory from the second purchase during the year, and so on.

As shown previously in Illustration 6–5 for Mario's Game Shop, 800 units were sold during the year. Using the FIFO method, we assume they were the *first* 800 units purchased. The remaining 200 units represent ending inventory. The calculations for cost of goods sold and ending inventory are shown in Illustration 6–6.

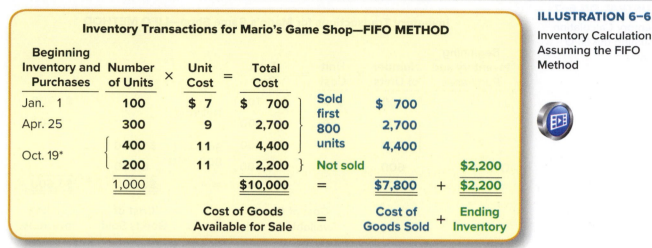

Inventory Transactions for Mario's Game Shop—FIFO METHOD

Beginning Inventory and Purchases	Number of Units	×	Unit Cost	=	Total Cost			
Jan. 1	100		$ 7		$ 700	Sold first 800 units	$ 700	
Apr. 25	300		9		2,700		2,700	
Oct. 19*	400		11		4,400		4,400	
	200		11		2,200 }	Not sold		$2,200
	1,000				$10,000	=	$7,800	+ $2,200

| | Cost of Goods Available for Sale | = | Cost of Goods Sold | + | Ending Inventory |

*Total of 600 units were purchased on October 19.

ILLUSTRATION 6–6

Inventory Calculation Assuming the FIFO Method

Cost of Goods Sold.   The first 800 units assumed sold include 100 units of beginning inventory, 300 units from the April 25 purchase, and 400 units from the October 19 purchase. Multiplying these units by their respective unit costs, Mario's reports cost of goods sold in the income statement as **$7,800**.

Ending Inventory.   Of the 600 units purchased on October 19, 200 are assumed not to be sold. These units cost $11 each, so the amount of ending inventory Mario's reports in the balance sheet will be **$2,200**.

 COMMON MISTAKE

When calculating cost of goods sold using FIFO, students sometimes forget to count beginning inventory as the first purchase. These units were purchased last period, which was before any purchases this period, so they are assumed to be the first units sold.

You may have noticed that we don't actually need to directly calculate both cost of goods sold and inventory. Once we calculate one, the other is apparent. Because the two amounts always add up to the cost of goods available for sale (**$10,000** in our example), knowing either amount allows us to subtract to find the other.

LAST-IN, FIRST-OUT

Using the **last-in, first-out (LIFO) method**, we assume that the last units purchased (the last in) are the first ones sold (the first out). In other words, the very *last unit purchased* for the year is assumed to be the very *first unit sold*. While this pattern of inventory flow is unrealistic for nearly all companies, LIFO is an allowable reporting practice. **Companies that use LIFO for reporting purposes calculate cost of goods sold and ending inventory only once per period—at the end.** This means that companies don't keep a continual record of LIFO amounts throughout the year.

Recall Mario's Game Shop sold 800 units during the year. Using the LIFO method, we assume they were the *last* 800 units purchased. The remaining 200 units represent ending inventory. The calculations for cost of goods sold and ending inventory are shown in Illustration 6–7.

ILLUSTRATION 6–7

Inventory Calculation Assuming the LIFO Method

Inventory Transactions for Mario's Game Shop—LIFO METHOD

Beginning Inventory and Purchases	Number of Units	×	Unit Cost	=	Total Cost			
Jan. 1	100		$ 7		$ 700 ⎫ Not sold			$ 700
Apr. 25*	100		9		900 ⎭			900
	200		9		1,800 ⎫ Sold last	$1,800		
Oct. 19	600		11		6,600 ⎭ 800 units	6,600		
	1,000				$10,000 =	$8,400	+	$1,600
					Cost of Goods Available for Sale	=	Cost of Goods Sold	+	Ending Inventory

*Total of 300 units were purchased on April 25.

Cost of Goods Sold.   The last 800 units assumed sold include the 600 units purchased on October 19 and 200 from the units purchased on April 25. Multiplying these units by their respective unit costs, Mario's reports cost of goods sold in the income statement as **$8,400**.

Ending Inventory.   Of the units purchased on April 25, 100 are assumed not to be sold. These units, along with the 100 units of beginning inventory, will be multiplied by their respective unit costs to reporting ending inventory of **$1,600**.

 COMMON MISTAKE

Many students find it surprising that companies are allowed to report inventory costs using assumed amounts rather than actual amounts. Nearly all companies sell their actual inventory in a FIFO manner, but they are allowed to report it as if they sold it in a LIFO manner. Later, we'll see why that's advantageous.

WEIGHTED-AVERAGE COST

Using the **weighted-average cost method**, we assume that both cost of goods sold and ending inventory consist of a random mixture of all the goods available for sale. We assume each unit of inventory has a cost equal to the weighted-average unit cost of all inventory items. We calculate that cost at the end of the year as

$$\text{Weighted-average unit cost} = \frac{\text{Cost of goods available for sale}}{\text{Number of units available for sale}}$$

Illustration 6–8 demonstrates the calculation of cost of goods sold and ending inventory using the weighted-average cost method. Notice that the weighted-average cost of each unit is $10, even though none of the units actually cost $10. However, on average, all the units cost $10, and this is the amount we use to calculate cost of goods sold and ending inventory under the weighted-average cost method.

ILLUSTRATION 6–8

Inventory Calculation Assuming the Weighted-Average Cost Method

Inventory Transactions for Mario's Game Shop— WEIGHTED-AVERAGE COST METHOD

		Cost of Goods Available for Sale		
Date	Transaction	Number of Units ×	Unit Cost =	Total Cost
Jan. 1	Beginning inventory	100	$ 7	$ 700
Apr. 25	Purchase	300	9	2,700
Oct. 19	Purchase	600	11	6,600
		1,000		$10,000

$$\text{Weighted-average unit cost} = \frac{\$10,000}{1,000 \text{ units}} = \$10 \text{ per unit}$$

Cost of goods sold	=	800 sold	×	$10	=	$ 8,000
Ending inventory	=	200 not sold	×	10	=	2,000
						$10,000

COMMON MISTAKE

In calculating the weighted-average unit cost, be sure to use a *weighted* average of the unit cost instead of the *simple* average. In the example above, there are three unit costs: $7, $9, and $11. A simple average of these amounts is $9 [= ($7 + $9 + $11) ÷ 3]. The simple average, though, fails to take into account that more units were purchased at $11 than at $7 or $9. So we need to *weight* the unit costs by the number of units purchased. We do that by taking the total cost of goods available for sale ($10,000) divided by the total number of units available for sale (1,000) for a weighted average of $10.

Illustration 6–9 depicts the concept behind the three inventory cost flow assumptions for Mario's Game Shop. If Mario sells 800 units of inventory, which 800 are they?

- Using FIFO, we assume inventory is sold in the order purchased: Beginning inventory is sold first, the first purchase during the year is sold second, and part of the second purchase during the year is sold third.
- Using LIFO, we assume inventory is sold in the opposite order that we purchased it: The last purchase is sold first, and part of the second-to-last purchase is sold second.
- Using average cost, we assume inventory is sold using an average of all inventory purchased, including the beginning inventory.

COMMON MISTAKE

FIFO and LIFO describe more directly the calculation of *cost of goods sold,* rather than ending inventory. For example, FIFO (first-in, first-out) directly suggests which inventory units are assumed sold (the first ones in) and therefore used to calculate cost of goods sold. It is implicit under FIFO that the inventory units *not* sold are the last ones in and are used to calculate ending inventory.

KEY POINT

Companies are allowed to report inventory costs by *assuming* which specific units of inventory are sold and not sold, even if this does not match the *actual* flow. The three major inventory cost flow assumptions are FIFO (first-in, first-out), LIFO (last-in, first-out), and weighted-average cost.

ILLUSTRATION 6–9

Comparison of Cost of Goods Sold and Ending Inventory under the Three Inventory Cost Flow Assumptions for Mario's Game Shop

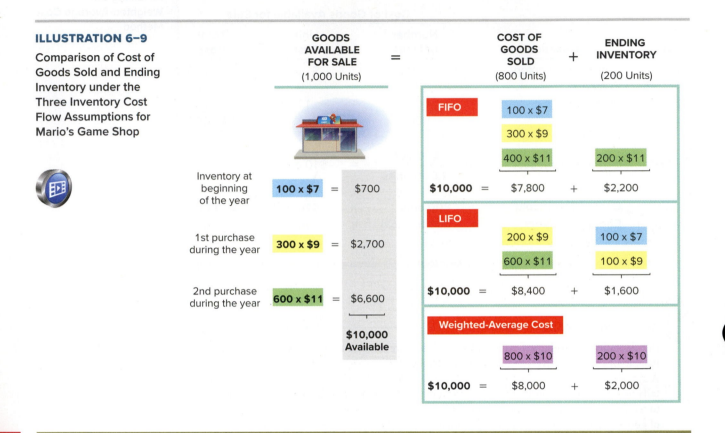

Let's Review

NASCAR Unlimited sells remote-control cars. The company has the following beginning inventory and purchase for the year.

Date	Transaction	Number of Units	Unit Cost	Total Cost
Jan. 1	Beginning inventory	120	$20	$2,400
Aug. 15	Purchase	180	15	2,700
	Total	300		$5,100

Because of technological advances, NASCAR Unlimited has seen a decrease in the unit cost of its inventory. Throughout the year, the company maintained a selling price of $30 for each remote-control car and sold a total of 280 units, which leaves 20 units in ending inventory.

Required:

1. Calculate cost of goods sold and ending inventory using the FIFO method.
2. Calculate cost of goods sold and ending inventory using the LIFO method.
3. Calculate cost of goods sold and ending inventory using the weighted-average cost method.

Solution:

1. Cost of goods sold and ending inventory using the **FIFO method**:

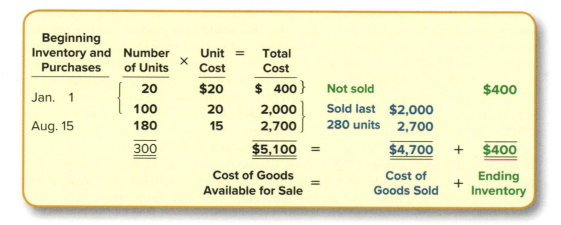

Beginning Inventory and Purchases	Number of Units	×	Unit Cost	=	Total Cost				
Jan. 1	120		$20		$2,400 ⎱	Sold first	$2,400		
Aug. 15	160		15		2,400 ⎰	280 units	2,400		
	20		15		300 ⎱	Not sold			$300
	300				$5,100	=	$4,800	+	$300
					Cost of Goods Available for Sale	=	Cost of Goods Sold	+	Ending Inventory

2. Cost of goods sold and ending inventory using the **LIFO method**:

Beginning Inventory and Purchases	Number of Units	×	Unit Cost	=	Total Cost				
Jan. 1	20		$20		$ 400 ⎰	Not sold			$400
	100		20		2,000 ⎱	Sold last	$2,000		
Aug. 15	180		15		2,700 ⎰	280 units	2,700		
	300				$5,100	=	$4,700	+	$400
					Cost of Goods Available for Sale	=	Cost of Goods Sold	+	Ending Inventory

3. Cost of goods sold and ending inventory using the **weighted-average cost method**:

$$\text{Weighted-average unit cost} = \frac{\$5,100}{300 \text{ units}} = \$17 \text{ per unit}$$

Cost of goods sold	=	280 **sold**	×	$17	=	$4,760
Ending inventory	=	20 not sold	×	17	=	340
		300				$5,100

Suggested Homework:
BE6–5, BE6–6;
E6–4, E6–5;
P6–1A&B, P6–2A&B

Effects of Inventory Cost Methods

Companies are free to choose FIFO, LIFO, or weighted-average cost to report inventory and cost of goods sold. However, because inventory costs generally change over time, the reported amounts for ending inventory and cost of goods sold will not be the same across inventory reporting methods. These differences could mislead investors and creditors if they are not aware of differences in inventory assumptions.

Illustration 6–10 compares the FIFO, LIFO, and weighted-average cost methods for Mario's Game Shop. (Recall from earlier discussion in this chapter that *gross profit* is a key measure of profitability, calculated as the difference between revenues and cost of goods sold.)

■ **LO6–4**
Explain the financial statement effects and tax effects of inventory cost methods.

ILLUSTRATION 6–10

Comparison of Inventory Cost Methods, when Costs Are Rising

	FIFO	LIFO	Weighted-Average
Balance sheet:			
Ending inventory	$ 2,200	$ 1,600	$ 2,000
Income statement:			
Sales revenue (800 × $15)	$12,000	$12,000	$12,000
Cost of goods sold	7,800	8,400	8,000
Gross profit	$ 4,200	$ 3,600	$ 4,000

When inventory costs are *rising* (as in our example), FIFO results in

1. Higher reported amount for inventory in the balance sheet.
2. Higher reported gross profit in the income statement.

The reason is that FIFO assumes the lower costs of the earlier purchases become cost of goods sold first. This leaves the higher costs of the later purchases in ending inventory. **If inventory costs had been** *falling*, then it's LIFO that would have produced higher reported inventory and gross profit. The weighted-average cost method typically produces amounts that fall between the FIFO and LIFO amounts for both cost of goods sold and ending inventory.

FIFO has a balance-sheet focus.

Accountants often call FIFO the *balance-sheet approach:* The amount it reports for ending inventory (which appears in the *balance sheet*) better approximates the current cost of inventory. The ending inventory amount reported under LIFO, in contrast, generally includes "old" inventory costs that do not realistically represent the cost of today's inventory.

LIFO has an income-statement focus.

Accountants often call LIFO the *income-statement approach:* The amount it reports for cost of goods sold (which appears in the *income statement*) more realistically matches the current costs of inventory needed to produce current revenues. Recall that LIFO assumes the last purchases are sold first, reporting the most recent inventory cost in cost of goods sold. However, also note that the most recent cost is not the same as the actual cost. FIFO better approximates actual cost of goods sold for most companies, since most companies' actual physical flow follows FIFO.

Decision Maker's Perspective

FIFO or LIFO?

Management must weigh the benefits of FIFO and LIFO when deciding which inventory cost flow assumption will produce a better outcome for the company. Here we review the logic behind that decision.

Why Choose FIFO?

FIFO matches physical flow for most companies.

Most companies' actual physical flow follows FIFO. Think about a supermarket, sporting goods store, clothing shop, electronics store, or just about any company with whom you're familiar. These companies generally sell their oldest inventory first (first-in, first-out). If a company wants to choose an inventory method that most closely approximates its *actual physical flow* of inventory, then for most companies, FIFO makes the most sense.

FIFO generally results in higher assets and higher net income when inventory costs are rising.

Another reason managers may want to use FIFO relates to its effect on the financial statements. **During periods of rising costs, which is the case for most companies (including our example for Mario's Game Shop), FIFO results in a (1)** *higher* **ending inventory, (2)** *lower* **cost of goods sold, and (3)** *higher* **reported profit than does LIFO.** Managers may want to report higher assets and profitability to increase their bonus compensation, decrease unemployment risk, satisfy shareholders, meet lending agreements, or increase stock price.

Why Choose LIFO?

If FIFO results in higher total assets and higher net income and produces amounts that most closely follow the actual flow of inventory, why would any company choose LIFO? **The primary benefit of choosing LIFO is tax savings.** LIFO results in the lowest amount of reported profits (when inventory costs are rising). While that might not look so good in the income statement, it's a welcome outcome in the tax return. When taxable income is lower, the company owes less in taxes to the Internal Revenue Service (IRS).

Can a company have its cake and eat it too by using FIFO for financial reporting and LIFO for the tax return? No. The IRS established the LIFO conformity rule, which requires a company that uses LIFO for tax reporting to also use LIFO for financial reporting.

REPORTING THE LIFO DIFFERENCE

As Mario's Game Shop demonstrates, the choice between FIFO and LIFO results in different amounts for ending inventory in the balance sheet and cost of goods sold in the income statement. This complicates the way we compare financial statements: One company may be using FIFO, while a competing company may be using LIFO. **To better compare each company's inventory and profitability, investors must adjust for the fact that managers' choice of inventory method has an effect on reported amounts.**

Companies that report using LIFO must also report the difference between the LIFO amount and what that amount would have been if they had used FIFO. This difference is often referred to as the *LIFO reserve.*

For example, Illustration 6–11 shows the current asset section of **Kroger Company**'s balance sheet. Kroger is a retail company that serves millions of people each day in its supermarkets. Supermarkets don't actually sell the last units first, but they are allowed to report inventory under that assumption. Kroger maintains its internal inventory records throughout the year using FIFO. This results in ending inventory of $8,464 million. Kroger then uses a year-end adjusting entry to convert that FIFO amount to LIFO for financial reporting purposes. Its LIFO inventory is lower by $1,380 million.

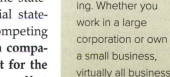 CAREER CORNER

Many career opportunities are available in tax accounting. Because tax laws constantly change and are complex, tax accountants provide services to their clients not only through income tax statement preparation but also by formulating tax strategies to minimize tax payments. The choice of LIFO versus FIFO is one such example.

Tax accountants need a thorough understanding of legal matters, business transactions, and the tax code. Large corporations increasingly are looking to hire individuals with both an accounting and a legal background in tax. For example, someone who is a Certified Public Accountant (CPA) and has a law degree is especially desirable in the job market. In addition, people in non-accounting positions also benefit greatly from an understanding of tax accounting. Whether you work in a large corporation or own a small business, virtually all business decisions have tax consequences.

Design Pics/Darren Greenwood

LIFO generally results in greater tax savings.

KROGER COMPANY Balance Sheet (partial)	
($ in millions)	2020
Current assets	
Cash and temporary cash investments	$ 399
Store deposits in-transit	1,179
Receivables	1,706
FIFO inventory	8,464
LIFO reserve	(1,380)
Prepaid and other current assets	522
Total current assets	$10,890

ILLUSTRATION 6–11

Impact of the LIFO Difference on Reported Inventory of Kroger Company

Decision Point

Question 	Accounting information	Analysis
When comparing inventory amounts between two companies, does the choice of inventory method matter?	The LIFO difference reported in the balance sheet or notes to the financial statements	When inventory costs are rising, FIFO results in a *higher* reported inventory. The LIFO difference can be used to compare inventory of two companies if one uses FIFO and the other uses LIFO.

CONSISTENCY IN REPORTING

Companies can choose which inventory method they prefer, even if the method does not match the actual physical flow of goods. However, once the company chooses a method, it is not allowed to frequently change to another one.[1] For example, a retail store cannot use FIFO in the current year because inventory costs are rising and then switch to LIFO in the following year because inventory costs are now falling.

However, a company need not use the same method for all its inventory. **International Paper Company**, for instance, uses LIFO for its raw materials and finished pulp and paper products, and both FIFO and weighted-average cost for other inventories. Because of the importance of inventories and the possible differential effects of different methods on the financial statements, a company informs its stockholders of the inventory method(s) being used in a note to the financial statements.

 KEY POINT

Generally, FIFO more closely resembles the actual physical flow of inventory. When inventory costs are rising, FIFO results in higher reported inventory in the balance sheet and higher reported income in the income statement. Conversely, LIFO results in a lower reported inventory and net income, reducing the company's income tax obligation.

 INTERNATIONAL FINANCIAL REPORTING STANDARDS (IFRS)

SHOULD LIFO BE ELIMINATED?

LIFO is *not* allowed under IFRS because it tends not to match the actual physical flow of inventory. FIFO and weighted-average cost are allowable inventory cost methods under IFRS. This distinction will become increasingly important as the United States continues to consider whether to accept IFRS for financial reporting. Will LIFO eventually disappear as a permitted inventory cost flow method? Perhaps so . . . stay tuned.

For more discussion, see Appendix E.

PART B   RECORDING INVENTORY TRANSACTIONS

So far, we've talked about purchases and sales of inventories and how to track their costs. We have not yet discussed how to *record* inventory transactions. We turn to that topic now.

A **perpetual inventory system** is used by nearly all companies to record inventory transactions. This system involves recording inventory purchases and sales on a *perpetual*

---

[1]When a company changes from LIFO for tax purposes, it cannot change back to LIFO until it has filed five tax returns using the non-LIFO method.

(continual) basis. Managers know that to make good decisions related to purchase orders, pricing, product development, and employee management, maintaining inventory records on a continual basis is necessary. Technological advances in recent years to instantly track inventory purchases and sales have made the perpetual system simpler and more cost-effective for most companies.

In contrast, a **periodic inventory system** does not continually record inventory amounts. Instead, it calculates the balance of inventory once per *period,* at the end, based on a physical count of inventory on hand. Appendix A to the chapter shows how to record transactions using the periodic inventory system.

As we'll see in the next example, **for companies that report using FIFO, recording transactions on a continual basis under a perpetual inventory system will produce the same amounts for cost of goods sold and ending inventory as under a periodic system** (computed previously in Illustration 6–6). However, this would not be true for LIFO. In practice, companies that report using LIFO typically maintain their own inventory records on a perpetual FIFO basis (as demonstrated in the example below) and then prepare a year-end adjusting entry to convert to LIFO periodic amounts (as computed previously in Illustration 6–7). We'll show this simple LIFO adjustment below. **The inventory recording and reporting procedures we demonstrate below most closely reflect those used in actual practice.**[2]

Perpetual Inventory System

To see how to record inventory transactions using a perpetual inventory system, let's look again at the inventory transactions for Mario's Game Shop, shown below in Illustration 6–12. These are the same transactions shown previously in Illustration 6–5.

■ **LO6–5**
Record inventory transactions using a perpetual inventory system.

ILLUSTRATION 6–12
Inventory Transactions for Mario's Game Shop

Date	Transaction	Details	Total Cost	Total Revenue
Jan. 1	Beginning inventory	100 units for $7 each	$ 700	
Apr. 25	Purchase	300 units for $9 each	2,700	
Jul. 17	Sale	300 units for $15 each		$ 4,500
Oct. 19	Purchase	600 units for $11 each	6,600	
Dec. 15	Sale	500 units for $15 each		7,500
	Totals		$10,000	$12,000

INVENTORY PURCHASES AND SALES

Purchase.   The purchase of inventory on account for $2,700 on April 25 would be recorded as

April 25	Debit	Credit
Inventory	**2,700**	
Accounts Payable		**2,700**
(Purchase inventory on account)		

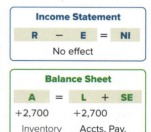

Income Statement

R	−	E	=	NI
		No effect		

Balance Sheet

A	=	L	+	SE
+2,700		+2,700		
Inventory		Accts. Pay.		

The purchase is recorded as an increase to Inventory (an asset) and an increase to Accounts Payable (a liability). If the purchase was paid in cash, we would have recorded Cash instead of Accounts Payable.

---

[2]Some companies use the weighted-average method with a perpetual inventory system for their inventory records. This means the company must recalculate the average cost of remaining inventory each time a new purchase is made during the year. Each sale could then potentially be assigned a different average cost—unlike our example in Illustration 6–8, which assumes a periodic system (a single average cost for the entire period). For this reason, the weighted-average method using a perpetual inventory system is often referred to as the *moving-average* method. With the help of computers and electronic scanners, such tedious calculations throughout the period are possible. However, for this introductory course, we focus on conceptual understanding from the weighted-average method and leave the moving-average method for more advanced accounting classes.

Sale.   On July 17, Mario sold 300 units of inventory on account for $15 each, resulting in total sales of $4,500. We make two entries to record the sale.

Income Statement		
R	**– E =**	**NI**
+4,500	+2,500	+2,000
Sales Rev.	COGS	

Balance Sheet		
A =	**L +**	**SE**
+4,500		+2,000
Accts. Rec.		
−2,500		
Inventory		

July 17	Debit	Credit
Accounts Receivable	4,500	
Sales Revenue		4,500
(Sell inventory on account)		
($4,500 = 300 units × $15)		
Cost of Goods Sold	2,500	
Inventory		2,500
(Record cost of inventory sold)		
($2,500 = [100 units × $7] + [200 units × $9])		

1. The first entry records an increase to an asset account (in this case, Accounts Receivable) and an increase to Sales Revenue. The amount to record is the price charged to the customer. Customers were charged $15 for each of the 300 units (or $4,500 total).

2. The second entry records an increase to Cost of Goods Sold and a decrease to Inventory. The amount to record is the assumed cost of the units sold. Assuming Mario's uses FIFO, the cost of the *first* 300 units purchased includes $700 of beginning inventory (100 units × $7) plus $1,800 of the April 25 purchase (200 units × $9).

By recording the sales revenue and the cost of goods sold at the same time, we can see that Mario's profit on the sale is $2,000.

Additional Purchase and Sale.   On October 19, Mario purchased 600 additional units of inventory for $6,600 on account. We record that purchase as

Income Statement		
R	**– E =**	**NI**
	No effect	

Balance Sheet		
A =	**L +**	**SE**
+6,600	+6,600	
Inventory	Accts. Pay.	

October 19	Debit	Credit
Inventory	6,600	
Accounts Payable		6,600
(Purchase inventory on account)		

On December 15, Mario sold another 500 units for $15 each on account. Again, we make two entries to record the sale. The first entry increases Accounts Receivable and Sales Revenue for $7,500 (500 units × $15). The second entry adjusts the Cost of Goods Sold and Inventory accounts. What did the inventory sold on December 15 cost Mario? Using the FIFO assumption, the cost of the 500 units sold is $5,300. This includes $900 of remaining units from the April 25 purchase (100 units × $9) plus $4,400 from the October 19 purchase (400 units × $11).

Income Statement		
R	**– E =**	**NI**
+7,500	+5,300	+2,200
Sales Rev.	COGS	

Balance Sheet		
A =	**L +**	**SE**
+7,500		+2,200
Accts. Rec.		
−5,300		
Inventory		

December 15	Debit	Credit
Accounts Receivable..	7,500	
Sales Revenue		7,500
(Sell inventory on account)		
($7,500 = 500 units × $15)		
Cost of Goods Sold..	5,300	
Inventory..		5,300
(Record cost of inventory sold)		
($5,300 = [100 units × $9] + [400 units × $11])		

After recording all purchases and sales of inventory for the year, we can determine the ending balance of Inventory by examining the postings to the account. Thus, Mario's ending Inventory balance is $2,200, as shown in Illustration 6–13. Refer back to Illustration 6–6 to verify the ending balance of inventory using FIFO.

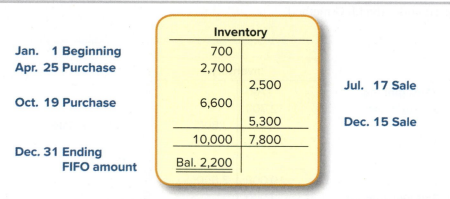

ILLUSTRATION 6–13

Inventory Account for Mario's Game Shop

You can also verify the balance of cost of goods sold. In the two preceding transactions, the Cost of Goods Sold account was debited for $2,500 and $5,300. That's an ending balance of $7,800, and that's the same amount calculated in Illustration 6–6 as the cost of the first 800 units sold.

 KEY POINT

The perpetual inventory system maintains a continual—or *perpetual*—record of inventory purchased and sold. When companies *purchase* inventory using a perpetual inventory system, they increase the Inventory account and either decrease Cash or increase Accounts Payable. When companies *sell* inventory, they make two entries: (1) They increase an asset account (Cash or Accounts Receivable) and increase Sales Revenue, and (2) they increase Cost of Goods Sold and decrease Inventory.

Simple Year-End Adjustment from FIFO to LIFO.   In the example above, we recorded inventory transactions using the FIFO assumption. Thus, Mario assumed that the 800 units sold during the year came from the first 800 units purchased. **In practice, most companies maintain their own inventory records throughout the year using the FIFO assumption, because that's how they typically sell their actual inventory.** However, as discussed earlier in the chapter, for preparing financial statements, many companies choose to report their inventory using the LIFO assumption. So, at the end of the year how does a company adjust its own FIFO inventory records to a LIFO basis for preparing financial statements? The company must make a year-end LIFO adjustment.

To see how easy the year-end LIFO adjustment can be, let's refer back to our example involving Mario's Game Shop. As summarized in Illustration 6–13, Mario's ending balance of Inventory using FIFO is $2,200. Under LIFO, it would be only $1,600 (see Illustration 6–7). As a result, if Mario's Game Shop wants to adjust its FIFO inventory records to LIFO for preparing financial statements, it needs to adjust the Inventory account downward by $600 (decreasing the balance from $2,200 to $1,600). In this case, we record the LIFO adjustment at the end of the period through a decrease to Inventory and an increase to Cost of Goods Sold:[3]

December 31	Debit	Credit
Cost of Goods Sold..	600	
Inventory..		600
(Record the LIFO adjustment)		

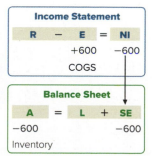

[3]Some companies credit a contra asset account called LIFO Reserve instead of the Inventory account. A credit to either account reduces the reported amount of inventory in the balance sheet.

In rare situations where the LIFO Inventory balance is *greater* than the FIFO Inventory balance (such as when inventory costs are declining), the entry for the LIFO adjustment would be reversed.

Illustration 6–14 shows the Inventory account for Mario's Game Shop after the year-end LIFO adjustment. Notice that the balance of Inventory has decreased to reflect the amount reported under the LIFO method.

ILLUSTRATION 6–14

Inventory Account for Mario's Game Shop, after LIFO Adjustment

Inventory		
Jan. 1 Beginning	700	
Apr. 25 Purchase	2,700	
		2,500 Jul. 17 Sale
Oct. 19 Purchase	6,600	
		5,300 Dec. 15 Sale
	10,000	7,800
Dec. 31 FIFO amount	2,200	
		600 Dec. 31 LIFO adjustment
Dec. 31 Ending LIFO amount	Bal. 1,600	

KEY POINT

Most companies maintain their own inventory records on a FIFO basis, and then some prepare financial statements on a LIFO basis. To adjust their FIFO inventory records to LIFO for financial reporting, companies use a LIFO adjustment at the end of the year.

ADDITIONAL INVENTORY TRANSACTIONS

To this point, we've recorded inventory purchases and inventory sales transactions. Let's add three more inventory-related transactions to our Mario's Game Shop example, as follows:

1. On April 25, pays freight charges of $300 for inventory purchased on April 25.
2. On April 30, pays for the units purchased on April 25, less a 2% purchase discount.
3. On October 22, returns 50 defective units from the October 19 purchase.

Next, we discuss how to record each of these three transactions.

Freight Charges.   A significant cost associated with inventory for most merchandising companies includes freight (also called shipping or delivery) charges. This includes the cost of shipments of inventory from suppliers, as well as the cost of shipments to customers. When goods are shipped, they are shipped with terms *FOB shipping point* or *FOB destination.* FOB stands for "free on board" and indicates *when* title (ownership) passes from the seller to the buyer.

1. **FOB** *shipping point* means title passes when the seller *ships* the inventory.
2. **FOB** *destination* means title passes when the inventory reaches the buyer's *destination.*

For example, suppose that when Mario purchased 300 units for $2,700 ($9 per unit) on April 25, the terms of the purchase were FOB shipping point. The inventory was shipped from the supplier's warehouse on April 25 but did not arrive at Mario's location until April 29. Mario would record the purchase when title passes—April 25—even though Mario does not have actual physical possession of the inventory until April 29. If, instead, the terms of the purchase were FOB destination, Mario would have waited until the inventory was received on April 29 to record the purchase. This idea is demonstrated in Illustration 6–15.

ILLUSTRATION 6–15

Shipping Terms

Supplier

300 units × $9

Mario's Game Shop

In transit

April 25

April 29

1. FOB Shipping Point. Title passes at shipping point (when inventory leaves the supplier's warehouse). Mario would record the purchase on April 25.

Shipping Terms

2. FOB Destination. Title passes at destination (when inventory arrives at Mario's). Mario would record the purchase on April 29.

Freight charges on incoming shipments from suppliers are commonly referred to as **freight-in**. **We add the cost of freight-in to the balance of Inventory.** In this case, the cost of freight is considered a cost of the purchased inventory. When Mario pays $300 for freight charges associated with the purchase of inventory on April 25, those charges would be recorded as part of the inventory cost.

April 25	Debit	Credit
Inventory..	300	
Cash		300
(Pay freight-in charges)		

Income Statement

R	–	E	=	NI
		No effect		

Balance Sheet

A	=	L	+	SE
+300				
Inventory				
–300				
Cash				

Later, when that inventory is sold, those freight charges become part of the cost of goods sold. In Mario's case, all of the units purchased on April 25 are sold by the end of the year, so the $300 freight charge would be reported as part of cost of goods sold in the income statement at the end of the year.

The cost of freight on shipments *to* customers is called **freight-out**. Shipping charges for outgoing inventory are reported in the income statement either as part of cost of goods sold or as an operating expense, usually among selling expenses. If a company adopts a policy of not including shipping charges in cost of goods sold, both the amounts incurred during the period as well as the income statement classification of the expense must be disclosed.[4]

To see an example of how **Amazon.com** accounts for freight charges, look at Illustration 6–16.

ILLUSTRATION 6–16

Accounting for Shipping Costs by **Amazon.com**

AMAZON.COM, INC.
Notes to the Financial Statements (excerpt)

Cost of sales primarily consists of the purchase price of consumer products, **inbound and outbound shipping costs**, including costs related to sortation and delivery centers and where we are the transportation service provider...

---

[4]FASB ASC 605–45–50–2: Revenue Recognition–Principal Agent Considerations–Disclosure–Shipping and Handling Fees and Costs (previously "Accounting for Shipping and Handling Fees and Costs," *EITF Issue No. 00–10* [Norwalk, Conn.: FASB, 2000] par. 6).

302 CHAPTER 6 Inventory and Cost of Goods Sold

Purchase Discounts. As discussed in Chapter 5, sellers often encourage prompt payment by offering *discounts* to buyers. From the seller's point of view, these are sales discounts; from the buyer's point of view, they are *purchase discounts*. **Purchase discounts allow buyers to trim a portion of the cost of the purchase in exchange for payment within a certain period of time.** Buyers are not required to take purchase discounts, but many find it advantageous to do so.

Let's assume that Mario's supplier, Luigi Software, Inc., offers terms 2/10, n/30 for the April 25 purchase on account. This means that Mario can receive a 2% discount if payment is made within 10 days, but the total invoice is due within 30 days.

Recall that on April 25 Mario purchased 300 units on account for $9 each (or $2,700 total). When Mario makes payment on April 30, the discount would be $54 (= $2,700 × 2%). Mario has to pay only $2,646 (= $2,700 − $54) to eliminate the $2,700 amount owed. To account for the purchase discount, we subtract the discount from the balance in the Inventory account.

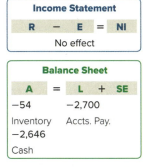

April 30	Debit	Credit
Accounts Payable	2,700	
Inventory		54
Cash		2,646
(Pay on account with a 2% purchase discount of $54)		
($54 = $2,700 × 2%)		

Just as freight charges *add* to the cost of inventory and therefore increase the cost of goods sold once those items are sold, purchase discounts *subtract* from the cost of inventory and therefore reduce cost of goods sold once those items are sold. When Mario sells the 300 units purchased on April 25, the cost of goods sold associated with those items will be the cost of the actual units ($2,700) plus freight charges ($300) less the purchase discount ($54), totaling $2,946.

Purchase Returns. Occasionally, a company will find inventory items to be unacceptable for some reason—perhaps they are damaged or are different from what was ordered. In those cases, the company returns the items to the supplier and records the purchase return as a reduction in both Inventory and Accounts Payable. For example, when Mario decides on October 22 to return 50 defective units from the 600 units purchased on October 19 for $11 each, the company would record the following transaction:

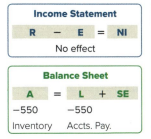

October 22	Debit	Credit
Accounts Payable	550	
Inventory		550
(Return inventory previously purchased on account)		
($550 = 50 defective units × $11)		

Let's recalculate Mario's gross profit after accounting for the additional inventory transactions related to freight charges and the purchase discount. The calculations are demonstrated in Illustration 6–17. Recall that Mario sold 800 units during the year for $15 each (or $12,000 total). This is the amount reported as sales revenue. From sales revenue, we subtract the cost of the 800 units sold. To calculate this amount, we need to look back at transactions related to the purchase cost of those 800 units, including the cost of freight charges and the purchase discount associated with the purchase on April 25. Mario would report $8,046 as the cost of goods sold, resulting in a gross profit of $3,954.

	Units	Unit Price	Total
Sales revenue	800	$15	$12,000

	Units	Unit Cost	Total
Cost of goods sold:			
Beginning inventory	100	$ 7	$ 700
Purchase on April 25	300	9	2,700
Freight charges			300
Purchase discount			(54)
Purchase on October 19	400	11	4,400
	800		$ 8,046
Gross profit			$ 3,954

ILLUSTRATION 6–17

Gross Profit for Mario's Game Shop after Additional Inventory Transactions

KEY POINT

For most companies, freight charges are added to the cost of inventory, whereas purchase returns and purchase discounts are deducted from the cost of inventory. Some companies choose to report freight charges on outgoing shipments as part of selling expenses instead of cost of goods sold.

Let's Review

Camcorder Central sells high-end **Sony** camcorders and accounts for its inventory using FIFO with a perpetual system. At the beginning of March, the company has camcorder inventory of $24,000 (= $240 × 100 units).

Required:

Record the following inventory transactions for Camcorder Central.
1. On March 7, Camcorder Central purchases on account 210 camcorders from Sony Corporation for $250 each, terms 2/10, n/30.
2. On March 8, Camcorder Central pays $2,000 for freight charges associated with the 210 camcorders purchased on March 7.
3. On March 10, Camcorder Central returns to Sony 10 defective camcorders from the March 7 purchase, receiving a credit of $250 for each camcorder.
4. On March 16, Camcorder Central makes full payment for inventory purchased on March 7, excluding the 10 defective camcorders returned and the 2% discount received.
5. On March 20, Camcorder Central sells 300 camcorders for $90,000 ($300 each). All sales are for cash.

Solution:

1. Camcorder Central's March 7 purchase on account of 210 camcorders from Sony Corporation for $250 each, terms 2/10, n/30:

March 7	Debit	Credit
Inventory	52,500	
Accounts Payable		52,500
(Purchase camcorders on account)		
($52,500 = $250 × 210 camcorders)		

2. Camcorder Central's March 8 payment for freight charges associated with the camcorders purchased on March 7:

March 8	Debit	Credit
Inventory..	2,000	
Cash..		2,000
(Pay for freight charges)		

3. Camcorder Central's March 10 return of 10 defective camcorders from the March 7 purchase, for a credit of $250 per camcorder:

March 10	Debit	Credit
Accounts Payable	2,500	
Inventory..		2,500
(Return defective camcorders)		

4. Camcorder Central's March 16 payment for inventory purchased on March 7, excluding the returned camcorders and less the 2% discount:

March 16	Debit	Credit
Accounts Payable	50,000	
Inventory..		1,000
Cash..		49,000
(Make full payment for March 7 purchase)		
($1,000 = $50,000 × 2%)		

5. Camcorder Central's cash sale on March 20 of 300 camcorders for $300 each:

March 20	Debit	Credit
Cash..	90,000	
Sales Revenue		90,000
(Sell 300 camcorders for cash)		
($90,000 = $300 × 300 camcorders)		
Cost of Goods Sold..	75,000	
Inventory..		75,000
(Record cost of camcorders sold)		
(Cost of 100 camcorders in beginning inventory = $24,000)		
(Cost of 200 camcorders purchased = $52,500 + $2,000 − $2,500 − $1,000 = $51,000)		

Suggested Homework:
BE6–10, BE6–12;
E6–9, E6–10;
P6–3A&B, P6–6A&B

SALES TRANSACTIONS: THE OTHER SIDE OF PURCHASE TRANSACTIONS

Flip Side

For every purchase transaction, there is a sales transaction for another party. Sometimes, seeing the other side of the transaction helps us understand the economic events we are recording. In the Let's Review exercise above, Camcorder Central made a $52,500 purchase of inventory on account from Sony Corporation. Camcorder Central then returned inventory of $2,500 and received a $1,000 purchase discount for quick payment. Camcorder Central is the purchaser and Sony is the seller.

We discussed returns and discounts from the seller's viewpoint in Chapter 5; here, let's briefly reexamine the transactions between Sony and Camcorder Central so we can

Purchaser			Seller		
Camcorder Central			**Sony Corporation**		
Purchase on Account			**Sale on Account***		
Inventory	52,500		Accounts Receivable	52,500	
Accounts Payable		52,500	Sales Revenue		52,500
Purchase Return			**Sales Return**		
Accounts Payable	2,500		Sales Return	2,500	
Inventory		2,500	Accounts Receivable		2,500
Payment on Account with Discount			**Receipt on Account with Discount**		
Accounts Payable	50,000		Cash	49,000	
Inventory		1,000	Sales Discounts	1,000	
Cash		49,000	Accounts Receivable		50,000

ILLUSTRATION 6–18

Comparison of Purchase and Sale of Inventory Transactions

*In practice, Sony also records the cost of inventory sold at the time of the sale. For simplicity, we omit this part of the transaction since Camcorder Central has no comparable transaction. We have also omitted Camcorder Central's March 20 sale of camcorders, since Sony is not party to that transaction.

see a side-by-side comparison of purchase and sales transactions. Illustration 6–18 shows these entries.

LOWER OF COST AND NET REALIZABLE VALUE

PART C

■ **LO6–6**
Apply the lower of cost and net realizable value rule for inventories.

Think about the store where you usually buy your clothes. You've probably noticed the store selling leftover inventory at deeply discounted prices after the end of each selling season to make room for the next season's clothing line. The value of the company's old clothing inventory has likely fallen below its original cost. Is it appropriate to still report the reduced-value inventory at its original cost?

When the value of inventory falls below its original cost, companies are required to report inventory at the lower **net realizable value** of that inventory. Net realizable value is the estimated selling price of the inventory in the ordinary course of business less any costs of completion, disposal, and transportation. In other words, it's the *net* amount a company expects to *realize* in cash from the sale of the inventory.

Once a company has determined both the cost and the net realizable value of inventory, it reports ending inventory in the balance sheet at the *lower* of the two amounts. This method of recording inventory is **lower of cost and net realizable value**.[5]

Illustration 6–19 demonstrates the concept behind the lower of cost and net realizable value (NRV).

To see how we apply the lower of cost and net realizable value to inventory amounts, assume Mario's Game Shop sells FunStation 2 and FunStation 3. Illustration 6–20 shows information related to ending inventory at the end of the year.

Mario reports the FunStation 2 in ending inventory at net realizable value ($200 per unit) because that's lower than its original cost ($300 per unit). The 15 FunStation 2s were originally reported in inventory at their cost of $4,500 (= 15 × $300). To reduce the inventory from that original cost of $4,500 to its lower net realizable value of $3,000 (= 15 × $200), Mario records a $1,500 reduction in inventory with the following year-end adjusting entry.

---

[5]The method of reporting inventory using the lower of cost and net realizable value applies to companies that use FIFO and weighted-average, but not LIFO. For LIFO, companies report inventory using the lower of cost or market, where market is typically defined as replacement cost. Market value is never greater than net realizable value. The lower of cost or market method is covered in intermediate accounting books.

ILLUSTRATION 6–19

Lower of Cost and Net Realizable Value

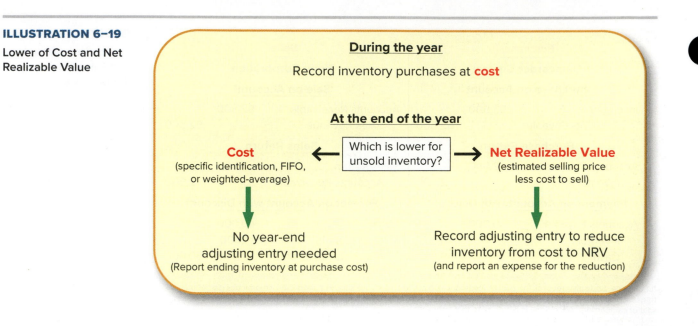

During the year

Record inventory purchases at **cost**

At the end of the year

| **Cost** (specific identification, FIFO, or weighted-average) | ← | Which is lower for unsold inventory? | → | **Net Realizable Value** (estimated selling price less cost to sell) |

No year-end adjusting entry needed
(Report ending inventory at purchase cost)

Record adjusting entry to reduce inventory from cost to NRV
(and report an expense for the reduction)

ILLUSTRATION 6–20

Calculating the Lower of Cost and Net Realizable Value

Inventory Items	Quantity	Cost Per unit	Cost Total	NRV Per unit	NRV Total	Lower of Cost and NRV	Year-end Adjustment Needed*
FunStation 2	15	$300	$ 4,500	$200	$3,000	= $ 3,000	$1,500
FunStation 3	20	400	8,000	450	9,000	= 8,000	0
			$12,500			$11,000	$1,500

Recorded Cost   Ending Inventory

* The year-end adjusting entry is needed when NRV is below cost. The adjustment equals the difference between cost and net realizable value.

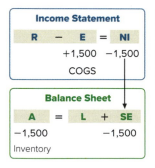

Income Statement

R	−	E	=	NI
		+1,500		−1,500
		COGS		

Balance Sheet

A	=	L	+	SE
−1,500				−1,500
Inventory				

December 31	Debit	Credit
Cost of Goods Sold (expense)..	**1,500**	
Inventory..		**1,500**
(Adjust inventory down to net realizable value)		

Notice that the write-down of inventory has the effect not only of reducing total assets, but also of reducing net income and retained earnings.

The FunStation 3 inventory, on the other hand, remains on the books at its original cost of $8,000 (= $400 × 20), since cost is less than net realizable value. Mario does not need to make any adjustment for these inventory items.

After adjusting inventory to the lower of cost and net realizable value, the store calculates its ending balance of inventory as follows:

Balance before adjustment

Inventory	
12,500	
	1,500 **Adjustment to NRV**

Ending balance   Bal. 11,000

Decision Maker's Perspective

Conservatism and the Lower of Cost and Net Realizable Value Method

Firms are required to report the falling value of inventory, but they are not allowed to report any increasing value of inventory. Why is this? The answer lies in the conservative nature of some accounting procedures. A *conservative* approach in accounting implies that there is more potential harm to users of financial statements if estimated *gains* turn out to be wrong than if estimated *losses* turn out to be wrong. It also guides companies, when faced with a choice, to select accounting methods that are less likely to overstate assets and net income. Therefore, companies typically do not report estimated gains.

KEY POINT

We report inventory at the lower of cost and net realizable value; that is, at cost (specific identification, FIFO, or weighted-average cost) or net realizable value (selling price minus cost of completion, disposal, and transportation), whichever is lower. When net realizable value falls below cost, we adjust downward the balance of inventory from cost to net realizable value.

Auto Adrenaline provides specialty car products—satellite radios, GPS navigation systems, and subwoofers. At the end of the year, the company's records show the following amounts in ending inventory.

Let's Review

Inventory Items	Quantity	Cost per Unit	NRV per Unit
Satellite radios	10	$100	$120
GPS navigators	20	300	350
Subwoofers	40	70	50

Required:

1. Determine ending inventory using the lower of cost and net realizable value method.
2. Record any necessary year-end adjusting entry associated with the lower of cost and net realizable value.

Solution:

1. Ending inventory, lower of cost and net realizable value:

Inventory Items	Quantity	Cost Per unit	Cost Total	NRV Per unit	NRV Total	Lower of Cost and NRV	Year-end Adjustment Needed
Satellite radios	10	$100	$1,000	$120	$1,200	= $1,000	$ 0
GPS navigators	20	300	6,000	350	7,000	= 6,000	0
Subwoofers	40	70	2,800	50	2,000	= 2,000	800
			$9,800			$9,000	$800
			Recorded Cost			Ending Inventory	

Cost is lower than net realizable value for satellite radios and GPS navigators. We get lower of cost and net realizable value by multiplying the *cost* per unit times the quantity. However, net realizable value is lower than cost for subwoofers. In that case, we get lower of cost and net realizable by multiplying the *net realizable value* per unit times quantity.

2. Year-end adjusting entry associated with the lower of cost and net realizable value:

December 31	Debit	Credit
Cost of Goods Sold..	**800**	
Inventory..		**800**
(Adjust inventory down to net realizable value)		
($800 = 40 subwoofers × $20 decline in net realizable value below cost)		

Suggested Homework:
BE6–14, BE6–15;
E6–13, E6–14;
P6–4A&B

We need the $800 adjustment to reduce the reported Inventory balance of the 40 subwoofers by $20 each (from $70 to $50).

ETHICAL DILEMMA

Cultura Creative RF/Alamy Stock Photo

Diamond Computers, which is owned and operated by Dale Diamond, manufactures and sells different types of computers. The company has reported profits every year since its inception in 2000 and has applied for a bank loan near the end of 2024 to upgrade manufacturing facilities. These upgrades should significantly boost future productivity and profitability.

In preparing the financial statements for the year, the chief accountant, Fatima Patel, mentions to Dale that approximately $80,000 of computer inventory has become obsolete and a write-down of inventory should be recorded in 2024.

Dale understands that the write-down would result in a net loss being reported for company operations in 2024. This could jeopardize the company's application for the bank loan, which would lead to employee layoffs. Dale is a very kind, older gentleman who cares little for his personal wealth but who is deeply devoted to his employees' well-being. He truly believes the loan is necessary for the company's sustained viability. Dale suggests Fatima wait until 2025 to write down the inventory so that profitable financial statements can be presented to the bank this year.

Explain how failing to record the write-down in 2024 inflates profit in that year. How would this type of financial accounting manipulation potentially harm the bank? Can Fatima justify the manipulation based on Dale's kind heart for his employees?

ANALYSIS

INVENTORY ANALYSIS
Best Buy vs. Tiffany

■ **LO6–7**
Analyze management of inventory using the inventory turnover ratio and gross profit ratio.

As discussed in the previous section, if managers purchase too much inventory, the company runs the risk of the inventory becoming outdated, resulting in inventory write-downs. Outside analysts as well as managers often use the *inventory turnover ratio* to evaluate a company's effectiveness in managing its investment in inventory. In addition, investors often rely on the *gross profit ratio* to determine the core profitability of a merchandising company's operations. We discuss these ratios next.

INVENTORY TURNOVER RATIO

The **inventory turnover ratio** shows the *number of times* the firm sells its average inventory balance during a reporting period. It is calculated as cost of goods sold divided by average inventory.

$$\text{Inventory turnover ratio} = \frac{\text{Cost of goods sold}}{\text{Average inventory}}$$

The amount for cost of goods sold is obtained from the current period's income statement; average inventory equals the average of inventory reported in this period's and last period's balance sheets. Last period's ending inventory is this period's beginning inventory. The more frequently a business is able to sell or "turn over" its average inventory balance, the less the company needs to invest in inventory for a given level of sales. Other things equal, a higher ratio indicates greater effectiveness of a company in managing its investment in inventory.

AVERAGE DAYS IN INVENTORY

Another way to measure the same activity is to calculate the **average days in inventory**. This ratio indicates the approximate *number of days* the average inventory is held. It is calculated as 365 days divided by the inventory turnover ratio.

$$\text{Average days in inventory} = \frac{365}{\text{Inventory turnover ratio}}$$

We can analyze the inventory of **Best Buy** and **Tiffany** by calculating these ratios for both companies. Best Buy sells a large volume of commonly purchased products. In contrast, Tiffany is a specialty retailer of luxury jewelry, watches, and other accessories. Below are relevant amounts for each company.

($ in millions)	Cost of Goods Sold	Beginning Inventory	Ending Inventory
Best Buy	$33,590	$5,409	$5,174
Tiffany	1,662	2,428	2,464

To compute the inventory turnover ratio we need the *average* inventory, which is the beginning amount of inventory plus the ending amount, divided by 2.

Best Buy   Average inventory = ($5,409 + $5,174) ÷ 2 = **$5,291.5**
Tiffany   Average inventory = ($2,428 + $2,464) ÷ 2 = **$2,446.0**

We put average inventory in the denominator to compute the inventory turnover ratio, as shown in Illustration 6–21.

	Inventory Turnover Ratio	Average Days in Inventory
Best Buy	$33,590 ÷ **$5,291.5** = 6.3 times	$\dfrac{365}{6.3}$ = 58 days
Tiffany	$1,662 ÷ **$2,446.0** = 0.7 times	$\dfrac{365}{0.7}$ = 521 days

ILLUSTRATION 6–21

Inventory Turnover Ratios for Best Buy and Tiffany

The turnover ratio is much higher for Best Buy. On average, each dollar of inventory is sold in 58 days. In contrast, each dollar of inventory at Tiffany is sold every 521 days. If the two companies had the same business strategies, this would indicate that Best Buy is better at managing inventory. In this case, though, the difference in inventory turnover relates to the products the two companies sell. Best Buy sells mostly common household electronics and accessories, while Tiffany has some very expensive jewelry (like engagement rings) that takes time to sell to the right customer. As we see in the next section, Tiffany offsets its low inventory turnover with a higher profit margin.

Decision Point

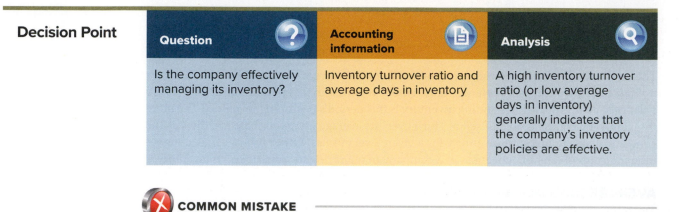

Question	Accounting information	Analysis
Is the company effectively managing its inventory?	Inventory turnover ratio and average days in inventory	A high inventory turnover ratio (or low average days in inventory) generally indicates that the company's inventory policies are effective.

✖ COMMON MISTAKE

Many students use ending inventory rather than average inventory in calculating the inventory turnover ratio. Generally, when you calculate a ratio that includes an income statement item (an amount generated over a period) with a balance sheet item (an amount at a particular date), the balance sheet item needs to be converted to an amount *over the same period*. This is done by averaging the beginning and ending balances of the balance sheet item.

GROSS PROFIT RATIO

Another important indicator of the company's successful management of inventory is the **gross profit ratio** (also called *gross profit percentage*). It measures the amount by which the sale of inventory exceeds its cost per dollar of sales. We calculate the gross profit ratio as gross profit divided by net sales. (Net sales equal total sales revenue less sales discounts, returns, and allowances.)

$$\text{Gross profit ratio} = \frac{\text{Gross profit}}{\text{Net sales}}$$

The higher the gross profit ratio, the higher is the "markup" a company is able to achieve on its inventories. Best Buy and Tiffany report the following information.

($ in millions)	Net Sales	−	Cost of Goods Sold	=	Gross Profit
Best Buy	$43,638		$33,590		$10,048
Tiffany	4,424		1,662		2,762

Illustration 6–22 shows calculation of the gross profit ratio for Best Buy and Tiffany.

ILLUSTRATION 6–22

Gross Profit Ratios for Best Buy and Tiffany

	Gross Profit/Net Sales	=	Gross Profit Ratio
Best Buy	$10,048/$43,638	=	23%
Tiffany	$2,762/$4,424	=	62%

For Best Buy, this means that for every $1 of net sales, the company spends $0.77 on inventory, resulting in a gross profit of $0.23. In contrast, the gross profit ratio for Tiffany is 62%. We saw earlier that Tiffany inventory turnover is much lower than that of Best Buy.

But, we see now that Tiffany makes up for that lower turnover with a much higher gross profit margin. The products Best Buy sells are familiar goods, and competition from companies like **Walmart**, **Target**, and **Amazon** for these high-volume items keeps sale prices low compared to costs. Because Tiffany specializes in custom jewelry and other expensive accessories, there is less competition, allowing greater price markups.

 KEY POINT

The inventory turnover ratio indicates the number of times the firm sells, or turns over, its average inventory balance during a reporting period. The gross profit ratio measures the amount by which the sale of inventory exceeds its cost per dollar of sales.

Decision Point

Question	Accounting information 	Analysis
For how much is a company able to sell a product above its cost?	Gross profit and net sales	The ratio of gross profit to net sales indicates how much inventory sales exceeds inventory costs for each $1 of sales.

RECORDING INVENTORY TRANSACTIONS USING A PERIODIC INVENTORY SYSTEM

APPENDIX A

■ **LO6–8**
Record inventory transactions using a periodic inventory system.

In this chapter, we discussed how to record inventory transactions using a *perpetual* inventory system. Here we discuss how to record inventory transactions using a *periodic* inventory system.

Recall that under a **perpetual inventory system** we maintain a continual—or *perpetual*—record of inventory purchased and sold. In contrast, using a **periodic inventory system** we do not continually modify inventory amounts. Instead, we *periodically* adjust for purchases and sales of inventory at the end of the reporting period, based on a physical count of inventory on hand.

To demonstrate the differences in these two systems, let's record inventory transactions under the periodic system using the same information (from Illustration 6–12) that we used to demonstrate the perpetual inventory system. We repeat those transactions in Illustration 6–23.

ILLUSTRATION 6–23
Inventory Transactions for Mario's Game Shop

Date	Transaction	Details	Total Cost	Total Revenue
Jan. 1	Beginning inventory	100 units for $7 each	$ 700	
Apr. 25	Purchase	300 units for $9 each	2,700	
Jul. 17	Sale	300 units for $15 each		$ 4,500
Oct. 19	Purchase	600 units for $11 each	6,600	
Dec. 15	Sale	500 units for $15 each		7,500
	Totals		$10,000	$12,000

To make the distinction between the perpetual system and the periodic system easier, in the next section we look at side-by-side comparisons. The perpetual entries are repeated from those in the chapter and shown on the left side of each comparison.

INVENTORY PURCHASES AND SALES

The first transaction on April 25 involves the purchase of $2,700 of inventory on account. Under the periodic system, instead of debiting the Inventory account, we debit a Purchases account. Remember, we're not continually adjusting the Inventory account under the periodic method. We use the Purchases account to temporarily track increases in inventory.

Perpetual System			Periodic System		
Inventory	2,700		Purchases	2,700	
Accounts Payable		2,700	Accounts Payable		2,700

The transaction on July 17 involves the sale on account of 300 units of inventory for $4,500. We record that transaction as follows.

Perpetual System			Periodic System		
Accounts Receivable	4,500		Accounts Receivable	4,500	
Sales Revenue		4,500	Sales Revenue		4,500
Cost of Goods Sold	2,500				
Inventory		2,500	No entry for cost of goods sold		

Notice that under the periodic system, we record the sales revenue, but we don't record the reduction in inventory or the increase in cost of goods sold at the time of the sale. Instead, we will record these at the end of the period.

The final two transactions are (1) the purchase of 600 additional units of inventory for $6,600 on account on October 19 and (2) the sale of 500 units for $7,500 on account on December 15. We record that transaction as follows.

Perpetual System			Periodic System		
Inventory	6,600		Purchases	6,600	
Accounts Payable		6,600	Accounts Payable		6,600

Perpetual System			Periodic System		
Accounts Receivable	7,500		Accounts Receivable	7,500	
Sales Revenue		7,500	Sales Revenue		7,500
Cost of Goods Sold	5,300				
Inventory		5,300	No entry for cost of goods sold		

In addition to purchases and sales of inventory, we also looked at additional inventory transactions for Mario's Game Shop that related to freight charges, purchase discounts, and purchase returns:

1. On April 25, Mario pays freight charges of $300 for inventory purchased on April 25.
2. On April 30, Mario pays for the units purchased on April 25, less a 2% purchase discount.
3. On October 22, Mario returns 50 defective units from the October 19 purchase.

Next, let's also compare the perpetual system and periodic system for these transactions.

FREIGHT CHARGES

Under the perpetual system discussed in the chapter, we saw that freight charges are included as an additional cost of inventory. Here we'll see that under the periodic system, we record these charges in a separate account called Freight-in. That account will later be closed in a period-end adjusting entry. For freight charges of $300 associated with the April 25 purchase, we record the following transaction.

Perpetual System		Periodic System		
Inventory	300	Freight-in	300	
Cash	300	Cash	300	

Pay freight-in charges.

PURCHASE DISCOUNTS AND RETURNS

Under the perpetual system, purchase discounts and purchase returns are recorded as a reduction in inventory cost. Under the periodic system, these transactions are recorded in separate accounts—Purchase Discounts and Purchase Returns. In the perpetual system, we credit purchase returns and purchase discounts to Inventory. The Purchase Returns and Purchase Discounts accounts used in the periodic system are referred to as *contra purchases accounts*.

For our examples in the chapter, Mario (1) makes payment on April 30 for inventory purchased on April 25 for $2,700, receiving a $54 discount and (2) returns 50 defective units on October 22 from the 600 units purchased on account on October 19 for $11 each.

Perpetual System		Periodic System		
Accounts Payable	2,700	Accounts Payable	2,700	
Inventory	54	Purchase Discounts	54	
Cash	2,646	Cash	2,646	

Perpetual System		Periodic System		
Accounts Payable	550	Accounts Payable	550	
Inventory	550	Purchase Returns	550	

PERIOD-END ADJUSTING ENTRY

A period-end adjusting entry is needed only under the periodic system. The adjusting entry serves the following purposes:

1. Adjusts the balance of inventory to its proper ending balance.
2. Records the cost of goods sold for the period, to match inventory costs with the related sales revenue.
3. Closes (or zeros out) the temporary purchases accounts (Purchases, Freight-in, Purchase Discounts, and Purchase Returns).

Let's see what the period-end adjusting entry would look like for Mario's Game Shop using the transactions described in this appendix. In addition, recall that beginning inventory equals $700 (= 100 units × $7 unit cost) and ending inventory equals $1,650 (= 150 units × $11 unit cost).

Perpetual System	Periodic System		
No entry	Inventory (ending)	1,650	
	Cost of Goods Sold	8,046	
	Purchase Discounts	54	
	Purchase Returns	550	
	Purchases		9,300
	Freight-in		300
	Inventory (beginning)		700

Temporary accounts closed

Notice that (1) the balance of Inventory is updated for its ending amount of $1,650, while its beginning balance of $700 is eliminated, (2) Cost of Goods Sold is recorded for $8,046, and (3) temporary accounts related to purchases are closed to zero. Purchase Discounts and Purchase Returns are credit balance accounts so they need to be debited to close them. Likewise, Purchases and Freight-in are debit balance accounts so they need to be credited to close them.

If you look carefully, you may notice that the amount of cost of goods sold above calculated under the periodic system is exactly the same as that calculated under the perpetual system (in Illustration 6–17). To see a detailed example of this, let's examine the first section of the multiple-step income statement, shown again in Illustration 6–24.

ILLUSTRATION 6–24

Calculation of Gross Profit in a Multiple-Step Income Statement

MARIO'S GAME SHOP		
Multiple-Step Income Statement (partial)		
For the year ended December 31, 2024		
Sales revenue		$12,000
Cost of goods sold:		
Beginning inventory	$ 700	
Add: Purchases	9,300	
Freight-in	300	
Less: Purchase discounts	(54)	
Purchase returns	(550)	
Cost of goods available for sale	9,696	
Less: Ending inventory	(1,650)	
Cost of goods sold		8,046
Gross profit		$ 3,954

The periodic system and perpetual system will always produce the same amounts for cost of goods sold (and therefore also ending inventory) when the FIFO inventory method is used.

However, when using LIFO or weighted-average, the amounts for cost of goods sold may differ between the periodic system and perpetual system. The reason for this difference is discussed further in more advanced accounting courses; it happens because determining which units of inventory are assumed sold occurs at the time of each sale throughout the period using a perpetual system but just once at the end of the period using a periodic system. For those interested, the book's online resources include additional discussion and problems related to FIFO, LIFO, and weighted-average using the perpetual inventory system.

As discussed in Part B of the chapter, some companies maintain their own records on a FIFO basis and then adjust for the LIFO difference in preparing financial statements. **The inventory recording and reporting procedures discussed in Part B of the chapter most closely reflect those used in actual practice.**

 KEY POINT

Using the periodic inventory system, we record purchases, freight-in, purchase returns, and purchase discounts to *temporary accounts* rather than directly to Inventory. These temporary accounts are closed in a period-end adjusting entry. In addition, at the time inventory is sold, we do not record a decrease in inventory sold; instead, we update the balance of Inventory in the period-end adjusting entry.

APPENDIX B

INVENTORY ERRORS

■ **LO6–9**

Determine the financial statement effects of inventory errors.

Nobody's perfect, and even accountants make mistakes. When we discover accounting errors, we correct them. However, we don't always know when we've made an error. Errors can unknowingly occur in inventory amounts if there are mistakes in a physical count of inventory or in the pricing of inventory quantities.

EFFECTS IN THE CURRENT YEAR

To understand the effects of an inventory error in the financial statements, let's think again about the formula for cost of goods sold, shown in Illustration 6–25.

Notice that an error in calculating ending inventory (an asset in the balance sheet) causes an error in calculating cost of goods sold (an expense in the income statement). If cost of goods sold is misstated, gross profit will be misstated as well, but in the opposite direction. This is true because gross profit equals sales *minus* cost of goods sold. Furthermore, if gross profit is misstated, then net income and retained earnings will be misstated in the same direction; any mistake in net income is closed to retained earnings. The effect of the inventory error in the current year is summarized in Illustration 6–26.

Inventory Error	Cost of Goods Sold	Gross Profit	Net Income	Retained Earning
Overstate ending inventory	Understate	Overstate	Overstate	Overstate
Understate ending inventory	Overstate	Understate	Understate	Understate

ILLUSTRATION 6–26
Summary of Effects of Inventory Error in the Current Year

EFFECTS IN THE FOLLOWING YEAR

To understand the effects of a current-year inventory error on financial statements in the following year, remember that the amount of ending inventory this year is the amount of beginning inventory next year. An error in ending inventory this year will create an error in beginning inventory next year. This is demonstrated in Illustration 6–27.

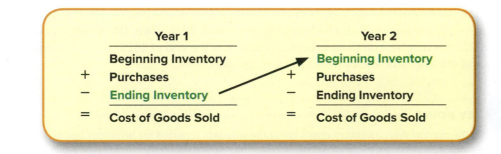

ILLUSTRATION 6–27
Relationship between Cost of Goods Sold in the Current Year and the Following Year

Notice that ending inventory is *subtracted* in calculating cost of goods sold in year 1 (the year of the inventory error). That same amount becomes beginning inventory in the following year and is *added* in calculating cost of goods sold. Because of this, **an error in calculating ending inventory in the current year will automatically affect cost of goods sold in the following year** *in the opposite direction.*

Consider a simple example to see how this works. Illustration 6–28 shows the correct inventory amounts for 2024 and 2025.

ILLUSTRATION 6–28

Correct Inventory
Amounts

		2024	2025
	Beginning Inventory	$ 600	$ 500
+	Purchases	3,000	4,000
−	Ending Inventory	500	800
	Cost of Goods Sold	$3,100	$3,700

$6,800

Now, assume the company mistakenly reports ending inventory in 2024 as **$400**, instead of $500. The effect of the mistake is shown in Illustration 6–29.

ILLUSTRATION 6–29

Incorrect Inventory
Amounts

		2024	2025
	Beginning Inventory	$ 600	$ 400
+	Purchases	3,000	4,000
−	Ending Inventory	400	800
	Cost of Goods Sold	$3,200	$3,600

$6,800

Notice three things:

1. The amount reported for inventory is correct by the end of the second year, $800. This is true *even if the company had never discovered its inventory mistake* in 2024.

2. The total amount reported for cost of goods sold over the two-year period from 2024 to 2025 is the same ($6,800) whether the error occurs or not. That's because the overstatement to cost of goods sold of $100 in 2024 is offset by an understatement to cost of goods sold of $100 in 2025. This also means that the inventory error affects gross profit in each of the two years, but the combined two-year gross profit amount is unaffected.

3. If the combined two-year gross profit (and therefore net income) is correct, then retained earnings will also be correct by the end of 2025. Thus, the inventory error in 2024 has no effect on the accounting equation at the end of 2025. Assets (inventory) and stockholders' equity (retained earnings) are correctly stated.

 KEY POINT

In the current year, inventory errors affect the amounts reported for inventory and retained earnings in the balance sheet and amounts reported for cost of goods sold and gross profit in the income statement. At the end of the following year, the error has no effect on ending inventory or retained earnings but reverses for cost of goods sold and gross profit.

CHAPTER FRAMEWORK

This chapter discusses accounting for inventory transactions (purchases and sales) and the different methods used to calculate cost of goods sold and ending inventory. Inventory transactions **during the year** and their related adjusting entries at the **end of the year** affect amounts reported in the financial statements.

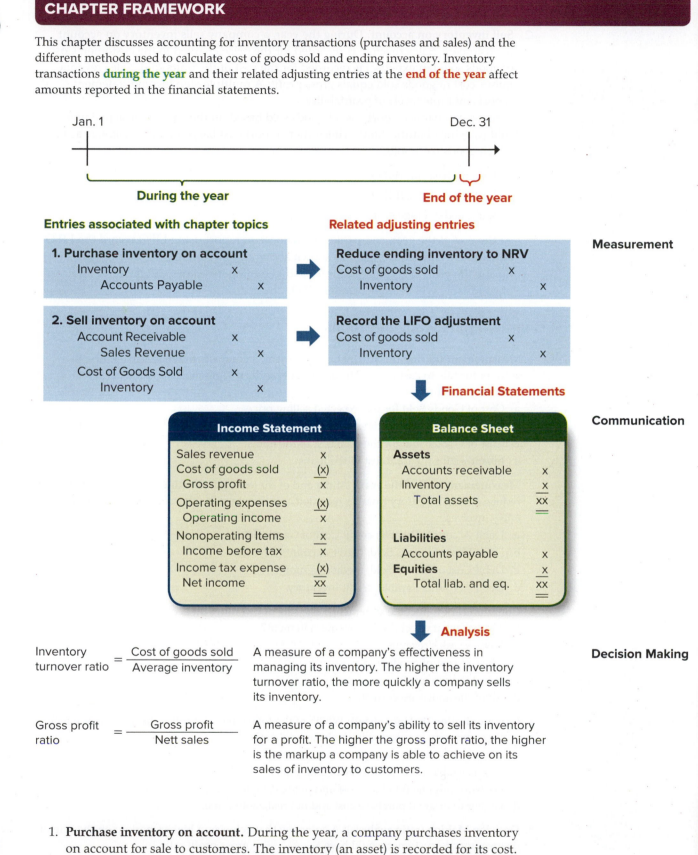

Jan. 1   Dec. 31

During the year   **End of the year**

Entries associated with chapter topics   **Related adjusting entries**   **Measurement**

1. Purchase inventory on account
| Inventory | X | |
| Accounts Payable | | X |

Reduce ending inventory to NRV
| Cost of goods sold | X | |
| Inventory | | X |

2. Sell inventory on account
Account Receivable	X	
Sales Revenue		X
Cost of Goods Sold	X	
Inventory		X

Record the LIFO adjustment
| Cost of goods sold | X | |
| Inventory | | X |

Financial Statements

Income Statement

Sales revenue	X
Cost of goods sold	(X)
Gross profit	X
Operating expenses	(X)
Operating income	X
Nonoperating Items	X
Income before tax	X
Income tax expense	(X)
Net income	XX

Balance Sheet

Assets
Accounts receivable	X
Inventory	X
Total assets	XX

Liabilities
| Accounts payable | X |

Equities
| Total liab. and eq. | XX |

Communication

Analysis

Decision Making

$$\text{Inventory turnover ratio} = \frac{\text{Cost of goods sold}}{\text{Average inventory}}$$

A measure of a company's effectiveness in managing its inventory. The higher the inventory turnover ratio, the more quickly a company sells its inventory.

$$\text{Gross profit ratio} = \frac{\text{Gross profit}}{\text{Nett sales}}$$

A measure of a company's ability to sell its inventory for a profit. The higher the gross profit ratio, the higher is the markup a company is able to achieve on its sales of inventory to customers.

1. **Purchase inventory on account.** During the year, a company purchases inventory on account for sale to customers. The inventory (an asset) is recorded for its cost. The recorded cost of inventory increases with freight charges and decreases with purchase discounts and purchase returns. At the end of the year, an adjusting entry is made to **reduce ending inventory to net realizable value (NRV),** if NRV has

fallen below ending inventory's recorded cost. NRV is the estimated selling price of inventory less its cost to sell.

2. **Sell inventory on account.** During the year, a company sells inventory on account to customers. Sales revenue is recorded for the price charged to the customer. Cost of goods sold (an expense) is recorded for the cost of the units sold. Sales revenue minus cost of goods sold equals gross profit. A multiple-step income statement reports multiple levels of profitability.

   Some companies report cost of goods sold based on the cost of the actual units sold (specific identification), while others report cost based on an *assumption* as to which goods were sold:

   a. First-in, first-out (FIFO)

   b. Last-in, first-out (LIFO)

   c. Weighted-average cost

   At the end of the year, companies that choose to report using LIFO **record the LIFO adjustment.** The adjusting entry shown above assumes increasing inventory costs during the year, suggesting in this case that ending inventory will be lower and cost of goods sold will be higher under LIFO.

Chapter Framework Questions

1. **Measurement (during the year):** During the year, a company purchases inventory on account for sale to customers. The company records the purchase (under a perpetual inventory system) to
   a. Cost of Goods Sold for the expected selling price.
   b. Inventory for the expected selling price.
   c. Cost of Goods Sold for the total cost of the items.
   d. Inventory for the total cost of the items.

2. **Measurement (end of the year):** At the end of the year, an adjusting entry is recorded to reduce ending inventory from its recorded cost to net realizable value (NRV). The adjusting entry involves
   a. Debit Accounts Payable; credit Cost of Goods Sold.
   b. Debit Cost of Goods Sold; credit Accounts Payable.
   c. Debit Cost of Goods Sold; credit Inventory.
   d. Debit Accounts Payable; credit Inventory.

3. **Communication (income statement):** The sale of inventory on account for an amount above its cost has what effect on the income statement?
   a. Increase sales revenue.
   b. Increase cost of goods sold.
   c. Increase gross profit.
   d. All of the above are correct.

4. **Communication (balance sheet):** Which of the follow best describes the amount at which ending inventory is reported in the balance sheet?
   a. Original purchase cost.
   b. Net realizable value (estimated selling price).
   c. Lower of original purchase cost and net realizable value.
   d. Higher of original purchase cost and net realizable value.

5. **Decision Making (ratio analysis):** A company that achieves a higher markup on the sale of its inventory to customer would have a _____ gross profit ratio.
   a. Higher.
   b. Lower.

Note: For answers, see the last page of the chapter.

KEY POINTS BY LEARNING OBJECTIVE

LO6–1 Understand that inventory flows from manufacturing companies to merchandising companies and is reported as an asset in the balance sheet.

Service companies record revenues when providing services to customers. Merchandising and manufacturing companies record revenues when selling inventory to customers.

LO6–2 Understand how cost of goods sold is reported in a multiple-step income statement.

Inventory is a current asset reported in the balance sheet and represents the cost of inventory *not yet sold* at the end of the period. Cost of goods sold is an expense reported in the income statement and represents the cost of inventory *sold.*

A multiple-step income statement reports multiple levels of profitability. **Gross profit** equals net revenues (or net sales) minus cost of goods sold. **Operating income** equals gross profit minus operating expenses. **Income before income taxes** equals operating income plus nonoperating revenues and minus nonoperating expenses. **Net income** equals all revenues minus all expenses.

LO6–3 Determine the cost of goods sold and ending inventory using different inventory cost methods.

Companies are allowed to report inventory costs by *assuming* which specific units of inventory are sold and not sold, even if this does not match the *actual* flow. The three major inventory cost flow assumptions are FIFO (first-in, first-out), LIFO (last-in, first-out), and weighted-average cost.

LO6–4 Explain the financial statement effects and tax effects of inventory cost methods.

Generally, FIFO more closely resembles the actual physical flow of inventory. When inventory costs are rising, FIFO results in higher reported inventory in the balance sheet and higher reported income in the income statement. Conversely, LIFO results in a lower reported inventory and net income, reducing the company's income tax obligation.

LO6–5 Record inventory transactions using a perpetual inventory system.

The perpetual inventory system maintains a continual—or *perpetual*—record of inventory purchased and sold. When companies *purchase* inventory using a perpetual inventory system, they increase the Inventory account and either decrease Cash or increase Accounts Payable. When companies *sell* inventory, they make two entries: (1) They increase an asset account (Cash or Accounts Receivable) and increase Sales Revenue, and (2) they increase Cost of Goods Sold and decrease Inventory.

Most companies maintain their own inventory records on a FIFO basis, and then some prepare financial statements on a LIFO basis. To adjust their FIFO inventory records to LIFO for financial reporting, companies use a LIFO adjustment at the end of the year.

For most companies, freight charges are added to the cost of inventory, whereas purchase returns and purchase discounts are deducted from the cost of inventory. Some companies choose to report freight charges on outgoing shipments as part of selling expenses instead of cost of goods sold.

LO6–6 Apply the lower of cost and net realizable value rule for inventories.

We report inventory at the lower of cost and net realizable value; that is, at cost (specific identification, FIFO, or weighted-average cost) or net realizable value (selling price minus cost of completion, disposal, and transportation), whichever is lower. When net realizable value falls below cost, we adjust downward the balance of inventory from cost to net realizable value.

Analysis

LO6–7 Analyze management of inventory using the inventory turnover ratio and gross profit ratio.

The inventory turnover ratio indicates the number of times the firm sells, or turns over, its average inventory balance during a reporting period. The gross profit ratio measures the amount by which the sale of inventory exceeds its cost per dollar of sales.

Appendixes

LO6–8 Record inventory transactions using a periodic inventory system.

Using the periodic inventory system, we record purchases, freight-in, purchase returns, and purchase discounts to *temporary accounts* rather than directly to Inventory. These temporary accounts are closed in a period-end adjusting entry. In addition, at the time inventory is sold, we do not record a decrease in inventory sold; instead, we update the balance of Inventory in the period-end adjusting entry.

LO6–9 Determine the financial statement effects of inventory errors.

In the current year, inventory errors affect the amounts reported for inventory and retained earnings in the balance sheet and amounts reported for cost of goods sold and gross profit in the income statement. At the end of the following year, the error has no effect on ending inventory or retained earnings but reverses for cost of goods sold and gross profit.

GLOSSARY

Average days in inventory: Approximate number of days the average inventory is held. It equals 365 days divided by the inventory turnover ratio. **p. 309**

Cost of goods sold: Cost of the inventory that was sold during the period. **p. 284**

First-in, first-out method (FIFO): Inventory costing method that assumes the first units purchased (the first in) are the first ones sold (the first out). **p. 288**

Freight-in: Cost to transport inventory to the company, which is included as part of inventory cost. **p. 301**

Freight-out: Cost of freight on shipments to customers, which is included in the income statement either as part of cost of goods sold or as a selling expense. **p. 301**

Gross profit: The difference between net sales and cost of goods sold. **p. 286**

Gross profit ratio: Measure of the amount by which the sale of inventory exceeds its cost per dollar of sales. It equals gross profit divided by net sales. **p. 310**

Income before income taxes: Operating income plus nonoperating revenues less nonoperating expenses. **p. 286**

Inventory: Items a company intends for sale to customers in the ordinary course of business. **p. 282**

Inventory turnover ratio: The number of times a firm sells its average inventory balance during a reporting period. It equals cost of goods sold divided by average inventory. **p. 309**

Last-in, first-out method (LIFO): Inventory costing method that assumes the last units purchased (the last in) are the first ones sold (the first out). **p. 289**

LIFO adjustment: An adjustment used to convert a company's own inventory records maintained throughout the year on a FIFO basis to LIFO basis for preparing financial statements at the end of the year. **p. 299**

LIFO conformity rule: IRS rule requiring a company that uses LIFO for tax reporting to also use LIFO for financial reporting. **p. 295**

Lower of cost and net realizable value: Method where companies report inventory in the balance sheet at the lower of cost and net realizable value, where net realizable value equals estimated selling price of the inventory in the ordinary course of business less any costs of completion, disposal, and transportation. **p. 305**

Multiple-step income statement: An income statement that reports *multiple* levels of income (or profitability). **p. 285**

Net income: Difference between all revenues and all expenses for the period. **p. 286**

Net realizable value: Estimated selling price of the inventory in the ordinary course of business less any costs of completion, disposal, and transportation. **p. 305**

Operating income: Profitability from normal operations that equals gross profit less operating expenses. **p. 286**

Periodic inventory system: Inventory system that periodically adjusts for purchases and sales of inventory at the end of the reporting period based on a physical count of inventory on hand. **p. 297**

Perpetual inventory system: Inventory system that maintains a continual record of inventory purchased and sold. **p. 296**

Specific identification method: Inventory costing method that matches or identifies each unit of inventory with its actual cost. **p. 288**

Weighted-average cost method: Inventory costing method that assumes both cost of goods sold and ending inventory consist of a random mixture of all the goods available for sale. **p. 290**

SELF-STUDY QUESTIONS

1. Which of following companies record revenues when selling inventory? **(LO6–1)**
   a. Service companies.
   b. Manufacturing companies.
   c. Merchandising companies.
   d. Both manufacturing and merchandising companies.

2. At the beginning of the year, Bennett Supply has inventory of $3,500. During the year, the company purchases an additional $12,000 of inventory. An inventory count at the end of the year reveals remaining inventory of $4,000. What amount will Bennett report for cost of goods sold? **(LO6–2)**
   a. $11,000.
   b. $11,500.
   c. $12,000.
   d. $12,500.

3. Which of the following levels of profitability in a multiple-step income statement represents revenues from the sale of inventory less the cost of that inventory? **(LO6–2)**
   a. Gross profit.
   b. Operating income.
   c. Income before income taxes.
   d. Net income.

4. Madison Outlet has the following inventory transactions for the year: **(LO6–3)**

Date	Transaction	Number of Units	Unit Cost	Total Cost
Jan. 1	Beginning inventory	10	$200	$2,000
Mar. 14	Purchase	15	300	4,500
				$6,500
Jan. 1–Dec. 31	Total sales to customers	12		

What amount would Madison report for *cost of goods sold* using FIFO?

a. $2,600.

b. $2,900.

c. $3,600.

d. $3,900.

5. Using the information in *Self-Study Question 4*, what amount would Madison report for *ending inventory* using FIFO? **(LO6–3)**

a. $2,600.

b. $2,900.

c. $3,600.

d. $3,900.

6. Using the information in *Self-Study Question 4*, what amount would Madison report for *cost of goods sold* using LIFO? **(LO6–3)**

a. $2,600.

b. $2,900.

c. $3,600.

d. $3,900.

7. Using the information in *Self-Study Question 4*, what amount would Madison report for *ending inventory* using weighted-average cost? **(LO6–3)**

a. $3,380.

b. $3,250.

c. $3,120.

d. $3,000.

8. Which inventory cost flow assumption generally results in the lowest reported amount for cost of goods sold when inventory costs are rising? **(LO6–4)**

a. Lower of cost and net realizable value.

b. First-in, first-out (FIFO).

c. Last-in, first-out (LIFO).

d. Weighted-average cost.

9. Using a *perpetual* inventory system, the purchase of inventory on account would be recorded as **(LO6–5)**

a. Debit Cost of Goods Sold; credit Inventory.

b. Debit Inventory; credit Sales Revenue.

c. Debit Purchases; credit Accounts Payable.

d. Debit Inventory; credit Accounts Payable.

10. Using a *perpetual* inventory system, the sale of inventory on account would be recorded as **(LO6–5)**

a. Debit Cost of Goods Sold; credit Inventory.

b. Debit Inventory; credit Sales Revenue.

c. Debit Accounts Receivable; credit Sales Revenue.

d. Both *a.* and *c.* are correct.

11. Maxwell Corporation has the following inventory information at the end of the year: **(LO6–6)**

Inventory	Quantity	Unit Cost	Unit NRV
Item A	20	$20	$35
Item B	50	30	25
Item C	40	10	15

Using the lower of cost and net realizable method, for what amount would Maxwell report ending inventory?

a. $2,050.

b. $2,300.

c. $2,550.

d $2,800.

12. When a company determines that the net realizable value of its ending inventory is lower than its cost, what would be the effect(s) of the adjusting entry to write down inventory to net realizable value? **(LO6–6)**

a. Decrease total assets.

b. Decrease net income.

c. Decrease retained earnings.

d. All of these answer choices are correct.

13. For the year, Marvell Incorporated reports net sales of $100,000, cost of goods sold of $80,000, and an average inventory balance of $40,000. What is Marvell's gross profit ratio? **(LO6–7)**

a. 20%.

b. 25%.

c. 40%.

d. 50%.

14. Using a *periodic* inventory system, the purchase of inventory on account would be recorded as **(LO6–8)**

a. Debit Cost of Goods Sold; credit Inventory.

b. Debit Inventory; credit Sales Revenue.

c. Debit Purchases; credit Accounts Payable.

d. Debit Inventory; credit Accounts Payable.

15. Suppose Ajax Corporation overstates its ending inventory amount. What effect will this have on the reported amount of cost of goods sold in the year of the error? **(LO6–9)**

a. Overstate cost of goods sold.

b. Understate cost of goods sold.

c. Have no effect on cost of goods sold.

d. Not possible to determine with information given.

Note: For answers, see the last page of the chapter.

DATA ANALYTICS & EXCEL

Visit Connect to find a variety of Data Analytics questions that help build Excel, Tableau, and data visualization skills. Assignable materials include **Integrated Excel**, **Applying Excel**, **Data Visualizations**, **Tableau Dashboard Activities**, and **Applying Tableau Cases**.

REVIEW QUESTIONS

■ **LO6–1**   1. What is inventory? Where in the financial statements is inventory reported?

■ **LO6–1**   2. What is the primary distinction between a service company and a manufacturing or merchandising company?

■ **LO6–1**   3. What is the difference among raw materials inventory, work-in-process inventory, and finished goods inventory?

■ **LO6–2**   4. Define the cost of goods available for sale. How does it relate to cost of goods sold and ending inventory?

■ **LO6–2**   5. For a company like **Best Buy**, what does the balance of Cost of Goods Sold in the income statement represent? What does the balance of Inventory in the balance sheet represent?

■ **LO6–2**   6. What is a multiple-step income statement? What information does it provide beyond "bottom-line" net income?

■ **LO6–3**   7. Cheryl believes that companies report cost of goods sold and ending inventory based on *actual* units sold and not sold. Her accounting instructor explains that most companies account for cost of goods sold and ending inventory based on *assumed* units sold and not sold. Help her understand why companies are allowed to do this.

■ **LO6–3**   8. What are the three primary cost flow assumptions? How does the specific identification method differ from these three primary cost flow assumptions?

■ **LO6–4**   9. Which cost flow assumption generally results in the highest reported amount for ending inventory when inventory costs are rising? Explain.

■ **LO6–4**   10. Which cost flow assumption generally results in the highest reported amount of net income when inventory costs are rising? Explain.

■ **LO6–4**   11. What does it mean that FIFO has a balance-sheet focus and LIFO has an income-statement focus?

■ **LO6–4**   12. Explain how LIFO generally results in lower income taxes payable when inventory costs are increasing. What is the LIFO conformity rule?

■ **LO6–5**   13. What is the difference between the *timing* of recording inventory transactions under the perpetual and periodic inventory systems?

■ **LO6–5**   14. Explain how freight charges, purchase returns, and purchase discounts affect the cost of inventory.

■ **LO6–6**   15. Explain the method of reporting inventory at lower of cost and net realizable value.

■ **LO6–6**   16. How is cost of inventory determined? How is net realizable value determined?

■ **LO6–6**   17. Describe the entry to adjust from cost to net realizable value for inventory write-downs. What effects does this adjusting entry have on (a) assets, (b) liabilities, (c) stockholders' equity (or retained earnings), (d) revenues, (e) expenses, and (f) net income?

■ **LO6–6**   18. What is meant by the assertion that an example of conservatism in accounting is recording inventory at the lower of cost and net realizable value?

■ **LO6–7**   19. What is the inventory turnover ratio? What is it designed to measure?

■ **LO6–7**   20. How is gross profit calculated? What is the gross profit ratio? What is it designed to measure?

■ **LO6–8**   21. Explain how the sale of inventory on account is recorded under a periodic system. How does this differ from the recording under a perpetual system?

22. What are the purposes of the period-end adjusting entries under the periodic inventory system?   ■ **LO6–8**

23. Jeff is the new inventory manager for Alan Company. During the year-end inventory count,   ■ **LO6–9**
    Jeff forgets that the company stores additional inventory in a back room, causing his final
    ending inventory count to be understated.
    Explain what effect this error will have on the reported amounts for (a) assets, (b) liabilities,
    (c) stockholders' equity (or retained earnings), (d) revenues, (e) expenses, and (f) net
    income in the current year.

24. Refer to the inventory error in *Question* 23. Explain what effect Jeff's error will have on   ■ **LO6–9**
    reported amounts at the end of the following year, assuming the mistake is not corrected
    and no further mistakes are made.

BRIEF EXERCISES

BE6–1 Match each of the following types of companies with its definition.   Understand terms
                                                                                                       related to types of
                                                                                                       companies **(LO6–1)**

Types of Companies	Definitions
1. _____ Service company	a. Purchases goods that are primarily in finished form for resale to customers.
2. _____ Merchandising company	b. Records revenues when providing services to customers.
3. _____ Manufacturing company	c. Produces the goods they sell to customers.

BE6–2 Match each of the following inventory classifications with its definition.   Understand terms related
                                                                                                       to inventory **(LO6–1)**

Inventory Classifications	Definitions
1. _____ Raw materials	a. Cost of items not yet complete by the end of the period.
2. _____ Work-in-process	b. Inventory that has been substantially completed.
3. _____ Finished goods	c. Basic components used to build a product.

BE6–3 At the beginning of the year, Bryers Incorporated reports inventory of $8,000. During   Calculate cost of goods
the year, the company purchases additional inventory for $23,000. At the end of the year, the   sold **(LO6–2)**
cost of inventory remaining is $10,000. Calculate cost of goods sold for for the year.

BE6–4 For each company, calculate the missing income statement amount.   Calculate amounts related
                                                                                                       to the multiple-step
                                                                                                       income statement **(LO6–2)**

Company	Sales Revenue	Cost of Goods Sold	Gross Profit	Operating Expenses	Net Income
Lennon	$18,000	(a)	$ 8,000	$3,500	$4,500
Harrison	20,000	$11,000	(b)	6,000	3,000
McCartney	13,000	9,000	4,000	(c)	1,500
Starr	16,000	6,000	10,000	6,500	(d)

BE6–5 During the year, Wright Company sells 470 remote-control airplanes for $110 each. The   Calculate ending inventory
company has the following inventory purchase transactions for the year.   and cost of goods sold
                                                                                                       using FIFO **(LO6–3)**

Date	Transaction	Number of Units	Unit Cost	Total Cost
Jan. 1	Beginning inventory	60	$82	$ 4,920
May 5	Purchase	250	85	21,250
Nov. 3	Purchase	200	90	18,000
		510		$44,170

Calculate ending inventory and cost of goods sold for the year, assuming the company uses FIFO.

Calculate ending inventory and cost of goods sold using LIFO (LO6–3)

BE6–6 Refer to the information in BE6–5. Calculate ending inventory and cost of goods sold for the year, assuming the company uses LIFO.

Calculate ending inventory and cost of goods sold using weighted-average cost (LO6–3)

BE6–7 Refer to the information in BE6–5. Calculate ending inventory and cost of goods sold for the year, assuming the company uses weighted-average cost.

Calculate ending inventory and cost of goods sold using specific identification (LO6–3)

BE6–8 Refer to the information in BE6–5. Calculate ending inventory and cost of goods sold for the year, assuming the company uses specific identification. Actual sales by the company include its entire beginning inventory, 230 units of inventory from the May 5 purchase, and 180 units from the November 3 purchase.

Identify financial statement effects of FIFO and LIFO (LO6–4)

BE6–9 For each item below, indicate whether FIFO or LIFO will generally result in a higher reported amount when inventory costs are rising versus falling. The first answer is provided as an example.

Inventory Costs	Higher Total Assets	Higher Cost of Goods Sold	Higher Net Income
Rising	FIFO		
Declining			

Record inventory purchases and sales using a perpetual system (LO6–5)

BE6–10 Shankar Company uses a perpetual system to record inventory transactions. The company purchases inventory on account on February 2 for $40,000 and then sells this inventory on account on March 17 for $60,000. Record transactions for (a) the purchase of inventory on account and (b) the sale of inventory on account.

Record freight charges for inventory using a perpetual system (LO6–5)

BE6–11 Shankar Company uses a perpetual system to record inventory transactions. The company purchases inventory on account on February 2 for $40,000.

In addition to the cost of inventory, the company also pays $600 for freight charges associated with the purchase on the same day. Record (a) the purchase of inventory on account and (b) payment of freight charges.

Record purchase returns of inventory using a perpetual system (LO6–5)

BE6–12 Shankar Company uses a perpetual system to record inventory transactions. The company purchases 1,500 units of inventory on account on February 2 for $60,000 ($40 per unit) but then returns 100 defective units on February 5. Record (a) the inventory purchase on account on February 2 and (b) the inventory return on February 5.

Record purchase discounts of inventory using a perpetual system (LO6–5)

BE6–13 Shankar Company uses a perpetual system to record inventory transactions. The company purchases inventory on account on February 2 for $40,000, with terms 3/10, n/30. On February 10, the company pays on account for the inventory. Record (a) the inventory purchase on account on February 2 and (b) the payment on February 10.

Calculate ending inventory using lower of cost and net realizable value (LO6–6)

BE6–14 Powder Ski Shop reports inventory using the lower of cost and net realizable value (NRV). Information related to its year-end inventory appears below. Calculate the total amount to be reported for ending inventory in the balance sheet.

Inventory	Quantity	Unit Cost	Unit NRV
Ski jackets	20	$115	$ 95
Skis	25	300	350

Record lower of cost and net realizable value (LO6–6)

BE6–15 Refer to the information in BE6–14. Record any necessary adjusting entry for the lower of cost and net realizable value.

BE6–16 Creative Technology reports inventory using the lower of cost and net realizable value (NRV). Below is information related to its year-end inventory. Calculate the total amount to be reported for ending inventory in the balance sheet.

Calculate ending inventory using the lower of cost and net realizable value (LO6–6)

Inventory	Quantity	Unit Cost	Unit NRV
Optima cameras	110	$45	$75
Inspire speakers	50	55	45

BE6–17 Using the amounts below, calculate the inventory turnover ratio, average days in inventory, and gross profit ratio.

Calculate inventory ratios (LO6–7)

Net sales	$250,000
Cost of goods sold	180,000
Beginning inventory	55,000
Ending inventory	45,000

BE6–18 Refer to the information in BE6–10, but now assume that Shankar uses a periodic system to record inventory transactions. Record transactions for the purchase and sale of inventory.

Record inventory purchases and sales using a periodic system (LO6–8)

BE6–19 Refer to the information in BE6–11, but now assume that Shankar uses a periodic system to record inventory transactions. Record the purchase of inventory on February 2, including the freight charges.

Record freight charges for inventory using a periodic system (LO6–8)

BE6–20 Refer to the information in BE6–12, but now assume that Shankar uses a periodic system to record inventory transactions. Record the inventory purchase on February 2 and the inventory return on February 5.

Record purchase returns of inventory using a periodic system (LO6–8)

BE6–21 Refer to the information in BE6–13, but now assume that Shankar uses a periodic system to record inventory transactions. Record the inventory purchase on February 2 and the payment on February 10.

Record purchase discounts of inventory using a periodic system (LO6–8)

BE6–22 Ebbers Corporation overstated its ending inventory balance by $15,000 in the current year. What impact will this error have on cost of goods sold and gross profit in the current year and following year?

Find income statement effects of overstatement in ending inventory (LO6–9)

BE6–23 Refer to the information in BE6–22. What impact will this error have on ending inventory and retained earnings in the current year and following year? Ignore any tax effects.

Find balance sheet effects of overstatement in ending inventory (LO6–9)

BE6–24 Refer to the information in BE6–10. Determine the financial statement effects for (a) the purchase of inventory on account and (b) the sale of inventory on account.

Determine financial statement effects of inventory purchases and sales (LO6–5)

BE6–25 Refer to the information in BE6–11. Determine the financial statement effects for (a) the purchase of inventory on account and (b) payment of freight charges.

Determine financial statement effects of freight charges for inventory (LO6–5)

BE6–26 Refer to the information in BE6–12. Determine the financial statement effects for (a) the inventory purchase on account on February 2 and (b) the inventory return on February 5.

Determine financial statement effects of purchase returns of inventory (LO6–5)

BE6–27 Refer to the information in BE6–13. Determine the financial statement effects for (a) the inventory purchase on account on February 2 and (b) the payment on February 10.

Determine financial statement effects of purchase discounts on inventory (LO6–5)

Determine financial statement effects of lower of cost and net realizable value **(LO6–5)**

BE6–28 Refer to the information in BE6–15. Determine the financial statement effects of adjusting inventory for the lower of cost and net realizable value.

EXERCISES

Calculate cost of goods sold **(LO6–2)**

E6–1 Quality Retail Group begins the year with inventory of $55,000 and ends the year with inventory of $45,000. During the year, the company has four purchases for the following amounts.

Purchase on February 17	$210,000
Purchase on May 6	130,000
Purchase on September 8	160,000
Purchase on December 4	410,000

Required:
Calculate cost of goods sold for the year.

Prepare a multiple-step income statement **(LO6–2)**

E6–2 Wayman Corporation reports the following amounts in its December 31, 2024, income statement.

Sales revenue	$390,000	Income tax expense	$ 50,000
Interest expense	20,000	Cost of goods sold	130,000
Salaries expense	40,000	Advertising expense	30,000
Utilities expense	50,000		

Required:
Prepare a multiple-step income statement.

Prepare a multiple-step income statement and analyze profitability **(LO6–2)**

E6–3 Tisdale Incorporated reports the following amount in its December 31, 2024, income statement.

Sales revenue	$300,000	Income tax expense	$ 30,000
Nonoperating revenue	110,000	Cost of goods sold	190,000
Selling expenses	60,000	Administrative expenses	40,000
General expenses	50,000		

Required:
1. Prepare a multiple-step income statement.
2. Explain how analyzing the multiple levels of profitability can help in understanding the future profit-generating potential of Tisdale Incorporated.

Calculate inventory amounts when costs are rising **(LO6–3)**

E6–4 During the year, TRC Corporation has the following inventory transactions.

Date	Transaction	Number of Units	Unit Cost	Total Cost
Jan. 1	Beginning inventory	60	$52	$ 3,120
Apr. 7	Purchase	140	54	7,560
Jul. 16	Purchase	210	57	11,970
Oct. 6	Purchase	120	58	6,960
		530		$29,610

For the entire year, the company sells 450 units of inventory for $70 each.

Required:
1. Using FIFO, calculate (a) ending inventory, (b) cost of goods sold, (c) sales revenue, and (d) gross profit.
2. Using LIFO, calculate (a) ending inventory, (b) cost of goods sold, (c) sales revenue, and (d) gross profit.
3. Using weighted-average cost, calculate (a) ending inventory, (b) cost of goods sold, (c) sales revenue, and (d) gross profit.
4. Determine which method will result in higher profitability when inventory costs are rising.

E6–5 During the year, Triumph Incorporated has the following inventory transactions.

Calculate inventory amounts when costs are declining **(LO6–3)**

Date	Transaction	Number of Units	Unit Cost	Total Cost
Jan. 1	Beginning inventory	20	$22	$ 440
Mar. 4	Purchase	25	21	525
Jun. 9	Purchase	30	20	600
Nov. 11	Purchase	30	18	540
		105		$2,105

For the entire year, the company sells 81 units of inventory for $30 each.

Required:
1. Using FIFO, calculate (a) ending inventory, (b) cost of goods sold, (c) sales revenue, and (d) gross profit.
2. Using LIFO, calculate (a) ending inventory, (b) cost of goods sold, (c) sales revenue, and (d) gross profit.
3. Using weighted-average cost, calculate (a) ending inventory, (b) cost of goods sold, (c) sales revenue, and (d) gross profit.
4. Determine which method will result in higher profitability when inventory costs are declining.

E6–6 Bingerton Industries began the year with inventory of $85,000. Purchases of inventory on account during the year totaled $310,000. Inventory costing $335,000 was sold on account for $520,000.

Record inventory transactions using a perpetual system **(LO6–5)**

Required:
Record transactions for the (a) purchase of inventory on account and (b) the sale of inventory on account using a perpetual system.

E6–7 On June 5, Staley Electronics purchases 200 units of inventory on account for $20 each. After closer examination, Staley determines 40 units are defective and returns them to its supplier for full credit on June 9. All remaining inventory is sold on account on June 16 for $35 each.

Record inventory purchase and purchase return using a perpetual system **(LO6–5)**

Required:
Record transactions for (a) the purchase of inventory on account, (b) the return of defective inventory, and (c) the sale of inventory on account using a perpetual system.

E6–8 On June 5, Staley Electronics purchases 200 units of inventory on account for $19 each, with terms 2/10, n/30. Staley pays for the inventory on June 12.

Record inventory purchase and purchase discount using a perpetual system **(LO6–5)**

Required:
1. Record transactions for the purchase of inventory on account and payment on account using a perpetual system.
2. Now assume payment is made on June 22. Record the payment on account.

E6–9 Littleton Books has the following transactions during May.

Record transactions using a perpetual system **(LO6–5)**

May 2   Purchases books on account from Readers Wholesale for $3,300, terms 1/10, n/30.
May 3   Pays cash for freight costs of $200 on books purchased from Readers.
May 5   Returns books with a cost of $400 to Readers because part of the order is incorrect.
May 10   Pays the full amount due to Readers.
May 30   Sells all books purchased on May 2 (less those returned on May 5) for $4,000 on account.

Required:
1. Record the transactions of Littleton Books, assuming the company uses a perpetual inventory system.
2. Assume that payment to Readers is made on May 24 instead of May 10. Record this payment.

Record transactions
using a perpetual
system (LO6–5)

E6–10 Sundance Systems has the following transactions during July.

July   5   Purchases 40 LCD televisions on account from Red River Supplies for $2,500 each, terms 3/10, n/30.
July   8   Returns to Red River two televisions that had defective sound.
July 13   Pays the full amount due to Red River.
July 28   Sells remaining 38 televisions from July 5 for $3,000 each on account.

Required:
Record the transactions of Sundance Systems, assuming the company uses a perpetual inventory system.

Record transactions
using a perpetual
system (LO6–5)

Flip Side of E6–12

E6–11 DS Unlimited has the following transactions during August.

August   6   Purchases 70 handheld game devices on account from GameGirl, Inc., for $200 each, terms 1/10, n/60.
August   7   Pays $400 to Sure Shipping for freight charges associated with the August 6 purchase.
August 10   Returns to GameGirl six game devices that were defective.
August 14   Pays the full amount due to GameGirl.
August 23   Sells 50 game devices purchased on August 6 for $220 each to customers on account. The total cost of the 50 game devices sold is $10,212.50.

Required:
Record the transactions of DS Unlimited, assuming the company uses a perpetual inventory system.

Record transactions
using a perpetual
system (LO6–5)

Flip Side of E6–11

E6–12 Refer to the transactions in E6–11.

Required:
Prepare the transactions for GameGirl, Inc., assuming the company uses a perpetual inventory system. Assume the 70 game devices sold on August 6 to DS Unlimited had a cost to GameGirl of $180 each. The items returned on August 10 were considered worthless to GameGirl and were discarded.

Calculate inventory using
lower of cost and net
realizable value (LO6–6)

E6–13 Home Furnishings reports inventory using the lower of cost and net realizable value (NRV). Below is information related to its year-end inventory.

Inventory	Quantity	Unit Cost	Unit NRV
Furniture	200	$ 85	$100
Electronics	50	400	300

Required:
1. Calculate the total recorded cost of ending inventory before any adjustments.
2. Calculate ending inventory using the lower of cost and net realizable value.
3. Record any necessary adjusting entry for inventory.
4. Determine the impact of the adjusting entry in the financial statements.

Calculate inventory using
lower of cost and net
realizable value (LO6–6)

E6–14 A company like **Golf USA** that sells golf-related inventory typically will have inventory items such as golf clothing and golf equipment. As technology advances the design and performance of the next generation of drivers, the older models become less marketable and therefore decline in value. Suppose that in the current year, **Ping** (a manufacturer of golf clubs) introduces the MegaDriver II, the new and improved version of the MegaDriver. Below are year-end amounts related to Golf USA's inventory.

Inventory	Quantity	Unit Cost	Unit NRV
Shirts	35	$ 60	$ 70
MegaDriver	15	360	250
MegaDriver II	30	350	420

Required:
1. Calculate the total recorded cost of ending inventory before any adjustments.
2. Calculate ending inventory using the lower of cost and net realizable value.
3. Record any necessary adjusting entry to inventory.
4. Determine the impact of the adjusting entry in the financial statements.

E6–15 Lewis Incorporated and Clark Enterprises report the following amounts for the year.

Calculate cost of goods sold, the inventory turnover ratio, and average days in inventory (LO6–2, 6–7)

	Lewis	Clark
Inventory (beginning)	$ 24,000	$ 50,000
Inventory (ending)	18,000	60,000
Purchases	261,000	235,000
Purchase returns	15,000	60,000

Required:
1. Calculate cost of goods sold for each company.
2. Calculate the inventory turnover ratio for each company.
3. Calculate the average days in inventory for each company.
4. Determine which company appears to be managing its inventory more efficiently.

E6–16 Below are amounts found in the income statements of three companies.

Calculate levels of profitability for a multiple-step income statement and the gross profit ratio (LO6–2, 6–7)

Company	Sales Revenue	Cost of Goods Sold	Operating Expenses	Nonoperating Expenses	Income Tax Expense
Henry	$32,000	$ 4,800	$ 5,000	$2,000	$2,000
Grace	35,000	24,500	13,100	7,000	0
James	40,000	24,800	3,000	0	3,000

Required:
1. For each company, calculate (a) gross profit, (b) operating income, (c) income before income taxes, and (d) net income.
2. For each company, calculate the gross profit ratio and indicate which company has the most favorable ratio.

E6–17 Refer to the transactions in E6–9.

Record transactions using a periodic system (LO6–8)

Required:
1. Record the transactions of Littleton Books, assuming the company uses a periodic inventory system.
2. Record the period-end adjusting entry to cost of goods sold on May 31, assuming the company has no beginning or ending inventory.

E6–18 Refer to the transactions in E6–10.

Record transactions using a periodic system (LO6–8)

Required:
1. Record the transactions of Sundance Systems, assuming the company uses a periodic inventory system.
2. Record the period-end adjusting entry to cost of goods sold on July 31, assuming the company has no beginning inventory.

Record inventory
purchases and sales using
a periodic system **(LO6–8)**

E6–19 Refer to the transactions in E6–11.

Required:
1. Record the transactions of DS Unlimited, assuming the company uses a periodic inventory system.
2. Record the period-end adjusting entry to cost of goods sold on August 31, assuming the company has no beginning inventory and ending inventory has a cost of $2,859.50.

Find financial
statement effects of
understatement in ending
inventory **(LO6–9)**

E6–20 Mulligan Corporation purchases inventory on account with terms FOB shipping point. The goods are shipped on December 30, 2024, but do not reach Mulligan until January 5, 2025. Mulligan correctly records accounts payable associated with the purchase but does not include this inventory in its 2024 ending inventory count.

Required:
1. If an error has been made, explain why.
2. If an error has been made, indicate whether there is an understatement (U), overstatement (O), or no effect (N) on the reported amount of each financial statement element in the current year and following year. Ignore any tax effects.

	Balance Sheet			Income Statement		
Year	Assets	Liabilities	Stockholders' Equity	Revenues	Cost of Goods Sold	Gross Profit
Current						
Following						

Complete the accounting
cycle using inventory
transactions **(LO 6–2,
6–3, 6–5, 6–6, 6–7)**

E6–21 On January 1, 2024, the general ledger of Big Blast Fireworks includes the following account balances:

Accounts	Debit	Credit
Cash	$ 21,900	
Accounts Receivable	36,500	
Allowance for Uncollectible Accounts		$ 3,100
Inventory	30,000	
Land	61,600	
Accounts Payable		32,400
Notes Payable (8%, due in 3 years)		30,000
Common Stock		56,000
Retained Earnings		28,500
Totals	$150,000	$150,000

The $30,000 beginning balance of inventory consists of 300 units, each costing $100. During January 2024, Big Blast Fireworks had the following inventory transactions:

January 3	Purchase 1,200 units for $126,000 on account ($105 each).
January 8	Purchase 1,300 units for $143,000 on account ($110 each).
January 12	Purchase 1,400 units for $161,000 on account ($115 each).
January 15	Return 100 of the units purchased on January 12 because of defects.
January 19	Sell 4,000 units on account for $600,000. The cost of the units sold is determined using a FIFO perpetual inventory system.
January 22	Receive $580,000 from customers on accounts receivable.
January 24	Pay $410,000 to inventory suppliers on accounts payable.
January 27	Write off accounts receivable as uncollectible, $2,500.
January 31	Pay cash for salaries during January, $128,000.

Required:

1. Record each of the transactions listed above, assuming a FIFO perpetual inventory system.
2. Record adjusting entries on January 31.
   a. At the end of January, the company estimates that the remaining units of inventory purchased on January 12 are expected to sell in February for only $100 each. Prepare the adjusting entry using the lower of cost and net realizable value method. [*Hint:* Determine the number of units remaining from January 12 after subtracting the units returned on January 15 and the units assumed sold (FIFO) on January 19.]
   b. The company records an adjusting entry for $3,000 for estimated future uncollectible accounts.
   c. The company accrues interest on notes payable for January. Interest is expected to be paid each December 31.
   d. The company accrues income taxes at the end of January of $12,300.
3. Prepare an adjusted trial balance as of January 31, 2024, after updating beginning balances (above) for transactions during January (*requirement* 1) and adjusting entries at the end of January (*requirement* 2).
4. Prepare a multiple-step income statement for the period ended January 31, 2024.
5. Prepare a classified balance sheet as of January 31, 2024.
6. Record closing entries.
7. Analyze how well Big Blast Fireworks' manages its inventory:
   a. Calculate the inventory turnover ratio for the month of January. If the industry average of the inventory turnover ratio for the month of January is 18.5 times, is the company managing its inventory *more* or *less* efficiently than other companies in the same industry?
   b. Calculate the gross profit ratio for the month of January. If the industry average gross profit ratio is 33%, is the company *more* or *less* profitable per dollar of sales than other companies in the same industry?
   c. Used together, what might the inventory turnover ratio and gross profit ratio suggest about Big Blast Fireworks' business strategy? Is the company's strategy to sell a *higher volume of less expensive* items or does the company appear to be selling a *lower volume of more expensive* items?

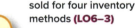

PROBLEMS: SET A

P6–1A Sandra's Purse Boutique has the following transactions related to its top-selling **Gucci** purse for the month of October.

Calculate ending inventory and cost of goods sold for four inventory methods **(LO6–3)**

Date	Transactions	Units	Unit Cost	Total Cost
October 1	Beginning inventory	6	$900	$ 5,400
October 4	Sale	4		
October 10	Purchase	5	910	4,550
October 13	Sale	3		
October 20	Purchase	4	920	3,680
October 28	Sale	7		
October 30	Purchase	7	930	6,510
				$20,140

Required:

1. Calculate ending inventory and cost of goods sold at October 31, using the specific identification method. The October 4 sale consists of purses from beginning inventory, the October 13 sale consists of one purse from beginning inventory and two purses from the October 10 purchase, and the October 28 sale consists of three purses from the October 10 purchase and four purses from the October 20 purchase.
2. Using FIFO, calculate ending inventory and cost of goods sold at October 31.
3. Using LIFO, calculate ending inventory and cost of goods sold at October 31.
4. Using weighted-average cost, calculate ending inventory and cost of goods sold at October 31.

Calculate ending
inventory, cost of goods
sold, sales revenue,
and gross profit for four
inventory methods
(LO6–3, 6–4, 6–5)

P6–2A Greg's Bicycle Shop has the following transactions related to its top-selling **Mongoose** mountain bike for the month of March.

Date	Transactions	Units	Unit Cost	Total Cost
March 1	Beginning inventory	20	$250	$ 5,000
March 5	Sale ($400 each)	15		
March 9	Purchase	10	270	2,700
March 17	Sale ($450 each)	8		
March 22	Purchase	10	280	2,800
March 27	Sale ($475 each)	12		
March 30	Purchase	9	300	2,700
				$13,200

Required:

1. Calculate ending inventory and cost of goods sold at March 31, using the specific identification method. The March 5 sale consists of bikes from beginning inventory, the March 17 sale consists of bikes from the March 9 purchase, and the March 27 sale consists of four bikes from beginning inventory and eight bikes from the March 22 purchase.
2. Using FIFO, calculate ending inventory and cost of goods sold at March 31.
3. Using LIFO, calculate ending inventory and cost of goods sold at March 31.
4. Using weighted-average cost, calculate ending inventory and cost of goods sold at March 31.
5. Calculate sales revenue and gross profit under each of the four methods.
6. Comparing FIFO and LIFO, which one provides the more meaningful measure of ending inventory? Explain.
7. If Greg's Bicycle Shop chooses to report inventory using LIFO instead of FIFO, record the LIFO adjustment.

Record transactions
and prepare a partial
income statement using
a perpetual inventory
system (LO6–2, 6–5)

P6–3A At the beginning of July, CD City has a balance in inventory of $3,400. The following transactions occur during the month of July.

July 3	Purchase CDs on account from Wholesale Music for $2,300, terms 1/10, n/30.
July 4	Pay cash for freight charges related to the July 3 purchase from Wholesale Music, $110.
July 9	Return incorrectly ordered CDs to Wholesale Music and receive credit, $200.
July 11	Pay Wholesale Music in full.
July 12	Sell CDs to customers on account, $5,800, that had a cost of $3,000.
July 15	Receive full payment from customers related to the sale on July 12.
July 18	Purchase CDs on account from Music Supply for $3,100, terms 1/10, n/30.
July 22	Sell CDs to customers for cash, $4,200, that had a cost of $2,500.
July 28	Return CDs to Music Supply and receive credit of $300.
July 30	Pay Music Supply in full.

Required:

1. Assuming that CD City uses a perpetual inventory system, record the transactions.
2. Prepare the top section of the multiple-step income statement through gross profit for the month of July.

Report inventory using
lower of cost and net
realizable value (LO6–6)

P6–4A A local **Chevrolet** dealership carries the following types of vehicles:

Inventory Items	Quantity	Unit Cost	Unit NRV	Lower of Cost and NRV
Vans	4	$27,000	$25,000	_____
Trucks	7	18,000	17,000	_____
2-door sedans	3	13,000	15,000	_____
4-door sedans	5	17,000	20,000	_____
Sports cars	1	37,000	40,000	_____
SUVs	6	30,000	28,000	_____
				_____

Because of recent increases in gasoline prices, the car dealership has noticed a reduced demand for its SUVs, vans, and trucks.

Required:

1. Compute the total cost of the entire inventory.
2. Determine whether each inventory item would be reported at cost or net realizable value (NRV). Multiply the quantity of each inventory item by the appropriate cost or NRV amount and place the total in the "Lower of Cost and NRV" column. Then determine the total for that column.
3. Compare your answers in *requirement* 1 and *requirement* 2 and then record any necessary adjusting entry to write down inventory from cost to net realizable value.
4. Determine the financial statement effects of using lower of cost and net realizable value to report inventory.

P6–5A For the current year, Parker Games has the following inventory transactions related to its traditional board games.

Calculate ending inventory and cost of goods sold using FIFO and LIFO and adjust inventory using lower of cost and net realizable value **(LO6–3, 6–6)**

Date	Transaction	Units	Unit Cost	Total Cost
Jan. 1	Beginning inventory	120	$21	$2,520
Mar. 12	Purchase	90	16	1,440
Sep. 17	Purchase	60	9	540
		270		$4,500
Jan. 1–Dec. 31	Sales	170		

Required:

1. Using FIFO, calculate ending inventory and cost of goods sold.
2. Using LIFO, calculate ending inventory and cost of goods sold.
3. Because of the increasing popularity of electronic video games, Parker Games continues to see a decline in the demand for board games. Sales prices have decreased by over 50% during the year. At the end of the year, Parker estimates the net realizable value of the 100 units of unsold inventory to be $500. Determine the amount of ending inventory to report using lower of cost and net realizable value under FIFO. Record any necessary adjusting entry.

P6–6A At the beginning of October, Bowser Co.'s inventory consists of 50 units with a cost per unit of $50. The following transactions occur during the month of October.

Record transactions using a perpetual system, prepare a partial income statement, and adjust for the lower of cost and net realizable value **(LO6–2, 6–3, 6–4, 6–5, 6–6)**

October 4	Purchase 130 units of inventory on account from Waluigi Co. for $50 per unit, terms 2/10, n/30.
October 5	Pay cash for freight charges related to the October 4 purchase, $600.
October 9	Return 10 defective units from the October 4 purchase and receive credit.
October 12	Pay Waluigi Co. in full.
October 15	Sell 160 units of inventory to customers on account, $12,800. (*Hint:* The cost of units sold from the October 4 purchase includes $50 unit cost plus $5 per unit for freight less $1 per unit for the purchase discount, or $54 per unit.)
October 19	Receive full payment from customers related to the sale on October 15.
October 20	Purchase 100 units of inventory from Waluigi Co. for $70 per unit.
October 22	Sell 100 units of inventory to customers for cash, $8,000.

Required:

1. Assuming that Bowser Co. uses a FIFO perpetual inventory system to maintain its inventory records, record the transactions.
2. Suppose by the end of October that the remaining inventory is estimated to have a net realizable value per unit of $35. Record any necessary adjusting entry for lower of cost and net realizable value.
3. Prepare the top section of the multiple-step income statement through gross profit for the month of October after the adjusting entry for lower of cost and net realizable value.

Prepare a multiple-step income statement and calculate the inventory turnover ratio and gross profit ratio (LO6–2, 6–7)

P6–7A **Baskin-Robbins** is one of the world's largest specialty ice cream shops. The company offers dozens of different flavors, from Very Berry Strawberry to lowfat Espresso 'n Cream. Assume that a local Baskin-Robbins in Raleigh, North Carolina, has the following amounts for the month of July 2024.

Salaries expense	$13,700	Sales revenue	$69,800
Inventory (July 1, 2024)	2,300	Interest income	3,300
Sales returns	1,100	Cost of goods sold	28,700
Utilities expense	3,600	Rent expense	6,700
Income tax expense	6,000	Interest expense	400
		Inventory (July 31, 2024)	1,100

Required:
1. Prepare a multiple-step income statement for the month ended July 31, 2024.
2. Calculate the inventory turnover ratio for the month of July. Would you expect this ratio to be higher or lower in December 2024? Explain.
3. Calculate the gross profit ratio for the month of July.

Use the inventory turnover ratio and gross profit ratio to analyze companies (LO6–7)

P6–8A **Wawa Food Markets** is a convenience store chain located primarily in the Northeast. The company sells gas, candy bars, drinks, and other grocery-related items. **St. Jude Medical Incorporated** sells medical devices related to cardiovascular needs. Suppose a local Wawa Food Market and St. Jude sales office report the following amounts in the same year (company names are disguised):

	Company 1	Company 2
Net sales	$400,000	$400,000
Cost of goods sold	180,000	330,000
Gross profit	$220,000	$ 70,000
Average inventory	$ 40,000	$ 30,000

Required:
1. For Company 1 and Company 2, calculate the inventory turnover ratio.
2. For Company 1 and Company 2, calculate the gross profit ratio.
3. After comparing the inventory turnover ratios and gross profit ratios, which company do you think is Wawa and which is St. Jude? Explain.

Record transactions and prepare a partial income statement using a periodic inventory system (LO6–8)

P6–9A Refer to the transactions of CD City in P6–3A.

Required:
1. Assuming that CD City uses a periodic inventory system, record the transactions.
2. Record the month-end adjusting entry to inventory, assuming that a final count reveals ending inventory with a cost of $2,889.
3. Prepare the top section of the multiple-step income statement through gross profit for the month of July.

Correct inventory understatement and calculate gross profit ratio (LO6–7, 6–9)

P6–10A Over a four-year period, Jackie Corporation reported the following series of gross profits.

	2021	2022	2023	2024
Net sales	$60,000	$66,000	$74,000	$90,000
Cost of goods sold	32,000	46,000	28,000	48,000
Gross profit	$28,000	$20,000	$46,000	$42,000

In 2024, the company performed a comprehensive review of its inventory accounting procedures. Based on this review, company records reveal that ending inventory was understated by $11,000 in 2022. Inventory in all other years is correct.

Required:
1. Calculate the gross profit ratio for each of the four years based on amounts originally reported.
2. Calculate the gross profit ratio for each of the four years based on corrected amounts. Describe the trend in the gross profit ratios based on the original amounts versus the corrected amounts.
3. Total gross profit over the four-year period based on the amounts originally reported equals $136,000 (= $28,000 + $20,000 + $46,000 + $42,000). Compare this amount to total gross profit over the four-year period based on the corrected amounts.

PROBLEMS: SET B

P6–1B Jimmie's Fishing Hole has the following transactions related to its top-selling **Shimano** fishing reel for the month of June:

Calculate ending inventory and cost of goods sold for four inventory methods **(LO6–3)**

Date	Transactions	Units	Unit Cost	Total Cost
June 1	Beginning inventory	16	$350	$ 5,600
June 7	Sale	11		
June 12	Purchase	10	340	3,400
June 15	Sale	12		
June 24	Purchase	10	330	3,300
June 27	Sale	8		
June 29	Purchase	9	320	2,880
				$15,180

Required:
1. Calculate ending inventory and cost of goods sold at June 30, using the specific identification method. The June 7 sale consists of fishing reels from beginning inventory, the June 15 sale consists of three fishing reels from beginning inventory and nine fishing reels from the June 12 purchase, and the June 27 sale consists of one fishing reel from beginning inventory and seven fishing reels from the June 24 purchase.
2. Using FIFO, calculate ending inventory and cost of goods sold at June 30.
3. Using LIFO, calculate ending inventory and cost of goods sold at June 30.
4. Using weighted-average cost, calculate ending inventory and cost of goods sold at June 30.

P6–2B Pete's Tennis Shop has the following transactions related to its top-selling **Wilson** tennis racket for the month of August:

Calculate ending inventory, cost of goods sold, sales revenue, and gross profit for four inventory methods **(LO6–3, 6–4, 6–5)**

Date	Transactions	Units	Unit Cost	Total Cost
August 1	Beginning inventory	8	$160	$1,280
August 4	Sale ($225 each)	5		
August 11	Purchase	10	150	1,500
August 13	Sale ($240 each)	8		
August 20	Purchase	10	140	1,400
August 26	Sale ($250 each)	11		
August 29	Purchase	11	130	1,430
				$5,610

Required:
1. Calculate ending inventory and cost of goods sold at August 31, using the specific identification method. The August 4 sale consists of rackets from beginning inventory, the August 13 sale consists of rackets from the August 11 purchase, and the August 26 sale consists of one racket from beginning inventory and 10 rackets from the August 20 purchase.

2. Using FIFO, calculate ending inventory and cost of goods sold at August 31.
3. Using LIFO, calculate ending inventory and cost of goods sold at August 31.
4. Using weighted-average cost, calculate ending inventory and cost of goods sold at August 31.
5. Calculate sales revenue and gross profit under each of the four methods.
6. Comparing FIFO and LIFO, which one provides the more meaningful measure of ending inventory? Explain.
7. If Pete's chooses to report inventory using LIFO, record the LIFO adjustment.

Record transactions and prepare a partial income statement using a perpetual inventory system (LO6–2, 6–5)

P6–3B At the beginning of June, Circuit Country has a balance in inventory of $3,000. The following transactions occur during the month of June.

June	2	Purchase radios on account from Radio World for $2,700, terms 1/15, n/45.
June	4	Pay cash for freight charges related to the June 2 purchase from Radio World, $400.
June	8	Return defective radios to Radio World and receive credit, $400.
June	10	Pay Radio World in full.
June	11	Sell radios to customers on account, $5,000, that had a cost of $3,200.
June	18	Receive payment on account from customers, $4,000.
June	20	Purchase radios on account from Sound Unlimited for $3,800, terms 3/10, n/30.
June	23	Sell radios to customers for cash, $5,300, that had a cost of $3,600.
June	26	Return damaged radios to Sound Unlimited and receive credit of $500.
June	28	Pay Sound Unlimited in full.

Required:
1. Assuming that Circuit Country uses a perpetual inventory system, record the transactions.
2. Prepare the top section of the multiple-step income statement through gross profit for the month of June.

Report inventory using lower of cost and net realizable value (LO6–6)

P6–4B A home improvement store, like **Lowe's**, carries the following items:

Inventory Items	Quantity	Unit Cost	Unit NRV	Lower of Cost and NRV
Hammers	110	$ 8.00	$ 8.50	_____
Saws	60	11.00	10.00	_____
Screwdrivers	140	3.00	3.60	_____
Drills	50	26.00	24.00	_____
One-gallon paint cans	170	6.50	6.00	_____
Paintbrushes	190	7.00	7.50	_____

Required:
1. Compute the total cost of inventory.
2. Determine whether each inventory item would be reported at cost or net realizable value. Multiply the quantity of each inventory item by the appropriate cost or NRV amount and place the total in the "Lower of Cost and NRV" column. Then determine the total of that column.
3. Compare your answers in *requirement* 1 and *requirement* 2 and then record any necessary adjusting entry to write down inventory from cost to net realizable value.
4. Determine the financial statement effects of using lower of cost and net realizable value to report inventory.

Calculate ending inventory and cost of goods sold using FIFO and LIFO and adjust inventory using lower of cost and net realizable value (LO6–3, 6–6)

P6–5B Trends by Tiffany sells high-end leather purses. The company has the following inventory transactions for the year.

Date	Transactions	Units	Unit Cost	Total Cost
Jan. 1	Beginning inventory	20	$500	$10,000
Apr. 9	Purchase	30	520	15,600
Oct. 4	Purchase	11	550	6,050
		61		$31,650
Jan. 1–Dec. 31	Sales	52		

Required:

1. Using FIFO, calculate ending inventory and cost of goods sold.
2. Using LIFO, calculate ending inventory and cost of goods sold.
3. Because trends in purses change frequently, Trends by Tiffany estimates that the remaining nine purses have a net realizable value at December 31 of only $350 each. Determine the amount of ending inventory to report using lower of cost and net realizable value under FIFO. Record any necessary adjusting entry.

P6–6B At the beginning of November, Yoshi Inc.'s inventory consists of 60 units with a cost per unit of $94. The following transactions occur during the month of November.

November 2	Purchase 90 units of inventory on account from Toad Inc. for $100 per unit, terms 3/10, n/30.
November 3	Pay cash for freight charges related to the November 2 purchase, $231.
November 9	Return 13 defective units from the November 2 purchase and receive credit.
November 11	Pay Toad Inc. in full.
November 16	Sell 100 units of inventory to customers on account, $14,000. (*Hint:* The cost of units sold from the November 2 purchase includes $100 unit cost plus $3 per unit for freight less $3 per unit for the purchase discount, or $100 per unit.)
November 20	Receive full payment from customers related to the sale on November 16.
November 21	Purchase 70 units of inventory from Toad Inc. for $104 per unit.
November 24	Sell 90 units of inventory to customers for cash, $12,600.

Record transactions using a perpetual system, prepare a partial income statement, and adjust for the lower of cost and net realizable value **(LO6–2, 6–3, 6–4, 6–5, 6–6)**

Required:

1. Assuming that Yoshi Inc. uses a FIFO perpetual inventory system to maintain its internal inventory records, record the transactions.
2. Suppose by the end of November that the remaining inventory is estimated to have a net realizable value per unit of $81, record any necessary adjusting entry for the lower of cost and net realizable value.
3. Prepare the top section of the multiple-step income statement through gross profit for the month of November after the adjusting entry for lower of cost and net realizable value.

P6–7B The Fun Zone sells a variety of children's toys, games, books, and accessories. Assume that a local store has the following amounts for the month of March 2024.

Prepare a multiple-step income statement and calculate the inventory turnover ratio and gross profit ratio **(LO6–2, 6–7)**

Sales revenue	$77,300	Inventory (Mar. 31, 2024)	$1,000
Advertising expense	6,400	Insurance expense	2,300
Rent expense	4,300	Sales discounts	3,000
Gain on sale of building	7,500	Salaries expense	9,400
Inventory (Mar. 1, 2024)	2,800	Income tax expense	4,200
Cost of goods sold	35,800		

Required:

1. Prepare a multiple-step income statement for the month ended March 31, 2024.
2. Calculate the inventory turnover ratio for the month of March. Would you expect this ratio to be higher or lower in December 2024? Explain.
3. Calculate the gross profit ratio for the month of March.

Use the inventory turnover ratio and gross profit ratio to analyze companies (LO6–7)

P6–8B **Payless ShoeSource** and **Dillard's** both offer men's formal footwear. Payless offers lower- to middle-priced footwear, whereas Dillard's offers more specialized, higher-end footwear. The average price for a pair of shoes in Payless may be about $50, whereas the average price in Dillard's may be about $175. The types of shoes offered by Dillard's are not sold by many other stores. Suppose a Payless store and a Dillard's store report the following amounts for men's shoes in the same year (company names are disguised):

	Company 1	Company 2
Net sales	$200,000	$200,000
Cost of goods sold	130,000	165,000
Gross profit	$ 70,000	$ 35,000
Average inventory	$ 35,000	$ 20,000

Required:
1. For Company 1 and Company 2, calculate the inventory turnover ratio.
2. For Company 1 and Company 2, calculate the gross profit ratio.
3. After comparing the inventory turnover ratios and gross profit ratios, which company do you think is Payless and which is Dillard's? Explain.

Record transactions and prepare a partial income statement using a periodic inventory system (LO6–8)

P6–9B Refer to the transactions of Circuit Country in P6–3B.

Required:
1. Assuming that Circuit Country uses a periodic inventory system, record the transactions.
2. Record the month-end adjusting entry to inventory, assuming that a final count reveals ending inventory with a cost of $2,078.
3. Prepare the top section of the multiple-step income statement through gross profit for the month of June.

Determine the effects of inventory errors using FIFO (LO6–3, 6–9)

P6–10B Sylvester has a bird shop that sells canaries. Sylvester maintains accurate records on the number of birds purchased from its suppliers and the number sold to customers. The records show the following purchases and sales during 2024.

Date	Transactions	Units	Cost per Unit	Total Cost
January 1	Beginning inventory	35	$40	$ 1,400
April 14	Purchase	80	42	3,360
August 22	Purchase	130	44	5,720
October 29	Purchase	95	46	4,370
		340		$14,850
Jan. 1–Dec. 31	Sales ($60 each)	280		

Sylvester uses a periodic inventory system and believes there are 60 birds remaining in ending inventory. However, Sylvester neglects to make a final inventory count at the end of the year. An employee accidentally left one of the cages open one night and 10 birds flew away, leaving only 50 birds in ending inventory. Sylvester is not aware of the lost canaries.

Required:
1. What amount will Sylvester calculate for ending inventory and cost of goods sold using FIFO, assuming he erroneously believes 60 canaries remain in ending inventory?
2. What amount would Sylvester calculate for ending inventory and cost of goods sold using FIFO if he knew that only 50 canaries remain in ending inventory?
3. What effect will the inventory error have on reported amounts for (a) ending inventory, (b) retained earnings, (c) cost of goods sold, and (d) net income (ignoring tax effects) in 2024?
4. Assuming that ending inventory is correctly counted at the end of 2025, what effect will the inventory error in 2024 have on reported amounts for (a) ending inventory, (b) retained earnings, (c) cost of goods sold, and (d) net income (ignoring tax effects) in 2025?

REAL-WORLD PERSPECTIVES

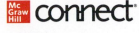

Data Analytics & Excel

Visit Connect to find a variety of Data Analytics questions that help build Excel, Tableau, and data visualization skills. Assignable materials include Integrated Excel, Applying Excel, Data Visualizations, Tableau Dashboard Activities, and Applying Tableau Cases.

Great Adventures

**General Ledger
Continuing Case**

(This is a continuation of the Great Adventures problem from earlier chapters.)

RWP6–1 Now that operations for outdoor clinics and TEAM events are running smoothly, Suzie thinks of another area for business expansion. She notices that a few clinic participants wear multiuse (MU) watches. Beyond the normal timekeeping features of most watches, MU watches are able to report temperature, altitude, and barometric pressure. MU watches are waterproof, so moisture from kayaking, rain, fishing, or even diving up to 100 feet won't damage them. Suzie decides to have MU watches available for sale at the start of each clinic. The following transactions relate to purchases and sales of watches during the second half of 2025. All watches are sold for $500 each.

Jul.	17	Purchased 50 watches for $7,500 ($150 per watch) on account.
Jul.	31	Sold 40 watches for $20,000 cash.
Aug.	12	Purchased 40 watches for $6,400 ($160 per watch) cash.
Aug.	22	Sold 30 watches for $15,000 on account.
Sep.	19	Paid for watches purchased on July 17.
Sep.	27	Receive cash of $9,000 for watches sold on account on August 22.
Oct.	27	Purchased 80 watches for $13,600 ($170 per watch) cash.
Nov.	20	Sold 90 watches for $45,000 cash.
Dec.	4	Purchased 100 watches for $18,000 ($180 per watch) on account.
Dec.	8	Sold 40 watches for $20,000 on account.

Required:
1. (a) Record each of these transactions, assuming a FIFO perpetual inventory system.
   (b) Calculate ending inventory as of December 31, 2025.
   (c) Prepare the gross profit section of a partial income statement for transactions related to MU watches.
2. Late in December, the next generation of multiuse (MU II) watches is released. In addition to all of the features of the MU watch, the MU II watches are equipped with a global positioning system (GPS) and have the ability to download and play songs and videos off the Internet. The demand for the original MU watches is greatly reduced. As of December 31, the estimated net realizable value of MU watches is only $100 per watch.
   (a) Record any necessary adjusting entry on December 31, for the lower of cost and net realizable value of inventory. (*Hint:* Determine the number of units remaining from the purchase on December 4 after subtracting the units assumed sold under FIFO.)
   (b) For what amount would MU inventory be reported in the December 31, 2025, balance sheet?
   (c) Prepare an updated gross profit section of a partial income statement accounting for this additional information. Compare your answer to *requirement* 1(b).

The Great Adventures continuing problem also can be assigned using the General Ledger software in Connect. Students will be given an existing trial balance and asked to prepare (1) the journal entries above, (2) financial statements, and (3) closing entries.

American Eagle Outfitters, Inc.

**Financial Analysis
Continuing Case**

RWP6–2 Financial information for American Eagle is presented in **Appendix A** at the end of the book.

Required:
1. For the most recent year, what is the amount of inventory in the balance sheet? What does this amount represent?
2. American Eagle refers to its cost of goods sold using a different name. What is it?

3. For the most recent year, what is the amount of cost of goods sold in the income statement? What does this amount represent?
4. Calculate American Eagle's inventory turnover ratio and average days in inventory for the most recent year.
5. Calculate American Eagle's gross profit ratio for each of the three years. Do you notice any trend?
6. For the most recent year, calculate American Eagle's ratio of operating expenses (other than cost of goods sold) to net sales. (*Hint:* These operating expenses include those amounts subtracted from gross profit to calculate operating income.)

Financial Analysis Continuing Case

The Buckle, Inc.

RWP6–3 Financial information for **Buckle** is presented in **Appendix B** at the end of the book.

Required:

1. For the most recent year, what is the amount of inventory in the balance sheet? What does this amount represent?
2. Buckle refers to its cost of goods sold using a different name. What is it?
3. For the most recent year, what is the amount of cost of goods sold in the income statement? What does this amount represent?
4. Calculate Buckle's inventory turnover ratio and average days in inventory for the most recent year.
5. Calculate Buckle's gross profit ratio for each of the three years. Do you notice any trend?
6. For the most recent year, calculate Buckle's ratio of operating expenses to net sales.

Comparative Analysis Continuing Case

American Eagle Outfitters, Inc. vs. The Buckle, Inc.

RWP6–4 Financial information for **American Eagle** is presented in **Appendix A** at the end of the book, and financial information for **Buckle** is presented in **Appendix B** at the end of the book.

Required:

1. Which company carries a greater inventory balance as a percentage of total assets?
2. Which company has a higher inventory turnover ratio and therefore lower average days in inventory?
3. Which company's operations are more profitable using the gross profit ratio?
4. Considering the companies' ratio of operating expenses to net sales, does your answer to *requirement* 3 change? Explain.

EDGAR Research

RWP6-5 Using EDGAR (Electronic Data Gathering, Analysis, and Retrieval system), find the annual report (10-K) for **Coca-Cola** and **Pepsico** for the year ended **December 2019.** Locate the "Consolidated Statements of Income" (income statement) and "Consolidated Balance Sheets." You may also find the annual reports at the companies' websites.

Required:

1. For each company, calculate the gross profit ratio, inventory turnover ratio, and average days in inventory.
2. Compare the management of each company's investment in inventory. Which company is more profitable and which company sells its inventory more quickly based on the ratios calculated in *requirement* 1?

Ethics

RWP6–6 Horizon Corporation manufactures personal computers. The company began operations in 2012 and reported profits for the years 2015 through 2022. Due primarily to increased competition and price slashing in the industry, 2023's income statement reported a loss of $20 million. Just before the end of the 2024 fiscal year, a memo from the company's chief financial officer (CFO) to Jim Fielding, the company controller, included the following comments:

> If we don't do something about the large amount of unsold computers already manufactured, our auditors will require us to record a write-down. The resulting loss for 2024 will cause a violation of our debt covenants and force the company into bankruptcy. I suggest that you ship half of our inventory to J.B. Sales, Inc., in Oklahoma City. I know the company's

president, and he will accept the inventory and acknowledge the shipment as a purchase. We can record the sale in 2024 which will boost our loss to a profit. Then J.B. Sales will simply return the inventory in 2025 after the financial statements have been issued.

Required:
1. Understand the reporting effect: What is the effect on income before taxes of the sales transaction requested by the CFO?
2. Specify the options: If Jim does not record the sales transaction requested by the CFO, what is the effect on total assets and income before taxes of the inventory write-down?
3. Identify the impact: Are investors and creditors potentially harmed by the CFO's suggestion?
4. Make a decision: Should Jim follow the CFO's suggestion?

Written Communication

RWP6–7 You have just been hired as a consultant to Gilbert Industries, a newly formed company. The company president, Mindy Grayson, is seeking your advice as to the appropriate inventory method Gilbert should use to value its inventory and cost of goods sold. Ms. Grayson has narrowed the choice to LIFO and FIFO. She has heard that LIFO might be better for tax purposes, but FIFO has certain advantages for financial reporting to investors and creditors. You have been told that the company will be profitable in its first year and for the foreseeable future.

Required:
Prepare a report for the president describing the factors that should be considered by Gilbert in choosing between LIFO and FIFO.

Earnings Management

RWP6–8 Eddie's Galleria sells billiard tables. The company has the following purchases and sales for 2024.

Date	Transactions	Units	Unit Cost	Total Cost
January 1	Beginning inventory	150	$540	$ 81,000
March 8	Purchase	120	570	68,400
August 22	Purchase	100	600	60,000
October 29	Purchase	80	640	51,200
		450		$260,600
Jan. 1–Dec. 31	Sales ($700 each)	400		

Eddie is worried about the company's financial performance. He has noticed an increase in the purchase cost of billiard tables, but at the same time, competition from other billiard table stores and other entertainment choices have prevented him from increasing the sales price. Eddie is worried that if the company's profitability is too low, stockholders will demand he be replaced. Eddie does not want to lose his job. Since 60 of the 400 billiard tables sold have not yet been picked up by the customers as of December 31, 2024, Eddie decides incorrectly to include these tables in ending inventory. He appropriately includes the sale of these 60 tables as part of total revenues in 2024.

Required:
1. What amount will Eddie calculate for ending inventory and cost of goods sold using FIFO, assuming he erroneously reports that 110 tables remain in ending inventory?
2. What amount would Eddie calculate for cost of goods sold using FIFO if he correctly reports that only 50 tables remain in ending inventory?
3. What effect will the inventory error have on reported amounts for (a) ending inventory, (b) retained earnings, (c) cost of goods sold, and (d) net income (ignoring tax effects) in 2024?
4. Assuming that ending inventory is correctly counted at the end of 2025, what effect will the inventory error in 2024 have on reported amounts for (a) ending inventory, (b) retained earnings, (c) cost of goods sold, and (d) net income (ignoring tax effects) in 2025?

Answers to Chapter Framework Questions
1. d   2. c   3. d   4. c   5. a

Answers to Self-Study Questions
1. d   2. b   3. a   4. a   5. d   6. c   7. a   8. b   9. d   10. d   11. a   12. d   13. a   14. c   15. b

CHAPTER 7

Long-Term Assets

Learning Objectives

PART A: ASSET ACQUISITIONS

- **LO7–1** Identify the major types of property, plant, and equipment.
- **LO7–2** Identify the major types of intangible assets.
- **LO7–3** Describe the accounting treatment of expenditures after acquisition.

PART B: DEPRECIATION AND AMORTIZATION

- **LO7–4** Calculate depreciation of property, plant, and equipment.
- **LO7–5** Calculate amortization of intangible assets.

PART C: ASSET DISPOSAL: SALE, RETIREMENT, OR EXCHANGE

- **LO7–6** Account for the disposal of long-term assets.

ANALYSIS: ASSET ANALYSIS

- **LO7–7** Describe the links among return on assets, profit margin, and asset turnover.

APPENDIX: IMPAIRMENT OF LONG-TERM ASSETS

- **LO7–8** Identify impairment situations and describe the two-step impairment process.

SELF-STUDY MATERIALS

- Let's Review—Expenditures after acquisition (p. 353).
- Let's Review—Depreciation methods (p. 363).
- Chapter Framework with questions and answers available (p. 374).
- Key Points by Learning Objective (p. 376).
- Glossary of Key Terms (p. 376).
- Self-Study Questions with answers available (p. 377).
- Videos including Concept Overview, Applying Excel, Let's Review, and Interactive Illustrations to demonstrate key topics (in Connect).

DISNEY: ASSETS ABOUND

The Walt Disney Company (hereafter: Disney) is an iconic worldwide entertainment company. If you're like most people, in the last month, you've probably watched a Disney movie, watched sports on its networks, streamed entertainment via its online services, taken a cruise on one of its cruise lines, or if you're very lucky, you've even gone to Disney World! Disney specializes in entertainment, with an incredible array of entertaining and iconic resources. Just think of the many icons related to Disney, including characters (Mickey and Minnie Mouse, Ironman, Luke Skywalker), physical properties (Magic Kingdom, Disneyland Parks and Resorts), cable networks (ESPN and ABC), and production studios (Marvel and Lucasfilms).

Many of these assets show up in Disney's balance sheet as **long-term assets.** However, measuring the value of the assets that Disney reports in the balance sheet can be challenging. For example, Disney has acquired dozens of other companies throughout the years, including **Pixar**, **Marvel**, **Lucasfilms**, **Hulu**, and, most recently, **21st Century Fox**. These acquisitions often lead to the creation of an intangible asset in the balance sheet called **goodwill,** an asset that is notoriously hard to value. Of its $100 billion in assets, Disney reports a whopping $31 billion in goodwill. Disney also has other **long-term assets,** such as amusement parks and resorts, which also are challenging to value. Disney reports that the historic cost of its parks is over $55 billion, but those parks have **accumulated depreciation** of nearly $31 billion over the years. Finally, Disney reports nearly $6 billion of other **intangible assets** (trademarks, licenses, etc.).

However, despite boasting $100 billion in assets in the balance sheet, Disney has many other assets that are *not* reported in the balance sheet, including the brand value of iconic figures like Mickey and Minnie Mouse. Other iconic characters, such as the brand value of Captain America and Thor are reported in the balance sheet. Why?

In this chapter, we'll answer that question and more related to how we account for the acquisition of long-term assets; allocate the cost of long-term assets through depreciation or amortization; and report the sale, retirement, or exchange of long-term assets at the end of their service life.

At the end of the chapter, we compare the return on assets for **Disney** and **Netflix**. We separate return on assets into two parts: profit margin (how much a company makes for each dollar in sales) and asset turnover (how much sales a company generates for each dollar in assets). We then examine whether the ratios support our expectations regarding Disney and Netflix, two close competitors in the entertainment industry.

ollyia/123RF

Hershey cannot make chocolate without its manufacturing facilities and the equipment in those facilities. In contrast, it's not physical assets but copyrights on its computer software that give **Alphabet** the ability to generate billions of dollars in revenue each year. Both of these types of revenue-producing assets are considered *long-term assets,* the topic of this chapter.

We classify long-term assets into two major categories:

1. **Tangible assets.** Assets in this category include land, land improvements, buildings, equipment, and natural resources. Hershey's land, buildings, and equipment fall into this category.

2. **Intangible assets.** Assets in this category include patents, trademarks, copyrights, franchises, and goodwill. We distinguish these assets from property, plant, and equipment by their lack of physical substance. The evidence of their existence often is based on a legal contract. Alphabet's copyrights are intangible assets.

Long-term assets often represent a significant portion of the total assets of a company. Illustration 7–1 presents a breakdown of the total assets for **Disney**. Notice that current assets represent only about 14.5% of total assets, and long-term assets make up the remaining 85.5%. Accounting for long-term assets, both tangible (such as investments, property, buildings, land, and equipment) and intangible, is important and is the primary focus in this chapter.

ILLUSTRATION 7–1

Asset Section of the Balance Sheet for **Disney**

THE WALT DISNEY COMPANY Balance Sheet (partial) ($ in thousands)	
Current assets	
Cash and cash equivalents	$ 5,418
Receivables	15,481
Inventories	1,649
Television costs and advances	4,597
Other current assets	979
Total current assets	28,124
Films and television costs	22,810
Investments	3,224
Parks, resorts and other property	
Attractions, buildings and equipment	58,589
Accumulated depreciation	(32,415)
	26,174
Projects in progress	4,264
Land	1,165
	31,603
Intangible assets, net	23,215
Goodwill	80,293
Other assets	4,715
Total assets	**$ 193,984**

To properly report both tangible and intangible assets, we need to address a variety of issues, including (1) which amounts to include in their initial cost, (2) how to expense their costs while using them, and (3) how to record their sale or disposal at the end of their useful life. These three issues are the basis for the three major parts of the chapter.

PART A

ASSET ACQUISITIONS

The first issue to consider in accounting for long-term assets is how to record their cost at the time of acquisition. To do this, we need to understand the major types of tangible and intangible assets. We begin with tangible assets, also referred to as property, plant, and equipment.

Property, Plant, and Equipment

The property, plant, and equipment category consists of land, land improvements, buildings, equipment, and natural resources. The general rule for recording all such long-term assets can be simply stated as: **We record a long-term asset at its cost *plus* all expenditures necessary to get the asset ready for use.** Thus, the initial cost of a long-term asset might be more than just its purchase price; it also will include any additional amounts the company paid to bring the asset to its desired condition and location for use.

To capitalize an expenditure means to record the expenditure as an asset. **The capitalized expenditure will be expensed *over time* as the asset is used in company operations.**

To **expense** an expenditure means to **record the full expenditure as an expense** *immediately*. We'll discuss both types of expenditures in this chapter. Whether management capitalizes an expenditure or expenses it fully in the current year can have a significant effect on a company's financial statements.

■ **LO7–1**
Identify the major types of property, plant, and equipment.

M_D_A/iStock/Getty Images

LAND

The Land account represents land a company is using in its operations. (In contrast, land purchased for investment purposes is reported in a separate investment account.) We capitalize to Land all expenditures necessary to get the land ready for its intended use.

Such capitalized costs include the purchase price of the land plus closing costs such as fees for the attorney, real estate agent commissions, title, title search, and recording fees. If the property is subject to back taxes or other obligations, we include these amounts as well. In fact, any additional expenditure such as clearing, filling, and leveling the land, or even removing existing buildings to prepare the land for its intended use, become part of the land's capitalized cost. If we receive any cash from selling salvaged building materials, we reduce the cost of land by that amount.

Assume, for instance, that **Olive Garden**, a restaurant chain owned by **Darden Restaurants**, purchases a two-acre tract of land and an existing building for $500,000. The company plans to remove the existing building and construct a new Olive Garden restaurant on the site. In addition to the purchase price, the company incurs several other costs, listed in Illustration 7–2. Using the guideline of **cost *plus* all expenditures necessary to get the asset ready for use,** at what amount should Olive Garden report as the total capitalized cost of the land?

Costs necessary to get the land ready for use	
Purchase price of land (and existing building)	$500,000
Commissions to sales agent	30,000
Back property taxes (seller's unpaid taxes)*	6,000
Property taxes for the current year ($2,000)*	—
Title insurance	3,000
Removing existing building	50,000
Less: Salvaged materials from existing building	(5,000)
Leveling the land	6,000
Total capitalized cost of land	$590,000

*Property taxes paid for the seller's unpaid taxes in previous years are necessary to get title clearance for the land. Any property taxes for the current period after the purchase are not included and instead expensed as incurred.

ILLUSTRATION 7–2

Computation of the Capitalized Cost of Land

 COMMON MISTAKE

Many students incorrectly add or ignore the cash received from the sale of salvaged materials. Cash received from the sale of salvaged materials *reduces* the total cost of land.

LAND IMPROVEMENTS

Beyond the cost of the land, **Olive Garden** likely will spend additional amounts to improve the land by adding a parking lot, sidewalks, driveways, landscaping, lighting systems, fences, sprinklers, and similar additions. These are land improvements. Because land improvements have limited useful lives (parking lots eventually wear out), and land has an unlimited useful life, we report land improvements separately from the land itself.

BUILDINGS

Buildings include administrative offices, retail stores, manufacturing facilities, and storage warehouses. **The cost of acquiring a building usually includes realtor commissions and legal fees in addition to the purchase price.** The new owner sometimes needs to remodel or otherwise modify the building to suit its needs. These additional costs are part of the building's acquisition cost.

Unique accounting issues arise when a firm constructs a building rather than purchasing it. Of course the cost of construction includes architect fees, material costs, and construction labor. New building construction likely also includes costs such as manager supervision, overhead (costs indirectly related to the construction), and interest costs incurred during construction.

Alistair Berg/Lifesize /Getty Images

EQUIPMENT

Equipment is a broad term that includes machinery used in manufacturing, computers and other office equipment, vehicles, furniture, and fixtures. **The cost of equipment is the actual purchase price plus all other costs necessary to prepare the asset for use.** These can be any of a variety of other costs, including sales tax, shipping, delivery insurance, assembly, installation, testing, and even legal fees incurred to establish title.

What about recurring costs related to equipment, such as annual property insurance and annual property taxes on vehicles? Rather than including recurring costs as part of the cost of the equipment, we expense them as we incur them. The question to ask yourself when deciding whether to add a cost to the asset account or record it as an expense of the current period is, *"Is this a cost of acquiring the asset and getting it ready for use, or is it a recurring cost that benefits the company in the current period?"*

Assume that **Olive Garden** purchases new restaurant equipment for $82,000 plus $6,500 in sales tax. It pays a freight company $800 to transport the equipment and $200 shipping insurance. The firm pays $1,600 for liability insurance on the equipment to cover the first year of operation. The equipment was also installed at an additional cost of $1,500. Illustration 7–3 shows the calculation of the amount at which Olive Garden should record the cost of the equipment.

ILLUSTRATION 7–3

Computation of the Capitalized Cost of Equipment

Costs necessary to get the equipment ready for use	
Purchase price	$82,000
Sales tax	6,500
Transportation	800
Shipping insurance	200
Installation	1,500
Annual insurance ($1,600)*	—
Total capitalized cost of equipment	$91,000

*The annual insurance of $1,600 will initially be recorded as Prepaid Insurance and allocated to Insurance Expense over the first year of coverage.

BASKET PURCHASES

Sometimes companies purchase more than one asset at the same time for one purchase price. This is known as a basket purchase. For example, assume **Olive Garden** purchases land, building, and equipment together for $900,000. We need to record land, building, and equipment in separate accounts. How much should we record in the separate accounts for land, building, and equipment? The simple answer is that **we allocate the total purchase price of $900,000 based on the estimated *fair values* of each of the individual assets.** The fair value of an asset is its estimated stand-alone selling price.

The difficulty, though, is that the estimated fair values of the individual assets often exceed the total purchase price, in this case, $900,000. Let's say the estimated fair values of the land, building, and equipment are $200,000, $700,000, and $100,000, respectively, for a total estimated fair value of $1 million. In that case, Olive Garden's total purchase of $900,000 will be allocated to the separate accounts for Land, Building, and Equipment based on their relative fair values, as shown in Illustration 7–4.

	Estimated Fair Value	Allocation Percentage	Amount of Basket Purchase	Recorded Amount
Land	$ 200,000	$200,000/$1,000,000 = 20% ×	$900,000	$180,000
Building	700,000	$700,000/$1,000,000 = 70% ×	$900,000	630,000
Equipment	100,000	$100,000/$1,000,000 = 10% ×	$900,000	90,000
Total	$1,000,000	100%		$900,000

ILLUSTRATION 7–4

Allocation of Cost in a Basket Purchase

NATURAL RESOURCES

Many companies depend heavily on natural resources, such as oil, natural gas, timber, and even salt. **ExxonMobil**, for example, maintains oil and natural gas deposits on six of the world's seven continents. **Weyerhaeuser** is one of the largest pulp and paper companies in the world with major investments in timber forests. Even salt is a natural resource, with the largest supply in the United States mined under the Great Lakes of North America.

We can distinguish natural resources from other property, plant, and equipment by the fact that we can physically use up, or *deplete,* natural resources. ExxonMobil's oil reserves are a natural resource that decreases as the firm extracts oil. Similarly, timber land is used to produce materials in the construction industry, and salt is extracted from salt mines for use in cooking and melting icy roads.

 KEY POINT

Tangible assets such as land, land improvements, buildings, equipment, and natural resources are recorded at cost plus all costs necessary to get the asset ready for its intended use.

Intangible Assets

The other major category of long-term assets, intangible assets, have no physical substance. Assets in this category include patents, trademarks, copyrights, franchises, and goodwill.

Despite their lack of physical substance, intangible assets can be very valuable indeed. One of the most valuable intangible assets for many companies is their trademark or brand. *Interbrand* publishes an annual list of the 100 most valuable brands. Illustration 7–5 summarizes the top 10 most valuable brands. As you can see, the **Apple** brand has an estimated value of $234.2 billion. Despite this value, Apple reports no intangible assets on its balance sheet. Later, we'll see why many intangible assets are *not* reported in the balance sheet at their estimated values.

Companies acquire intangible assets in two ways:

1. They *purchase* intangible assets like patents, copyrights, trademarks, or franchise rights from other companies. **We record purchased intangible assets at their original cost plus all other costs, such as legal fees, necessary to get the asset ready for use.**

■ **LO7–2**
Identify the major types of intangible assets.

ILLUSTRATION 7–5   World's Top 10 Brands

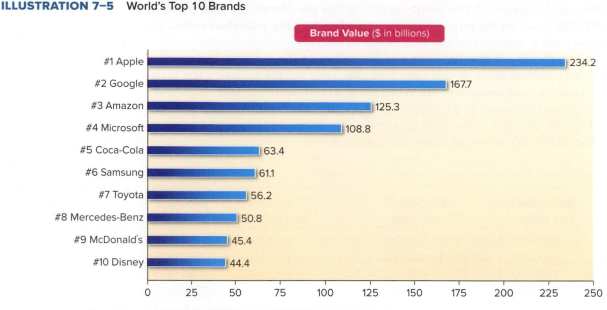

Source: "Best Gobal Brands 2019 Rankings," Interbrand.com, 2019, www.interbrand.com.

2. They *develop* intangible assets internally, for instance by developing a new product or process and obtaining a protective patent. Rather than reporting these in the balance sheet as intangible assets, **we expense in the income statement most of the costs for internally developed intangible assets in the period we incur those costs**.

Research and development costs are expensed as incurred.

Research and Development (R&D).   Costs incurred to conduct research and to develop a new product or process are not reported as an intangible asset in the balance sheet. Instead, they are expensed directly in the income statement. For example, Apple spends approximately $15–$20 billion in research and development every year. All of this cost is reported by Apple as an expense in the income statement rather than as an intangible asset in the balance sheet. The reason we expense all R&D costs is the difficulty in determining the portion of R&D that benefits future periods. Conceptually, we should report as an intangible asset the portion that benefits future periods. Due to the difficulties in arriving at this estimate, current U.S. accounting rules require firms to expense all R&D costs as incurred.

Advertising.   A similar argument about the difficulty of estimating benefits in future periods can be made for advertising expenses. Advertising at Apple clearly has made its trademark more valuable. Because we cannot tell what portion of today's advertising benefits future periods and how many periods it might benefit, advertising costs are not reported as an intangible asset in the balance sheet. Instead, advertising costs are reported as expenses in the income statement in the period incurred.

INTERNATIONAL FINANCIAL REPORTING STANDARDS (IFRS)

SHOULD R&D BE CLASSIFIED AS AN ASSET OR AN EXPENSE?

International accounting standards differ from U.S. accounting standards in the treatment of R&D costs. U.S. GAAP requires that we expense nearly all research and development expenditures in the period incurred. IFRS makes a distinction between *research* activities and *development* activities. Under IFRS, research expenditures are expensed in the period incurred, consistent with U.S. GAAP. However, development costs that benefit future periods can be recorded as an intangible asset.

For more discussion, see Appendix E.

KEY POINT

We record purchased intangibles as long-term assets at their purchase price plus all costs necessary to get the asset ready for use. We expense internally generated intangibles, such as R&D and advertising costs, as we incur them.

Let's look in more detail at some specific types of intangible assets that are reported in the balance sheet.

PATENTS

A **patent** is an exclusive right to manufacture a product or to use a process. The U.S. Patent and Trademark Office grants this right for a period of 20 years. **When a firm *purchases* a patent, it records the patent as an intangible asset at its purchase price plus other costs such as legal and filing fees to secure the patent.** Filing fees include items such as the fee to record a patent with the U.S. Patent and Trademark Office.

In contrast, when a firm engages in its own research activities to develop a new product or process, it expenses those costs as it incurs them. For example, major pharmaceutical companies like **Amgen** and **Gilead Sciences** spend over a billion dollars each year developing new drugs. Most of these research and development costs are recorded as operating expenses in the income statement. An exception to this rule is legal fees. The firm will record in the Patent asset account the legal and filing fees to secure a patent, even if it developed the patented item or process internally.

Let's look at an example of purchased versus internally developed patents in Illustration 7-6. Suppose a company obtains two patents during the year. Patent #1 was purchased from another company for $200,000, while Patent #2 was developed internally at a cost of $200,000 (cost of salaries, supplies, equipment, and facilities). Both patents had legal and filing fees of $40,000 and $5,000, respectively. While these two situations may seem similar, Patent #1 will result in an intangible asset being recorded for $245,000, while only the legal and filing fees would be recorded as an intangible asset for Patent #2. All internal costs for research and development would be expensed immediately.

	Patent #1 (*externally purchased*)	Patent #2 (*internally developed*)
Cash expenditures	$200,000	$200,000
Legal fees	40,000	40,000
Filing fees	5,000	5,000
Patent (intangible asset)	$245,000	$ 45,000
Research and development expense		$200,000

ILLUSTRATION 7–6

Computation of the Cost of Patent

COPYRIGHTS

A **copyright** is an exclusive right of protection given by the U.S. Copyright Office to the creator of a published work such as a song, film, painting, photograph, book, or computer software. Copyrights are protected by law and give the creator (and his or her heirs) the exclusive right to reproduce and sell the artistic or published work for the life of the creator plus 70 years. A copyright also allows the copyright holder to pursue legal action against anyone who attempts to infringe on the copyright. Accounting for the costs of copyrights is virtually identical to that of patents.

Cesare Ferrari/Alamy Stock Photo

TRADEMARKS

A **trademark**, like the name **Apple**, is a word, slogan, or symbol that distinctively identifies a company, product, or service. The firm can register its trademark with the U.S. Patent and Trademark Office to protect it from use by others for a period of 10 years. The registration can be renewed for an indefinite number of 10-year periods, so a trademark is an example of an intangible asset whose useful life can be indefinite.

Firms often acquire trademarks through acquisition. As an example, **Hewlett-Packard (HP)** acquired all the outstanding stock of **Compaq Computer Corporation** for $24 billion, of which $1.4 billion was assigned to the Compaq trademark.

A firm can record attorney fees, registration fees, design costs, successful legal defense, and other costs directly related to securing the trademark as an intangible asset in the Trademark asset account. This is how Apple Inc. can have a trademark valued at $181.2 billion, but reported in the balance sheet for much less. The estimated value of the trademark is not recorded in the Trademarks account; instead, only the legal, registration, and design fees are recorded. The advertising costs that help create value for the trademark are recorded as advertising expense.

FRANCHISES

Subway, **McDonald's**, and **Starbucks** are three of the world's largest franchises. Many popular retail businesses such as restaurants, auto dealerships, and hotels are set up as **franchises**. These are local outlets that pay for the exclusive right to use the franchisor company's name and to sell its products within a specified geographical area. Many franchisors provide other benefits to the franchisee, such as participating in the construction of the retail outlet, training employees, and purchasing national advertising.

To record the cost of a franchise, the franchisee records the initial fee as an intangible asset. Additional periodic payments to the franchisor usually are for services the franchisor provides on a continuing basis, and the franchisee will expense them as incurred.

GOODWILL

Goodwill often is the largest (and the most unique) intangible asset in the balance sheet. **It is recorded *only* when one company acquires another company.** **Goodwill** is reported by the acquiring company for the amount that the purchase price exceeds the fair value of the acquired company's identifiable net assets.

The calculation of goodwill is easiest to see with a simple example. Assume that Allied Foods acquires Ritz Produce by paying $36 million in cash. The fair values of Ritz Produce's identifiable assets and liabilities are as follows ($ in millions):

Accounts receivable	$10	Accounts payable	$ 9
Equipment	32	Long-term notes payable	15
Patent	8		
Total fair value of assets	$50	Total fair value of liabilities	$24

In this example, Ritz Produce has identifiable net assets of $26 million (= $50 million − $24 million). Why is Allied Foods willing to pay $36 million to acquire a company that has *identifiable* net assets of only $26 million? Allied Foods must believe that there are other benefits worth $10 million in the acquisition, but these benefits are *not identified* as assets in the balance sheet of Ritz Produce. Allied Food will record these unidentified assets as goodwill at the time it pays $36 million. Illustration 7–7 summarizes the calculation of goodwill ($10 million) that Allied Foods would report in its balance sheet.

ILLUSTRATION 7–7
**Business Acquisition
with Goodwill**

($ in millions)		
Purchase price		$ 36
Less:		
Fair value of assets acquired	$ 50	
Less: Fair value of liabilities assumed	(24)	
Fair value of identifiable net assets		(26)
Goodwill		**$ 10**

Allied Foods records the acquisition as follows:

	Debit	Credit
Accounts Receivable (at fair value)	10	
Equipment (at fair value)	32	
Patent (at fair value)	8	
Goodwill (remaining purchase price)	10	
Accounts Payable (at fair value)		9
Notes Payable (at fair value)		15
Cash (at purchase price)		36
(Acquire assets and liabilities of Ritz Produce)		

Income Statement

R	−	E	=	NI

No effect

Balance Sheet

A	=	L	+	SE
+10		+9		
Accts. Rec.		Accts. Pay.		
+32		+15		
Equipment		Notes Pay.		
+8				
Patent				
+10				
Goodwill				
−36				
Cash				

Most companies also create goodwill to some extent through advertising, employee training, and other efforts. However, as it does for other internally generated intangibles, a company must *expense* costs incurred in the internal generation of goodwill. Imagine how difficult it would be to estimate the amount and future benefits of internally generated goodwill. Due to this difficulty, we record goodwill only when it is part of the acquisition of another business.

 KEY POINT

Intangible assets have no physical substance and generally represent exclusive rights that provide benefits to owners. Common types include patents, copyrights, trademarks, franchises, and goodwill.

Expenditures after Acquisition

Over the life of a long-term asset, the owners often incur additional expenditures associated with the asset. Are these expenditures recorded as an asset or an expense?

■ **LO7–3**
Describe the accounting treatment of expenditures after acquisition.

1. We **capitalize** an expenditure as an asset if it increases **future** benefits.

2. We **expense** an expenditure if it benefits only the **current** period.

To see the choice more clearly, let's look at different types of expenditures: repairs and maintenance, additions, improvements, and litigation costs.

REPAIRS AND MAINTENANCE

The cost of an engine tune-up, oil change, or repair of a minor engine part for a delivery truck allows the truck to continue its productive activity in the *current* period. We expense repairs and maintenance expenditures like these in the period incurred because they maintain a given level of benefits. They also are likely to recur again in the following period. More extensive repairs that increase the *future* benefits of the delivery truck would be capitalized as assets. These include major repairs that are unlikely to recur each period, such as a new transmission or an engine overhaul.

CAREER CORNER

ADDITIONS

An **addition** occurs when we add a new major component to an existing asset. We should capitalize the cost of additions if they increase, rather than maintain, the future benefits from the expenditure. For example, adding a refrigeration unit to a delivery truck increases the capability of the truck beyond that originally anticipated, thus increasing its future benefits.

IMPROVEMENTS

An **improvement** is the cost of replacing a major component of an asset. The replacement can be a new component with the same characteristics as the old component, or a new component with enhanced operating capabilities. For example, we could replace an existing refrigeration unit in a delivery truck with a new but similar unit or with a new and improved refrigeration unit. In either case, the cost of the improvement usually increases future benefits, and we should capitalize it to the Equipment account.

LEGAL DEFENSE OF INTANGIBLE ASSETS

The expenditures after acquisition mentioned so far—repairs and maintenance, additions, and improvements—generally relate to property, plant, and equipment. Intangible assets, though, also can require expenditures after their acquisition, the most frequent being the cost of legally defending the right that gives the asset its value. For example, **Apple** spends millions of dollars every year defending its patents related to the iPhone and other products. The costs of successfully defending a patent, including attorneys' fees, are added to the Patent account. However, if the defense of an intangible right is unsuccessful, then the firm should expense the litigation costs as incurred because they provide no future benefit.

MATERIALITY

An item is said to be **material** if it is large enough to influence a decision. The decision to capitalize versus expense can have a material impact on financial statements. If a company incorrectly capitalizes rather than expenses a material expenditure, then in the current period, both total assets and net income will be overstated.

When an expenditure is not material, the item is typically recorded as an expense regardless of its expected period of benefit. For example, a $10 stapler may have a 20-year service life, but it would not be practical to capitalize such a small amount. Companies generally expense all costs under a certain dollar amount, say $1,000, regardless of whether future benefits are increased. It's important for a company to establish a policy for treating these expenditures and apply the policy consistently.

Illustration 7–8 provides a summary of expenditures after acquisition.

 KEY POINT

We capitalize (record as an asset) expenditures that benefit *future* periods. We expense items that benefit only the *current* period.

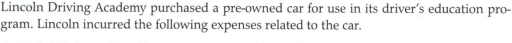

Type of Expenditure	Definition	Period Benefited	Usual Accounting Treatment
Repairs and maintenance	Maintaining a given level of benefits	Current	**Expense**
Repairs and maintenance	Making major repairs that increase future benefits	Future	**Capitalize**
Additions	Adding a new major component	Future	**Capitalize**
Improvements	Replacing a major component	Future	**Capitalize**
Legal defense of intangible assets	Incurring litigation costs to defend the legal right to the asset	Future	**Capitalize** (Expense if defense is unsuccessful)

ILLUSTRATION 7–8

Expenditures after Acquisition

Let's Review

Lincoln Driving Academy purchased a pre-owned car for use in its driver's education program. Lincoln incurred the following expenses related to the car.

1. Replaced the car's transmission at a cost of $4,100. The repairs are considered extensive and increase future benefits.
2. Installed a passenger side brake to be used by the instructor, if necessary, at a cost of $1,100.
3. Paid the annual registration fees of $185.
4. Changed the oil and had an engine tune-up at a cost of $350.
5. Overhauled the engine at a cost $2,200, increasing the service life of the car by an estimated four years.

Required:

Indicate whether Lincoln should capitalize or expense each of these expenditures. How could Lincoln fraudulently use expenditures like these to increase reported earnings?

Solution:

1. Capitalize. It benefits future periods.
2. Capitalize. It benefits future periods.
3. Expense. It benefits only the current period.
4. Expense. It benefits only the current period.
5. Capitalize. It benefits future periods.

Lincoln could increase reported earnings by improperly recording expenses as assets. For example, Lincoln could record maintenance and repair expense (like item 4) to the equipment asset account. This would lower expenses and increase earnings reported in the current year.

Suggested Homework:
BE7–6, BE7–7;
E7–9;
P7–4A&B

DEPRECIATION AND AMORTIZATION

PART B

When people talk about a car depreciating, they usually are talking about how much the value of the car has decreased. Depreciation in accounting, though, is different. The primary dictionary definition of depreciation differs from the definition of depreciation used in accounting:

Dictionary definition = Decrease in value (or selling price) of an asset.
Accounting definition = Allocation of an asset's cost to an expense over time.

If depreciation were calculated based on the dictionary definition, we would need to estimate the value of every long-term asset each period. Due to the difficulty and subjectivity involved, long-term assets are not adjusted to fair value each period. Rather, long-term assets are recorded at their cost, and then this cost is allocated to expense over time. We use the term *depreciation* to describe that process when it applies to property, plant, and equipment. For intangible assets, the cost allocation process is called *amortization*.

Depreciation of Property, Plant, and Equipment

■ **LO7–4**

Calculate depreciation of property, plant, and equipment.

Depreciation in accounting is allocating the cost of an asset to an expense over its service life. An asset provides benefits (revenues) to a company in future periods. We allocate a portion of the asset's cost to depreciation expense in each year the asset provides a benefit. If the asset will provide benefits to the company for four years, for example, then we allocate a portion of the asset's cost to depreciation expense in each year for four years. Illustration 7–9 portrays this concept of depreciating an asset's original purchase cost over the periods benefited.

ILLUSTRATION 7–9

Depreciation of
Long-Term Assets

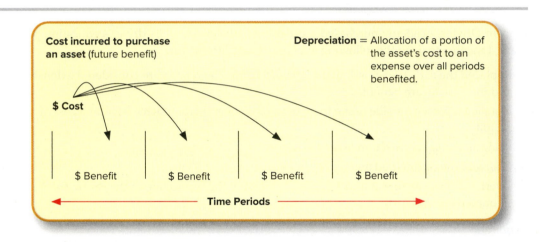

COMMON MISTAKE

Students sometimes mistake accounting depreciation as recording the decrease in value of an asset. Depreciation in accounting is *not* a valuation process. Rather, depreciation in accounting is an allocation of an asset's cost to expense over time.

For demonstration, let's assume the local **Starbucks** pays $1,200 for equipment—say, an espresso machine. The machine is expected to have a service life of four years. We record annual depreciation as shown below.

Income Statement		
R − **E** = **NI**		
+300 −300		
Depr Exp.		

Balance Sheet		
A = **L** + **SE**		
−300		−300
Accum		
Depr ↑		

	Debit	Credit
Depreciation Expense	**300**	
Accumulated Depreciation		**300**
(Depreciate equipment)		
($300 = $1,200 ÷ 4 years)		

The credit side of the entry requires some explanation. **Accumulated Depreciation** is a contra asset account, meaning that it reduces an asset account. Rather than credit the Equipment account directly, we instead credit its contra account, which we offset against the Equipment account in the balance sheet. In this manner, a company can keep track of the amount originally paid for the equipment and the amount of depreciation taken on the asset so far.

Most companies have separate accumulated depreciation accounts for each specific asset or asset class. For simplicity, we use one general account called Accumulated Depreciation. The name of the account comes from the fact that the depreciation we record each period *accumulates* in the account. After one year, for instance, we have

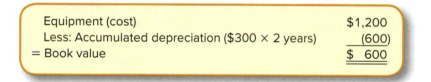

Equipment (cost)	$1,200
Less: Accumulated depreciation ($300 × 1 year)	(300)
= Book value	$ 900

Book value, also referred to as carrying value, equals the original cost of the asset minus the current balance in Accumulated Depreciation. Note that by increasing accumulated depreciation each period, we are reducing the book value of equipment. The Accumulated Depreciation account allows us to reduce the book value of assets through depreciation, while maintaining the original cost of each asset in the accounting records.

After two years, we have

Equipment (cost)	$1,200
Less: Accumulated depreciation ($300 × 2 years)	(600)
= Book value	$ 600

Each year the Accumulated Depreciation account increases by $300 and the book value decreases by $300. By the end of the fourth year, Accumulated Depreciation will be $1,200 and the book value will be $0.

 KEY POINT

Depreciation refers to the allocation of the asset's original cost to an expense during the periods benefited. Depreciation does *not* refer to the change in value or selling price.

Recording depreciation requires accountants to establish three factors at the time the asset is put into use:

1. **Service life** (or useful life)—The estimated use the company expects to receive from the asset before disposing of it.
2. **Residual value** (or salvage value)—The amount the company expects to receive from selling the asset at the end of its service life.
3. **Depreciation method**—The pattern in which the asset's depreciable cost (original cost minus residual value) is allocated over time.

Service Life. We can measure service life in units of time or in units of activity. For example, the estimated service life of a delivery truck might be either five years or 100,000 miles. We use the terms service life and useful life interchangeably, because both terms are used in practice.

Residual Value. At the end of an asset's service life, a company may sell or trade the asset for a new one. The residual value is the selling price or the trade-in value of the asset. A company might estimate residual value from prior experience or by researching the resale values of similar types of assets. Due to the difficulty in estimating residual value, it's not uncommon to assume a residual value of zero.

Depreciation Method.   In determining how much of an asset's cost to allocate to each year, a company should choose a depreciation method that corresponds to the pattern of benefits received from using the asset. The three most common depreciation methods used in practice are straight-line, declining-balance, and activity-based.[1]

1. **Straight-line.** This method allocates an equal amount of depreciation to each year. The implication is that the asset is used evenly over its service life. This method is by far the simplest and most common depreciation method used in financial accounting.
2. **Declining-balance.** This method is an accelerated method, meaning that more depreciation expense is taken in the earlier years than in the later years of an asset's life. Declining-balance methods are also used in calculating depreciation for tax purposes.
3. **Activity-based.** This method calculates depreciation based on the activity associated with the asset. For example, a vehicle can be depreciated based on the miles driven, or a machine can be depreciated based on the hours used. The method is commonly used to allocate the cost of natural resources.

Let's illustrate each of the three methods using the same business situation: Little King Sandwiches, a local submarine sandwich restaurant, purchased a new delivery truck. The specific details of that purchase are described in Illustration 7–10.

ILLUSTRATION 7–10

Data to Illustrate Depreciation Methods

Cost of the new truck	$40,000
Estimated residual value	$5,000
Estimated service life	5 years or 100,000 miles

STRAIGHT-LINE DEPRECIATION

By far the most easily understood and widely used depreciation method is straight-line. With the **straight-line method**, we allocate an *equal* amount of the depreciable cost to each year of the asset's service life. The *depreciable cost* is the asset's cost minus its estimated residual value. Depreciable cost represents the total depreciation to be taken over the asset's service life. To calculate depreciation expense for a given year, we divide the depreciable cost by the number of years in the asset's life, as shown in Illustration 7–11.

ILLUSTRATION 7–11

Formula for Straight-Line Depreciation

$$\text{Depreciation expense} = \frac{\text{Asset's cost} - \text{Residual value}}{\text{Service life}} = \frac{\text{Depreciable cost}}{\text{Service life}}$$

$$\text{Depreciation expense} = \frac{\$40,000 - \$5,000}{5 \text{ years}} = \$7,000 \text{ per year}$$

Note that dividing the depreciable cost each year by five is the same as multiplying the depreciable cost each year by 20% ($1/5 = 0.20$).

Illustration 7–12 provides a depreciation schedule using the straight-line method. Notice that the asset is depreciated until its book value equals the residual value ($5,000). **The residual value is never depreciated.**

---

[1] Some introductory financial accounting textbooks illustrate a fourth depreciation method called *sum-of-the-years'-digits*. However, use of this method has decreased dramatically over the years to the point that this method is now rarely seen in actual practice. A recent survey of depreciation methods used by large public companies is provided in Illustration 7–19.

LITTLE KING SANDWICHES
Depreciation Schedule—Straight-Line

Year	Depreciable Cost	×	Depreciation Rate	=	Depreciation Expense	Accumulated Depreciation	Book Value*
	Calculation					**End-of-Year Amounts**	
							$40,000
1	$35,000		0.20		$ 7,000	$ 7,000	33,000
2	35,000		0.20		7,000	14,000	26,000
3	35,000		0.20		7,000	21,000	19,000
4	35,000		0.20		7,000	28,000	12,000
5	35,000		0.20		7,000	35,000	**5,000**
Total					**$35,000**		

ILLUSTRATION 7–12

Straight-Line Depreciation Schedule

*Book value is the original cost of the asset ($40,000) minus accumulated depreciation. Book value of $33,000 at the end of year 1, for example, is $40,000 minus $7,000 in accumulated depreciation.

Partial-Year Depreciation. In the example above, we assumed Little King Sandwiches bought the truck *at the beginning of Year 1*. What if the company bought the truck *partially through Year 1?* In this case, the truck should be depreciated only for the portion of Year 1 it was used. For example, if Little King bought the truck on November 1 and its year-end is December 31, depreciation in Year 1 is calculated for only two of the 12 months. This calculation is shown in Illustration 7–13. Notice that we depreciate the truck in Year 1 for only 2/12 of the full-year amount because we've used the truck for only 2/12 of the year.

ILLUSTRATION 7–13

Partial-Year Straight-Line Depreciation

Year	Depreciable Cost	×	Depreciation Rate*	=	Depreciation Expense	Accumulated Depreciation	Book Value
	Calculation					**End-of-Year Amounts**	
							$40,000
1	$35,000		0.20 × **2/12**		$ 1,167	$ 1,167	38,833
2	35,000		0.20		7,000	8,167	31,833
3	35,000		0.20		7,000	15,167	24,833
4	35,000		0.20		7,000	22,167	17,833
5	35,000		0.20		7,000	29,167	10,833
6	35,000		0.20 × **10/12**		5,833	35,000	**5,000**
Total					**$35,000**		

*Depreciation in Year 1 assumes the asset is purchased on November 1. The asset is depreciated using the straight-line method, assuming a five-year service life and residual value of $5,000.

Depreciation for the second, third, fourth and fifth years is for the full-year amount. The partial-year depreciation for the first year doesn't affect depreciation in those subsequent years because the truck is utilized for those entire years.

The truck's five-year service life will extend to Year 6. Since the company depreciated the truck for only two months in Year 1, the final 10 months of depreciation will occur in Year 6. The amount of depreciation expense in Year 6 is 10/12 of the full-year amount. By the end of Year 6, the truck has been fully depreciated (from its original cost of $40,000 down to its residual value of $5,000).

You can determine partial year depreciation for any month. If an asset is purchased at the beginning of April (nine months until the year end), its first year of annual depreciation will be multiplied by 9/12, and its final year of annual depreciation will be multiplied by 3/12.

COMMON MISTAKE

Many students think March 1 to the end of the year is nine months because December is the twelfth month and March is the third month. March 1 to the end of the year is actually *ten* months; it is every month except January and February.

Land.   We record depreciation for land improvements, buildings, and equipment, but we *don't* record depreciation for land. Unlike other long-term assets, land is not "used up" over time.

 COMMON MISTAKE

Some students mistakenly depreciate land because it's part of property, plant, and equipment. Land is *property*, but it is *not* depreciated because its service life never ends.

Change in Depreciation Estimate.   Depreciation is an *estimate*. Remember that the amount of depreciation allocated to each period is based on management's estimates of service life and of residual value—as well as the depreciation method chosen. Management needs to periodically review these estimates. If a change in estimate is required, the company changes depreciation in current and future years, but not in prior periods.

For example, assume that after three years Little King Sandwiches estimates the remaining service life of the delivery truck to be four more years, for a total service life of seven years rather than the original five. At this time, Little King also changes the estimated residual value to $3,000 from the original estimate of $5,000. How much should Little King report each year for depreciation in years 4 to 7? Take the book value at the end of year 3 ($19,000), subtract the new estimated residual value ($3,000), and then divide by the new remaining service life (four more years). Little King Sandwiches will report depreciation in years 4 to 7 as $4,000 per year. Illustration 7–14 shows the calculations.

ILLUSTRATION 7–14

Change in Depreciation Estimate

Book value, end of year 3	$19,000
− New residual value	(3,000)
New depreciable cost	16,000
÷ New remaining service life	4
Annual depreciation in years 4 to 7	$ 4,000

Notice that Little King Sandwiches makes all the changes in years 4 to 7. The company does not go back and change the calculations for depreciation already reported during the first three years.

Straight-line depreciation assumes that the benefits we derive from the use of an asset are the same each year. In some situations, it might be more reasonable to assume that the asset will provide greater benefits in the earlier years of its life than in the later years. In these cases, we achieve a better matching of depreciation with revenues by using an accelerated depreciation method, with higher depreciation in the earlier years of the asset's life and lower depreciation in later years. We look at one such method next.

DECLINING-BALANCE DEPRECIATION

The declining-balance method is an accelerated depreciation method. Declining-balance depreciation will be higher than straight-line depreciation in earlier years, but lower in later years. **However, both declining-balance and straight-line will result in the same total depreciation over the asset's service life.** No matter what allocation method we use, total depreciation over the asset's service life will be equal to the depreciable cost (asset cost minus residual value).

9nong/Shutterstock

James Wright is the chief financial officer (CFO) for The Butcher Block, a major steakhouse restaurant chain. As CFO, James has the final responsibility for all aspects of financial reporting. James tells investors that The Butcher Block should post earnings of at least $1 million.

In examining the preliminary year-end numbers, James notices that earnings are coming in at $950,000. He also is aware that The Butcher Block has been depreciating most of its restaurant equipment over a five-year service life. He proposes to change the estimated service life for a subset of the equipment to a service life of seven, rather than five, years. By depreciating over a longer service life, depreciation expense will be lower in the current year, increasing earnings to just over $1 million. It looks like The Butcher Block is going to exceed earnings of $1 million after all.

Do you think James Wright's change in the depreciable life of assets is ethical? What concerns might you have?

The depreciation rate we use under the declining-balance method is a multiple of the straight-line rate, such as 125%, 150%, or 200% of the straight-line rate. The most common declining-balance rate is 200%, which we refer to as the *double*-declining-balance method since the rate is double the straight-line rate. In our illustration for Little King Sandwiches, the double-declining-balance rate would be 40% (double the straight-line rate of 20%). Illustration 7–15 provides a depreciation schedule using the double-declining-balance method.

ILLUSTRATION 7–15

Double-Declining-Balance Depreciation Schedule

LITTLE KING SANDWICHES
Depreciation Schedule—Double-Declining-Balance

| | | Calculation | | | End-of-Year Amounts | |
Year	Beginning Book Value	× Depreciation Rate	=	Depreciation Expense	Accumulated Depreciation	Book Value*
						$40,000
1	$40,000	0.40		$16,000	$16,000	24,000
2	24,000	0.40		9,600	25,600	14,400
3	14,400	0.40		5,760	31,360	8,640
4	8,640	0.40		3,456	34,816	5,184
5	5,184			184**	35,000	5,000
Total				$35,000		

*Book value is the original cost of the asset minus accumulated depreciation. Book value at the end of year 1 is $24,000, equal to the cost of $40,000 minus accumulated depreciation of $16,000. Book value at the end of **year 1** in the last column is equal to book value at the beginning of **year 2** in the second column of the schedule.
**Amount necessary to reduce book value to residual value.

A simple way to get the depreciation rate for double-declining-balance is to divide the number 2 by the estimated service life. In our example of a five-year asset, that would be 2 divided by 5, which equals 0.40. The depreciation rate for double-declining-balance depreciation is determined by the following general equation:

$$\text{Double-declining depreciation rate} = 2/\text{Estimated service life}$$

If the service life had been four years instead of five, what depreciation rates would we use under straight-line and under double-declining-balance? The straight-line rate is 1 divided by the four-year service life, or 1/4 = 0.25. The double-declining-balance rate is 2 divided by the four-year service life, or 2/4 = 0.50.

Notice two unusual features of declining-balance depreciation.

1. We multiply the rate by *book value* (cost minus accumulated depreciation), rather than by the depreciable cost (cost minus residual value).

2. In year 5, we are not able to record depreciation expense for the entire $5,184 times 0.40, because doing so would cause the book value to fall below the expected residual value. Instead, depreciation expense in the final year is the amount that reduces book value to the estimated residual value (book value beginning of year, $5,184, minus estimated residual value, $5,000, = $184).

If the estimated residual value is high enough, the asset will reach its residual value in fewer years than its expected service life. For instance, if the estimated residual value had been $10,000 rather than $5,000, the delivery truck would be fully depreciated under the double-declining-balance method in only three years, even though we used a five-year life in determining the depreciation rate.

 COMMON MISTAKE

When using the declining-balance method, mistakes are commonly made in the first and last year of the calculation. In the first year, students sometimes calculate depreciation incorrectly as cost minus residual value times the depreciation rate. The correct way in the first year is to multiply cost times the depreciation rate. In the final year, some students incorrectly calculate depreciation expense in the same manner as in earlier years, multiplying book value by the depreciation rate. However, under the declining-balance method, depreciation expense in the final year is the amount necessary to reduce book value down to residual value.

ACTIVITY-BASED DEPRECIATION

Common Terms Activity-based depreciation is also called *units of production* or *units of output.*

Straight-line and declining-balance methods measure depreciation based on time. In an **activity-based method**, we instead allocate an asset's cost based on its *use.* For example, we could measure the service life of a machine in terms of its output (units, pounds, barrels). This method also works for vehicles such as our delivery truck, whose use we measure in miles.

We first compute the average *depreciation rate per unit* by dividing the depreciable cost (cost minus residual value) by the number of units expected to be produced. In our illustration, the depreciation rate is $0.35 per mile, calculated as shown in Illustration 7–16.

ILLUSTRATION 7–16

Formula for Activity-Based Depreciation

$$\text{Depreciation rate per unit} = \frac{\text{Depreciable cost}}{\text{Total units expected to be produced}}$$

$$\text{Depreciation rate} = \frac{\$40,000 - \$5,000}{100,000 \text{ expected miles}} = \$0.35 \text{ per mile}$$

To calculate the depreciation expense for the reporting period, we then multiply the per unit rate by the number of units of activity each period. Illustration 7–17 shows a depreciation schedule using the activity-based method. The actual miles driven in years 1 to 5 were 30,000, 22,000, 15,000, 20,000, and 13,000. Notice that the activity-based method is very similar to the straight-line method, except that rather than dividing the depreciable cost by the service life in years, we divide it by the service life in expected miles.

					End-of-Year Amounts	

LITTLE KING SANDWICHES
Depreciation Schedule—Activity-Based

	Calculation				End-of-Year Amounts	
Year	Miles Driven	×	Depreciation Rate	= Depreciation Expense	Accumulated Depreciation	Book Value*
						$40,000
1	30,000		$0.35	**$10,500**	$10,500	29,500
2	22,000		0.35	**7,700**	18,200	21,800
3	15,000		0.35	**5,250**	23,450	16,550
4	20,000		0.35	**7,000**	30,450	9,550
5	13,000		0.35	**4,550**	35,000	**5,000**
Total				**$35,000**		

ILLUSTRATION 7–17

Activity-Based Depreciation Schedule

*Book value is the original cost of the asset ($40,000) minus accumulated depreciation. Book value of $29,500 in year 1 is $40,000 minus $10,500 in accumulated depreciation.

In our illustration, the delivery truck is driven exactly 100,000 miles over the five years. What if we drive the delivery truck *less than* 100,000 miles by the end of the fifth year? Then we will continue to depreciate the truck past five years until we reach 100,000 miles. Similarly, if we drive the delivery truck *more than* 100,000 miles by the end of the fifth year, we will stop depreciating the truck at 100,000 miles before the five years are up. In either case, we need to depreciate the asset until the book value (cost minus accumulated depreciation) declines to the estimated residual value.

Decision Maker's Perspective

Selecting a Depreciation Method

Assume you are the chief financial officer (CFO) responsible for your company's accounting and reporting policies. Which depreciation method would you choose? Illustration 7–18 compares annual depreciation under the three alternatives we discussed.

Year	Straight-Line	Double-Declining-Balance	Activity-Based
1	$ 7,000	$16,000	$10,500
2	7,000	9,600	7,700
3	7,000	5,760	5,250
4	7,000	3,456	7,000
5	7,000	184	4,550
Total	$35,000	$35,000	$35,000

ILLUSTRATION 7–18

Comparison of Depreciation Methods

Comparing methods, we see that all three alternatives result in total depreciation of $35,000 ($40,000 cost minus $5,000 residual value). Straight-line creates an equal amount of depreciation each year. Double-declining-balance creates more depreciation in earlier years and less depreciation in later years. Activity-based depreciation varies depending on the miles driven each year. Illustration 7–19 provides a graph that shows depreciation expense over time for each of these three methods.

ILLUSTRATION 7–19

Depreciation Expense Over Time for Three Depreciation Methods

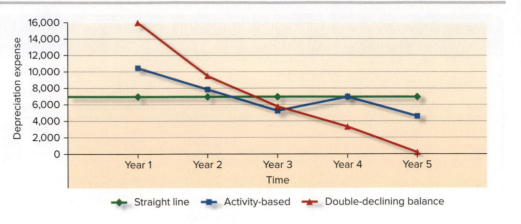

Companies are free to choose the depreciation method they believe best reflects the pattern of an asset's use and the revenues it creates. Illustration 7–20 shows the results of a recent survey of depreciation methods used by large public companies.

ILLUSTRATION 7–20

Use of Various Depreciation Methods

Other (1%)
Activity-Based (3%)
Declining-Balance (4%)
Straight-Line (92%)

Why do so many companies use the straight-line method? Many probably believe they realize benefits from their plant assets approximately evenly over these assets' service lives. Certainly another motivating factor is that straight-line is the easiest method to apply. One more important motivation is straight-line's positive effect on reported income. Straight-line produces a higher net income than accelerated methods in the earlier years of an asset's life. Higher net income can improve bonuses paid to management, increase stock prices, and reduce the likelihood of violating debt agreements with lenders.

TAX DEPRECIATION

Conflicting with the desire to report higher net income is the desire to reduce taxes by *reducing* taxable income. An accelerated method serves this objective by reducing taxable income more in the earlier years of an asset's life than does straight-line. As a result, most companies use the straight-line method for financial reporting and the Internal Revenue Service's prescribed accelerated method (called MACRS[2]) for income tax purposes. Thus, companies record higher net income using straight-line depreciation and lower taxable income using MACRS depreciation. MACRS combines declining-balance methods in earlier years with straight-line in later years to allow for a more advantageous tax depreciation deduction. Congress, not accountants, approved MACRS rules to encourage greater investment in long-term assets by U.S. companies.

 KEY POINT

Straight-line, declining-balance, and activity-based depreciation all are acceptable depreciation methods for financial reporting. Most companies use straight-line depreciation for financial reporting and an accelerated method called MACRS for tax reporting.

[2] Modified Accelerated Cost Recovery System.

Let's Review

University Hero purchases new bread ovens at a cost of $110,000. On the date of purchase, the company estimates the ovens will have a residual value of $20,000. University Hero expects to use the ovens for four years or about 9,000 total hours.

Required:

Prepare a depreciation schedule using each of the following methods:

1. Straight-line.
2. Double-declining-balance.
3. Activity-based.

   Actual oven use per year was as follows:

Year	Hours Used
1	2,200
2	2,600
3	2,300
4	2,100
Total	9,200

Solution:

1. Straight-line:

UNIVERSITY HERO
Depreciation Schedule—Straight-Line

	Calculation			End-of-Year Amounts	
Year	Depreciable Cost	× Depreciation Rate*	= Depreciation Expense	Accumulated Depreciation	Book Value**
1	$90,000	0.25	**$22,500**	$22,500	$87,500
2	90,000	0.25	**22,500**	45,000	65,000
3	90,000	0.25	**22,500**	67,500	42,500
4	90,000	0.25	**22,500**	90,000	20,000
Total			**$90,000**		

*1 ÷ 4 years = 0.25 per year
**$110,000 cost minus accumulated depreciation.

2. Double-declining-balance:

UNIVERSITY HERO
Depreciation Schedule—Double-Declining-Balance

	Calculation			End-of-Year Amounts	
Year	Beginning Book Value	× Depreciation Rate*	= Depreciation Expense	Accumulated Depreciation	Book Value**
1	$110,000	0.50	**$55,000**	$55,000	$55,000
2	55,000	0.50	**27,500**	82,500	27,500
3	27,500	0.50	**7,500***	90,000	20,000
4			**0**	90,000	20,000
Total			**$90,000**		

*2 ÷ 4 years = 0.50 per year
**$110,000 cost minus accumulated depreciation.
***Amount needed to reduce book value to residual value.

3. Activity-based:

		Calculation				End-of-Year Amounts	
UNIVERSITY HERO **Depreciation Schedule—Activity-Based**							
Year	Hours Used	×	Depreciation Rate*	=	Depreciation Expense	Accumulated Depreciation	Book Value**
1	2,200		$10		**$22,000**	$22,000	$88,000
2	2,600		10		**26,000**	48,000	62,000
3	2,300		10		**23,000**	71,000	39,000
4	2,100				**19,000***	90,000	**20,000**
Total	9,200				**$90,000**		

Suggested Homework:
BE7–10, BE7–12;
E7–10, E7–11;
P7–5A&B, P7–7A&B

*$90,000 ÷ 9,000 hours = $10/hour
**$110,000 cost minus accumulated depreciation.
***Amount needed to reduce book value to residual value.

Amortization of Intangible Assets

Allocating the cost of property, plant, and equipment to expense is called depreciation. Similarly, allocating the cost of *intangible* assets to expense is called **amortization**.

INTANGIBLE ASSETS SUBJECT TO AMORTIZATION

■ LO7–5
Calculate amortization of intangible assets.

Most intangible assets have a finite useful life that we can estimate. The service life of an intangible asset usually is limited by legal, regulatory, or contractual provisions. For example, the legal life of a patent is 20 years. However, the estimated useful life of a patent often is less than 20 years if the benefits are not expected to continue for the patent's entire legal life. The patent for the Apple Watch, for example, is amortized over fewer than 20 years, since new technology will cause the watch to become outdated in a shorter period.

The expected residual value of most intangible assets is zero. This might not be the case, though, if at the end of its useful life to the reporting entity, the asset will benefit another entity. For example, if **Apple** has a commitment from another company to purchase one of its patents at the end of the patent's useful life at a determinable price, we use that price as the patent's residual value.

Most companies use *straight-line amortization* for intangibles. Also, many companies credit amortization to the intangible asset account itself rather than to accumulated amortization. That's the approach illustrated in the chapter and the approach to be used for homework in Connect. However, using a contra account such as Accumulated Amortization is also acceptable in practice.

Example.   In early January, Little King Sandwiches acquires from University Hero two intangible assets—franchise and patent. The details of the transaction include:

- Purchase price of the franchise is $800,000, and the agreement is for a period of 20 years.
- Purchase price of the patent is $72,000. The original legal life of the patent was 20 years, and there are 12 years remaining. However, due to expected technological obsolescence, the Little King estimates that the useful life of the patent is only 8 more years. Little King uses straight-line amortization for all intangible assets. The company's fiscal year-end is December 31. Little King records the amortization expense for the franchise and the patent as follows.

	Debit	Credit
Amortization Expense	40,000	
Franchises		40,000
(Amortize franchise)		
($40,000 = $800,000/20 years)		
Amortization Expense	9,000	
Patents		9,000
(Amortize patent)		
($9,000 = $72,000/8 years)		

Income Statement

R	−	E	=	NI
		+40,000		−49,000
		Amor Exp.		
		+9,000		
		Amor Exp.		

Balance Sheet

A	=	L	+	SE
−40,000				−49,000
Franchises				
−9,000				
Patents				

INTANGIBLE ASSETS NOT SUBJECT TO AMORTIZATION

We don't depreciate land because it has an unlimited life. Similarly, we do *not* amortize intangible assets with indefinite (unknown or not determinable) useful lives. Illustration 7–21 provides a summary of intangible assets that are amortized and those that are not amortized. An asset's useful life is indefinite if there is no foreseeable limit on the period of time over which we expect it to contribute to the cash flows of the entity. For example, suppose Little King acquired a trademark for its name. Registered trademarks have a legal life of 10 years, but the trademark registration is renewable for an indefinite number of 10-year periods. We consider the life of Little King's trademark for its name to be indefinite, so we don't amortize it.

Intangible Assets Subject to Amortization (those with finite useful life)	Intangible Assets Not Subject to Amortization (those with indefinite useful life)
• Patents • Copyrights • Trademarks (with finite life) • Franchises	• Goodwill • Trademarks (with indefinite life)

ILLUSTRATION 7–21

Amortization Treatment of Intangible Assets

Goodwill is the most common intangible asset with an indefinite useful life. Recall that we measure goodwill as the difference between the purchase price of a company and the fair value of all its identifiable net assets (tangible and intangible assets minus the liabilities assumed). Does this mean that goodwill and other intangible assets with indefinite useful lives will remain on a company's balance sheet at their original cost forever? Probably not. **Management must review long-term assets for a potential write-down when events or changes in circumstances indicate the asset's "recoverable amount" is *less than* its "recorded amount" in the accounting records.** The recoverable amount is the cash expected to be received from using the asset over its remaining useful life. All long-term assets are subject to these impairment rules, which we discuss in more detail in the appendix to this chapter.

 KEY POINT

Amortization is a process, similar to depreciation, in which we allocate the cost of intangible assets over their estimated service lives. Intangible assets with an indefinite useful life (goodwill and most trademarks) are *not* amortized.

ASSET DISPOSAL: SALE, RETIREMENT, OR EXCHANGE

PART C

Few things last forever. In this section, we discuss what to do when we no longer use a long-term asset. Illustration 7–22 shows three different ways an asset can be disposed of. A *sale* is the most common method to dispose of an asset. When a long-term asset is no longer useful but cannot be sold, we have a *retirement*. For example, Little King Sandwiches might

■ **LO7–6**

Account for the disposal of long-term assets.

physically remove a baking oven that no longer works and also remove it from the accounting records through a retirement entry. An *exchange* occurs when two companies trade assets. In an exchange, we often use cash to make up for any difference in fair value between the assets.

ILLUSTRATION 7–22

Three Methods of Asset Disposal

Sale of Long-Term Assets

The sale of a long-term asset typically involves a transaction in which cash is received for the asset given up. The difference between the cash received and the book value of the asset given up is reported as a gain or loss in the income statement.

Gains increase net income.

A **gain** occurs when we sell an asset for *more than its book value.* In this case, the cash received is greater than the book value of the asset sold. The amount of the gain equals the net increase in assets. Gains, like revenues, have a credit balance and are reported as an increase to net income.

Losses decrease net income.

A **loss** occurs when we sell an asset for *less than its book value.* In this case, the cash received is less than the book value of the asset sold. The amount of the loss equals the net decrease in assets. Losses, like expenses, have a debit balance and are reported as a decrease to net income.

Remember, book value is the cost of the asset minus accumulated depreciation. In order to have the correct book value, it's important to record depreciation up to the date of the sale.

 COMMON MISTAKE

Some students forget to update depreciation prior to recording the disposal of the asset. Depreciation must be recorded up to the date of the sale, retirement, or exchange. Otherwise, the book value will be overstated, and the resulting gain or loss on disposal will be in error as well.

To illustrate the sale of an asset, let's return to our delivery truck example for Little King Sandwiches. Assume Little King uses straight-line depreciation and records the delivery truck in the Equipment account. The specific details are summarized again in Illustration 7–23.

ILLUSTRATION 7–23

Data to Illustrate Long-Term Asset Disposals

Original cost of the truck	$40,000
Estimated residual value	$5,000
Estimated service life	5 years
Depreciation/year	$7,000

If we assume that Little King sells the delivery truck at the end of year 3 for $22,000, we can calculate the gain as $3,000. The gain is equal to the cash received of $22,000 less the truck's book value of $19,000. Illustration 7–24 shows the calculation.

ILLUSTRATION 7–24

Gain on Sale

Sale amount		$22,000
Less:		
Original cost of the truck	$40,000	
Less: Accumulated depreciation (3 years × $7,000/year)	(21,000)	
Book value at the end of year 3		19,000
Gain		**$ 3,000**

We record the sale by removing the delivery truck accounts (both Equipment and Accumulated Depreciation) from the accounting records and recording the cash collected. The gain is the difference between the sale amount and the book value of the truck.

	Debit	Credit
Cash	22,000	
Accumulated Depreciation	21,000	
Equipment		40,000
Gain		3,000
(Sell equipment for a gain)		

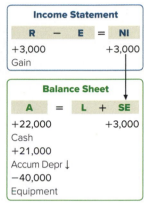

Income Statement

R	−	E	=	NI
+3,000 Gain				+3,000

Balance Sheet

A	=	L	+	SE
+22,000 Cash				+3,000
+21,000 Accum Depr ↓				
−40,000 Equipment				

COMMON MISTAKE

Be careful not to combine the delivery truck ($40,000) and accumulated depreciation ($21,000) and credit the $19,000 difference to the Equipment account. Instead, remove the delivery truck and accumulated depreciation from the accounting records separately. Otherwise, the Equipment and the Accumulated Depreciation accounts will incorrectly have a remaining balance after the asset has been sold.

If we assume that Little King sells the delivery truck at the end of year 3 for only $17,000 instead of $22,000, we have a $2,000 loss as calculated in Illustration 7–25. In this case, the sale amount is less than the truck's book value.

ILLUSTRATION 7–25

Loss on Sale

Sale amount		$17,000
Less:		
Original cost of the truck	$40,000	
Less: Accumulated depreciation (3 years × $7,000/year)	(21,000)	
Book value at the end of year 3		19,000
Loss		**$(2,000)**

We record the loss on sale as

	Debit	Credit
Cash	17,000	
Accumulated Depreciation	21,000	
Loss	2,000	
Equipment		40,000
(Sell equipment for a loss)		

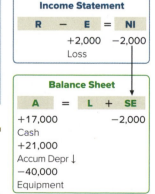

Income Statement

R	−	E	=	NI
		+2,000 Loss		−2,000

Balance Sheet

A	=	L	+	SE
+17,000 Cash				−2,000
+21,000 Accum Depr ↓				
−40,000 Equipment				

Decision Maker's Perspective

Understanding Gains and Losses

It's tempting to think of a "gain" and "loss" on the sale of a depreciable asset as "good" and "bad" news. For example, we commonly use the term "gain" in everyday language to mean we sold something for more than we bought it. Gain could also be misinterpreted to mean the asset was sold for more than its fair value (we got a "good deal"). However, neither of these represents the meaning of a gain on the sale of assets. Refer back to our example in Illustration 7–24. The sale of the truck resulted in a gain, but the truck was sold for *less than* its original cost, and there is no indication that Little King sold the machine for more than its fair value.

A gain on the sale of a depreciable asset simply means the asset was sold for more than its book value. In other words, the asset received and recorded (such as cash) is greater than the book value of the asset that was sold and removed from the accounting records. The net increase in the book value of total assets is an accounting gain (not an economic gain).

The same is true for losses. A loss signifies that the cash received is less than the book value of the asset that was sold; there is a net decrease in the book value of total assets.

Retirement of Long-Term Assets

Now assume that Little King retires the delivery truck instead of selling it. If, for example, the truck is totaled in an accident at the end of year 3, we have a $19,000 loss on retirement as calculated in Illustration 7–26.

ILLUSTRATION 7–26

Loss on Retirement

Sale amount		$　　0
Less:		
Original cost of the truck	$40,000	
Less: Accumulated depreciation (3 years × $7,000/year)	(21,000)	
Book value at the end of year 3		19,000
Loss		**$(19,000)**

We record the loss on retirement as

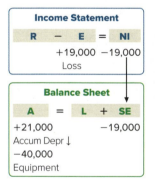

	Debit	Credit
Accumulated Depreciation	**21,000**	
Loss	**19,000**	
Equipment		**40,000**
(Retire equipment for a loss)		

Income Statement

R	−	E	=	NI
	+19,000	−19,000		
		Loss		

Balance Sheet

A	=	L	+	SE
+21,000				−19,000
Accum Depr ↓				
−40,000				
Equipment				

The above entry assumes Little King did not have collision insurance coverage. If Little King had insured the truck and collected $17,000 in insurance money for the totaled vehicle, the entry would be identical to the sale for $17,000 in Illustration 7–25.

Exchange of Long-Term Assets

Now assume that Little King exchanges the delivery truck at the end of year 3 for a new truck valued at $45,000. The dealership gives Little King a trade-in allowance of $23,000 on the exchange, with the remaining $22,000 paid in cash. We have a $4,000 gain, as calculated in Illustration 7–27.[3]

ILLUSTRATION 7–27

Gain on Exchange

Trade-in allowance		$23,000
Less:		
Original cost of the truck	$ 40,000	
Less: Accumulated depreciation (3 years × $7,000/year)	(21,000)	
Book value at the end of year 3		19,000
Gain		**$ 4,000**

---

[3] In 2005, a new accounting standard (FASB ASC 845: Nonmonetary Transactions) simplified accounting for exchanges by requiring the new asset acquired in an exchange be recorded at fair value. This eliminates the deferred gain on exchange recorded under previous standards.

We record the gain on exchange as

	Debit	Credit
Equipment (new)	**45,000**	
Accumulated Depreciation (old)	**21,000**	
Equipment (old)		**40,000**
Cash		**22,000**
Gain		**4,000**
(Exchange equipment for a gain)		

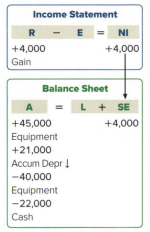

Income Statement

R	−	E	=	NI
+4,000				+4,000
Gain				

Balance Sheet

A	=	L	+	SE
+45,000				+4,000
Equipment				
+21,000				
Accum Depr ↓				
−40,000				
Equipment				
−22,000				
Cash				

KEY POINT

If we dispose of an asset for *more* than its book value, we record a gain. If we dispose of an asset for *less* than its book value, we record a loss.

ASSET ANALYSIS
Disney vs. Netflix

■ **LO7–7**
Describe the links among return on assets, profit margin, and asset turnover.

We have discussed the purchase, depreciation, and disposal of long-term assets. In this final section, we see how to use actual financial statement information to analyze the profitability of a company's assets. Illustration 7–28 provides selected financial data reported from **Disney** and **Netflix** for use in our analysis.

ANALYSIS

ILLUSTRATION 7–28
Selected Financial Data for Disney and Netflix

($ in millions)	
Disney	
Net sales	$ 69,570
Net income	11,584
Total assets, beginning	98,598
Total assets, ending	193,984
Netflix	
Net sales	$ 20,156
Net income	1,867
Total assets, beginning	25,974
Total assets, ending	33,976

RETURN ON ASSETS

Disney had net income of $11,584 million and Netflix had net income of $1,867 million. Since Disney's net income is so much larger, is Disney more profitable? Not necessarily. Disney is also a much larger company as indicated by total assets. Disney's ending total assets were $193,984 million compared to $33,976 billion for Netflix. A more comparable measure of profitability than net income is **return on assets**, or ROA for short, which equals net income divided by *average* total assets.

$$\text{Return on assets} = \frac{\text{Net income}}{\text{Average total assets}}$$

The average is calculated as the beginning amount plus the ending amount, divided by 2. Dividing net income by average total assets adjusts net income for differences in company size.

COMMON MISTAKE

Students sometimes divide by ending total assets rather than by average total assets. However, there is a good reason to use average total assets in the denominator: to align the *timing* of the numerator and denominator. That is, given that net income (the numerator) is measured over a fiscal period, we want total assets (the denominator) to reflect that same time period, so we use the *average* total assets over that time period. This is the standard approach in ratio analysis: whenever we divide a number in the income statement by a number in the balance sheet, we use an average balance sheet number in the denominator so that both the numerator and denominator are aligned in time.

The return on assets ratio is calculated for Disney and Netflix in Illustration 7–29.

ILLUSTRATION 7–29

Return on Assets for Disney and Netflix

($ in millions)	Net Income	÷	Average Total Assets	=	Return on Assets
Disney	$11,584	÷	($98,598 + $193,984)/2	=	7.9%
Netflix	$ 1,867	÷	($25,974 + $33,976)/2	=	6.2%

Return on assets indicates the amount of net income generated for each dollar invested in assets. With an ROA of 7.9%, Disney generates 7.9 cents of profit for every dollar of assets. Netflix's 6.2% ROA indicates that it generates 6.2 cents of profit for every dollar of assets. Disney is more profitable than Netflix.

Decision Point

Question ❓	Accounting information 📄	Analysis 🔍
How effectively is the company using its assets?	Return on assets ratio	A higher return on assets generally indicates a more effective use of assets.

PROFIT MARGIN AND ASSET TURNOVER

We can explore profitability further by separating return on assets into two components: profit margin and asset turnover, as shown in Illustration 7–30.

ILLUSTRATION 7–30

Components of Return on Assets

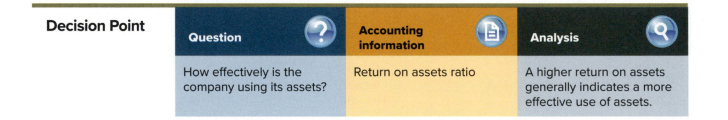

$$\frac{\text{Return on assets}}{\frac{\text{Net income}}{\text{Average total assets}}} = \frac{\text{Profit margin}}{\frac{\text{Net income}}{\text{Net sales}}} \times \frac{\text{Asset turnover}}{\frac{\text{Net sales}}{\text{Average total assets}}}$$

As the second row in Illustration 7–30 indicates, **profit margin** is calculated as net income divided by net sales. This ratio indicates the earnings per dollar of sales. **Asset turnover** is calculated as net sales divided by average total assets. This ratio measures the sales per dollar of assets invested.

Decision Maker's Perspective

Strategies for Increasing Return on Assets

Companies have two primary strategies for increasing their return on assets: increasing profit margin and increasing asset turnover. Some companies pursue a higher profit margin through *product differentiation* and *premium pricing*. They set higher selling prices, giving them more profit per dollar of sales. Other companies pursue a higher asset turnover by charging *lower prices*. They increase sales volume, giving them more sales per dollar invested in assets.

Comparing Disney and Netflix, we might expect Disney to have a higher profit margin and a lower asset turnover than Netflix. Disney's operating results include both its traditional high-end theme parks and its media and studio business. Netflix is in the highly competitive streaming entertainment business, forced to offer lower prices to customers with higher sales volume. In Illustrations 7–31 and 7–32 we calculate profit margin and asset turnover for both companies.

($ in millions)	Net Income	÷	Net Sales	=	Profit Margin
Disney	$11,584	÷	$69,570	=	16.7%
Netflix	$ 1,867	÷	$20,156	=	9.3%

ILLUSTRATION 7–31

Profit Margin for Disney and Netflix

($ in millions)	Net Sales	÷	Average Total Assets	=	Asset Turnover
Disney	$69,570	÷	($98,598 + $193,984)/2	=	0.48 times
Netflix	$20,156	÷	($25,974 + $33,976)/2	=	0.67 times

ILLUSTRATION 7–32

Asset Turnover for Disney and Netflix

Illustration 7–31 indicates that Disney's profit margin is higher than Netflix's. Illustration 7–32, however, shows that Netflix has the higher asset turnover. These accounting ratios support expectations regarding the business strategies Disney and Netflix are pursuing. To maximize profitability, a company ideally strives to increase *both* net income per dollar of sales (profit margin) and sales per dollar of assets invested (asset turnover).

Question	Accounting information	Analysis
How much profit is being generated from sales?	Profit margin	A higher profit margin indicates a company generates a higher net income per dollar of sales.
Is the company effectively generating sales from its assets?	Asset turnover ratio	A higher asset turnover indicates a company generates a higher sales volume per dollar of assets invested.

Decision Point

Impact of Estimates on Financial Ratios. To calculate depreciation, managers must estimate the service life and residual value of an asset. By purposely *overestimating* the service life and/or residual value of an asset, a manager reduces the reported amount of depreciation expense and thereby inflates net income in the earlier years of an asset's life. This causes financial ratios—such as return on assets and profit margin—to create the appearance of better company performance.

KEY POINT

Return on assets indicates the amount of net income generated for each dollar invested in assets. Return on assets can be separated to examine two important business strategies: profit margin and asset turnover.

APPENDIX

IMPAIRMENT OF LONG-TERM ASSETS

■ **LO7–8**

Identify impairment situations and describe the two-step impairment process.

Depreciation and amortization represent a gradual consumption of the benefits inherent in property, plant, and equipment and intangible assets. Situations can arise, however, that cause a significant decline or impairment of the total benefits or service potential of specific long-term assets. For example, if a retail chain closed several stores and no longer used them in operations, the buildings and equipment may be subject to impairment. **Michael Kors**, designer of luxury accessories, recently recorded impairment charges of $198 million related to the closing of selected stores.

When operating conditions suggest a potential reduction in an asset's benefit or service potential, management must review the asset for impairment. **Impairment** occurs when the expected future cash flows (expected future benefits) generated for a long-term asset fall below its book value (original cost minus accumulated depreciation).

Reporting for impairment losses is a two-step process summarized in Illustration 7–33.

ILLUSTRATION 7–33

Two-Step Impairment Process

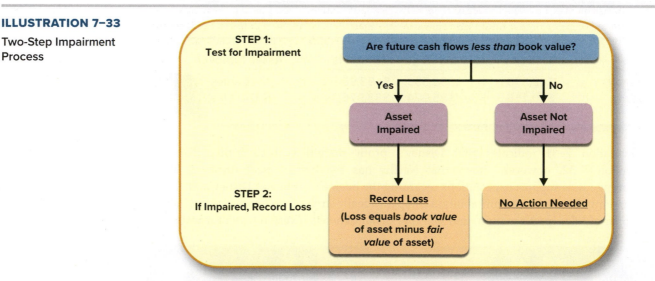

To illustrate asset impairment, suppose Little King pays $60,000 for the trademark rights to a line of specialty sandwiches. After several years, the book value is now $50,000, based on the initial cost of $60,000 less $10,000 in accumulated amortization. Unfortunately, sales for this line of specialty sandwiches are disappointing, and management estimates the total future cash flows from sales will be only $20,000. Due to the disappointing sales, the estimated fair value of the trademark is now only $12,000. Here's how Little King determines and records the impairment loss.

STEP 1: TEST FOR IMPAIRMENT

The long-term asset is impaired since future cash flows ($20,000) are less than book value ($50,000).

STEP 2: IF IMPAIRED, RECORD THE LOSS

The loss is $38,000, calculated as the amount by which book value ($50,000) exceeds fair value ($12,000). We record the impairment loss as follows:

	Debit	Credit
Loss	38,000	
Trademarks		38,000
(Record impairment of trademark) ($50,000 book value less $12,000 fair value)		

Income Statement

R	−	E	=	NI
		+38,000		−38,000
		Loss		

Balance Sheet

A	=	L	+	SE
−38,000				−38,000
Trademarks				

⊗ COMMON MISTAKE

Some students forget step 1 when considering impairment. Record an impairment loss only when book value exceeds *both* future cash flows and fair value.

What is the overall financial statement effect of an impairment loss? The impairment entry reduces net income in the income statement by $38,000 and reduces total assets in the balance sheet by $38,000. The new balance in the Trademarks account is $12,000, which equals its current fair value. We can write down the trademark further through impairment in future years, but we cannot write it back up under current accounting rules.

We covered the basic impairment rules in this appendix. The two-step impairment process applies to property, plant, and equipment and to intangible assets with *finite* useful lives. For intangible assets with *indefinite* useful lives (such as goodwill and certain trademarks), we omit step 1. We omit step 1 for these types of intangible assets because they are presumed to provide cash flows indefinitely, so estimated future cash flows are not a good indicator of impairment in the current period.

🔑 KEY POINT

Impairment is a two-step process: **Step 1: Test for impairment:** A long-term asset with a finite life is impaired if future cash flows are less than book value. **Step 2: If impaired, record impairment loss:** The impairment loss is the amount by which book value exceeds fair value.

🌐 INTERNATIONAL FINANCIAL REPORTING STANDARDS (IFRS)

CAN IMPAIRMENT LOSSES BE REVERSED?

International accounting standards also record impairments based on a two-step impairment process. However, one important difference is this: Impairments under U.S. GAAP are permanent—the asset cannot be written back up in future periods. In contrast, impairments under IFRS rules can be reversed. Thus, under IFRS a company can record an impairment loss in one period and then write the asset back up with a corresponding gain in a later period.

For more discussion, see Appendix E.

Decision Maker's Perspective

Taking a Big Bath

In practice, determining impairment losses can be subjective. Accounting research suggests that managers sometimes use the recording of impairment losses to their advantage. Some companies time their impairment losses with other one-time losses such as losses on sales of assets, inventory write-downs, and restructuring charges, to record a big loss in one year. We refer to this practice as taking a **big bath**—recording all losses in one year to make a bad year even worse. Management thus cleans its slate and is able to report higher earnings in future years. Future earnings are higher because the write-down of assets in this year results in lower depreciation and amortization charges in the future. When analyzing financial statements, investors should be alert to this kind of manipulation.

CHAPTER FRAMEWORK

This chapter discusses transactions over the useful life of a long-term asset: (1) acquisition, (2) expenditures after acquisition, (3) depreciation over time, and (4) eventual sale or retirement. Long-term asset transactions **during the year** and their related adjusting entries at the **end of the year** affect amounts reported in the financial statements.

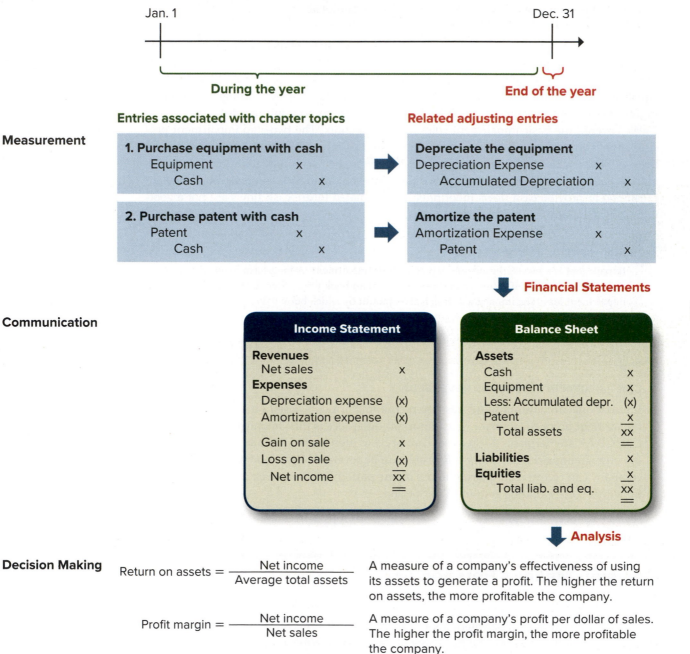

Measurement

Entries associated with chapter topics

Related adjusting entries

1. Purchase equipment with cash
Equipment   x
    Cash   x

Depreciate the equipment
Depreciation Expense   x
    Accumulated Depreciation   x

2. Purchase patent with cash
Patent   x
    Cash   x

Amortize the patent
Amortization Expense   x
    Patent   x

Financial Statements

Communication

Income Statement

Revenues	
Net sales	x
Expenses	
Depreciation expense	(x)
Amortization expense	(x)
Gain on sale	x
Loss on sale	(x)
Net income	xx

Balance Sheet

Assets	
Cash	x
Equipment	x
Less: Accumulated depr.	(x)
Patent	x
Total assets	xx
Liabilities	x
Equities	x
Total liab. and eq.	xx

Analysis

Decision Making

$$\text{Return on assets} = \frac{\text{Net income}}{\text{Average total assets}}$$

A measure of a company's effectiveness of using its assets to generate a profit. The higher the return on assets, the more profitable the company.

$$\text{Profit margin} = \frac{\text{Net income}}{\text{Net sales}}$$

A measure of a company's profit per dollar of sales. The higher the profit margin, the more profitable the company.

$$\text{Asset turnover} = \frac{\text{Net sales}}{\text{Average total assets}}$$

A measure of a company's effectiveness of using its assets to generate sales. The higher the asset turnover, the better a company uses its assets.

1. **Purchase equipment with cash.** During the year, a company purchases equipment, a tangible asset, that is expected to be used for several years. At the end of the year, an adjusting entry is made to **depreciate the equipment** (expense a portion of the equipment's cost in the current year). Depreciation expense each year accumulates over time in Accumulated Depreciation, a contra (or negative) asset account.

2. **Purchase patent with cash.** During the year, a company purchases a patent, an intangible asset, that is expected to be used for several years. At the end of the year, an adjusting entry is made to **amortize the patent** (expense a portion of the patent's cost in the current year). Amortization is typically an even amount (straight-line) in each year. The balance of the Patent account is reduced from its original cost by the amount of amortization since the patent was purchased.

If a long-term asset is sold for more than its book value (original cost less accumulated depreciation to date), a **gain** is reported in the income statement. If the asset is sold for less than its book value, a **loss** is reported.

Chapter Framework Questions

1. **Measurement (during the year):** During the year, a company purchases equipment that is expected to be used for several years. The company records
   a. Debit Equipment; credit Cash.
   b. Debit Equipment Expense; credit Cash.
   c. Debit Cash; credit Equipment.
   d. Debit Cash; credit Equipment Expense.

2. **Measurement (end of the year):** At the end of the year, the adjusting entry to depreciate equipment involves
   a. Debit Accumulated Depreciation; credit Equipment.
   b. Debit Depreciation Expense; credit Accumulated Depreciation.
   c. Debit Depreciation Expense; credit Equipment.
   d. Debit Accumulated Depreciation; credit Depreciation Expense.

3. **Communication (income statement):** Depreciation of equipment each year has what effect on the income statement?
   a. Decrease expenses for the amount of depreciation for the current year only.
   b. Decrease expenses for the amount of depreciation since the asset was purchased.
   c. Increase expenses for the amount of depreciation for the current year only.
   d. Increase expenses for the amount of depreciation since the asset was purchased.

4. **Communication (balance sheet):** Which of the following is true about Accumulated Depreciation reported in the balance sheet related to equipment?
   a. An asset account that maintains a record of the equipment's original cost.
   b. A contra (or negative) asset account that represents depreciation of the equipment for the current year only.
   c. A liability account that represents total depreciation since the equipment was purchased.
   d. A contra (or negative) asset account that represents total depreciation since the equipment was purchased.

5. **Decision Making (ratio analysis):** A company that is less effective at using its assets to generate sales would have a _____ asset turnover ratio.
   a. Higher.
   b. Lower.

Note: For answers, see the last page of the chapter.

KEY POINTS BY LEARNING OBJECTIVE

LO7–1   Identify the major types of property, plant, and equipment.

Tangible assets such as land, land improvements, buildings, equipment, and natural resources are recorded at cost plus all costs necessary to get the asset ready for its intended use.

LO7–2   Identify the major types of intangible assets.

We record purchased intangibles as long-term assets at their purchase price plus all costs necessary to get the asset ready for use. We expense internally generated intangibles, such as R&D and advertising costs, as we incur those costs.

Intangible assets have no physical substance and generally represent exclusive rights that provide benefits to owners. Common types include patents, copyrights, trademarks, franchises, and goodwill.

LO7–3   Describe the accounting treatment of expenditures after acquisition.

We capitalize (record as an asset) expenditures that benefit *future* periods. We expense items that benefit only the *current* period.

LO7–4   Calculate depreciation of property, plant, and equipment.

Depreciation refers to the allocation of an asset's original cost to an expense during the periods benefited. Depreciation does *not* refer to the change in value or selling price.

Straight-line, declining-balance, and activity-based depreciation all are acceptable depreciation methods for financial reporting. Most companies use straight-line depreciation for financial

reporting and an accelerated method called MACRS for tax reporting.

LO7–5   Calculate amortization of intangible assets.

Amortization is a process, similar to depreciation, in which we allocate the cost of intangible assets over their estimated service life. Intangible assets with an indefinite useful life (goodwill and most trademarks) are *not* amortized.

LO7–6   Account for the disposal of long-term assets.

If we dispose of an asset for *more* than its book value, we record a gain. If we dispose of an asset for *less* than its book value, we record a loss.

Analysis

LO7–7   Describe the links among return on assets, profit margin, and asset turnover.

Return on assets indicates the amount of net income generated for each dollar invested in assets. Return on assets can be separated to examine two important business strategies: profit margin and asset turnover.

Appendix

LO7–8   Identify impairment situations and describe the two-step impairment process.

Impairment is a two-step process. **Step 1: Test for impairment:** A long-term asset with a finite life is impaired if future cash flows are less than book value. **Step 2: If impaired, record loss:** The impairment loss is the amount by which book value exceeds fair value.

GLOSSARY

Accelerated depreciation method: Allocates a higher depreciation in the earlier years of the asset's life and lower depreciation in later years. **p. 358**

Accumulated Depreciation: A contra asset account representing the total depreciation taken to date. **p. 354**

Activity-based method: Allocates an asset's cost based on its use. **p. 360**

Addition: Occurs when a new major component is added to an existing asset. **p. 352**

Amortization: Allocation of the cost of an intangible asset over its service life. **p. 364**

Asset turnover: Net sales divided by average total assets, which measures the sales per dollar of assets invested. **p. 370**

Basket purchase: Purchase of more than one asset at the same time for one purchase price. **p. 346**

Big bath: Recording all losses in one year to make a bad year even worse. **p. 373**

Book value: An asset's original cost less accumulated depreciation. **p. 355**

Capitalize: Record an expenditure as an asset. **p. 345**

Copyright: An exclusive right of protection given to the creator of a published work such as a song, film, painting, photograph, book, or computer software. **p. 349**

Declining-balance method: An accelerated depreciation method that records more depreciation in earlier years and less depreciation in later years. **p. 358**

Depreciation: Allocating the cost of a long-term asset to an expense over its service life. **p. 354**

Depreciation method: The pattern in which the asset's depreciable cost (original cost minus residual value) is allocated over time. **p. 355**

Franchise: Local outlets that pay for the exclusive right to use the franchisor company's name and to sell its products within a specified geographical area. **p. 350**

Goodwill: Goodwill equals the purchase price less the fair value of the net assets acquired. **p. 350**

Impairment: Occurs when the future cash flows (future benefits) generated for a long-term asset fall below its book value (cost minus accumulated depreciation). **p. 372**

Improvement: The cost of replacing a major component of an asset. **p. 352**

Intangible assets: Long-term assets that lack physical substance, and whose existence is often based on a legal contract. **p. 347**

Land improvements: Improvements to land such as paving, lighting, and landscaping that, unlike land itself, are subject to depreciation. **p. 346**

Material: Large enough to influence a decision. **p. 352**

Natural resources: Assets like oil, natural gas, and timber that we can physically use up or deplete. **p. 347**

Patent: An exclusive right to manufacture a product or to use a process. **p. 349**

Profit margin: Net income divided by net sales; indicates the earnings per dollar of sales. **p. 370**

Repairs and maintenance: Expenses that maintain a given level of benefits in the period incurred. **p. 351**

Residual value: The amount the company expects to receive from selling the asset at the end of its service life; also referred to as *salvage value.* **p. 355**

Return on assets: Net income divided by average total assets; measures the amount of net income generated for each dollar invested in assets. **p. 369**

Service life: How long the company expects to receive benefits from the asset before disposing of it; also referred to as *useful life.* **p. 355**

Straight-line method: Allocates an equal amount of depreciation to each year of the asset's service life. **p. 356**

Trademark: A word, slogan, or symbol that distinctively identifies a company, product, or service. **p. 350**

SELF-STUDY QUESTIONS

1. We normally record a long-term asset at the **(LO7–1)**
   a. Cost of the asset only.
   b. Cost of the asset plus all costs necessary to get the asset ready for use.
   c. Appraised value.
   d. Cost of the asset, but subsequently adjust it up or down to appraised value.

2. Sandwich Express incurred the following costs related to its purchase of a bread machine. **(LO7–1)**

Cost of the equipment	$20,000
Sales tax (8%)	1,600
Shipping	2,200
Installation	1,400
Total costs	$25,200

   At what amount should Sandwich Express record the bread machine?
   a. $20,000.
   b. $21,600.
   c. $23,800.
   d. $25,200.

3. Research and development costs **(LO7–2)**
   a. Are recorded as research and development assets.
   b. Are capitalized and then amortized.
   c. Should be included in the cost of the patent they relate to.
   d. Should be expensed.

4. Bryer Co. purchases all of the assets and liabilities of Stellar Co. for $1,500,000. The fair value of Stellar's assets is $2,000,000, and its liabilities have a fair value of $1,200,000. The book value of Stellar's assets and liabilities are not known. For what amount would Bryer record goodwill associated with the purchase? **(LO7–2)**
   a. $800,000.
   b. $500,000.
   c. $700,000.
   d. $0.

5. Which of the following expenditures should be recorded as an expense? **(LO7–3)**
   a. Repairs and maintenance that maintain current benefits.
   b. Adding a major new component to an existing asset.
   c. Replacing a major component of an existing asset.
   d. Successful legal defense of an intangible asset.

6. Which of the following will maximize net income by minimizing depreciation expense in the first year of the asset's life? **(LO7–4)**
   a. Short service life, high residual value, and straight-line depreciation.
   b. Long service life, high residual value, and straight-line depreciation.
   c. Short service life, low residual value, and double-declining-balance depreciation.
   d. Long service life, high residual value, and double-declining-balance depreciation.

7. The balance in the Accumulated Depreciation account represents **(LO7–4)**
   a. The amount charged to expense in the current period.
   b. A contra expense account.
   c. A cash fund to be used to replace plant assets.
   d. The amount charged to depreciation expense since the acquisition of the plant asset.

8. The book value of an asset is equal to the **(LO7–4)**
   a. Replacement cost.
   b. Asset's cost less accumulated depreciation.
   c. Asset's fair value less its historical cost.
   d. Historical cost plus accumulated depreciation.

9. Equipment was purchased for $50,000. At that time, the equipment was expected to be used eight years and have a residual value of $10,000. The company uses straight-line depreciation. At the beginning of the third year, the company changed its estimated service life to a total of six years (four years remaining) and the residual value to $8,000. What is depreciation expense in the third year? **(LO7–4)**
   a. $8,000.
   b. $5,000.
   c. $7,000.
   d. $5,500.

10. Equipment was purchased for $50,000. The equipment is expected to be used 15,000 hours over its service life and then have a residual value of $10,000. In the first two years of operation, the equipment was used 2,700 hours and 3,300 hours, respectively. What is the equipment's accumulated depreciation at the end of the second year using the activity-based method? **(LO7–4)**
   a. $16,000.
   b. $7,200.
   c. $8,800.
   d. $20,000.

11. Which of the following statements is *true* regarding the amortization of intangible assets? **(LO7–5)**
   a. Intangible assets with a limited useful life are not amortized.
   b. The useful life of an intangible asset is always equal to its legal life.
   c. The expected residual value of most intangible assets is zero.
   d. In recording amortization, Accumulated Amortization is always credited.

12. Equipment originally costing $95,000 has accumulated depreciation of $30,000. If the equipment is sold for $55,000, the company should record **(LO7–6)**
   a. No gain or loss.
   b. A gain of $10,000.
   c. A loss of $10,000.
   d. A loss of $40,000.

13. The company's profitability on each dollar invested in assets is represented by which of the following ratios: **(LO7–7)**
   a. Profit margin.
   b. Asset turnover.
   c. Return on assets.
   d. Return on equity.

14. A company has a profit margin of 10% and reports net sales of $4,000,000 and average total assets of $5,000,000. Calculate the company's return on assets. **(LO7–7)**
   a. 12.5%.
   b. 8.0%.
   c. 4.5%.
   d. 5.0%.

15. A company has the following three assets with the information provided: **(LO7–8)**

($ in millions)	Equipment	Land	Building
Book value	$8	$20	$12
Estimated total future cash flows	6	35	14
Fair value	5	30	10

Determine the amount of the impairment loss, if any.
   a. $0.
   b. $5 million.
   c. $10 million.
   d. $3 million.

Note: For answers, see the last page of the chapter.

DATA ANALYTICS & EXCEL

 **Mc Graw Hill** **connect**

 **Visit Connect to find a variety of Data Analytics questions that help build Excel, Tableau, and data visualization skills. Assignable materials include Integrated Excel, Applying Excel, Data Visualizations, Tableau Dashboard Activities, and Applying Tableau cases.**

REVIEW QUESTIONS

■ **LO7–1**   1. **Disney** has several types of long-term assets. What are the primary ones shown in its balance sheet?

■ **LO7–1**   2. What are the two major categories of long-term assets? How do these two categories differ?

3. Explain how we initially record a long-term asset. ■ **LO7–1**

4. If University Hero initially records an expense incorrectly as an asset, how does this mistake affect the income statement and the balance sheet? ■ **LO7–1**

5. Little King acquires land and an old building across the street from Northwestern State University. Little King intends to remove the old building and build a new sandwich shop on the land. What costs might the firm incur to make the land ready for its intended use? ■ **LO7–1**

6. Why don't we depreciate land? What are land improvements? Why do we record land and land improvements separately? ■ **LO7–1**

7. Equipment includes machinery used in manufacturing, computers and other office equipment, vehicles, furniture, and fixtures. What costs might we incur to get equipment ready for use? ■ **LO7–1**

8. Where in the balance sheet do we report natural resources? Provide three examples of natural resource assets. ■ **LO7–1**

9. Explain how the accounting treatment differs between purchased and internally developed intangible assets. ■ **LO7–2**

10. What are the differences among a patent, a copyright, and a trademark? ■ **LO7–2**

11. What is goodwill and how do we measure it? Can we sell goodwill separately from the business? ■ **LO7–2**

12. How do we decide whether to capitalize (record as an asset) or expense a particular cost? ■ **LO7–3**

13. Explain the usual accounting treatment for repairs and maintenance, additions, and improvements. ■ **LO7–3**

14. Are litigation costs to defend an intangible asset capitalized or expensed? Explain your answer. ■ **LO7–3**

15. How is the dictionary definition different from the accounting definition of depreciation? ■ **LO7–4**

16. What factors must we estimate in allocating the cost of a long-term asset over its service life? ■ **LO7–4**

17. What is the service life of an asset? How do we determine service life under the straight-line and the activity-based depreciation methods? ■ **LO7–4**

18. What is residual value? How do we use residual value in calculating depreciation under the straight-line method? ■ **LO7–4**

19. Contrast the effects of the straight-line, declining-balance, and activity-based methods on annual depreciation expense. ■ **LO7–4**

20. Assume that Little King Sandwiches uses straight-line depreciation and University Hero uses double-declining-balance depreciation. Explain the difficulties in comparing the income statements and balance sheets of the two companies. ■ **LO7–4**

21. Assume Little King Sandwiches depreciates a building over 40 years and University Hero depreciates a similar building over 20 years, and both companies use the straight-line depreciation method. Explain the difficulties in comparing the income statements and balance sheets of the two companies. ■ **LO7–4**

22. Which depreciation method is most common for financial reporting? Which depreciation method is most common for tax reporting? Why do companies choose these methods? ■ **LO7–4**

23. Justin Time is confident that firms amortize all intangible assets. Is he right? If amortized, are intangible assets always amortized over their legal life? Explain. ■ **LO7–5**

24. What is book value? How do we compute the gain or loss on the sale of long-term assets? ■ **LO7–6**

25. Describe return on assets, profit margin, and asset turnover. ■ **LO7–7**

26. Provide an example of a company with a high-profit margin. Provide an example of a company with a high asset turnover. ■ **LO7–7**

27. What is an asset impairment? Describe the two-step process for recording impairments. How does recording an impairment loss affect the income statement and the balance sheet? ■ **LO7–8**

28. How do companies take a *big bath*? Explain the effect of a big bath on the current year's and future years' net income. ■ **LO7–8**

BRIEF EXERCISES

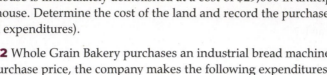

Record the initial cost of land (LO7–1)

BE7–1 Fresh Veggies, Inc. (FVI), purchases land and a warehouse for $490,000. In addition to the purchase price, FVI makes the following expenditures related to the acquisition: broker's commission, $29,000; title insurance, $1,900; and miscellaneous closing costs, $6,000. The warehouse is immediately demolished at a cost of $29,000 in anticipation of building a new warehouse. Determine the cost of the land and record the purchase (assuming cash was paid for all expenditures).

Determine the initial cost of equipment (LO7–1)

BE7–2 Whole Grain Bakery purchases an industrial bread machine for $30,000. In addition to the purchase price, the company makes the following expenditures: freight, $2,000; installation, $4,000; testing, $1,500; and property tax on the machine for the first year, $600. What is the initial cost of the bread machine?

Allocate cost in a basket purchase (LO7–1)

BE7–3 Finley Co. is looking for a new office location and sees a building with a fair value of $400,000. Finley also notices that much of the equipment in the existing building would be useful to its own operations. Finley estimates the fair value of the equipment to be $80,000. Finley offers to buy both the building and the equipment for $450,000, and the offer is accepted. Determine the amounts Finley should record in the separate accounts for building and equipment.

Calculate goodwill (LO7–2)

BE7–4 Kosher Pickle Company acquires all the outstanding stock of Midwest Produce for $19 million. The fair value of Midwest's assets is $14.3 million. The fair value of Midwest's liabilities is $2.5 million. Calculate the amount paid for goodwill.

Compute research and development expense (LO7–2)

BE7–5 West Coast Growers incurs the following costs during the year related to the creation of a new disease-resistant tomato plant.

Salaries for R&D	$540,000
Depreciation on R&D facilities and equipment	145,000
Utilities incurred for the R&D facilities	7,000
Patent filing and related legal costs	27,000
Payment to another company for part of the development work	13,000

What amount should West Coast Growers report as research and development (R&D) expense in its income statement?

Account for expenditures after acquisition (LO7–3)

BE7–6 Hanoi Foods incurs the following expenditures during the current fiscal year: (1) annual maintenance on its machinery, $8,900; (2) remodeling of offices, $42,000; (3) improvement of the shipping and receiving area, resulting in an increase in productivity, $25,000; and (4) addition of a security system to the manufacturing facility, $35,000. How should Hanoi account for each of these expenditures?

Legal defense of intangible asset (LO7–3)

BE7–7 Betty Foods has separate patents for its chocolate chip cookie dough and vanilla ice cream. In the current year, both patents were challenged in court. Betty Foods spent $240,000 in legal fees to successfully defend its cookie dough, and $300,000 in legal fees in an unsuccessful defense of its vanilla ice cream. For what amount can Betty Foods capitalize these costs?

Explain the accounting definition of depreciation (LO7–4)

BE7–8 Early in the fiscal year, The Beanery purchases a delivery vehicle for $40,000. At the end of the year, the vehicle has a fair value of $33,000. The company controller records depreciation expense of $7,000 for the year, the decline in the vehicle's value. Is the company controller's approach to recording depreciation expense correct?

Calculate partial-year depreciation (LO7–4)

BE7–9 El Tapitio purchased restaurant furniture on September 1, 2024, for $45,000. Residual value at the end of an estimated 10-year service life is expected to be $6,000. Calculate depreciation expense for 2024 and 2025, using the straight-line method and assuming a December 31 year-end.

Calculate depreciation (LO7–4)

BE7–10 On January 1, Hawaiian Specialty Foods purchased equipment for $30,000. Residual value at the end of an estimated four-year service life is expected to be $3,000. The machine operated for 3,100 hours in the first year, and the company expects the machine to operate for a total of 20,000 hours. Calculate depreciation expense for the first year using each of the following depreciation methods: (1) straight-line, (2) double-declining-balance, and (3) activity-based.

BE7–11 Refer to the information in BE7-10. Record depreciation expense for each of the first two years using the straight-line method.

Record depreciation using straight-line method (LO7-4)

BE7–12 Refer to the information in BE7-10. In addition, assume the machine operated for an additional 3,400 hours in the second year. Record depreciation expense for the first two years using the activity-based method.

Record depreciation using activity-based method (LO7-4)

BE7–13 Omaha Beef Co. purchased a delivery truck for $50,000. The residual value at the end of an estimated eight-year service life is expected to be $10,000. The company uses straight-line depreciation for the first six years. In the seventh year, the company now believes the truck will be useful for a total of 10 years (four more years), and the residual value will remain at $10,000. Calculate depreciation expense for the seventh year.

Change in depreciation estimate (LO7–4)

BE7–14 In early January, Burger Mania acquired 100% of the common stock of the Crispy Taco restaurant chain. The purchase price allocation included the following items: $4 million, patent; $5 million, trademark considered to have an indefinite useful life; and $6 million, goodwill. Burger Mania's policy is to amortize intangible assets with finite useful lives using the straight-line method, no residual value, and a five-year service life. What is the total amount of amortization expense that would appear in Burger Mania's income statement for the first year ended December 31 related to these items?

Calculate amortization expense (LO7–5)

BE7–15 Granite Stone Creamery sold ice cream equipment for $16,000. Granite Stone originally purchased the equipment for $90,000, and depreciation through the date of sale totaled $71,000. Record the gain or loss on the sale of the equipment.

Record the sale of long-term assets (LO7–6)

BE7–16 Piper's Pizza sold baking equipment for $25,000. The equipment was originally purchased for $72,000, and depreciation through the date of sale totaled $51,000. Record the gain or loss on the sale of the equipment.

Record the sale of long-term assets (LO7–6)

BE7–17 On January 1, Masterson Supply purchased a small storage building for $20,000 to be used over a five-year period. The building has no residual value. Early in the fourth year, the storage building burned down. Record the retirement of the remaining book value of the storage building.

Account for the retirement of long-term assets (LO7–6)

Flip Side of BE7–19

BE7–18 China Inn and Midwest Chicken exchanged assets. China Inn received delivery equipment and gave restaurant equipment. The fair value and book value of the restaurant equipment were $22,000 and $12,000 (original cost of $45,000 less accumulated depreciation of $33,000), respectively. To equalize market values of the exchanged assets, China Inn paid $9,000 in cash to Midwest Chicken. Record the gain or loss for China Inn on the exchange of the equipment.

Account for the exchange of long-term assets (LO7–6)

Flip Side of BE7–18

BE7–19 China Inn and Midwest Chicken exchanged assets. Midwest Chicken received restaurant equipment and gave delivery equipment. The fair value and book value of the delivery equipment given were $31,000 and $32,600 (original cost of $37,000 less accumulated depreciation of $4,400), respectively. To equalize market values of the exchanged assets, Midwest Chicken received $9,000 in cash from China Inn. Record the gain or loss for Midwest Chicken on the exchange of the equipment.

Account for the exchange of long-term assets (LO7–6)

BE7–20 The balance sheet of Cedar Crest Resort reports total assets of $840,000 and $930,000 at the beginning and end of the year, respectively. The return on assets for the year is 20%. Calculate Cedar Crest's net income for the year.

Use the return on assets ratio (LO7–7)

BE7–21 Vegetarian Delights has been experiencing declining market conditions for its specialty foods division. Management decided to test the operational assets of the division for possible

Determine the impairment loss (LO7–8)

impairment. The test revealed the following: book value of the division's assets, $33.5 million; fair value of the division's assets, $30 million; sum of estimated future cash flows generated from the division's assets, $38 million. What amount of impairment loss, if any, should Vegetarian Delights record?

Determine the impairment loss (LO7–8)

BE7–22 Refer to the situation described in BE7–21. Assume the sum of estimated future cash flows is $32 million instead of $38 million. What amount of impairment loss should Vegetarian Delights record?

Determine financial statement effects of purchasing land (LO7–1)

BE7–23 Refer to the information in BE7–1. Determine the financial statement effects of the purchase of land.

Determine financial statement effects of straight-line depreciation (LO10–4)

BE7–24 Refer to the information in BE7–11. Determine the financial statement effects of depreciation for each of the first two years using the straight-line method.

Determine financial statement effects of activity-based depreciation (LO10–4)

BE7–25 Refer to the information in BE7–12. Determine the financial statement effects of depreciation using the activity-based method.

Determine financial statement effects of sale of long-term assets (LO10–6)

BE7–26 Refer to the information in BE7–15. Determine the financial statement effects of the gain or loss on the sale of the equipment.

Determine financial statement effects of sale of long-term assets (LO10–6)

BE7–27 Refer to the information in BE7–16. Determine the financial statement effects of the gain or loss on the sale of the equipment.

EXERCISES

Mc Graw Hill connect®

Record purchase of land (LO7–1)

E7–1 McCoy's Fish House purchases a tract of land and an existing building for $1,000,000. The company plans to remove the old building and construct a new restaurant on the site. In addition to the purchase price, McCoy pays closing costs, including title insurance of $3,000. The company also pays $14,000 in property taxes, which includes $9,000 of back taxes (unpaid taxes from previous years) paid by McCoy on behalf of the seller and $5,000 due for the current fiscal year after the purchase date. Shortly after closing, the company pays a contractor $50,000 to tear down the old building and remove it from the site. McCoy is able to sell salvaged materials from the old building for $5,000 and pays an additional $11,000 to level the land.

Required:
Determine the amount McCoy's Fish House should record as the cost of the land.

Record purchase of equipment (LO7–1)

E7–2 Orion Flour Mills purchased new equipment and made the following expenditures:

Purchase price	$75,000
Sales tax	6,000
Shipment of equipment	1,000
Insurance on the equipment for the first year	700
Installation of equipment	2,000

Required:
Record the expenditures. All expenditures were paid in cash.

Allocate costs in a basket purchase (LO7–1)

E7–3 Red Rock Bakery purchases land, building, and equipment for a single purchase price of $600,000. However, the estimated fair values of the land, building, and equipment are $175,000, $455,000, and $70,000, respectively, for a total estimated fair value of $700,000.

Required:

Determine the amounts Red Rock should record in the separate accounts for the land, the building, and the equipment.

E7–4 Micro Facilities incurs the following costs during the year.

- A new patent is purchased for $600,000 from Techno Company. The patent gives Micro exclusive right to sell specialized data storage units.
- Internal costs of $500,000 were used to research and develop a new high-resolution monitor. The company expects production to begin next year, and sales to customers to occur over the next five years.
- An integrated sound component for video capture processes is developed using internal resources at a cost of $450,000. By the end of the year, the company applies for and receives a patent on the sound component.
- Advertising costs of $250,000 were used in the current year to promote the company's products and services, including those expected to be released next year.

Required:

Record the expenditures. Assume all expenditures were paid in cash.

E7–5 Brick Oven Corporation made the following expenditures during the first month of operations:

Attorneys' fees to organize the corporation	$ 9,000
Purchase of a patent	40,000
Legal and other fees for transfer of the patent	2,500
Advertising	80,000
Total	$131,500

Required:

Record the $131,500 in cash expenditures.

E7–6 Mainline Produce Corporation acquired all the outstanding common stock of Iceberg Lettuce Corporation for $30,000,000 in cash. The book values and fair values of Iceberg's assets and liabilities were as follows:

	Book Value	Fair Value
Current assets	$11,400,000	$14,400,000
Property, plant, and equipment	20,200,000	26,200,000
Other assets	3,400,000	4,400,000
Current liabilities	7,800,000	7,800,000
Long-term liabilities	13,200,000	12,200,000

Required:

Calculate the amount paid for goodwill.

E7–7 Satellite Systems modified its model Z2 satellite to incorporate a new communication device. The company made the following expenditures:

Basic research to develop the technology	$3,900,000
Engineering design work	1,180,000
Development of a prototype device	590,000
Testing and modification of the prototype	390,000
Legal fees for patent application	79,000
Legal fees for successful defense of the new patent	39,000
Total	$6,178,000

Margin notes:

Record expenditures related to intangibles **(LO7–2)**

Record intangible assets **(LO7–2)**

Calculate the amount of goodwill **(LO7–2)**

Report patent and research and development expense **(LO7–2)**

During your year-end review of the accounts related to intangibles, you discover that the company has capitalized all costs of the patent. Management contends that the device represents an improvement of the existing communication system of the satellite and, therefore, should be capitalized.

Required:
1. Which of the costs should Satellite Systems capitalize to the Patent account in the balance sheet?
2. Which of the costs should Satellite Systems report as research and development expense in the income statement?
3. What are the basic criteria for determining whether to capitalize or expense intangible related costs?

Match terms used in the chapter (LO7–2, 7–4)

E7–8 Listed below are several terms and phrases associated with operational assets. Pair each item from List A (by letter) with the item from List B that is most appropriately associated with it.

List A	List B
_____ 1. Depreciation	a. Exclusive right to display a word, a symbol, or an emblem.
_____ 2. Goodwill	
_____ 3. Amortization	b. Exclusive right to benefit from a creative work.
_____ 4. Natural resources	c. Assets that represent contractual rights.
_____ 5. Intangible assets	d. Oil and gas deposits, timber tracts, and mineral deposits.
_____ 6. Copyright	e. Purchase price less fair value of net identifiable assets.
_____ 7. Trademark	f. The allocation of cost for plant and equipment.
	g. The allocation of cost for intangible assets.

Record expenditures after acquisition (LO7–3)

E7–9 Sub Sandwiches of America made the following expenditures related to its restaurant:
1. Replaced the heating equipment at a cost of $250,000.
2. Covered the patio area with a clear plastic dome and enclosed it with glass for use during the winter months. The total cost of the project was $750,000.
3. Performed annual building maintenance at a cost of $24,000.
4. Paid for annual insurance for the facility at $8,800.
5. Built a new sign above the restaurant, putting the company name in bright neon lights, for $9,900.
6. Paved a gravel parking lot at a cost of $65,000.

Required:
Sub Sandwiches of America credits Cash for each of these expenditures. Indicate the account it debits for each.

Determine depreciation for the first year under three methods (LO7–4)

E7–10 On January 1, Super Saver Groceries purchased store equipment for $29,500. Super Saver estimates that at the end of its 10-year service life, the equipment will be worth $3,500. During the 10-year period, the company expects to use the equipment for a total of 13,000 hours. Super Saver used the equipment for 1,700 hours the first year.

Required:
Calculate depreciation expense for the first year, using each of the following methods. Round all amounts to the nearest dollar.
1. Straight-line.
2. Double-declining-balance.
3. Activity-based.

Determine depreciation under three methods (LO7–4)

E7–11 On January 1, Speedy Delivery Company purchases a delivery van for $90,000. Speedy estimates that at the end of its six-year service life, the van will be worth $30,000. During the six-year period, the company expects to drive the van 200,000 miles.

Required:
Calculate annual depreciation for the first two years using each of the following methods. Round all amounts to the nearest dollar.
1. Straight-line.
2. Double-declining-balance.
3. Activity-based.
    Actual miles driven each year were 32,000 miles in year 1 and 35,000 miles in year 2.

E7–12 Togo's Sandwiches acquired equipment on April 1, 2024, for $18,000. The company estimates a residual value of $2,000 and a five-year service life.

Required:

Calculate depreciation expense using the straight-line method for 2024 and 2025, assuming a December 31 year-end.

Determine straight-line depreciation for partial periods **(LO7–4)**

E7–13 Tasty Subs acquired a food-service truck on October 1, 2024, for $120,000. The company estimates residual value of $40,000 and a four-year service life.

Required:

Calculate depreciation expense using the straight-line method for 2024 and 2025, assuming a December 31 year-end.

Determine straight-line depreciation for partial periods **(LO7–4)**

E7–14 The Donut Stop acquired equipment for $19,000. The company uses straight-line depreciation and estimates a residual value of $3,000 and a four-year service life. At the end of the second year, the company estimates that the equipment will be useful for four additional years, for a total service life of six years rather than the original four. At the same time, the company also changed the estimated residual value to $1,200 from the original estimate of $3,000.

Required:

Calculate how much The Donut Stop should record each year for depreciation in years 3 to 6.

Determine depreciation expense for a change in depreciation estimate **(LO7–4)**

E7–15 Tasty Subs acquired a food service truck on October 1, 2024, for $120,000. The company estimates a residual value of $40,000 and a four-year service life. It expects to drive the truck 100,000 miles. Actual mileage was 5,000 miles in 2024 and 28,000 miles in 2025.

Required:

Calculate depreciation expense using the activity-based method for 2024 and 2025, assuming a December 31 year-end.

Determine activity-based depreciation **(LO7–4)**

E7–16 On January 1, 2024, Weaver Corporation purchased a patent for $237,000. The remaining legal life is 20 years, but the company estimates the patent will be useful for only six more years. In January 2026, the company incurred legal fees of $57,000 in successfully defending a patent infringement suit. The successful defense did not change the company's estimate of useful life. Weaver Corporation's year-end is December 31.

Required:

1. Record the purchase in 2024; amortization in 2024; amortization in 2025; legal fees in 2026; and amortization in 2026.
2. What is the balance in the Patent account at the end of 2026?

Record amortization expense **(LO7–5)**

E7–17 Abbott Landscaping purchased a tractor at a cost of $42,000 and sold it three years later for $21,600. Abbott recorded depreciation using the straight-line method, a five-year service life, and a $3,000 residual value. Tractors are included in the Equipment account.

Required:

1. Record the sale.
2. Assume the tractor was sold for $13,600 instead of $21,600. Record the sale.

Record the sale of equipment **(LO7–6)**

E7–18 Salad Express exchanged land it had been holding for future plant expansion for a more suitable parcel of land along distribution routes. Salad Express reported the old land on the previously issued balance sheet at its original cost of $70,000. According to an independent appraisal, the old land currently is worth $132,000. Salad Express paid $19,000 in cash to complete the transaction.

Required:

1. What is the fair value of the new parcel of land received by Salad Express?
2. Record the exchange.

Record an exchange of land **(LO7–6)**

E7–19 Brad's BBQ reported sales of $735,000 and net income of $28,000. Brad's also reported ending total assets of $496,000 and beginning total assets of $389,000.

Required:

Calculate the return on assets, the profit margin, and the asset turnover ratio for Brad's BBQ.

Calculate ratios **(LO7–7)**

Calculate impairment loss (LO7–8)

E7–20 Midwest Services, Inc., operates several restaurant chains throughout the Midwest. One restaurant chain has experienced sharply declining profits. The company's management has decided to test the operational assets of the restaurants for possible impairment. The relevant information for these assets is presented below.

Book value	$8.6 million
Estimated total future cash flows	7.1 million
Fair value	5.9 million

Required:

1. Determine the amount of the impairment loss, if any.
2. Repeat *requirement* 1 assuming that the estimated total future cash flows are $10 million and the fair value is $8.2 million.

Complete the accounting cycle using long-term asset transactions (LO7–4, 7–7)

E7–21 On January 1, 2024, the general ledger of TNT Fireworks includes the following account balances:

Accounts	Debit	Credit
Cash	$ 58,700	
Accounts Receivable	25,000	
Allowance for Uncollectible Accounts		$ 2,200
Inventory	36,300	
Notes Receivable (5%, due in 2 years)	12,000	
Land	155,000	
Accounts Payable		14,800
Common Stock		220,000
Retained Earnings		50,000
Totals	$287,000	$287,000

During January 2024, the following transactions occur:

January 1	Purchase equipment for $19,500. The company estimates a residual value of $1,500 and a five-year service life.
January 4	Pay cash on accounts payable, $9,500.
January 8	Purchase additional inventory on account, $82,900.
January 15	Receive cash on accounts receivable, $22,000
January 19	Pay cash for salaries, $29,800.
January 28	Pay cash for January utilities, $16,500.
January 30	Firework sales for January total $220,000. All of these sales are on account. The cost of the units sold is $115,000.

Required:

1. Record each of the transactions listed.
2. Record adjusting entries on January 31.
   a. Depreciation on the equipment for the month of January is calculated using the straight-line method.
   b. The company records an adjusting entry for $5,900 for estimated future uncollectible accounts.
   c. The company has accrued interest on notes receivable for January.
   d. Unpaid salaries owed to employees at the end of January are $32,600.
   e. The company accrued income taxes at the end of January of $9,000.
3. Prepare an adjusted trial balance as of January 31, 2024, after updating beginning balances (above) for transactions during January (*requirement* 1) and adjusting entries at the end of January (*requirement* 2).
4. Prepare a multiple-step income statement for the period ended January 31, 2024.
5. Prepare a classified balance sheet as of January 31, 2024.

6. Record closing entries.
7. Analyze how well TNT Fireworks manages its assets:
    a. Calculate the return on assets ratio for the month of January. If the average return on assets for the industry in January is 2%, is the company *more* or *less* profitable than other companies in the same industry?
    b. Calculate the profit margin for the month of January. If the industry average profit margin is 4%, is the company *more* or *less* efficient at converting sales to profit than other companies in the same industry?
    c. Calculate the asset turnover ratio for the month of January. If the industry average asset turnover is 0.5 times per month, is the company more or less efficient at producing revenues with its assets than other companies in the same industry?

PROBLEMS: SET A

P7–1A The Italian Bread Company purchased land as a factory site for $70,000. An old building on the property was demolished, and construction began on a new building. Costs incurred during the first year are listed as follows:

Determine the acquisition cost of land and building **(LO7–1)**

Demolition of old building	$ 9,000
Sale of salvaged materials	(1,100)
Architect fees (for new building)	20,000
Legal fees (for title investigation of land)	3,000
Property taxes on the land (for the first year)	4,000
Building construction costs	600,000
Interest costs related to the construction	23,000

Required:
Determine the amounts that the company should record in the Land and the Building accounts.

P7–2A Great Harvest Bakery purchased bread ovens from New Morning Bakery. New Morning Bakery was closing its bakery business and sold its two-year-old ovens at a discount for $700,000. Great Harvest incurred and paid freight costs of $35,000, and its employees ran special electrical connections to the ovens at a cost of $5,000. Labor costs were $37,800. Unfortunately, one of the ovens was damaged during installation, and repairs cost $4,000. Great Harvest then consumed $900 of bread dough in testing the ovens. It installed safety guards on the ovens at a cost of $1,500 and placed the machines in operation.

Determine the acquisition cost of equipment **(LO7–1)**

Flip Side of P7–8A

Required:
1. Prepare a schedule showing the amount at which the ovens should be recorded in Great Harvest's Equipment account.
2. Indicate where any amounts not included in the Equipment account should be recorded.

P7–3A Fresh Cut Corporation purchased all the outstanding common stock of Premium Meats for $12,000,000 in cash. The book values and fair values of Premium Meats' assets and liabilities were as follows:

Calculate and record goodwill **(LO7–2)**

	Book Value	Fair Value
Accounts Receivable	$ 1,800,000	$ 1,600,000
Equipment	8,500,000	9,900,000
Patents	300,000	1,700,000
Notes Payable	(2,700,000)	(2,700,000)
Net assets	$ 7,900,000	$10,500,000

Required:
1. Calculate the amount Fresh Cut should report for goodwill.
2. Record Fresh Cut's acquisition of Premium Meats.

Record expenditures after acquisition (LO7–3)

P7–4A Several years ago, Health Services acquired a helicopter for use in emergency situations. Health Services incurred the following expenditures related to the helicopter delivery operations in the current year:

1. Overhauled the engine at a cost of $7,500. Health Services estimated the work would increase the service life for an additional five years.
2. Cleaned, repacked, and sealed the bearings on the helicopter at a cost of $800. This repair is performed annually.
3. Added new emergency health equipment to the helicopter for $25,000.
4. Modified the helicopter to reduce cabin noise by installing new sound barrier technology at a cost of $15,000.
5. Paid insurance on the helicopter for the current year, which increased 15% over the prior year to $9,000.
6. Performed annual maintenance and repairs at a cost of $39,000.

Required:

Indicate whether Health Services should capitalize or expense each of these expenditures.

Determine depreciation under three methods (LO7–4)

P7–5A University Car Wash purchased new soap dispensing equipment that cost $270,000 including installation. The company estimates that the equipment will have a residual value of $24,000. University Car Wash also estimates it will use the machine for six years or about 12,000 total hours.

Required:

Prepare a depreciation schedule for six years using the following methods:

1. Straight-line.
2. Double-declining-balance.
3. Activity-based.

Actual use per year was as follows:

Year	Hours Used
1	3,100
2	1,100
3	1,200
4	2,800
5	2,600
6	1,200

Record amortization and prepare the intangible assets section (LO7–5)

P7–6A The following information relates to the intangible assets of University Testing Services (UTS):

a. On January 1, 2024, UTS completed the purchase of Heinrich Corporation for $3,510,000 in cash. The fair value of the net identifiable assets of Heinrich was $3,200,000.
b. Included in the assets purchased from Heinrich was a patent valued at $82,250. The original legal life of the patent was 20 years; there are 12 years remaining, but UTS believes the patent will be useful for only 7 more years.
c. UTS acquired a franchise on July 1, 2024, by paying an initial franchise fee of $333,000. The contractual life of the franchise is nine years.

Required:

1. Record amortization expense for the intangible assets at December 31, 2024.
2. Prepare the intangible asset section of the December 31, 2024, balance sheet.

Compute depreciation, amortization, and book value of long-term assets (LO7–4, 7–5)

P7–7A Solich Sandwich Shop had the following long-term asset balances as of January 1, 2024:

	Cost	Accumulated Depreciation	Book Value
Land	$ 95,000	–	$ 95,000
Building	460,000	$(165,600)	294,400
Equipment	235,000	(50,000)	185,000
Patent	250,000	(100,000)	150,000

Additional information:

- Solich purchased all the assets at the beginning of 2022.
- The building is depreciated over a 10-year service life using the double-declining-balance method and estimating no residual value.
- The equipment is depreciated over a nine-year service life using the straight-line method with an estimated residual value of $10,000.
- The patent is estimated to have a five-year useful life with no residual value and is amortized using the straight-line method.
- Depreciation and amortization have been recorded for 2022 and 2023 (first two years).

Required:

1. For the year ended December 31, 2024 (third year), record depreciation expense for buildings and equipment. Land is not depreciated.
2. For the year ended December 31, 2024, record amortization expense for the patent.
3. Calculate the book value for each of the four long-term assets at December 31, 2024.

P7–8A New Morning Bakery is in the process of closing its operations. It sold its two-year-old bakery ovens to Great Harvest Bakery for $700,000. The ovens originally cost $910,000, had an estimated service life of 10 years, had an estimated residual value of $60,000, and were depreciated using straight-line depreciation. Complete the requirements below for New Morning Bakery.

Record the disposal of equipment **(LO7–6)**

Required:

1. Calculate the balance in the Accumulated Depreciation account at the end of the second year.
2. Calculate the book value of the ovens at the end of the second year.
3. What is the gain or loss on the sale of the ovens at the end of the second year?
4. Record the sale of the ovens at the end of the second year.

Flip Side of P7–2A

P7–9A Sub Station and Planet Sub reported the following selected financial data ($ in thousands). Sub Station's business strategy is to sell the best-tasting sandwich with the highest-quality ingredients. Planet Sub's business strategy is to sell the lowest-cost sub on the planet.

Calculate and interpret ratios **(LO7–7)**

	Sub Station	Planet Sub
Net sales	$108,249	$62,071
Net income	25,922	3,492
Total assets, beginning	75,183	38,599
Total assets, ending	116,371	44,533

Required:

1. Calculate Sub Station's return on assets, profit margin, and asset turnover ratio.
2. Calculate Planet Sub's return on assets, profit margin, and asset turnover ratio.
3. Which company has the more favorable profit margin and which company has the more favorable asset turnover? Is this consistent with the primary business strategies of these two companies?

Calculate and interpret ratios (LO7–7)

P7–10A University Hero is considering expanding operations beyond its healthy sandwiches. Jim Axelrod, vice president of marketing, would like to add a line of smoothies with a similar health emphasis. Each smoothie would include two free health supplements, such as vitamins, antioxidants, and protein. Jim believes smoothie sales should help fill the slow mid-afternoon period. Adding the line of smoothies would require purchasing additional freezer space, machinery, and equipment. Jim provides the following projections of net sales, net income, and average total assets in support of his proposal.

	Sandwiches Only	Sandwiches and Smoothies
Net sales	$900,000	$1,500,000
Net income	170,000	260,000
Average total assets	500,000	900,000

Required:

1. Calculate University Hero's return on assets, profit margin, and asset turnover for sandwiches only.
2. Calculate University Hero's return on assets, profit margin, and asset turnover for sandwiches and smoothies.
3. Based on these ratios, what recommendation would you make?

PROBLEMS: SET B

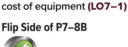

Determine the acquisition cost of land and building (LO7–1)

P7–1B The Italian Pizza Company purchased land as a factory site for $90,000. Prior to construction of the new building, the land had to be cleared of trees and brush. Construction costs incurred during the first year are listed below:

Land clearing costs	$ 5,000
Sale of firewood to a worker	(400)
Architect fees (for new building)	30,000
Title investigation of land	3,500
Property taxes on land (for the first year)	3,000
Building construction costs	400,000

Required:
Determine the amounts that the company should record in the Land and the Building accounts.

Determine the acquisition cost of equipment (LO7–1)

Flip Side of P7–8B

P7–2B Sicily Pizza purchased baking ovens from New World Deli. New World Deli was closing its bakery business and sold its three-year-old ovens for $341,000. In addition to the purchase price, Sicily Pizza paid shipping costs of $16,000. Employees of Sicily Pizza installed the ovens; labor costs were $17,000. An outside contractor performed some of the electrical work for $3,800. Sicily Pizza consumed pizza dough with a cost of $1,300 in testing the ovens. It then installed new timers on the ovens at a cost of $800 and placed the machines in operation.

Required:

1. Prepare a schedule showing the amount at which Sicily Pizza should record the ovens in the Equipment account.
2. Indicate where any amounts not included in the Equipment account should be recorded.

Calculate and record goodwill (LO7–2)

P7–3B Northern Equipment Corporation purchased all the outstanding common stock of Pioneer Equipment Rental for $5,600,000 in cash. The book values and fair values of Pioneer's assets and liabilities were as follows:

	Book Value	Fair Value
Accounts Receivable	$ 750,000	$ 650,000
Buildings	4,100,000	4,800,000
Equipment	110,000	200,000
Accounts Payable	(750,000)	(750,000)
Net assets	$4,210,000	$4,900,000

Required:

1. Calculate the amount Northern Equipment should report for goodwill.
2. Record Northern Equipment's acquisition of Pioneer Equipment Rental.

P7–4B Stillwater Youth Programs (SYP) purchased a used school bus to transport children for its after-school program. SYP incurred the following expenses related to the bus for the current year:

Record expenditures after acquisition (LO7–3)

1. Replaced a blown tire on the bus for $175.
2. Installed new seats on the bus at a cost of $5,000.
3. Installed a sound system to entertain the children in-transit and announce upcoming events at a cost of $1,000.
4. Paid insurance on the school bus for the current year, which increased 10% over the prior year to an annual premium of $2,800.
5. Performed annual maintenance and repairs for $1,400.
6. Overhauled the engine at a cost of $6,500, increasing the service life of the bus by an estimated three years.

Required:

Indicate whether SYP should capitalize or expense each of these expenditures.

P7–5B Cheetah Copy purchased a new copy machine. The new machine cost $140,000 including installation. The company estimates the equipment will have a residual value of $35,000. Cheetah Copy also estimates it will use the machine for four years or about 8,000 total hours.

Determine depreciation under three methods (LO7–4)

Required:

Prepare a depreciation schedule for four years using the following methods:

1. Straight-line.
2. Double-declining-balance. (*Hint:* The asset will be depreciated in only two years.)
3. Activity-based.
   Actual use per year was as follows:

Year	Hours Used
1	3,000
2	2,000
3	2,000
4	2,000

P7–6B The following information relates to the intangible assets of Lettuce Express:

Record amortization and prepare the intangible assets section (LO7–5)

a. On January 1, 2024, Lettuce Express completed the purchase of Farmers Produce, Inc., for $1,600,000 in cash. The fair value of the identifiable net assets of Farmers Produce was $1,440,000.
b. Included in the assets purchased from Farmers Produce was a patent for a method of processing lettuce valued at $49,500. The original legal life of the patent was 20 years. There are still 17 years left on the patent, but Lettuce Express estimates the patent will be useful for only 9 more years.
c. Lettuce Express acquired a franchise on July 1, 2024, by paying an initial franchise fee of $216,000. The contractual life of the franchise is eight years.

Required:

1. Record amortization expense for the intangible assets at December 31, 2024.
2. Prepare the intangible asset section of the December 31, 2024, balance sheet.

Compute depreciation, amortization, and book value of long-term assets (LO7–4, 7–5)

P7–7B Togo's Sandwich Shop had the following long-term asset balances as of January 1, 2024:

	Cost	Accumulated Depreciation	Book Value
Land	$ 85,000	–	$ 85,000
Building	560,000	$(201,600)	358,400
Equipment	145,000	(30,000)	115,000
Patent	125,000	(50,000)	75,000

Additional information:

- Togo's purchased all the assets at the beginning of 2022.
- The building is depreciated over a 10-year service life using the double-declining-balance method and estimating no residual value.
- The equipment is depreciated over a nine-year service life using the straight-line method with an estimated residual value of $10,000.
- The patent is estimated to have a five-year useful life with no residual value and is amortized using the straight-line method.
- Depreciation and amortization have been recorded for 2022 and 2023 (first two years).

Required:

1. For the year ended December 31, 2024 (third year), record depreciation expense for buildings and equipment. Land is not depreciated.
2. For the year ended December 31, 2024, record amortization expense for the patent.
3. Calculate the book value for each of the four long-term assets at December 31, 2024.

Record the disposal of equipment (LO7–6)

Flip Side of P7–2B

P7–8B New Deli is in the process of closing its operations. It sold its three-year-old ovens to Sicily Pizza for $341,000. The ovens originally cost $455,000, had an estimated service life of 10 years, had an estimated residual value of $30,000, and were depreciated using straight-line depreciation. Complete the requirements below for New Deli.

Required:

1. Calculate the balance in the Accumulated Depreciation account at the end of the third year.
2. Calculate the book value of the ovens at the end of the third year.
3. What is the gain or loss on the sale of the ovens at the end of the third year?
4. Record the sale of the ovens at the end of the third year.

Calculate and interpret ratios (LO7–7)

P7–9B Papa's Pizza is the market leader and Pizza Prince is an up-and-coming player in the highly competitive delivery pizza business. The companies reported the following selected financial data ($ in thousands):

	Papa's Pizza	Pizza Prince
Net sales	$24,128	$1,835
Net income	2,223	129
Total assets, beginning	14,998	919
Total assets, ending	15,465	1,157

Required:

1. Calculate the return on assets, profit margin, and asset turnover ratio for Papa's Pizza.
2. Calculate the return on assets, profit margin, and asset turnover ratio for Pizza Prince.
3. Which company has the more favorable profit margin and which company has the more favorable asset turnover?

P7–10B Barry Sanders, likely the best running back to ever play football, has opened a successful used-car dealership. He has noted a higher than normal percentage of sales for trucks and SUVs with hauling capacity at his dealership. He is also aware that several of the best recreational lakes in the state are located nearby. Barry is considering expanding his dealership to include the sale of recreational boats. Barry provides the following projections of net sales, net income, and average total assets in support of his proposal.

Calculate and interpret ratios (LO7–7)

	Cars Only	Cars and Boats
Net sales	$6,500,000	$7,700,000
Net income	500,000	700,000
Average total assets	1,700,000	1,900,000

Required:

1. Calculate Barry's return on assets, profit margin, and asset turnover for cars only.
2. Calculate Barry's return on assets, profit margin, and asset turnover for cars and boats.
3. Based on these ratios, what recommendation would you make?

REAL-WORLD PERSPECTIVES

Data Analytics & Excel

Visit Connect to find a variety of Data Analytics questions that help build Excel, Tableau, and data visualization skills. Assignable materials include Integrated Excel, Applying Excel, Data Visualizations, Tableau Dashboard Activities, and Applying Tableau cases.

Great Adventures

General Ledger
Continuing Case

(This is a continuation of the Great Adventures problem from earlier chapters.)

RWP7–1 Tony and Suzie see the need for a rugged all-terrain vehicle to transport participants and supplies. They decide to purchase a used Suburban on July 1, 2025, for $12,000. They expect to use the Suburban for five years and then sell the vehicle for $4,500. The following expenditures related to the vehicle were also made on July 1, 2025:

- The company pays $1,800 to **GEICO** for a one-year insurance policy.
- The company spends an extra $3,000 to repaint the vehicle, placing the Great Adventures logo on the front hood, back, and both sides.
- An additional $2,000 is spent on a deluxe roof rack and a trailer hitch.

The painting, roof rack, and hitch are all expected to increase the future benefits of the vehicle for Great Adventures. In addition, on October 22, 2025, the company pays $400 for basic vehicle maintenance related to changing the oil, replacing the windshield wipers, rotating the tires, and inserting a new air filter.

Required:

1. Record the expenditures related to the vehicle on July 1, 2025. Note: The capitalized cost of the vehicle is recorded in the Equipment account.
2. Record the expenditure related to vehicle maintenance on October 22, 2025.
3. Prepare a depreciation schedule using the straight-line method. Follow the example in Illustration 7–12, except the calendar years 2025 (first year) and 2030 (last year) will have a half-year of depreciation to reflect the five-year service life beginning on July 1, 2025.
4. Record the depreciation expense and any other adjusting entries related to the vehicle on December 31, 2025.
5. Record the sale of the vehicle two years later on July 1, 2027, for $10,000.

The Great Adventures continuing problem also can be assigned using the General Ledger software in Connect. Students will be given an existing trial balance and asked to prepare (1) the journal entries for the transactions in 2025, (2) financial statements, and (3) closing entries.

Financial Analysis
Continuing Case

American Eagle Outfitters, Inc.

RWP7–2 Financial information for **American Eagle** is presented in **Appendix A** at the end of the book.

Required:

1. The summary of significant accounting policies is located in note 2 to the financial statements. Locate the section on property and equipment. What depreciation method does American Eagle use? What are the estimated useful lives for buildings and for fixtures and equipment?
2. Find note 7 for Property and Equipment. What are the cost and the book value of property and equipment for the most recent year? What is the trend in depreciation expense for the past three years?
3. Find note 8 for Intangible Assets. What intangible asset is listed? What are listed as the cost and the book value of intangible assets for the most recent year? What is the trend in amortization expense for the past three years?

Financial Analysis
Continuing Case

The Buckle, Inc.

RWP7–3 Financial information for **Buckle** is presented in **Appendix B** at the end of the book.

Required:

1. The summary of significant accounting policies is located in note A to the financial statements. Locate the section on property and equipment. What depreciation method does Buckle use? What are the estimated useful lives for property and equipment? What are the estimated useful lives for buildings?
2. Find note D entitled Property and Equipment. What is the cost of property and equipment for the most recent year? What is the trend in property and equipment for the past two years?
3. From the balance sheet, what three other types of long-term assets are listed?

Comparative Analysis
Continuing Case

American Eagle Outfitters, Inc. vs. The Buckle, Inc.

RWP7–4 Financial information for **American Eagle** is presented in **Appendix A** at the end of the book, and financial information for **Buckle** is presented in **Appendix B** at the end of the book.

Required:

1. Calculate American Eagle's return on assets, profit margin, and asset turnover ratio for the most recent year.
2. Calculate Buckle's return on assets, profit margin, and asset turnover ratio for the most recent year.
3. Which company is doing better based on return on assets? Which company has the higher profit margin? Which company has the higher asset turnover?

EDGAR Research

RWP7–5 Using EDGAR (Electronic Data Gathering, Analysis, and Retrieval system), find the annual report (10-K) for **Facebook** for the year ended **December 31, 2019.** Locate the "Consolidated Statements of Income" (income statement) and "Consolidated Balance Sheets." You may also find the annual report at the company's website.

Required:

1. What is the net balance in property and equipment in the most recent year?
2. What are the amounts reported for (a) goodwill and (b) intangible assets net?
3. What are the balances of (a) gross property and equipment and (b) accumulated depreciation? (*Hint:* These are in a note about property and equipment.)
4. Which method of depreciation is used? (*Hint:* Look in the Summary of Significant Accounting Policies for the note on Property and Equipment.)
5. Calculate the profit margin ratio for the current year and last year. Is the company's profitability increasing or decreasing?

Ethics

RWP7–6 Companies often are under pressure to meet or beat Wall Street earnings projections in order to increase stock prices and also to increase the value of stock options. Such pressure may cause some managers to alter their estimates for depreciation to artificially create desired results.

Required:

1. Understand the reporting effect: Do estimates by management affect the amount of depreciation in its company's financial statements?
2. Specify the options: To increase earnings in the initial years following the purchase of a depreciable asset, would management (a) choose straight-line or double-declining balance, (b) estimate a longer or shorter service life, and (c) estimate a higher or lower residual value?
3. Identify the impact: Are decisions of investors and creditors affected by accounting estimates?
4. Make a decision: Should a company alter depreciation estimates for the sole purpose of meeting expectations of Wall Street analysts?

Written Communication

RWP7–7 At a recent luncheon, you were seated next to Mr. Fogle, the president of a local company that manufactures food processors. He heard you were in a financial accounting class and asked:

> "Why is it that I'm forced to record depreciation expense on my property when I could sell it for more than I originally paid? I thought that the purpose of the balance sheet is to reflect the value of my business and that the purpose of the income statement is to report the net change in value or wealth of a company. It just doesn't make sense to penalize my profits when the building hasn't lost any value."

At the conclusion of the luncheon, you promised to send him a short explanation of the rationale for current depreciation practices.

Required:

Prepare a memo to Mr. Fogle. Explain the accounting concept of depreciation and contrast this with the dictionary definition of depreciation.

Earnings Management

RWP7–8 Edward L. Vincent is CFO of Energy Resources, Inc. The company specializes in the exploration and development of natural gas. It's near year-end, and Edward is feeling terrific. Natural gas prices have risen throughout the year, and Energy Resources is set to report record-breaking performance that will greatly exceed analysts' expectations. However, during an executive meeting this morning, management agreed to "tone down" profits due to concerns that reporting excess profits could encourage additional government regulations in the industry, hindering future profitability.

At the beginning of the current year, the company purchased equipment for $4,200,000. The company's standard practice for equipment like this is to use straight-line depreciation over 12 years using an estimated residual value of $600,000. To address the issue discussed in the meeting, Edward is considering three options. Option 1: Adjust the estimated service life of the equipment from 12 years to 6 years. Option 2: Adjust estimated residual values on the equipment from $600,000 to $0. Option 3: Make both adjustments.

Required:

1. Calculate annual depreciation using the company's standard practice.
2. Calculate annual depreciation for each of the three options and state whether the option would increase or decrease net income.
3. Which option has the biggest effect on net income?

Answers to Chapter Framework Questions
1. a   2. b   3. c   4. d   5. b

Answers to Self-Study Questions
1. b   2. d   3. d   4. c   5. a   6. b   7. d   8. b   9. a   10. a   11. c   12. c   13. c   14. b   15. d

Current Liabilities

PART A: CURRENT LIABILITIES

- ■ **LO8–1** Distinguish between current and long-term liabilities.
- ■ **LO8–2** Account for notes payable and interest expense.
- ■ **LO8–3** Account for employee and employer payroll liabilities.
- ■ **LO8–4** Explain the accounting for other current liabilities.

PART B: CONTINGENCIES

- ■ **LO8–5** Apply the appropriate accounting treatment for contingencies.

ANALYSIS: LIQUIDITY ANALYSIS

- ■ **LO8–6** Assess liquidity using current liability ratios.

SELF-STUDY MATERIALS

- ■ Let's Review—Notes payable and interest (p. 401).
- ■ Let's Review—Deferred revenue (p. 407).
- ■ Let's Review—Liquidity analysis (p. 416).
- ■ Chapter Framework with questions and answers available (p. 419).
- ■ Key Points by Learning Objective (p. 420).
- ■ Glossary of Key Terms (p. 421).
- ■ Self-Study Questions with answers available (p. 422).
- ■ Videos including Concept Overview, Applying Excel, Let's Review, and Interactive Illustrations to demonstrate key topics (in Connect).

UNITED AIRLINES: A FUTURE UP IN THE AIR

You might think that airlines like American, Delta, or United are highly profitable, low-risk companies. Commercial airlines typically fly more than 40,000 flights each day. However, American, Delta, and United Airlines have all filed for bankruptcy over the years, and external factors such as COVID-19 represent significant operating risks to their ability to pay debts.

Companies must file for bankruptcy protection when they are no longer able to pay their liabilities as they become due. By carefully examining information in financial statements, investors and creditors can assess a company's profitability and its *liquidity*—its ability to pay currently maturing debt. Both profitability and liquidity help indicate a company's risk of filing for bankruptcy.

Feature Story

What are some of the current liabilities reported by companies in the airline industry? The airline industry is very labor-intensive, resulting in extensive payroll liabilities. Another substantial current liability for airlines is advance ticket sales. This liability, representing tickets sold for future flights, is in the billions of dollars for several major U.S. airlines. Airlines are also well known for their frequent-flyer programs. These programs have created liabilities for frequent-flyer incentives exceeding $100 million. Finally, a somewhat different type of liability airlines face is contingent liabilities. A *contingent liability* is a possible liability for which payment is contingent upon another event. An example is pending litigation. All of the major airlines report contingent liabilities related to unsettled litigation. With airlines incurring so many types of liabilities, it is no wonder many airlines have filed for bankruptcy.

In this chapter, we adopt an airline and travel theme in exploring current liabilities such as notes payable, payroll liabilities, deferred revenues, and contingent liabilities. At the end of the chapter, we compare liquidity ratios between United Airlines and American Airlines to explore whether United or American is in a better position to pay its current liabilities as they come due.

Philip Lange/Shutterstock

PART A

■ **LO8–1**
Distinguish between current and long-term liabilities.

CURRENT LIABILITIES

In the four preceding chapters, we worked our way down the asset side of the balance sheet, examining cash, accounts receivable, inventory, and long-term assets. We now turn to the other half of the balance sheet. In these next three chapters, we look at current liabilities (Chapter 8), long-term liabilities (Chapter 9), and stockholders' equity (Chapter 10).

A liability is an obligation of a company to transfer some economic benefit in the future. Most liabilities require the payment of cash in the future. For instance, accounts payable, notes payable, and salaries payable usually are paid in cash. Other liabilities, such as deferred revenue, arise when a company receives cash in advance from customers. These liabilities represent an obligation of the company to transfer inventory or services to those customers in the future.

Current vs. Long-Term Classification

Common Terms Current liabilities are also sometimes called *short-term liabilities* or *short-term debt*.

In a classified balance sheet, we categorize liabilities as either current or long-term. **In most cases, current liabilities are payable within one year from the balance sheet date, and long-term liabilities are payable in more than one year.**

Current liabilities are *usually*, but not always, due within one year. If a company has an operating cycle longer than one year (a winery, for example), its current liabilities are defined by the operating cycle rather than by the length of a year. An *operating cycle* is the length of time from spending cash to provide goods and services to a customer until collection of cash from that customer. For now, remember that in most cases (but not all), current liabilities are due within one year.

Distinguishing between current and long-term liabilities is important in helping investors and creditors assess risk. Given a choice, most companies would prefer to report a liability as long-term rather than current, because doing so may cause the company to appear less risky. In turn, less-risky companies may enjoy lower interest rates on borrowing and command higher stock prices for new stock listings.

The Feature Story at the beginning of this chapter pointed out that the U.S. airline industry has experienced financial difficulties over the years, resulting in greater risk to investors. Several major airlines were forced into bankruptcy because they were unable to pay current liabilities as they became due. In Illustration 8–1, an excerpt from the annual report of **United Airlines** discusses some of the risk factors faced by the airline industry.

What obligations do companies most frequently report as current liabilities? Notes payable, accounts payable, and payroll liabilities are three main categories. In addition, companies report a variety of other current liabilities, including deferred revenue, sales tax payable, and the current portion of long-term debt.

There is no prescribed order for presenting accounts within the current liabilities section of the balance sheet. Illustration 8–2 presents the current liabilities section for **Southwest Airlines**.

For a company like Southwest Airlines, accounts payable and accrued liabilities consist of amounts owed for items such as employee compensation, taxes, airplane maintenance, and fuel. Air traffic liability is a liability recorded when tickets are first sold (deferred revenue). Southwest Airlines owes the customer a service until that flight is provided. Long-term debt is sometimes referred to as a note. When a note (or a portion of a long-term note) becomes due in the next year, the amount due is classified as a current liability.

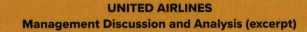

UNITED AIRLINES
Management Discussion and Analysis (excerpt)

The global pandemic resulting from a novel strain of coronavirus has had an adverse impact that has been material to the Company's business, operating results, financial condition, and liquidity, and the duration and spread of the pandemic could result in additional adverse impacts. The outbreak of another disease or similar public health threat in the future could also have an adverse effect on the Company's business, operating results, financial condition, and liquidity.

  The Company has a significant amount of financial leverage from fixed obligations and intends to seek material amounts of additional financial liquidity in the short-term, and insufficient liquidity may have a material adverse effect on the Company's financial condition and business.

ILLUSTRATION 8–1

Risk Factors of United Airlines

SOUTHWEST AIRLINES
Balance Sheet (partial)
($ in millions)

Current liabilities:	
Accounts payable	$1,574
Accrued liabilities	1,749
Current operating lease liabilities	353
Air traffic liability	4,457
Current maturities of long-term debt	819
Total current liabilities	$8,952

ILLUSTRATION 8–2

Current Liabilities Section for Southwest Airlines

KEY POINT

In most cases, current liabilities are payable within one year from the balance sheet date, and long-term liabilities are payable in more than one year.

Notes Payable

When a company borrows cash from a bank, the bank requires the company to sign a note promising to repay the amount borrowed plus interest. The borrower reports its liability as notes payable. About two-thirds of bank loans are short-term. Companies often use short-term debt because it usually offers lower interest rates than does long-term debt, because the risk of default is lower with loans of shorter durations.

■ **LO8–2**
Account for notes payable and interest expense.

Example. Assume Southwest Airlines borrows $100,000 from Bank of America on September 1, 2024, signing a 6%, six-month note for the amount borrowed plus accrued interest due six months later on March 1, 2025. On September 1, 2024, Southwest will receive $100,000 in cash and record the following:

September 1, 2024	Debit	Credit
Cash..	100,000	
Notes Payable...		100,000
(*Issue note payable*)		

Income Statement			
R	− E	=	NI
No Effect			

Balance Sheet			
A	=	L	+ SE
+100,000		+100,000	
Cash		Notes Pay.	

When a company borrows money, it pays the lender **interest** in return for using the lender's money during the term of the loan. Interest is stated in terms of an annual percentage rate to be applied to the face value of the loan. Because the stated interest rate is an *annual* rate, when calculating interest for a current note payable, we must adjust for the fraction of the year the loan spans. We calculate interest on notes as

$$\text{Interest} = \frac{\text{Face}}{\text{value}} \times \frac{\text{Annual}}{\text{interest rate}} \times \frac{\text{Fraction}}{\text{of the year}}$$

In the example above, how much interest cost does Southwest incur for the six-month period of the note from September 1, 2024, to March 1, 2025?

$$\$3,000 = \$100,000 \times 6\% \times 6/12$$

However, if Southwest's reporting period ends on December 31, 2024, then the company should not wait until March 1, 2025, to record interest cost. Instead, the company reports the four months' interest incurred during 2024 (September, October, November, and December) in its 2024 financial statements. The remaining $1,000 of interest (for January and February) will be reported in its 2025 financial statements. In addition, because the company will not pay the 2024 interest until the note becomes due next year (March 1, 2025), the 2024 financial statements need to report the four months of **interest payable** as of December 31, 2024. The adjusting entry to record interest is:

Income Statement

R	–	E	=	NI
		+2,000		−2,000
		Interest Exp.		

Balance Sheet

A	=	L	+	SE
		+2,000		−2,000
		Interest Pay.		

December 31, 2024	Debit	Credit
Interest Expense (= $100,000 × 6% × 4/12)	2,000	
Interest Payable		2,000
(*Record interest incurred, but not paid*)		

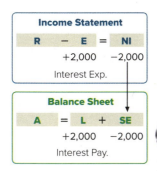 **COMMON MISTAKE**

When calculating the number of months of interest, students sometimes mistakenly subtract December (month 12) from September (month 9) and get three months. However, the time from September 1 to December 31 includes both September and December, so there are four months.

When the note comes due on March 1, 2025, Southwest Airlines will pay the face value of the loan ($100,000) plus the entire $3,000 interest incurred ($100,000 × 6% × 6/12). The $3,000 represents six months of interest—the four months of interest ($2,000) in 2024 previously recorded as interest payable and two months of interest ($1,000) in 2025. Southwest records the repayment of the note and interest as follows:

Income Statement

R	–	E	=	NI
		+1,000		−1,000
		Interest Exp.		

Balance Sheet

A	=	L	+	SE
−103,000		−100,000		−1,000
Cash		Notes Pay.		
		−2,000		
		Interest Pay.		

March 1, 2025	Debit	Credit
Notes Payable (face value)	100,000	
Interest Payable (from 2024)	2,000	
Interest Expense (= $100,000 × 6% × 2/12)	1,000	
Cash		103,000
(*Pay note payable and interest*)		

The entry on March 1, 2025, does the following:

• Removes the note payable recorded on September 1, 2024 ($100,000).

- Removes the interest payable recorded in the December 31, 2024 adjusting entry ($2,000).
- Records interest expense for January and February 2025 ($1,000).
- Reduces cash for the total amount paid ($103,000).

Notice that we record interest expense incurred for four months in 2024 and two months in 2025 rather than recording all six months' interest expense in 2025 when we pay it.

 KEY POINT

We record interest expense in the period in which we *incur* it, rather than in the period in which we pay it.

Flip Side

How would the lender, Bank of America, record this note? For the bank, it's a **note receivable** rather than a note payable, and it generates **interest revenue** rather than interest expense. (You may want to review the discussion of notes receivable in Chapter 5.) The entries for Bank of America's loan are as follows:

September 1, 2024	Debit	Credit
Notes Receivable	100,000	
Cash		100,000
(Accept note receivable)		

Income Statement 2024

R	–	E	=	NI
+2,000				+2,000
Interest Rev.				

Balance Sheet 2024

A	=	L	+	SE
+100,000				+2,000
Notes Rec.				
−100,000				
Cash				
+2,000				
Interest Rec.				

December 31, 2024	Debit	Credit
Interest Receivable..	2,000	
Interest Revenue (= $100,000 × 6% × 4/12)............................		2,000
(Record interest earned, but not received)		

Income Statement 2025

R	–	E	=	NI
+1,000				+1,000
Interest Rev.				

March 1, 2025	Debit	Credit
Cash...	103,000	
Notes Receivable (face value)		100,000
Interest Receivable (from 2024)		2,000
Interest Revenue (= $100,000 × 6% × 2/12)............................		1,000
(Collect note receivable and interest)		

Balance Sheet 2025

A	=	L	+	SE
+103,000				+1,000
Cash				
−100,000				
Notes Rec.				
−2,000				
Interest Rec.				

Assume **Delta Airlines** borrows $500,000 from **Chase Bank** on November 1, 2024, signing a 9%, six-month note payable.

Let's Review

Required:

1. Record the issuance of the note payable.
2. Record the adjusting entry for interest payable on December 31, 2024.
3. Record the payment of the note and interest at maturity.

Solution:

1. Record the issuance of the note payable.

November 1, 2024	Debit	Credit
Cash...	500,000	
Notes Payable..		500,000
(Issue note payable)		

2. Record the adjusting entry for interest payable on December 31, 2024.

December 31, 2024	Debit	Credit
Interest Expense (= $500,000 × 9% × 2/12)	**7,500**	
Interest Payable		**7,500**
(Record interest incurred, but not paid)		

3. Record the payment of the note and interest at maturity.

May 1, 2025	Debit	Credit
Notes Payable	**500,000**	
Interest Payable (from 2024)	**7,500**	
Interest Expense (= $500,000 × 9% × 4/12)	**15,000**	
Cash		**522,500**
(Pay note payable and interest)		

Suggested Homework:
BE8–1, BE8–2;
E8–2, E8–3;
P8–2A&B

Many companies prearrange the terms of a note payable by establishing a line of credit with a bank. A **line of credit** is an informal agreement that permits a company to borrow up to a prearranged limit without having to follow formal loan procedures and prepare paperwork. Notes payable is recorded each time the company borrows money under the line of credit. However, no entry is made up front when the line of credit is first negotiated, since no money has yet been borrowed.

Decision Point

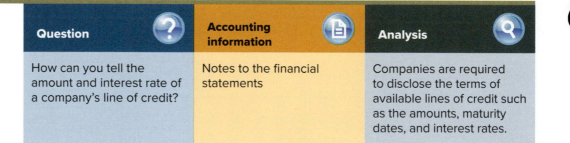

Question	Accounting information	Analysis
How can you tell the amount and interest rate of a company's line of credit?	Notes to the financial statements	Companies are required to disclose the terms of available lines of credit such as the amounts, maturity dates, and interest rates.

If a company borrows from another company rather than from a bank, the note is referred to as **commercial paper**. The recording for commercial paper is exactly the same as the recording for notes payable described earlier. Commercial paper is sold with maturities normally ranging from 30 to 270 days. Since a company is borrowing directly from another company, the interest rate on commercial paper is usually lower than on a bank loan. Because of this, commercial paper has thus become an increasingly popular way for large companies to raise funds.

 KEY POINT

Many short-term loans are arranged under an existing line of credit with a bank, or for larger corporations in the form of commercial paper, a loan from one company to another.

Accounts Payable

Accounts payable, sometimes called *trade accounts payable,* are amounts the company owes to suppliers of merchandise or services that it has bought on credit. We previously discussed accounts payable when we studied inventory purchases in Chapter 6. Briefly, recall that when a company purchases inventory on account (if it does not pay immediately with cash), it increases Inventory and Accounts Payable. Later, when the company pays the amount owed, it decreases both Cash and Accounts Payable. Most accounts are payable within one year and are therefore classified as current liabilities. Any accounts payable in more than one year would be classified as long-term liabilities.

Accounts payable are an attractive form of financing for companies because suppliers generally do not charge interest on the amount owed. Large retailers, such as **Target** and **Walmart**, rely heavily on this type of free supplier financing. In its recent balance sheet, Walmart reports accounts payable of approximately $47 billion, representing 33% of its total liabilities.

Payroll Liabilities

Many companies, including those in the airline industry, are very labor-intensive. Payroll liabilities make up a significant portion of current liabilities for these companies. Here, we will look at how payroll is calculated for both the employee and the employer.

Let's assume you are hired at a $60,000 annual salary with salary payments of $5,000 per month. Before making any spending plans, though, you need to realize that your paycheck will be much *less* than $5,000 a month. For instance, your employer will "withhold" amounts for (1) federal and state income taxes; (2) Social Security and Medicare; (3) health, dental, disability, and life insurance premiums; and (4) *employee* investments to retirement or savings plans. Realistically, then, your $5,000 monthly salary translates to much less in actual take-home pay, as summarized next.

■ LO8–3
Account for employee and employer payroll liabilities.

Monthly salary	$5,000
Less:	
Federal income taxes	(750)
State income taxes	(300)
Social Security and Medicare	(383)
Employee contributions for health insurance	(197)
Employee investments in retirement plan	(220)
= Actual take-home pay	$3,150

Now assume you hire an employee at a starting annual salary of $60,000. Your costs for this employee will be much *more* than $5,000 per month. Besides the $5,000 monthly salary, you will incur significant costs for (1) federal and state unemployment taxes; (2) the *employer* portion of Social Security and Medicare; (3) *employer* contributions for health, dental, disability, and life insurance; and (4) *employer* contributions to retirement or savings plans. With these additional costs, a $5,000 monthly salary could very easily create total costs in excess of $6,000 per month. Illustration 8–3 summarizes payroll costs for employees and employers. We discuss these costs next.

ILLUSTRATION 8–3
Payroll Costs for Employees and Employers

Employee Costs	Employer Costs
• Federal and state income taxes	• Federal and state unemployment taxes
• Employee portion of Social Security and Medicare (FICA taxes)	• Employer matching portion of Social Security and Medicare
• Employee contributions for health, dental, disability, and life insurance	• Employer contributions for health, dental, disability, and life insurance
• Employee investments in retirement or savings plans	• Employer contributions to retirement or savings plans

EMPLOYEE COSTS

Companies are required by law to withhold federal and state income taxes from employees' paychecks and remit these taxes to the government. The amount withheld varies according to the amount the employee earns and the number of exemptions the employee claims.

CAREER CORNER

When comparing compensation among different career opportunities, don't base your final decision on salary alone. Various employers offer *fringe benefits*—also called "perquisites" or "perks"—that catch the attention of would-be employees: a pound of coffee every month at Starbucks, free skiing for employees at Vail Ski Resort, or scuba and kayaking in the pool at Nike's Athletic Village in Beaverton, Oregon. More common fringe benefits include employer coverage of family health insurance, educational benefits, and contributions to retirement or savings plans.

However, even more important than either salary *or* benefits are the training and experience the position offers. Training and experience can provide you with the skills necessary to land that big promotion or dream job in the future.

Jim Arbogast/Photodisc/Getty Image

IRS Publication 15, also called Circular E, is a valuable tool for employers, answering important payroll tax withholding questions as well as providing the individual tax tables. If you are able to claim more exemptions, you will have less tax withheld from your paycheck. Not all states require the payment of personal income taxes: Alaska, Florida, Nevada, South Dakota, Texas, Washington, and Wyoming have no state income tax. Two others, New Hampshire and Tennessee, tax only dividend and interest income.

Employers also withhold Social Security and Medicare taxes from employees' paychecks. Collectively, Social Security and Medicare taxes are referred to as **FICA taxes**, named for the Federal Insurance Contributions Act (FICA). This act requires employers to withhold a 6.2% Social Security tax up to a maximum base amount plus a 1.45% Medicare tax with no maximum. Therefore, the total FICA tax is 7.65% (6.2% + 1.45%) on income up to a base amount ($142,800 in 2021) and 1.45% on all income earned. For example, if you earn less than $142,800, you will have 7.65% withheld from your check all year. However, if you earn, let's say, $192,800, you would have 7.65%

withheld for FICA on the first $142,800 of your annual salary and then only 1.45% withheld on the remaining $50,000 earned during the rest of the year.[1]

Besides the required deductions for income tax and FICA taxes, employees may opt to have additional amounts withheld from their paychecks. These might include the employee portion of insurance premiums, employee investments in retirement or savings plans, and contributions to charitable organizations such as **United Way**. The employer records the amounts deducted from employee payroll as liabilities until it pays them to the appropriate organizations.

EMPLOYER COSTS

By law, the employer pays matching FICA tax on behalf of the employee. The employer's limits on FICA tax are the same as the employee's. Thus, the government actually collects 15.3% (7.65% employee + 7.65% employer) on each employee's salary.

In addition to FICA, the employer also must pay federal and state **unemployment taxes** on behalf of its employees. The *Federal Unemployment Tax Act* (FUTA) requires a tax of 6.2% on the first $7,000 earned by each employee. This amount is reduced by a 5.4% (maximum) credit for contributions to state unemployment programs, so the net federal rate often is 0.8%. Under the *State Unemployment Tax Act* (SUTA), in many states the maximum state unemployment tax rate is 5.4%, but many companies pay a lower rate based on past employment history.[2]

 COMMON MISTAKE

Many people think FICA taxes are paid only by the employee. The employer is required to match the amount withheld for each employee, effectively doubling the amount paid into Social Security.

---

[1]High-income earners pay an additional 0.9% for Medicare taxes above a certain income threshold. The threshold for this additional amount depends on the taxpayer's filing status. This additional amount is not matched by the employer.

[2]Employers also pay workers' comp (workers' compensation), a form of insurance providing wage replacement and medical benefits to employees injured on the job. Workers' comp is recorded as Insurance Expense. In three states (Alaska, New Jersey, and Pennsylvania), state unemployment tax is also paid by employees.

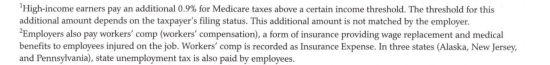

Additional employee benefits paid for by the employer are referred to as **fringe benefits**. Employers often pay all or part of employees' insurance premiums and make contributions to retirement or savings plans. Many companies provide additional fringe benefits specific to the company or the industry. For instance, a fringe benefit in the airline industry is free flights for employees and their families. Some fringe benefits, like free skiing for employees of a ski resort, are usually not recorded in the accounting records.

Example. To understand how employee and employer payroll costs are recorded, assume that Hawaiian Travel Agency has a total payroll for the month of January of $100,000 for its 20 employees. Its withholdings and payroll taxes are shown in Illustration 8–4.

Federal and state income tax withheld	$24,000
FICA tax rate (Social Security and Medicare)	7.65%
Health insurance premiums (Blue Cross) paid by employer	$ 5,000
Contribution to retirement plan (Fidelity) paid by employer	$10,000
Federal and state unemployment tax rate	6.2%

ILLUSTRATION 8–4

Payroll Example, Hawaiian Travel Agency

Hawaiian Travel Agency records the *employee* salary expense, withholdings, and salaries payable on January 31 as follows:

January 31	Debit	Credit
Salaries Expense	**100,000**	
Employee Income Tax Payable		**24,000**
FICA Tax Payable (= 0.0765 × $100,000)		**7,650**
Salaries Payable (to employees)		**68,350**
(Record employee salary expense and withholdings)		

Income Statement

R	−	E	=	NI
+100,000				−128,850
Salaries Exp.				
+15,000				
Salaries Exp.				
+13,850				
Pay Tax Exp.				

Hawaiian Travel Agency also records its employer-provided fringe benefits as Salaries Expense and records the related credit balances to Fringe Benefits Payable:

January 31	Debit	Credit
Salaries Expense (fringe benefits)	**15,000**	
Fringe Benefits Payable (to Blue Cross)		**5,000**
Fringe Benefits Payable (to Fidelity)		**10,000**
(Record employer-provided fringe benefits)		

Balance Sheet

A	=	L	+	SE
+24,000				−128,850
Empl. IT Pay				
+7,650				
FICA Pay				
+68,350				
Salaries Pay				
+5,000				
Fringe Pay				
+10,000				
Fringe Pay				
+7,650				
FICA Pay				
+6,200				
Unempl. Pay				

Hawaiian Travel Agency pays employer's FICA taxes at the same rate that the employees pay (7.65%) and also pays unemployment taxes at the rate of 6.2%. The agency records its *employer's* payroll taxes as follows:

December 31	Debit	Credit
Payroll Tax Expense (total)	**13,850**	
FICA Tax Payable (= 0.0765 × $100,000)		**7,650**
Unemployment Tax Payable (= 0.062 × $100,000)		**6,200**
(Record employer payroll taxes)		

Hawaiian Travel Agency incurred an additional $28,850 in expenses ($15,000 for fringe benefits plus $13,850 for employer payroll taxes) beyond the $100,000 salary expense. Also notice that the FICA tax payable in the *employee* withholding is the same amount recorded for *employer* payroll tax. That's because the employee pays 7.65% and the employer matches this amount with an additional 7.65%. The amounts withheld are then transferred at regular intervals, monthly or quarterly, to their designated recipients. Income taxes, FICA taxes, and unemployment taxes are transferred to various government agencies, and fringe benefits are paid to the company's contractual suppliers.

 KEY POINT

> Employee salaries are reduced by withholdings for federal and state income taxes, FICA taxes, and the employee portion of insurance and retirement contributions. The employer, too, incurs additional payroll expenses for unemployment taxes, the employer portion of FICA taxes, and employer insurance and retirement contributions.

Other Current Liabilities

■ LO8–4
Explain the accounting for other current liabilities.

Additional current liabilities companies might report include deferred revenues, sales tax payable, and the current portion of long-term debt. We explore each of these in more detail next.

DEFERRED REVENUES

United Airlines sells tickets and collects the cash price several days, weeks, or sometimes months before the actual flight. Do you think United Airlines records passenger revenue when it sells the ticket or when the flight actually takes place? Illustration 8–5 provides the answer in United's disclosure of its revenue recognition policies.

ILLUSTRATION 8–5
Revenue Recognition Policy of United Airlines

> **UNITED AIRLINES**
> **Notes to the Financial Statements (excerpt)**
>
> The Company presents Passenger revenue, Cargo revenue, and Other operating revenue on its income statement. **Passenger revenue is recognized when transportation is provided**, and Cargo revenue is recognized when shipments arrive at their destination. Other operating revenue is recognized as the related performance obligations are satisfied.

As you can see, United waits until the actual flight occurs to record passenger revenues. United's situation is not unique. It's not uncommon for companies to require advance payments from customers that will be applied to the purchase price when they deliver goods or provide services. You've likely been one of these customers. Examples of advance payments are gift cards from clothing stores like **American Eagle** or restaurants like **Chili's**, movie tickets from **Fandango**, room deposits at hotels like **Holiday Inn Express**, and subscriptions for magazines like *Sports Illustrated*. How do these companies account for the cash they receive in advance? We initially discussed deferred revenue in Chapter 3, but let's review with an example.

Example.   Assume **Apple Inc.** sells an iTunes gift card to a customer for $100. Apple records the sale of the gift card as follows:

Income Statement		
R	− E =	NI
No Effect		

Balance Sheet		
A	= L +	SE
+100	+100	
Cash	Def. Rev.	

	Debit	Credit
Cash..	100	
Deferred Revenue..		100
(Receive cash for gift card)		

As you can see, Apple records the receipt of cash, but does not credit Sales Revenue. Rather, since the music has not been downloaded yet, the company credits Deferred Revenue, a liability account. While it may seem unusual for an account called Deferred Revenue to be a liability, think of it this way: Having already collected the cash, the company now has the *obligation* to provide a good or service.

COMMON MISTAKE

Some students incorrectly think the Deferred Revenue account is a revenue account, since the account has the word "Revenue" in the title. As indicated above, Deferred Revenue is a liability account, not a revenue account.

When the customer purchases and downloads, say, $15 worth of music, Apple records the following:

	Debit	Credit
Deferred Revenue..	15	
Sales Revenue		15
(Record revenue from music downloaded)		

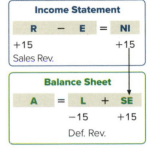

As the company provides music downloads, it decreases (debits) Deferred Revenue and increases (credits) Sales Revenue. The customer has a balance of $85 on his gift card, and Apple has a balance in Deferred Revenue, a liability account, of $85 for future music downloads.

Gift Card Breakage.   Some gift cards may expire, say, within one year after purchase, and others may have no expiration date. Companies reduce deferred revenue and recognize sales revenue when gift cards are redeemed by customers or when those gift cards are considered "broken." **Gift card breakage** refers to the point in time when gift cards expire or when the likelihood of redemption by customers is viewed as remote.

Record revenue for gift card breakage.

 KEY POINT

When a company receives cash in advance from customers, it debits Cash and credits Deferred Revenue, a current liability account. When the company provides those goods to its customers, it debits Deferred Revenue and credits Sales Revenue.

Let's Review

The **Dallas Cowboys** football stadium has a seating capacity of 80,000, expandable to 111,000 with standing-room-only capacity. The new stadium cost $1.15 billion, making it one of the most expensive sports stadiums ever built. The Cowboys hold eight regular season games at home; an average ticket sells for about $100 a game. Assume the Cowboys collect $48 million in season ticket sales prior to the beginning of the season. For eight home games, that's $6 million per game ($48 million ÷ 8 games).

Required:

1. Record the sale of $48 million in season tickets prior to the beginning of the season.
2. Record the $6 million in revenue recognized after the first game.

Solution:

1. Sale of $48 million in season ticket sales:

($ in millions)	Debit	Credit
Cash..	48	
Deferred Revenue...		48
(Sell season tickets prior to the beginning of the season)		

2. $6 million in revenue recognized after the first game:

($ in millions)	Debit	Credit
Deferred Revenue..	6	
Sales Revenue		6
(*Recognize revenue for each home game played*)		

Suggested Homework:
BE8–6, BE8–7;
E8–10, E8–11;
P8–5A&B

The Cowboys would make similar entries after each home game.

SALES TAX PAYABLE

Most states impose a state sales tax, and many areas include a local sales tax as well. Yet, some states do not have a sales tax, including Alaska, Delaware, Montana, New Hampshire, and Oregon. However, many cities in Alaska have local sales taxes. The other four states impose sales-type taxes on specific transactions such as lodging, tobacco, or gasoline sales.

Each company selling products subject to sales tax is responsible for collecting the sales tax directly from customers and periodically sending the sales taxes collected to the state and local governments. The selling company records sales revenue in one account and **sales tax payable** in another. **When the company collects the sales taxes, it increases (debits) Cash and increases (credits) Sales Tax Payable.**

COMMON MISTAKE

Some students want to debit Sales Tax Expense. Note that a Sales Tax Expense account does not even exist. That's because, while sales tax is an expense for the consumer, it is not an expense for the company selling the goods or service. For the company, sales taxes are simply additional cash collected for taxes owed to the local or state government.

Let's look at an example. Suppose you buy lunch in the airport for $15 plus 10% sales tax. The airport restaurant records the transaction this way:

Income Statement		
R – **E** = **NI**		
+15.00		+15.00
Sales Rev.		

Balance Sheet		
A = **L** + **SE**		
+16.50	+1.50	+15.00
Cash	Sales Tax Pay.	

	Debit	Credit
Cash..	16.50	
Sales Revenue		15.00
Sales Tax Payable (= $15 × 10%)		1.50
(*Record sales and sales tax*)		

When a company collects $16.50 from the customer, it owes $1.50 of that to the government for sales taxes. Only $15.00 represents revenue the company has generated from sales to customers.

The amount of sales tax can also be computed by knowing the total cash for the transaction and the sales tax rate. For example, when the cashier at the airport asked you to pay $16.50 for lunch, you could have figured the amount of the sale versus the amount of the sales taxes if you knew the sales tax rate was 10%. If we divide the total cash of $16.50 by 1.10 (1 + 10% sales tax rate), we get $15 (= $16.50 ÷ 1.10) for the actual sale, leaving $1.50 as sales tax. In this situation, the general formula to determine sales tax can be stated as

$$\text{Sales tax} = \text{Total cash paid} - \frac{\text{Total cash paid}}{1 + \text{Sales tax rate}}$$

KEY POINT

Sales taxes collected from customers by the seller are not an expense. Instead, they represent current liabilities payable to the government.

CURRENT PORTION OF LONG-TERM DEBT

The **current portion of long-term debt** is the amount that will be paid within one year from the balance sheet date. Management needs to know this amount in order to budget the cash flow necessary to pay the current portion as it comes due. Investors and lenders also pay attention to current debt because it provides information about a company's bankruptcy risk.

Reclassification.   Long-term obligations (notes, mortgages, leases, bonds) are reclassified and reported as current liabilities when they become payable within the upcoming year (or operating cycle, if longer than a year). The reclassification is a simple entry made at the balance sheet date.

For example, suppose a company has a long-term note payable of $1,000,000. At the balance sheet date (December 31, 2024), the company determines that $200,000 of the note is due within the next 12 months (2025), while the remaining $800,000 is due in later periods (2026 and beyond). The company needs to reclassify $200,000 of the long-term note to current notes payable. We do that by decreasing the balance of long-term notes payable and increasing the balance of current notes payable.

December 31, 2024	Debit	Credit
Notes Payable (long-term)	200,000	
Notes Payable (current)		200,000
(Reclassify long-term portion of note as current)		

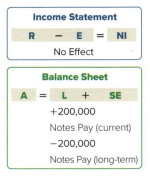

Income Statement

R	–	E	=	NI

No Effect

Balance Sheet

A	=	L	+	SE

+200,000
Notes Pay (current)
–200,000
Notes Pay (long-term)

The entry has no effect on total liabilities. Instead of reporting long-term notes payable of $1,000,000, the company will now report long-term notes payable of $800,000 and current notes payable of $200,000.

Southwest Airlines had total borrowings of $3,387 million. Of that amount, $566 million is due in the next year and the remaining $2,821 million is due in more than a year. In its balance sheet, the company reports these amounts separately, as shown in Illustration 8–6.

SOUTHWEST AIRLINES
Balance Sheet (partial)
($ in millions)

Current liabilities:	
Current maturities of long-term debt	$ 566
Long-term liabilities:	
Long-term debt less current maturities	2,821
Total borrowings	$3,387

ILLUSTRATION 8–6

Current Portion of Long-Term Debt

🔑 KEY POINT

We report the currently maturing portion of a long-term debt as a current liability in the balance sheet.

Decision Maker's Perspective

Current or Long-Term?

Given a choice, do you suppose management would prefer to report an obligation as a current liability or a long-term liability? Other things being equal, most managers would choose the long-term classification. The reason is that outsiders such as banks, bondholders, and shareholders usually consider debt that is due currently to be riskier than debt that is not due for some time. Riskier debt means paying higher interest rates for borrowing. So, be aware that management has incentives to report current obligations as long-term.

PART B

CONTINGENCIES

Many companies are involved in litigation disputes, in which the final outcome is uncertain. In its financial statements, does the company wait until the lawsuit is settled, or does it go ahead and report the details of the unsettled case? In this section, we discuss how to report these uncertain situations, which are broadly called **contingencies**. We look at contingent liabilities first and then their flip side, contingent gains.

Contingent Liabilities

A **contingent liability** is an existing uncertain situation that *might* result in a loss depending on the outcome of a future event. Examples include lawsuits, product warranties, environmental problems, and premium offers. **Philip Morris**'s tobacco litigation, **Motorola**'s cell phone warranties, **BP**'s environmental obligations, and **United**'s frequent-flyer program are all contingent liabilities. Let's consider a litigation example.

LITIGATION AND OTHER CAUSES

Deloitte was the auditor for a client we'll call Jeeps, Inc. The client sold accessories for jeeps, such as tops, lights, cargo carriers, and hitches. One of the major issues that appeared in Deloitte's audit of Jeeps, Inc., was outstanding litigation. Several lawsuits against the company alleged that the jeep top (made of vinyl) did not hold in a major collision. The jeep manufacturer, **Chrysler**, also was named in the lawsuits. The damages claimed were quite large, about $100 million. Although the company had litigation insurance, there was some question whether the insurance company could pay because the insurance carrier was undergoing financial difficulty. The auditor discussed the situation with the outside legal counsel representing Jeeps, Inc.

What, if anything, should the auditor require Jeeps, Inc., to report because of the litigation? The outcome of the litigation was not settled by the end of the year, so no amount is yet legally owed. There are three options to consider for Jeeps, Inc.

1. Report a liability in the balance sheet for the full $100 million (or perhaps some lesser amount that is more likely to be owed),
2. Do not report a liability in the balance sheet, but provide full disclosure of the litigation in a note to the financial statements, or
3. Do not report a liability in the balance sheet and provide no disclosure in a note.

The option we choose depends on (1) the likelihood of payment and (2) the ability to estimate the amount of payment. Illustration 8–7 provides details for each of these criteria.

ILLUSTRATION 8–7

Criteria for Reporting a Contingent Liability

1. **The likelihood of payment is**
   a. *Probable*—likely to occur;
   b. *Reasonably possible*—more than remote but less than probable; or
   c. *Remote*—the chance is slight.

2. **The amount of payment is**
   a. *Reasonably estimable;* or
   b. *Not reasonably estimable.*

A contingent liability is recorded only if a loss is probable *and* the amount is reasonably estimable. In the case of Jeeps, Inc., above, if the auditor believes it is probable that Jeeps, Inc., will lose the $100 million lawsuit at some point in the future, Jeeps, Inc., would report a contingent liability for $100 million at the end of the year.

December 31 ($ in millions)	Debit	Credit
Loss	100	
Contingent Liability		100
(*Record a contingent liability*)		

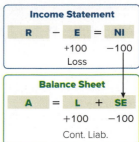

The loss is reported in the income statement as either an operating or a nonoperating expense. The contingent liability is reported in the balance sheet as either a current or a long-term liability depending on when management expects the probable loss to be paid.

If the likelihood of payment is probable and if one amount within a range appears more likely, we record that amount. When no amount within the range appears more likely than others, we record the *minimum* amount and disclose the range of potential loss.

If the likelihood of payment is only *reasonably possible* rather than probable, we record no entry but make full disclosure in a note to the financial statements to describe the contingency. Finally, if the likelihood of payment is *remote*, disclosure usually is not required. Illustration 8–8 provides a summary of the accounting for contingent liabilities.

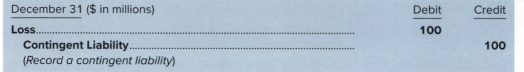

INTERNATIONAL FINANCIAL REPORTING STANDARDS (IFRS)

WHEN SHOULD CONTINGENT LIABILITIES BE REPORTED?

We record a contingent liability under U.S. GAAP if it's both probable and the amount is reasonably estimable. IFRS rules are similar, but the threshold is "more likely than not." This is a lower threshold than "probable," and thus, contingent liabilities are more likely to be recorded under IFRS rules than under U.S. GAAP.

For more discussion, see Appendix E.

	Amount of payment is:	
Likelihood of payment is:	*Reasonably Estimable*	*Not Reasonably Estimable*
Probable	Liability recorded	Disclosure required
Reasonably possible	Disclosure required	Disclosure required
Remote	Disclosure not required	Disclosure not required

ILLUSTRATION 8–8
Accounting Treatment of Contingent Liabilities

KEY POINT

A contingent liability is recorded only if a loss is **probable** *and* the amount is **reasonably estimable.**

Back to the example of Jeeps, Inc.: How do you think Deloitte, as the auditor of Jeeps, Inc., treated the litigation described earlier? Based on the response of legal counsel, the likelihood of the payment occurring was considered to be remote, so disclosure was not required. Although this additional disclosure may not be required, it still may prove useful to investors and creditors evaluating the financial stability of a company involved in litigation. Since the amount was so large, and because there were concerns about the company's primary insurance carrier undergoing financial difficulty, Deloitte insisted on full disclosure of the litigation in the notes to the financial statements.

Decision Point

Question	Accounting information	Analysis
Is the company involved in any litigation?	Notes to the financial statements	Companies are required to disclose all contingencies, including litigation, with at least a reasonable possibility of payment. This information can then be used to help estimate their potential financial impact.

Illustration 8–9 provides an excerpt from the disclosure of contingencies made by **United Airlines**.

ILLUSTRATION 8–9

Disclosure of Contingencies by United Airlines

UNITED AIRLINES
Notes to the Financial Statements (excerpt)

Legal and Environmental Contingencies. The Company has certain contingencies resulting from litigation and claims incident to the ordinary course of business. Management believes, after considering a number of factors, including (but not limited to) the information currently available, the views of legal counsel, the nature of contingencies to which the Company is subject and prior experience, that the ultimate disposition of the litigation and claims will not materially affect the Company's consolidated financial position or results of operations. The Company records liabilities for legal and environmental claims when a loss is probable and reasonably estimable. These amounts are recorded based on the Company's assessments of the likelihood of their eventual disposition.

WARRANTIES

Warranties are perhaps the most common example of contingent liabilities. When you buy a new **Dell** laptop, it comes with a warranty covering the hardware from defect for either a 90-day, one-year, or two-year period depending on the product. Dell offers such warranties to increase sales.

The warranty for the computer represents a liability for Dell at the time of the sale because it meets the criteria for recording a contingent liability.

1. **Probable.** Warranties almost always entail an eventual expenditure.
2. **Reasonably estimable.** Even though Dell doesn't know precisely what the warranty costs will be next year, it can formulate a reasonable prediction from past experiences, industry statistics, and other current business conditions.

Example. Suppose Dell introduces a new laptop computer in December 2024 that carries a one-year warranty against manufacturer's defects. Suppose new laptop sales for the entire month of December are $1.5 million. How much does Dell "owe" these customers? Even though no laptops are currently needing warranty work, Dell expects future warranty costs to be 3% of sales. This means the probable warranty cost in the next year is estimated to be $45,000 (= $1.5 million × 3%). This contingent liability is recorded in an adjusting entry at the end of 2024, the year of the sales:

December 31, 2024	Debit	Credit
Warranty Expense...	45,000	
Warranty Liability..		45,000
(Record liability for warranties) ($45,000 = $1.5 million × 3%)		

Income Statement

R	–	E	=	NI
		+45,000		–45,000
		Warr. Exp.		

Balance Sheet

A	=	L	+	SE
		+45,000		–45,000
		Warr. Liab.		

When customers make warranty claims and Dell incurs costs to satisfy those claims, the liability is reduced. Let's say that customers make warranty claims costing Dell $12,000 in January of 2025 (the following year). We record the payment for warranty work performed as follows:

January 31, 2025	Debit	Credit
Warranty Liability	12,000	
Cash		12,000
(Record actual warranty expenditures)		

Income Statement

R	–	E	=	NI
		No Effect		

Balance Sheet

A	=	L	+	SE
–12,000		–12,000		
Cash		Warr. Liab.		

The entry above assumes Dell pays for all warranty costs with cash to simplify the transaction. Companies may also use employee labor hours, inventory parts, or supplies in satisfying warranty claims. In that more complex case, we might credit Salaries Payable, Inventory, or Supplies rather than Cash.

The balance in the Warranty Liability account at the end of January is $33,000.

	Warranty Liability	
		45,000 → Estimated expense
Actual payment → 12,000		
		33,000 → Current balance

Because Dell provides a one-year warranty, any balance remaining in Warranty Liability will expire at the end of one year and can be written off. However, it's likely that Dell will have additional laptop sales in the following year, and those laptops also have a one-year warranty. Any remaining balance in Warranty Liability at the end of the year is adjusted for whatever amount is needed to equal Dell's new estimate of future warranty costs.

 COMMON MISTAKE

Some students think the balance in the Warranty Liability account is always equal to Warranty Expense. Remember, the Warranty Liability account is increased when the estimated warranty liability is recorded, but then is reduced over time by actual warranty expenditures.

Contingent Gains

A **contingent gain** is an existing uncertain situation that might result in a gain, which often is the flip side of contingent liabilities. In a pending lawsuit, one side—the defendant—faces a contingent liability, while the other side—the plaintiff—has a contingent gain. For example, **Polaroid** sued **Kodak** for patent infringement of its instant photography technology. Polaroid had a contingent gain, while Kodak faced a contingent loss.

Companies usually do not record contingent gains until the gain is known with certainty. This is different from contingent liabilities that are reported when the loss is *probable* and the amount is reasonably estimable. The nonparallel treatment of contingent gains and contingent losses reflects a general tendency toward conservatism in financial reporting through more timely recognition of losses.

Flip Side

ColorBlind Images/Blend Images/Getty Images

KEY POINT

Unlike contingent liabilities, contingent gains are not recorded until the gain is certain and no longer a contingency.

ANALYSIS

■ **LO8–6**
Assess liquidity using current liability ratios.

LIQUIDITY ANALYSIS
United Airlines vs. American Airlines

Liquidity refers to having sufficient cash (or other current assets convertible to cash in a relatively short time) to pay currently maturing debts. Because a lack of liquidity can result in financial difficulties or even bankruptcy, it is critical that managers, as well as outside investors and lenders, maintain a close watch on this aspect of a company's well being. Here we look at three liquidity measures: working capital, the current ratio, and the acid-test ratio. All three measures are calculated using current assets and current liabilities.

WORKING CAPITAL

The concept of working capital is straightforward. It is simply the difference between current assets and current liabilities.

$$\text{Working capital} = \text{Current assets} - \text{Current liabilities}$$

Working capital answers the question, "After paying our current obligations, how much in current assets will we have to work with?" For example, if you have $20 in your pocket and you know that you still owe $10 to your friend and $3 for parking, your working capital is $7. A large positive working capital is an indicator of liquidity—whether a company will be able to pay its current obligations on time.

However, working capital is not the best measure of liquidity when comparing one company with another, because it does not control for the relative size of each company. In comparing companies, the current ratio and the acid-test ratio are better measures of a company's ability to pay its obligations on time.

CURRENT RATIO

We calculate the current ratio by dividing current assets by current liabilities.

$$\text{Current ratio} = \frac{\text{Current assets}}{\text{Current liabilities}}$$

A current ratio greater than 1 indicates that there are more current assets than current liabilities. Recall that current assets include cash, current investments, accounts receivable, inventories, and prepaid expenses. A current ratio of, say, 1.5 indicates that for every $1 of current liabilities, the company has $1.50 of current assets.

In general, the higher the current ratio, the greater the company's liquidity. But we should evaluate the current ratio, like other ratios, in the context of the industry in which the company operates. Keep in mind, though, that not all current assets are equally liquid, which leads us to another, more specific ratio for measuring liquidity.

ETHICAL DILEMMA

Airport Accessories (AA) has several loans outstanding with a local bank. The loan contract contains an agreement that AA must maintain a current ratio of at least 0.90. Micah, the assistant controller, estimates that the year-end current assets and current liabilities will be $2,100,000 and $2,400,000, respectively. These estimates provide a current ratio of only 0.875. Violation of the debt agreement will increase AA's borrowing costs because the loans will be renegotiated at higher interest rates.

Litvinov/Shutterstock

Micah proposes that AA purchase inventory of $600,000 on credit before year-end. This will cause both current assets and current liabilities to increase by the same amount, but the current ratio will increase to 0.90. The extra $600,000 in inventory will be used over the next year. However, the purchase will cause warehousing costs and financing costs to increase.

Micah is concerned about the ethics of his proposal. What do you think?

ACID-TEST RATIO

The **acid-test ratio**, or *quick ratio,* is similar to the current ratio but is based on a more conservative measure of current assets available to pay current liabilities. We calculate it by dividing "quick assets" by current liabilities. **Quick assets** include only cash, current investments, and accounts receivable.

Common Terms The acid-test ratio is also called the *quick ratio.*

Because the numerator contains only a portion of the current assets used in the current ratio, the acid-test ratio will be smaller than the current ratio. By eliminating other current assets, such as inventory and prepaid expenses, that are less readily convertible into cash, the acid-test ratio may provide a better indication of a company's liquidity than does the current ratio.

$$\text{Acid-test ratio} = \frac{\text{Cash} + \text{Current investments} + \text{Accounts receivable}}{\text{Current liabilities}}$$

We interpret the acid-test ratio much like the current ratio, with one difference: We know that current assets in the numerator are only those that can be quickly converted to cash. Thus, an acid-test ratio of, say, 1.5 would indicate that for every $1 of current liabilities, the company has $1.50 of current assets that are easily convertible to cash that might be used to help pay the current liabilities as they come due. As is true for other ratios, be sure to evaluate the acid-test ratio in the context of the industry in which the company operates.

KEY POINT

Working capital is the difference between current assets and current liabilities. The current ratio is equal to current assets divided by current liabilities. The acid-test ratio is equal to quick assets (cash, current investments, and accounts receivable) divided by current liabilities. Each measures a company's liquidity, its ability to pay currently maturing debts.

Decision Point

Question	Accounting information	Analysis
Does the company have enough cash to pay current liabilities as they come due?	Working capital, current ratio, and acid-test ratio	A high working capital, current ratio, or acid-test ratio generally indicates the ability to pay current liabilities on a timely basis.

Many companies in the airline industry struggle to maintain adequate liquidity. United Airlines declared bankruptcy in 2002 and emerged from bankruptcy in 2006. Similarly, American Airlines declared bankruptcy in 2011 and came out of bankruptcy two years later in late 2013. The recovery by American Airlines has been remarkable. Their share price increased from around $25 per share when they first came out of bankruptcy in December 2013 to over $50 per share, just one year later.

Let's Review

Let's compare **United Airlines**' liquidity ratios to those of **American Airlines** and see if the recovery from bankruptcy of American Airlines is reflected in stronger liquidity ratios. Selected financial data regarding current assets and current liabilities for United and American Airlines are as follows:

($ in millions)	United	American
Current assets:		
Cash and cash equivalents	$2,756	$ 280
Current investments	2,182	3,704
Net receivables	1,364	1,750
Inventory	1,072	1,851
Other current assets	814	621
Total current assets	$8,188	$8,206

($ in millions)	United	American
Current liabilities:		
Current debt	$ 2,139	$ 2,861
Accounts payable	2,703	2,062
Salaries payable	2,271	1,541
Deferred revenue	7,259	8,001
Other current liabilities	571	3,846
Total current liabilities	$14,943	$18,311

Required:

1. Calculate and compare working capital for United Airlines and American Airlines.

2. Calculate the current ratio for United Airlines and American Airlines. Which company has a higher current ratio?

3. Calculate the acid-test (quick) ratio for United Airlines and American Airlines. Which company has a higher acid-test ratio?

Solution:

1. Working capital:

($ in millions)	Current Assets	–	Current Liabilities	=	Working Capital
United	$8,188	–	$14,943	=	$ (6,755)
American	$8,206	–	$18,311	=	$(10,105)

Both companies have a negative working capital, in which current liabilities exceed current assets. United has a smaller negative working capital of $6,755 million.

2. Current ratio:

($ in millions)	Current Assets	÷	Current Liabilities	=	Current Ratio
United	$8,188	÷	$14,943	=	0.55
American	$8,206	÷	$18,311	=	0.45

United has a higher current ratio, which would indicate better liquidity than American.

3. Acid-test (quick) ratio:

($ in millions)	Quick Assets	÷	Current Liabilities	=	Acid-Test Ratio
United	$6,302	÷	$14,943	=	0.42
American	$5,734	÷	$18,311	=	0.31

Remember that *quick assets* equal cash + current investments + net receivables.

By eliminating less-liquid current assets such as inventory and other current assets, the acid-test ratio often provides a better indicator of liquidity. Again, United has a higher acid-test ratio.

We should be careful to evaluate liquidity measures in the context of an industry. The airlines have faced tough times and many airlines have struggled to maintain adequate liquidity. So, while United's current ratio and acid-test ratio exceed those for American, the liquidity for both companies likely does not compare well with companies in most other industries.

Suggested Homework:
BE8–17, BE8–18;
E8–18;
P8–9A&B

Decision Maker's Perspective

Indicators of Liquidity

If the company's current ratio or acid-test ratio is lower than that of the industry as a whole, does that mean liquidity is a problem? Perhaps, but perhaps not. It does, though, raise a red flag that suggests caution when assessing other aspects of the company.

It's important to remember that each ratio is but one piece of the puzzle. For example, profitability is probably the best long-run indicator of liquidity. It is difficult to maintain liquidity over a string of consecutive loss years. Another consideration is that management may be very efficient in managing current assets so that some current assets—receivables or inventory—remain at minimum amounts. This is good for the company overall, but it may result in less-impressive current and acid-test ratios. The turnover ratios we discussed in Chapters 5 and 6, such as receivables turnover and inventory turnover, help measure the efficiency of asset management in this regard.

COMMON MISTAKE

As a general rule, a higher current ratio is better. However, a high current ratio is not always a positive signal. Companies having difficulty collecting receivables or holding excessive inventory will also have a higher current ratio. Managers must balance the incentive for strong liquidity (yielding a higher current ratio) with the need to minimize levels of receivables and inventory (yielding a lower current ratio).

Effect of Transactions on Liquidity Ratios

How are the ratios affected by changes in current assets? It depends on which current asset changes. Both ratios include cash, current investments, and accounts receivable. An increase in any of those will increase *both* ratios. However, only the current ratio includes inventory and other current assets. An increase in inventory or other current assets will increase the current ratio, but not the acid-test ratio.

What about changes in current liabilities? Current liabilities are in the bottom half of the fraction (the denominator) for both ratios. Therefore, an increase in current liabilities will decrease both ratios, since we are dividing by a larger amount. Illustration 8–10 summarizes the effect of changes in current assets and current liabilities on the liquidity ratios.

ILLUSTRATION 8–10

Effect of Various Changes on the Liquidity Ratios

	Changes that Increase the Ratio	Changes that Decrease the Ratio
Current Ratio	• Increase in current assets	• Decrease in current assets
	• Decrease in current liabilities	• Increase in current liabilities
Acid-Test Ratio	• Increase in quick assets	• Decrease in quick assets
	• Decrease in current liabilities	• Increase in current liabilities

LIQUIDITY MANAGEMENT

Can management influence the ratios that measure liquidity? Yes, at least to some extent. A company can influence the timing of inventory and accounts payable recognition by asking suppliers to change their delivery schedules. For instance, a large airplane manufacturer like Boeing might delay the shipment and billing of certain inventory parts to receive them in early January rather than late December, reducing inventory and accounts payable at year-end. It can also choose to make additional purchases in late December, increasing inventory and accounts payable at year-end. Let's see how changes in the delivery of inventory affect the current ratio.

Assume a company with a current ratio of 1.25 (current assets of $5 million and current liabilities of $4 million) has a *debt covenant* with its bank that requires a minimum current ratio exceeding 1.25. A **debt covenant** is an agreement between a borrower and a lender that requires certain minimum financial measures be met, or the lender can recall the debt. By delaying the receipt of $1 million in goods until early January, inventory and accounts payable would both be lower by $1 million than they would be without the delay. This, in turn, increases the current ratio to 1.33 (current assets of $4 million and current liabilities of $3 million), and the requirement of the debt covenant is met.

Now, let's look at what happens when the current ratio is less than 1.00. Assume the company has a current ratio of 0.75 (current assets of $3 million and current liabilities of $4 million) and has a *debt covenant* with its bank that requires a minimum current ratio exceeding 0.75. In this situation, delaying the delivery of $1 million decreases the current ratio even further to 0.67 (current assets of $2 million and current liabilities of $3 million).

Rather than delay delivery, the company could choose instead to purchase $1 million in additional inventory on credit. Then, inventory and accounts payable both increase by $1 million, raising the current ratio from 0.75 to 0.80 (current assets of $4 million and current liabilities of $5 million). This is what was proposed in the ethical dilemma presented earlier in the chapter. Investors and creditors should be aware of managerial activities that increase liquidity ratios, such as large fluctuations in inventory purchases near year-end or unusual variations in accounts payable balances.

CHAPTER FRAMEWORK

This chapter discusses the different types of current liabilities, those due in less than one year from the balance sheet date. Current liability transactions **during the year** and their related adjusting entries at the **end of the year** affect amounts reported in the financial statements.

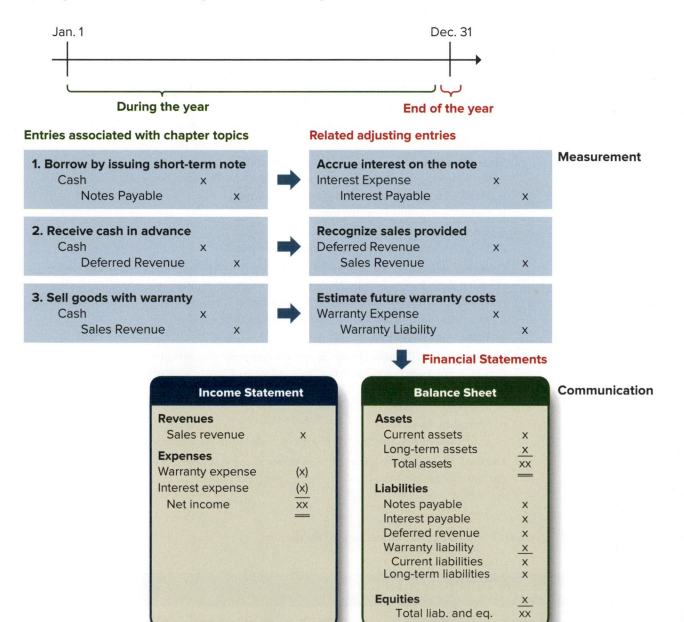

Entries associated with chapter topics	Related adjusting entries	
1. Borrow by issuing short-term note	**Accrue interest on the note**	Measurement
Cash x	Interest Expense x	
Notes Payable x	Interest Payable x	
2. Receive cash in advance	**Recognize sales provided**	
Cash x	Deferred Revenue x	
Deferred Revenue x	Sales Revenue x	
3. Sell goods with warranty	**Estimate future warranty costs**	
Cash x	Warranty Expense x	
Sales Revenue x	Warranty Liability x	

Financial Statements

Income Statement

Revenues	
Sales revenue	x
Expenses	
Warranty expense	(x)
Interest expense	(x)
Net income	xx

Balance Sheet   Communication

Assets	
Current assets	x
Long-term assets	x
Total assets	xx
Liabilities	
Notes payable	x
Interest payable	x
Deferred revenue	x
Warranty liability	x
Current liabilities	x
Long-term liabilities	x
Equities	x
Total liab. and eq.	xx

Analysis

$$\text{Current ratio} = \frac{\text{Current assets}}{\text{Current liabilities}}$$

A measure of a company's current liquidity risk (the risk of not being able to pay current obligations). The lower the current ratio, the higher a company's liquidity risk.

Decision Making

1. **Borrow by issuing short-term note.** During the year, a company borrows by issuing a note payable due in less than one year. At the end of the year, an adjusting entry is made to **accrue interest on the note** for the interest charged during the year.

2. **Receive cash in advance.** During the year, a company receives cash in advance from customers. This creates an obligation for the company to provide goods or services in the future. At the end of the year, an adjusting entry is made to **recognize sales provided** to customers who paid in advance.

3. **Sell goods with a warranty.** During the year, a company has sales to customers and offers a warranty (guarantee by the company on quality of product or service). At the end of the year, an adjusting entry is made to **estimate future warranty costs** related to sales in the current year.

Chapter Framework Questions

1. **Measurement (during the year):** During the year, a company receives cash in advance from customers for services to be provided in the future. Which of the following is recorded at the time cash is received?
   a. Service Revenue for the amount of services expected to be provided.
   b. Service Revenue for the amount of cash received.
   c. Deferred Revenue (a liability account) for the amount of cash received.
   d. No transaction is recorded until the services are actually provided.

2. **Measurement (end of the year):** At the end of the year, an adjusting entry is recorded for services provided to customers who paid in advance. The adjusting entry involves
   a. Debit Deferred Revenue; credit Service Revenue.
   b. Debit Cash; credit Deferred Revenue.
   c. Debit Cash; credit Service Revenue.
   d. Debit Service Revenue; credit Deferred Revenue.

3. **Communication (income statement):** Suppose a company sells inventory in the current year that includes a warranty. The company's estimate of future warranty costs will be reported in the income statement as an expense
   a. In a future year when the expense actually occurs.
   b. In the current year.

4. **Communication (balance sheet):** Suppose a company sells inventory in the current year that includes a warranty. The company's estimate of future warranty costs will be reported in the balance sheet as
   a. Warranty Liability.
   b. Warranty Asset.
   c. Estimated future warranty costs are not reported in the balance sheet.

5. **Decision Making (ratio analysis):** A company that has a higher risk of not being able to pay current obligations would have a _____ current ratio.
   a. Higher.
   b. Lower.

Note: For answers, see the last page of the chapter.

KEY POINTS BY LEARNING OBJECTIVE

LO8–1 Distinguish between current and long-term liabilities.

In most cases, current liabilities are payable within one year from the balance sheet date, and long-term liabilities are payable in more than one year.

LO8–2 Account for notes payable and interest expense.

We record interest expense in the period we incur it, rather than in the period in which we pay it.

Many short-term loans are arranged under an existing line of credit with a bank, or for larger corporations in the form of commercial paper, a loan from one company to another.

LO8–3 Account for employee and employer payroll liabilities.

Employee salaries are reduced by withholdings for federal and state income taxes, FICA taxes, and the employee portion of insurance and retirement contributions. The employer, too, incurs additional payroll expenses for unemployment taxes, the employer portion of FICA taxes, and employer insurance and retirement contributions.

LO8–4 Explain the accounting for other current liabilities.

When a company receives cash in advance from customers, it debits Cash and credits Deferred Revenue, a current liability account. When the company provides those goods to its customers, it debits Deferred Revenue and credits Sales Revenue.

Sales taxes collected from customers by the seller are not an expense. Instead, they represent current liabilities payable to the government.

We report the currently maturing portion of a long-term debt as a current liability in the balance sheet.

LO8–5 Apply the appropriate accounting treatment for contingencies.

A contingent liability is recorded only if a loss is **probable** *and* the amount is **reasonably estimable**.

Unlike contingent liabilities, contingent gains are not recorded until the gain is certain and no longer a contingency.

Analysis

LO8–6 Assess liquidity using current liability ratios.

Working capital is the difference between current assets and current liabilities. The current ratio is equal to current assets divided by current liabilities. The acid-test ratio is equal to quick assets (cash, short-term investments, and accounts receivable) divided by current liabilities. Each measures a company's liquidity, its ability to pay currently maturing obligations.

GLOSSARY

Acid-test ratio: Cash, current investments, and accounts receivable divided by current liabilities; measures the availability of liquid current assets to pay current liabilities. **p. 415**

Commercial paper: Borrowing from another company rather than from a bank. **p. 402**

Contingencies: Uncertain situations that can result in a gain or a loss for a company. **p. 410**

Contingent gain: An existing uncertain situation that might result in a gain. **p. 413**

Contingent liability: An existing uncertain situation that might result in a loss. **p. 410**

Current liabilities: Obligations that, in most cases, are due within one year from the balance sheet date. However, when a company has an operating cycle of longer than a year, its current liabilities are defined by the length of the operating cycle, rather than by the length of one year. **p. 398**

Current portion of long-term debt: Debt that will be paid within one year from the balance sheet date. **p. 409**

Current ratio: Current assets divided by current liabilities; measures the availability of current assets to pay current liabilities. **p. 414**

Debt covenant: An agreement between a borrower and a lender requiring certain minimum financial measures be met or the lender can recall the debt. **p. 418**

Deferred revenue: Cash received in advance from a customer for products or services to be provided in the future. **p. 406**

FICA taxes: Based on the Federal Insurance Contributions Act; tax withheld from employees' paychecks

and matched by employers for Social Security and Medicare. **p. 404**

Fringe benefits: Additional employee benefits paid for by the employer. **p. 405**

Gift card breakage: The point in time when gift cards expire or when the likelihood of redemption by customers is viewed as remote. **p. 407**

Liability: An obligation of a company to transfer some economic benefit in the future. **p. 398**

Line of credit: An informal agreement that permits a company to borrow up to a prearranged limit without having to follow formal loan procedures and prepare paperwork. **p. 402**

Liquidity: Having sufficient cash (or other assets convertible to cash in a relatively short time) to pay currently maturing debts. **p. 414**

Notes payable: Written promises to repay amounts borrowed plus interest. **p. 399**

Quick assets: Includes only cash, current investments, and accounts receivable. **p. 415**

Sales tax payable: Sales tax collected from customers by the seller, representing current liabilities payable to the government. **p. 408**

Unemployment taxes: A tax to cover federal and state unemployment costs paid by the employer on behalf of its employees. **p. 404**

Working capital: The difference between current assets and current liabilities. **p. 414**

SELF-STUDY QUESTIONS

1. Which of the following statements regarding liabilities is *not* true? **(LO8–1)**
   a. Liabilities can be for services rather than cash.
   b. Liabilities are reported in the balance sheet for almost every business.
   c. Liabilities result from future transactions.
   d. Liabilities represent probable future sacrifices of benefits.

2. Current liabilities **(LO8–1)**
   a. May include contingent liabilities.
   b. Include obligations payable within one year or one operating cycle, whichever is shorter.
   c. Can be satisfied only with the payment of cash.
   d. Are preferred by most companies over long-term liabilities.

3. Express Jet borrows $100 million on October 1, 2024, for one year at 6% interest. For what amount does Express Jet report interest payable for the year ended December 31, 2024? **(LO8–2)**
   a. $0.
   b. $4.5 million.
   c. $1.5 million.
   d. $6 million.

4. Express Jet borrows $100 million on October 1, 2024, for one year at 6% interest. For what amount does Express Jet report interest expense for the year ended December 31, 2025? **(LO8–2)**
   a. $0.
   b. $4.5 million.
   c. $1.5 million.
   d. $6 million.

5. We record interest expense on a note payable in the period in which **(LO8–2)**
   a. We pay cash for interest.
   b. We incur interest.
   c. We pay cash and incur interest.
   d. We pay cash or incur interest.

6. Which of the following is *not* deducted from an employee's salary? **(LO8–3)**
   a. FICA taxes.
   b. Unemployment taxes.
   c. Income taxes.
   d. Employee portion of insurance and retirement payments.

7. A local **Starbucks** sells gift cards of $10,000 during the year. By the end of the year, customers have redeemed $8,000 of gift cards. What will be the year-end balance in the Deferred Revenue account? **(LO8–4)**
   a. $0.
   b. $2,000.
   c. $8,000.
   d. $10,000.

8. The seller collects sales taxes from the customer at the time of sale and reports the sales taxes as **(LO8–4)**
   a. Sales tax expense.
   b. Sales tax revenue.
   c. Sales tax receivable.
   d. Sales tax payable.

9. The city of Summerton has a sales tax rate of 8%. A local convenience store sells merchandise, and the customer pays a total of $38.34. What effect does this transaction have on total liabilities? **(LO8–4)**
   a. Increase of $3.07.
   b. Decrease of $38.34.
   c. Increase of $2.84.
   d. No effect.

10. Management can estimate the amount of loss that will occur due to litigation against the company. If the likelihood of loss is reasonably possible, a contingent liability should be **(LO8–5)**
    a. Disclosed but not reported as a liability.
    b. Disclosed and reported as a liability.
    c. Neither disclosed nor reported as a liability.
    d. Reported as a liability but not disclosed.

11. Smith Co. filed suit against Western, Inc., seeking damages for patent infringement. Western's legal counsel believes it is probable that Western will have to pay an estimated amount in the range of $75,000 to $175,000, with all amounts in the range considered equally likely. How should Western report this litigation? **(LO8–5)**
    a. As a liability for $75,000 with disclosure of the range.
    b. As a liability for $125,000 with disclosure of the range.
    c. As a liability for $175,000 with disclosure of the range.
    d. As a disclosure only. No liability is reported.

12. Smith Co. filed suit against Western, Inc., seeking damages for patent infringement. Smith's legal counsel believes it is probable that Western will have to pay $125,000, although no final settlement has yet been reached. How should Smith report this litigation? **(LO8–5)**
    a. As an asset for $125,000.
    b. As a gain for $125,000.
    c. As both an asset and a gain for $125,000.
    d. No asset or gain is reported.

13. Pizza Shop sells toaster ovens with a one-year warranty to fix any defects. For the current year, 100 toaster ovens have been sold. By the end of the year four ovens have been fixed for an average of $80 each. Management estimates that five more of the 100 sold will need to be fixed next year for an estimated $80 each. For how much should Pizza Shop report warranty liability at the end of the current year? **(LO8–5)**
    a. $400.
    b. $320.
    c. $720.
    d. $0.

14. The acid-test ratio is **(LO8–6)**
    a. Current assets divided by current liabilities.
    b. Cash and current investments divided by current liabilities.
    c. Cash, current investments, and accounts receivable divided by current liabilities.
    d. Cash, current investments, accounts receivable, and inventory divided by current liabilities.

15. Assuming a current ratio of 1.00 and an acid-test ratio of 0.75, how will the purchase of inventory with cash affect each ratio? **(LO8–6)**
    a. Increase the current ratio and increase the acid-test ratio.
    b. No change to the current ratio and decrease the acid-test ratio.
    c. Decrease the current ratio and decrease the acid-test ratio.
    d. Increase the current ratio and decrease the acid-test ratio.

Note: For answers, see the last page of the chapter.

DATA ANALYTICS & EXCEL

Visit Connect to find a variety of Data Analytics questions that help build Excel, Tableau, and data visualization skills. Assignable materials include Integrated Excel, Applying Excel, Data Visualizations, Tableau Dashboard Activities, and Applying Tableau cases.

REVIEW QUESTIONS

1. What is the definition of a liability? ■ **LO8–1**

2. How do we define current liabilities? Long-term liabilities? ■ **LO8–1**

3. Why is it important to distinguish between current and long-term liabilities? ■ **LO8–1**

4. Provide examples of current liabilities in the airline industry. ■ **LO8–1**

5. Explain why we record interest in the period in which we incur it rather than in the period in which we pay it. ■ **LO8–2**

6. Bank loans often are arranged under existing lines of credit. What is a line of credit? How does a line of credit work? ■ **LO8–2**

7. How does commercial paper differ from a normal bank loan? Why is the interest rate often less for commercial paper? ■ **LO8–2**

8. Name at least four items withheld from employee payroll checks. Which deductions are required by law and which are voluntary? ■ **LO8–3**

9. Name at least four employer costs in addition to the employee's salary. Which costs are required by law and which are voluntary? ■ **LO8–3**

10. Who pays Social Security taxes: the employer, the employee, or both? How is the deduction for Social Security and Medicare (FICA) computed? ■ **LO8–3**

11. How do retailers like **McDonald's**, **American Eagle**, and **Apple Inc.** account for the sale of gift cards? ■ **LO8–4**

12. *Sports Illustrated* sells magazine subscriptions in advance of their distribution. (a) What journal entry would the company make at the time it sells subscriptions? (b) What journal entry would the company make each time it distributes a magazine? ■ **LO8–4**

13. Like all retailers, **Hollister** is required to collect sales tax to be remitted to state and local government authorities. Assume a local store has cash proceeds from sales of $5,325, including $325 in sales tax. What is the sales tax rate? Provide the journal entry to record the proceeds. ■ **LO8–4**

14. If $10 million of **Dell Inc.**'s $130 million notes payable is due in the next year, how will the company present this debt within the current and long-term liabilities sections of the current year's balance sheet? ■ **LO8–4**

15. Define contingent liability. Provide three common examples. ■ **LO8–5**

16. List and briefly describe the three categories of likelihood that a payment for a contingent liability will need to be made. ■ **LO8–5**

■ **LO8–5**   17. Under what circumstances should a company report a contingent liability?

■ **LO8–5**   18. Suppose the company's analysis of a contingent liability indicates that an obligation is not probable. What accounting treatment, if any, is warranted?

■ **LO8–5**   19. If a contingent liability is probable but estimable only within a range, what amount, if any, should the company report?

■ **LO8–5**   20. Your company is the plaintiff in a lawsuit. Legal counsel advises you that your eventual victory is inevitable. "You will be awarded $2 million," your attorney confidently asserts. Describe the appropriate accounting treatment.

■ **LO8–6**   21. Current liabilities affect a company's liquidity. What is liquidity, and how do we evaluate it?

■ **LO8–6**   22. Explain the differences among working capital, the current ratio, and the acid-test ratio.

■ **LO8–6**   23. How would the following transactions affect the current ratio and the acid-test ratio? (a) Purchase of inventory with cash; and (b) sale of inventory for more than its cost. Assume that prior to these transactions the current ratio and acid-test ratio are both less than one.

BRIEF EXERCISES

Record notes payable (LO8–2)
Flip Side of BE8–2

BE8–1 On November 1, Bahama Cruise Lines borrows $4 million and issues a six-month, 6% note payable. Interest is payable at maturity. Record the issuance of the note and the appropriate adjusting entry for interest owed by December 31, the end of the reporting period.

Record notes receivable (LO8–2)
Flip Side of BE8–1

BE8–2 On November 1, Bahama National Bank lends $4 million and accepts a six-month, 6% note receivable. Interest is due at maturity. Record the acceptance of the note and the appropriate adjusting entry for interest revenue at December 31, the end of the reporting period.

Determine interest expense (LO8–2)

BE8–3 On July 1, Alaskan Adventures issues a $160,000, eight-month, 6% note. Interest is payable at maturity. What is the amount of interest expense that the company would record in a year-end adjusting entry on December 31?

Record commercial paper (LO8–2)

BE8–4 On April 1, Online Travel issues $13 million of commercial paper with a maturity on December 31 and a 9% interest rate. Record the issuance of the commercial paper and its repayment at maturity.

Calculate FICA taxes (LO8–3)

BE8–5 Mike Samson is a college football coach making a base salary of $652,800 a year ($54,400 per month). Employers are required to withhold a 6.2% Social Security tax up to a maximum base amount and a 1.45% Medicare tax with no maximum. Assuming the FICA base amount is $142,800, compute how much will be withheld during the year for Coach Samson's Social Security and Medicare. What matching amount will the employer need to contribute?

Record deferred revenues (LO8–4)

BE8–6 On December 18, Intel receives $260,000 from a customer as down payment on a total sale of $2.6 million for computer chips to be completed on January 23. On January 23, the computer chips were delivered and the remaining cash was received from the customer. What journal entries should Intel record on December 18 and January 23? Assume Intel uses the perpetual inventory system, and the computer chips had a total production cost of $1.6 million.

Calculate gift card revenue (LO8–4)

BE8–7 On May 31, Marty's Ice Cream Shop sells gift cards for $5,000. Customers redeem $1,200 in June, $2,100 in July, and $1,400 in August. Marty's experience is that any unredeemed gift cards as of August 31 are not likely to be redeemed. Calculate the amount of gift card revenue each month.

Record sales tax (LO8–4)

BE8–8 During December, Far West Services makes a credit sale of $3,200 (before sales taxes). The state sales tax rate is 6% and the local sales tax rate is 2.5%. Record sales and sales tax payable.

Reclassify current portion of long-term debt (LO8–4)

BE8-9 On September 1, 2024, Southwest Airlines borrows $41 million, and records the full amount as Notes Payable (long-term). On December 31, 2024 (balance sheet date), Southwest determines $10 million of the note is due next year, while the remaining $31 million is due in two years. Record the entry to reclassify the current portion of long-term debt.

BE8–10 On September 1, 2024, **Southwest Airlines** borrows $41 million, of which $10 million is due next year. Show how Southwest Airlines would report the $41 million debt on its December 31, 2024, balance sheet.

BE8–11 **Sony** introduces a new compact music player that carries a two-year warranty against manufacturer's defects. Based on industry experience with similar product introductions, warranty costs are expected to be approximately 3% of sales. By the end of the first year of selling the product, total sales are $31 million, and actual warranty expenditures are $300,000. Record the adjusting entry for the remaining expected future warranty costs as of December 31, the end of the reporting period.

BE8–12 Consultants notify management of Discount Pharmaceuticals that a stroke medication poses a potential health hazard. Counsel indicates that a product recall is probable and is estimated to cost the company $8 million. Determine how the estimated cost of the product recall will affect the current financial statements.

BE8–13 Electronic Innovators is the defendant in a $10 million lawsuit filed by one of its customers, Aviation Systems. The litigation is in final appeal, and legal counsel advises that it is probable that Electronic Innovators will lose the lawsuit. The estimated amount is somewhere between $6 and $10 million. How should Electronic Innovators account for this event?

BE8–14 Aviation Systems is involved in a $10 million lawsuit filed against one of its suppliers, Electronic Innovators. The litigation is in final appeal, and legal counsel advises that it is probable that Aviation Systems will win the lawsuit and be awarded somewhere between $6 and $10 million. How should Aviation Systems account for this event?

BE8–15 The Environmental Protection Agency (EPA) is in the process of investigating a possible water contamination issue at the manufacturing facility of Northwest Forest Products. The EPA has not yet proposed a penalty assessment. Management feels an assessment is reasonably possible, and if an assessment is made, an unfavorable settlement is estimated to be $25 million. Determine how the estimated cost of the settlement will affect the current financial statements.

BE8–16 **Motorola** is a world leader in the development of cellular phone technology. During the year, the company becomes aware of potential costs due to (1) a product defect that is reasonably possible and is reasonably estimable, (2) a safety hazard that is probable and cannot be reasonably estimated, and (3) a new product warranty that is probable and can be reasonably estimated. Which of these potential costs, if any, should Motorola report?

BE8–17 Airline Accessories has the following current assets: cash, $112 million; receivables, $104 million; inventory, $192 million; and other current assets, $28 million. Airline Accessories has the following liabilities: accounts payable, $118 million; current portion of long-term debt, $45 million; and long-term debt, $33 million. Based on these amounts, calculate the current ratio and the acid-test ratio for Airline Accessories.

BE8–18 For each of the transactions below, determine the effect on (a) the current ratio and (b) the acid-test ratio.
1. Provide services to customers on account.
2. Borrow cash from the bank by signing a long-term note payable.
3. Purchase office supplies with cash.
4. Pay rent for the current period.

BE8–19 Refer to the information in BE8–1. Determine the financial statement effects of (1) the issuance of the note and (2) the adjusting entry for interest owed by December 31, the end of the reporting period.

BE8–20 Refer to the information in BE8–6. Determine the financial statement effects of (1) the collection of the down payment on December 18 and (2) the delivery of inventory and collection of remaining cash on January 23.

BE8–21 Refer to the information in BE8–8. Determine the financial statement effects of sales and sales tax payable.

BE8–22 Refer to the information in BE8–11. Determine the financial statement effects of accounting for expected future warranty costs.

Report current portion of long-term debt **(LO8–4)**

Record warranty liability **(LO8–5)**

Determine the financial statement effects of a contingent liability **(LO8–5)**

Account for a contingent liability **(LO8–5)**
Flip Side of BE8–14

Account for a contingent gain **(LO8–5)**
Flip Side of BE8–13

Determine the financial statement effects of a contingent liability **(LO8–5)**

Account for contingent liabilities **(LO8–5)**

Calculate current ratio and acid-test ratio **(LO8–6)**

Determine effect of transactions on liquidity ratios **(LO8–6)**

Determine financial statement effects of notes payable and interest **(LO8–2)**

Determine financial statement effects of deferred revenues **(LO8–4)**

Determine financial statement effects of sales tax **(LO8–4)**

Determine financial statement effects of warranties **(LO8–5)**

EXERCISES

Determine proper classification of liabilities (LO8–1)

E8–1 Match (by letter) the correct reporting method for each of the items listed below.

Reporting Method

C = Current liability
L = Long-term liability
D = Disclosure note only
N = Not reported

Item

_____   1. Accounts payable.
_____   2. Current portion of long-term debt.
_____   3. Sales tax collected from customers.
_____   4. Notes payable due next year.
_____   5. Notes payable due in two years.
_____   6. Advance payments from customers.
_____   7. Commercial paper.
_____   8. Unused line of credit.
_____   9. A contingent liability with a *probable* likelihood of occurring within the next year and can be estimated.
_____   10. A contingent liability with a *reasonably possible* likelihood of occurring within the next year and can be estimated.

Record notes payable (LO8–2)

E8–2 On November 1, 2024, Aviation Training Corp. borrows $60,000 cash from Community Savings and Loan. Aviation Training signs a three-month, 7% note payable. Interest is payable at maturity. Aviation's year-end is December 31.

Required:
1. Record the note payable by Aviation Training.
2. Record the appropriate adjusting entry for the note by Aviation Training on December 31, 2024.
3. Record the payment of the note at maturity.

Record notes payable (LO8–2)

Flip Side of E8–4

E8–3 On August 1, 2024, Trico Technologies, an aeronautic electronics company, borrows $21 million cash to expand operations. The loan is made by FirstBanc Corp. under a short-term line of credit arrangement. Trico signs a six-month, 9% promissory note. Interest is payable at maturity. Trico's year-end is December 31.

Required:
1. Record the issuance of the note by Trico Technologies.
2. Record the appropriate adjusting entry for the note by Trico on December 31, 2024.
3. Record the payment of the note by Trico at maturity.

Record notes receivable (LO8–2)

Flip Side of E8–3

E8–4 On August 1, 2024, Trico Technologies, an aeronautic electronics company, borrows $21 million cash to expand operations. The loan is made by FirstBanc Corp. under a short-term line of credit arrangement. Trico signs a six-month, 9% promissory note. Interest is payable at maturity. FirstBanc Corp.'s year-end is December 31.

Required:
1. Record the acceptance of the note by FirstBanc Corp.
2. Record the appropriate adjusting entry for the note by FirstBanc Corp. on December 31, 2024.
3. Record the receipt of cash by FirstBanc Corp. at maturity.

Determine interest expense (LO8–2)

E8–5 OS Environmental provides cost-effective solutions for managing regulatory requirements and environmental needs specific to the airline industry. Assume that on July 1 the company issues a one-year note for the amount of $6 million. Interest is payable at maturity.

Required:
Determine the amount of interest expense that should be reported in the year-end income statement under each of the following independent assumptions:

Interest Rate	Fiscal Year-End
1. 11%	December 31
2. 9%	September 30
3. 10%	October 31
4. 7%	January 31

E8–6 The following selected transactions relate to liabilities of Rocky Mountain Adventures. Rocky Mountain's fiscal year ends on December 31.

Record a line of credit (LO8–2)

January 13	Negotiate a revolving credit agreement with First Bank that can be renewed annually upon bank approval. The amount available under the line of credit is $10 million at the banks prime rate.
February 1	Arrange a three-month bank loan of $5 million with First Bank under the line of credit agreement. Interest at the prime rate of 7% is payable at maturity.
May 1	Pay the 7% note at maturity.

Required:
Record the appropriate entries, if any, on January 13, February 1, and May 1.

E8–7 Aspen Ski Resorts has 100 employees, each working 40 hours per week and earning $20 an hour. Although the company does not pay any health or retirement benefits, one of the perks of working at Aspen is that employees are allowed free skiing on their days off. Federal income taxes are withheld at 15% and state income taxes at 5%. FICA taxes are 7.65% of the first $128,400 earned per employee and 1.45% thereafter. Unemployment taxes are 6.2% of the first $7,000 earned per employee.

Calculate payroll withholdings and payroll taxes (LO8–3)

Required:
1. Compute the total salary expense, the total withholdings from employee salaries, and the actual direct deposit of payroll for the first week of January.
2. Compute the total payroll tax expense Aspen Ski Resorts will pay for the first week of January in addition to the total salary expense and employee withholdings calculated in *requirement* 1.
3. How should Aspen Ski Resorts account for the free skiing given to employees on their days off?

E8–8 During January, Luxury Cruise Lines incurs employee salaries of $3 million. Withholdings in January are $229,500 for the employee portion of FICA, and $667,500 for employee federal and state. The company incurs an additional $186,000 for federal and state unemployment tax and $90,000 for the employer portion of health insurance (fringe benefits payable to **Blue Cross Blue Shield**).

Record payroll (LO8–3)

Required:
1. Record the employee salary expense, withholdings, and salaries payable.
2. Record the employer-provided fringe benefits.
3. Record the employer payroll taxes.

E8–9 Airline Temporary Services (ATS) pays employees monthly. Payroll information is listed below for January, the first month of ATS's fiscal year. Assume that none of the employees exceeds the federal unemployment tax maximum salary of $7,000 in January.

Record payroll (LO8–3)

Salaries expense	$600,000
Federal and state income tax withheld	120,000
Federal unemployment tax rate	0.80%
State unemployment tax rate (after FUTA deduction)	5.40%
Social Security (FICA) tax rate	7.65%

Required:
Record salaries expense and payroll tax expense for the January pay period.

Analyze and record deferred revenues (LO8–4)

E8–10 Apple Inc. is one of the top online music retailers through its iTunes music store. Assume Apple sells $21 million in iTunes gift cards in November, and customers redeem $14 million of the gift cards in December.

Required:
1. Record the advance collection of $21 million for iTunes gift cards in November.
2. Record the revenue recognized when $14 million in gift cards is redeemed in December.
3. What is the ending balance in the Deferred Revenue account?

Record gift card transactions (LO8–4)

E8–11 Vail is one of the largest ski resorts in the United States. Suppose that on October 1, 2024, Vail sells gift cards (lift passes) for $100,000. The gift cards are redeemable for one day of skiing during the upcoming winter season. The gift cards expire on April 1, 2025. Customers redeem gift cards of $20,000 in December, $30,000 in January, $25,000 in February, and $15,000 in March.

Required:
1. Record the sale of gift cards on October 1, 2024.
2. Record the redemption of gift cards as of December 31, 2024.
3. Record the redemption of gift cards in 2025 by preparing a summary entry as of March 31, 2025.
4. Record the expiration (breakage) of gift cards on April 1, 2025.

Record notes payable and reclassify debt (LO8-2, 8-4)

E8-12 On September 1, 2024, Lindsey Engineering borrows $400,000 cash. The loan is made by FirstLending, under the agreement that Lindsey will repay the principal with four payments of $100,000. Payments are due by October 1 each year, with the first payment being due October 1, 2025 (next year). Interest on the borrowing is 6%, and Lindsey's year-end is December 31.

Required:
1. Record the long-term note payable by Lindsey Engineering.
2. Record the adjusting entry for interest on December 31, 2024.
3. Record the entry to reclassify the current portion of the note on December 31, 2024.

Analyze and record a contingent liability (LO8–5)

E8-13 Top Sound International designs and sells high-end stereo equipment for auto and home use. Engineers notified management in December 2024 of a circuit flaw in an amplifier that poses a potential fire hazard. Further investigation indicates that a product recall is probable, estimated to cost the company $4 million. The fiscal year ends on December 31.

Required:
1. Should this contingent liability be reported, disclosed in a note only, or neither? Explain.
2. What loss, if any, should Top Sound report in its 2024 income statement?
3. What liability, if any, should Top Sound report in its 2024 balance sheet?
4. What entry, if any, should be recorded?

Determine proper treatment of a contingent liability (LO8–5)

E8-14 Pacific Cruise Lines is a defendant in litigation involving a swimming accident on one of its three cruise ships.

Required:
For each of the following scenarios, determine the appropriate way to report the situation. Explain your reasoning and record any necessary entry.
1. The likelihood of a payment occurring is probable, and the estimated amount is $1.3 million.
2. The likelihood of a payment occurring is probable, and the amount is estimated to be in the range of $1.1 to $1.6 million.
3. The likelihood of a payment occurring is reasonably possible, and the estimated amount is $1.3 million.
4. The likelihood of a payment occurring is remote, while the estimated potential amount is $1.3 million.

Record warranties (LO8–5)

E8-15 Computer Wholesalers restores and resells notebook computers. It originally acquires the notebook computers from corporations upgrading their computer systems, and it backs each notebook it sells with a 90-day warranty against defects. Based on previous experience, Computer Wholesalers expects warranty costs to be approximately 6% of sales. Sales for the month of December are $600,000. Actual warranty expenditures in January of the following year were $13,000.

Required:

1. Does this situation represent a contingent liability? Why or why not?
2. Record warranty expense and warranty liability for the month of December based on 6% of sales.
3. Record the payment of the actual warranty expenditures of $13,000 in January of the following year.
4. What is the balance in the Warranty Liability account after the entries in *requirements* 2 and 3?

E8–16 Lindy Appliance begins operations in 2024 and offers a one-year warranty on all products sold. Total appliance sales in 2024 are $1,600,000, and Lindy estimates future warranty costs in 2025 to be 2% of current sales. Actual warranty costs in 2025 are $25,000. Also in 2025, Lindy has additional sales of $2,400,000 and revises its estimate of warranty costs associated with sales in 2025 to be 1.5%.

Record warranties over two years **(LO8–5)**

Required:

1. Record the adjusting entry for estimated warranty costs at the end of 2024.
2. Record the summary entry for actual warranty expenditures in 2025, assuming all costs were paid in cash.
3. Record the adjusting entry for estimated warranty costs at the end of 2025.
4. What is the balance in Warranty Liability at the end of 2024 and 2025?

E8–17 **Dow Chemical Company** provides chemical, plastic, and agricultural products and services to various consumer markets. The following excerpt is taken from the disclosure notes of Dow's annual report.

Analyze disclosure of contingent liabilities **(LO8–5)**

DOW CHEMICAL
Notes to the Financial Statements (excerpt)

Dow Chemical had accrued obligations of $381 million for environmental remediation and restoration costs, including $40 million for the remediation of Superfund sites. This is management's best estimate of the costs for remediation and restoration with respect to environmental matters for which the Company has accrued liabilities, although the ultimate cost with respect to these particular matters could range up to twice that amount. Inherent uncertainties exist in these estimates primarily due to unknown conditions, changing governmental regulations and legal standards regarding liability, and evolving technologies for handling site remediation and restoration.

Required:

1. Does the excerpt describe a contingent liability?
2. Under what conditions would Dow record such a contingency?
3. How did Dow record the $381 million?

E8–18 Selected financial data regarding current assets and current liabilities for Queen's Line, a competitor in the cruise line industry, is provided:

Calculate and analyze liquidity ratios **(LO8–6)**

($ in millions)	
Current assets:	
Cash and cash equivalents	$ 331
Current investments	63
Net receivables	230
Inventory	116
Other current assets	135
Total current assets	$ 875
Current liabilities:	
Accounts payable	$1,025
Short-term debt	694
Other current liabilities	919
Total current liabilities	$2,638

Required:

1. Calculate the current ratio and the acid-test ratio for Queen's Line.
2. Compare your calculations with those for United Airlines and American Airlines reported in the chapter text. Which company appears more likely to have difficulty paying its currently maturing debts?

Complete the accounting cycle using current liability transactions (LO 8-1, 8-2, 8-4, 8-6)

E8–19 On January 1, 2024, the general ledger of ACME Fireworks includes the following account balances:

Accounts	Debit	Credit
Cash	$ 25,100	
Accounts Receivable	46,200	
Allowance for Uncollectible Accounts		$ 4,200
Inventory	20,000	
Land	46,000	
Equipment	15,000	
Accumulated Depreciation		1,500
Accounts Payable		28,500
Notes Payable (6%, due April 1, 2025)		50,000
Common Stock		35,000
Retained Earnings		33,100
Totals	$152,300	$152,300

During January 2024, the following transactions occur:

January 2	Sold gift cards totaling $8,000. The cards are redeemable for merchandise within one year of the purchase date.
January 6	Purchase additional inventory on account, $147,000. ACME uses the perpetual inventory system.
January 15	Firework sales for the first half of the month total $135,000. All of these sales are on account. The cost of the units sold is $73,800.
January 23	Receive $125,400 from customers on accounts receivable.
January 25	Pay $90,000 to inventory suppliers on accounts payable.
January 28	Write off accounts receivable as uncollectible, $4,800.
January 30	Firework sales for the second half of the month total $143,000. Sales include $11,000 for cash and $132,000 on account. The cost of the units sold is $79,500.
January 31	Pay cash for monthly salaries, $52,000.

Required:

1. Record each of the transactions listed above.
2. Record adjusting entries on January 31.
    a. Depreciation on the equipment for the month of January is calculated using the straight-line method. At the time the equipment was purchased, the company estimated a residual value of $3,000 and a two-year service life.
    b. The company records an adjusting entry for $12,500 for estimated future uncollectible accounts.
    c. The company has accrued interest on notes payable for January.
    d. The company has accrued income taxes at the end of January of $13,000.
    e. By the end of January, $3,000 of the gift cards sold on January 2 have been redeemed (ignore cost of goods sold).
3. Prepare an adjusted trial balance as of January 31, 2024, after updating beginning balances (above) for transactions during January (*requirement* 1) and adjusting entries at the end of January (*requirement* 2).
4. Prepare a multiple-step income statement for the period ended January 31, 2024.
5. Prepare a classified balance sheet as of January 31, 2024.
6. Record closing entries.

7. Analyze the following for ACME Fireworks:
   a. Calculate the current ratio at the end of January. If the average current ratio for the industry is 1.8, is ACME Fireworks more or less liquid than the industry average?
   b. Calculate the acid-test ratio at the end of January. If the average acid-test ratio for the industry is 1.5, is ACME Fireworks more or less likely to have difficulty paying its currently maturing debts (compared to the industry average)?
   c. Assume the notes payable were due on April 1, 2024, rather than April 1, 2025. Calculate the revised current ratio at the end of January, and indicate whether the revised ratio would *increase, decrease,* or remain *unchanged* compared to your answer in (a).

PROBLEMS: SET A

Review current liability terms and concepts (LO8–1)

P8–1A Listed below are several terms and phrases associated with current liabilities. Pair each item from List A (by letter) with the item from List B that is most appropriately associated with it.

List A	List B
_____ 1. An IOU promising to repay the amount borrowed plus interest.	a. Recording of a contingent liability
_____ 2. Payment amount is reasonably possible and is reasonably estimable.	b. Deferred revenue
_____ 3. Mixture of liabilities and equity a business uses.	c. The riskiness of a business's obligations
_____ 4. Payment amount is probable and is reasonably estimable.	d. Disclosure of a contingent liability
_____ 5. A liability that requires the sacrifice of something other than cash.	e. Interest on debt
_____ 6. Long-term debt maturing within one year.	f. Payroll taxes
_____ 7. FICA and FUTA.	g. Line of credit
_____ 8. Informal agreement that permits a company to borrow up to a prearranged limit.	h. Capital structure
_____ 9. Classifying liabilities as either current or long-term helps investors and creditors assess this.	i. Note payable
_____ 10. Amount of note payable × annual interest rate × fraction of the year.	j. Current portion of long-term debt

Record notes payable and notes receivable (LO8–2)

P8–2A Precision Castparts, a manufacturer of processed engine parts in the automotive and airline industries, borrows $41 million cash on October 1, 2024, to provide working capital for anticipated expansion. Precision signs a one-year, 9% promissory note to Midwest Bank under a prearranged short-term line of credit. Interest on the note is payable at maturity. Each company has a December 31 year-end.

Required:
1. Prepare the journal entries on October 1, 2024, to record (a) the notes payable for Precision Castparts and (b) the notes receivable for Midwest Bank.
2. Record the adjusting entry on December 31, 2024, for (a) Precision Castparts and (b) Midwest Bank.
3. Prepare the journal entries on September 30, 2025, to record payment of (a) the notes payable for Precision Castparts and (b) the notes receivable for Midwest Bank.

Record payroll (LO8–3)

P8–3A Caribbean Tours' total payroll for the month of January was $600,000. The following withholdings, fringe benefits, and payroll taxes apply:

Federal and state income tax withheld	$60,000
Health insurance premiums paid by employer (payable to **Blue Cross**)	10,800
Contribution to retirement plan paid by employer (payable to **Fidelity**)	24,000
FICA tax rate (Social Security and Medicare)	7.65%
Federal and state unemployment tax rate	6.20%

Assume that none of the withholdings or payroll taxes has been paid by the end of January (record them as payables), and no employee's cumulative wages exceed the relevant wage bases.

Required:
1. Record the employee salary expense, withholdings, and salaries payable.
2. Record the employer-provided fringe benefits.
3. Record the employer payroll taxes.

Record payroll (LO8–3)

P8–4A Vacation Destinations offers its employees the option of contributing up to 7% of their salaries to a voluntary retirement plan, with the employer matching their contribution. The company also pays 100% of medical and life insurance premiums. Assume that no employee's cumulative wages exceed the relevant wage bases. Payroll information for the first biweekly payroll period ending February 14 is listed below.

Wages and salaries	$1,500,000
Employee contribution to voluntary retirement plan	63,000
Medical insurance premiums paid by employer	31,500
Life insurance premiums paid by employer	6,000
Federal and state income tax withheld	375,000
Social Security tax rate	6.20%
Medicare tax rate	1.45%
Federal and state unemployment tax rate	6.20%

Required:
1. Record the employee salary expense, withholdings, and salaries payable.
2. Record the employer-provided fringe benefits.
3. Record the employer payroll taxes.

Record deferred revenues (LO8–4)

P8–5A The University of Michigan football stadium, built in 1927, is one of the largest stadiums in America. Assume the university sells 100,000 season tickets to all six home games before the season begins, and the athletic department collects $102.6 million in ticket sales.

Required:
1. What is the average price per season ticket and average price per individual game ticket sold?
2. Record the advance collection of $102.6 million in ticket sales.
3. Record the revenue recognized after the first home game is completed.

Record deferred revenues and sales taxes (LO8–4)

P8–6A Texas Roadhouse opened a new restaurant in October. During its first three months of operation, the restaurant sold gift cards in various amounts totaling $3,500. The cards are redeemable for meals within one year of the purchase date. Gift cards totaling $728 were presented for redemption during the first three months of operation prior to year-end on December 31. The sales tax rate on restaurant sales is 4%, assessed at the time meals (not gift cards) are purchased. Texas Roadhouse will remit sales taxes in January.

Required:
1. Record (in summary form) the $3,500 in gift cards sold (keeping in mind that, in actuality, the company would record each sale of a gift card individually).
2. Record the $728 in gift cards redeemed. (*Hint:* The $728 includes a 4% sales tax of $28.)
3. Determine the balance in the Deferred Revenue account (remaining liability for gift cards) Texas Roadhouse will report on the December 31 balance sheet.

Record contingencies (LO8–5)

P8–7A The ink-jet printing division of Environmental Printing has grown tremendously in recent years. Assume the following transactions related to the ink-jet division occur during the year ended December 31, 2024.

Required:
Determine the appropriate way Environmental Printing would report the contingencies. Record any amounts as a result of each of these contingencies if required.

1. Environmental Printing is being sued for $11 million by Addamax. Plaintiff alleges that the defendants formed an unlawful joint venture and drove it out of business. The case is expected to go to trial later this year. The likelihood of payment is reasonably possible.
2. Environmental Printing is the plaintiff in an $9 million lawsuit filed against a competitor in the high-end color-printer market. Environmental Printing expects to win the case and be awarded between $6.5 and $9 million.
3. Environmental Printing recently became aware of a design flaw in one of its ink-jet printers. A product recall appears probable. Such an action would likely cost the company between $500,000 and $900,000.

P8–8A Dinoco Petroleum faces three potential contingency situations, described below. Dinoco's fiscal year ends December 31, 2024, and it issues its 2024 financial statements on March 15, 2025.

Record contingencies (LO8–5)

Required:
Determine the appropriate means of reporting each situation for the year ended December 31, 2024, and record any necessary entries. Explain your reasoning.
1. In the initial trial in October, Dinoco lost a $130 million lawsuit resulting from a dispute with a supplier. Although Dinoco feels it is probable it will have to pay the full amount, the case is under appeal at the end of the year. Dinoco does not expect the case to have a material adverse effect on the company.
2. In November 2023, the state of Texas filed suit against Dinoco, seeking civil penalties and injunctive relief for violations of environmental laws regulating hazardous waste. On January 12, 2025, Dinoco reached a settlement with state authorities. Based upon discussions with legal counsel, it is probable that Dinoco will require $150 million to cover the cost of violations.
3. Dinoco is the plaintiff in a $300 million lawsuit filed against a customer for damages due to lost profits from rejected contracts and for unpaid receivables. The case is in final appeal, and legal counsel advises that it is probable Dinoco will prevail and be awarded $150 million.

P8–9A Selected financial data regarding current assets and current liabilities for ACME Corporation and Wayne Enterprises, are as follows:

Calculate and analyze ratios (LO8–6)

($ in millions)	ACME Corporation	Wayne Enterprises
Current assets:		
Cash and cash equivalents	$ 2,494	$ 541
Current investments		125
Net receivables	1,395	217
Inventory	10,710	8,600
Other current assets	773	301
Total current assets	$15,372	$9,784
Current liabilities		
Current debt	$ 1,321	$ 47
Accounts payable	8,871	5,327
Other current liabilities	1,270	2,334
Total current liabilities	$11,462	$7,708

Required:
1. Calculate the current ratio for ACME Corporation and Wayne Enterprises. Which company has the more favorable ratio?
2. Calculate the acid-test (quick) ratio for ACME Corporation and Wayne Enterprises. Which company has the more favorable ratio?
3. How would the purchase of additional inventory on credit affect the current ratio? How would it affect the acid-test ratio?

PROBLEMS: SET B

Mc Graw Hill connect

Review current liability terms and concepts (LO8–1)

P8–1B Listed below are several terms and phrases associated with current liabilities. Pair each item from List A (by letter) with the item from List B that is most appropriately associated with it.

List A	List B
_____ 1. Interest expense is recorded in the period interest is incurred rather than in the period interest is paid.	a. The riskiness of a business's obligations
_____ 2. Payment is reasonably possible and is reasonably estimable.	b. Current portion of long-term debt
_____ 3. Cash, current investments, and accounts receivable all divided by current liabilities.	c. Recording a contingent liability
	d. Disclosure of a contingent liability
_____ 4. Payment is probable and is reasonably estimable.	e. Interest expense
_____ 5. Gift cards.	f. FICA
_____ 6. Long-term debt maturing within one year.	g. Commercial paper
_____ 7. Social Security and Medicare.	h. Acid-test ratio
_____ 8. Unsecured notes sold in minimum denominations of $25,000 with maturities up to 270 days.	i. Accrual accounting
	j. Deferred revenue
_____ 9. Classifying liabilities as either current or long-term helps investors and creditors assess this.	
_____ 10. Incurred on notes payable.	

Record notes payable and notes receivable (LO8–2)

P8–2B Eskimo Joe's, designer of the world's second best-selling T-shirt (just behind Hard Rock Cafe), borrows $21 million cash on November 1, 2024. Eskimo Joe's signs a six-month, 7% promissory note to Stillwater National Bank under a prearranged short-term line of credit. Interest on the note is payable at maturity. Each company has a December 31 year-end.

Required:
1. Prepare the journal entries on November 1, 2024, to record (a) the notes payable for Eskimo Joe's and (b) the notes receivable for Stillwater National Bank.
2. Record the adjusting entry on December 31, 2024, for (a) Eskimo Joe's and (b) Stillwater National Bank.
3. Prepare the journal entries on April 30, 2025, to record payment of (a) the notes payable for Eskimo Joe's and (b) the notes receivable for Stillwater National Bank.

Record payroll (LO8–3)

P8–3B Kashi Sales, L.L.C., produces healthy, whole-grain foods such as breakfast cereals, frozen dinners, and granola bars. Assume payroll for the month of January was $500,000 and the following withholdings, fringe benefits, and payroll taxes apply:

Federal and state income tax withheld	$135,000
Health insurance premiums (Blue Cross) paid by employer	13,000
Contribution to retirement plan (Fidelity) paid by employer	60,000
FICA tax rate (Social Security and Medicare)	7.65%
Federal and state unemployment tax rate	6.20%

Assume that Kashi has paid none of the withholdings or payroll taxes by the end of January (record them as payables), and no employee's cumulative wages exceed the relevant wage bases.

Required:
1. Record the employee salary expense, withholdings, and salaries payable.

2. Record the employer-provided fringe benefits.
3. Record the employer payroll taxes.

Record payroll (LO8–3)

P8–4B Emily Turnbull, president of Aerobic Equipment Corporation, is concerned about her employees' well-being. The company offers its employees free medical, dental, and life insurance coverage. It also matches employee contributions to a voluntary retirement plan up to 6% of their salaries. Assume that no employee's cumulative wages exceed the relevant wage bases. Payroll information for the biweekly payroll period ending January 24 is listed below.

Wages and salaries	$2,500,000
Employee contribution to voluntary retirement plan	125,000
Medical insurance premiums paid by employer	50,000
Dental insurance premiums paid by employer	17,500
Life insurance premiums paid by employer	8,750
Federal and state income tax withheld	537,500
FICA tax rate	7.65%
Federal and state unemployment tax rate	6.20%

Required:
1. Record the employee salary expense, withholdings, and salaries payable.
2. Record the employer-provided fringe benefits.
3. Record the employer payroll taxes.

Record deferred revenues (LO8–4)

P8–5B Named in honor of the late Dr. F. C. "Phog" Allen, the Kansas Jayhawks' head coach for 39 years, Allen Fieldhouse is labeled by many as one of the best places in America to watch a college basketball game. Allen Fieldhouse has a seating capacity of 16,300. Assume the basketball arena sells out all 16 home games before the season begins, and the athletic department collects $9,128,000 in ticket sales.

Required:
1. What is the average price per season ticket and average price per individual game ticket sold?
2. Record the advance collection of $9,128,000 in ticket sales.
3. Record the revenue recognized after the first home game is completed.

Record deferred revenues and sales taxes (LO8–4)

P8–6B Logan's Roadhouse opened a new restaurant in November. During its first two months of operation, the restaurant sold gift cards in various amounts totaling $2,300. The cards are redeemable for meals within one year of the purchase date. Gift cards totaling $742 were presented for redemption during the first two months of operation prior to year-end on December 31. The sales tax rate on restaurant sales is 6%, assessed at the time meals (not gift cards) are purchased. Logan's will remit sales taxes in January.

Required:
1. Record (in summary form) the $2,300 in gift cards sold (keeping in mind that, in actuality, each sale of a gift card or a meal would be recorded individually).
2. Record the $742 in gift cards redeemed. (*Hint:* The $742 includes a 6% sales tax of $42.)
3. Determine the balance in the Deferred Revenue account (remaining liability for gift cards) to be reported on the December 31 balance sheet.

Record contingencies (LO8–5)

P8–7B Compact Electronics is a leading manufacturer of digital camera equipment. Assume the following transactions occur during the year ended December 31, 2024.

Required:
Determine the appropriate way Compact Electronics would report the contingencies. Record any amounts as a result of each of these contingencies if required.
1. Accounts receivable were $29 million (all credit) at the end of 2024. Although no specific customer accounts have been shown to be uncollectible, the company estimates that 3% of accounts receivable will eventually prove uncollectible.
2. Compact Electronics is the plaintiff in a $5 million lawsuit filed against a supplier. The suit is in final appeal, and attorneys advise it is virtually certain that Compact Electronics will win and be awarded $3.5 million.

3. In November 2024, Compact Electronics became aware of a design flaw in one of its digital camera models. A product recall appears probable and would likely cost the company $600,000.
4. Compact Electronics is the defendant in a patent infringement lawsuit brought by a competitor. It appears reasonably likely Compact Electronics will lose the case, and potential losses are estimated to be in the range of $2.5 to $3.5 million.

Record contingencies (LO8–5)

P8–8B Authors Academic Press faces three potential contingency situations, described below. Authors' fiscal year ends December 31, 2024.

Required:

Determine the appropriate means of reporting each situation for the year ended December 31, 2024, and record any necessary entries. Explain your reasoning.

1. In August 2024, a worker was injured in an accident, partially as a result of his own negligence. The worker has sued the company for $1.2 million. Legal counsel believes it is reasonably possible that the outcome of the suit will be unfavorable, and that the settlement would cost the company from $300,000 to $600,000.
2. A suit for breach of contract seeking damages of $3 million was filed by an author on October 4, 2024. Legal counsel believes an unfavorable outcome is probable. A reasonable estimate of the award to the plaintiff is between $1.5 million and $2.25 million. No amount within this range is a better estimate of potential damages than any other amount.
3. Authors is the plaintiff in a pending court case. Its lawyers believe it is probable that Authors will be awarded damages of $3 million.

Calculate and analyze ratios (LO8–6)

P8–9B Selected financial data regarding current assets and current liabilities for Ferris Air and Oceanic Airlines are provided as follows:

($ in millions)	Ferris Air	Oceanic Airlines
Current assets:		
Cash and cash equivalents	$1,113	$ 2,791
Current investments	1,857	958
Net receivables	578	2,156
Inventory	469	1,023
Other current assets	210	1,344
Total current assets	$4,227	$ 8,272
Current liabilities:		
Current debt	$ 271	$ 1,627
Accounts payable	2,209	5,686
Other current liabilities	2,170	5,957
Total current liabilities	$4,650	$13,270

Required:

1. Calculate the current ratio for Ferris Air and Oceanic Airlines. Which company has the more favorable current ratio?
2. Calculate the acid-test (quick) ratio for Ferris Air and Oceanic Airlines. Which company has the more favorable acid-test ratio?
3. How would the purchase of additional inventory with cash affect the current ratio? How would it affect the acid-test ratio?

REAL-WORLD PERSPECTIVES

Continuing Problem

Data Analytics & Excel

Visit Connect to find a variety of Data Analytics questions that help build Excel, Tableau, and data visualization skills. Assignable materials include Integrated Excel, Applying Excel, Data Visualizations, Tableau Dashboard Activities, and Applying Tableau cases.

Great Adventures

(This is a continuation of the Great Adventures problem from earlier chapters.)

RWP8–1 At the end of 2025, the following information is available for Great Adventures.

- Additional interest for five months needs to be accrued on the $30,000, 6% note payable obtained on August 1, 2024. Recall that annual interest is paid each July 31.
- Assume that $10,000 of the $30,000 note discussed above is due next year. Record the entry to reclassify the current portion of the long-term note.
- By the end of the year, $20,000 in gift cards have been redeemed. The company had sold gift cards of $25,000 during the year and recorded those as Deferred Revenue.
- Great Adventures is a defendant in litigation involving a biking accident during one of its adventure races. The company believes the likelihood of payment occurring is probable, and the estimated amount to be paid is $12,000.
- For sales of MU watches, Great Adventures offers a warranty against defect for one year. At the end of the year, the company estimates future warranty costs to be $4,000.

Required:

1. Record each of the transactions above on December 31, 2025.
2. If the likelihood of payment for the litigation is determined to be reasonably possible, what should Great Adventures record for this possible payment?

The Great Adventures continuing problem also can be assigned using the General Ledger software in Connect. Students will be given an existing trial balance and asked to prepare (1) the journal entries for the transactions above in 2025, (2) financial statements, and (3) closing entries.

American Eagle Outfitters, Inc.

RWP8–2 Financial information for **American Eagle** is presented in **Appendix A** at the end of the book.

Required:

1. Calculate the current ratio for the past two years. Did the current ratio improve or weaken in the more recent year?
2. Calculate the acid-test (quick) ratio for the past two years. Did the acid-test ratio improve or weaken in the more recent year?
3. If American Eagle used $100 million in cash to pay $100 million in accounts payable, how would its current ratio and acid-test ratio change? Show your calculations.

The Buckle, Inc.

RWP8–3 Financial information for **Buckle** is presented in **Appendix B** at the end of the book.

Required:

1. Calculate the current ratio for the past two years. Did the current ratio improve or weaken in the more recent year?
2. Calculate the acid-test (quick) ratio for the past two years. Did the acid-test ratio improve or weaken in the more recent year?
3. If Buckle purchased $50 million of inventory by debiting Inventory and crediting Accounts Payable, how would its current ratio and acid-test ratio change? Show your calculations.

American Eagle Outfitters, Inc. vs. The Buckle, Inc.

RWP8–4 Financial information for **American Eagle** is presented in **Appendix A** at the end of the book, and financial information for **Buckle** is presented in **Appendix B** at the end of the book.

Required:

1. Calculate the current ratio for both companies for the most recent year. Which company has the more favorable ratio? Compare your calculations with those for **United Airlines** and **American Airlines** reported in the chapter text. Which industry maintains a higher current ratio?

2. Calculate the acid-test (quick) ratio for both companies for the most recent year, 2021. Which company has the more favorable ratio? Compare your calculations with those for United Airlines and American Airlines reported in the chapter text. Which industry maintains a higher acid-test ratio?

3. How would the purchase of additional inventory with accounts payable affect the current ratio for these two companies?

EDGAR Research

RWP8–5 Using EDGAR (Electronic Data Gathering, Analysis, and Retrieval system), find the annual report (10-K) for **Target Corporation** for the year ended **February 1, 2020.** Locate the "Consolidated Statements of Financial Position" (balance sheet). You may also find the annual report at the company's website.

Required:
1. What amount does the company report for current liabilities in the most recent year?
2. What amount does the company report for current assets in the most recent year?
3. Calculate the current ratio. Using 1.1 as the industry average, is Target more or less liquid than its industry peers?
4. What amount does the company report as a current liability associated with gift cards, net of estimated breakage? (*Hint*: See Note 13.)
5. The company owes for "debt and other borrowings." What amount is due to be paid back within the next 12 months?

Ethics

RWP8–6 Eugene Wright is CFO of Caribbean Cruise Lines. The company offers luxury cruises. It's near year-end, and Eugene is feeling kind of queasy. The economy is in a recession, and demand for luxury cruises is way down. Eugene doesn't want the company's current ratio to fall below the 1.0 minimum stated in its debt covenant with First Federal Bank. If the company reports a current ratio below 1.0 at year-end, First Federal may require immediate repayment of its $8 million loan, which is not due for another two years.

At the end of the year, Caribbean Cruise Lines reports current assets of $10.1 million and current liabilities of $10 million. These amounts include advanced payments of $1 million from customers in December for cruises to be provided the following summer. Instead of treating the $1 million as deferred revenue, Eugene decided to count the cash received as revenue. He reasoned that cash has already been collected, and the company has a long history of providing cruises, so customers will be provided their cruise as scheduled, and the company will have cash to pay the bank in the future.

Required:
1. Understand the reporting effect: How does Eugene's decision affect the reported amount of current assets and current liabilities at the end of December?
2. Specify the options: Calculate the current ratio assuming the $1 million is treated as (a) service revenue or (b) deferred revenue.
3. Identify the impact: Does Eugene's decision have an effect on First Federal Bank?
4. Make a decision: Should Eugene record the $1 million as service revenue?

Written Communication

RWP8–7 Western Manufacturing is involved with several potential contingent liabilities. Your assignment is to draft the appropriate accounting treatment for each situation described below. Western's fiscal year-end is December 31, 2024, and the financial statements will be issued in early February 2025.

a. During 2024, Western experienced labor disputes at three of its plants. Management hopes an agreement will soon be reached. However, negotiations between the company and the unions have not produced an acceptable settlement, and employee strikes are currently under way. It is virtually certain that material costs will be incurred, but the amount of possible costs cannot be reasonably estimated.

b. Western warrants most products it sells against defects in materials and workmanship for a period of a year. Based on its experience with previous product introductions, warranty costs are expected to approximate 2% of sales. A new product introduced in 2024 had sales of $2 million, and actual warranty expenditures incurred so far on the product are $25,000. The only entry made so far relating to warranties on this new product was to debit Warranty Expense $25,000 and credit Cash $25,000.

c. Western is involved in a suit filed in January 2025 by Crump Holdings seeking $88 million as an adjustment to the purchase price in connection with the company's sale of its textile business in 2024. The suit alleges that Western misstated the assets and liabilities used to calculate the purchase price for the textile division. Legal counsel advises that it is reasonably possible that Western could lose up to $88 million.

Required:

In a memo, describe the appropriate means of reporting each situation and explain your reasoning.

Earnings Management

RWP8–8 Quattro Technologies, a hydraulic manufacturer in the aeronautics industry, has reported steadily increasing net income over the past few years. The company reported net income of $120 million in 2022 and $140 million in 2023. The stock is receiving increasing analyst attention because many investors expect the steady growth in net income to continue well into the future.

One of the factors increasing sales is the superior warranty Quattro offers. Based on experience, warranty expense in 2024 should be around $40 million. However, in a recent executive meeting, it was suggested that the CFO report a larger, more conservative estimate of warranty expense of $50 million this year.

Required:

1. Can Quattro use warranty expense to manage its reported amount of net income?
2. Assume net income before warranty expense is $210 million in 2024 and $210 million in 2025, and total warranty expense over the two years is $80 million. Calculate net income after warranty expense based on the suggestion in the executive meeting to report $50 million in warranty expense in 2024. Calculate net income after warranty expense in 2025.
3. Does reporting warranty expense of $50 million in 2024 and $30 million in 2025 produce a steadier growth in net income than does reporting $40 million in each year?

Answers to Chapter Framework Questions

1. c   2. a   3. b   4. a   5. b

Answers to Self-Study Questions

1. c   2. a   3. c   4. b   5. b   6. b   7. b   8. d   9. c   10. a   11. a   12. d   13. a   14. c   15. b

9

Long-Term Liabilities

Learning Objectives

PART A: TYPES OF LONG-TERM DEBT

- **LO9–1** Explain financing alternatives.
- **LO9–2** Account for installment notes payable.
- **LO9–3** Understand how leases are recorded.
- **LO9–4** Account for the issuance of bonds at face amount.

PART B: BONDS ISSUED AT DISCOUNT OR PREMIUM

- **LO9–5** Account for the issuance of bonds at a discount or premium.
- **LO9–6** Record gain or loss on retirement of bonds.

PART C: PRICING A BOND

- **LO9–7** Calculate the issue price of a bond.

ANALYSIS: DEBT ANALYSIS

- **LO9–8** Assess the impact of long-term debt on risk and return.

SELF-STUDY MATERIALS

- Let's Review—Record the issuance of bonds at face amount and related interest (p. 448).
- Let's Review—Record issuance of bonds at discount and premium and related interest (p. 455).
- Let's Review—Calculate the issue price of a bond (p. 462).
- Chapter Framework with questions and answers available (p. 469).
- Key Points by Learning Objective (p. 470).
- Glossary of Key Terms (p. 471).
- Self-Study Questions with answers available (p. 472).
- Videos including Concept Overview, Applying Excel, Let's Review, and Interactive Illustrations to demonstrate key topics (in Connect).

SIX FLAGS: THE UPS AND DOWNS OF BORROWING

Can you name the largest chain of amusement parks in the world? Would you guess **Disney**? **Six Flags** actually is larger, with 26 amusement parks and water parks across North America. The first Six Flags amusement park, *Six Flags Over Texas*, was built in 1961 in Arlington, between Dallas and Fort Worth. The park is named for the six different flags that have flown over the state of Texas during its history—the flags of Spain, France, Mexico, the Republic of Texas, the Confederate States of America, and the United States.

Feature Story

Cedar Point, in Sandusky, Ohio, is known as the roller-coaster capital of the world. With a lineup that includes three of the top 10 steel roller coasters, Cedar Point is a coaster lover's dream come true. Its parent firm, **Cedar Fair Entertainment Company**, owns and operates 13 amusement parks and water parks across North America.

Both Six Flags and Cedar Fair carry a very high level of long-term debt to finance their extensive investments in physical properties. By updating and building rides and facilities in their parks, debt financing is used to spur additional sales and earnings growth. The goal is to earn a rate of return on assets higher than the interest rate on borrowing. However, high debt also increases their risk of bankruptcy. In fact, Six Flags entered into bankruptcy in 2009 and successfully restructured the company, coming out of bankruptcy in 2010.

In this chapter, we'll discuss three types of long-term debt— installment notes, leases, and bonds. The first two (notes and leases) are used by most companies, and these are the ones you'll likely encounter in your own life. For example, you may decide whether to buy a car by borrowing (installment note) or instead commit to lease payments over a specified number of years. Perhaps you or someone you know has considered whether to buy a house using a mortgage (installment note) or instead lease the property for a period of time. But just like companies, people need to consider not only the potential advantages that long-term debt offers, but also its risks. At the end of the chapter, we look at at how debt affects the riskiness and profitability of **Coca-Cola** and **Pepsi**.

Chuck Eckert/Alamy Stock Photo

PART A

TYPES OF LONG-TERM DEBT

Suppose you are the chief financial officer (CFO) for California Coasters, a company that designs, manufactures, and installs roller coasters. The executives at your company have an idea for a new ride that could revolutionize the amusement park industry. A ride like this could generate a huge increase in sales volume and create the opportunity to expand the idea to amusement parks around the world. But growth requires funding. Let's consider the financing alternatives available.

Financing Alternatives

■ **LO9–1**
Explain financing alternatives.

Some of the funds needed to pay for a company's growth can come from the profits generated by operations. Profits generated by the company are a source of *internal financing*. Frequently, though, companies must rely on funds from those outside the company to pay for operations and expansion. Funds coming from those outside of the company are sources of *external financing*. Let's look back at the basic accounting equation:

Assets	=	Liabilities	+	Stockholders' Equity
(resources)		(creditors' claims)		(owners' claims)

The right side of the accounting equation reveals the two sources of external financing—debt financing and equity financing. **Debt financing** refers to borrowing money from creditors (liabilities). **Equity financing** refers to obtaining investment from stockholders (stockholders' equity).

Amusement parks, like **Six Flags** or **Cedar Fair**, typically use debt financing to a greater extent for their financing. High-tech companies, like **Alphabet** or **Microsoft**, use equity financing to a greater extent to finance their asset growth. The mixture of liabilities and stockholders' equity a business uses is called its **capital structure**.

Decision Point

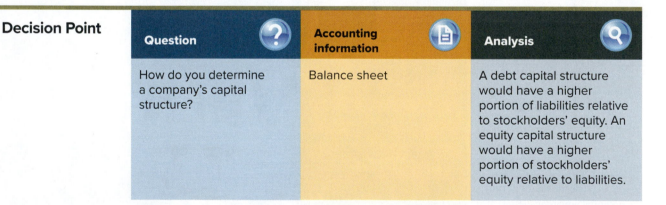

Question	Accounting information	Analysis
How do you determine a company's capital structure?	Balance sheet	A debt capital structure would have a higher portion of liabilities relative to stockholders' equity. An equity capital structure would have a higher portion of stockholders' equity relative to liabilities.

Why would a company choose to borrow money rather than issue additional stock in the company? One of the primary reasons relates to taxes. **Interest expense incurred when borrowing money is tax-deductible, whereas dividends paid to stockholders are *not* tax-deductible.** Interest expense incurred on debt reduces taxable income; paying dividends to stockholders does not reduce taxable income because dividends are not an expense. Therefore, debt can be a less costly source of external financing.

 KEY POINT

Companies obtain external funds through debt financing (liabilities) and equity financing (stockholders' equity). One advantage of debt financing is that interest on borrowed funds is tax-deductible.

Companies have three primary sources of long-term debt financing: notes, leases, and bonds. We discuss each of these sources of long-term debt financing next. **The first two (notes and leases) are types of debt financing you'll likely encounter in your own life.**

Installment Notes

You may have purchased a car or maybe even a house. If so, unless you paid cash, you signed a note promising to pay the purchase price over, say, 4 years for the car or 30 years for the house. Car loans and home loans usually call for payment in monthly installments rather than by a single amount at maturity. Companies, too, often borrow cash using installment notes. **Each installment payment includes both an amount that represents interest and an amount that represents a reduction of the outstanding loan balance.** The periodic reduction of the balance is enough that at maturity the note is completely paid.

■ **LO9–2**
Account for installment notes payable.

To illustrate, assume that California Coasters obtains a $25,000, 6%, four-year loan for the purchase of a new delivery truck on November 1, 2024. Payments of $587.13 (rounded) are required at the end of each month for 48 months.[1] An **amortization schedule** provides a table format detailing the cash payment each period, the portions of each cash payment that represent interest and the change in carrying value, and the balance of the carrying value. For an installment note payable, the interest portion is recorded as interest expense and the **carrying value** is the loan's remaining balance. Illustration 9–1 provides a partial amortization schedule. The full amortization schedule would have a row for each of the 48 payments. We use asterisks to denote periods omitted.

ILLUSTRATION 9–1

Amortization Schedule for an Installment Note

(1) Date	(2) Cash Paid	(3) Interest Expense	(4) Decrease in Carrying Value	(5) Carrying Value
		Carrying Value × Interest Rate	(2) − (3)	Prior Carrying Value − (4)
11/1/2024				$25,000.00
11/30/2024	$ 587.13	$ 125.00	$ 462.13	24,537.87
12/31/2024	587.13	122.69	464.44	24,073.43
*	*	*	*	*
12/31/2025	587.13	94.04	493.09	18,315.65
*	*	*	*	*
9/30/2028	587.13	5.83	581.30	584.21
10/31/2028	587.13	2.92	584.21	0
Total	$28,182.24 =	$3,182.24 +	$25,000.00	

Notice the following features of the amortization schedule:

1. **Date.** Payments are made at the end of each month.
2. **Cash Paid.** Monthly payments remain the same over the loan period. Notice the 48 payments of $587.13 add up to $28,182.24. This amount represents total interest on borrowing ($3,182.24) plus repayment of the loan amount ($25,000).
3. **Interest Expense.** Interest expense equals the prior month's carrying value times the interest rate (in this example, the monthly interest rate is 0.5% = 6% annual rate × 1/12).
4. **Decrease in Carrying Value.** The cash paid in excess of interest expense reduces the carrying value (remaining loan balance).
5. **Carrying Value.** The carrying value begins at $25,000, the original amount of the loan. With each monthly cash payment, the portion assigned to interest expense becomes

---

[1]The monthly payment of $587.13 is based on the following financial calculator inputs: future value, $0; present value, $25,000; interest rate, 0.5% (6% ÷ 12 periods each year); periods to maturity, 48 (4 years × 12 periods each year)—and solving for the monthly payment (PMT).

less and the portion that reduces the carrying value becomes more. By the end of the four-year loan, the $25,000 loan has been paid off and the carrying value equals $0.

California Coasters records the issuance of the $25,000 note as follows:

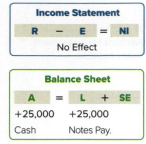

November 1, 2024	Debit	Credit
Cash	25,000	
Notes Payable		25,000
(Issue a note payable)		

California Coasters will make its first monthly payment on November 30, another monthly payment on December 31, and so on. The amounts used in recording the monthly payments come directly from the amortization schedule. Notice that the amount of cash paid is the same for each payment but (a) the amount of interest expense is decreasing and (b) the amount paid on the note's principal balance is increasing. After the second payment, the note will have a balance of $24,073.43.

November 30, 2024	Debit	Credit
Interest Expense (= $25,000 × 6% × 1/12)	125.00	
Notes Payable (difference)	462.13	
Cash (monthly payment)		587.13
(Pay monthly installment on note)		
December 31, 2024		
Interest Expense (= $24,537.87 × 6% × 1/12)	122.69	
Notes Payable (difference)	464.44	
Cash (monthly payment)		587.13
(Pay monthly installment on note)		

In the example above, we received cash at the time the note was issued. If we instead used the note to purchase a noncash asset, such as equipment, buildings, or land, we would record that asset account instead.

Reclassification of Debt.   By the end of 2024, the remaining balance of the note is $24,073.43. For financial reporting, this amount needs to be split into its current and long-term portions.

- The *current portion* is the amount of the loan that will be settled *within one year* of the balance sheet date ($5,757.78).
- The *long-term portion* is the remaining amount of the loan not classified as current ($18,315.65).

We can determine these amounts by looking back at Illustration 9–1. Over the next year (2025), the note's carrying value will decrease from $24,073.43 to $18,315.65. That means after 12 more monthly payments in 2025, $5,757.78 of the loan's balance (= $24,073.43 − $18,315.65) will be settled. California Coasters needs to reclassify $5,757.78 of the note payable by decreasing Notes Payable (long-term) and increasing Notes Payable (current). This entry to reclassify the current portion of long-term debt was covered in Chapter 8.

 KEY POINT

Most notes payable require periodic installment payments. Each installment payment includes an amount that represents interest expense and an amount that represents a reduction of the carrying value (remaining loan balance).

Leases

It's important that you understand how companies report their leases because **leasing has become the number one method of external financing by U.S. companies.** You are already familiar with a lease if you've ever leased a car or an apartment. A **lease** is a contractual arrangement by which the *lessor* (owner) provides the *lessee* (user) the right to use an asset for a specified period of time. The airplane in which you last flew probably was leased, as was the gate from which it departed. Your cell phone service provider likely leases the space in which it operates. Many of the stores where you shop and the last hotel you stayed in were probably leased buildings. So, why the popularity?

■ **LO9–3**
Understand how leases are recorded.

Decision Maker's Perspective

Why Do Many Companies Lease Rather Than Buy?

1. **Leasing reduces the upfront cash needed to use an asset.** Instead of paying cash upfront for the full purchase of an asset, only the first month's lease payment is needed to begin using the asset. This is especially important for companies that have high credit risk and may not be able to borrow enough cash to purchase an asset.

2. **Lease payments often are lower than installment payments.** Lease payments often are tied only to the portion of value related to the period of use, while the installment payments are tied to the entire value of the asset regardless of the borrower's intended period of use. This means the monthly payments associated with leasing often are lower.

3. **Leasing offers flexibility and lower costs when disposing of an asset.** Returning a leased asset at the end of the lease term requires little effort or cost. Selling an asset, however, may require more time to find a buyer, especially for unique assets. Selling an asset also can require significant costs, such as selling commissions and legal fees.

4. **Leasing may offer protection against the risk of declining asset values.** In certain lease agreements, lessees don't have to worry about declining fair values (selling prices) while they are using the asset. Of course, the lessee also misses out on any increase in fair value.

RECORDING A LEASE

The lease arrangement gives the lessee (user) the right to use an asset for a period of time. This right is recorded as an *asset*. The user also has an obligation to make payments over the lease period. This obligation is recorded as a *liability*.

A long-term lease creates an asset and a liability for the lessee (user).

Let's look at an example of recording a lease by modifying our earlier example of California Coasters. Instead of purchasing a new delivery truck, California Coasters agrees to make lease payments of $352.28 at the end of each month for 48 months. California Coasters doesn't own the leased truck, but the company has the right to use the truck by agreeing to terms of the lease. At the beginning of the lease period, California Coasters records a lease asset and lease payable for the *present value of the lease payments*. In this example, the present value of the 48 lease payments using a 6% borrowing rate is $15,000 (calculation discussed below).

Record a long-term lease for the present value of payments.

November 1, 2024	Debit	Credit
Lease Asset	**15,000**	
Lease Payable		**15,000**
(Record the lease)		
($15,000 = present value of lease payments*)		

*present value of ordinary annuity; $n = 48$, $i = 6\% \div 12$.

Income Statement

R	–	E	=	NI
No Effect				

Balance Sheet

A	=	L	+	SE
+15,000		+15,000		
Lease Asset		Lease Payable		

Even though lease payments total $16,909.44 over the four-year period ($352.28 × 48 payments), we record the lease payable for only $15,000, the present value of those future payments. The additional payment of $1,909.44 essentially represents the cost of borrowing for four years. As lease payments are made over time, the carrying values of the asset and the liability will be reduced to zero. These adjustments are covered in intermediate accounting textbooks.

Calculating the Present Value of Lease Payments (Annuity).   Table 4 at the back of this book provides present values of annuities of $1 for many variations in number of periods (n) and interest rates (i). These values are multiplied by the monthly lease payment to get the present value of the total lease payments. For combinations of n and i not shown, you can calculate the present value of the lease payments using a financial calculator or Excel.

In our example, the lease period is 48 months, and the interest rate per month is 0.5% (= 6% annual rate ÷ 12). Illustration 9–2 shows the calculator inputs used to obtain the present value of $15,000.

ILLUSTRATION 9–2

Present Value of Lease Payments Using a Financial Calculator

	CALCULATOR INPUT	
Lease Characteristics	**Key**	**Amount**
1. Future value	FV	$0
2. Lease payment	PMT	$352.28
3. Number of payments	N	48 = 4 years × 12 periods each year
4. Interest rate	I	0.5 = 6% ÷ 12 periods each year
	CALCULATOR OUTPUT	
Present value of payments	PV	$15,000

An alternative to using a financial calculator is to use Excel. Illustration 9–3 demonstrates the inputs and the formula used to calculate the present value of lease payments.

ILLUSTRATION 9–3

Present Value of Lease Payments Using Excel

B7			f_x	=-PV(B5,B4,B3,B2,0)		
	A			B	C	D
1						
2	Future value			$0		
3	Lease payment			$352.28		
4	Number of payments			48		
5	Interest rate			0.005		
6						
7	Present value of payments			$15,000		
8						
9						

Microsoft Corporation

Initial Down Payment.   In addition to having the obligation of future lease payments, companies often are required to pay an initial amount at the beginning of the lease. In this case, the entry to record the lease would include a credit to Cash for the down payment and a credit to Lease Payable for the present value of the future lease payments. Lease Asset would be debited for an amount equal to Cash and Lease Payable.

KEY POINT

> While not transferring ownership as in a purchase, a lease gives the lessee (user) the right to use the asset over the lease period. This right is recorded as an asset, and the obligation to make lease payments is recorded as a liability.

Bonds Issued at Face Amount

A **bond** is a formal debt instrument issued by a company to borrow money. The issuing company (borrower) receives cash by selling a bond to an investor (lender). In return, the issuing company promises to pay back to the investor: (1) a stated amount, referred to as the *principal* or *face amount,* at a specified maturity date and (2) periodic interest payments over the life of the bond. Bonds are very similar to notes. Bonds, though, usually are for greater amounts and are issued to many lenders, while notes most often are issued to a single lender such as a bank. Traditionally, interest on bonds is paid twice a year (semiannually) on designated interest dates, beginning six months after the original bond issue date.

Perhaps your local school board issued bonds to build a new football stadium for the high school, or maybe your hometown issued bonds to build a new library. To build the stadium or library, a city needs external financing, so it borrows money from people in the community. In return, those people receive interest over the life of the bonds, say 20 years, and repayment of the principal amount at the end of the bonds' life.

Why do some companies issue bonds rather than borrow money directly from a bank? A company that borrows by issuing bonds is effectively bypassing the bank and borrowing directly from the investing public—usually at a lower interest rate than it would in a bank loan. However, issuing bonds entails significant bond issue costs that can exceed 5% of the amount borrowed. For smaller loans, the additional bond issuance costs exceed the savings from a lower interest rate, making it more economical to borrow from a bank. For loans of $20 million or more, the interest rate savings often exceed the additional bond issuance costs, making a bond issue more attractive.

■ **LO9–4**
Account for the issuance of bonds at face amount.

Katherine Welles/Shutterstock

RECORDING A BOND ISSUANCE AND INTEREST PAYMENTS

Corporations normally issue bonds in the millions of dollars. However, to simplify the illustrations in this chapter, we drop three digits and illustrate the issuance of bonds in thousands rather than in millions. We begin with the following example and build upon it as we progress through the bonds section of this chapter.

Assume that on January 1, 2024, California Coasters decides to raise money for development of its new roller coaster by issuing $100,000 of bonds paying interest of 7% each year. The bonds are due in 10 years, with interest payable semiannually on June 30 and December 31 each year. **In practice, most corporate bonds pay interest semiannually (every six months) rather than paying interest monthly, quarterly, or annually.**

In this example, California Coasters will receive cash of **$100,000** on the issue date. In return, California Coasters promises the following cash payments back to investors:

1. **Face amount** of $100,000 at the end of 10 years, plus
2. **Interest payments** of $3,500 (= $100,000 × 7% × 1/2 year) every six months for 10 years. That's a total of 20 interest payments of $3,500 each (= $70,000).

Illustration 9–4 provides a timeline of the cash flows related to the bond issue.

Over the 10-year period, investors will receive a total of $170,000, which is the face amount of $100,000 due at maturity plus 20 semiannual interest payments of $3,500, totaling $70,000. California Coasters records the bonds at their issue price of $100,000.

January 1, 2024	Debit	Credit
Cash	**100,000**	
Bonds Payable		**100,000**
(Issue bonds at face amount)		

Income Statement

R	–	E	=	NI
		No Effect		

Balance Sheet

A	=	L	+	SE
+100,000		+100,000		
Cash		Bonds Payable		

ILLUSTRATION 9–4

Timeline of a Bond
Issue

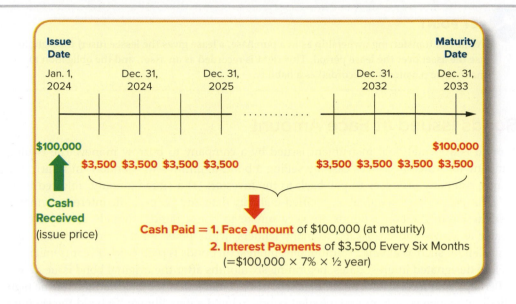

California Coasters reports bonds payable in the long-term liabilities section of the balance sheet. Nine years from now, when the bonds are within one year of maturity, the firm will reclassify the bonds as current liabilities.

On June 30, 2024, California Coasters records the first semiannual interest payment based on the bond's stated interest rate. The **stated interest rate** is the rate specified in the bond contract used to calculate the cash payments for interest.

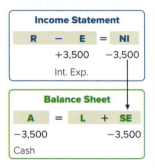

Income Statement		
R	− E =	NI
	+3,500	−3,500
	Int. Exp.	

Balance Sheet		
A	= L +	SE
−3,500		−3,500
Cash		

June 30, 2024	Debit	Credit
Interest Expense	3,500	
Cash		3,500
(Pay semiannual interest)		
($3,500 = $100,000 × 7% × 1/2)		

The firm will record another semiannual interest payment on December 31, 2024. In fact, it will record this same semiannual interest payment at the end of every six-month period for the next 10 years.

Let's Review

Assume that on January 1, 2024, Water World issues $200,000 of 9% bonds, due in 10 years, with interest payable semiannually on June 30 and December 31 each year.

Required:

1. Record the bond issue on January 1, 2024, for $200,000.

2. Record the first two semiannual interest payments on June 30, 2024, and December 31, 2024.

Solution:

1. Record the bond issue on January 1, 2024, for $200,000.

January 1, 2024	Debit	Credit
Cash	200,000	
Bonds Payable		200,000
(Issue bonds at face amount)		

2. Record the first two semiannual interest payments on June 30, 2024, and December 31, 2024.

June 30, 2024	Debit	Credit
Interest Expense	9,000	
Cash (= $200,000 × 9% × 1/2)		9,000
(Pay semiannual interest)		
December 31, 2024		
Interest Expense	9,000	
Cash (= $200,000 × 9% × 1/2)		9,000
(Pay semiannual interest)		

Suggested Homework:
BE9–8, BE9–10;
E9–10, E9–13;
P9–5A&B (Req. 1)

RETIRING A BOND

When the issuing company buys back its bonds from the investors, we say the company has retired those bonds. The company may wait until the bonds mature to retire them or choose to buy back the bonds from the investors early. At retirement, California Coasters would pay cash of $100,000 to eliminate its bonds payable liability.

December 31, 2033	Debit	Credit
Bonds Payable	100,000	
Cash		100,000
(Retire bonds at maturity)		

Income Statement

R	–	E	=	NI
		No Effect		

Balance Sheet

A	=	L	+	SE
−100,000		−100,000		
Cash		Bonds		
		Payable		

BOND CHARACTERISTICS

For most large corporations, bonds are sold, or *underwritten,* by investment houses. The three largest bond underwriters are **JPMorgan Chase**, **Citigroup**, and **Bank of America**. A company issuing a bond pays a fee for these underwriting services. Other costs include legal, accounting, registration, and printing fees. To keep costs down, the issuing company may choose to sell the bonds directly to a single investor, such as a large investment fund or an insurance company. This is referred to as a **private placement**.

Bonds may be secured or unsecured, term or serial, callable, or convertible. Illustration 9–5 provides a summary. We'll discuss each of these characteristics next.

ILLUSTRATION 9–5

Summary of Bond Characteristics

Bond Characteristic	Definition
Secured	Bonds are backed by collateral.
Unsecured	Bonds are not backed by collateral.
Term	Bond issue matures on a single date.
Serial	Bond issue matures in installments.
Callable	Issuing company can pay off bonds early.
Convertible	Investor can convert bonds to common stock.

Secured and Unsecured Bonds.   **Secured bonds** are supported by specific assets the issuing company has pledged as collateral. If the company defaults on the payments, the investor is entitled to the assets pledged as collateral.

Unsecured bonds, also referred to as *debentures,* are not backed by a specific asset. These bonds are secured only by the "full faith and credit" of the issuing company. Most bonds are unsecured.

Term and Serial Bonds.   **Term bonds** require payment of the full principal amount of the bond at a single maturity date. To ensure that sufficient funds are available to pay back the bonds at the end of the loan term, the issuing company usually sets aside money in a "sinking

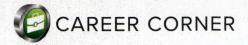

CAREER CORNER

Financing alternatives, capital structure, notes, leases, and bonds are topics covered in both accounting and finance. How do you decide whether to major in accounting or finance? Some students choose finance because they consider accounting more of a "desk job" and finance more "people-oriented." This just isn't true! Both accounting and finance positions require strong communication skills. Other students avoid accounting because they heard it was more difficult. Although an accounting degree is not easy, remember **Nike**'s famous slogan, "No pain, no gain." Accounting majors can apply for most entry-level finance positions, while finance majors do not have the accounting coursework to apply for most entry-level accounting positions.

Diego Cervo/Shutterstock

fund." A **sinking fund** is an investment fund to which an organization makes payments each year over the life of its outstanding debt. **Since most bonds are term bonds, we focus on term bonds in this chapter.** The example we covered using California Coasters in the previous section involved term bonds.

Serial bonds require payments in installments over a series of years. Rather than issuing $20 million in bonds that will be due at the *end* of the 10th year, the company may issue $20 million in serial bonds, of which $2 million is due *each year* for the next 10 years. This makes it easier to meet its bond obligations as they become due.

Callable Bonds. Suppose your company issued bonds a few years ago that pay 10% interest. Now market interest rates have declined to 6%, but you're obligated to pay 10% interest for the remaining time to maturity. How can you avoid this unfortunate situation?

Most corporate bonds are **callable**, or redeemable. This feature allows the issuing company to repay the bonds before their scheduled maturity date at a specified call price, usually at an amount just above face value. Callable bonds protect the issuing company against future decreases in interest rates. If interest rates decline, the company can buy back the high-interest-rate bonds at a fixed price and issue new bonds at the new, lower interest rate.

Convertible Bonds. **Convertible** bonds allow the investor to convert each bond into a specified number of shares of common stock. For example, let's say a $1,000 convertible bond can be converted into 20 shares of common stock. In this case, investors in the convertible bonds benefit if the market price of the common stock goes above $50 per share (= $1,000 ÷ 20 shares), assuming the current market price of the bond is $1,000. If the company's stock price goes to $60 per share, the investors can trade the $1,000 bond for 20 shares of stock worth $60 per share (or $1,200). Prior to conversion, the investor still receives interest on the convertible bond. While a bond could be both callable and convertible, **a call feature is more common than a conversion feature.**

 KEY POINT

The distinguishing characteristics of bonds include whether they are backed by collateral (secured or unsecured), become due at a single specified date or over a series of years (term or serial), can be redeemed prior to maturity (callable), or can be converted into common stock (convertible).

PART B

■ **LO9–5**

Account for the issuance of bonds at a discount or premium.

BONDS ISSUED AT DISCOUNT OR PREMIUM

As discussed above, the *stated interest rate* is specified in the bond contract as the interest rate to be paid by the company to investors in the bond. The **market interest rate** is not specified in the bond contract. The market rate is an implied rate based on the price investors pay to purchase a bond in return for the right to receive the face amount at maturity and periodic interest payments over the remaining life of the bond.

All else equal, investors demand a higher market rate for bonds that have a higher default risk. **Default risk** refers to the possibility that a company will be unable to pay the bond's face amount or interest payments as they become due. **As the default risk of the bond increases, investors can *increase* their rate of return over the life of the bond by paying a *lower* price at the issue date.**

In the preceding section, we assumed the issuance of bonds at face amount. This will occur when the bond's stated interest rate (7%) equals the market interest rate (7%). But often, depending on the market interest rate, bonds will issue for more than or less than the face amount. If the bonds' stated interest rate is *less than* the market interest rate, then the bonds will issue below face amount (**discount**). If the bonds' stated interest rate is *more than* the market interest rate, the bonds will issue above face amount (**premium**). Now we will proceed to describe the issuance of bonds and the related interest for bonds issued at a discount, and then we will describe the same but for bonds issued at a premium.

Bonds Issued at a Discount

Let's assume that California Coasters issues the same $100,000 of 7% bonds, but due to the company's higher default risk, investors require a market rate of return of 8%. California Coasters' bonds are less attractive to investors because they will receive a stated interest rate of 7% per year, which is less than their required rate of 8%. Because of the unfavorable interest rate, investors will pay less than $100,000 to purchase the bonds. These bonds will issue at a discount of $93,205.[2]

California Coasters records the cash received of $93,205. The company records Bonds Payable for the full face amount of $100,000 that must be paid to investors in 10 years. The difference between these two amounts is Discount on Bonds Payable.

January 1, 2024	Debit	Credit
Cash	93,205	
Discount on Bonds Payable	6,795	
Bonds Payable		100,000
(Issue bonds at a discount)		

Income Statement

R	−	E	=	NI

No Effect

Balance Sheet

A	=	L	+	SE
+93,205		+100,000		
Cash		Bonds Pay.		
		−6,795		
		Discount ↑		

The Discount account is a contra liability, which is deducted from Bonds Payable in the balance sheet as shown below:

Long-term liabilities:
Bonds payable	$100,000
Less: Discount on bonds payable	(6,795)
Carrying value	$ 93,205

These bonds initially will be reported in the balance sheet at their carrying value of $93,205, which equals bonds payable less the bond discount. The amount of the discount ($6,795 in this example) effectively represents the additional cost of borrowing when issuing bonds for $93,205 but being required to pay back principal of $100,000. We'll report this amount as additional interest expense over the 10-year life of the bonds as we record each period's interest payment, as shown next.

Interest Paid Versus Interest Expense. The bond agreement specifies that cash paid for interest will be the same every six months—the face amount times the stated rate:

Cash paid for interest	=	Face amount of bond	×	Stated interest rate per period
$3,500	=	$100,000	×	7% × 1/2

However, interest expense is not based on the *stated* rate. The amount to record for interest expense equals the current carrying value times the *market* rate (4% semiannually or 8%

---

[2]In this example, the issue price of $93,205 is given. To see the details of how the issue price is calculated, see Illustration 9–12, 9–13, or 9–14 in Part C of this chapter.

annually, in our example). This method of calculating interest is referred to as the *effective-interest method*.[3] For the first interest payment, interest expense is calculated as

$$
\begin{array}{ccccc}
\text{Interest} & = & \text{Carrying value} & \times & \text{Market interest rate} \\
\text{expense} & & \text{of bond} & & \text{per period} \\
\$3{,}728 & = & \$93{,}205 & \times & 8\% \times 1/2
\end{array}
$$

When a bond sells at a discount, interest expense ($3,728) will be more than the cash paid for interest ($3,500). The difference represents the reduction in the discount. On June 30, 2024, California Coasters records the first semiannual interest payment as

Income Statement

R	–	E	=	NI
		+3,728		–3,728
		Int. Exp.		

Balance Sheet

A	=	L	+	SE
–3,500		+228		–3,728
Cash		Discount ↓		

June 30, 2024	Debit	Credit
Interest Expense (= $93,205 × 8% × 1/2)	**3,728**	
Discount on Bonds Payable (difference)		**228**
Cash (= $100,000 × 7% × 1/2)		**3,500**
(Pay semiannual interest)		

 COMMON MISTAKE

> Students sometimes incorrectly record interest expense using the stated rate rather than the market rate. Remember that interest expense is the carrying value times the market rate, while the cash paid for interest is the face amount times the stated rate.

After the first interest payment, the balance of the discount has decreased by $228, which increases the bond's carrying value to $93,433 (= $93,205 + $228). We use the revised carrying value to calculate interest expense for the second semiannual interest period on December 31, 2024:

Income Statement

R	–	E	=	NI
		+3,737		–3,737
		Int. Exp.		

Balance Sheet

A	=	L	+	SE
–3,500		+237		–3,737
Cash		Discount ↓		

December 31, 2024	Debit	Credit
Interest Expense (= [$93,205 + $228] × 8% × 1/2)	**3,737**	
Discount on Bonds Payable (difference)		**237**
Cash (= $100,000 × 7% × 1/2)		**3,500**
(Pay semiannual interest)		

A bond amortization schedule summarizes the cash paid for interest, interest expense, and changes in the bond's carrying value for each semiannual interest period. Illustration 9–6 provides an amortization schedule for the bonds issued at a discount. Note that the amounts for the June 30, 2024, and the December 31, 2024, semiannual interest payments shown above can be taken directly from the amortization schedule.

ILLUSTRATION 9–6

Amortization Schedule for Bonds Issued at a Discount

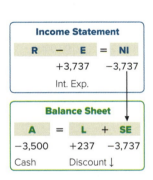

(1)	(2)	(3)	(4)	(5)
		Interest	Increase in	Carrying
Date	Cash Paid	Expense	Carrying Value	Value
	Face Amount × Stated Rate	Carrying Value × Market Rate	(3) − (2)	Prior Carrying Value + (4)
1/1/2024				$ 93,205
6/30/2024	$3,500	$3,728	$228	93,433
12/31/2024	3,500	3,737	237	93,670
*	*	*	*	*
*	*	*	*	99,057
6/30/2033	3,500	3,962	462	99,519
12/31/2033	3,500	3,981	481	100,000

---

[3] We cover the effective-interest method, as this is the generally accepted method under both U.S. GAAP and IFRS. The straight-line amortization method, which is allowed only if it does not materially differ from the effective-interest method, is discussed as an alternative approach in intermediate accounting.

The amortization schedule shows interest calculations every six months because interest is paid semiannually. The entire amortization schedule would include 20 more rows (10 years × 2 periods per year) after the initial balance on January 1, 2024. To save space, we show only the amortization for the first and last years. The eight years in the middle are represented by asterisks. Cash paid is $3,500 (= $100,000 × 7% × 1/2) every six months. Interest expense is the carrying value times the market rate. Interest expense for the six months ended June 30, 2024, is $3,728 (= $93,205 × 8% × 1/2). The difference between interest expense and the cash paid increases the carrying value of the bonds. At the maturity date, the carrying value will equal the face amount of $100,000.

Decision Maker's Perspective

Carrying Value and Market Value

Is the carrying value of bonds payable reported in the balance sheet really what the bonds are worth? Yes, but only on the date issued and on the final maturity date. Between these two dates, the carrying value of bonds payable reported in the balance sheet can vary considerably from the true underlying market value of the liability. The reason is that the market interest rate is constantly changing. The market value of bonds moves in the opposite direction of interest rates: When market interest rates go up, the market value of bonds goes down. However, the carrying value of bonds is not adjusted for changes in market interest rates after the issue date.

Bonds Issued at a Premium

Now let's assume that California Coasters issues the same $100,000 of 7% bonds, but, for this example, investors require a rate of return of only 6%. Investors will pay *more* than $100,000 for these bonds since the bonds' 7% stated rate is relatively attractive to investors requiring only 6%. The bonds will issue at a premium of $107,439.

California Coasters records the cash received of $107,439. The company records Bonds Payable for the full face amount of $100,000 that must be paid to investors in 10 years. The difference is Premium on Bonds Payable. The amount of the Premium ($7,439 in this example) effectively represents the reduction in total interest paid when issuing bonds for $107,439 but being required to pay back principal of only $100,000.

January 1, 2024	Debit	Credit
Cash	107,439	
Bonds Payable		100,000
Premium on Bonds Payable		7,439
(Issue bonds at a premium)		

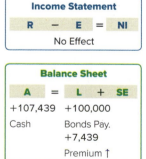

Income Statement

R	–	E	=	NI
No Effect				

Balance Sheet

A	=	L	+	SE
+107,439		+100,000		
Cash		Bonds Pay.		
		+7,439		
		Premium ↑		

The balance of Premium on Bonds Payable is added to Bonds Payable in the balance sheet as shown below:

Long-term liabilities:	
Bonds payable	$100,000
Add: Premium on bonds payable	7,439
Carrying value	$107,439

Initially, the bonds will be reported in the balance sheet at their carrying value of $107,439. However, California Coasters will need to pay back only $100,000 when the bonds mature in 10 years. Therefore, the carrying value will decrease from $107,439 (issue price) to $100,000 (face amount) over the 10-year life of the bonds. We decrease the carrying amount by eliminating the premium as we record each period's interest payment.

When a bond sells at a premium, interest expense ($3,223) will be less than the cash paid for interest ($3,500). The difference represents the reduction in the premium. On June 30, 2024, California Coasters records the first semiannual interest payment as

Income Statement

R	−	E	=	NI
		+3,223		−3,223
		Int. Exp.		

Balance Sheet

A	=	L	+	SE
−3,500		−277		−3,223
Cash		Premium ↓		

June 30, 2024	Debit	Credit
Interest Expense (= $107,439 × 6% × 1/2)	3,223	
Premium on Bonds Payable (difference)	277	
Cash (= $100,000 × 7% × 1/2)		3,500
(Pay semiannual interest)		

After the first interest payment, the balance of the premium has decreased by $277, which decreases the bond's carrying value to $107,162 (= $107,439 − $277). We use the revised carrying value to calculate interest expense for the second semiannual interest period on December 31, 2024:

Income Statement

R	−	E	=	NI
		+3,215		−3,215
		Int. Exp.		

Balance Sheet

A	=	L	+	SE
−3,500		−285		−3,215
Cash		Premium ↓		

December 31, 2024	Debit	Credit
Interest Expense (= [$107,439 − $277] × 6% × 1/2)	3,215	
Premium on Bonds Payable (difference)	285	
Cash (= $100,000 × 7% × 1/2)		3,500
(Pay semiannual interest)		

The amortization schedule in Illustration 9–7 summarizes the recording of interest expense for the bonds issued at a premium.

ILLUSTRATION 9–7

Amortization Schedule for Bonds Issued at a Premium

(1)	(2)	(3)	(4)	(5)
		Interest	Decrease in	Carrying
Date	Cash Paid	Expense	Carrying Value	Value
	Face Amount × Stated Rate	Carrying Value × Market Rate	(2) − (3)	Prior Carrying Value − (4)
1/1/2024				$107,439
6/30/2024	$3,500	$3,223	$277	107,162
12/31/2024	3,500	3,215	285	106,877
*	*	*	*	*
*	*	*	*	100,956
6/30/2033	3,500	3,029	471	100,485
12/31/2033	3,500	3,015	485	100,000

Just as in the discount example, the amounts for the June 30, 2024, and the December 31, 2024, semiannual interest payments can be obtained directly from the amortization schedule. Now, however, with a bond premium, the difference between cash paid and interest expense *decreases* the carrying value each period from $107,439 at bond issue down to $100,000 (the face amount) at bond maturity.

Illustration 9–8 shows how carrying value changes as a bond approaches its maturity date.

 KEY POINT

When bonds issue at a discount (below face amount), the carrying value and the corresponding interest expense *increase* over time. When bonds issue at a premium (above face amount), the carrying value and the corresponding interest expense *decrease* over time.

ILLUSTRATION 9–8

Changes in Carrying Value over Time

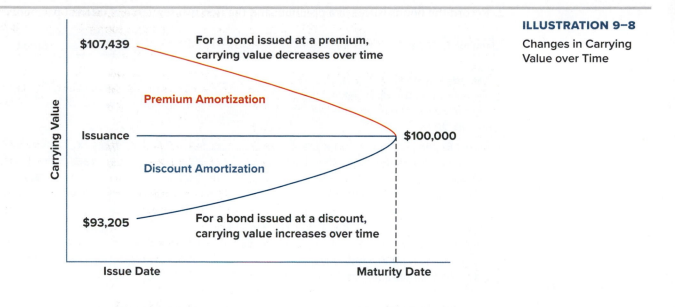

Assume that on January 1, 2024, Water World issues $200,000 of 9% bonds, due in 10 years, with interest payable semiannually on June 30 and December 31 each year.

Let's Review

Required:

1. If the market rate is 10%, the bonds will issue at $187,538. Record the bond issue on January 1, 2024, and the first two semiannual interest payments on June 30, 2024, and December 31, 2024.

2. If the market rate is 8%, the bonds will issue at $213,590. Record the bond issue on January 1, 2024, and the first two semiannual interest payments on June 30, 2024, and December 31, 2024.

Solution:

1. Record the bonds issued at a discount and the first two semiannual interest payments:

January 1, 2024	Debit	Credit
Cash	187,538	
Discount on Bonds Payable	12,462	
Bonds Payable		200,000
(Issue bonds at a discount)		
June 30, 2024		
Interest Expense (= $187,538 × 10% × 1/2)	9,377	
Discount on Bonds Payable (difference)		377
Cash (= $200,000 × 9% × 1/2)		9,000
(Pay semiannual interest)		
December 31, 2024		
Interest Expense (= [$187,538 + $377] × 10% × 1/2)	9,396	
Discount on Bonds Payable (difference)		396
Cash (= $200,000 × 9% × 1/2)		9,000
(Pay semiannual interest)		

2. Record the bonds issued at a premium and the first two semiannual interest payments:

January 1, 2024	Debit	Credit
Cash	213,590	
Bonds Payable		200,000
Premium on Bonds Payable		13,590
(Issue bonds at a premium)		
June 30, 2024		
Interest Expense (= $213,590 \times 8\% \times 1/2$)	8,544	
Premium on Bonds Payable (difference)	456	
Cash (= $200,000 \times 9\% \times 1/2$)		9,000
(Pay semiannual interest)		
December 31, 2024		
Interest Expense ($= [\$213,590 - \$456] \times 8\% \times 1/2$)	8,525	
Premium on Bonds Payable (difference)	475	
Cash ($= \$200,000 \times 9\% \times 1/2$)		9,000
(Pay semiannual interest)		

Suggested Homework:
BE9–9, BE9–10;
E9–11, E9–12;
P9–7A&B, P9–8A&B

Gains and Losses on Retirement of Bonds

■ **LO9–6**

Record gain or loss on retirement of bonds.

A company can wait until the bonds mature to retire them, or frequently (for reasons we describe below), the issuing company will choose to buy the bonds back from the investors early.

BOND RETIREMENTS AT MATURITY

Regardless of whether bonds are issued at face amount, at a discount, or at a premium, **their carrying value at maturity will equal their face amount.** California Coasters records the retirement of its bonds at maturity (December 31, 2033) as follows:

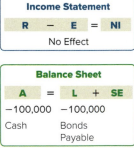

Income Statement
R – E = NI
No Effect

Balance Sheet
A = L + SE
−100,000 −100,000
Cash   Bonds
Payable

December 31, 2033	Debit	Credit
Bonds Payable	100,000	
Cash		100,000
(Retire bonds at maturity)		

BOND RETIREMENTS BEFORE MATURITY

Earlier we noted that a call feature accompanies most bonds, allowing the issuing company to buy back bonds at a fixed price. Even when bonds are not callable in this way, the issuing company can retire bonds early by purchasing them on the open market. Regardless of the method, when the issuing company retires debt of any type before its scheduled maturity date, the transaction is an **early extinguishment of debt**.

A simple example of an early extinguishment of debt is paying off your car loan early. If you owe $5,000 on your car loan and you have to pay $5,200 to pay it off early, we would record a $200 loss on the early retirement of your debt. If you have to pay only $4,700, we would record a $300 gain on the early retirement of your debt. The same scenario holds true for bonds.

Let's return to our example of California Coasters issuing $100,000 of 7% bonds maturing in 10 years with a market interest rate of 6%. The bonds were issued on January 1, 2024, above face amount (at a premium) at $107,439. The carrying value of the bonds one year later on December 31, 2024, is $106,877 (see the amortization table in Illustration 9–7).

When interest rates go down, bond prices go up. If the market rate drops to 5%, it will now cost $114,353 to retire the bonds on December 31, 2024.[4] The bonds have a carrying value on December 31, 2024, of $106,877, but it will cost the issuing company $114,353 to retire them. California Coasters will record a loss for the difference between the price paid to repurchase the bonds and the bonds' carrying value. California Coasters records the retirement as follows:

December 31, 2024	Debit	Credit
Bonds Payable (account balance)	100,000	
Premium on Bonds Payable	6,877	
Loss (difference)	7,476	
Cash (amount paid)		114,353
(Retire bonds before maturity)		

Income Statement

R	−	E	=	NI
		+7,476		−7,476
		Loss		

Balance Sheet

A	=	L	+	SE
−114,353		−100,000		−7,476
Cash		Bonds Pay.		
		−6,877		
		Premium ↓		

If California Coasters paid less than $106,877 to retire the bonds, a gain would have been recorded instead of a loss. Gains and losses on the early extinguishment of debt are reported in the income statement. This is similar to gains and losses on the sale of long-term assets, discussed in Chapter 7.

Decision Maker's Perspective

Why Buy Back Debt Early?

In the example above, California Coasters recorded a loss of $7,476 due to a decrease in market interest rates of 1%. One way a company can protect itself from decreases in interest rates is to include a call feature allowing the company to repurchase bonds at a fixed price (such as 2% over face amount, which in our example would be $102,000). When interest rates decrease, companies with a call feature are more likely to repurchase higher-cost debt and then reissue debt at new, lower interest rates. This type of buyback and reissue lowers future interest expense.

Another reason to repay debt early is to improve the company's debt ratios (discussed later in the chapter). **Six Flags** sold seven amusement parks for just over $300 million and used the proceeds to reduce its overall debt.

Early extinguishment of debt can also be timed to manage reported earnings. Since bonds payable are reported at carrying values and not market values, firms can time their repurchase of bonds to help meet earnings expectations. For instance, when interest rates go up, bond prices go down. In this case, California Coasters will record a gain rather than a loss on early extinguishment.

 KEY POINT

No gain or loss is recorded on bonds retired at maturity. For bonds retired before maturity, we record a gain or loss on early extinguishment equal to the difference between the price paid to repurchase the bonds and the bonds' carrying value.

---

[4]The repurchase price of $114,353 is based on the following financial calculator inputs: future value, $100,000; interest payment each period, $3,500; market interest rate each period, 2.5% (5% ÷ 2 semiannual periods); and periods to maturity, 18 (9 years left × 2 periods each year).

ETHICAL DILEMMA

On January 1, 2023, West-Tex Oil issued $50 million of 8% bonds maturing in 10 years. The market interest rate on the issue date was 9%, which resulted in the bonds being issued at a discount. In December 2024, Tex Winters, the company CFO, notes that in the two years since the bonds were issued, interest rates have fallen almost 3%. Tex suggests that West-Tex might consider repurchasing the 8% bonds and reissuing new bonds at the lower current interest rates.

Another executive, Will Bright, asks, "Won't the repurchase result in a large loss to our financial statements?" Tex agrees, indicating that West-Tex is likely to just meet earnings targets for 2024. The company would probably not meet its targets with a multimillion-dollar loss on a bond repurchase. However, 2025 looks to be a record-breaking year. They decide that maybe they should wait until 2025 to repurchase the bonds.

How could the repurchase of debt cause a loss to be reported in net income? Explain how the repurchase of debt might be timed to manage reported earnings. Is it ethical to time the repurchase of bonds to help meet earnings targets?

PART C

■ **LO9–7**
Calculate the issue price of a bond.

PRICING A BOND

In Part B of this chapter, the issue price of the bond was given. In this section, we demonstrate how that issue price is calculated. **The issue price of a bond equals the *present value* of the bond's face amount plus the *present value* of its periodic interest payments.** To calculate these present values, we need to know

1. The face amount of the bond.
2. The interest payment each period based on the stated interest rate of the bond.
3. The number of periods until the bond matures.
4. The market interest rate per period.

The first three items are stated in the bond contract. In our example for California Coasters, the *face amount* equals $100,000. The *interest payment* every six months is $3,500 (= $100,000 × 7% × 1/2 year) based on the bond's stated interest rate of 7%. The *number of periods* to maturity is 20 because the bonds pay interest semiannually (twice per year) for 10 years.

As discussed previously, the *market interest rate* is not stated in the bond contract. This rate is implied based on the issue price of the bond. **It's the market rate that we'll use to determine the present value of the face amount and the present value of the interest payments.** When the market rate equals the bond's stated rate, the issue price equals the face amount. When the market rate is greater than (less than) the stated rate, the bonds will issue at a discount (premium).

Bonds Issued at Face Amount

Let's first assume the market interest rate is 7%, the same as the issuing company's stated interest rate. One way to determine the issue price of bonds is to use your financial calculator. Illustration 9–9 shows the calculator inputs used to obtain an issue price at the face amount of $100,000.

ILLUSTRATION 9–9
Pricing Bonds Issued at Face Amount Using a Financial Calculator

CALCULATOR INPUT

Bond Characteristics	Key	Amount
1. Face amount	FV	$100,000
2. Interest payment	PMT	$3,500 = 100,000 × 7% × 1/2 year
3. Number of periods	N	20 = 10 years × 2 periods each year
4. Market interest rate	I	3.5 = 7% ÷ 2 periods each year

CALCULATOR OUTPUT

Issue price	PV	$100,000

An alternative to using a financial calculator is to calculate the price of bonds in Excel. Illustration 9–10 demonstrates the inputs and the formula used to calculate the issue price.

ILLUSTRATION 9–10
Pricing Bonds Issued at Face Amount Using Excel

B7   fx   =-PV(B5,B4,B3,B2,0)

	A	B
1		
2	Face amount	$100,000
3	Interest payment	$3,500
4	Number of periods	20
5	Market interest rate	0.035
6		
7	Issue price	$100,000
8		
9		

Sheet1   READY   100%

Microsoft Corporation

A third alternative is to calculate the price of the bonds using present value tables. In Illustration 9–11 we calculate the price of the bonds using the present value tables provided at the back of this book.

ILLUSTRATION 9–11
Pricing Bonds Issued at Face Amount Using Present Value Tables

Present value of face amount	= $100,000 × 0.50257*	=	$ 50,257
Present value of interest payments	= $3,500† × 14.21240**	=	49,743
Issue price of the bonds			$100,000

†$100,000 × 7% × 1/2 year = $3,500
*Table 2, i = 3.5%, n = 20
**Table 4, i = 3.5%, n = 20

We use Table 2, the present value of $1, to calculate the present value of the face amount since it's just one amount ($100,000) due at maturity. We use Table 4, the present value of an ordinary annuity of $1, to calculate the present value of the interest payments since they are a series of equal amounts ($3,500 each) paid every semiannual interest period. A series of equal amounts over equal time periods is called an **annuity**.

Using any of these three alternatives, the issue price of the bonds is equal to $100,000. All three methods have their advantages. A financial calculator and Excel are simple to use and provide greater flexibility regarding the choice of different interest rates and time periods. On the other hand, present value tables provide a more detailed understanding of how bond prices are determined.

Bonds Issued at a Discount

Now let's assume that California Coasters issues the same $100,000 of 7% bonds but investors require a market rate of return of 8%. These bonds will issue for less than $100,000 (at a *discount*). Illustration 9–12 shows the calculation of this issue price using a market rate of 8% (4% every semiannual period).

ILLUSTRATION 9–12

Pricing Bonds Issued at a Discount Using a Financial Calculator

	CALCULATOR INPUT		
Bond Characteristics	**Key**	**Amount**	
1. Face amount	FV	$100,000	
2. Interest payment	PMT	$3,500 = $100,000 × 7% × 1/2 year	
3. Number of periods	N	20 = 10 years × 2 periods each year	
4. Market interest rate	I	4 = 8% ÷ 2 periods each year	
	CALCULATOR OUTPUT		
Issue price	PV	$93,205	

Illustration 9–13 demonstrates how to use Excel to determine the issue price.

ILLUSTRATION 9–13

Pricing Bonds Issued at a Discount Using Excel

Microsoft Corporation

In Illustration 9–14, we calculate the price of the bonds using the present value tables provided at the back of this textbook, assuming the market rate of interest is 8% per year, or 4% every semiannual period.

ILLUSTRATION 9–14

Pricing Bonds Issued at a Discount Using Present Value Tables

Present value of principal	= $100,000 × 0.45639*	= $45,639
Present value of interest payments	= $3,500¹ × 13.59033**	= 47,566
Issue price of the bonds		$93,205

¹$100,000 × 7% × 1/2 year = $3,500
*Table 2, $i = 4\%$, $n = 20$
**Table 4, $i = 4\%$, $n = 20$

By investing only $93,205 to receive the face amount of $100,000 and semiannual interest payments of $3,500, investors *effectively* earn the market rate of 8% on their investment. **In other words, an investor paying $93,205 for the 7% bonds will earn the same rate of return (8%) as an investor paying $100,000 for bonds with a stated rate of 8%.**

COMMON MISTAKE

The interest rate we use to calculate the bond issue price is always the *market* rate, never the stated rate. Some students get confused and incorrectly use the stated rate to calculate present value. Use the stated rate to calculate the interest payment each period, but use the market rate to calculate the present value of the cash flows.

Bonds Issued at a Premium

Now let's assume that California Coasters issues $100,000 of 7% bonds when investors require a rate of only 6%. These bonds will issue for more than $100,000 (a *premium*). Illustration 9–15 shows the calculation of this issue price using a market rate of 6% (3% every semiannual period).

ILLUSTRATION 9–15

Pricing Bonds Issued at a Premium Using a Financial Calculator

CALCULATOR INPUT		
Bond Characteristics	**Key**	**Amount**
1. Face amount	FV	$100,000
2. Interest payment	PMT	$3,500 = $100,000 × 7% × 1/2 year
3. Number of periods	N	20 = 10 years × 2 periods each year
4. Market interest rate	I	3 = 6% ÷ 2 periods each year
CALCULATOR OUTPUT		
Issue price	PV	$107,439

Illustration 9–16 demonstrates how to use Excel to determine the issue price.

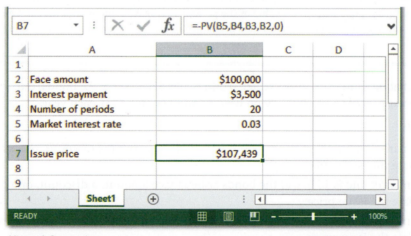

Microsoft Corporation

ILLUSTRATION 9–16

Pricing Bonds Issued at a Premium Using Excel

Illustration 9–17 calculates the price of the bonds using the present value tables provided at the back of this book, again assuming the market rate of interest is 6% (3% semiannually).

ILLUSTRATION 9–17

Pricing Bonds Issued at a Premium Using Present Value Tables

Present value of principal	= $100,000 × 0.55368*	=	$ 55,368
Present value of interest payments	= $3,500[1] × 14.87747**	=	52,071
Issue price of the bonds			$107,439

[1]$100,000 × 7% × 1/2 year = $3,500
*Table 2, *i* = 3%, *n* = 20
**Table 4, *i* = 3%, *n* = 20

By investing $107,439 to receive the face amount of $100,000 and semiannual interest payments of $3,500, investors *effectively* earn the market rate of 6% on their investment.

In other words, an investor paying $107,439 for the 7% bonds will earn the same rate of return (6%) as an investor paying $100,000 for bonds with a stated rate of 6%.

Illustration 9–18 shows the relation between the stated interest rate, the market interest rate, and the bond issue price.

ILLUSTRATION 9–18

Stated Rate, Market Rate, and the Bond Issue Price

Bonds Issued at a Discount	Bonds Issued at Face Amount	Bonds Issued at a Premium
Stated rate (7%) less than **Market rate (8%)**	Stated rate (7%) equal to **Market rate (7%)**	Stated rate (7%) greater than **Market rate (6%)**

If the bonds' stated interest rate is less than the market interest rate, then the bonds will issue below face amount (discount). If the bonds' stated interest rate equals the market interest rate, then the bonds will issue at face amount. Finally, if the bonds' stated interest rate is more than the market interest rate, the bonds will issue above face amount (premium).

Which is most common in practice—bonds issued at face amount, a discount, or a premium? Most bonds initially are issued at a slight discount. Because there is a delay between when the company determines the characteristics of the bonds and when the bonds actually are issued, the company must estimate the market rate of interest. Bond issuers usually adopt a stated interest rate that is close to, but just under, the expected market interest rate. However, in future periods, the bonds may trade at either a discount or a premium depending on changes in market interest rates.

 KEY POINT

The issue price of a bond is equal to the present value of the face amount (principal) payable at maturity, plus the present value of the periodic interest payments. Bonds can be issued at face amount, below face amount (at a discount), or above face amount (at a premium).

Let's Review

Assume that on January 1, 2024, Water World issues $200,000 of 9% bonds, due in 10 years, with interest payable semiannually on June 30 and December 31 each year.

Required:

1. If the market rate is 9%, will the bonds issue at face amount, a discount, or a premium? Calculate the issue price.

2. If the market rate is 10%, will the bonds issue at face amount, a discount, or a premium? Calculate the issue price.

3. If the market rate is 8%, will the bonds issue at face amount, a discount, or a premium? Calculate the issue price.

Solution:

1. If the market rate is 9%, the bonds will issue at face amount.

CALCULATOR INPUT		
Bond Characteristics	**Key**	**Amount**
1. Face amount	FV	$200,000
2. Interest payment	PMT	$9,000 = $200,000 × 9% × 1/2 year
3. Number of periods	N	20 = 10 years × 2 periods each year
4. Market interest rate	I	4.5 = 9% ÷ 2 periods each year
CALCULATOR OUTPUT		
Issue price	PV	$200,000

C7	▾	:	×	✓	*fx*	=-PV(C5,C4,C3,C2,0)			▾

◢	A	B	C	D	E	F	▲
1							
2	Face amount		$200,000				
3	Interest payment		$9,000				
4	Number of periods		20				
5	Market interest rate		0.045				
6							
7	Issue price		$200,000				
8							
9							▾

Sheet1   ⊕

READY   ⊞ ▣ 🗖 − ▬ +   100%

Microsoft Corporation

PRESENT VALUE TABLES

Present value of principal	= $200,000 × 0.41464*	=	$ 82,928
Present value of interest payments	= $9,000[†] × 13.00794**	=	117,072
Issue price of the bonds			$200,000

[†]$200,000 × 9% × 1/2 year = $9,000
*Table 2, i = 4.5%, n = 20
**Table 4, i = 4.5%, n = 20

2. If the market rate is 10%, the bonds will issue at a discount. The only change we make in the calculation is that now I = 5 rather than 4.5.

CALCULATOR INPUT

Bond Characteristics	Key	Amount
1. Face amount	FV	$200,000
2. Interest payment	PMT	$9,000 = $200,000 × 9% × 1/2 year
3. Number of periods	N	20 = 10 years × 2 periods each year
4. Market interest rate	I	5 = 10% ÷ 2 periods each year

CALCULATOR OUTPUT

Issue price	PV	$187,538

C7	▾	:	×	✓	*fx*	=-PV(C5,C4,C3,C2,0)			▾

◢	A	B	C	D	E	F	▲
1							
2	Face amount		$200,000				
3	Interest payment		$9,000				
4	Number of periods		20				
5	Market interest rate		0.05				
6							
7	Issue price		$187,538				
8							
9							▾

Sheet1   ⊕

READY   ⊞ ▣ 🗖 − ▬ +   100%

Microsoft Corporation

PRESENT VALUE TABLES

Present value of principal	= $200,000 × 0.37689*	=	$ 75,378
Present value of interest payments	= $9,000† × 12.46221**	=	112,160
Issue price of the bonds			$187,538

†$200,000 × 9% × 1/2 year = $9,000
*Table 2, $i = 5\%$, $n = 20$
**Table 4, $i = 5\%$, $n = 20$

3. If the market rate is 8%, the bonds will issue at a premium. The only change we make in the calculation is that now I = 4.

CALCULATOR INPUT

Bond Characteristics	Key	Amount
1. Face amount	FV	$200,000
2. Interest payment	PMT	$9,000 = $200,000 × 9% × 1/2 year
3. Number of periods	N	20 = 10 years × 2 periods each year
4. Market interest rate	I	4 = 8% ÷ 2 periods each year

CALCULATOR OUTPUT

Issue price	PV	$213,590

C7   fx   =-PV(C5,C4,C3,C2,0)

	A	B	C	D	E	F
1						
2	Face amount		$200,000			
3	Interest payment		$9,000			
4	Number of periods		20			
5	Market interest rate		0.04			
6						
7	Issue price		$213,590			
8						
9						

Sheet1   READY   100%

Microsoft Corporation

PRESENT VALUE TABLES

Present value of principal	= $200,000 × 0.45639*	=	$ 91,278
Present value of interest payments	= $9,000† × 13.59033**	=	122,312
Issue price of the bonds			$213,590

†$200,000 × 9% × 1/2 year = $9,000
*Table 2, $i = 4\%$, $n = 20$
**Table 4, $i = 4\%$, $n = 20$

Suggested Homework:
BE9–21, BE9–22;
E9–21, E9–22;
P9–8A&B

DEBT ANALYSIS
Coca-Cola vs. PepsiCo

A company's level of debt is one of the first places decision makers look when trying to get a handle on solvency risk. **Solvency** refers to a company's ability to pays its current and long-term obligations. The year before **Toys R Us** declared bankruptcy, the company described in its annual report the risks of its growing debt. Excerpts are provided in Illustration 9–19.

■ **LO9–8**

Assess the impact of long-term debt on risk and return.

ANALYSIS

**Toys R Us
Notes to the Financial Statements (excerpt)**

Our substantial indebtedness could have significant consequences, including, among others,

*   increasing our vulnerability to general economic and industry conditions;
*   reducing our ability to fund our operations and capital expenditures, capitalize on future business opportunities, expand our business and execute our strategy;
*   increasing the difficulty for us to make scheduled payments on our outstanding debt;
*   exposing us to the risk of increased interest expense;
*   causing us to make non-strategic divestitures;
*   limiting our ability to obtain additional financing;
*   limiting our ability to adjust to changing market conditions and reacting to competitive pressure, placing us at a competitive disadvantage compared to our competitors who are less leveraged.

ILLUSTRATION 9–19

Toys R Us Notes to the Financial Statements (excerpt)

Here, we look at two ratios frequently used to measure financial risk: (1) debt to equity and (2) times interest earned.

DEBT TO EQUITY RATIO

To measure a company's risk, we often calculate the **debt to equity ratio**:

$$\text{Debt to equity ratio} = \frac{\text{Total liabilities}}{\text{Stockholders' equity}}$$

Debt requires payment on specific dates. Failure to repay debt or the interest associated with the debt on a timely basis may result in default and perhaps even bankruptcy for a company. Other things being equal, the higher the debt to equity ratio, the higher the risk of bankruptcy. When a company assumes more debt, risk increases.

Debt also can be an advantage. It can enhance the return to stockholders. If a company earns a return in excess of the cost of borrowing the funds, shareholders are provided with a total return greater than what could have been earned with equity funds alone. Unfortunately, borrowing is not always favorable. Sometimes the cost of borrowing the funds exceeds the returns they generate. This illustrates the risk–reward trade-off faced by shareholders.

Have you ever ordered a Pepsi and then found out the place serves only Coke products? Amusement parks often have exclusive contracts for soft drinks. The official soft drink of **Six Flags** is Coca-Cola. **Cedar Point** used to serve only Pepsi products, but now also has an exclusive deal with Coca-Cola. Illustration 9–20 provides selected financial data for **Coca-Cola** and **PepsiCo.**

ILLUSTRATION 9–20

Financial Information for Coca-Cola and PepsiCo

SELECTED BALANCE SHEET DATA ($ in millions)		
	Coca-Cola	**PepsiCo**
Total assets*	$86,381	$78,547
Total liabilities	$65,283	$63,679
Stockholders' equity	21,098	14,868
Total liabilities and equity	$86,381	$78,547

* Amounts shown are total assets at the end of the year. Beginning total assets are $83,216 (for Coca-Cola) and $77,468 (for PepsiCo).

INCOME STATEMENTS ($ in millions)		
	Coca-Cola	**PepsiCo**
Net sales	$37,266	$67,161
Cost of goods sold	14,619	30,132
Gross profit	22,647	37,029
Operating expenses	12,561	26,738
Other income	1,646	156
Interest expense	946	1,135
Income tax expense	1,801	1,959
Net income	$ 8,985	$ 7,353

Illustration 9–21 compares the debt to equity ratio for Coca-Cola and PepsiCo.

ILLUSTRATION 9–21

Debt to Equity Ratio for Coca-Cola and PepsiCo

($ in millions)	Total Liabilities	÷	Stockholders' Equity	=	Debt to Equity Ratio
Coca-Cola	$65,283	÷	$21,098	=	3.09
PepsiCo	$63,679	÷	$14,868	=	4.28

The debt to equity ratio is higher for PepsiCo. Debt to equity is a measure of financial leverage. Thus, PepsiCo has higher leverage than Coca-Cola. Leverage enables a company to earn a higher return using debt than without debt, in the same way a person can lift more weight with a lever than without it.

Decision Point

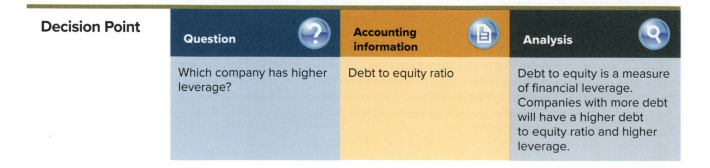

Question	Accounting information	Analysis
Which company has higher leverage?	Debt to equity ratio	Debt to equity is a measure of financial leverage. Companies with more debt will have a higher debt to equity ratio and higher leverage.

PepsiCo is assuming more debt, and therefore its investors are assuming more risk. Remember, this added debt could be good or bad depending on whether the company earns a return in excess of the cost of borrowed funds. Let's explore this further by revisiting the return on assets introduced in Chapter 7. Recall that **return on assets** measures the amount of income generated for each dollar of assets. In Illustration 9–22, we calculate the return on assets for Coca-Cola and PepsiCo.

$$\text{Return on assets} = \frac{\text{Net income}}{\text{Average total assets}}$$

($ in millions)	Net Income	÷	Average Total Assets	=	Return on Assets
Coca-Cola	$8,985	÷	$84,798.5*	=	10.6%
PepsiCo	$7,353	÷	$78,097.5**	=	9.4%

ILLUSTRATION 9–22

Return on Assets for Coca-Cola and PepsiCo

*($86,381 + $83,216)/2
**($78,547 + $77,648)/2

Coca-Cola returns 10.6 cents for each dollar of assets, compared with 9.4 cents for PepsiCo. For both companies, the return on assets exceeds the cost of borrowing (each company's borrowing rate is less than 4%). Therefore, both companies increase their total return by borrowing at a low rate and then earning a higher return on those borrowed funds. This illustrates the power of leverage to increase a company's profits. This is especially true for PepsiCo because its return on assets is similar to Coca-Cola's, but Pepsi's leverage is much higher. If return on assets should fall below the rate charged on borrowed funds, PepsiCo's greater leverage will result in a lower overall return to shareholders. That's where the risk comes in.

TIMES INTEREST EARNED RATIO

Lenders require interest payments in return for the use of their money. Failure to pay interest when it is due may invoke penalties, possibly leading to bankruptcy. A ratio often used to measure this risk is the **times interest earned ratio**. This ratio provides an indication to creditors of how many "times" greater earnings are than interest expense. A company's earnings (or profitability) provide an indication of its ability to generate cash from operations in the current year and in future years, and its cash that will be used to pay interest payments. So, **the higher a company's earnings relative to its interest expense, the more likely it will be able to make current and future interest payments.**

At first glance, you might think we can calculate the times interest earned ratio as net income divided by interest expense. But remember, interest is one of the expenses subtracted in determining net income. So, to measure how many times greater earnings are than interest expense, we need to add interest expense back to net income. Similarly, because interest is deductible for income tax purposes, we also need to add back income tax expense to get a measure of earnings *before* the effects of interest and taxes. We compute the times interest earned ratio as

$$\text{Times interest earned ratio} = \frac{\text{Net income} + \text{Interest expense} + \text{Income tax expense}}{\text{Interest expense}}$$

To further understand why we need to add back interest expense and income tax expense to net income, assume a company has the following income statement:

Income before interest and taxes	$ 90,000
Interest expense	**(10,000)**
Income before taxes	80,000
Income tax expense (25%)	(20,000)
Net income	$ 60,000

How many times greater is the company's earnings than interest expense? Is it 6.0 times greater (= $60,000 ÷ $10,000)? No, it's 9.0 times greater (= $90,000 ÷ $10,000). If current earnings provide an indication of the ability of a company to generate cash from operations in the current year and in future years, then a ratio of 9.0 suggests that the company will have plenty of cash available to pay current and future interest payments.

Illustration 9–23 computes the times interest earned ratios for Coca-Cola and PepsiCo to compare the companies' ability to make interest payments.

ILLUSTRATION 9–23

Times Interest Earned Ratio for Coca-Cola and PepsiCo

($ in millions)	Net Income + Interest Expense + Income Tax Expense	÷	Interest Expense	=	Times Interest Earned Ratio
Coca-Cola	$11,732	÷	$ 946	=	12.4
PepsiCo	$10,447	÷	$1,135	=	9.2

Coca-Cola has a higher times interest earned ratio than PepsiCo, indicating Coca-Cola is better able to meet its long-term interest obligations. However, both companies exhibit strong earnings in relation to their interest expense, and both companies appear well able to meet interest payments as they become due.

KEY POINT

The debt to equity ratio is a measure of financial leverage. Taking on more debt (higher leverage) can be good or bad depending on whether the company earns a return in excess of the cost of borrowed funds. The times interest earned ratio measures a company's ability to meet interest payments as they become due.

Decision Point

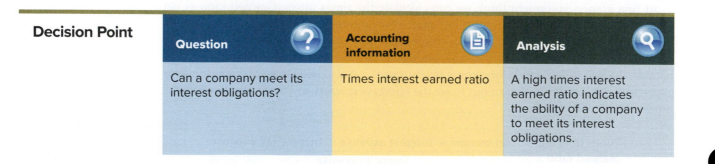

Question ❓	Accounting information 📄	Analysis 🔍
Can a company meet its interest obligations?	Times interest earned ratio	A high times interest earned ratio indicates the ability of a company to meet its interest obligations.

CHAPTER FRAMEWORK

This chapter discusses the different types of long-term liabilities—installment notes, leases, and bonds. Long-term liability transactions affect amounts reported in the financial statements.

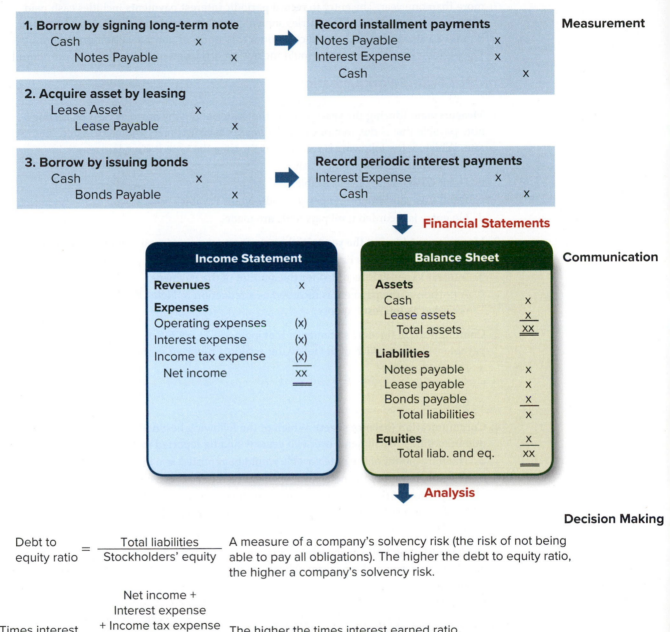

1. Borrow by signing long-term note		
Cash	x	
Notes Payable		x

2. Acquire asset by leasing		
Lease Asset	x	
Lease Payable		x

3. Borrow by issuing bonds		
Cash	x	
Bonds Payable		x

Measurement

Record installment payments		
Notes Payable	x	
Interest Expense	x	
Cash		x

Record periodic interest payments		
Interest Expense	x	
Cash		x

Financial Statements

Communication

Income Statement	
Revenues	x
Expenses	
Operating expenses	(x)
Interest expense	(x)
Income tax expense	(x)
Net income	xx

Balance Sheet	
Assets	
Cash	x
Lease assets	x
Total assets	xx
Liabilities	
Notes payable	x
Lease payable	x
Bonds payable	x
Total liabilities	x
Equities	x
Total liab. and eq.	xx

Analysis

Decision Making

$$\text{Debt to equity ratio} = \frac{\text{Total liabilities}}{\text{Stockholders' equity}}$$

A measure of a company's solvency risk (the risk of not being able to pay all obligations). The higher the debt to equity ratio, the higher a company's solvency risk.

$$\text{Times interest earned ratio} = \frac{\text{Net income} + \text{Interest expense} + \text{Income tax expense}}{\text{Interest expense}}$$

The higher the times interest earned ratio, the lower a company's solvency risk.

1. **Borrow by signing long-term note.** A company borrows by issuing a note payable due in more than one year. These notes often have payments that are due in installments over the life of the note. The entry to **record installment payments** includes both an amount that represents interest and an amount that represents a reduction of the outstanding loan balance. The portion of the note due over the next year would be reported as a current liability, and the portion due in more than one year would be reported as a long-term liability.

2. **Acquire asset by leasing.** During the year, a company acquires an asset by leasing. Leasing does not transfer ownership, but the right of use is recorded as an asset, and the obligation to make lease payments is recorded as a liability. The amount to record is the present value of the lease payments. (Note: The entry to record each lease payment over the lease period is not covered.)

3. **Borrow by issuing bonds.** During the year, a company borrows by issuing bonds due in more than one year. The entry to **record periodic interest payments** includes cash paid at the bond's stated rate. [The entries shown above are for bonds issued at face amount. Bonds can also be issued below face amount (discount) or above face amount (premium). The periodic interest payments would include amortization of the discount or premium.]

Chapter Framework Questions

1. **Measurement (during the year):** During the year, a company borrows cash by issuing a note payable that is due in monthly installments over two years and has a stated interest rate. Which of the following is recorded at the time the note is issued?
   a. Debit Notes Payable; credit Cash.
   b. Debit Cash; credit Notes Payable.
   c. Debit Cash and Interest Expense; credit Notes Payable.
   d. No entry is recorded until payments are made.

2. **Measurement (during the year):** With each payment on an installment note payable
   a. The balance of Notes Payable decreases by the amount of the payment.
   b. Interest Expense is recorded for the amount of the payment.
   c. A portion of the payment is recorded as a reduction in Notes Payable and a portion is recorded as Interest Expense.

3. **Communication (income statement):** Making periodic payments on an installment note payable will affect which of the following accounts reported in the income statement?
   a. Interest Expense.
   b. Notes Payable.
   c. Cash.

4. **Communication (balance sheet):** Which of the following best describes how a note payable due in monthly installments over two years would be reported in the balance sheet?
   a. The full amount of the note payable would be reported as a long-term liability.
   b. The full amount of the note payable would be reported as a current liability.
   c. The portion of the note payable due over the next year would be reported as a current liability, and the portion due in more than one year would be reported as a long-term liability.

5. **Decision Making (ratio analysis):** Companies that are likely to have higher risk of not being able to pay current and long-term obligations would have a _____ debt to equity ratio.
   a. Higher.
   b. Lower.

Note: For answers, see the last page of the chapter.

KEY POINTS BY LEARNING OBJECTIVE

LO9–1 Explain financing alternatives.

Companies obtain external funds through debt financing (liabilities) and equity financing (stockholders' equity). One advantage of debt financing is that interest on borrowed funds is tax-deductible.

LO9–2 Account for installment notes payable.

Most notes payable require periodic installment payments. Each installment payment includes an amount that represents interest expense and an amount that represents a reduction of the carrying value (remaining loan balance).

LO9–3 Understand how leases are recorded.

While not transferring ownership as in a purchase, a lease gives the lessee (user) the right to use the asset over the lease period. This right is recorded as an asset, and the obligation to make lease payments is recorded as a liability.

LO9–4 Account for the issuance of bonds at face amount.

The distinguishing characteristics of bonds include whether they are backed by collateral (secured or unsecured), become due at a single specified date or over a series of years (term or serial), can be redeemed prior to maturity (callable), or can be converted into common stock (convertible).

LO9–5 Account for the issuance of bonds at a discount or premium.

When bonds issue at a discount (below face amount), the carrying value and the corresponding interest expense *increase* over time. When bonds issue at a premium (above face amount), the carrying value and the corresponding interest expense *decrease* over time.

LO9–6 Record gain or loss on retirement of bonds.

No gain or loss is recorded on bonds retired at maturity. For bonds retired before maturity, we record a gain or loss on early extinguishment equal to the difference between the price paid to repurchase the bonds and the bonds' carrying value.

LO9–7 Calculate the issue price of a bond.

The issue price of a bond is equal to the present value of the face amount (principal) payable at maturity, plus the present value of the periodic interest payments. Bonds can be issued at face amount, below face amount (at a discount), or above face amount (at a premium).

Analysis

LO9–8 Assess the impact of long-term debt on risk and return.

The debt to equity ratio is a measure of financial leverage. Assuming more debt (higher leverage) can be good or bad depending on whether the company earns a return in excess of the cost of borrowed funds. The times interest earned ratio measures a company's ability to meet interest payments as they become due.

GLOSSARY

Amortization schedule: Provides a table format detailing the cash payment each period, the portions of each cash payment that represents interest and the change in carrying value, and balance of the carrying value. **p. 443**

Annuity: Cash payments of equal amounts over equal time periods. **p. 459**

Bond: A formal debt instrument issued by a company to borrow money. The issuing company (borrower) is obligated to pay back to the investor (lender): (1) a stated amount, referred to as the *principal* or *face amount,* at a specified maturity date and (2) periodic interest payments over the life of the bond. **p. 447**

Callable: A bond feature that allows the borrower to repay the bonds before their scheduled maturity date at a specified call price. **p. 450**

Capital structure: The mixture of liabilities and stockholders' equity in a business. **p. 442**

Carrying value: The amount for which a liability is reported in the balance sheet. **p. 443**

Convertible: A bond feature that allows the lender (or investor) to convert each bond into a specified number of shares of common stock. **p. 450**

Debt financing: Borrowing money from creditors (liabilities). **p. 442**

Debt to equity ratio: Total liabilities divided by total stockholders' equity; measures a company's risk. **p. 465**

Default risk: The risk that a company will be unable to pay the bond's face amount or interest payments as they become due. **p. 450**

Discount: A bond's issue price is below the face amount. **p. 451**

Early extinguishment of debt: The issuer retires debt before its scheduled maturity date. **p. 456**

Equity financing: Obtaining investment from stockholders (stockholders' equity). **p. 442**

Installment payment: Includes both an amount that represents interest and an amount that represents a reduction of the carrying value. **p. 443**

Lease: A contractual arrangement by which the lessor (owner) provides the lessee (user) the right to use an asset for a specified period of time. **p. 445**

Market interest rate: An implied rate based on the price investors are willing to pay to purchase a bond in return for the right to receive the face amount at maturity and periodic interest payments over the remaining life of the bond. **p. 450**

Premium: A bond's issue price is above the face amount. **p. 451**

Private placement: Sale of debt securities directly to a single investor. **p. 449**

Return on assets: Net income divided by average total assets; measures the amount of net income generated for each dollar invested in assets. **p. 467**

Secured bonds: Bonds that are supported by specific assets pledged as collateral. **p. 449**

Serial bonds: Bonds that require payment of the principal amount of the bond over a series of maturity dates. **p. 450**

Sinking fund: An investment fund used to set aside money to be used to pay debts as they come due. **p. 450**

Solvency: Refers to a company's ability to pay its current and long-term obligations. **p. 465**

Stated interest rate: The rate specified in the bond contract used to calculate the cash payments for interest. **p. 448**

Term bonds: Bonds that require payment of the full principal amount at a single maturity date. **p. 449**

Times interest earned ratio: Ratio that compares interest expense with income available to pay those charges. **p. 467**

Unsecured bonds: Bonds that are *not* supported by specific assets pledged as collateral. **p. 449**

SELF-STUDY QUESTIONS

1. Which of the following is *not* a primary source of corporate debt financing? **(LO9–1)**
   a. Bonds.
   b. Notes.
   c. Leases.
   d. Receivables.

2. A company purchased new equipment for $31,000 with a two-year installment note requiring 5% interest. The required monthly payment is $1,360. For the first month's payment, what is the amount to record for interest expense? **(LO9–2)**
   a. $120.
   b. $129.
   c. $68.
   d. $155.

3. A company purchased new equipment for $31,000 with a two-year installment note requiring 5% interest. The required monthly payment is $1,360. After the first month's payment, what is the balance of the note? **(LO9–2)**
   a. $30,723.
   b. $29,640.
   c. $29,769.
   d. $30,871.

4. Which of the following typically represents an advantage of leasing over purchasing an asset with an installment note? **(LO9–3)**
   a. Lease payments often are lower than installment payments.
   b. Leasing generally requires less cash upfront.
   c. Leasing typically offers greater flexibility and lower costs in disposing of an asset.
   d. All of the above are advantages of leasing.

5. A company needs construction equipment to complete a project over the next 20 months. The equipment costs $10,000. Instead of purchasing the equipment with a 12% note, the company leases the equipment with payments of $300 due at the end of each month. For what amount would the company record the lease liability at the beginning of the lease? **(LO9–3)**
   a. $5,414.
   b. $6,000.
   c. $4,586.
   d. $10,000.

6. Suppose a company issues five-year bonds for face amount of $80,000 with 6% semiannual interest. On the issue date, the company will record Bonds Payable for **(LO9–4)**
   a. $84,800.
   b. $80,000.
   c. $82,400.
   d. $104,000.

7. Suppose a company issues five-year bonds for face amount of $80,000 with 6% semiannual interest. On the first interest payment date, the company records Interest Expense of **(LO9–4)**
   a. $0.
   b. $4,800.
   c. $2,400.
   d. $24,000.

8. Which of the following is true for bonds issued at a discount? **(LO9–5)**
   a. The stated interest rate is greater than the market interest rate.
   b. The market interest rate is greater than the stated interest rate.
   c. The stated interest rate and the market interest rate are equal.
   d. The stated interest rate and the market interest rate are unrelated.

9. When bonds are issued at a premium, what happens to the carrying value and interest expense each period over the life of the bonds? **(LO9–5)**
   a. Carrying value and interest expense increase.
   b. Carrying value and interest expense decrease.
   c. Carrying value decreases and interest expense increases.
   d. Carrying value increases and interest expense decreases.

10. A company issues $50,000 of 4% bonds, due in five years, with interest payable semiannually. Assuming a market rate of 3%, the bonds issue for $52,306. Calculate interest expense as of the first semiannual interest payment. **(LO9–5)**

    a. $1,570.

    b. $1,000.

    c. $785.

    d. $375.

11. A company issues $50,000 of 4% bonds, due in five years, with interest payable semiannually. Assuming a market rate of 3%, the bonds issue for $52,306. Calculate the carrying value of the bonds after the first semiannual interest payment. **(LO9–5)**

    a. $51,306.

    b. $52,091.

    c. $49,000.

    d. $51,521.

12. Lincoln County retires a $50 million bond issue when the carrying value of the bonds is $48 million, but the market value of the bonds is $54 million. Lincoln County will record the retirement as **(LO9–6)**

    a. A debit of $6 million to Loss due to early extinguishment.

    b. A credit of $6 million to Gain due to early extinguishment.

    c. No gain or loss on retirement.

    d. A debit to Cash for $54 million.

13. The price of a bond is equal to **(LO9–7)**

    a. The present value of the face amount plus the present value of the stated interest payments.

    b. The future value of the face amount plus the future value of the stated interest payments.

    c. The present value of the face amount only.

    d. The present value of the interest only.

14. A company issues $50,000 of 4% bonds, due in five years, with interest payable semiannually. Calculate the issue price of the bonds, assuming a market interest rate of 5%. **(LO9–7)**

    a. $47,835.

    b. $52,246.

    c. $58,983.

    d. $47,812.

15. Which of the following ratios measures financial leverage? **(LO9–8)**

    a. The return on assets ratio.

    b. The inventory turnover ratio.

    c. The times interest earned ratio.

    d. The debt to equity ratio.

Note: For answers, see the last page of the chapter.

DATA ANALYTICS & EXCEL

Visit Connect to find a variety of Data Analytics questions that help build Excel, Tableau, and data visualization skills. Assignable materials include Integrated Excel, Applying Excel, Data Visualizations, Tableau Dashboard Activities, and Applying Tableau Cases.

REVIEW QUESTIONS

1. What is capital structure? How do the capital structures of Ford and Microsoft differ?   ■ **LO9–1**

2. Why would a company choose to borrow money rather than issue additional stock?   ■ **LO9–1**

3. How do interest expense and the carrying value of the note change over time for an installment note with fixed monthly loan payments?   ■ **LO9–2**

4. What is a lease and how does a lease affect a company's balance sheet?   ■ **LO9–3**

5. What are bond issue costs? What is an underwriter?   ■ **LO9–4**

6. Why do some companies issue bonds rather than borrow money directly from a bank?   ■ **LO9–4**

7. Contrast the following types of bonds: ■ **LO9–4**

    a. Secured and unsecured.

    b. Term and serial.

    c. Callable and convertible.

8. What are convertible bonds? How do they benefit both the investor and the issuer?   ■ **LO9–4**

9. Explain the difference in each of these terms used for bonds: ■ **LO9–5**

    a. Face amount and carrying value.

    b. Stated interest rate and market interest rate.

■ **LO9–5**	10. If bonds issue at a *discount,* is the stated interest rate less than, equal to, or more than the market interest rate? Explain.
■ **LO9–5**	11. If bonds issue at a *premium,* is the stated interest rate less than, equal to, or more than the market interest rate? Explain.
■ **LO9–5**	12. If bonds issue at a *discount,* what happens to the carrying value of bonds payable and the amount recorded for interest expense over time?
■ **LO9–5**	13. If bonds issue at a *premium,* what happens to the carrying value of bonds payable and the amount recorded for interest expense over time?
■ **LO9–5**	14. Explain how each of the columns in an amortization schedule is calculated, assuming the bonds are issued at a discount. How is the amortization schedule different if bonds are issued at a premium?
■ **LO9–6**	15. Why would a company choose to buy back bonds before their maturity date?
■ **LO9–6**	16. If bonds with a face amount of $250,000 and a carrying value of $280,000 are retired early at a cost of $330,000, is a gain or loss recorded by the issuer retiring the bonds? How does the issuer record the retirement?
■ **LO9–7**	17. How do we calculate the issue price of bonds? Is it equal to the present value of the principal? Explain.
■ **LO9–7**	18. Extreme Motion issues $500,000 of 6% bonds due in 20 years with interest payable semiannually on June 30 and December 31. What is the amount of the cash payment for interest every six months? How many interest payments will there be?
■ **LO9–7**	19. Extreme Motion issues $500,000 of 6% bonds due in 20 years with interest payable semiannually on June 30 and December 31. Calculate the issue price of the bonds assuming a market interest rate of a. 5%. b. 6%. c. 7%.
■ **LO9–8**	20. What are the potential risks and rewards of carrying additional debt?

BRIEF EXERCISES

Record installment notes (LO9–2)

BE9–1 On January 1, 2024, Corvallis Carnivals borrows $30,000 to purchase a delivery truck by agreeing to a 5%, five-year loan with the bank. Payments of $566.14 are due at the end of each month, with the first installment due on January 31, 2024. Record the issuance of the installment note payable and the first monthly payment.

Record installment notes (LO9–2)

BE9–2 On January 1, 2024, Beaver Tours financed the purchase of a new building by borrowing $600,000 from the bank using a 30-year, 6% note payable. Payments of $3,597.30 are due at the end of each month, with the first installment due on January 31, 2024. Record the issuance of the installment note payable and the first monthly payment.

Interpret an amortization schedule for an installment note (LO9–2)

BE9–3 Presented below is a partial amortization schedule for a three-year installment note requiring monthly payments of $1,128.11.

	(1)	(2)	(3)	(4)	(5)
			Interest	**Decrease in**	
	Date	**Cash Paid**	**Expense**	**Carrying Value**	**Carrying Value**
			Carrying Value × Interest Rate	(2) − (3)	Prior Carrying Value − (4)
	11/1/2024				$36,000.00
	11/30/2024	$1,128.11	$240.00	$ 888.11	35,111.89
	12/31/2024	1,128.11	234.08	894.03	34,217.86
	*	*	*	*	*
	10/31/2027	1,128.11	7.47	1,120.64	0.00

1. What is the principal amount of the note?
2. What is the total number of monthly payments?
3. What is the total cash paid over the entire period of the note?
4. What is the total amount of interest paid over the entire period of the note?
5. The portion of the monthly payment that reduces the carrying value (increases/decreases) over time.

BE9–4 A company purchases a small office building as its new headquarters. The building cost $750,000. To purchase the building, the company issues a 15-year installment note with 5% interest. The company is considering two options:

a. Pay $0 down and make monthly payments of $5,930.95 over 15 years.

b. Pay $150,000 down and make payments of $4,744.76 over 15 years.

For each option, determine (1) the total cash paid for the building over 15 years, including the down payment, and (2) total interest paid over 15 years.

Compute total interest on installment notes (LO9–2)

BE9–5 On April 1, 2024, Primer Corp. signs a five-year lease to use office space. The present value of the monthly lease payments is $100,000. Record the lease.

Record leases (LO9–3)

BE9–6 Suppose a company signs a three-year lease agreement. The lease payments have a present value of $40,000. Prior to signing the lease, the company had total assets of $600,000, total liabilities of $400,000, and total stockholders' equity of $200,000. Calculate the balance of total assets, total liabilities, and total stockholders' equity immediately after signing the lease.

Understand balance sheet effect of leases (LO9–3)

BE9–7 Listed below are terms and definitions associated with bonds. Match (by letter) the bond terms with their definitions. Each letter is used only once.

Match bond terms with their definitions (LO9–4)

Terms	Definitions
_____ 1. Sinking fund	a. Allows the issuer to pay off the bonds early at a fixed price.
_____ 2. Secured bond	b. Matures in installments.
_____ 3. Unsecured bond	c. Secured only by the "full faith and credit" of the issuing corporation.
_____ 4. Term bond	d. Allows the investor to transfer each bond into shares of common stock.
_____ 5. Serial bond	e. Money set aside to pay debts as they come due.
_____ 6. Callable bond	f. Matures on a single date.
_____ 7. Convertible bond	g. Supported by specific assets pledged as collateral by the issuer.
_____ 8. Bond issue costs	h. Includes underwriting, legal, accounting, registration, and printing fees.

BE9–8 Pretzelmania, Inc., issues 7%, 10-year bonds with a face amount of $70,000 for $70,000 on January 1, 2024. Interest is paid semiannually on June 30 and December 31.
1. Record the bond issue on January 1, 2024.
2. Record the first interest payment on June 30, 2024.

Record bond issue at face amount and related semiannual interest (LO9–4)

BE9–9 Pretzelmania, Inc., issues 7%, 15-year bonds with a face amount of $70,000 for $63,948 on January 1, 2024. The market interest rate for bonds of similar risk and maturity is 8%. Interest is paid semiannually on June 30 and December 31.
1. Record the bond issue on January 1, 2024.
2. Record the first interest payment on June 30, 2024.

Record bond issue at a discount and related semiannual interest (LO9–5)

BE9–10 Pretzelmania, Inc., issues 7%, 15-year bonds with a face amount of $70,000 for $76,860 on January 1, 2024. The market interest rate for bonds of similar risk and maturity is 6%. Interest is paid semiannually on June 30 and December 31.
1. Record the bond issue on January 1, 2024.
2. Record the first interest payment on June 30, 2024.

Record bond issue at a premium and related semiannual interest (LO9–5)

Record bond issue at face amount and related *annual* interest (LO9–4)

BE9–11 Pretzelmania, Inc., issues 7%, 10-year bonds with a face amount of $70,000 for $70,000 on January 1, 2024. Interest is paid *annually* on December 31.
1. Record the bond issue on January 1, 2024.
2. Record the first interest payment on December 31, 2024.

Record bond issue at a discount and related *annual* interest (LO9–5)

BE9–12 Pretzelmania, Inc., issues 7%, 15-year bonds with a face amount of $70,000 for $64,008 on January 1, 2024. The market interest rate for bonds of similar risk and maturity is 8%. Interest is paid *annually* on December 31.
1. Record the bond issue on January 1, 2024.
2. Record the first interest payment on December 31, 2024. (*Hint:* Interest expense is 8% times the carrying value of $64,008.)

Record bond issue at a premium and related *annual* interest (LO9–5)

BE9–13 Pretzelmania, Inc., issues 7%, 15-year bonds with a face amount of $70,000 for $76,799 on January 1, 2024. The market interest rate for bonds of similar risk and maturity is 6%. Interest is paid *annually* on December 31.
1. Record the bond issue on January 1, 2024.
2. Record the first interest payment on December 31, 2024. (*Hint:* Interest expense is 6% times the carrying value of $76,799.)

Calculate interest expense (LO9–5)

BE9–14 On January 1, 2024, Lizzy's Lemonade issues 5%, 20-year bonds with a face amount of $100,000 for $88,443, priced to yield 6%. Interest is paid semiannually. What amount of interest expense will be recorded on June 30, 2024, the first interest payment date?

Calculate interest expense (LO9–5)

BE9–15 On January 1, 2024, Lyle's Limeade issues 4%, 10-year bonds with a face amount of $90,000 for $82,985, priced to yield 5%. Interest is paid semiannually. What amount of interest expense will be recorded in the December 31, 2024, annual income statement?

Interpret a bond amortization schedule (LO9–5)

BE9–16 Presented below is a partial amortization schedule for Discount Pizza.

(1) Period	(2) Cash Paid for Interest	(3) Interest Expense	(4) Increase in Carrying Value	(5) Carrying Value
Issue date				$63,948
1	$2,450	$2,558	$108	64,056
2	2,450	2,562	112	64,168

1. Record the bond issue assuming the face amount of bonds payable is $70,000.
2. Record the first interest payment.
3. Explain why interest expense increases each period.

Interpret a bond amortization schedule (LO9–5)

BE9–17 Presented below is a partial amortization schedule for Premium Pizza.

(1) Period	(2) Cash Paid for Interest	(3) Interest Expense	(4) Decrease in Carrying Value	(5) Carrying Value
Issue date				$76,860
1	$2,450	$2,306	$144	76,716
2	2,450	2,301	149	76,567

1. Record the bond issue assuming the face amount of bonds payable is $70,000.
2. Record the first interest payment.
3. Explain why interest expense decreases each period.

Record early retirement of bonds issued at a discount (LO9–6)

BE9–18 Discount Pizza retires its 7% bonds for $68,000 before their scheduled maturity. At the time, the bonds have a face amount of $70,000 and a carrying value of $64,168. Record the early retirement of the bonds.

BE9–19 Premium Pizza retires its 7% bonds for $72,000 before their scheduled maturity. At the time, the bonds have a face amount of $70,000 and a carrying value of $76,567. Record the early retirement of the bonds.

Record early retirement of bonds issued at a premium (LO9–6)

BE9–20 Ultimate Butter Popcorn issues 7%, 10-year bonds with a face amount of $60,000. The market interest rate for bonds of similar risk and maturity is 7%. Interest is paid semiannually. At what price will the bonds issue?

Calculate the issue price of bonds (LO9–7)

BE9–21 Ultimate Butter Popcorn issues 7%, 15-year bonds with a face amount of $60,000. The market interest rate for bonds of similar risk and maturity is 8%. Interest is paid semiannually. At what price will the bonds issue?

Calculate the issue price of bonds (LO9–7)

BE9–22 Ultimate Butter Popcorn issues 7%, 20-year bonds with a face amount of $60,000. The market interest rate for bonds of similar risk and maturity is 6%. Interest is paid semiannually. At what price will the bonds issue?

Calculate the issue price of bonds (LO9–7)

BE9–23 Surf's Up, a manufacturer of surfing supplies and training equipment, has the following selected data ($ in millions):

Calculate ratios (LO9–8)

SURF'S UP Selected Balance Sheet Data		
	2024	**2023**
Total assets	$727	$718
Total liabilities	628	530
Total stockholders' equity	99	188

SURF'S UP Selected Income Statement Data	
	2024
Sales revenue	$795
Interest expense	15
Income tax expense	44
Net income	66

Based on these amounts, calculate the following ratios for 2024:
1. Debt to equity ratio.
2. Return on assets ratio.
3. Times interest earned ratio.

BE9–24 Refer to the information in BE9–1. Determine the financial statement effects of the issuance of the installment note and the first monthly payment.

Determine financial statement effects of installment notes (LO9–2)

BE9–25 Refer to the information in BE9–5. Determine the financial statement effects of the lease.

Determine financial statement effects of leases (LO9–3)

BE9–26 Refer to the information in BE9–8. Determine the financial statement effects of (1) the bond issue on January 1, 2024, and (2) the first interest payment on June 30, 2024.

Determine financial statement effects of bonds issued at face amount (LO9–4)

EXERCISES

E9–1 Penny Arcades, Inc., is trying to decide between the following two alternatives to finance its new $35 million gaming center:

Compare financing alternatives (LO9–1)

a. Issue $35 million, 7% note.
b. Issue 1 million shares of common stock for $35 per share with expected annual dividends of $2.45 per share.

	Issue Note	Issue Stock
Operating income	$11,000,000	$11,000,000
Interest expense (on note only)		
Income before tax		
Income tax expense (25%)		
Net income	$	$
Number of shares	4,000,000	5,000,000
Earnings per share (Net income/# of shares)	$	$

Required:

1. Assuming the note or shares of stock are issued at the beginning of the year, complete the income statement for each alternative.
2. Answer the following questions for the current year:
   (a) By how much are interest payments higher if issuing the note?
   (b) By how much are dividend payments higher by issuing stock?
   (c) Which alternative results in higher earnings per share?

Record installment notes **(LO9–2)**

E9–2 On January 1, 2024, Tropical Paradise borrows $50,000 by agreeing to a 6%, six-year note with the bank. Loan payments of $828.64 are due at the end of each month with the first installment due on January 31, 2024.

Required:

Record the issuance of the installment note payable and the first two monthly payments.

Record installment notes **(LO9–2)**

E9–3 On January 1, 2024, Jalen Company purchased land costing $800,000. Instead of paying cash at the time of purchase, Jalen plans to make four installment payments of $215,221.64 on June 30 and December 31 in 2024 and 2025. The payments include interest at a rate of 6%.

Required:

1. Record the purchase of land when the note is issued.
2. Record the first installment payment on June 30, 2024, and the second installment payment on December 31, 2024.
3. Calculate the balance of Notes Payable and Interest Expense on December 31, 2024.

Record installment note with down payment **(LO9–2)**

E9–4 On January 1, 2024, Mitchell Company purchases new equipment for $700,000. Mitchell is required to make a down payment of $100,000 and issue an installment note for the remaining balance of $600,000. The note requires payments of $81,905.88 every three months, beginning March 31, 2024, over the next two years. The interest rate on the note is 8% annually (or 2% every three months).

Required:

1. Record the purchase of equipment with down payment of $100,000 and the installment note of $600,000 on January 1, 2024.
2. Record the first payment of $81,905.88 on March 31, 2024.

Compute total interest and record installment notes **(LO9–2)**

E9–5 A company decides to obtain a small-business loan of $200,000. The financial institution from which the company borrows offers two options:

a. Borrow $200,000 at 6% with monthly payments of $3,866.56 over 5 years.
b. Borrow $200,000 at 7% with monthly payments of $2,322.17 over 10 years.

Required:

1. Record the issuance of an installment note payable under each option.
2. Record the payments for the first and second month under each option.
3. Determine the total amount of interest paid under each option over the full period of the note.

Understand the effect of leases on financial ratios **(LO9–3, LO9–8)**

E9–6 Coney Island enters into a lease agreement for a new ride. The lease payments have a present value of $2 million. Prior to this agreement, the company's total assets are $25 million and its total liabilities are $15 million.

Required:

1. Calculate total stockholders' equity prior to the lease agreement.
2. Prior to the lease being signed, calculate the debt to equity ratio.
3. Immediately after the lease being signed, calculate the debt to equity ratio.
4. Does the direction of the change in the debt to equity ratio typically indicate that the company has higher leverage risk?

Record leases **(LO9–3)**

E9–7 On June 1, 2024, Florida National leased a building. The lease agreement calls for Florida National to make lease payments of $3,618.18 each month for the next two years, with the first lease payment beginning June 30. The company's normal borrowing rate is 8%.

Required:

Calculate the present value of the lease payments and record the lease on June 1, 2024. Round to the nearest whole dollar. (*Hint:* Use a financial calculator or Excel.)

E9–8 On June 30, 2024, Exploration Inc. signs a lease requiring quarterly payments each year for the next five years. Each of the 20 quarterly payments is $29,122.87, with the first lease payment beginning September 30. The company's normal borrowing rate is 6%.

Record leases **(LO9–3)**

Required:

Calculate the present value of the lease payments and record the lease on June 30, 2024. Round to the nearest whole dollar.

E9–9 January 1, 2024, Paradise Partners decides to upgrade recreational equipment at its resorts. The company is contemplating whether to purchase or lease the new equipment.

Compare installment notes and leases **(LO9–2, 9–3)**

Required:

1. The company can purchase the equipment by borrowing $250,000 with a 30-month, 12% installment note. Payments of $9,687.03 are due at the end of each month, and the first installment is due on January 31, 2024. Record the issuance of the installment note payable for the purchase of the equipment.
2. The company can sign a 30-month lease for the equipment by agreeing to pay $7,749.62 at the end of each month, beginning January 31, 2024. At the end of the lease, the equipment must be returned. Assuming a borrowing rate of 12%, record the lease.
3. As of January 1, 2024, does the installment note or the lease have a greater effect on increasing the company's amount of reported debt, and by how much?
4. Suppose the equipment has a total value of $100,000 at the end of the 30-month period, which option (purchasing with installment note or leasing) would likely be better?

E9–10 On January 1, 2024, Splash City issues $500,000 of 9% bonds, due in 20 years, with interest payable semiannually on June 30 and December 31 each year.

Record bonds issued at face amount and related *semiannual* interest **(LO9–4)**

Required:

Assuming the bonds issue for $500,000, record the bond issue on January 1, 2024, and the first two semiannual interest payments on June 30, 2024, and December 31, 2024.

E9–11 On January 1, 2024, Splash City issues $500,000 of 9% bonds, due in 20 years, with interest payable semiannually on June 30 and December 31 each year.

Record bonds issued at a discount and related *semiannual* interest **(LO9–5)**

Required:

Assuming the market interest rate on the issue date is 10%, the bonds will issue at $457,102.
1. Complete the first three rows of an amortization schedule.
2. Record the bond issue on January 1, 2024, and the first two semiannual interest payments on June 30, 2024, and December 31, 2024.

E9–12 On January 1, 2024, Splash City issues $500,000 of 9% bonds, due in 20 years, with interest payable semiannually on June 30 and December 31 each year.

Record bonds issued at a premium and related *semiannual* interest **(LO9–5)**

Required:

Assuming the market interest rate on the issue date is 8%, the bonds will issue at $549,482.
1. Complete the first three rows of an amortization schedule.
2. Record the bond issue on January 1, 2024, and the first two semiannual interest payments on June 30, 2024, and December 31, 2024.

E9–13 On January 1, 2024, White Water issues $600,000 of 7% bonds, due in 10 years, with interest payable semiannually on June 30 and December 31 each year.

Record bonds issued at face amount and related *semiannual* interest **(LO9–4)**

Required:

Assuming the bonds issue for $600,000, record the bond issue on January 1, 2024, and the first two semiannual interest payments on June 30, 2024, and December 31, 2024.

E9–14 On January 1, 2024, White Water issues $600,000 of 7% bonds, due in 10 years, with interest payable semiannually on June 30 and December 31 each year.

Required:

Assuming the market interest rate on the issue date is 8%, the bonds will issue at $559,229.
1. Complete the first three rows of an amortization schedule.
2. Record the bond issue on January 1, 2024, and the first two semiannual interest payments on June 30, 2024, and December 31, 2024.

E9–15 On January 1, 2024, White Water issues $600,000 of 7% bonds, due in 10 years, with interest payable semiannually on June 30 and December 31 each year.

Required:

Assuming the market interest rate on the issue date is 6%, the bonds will issue at $644,632.
1. Complete the first three rows of an amortization schedule.
2. Record the bond issue on January 1, 2024, and the first two semiannual interest payments on June 30, 2024, and December 31, 2024.

E9–16 On January 1, 2024, White Water issues $600,000 of 7% bonds, due in 10 years, with interest payable annually on December 31 each year.

Required:

Assuming the bonds issue for $600,000, record the bond issue on January 1, 2024, and the first two interest payments on December 31, 2024, to December 31, 2025.

E9–17 On January 1, 2024, White Water issues $600,000 of 7% bonds, due in 10 years, with interest payable annually on December 31 each year.

Required:

Assuming the market interest rate on the issue date is 8%, the bonds will issue at $559,740.
1. Complete the first three rows of an amortization schedule. (*Hint:* Use Illustration 9–6, except the dates for the first three rows will be 1/1/2024, 12/31/2024, and 12/31/2025 since interest is payable *annually* rather than semiannually. Interest expense for the period ended December 31, 2024, is calculated as the carrying value of $559,740 times the market rate of 8%.)
2. Record the bond issue on January 1, 2024, and the first two interest payments on December 31, 2024, and December 31, 2025.

E9–18 On January 1, 2024, White Water issues $600,000 of 7% bonds, due in 10 years, with interest payable annually on December 31 each year.

Required:

Assuming the market interest rate on the issue date is 6%, the bonds will issue at $644,161.
1. Complete the first three rows of an amortization schedule. (*Hint:* Use Illustration 9–7, except the dates for the first three rows will be 1/1/2024, 12/31/2024, and 12/31/2025 since interest is payable *annually* rather than semiannually. Interest expense for the period ended December 31, 2024, is calculated as the carrying value of $644,161 times the market rate of 6%.)
2. Record the bond issue on January 1, 2024, and the first two interest payments on December 31, 2024, and December 31, 2025.

E9–19 On January 1, 2024, Splash City issues $500,000 of 9% bonds, due in 20 years, with interest payable semiannually on June 30 and December 31 each year. The market interest rate on the issue date is 10% and the bonds issued at $457,102.

Required:

1. Using an amortization schedule, show that the bonds have a carrying value of $458,633 on December 31, 2025.
2. If the market interest rate drops to 7% on December 31, 2025, it will cost $601,452 to retire the bonds. Record the retirement of the bonds on December 31, 2025.

E9–20 On January 1, 2024, White Water issues $600,000 of 7% bonds, due in 10 years, with interest payable semiannually on June 30 and December 31 each year. The market interest rate on the issue date is 6% and the bonds issued at $644,632.

Record the early retirement of bonds issued at a premium (LO9–6)

Required:

1. Using an amortization schedule, show that the bonds have a carrying value of $633,887 on December 31, 2026.
2. If the market interest rate increases to 8% on December 31, 2026, it will cost $568,311 to retire the bonds. Record the retirement of the bonds on December 31, 2026.

E9–21 On January 1, 2024, Frontier World issues $41 million of 9% bonds, due in 20 years, with interest payable semiannually on June 30 and December 31 each year. The proceeds will be used to build a new ride that combines a roller coaster, a water ride, a dark tunnel, and the great smell of outdoor barbeque, all in one ride.

Calculate the issue price of bonds (LO9–7)

Required:

1. If the market rate is 8%, will the bonds issue at face amount, a discount, or a premium? Calculate the issue price.
2. If the market rate is 9%, will the bonds issue at face amount, a discount, or a premium? Calculate the issue price.
3. If the market rate is 10%, will the bonds issue at face amount, a discount, or a premium? Calculate the issue price.

E9–22 On January 1, 2024, Water World issues $26 million of 7% bonds, due in 10 years, with interest payable semiannually on June 30 and December 31 each year. Water World intends to use the funds to build the world's largest water avalanche and the "tornado"—a giant outdoor vortex in which riders spin in progressively smaller and faster circles until they drop through a small tunnel at the bottom.

Calculate the issue price of bonds (LO9–7)

Required:

1. If the market rate is 6%, will the bonds issue at face amount, a discount, or a premium? Calculate the issue price.
2. If the market rate is 7%, will the bonds issue at face amount, a discount, or a premium? Calculate the issue price.
3. If the market rate is 8%, will the bonds issue at face amount, a discount, or a premium? Calculate the issue price.

E9–23 Two online travel companies, E-Travel and Pricecheck, provide the following selected financial data:

Calculate and analyze ratios (LO9–8)

	E-Travel	Pricecheck
Total assets	$7,437,156	$2,094,224
Total liabilities	4,254,475	486,610
Total stockholders' equity	3,182,681	1,607,614
Sales revenue	$3,455,426	$2,838,212
Interest expense	94,233	34,084
Income tax expense	174,400	57,168
Net income	319,526	509,472

Required:

1. Calculate the debt to equity ratio for E-Travel and Pricecheck. Which company has higher leverage risk?
2. Calculate the times interest earned ratio for E-Travel and Pricecheck. Which company is better able to meet interest payments as they become due?

Complete the accounting cycle using long-term liability transactions (LO9–2, LO9–8)

E9–24 On January 1, 2024, the general ledger of Freedom Fireworks includes the following account balances:

Accounts	Debit	Credit
Cash	$ 11,200	
Accounts Receivable	34,000	
Allowance for Uncollectible Accounts		$ 1,800
Inventory	152,000	
Land	67,300	
Buildings	120,000	
Accumulated Depreciation		9,600
Accounts Payable		17,700
Common Stock		200,000
Retained Earnings		155,400
Totals	$384,500	$384,500

During January 2024, the following transactions occur:

January 1   Borrow $100,000 from Captive Credit Corporation. The installment note bears interest at 7% annually and matures in five years. Payments of $1,980 are required at the end of each month for 60 months.

January 4   Receive $31,000 from customers on accounts receivable.

January 10   Pay cash on accounts payable, $11,000.

January 15   Pay cash for salaries, $28,900.

January 30   Firework sales for the month total $195,000. Sales include $65,000 for cash and $130,000 on account. The cost of the units sold is $112,500.

January 31   Pay the first monthly installment of $1,980 related to the $100,000 borrowed on January 1. Round your interest calculation to the nearest dollar.

Required:

1. Record each of the transactions listed above.
2. Record adjusting entries on January 31.
   a. Depreciation on the building for the month of January is calculated using the straight-line method. At the time the building was purchased, the company estimated a service life of 10 years and a residual value of $24,000.
   b. The company estimates additional future uncollectible accounts of $2,300.
   c. Unpaid salaries at the end of January are $26,100.
   d. Accrued income taxes at the end of January are $8,000.
   e. The portion of Notes Payable (long-term) due within the next 12 months is reclassified as Notes Payable (current). The amount of the reclassification is $17,411.
3. Prepare an adjusted trial balance as of January 31, 2024, after updating beginning balances (above) for transactions during January (*requirement* 1) and adjusting entries at the end of January (*requirement* 2).
4. Prepare a multiple-step income statement for the period ended January 31, 2024.
5. Prepare a classified balance sheet as of January 31, 2024.
6. Record closing entries.
7. Analyze the following for Freedom Fireworks:
   a. Calculate the debt to equity ratio. If the average debt to equity ratio for the industry is 1.0, is Freedom Fireworks more or less leveraged than other companies in the same industry?
   b. Calculate the times interest earned ratio. If the average times interest earned ratio for the industry is 20 times, is the company more or less able to meet interest payments than other companies in the same industry?
   c. Based on the ratios calculated in (a) and (b), would Freedom Fireworks be more likely to receive a higher or lower interest rate than the average borrowing rate in the industry?

PROBLEMS: SET A

P9–1A On January 1, 2024, Gundy Enterprises purchases an office for $360,000, paying $60,000 down and borrowing the remaining $300,000, signing a 7%, 10-year mortgage. Installment payments of $3,483.25 are due at the end of each month, with the first payment due on January 31, 2024.

Record and analyze installment notes (LO9–2)

Required:
1. Record the purchase of the building on January 1, 2024.
2. Complete the first three rows of an amortization schedule similar to Illustration 9–1.
3. Record the first monthly mortgage payment on January 31, 2024. How much of the first payment goes to interest expense and how much goes to reducing the carrying value of the loan?
4. Total payments over the 10 years are $417,990 ($3,483.25 × 120 monthly payments). How much of this is interest expense and how much is actual payment of the loan?

P9–2A On January 1, 2024, Strato Corporation borrowed $2 million from a local bank to construct a new building over the next three years. The loan will be paid back in three equal installments of $776,067 on December 31 of each year. The payments include interest at a rate of 8%.

Prepare amortization schedule and record installment notes (LO9–2)

Required:
1. Record the cash received when the note is issued.
2. Prepare an amortization schedule over the three-year life of the installment note. Round answers to the nearest dollar.
3. Use amounts from the amortization schedule to record each installment payment.

P9–3A On September 1, 2024, a company decides to lease office space in a building. The building's owner offers the company the following options, with the first monthly payment beginning September 30, 2024:
1. Sign a two-year lease with monthly payments of $3,000.
2. Sign a three-year lease with monthly payments of $2,750.
3. Sign a four-year lease with monthly payments of $2,500.

Record leases (LO9–3)

Required:
1. For each option, calculate the present value of the lease payments using an interest rate of 6%. Round to the nearest whole dollar. (*Hint:* Use a financial calculator or Excel.)
2. Record each lease on September 1, 2024.
3. For which option is the lease payable recorded for the highest amount?

P9–4A Thrillville has $41 million in bonds payable. One of the contractual agreements in the bond is that the debt to equity ratio cannot exceed 2.0. Thrillville's total assets are $81 million, and its liabilities other than the bonds payable are $11 million. The company is considering some additional financing through leasing.

Explore the impact of leases on the debt to equity ratio (LO9–3, LO9–8)

Required:
1. Calculate total stockholders' equity using the balance sheet equation.
2. Calculate the debt to equity ratio.
3. The company enters a lease agreement requiring lease payments with a present value of $16 million. Record the lease.
4. Will entering into the lease cause the debt to equity ratio to be in violation of the contractual agreement in the bond? Determine your answer by calculating the debt to equity ratio after recording the lease.

P9–5A On January 1, 2024, Twister Enterprises, a manufacturer of a variety of transportable spin rides, issues $600,000 of 8% bonds, due in 20 years, with interest payable semiannually on June 30 and December 31 each year.

Record bond issue and related interest (LO9–4)

Required:
1. If the market interest rate is 8%, the bonds will issue at $600,000. Record the bond issue on January 1, 2024, and the first two semiannual interest payments on June 30, 2024, and December 31, 2024.

2. If the market interest rate is 9%, the bonds will issue at $544,795. Record the bond issue on January 1, 2024, and the first two semiannual interest payments on June 30, 2024, and December 31, 2024.

3. If the market interest rate is 7%, the bonds will issue at $664,065. Record the bond issue on January 1, 2024, and the first two semiannual interest payments on June 30, 2024, and December 31, 2024.

Understand a bond amortization schedule (LO9–5)

P9–6A On January 1, 2024, Vacation Destinations issues $40 million of bonds that pay interest semiannually on June 30 and December 31. Portions of the bond amortization schedule appear below:

(1) Date	(2) Cash Paid for Interest	(3) Interest Expense	(4) Increase in Carrying Value	(5) Carrying Value
1/1/2024				$37,281,935
6/30/2024	$1,400,000	$1,491,277	$91,277	37,373,212
12/31/2024	1,400,000	1,494,928	94,928	37,468,140

Required:
1. Were the bonds issued at face amount, a discount, or a premium?
2. What is the original issue price of the bonds?
3. What is the face amount of the bonds?
4. What is the stated annual interest rate?
5. What is the market annual interest rate?
6. What is the total cash paid for interest assuming the bonds mature in 10 years?

Prepare a bond amortization schedule and record transactions for the bond issuer (LO9–5)

P9–7A On January 1, 2024, Universe of Fun issues $900,000, 8% bonds that mature in 10 years. The market interest rate for bonds of similar risk and maturity is 9%, and the bonds issue for $841,464. Interest is paid semiannually on June 30 and December 31.

Required:
1. Complete the first three rows of an amortization schedule.
2. Record the issuance of the bonds on January 1, 2024.
3. Record the interest payments on June 30, 2024, and December 31, 2024.

Calculate the issue price of a bond and prepare amortization schedules (LO9–5, LO9–7)

P9–8A On January 1, 2024, Coney Island Entertainment issues $1,300,000 of 7% bonds, due in 15 years, with interest payable semiannually on June 30 and December 31 each year.

Required:
Calculate the issue price of a bond and complete the first three rows of an amortization schedule when
1. The market interest rate is 7% and the bonds issue at face amount.
2. The market interest rate is 8% and the bonds issue at a discount.
3. The market interest rate is 6% and the bonds issue at a premium.

Calculate and analyze ratios (LO9–8)

P9–9A Selected financial data for Bahama Bay and Caribbean Key are as follows:

($ in millions)	Bahama Bay		Caribbean Key	
	2024	**2023**	**2024**	**2023**
Total assets	$8,861	$9,560	$7,640	$7,507
Total liabilities	5,724	6,606	2,819	2,689
Total stockholders' equity	3,137	2,954	4,821	4,818
Sales revenue	$6,321		$3,949	
Interest expense	170		70	
Income tax expense	148		8	
Net income	562		88	

Required:
1. Calculate the debt to equity ratio for Bahama Bay and Caribbean Key for the most recent year. Which company has the higher ratio?
2. Calculate the return on assets for Bahama Bay and Caribbean Key. Which company appears more profitable?
3. Calculate the times interest earned ratio for Bahama Bay and Caribbean Key. Which company is better able to meet interest payments as they become due?

PROBLEMS: SET B

P9–1B On January 1, 2024, Stoops Entertainment purchases a building for $610,000, paying $110,000 down and borrowing the remaining $500,000, signing a 9%, 15-year mortgage. Installment payments of $5,071.33 are due at the end of each month, with the first payment due on January 31, 2024.

Record and analyze installment notes (LO9–2)

Required:
1. Record the purchase of the building on January 1, 2024.
2. Complete the first three rows of an amortization schedule similar to Illustration 9–1.
3. Record the first monthly mortgage payment on January 31, 2024. How much of the first payment goes to interest expense and how much goes to reducing the carrying value of the loan?
4. Total payments over the 15 years are $912,839 ($5,071.33 × 180 monthly payments). How much of this is interest expense and how much is actual payment of the loan?

P9–2B On January 1, 2024, Monster Corporation borrowed $9 million from a local bank to construct a new highway over the next four years. The loan will be paid back in four equal installments of $2,657,053 on December 31 of each year. The payments include interest at a rate of 7%.

Prepare amortization schedule and record installment notes (LO9–2)

Required:
1. Record the cash received when the note is issued.
2. Prepare an amortization schedule over the four-year life of the installment note. Round answers to the nearest dollar.
3. Use amounts from the amortization schedule to record each installment payment.

P9–3B On September 1, 2024, a company decides to lease a new delivery truck for three years. The truck dealership offers the company the following options, with the first monthly lease payment beginning September 30, 2024:
1. Pay $0 down and monthly lease payments of $2,000.
2. Pay $20,000 down and monthly lease payments of $1,300.
3. Pay $40,000 down and monthly lease payments of $600.

Required:
1. For each option, calculate the present value of the lease payments using an interest rate of 5%. Round to the nearest whole dollar. (*Hint:* Use a financial calculator or Excel.)
2. Record each lease on September 1, 2024.
3. For which option is the lease asset recorded for the highest amount? (*Hint:* Include any downpayment in determining your answer.)

P9–4B Chunky Cheese Pizza has $61 million in bonds payable. The bond agreement states that the debt to equity ratio cannot exceed 3.25. Chunky's total assets are $201 million, and its liabilities other than the bonds payable are $91 million. The company is considering some additional financing through leasing.

Explore the impact of leases on the debt to equity ratio (LO9–3, LO9–8)

Required:
1. Calculate total stockholders' equity using the balance sheet equation.
2. Calculate the debt to equity ratio.
3. The company enters a lease agreement requiring lease payments with a present value of $26 million. Record the lease.

4. Will entering into the lease cause the debt to equity ratio to be in violation of the bond agreement? Determine your answer by calculating the debt to equity ratio after recording the lease.

Record bond issue and related interest (LO9–4)

P9–5B Viking Voyager specializes in the design and production of replica Viking boats. On January 1, 2024, the company issues $3,000,000 of 9% bonds, due in 10 years, with interest payable semiannually on June 30 and December 31 each year.

Required:
1. If the market interest rate is 9%, the bonds will issue at $3,000,000. Record the bond issue on January 1, 2024, and the first two semiannual interest payments on June 30, 2024, and December 31, 2024.
2. If the market interest rate is 10%, the bonds will issue at $2,813,067. Record the bond issue on January 1, 2024, and the first two semiannual interest payments on June 30, 2024, and December 31, 2024.
3. If the market interest rate is 8%, the bonds will issue at $3,203,855. Record the bond issue on January 1, 2024, and the first two semiannual interest payments on June 30, 2024, and December 31, 2024.

Understand a bond amortization schedule (LO9–5)

P9–6B Temptation Vacations issues $60 million in bonds on January 1, 2024, that pay interest semiannually on June 30 and December 31. Portions of the bond amortization schedule appear below:

(1) Date	(2) Cash Paid for Interest	(3) Interest Expense	(4) Decrease in Carrying Value	(5) Carrying Value
1/1/2024				$66,934,432
6/30/2024	$2,100,000	$2,008,033	$91,967	66,842,465
12/31/2024	2,100,000	2,005,274	94,726	66,747,739

Required:
1. Were the bonds issued at face amount, a discount, or a premium?
2. What is the original issue price of the bonds?
3. What is the face amount of the bonds?
4. What is the stated annual interest rate?
5. What is the market annual interest rate?
6. What is the total cash paid for interest assuming the bonds mature in 20 years?

Prepare a bond amortization schedule and record transactions for the bond issuer (LO9–5)

P9–7B Super Splash issues $1,000,000, 7% bonds on January 1, 2024, that mature in 15 years. The market interest rate for bonds of similar risk and maturity is 6%, and the bonds issue for $1,098,002. Interest is paid semiannually on June 30 and December 31.

Required:
1. Complete the first three rows of an amortization schedule.
2. Record the issuance of the bonds on January 1, 2024.
3. Record the interest payments on June 30, 2024, and December 31, 2024.

Calculate the issue price of a bond and prepare amortization schedules (LO9–5, LO9–7)

P9–8B On January 1, 2024, Christmas Anytime issues $850,000 of 6% bonds, due in 10 years, with interest payable semiannually on June 30 and December 31 each year.

Required:
Calculate the issue price of a bond and complete the first three rows of an amortization schedule when
1. The market interest rate is 6% and the bonds issue at face amount.
2. The market interest rate is 7% and the bonds issue at a discount.
3. The market interest rate is 5% and the bonds issue at a premium.

P9–9B Selected financial data for Surf City and Paradise Falls are as follows:

Calculate and analyze
ratios **(LO9–8)**

($ in millions)	Surf City		Paradise Falls	
	2024	**2023**	**2024**	**2023**
Total assets	$19,828	$19,804	$39,161	$38,637
Total liabilities	11,519	11,396	15,232	14,805
Total stockholders' equity	8,309	8,408	23,929	23,832
Sales revenue	$ 7,688		$15,382	
Interest expense	356		336	
Income tax expense	–		4	
Net income	18		1,298	

Required:
1. Calculate the debt to equity ratio for Surf City and Paradise Falls for the most recent year. Which company has the higher ratio?
2. Calculate the return on assets for Surf City and Paradise Falls. Which company appears more profitable?
3. Calculate the times interest earned ratio for Surf City and Paradise Falls. Which company is better able to meet interest payments as they become due?

REAL-WORLD PERSPECTIVES

Data Analytics & Excel

Visit Connect to find a variety of Data Analytics questions that help build Excel, Tableau, and data visualization skills. Assignable materials include Integrated Excel, Applying Excel, Data Visualizations, Tableau Dashboard Activities, and Applying Tableau Cases.

Great Adventures

General Ledger
Continuing Case

(This is a continuation of the Great Adventures problem from earlier chapters.)

RWP9–1 Tony's favorite memories of his childhood were the times he spent with his dad at camp. Tony was daydreaming of those days a bit as he and Suzie jogged along a nature trail and came across a wonderful piece of property for sale. He turned to Suzie and said, "I've always wanted to start a camp where families could get away and spend some quality time together. If we just had the money, I know this would be the perfect place." On November 1, 2025, Great Adventures purchased the land by issuing a $500,000, 6%, 10-year installment note to the seller. Payments of $5,551 are required at the end of each month over the life of the 10-year loan. Each monthly payment of $5,551 includes both interest expense and principal payments (i.e., reduction of the loan amount).

Late that night, Tony exclaimed, "We now have land for our new camp; this has to be the best news ever!" Suzie said, "There's something else I need to tell you. I'm expecting!"

Required:
1. Complete the first three rows of an amortization schedule.
2. Record the purchase of land with the issuance of a long-term note payable on November 1, 2025.
3. Record the first two payments on November 30, 2025, and December 31, 2025, and calculate the remaining balance of the note payable as of December 31, 2025.
4. The 12 monthly payments in 2026 (following year) will reduce the note's balance by an additional $38,014. Record the reclassification of this amount from Notes Payable (long-term) to Notes Payable (current).

The Great Adventures continuing problem also can be assigned using the General Ledger software in Connect. Students will be given an existing trial balance and asked to prepare (1) the journal entries for the transactions above in 2025, (2) financial statements, and (3) closing entries.

American Eagle Outfitters, Inc.

RWP9–2 Financial information for **American Eagle** is presented in **Appendix A** at the end of the book.

Required:
1. Calculate the debt to equity ratio for the past two years. Did the ratio increase or decrease the more recent year?
2. Calculate the return on assets for the most recent year. Does the return on assets exceed the cost of borrowing of approximately 4%?
3. *Review the balance sheet and note 9 to the financial statements.* Based on this information, how would you rate the bankruptcy risk of American Eagle?

The Buckle, Inc.

RWP9–3 Financial information for **Buckle** is presented in **Appendix B** at the end of the book.

Required:
1. Calculate the debt to equity ratio for the past two years. Did the ratio increase or decrease in the more recent year?
2. Calculate the return on assets for the most recent year. Does the return on assets exceed the cost of borrowing of approximately 4%?
3. *Review the balance sheet and note E to the financial statements.* Based on this information, how would you rate the bankruptcy risk of Buckle?

American Eagle Outfitters, Inc., vs. The Buckle, Inc.

RWP9–4 Financial information for **American Eagle** is presented in **Appendix A** at the end of the book, and financial information for **Buckle** is presented in **Appendix B** at the end of the book.

Required:
1. Calculate the debt to equity ratio for American Eagle and Buckle for the most recent year. Which company has the riskier ratio? Compare your calculations with those for **Coca-Cola** and **PepsiCo** reported earlier in the chapter. Which industry maintains a higher debt to equity ratio?
2. Calculate the return on assets for American Eagle and Buckle for the most recent year. Which company appears more profitable?

EDGAR Research

RWP9–5 Using EDGAR (Electronic Data Gathering, Analysis, and Retrieval system), find the annual report (10-K) for **Six Flags Entertainment Corporation** for the year ended **December 31, 2019.** Locate the "Consolidated Statement of Operations" (income statement) and "Consolidated Balance Sheets." You may also find the annual report at the company's website.

Required:
1. What amount does the company report for total liabilities in the current year?
2. What amount does the company report for current liabilities and long-term liabilities?
3. Determine the amount the company reports for short-term lease liabilities and long-term lease liabilities.
4. Find Note 8. Long-Term Indebtedness. What amount does the company report for 2024 notes and 2027 notes?
5. What is the approximate interest rate the company is paying on its debt? (*Hint:* Divide interest expense in the income statement by the amount of long-term debt plus the current portion of long-term debt.)

Ethics

RWP9–6 The Tony Hawk Skate Park was built in early 2024. The construction was financed by a $3,000,000, 7% note due in six years, with payments of $51,147 required each month. The first year has not been as profitable as hoped. The discussion at the executive board meeting at the end of 2024 focused on the potential need to obtain additional financing. However, board members are concerned that the company's debt level at the end of 2024 will make the company appear too risky to additional lenders. The balance of the note at the end of 2024 is $2,583,026. By the end of 2025, the 12 monthly payments will reduce the balance by an additional $447,116. Separate from the note, the company has the following amounts at the end of 2024: current assets of $3,100,000; current liabilities of $2,700,000; total equity of $4,000,000.

Jim Trost, the VP of finance, tells board members that he plans to classify the full balance of the note at the end of 2024 as long-term because the full length of the note is six years. He explains that lenders will be more willing to let the company borrow and will offer a lower interest rate if the company reports fewer current liabilities. Plus, he plans to tell lenders that there is no problem with long-term solvency because the company long-term profits will be used to pay its long-term debt.

Required:
1. Understand the reporting effect: How does Jim's decision affect the reported amount of current liabilities versus long-term liabilities as of December 31, 2024?
2. Specify the options: Calculate the current ratio and the debt to equity ratio at the end of 2024 (a) with and (b) without Jim's assumption.
3. Identify the impact: Can Jim's decision affect lenders?
4. Make a decision: Should Jim record the full balance of the note as a long-term liability in its balance sheet as of December 31, 2024?

Written Communication

RWP9–7 Western Entertainment is considering issuing bonds to finance its business expansion. The company contacts you, a business consultant charging $200 an hour, to answer the following questions.
1. What are the advantages of issuing bonds over borrowing funds from a bank?
2. What are the advantages of issuing bonds over issuing common stock?
3. How is a bond price determined?

Required:
Write a memo providing answers worthy of your billing rate.

Earnings Management

RWP9–8 Adrenaline Entertainment is struggling financially and its CFO, David Plesko, is starting to feel the heat. Back on January 1, 2020, Adrenaline Entertainment issued $100 million of 6% bonds, due in 15 years, with interest payable semiannually on June 30 and December 31 each year. The market interest rate on the date of issue was 5%.

It is now the end of 2024, and David has a plan to increase reported net income in 2024. The market interest rate has risen to 9% by the end of 2024. David wants to retire the $100 million, 6% bonds and reissue new 9% bonds instead.

Required:
1. Calculate the issue price of the bonds on January 1, 2020. [*Hint:* Use a market rate of 2.5% (5% ÷ 2), and the number of periods is 30 semiannual periods.]
2. Calculate the carrying value of the bonds five years later on December 31, 2024. [*Hint:* Use a market rate of 2.5% (5% ÷ 2), and the number of periods is now 20 semiannual periods.]
3. Calculate the market value of the bonds five years later on December 31, 2024. [*Hint:* The market rate is now 4.5% (9% ÷ 2) rather than 2.5% (5% ÷ 2), and the number of periods is now 20 semiannual periods.]
4. Record the early retirement of the bonds on December 31, 2024. Does the transaction increase net income? By how much (ignoring any tax effect)?
5. Do you think investors would likely agree with David Plesko that the retirement of the 6% bonds and the reissue of 9% bonds is a good idea? Explain why or why not.

Answers to Chapter Framework Questions
1. b   2. c   3. a   4. c   5. a

Answers to Self-Study Questions
1. d   2. b   3. c   4. d   5. a   6. b   7. c   8. b   9. b   10. c   11. b   12. a   13. a   14. d   15. d

Stockholders' Equity

Learning Objectives

PART A: INVESTED CAPITAL

- **LO10–1** Identify the advantages and disadvantages of the corporate form of ownership.
- **LO10–2** Record the issuance of common stock.
- **LO10–3** Understand unique features and recording of preferred stock.
- **LO10–4** Account for treasury stock.

PART B: EARNED CAPITAL

- **LO10–5** Describe retained earnings and record cash dividends.
- **LO10–6** Explain the effect of stock dividends and stock splits.

PART C: REPORTING STOCKHOLDERS' EQUITY

- **LO10–7** Prepare and analyze the stockholders' equity section of a balance sheet and the statement of stockholders' equity.

ANALYSIS: EQUITY ANALYSIS

- **LO10–8** Evaluate company performance using information on stockholders' equity.

SELF-STUDY MATERIALS

- Let's Review—Equity transactions (p. 507).
- Let's Review—Statement of stockholders' equity (p. 514).
- Chapter Framework with questions and answers available (p. 518).
- Key Points by Learning Objective (p. 519).
- Glossary of Key Terms (p. 520).
- Self-Study Questions with answers available (p. 521).
- Videos including Concept Overview, Applying Excel, Let's Review, and Interactive Illustrations to demonstrate key topics (in Connect).

ZOOM: OFF TO THE RACES

Have you ever wanted to start your own business? What product could you sell for more than its cost? What unique service could you provide that's worth your time? What need in the market is unmet by existing products and services? These are the questions faced by countless entrepreneurs.

In 2011, Eric Yuan was working for Cisco Corporation as vice president for engineering. He noticed that many of his customers weren't happy with their videoconferencing services. He knew there was a need for an easier-to-use videoconferencing system that could also work on mobile phones and allow screen sharing. He, along with 40 other software engineers, left Cisco and started a new company. In 2012, the company was named **Zoom**. By May 2013, the company had acquired more than 1 million users. By 2020, Zoom had well over 200 million users throughout the world.

To help finance its current and future growth, Zoom had its initial public offering (IPO) in 2019. An IPO is a form of equity financing, where the company receives cash from outside investors, and in return, these investors receive ownership shares in the company's profits. By the end of the first day of trading, Zoom's stock had risen from $36 per share to $62 per share. The company was valued at more than $15 billion. Eric Yuan, who owned about 20% of the company, saw his net worth increase by $3 billion that day.

During the COVID-19 pandemic, demand for Zoom soared. In 2020, the company's annual revenue quadrupled, and its stock price rose by over 300%. By the end of 2020, Eric Yuan's ownership stake in Zoom had reached approximately $15 billion.

Like Zoom, many technology companies have financed their growth through equity. Other companies tend to rely more on debt financing, as we discussed in Chapter 9. While Zoom has shown the ability to generate profits in the past and investors expect these profits to grow, there is no guarantee they will. Zoom has faced potential security and performance issues, and the company competes against tech giants such as Cisco, Microsoft, and Alphabet. These risks, as well as others in the fast-changing technology industry, potentially jeopardize those future profits. At the end of this chapter, we'll analyze the equity and performance of **Zoom** versus **Microsoft**.

Feature Story

REUTERS/Carlo Allegri/Alamy Stock Photo

Common Terms
Stockholders' equity sometimes is referred to as *shareholders' equity*.

A major decision for a manager is how to raise capital for the company. The manager must consider whether to finance the company via debt, equity, or most commonly, both. The previous chapter discusses financing with debt, such as notes, leases, and bonds. In this chapter, we'll examine financing with equity, which entails exchanging ownership of the company for capital. We focus on the financial statement impact of major equity transactions, including issuing stock, stock repurchases, paying dividends, and stock splits.

Recall the accounting equation, which captures the intuition that a company's assets arise from one of two forms of financing: debt financing or equity financing. Illustration 10–1 shows the primary components of stockholders' equity.

ILLUSTRATION 10–1

Accounting Equation and Components of Stockholders' Equity

Assets	=	**Liabilities**	+	**Stockholders' Equity**
(resources)		(creditors' claims)		(owners' claims)

Primary Components of Stockholders' Equity

1. **Paid-in capital** is the amount stockholders have invested in the company.

2. **Retained earnings** is the amount of earnings the company has kept or retained—that is, the earnings not distributed in dividends to stockholders over the life of the company.

3. **Treasury stock** is a company's own issued stock that it has repurchased.

In Part A of the chapter, we discuss transactions involving paid-in capital. A better description might be "invested capital" since it's the amount stockholders invest when they purchase a company's stock. This discussion will include treasury stock for company purchases of its own shares. In Part B, we examine transactions involving retained earnings. A better description might be "earned capital," since it's the amount the company has *earned* for the stockholders and has been retained in the business. In Part C, we look at the reporting of total stockholders' equity.

PART A

INVESTED CAPITAL

Paid-in capital (or **invested capital**) is the amount of money paid into a company by its owners. Recall from Chapter 1 that a company can be formed as a sole proprietorship, a partnership, or a corporation. A sole proprietorship is a business owned by one person, whereas a partnership is a business owned by two or more persons. A **corporation** is an entity that is legally separate from its owners and even pays its own income taxes. Most corporations are owned by many stockholders, although some corporations are owned entirely by one individual. While sole proprietorships are the most common form of business, corporations are typically far larger in terms of total sales, assets, earnings, and employees.

Corporations

■ **LO10–1**
Identify the advantages and disadvantages of the corporate form of ownership.

Corporations are formed in accordance with the laws of individual states. The state incorporation laws guide corporations as they write their **articles of incorporation** (sometimes called the *corporate charter*). The articles of incorporation describe (a) the nature of the firm's business activities, (b) the shares of stock to be issued, and (c) the initial board of directors. The board of directors establishes corporate policies and appoints officers who manage the corporation. Illustration 10–2 presents an **organization chart** tracing the line of authority for a typical corporation.

Ultimately, a corporation's stockholders control the company. They are the owners of the corporation. By voting their shares, stockholders determine the makeup of the board of directors—which in turn appoints the management to run the company.

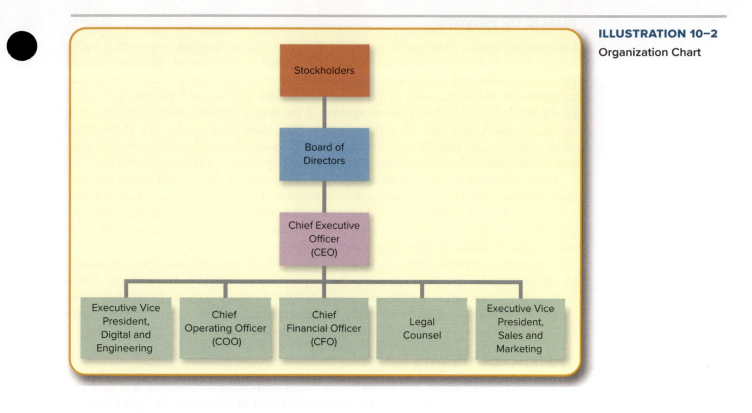

ILLUSTRATION 10–2
Organization Chart

STAGES OF EQUITY FINANCING

Most corporations that end up selling stock on a major stock exchange don't begin that way. Instead, there's usually a progression of equity financing stages leading to a public offering, as summarized in Illustration 10–3.

ILLUSTRATION 10–3 Stages of Equity Financing

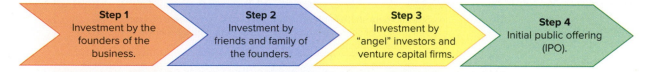

Most corporations first raise money by selling stock to the founders of the business and to their friends and family. As the equity financing needs of the corporation grow, companies prepare a business plan and seek outside investment from "angel" investors and venture capital firms. **Angel investors** are wealthy individuals in the business community, like those featured in the television show *Shark Tank*, willing to risk investment funds on a promising business venture. Individual angel investors may invest from a few thousand dollars to millions of dollars in the corporation. **Venture capital firms** provide additional financing, often in the millions, for a percentage ownership in the company. Many venture capital firms look to invest in promising companies to which they can add value through business contacts, financial expertise, or marketing channels. Most corporations do not consider issuing stock to the general public ("going public") until their equity financing needs exceed $20 million.

The first time a corporation issues stock to the public is called an **initial public offering (IPO)**. Like the issuance of bonds in Chapter 9, the public issuance of stock is a major event requiring the assistance of an investment banking firm (underwriter), lawyers, and public accountants. Major investment bankers, such as **Citigroup**, **Morgan Stanley**, and **Goldman Sachs**, charge up to 6% of the issue proceeds for their services. Legal and accounting fees also are not cheap, costing several hundred dollars per hour for services performed in preparation for a public stock offering.

PUBLIC OR PRIVATE

Corporations may be either public or private. The stock of a **publicly held corporation** trades on the New York Stock Exchange (NYSE) or National Association of Securities Dealers Automated Quotations (NASDAQ), or by over-the-counter (OTC) trading. Many of the largest companies in the world, such as **Walmart**, **ExxonMobil**, and **General Electric**, are traded on the NYSE. The NASDAQ is home to many of the largest high-tech companies, including **Apple**, **Microsoft**, and **Intel**. Over-the-counter trading takes place outside one of the major stock exchanges. All publicly held corporations are regulated by the Securities and Exchange Commission (SEC), resulting in significant additional reporting and filing requirements.

A **privately held corporation** does not allow investment by the general public and normally has fewer stockholders than a public corporation. Three of the largest private corporations in the United States are **Cargill** (agricultural commodities), **Koch Industries** (oil and gas), and **Mars** (food and candy). Generally, corporations whose stock is privately held do not need to file financial statements with the SEC.

Frequently, companies begin as smaller, privately held corporations. Then, as success broadens opportunities for expansion, the corporation goes public. For example, **Zoom** was a private corporation until it went public in 2019. Similarly, **Alibaba** (a Chinese online commerce company similar to **eBay** in the United States) went public in 2014 and raised $25 billion of outside investment funds. The result was the largest technology IPO ever.

STOCKHOLDER RIGHTS

Whether public or private, stockholders are the owners of the corporation and have certain rights: the right to vote (including electing the board of directors), the right to receive dividends, and the right to share in the distribution of assets if the company is dissolved. Illustration 10–4 further explains these stockholder rights.

ILLUSTRATION 10–4

Stockholder Rights

Right to Vote
- Stockholders vote on matters, including the election of corporate directors.

Right to Receive Dividends
- Stockholders share in profits when the company declares dividends. The percentage of shares a stockholder owns determines his or her share of the dividends distributed.

Right to Share in the Distribution of Assets
- Stockholders share in the distribution of assets if the company is dissolved. The percentage of shares a stockholder owns determines his or her share of the assets, which are distributed after creditors and preferred stockholders are paid.

ADVANTAGES OF A CORPORATION

A corporation offers two primary advantages over sole proprietorships and partnerships: limited liability and the ability to raise capital and transfer ownership.

Limited Liability.   **Limited liability** guarantees that stockholders in a corporation can lose no more than the amount they invested in the company, even in the event of bankruptcy. In contrast, owners in a sole proprietorship or a partnership can be held personally liable for debts the company has incurred, above and beyond the investment they have made.

Ability to Raise Capital and Transfer Ownership.   Because corporations sell ownership interest in the form of shares of stock, ownership rights are easily transferred. An investor can sell his or her ownership interest (shares of stock) at any time and without affecting the structure of the corporation or its operations. As a result, attracting outside investment is easier for a corporation than for a sole proprietorship or a partnership.

DISADVANTAGES OF A CORPORATION

A corporation has two primary disadvantages relative to sole proprietorships and partnerships: additional taxes and more paperwork.

Additional Taxes. Owners of sole proprietorships and partnerships are taxed once, when they include their share of earnings in their personal income tax returns. However, corporations have double taxation: As a legal entity separate from its owners, a corporation pays income taxes on its earnings. Then, when it distributes the earnings to stockholders in dividends, the stockholders—the company's owners—pay taxes a second time on the corporate dividends they receive. In other words, corporate income is taxed once on earnings at the corporate level and again on dividends at the individual level.

More Paperwork. To protect the rights of those who buy a corporation's stock or who lend money to a corporation, the federal and state governments impose extensive reporting requirements on the company. The additional paperwork is intended to ensure adequate disclosure of the information investors and creditors need.

Illustration 10–5 summarizes the primary advantages and disadvantages of a corporation compared to a sole proprietorship or partnership.

Advantages	Disadvantages
Limited liability A stockholder can lose no more than the amount invested.	**Additional taxes** Corporate earnings are taxed twice—at the corporate level and individual stockholder level.
Ability to raise capital and transfer ownership Attracting outside investment and transferring ownership is easier for a corporation.	**More paperwork** Federal and state governments impose additional reporting requirements.

ILLUSTRATION 10–5

Advantages and Disadvantages of a Corporation

Decision Maker's Perspective

Limited Liability *and* Beneficial Tax Treatment

Wouldn't it be nice to get the best of both worlds—enjoy the limited liability of a corporation and the tax benefits of a sole proprietorship or partnership? An S corporation allows a company to enjoy limited liability as a corporation, but tax treatment as a partnership. Because of these benefits, many companies that qualify choose to incorporate as S corporations. One of the major restrictions is that the corporation cannot have more than 100 stockholders, so S corporations appeal more to smaller, less widely held businesses.

Two additional business forms have evolved in response to liability issues and tax treatment—*limited liability companies* (LLCs) and *limited liability partnerships* (LLPs). Most accounting firms in the United States adopt one of these two business forms because they offer limited liability and avoid double taxation, but with no limits on the number of owners as in an S corporation.

 KEY POINT

The primary advantages of the corporate form of business are limited liability and the ability to raise capital. The primary disadvantages are additional taxes and more paperwork.

■ **LO10–2**
Record the issuance of common stock.

Common Stock

We can think of the common stockholders as the "true owners" of the business. In most cases, each share of common stock represents one unit of ownership.

AUTHORIZED, ISSUED, OUTSTANDING, AND TREASURY STOCK

For our discussion in this chapter, we need to make clear the different types of shares.

- **Authorized stock** is the total number of shares available to sell, stated in the company's articles of incorporation.
- **Issued stock** is the number of shares that have been sold to investors. A company usually does not issue all its authorized stock.

The total number of issued shares can then be divided into two categories.

- **Outstanding stock** is the number of issued shares held *by investors.* Only these shares receive dividends.
- **Treasury stock** is the number of issued shares repurchased *by the company.*

Illustration 10–6 summarizes the differences between authorized, issued, outstanding, and treasury stock.

ILLUSTRATION 10–6

Authorized, Issued, Outstanding, and Treasury Stock

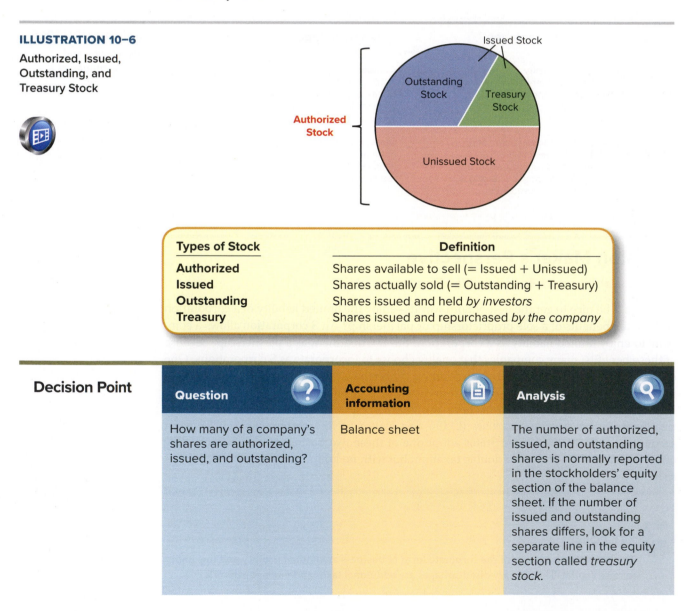

Types of Stock	Definition
Authorized	Shares available to sell (= Issued + Unissued)
Issued	Shares actually sold (= Outstanding + Treasury)
Outstanding	Shares issued and held *by investors*
Treasury	Shares issued and repurchased *by the company*

Decision Point

Question ❓	Accounting information 📄	Analysis 🔍
How many of a company's shares are authorized, issued, and outstanding?	Balance sheet	The number of authorized, issued, and outstanding shares is normally reported in the stockholders' equity section of the balance sheet. If the number of issued and outstanding shares differs, look for a separate line in the equity section called *treasury stock.*

PAR VALUE

Par value is the legal capital per share of stock that's assigned when the corporation is first established. Par value originally indicated the real value of a company's shares of stock. Today, **par value has no relationship to the market value of the common stock.** For instance, **Zoom**'s common stock originally was issued at $36 per share and in 2020 was trading as high as $568 per share, but it has a par value of $0.001 per share.

No-par value stock is common stock that has not been assigned a par value. Laws in many states permit corporations to issue no-par stock. Most new corporations, and even some established corporations such as **Nike** or **Procter & Gamble**, issue no-par value common stock. In some cases, a corporation assigns a **stated value** to the shares. Stated value is treated and recorded in the same manner as par value shares.

 COMMON MISTAKE

Some students confuse par value with market value. Par value is the legal capital per share that is set when the corporation is first established and actually is unrelated to "value." The market value per share is equal to the current share price. In most cases, the market value per share will far exceed the par value.

ACCOUNTING FOR COMMON STOCK ISSUES

When a company issues no-par value stock, the corporation records the equity account entitled Common Stock. For example, let's assume Canadian Falcon, an online retail company, issues 1,000 shares of no-par value common stock at $30 per share. We record this transaction as follows:

	Debit	Credit
Cash (= 1,000 shares × $30)	**30,000**	
Common Stock		**30,000**
(Issue no-par value common stock)		

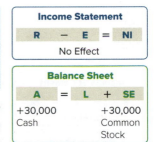

If the company issues par value stock rather than no-par value stock, we credit two equity accounts. We credit the Common Stock account for the number of shares issued times the par value per share, *and* we credit **Additional Paid-in Capital** for the portion of the cash proceeds above par value.

For example, assume that Canadian Falcon issues 1,000 shares of $0.01 par value common stock at $30 per share. The company credits the Common Stock account for par value. One thousand shares issued times $0.01 per share is $10. The company credits Additional Paid-in Capital for the portion of the cash proceeds above par value.

Common Terms
Additional paid-in capital is simply the amount paid for stock over par value. It is also called paid-in capital in excess of par.

	Debit	Credit
Cash (= 1,000 shares × $30)	**30,000**	
Common Stock (= 1,000 shares × $0.01)		**10**
Additional Paid-in Capital (difference)		**29,990**
(Issue common stock above par)		

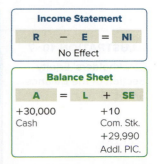

What if the common stock had a *stated value* of $0.01, rather than a *par value* of $0.01? We would record the same entry as in the par value example. For accounting purposes, **stated value is treated in the same manner as par value.**

Occasionally, a company will issue shares of stock in exchange for noncash goods or services. For example, what if 1,000 shares of common stock were issued to an attorney in payment for $30,000 in legal services? We would record the transaction in the same way as above, except we debit Legal Fees Expense, rather than Cash, for $30,000. The noncash exchange of stock, in this case for legal services, must be recorded at the fair value of the goods or services received.

KEY POINT

If no-par value stock is issued, the corporation records the full amount to Common Stock. If par value or stated value stock is issued, the corporation records two equity accounts—Common Stock at the par value or stated value per share and Additional Paid-in Capital for the portion above par or stated value.

■ **LO10–3**
Understand unique features and recording of preferred stock.

Preferred Stock

In order to attract wider investment, some corporations issue preferred stock in addition to common stock. For example, **Wells Fargo** has issued over $23 billion in preferred stock. **Preferred stock** is "preferred" over common stock in two ways:

1. Preferred stockholders usually have first rights to a specified amount of dividends (a stated dollar amount per share or a percentage of par value per share). If the board of directors declares dividends, preferred shareholders will receive the designated dividend before common shareholders receive any.

2. Preferred stockholders receive preference over common stockholders in the distribution of assets in the event the corporation is dissolved.

About 20% of the largest U.S. companies have preferred stock outstanding. However, unlike common stock, most preferred stock does not have voting rights. Control of the company remains with common stockholders.

ACCOUNTING FOR PREFERRED STOCK ISSUES

We record the issuance of preferred stock similar to the way we did for the issue of common stock. Assume that Canadian Falcon issues 1,000 shares of $30 par value preferred stock for $40 per share. We record the transaction as follows:

Income Statement		
R	– E =	NI
No Effect		

Balance Sheet		
A	= L +	SE
+40,000		+30,000
Cash		Pref. Stk.
		+10,000
		Addl. PIC.

	Debit	Credit
Cash (= 1,000 shares × $40)	40,000	
Preferred Stock (= 1,000 shares × $30)		30,000
Additional Paid-in Capital (difference)		10,000
(Issue preferred stock above par)		

Illustration 10–7 displays the stockholders' equity section of the balance sheet for Canadian Falcon following the issuance of both common and preferred stock. The balance of retained earnings is discussed later in this chapter.

ILLUSTRATION 10–7

Stockholders' Equity Section of the Balance Sheet

CANADIAN FALCON Balance Sheet (partial)	
Stockholders' equity:	
Preferred stock, $30 par value; 100,000 shares authorized; 1,000 shares issued and outstanding	$ 30,000
Common stock, $0.01 par value; 1 million shares authorized; 1,000 shares issued and outstanding	10
Additional paid-in capital	39,990
Total paid-in capital	70,000
Retained earnings	30,000
Total stockholders' equity	$100,000

FEATURES OF PREFERRED STOCK

Preferred stock is especially interesting due to the flexibility allowed in its contractual provisions. For instance, preferred stock might be convertible, redeemable, and/or cumulative:

Convertible	Shares can be converted into common stock.
Redeemable	Shares can be returned to (or redeemed by) the corporation at a fixed price.
Cumulative	Shares receive priority for future dividends, if dividends are not declared in a given year.

Preferred stock may be **convertible**, which allows the stockholder to exchange shares of preferred stock for common stock at a specified conversion ratio. Occasionally, preferred stock is **redeemable** at the option of either stockholders or the corporation. A redemption privilege might allow preferred stockholders the option, under specified conditions, to return their shares for a predetermined redemption price. Similarly, shares may be redeemable at the option of the issuing corporation.

Preferred stock usually is **cumulative**. If the specified dividends are not declared in a given year, they become **dividends in arrears**, and they accumulate until the company does declare dividends. We'll go through an example of dividends on cumulative preferred stock later in this section.

Debt or Equity.   These features of preferred stock give it attributes somewhere between common stock (equity) and long-term debt (liabilities). Investors in common stock are the owners of the corporation because they have voting rights, and some preferred stock may be convertible to common stock. Investors in long-term debt, such as bonds, are creditors who have loaned money to the corporation. These investors have the right to interest payments each year and then the face amount of the bond at maturity. This financing arrangement is similar to preferred stock that pays cumulative dividends and is redeemable by stockholders. Illustration 10–8 provides a comparison of common stock, preferred stock, and bonds along several dimensions. Note that preferred stock falls in the middle between common stock and bonds for each of these factors.

ILLUSTRATION 10–8

Comparison of Financing Alternatives

Factor	Common Stock	Preferred Stock	Bonds
Voting rights	Yes	Usually no	No
Risk to the investor	Highest	Middle	Lowest
Expected return to the investor	Highest	Middle	Lowest
Preference for dividends/interest	Lowest	Middle	Highest
Preference in distribution of assets	Lowest	Middle	Highest
Tax deductibility of payments	No	Usually no	Yes

INTERNATIONAL FINANCIAL REPORTING STANDARDS (IFRS)

SHOULD PREFERRED STOCK BE CLASSIFIED AS DEBT RATHER THAN EQUITY?

Under U.S. accounting rules, we usually record preferred stock in the stockholders' equity section of the balance sheet just above common stock. However, sometimes preferred stock shares features with debt. Redeemable preferred stock with a fixed redemption date (called *mandatorily redeemable*) is reported, like bonds payable, in the liability section of the balance sheet.[1] However, under IFRS, most preferred stock is reported as debt, with the dividends reported in the income statement as interest expense. Under U.S. GAAP, that's the case only for "mandatorily redeemable" preferred stock.

For more discussion, see Appendix E.

DIVIDENDS FOR PREFERRED STOCK

As discussed previously, preferred stock usually is *cumulative.* For this type of preferred stock, if dividends are not declared in a given year, they accumulate until the company does declare dividends. Common stockholders are not entitled to dividends in any year until stockholders of cumulative preferred stock are attributed all dividends to which they are entitled.

Assume that a company issues 1,000 shares of 8%, $30 par value preferred stock and 1,000 shares of $1 par value common stock at the beginning of 2022. If the preferred stock is *cumulative,* the company owes a dividend on the preferred stock of $2,400 each year (= 1,000 shares × 8% × $30 par value). If the preferred dividend is not declared in 2022 or 2023, dividends in arrears for the two years will total $4,800, and this amount is expected to be paid in some future year. If the preferred stock is *noncumulative,* then there will not be any dividends in arrears for 2022 and 2023.

Now, let's say in 2024 the company declares a total dividend of $10,000. How will the total dividend of $10,000 be distributed between preferred stockholders and common stockholders? As shown in Illustration 10–9, the answer depends on whether the preferred stock is cumulative or noncumulative.

ILLUSTRATION 10–9

Allocate Dividends between Preferred and Common Stock

If the preferred stock is *cumulative:*	
Preferred dividends in arrears for 2022 and 2023	$ 4,800
Preferred dividends for 2024 (1,000 shares × 8% × $30 par value)	2,400
Remaining dividends to common stockholders	2,800
Total dividends paid in 2024	$10,000
If the preferred stock is *noncumulative:*	
No preferred dividends in arrears for 2022 and 2023	—
Preferred dividends for 2024 (1,000 shares × 8% × $30 par value)	$ 2,400
Remaining dividends to common stockholders	7,600
Total dividends paid in 2024	$10,000

Before the company can pay dividends to common stockholders, if the preferred stock is cumulative, the company must pay the $4,800 in unpaid dividends for 2022 and 2023 and then the current dividend on preferred stock of $2,400 in 2024. After paying the preferred stock dividends, the company can pay the remaining balance of $2,800 (= $10,000 − $4,800 − $2,400) in dividends on common stock. However, if the preferred stock is noncumulative, there are no dividends in arrears to consider. The dividend of $10,000 in 2024 will be split, with $2,400 paid first to preferred stockholders for the current year and then the remaining $7,600 paid to common stockholders.

---

[1]The stock exchange on which the company's stock is traded sets an ex-dividend date, which typically is one business day before the record date. Investors must own the stock at least one day prior to the ex-dividend date to receive the dividend. The reason the ex-dividend date is one day before the record date is that in the United States, the Securities and Exchange Commission (SEC) requires stock trades to settle two days after purchase. So, to own the stock by the record date and have the right to receive the dividend, an investor would need to purchase the stock at least two business days before the date of record, which is one day before the ex-dividend date.

Because dividends are not an actual liability until they are declared by the board of directors, dividends in arrears for cumulative preferred stockholders are not reported as a liability in the balance sheet. However, information regarding any dividends in arrears is disclosed in the notes to the financial statements.

 KEY POINT

Preferred stock has preference over common stock in receiving dividends and in the distribution of assets in the event the corporation is dissolved. We record the issuance of preferred stock similar to the way we did for the issuance of common stock. Some preferred stock is cumulative, meaning any dividends not declared in a given year accumulate to be paid in a later year.

Treasury Stock

We just examined the issuance of common and preferred stock. Next, we look at what happens when companies buy back shares they have previously issued. Treasury stock is the name given to a company's own issued stock that it has purchased.

Over two-thirds of all publicly traded companies report treasury stock in their balance sheets. Illustration 10–10 provides a summary of cash dividends and stock purchases for the 1,000 largest companies in the U.S.

For the 1,000 largest U.S. companies, stock purchases are larger than cash dividends paid in recent years. In addition, cash dividends are relatively steady over time, while stock purchases are more volatile. Both cash dividends and stock purchases return cash to investors, but companies have different reasons for choosing which method to return that cash.

■ **LO10–4**
Account for treasury stock.

Common Terms
Purchases of treasury stock are commonly referred to as *buybacks*, *acquisitions*, or *repurchases* of treasury stock.

ILLUSTRATION 10–10   Cash Dividends versus Stock Purchases

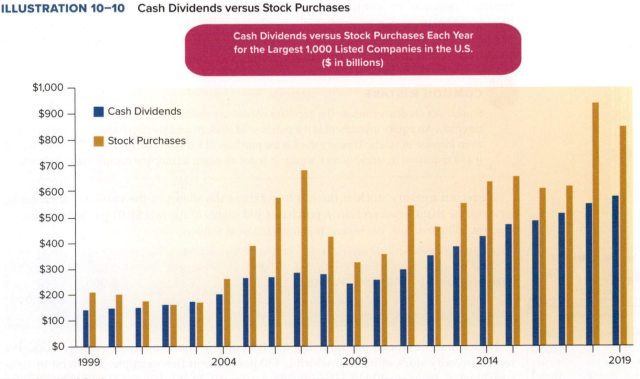

Cash Dividends versus Stock Purchases Each Year
for the Largest 1,000 Listed Companies in the U.S.
($ in billions)

Source: Standard & Poor's

Decision Maker's Perspective

Why Corporations Purchase Their Stock

What would motivate a company to buy back its own stock? Companies acquire their own stock for various reasons:

1. **To boost underpriced stock.** When company management feels the market price of its stock is too low, it may attempt to support the price by decreasing the supply of stock in the marketplace. An announcement by Johnson & Johnson that it planned to buy up to $5 billion of its outstanding shares triggered a public buying spree that pushed the stock price up by more than 3%.

2. **To distribute surplus cash without paying dividends.** While dividends usually are a good thing, investors do pay personal income tax on them. Another way for a firm to distribute surplus cash to shareholders without giving them taxable *dividend* income is to use the excess cash to purchase its own stock. Under a stock purchase, only shareholders selling back their stock to the company at a profit incur taxable income.

3. **To boost earnings per share.** Earnings per share is calculated as earnings divided by the number of shares outstanding. Stock purchases reduce the number of shares outstanding, thereby increasing earnings per share. However, with less cash in the company, it's more difficult for companies to maintain the same level of earnings following a share purchase.

4. **To satisfy employee stock ownership plans.** Another motivation for stock purchases is to acquire shares used in employee stock award and stock option compensation programs. Microsoft, for example, reported that its board of directors had approved a program to purchase shares of its common stock to offset the increase in shares from stock option and stock purchase plans.

ACCOUNTING FOR TREASURY STOCK

Treasury stock is the purchase of a company's own issued stock. **Just as issuing shares increases stockholders' equity, buying back those shares decreases stockholders' equity.** Rather than reducing the stock accounts directly, though, we record treasury stock as a separate "negative" or "contra" account. Recall that stockholders' equity accounts normally have credit balances. So, treasury stock is included in the stockholders' equity section of the balance sheet with an opposite, or debit, balance. When a corporation purchases its own stock, it increases (debits) Treasury Stock, while it decreases (credits) Cash.

 COMMON MISTAKE

Sometimes students confuse the purchase of treasury stock with investments in another company. An equity investment is the purchase of stock *in another corporation,* and we record it as an increase in assets. Treasury stock is the purchase of a *corporation's own stock,* and we record it as a reduction in stockholders' equity. It is not an asset; a company cannot invest in itself.

We record treasury stock at the *cost* to purchase the shares in the market. For example, let's assume that Canadian Falcon purchases 100 shares of its own $0.01 par value common stock at $30 per share. We record this transaction as follows:

Income Statement

R	−	E	=	NI
		No Effect		

Balance Sheet

A	=	L	+	SE
−3,000				−3,000
Cash				Treasury Stock ↑

	Debit	Credit
Treasury Stock (= 100 shares × $30)	**3,000**	
Cash		**3,000**
(Purchase treasury stock)		

Notice that the stock's par value has no effect on the entry to record treasury stock. We record treasury stock at its cost, which is $30 per share in this example. The debit to Treasury Stock reduces stockholders' equity. Illustration 10–11 displays the stockholders' equity section of the balance sheet before and after the purchase of treasury stock.

CANADIAN FALCON
Balance Sheet (partial)

Stockholders' equity:	Before	After
Preferred stock, $30 par value; 100,000 shares authorized; 1,000 shares issued and outstanding	$ 30,000	$30,000
Common stock, $0.01 par value; 1 million shares authorized; 1,000 shares issued and 900 shares outstanding	10	10
Additional paid-in capital	39,990	39,990
Total paid-in capital	70,000	70,000
Retained earnings	30,000	30,000
Treasury stock, 100 shares	**0**	**(3,000)**
Total stockholders' equity	$100,000	$97,000

Treasury stock is reported as a contra equity, or negative amount, because treasury stock reduces total stockholders' equity.

Now let's assume that Canadian Falcon resells the 100 shares of treasury stock for $35. Recall that these shares originally were purchased for $30 per share, so the $35 resale price represents a $5 per share increase in additional paid-in capital. It's *not* recorded as a $5 per share gain in the income statement, as we would for the sale of an investment in another company, since the company is reselling its own stock. We record this transaction as follows:

	Debit	Credit
Cash (= 100 shares × $35)	**3,500**	
Treasury Stock (= 100 shares × $30)		**3,000**
Additional Paid-in Capital[2] (= 100 shares × $5)		**500**
(Resell treasury stock above cost)		

Income Statement

R	–	E	=	NI
	No Effect			

Balance Sheet

A	=	L	+	SE
+3,500 Cash				+3,000 Treas. Stk. ↓ +500 Addl. PIC.

We debit Cash for $35 per share to record the inflow of cash from reselling treasury stock. We recorded the 100 shares of treasury stock in the accounting records at a cost of $30 per share at the time of purchase. Now, when we resell the treasury shares, we must reduce the Treasury Stock account at the same $30 per share. We record the $500 difference (= 100 shares × $5 per share) as Additional Paid-in Capital. Illustration 10–12 presents the stockholders' equity section of the balance sheet before and immediately after the sale of treasury stock.

CANADIAN FALCON
Balance Sheet (partial)

Stockholders' equity:	Before	After
Preferred stock, $30 par value; 100,000 shares authorized; 1,000 shares issued and outstanding	$30,000	$ 30,000
Common stock, $0.01 par value; 1 million shares authorized; 1,000 shares issued and 900 shares outstanding	10	10
Additional paid-in capital	**39,990**	**40,490**
Total paid-in capital	70,000	70,500
Retained earnings	30,000	30,000
Treasury stock, 100 shares	**(3,000)**	**0**
Total stockholders' equity	$97,000	$100,500

---

[2]Some companies credit "Additional Paid-in Capital from Treasury Stock Transactions" as a separate account from "Additional Paid-in Capital from Common Stock Transactions." We combine all additional paid-in capital entries into one "Additional Paid-in Capital" account, similar to how most companies report additional paid-in capital on the balance sheet.

What if the stock price goes down, and we resell the treasury stock for less than the $30 per share we paid to buy back the shares? Let's assume Canadian Falcon resells the 100 shares of treasury stock for only $25. It records the resale as follows:

Income Statement

R	−	E	=	NI

No Effect

Balance Sheet

A	=	L	+	SE

+2,500 Cash			+3,000 Treas. Stk. ↓ −500 Addl. PIC.

	Debit	Credit
Cash (= 100 × $25)	2,500	
Additional Paid-in Capital[3] (= 100 × $5)	500	
Treasury Stock (= 100 × $30)		3,000
(Resell treasury stock below cost)		

By purchasing 100 shares of its own stock for $30 per share and reselling them for only $25 per share, Canadian Falcon experienced a decrease in additional paid-in capital. This is reflected in the entry as a debit to the Additional Paid-in Capital account. It's not recorded as a $5 per share loss in the income statement, as we would for the sale of an investment in another company, because the company is reselling its own stock.

 **KEY POINT**

We include treasury stock in the stockholders' equity section of the balance sheet as a reduction in stockholders' equity (increases in treasury stock will decrease stockholders' equity). When we resell treasury stock, the amount of the sale price above (below) the stock's original purchase cost is reported as an increase (decrease) in additional paid-in capital.

PART B

■ LO10–5
Describe retained earnings and record cash dividends.

EARNED CAPITAL

In Part A of the chapter, we discussed transactions involving "invested capital," because when investors buy a corporation's stock, they are investing in the company. Here, in Part B, we examine transactions involving "earned capital." This component of equity represents the net assets of the company that have been *earned* for the stockholders rather than *invested* by the stockholders. We'll also see that some of this earned capital is distributed back to stockholders in the form of dividends. Thus, we end up with a component of equity that represents earned capital that has been retained in the company, commonly referred to as *retained earnings*.

Retained Earnings

As noted at the beginning of the chapter, **retained earnings** represent the earnings retained in the company—earnings not distributed as dividends to stockholders over the life of the company. In other words, the balance in retained earnings equals all net income, less all dividends, since the company began operations.

$$\text{Retained earnings} = \text{All net income since the company began} - \text{All dividends since the company began}$$

Let's look at an example. Illustration 10–13 shows how net income and dividends impact the balance in retained earnings over a four year period.

ILLUSTRATION 10–13

Retained Earnings over a Four-Year Period

	Net Income (Net Loss)	Dividends	Balance in Retained Earnings
Year 1	$ (1,000)	$ 0	$ (1,000)
Year 2	3,000	0	2,000
Year 3	4,000	1,000	5,000
Year 4	10,000	3,000	12,000

---

[3]Companies debit Retained Earnings rather than Additional Paid-in Capital if there is not a sufficient prior credit balance in Additional Paid-in Capital from treasury stock transactions. The details are covered in intermediate financial accounting courses.

- Year 1 (first year of operations): The company reports a net loss of $1,000. The net loss results in a balance of −$1,000 in retained earnings.
- Year 2: The company reports net income of $3,000. This means that by the end of year 2, all net income (−$1,000 in year 1 and $3,000 in year 2) minus all dividends ($0 in years 1 and 2) results in a cumulative balance in retained earnings of $2,000.
- Year 3: The difference between net income and dividends is $3,000 (= $4,000 − $1,000), and this amount adds to the cumulative balance of retained earnings from year 2.
- Year 4: The difference between net income and dividends is $7,000 and adds to the cumulative balance of retained earnings in year 3.

This process of adding net income and subtracting dividends each year to calculate the cumulative balance of retained earnings continues over the life of the company.

COMMON MISTAKE

Some students think, incorrectly, that retained earnings represents a *cash* balance set aside by the company. In fact, the size of retained earnings can differ greatly from the balance in the Cash account.

Negative Retained Earnings (or Accumulated Deficit).   In a company's early years, the balance in retained earnings tends to be small, and total paid-in capital—money invested into the corporation—tends to be large. As the years go by, the earnings retained in the business continue to grow and, for many profitable companies, can exceed the total amount originally invested in the corporation. Unfortunately, for some companies, expenses sometimes are more than revenues, so a net loss rather than net income is recorded. Just as net income increases retained earnings, a net loss *decreases* retained earnings.

If losses exceed income since the company began, Retained Earnings will have a negative balance. A negative balance in Retained Earnings is called an **accumulated deficit**. In Illustration 10–13, we saw an example of an accumulated deficit in year 1. We subtract an accumulated deficit from total paid-in capital in the balance sheet to arrive at total stockholders' equity. Many companies in the start-up phase or when experiencing financial difficulties report an accumulated deficit.

KEY POINT

Retained earnings represent all net income, less all dividends, since the company began operations.

Cash Dividends

Dividends are distributions by a corporation to its stockholders. Investors pay careful attention to cash dividends. A change in the quarterly or annual cash dividend paid by a company can provide useful information about its future prospects. For instance, an increase in dividends often is perceived as good news. Companies tend to increase dividends when the company is doing well and future prospects look bright.

Decision Maker's Perspective

Why Don't Some Companies Pay Dividends?

Many companies that are unprofitable choose not to pay dividends. Management of these companies may instead need to use that cash for strategic purposes to keep the company from bankruptcy. However, many profitable companies also choose not to pay cash dividends. Companies with large expansion plans, called *growth companies,* prefer to reinvest earnings in the growth of the company rather than distribute earnings back to investors in the form of cash dividends. **Facebook, Alphabet** (Google), and **Berkshire Hathaway** are highly profitable companies that have yet to pay any dividends, although these companies may buy back their own stock from time to time.

As companies mature and their growth opportunities diminish, they tend to pay out more dividends. **Microsoft** and **Apple** did not pay dividends in their early growth years, but have been paying them in more recent years.

Why do investors buy stock in companies like **Facebook** if they do not receive dividends? Investors hope a company's share price increases and then they can sell the stock for a profit. Illustration 10–14 presents the disclosure of Facebook's dividend policy.

For companies that do pay dividends, the date the board of directors announces the next dividend to be paid is known as the **declaration date**. The declaration of a dividend creates a binding legal obligation for the company declaring the dividend. On that date, we (a) increase Dividends, a temporary account that is closed into Retained Earnings at the end of each period, and (b) increase a liability account, Dividends Payable.

ILLUSTRATION 10–14

Facebook's Dividend Policy

> ### FACEBOOK, INC.
> #### Notes to the Financial Statements (excerpt)
>
> We have never declared or paid cash dividends on our capital stock. We currently intend to retain any future earnings to finance the operation and expansion of our business, and we do not expect to declare or pay any cash dividends in the foreseeable future. As a result, you may only receive a return on your investment in our Class A common stock and, if issued, our Class C capital stock if the trading price of your shares increases.

Source: Facebook, Inc.

The board of directors also indicates a specific date on which the company looks at its records to determine who the stockholders of the company are. This date is called the **record date**. An investor must be a stockholder on the record date to have the right to receive the dividend.[4] The date of the actual distribution is the **payment date**. Dividends are paid only on shares outstanding. **Dividends are not paid on treasury shares.**

To illustrate the payment of a cash dividend, assume that on March 15 Canadian Falcon declares a $0.25 per share dividend on its 2,000 outstanding shares—1,000 shares of common stock and 1,000 shares of preferred stock. We record the declaration of cash dividends as follows:

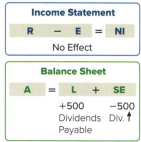

Income Statement

R	–	E	=	NI

No Effect

Balance Sheet

A	=	L	+	SE
		+500		–500
		Dividends Payable		Div. ↑

March 15 (declaration date)	Debit	Credit
Dividends (= 2,000 shares × $0.25)	**500**	
Dividends Payable		**500**
(Declare cash dividends)		

The Dividends account is a *temporary* stockholders' equity account that is closed into Retained Earnings at the end of each period. Dividends are legally payable, once declared by the board of directors, so Dividends Payable is credited. Dividends Payable is classified as a current liability in the balance sheet because once they are declared, the company is legally obligated to pay them in the near future.

---

[4]The stock exchange on which the company's stock is traded sets an ex-dividend date, which typically is one business day before the record date. Investors must own the stock at least one day prior to the ex-dividend date to receive the dividend. The reason the ex-dividend date is one day before the record date is that in the United States, the Securities and Exchange Commission (SEC) requires stock trades to settle two days after purchase. So, to own the stock by the record date and have the right to receive the dividend, an investor would need to purchase the stock at least two business days before the date of record, which is one day before the ex-dividend date.

COMMON MISTAKE

Some students incorrectly calculate dividends based on the number of issued shares. Dividends are based on the number of outstanding shares since dividends are not paid on treasury stock.

Let's continue our example and assume that the dividend declared by Canadian Falcon is payable to stockholders of record at March 31. We make no entry on March 31, the record date.

April 15 is the payment date and we record the cash paid and the reduction in Dividends Payable.

April 15 (payment date)	Debit	Credit
Dividends Payable (= 2,000 shares × $0.25)	500	
Cash		500
(Pay cash dividends)		

Income Statement

R	–	E	=	NI
		No Effect		

Balance Sheet

A	=	L	+	SE
−500		−500		
Cash		Dividends		
		Payable		

Because cash is the asset most easily distributed to stockholders, most corporate dividends are cash dividends. In concept, though, any asset can be distributed to stockholders as a dividend. When a noncash asset is distributed to stockholders, it is referred to as a **property dividend**. Securities held as investments are the assets most often distributed in a property dividend. The actual recording of property dividends is covered in intermediate accounting.

KEY POINT

The declaration of cash dividends decreases Retained Earnings and increases Dividends Payable. The payment of cash dividends decreases Dividends Payable and decreases Cash. The net effect, then, is a reduction in both Retained Earnings and Cash.

Decision Point

Question ?	**Accounting information** 📄	**Analysis** 🔍
How much profit has the company made for its stockholders that has not been distributed back to them in dividends?	Balance in Retained Earnings	The balance in Retained Earnings shows all net income less dividends since the company began operations.

Let's Review

Slacks 5th Avenue has two classes of stock authorized: $100 par preferred and $1 par common. As of the beginning of the year, 1,000 shares of common stock and no preferred shares have been issued. The following transactions affect stockholders' equity during the year:

January	15	Issue 2,000 additional shares of common stock for $20 per share.
February	1	Issue 100 shares of preferred stock for $110 per share.
June	1	Declare a cash dividend of $5 per share on preferred stock and $1 per share on common stock to all stockholders of record on June 15.
June	30	Pay the cash dividend declared on June 1.
October	1	Purchase 200 shares of treasury stock for $25 per share.
November	1	Resell 100 shares of the treasury stock purchased on October 1 for $28 per share.

Required:

1. Record each transaction.

2. Indicate whether each transaction increases (+), decreases (−), or has no effect (NE), on total assets, total liabilities, and total stockholders' equity.

Solution:

1. Entries to record each transaction:

January 15	Debit	Credit
Cash (= 2,000 × $20)	40,000	
Common Stock (= 2,000 × $1)		2,000
Additional Paid-in Capital (difference)		38,000
(Issue common stock above par)		
February 1		
Cash (= 100 × $110)	11,000	
Preferred Stock (= 100 × $100)		10,000
Additional Paid-in Capital (difference)		1,000
(Issue preferred stock above par)		
June 1		
Dividends*	3,500	
Dividends Payable		3,500
(Declare cash dividends)		
= (100 preferred shares × $5) + (3,000 common shares × $1)		
June 30		
Dividends Payable	3,500	
Cash		3,500
(Pay cash dividends)		
October 1		
Treasury Stock (= 200 shares × $25)	5,000	
Cash		5,000
(Purchase treasury stock)		
November 1		
Cash (= 100 shares × $28)	2,800	
Treasury Stock (= 100 shares × $25)		2,500
Additional Paid-in Capital (= 100 × $3)		300
(Resell treasury stock above cost)		

2. Effects of transactions on the components of the accounting equation:

Transaction	Total Assets	Total Liabilities	Total Stockholders' Equity
Issue common stock	+	NE	+
Issue preferred stock	+	NE	+
Declare cash dividends	NE	+	−
Pay cash dividends	−	−	NE
Purchase treasury stock	−	NE	−
Resell treasury stock	+	NE	+

Suggested Homework:
BE10–3, BE10–4;
E10–5, E10–6;
P10–2A&B

Stock Dividends and Stock Splits

■ **LO10–6**

Explain the effect of stock dividends and stock splits.

Sometimes corporations distribute additional shares of their own stock to shareholders rather than cash. These are known as **stock dividends** or **stock splits**, depending on the size of the stock distribution. Suppose you own 100 shares of stock. Assuming a 10% stock dividend, you'll get 10 additional shares. A 100% stock dividend, equivalent to a 2-for-1 stock split, means 100 more shares.

Large stock dividends (25% or more of the shares outstanding) and stock splits are declared primarily due to the effect they have on stock prices. Let's say that before the 100% stock dividend, your shares are trading at $40 a share, so your 100 shares are worth $4,000. After the 100% stock dividend, you will have twice as many shares. It sounds good, but let's look closer. Since the company as a whole still has the same value, each share of stock is now worth one-half what it was worth before the stock dividend. Your 200 shares still have a value of $4,000, the same as your 100 shares before the stock dividend. However, now each share is worth half as much—$20 rather than $40 per share.

Think of the company as a pizza. A 100% stock dividend is like changing an 8-slice pizza into 16 slices by cutting each slice in half. You are no better off with 16 half-slices than with the original 8 slices. Whether it's cut in 8 large slices or 16 smaller slices, it's still the same-sized pizza. Whether a company is represented by 1 million shares worth $40 each or 2 million shares worth $20 each, it's the same $40 million company. **Total assets, total liabilities, and total stockholders' equity do not change as a result of a stock dividend.**

Vasko/E+/Getty Images

Decision Maker's Perspective

Why Declare a Stock Split?

Why would a company declare a 2-for-1 stock split when the stockholders are not really receiving anything of substance? The primary reason is to lower the trading price of the stock to a more acceptable trading range, making it attractive to a larger number of potential investors. Many companies like their stock to trade under $100 per share—$20 to $40 per share is common. For instance, after a company declares a 2-for-1 stock split with a per share market price of $80, it then has twice the number of shares outstanding, each with an approximate market value reduced to a more marketable trading range of $40. Apple recently announced a 4-for-1 stock split, lowering its stock price at that time from about $500 to $125.

However, there are exceptions to the normal trading range. **Amazon**'s stock traded at over $3,000 per share in 2021. **Berkshire Hathaway**'s "A" shares traded at over $300,000 per share in 2021, making it accessible only to wealthier investors. Berkshire Hathaway is founded by billionaire investor Warren Buffett. While still an outspoken critic of stock dividends and stock splits, even Warren Buffett is giving in a little. Berkshire Hathaway created "B" shares, designed for general public investment. B shares trade at a ratio of 1,500-to-1 relative to A shares.

Accounting standards distinguish between stock splits, large stock dividends, and small stock dividends. We look first at the accounting for stock splits and large stock dividends because they are more common in practice.

STOCK SPLITS/LARGE STOCK DIVIDENDS

When a company declares a stock split, we do not record a transaction. After a 2-for-1 stock split, the Common Stock account balance (total par value) represents twice as many shares. For instance, assume Canadian Falcon declares a 2-for-1 stock split on its 1,000 shares of $0.01 par value common stock. The balance in the Common Stock account is 1,000 shares times $0.01 par value per share, which equals $10. With no journal entry, the balance remains $10 despite the number of shares doubling. As a result, the par value *per share* is reduced by one-half to $0.005 (2,000 shares times $0.005 par per share still equals $10).

As you might expect, having the par value per share change in this way is cumbersome and expensive. All records, printed or electronic, that refer to the previous amount must be changed to reflect the new amount. To avoid changing the par value per share, most companies report stock splits in the same way as a large stock dividend. We account for a large stock dividend by recording an increase in the Common Stock account in the amount of the par value of the additional shares distributed, as presented below:

Income Statement
R   −   E   =   NI
No Effect

Balance Sheet
A   =   L   +   SE
+10
Com. Stk.
−10
Stk. Div. ↑

	Debit	Credit
Stock Dividends (= 1,000 shares × $0.01)	10	
Common Stock		10
(Record 100% [large] stock dividend)		

Similar to cash dividends, the Stock Dividends account is a temporary stockholders' equity account that is closed into Retained Earnings. The debit to Stock Dividends reduces Retained Earnings. So, a stock dividend entry decreases one equity account, Retained Earnings, and increases another equity account, Common Stock. **Note that the above entry does not change total assets, total liabilities, or total stockholders' equity.** Illustration 10–15 presents the stockholders' equity section of the balance sheet for Canadian Falcon before and after the 2-for-1 stock split accounted for as a 100% stock dividend.

ILLUSTRATION 10–15

Stockholders' Equity before and after a 2-for-1 Stock Split Accounted for as a 100% Stock Dividend

CANADIAN FALCON **Balance Sheet (partial)**		
	Before 100% **Stock Dividend**	**After 100%** **Stock Dividend**
Stockholders' equity:		
Preferred stock, $30 par value	$ 30,000	$ 30,000
Common stock, $0.01 par value	10	20
Additional paid-in capital	40,490	40,490
Total paid-in capital	70,500	70,510
Retained earnings	29,500	29,490
Total stockholders' equity	$100,000	$100,000
Common shares outstanding	1,000	2,000
Par value per share	$ 0.01	$ 0.01
Share price	$ 30	$ 15

Notice that total stockholders' equity remains at $100,000 before and after the stock distribution. Common stock increased by $10, while retained earnings decreased by $10. Illustration 10–16 summarizes the effects of a stock split and a stock dividend.

ILLUSTRATION 10–16

Effects of a Stock Split and a Stock Dividend

	Stock Split	Stock Dividend
Total stockholders' equity	No change	No change
Common stock	No change	Increase
Retained earnings	No change	Decrease
Par value per share	Decrease	No change

Illustration 10–17 presents the disclosure of **Apple**'s 4-for-1 stock split.

ILLUSTRATION 10–17

Apple's Stock Split

APPLE INC.
The Board of Directors has also approved a four-for-one stock split to make the stock more accessible to a broader base of investors. Each Apple shareholder of record at the close of business on August 24, 2020, will receive three additional shares for every share held on the record date, and trading will begin on a split-adjusted basis on August 31, 2020.

Source: Apple Inc.

SMALL STOCK DIVIDENDS

Recall that we record large stock dividends at the *par value* per share. We record small stock dividends at the *market value,* rather than the par value per share. Assume, for example, the market value of Canadian Falcon common stock is $30 per share when Canadian Falcon declares a 10% dividend on its 1,000 shares outstanding of $0.01 par value common stock. After the 10% stock dividend, Canadian Falcon will have an additional 100 shares outstanding. The company records this small stock dividend as follows:

	Debit	Credit
Stock Dividends (= 1,000 × 10% × $30)	**3,000**	
Common Stock (= 1,000 × 10% × $0.01)		1
Additional Paid-in Capital (difference)		**2,999**
(Distribute 10% [small] stock dividend)		

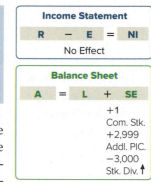

Income Statement

R	−	E	=	NI

No Effect

Balance Sheet

A	=	L	+	SE

+1
Com. Stk.
+2,999
Addl. PIC.
−3,000
Stk. Div. ↑

So, small stock dividends are recorded at the market value per new share, while large stock dividends are recorded at the par value per share. Why the inconsistency? Some believe that a small stock dividend will have little impact on the market price of shares currently outstanding, arguing for the recording of small stock dividends at market value. However, this reasoning is contrary to research evidence, which finds the market price adjusts for both large and small stock dividends.[5] A 10% stock dividend will result in 10% more shares, but each share will be worth 10% less, so the investor is no better off. **Note that the above entry still does not change total assets, total liabilities, or total stockholders' equity.** The debit to Stock Dividends simply decreases one equity account, Retained Earnings, while the credits increase two other equity accounts, Common Stock and Additional Paid-in Capital.

ETHICAL DILEMMA

Take A Pix Media/Shutterstock

Intercontinental Clothing Distributors has paid cash dividends every year since the company was founded in 1990. The dividends have steadily increased from $0.05 per share to the latest dividend declaration of $1.00 per share. The board of directors is eager to continue this trend despite the fact that earnings fell significantly during the recent quarter. The chair of the board proposes a solution. He suggests a 5% stock dividend in lieu of a cash dividend, to be accompanied by the following press announcement: "In place of our regular $1.00 per share cash dividend, Intercontinental will distribute a 5% stock dividend on its common shares, currently trading at $20 per share. Changing the form of the dividend will permit the company to direct available cash resources to the modernization of facilities and other capital improvements.a

Is a 5% stock dividend on shares trading at $20 per share equivalent to a $1.00 per share cash dividend? Is the chair's suggestion ethical?

KEY POINT

Declaring stock dividends and stock splits is like cutting a pizza into more slices. Everyone has more shares, but each share is worth proportionately less than before.

---

[5]Taylor W. Foster and Don Vickrey. 1978. "The Information Content of Stock Dividend Announcements." *Accounting Review* 53, no. 2 (April), pp. 360–70; and J. David Spiceland and Alan J. Winters. 1986. "The Market Reaction to Stock Distributions: The Effect of Market Anticipation and Cash Returns." *Accounting and Business Research 16,* no. 63 (Summer), pp. 211–25.

PART C

We now can apply what we've learned so far in the chapter to analyze the stockholders' equity of an actual company—**Citigroup**. In this section, we show the financial statement presentation of stockholders' equity in the balance sheet and differentiate it from the statement of stockholders' equity.

■ **LO10–7**

Prepare and analyze the stockholders' equity section of a balance sheet and the statement of stockholders' equity.

Stockholders' Equity in the Balance Sheet

Illustration 10–18 presents the stockholders' equity section of the balance sheet for **Citigroup**, an investment bank and financial services corporation headquartered in New York City.

ILLUSTRATION 10–18

Stockholders' Equity Section for Citigroup

CITIGROUP ($ and shares in millions)	
Preferred stock ($1.00 par value; issued shares):	$ 17,980
Common stock ($0.01 par value; issued shares): 3,099,602,856	31
Additional paid-in capital	107,840
Retained earnings	165,369
Treasury stock, at cost: 985,479,501 shares	(61,660)
Accumulated other comprehensive income (loss)	(36,318)
Total stockholders' equity	$193,242

Preferred stock is usually listed before common stock in the balance sheet, given its preference over common stock. The dollar amounts shown for common stock and preferred stock are based on the number of shares issued times their par value. The company has issued 719,200 shares of preferred stock with a par value of $1.00 (reported at liquidation value). The company has issued nearly 3.1 billion shares of common stock. With a par value of $0.01, that rounds to a common stock balance of $31 million.

Additional paid-in capital represents amounts above par value that have been received from investors. For Citigroup, this balance is much larger than the Common Stock account balance. This is to be expected. Remember, Citigroup has a par value of only $0.01 per share, so most of the money invested in the company was credited to Additional Paid-in Capital rather than Common Stock.

Now look at retained earnings. When a company is started, most of the equity is in the paid-in capital section because that's the amount invested by stockholders. But then, if a company is profitable, like Citigroup the retained earnings section of equity grows. For Citigroup, the balance in retained earnings is nearly as large as total stockholders' equity. How can this happen? Citigroup has used a portion of cash generated from earnings to buy back treasury shares, which decreases stockholders' equity.

Decision Maker's Perspective

Why Doesn't Stockholders' Equity Equal the Market Value of Equity?

The *market* value of equity is the price investors are willing to pay for a company's stock. The market value of equity equals the stock price times the number of shares outstanding. On the other hand, the *book* value of equity equals total stockholders' equity reported in the balance sheet. Market value and book value generally are not the same and often are vastly different. For example, Nvidia reported total stockholders' equity of about $12 billion, yet its market value at this same time was over $144 billion. Why?

Keep in mind that stockholders' equity is equal to assets minus liabilities. An asset's book value usually equals its market value *on the date it's purchased*. However, the two aren't necessarily the same after that. For instance, an asset such as a building often increases in value over time, but it continues to be reported in the balance sheet at historical cost minus accumulated depreciation. Consider another example. Nvidia spends over $3 billion each year on research and development (R&D). These activities increase the long-term profit-generating ability of the company, but under accounting rules, it expenses all its R&D costs as it incurs them. This causes the true market value of assets and stockholders' equity to be greater than the amount recorded for assets and stockholders' equity in the accounting records. Even when investors see the increase in a company's value and its stock price moves higher, common stock in the company's balance sheet continues to be reported at its original issue price rather than its higher market value.

Statement of Stockholders' Equity

The stockholders' equity section of the balance sheet, like the one we just examined for Citigroup, shows the balance in each equity account *at a point in time.* In contrast, the **statement of stockholders' equity** summarizes the *changes* in the balance in each stockholders' equity account *over time.*

To contrast the *stockholders' equity section* of the balance sheet and the *statement of stockholders' equity,* let's compare both for Canadian Falcon. Illustration 10–19 shows the stockholders' equity section reported in Canadian Falcon's balance sheet.

ILLUSTRATION 10–19

Stockholders' Equity Section—Canadian Falcon

CANADIAN FALCON
Balance Sheet (partial)
December 31, 2024

Stockholders' equity:	
Preferred stock, $30 par value; 100,000 shares authorized;	
1,000 shares issued and outstanding	$ 30,000
Common stock, $0.01 par value; 1 million shares authorized;	
2,000 shares issued and outstanding	20
Additional paid-in capital	40,490
Total paid-in capital	70,510
Retained earnings	29,490
Treasury stock	–0–
Total stockholders' equity	$100,000

Compare that snapshot of stockholders' equity at the end of 2024 with Illustration 10–20, showing the statement of stockholders' equity for Canadian Falcon.

ILLUSTRATION 10–20

Statement of Stockholders' Equity—Canadian Falcon

CANADIAN FALCON
Statement of Stockholders' Equity
For the year ended December 31, 2024

	Preferred Stock	Common Stock	Additional Paid-in Capital	Retained Earnings	Treasury Stock	Total Stockholders' Equity
Balance, January 1	$ –0–	$–0–	$ –0–	$ –0–	$ –0–	$ –0–
Issue common stock		10	29,990			30,000
Issue preferred stock	30,000		10,000			40,000
Purchase treasury stock					(3,000)	(3,000)
Resell treasury stock			500		3,000	3,500
Cash dividends				(500)		(500)
100% stock dividend		10		(10)		–0–
Net income				30,000		30,000
Balance, December 31	**$30,000**	**$ 20**	**$40,490**	**$29,490**	**$ –0–**	**$100,000**

The statement of stockholders' equity reports how each equity account changed during the year. The beginning balances in Illustration 10–20 are zero because this is the first year of operations.

- Common Stock increased because Canadian Falcon issued common stock during the year. There was also a common stock dividend.
- Additional Paid-in Capital account increased from the issuance of common stock, the issuance of preferred stock, and the sale of treasury stock for more than its original cost.
- Retained Earnings increased due to net income and decreased due to cash dividends and stock dividends. The retained earnings column is sometimes shown separately and referred to as a statement of retained earnings.
- Treasury stock was initially purchased, reducing total stockholders' equity. The treasury stock was then resold by the end of the year, eliminating its negative effect.

The ending balances of each stockholders' equity account are shown in the stockholders' equity section of the balance sheet. These ending balances will be the beginning balances next year in the statement of stockholders' equity.

KEY POINT

The stockholders' equity section of the balance sheet presents the balance of each equity account *at a point in time.* The statement of stockholders' equity shows the change in each equity account balance *over time.*

Let's Review

This is a continuation of the Let's Review exercise presented earlier in the chapter. Recall that Slacks 5th Avenue has two classes of stock authorized: $100 par preferred and $1 par value common. As of the beginning of 2024, 1,000 shares of common stock have been issued and no shares of preferred stock have been issued. The following transactions affect stockholders' equity during 2024:

January	15	Issue 2,000 additional shares of common stock for $20 per share.
February	1	Issue 100 shares of preferred stock for $110 per share.
June	1	Declare a cash dividend of $5 per share on preferred stock and $1 per share on common stock to all stockholders of record on June 15.
June	30	Pay the cash dividend declared on June 1.
October	1	Purchase 200 shares of common treasury stock for $25 per share.
November 1		Resell 100 shares of treasury stock purchased on October 1 for $28 per share.

Slacks 5th Avenue has the following beginning balances in its stockholders' equity accounts on January 1, 2024: Preferred Stock, $0; Common Stock, $1,000; Additional Paid-in Capital, $14,000; and Retained Earnings, $5,000. Net income for the year ended December 31, 2024, is $4,000.

Required:

Taking into consideration the beginning balances and all of the transactions during 2024, prepare the following for Slacks 5th Avenue:

1. The stockholders' equity section as of December 31, 2024.
2. The statement of stockholders' equity for the year ended December 31, 2024.

Solution:

1. Stockholders' equity section:

SLACKS 5TH AVENUE Balance Sheet (partial) December 31, 2024	
Stockholders' equity:	
Preferred stock, $100 par value	$10,000
Common stock, $1 par value	3,000
Additional paid-in capital	53,300
Total paid-in capital	66,300
Retained earnings	5,500
Treasury stock	(2,500)
Total stockholders' equity	$69,300

2. Statement of stockholders' equity:

SLACKS 5TH AVENUE Statement of Stockholders' Equity For the year ended December 31, 2024						
	Preferred Stock	Common Stock	Additional Paid-in Capital	Retained Earnings	Treasury Stock	Total Stockholders' Equity
Balance, January 1	$ –0–	$1,000	$14,000	$5,000	$ –0–	$20,000
Issue common stock		2,000	38,000			40,000
Issue preferred stock	10,000		1,000			11,000
Dividends				(3,500)		(3,500)
Purchase treasury stock					(5,000)	(5,000)
Resell treasury stock			300		2,500	2,800
Net income				4,000		4,000
Balance, December 31	$10,000	$3,000	$53,300	$5,500	$(2,500)	$69,300

Suggested Homework:
BE10–15, BE10–16;
E10–14, E10–15;
P10–5A&B

EQUITY ANALYSIS
Zoom vs. Microsoft

ANALYSIS

Earnings are the key to a company's long-run survival. However, we need to evaluate earnings in comparison to the size of the investment. For instance, earnings of $500,000 may be quite large for a small business but would be a rather disappointing outcome for a major corporation like **Microsoft**. A useful summary measure of earnings that considers the relative size of the business is the return on equity.

■ **LO10–8**
Evaluate company performance using information on stockholders' equity.

RETURN ON EQUITY

The **return on equity (ROE)** measures the ability of company management to generate profits from the resources provided by owners. We compute the ratio by dividing net income by average stockholders' equity.

$$\text{Return on equity} = \frac{\text{Net income}}{\text{Average stockholders' equity}}$$

Let's compare the profitability of **Zoom** and **Microsoft**. Illustration 10–21 provides selected financial data for each company.

$ in millions except per share data	Zoom	Microsoft
Net sales	$ 623	$143,015
Net income	$ 22	$ 44,281
Total liabilities	$ 456	$183,007
Stockholders' equity, beginning	$ −7	$102,330
Stockholders' equity, ending	$ 834	$118,304
Stock price, ending	$76.30	$ 203.51
Dividends per share	$ 0	$ 1.99
Average shares outstanding	234 million	7,610 million

The return on equity for both companies is calculated in Illustration 10–22.

ILLUSTRATION 10–22

Return on Equity for
Zoom and Microsoft

	Net Income	÷	Average Stockholders' Equity	=	Return on Equity
Zoom	$ 22	÷	($−7 + $834)/2	=	5.3%
Microsoft	$44,281	÷	($102,330 + $118,304)/2	=	40.1%

Zoom has a return on equity of 5.3%, compared to 40.1% for Microsoft. At first, you might think this means that Zoom is less profitable, and in terms of return on equity, that is true. However, a key reason for the difference in return on equity is that Zoom relies to a greater extent on equity financing, while Microsoft relies on debt financing. The ratio of debt to equity for Zoom is only 54.7% (= $456 / $834) compared to that of Microsoft of 154.7% (=$183,007 / $118,304).

DIVIDEND YIELD

Investors are also interested in knowing how much a company pays out in dividends relative to its share price. The **dividend yield** is computed as dividends per share divided by the stock price.

$$\text{Dividend yield} = \frac{\text{Dividends per share}}{\text{Stock price}}$$

Dividend yield for Zoom and Microsoft is shown in Illustration 10–23.

ILLUSTRATION 10–23

Dividend Yield for
Zoom and Microsoft

	Dividends Per Share	÷	Stock Price	=	Dividend Yield
Zoom	$0.00	÷	$ 76.30	=	0.0%
Microsoft	$1.99	÷	$203.51	=	1.0%

Small growth companies tend not to pay dividends, while larger, more mature companies do. Zoom does not pay dividends, so its dividend yield is 0%. Microsoft pays a dividend yield of 1.0%. Shareholders of Zoom earn a total stock return equal to the change in stock price for the year. Shareholders of Microsoft earn a total stock return equal to the change in stock price for the year plus dividends.

EARNINGS PER SHARE

Earnings per share (EPS) measures the net income per share of common stock. We calculate earnings per share as net income minus preferred stock dividends divided by the average shares outstanding during the period:

$$\text{Earnings per share} = \frac{\text{Net income} - \text{Dividends on preferred stock}}{\text{Average shares of common stock outstanding}}$$

The upper half of the fraction measures the income available to common stockholders. We subtract any dividends on preferred stock from net income to arrive at the income available to the true owners of the company—the common stockholders. If a company does not issue preferred stock, the top half of the fraction is simply net income. We then divide income available to common stockholders by the average shares outstanding during the period to calculate earnings per share.

Earnings per share is useful in comparing earnings performance for the same company over time. It is *not* useful for comparing earnings performance of one company with another because of wide differences in the number of shares outstanding among companies. For instance, assume two companies, Alpha and Beta, both report net income of $1 million and are valued by the market at $20 million. Quite comparable, right? Not if we are talking about their earnings per share. If Alpha has one million shares outstanding and Beta has two million shares outstanding, their earnings per share amounts will not be comparable. Alpha will have a share price of $20 (= $20 million ÷ 1 million shares) and an EPS of $1.00 (= $1 million in earnings ÷ 1 million shares). Beta, on the other hand, will have a share price of $10 ($20 million ÷ 2 million shares) and an EPS of $0.50 ($1 million in earnings ÷ 2 million shares). Is the earnings performance for Alpha better than that for Beta? Of course not. They both earned $1 million. Alpha's earnings per share is higher simply because it has half as many shares outstanding. (Same pizza, fewer slices.)

If Alpha declared a 2-for-1 stock split, its earnings per share would match Beta's exactly. The key point is that earnings per share is useful in comparing either Alpha's earnings over time or Beta's earnings over time, but it is not useful in comparing the companies with each other.

Investors use earnings per share extensively in evaluating the earnings performance of a company over time. Investors are looking for companies with the potential to increase earnings per share. Analysts also forecast earnings on a per share basis. If reported earnings per share fall short of analysts' forecasts, this is considered negative news, usually resulting in a decline in a company's stock price.

PRICE-EARNINGS RATIO

Another measure widely used by analysts is the **price-earnings ratio** (PE ratio). It indicates how the stock is trading relative to current earnings. We calculate the PE ratio as the stock price divided by earnings per share, so that both stock price and earnings are expressed on a per share basis:

$$\text{Price-earnings ratio} = \frac{\text{Stock price}}{\text{Earnings per share}}$$

Price-earnings ratios commonly are in the range of 20 to 25 in recent years. A high PE ratio indicates that the market has high hopes for a company's stock and has bid up the price. **Growth stocks** are stocks whose future earnings investors expect to be higher. Their stock prices are high in relation to current earnings because investors expect future earnings to be higher. On the other hand, **value stocks** are stocks that are priced low in relation to current earnings. The low price in relation to earnings may be justified due to poor future prospects, or it might suggest an underpriced stock that could boom in the future. Illustration 10–24 calculates the price-earnings ratios for Zoom and Microsoft.

	Stock Price	÷	Earnings per Share	=	Price-Earnings Ratio
Zoom	$ 76.30	÷	$22/234	=	811.6
Microsoft	$203.51	÷	$44,281/7,610	=	35.0

ILLUSTRATION 10–24

Price-Earnings Ratios for Zoom and Microsoft

The price-earnings ratios for Zoom is much higher, indicating that investors expect greater growth in future earnings. Only time will tell whether those growth expectations are correct.

 KEY POINT

The return on equity measures the ability to generate earnings from the owners' investment. It is calculated as net income divided by average stockholders' equity. The dividend yield measures how much a company pays out in dividends in relation to its stock price. Earnings per share measures the net income per share of common stock. The price-earnings ratio indicates how the stock is trading relative to current earnings.

Decision Point

Question	Accounting information	Analysis
Do investors expect future earnings to grow?	Price-earnings ratio (PE ratio)	A high PE ratio indicates investors expect future earnings to be higher. A low PE ratio indicates investors' lack of confidence in future earnings growth.

CHAPTER FRAMEWORK

This chapter discusses the three primary components of stockholders' equity—paid-in capital, retained earnings, and treasury stock. Equity transactions affect amounts reported in the financial statements.

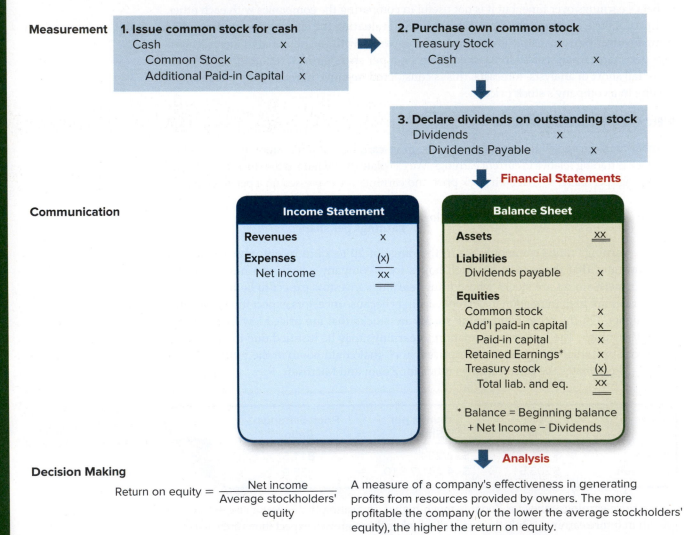

Measurement

1. Issue common stock for cash

Cash	x	
Common Stock		x
Additional Paid-in Capital		x

2. Purchase own common stock

Treasury Stock	x	
Cash		x

3. Declare dividends on outstanding stock

Dividends	x	
Dividends Payable		x

Financial Statements

Communication

Income Statement

Revenues	x
Expenses	(x)
Net income	xx

Balance Sheet

Assets	xx
Liabilities	
Dividends payable	x
Equities	
Common stock	x
Add'l paid-in capital	x
Paid-in capital	x
Retained Earnings*	x
Treasury stock	(x)
Total liab. and eq.	xx

* Balance = Beginning balance + Net Income − Dividends

Analysis

Decision Making

$$\text{Return on equity} = \frac{\text{Net income}}{\text{Average stockholders' equity}}$$

A measure of a company's effectiveness in generating profits from resources provided by owners. The more profitable the company (or the lower the average stockholders' equity), the higher the return on equity.

1. **Issue common stock for cash.** A company issues common stock and receives cash from stockholders. Common stock is recorded for par value, and additional paid-in capital is the issue price of the stock above par value.

2. **Purchase own common stock.** A company buys back its own common stock that previously was issued. Rather than reducing the common stock account directly, treasury stock is recorded as a separate contra (or negative) equity account for the cost to acquire the shares.

3. **Declare dividends on outstanding stock.** A company declares dividends to be paid to its outstanding stockholders. Outstanding stock includes all issued shares other than treasury stock. At the time of declaration, the dividends are legally payable. Those dividends typically are paid in the near future.

Chapter Framework Questions

1. **Measurement:** Which of the following is recorded when a company issues stock above par value?
   a. Cash is recorded for the total issue price.
   b. Common Stock is recorded for the amount of par value.
   c. Additional Paid-in Capital is recorded for the issue price above par value.
   d. All of the choices above are correct.

2. **Measurement:** Which of the following is recorded when a company purchases its own common stock.
   a. Common Stock is recorded for par value.
   b. Treasury Stock is recorded for the cost to acquire the shares.
   c. Common Stock is recorded for the cost to acquire the shares above par value.
   d. Treasury Stock is recorded for par value.

3. **Communication (income statement):** The (a) issuance of common stock and (b) purchase of treasury stock have what effects on total expenses reported in the income statement?
   a. Issuing common stock increases total revenues.
   b. Purchasing treasury stock increases total expenses.
   c. Both *a.* and *b.* are correct.
   d. Neither *a.* or *b.* is correct.

4. **Communication (balance sheet):** Which of following best describes how treasury stock is reported in the balance sheet?
   a. A separate contra (or negative) equity account.
   b. Reduction in the Common Stock account.
   c. A separate asset account.
   d. A separate contra (or negative) liability account.

5. **Decision Making (ratio analysis):** Companies that are better able to generate profits for their owners would have a _____ return on equity ratio.
   a. Higher.
   b. Lower.

Note: For answers, see the last page of the chapter.

KEY POINTS BY LEARNING OBJECTIVE

LO10–1 Identify the advantages and disadvantages of the corporate form of ownership.

The primary advantages of the corporate form of business are limited liability and the ability to raise capital. The primary disadvantages are additional taxes and more paperwork.

LO10–2 Record the issuance of common stock.

If no-par value stock is issued, the corporation records the full amount to Common Stock. If par value or stated value stock is issued, the corporation records two equity accounts— Common Stock at the par value or stated value per share and Additional Paid-in Capital for the portion above par or stated value.

LO10–3 Understand unique features and recording of preferred stock.

Preferred stock has preference over common stock in receiving dividends and in the distribution of assets in the event the corporation is dissolved. We record the issuance of preferred stock similar to the way we do for the issuance of common stock. Some preferred stock is cumulative, meaning any dividends not declared in a given year accumulate to be paid in a later year.

LO10–4 Account for treasury stock.

We include treasury stock in the stockholders' equity section of the balance sheet as a reduction in stockholders' equity (increases in treasury stock will decrease stockholders' equity). When we resell treasury stock, the amount of the sale price above (below) the stock's original purchase cost is reported as an increase (decrease) in additional paid-in capital.

LO10–5 Describe retained earnings and record cash dividends.

Retained earnings represent all net income, less all dividends, since the company began operations.

The declaration of cash dividends decreases Retained Earnings and increases Dividends Payable. The payment of cash dividends decreases Dividends Payable and decreases Cash. The net effect, then, is a reduction in both Retained Earnings and Cash.

LO10–6 Explain the effect of stock dividends and stock splits.

Declaring stock dividends and stock splits is like cutting a pizza into more slices. Everyone has more shares, but each share is worth proportionately less than before.

LO10–7 Prepare and analyze the stockholders' equity section of a balance sheet and the statement of stockholders' equity.

The stockholders' equity section of the balance sheet presents the balance of each equity account *at a point in time.* The statement of stockholders' equity shows the change in each equity account balance *over time.*

Analysis

LO10–8 Evaluate company performance using information on stockholders' equity.

The return on equity measures the ability to generate earnings from the owners' investment. It is calculated as net income divided by average stockholders' equity. The dividend yield measures how much a company pays out in dividends in relation to its stock price. Earnings per share measures the net income per share of common stock. The price-earnings ratio indicates how the stock is trading relative to current earnings.

GLOSSARY

Accumulated deficit: A negative balance in Retained Earnings. **p. 505**

Additional paid-in capital: The portion of the cash proceeds from issuing stock above par value. **p. 497**

Angel investors: Wealthy individuals in the business community willing to risk investment funds on a promising business venture. **p. 493**

Articles of incorporation: Describes the nature of the firm's business activities, the shares to be issued, and the composition of the initial board of directors. **p. 492**

Authorized stock: Shares available to sell, as stated in the company's articles of incorporation. **p. 496**

Convertible: Shares can be exchanged for common stock. **p. 499**

Corporation: An entity that is legally separate from its owners and even pays its own income taxes. **p. 492**

Cumulative: Preferred stock shares receive priority for future dividends, if dividends are not declared in a given year. **p. 499**

Declaration date: The date the board of directors announces the next dividend to be paid. **p. 506**

Dividends: Distributions to stockholders, typically in the form of cash. **p. 505**

Dividends in arrears: Unpaid dividends on cumulative preferred stock. **p. 499**

Dividend yield: Dividends per share divided by the stock price. **p. 516**

Double taxation: Corporate income is taxed once on earnings at the corporate level and again on dividends at the individual level. **p. 495**

Earnings per share (EPS): Net income available to common shareholders divided by average shares of common stock outstanding. **p. 516**

Growth stocks: Stocks that tend to have higher price-earnings ratios and are expected to have higher future earnings. **p. 517**

Initial public offering (IPO): The first time a corporation issues stock to the public. **p. 493**

Issued stock: Shares sold to investors; includes treasury shares. **p. 496**

Limited liability: Stockholders in a corporation can lose no more than the amount they invested in the company. **p. 494**

No-par value stock: Common stock that has not been assigned a par value. **p. 497**

Organization chart: Traces the line of authority within the corporation. **p. 492**

Outstanding stock: Issued shares that currently are held by investors; does not include treasury shares. **p. 496**

Paid-in capital: The amount stockholders have invested in the company. **p. 492**

Par value: The legal capital assigned per share of stock. **p. 497**

Payment date: The date of the actual distribution of dividends. **p. 506**

Preferred stock: Stock with preference over common stock in the payment of dividends and the distribution of assets. **p. 498**

Price-earnings ratio: The stock price divided by earnings per share so that both stock price and earnings are expressed on a per share basis. **p. 517**

Privately held corporation: Does not allow investment by the general public and normally has fewer stockholders. **p. 494**

Property dividend: The distribution of a noncash asset to stockholders. **p. 507**

Publicly held corporation: Allows investment by the general public and is regulated by the Securities and Exchange Commission. **p. 494**

Record date: The date on which a company looks at its records to determine who the stockholders of the company are. **p. 506**

Redeemable: Shares can be returned to the corporation at a fixed price. **p. 499**

Retained earnings: Earnings not distributed as dividends to stockholders over the life of the company. **pp. 492, 504**

Return on equity (ROE): Net income divided by average stockholders' equity; measures the income generated per dollar of equity. **p. 515**

S corporation: Allows a company to enjoy limited liability as a corporation, but tax treatment as a partnership. **p. 495**

Stated value: The legal capital assigned per share to no-par stock. **p. 497**

Statement of stockholders' equity: A financial statement that summarizes the changes in stockholders' equity over time. **p. 513**

Stock dividends: Additional shares of a company's own stock given to stockholders. **p. 508**

Stock split: A large stock dividend that includes a reduction in the par or stated value per share. **p. 508**

Treasury stock: A company's own issued stock that it has purchased. **pp. 492, 496, 501**

Value stocks: Stocks that tend to have lower price-earnings ratios and are priced low in relation to current earnings. **p. 517**

Venture capital firms: Provide additional financing, often in the millions, for a percentage ownership in the company. **p. 493**

SELF-STUDY QUESTIONS

1. Which of the following is a publicly traded company? **(LO10–1)**
   a. Zoom.
   b. Cargill.
   c. Ernst & Young.
   d. Koch Industries.

2. The advantages of owning a corporation include **(LO10–1)**
   a. Difficulty in transferring ownership.
   b. Limited liability.
   c. Lower taxes.
   d. Less paperwork.

3. The correct order from the smallest number of shares to the largest number of shares is **(LO10–2)**
   a. Authorized, issued, and outstanding.
   b. Outstanding, issued, and authorized.
   c. Issued, outstanding, and authorized.
   d. Issued, authorized, and outstanding.

4. A company issues 10,000 shares of $0.05 par value common stock for $25 per share. Which of the following is recorded at issuance? **(LO10–2)**
   a. Credit Common Stock for $250,000.
   b. Credit Additional Paid-in Capital for $250,000.
   c. Credit Common Stock for $500.
   d. Credit Additional Paid-in Capital for $500.

5. Preferred stock **(LO10–3)**
   a. Is always recorded as a liability.
   b. Is always recorded as part of stockholders' equity.
   c. Can have features of both liabilities and stockholders' equity.
   d. Is not included in either liabilities or stockholders' equity.

6. Treasury stock **(LO10–4)**
   a. Has a normal credit balance.
   b. Decreases stockholders' equity.
   c. Is recorded as an investment.
   d. Increases stockholders' equity.

7. Suppose a company purchases 2,000 shares of its own $1 par value common stock for $16 per share. Which of the following is recorded at the time of the purchase? **(LO10–4)**
   a. Debit Treasury Stock for $32,000.
   b. Debit Common Stock for $30,000.
   c. Debit Common Stock for $32,000.
   d. Debit Treasury Stock for $2,000.

8. Suppose a company purchases 2,000 shares of its own $1 par value common stock for $16 per share. The company then resells 400 of these shares for $20 per share. Which of the following is recorded at the time of the resale? **(LO10–4)**

a. Credit Common Stock for $400.

b. Credit Treasury Stock for $8,000.

c. Credit Common Stock for $8,000.

d. Credit Additional Paid-in Capital for $1,600.

9. Retained earnings **(LO10–5)**

   a. Has a normal debit balance.

   b. Decreases stockholders' equity.

   c. Is equal to the balance in cash.

   d. Increases stockholders' equity.

10. In its first three years of operations, a company has net income of $2,000, $5,000, and $8,000. It also pays dividends of $1,000 in the second year and $3,000 in the third year. What is the balance of Retained Earnings at the end of the third year? **(LO10–5)**

    a. $5,000.

    b. $11,000.

    c. $15,000.

    d. $4,000.

11. We credit Dividends Payable on **(LO10–5)**

    a. Payment date.

    b. Record date.

    c. Declaration date.

    d. Never.

12. Suppose a company declares a dividend of $0.50 per share. At the time of declaration, the company has 100,000 shares issued and 90,000 shares outstanding. On the declaration date, Dividends would be recorded for **(LO10–5)**

a. $0.

b. $50,000.

c. $45,000.

d. $95,000.

13. Both cash dividends and stock dividends **(LO10–6)**

    a. Reduce total assets.

    b. Reduce total liabilities.

    c. Reduce total stockholders' equity.

    d. Reduce retained earnings.

14. How does the stockholders' equity section in the balance sheet differ from the statement of stockholders' equity? **(LO10–7)**

    a. The stockholders' equity section shows balances at a point in time, whereas the statement of stockholders' equity shows activity over a period of time.

    b. The stockholders' equity section shows activity over a period of time, whereas the statement of stockholders' equity is at a point in time.

    c. There are no differences between them.

    d. The stockholders' equity section is more detailed than the statement of stockholders' equity.

15. The PE ratio **(LO10–8)**

    a. Measures a company's profitability per share.

    b. Tends to be higher for value stocks.

    c. Tends to be higher for growth stocks.

    d. Typically is less than 1.

Note: For answers, see the last page of the chapter.

DATA ANALYTICS & EXCEL

Visit Connect to find a variety of Data Analytics questions that help build Excel, Tableau, and data visualization skills. Assignable materials include Integrated Excel, Applying Excel, Data Visualizations, Tableau Dashboard Activities, and Applying Tableau Cases.

REVIEW QUESTIONS

■ **LO10–1**   1. Corporations typically do not first raise capital by issuing stock to the general public. What are the common stages of equity financing leading to an initial public offering (IPO)?

■ **LO10–1**   2. What is the difference between a public and a private corporation? Provide an example of each.

■ **LO10–1**   3. What are the basic ownership rights of common stockholders?

■ **LO10–1**   4. Which form of business organization is most common? Which form of business organization is larger in terms of total sales, total assets, earnings, and number of employees?

■ **LO10–1**   5. Describe the primary advantages and disadvantages of a corporation.

■ **LO10–1**   6. Explain how an LLC or an S corporation represents the "best of both worlds" in terms of business ownership.

7. Explain the difference among authorized, issued, and outstanding shares. ■ **LO10–2**

8. The articles of incorporation allow for the issuance of 1 million shares of common stock. During its first year, California Clothing issued 100,000 shares and reacquired 10,000 shares it held as treasury stock. At the end of the first year, how many shares are authorized, issued, and outstanding? ■ **LO10–2**

9. What is par value? How is it related to market value? How is it used in recording the issuance of stock? ■ **LO10–2**

10. What are the three potential features of preferred stock? Indicate whether each feature makes the preferred stock appear more like stockholders' equity or more like long-term liabilities. ■ **LO10–3**

11. Explain why preferred stock often is said to be a mixture of attributes somewhere between common stock and bonds. ■ **LO10–3**

12. What would motivate a company to buy back its own stock? ■ **LO10–4**

13. How is the accounting for a purchase of a company's own stock (treasury stock) different from the purchase of stock in another corporation? ■ **LO10–4**

14. Explain why some companies choose not to pay cash dividends. Why do investors purchase stock in companies that do not pay cash dividends? ■ **LO10–5**

15. Describe the declaration date, record date, and payment date for a cash dividend. ■ **LO10–5**

16. How does a 100% stock dividend or a 2-for-1 stock split affect total assets, total liabilities, and total stockholders' equity? ■ **LO10–6**

17. Contrast the effects of a cash dividend and a stock dividend on total assets, total liabilities, and total stockholders' equity. ■ **LO10–6**

18. What happens to the par value, the share's trading price, and the number of shares outstanding in a 2-for-1 stock split? ■ **LO10–6**

19. Indicate the correct order in which to report the following accounts in the stockholders' equity section of the balance sheet: Additional Paid-in Capital, Common Stock, Preferred Stock, Treasury Stock, and Retained Earnings. ■ **LO10–7**

20. How is the stockholders' equity section of the balance sheet different from the statement of stockholders' equity? ■ **LO10–7**

21. Why doesn't total stockholders' equity equal the market value of the firm? ■ **LO10–7**

22. Explain why earnings per share is useful for comparing earnings performance for the same company over time, but is not useful for comparing earnings performance between two competing companies. ■ **LO10–8**

23. What does "PE" stand for in the PE ratio, and how do investors use this ratio? ■ **LO10–8**

BRIEF EXERCISES

BE10–1 Waldo is planning to start a clothing store helping big and tall men blend in with the crowd. Explain to Waldo the advantages and disadvantages of a corporation in comparison to a sole proprietorship or partnership.

Cite advantages and disadvantages of a corporation **(LO10–1)**

BE10–2 Renaldo heard that an S corporation combines the benefits of a corporation with the benefits of a partnership. Explain to Renaldo the specific benefits of an S corporation and any drawbacks to organizing as an S corporation.

Understand an S corporation **(LO10–1)**

BE10–3 Western Wear Clothing issues 3,000 shares of its $0.01 par value common stock to provide funds for further expansion. Assuming the issue price is $11 per share, record the issuance of common stock.

Record issuance of common stock **(LO10–2)**

BE10–4 Gothic Architecture is a new chain of clothing stores. Gothic issues 1,000 shares of its $1 par value common stock at $30 per share. Record the issuance of the stock. How would the entry differ if Gothic issued no-par value stock?

Record issuance of common stock **(LO10–2)**

Record issuance of preferred stock (LO10–3)

BE10–5 Equinox Outdoor Wear issues 1,000 shares of its $0.01 par value preferred stock for cash at $32 per share. Record the issuance of the preferred shares.

Recognize preferred stock features (LO10–3)

BE10–6 Match each of the following preferred stock features with its description.

Preferred Stock Features	Description
1. Convertible	a. Prior unpaid dividends receive priority.
2. Redeemable	b. Shares can be sold at a predetermined price.
3. Cumulative	c. Shares can be exchanged for common stock.

Determine the amount of preferred stock dividends on (LO10–3)

BE10–7 Rachel's Designs has 2,000 shares of 7%, $50 par value cumulative preferred stock issued at the beginning of 2022. All remaining shares are common stock. Due to cash flow difficulties, the company was not able to pay dividends in 2022 or 2023. The company plans to pay total dividends of $23,000 in 2024. How much of the $23,000 dividend will be paid to preferred stockholders and how much will be paid to common stockholders?

Record purchase of treasury stock (LO10–4)

BE10–8 California Surf Clothing Company issues 1,000 shares of $1 par value common stock at $35 per share. Later in the year, the company decides to purchase 100 shares at a cost of $38 per share. Record the purchase of treasury stock.

Record sale of treasury stock (LO10–4)

BE10–9 Refer to the situation described in BE10–8. Record the transaction if California Surf resells the 100 shares of treasury stock at $40 per share.

Record sale of treasury stock (LO10–4)

BE10-10 Refer to the situation described in BE10-8. Record the transaction if California Surf resells the 100 shares of treasury stock at $35 per share.

Calculate retained earnings (LO10–5)

BE10-11 Diamond Dresses began the year with a balance of $425,000 in Retained Earnings. During the year, the company had net income of $100,000 and declared no dividends. (a) Calculate the ending balance of Retained Earnings. (b) Now assume the company declared dividends of $25,000. Calculate the ending balance of Retained Earnings.

Record cash dividends (LO10–5)

BE10–12 Divine Apparel has 4,000 shares of common stock outstanding. On October 1, the company declares a $0.75 per share dividend to stockholders of record on October 15. The dividend is paid on October 31. Record all transactions on the appropriate dates for cash dividends.

Record stock dividends (LO10–6)

BE10–13 On June 30, the board of directors of Sandals, Inc., declares and issues a 100% stock dividend on its 30,000, $1 par, common shares. The market price of Sandals common stock is $35 on June 30. Record the stock dividend.

Analyze a stock split (LO10–6)

BE10–14 Refer to the situation described in BE10–13, but assume a 2-for-1 stock split instead of the 100% stock dividend. Explain why Sandals did not record a 2-for-1 stock split. What are the number of shares, par value per share, and market price per share immediately after the 2-for-1 stock split?

Indicate effects on total stockholders' equity (LO10–7)

BE10–15 Indicate whether each of the following transactions increases (+), decreases (−), or has no effect (NE) on total assets, total liabilities, and total stockholders' equity. The first transaction is completed as an example.

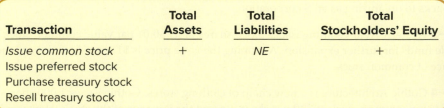

Transaction	Total Assets	Total Liabilities	Total Stockholders' Equity
Issue common stock	+	NE	+
Issue preferred stock			
Purchase treasury stock			
Resell treasury stock			

BE10–16 Summit Apparel has the following accounts at December 31: Common Stock, $1 par value, 2,000,000 shares issued; Additional Paid-in Capital, $18 million; Retained Earnings, $11 million; and Treasury Stock, 60,000 shares, $1.32 million. Prepare the stockholders' equity section of the balance sheet.

Prepare the stockholders' equity section (LO10–7)

BE10–17 The financial statements of Colorado Outfitters include the following selected data ($ in millions): sales, $9,543; net income, $320; beginning stockholders' equity, $3,219; and ending stockholders' equity, $2,374. Calculate the return on equity.

Calculate the return on equity (LO10–8)

BE10-18 Refer to the information in BE10-3. Determine the financial statement effects of the issuance of common stock.

Determine financial statement effects of issuing common stock (LO10–2)

BE10-19 Refer to the information in BE10-8. Determine the financial statement effects of the purchase of treasury stock.

Determine financial statement effects of purchasing treasury stock (LO10-4)

BE10-20 Refer to the information in BE10-9. Determine the financial statement effects of the sale of treasury stock.

Determine financial statement effects of selling treasury stock (LO10-4)

BE10-21 Refer to the information in BE10-10. Determine the financial statement effects of the sale of treasury stock.

Determine financial statement effects of selling treasury stock (LO10-4)

BE10-22 Refer to the information in BE10-12. Determine the financial statement effects for (1) the declaration of dividends on October 1 and (2) the payment of dividends on October 31.

Determine financial statement effects of cash dividends (LO10-5)

EXERCISES

E10–1 Match (by letter) the following terms with their definitions. Each letter is used only once.

Match terms with their definitions (LO10–1)

Terms	Definitions
_____ 1. Publicly held corporation	a. Shareholders can lose no more than the amount they invest in the company.
_____ 2. Organization chart	b. Corporate earnings are taxed twice—at the corporate level and individual shareholder level.
_____ 3. Articles of incorporation	c. Like an S corporation, but there are no limitations on the number of owners as in an S corporation.
_____ 4. Limited liability	d. Traces the line of authority within the corporation.
_____ 5. Initial public offering	e. Allows for legal treatment as a corporation, but tax treatment as a partnership.
_____ 6. Double taxation	f. Has stock traded on a stock exchange such as the New York Stock Exchange (NYSE).
_____ 7. S corporation	g. The first time a corporation issues stock to the public.
_____ 8. Limited liability company	h. Describes (a) the nature of the firm's business activities, (b) the shares to be issued, and (c) the composition of the initial board of directors.

Match terms with their definitions (LO10–2, 10–3, 10–4)

E10–2 Match (by letter) the following terms with their definitions. Each letter is used only once.

Terms	Description
_____ 1. Authorized Stock	a. Shares held by investors (shares issued that have not been repurchased by the corporation).
_____ 2. Issued Stock	
_____ 3. Outstanding Stock	
_____ 4. Preferred Stock	b. Shares that have been sold to investors.
_____ 5. Treasure Stock	c. Shares of a company's own stock that it has purchased.
	d. Shares available to sell, stated in the company's articles of incorporation.
	e. Shares that have preference over common stockholders to receive dividends.

Record the issuance of common stock (LO10–2)

E10–3 Clothing Frontiers began operations on January 1 and engages in the following transactions during the year related to stockholders' equity.

January 1   Issues 700 shares of common stock for $50 per share.
April   1   Issues 110 additional shares of common stock for $54 per share.

Required:
1. Record the transactions, assuming Clothing Frontiers has no-par common stock.
2. Record the transactions, assuming Clothing Frontiers has either $1 par value or $1 stated value common stock.

Record the issuance of common stock (LO10–2)

E10–4 Major Sports plans to raise $5,000,000 in an initial public offering of its common stock. The company is considering three options:
  a. Issue 100,000 shares of $1 par value common stock for $50 per share.
  b. Issue 500,000 shares of $1 par value common stock for $10 per share.
  c. Issue 1,000,000 shares of $1 par value common stock for $5 per share.

Required:
Record the issuance of common stock for each option.

Determine the amount of dividends on preferred stock (LO10–3)

E10–5 Nathan's Athletic Apparel has 2,000 shares of 5%, $100 par value preferred stock the company issued at the beginning of 2023. All remaining shares are common stock. The company was not able to pay dividends in 2023, but plans to pay dividends of $22,000 in 2024.

Required:
1. Assuming the preferred stock is cumulative, how much of the $22,000 dividend will be paid to preferred stockholders and how much will be paid to common stockholders in 2024?
2. Assuming the preferred stock is noncumulative, how much of the $22,000 dividend will be paid to preferred stockholders and how much will be paid to common stockholders in 2024?

Record common stock, preferred stock, and dividend transactions (LO10–2, 10–3, 10–5)

E10–6 Italian Stallion has the following transactions during the year related to stockholders' equity.

February 1   Issues 6,000 shares of no-par common stock for $16 per share.
May   15   Issues 700 shares of $10 par value, 12.5% preferred stock for $13 per share.
October   1   Declares a cash dividend of $1.25 per share to all stockholders of record (both common and preferred) on October 15.
October 15   Date of record.
October 31   Pays the cash dividend declared on October 1.

Required:
Record each of these transactions.

E10–7 Finishing Touches has two classes of stock authorized: 8%, $10 par preferred, and $1 par value common. The following transactions affect stockholders' equity during 2024, its first year of operations:

Record issuance of stock and treasury stock transactions (LO10–2, 10–3, 10–4)

January	2	Issues 100,000 shares of common stock for $35 per share.
February	6	Issues 3,000 shares of 8% preferred stock for $11 per share.
September	10	Purchases 11,000 shares of its own common stock for $40 per share.
December	15	Resells 5,500 shares of treasury stock at $45 per share.

Required:

Record each of these transactions.

E10–8 Refer to the information in E10–7. In its first year of operations, Finishing Touches has net income of $160,000 and pays dividends at the end of the year of $94,500 ($1 per share) on all common shares outstanding and $2,400 on all preferred shares outstanding.

Prepare the stockholders' equity section (LO10–7)

Required:

Prepare the stockholders' equity section of the balance sheet for Finishing Touches as of December 31, 2024.

E10-9 Consider each of the following independent situations:

Find missing amounts for retained earnings (LO10-5)

	Beginning Retained Earnings	Net Income for the Year	Dividends for the Year	Ending Retained Earnings
a.	$320,000	$120,000	$20,000	_____
b.	$540,000	$230,000	_____	$700,000
c.	$290,000	_____	$50,000	$360,000
d.	_____	$170,000	$30,000	$490,000

Required:

For each situation, calculate the missing amount.

E10-10 In its first five years of operations, Monster Hats reports the following net income and dividends (the first year is a net loss).

Calculate retained earnings each year (LO10-5)

Year	Net Income (Loss) for the Year	Dividends for the Year	Ending Retained Earnings
1	$(35,000)	$ 0	_____
2	52,000	0	_____
3	87,000	20,000	_____
4	128,000	20,000	_____
5	153,000	25,000	_____

Required:

Calculate the balance of Retained Earnings at the end of each year.

E10–11 On March 15, **American Eagle** declares a quarterly cash dividend of $0.125 per share payable on April 13 to all stockholders of record on March 30.

Record cash dividends (LO10–5)

Required:

Record American Eagle's declaration and payment of cash dividends for its 210 million shares.

E10–12 Power Drive Corporation designs and produces a line of golf equipment and golf apparel. Power Drive has 100,000 shares of common stock outstanding as of the beginning of 2024. Power Drive has the following transactions affecting stockholders' equity in 2024.

Record common stock, treasury stock, and cash dividends (LO10–2, 10–4, 10–5)

March	1	Issues 65,000 additional shares of $1 par value common stock for $62 per share.
May	10	Purchases 6,000 shares of treasury stock for $65 per share.
June	1	Declares a cash dividend of $2.00 per share to all stockholders of record on June 15. (*Hint:* Dividends are not paid on treasury stock.)
July	1	Pays the cash dividend declared on June 1.
October	21	Resells 3,000 shares of treasury stock purchased on May 10 for $70 per share.

Required:

Record each of these transactions.

Record stock dividends and stock splits (LO10–6)

E10–13 On September 1, the board of directors of Colorado Outfitters, Inc., declares and issues a stock dividend on its 10,000, $1 par, common shares. The market price of the common stock is $30 on this date.

Required:

1. Record the stock dividend assuming a small (10%) stock dividend.
2. Record the stock dividend assuming a large (100%) stock dividend.
3. Record the transaction assuming a 2-for-1 stock split.

Prepare the stockholders' equity section of the balance sheet (LO10–7)

E10–14 Refer to the information in E10–12. Power Drive Corporation has the following beginning balances in its stockholders' equity accounts on January 1, 2024: Common Stock, $100,000; Additional Paid-in Capital, $5,500,000; and Retained Earnings, $3,000,000. Net income for the year ended December 31, 2024, is $700,000.

Required:

Taking into consideration all of the transactions recorded in E10–12, prepare the stockholders' equity section of the balance sheet for Power Drive Corporation as of December 31, 2024.

Prepare a statement of stockholders' equity (LO10–7)

E10–15 Refer to the information in E10–12. Power Drive Corporation has the following beginning balances in its stockholders' equity accounts on January 1, 2024: Common Stock, $100,000; Additional Paid-in Capital, $5,500,000; and Retained Earnings, $3,000,000. Net income for the year ended December 31, 2024, is $700,000.

Required:

Taking into consideration all the transactions recorded in E10–12, prepare the statement of stockholders' equity for Power Drive Corporation for the year ended December 31, 2024, using the format provided.

POWER DRIVE CORPORATION
Statement of Stockholders' Equity
For the year ended December 31, 2024

	Common Stock	Additional Paid-in Capital	Retained Earnings	Treasury Stock	Total Stockholders' Equity
Balance, January 1	$100,000	$5,500,000	$3,000,000	$ -0-	$8,600,000
Issue common stock					
Purchase treasury stock					
Declare dividends					
Resell treasury stock					
Net income					
Balance, December 31					

Indicate effects on total stockholders' equity (LO10–7)

E10–16 Indicate whether each of the following transactions increases (+), decreases (−), or has no effect (NE) on total assets, total liabilities, and total stockholders' equity. The first transaction is completed as an example.

Transaction	Total Assets	Total Liabilities	Total Stockholders' Equity
Issue common stock	+	NE	+
Issue preferred stock			
Purchase treasury stock			
Resell treasury stock			
Declare cash dividend			
Pay cash dividend			
100% stock dividend			
2-for-1 stock split			

E10–17 United Apparel has the following balances in its stockholders' equity accounts on December 31, 2024: Treasury Stock, $850,000; Common Stock, $600,000; Preferred Stock, $3,600,000; Retained Earnings, $2,200,000; and Additional Paid-in Capital, $8,800,000.

Prepare the stockholders' equity section (LO10–7)

Required:
Prepare the stockholders' equity section of the balance sheet for United Apparel as of December 31, 2024.

E10–18 The financial statements of Friendly Fashions include the following selected data (in millions):

Calculate and analyze ratios (LO10–8)

($ in millions)	2024	2023
Sales	$10,043	$11,134
Net income	$ 312	$ 818
Stockholders' equity	$ 1,850	$ 2,310
Average shares outstanding (in millions)	675	–
Dividends per share	$ 0.31	–
Stock price	$ 6.20	–

Required:
1. Calculate the return on equity in 2024.
2. Calculate the dividend yield in 2024.
3. Calculate earnings per share in 2024.
4. Calculate the price-earnings ratio in 2024.

E10–19 Financial information for Forever 18 includes the following selected data:

Calculate and analyze ratios (LO10–8)

($ in millions)	2024	2023
Net income	$ 129	$ 308
Dividends on preferred stock	$ 20	$ 15
Average shares outstanding	150	400
Stock price	$12.02	$10.97

Required:
1. Calculate earnings per share in 2023 and 2024. Did earnings per share increase in 2024?
2. Calculate the price-earnings ratio in 2023 and 2024. In which year is the stock priced lower in relation to reported earnings?

E10–20 On January 1, 2024, the general ledger of Grand Finale Fireworks includes the following account balances:

Complete the accounting cycle using stockholders' equity transactions (LO 10–2, 10–4, 10–5, 10–8)

Accounts	Debit	Credit
Cash	$ 42,700	
Accounts Receivable	44,500	
Supplies	7,500	
Equipment	64,000	
Accumulated Depreciation		$ 9,000
Accounts Payable		14,600
Common Stock, $1 par value		10,000
Additional Paid-in Capital		80,000
Retained Earnings		45,100
Totals	$158,700	$158,700

During January 2024, the following transactions occur:

January	2	Issue an additional 2,000 shares of $1 par value common stock for $40,000.
January	9	Provide services to customers on account, $14,300.
January	10	Purchase additional supplies on account, $4,900.
January	12	Purchase 1,000 shares of treasury stock for $18 per share.
January	15	Pay cash on accounts payable, $16,500.
January	21	Provide services to customers for cash, $49,100.
January	22	Receive cash on accounts receivable, $16,600.
January	29	Declare a cash dividend of $0.30 per share to all shares outstanding on January 29. The dividend is payable on February 15. (*Hint:* Grand Finale Fireworks had 10,000 shares outstanding on January 1, 2024, and dividends are not paid on treasury stock.)
January	30	Resell 600 shares of treasury stock for $20 per share.
January	31	Pay cash for salaries during January, $42,000.

Required:

1. Record each of the transactions listed above.
2. Record adjusting entries on January 31.
   a. Unpaid utilities for the month of January are $6,200.
   b. Supplies at the end of January total $5,100.
   c. Depreciation on the equipment for the month of January is calculated using the straightline method. At the time the equipment was purchased, the company estimated a service life of three years and a residual value of $10,000.
   d. Accrued income taxes at the end of January are $2,000.
3. Prepare an adjusted trial balance as of January 31, 2024, after updating beginning balances (above) for transactions during January (*requirement* 1) and adjusting entries at the end of January (*requirement* 2).
4. Prepare a multiple-step income statement for the period ended January 31, 2024.
5. Prepare a classified balance sheet as of January 31, 2024.
6. Record closing entries.
7. Analyze the following for Grand Finale Fireworks:
   a. Calculate the return on equity for the month of January. If the average return on equity for the industry for January is 2.5%, is the company *more* or *less* profitable than other companies in the same industry?
   b. How many shares of common stock are outstanding as of January 31, 2024?
   c. Calculate earnings per share for the month of January. (*Hint:* To calculate average shares of common stock outstanding take the beginning shares outstanding plus the ending shares outstanding and divide the total by 2.) If earnings per share was $3.60 last year (i.e., an average of $0.30 per month), is earnings per share for January 2024 *better* or *worse* than last year's average?

PROBLEMS: SET A

Match terms with their definitions (LO10–1)

P10–1A Match (by letter) the following terms with their definitions. Each letter is used only once.

Terms	Definitions
_____ 1. Cumulative	a. The amount invested by stockholders.
_____ 2. Retained earnings	b. Shares available to sell.
_____ 3. Outstanding stock	c. Shares can be returned to the corporation at a predetermined price.
_____ 4. Limited liability	d. The earnings not paid out in dividends.
_____ 5. Treasury stock	e. Shares actually sold.
_____ 6. Issued stock	f. Shares receive priority for future dividends if dividends are not paid in a given year.
_____ 7. Angel investors	

_____ 8. Paid-in capital
_____ 9. Authorized stock
_____ 10. Redeemable

g. Shares held by investors.
h. Shareholders can lose no more than the amount they invested in the company.
i. Wealthy individuals in the business community willing to risk investment funds on a promising business venture.
j. The corporation's own stock that it acquired.

P10–2A Donnie Hilfiger has two classes of stock authorized: $1 par preferred and $0.01 par value common. As of the beginning of 2024, 300 shares of preferred stock and 4,000 shares of common stock have been issued. The following transactions affect stockholders' equity during 2024:

Record equity transactions and indicate the effect on the balance sheet equation (LO10–2, 10–3, 10–4, 10–5)

March	1	Issue 1,100 shares of common stock for $42 per share.
May	15	Purchase 400 shares of treasury stock for $35 per share.
July	10	Resell 200 shares of treasury stock purchased on May 15 for $40 per share.
October	15	Issue 200 shares of preferred stock for $45 per share.
December	1	Declare a cash dividend on both common and preferred stock of $0.50 per share to all stockholders of record on December 15. (_Hint:_ Dividends are not paid on treasury stock.)
December	31	Pay the cash dividends declared on December 1.

Donnie Hilfiger has the following beginning balances in its stockholders' equity accounts on January 1, 2024: Preferred Stock, $300; Common Stock, $40; Additional Paid-in Capital, $76,000; and Retained Earnings, $30,500. Net income for the year ended December 31, 2024, is $10,800.

Required:

1. Record each of these transactions.
2. Indicate whether each of these transactions would increase (+), decrease (−), or have no effect (NE) on total assets, total liabilities, and total stockholders' equity by completing the following chart.

Transaction	Total Assets	Total Liabilities	Total Stockholders' Equity
Issue common stock			
Purchase treasury stock			
Resell treasury stock			
Issue preferred stock			
Declare cash dividends			
Pay cash dividends			

P10–3A Sammy's Sportshops has been very profitable in recent years and has seen its stock price steadily increase to over $100 per share. The CFO thinks the company should consider either a 100% stock dividend or a 2-for-1 stock split.

Indicate effect of stock dividends and stock splits (LO10–6)

Required:

1. Complete the following chart comparing the effects of a 100% stock dividend versus a 2-for-1 stock split on the stockholders' equity accounts, shares outstanding, par value, and share price.

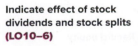

	Before	After 100% Stock Dividend	After 2-for-1 Stock Split
Common stock, $1 par value	$ 1,100		
Additional paid-in capital	59,000		
Total paid-in capital	60,100		
Retained earnings	23,850		
Total stockholders' equity	$83,950		
Shares outstanding	1,100		
Par value per share	$ 1		
Share price	$ 130		

2. What is the primary reason companies declare a large stock dividend or a stock split?

Analyze the stockholders' equity section (LO10–7)

P10–4A The stockholders' equity section of Velcro World is presented here.

VELCRO WORLD
Balance Sheet (partial)

($ and shares in thousands)	
Stockholders' equity:	
Preferred stock, $1 par value	$ 6,000
Common stock, $1 par value	30,000
Additional paid-in capital	1,164,000
Total paid-in capital	1,200,000
Retained earnings	288,000
Treasury stock, 11,000 common shares	(352,000)
Total stockholders' equity	$1,136,000

Required:

Based on the stockholders' equity section of Velcro World, answer the following questions. Remember that all amounts are presented in thousands.
1. How many shares of preferred stock have been issued?
2. How many shares of common stock have been issued?
3. If the common shares were issued at $30 per share, at what average price per share were the preferred shares issued?
4. If retained earnings at the beginning of the period was $250 million and $30 million was paid in dividends during the year, what was the net income for the year?
5. What was the average cost per share of the treasury stock acquired?

Understand stockholders' equity and the statement of stockholders' equity (LO10–7)

P10–5A Refer to the information provided in P10–2A.

Required:

Taking into consideration the beginning balances on January 1, 2024 and all the transactions during 2024, respond to the following for Donnie Hilfiger:
1. Prepare the stockholders' equity section of the balance sheet as of December 31, 2024.
2. Prepare the statement of stockholders' equity for the year ended December 31, 2024.
3. Explain how *requirements* 1 and 2 are similar and how they are different.

Record equity transactions and prepare the stockholders' equity section (LO10–2, 10–3, 10–4, 10–5, 10–7)

P10–6A Major League Apparel has two classes of stock authorized: 6%, $10 par preferred, and $1 par value common. The following transactions affect stockholders' equity during 2024, its first year of operations:

January	2	Issue 110,000 shares of common stock for $70 per share.
February	14	Issue 60,000 shares of preferred stock for $12 per share.
May	8	Purchase 11,000 shares of its own common stock for $60 per share.
May	31	Resell 5,500 shares of treasury stock for $65 per share.

December   1   Declare a cash dividend on its common stock of $0.25 per share and a
               $36,000 (6% of par value) cash dividend on its preferred stock payable to
               all stockholders of record on December 15. The dividend is payable on
               December 30. (*Hint:* Dividends are not paid on treasury stock.)

December 30   Pay the cash dividends declared on December 1.

Required:
1. Record each of these transactions.
2. Prepare the stockholders' equity section of the balance sheet as of December 31, 2024. Net
   income for the year was $490,000.

P10–7A Khaki Republic sells clothing and accessories through premium outlet locations and
online. Selected financial data for Khaki Republic is provided as follows:

*Calculate and analyze
ratios (LO10–8)*

($ in millions)	
Sales	$4,158
Net income	$ 144
Stockholders' equity, beginning	$1,890
Stockholders' equity, ending	$1,931
Average shares outstanding	85.6
Dividends per share	$ 0.75
Stock price, ending	$47.23

Required:
1. Calculate the return on equity for Khaki Republic. How does it compare with the return on
   equity for Zoom and Microsoft reported in the chapter?
2. Calculate the dividend yield for Khaki Republic. How does it compare with the dividend
   yield for Zoom and Microsoft reported in the chapter?
3. Calculate the price-earnings ratio for Khaki Republic. How does it compare with the price-
   earnings ratio for Zoom and Microsoft reported in the chapter?

PROBLEMS: SET B

P10–1B Match (by letter) the following terms with their definitions. Each letter is used only once.

*Match terms with their
definitions (LO10–1 to
10–8)*

Terms	Definitions
_____ 1. PE ratio	a. A debit balance in Retained Earnings.
_____ 2. Stockholders' equity section of the balance sheet	b. Priced high in relation to current earnings as investors expect future earnings to be higher.
_____ 3. Accumulated deficit	c. Effectively the same as a 2-for-1 stock split.
_____ 4. Growth stocks	d. The earnings not paid out in dividends.
_____ 5. 100% stock dividend	e. The stock price divided by earnings per share.
_____ 6. Statement of stockholders' equity	f. Summarizes the *changes* in the balance in each stockholders' equity account *over a period of time.*
_____ 7. Treasury stock	
_____ 8. Value stocks	g. Priced low in relation to current earnings.
_____ 9. Return on equity	h. Measures the ability of company management to generate earnings from the resources that owners provide.
_____ 10. Retained earnings	i. Shows the balance in each equity account *at a point in time.*
	j. The corporation's own stock that it acquired.

P10–2B Nautical has two classes of stock authorized: $10 par preferred, and $1 par value common. As of the beginning of 2024, 125 shares of preferred stock and 3,000 shares of common stock have been issued. The following transactions affect stockholders' equity during 2024:

March	1	Issue 3,000 additional shares of common stock for $10 per share.
April	1	Issue 175 additional shares of preferred stock for $40 per share.
June	1	Declare a cash dividend on both common and preferred stock of $0.25 per share to all stockholders of record on June 15.
June	30	Pay the cash dividends declared on June 1.
August	1	Purchase 175 shares of common treasury stock for $7 per share.
October	1	Resell 125 shares of treasury stock purchased on August 1 for $9 per share.

Nautical has the following beginning balances in its stockholders' equity accounts on January 1, 2024: Preferred Stock, $1,250; Common Stock, $3,000; Additional Paid-in Capital, $19,500; and Retained Earnings, $11,500. Net income for the year ended December 31, 2024, is $7,650.

Required:

1. Record each of these transactions.
2. Indicate whether each of these transactions would increase (+), decrease (−), or have no effect (NE) on total assets, total liabilities, and total stockholders' equity by completing the following chart.

Transaction	Total Assets	Total Liabilities	Total Stockholders' Equity
Issue common stock			
Issue preferred stock			
Declare cash dividends			
Pay cash dividends			
Purchase treasury stock			
Resell treasury stock			

P10–3B The Athletic Village has done very well the past year, and its stock price is now trading at $102 per share. Management is considering either a 100% stock dividend or a 2-for-1 stock split.

Required:

Complete the following chart comparing the effects of a 100% stock dividend versus a 2-for-1 stock split on the stockholders' equity accounts, shares outstanding, par value, and share price.

	Before	After 100% Stock Dividend	After 2-for-1 Stock Split
Common stock, $0.01 par value	$ 11		
Additional paid-in capital	34,990		
Total paid-in capital	35,001		
Retained earnings	16,000		
Total stockholders' equity	$51,001		
Shares outstanding	1,100		
Par value per share	$ 0.01		
Share price	$ 102		

Analyze the stockholders'
equity section (LO10–7)

P10–4B The stockholders' equity section of The Seventies Shop is presented here.

THE SEVENTIES SHOP
Balance Sheet (partial)

($ in thousands)	
Stockholders' equity:	
Preferred stock, $50 par value	$ –0–
Common stock, $5 par value	20,000
Additional paid-in capital	100,000
Total paid-in capital	120,000
Retained earnings	53,000
Treasury stock	(3,700)
Total stockholders' equity	$169,300

Required:

Based on the stockholders' equity section of The Seventies Shop, answer the following
questions. Remember that all amounts are presented in thousands.
1. How many shares of preferred stock have been issued?
2. How many shares of common stock have been issued?
3. Total paid-in capital is $120 million. At what average price per share were the common
   shares issued?
4. If retained earnings at the beginning of the period was $45 million and net income during
   the year was $9,907,500, how much was paid in dividends for the year?
5. If the treasury stock was purchased for $20 per share, how many shares were purchased?
6. How much was the dividend per share? (*Hint:* Dividends are not paid on treasury stock.)

Understand stockholders'
equity and the statement
of stockholders'
equity (LO10–7)

P10–5B Refer to the information provided in P10–2B.

Required:

Taking into consideration the beginning balances on January 1, 2024 and all the transactions
during 2024, respond to the following for Nautical:
1. Prepare the stockholders' equity section of the balance sheet as of December 31, 2024.
2. Prepare the statement of stockholders' equity for the year ended December 31, 2024.
3. Explain how *requirements* 1 and 2 are similar and how they are different.

Record equity
transactions and prepare
the stockholders' equity
section (LO10–2, 10–3,
10–4, 10–5, 10–7)

P10–6B National League Gear has two classes of stock authorized: 4%, $20 par preferred,
and $5 par value common. The following transactions affect stockholders' equity during 2024,
National League's first year of operations:

February	2	Issue 1.5 million shares of common stock for $35 per share.
February	4	Issue 600,000 shares of preferred stock for $23 per share.
June	15	Purchase 150,000 shares of its own common stock for $30 per share.
August	15	Resell 112,500 shares of treasury stock for $45 per share.
November	1	Declare a cash dividend on its common stock of $1.50 per share and a $480,000 (4% of par value) cash dividend on its preferred stock payable to all stockholders of record on November 15. (*Hint:* Dividends are not paid on treasury stock.)
November	30	Pay the dividends declared on November 1.

Required:

1. Record each of these transactions.
2. Prepare the stockholders' equity section of the balance sheet as of December 31, 2024. Net
   income for the year was $4,900,000.

Calculate and analyze ratios (LO10–8)

P10–7B Selected financial data for DC Menswear is provided as follows:

($ in millions)	
Sales	$14,549
Net income	$ 833
Stockholders' equity, beginning	$ 4,080
Stockholders' equity, ending	$ 2,755
Average shares outstanding	485
Dividends per share	$ 1.00
Stock price, ending	$ 18.93

Required:

1. Calculate the return on equity for DC Menswear. How does it compare with the return on equity for Zoom and Microsoft reported in the chapter?
2. Calculate the dividend yield for DC Menswear. How does it compare with the dividend yield for Zoom and Microsoft reported in the chapter?
3. Calculate the price-earnings ratio for DC Menswear. How does it compare with the price-earnings ratio for Zoom and Microsoft reported in the chapter?

REAL-WORLD PERSPECTIVES

McGraw Hill **connect**

Data Analytics & Excel

Visit Connect to find a variety of Data Analytics questions that help build Excel, Tableau, and data visualization skills. Assignable materials include **Integrated Excel**, **Applying Excel**, **Data Visualizations**, **Tableau Dashboard Activities**, and **Applying Tableau Cases**.

General Ledger Continuing Case

Great Adventures

(This is a continuation of the Great Adventures problem from earlier chapters.)

RWP10–1 Tony and Suzie have purchased land for a new camp. Now they need money to build the cabins, dining facility, a ropes course, and an outdoor swimming pool. Tony and Suzie first checked with Summit Bank to see if they could borrow an additional $1 million, but unfortunately the bank turned them down as too risky. Undeterred, they promoted their idea to close friends they had made through the outdoor clinics and TEAM events. They decided to go ahead and sell shares of stock in the company to raise the additional funds for the camp.

Great Adventures has authorized $1 par value common stock. When the company began on July 1, 2024, Tony and Suzie each purchased 10,000 shares (20,000 shares total) of $1 par value common stock at $1 per share. The following transactions affect stockholders' equity during the remainder of 2025:

November 5	Issue an additional 100,000 shares of common stock for $10 per share.
November 16	Purchase 10,000 shares of its own common stock (i.e., treasury stock) for $15 per share.
November 24	Resell 4,000 shares of treasury stock at $16 per share.
December 1	Declare a cash dividend on its common stock of $11,400 ($0.10 per share) to all stockholders of record on December 15.
December 20	Pay the cash dividend declared on December 1.
December 30	Pay $800,000 for construction of new cabins and other facilities. The entire expenditure is recorded in the Buildings account.

Required:

1. Record each of these transactions.
2. Great Adventures has net income of $35,835 in 2025. Retained earnings at the beginning of 2025 was $33,450. Prepare the stockholders' equity section of the balance sheet for Great Adventures as of December 31, 2025.

The Great Adventures continuing problem also can be assigned using the General Ledger software in Connect. Students will be given an existing trial balance and asked to prepare (1) the journal entries for the transactions above in 2025, (2) financial statements, and (3) closing entries.

American Eagle Outfitters, Inc.

Financial Analysis Continuing Case

RWP10–2 Financial information for **American Eagle** is presented in **Appendix A** at the end of the book. Using the financial information presented in **Appendix A,** answer the following.

Required:

1. What is the par value per share for the common stock?
2. How many common shares were issued at the end of the most recent year?
3. Did the company have any treasury stock? How many shares?
4. How much did the company pay in cash dividends in the most recent year? (*Hint:* Look in the statement of stockholders' equity in the retained earnings column.)

The Buckle, Inc.

Financial Analysis Continuing Case

RWP10–3 Financial information for **Buckle** is presented in **Appendix B** at the end of the book.

Required:

1. What is the par value per share for the common stock?
2. How many common shares were issued at the end of the most recent year?
3. Did the company have any treasury stock? How many shares?
4. How much did the company pay in cash dividends in the most recent year? (*Hint:* Look in the statement of stockholders' equity in the retained earnings column.)

American Eagle Outfitters, Inc. vs. The Buckle, Inc.

Comparative Analysis Continuing Case

RWP10–4 Financial information for **American Eagle** is presented in **Appendix A** at the end of the book, and financial information for **Buckle** is presented in **Appendix B** at the end of the book.

Required:

1. Calculate the return on equity for American Eagle and Buckle for the most recent year. Which company is more profitable?
2. Determine the amount reported for basic earnings per share (or net income per share) for the most recent year for each company. Basic earnings per share are provided for each company near the bottom of the income statement.
3. Determine the amount of dividends per share for the most recent year for each company. (Hint: Find dividends per share in the statement of stockholders' equity). Using your answers for requirement 2, which company has a higher ratio of cash dividends to earnings? Which company has more treasury stock purchases?

EDGAR Research

RWP10–5 Using EDGAR (Electronic Data Gathering, Analysis, and Retrieval system), find the annual report (10-K) for **Abercrombie & Fitch Co**. for the year ended **February 1, 2020.** Locate the "Consolidated Statements of Operations and Comprehensive Income" (income statement) and "Consolidated Balance Sheets." You may also find the annual report at the company's website.

Required:

1. From the equity section of the balance sheet, determine the par value of the company's common stock.
2. How many shares of common stock have been issued?
3. What is the reported amount of common stock and additional paid-in capital (listed as "paid-in capital")?
4. Using your answers in *requirements* 2 and 3, determine the average issue price of common stock.
5. How many shares of treasury stock is the company holding by the end of the most recent year?
6. Using the balance of treasury stock and your answer in *requirement* 5, determine the average cost per share of treasury stock.
7. If the company were to sell all of its treasury stock for $2,000,000 (in thousands), by how much would net income increase/decrease?

Ethics

RWP10–6 Brooke Remming is the Chief Executive Officer of Dundem Corp. The board of directors has agreed to pay Brooke a salary of $400,000 plus a 15% bonus if the company's pretax income increases by at least 10% from the prior year. In the prior year, Dundem reported pretax income of $3,000,000.

In the final week of the current year, Brooke projects that pretax income will be $3,250,000. While this is a nice increase over the prior year, she realizes that the increase is below the 10% required for her bonus. Brooke has devoted many years to the company and feels that the company has had another successful year thanks to her efforts and good decisions.

As one example of a good decision, Brooke noticed earlier in the year that the company's stock price had fallen to $42 per share. She felt that price was too low, so she used some of the company's available cash to purchase 10,000 shares. The current price has risen to $50 per share, and she is considering whether to sell the stock. She calculates that the company will make a profit of $80,000 (= 10,000 shares × $8 increase per share) on the sale, and she would include the gain in pretax income. She feels this profit is possible only because of her good intuition, so it should be used in calculating whether she gets a bonus.

Required:

1. Understand the reporting effect: If Brooke sells the stock and includes the $80,000 gain in pretax income, will she get her bonus? Assume any bonus paid to Brooke is not included in calculating pretax income.
2. Specify the options: Instead of reporting the gain as part of pretax income, how else might Brooke report the gain on the sale?
3. Identify the impact: Does Brooke's decision affect the company?
4. Make a decision: Should Brooke record the gain on the sale of stock as part of pretax income?

Written Communication

RWP10–7 Preferred stock has characteristics of both liabilities and stockholders' equity. Convertible bonds are another example of a financing arrangement that blurs the line between liabilities and stockholders' equity. Items like these have led some to conclude that the present distinction between liabilities and equity should be eliminated. Under this approach, liabilities and equity would be combined into one category that includes both creditor and owner claims to resources.

Required:

1. Define liabilities and stockholders' equity.
2. Provide arguments in support of maintaining the distinction between liabilities and stockholders' equity in the balance sheet.
3. Provide arguments in support of eliminating the distinction between liabilities and stockholders' equity in the balance sheet.
4. Which do you recommend? Why?

Earnings Management

RWP10–8 Renegade Clothing is struggling to meet analysts' forecasts. It's early December 2024, and the year-end projections are in. Listed below are the projections for the year ended 2024 and the comparable actual amounts for 2023.

	Projected 2024	Actual 2023
Sales	$14,000,000	$16,023,000
Net income	878,000	1,113,000
Total assets	$ 6,500,000	$ 6,821,000
Total liabilities	$ 2,500,000	$ 2,396,000
Stockholders' equity	4,000,000	4,425,000
Total liabilities and stockholders' equity	$ 6,500,000	$ 6,821,000
Shares outstanding at year-end	950,000	950,000

Analysts forecast earnings per share for 2024 to be $0.95 per share. It looks like earnings per share will fall short of expectations in 2024.

Ronald Outlaw, the director of marketing, has a creative idea to improve earnings per share and the return on equity. He proposes the company borrow additional funds and use the proceeds to purchase some of its own stock—treasury shares. Is this a good idea?

Required:

1. Calculate the projected earnings per share and return on equity for 2024 before any purchase of stock.

Now assume Renegade Clothing borrows $1 million and uses the money to purchase 100,000 shares of its own stock at $10 per share. The projections for 2024 will change as follows:

	2024	2023
Sales	$14,000,000	$16,023,000
Net income	878,000	1,113,000
Total assets	$ 6,500,000	$ 6,821,000
Total liabilities	$ 3,500,000	$ 2,396,000
Stockholders' equity	3,000,000	4,425,000
Total liabilities and stockholders' equity	$ 6,500,000	$ 6,821,000
Shares outstanding at year-end	850,000	950,000

2. Calculate the new projected earnings per share and return on equity for 2024, assuming the company goes through with the treasury stock purchase. [*Hint:* In computing earnings per share, average shares outstanding is now 900,000 = (850,000 + 950,000)/2.]
3. Does the purchase of treasury stock near year-end improve earnings per share and the return on equity ratio? Explain.

Answers to Chapter Framework Questions
1. d   2. b   3. d   4. a   5. a

Answers to Self-Study Questions
1. a   2. b   3. b   4. c   5. c   6. b   7. a   8. d   9. d   10. b   11. c   12. c   13. d   14. a   15. c

11

Statement of Cash Flows

Learning Objectives

PART A: CLASSIFICATION OF CASH FLOW ACTIVITIES

■ **LO11–1** Classify cash transactions as operating, investing, or financing activities.

PART B: PREPARING THE STATEMENT OF CASH FLOWS

■ **LO11–2** Understand the steps and basic format in preparing the statement of cash flows.

■ **LO11–3** Prepare the operating activities section of the statement of cash flows using the indirect method.

■ **LO11–4** Prepare the investing activities section of the statement of cash flows.

■ **LO11–5** Prepare the financing activities section of the statement of cash flows.

ANALYSIS: CASH FLOW ANALYSIS

■ **LO11–6** Perform financial analysis using the statement of cash flows.

APPENDIX: OPERATING ACTIVITIES—DIRECT METHOD

■ **LO11–7** Prepare the operating activities section of the statement of cash flows using the direct method.

SELF-STUDY MATERIALS

■ Let's Review—Types of cash flows (p. 545).

■ Let's Review—Indirect method for operating cash flows (p. 555).

■ Let's Review—Indirect method for the statement of cash flows (p. 559).

■ Let's Review—Direct method for the statement of cash flows (p. 570).

■ Chapter Framework with questions and answers available (p. 572).

■ Key Points by Learning Objective (p. 574).

■ Glossary of Key Terms (p. 575).

■ Self-Study Questions with answers available (p. 575).

■ Videos including Concept Overview, Applying Excel, Let's Review, and Interactive Illustrations to demonstrate key topics (in Connect).

APPLE INC.: CASH FLOWS AT THE CORE

Net income represents all revenues less expenses of a company during a reporting period. Operating cash flows represent the cash inflows less cash outflows related to the very same revenue and expense activities. Although you might expect these two amounts to be similar, fairly large differences can occur. Below are the net income and operating cash flows for three well-known companies in the technology industry ($ in millions):

Company Name	Net Income	Operating Cash Flows
Apple	$55,256	$69,391
Alphabet	34,343	54,520
Amazon	11,588	38,514

All three companies report much higher operating cash flows than net income. One reason that operating cash flows are often higher than net income is that certain items, like depreciation expense, decrease net income but have no effect on operating cash flows. Both net income and operating cash flows are important indicators in explaining stock prices, but which is more important to investors?

In comparing net income with operating cash flows, research consistently finds that net income is more important. Net income works better than operating cash flow in forecasting not only future net income, but also future cash flow. Research also finds that stock returns (the change in stock price plus dividends) are more closely related to net income than to operating cash flow. Net income helps smooth out the unevenness or lumpiness in year-to-year operating cash flow, producing a better estimate of ongoing profitability.

It's important to remember that both net income and operating cash flow provide important information. An investor or creditor who analyzes both net income and operating cash flow will do better than one who focuses solely on one or the other. In this chapter, we will learn how to prepare and analyze the operating, investing, and financing sections of the statement of cash flows. At the end of the chapter, we'll perform a cash flow analysis for **Apple** vs. **Alphabet**.

Prostock-studio/Alamy Stock Photo

PART A

CLASSIFICATION OF CASH FLOW ACTIVITIES

A **statement of cash flows** provides a summary of cash inflows and cash outflows during the reporting period. A cash *inflow* simply means cash received by the company during the period. Similarly, a cash *outflow* is cash paid by the company during the period. The difference between cash inflows and cash outflows is called *net cash flows*. The statement of cash flows reports separately the net cash flows from operating, investing, and financing activities. The sum of the net cash flows from those three activities equals the change in total cash for the period. Illustration 11–1 presents the statement of cash flows for E-Games, Inc.

ILLUSTRATION 11–1

Statement of Cash Flows

E-GAMES, INC.
Statement of Cash Flows
For the year ended December 31, 2024

Cash Flows from Operating Activities		
Net income	$42,000	
Adjustments to reconcile net income to net cash flows from operating activities:		
Depreciation expense	9,000	
Loss on sale of land	4,000	
Increase in accounts receivable	(7,000)	
Decrease in inventory	10,000	
Increase in prepaid rent	(2,000)	
Decrease in accounts payable	(5,000)	
Increase in interest payable	1,000	
Decrease in income tax payable	(2,000)	
Net cash flows from operating activities		$50,000
Cash Flows from Investing Activities		
Purchase of investments	(35,000)	
Sale of land	6,000	
Net cash flows from investing activities		(29,000)
Cash Flows from Financing Activities		
Issuance of common stock	5,000	
Payment of cash dividends	(12,000)	
Net cash flows from financing activities		(7,000)
Net increase (decrease) in cash		14,000
Cash at the beginning of the period		48,000
Cash at the end of the period		$62,000
Note: Noncash Activities		
Purchased equipment by issuing a note payable		$20,000

We will use this statement as an example throughout the chapter. Don't be concerned about the details yet. That's what the rest of the chapter is all about.

Classification of Transactions

■ **LO11–1**

Classify cash transactions as operating, investing, or financing activities.

The three primary categories of cash flows are (1) cash flows from operating activities, (2) cash flows from investing activities, and (3) cash flows from financing activities. Classifying each cash flow by source (operating, investing, or financing activities) is more informative than simply listing the various cash flows.

CASH FLOW ACTIVITIES

Operating activities include cash receipts and cash payments for transactions involving revenue and expense activities during the period. In other words, operating activities include the cash effects of the same activities that are reported in the income statement to calculate net income. Common examples of operating activities include the collection of cash from customers or the payment of cash for inventory, salaries, and rent.

Investing activities include transactions involving the purchase and sale of long-term assets and current investments. Companies periodically invest cash to replace or expand productive facilities such as buildings, land, and equipment. These are included in investing activities because they represent investments in capital assets, often referred to as **capital expenditures,** or **CAPEX**. Companies also might invest cash in other assets, such as stocks or bonds of other companies, with the expectation of a return on those investments. Eventually, many of these assets are sold. The purchase and sale of long-term assets and investments are common examples of investing activities.

Financing activities include transactions with lenders, such as borrowing money and repaying debt, and with stockholders, such as issuing stock, paying dividends, and purchasing treasury stock. It's the lenders and stockholders who provide external financing to the company.

The total net cash flows from operating, investing, and financing activities equal the increase or decrease in total cash for the year. That is, the balance of cash at the beginning of the year, plus or minus net cash flows as reported in the statement of cash flows, equals the ending balance of cash reported in the balance sheet.

Illustration 11–2 lists common cash receipts and cash payments for operating, investing, and financing activities. **Review this illustration carefully** (you may even want to bookmark it); it will come in handy in solving many of the homework problems at the end of the chapter.

ILLUSTRATION 11–2

Operating, Investing, and Financing Activities

Cash Flows from Operating Activities

Cash Inflows	**Cash Outflows**
Sale of goods or services	Purchase of inventory
Collection of interest and dividends	Payment for operating expenses
	Payment of interest
	Payment of income taxes

Cash Flows from Investing Activities

Cash Inflows	**Cash Outflows**
Sale of investments	Purchase of investments
Sale of long-term assets	Purchase of long-term assets
Collection of notes receivable	Lending with notes receivable

Cash Flows from Financing Activities

Cash Inflows	**Cash Outflows**
Issuance of bonds or notes payable	Repayment of bonds or notes payable
Issuance of stock	Acquisition of treasury stock
	Payment of dividends

Let's look at a few of the cash flows. For example, we report interest and dividends received from investments with operating activities rather than investing activities. Similarly, we report interest paid on bonds or notes payable with operating activities rather than financing activities. Why are these classified as operating activities? They are included in operating activities because each is a cash flow from an activity reported in the income statement—interest revenue, dividend revenue, and interest expense. As we discussed earlier, operating activities are those we report in the income statement.

On the other hand, we record dividends paid as a financing activity. Recall that dividends are not an expense and, therefore, paying dividends has no effect on net income. The payment of dividends simply reduces assets (cash) and stockholders' equity (retained earnings).

COMMON MISTAKE

Students sometimes misclassify dividends in preparing the statement of cash flows. Dividends *received* are included in operating activities. Dividends *paid* are included in financing activities.

As we saw in Chapter 3, we prepare the income statement, the statement of stockholders' equity, and the balance sheet directly from the adjusted trial balance. However, the accounts listed on the adjusted trial balance do not directly provide the cash inflows and cash outflows we report in the statement of cash flows. We need to rely on other information sources to determine the amounts necessary to prepare the statement of cash flows. Illustration 11–3 outlines the three primary sources.

ILLUSTRATION 11–3

Information Sources for Preparing the Statement of Cash Flows

Information Sources	Explanation
1. Income statement	Revenues and expenses provide information in determining cash flows from operating activities.
2. Balance sheet	Changes in assets, liabilities, and stockholders' equity from the end of the last period to the end of this period help to identify cash flows from operating, investing, and financing activities.
3. Detailed accounting records	Sometimes additional information from the accounting records is needed to determine specific cash inflows or cash outflows for the period.

Illustration 11–4 summarizes the relationship of the income statement and balance sheet to the operating, investing, and financing sections in the statement of cash flows.

ILLUSTRATION 11–4

Relationship of the Income Statement and Balance Sheet to the Statement of Cash Flows

Income Statement

Revenues
Expenses

Balance Sheet

Assets:
  Change in cash
  Changes in other current assets
  Changes in long-term assets
Liabilities:
  Changes in current liabilities
  Changes in long-term liabilities
Stockholders' Equity:
  Changes in common stock
  Changes in retained earnings (dividends paid)

Statement of Cash Flows

Operating Activities:

Investing Activities:

Financing Activities:

Net cash flows = Change in cash

KEY POINT

Operating activities generally relate to income statement items and changes in current assets and current liabilities. Investing activities primarily involve changes in long-term assets. Financing activities primarily involve changes in long-term liabilities and stockholders' equity.

NONCASH ACTIVITIES

Suppose a company borrows $200,000 in cash from a bank, issuing a long-term note payable for that amount. The company reports this transaction in a statement of cash flows as a *financing activity*. Suppose the company then uses that cash to purchase new equipment. The company reports this second transaction as an *investing activity*. But what if, instead of two separate transactions, the company had a *single transaction* that involved acquiring $200,000 of new equipment by issuing a $200,000 long-term note payable to the seller? **Since this single transaction does not affect cash, there are no investing or financing activities to report in the statement of cash flows.**

However, transactions that do not increase or decrease cash, but that result in significant investing and financing activities, are reported as **noncash activities** either directly after the cash flow statement or in a note to the financial statements. Examples of significant noncash investing and financing activities include

1. Purchase of long-term assets by issuing debt.
2. Purchase of long-term assets by issuing stock.
3. Conversion of bonds payable into common stock.
4. Exchange of long-term assets.

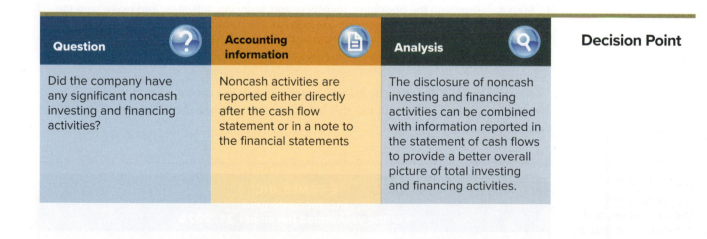

Decision Point

Question	Accounting information	Analysis
Did the company have any significant noncash investing and financing activities?	Noncash activities are reported either directly after the cash flow statement or in a note to the financial statements	The disclosure of noncash investing and financing activities can be combined with information reported in the statement of cash flows to provide a better overall picture of total investing and financing activities.

Let's Review

Indicate whether each of the following items is classified as an operating activity, investing activity, financing activity, or a significant noncash activity.

1. Dividends received from an investment.
2. Dividends paid to shareholders.
3. Property, plant, and equipment purchased for cash.
4. Property, plant, and equipment purchased by issuing stock.
5. Notes receivable accepted for lending cash.
6. Notes payable issued for borrowing cash.

Solution:

1. Operating.
2. Financing.
3. Investing.
4. Noncash.
5. Investing.
6. Financing.

Suggested Homework:
BE11–1, BE11–2;
E11–2, E11–3;
P11–1A&B

PART B

PREPARING THE STATEMENT OF CASH FLOWS

In this section, we first look at the steps involved in preparing the statement of cash flows, and its basic format. Then we work through these steps in preparing the operating, investing, and financing sections of the statement of cash flows.

■ **LO11–2**
Understand the steps and basic format in preparing the statement of cash flows.

Steps in Preparing the Statement of Cash Flows

Illustration 11–5 summarizes the four basic steps in preparing the statement of cash flows.

ILLUSTRATION 11–5

Steps in Preparing the Statement of Cash Flows

Step 1. Calculate net cash flows from *operating activities,* using information from the income statement and changes in current assets (other than cash) and changes in current liabilities from the balance sheet.

Step 2. Determine the net cash flows from *investing activities,* by analyzing changes in long-term asset accounts from the balance sheet.

Step 3. Determine the net cash flows from *financing activities,* by analyzing changes in long-term liabilities and stockholders' equity accounts from the balance sheet.

Step 4. Combine the operating, investing, and financing activities, and make sure the total from these three activities equals the amount of cash reported in the balance sheet this year versus last year (the change in cash).

Illustration 11–6 provides the income statement, balance sheets, and additional information for E-Games, Inc. We will use this information to prepare the statement of cash flows following the four basic steps.

ILLUSTRATION 11–6

Income Statement, Balance Sheets, and Additional Information for E-Games, Inc.

E-GAMES, INC. Income Statement For the year ended December 31, 2024		
Net sales		$1,012,000
Expenses:		
Cost of goods sold	$650,000	
Operating expenses (salaries, rent, utilities)	286,000	
Depreciation expense	9,000	
Loss on sale of land	4,000	
Interest expense	5,000	
Income tax expense	16,000	
Total expenses		970,000
Net income		$ 42,000

ILLUSTRATION 11–6

(concluded)

E-GAMES, INC.
Balance Sheets
December 31, 2024 and 2023

	2024	2023	Increase (I) or Decrease (D)
Assets			
Current assets:			
Cash	$ 62,000	$ 48,000	$14,000 (I)
Accounts receivable	27,000	20,000	7,000 (I)
Inventory	35,000	45,000	10,000 (D)
Prepaid rent	4,000	2,000	2,000 (I)
Long-term assets:			
Investments	35,000	0	35,000 (I)
Land	70,000	80,000	10,000 (D)
Equipment	90,000	70,000	20,000 (I)
Accumulated depreciation	(23,000)	(14,000)	9,000 (I)
Total assets	$300,000	$251,000	
Liabilities and Stockholders' Equity			
Current liabilities:			
Accounts payable	$ 22,000	$ 27,000	$ 5,000 (D)
Interest payable	2,000	1,000	1,000 (I)
Income tax payable	5,000	7,000	2,000 (D)
Long-term liabilities:			
Notes payable	95,000	75,000	20,000 (I)
Stockholders' equity:			
Common stock	105,000	100,000	5,000 (I)
Retained earnings	71,000	41,000	30,000 (I)
Total liabilities and stockholders' equity	$300,000	$251,000	

Additional Information for 2024:

1. Purchased stock in Intendo Corporation for $35,000.

2. Sold land for $6,000. The land originally was purchased for $10,000, resulting in a $4,000 loss being recorded at the time of the sale.

3. Purchased $20,000 in equipment by issuing a $20,000 note payable due in three years to the seller. No cash was exchanged in the transaction.

4. Issued common stock for $5,000 cash.

5. Declared and paid a cash dividend of $12,000.

Notice the first line of the balance sheets in 2023 and 2024. Cash increased from $48,000 in 2023 to $62,000 in 2024. That's an increase in cash of **$14,000** in 2024. **The purpose of the statement of cash flows is to report the activities that caused the change in cash balances reported in the balance sheets from period to period.** Those activities are listed by type—operating, investing, or financing.

 KEY POINT

The steps in preparing the statement of cash flows involve calculating (1) net cash flows from operating activities, (2) net cash flows from investing activities, (3) net cash flows from financing activities, and (4) the sum of these three activities to verify it equals the amount of cash reported in the balance sheet this year versus last year (the change in cash).

Basic Format

In preparing the statement of cash flows, it's helpful to first set up the basic format. As Illustration 11–7 shows, the statement of cash flows will always contain three sections, each of which has a total dollar amount for the section items listed. Thus, there will be a total for net cash flows from operating activities, from investing activities, and from financing activities. The total of these three net cash flow amounts will equal the net increase or net decrease in cash for the period. For our E-Games example, the **$14,000** change in the cash balance will be our "check figure," which means the cash inflows and cash outflows we identify must net to this amount.

After determining the net increase or decrease in cash for the period, we add cash at the beginning of the period to calculate cash at the end of the period. The amount of ending cash shown in the statement of cash flows will match the balance of cash shown in the balance sheet.

OPERATING ACTIVITIES FORMAT—INDIRECT AND DIRECT METHODS

We have two ways to determine and report cash flows from operating activities in a statement of cash flows—the indirect method and the direct method.

Using the **indirect method**, we begin with net income and then list adjustments to net income in order to arrive at operating cash flows. An example of the indirect method was presented in Illustration 11–1 and the basic format is shown in Illustration 11–7. The indirect method is more popular because it is generally easier and less costly to prepare. In fact, nearly all major companies in the United States (about 99%) prepare the statement of cash flows using the indirect method.[1] For this reason, we emphasize the indirect method.

Using the **direct method**, we adjust the items in the income statement to directly show the cash inflows and outflows from operations such as cash received from customers and cash paid for inventory, salaries, rent, interest, and taxes. If a company decides to use the direct method to report operating activities, it must also report the indirect method either along with the statement of cash flows or in a separate note to the financial statements.

ILLUSTRATION 11–7

Basic Format for the Statement of Cash Flows—Indirect Method

E-GAMES, INC. Statement of Cash Flows For the year ended December 31, 2024		
Cash Flows from Operating Activities		
Net income	$42,000	
Adjustments to reconcile net income to net cash flows from operating activities:		
(List individual reconciling items)	_____	
Net cash flows from operating activities		$ XXX
Cash Flows from Investing Activities		
(List individual inflows and outflows)	_____	
Net cash flows from investing activities		XXX
Cash Flows from Financing Activities		
(List individual inflows and outflows)	_____	
Net cash flows from financing activities		XXX
Net increase (decrease) in cash		**14,000**
Cash at the beginning of the period		48,000
Cash at the end of the period		$62,000

[1]*Accounting Trends and Techniques–2011* (New York: American Institute of Certified Public Accountants).

The total net cash flows from operating activities are identical under both methods. The methods differ only in the presentation format for operating activities. We discuss the indirect method in the next section. We present the direct method using the same example in an appendix to this chapter. Investing, financing, and noncash activities are reported identically under both methods.

KEY POINT

Companies choose between the indirect method and the direct method in reporting operating activities in the statement of cash flows. The indirect method begins with net income and then lists adjustments to net income in order to arrive at operating cash flows. The direct method specifically lists the various cash inflows and outflows from operations. The investing and financing sections of the statement of cash flows are identical under both methods.

Operating Activities—Indirect Method

As summarized in Illustration 11–5, the first step in preparing the statement of cash flows is to calculate net cash flows from operating activities. To do so, we start with net income. Net income includes all revenue and expense activities reported on an *accrual basis*. We need to remove the accruals from accrual-basis net income so that only the cash portion remains. Adjustments to net income include the following:

■ **LO11–3**
Prepare the operating activities section of the statement of cash flows using the indirect method.

1. **Income statement items.** (a) Remove noncash revenues and noncash expenses, such as depreciation expense and amortization expense, and (b) remove nonoperating gains and nonoperating losses, such as gains and losses on the sale of land, buildings, and equipment.

2. **Balance sheet items.** Adjust for changes in current assets and current liabilities. These changes represent differences between accrual-basis revenues/expenses and their corresponding operating cash flows. For example, an *increase* in accounts receivable represents sales to customers (accrual-basis revenue) that have not yet been collected (no operating cash inflow). We need to remove this amount of revenue from net income so that only the cash portion of sales revenue remains.

In the pages that follow, we'll cover many examples of both types of adjustments to net income. For now, understand the big picture—under the indirect method, the operating cash flows section provides a reconciliation from net income (accrual basis) to operating cash flows (cash basis). The adjustments are summarized in Illustration 11–8.

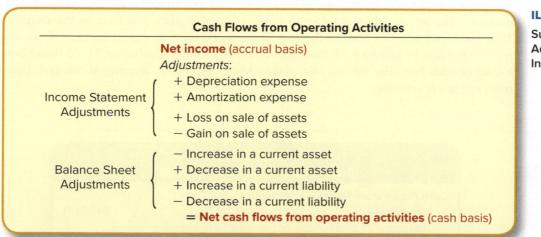

Cash Flows from Operating Activities	
Net income (accrual basis)	
Adjustments:	
Income Statement Adjustments	+ Depreciation expense
	+ Amortization expense
	+ Loss on sale of assets
	− Gain on sale of assets
Balance Sheet Adjustments	− Increase in a current asset
	+ Decrease in a current asset
	+ Increase in a current liability
	− Decrease in a current liability
	= **Net cash flows from operating activities** (cash basis)

ILLUSTRATION 11–8
Summary of Adjustments to Net Income

This illustration is a helpful reference when completing the homework at the end of the chapter.

NONCASH INCOME STATEMENT ADJUSTMENTS

To calculate operating cash flows using the indirect method, we first adjust net income for income statement items. Two of the most common adjustments relate to (1) **noncash items,** such as depreciation expense and amortization expense, and (2) **nonoperating items,** such as gains and losses on the sale of land, equipment, and buildings. We'll discuss both of these next.

Depreciation Expense. Depreciation expense reduces net income without any related cash outflows in the current period. Because we *deducted* this noncash item in the determination of net income, we need to *add back* that amount in calculating operating cash flows. Adding back the amount of depreciation eliminates the deduction of this noncash expense in net income.

E-Games, Inc., reports net income of $42,000 in its income statement. Included in this amount is depreciation expense of $9,000. Because depreciation expense reduces net income by $9,000 but has no affect on cash, E-Games will add back the $9,000 to net income in arriving at net cash flows from operations. Illustration 11–9 shows how E-Games reports depreciation expense in the statement of cash flows under the indirect method.

ILLUSTRATION 11–9

Adjustment for
Depreciation Expense

E-GAMES, INC. Statement of Cash Flows (partial)	
Cash Flows from Operating Activities	
Net income	$42,000
Adjustments to reconcile net income to net cash flows from operating activities:	
Depreciation expense	**9,000**

Next, we adjust for gains and losses that do not affect operating cash flows. These gains and losses typically relate to investing activities, such as the sale of land, equipment and buildings.

Loss on Sale of Land. Losses on the sale of long-term assets decrease net income, while gains on the sale of those assets increase net income. Included in E-Games' net income is a $4,000 loss on the sale of land. The loss is not an *operating* cash inflow or cash outflow. (The actual sale of land is an *investing* activity discussed later in the chapter.) This means we need to remove the loss in the calculation of operating cash flows. We remove the loss by adding back that amount to net income. Illustration 11–10 shows how E-Games adds back the loss on sale of land to net income in arriving at net cash flows from operating activities.

ILLUSTRATION 11–10

Adjustment for Loss on
Sale of Land

E-GAMES, INC. Statement of Cash Flows (partial)	
Cash Flows from Operating Activities	
Net income	$42,000
Adjustments to reconcile net income to net cash flows from operating activities:	
Depreciation expense	9,000
Loss on sale of land	**4,000**

What if E-Games, Inc., had a gain of $4,000, rather than a loss, on the sale of land? Because we would have added the $4,000 gain in the determination of net income, we would need to subtract that amount from net income to calculate operating cash flows.

⊗ COMMON MISTAKE

Students sometimes are unsure whether to add or subtract a loss on the sale of assets. Just remember that a loss is like an expense—both reduce net income. Treat a loss on the sale of assets like depreciation expense and add back that amount to net income. A gain on the sale of long-term assets is the opposite of an expense, so we subtract that amount from net income to arrive at net cash flows from operating activities.

BALANCE SHEET ADJUSTMENTS

To reconcile net income to operating cash flows, we also adjust for changes in the balances of related balance sheet accounts. These accounts predominantly include current assets other than investments and notes receivable, and current liabilities other than various forms of borrowing. Adjusting for these changes in current assets and current liabilities helps to adjust accrual-basis revenues and expenses (within net income) to their related cash flow amounts. Let's look at the changes in current assets and current liabilities for E-Games to see how this works.

Increase in Accounts Receivable.   E-Games reports sales revenue of $1,012,000 in its income statement. This does not mean, however, that E-Games collected $1,012,000 cash from its customers during the reporting period. We know this because E-Games' accounts receivable increased $7,000 during the year (from $20,000 in 2023 to $27,000 in 2024). This tells us that the company must have collected less cash than its $1,012,000 in sales revenue. Why? Because customers owe the company $7,000 more than before. Here's a summary.

Sales Revenue	$1,012,000
− Increase in Accounts Receivable	− 7,000
= Cash inflow from customers	$1,005,000

The $7,000 increase in accounts receivable represents $7,000 of sales revenue that E-Games reported as part of net income, but that did not result in operating cash inflows. Therefore, to adjust the sales revenue portion of net income (accrual basis = $1,012,000) to operating cash inflows from customers (cash basis = $1,005,000), we need to subtract the $7,000 increase in accounts receivable from net income, as shown in Illustration 11–11.

ILLUSTRATION 11–11

Adjustment for Change in Accounts Receivable

E-GAMES, INC. Statement of Cash Flows (partial)	
Cash Flows from Operating Activities	
Net income	$42,000
Adjustments to reconcile net income to net cash flows from operating activities:	
Depreciation expense	9,000
Loss on sale of land	4,000
Increase in accounts receivable	**(7,000)**

Net income
− Incr. in A/R
+ Decr. in A/R
Oper. cash flows

A decrease in accounts receivable would have the opposite effect. We would *add* a decrease in accounts receivable to net income to arrive at net cash flows from operating activities. A decrease in accounts receivable indicates that we collected more cash from customers than we recorded as sales revenue.

Decrease in Inventory.   E-Games' inventory balance decreased by $10,000 during the year. This tells us that the company sold $10,000 of inventory that was not replaced. This $10,000 is reported as cost of goods sold (an expense) in the income statement, reducing net income, but that amount had no effect on cash. To adjust for cash being greater by $10,000, we add the decrease in inventory to net income. Stated another way, we remove the $10,000 noncash portion of cost of goods sold by adding back that amount to net income. Illustration 11–12 shows the adjustment.

ILLUSTRATION 11–12

Adjustment for Change in Inventory

Net income
− Incr. in Inventory
+ Decr. in Inventory
Oper. cash flows

E-GAMES, INC.
Statement of Cash Flows (partial)

Cash Flows from Operating Activities	
Net income	$42,000
Adjustments to reconcile net income to net cash flows from operating activities:	
Depreciation expense	9,000
Loss on sale of land	4,000
Increase in accounts receivable	(7,000)
Decrease in inventory	**10,000**

If inventory had instead increased from year to year, the change in the balance would have been subtracted from net income to convert cost of goods sold from an accrual basis to a cash basis.

Increase in Prepaid Rent.   E-Games' prepaid rent increased $2,000 during the year. This means the company paid $2,000 cash for an asset (prepaid rent) for which there is no corresponding expense (rent expense). In other words, the cash outflow to increase prepaid rent caused cash to decrease by $2,000, but net income remained unaffected. To adjust for cash being lower by $2,000, we subtract the increase in prepaid rent from net income. Illustration 11–13 shows this adjustment.

ILLUSTRATION 11–13

Adjustment for Change in Prepaid Rent

Net income
− Incr. in Ppd. Rent
+ Decr. in Ppd. Rent
Oper. cash flows

E-GAMES, INC.
Statement of Cash Flows (partial)

Cash Flows from Operating Activities	
Net income	$42,000
Adjustments to reconcile net income to net cash flows from operating activities:	
Depreciation expense	9,000
Loss on sale of land	4,000
Increase in accounts receivable	(7,000)
Decrease in inventory	10,000
Increase in prepaid rent	**(2,000)**

If prepaid rent had instead decreased from year to year, the change in the balance would have been added to net income to convert rent expense from an accrual basis to a cash basis.

Decrease in Accounts Payable.   E-Games' accounts payable decreased $5,000 during the year. The decrease in accounts payable indicates that the company paid $5,000 cash to reduce its liability (accounts payable) for which there was no corresponding expense (cost of goods sold) during the period. In other words, the cash outflow to reduce accounts payable caused cash to decrease by $5,000, but net income remained unaffected. To adjust for cash being lower by $5,000, we subtract the decrease in accounts payable from net income, as shown in Illustration 11–14.

ILLUSTRATION 11–14

Adjustment for Change in Accounts Payable

E-GAMES, INC. Statement of Cash Flows (partial)	
Cash Flows from Operating Activities	
Net income	$42,000
Adjustments to reconcile net income to net cash flows from operating activities:	
Depreciation expense	9,000
Loss on sale of land	4,000
Increase in accounts receivable	(7,000)
Decrease in inventory	10,000
Increase in prepaid rent	(2,000)
Decrease in accounts payable	**(5,000)**

Net income
+ Incr. in A/P
− Decr. in A/P
Oper. cash flows

If accounts payable had instead increased from year to year, the change in the balance would have been added to net income to convert associated expenses from an accrual basis to a cash basis. The expense most often associated with accounts payable is cost of goods sold.

Increase in Interest Payable.   E-Games' interest payable increased $1,000 during the year. An increase in interest payable indicates that the company recorded interest expense of $1,000 for which it did not pay cash. In other words, the $1,000 increase in interest payable reduces net income (because of interest expense) but has no effect on cash. To adjust for cash being greater by $1,000, we add the increase in interest payable to net income. This is shown in Illustration 11–15.

ILLUSTRATION 11–15

Adjustment for Change in Interest Payable

E-GAMES, INC. Statement of Cash Flows (partial)	
Cash Flows from Operating Activities	
Net income	$42,000
Adjustments to reconcile net income to net cash flows from operating activities:	
Depreciation expense	9,000
Loss on sale of land	4,000
Increase in accounts receivable	(7,000)
Decrease in inventory	10,000
Increase in prepaid rent	(2,000)
Decrease in accounts payable	(5,000)
Increase in interest payable	**1,000**

Net income
+ Incr. in Int. Pay.
− Decr. in Int. Pay.
Oper. cash flows

If interest payable had instead decreased from year to year, the change in the balance would have been subtracted from net income to convert interest expense from an accrual basis to a cash basis.

Decrease in Income Tax Payable.   E-Games' income tax payable decreased $2,000 during the year. The decrease in income tax payable indicates that the company paid $2,000 cash to reduce its liability (income tax payable) but reported no corresponding expense (income tax expense) during the period. In other words, the cash outflow to reduce income tax payable caused cash to decrease by $2,000, but net income remained unaffected. To adjust for cash being lower by $2,000, we subtract the decrease in income tax payable from net income. Illustration 11–16 shows this adjustment and calculates total net cash flows from operating activities of $50,000.

ILLUSTRATION 11–16

Adjustment for Change in Income Tax Payable

Net income
+ Incr. in Tax Pay.
− Decr. in Tax Pay.
Oper. cash flows

E-GAMES, INC.
Statement of Cash Flows (partial)

Cash Flows from Operating Activities

Net income	$42,000
Adjustments to reconcile net income to net cash flows from operating activities:	
Depreciation expense	9,000
Loss on sale of land	4,000
Increase in accounts receivable	(7,000)
Decrease in inventory	10,000
Increase in prepaid rent	(2,000)
Decrease in accounts payable	(5,000)
Increase in interest payable	1,000
Decrease in income tax payable	**(2,000)**
Net cash flows from operating activities	$50,000

If income tax payable had instead increased from year to year, the change in the balance would have been added to net income to convert operating activities from an accrual basis to a cash basis.

KEY POINT

Using the indirect method, we start with net income and adjust this number for income statement items (removing noncash revenues and noncash expenses and removing nonoperating gains and nonoperating losses), and we adjust net income for balance sheet items (changes in current assets and changes in current liabilities).

Decision Point

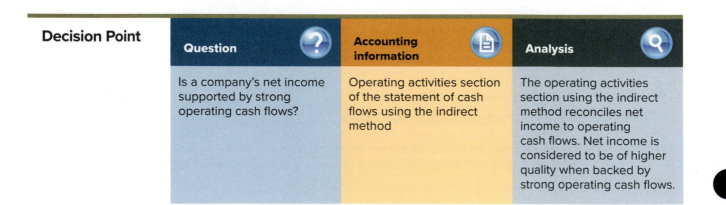

Question	Accounting information	Analysis
Is a company's net income supported by strong operating cash flows?	Operating activities section of the statement of cash flows using the indirect method	The operating activities section using the indirect method reconciles net income to operating cash flows. Net income is considered to be of higher quality when backed by strong operating cash flows.

Provided below are the income statement and partial balance sheet information for E-Phones, Inc.

Let's Review

E-PHONES, INC.
Income Statement
For the year ended December 31, 2024

Net sales		$2,200,000
Gain on sale of investment		5,000
Expenses:		
Cost of goods sold	$1,100,000	
Operating expenses	450,000	
Depreciation expense	25,000	
Income tax expense	217,000	
Total expenses		1,792,000
Net income		$ 413,000

Balance sheet information:	2024	2023	Increase (I) or Decrease (D)
Accounts receivable	$ 32,000	$40,000	$ 8,000 (D)
Inventory	100,000	70,000	30,000 (I)
Accounts payable	52,000	62,000	10,000 (D)
Income tax payable	55,000	12,000	43,000 (I)

Required:

Prepare the operating activities section of statement of cash flows for E-Phones using the *indirect method*.

Solution:

E-PHONES, INC.
Statement of Cash Flows—Indirect Method
For the year ended December 31, 2024

Cash Flows from Operating Activities	
Net income	$413,000
Adjustments to reconcile net income to net cash flows from operating activities:	
Depreciation expense	25,000
Gain on sale of investment	(5,000)
Decrease in accounts receivable	8,000
Increase in inventory	(30,000)
Decrease in accounts payable	(10,000)
Increase in income tax payable	43,000
Net cash flows from operating activities	$444,000

Suggested Homework:
BE11–4, BE11–5;
E11–6, E11–7, E11–11;
P11–3A&B

Investing Activities

■ **LO11–4**
Prepare the investing
activities section of the
statement of cash flows.

As noted earlier, we present the investing activities in the statement of cash flows the same way whether we use the indirect or the direct method. Here, we take a detailed look at how investing activities are determined, continuing our example of E-Games, Inc.

The second step in preparing the statement of cash flows is to determine the net cash flows from *investing* activities. Companies periodically invest cash to replace or expand productive facilities such as property, plant, and equipment. Information concerning these investing activities can provide valuable insight to decision makers regarding the nature and amount of assets being acquired for future use, as well as provide clues concerning the company's ambitions for the future. In the investing activities section of the statement of cash flows, companies list separately cash inflows and cash outflows from transactions such as buying and selling property, plant, and equipment, making and collecting loans, and buying and selling investments in other companies.

We can find a firm's investing activities by analyzing changes in long-term asset accounts from the balance sheet.[2] Looking at that section of E-Games' balance sheet, we determine the following cash flows from investing activities.

Increase in Investments.   Investments increased $35,000 during the year (from $0 in 2023 to $35,000 in 2024). In the absence of contrary evidence, it's logical to assume the increase is due to the purchase of investments during the year. Additional-information item (1) in Illustration 11–6 confirms this assumption. As Illustration 11–17 shows, we report the purchase of investments as a cash outflow of $35,000 from investing activities.

Decrease in Land.   The Land account decreased $10,000 during the year, indicating that E-Games sold land costing $10,000. Additional-information item (2) in Illustration 11–6 indicates that we originally recorded the land at a cost of $10,000 but sold it for only $6,000 (resulting in a loss on the sale of land of $4,000, as recorded in the operating activities section). We report the actual cash proceeds of $6,000 from the sale as a cash inflow from investing activities. (See Illustration 11–17 below.)

 COMMON MISTAKE

Some students mistakenly record a cash inflow from investing activities, like the sale of land for $6,000, at an amount that equals the change in the asset account, $10,000 in this case. Remember that the investing activities section reports the *actual* cash received or paid for an asset, which is usually not the same as the change in the asset account reported in the balance sheet.

ILLUSTRATION 11–17

Cash Flows from
Investing Activities

E-GAMES, INC. Statement of Cash Flows (partial)	
Cash Flows from Investing Activities	
Purchase of investments	$(35,000)
Sale of land	6,000
Net cash flows from investing activities	$ (29,000)
Note: Noncash Activities	
Purchased equipment by issuing a note payable	$ 20,000

---

[2]Although not used as an example in this chapter, it's also possible to have investing activities related to changes in current investments or current notes receivable.

Increase in Equipment. E-Games' Equipment account increased by $20,000 during the year. If E-Games purchased the equipment with cash, we would record a cash outflow from investing activities of $20,000. However, additional-information item (3) in Illustration 11–6 indicates that the firm paid for the equipment by issuing a $20,000 note payable to the seller. No cash was exchanged in the transaction. Therefore, the increase in equipment represents a noncash activity, which is disclosed either directly after the cash flow statement or in a note to the financial statements. Illustration 11–17 provides a summary of the cash flows from investing activities and disclosure of the noncash activity.

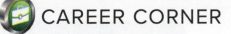

KEY POINT

Cash transactions (inflows and outflows) involving long-term assets and current investments are reported in the investing activities section of the statement of cash flows. Typical investing activities include buying and selling property, plant, and equipment, as well as making and collecting loans.

Financing Activities

The third step in preparing the statement of cash flows is to determine the net cash flows from *financing* activities. To fund its operating and investing activities, a company must often rely on external financing from two sources—creditors and shareholders. In the financing activities section of the statement of cash flows, companies list separately cash inflows, such as borrowing money and issuing stock, and cash outflows, such as repaying amounts borrowed and paying dividends to shareholders. And like investing activities, the presentation of financing activities is the same whether we use the indirect or the direct method for operating cash flows.

We can find a firm's financing activities by examining changes in long-term liabilities and stockholders' equity accounts from the balance sheet.[3] Referring back to E-Games' balance sheet, we find the following cash flows from financing activities.

Increase in Notes Payable. E-Games has only one long-term liability. The company reports an increase in notes payable of $20,000. As we saw earlier, this was in payment for equipment and represents a noncash activity disclosed in a note to the financial statements.

Increase in Common Stock. Common stock increased by $5,000 during the year. Item (4) of the additional information in Illustration 11–6 confirms that this was the result of issuing $5,000 of common stock. As Illustration 11–18 shows, the $5,000 inflow of cash is reported as a financing activity.

■ **LO11–5**
Prepare the financing activities section of the statement of cash flows.

---

[3]Although not used as an example in this chapter, it is also possible for financing activities to be indicated by changes in current liability accounts, such as current notes payable.

ILLUSTRATION 11–18

Cash Flows from
Financing Activities

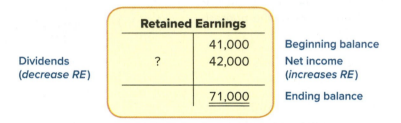

E-GAMES, INC.
Statement of Cash Flows (partial)

Cash Flows from Financing Activities	
Issuance of common stock	$ 5,000
Payment of cash dividends	(12,000)
Net cash flows from financing activities	(7,000)

Increase in Retained Earnings. E-Games' Retained Earnings balance increased by $30,000 during the year (from $41,000 to $71,000). Recall from earlier chapters that the balance of Retained Earnings increases with net income and decreases with dividends declared.

Retained Earnings

		41,000	Beginning balance
Dividends *(decrease RE)*	?	42,000	Net income *(increases RE)*
		71,000	Ending balance

Because net income is $42,000 and retained earnings increased by only $30,000, the company must have declared dividends of $12,000 during the year.

Retained earnings, beginning balance	$41,000
+ Net income	42,000
− **Dividends**	**(12,000)**
Retained earnings, ending balance	$71,000

Item (5), listed as additional information at the end of Illustration 11–6, confirms that E-Games declared and paid dividends of $12,000 during the year. As shown in Illustration 11–18, we report the payment of cash dividends as a cash outflow from financing activities.

Only the dividends actually paid in cash during the year are reported in the statement of cash flows. If the company declares dividends in 2024 but does not pay them until 2025, it will report the dividends paid as a cash outflow in 2025, not in 2024.

 KEY POINT

Cash transactions (inflows and outflows) with creditors and shareholders are reported in the financing activities section of the statement of cash flows. Typical financing activities include borrowing money and repaying amounts borrowed from creditors, as well as issuing stock and paying dividends to shareholders.

The fourth and final step in preparing the statement of cash flows is to combine the operating, investing, and financing activities and make sure the total of these three activities equals the net increase (decrease) in cash in the balance sheet. Illustration 11–19 shows the complete statement of cash flows for E-Games, with all three sections—operating, investing, and financing—included along with the note for noncash activities.

ILLUSTRATION 11–19

Complete Statement of Cash Flows for E-Games, Inc.

E-GAMES, INC.
Statement of Cash Flows
For the year ended December 31, 2024

Cash Flows from Operating Activities		
Net income	$42,000	
Adjustments to reconcile net income to net cash flows		
from operating activities:		
Depreciation expense	9,000	
Loss on sale of land	4,000	
Increase in accounts receivable	(7,000)	
Decrease in inventory	10,000	
Increase in prepaid rent	(2,000)	
Decrease in accounts payable	(5,000)	
Increase in interest payable	1,000	
Decrease in income tax payable	(2,000)	
Net cash flows from operating activities		$50,000
Cash Flows from Investing Activities		
Purchase of investments	(35,000)	
Sale of land	6,000	
Net cash flows from investing activities		(29,000)
Cash Flows from Financing Activities		
Issuance of common stock	5,000	
Payment of cash dividends	(12,000)	
Net cash flows from financing activities		(7,000)
Net increase (decrease) in cash		**14,000**
Cash at the beginning of the period		48,000
Cash at the end of the period		$62,000
Note: Noncash Activities		
Purchased equipment by issuing a note payable		$20,000

This is the moment of truth. The sum of the net cash flows from operating, investing, and financing activities should equal the net increase (decrease) in cash for the period. In Illustration 11–19, we see that the total of the cash flows from operating (+$50,000), investing (−$29,000), and financing (−$7,000) activities equals the net increase in cash of **$14,000**, reconciling cash from the two consecutive balance sheets originally reported in Illustration 11–6.

Let's Review

This is a continuation of the Let's Review exercise presented earlier in the chapter. Provided below are the income statement, balance sheets, and additional information for E-Phones, Inc.

E-PHONES, INC.
Income Statement
For the year ended December 31, 2024

Net sales		$2,200,000
Gain on sale of investment		5,000
Expenses:		
Cost of goods sold	$1,100,000	
Operating expenses	450,000	
Depreciation expense	25,000	
Income tax expense	217,000	
Total expenses		1,792,000
Net income		$ 413,000

E-PHONES, INC.
Balance Sheets
December 31, 2024 and 2023

	2024	2023	Increase (I) or Decrease (D)
Assets			
Current assets:			
Cash	$ 32,000	$ 48,000	$ 16,000 (D)
Accounts receivable	32,000	40,000	8,000 (D)
Inventory	100,000	70,000	30,000 (I)
Long-term assets:			
Investments	0	50,000	50,000 (D)
Land	280,000	180,000	100,000 (I)
Equipment	200,000	140,000	60,000 (I)
Accumulated depreciation	(53,000)	(28,000)	25,000 (I)
Total assets	$591,000	$500,000	
Liabilities and Stockholders' Equity			
Current liabilities:			
Accounts payable	$ 52,000	$ 62,000	$ 10,000 (D)
Income tax payable	55,000	12,000	43,000 (I)
Long-term liabilities:			
Bonds payable	0	200,000	200,000 (D)
Stockholders' equity:			
Common stock	200,000	100,000	100,000 (I)
Retained earnings	284,000	126,000	158,000 (I)
Total liabilities and stockholders' equity	$591,000	$500,000	

Additional Information for 2024:

1. Sold an investment in stock costing $50,000 for $55,000, resulting in a $5,000 gain on sale of investment.
2. Purchased $100,000 in land, issuing $100,000 of common stock as payment. No cash was exchanged in the transaction.
3. Purchased equipment for $60,000 cash.
4. Retired the $200,000 balance in bonds payable at the beginning of the year.
5. Declared and paid a cash dividend of $255,000.

Required:

Prepare the statement of cash flows using the *indirect method*. Disclose any noncash transactions in an accompanying note.

Solution:

E-PHONES, INC.
Statement of Cash Flows—Indirect Method
For the year ended December 31, 2024

Cash Flows from Operating Activities

Net income	$413,000
Adjustments to reconcile net income to net cash flows from operating activities:	
Depreciation expense	25,000

(continued)

(concluded)

E-PHONES, INC.
Statement of Cash Flows—Indirect Method
For the year ended December 31, 2024

Gain on sale of investment	(5,000)	
Decrease in accounts receivable	8,000	
Increase in inventory	(30,000)	
Decrease in accounts payable	(10,000)	
Increase in income tax payable	43,000	
Net cash flows from operating activities		$444,000
Cash Flows from Investing Activities		
Sale of investment	55,000	
Purchase of equipment	(60,000)	
Net cash flows from investing activities		(5,000)
Cash Flows from Financing Activities		
Retirement of bonds payable	(200,000)	
Payment of cash dividends	(255,000)	
Net cash flows from financing activities		(455,000)
Net increase (decrease) in cash		**(16,000)**
Cash at the beginning of the period		48,000
Cash at the end of the period		$ 32,000
Note: Noncash Activities		
Purchased land by issuing common stock		$100,000

Suggested Homework:
BE11–8, BE11–11;
E11–8; E11–9;
P11–2A&B; P11–4A&B

CASH FLOW ANALYSIS
Apple vs. Alphabet

Throughout this text, we have emphasized the analysis of financial statements from a decision maker's perspective. Often that analysis includes the development and comparison of financial ratios. The ratios discussed in Chapters 5 through 10 are all based on income statement and balance sheet amounts.

ANALYSIS

■ **LO11–6**
Perform financial analysis using the statement of cash flows.

Decision Maker's Perspective

Cash Flow Ratios

Analysts often supplement their investigation of income statement and balance sheet amounts with cash flow ratios. Some cash flow ratios are derived by substituting net cash flows from operating activities in place of net income—not to replace those ratios but to complement them. Substituting cash flow from operations in place of net income offers additional insight in the evaluation of a company's profitability and financial strength.[4] Positive cash flow from operations is important to a company's survival in the long run.

Now we reexamine the financial ratios introduced in Chapter 7—return on assets, profit margin, and asset turnover—substituting net cash flows from operating activities, also called **operating cash flows,** in place of net income. Illustration 11–20 provides selected financial data for **Apple** and **Alphabet**.

[4]Proposals for informative sets of cash flow ratios are offered by Charles A. Carslaw and John R. Mills. 1991. "Developing Ratios for Effective Cash Flow Statement Analysis." *Journal of Accountancy 172* (November), pp. 63–70; Don E. Giacomino and David E. Mielke. 1993. "Cash Flows: Another Approach to Ratio Analysis." *Journal of Accountancy 174* (March), pp. 55–58; and John Mills and Jeanne H. Yamamura. 1998. "The Power of Cash Flow Ratios." *Journal of Accountancy 186* (October), pp. 53–61.

ILLUSTRATION 11–20

Selected Financial Data

($ in millions)	Apple	Alphabet
Net sales	$260,174	$161,857
Net income	55,256	34,343
Operating cash flows	69,391	54,520
Total assets, beginning	365,725	232,792
Total assets, ending	338,516	275,909

RETURN ON ASSETS

Return on assets, introduced in Chapter 7, is calculated as net income divided by average total assets. Illustration 11–21 presents return on assets for Apple and Alphabet.

ILLUSTRATION 11–21

Return on Assets for Apple and Alphabet

($ in millions)	Net Income	÷	Average Total Assets	=	Return on Assets
Apple	$55,256	÷	($365,725 + $338,516)/2	=	15.7%
Alphabet	$34,343	÷	($232,792 + $275,909)/2	=	13.5%

Apple generated slightly more income for each dollar invested in assets.

CASH RETURN ON ASSETS

We can gain additional insights by examining a similar measure called the **cash return on assets** by substituting operating cash flows for net income. We calculate it as

$$\text{Cash return on assets} = \text{Operating cash flows} \div \text{Average total assets}$$

Illustration 11–22 presents the cash return on assets for Apple and Alphabet.

ILLUSTRATION 11–22

Cash Return on Assets for Apple and Alphabet

($ in millions)	Operating Cash Flows	÷	Average Total Assets	=	Cash Return on Assets
Apple	$69,391	÷	($365,725 + $338,516)/2	=	19.7%
Alphabet	$54,520	÷	($232,792 + $275,909)/2	=	21.4%

Now we see that it's Alphabet that shows a higher return on assets, in terms of operating cash flows. Do you think Alphabet's higher cash return on assets is due to higher pricing strategies or greater sales volume? We examine this question next.

COMPONENTS OF CASH RETURN ON ASSETS

Let's explore the cash return on assets further by separating the ratio into two separate parts, as shown in Illustration 11–23.

ILLUSTRATION 11–23

Components of Cash Return on Assets

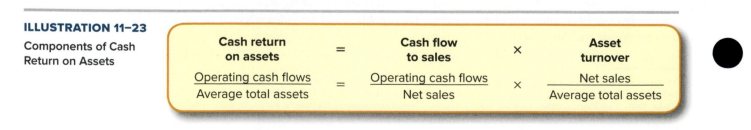

Cash return on assets can be separated into cash flow to sales and asset turnover. **Cash flow to sales** measures the operating cash flows generated for each dollar of sales. (It is the cash flow equivalent to profit margin, introduced in Chapter 7.) **Asset turnover**, also covered in Chapter 7, measures the sales revenue generated per dollar of assets. Cash flow to sales and asset turnover represent two primary strategies that companies have for increasing their cash return on assets. One strategy, pursued by both Apple and Alphabet, is to sell highly innovative products that yield very high cash inflows from customers in relationship to the cash outflows to produce their products. Another strategy is to pursue high asset turnover by selling at lower prices than the competition. In Illustrations 11–24 and 11–25, we calculate cash flow to sales and asset turnover for both companies.

ILLUSTRATION 11–24

Cash Flow to Sales for Apple and Alphabet

($ in millions)	Operating Cash Flows	÷	Net Sales	=	Cash Flow to Sales
Apple	$69,391	÷	$260,174	=	26.7%
Alphabet	$54,520	÷	$161,857	=	33.7%

ILLUSTRATION 11–25

Asset Turnover for Apple and Alphabet

($ in millions)	Net Sales	÷	Average Total Assets	=	Asset Turnover
Apple	$260,174	÷	($365,725 + $338,516)/2	=	0.74 times
Alphabet	$161,857	÷	($232,792 + $275,909)/2	=	0.64 times

Both companies have high cash flow to sales ratios, but Apple's is easily lower. This difference explains why Apple generates lower cash return on assets. However, this lower return is partially offset by Apple's higher asset turnover ratio. Apple uses its assets more efficiently to generate sales. To maximize cash flow from operations, a company strives to increase *both* cash flow per dollar of sales (cash flow to sales) and sales per dollar of assets invested (asset turnover).

 KEY POINT

Cash return on assets indicates the amount of operating cash flow generated for each dollar invested in assets. We can separate cash return on assets into two components—cash flow to sales and asset turnover—to examine two important business strategies.

Decision Point

Question	Accounting information	Analysis
Are the company's cash flows based more on selling at higher prices or on increasing sales volume?	Cash flow to sales and asset turnover ratios	Companies with high cash flow to sales ratios obtain high cash inflows from sales to customers in relation to the cash outflows to produce the products. Companies with high asset turnover ratios may not make as much on each sale, but they make money through higher sales volume.

ETHICAL DILEMMA

Ebenezer is CEO of a successful small business. One day he stops by to see Tim Cratchit, the new branch manager at First National Bank. Ebenezer and his partner Marley would like to double the size of their loan with the bank from $500,000 to $1 million. Ebenezer explains, "Business is booming, sales and earnings are up each of the past three years, and we could certainly use the funds for further business expansion." Tim Cratchit has a big heart, and Ebenezer has been a close friend of the family. He thinks to himself this loan decision will be easy, but he asks Ebenezer to e-mail the past three years' financial statements as required by bank policy.

In looking over the financial statements sent by Ebenezer, Tim becomes concerned. Sales and earnings have increased, just as Ebenezer said. However, receivables, inventory, and accounts payable have grown at a much faster rate than sales. Further, he notices a steady decrease in operating cash flows over the past three years, with negative operating cash flows in each of the past two years.

Who are the stakeholders, and what is the ethical dilemma? Do you think Tim should go ahead and approve the loan?

APPENDIX

■ **LO11–7**

Prepare the operating activities section of the statement of cash flows using the direct method.

OPERATING ACTIVITIES—DIRECT METHOD

There are two acceptable alternatives in reporting operating activities—the indirect method and the direct method. The presentation of operating activities in the main body of the chapter is referred to as the indirect method. By this method, we begin with reported net income and work backward to convert to a cash basis.

An alternative is the **direct method**, by which we report the cash inflows and cash outflows from operating activities directly in the statement of cash flows. For instance, we report *cash received from customers* as the cash effect of sales, and *cash paid to suppliers* as the cash effect of cost of goods sold. Income statement items that have *no* cash effect—such as depreciation expense or gains and losses on the sale of assets—are simply not reported under the direct method.

Here, we repeat the example for E-Games, Inc., this time presenting cash flows from operating activities using the direct method. For convenience, the income statement, balance sheets, and additional information for E-Games, Inc., are repeated in Illustration 11–26.

ILLUSTRATION 11–26

Income Statement, Balance Sheets, and Additional Information for E-Games, Inc.

E-GAMES, INC. Income Statement For the year ended December 31, 2024		
Net sales		$1,012,000
Expenses:		
Cost of goods sold	$650,000	
Operating expenses (salaries, rent, utilities)	286,000	
Depreciation expense	9,000	
Loss on sale of land	4,000	
Interest expense	5,000	
Income tax expense	16,000	
Total expenses		970,000
Net income		$ 42,000

(continued)

ILLUSTRATION 11–26
(concluded)

E-GAMES, INC.
Balance Sheets
December 31, 2024 and 2023

	2024	2023	Increase (I) or Decrease (D)
Assets			
Current assets:			
Cash	$ 62,000	$ 48,000	$14,000 (I)
Accounts receivable	27,000	20,000	7,000 (I)
Inventory	35,000	45,000	10,000 (D)
Prepaid rent	4,000	2,000	2,000 (I)
Long-term assets:			
Investments	35,000	0	35,000 (I)
Land	70,000	80,000	10,000 (D)
Equipment	90,000	70,000	20,000 (I)
Accumulated depreciation	(23,000)	(14,000)	9,000 (I)
Total assets	$300,000	$251,000	
Liabilities and Stockholders' Equity			
Current liabilities:			
Accounts payable	$ 22,000	$ 27,000	$ 5,000 (D)
Interest payable	2,000	1,000	1,000 (I)
Income tax payable	5,000	7,000	2,000 (D)
Long-term liabilities:			
Notes payable	95,000	75,000	20,000 (I)
Stockholders' equity:			
Common stock	105,000	100,000	5,000 (I)
Retained earnings	71,000	41,000	30,000 (I)
Total liabilities and stockholders' equity	$300,000	$251,000	

Additional Information for 2024:

1. Purchased stock in Intendo Corporation for $35,000.
2. Sold land for $6,000. The land originally was purchased for $10,000, resulting in a $4,000 loss being recorded at the time of the sale.
3. Purchased $20,000 in equipment by issuing a $20,000 note payable due in three years. No cash was exchanged in the transaction.
4. Issued common stock for $5,000 cash.
5. Declared and paid a cash dividend of $12,000.

Remember from Illustration 11–5 that the first step in preparing the statement of cash flows is to calculate net cash flows from *operating* activities using information from the income statement and changes in current assets and current liabilities from the balance sheet.

The income statement reports revenues recognized during the year, *regardless of when cash is received,* and the expenses incurred in generating those revenues, *regardless of when cash is paid.* This is the *accrual concept* of accounting that we've discussed throughout the book. Cash flows from operating activities, on the other hand, are both inflows and outflows of cash that result from activities reported in the income statement. In other words, it's the elements of net income, but **reported on a cash basis.** Using the direct method, we examine each account in the income statement and convert it from an accrual amount to a cash amount. We directly report the cash inflows and cash outflows. The relationships between items in the income statement and operating cash flows are shown in Illustration 11–27.

ILLUSTRATION 11–27

Relationship between the Income Statement and Cash Flows from Operating Activities— Direct Method

Income Statement	Cash Flows from Operating Activities
Revenues:	**Cash inflows:**
Sales and service revenue	➡ Cash received from customers
Investment revenue	➡ Cash received from interest and dividends
Noncash revenues and gains (gains on sale of assets)	➡ (Not reported)
Less: Expenses	**Less: Cash outflows**
Cost of goods sold	➡ Cash paid to suppliers for inventory
Operating expense	➡ Cash paid for salaries, rent, utilities, etc.
Noncash expenses and losses (loss on sale of assets, depreciation)	➡ (Not reported)
Interest expense	➡ Cash paid to creditors for interest
Income tax expense	➡ Cash paid to the government for taxes
= Net income	**= Net cash flows from operating activities**

The best way to apply the direct method is to convert each revenue and expense item to its cash-basis amount. We'll do this next using our E-Games example. Use the general guidelines in Illustration 11-27A for converting each income statement item to its operating cash flows.

ILLUSTRATION 11–27A

Convert Income Statement Items to Operating Cash Flows

Revenue	**Expense**
− Increase in related current asset	+ Increase in related current asset
+ Decrease in related current asset	− Decrease in related current asset
+ Increase in related current liability	− Increase in related current liability
− Decrease in related current liability	+ Decrease in related current liability
= Cash received	**= Cash paid**

Cash Received from Customers.   E-Games reports net sales of $1,012,000 as the first item in its income statement. Did E-Games receive $1,012,000 in cash from those sales? We can answer this by looking at the change in accounts receivable. If accounts receivable increases, this indicates that net sales exceed cash receipts from customers. That's why customers owe more than they did before. If accounts receivable decreases, the opposite will be true. Recall that accounts receivable increased $7,000. Therefore, we deduct the $7,000 increase in accounts receivable from net sales to obtain cash received from customers of $1,005,000, as shown in Illustration 11–28.

ILLUSTRATION 11–28

Cash Received from Customers

Net sales	$ 1,012,000
− Increase in accounts receivable	(7,000)
= Cash received from customers	**$1,005,000**

Let's consider this again from a couple of different perspectives. Accounts receivable increases when customers buy on credit and decreases when we receive cash from customers. We can compare sales and the change in accounts receivable during the year to determine the amount of cash we received from customers. In T-account format the relationship looks like this:

	Accounts Receivable		
Beginning balance	20,000		
Credit sales (*increase A/R*)	1,012,000	?	Cash received (*decreases A/R*)
Ending balance	27,000		

We see from this analysis that *cash received from customers* must have been $1,005,000. Still another way to view the situation is to think about how E-Games recorded these selling and collection activities during the year.

	Debit	Credit
Cash (to balance)	1,005,000	
Accounts Receivable (= $27,000 – $20,000)	7,000	
Sales Revenue (from income statement)		1,012,000
(Receive cash from customers)		

We record an increase in Sales Revenue with a credit and an increase in Accounts Receivable with a debit. Cash received from customers must be $1,005,000 for debits to equal credits.

Cash Paid to Suppliers. Moving down the income statement, we see that E-Games reports cost of goods sold of $650,000. Did E-Games pay cash of $650,000 to suppliers of those goods during the year? To answer this, we look to the two current balance sheet accounts affected by merchandise purchases—Inventory and Accounts Payable.

First, compare cost of goods sold with the change in inventory to determine the cost of goods purchased (not necessarily cash paid) during the year. Inventory decreased by $10,000. We can visualize the relationship in T-account format.

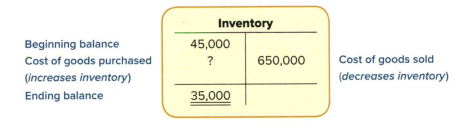

	Inventory		
Beginning balance	45,000		
Cost of goods purchased	?	650,000	Cost of goods sold
(increases inventory)			*(decreases inventory)*
Ending balance	35,000		

The number needed to explain the change is $640,000. That's the cost of goods *purchased* during the year. It's not necessarily true, though, that E-Games paid $640,000 cash to suppliers of these goods. We need to look at the change in accounts payable to determine the cash paid to suppliers.

	Accounts Payable		
		27,000	Beginning balance
Cash paid to suppliers	?	640,000	Cost of goods purchased
(decreases A/P)			*(increases A/P)*
		22,000	Ending balance

We now see that cash paid to suppliers must be $645,000. We can confirm this by looking at how E-Games recorded inventory purchases and sales during the year.

	Debit	Credit
Cost of Goods Sold (from income statement)	650,000	
Accounts Payable (= $27,000 – $22,000)	5,000	
Inventory (= $45,000 – $35,000)		10,000
Cash (to balance)		645,000
(Pay cash for inventory)		

We record an increase in Cost of Goods Sold with a debit, a decrease in Inventory with a credit, and a decrease in Accounts Payable with a debit. Cash paid to suppliers is the "plug" figure we need for debits to equal credits in the journal entry.

Alternatively, we can analyze the situation this way: Inventory decreased $10,000 for the year, so E-Games needed to purchase only $640,000 of goods in order to sell $650,000 of goods; $10,000 came from existing inventory. Because accounts payable decreased by $5,000, cash paid to suppliers must have been $5,000 more than purchases, so we add the decrease in accounts payable to purchases of $640,000 to arrive at cash paid to suppliers of $645,000, as shown in Illustration 11–29.

ILLUSTRATION 11–29

Cash Paid to Suppliers

Cost of goods sold	$650,000
− Decrease in inventory	(10,000)
= Purchases	640,000
+ Decrease in accounts payable	5,000
= Cash paid to suppliers	**$645,000**

Cash Paid for Operating Expenses.   Operating expenses of $286,000 appear next in the income statement. We examine the changes in current assets and current liabilities for any accounts related to operating expenses. Rent expense is included in operating expenses, so we must consider the change in prepaid rent. Increasing prepaid rent takes additional cash. Prepaid rent increased by $2,000, so we need to add this change to operating expenses to determine the cash paid for operating expenses, as shown in Illustration 11–30.

ILLUSTRATION 11–30

Cash Paid for Operating Expenses

Operating expenses	$286,000
+ Increase in prepaid rent	2,000
= Cash paid for operating expenses	**$288,000**

We see no current assets or current liabilities associated with other operating expenses such as salaries expense or utilities expense, so we make no adjustments to these operating expenses. Therefore, the amounts we report for these operating expenses in the income statement must equal the amount of cash we paid for these items.

Let's check our calculation by recording the payment for operating expenses during the year:

	Debit	Credit
Operating Expenses (from the income statement)	286,000	
Prepaid Rent (= $4,000 − $2,000)	2,000	
Cash (to balance)		288,000
(Pay operating expenses)		

Depreciation Expense and Loss on Sale of Land.   The next expense listed in the income statement is depreciation expense of $9,000. Depreciation expense has no effect on cash flows. It is merely an allocation in the current period of a prior cash expenditure (to acquire the depreciable asset). Therefore, unlike the other expenses to this point, depreciation is *not* reported on the statement of cash flows under the direct method.

Similar to depreciation expense, the loss on sale of land is *not* reported because it, too, has no effect on *operating* cash flows. Additional-information item (2) in Illustration 11–26 indicates that land we originally purchased at a cost of $10,000 was sold for $6,000, resulting in a loss on the sale of land of $4,000. E-Games records the sale as

	Debit	Credit
Cash (selling price)	6,000	
Loss (difference)	4,000	
Land (cost)		10,000
(Receive cash from sale of land)		

As we discussed previously, we report the $6,000 cash inflow as an investing activity, because both investing in land and later selling the land are considered investing activities. The original cost of the land, and thus the loss, has no effect on operating cash flows.

Cash Paid for Interest. E-Games next reports interest expense of $5,000 in the income statement. The related current asset or current liability in the balance sheet is interest payable. If interest payable increases, interest expense exceeds cash paid for interest. Interest payable increases $1,000. As shown in Illustration 11–31, we deduct the increase in interest payable from interest expense to arrive at cash paid for interest.

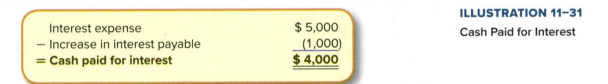

Interest expense	$ 5,000
− Increase in interest payable	(1,000)
= **Cash paid for interest**	**$ 4,000**

ILLUSTRATION 11–31

Cash Paid for Interest

We can check our calculation by recording the payment for interest during the year:

	Debit	Credit
Interest Expense (from income statement)	5,000	
Interest Payable (= $2,000 − $1,000)		1,000
Cash (to balance)		4,000
(Pay interest)		

Cash Paid for Income Taxes. The final item reported in the income statement is income tax expense of $16,000. The related current asset or current liability in the balance sheet is income tax payable. Income tax payable decreased $2,000. This means that E-Games paid $2,000 more than the income tax expense recorded. As shown in Illustration 11–32, we add the decrease in income tax payable to income tax expense to calculate cash paid for income taxes.

ILLUSTRATION 11–32

Cash Paid for Income Taxes

Income Tax Expense	$16,000
+ Decrease in income tax payable	2,000
= **Cash paid for income taxes**	**$18,000**

Recording the payment of taxes during the year confirms this.

	Debit	Credit
Income Tax Expense (from income statement)	16,000	
Income Tax Payable (= $7,000 − $5,000)	2,000	
Cash (to balance)		18,000
(Pay income taxes)		

Illustration 11–33 shows the completed operating activities section using the direct method.

E-GAMES, INC.
Statement of Cash Flows (partial)–Direct Method

Cash Flows from Operating Activities

Cash received from customers	$1,005,000
Cash paid to suppliers	(645,000)
Cash paid for operating expenses	(288,000)
Cash paid for interest	(4,000)
Cash paid for income taxes	(18,000)
Net cash flows from operating activities	$50,000

Note that the net cash flows from operating activities is $50,000—**the same amount we calculated earlier in Illustration 11–16 using the indirect method.** This will always be the case. The indirect method begins with net income, whereas the direct method considers each of the individual accounts that make up net income. Both methods take into consideration the *same changes* in current asset and current liability accounts.

KEY POINT

The indirect method and direct method differ only in the presentation of operating activities. In the indirect method, we start with net income and make adjustments to arrive at net cash flows from operating activities. In the direct method, we convert each individual line item in the income statement to its cash basis and directly list the cash inflows and cash outflows from operating activities. The net cash flows from operating activities are *the same under both methods.*

Let's Review

The income statement, balance sheets, and additional information from the accounting records of E-Phones, Inc., are provided below.

E-PHONES, INC.
Income Statement
For the year ended December 31, 2024

Net sales		$2,200,000
Gain on sale of investment		5,000
Expenses:		
Cost of goods sold	$1,100,000	
Operating expenses	450,000	
Depreciation expense	25,000	
Income tax expense	217,000	
Total expenses		1,792,000
Net income		$ 413,000

E-PHONES, INC.
Balance Sheets
December 31, 2024 and 2023

	2024	2023	Increase (I) or Decrease (D)
Assets			
Current assets:			
Cash	$ 32,000	$ 48,000	**$ 16,000 (D)**
Accounts receivable	32,000	40,000	8,000 (D)
Inventory	100,000	70,000	30,000 (I)
Long-term assets:			
Investments	0	50,000	50,000 (D)
Land	280,000	180,000	100,000 (I)
Equipment	200,000	140,000	60,000 (I)
Accumulated depreciation	(53,000)	(28,000)	25,000 (I)
Total assets	$591,000	$500,000	
Liabilities and Stockholders' Equity			
Current liabilities:			
Accounts payable	$ 52,000	$ 62,000	$ 10,000 (D)
Income tax payable	55,000	12,000	43,000 (I)
Long-term liabilities:			
Bonds payable	0	200,000	200,000 (D)
Stockholders' equity:			
Common stock	200,000	100,000	100,000 (I)
Retained earnings	284,000	126,000	158,000 (I)
Total liabilities and stockholders' equity	$591,000	$500,000	

Additional Information for 2024:

1. Sold an investment in stock costing $50,000 for $55,000, resulting in a $5,000 gain on sale of investment.
2. Purchased $100,000 in land, issuing $100,000 of common stock as payment. No cash was exchanged in the transaction.
3. Purchased equipment for $60,000 cash.
4. Retired the $200,000 balance in bonds payable at the beginning of the year.
5. Declared and paid a cash dividend of $255,000.

Required:

Prepare the statement of cash flows using the *direct method* for reporting operating activities. Disclose any noncash transactions in a note to the statement of cash flows.

Solution:

E-PHONES, INC.
Statement of Cash Flows—Direct Method
For the year ended December 31, 2024

Cash Flows from Operating Activities
Cash received from customers	$2,208,000
Cash paid to suppliers	(1,140,000)

(continued)

(concluded)

E-PHONES, INC.
Statement of Cash Flows—Direct Method
For the year ended December 31, 2024

Cash paid for operating expenses	(450,000)	
Cash paid for income taxes	(174,000)	
Net cash flows from operating activities		$444,000
Cash Flows from Investing Activities		
Sale of investment	55,000	
Purchase of equipment	(60,000)	
Net cash flows from investing activities		(5,000)
Cash Flows from Financing Activities		
Retirement of bonds payable	(200,000)	
Payment of cash dividends	(255,000)	
Net cash flows from financing activities		(455,000)
Net increase (decrease) in cash		**(16,000)**
Cash at the beginning of the period		48,000
Cash at the end of the period		$ 32,000
Note: Noncash Activities		
Purchased land by issuing common stock		$100,000

Here are the supporting calculations for cash flows from operating activities under the direct method:

Net sales	$ 2,200,000
+ Decrease in accounts receivable	8,000
= **Cash received from customers**	**$2,208,000**
Cost of goods sold	$ 1,100,000
+ Increase in inventory	30,000
= Purchases	1,130,000
+ Decrease in accounts payable	10,000
= **Cash paid to suppliers**	**$1,140,000**
Cash paid for operating expenses	**$ 450,000**
Income tax expense	$ 217,000
− Increase in income tax payable	(43,000)
= **Cash paid for income taxes**	**$ 174,000**

Suggested Homework:
BE11–16, BE11–17;
E11–15, E11–16;
P11–6A&B; P11–7A&B

CHAPTER FRAMEWORK

This chapter discusses the three types of cash flows reported in the statement of cash flows—operating, investing, and financing.

1. **Operating Cash Flows.** These include cash transactions related to revenue and expense activities. Accrual-basis revenues and expenses are reported in the income statement, and the statement of cash flows provides a reconciliation from net income (accrual basis) to operating cash flows (cash basis).

2. **Investing Cash Flows.** These include cash transactions involving the purchase and sale of long-term assets and current investments. Cash inflows are listed separately from cash outflows.

3. **Financing Cash Flows.** These include cash transactions involving external financing of a business with creditors and stockholders. Cash inflows are listed separately from cash outflows.

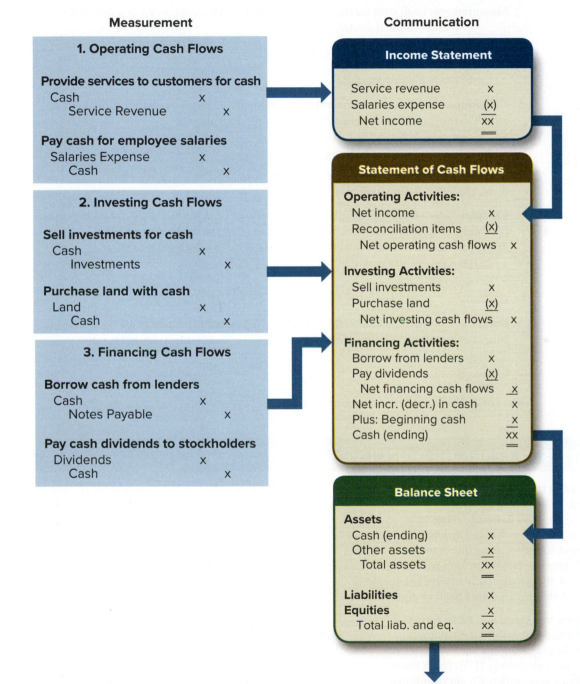

Cash return on assets $= \dfrac{\text{Operating cash flows}}{\text{Average total assets}}$

A measure of a company's effectiveness in using its assets to generate operating cash flows. The higher the cash return on assets, the greater the cash-generating ability of the company.

Chapter Framework Questions

1. **Measurement:** Cash received from providing services would be recorded as an increase to _____ and classified as a(n) _____.
   a. Cash; operating cash inflow.
   b. Cash; investing cash inflow.
   c. Cash; financing cash inflow.

2. **Measurement:** Cash paid for the purchase of land would be recorded as a decrease to _____ and classified as a(n) _____.
   a. Cash; operating cash outflow.
   b. Cash; investing cash outflow.
   c. Cash; financing cash outflow.

3. **Communication (income statement):** The statement of cash flows (indirect method) is linked to the income statement by reporting a reconciliation of _____ to _____.
   a. Operating cash flows; total assets.
   b. Net income; operating cash flows.
   c. Operating cash flows; total cash flows.
   d. Net income; ending cash balance.

4. **Communication (balance sheet):** In the statement of cash flows, the net cash flows from operating, investing, and financing activities are added to the beginning balance of cash. The resulting amount will equal the reported balance in which balance sheet account?
   a. Dividends.
   b. Retained Earnings.
   c. Cash.

5. **Decision Making (ratio analysis):** A company that is more effective in using its assets to generate operating cash flows would have a _____ cash return on assets ratio.
   a. Higher.
   b. Lower.

Note: For answers, see the last page of the chapter.

KEY POINTS BY LEARNING OBJECTIVE

LO11–1 Classify cash transactions as operating, investing, or financing activities.
Operating activities generally relate to income statement items and changes in current assets and current liabilities. Investing activities primarily involve changes in long-term assets. Financing activities primarily involve changes in long-term liabilities and stockholders' equity.

LO11–2 Understand the steps and basic format in preparing the statement of cash flows.
The steps in preparing the statement of cash flows involve calculating: (1) net cash flows from operating activities, (2) net cash flows from investing activities, (3) net cash flows from financing activities, and (4) the sum of these three activities to verify it equals the amount of cash reported in the balance sheet this year versus last year (the change in cash).

Companies choose between the indirect method and the direct method in reporting operating activities in the statement of cash flows. The indirect method begins with net income and then lists adjustments to net income, in order to arrive at operating cash flows. The direct method specifically lists the various cash inflows and outflows from operations. The investing and financing sections of the statement of cash flows are identical under both methods.

LO11–3 Prepare the operating activities section of the statement of cash flows using the indirect method.
Using the indirect method, we start with net income and adjust this number for income statement items (removing noncash revenues and noncash expenses and removing nonoperating gains and nonoperating losses), and we adjust net income for balance sheet items (changes in current assets and changes in current liabilities).

LO11–4 Prepare the investing activities section of the statement of cash flows.

Cash transactions (inflows and outflows) involving long-term assets and current investments are reported in the investing activities section of the statement of cash flows. Typical investing activities include buying and selling property, plant, and equipment, as well as making and collecting loans.

LO11–5 Prepare the financing activities section of the statement of cash flows.

Cash transactions (inflows and outflows) with creditors and shareholders are reported in the financing activities section of the statement of cash flows. Typical financing activities include borrowing money and repaying amounts borrowed from creditors, as well as issuing stock and paying dividends to shareholders.

Analysis

LO11–6 Perform financial analysis using the statement of cash flows.

Cash return on assets indicates the amount of operating cash flow generated for each dollar invested in assets. We can separate cash return on assets into two components—cash flow to sales and asset turnover—to examine two important business strategies.

Appendix

LO11–7 Prepare the operating activities section of the statement of cash flows using the direct method.

The indirect method and direct method differ only in the presentation of operating activities. In the indirect method, we start with net income and make adjustments to arrive at net cash flows from operating activities. In the direct method, we convert each individual line item in the income statement to its cash basis and directly list the cash inflows and cash outflows from operating activities. The net cash flows from operating activities are *the same under both methods.*

GLOSSARY

Asset turnover: Net sales divided by average total assets, which measures the sales per dollar of assets invested. **p. 563**

Cash flow to sales: Net cash flows from operating activities divided by sales revenue; measures the operating cash flow generated per dollar of sales. **p. 563**

Cash return on assets: Net cash flows from operating activities divided by average total assets; measures the operating cash flow generated per dollar of assets. **p. 562**

Direct method: Adjusts the items in the income statement to directly show the cash inflows and outflows from operations, such as cash received from customers and cash paid for inventory, salaries, rent, interest, and taxes. **pp. 548, 564**

Financing activities: Transactions with lenders, such as borrowing money and repaying debt, and with stockholders,

such as issuing stock, paying dividends, and purchasing treasury stock. **p. 543**

Indirect method: Begins with net income and then lists adjustments to net income in order to arrive at operating cash flows. **p. 548**

Investing activities: Transactions involving the purchase and sale of long-term assets and current investments. **p. 543**

Noncash activities: Significant investing and financing activities that do not affect cash. **p. 545**

Operating activities: Transactions involving revenue and expense activities. **p. 542**

Statement of cash flows: A financial statement that measures activities involving cash receipts and cash payments over a period of time. **p. 542**

SELF-STUDY QUESTIONS

1. The purchase of a long-term asset is classified in the statement of cash flows as a(n) **(LO11–1)**
   a. Operating activity.
   b. Investing activity.
   c. Financing activity.
   d. Noncash activity.

2. The issuance of common stock is classified in the statement of cash flows as a(n) **(LO11–1)**
   a. Operating activity.
   b. Investing activity.
   c. Financing activity.
   d. Noncash activity.

3. The issuance of notes payable is classified in the statement of cash flows as a(n) **(LO11–1)**
   a. Operating activity.
   b. Investing activity.
   c. Financing activity.
   d. Noncash activity.

4. Which of the following is an example of a noncash activity? **(LO11–1)**
   a. Cash received from the sale of land for more than its cost.
   b. Purchase of land by issuing common stock to the seller.

c. Cash received from the sale of land for less than its cost.

d. Purchase of land using cash proceeds from issuance of common stock.

5. The indirect and direct methods **(LO11–2)**

a. Are used by companies about equally in actual practice.

b. Affect the presentations of operating, investing, and financing activities.

c. Arrive at different amounts for net cash flows from operating activities.

d. Are two allowable methods to present operating activities in the statement of cash flows.

6. Which of the following best describes the indirect method of preparing the operating activities section of the statement of cash flows? **(LO11–3)**

a. Net income reconciled from accrual basis to cash basis.

b. A list of cash inflows and cash outflows from transactions involving the purchase and sale of long-term assets and current investments.

c. A list of cash inflows and cash outflows from transactions related to revenue and expense activities.

d. A list of cash inflows and cash outflows from transactions with lenders and stockholders.

7. Using the information below, calculate net cash flows from operating activities: **(LO11–3)**

Net income	$120,000
Receive cash from issuing stock	80,000
Pay cash for equipment	90,000
Increase in accounts receivable	10,000
Depreciation expense	$ 30,000
Increase in accounts payable	5,000
Receive cash from sale of land	75,000
Pay cash dividends	20,000

a. $115,000.

b. $155,000.

c. $145,000.

d. $190,000.

8. Which of the following is an example of a cash inflow from an investing activity? **(LO11–4)**

a. Receipt of cash from the issuance of common stock.

b. Receipt of cash from the sale of equipment.

c. Receipt of cash from the issuance of a note payable.

d. Receipt of cash from the sale of inventory.

Note: For answers, see the last page of the chapter.

9. Using the information in *Question 7*, calculate net cash flows from investing activities. **(LO11–4)**

a. $(165,000).

b. $15,000.

c. $60,000.

d. $(15,000).

10. Which of the following is an example of a cash outflow from a financing activity? **(LO11–5)**

a. Payment of interest.

b. Purchase of an intangible asset.

c. Payment of cash dividends.

d. Purchase of land.

11. Using the information in *Question 7*, calculate net cash flows from financing activities. **(LO11–5)**

a. $60,000.

b. $(15,000).

c. $100,000.

d. $80,000.

12. The balance of cash at the beginning of the year was $120,000, and at the end of the year was $140,000. Assuming operating cash flows equal $90,000 and investing cash flows equal $(40,000), calculate financing cash flows for the year. **(LO11–5)**

a. $50,000.

b. $(30,000).

c. $10,000.

d. $(70,000).

13. We can separate cash return on assets into **(LO11–6)**

a. Cash flow to sales and return on assets.

b. Profit margin and asset turnover.

c. Cash flow to sales and profit margin.

d. Cash flow to sales and asset turnover.

14. Which of the following items do we report in the statement of cash flows using the direct method? **(LO11–7)**

a. Depreciation expense.

b. Gain on sale of an asset.

c. Cash paid to suppliers.

d. Loss on sale of an asset.

15. Salaries expense for the year equals $240,000. Salaries payable at the beginning of the year were $25,000, and at the end of the year were $15,000. Calculate cash paid for salaries during the year. **(LO11–7)**

a. $225,000.

b. $250,000.

c. $230,000.

d. $265,000.

DATA ANALYTICS & EXCEL

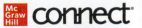

Visit Connect to find a variety of Data Analytics questions that help build Excel, Tableau, and data visualization skills. Assignable materials include Integrated Excel, Applying Excel, Data Visualizations, Tableau Dashboard Activities, and Applying Tableau cases.

REVIEW QUESTIONS

1. Identify and briefly describe the three categories of cash flows reported in the statement of cash flows. ■ **LO11–1**

2. Changes in current assets and current liabilities are used in determining net cash flows from operating activities. Changes in which balance sheet accounts are used in determining net cash flows from investing activities? Changes in which balance sheet accounts are used in determining net cash flows from financing activities? ■ **LO11–1**

3. Explain what we mean by noncash activities and provide an example. ■ **LO11–1**

4. Why is it necessary to use an income statement, balance sheet, and additional information to prepare a statement of cash flows? ■ **LO11–1**

5. Describe the basic format used in preparing a statement of cash flows, including the heading, the three major categories, and what is included in the last three lines of the statement. ■ **LO11–2**

6. Briefly describe the four steps outlined in the text for preparing a statement of cash flows. ■ **LO11–2**

7. Distinguish between the indirect method and the direct method for reporting net cash flows from operating activities. Which method is more common in practice? Which method provides a more logical presentation of cash flows? ■ **LO11–2**

8. Describe the most common adjustments we use to convert net income to net cash flows from operations under the indirect method. ■ **LO11–3**

9. The executives at Peach, Inc., are confused. The company reports a net loss of $200,000, and yet its net cash flow from operating activities increased $300,000 during the same period. Is this possible? Explain. ■ **LO11–3**

10. Explain how we report depreciation expense in the statement of cash flows using the indirect method. Why do we report it this way? ■ **LO11–3**

11. Describe how we report a gain or loss on the sale of an asset in the statement of cash flows using the indirect method. Why do we report it this way? ■ **LO11–3**

12. Indicate whether each of the following items would be added or subtracted from net income in preparing the statement of cash flows using the indirect method: (a) an increase in current assets, (b) a decrease in current assets, (c) an increase in current liabilities, and (d) a decrease in current liabilities. ■ **LO11–3**

13. How does an increase in accounts receivable affect net income in relation to operating cash flows? Why? How does a decrease in accounts receivable affect net income in relation to operating cash flows? Why? ■ **LO11–3**

14. A $10,000 investment on the books of a company is sold for $9,000. Under the indirect method, how does this transaction affect operating, investing, and financing activities? ■ **LO11–3, 11–4**

15. Provide three examples of financing activities reported in the statement of cash flows. ■ **LO11–5**

16. Bell Corporation purchases land by issuing its own common stock to the seller. No cash is exchanged. How do we report this transaction in the statement of cash flows, if at all? ■ **LO11–1, 11–4, 11–5**

17. Explain the difference between the calculation of return on assets and cash return on assets. How can cash-based ratios supplement the analysis of ratios based on income statement and balance sheet information? ■ **LO11–6**

18. Describe the two primary strategies firms use to increase cash return on assets. ■ **LO11–6**

19. What are the primary cash inflows and cash outflows under the direct method for determining net cash flows from operating activities? ■ **LO11–7**

20. Why do we exclude depreciation expense and the gain or loss on sale of an asset from the operating activities section of the statement of cash flows under the direct method? ■ **LO11–7**

BRIEF EXERCISES

Determine proper classification (LO11–1)

BE11–1 Classify each of the following items as an operating, investing, or financing activity.
1. Dividends paid.
2. Repayment of notes payable.
3. Payment for inventory.
4. Purchase of equipment.
5. Interest paid.

Determine proper classification (LO11–1)

BE11–2 The following selected transactions occur during the first year of operations. Determine how each should be reported in the statement of cash flows.
1. Issued one million shares of common stock at $20 per share.
2. Paid $75,000 to suppliers for inventory.
3. Paid a dividend of $1 per share to common stockholders.
4. Loaned $50,000 to an employee and accepted a note receivable.

Understand the basic format for the statement of cash flows (LO11–2)

BE11–3 Place the following items in the correct order as they would appear in the statement of cash flows.
Financing activities.
Net increase (decrease) in cash.
Operating activities.
Beginning cash balance.
Ending cash balance.
Investing activities.

Calculate operating activities—indirect method (LO11–3)

BE11–4 Laser World reports net income of $650,000. Depreciation expense is $50,000, accounts receivable increases $11,000, and accounts payable decreases $30,000. Calculate net cash flows from operating activities using the indirect method.

Calculate operating activities—indirect method (LO11–3)

BE11–5 Macrosoft Company reports net income of $75,000. The accounting records reveal depreciation expense of $90,000 as well as increases in prepaid rent, accounts payable, and income tax payable of $70,000, $10,000, and $23,000, respectively. Prepare the operating activities section of Macrosoft's statement of cash flows using the indirect method.

Calculate operating activities—indirect method (LO11–3)

BE11–6 Hi-Tech, Inc., reports net income of $70 million. Included in that number are depreciation expense of $6 million and a loss on the sale of equipment of $2 million. Records reveal increases in accounts receivable, accounts payable, and inventory of $3 million, $4 million, and $5 million, respectively. What are Hi-Tech's net cash flows from operating activities?

Calculate operating activities—indirect method (LO11–3)

BE11–7 Engineering Wonders reports net income of $70 million. Included in that number is building depreciation expense of $6 million and a gain on the sale of land of $2 million. Records reveal decreases in accounts receivable, accounts payable, and inventory of $3 million, $4 million, and $5 million, respectively. What are Engineering Wonders' net cash flows from operating activities?

Calculate net cash flows from investing activities (LO11–4)

BE11–8 Creative Sound Systems sold investments, land, and its own common stock for $40 million, $16 million, and $42 million, respectively. Creative Sound Systems also purchased treasury stock, equipment, and a patent for $22 million, $26 million, and $13 million, respectively. What amount should the company report as net cash flows from investing activities?

Determine investing cash flows from lending (LO11–4)

BE11–9 On April 1, 2023, Teleworks Company lent $100,000 to IT Industries. IT Industries pays back in full the note plus 10% interest on April 1, 2024. Determine the investing cash flows to be reported by Teleworks Company in 2024.

Determine investing cash flows from sale of land (LO11–4)

BE11–10 Technologies Worldwide purchased land for $850,000 in 2023 with the intent to expand operations. In 2024, the company decides the land is no longer needed, and the land is sold for $900,000. Determine the investing cash flows to be reported in 2024. Determine the investing cash flows to be reported in 2024 if the land was purchased in 2023 for $950,000?

Calculate net cash flows from financing activities (LO 11–5)

BE11–11 Refer to the situation described in BE11–8. What amount should Creative Sound Systems report as net cash flows from financing activities?

BE11–12 Refer to the situation described in BE11–9. Determine the financing cash flows to be reported by IT Industries in 2024.

Determine financing cash flows from borrowing (LO 11–5)

BE11–13 A-2-Z Design Services engaged in the following significant activities during the year:
a. The company issued common stock for $250,000. Management expects to use the proceeds to purchase land next year.
b. A new office building was purchased by issuing a $700,000 long-term note payable to the seller.
c. A-2-Z acquired equipment from one of its suppliers. In exchange, A-2-Z offers to provide design services to its supplier over the next two years. The services are valued at $90,000.

Determine the impact of each transaction on cash flows from investing and financing activities in the current year.

Understand significant noncash activities (LO11–1, 11–4, 11–5)

BE11–14 The balance sheet of Cranium Gaming reports total assets of $500,000 and $800,000 at the beginning and end of the year, respectively. Sales revenues are $2.10 million, net income is $75,000, and operating cash flows are $60,000. Calculate the cash return on assets, cash flow to sales, and asset turnover for Cranium Gaming.

Calculate the cash return on assets (LO11–6)

BE11–15 The balance sheet of Innovative Products reports total assets of $620,000 and $820,000 at the beginning and end of the year, respectively. The cash return on assets for the year is 25%. Calculate Innovative Products' net cash flows from operating activities (operating cash flows) for the year.

Calculate the net cash flows from operating activities (LO11–6)

BE11–16 Video Shack's accounts receivable decreases during the year by $9 million. What is the amount of cash received from customers during the reporting period if its net sales are $73 million?

Determine cash received from customers (LO11–7)

BE11–17 Electronic Superstore's inventory increases during the year by $5 million, and its accounts payable to suppliers increases by $7 million during the same period. What is the amount of cash paid to suppliers of merchandise during the reporting period if its cost of goods sold is $45 million?

Determine cash paid to suppliers (LO11–7)

BE11–18 Wireless Solutions reports operating expenses of $985,000. Operating expenses include both rent expense and salaries expense. Prepaid rent increases during the year by $30,000 and salaries payable increases by $20,000. What is the cash paid for operating expenses during the year?

Determine cash paid for operating expenses (LO11–7)

BE11–19 Computer World reports income tax expense of $340,000. Income taxes payable at the beginning and end of the year are $60,000 and $75,000, respectively. What is the cash paid for income taxes during the year?

Determine cash paid for income taxes (LO11–7)

BE11–20 Wifi Around reports net income for the year of $220,000. Retained earnings at the beginning and end of the year are $810,000 and $930,000, respectively. What is the cash paid for dividends during the year (assume any dividends declared were paid)?

Determine cash paid for dividends (LO 11–5, LO11–7)

EXERCISES

E11–1 Match (by letter) the following items with the description or example that best fits. Each letter is used only once.

Match terms with their definitions (LO11–1, 11–2, 11–3, 11–4, 11–5, 11–6, 11–7)

Terms

_____ 1. Operating activities
_____ 2. Investing activities
_____ 3. Financing activities
_____ 4. Noncash activities
_____ 5. Indirect method
_____ 6. Direct method
_____ 7. Depreciation expense
_____ 8. Cash return on assets

Descriptions

a. Begins with net income and then lists adjustments to net income in order to arrive at operating cash flows.

b. Item included in net income, but excluded from net operating cash flows.

c. Net cash flows from operating activities divided by average total assets.

d. Cash transactions involving lenders and investors.

e. Cash transactions involving net income.

f. Cash transactions for the purchase and sale of long-term assets.

g. Purchase of long-term assets by issuing stock to seller.

h. Shows the cash inflows and outflows from operations such as cash received from customers and cash paid for inventory, salaries, rent, interest, and taxes.

Determine proper classification (LO11–1)

E11–2 Analysis of an income statement, balance sheet, and additional information from the accounting records of Gadgets, Inc., reveals the following items.

1. Purchase of a patent.
2. Depreciation expense.
3. Decrease in accounts receivable.
4. Issuance of a note payable.
5. Increase in inventory.
6. Collection of notes receivable.
7. Purchase of equipment.
8. Exchange of long-term assets.
9. Decrease in accounts payable.
10. Payment of dividends.

Required:

Indicate in which section of the statement of cash flows each of these items would be reported: operating activities (indirect method), investing activities, financing activities, or a separate noncash activities note.

Determine proper classification (LO11–1)

E11–3 Wi-Fi, Inc., has the following selected transactions during the year.

1. Issues $20 million in bonds.
2. Purchases equipment for $80,000.
3. Pays a $20,000 account payable.
4. Collects a $15,000 account receivable.
5. Exchanges land for a new patent. Both are valued at $300,000.
6. Declares and pays a cash dividend of $100,000.
7. Loans $50,000 to a customer, accepting a note receivable.
8. Pays $75,000 to suppliers for inventory.

Required:

Indicate in which section of the statement of cash flows each of these items would be reported: operating activities (indirect method), investing activities, financing activities, or a separate noncash activities note.

Determine proper classification (LO11–1)

Flip Side of E11–5

E11–4 Ernie's Electronics had the following transactions with Bert's Bargain House:

1. Ernie sold Bert land for $195,000. Ernie originally purchased the land for $180,000, resulting in a $15,000 gain being recorded by Ernie at the time of the sale.
2. Ernie borrowed $100,000 from Bert, signing a three-year note payable.
3. Ernie purchased $1 million in common stock in Bert's Bargain House through a private placement.
4. Ernie received a dividend of $40,000 from the common stock investment in Bert's Bargain House.

Required:

Analyze each of the four transactions from the perspective of Ernie's Electronics. Indicate in which section of the statement of cash flows each of these items would be reported for Ernie's Electronics: operating activities (indirect method), investing activities, financing activities, or a separate noncash activities note.

E11–5 Refer to the transactions between Ernie's Electronics and Bert's Bargain House recorded in E11–4.

Determine proper classification (LO11–1)

Flip Side of E11–4

Required:

Analyze each of the four transactions from the perspective of Bert's Bargain House. Indicate in which section of the statement of cash flows each of these items would be reported for Bert's Bargain House: operating activities (indirect method), investing activities, financing activities, or a separate noncash activities note.

E11–6 Hardware Suppliers reports net income of $165,000. Included in net income is a gain on the sale of land of $20,000. A comparison of this year's and last year's balance sheets reveals an increase in accounts receivable of $35,000, an increase in inventory of $20,000, and a decrease in accounts payable of $55,000.

Calculate operating activities—indirect method (LO11–3)

Required:

Prepare the operating activities section of the statement of cash flows using the indirect method. Do you see a pattern in Hardware Suppliers' adjustments to net income to arrive at operating cash flows? What might this imply?

E11–7 Software Distributors reports net income of $65,000. Included in that number is depreciation expense of $15,000 and a loss on the sale of land of $6,000. A comparison of this year's and last year's balance sheets reveals a decrease in accounts receivable of $28,000, a decrease in inventory of $37,000, and an increase in accounts payable of $45,000.

Calculate operating activities—indirect method (LO11–3)

Required:

Prepare the operating activities section of the statement of cash flows using the indirect method. Do you see a pattern in Software Distributors' adjustments to net income to arrive at operating cash flows? What might this imply?

E11–8 The balance sheets for Plasma Screens Corporation, along with additional information, are provided below:

Prepare a statement of cash flows—indirect method (LO11–3, 11–4, 11–5)

PLASMA SCREENS CORPORATION
Balance Sheets
December 31, 2024 and 2023

	2024	2023
Assets		
Current assets:		
Cash	$ 108,900	$ 126,800
Accounts receivable	82,000	97,000
Inventory	105,000	89,000
Prepaid rent	6,000	3,000
Long-term assets:		
Land	530,000	530,000
Equipment	830,000	720,000
Accumulated depreciation	(438,000)	(288,000)
Total assets	$1,223,900	$1,277,800
Liabilities and Stockholders' Equity		
Current liabilities:		
Accounts payable	$ 109,000	$ 94,000
Interest payable	6,900	13,800
Income tax payable	10,000	6,000
Long-term liabilities:		
Notes payable	115,000	230,000
Stockholders' equity:		
Common stock	750,000	750,000
Retained earnings	233,000	184,000
Total liabilities and stockholders' equity	$1,223,900	$1,277,800

Additional Information for 2024:

1. Net income is $79,000.
2. The company purchases $110,000 in equipment. No equipment was sold.
3. Depreciation expense is $150,000.
4. The company repays $115,000 in notes payable.
5. The company declares and pays a cash dividend of $30,000.

Required:
Prepare the statement of cash flows using the indirect method.

Calculate operating activities—indirect method (LO11–3)

E11–9 Portions of the financial statements for Peach Computer are provided below.

PEACH COMPUTER
Income Statement
For the year ended December 31, 2024

Net sales		$2,050,000
Expenses:		
Cost of goods sold	$1,150,000	
Operating expenses	660,000	
Depreciation expense	60,000	
Income tax expense	50,000	
Total expenses		1,920,000
Net income		$ 130,000

PEACH COMPUTER
Selected Balance Sheet Data
December 31

	2024	2023	Increase (I) or Decrease (D)
Cash	$112,000	$90,000	$22,000 (I)
Accounts receivable	46,000	54,000	8,000 (D)
Inventory	85,000	60,000	25,000 (I)
Prepaid rent	4,000	7,000	3,000 (D)
Accounts payable	55,000	42,000	13,000 (I)
Income tax payable	6,000	15,000	9,000 (D)

Required:
Prepare the operating activities section of the statement of cash flows for Peach Computer using the *indirect* method.

Calculate investing cash flows (LO11–4)

E11–10 The following summary transactions occurred during the year for Bluebonnet.

Cash received from:	
Collections from customers	$380,000
Interest on notes receivable	6,000
Collection of notes receivable	50,000
Sale of investments	30,000
Issuance of notes payable	100,000
Cash paid for:	
Purchase of inventory	160,000
Interest on notes payable	5,000
Purchase of equipment	85,000
Salaries to employees	90,000
Payment of notes payable	25,000
Dividends to shareholders	20,000

Required:

Calculate net cash flows from investing activities.

E11–11 Refer to the information in E11-10.

Calculate financing cash flows **(LO11–5)**

Required:

Calculate net cash flows from financing activities.

E11–12 Dristell Inc. had the following activities during the year (all transactions are for cash unless stated otherwise):

Calculate investing cash flows **(LO11–4)**

a. A building with a book value of $400,000 was sold for $500,000.
b. Additional common stock was issued for $160,000.
c. Dristell purchased its own common stock as treasury stock at a cost of $75,000.
d. Land was acquired by issuing a 6%, 10-year, $750,000 note payable to the seller.
e. A dividend of $40,000 was paid to shareholders.
f. An investment in Fleet Corp.'s common stock was made for $120,000.
g. New equipment was purchased for $65,000.
h. A $90,000 note payable issued three years ago was paid in full.
i. A loan for $100,000 was made to one of Dristell's suppliers. The supplier plans to repay Dristell this amount plus 10% interest within 18 months.

Required:

Calculate net cash flows from investing activities.

E11–13 Refer to the information in E11–12.

Calculate financing cash flows **(LO11–5)**

Required:

Calculate net cash flows from financing activities.

E11–14 Zoogle has the following selected data ($ in millions):

Calculate financial ratios **(LO11–6)**

Net sales	$24,651
Net income	6,620
Operating cash flows	9,326
Total assets, beginning	41,768
Total assets, ending	50,497

Required:

1. Calculate the return on assets.
2. Calculate the cash return on assets.
3. Calculate the cash flow to sales ratio and the asset turnover ratio.

E11–15 Refer to the information provided for Peach Computer in E11–9.

Calculate operating activities—direct method **(LO11–7)**

Required:

Prepare the operating activities section of the statement of cash flows for Peach Computer using the *direct* method.

E11–16 Mega Screens, Inc., reports net sales of $3,200,000, cost of goods sold of $2,000,000, and income tax expense of $150,000 for the year ended December 31, 2024. Selected balance sheet accounts are as follows:

Calculate operating activities—direct method **(LO11–7)**

MEGA SCREENS, INC.
Selected Balance Sheet Data
December 31

	2024	2023	Increase (I) or Decrease (D)
Cash	$150,000	$195,000	$45,000 (D)
Accounts receivable	285,000	230,000	55,000 (I)
Inventory	125,000	165,000	40,000 (D)
Accounts payable	120,000	137,000	17,000 (D)
Income tax payable	25,000	16,000	9,000 (I)

Required:

Calculate cash received from customers, cash paid to suppliers, and cash paid for income taxes.

Calculate operating
activities—direct
method (LO11–7)

E11–17 The income statement for Electronic Wonders reports net sales of $91,758 million and cost of goods sold of $69,278 million. An examination of balance sheet amounts indicates accounts receivable increased $1,733 million, inventory increased $883 million, and accounts payable to suppliers decreased $1,967 million.

Required:

Using the direct method, calculate (1) cash received from customers and (2) cash paid to suppliers.

Determine cash received
from customers (LO11–7)

E11–18 Consider the three independent situations below (amounts are $ in millions):

Situation	Sales Revenue	Accounts Receivable Increase (Decrease)	Cash Received from Customers
1.	200	-0-	?
2.	200	30	?
3.	200	(30)	?

Required:

1. Calculate cash received from customers.
2. Prepare the summary journal entry for each situation.

Determine cash paid to
suppliers (LO11–7)

E11–19 Consider the four independent situations below.

Situation	Cost of Goods Sold	Inventory Increase (Decrease)	Accounts Payable Increase (Decrease)	Cash Paid to Suppliers
1.	150	25	20	?
2.	150	(25)	20	?
3.	150	25	(20)	?
4.	150	(25)	(20)	?

Required:

1. Calculate cash paid to suppliers.
2. Prepare the summary journal entry for each situation.

Determine cash
paid for operating
expenses (LO11–7)

E11–20 Consider the four independent situations below.

Situation	Operating Expenses	Prepaid Insurance Increase (Decrease)	Salaries Payable Increase (Decrease)	Cash Paid for Operating Expenses
1.	100	15	10	?
2.	100	(15)	10	?
3.	100	15	(10)	?
4.	100	(15)	(10)	?

Required:

1. Calculate cash paid for operating expenses.
2. Prepare the summary journal entry for each situation.

PROBLEMS: SET A

P11–1A Listed below are several transactions. For each transaction, indicate by letter whether the cash effect of each transaction is reported in a statement of cash flows as an operating (O), investing (I), financing (F), or noncash (NC) activity. Also, indicate whether the transaction is a cash inflow (CI) or cash outflow (CO), or has no effect on cash (NE). The first answer is provided as an example.

Determine proper classification (LO11–1)

Transaction	Type of Activity	Cash Inflow or Outflow
1. *Payment of employee salaries.*	O	CO
2. Sale of land for cash.		
3. Purchase of rent in advance.		
4. Collection of an account receivable.		
5. Issuance of common stock.		
6. Purchase of inventory.		
7. Collection of notes receivable.		
8. Payment of income taxes.		
9. Sale of equipment for a note receivable.		
10. Issuance of bonds.		
11. Loan to another company.		
12. Payment of a long-term note payable.		
13. Purchase of treasury stock.		
14. Payment of an account payable.		
15. Sale of equipment for cash.		

P11–2A Seth Erkenbeck, a recent college graduate, has just completed the basic format to be used in preparing the statement of cash flows (indirect method) for ATM Software Developers. All amounts are in thousands (000s).

Classify items and prepare the statement of cash flows (LO11–1, 11–3, 11–4, 11–5)

ATM SOFTWARE DEVELOPERS **Statement of Cash Flows** **For the year ended December 31, 2024**	
Cash Flows from Operating Activities	
Net income	
Adjustments to reconcile net income to net cash flows from operating activities:	
Net cash flows from operating activities	_____
Cash Flows from Investing Activities	
Net cash flows from investing activities	_____
Cash Flows from Financing Activities	
Net cash flows from financing activities	
Net increase (decrease) in cash	$ 3,765
Cash at the beginning of the period	7,510
Cash at the end of the period	$11,275

Listed below in random order are line items to be included in the statement of cash flows.

Cash received from the sale of land (no gain or loss)	$ 8,650
Issuance of common stock	13,075
Depreciation expense	5,465
Increase in accounts receivable	4,090
Decrease in accounts payable	1,760
Issuance of long-term notes payable	16,495
Purchase of equipment	39,865
Decrease in inventory	1,475
Decrease in prepaid rent	905
Payment of dividends	6,370
Net income	12,400
Purchase of treasury stock	2,615

Required:

Prepare the statement of cash flows for ATM Software Developers using the *indirect* method.

Calculate operating activities—indirect method (LO11–3)

P11–3A Portions of the financial statements for Alliance Technologies are provided below.

ALLIANCE TECHNOLOGIES
Income Statement
For the year ended December 31, 2024

Net sales		$405,000
Expenses:		
Cost of goods sold	$235,000	
Operating expenses	70,000	
Depreciation expense	17,000	
Income tax expense	27,000	
Total expenses		349,000
Net income		$ 56,000

ALLIANCE TECHNOLOGIES
Selected Balance Sheet Data
December 31, 2024, compared to December 31, 2023

Decrease in accounts receivable	$ 7,000
Increase in inventory	14,000
Decrease in prepaid rent	10,000
Increase in salaries payable	6,000
Decrease in accounts payable	9,000
Increase in income tax payable	24,000

Required:

Prepare the operating activities section of the statement of cash flows for Alliance Technologies using the *indirect* method.

P11–4A The income statement, balance sheets, and additional information for Video Phones, Inc., are provided.

Prepare a statement of cash flows—indirect method (LO11–2, 11–3, 11–4, 11–5)

VIDEO PHONES, INC.
Income Statement
For the year ended December 31, 2024

Net sales		$3,636,000
Expenses:		
Cost of goods sold	$2,450,000	
Operating expenses	958,000	
Depreciation expense	37,000	
Loss on sale of land	9,000	
Interest expense	20,000	
Income tax expense	58,000	
Total expenses		3,532,000
Net income		$ 104,000

VIDEO PHONES, INC.
Balance Sheets
December 31

	2024	2023
Assets		
Current assets:		
Cash	$ 254,600	$227,800
Accounts receivable	92,000	70,000
Inventory	105,000	145,000
Prepaid rent	14,400	7,200
Long-term assets:		
Investments	115,000	0
Land	220,000	260,000
Equipment	290,000	220,000
Accumulated depreciation	(81,000)	(44,000)
Total assets	$1,010,000	$886,000

VIDEO PHONES, INC.
Balance Sheets
December 31

	2024	2023
Liabilities and Stockholders' Equity		
Current liabilities:		
Accounts payable	$ 75,000	$ 91,000
Interest payable	7,000	12,000
Income tax payable	16,000	15,000
Long-term liabilities:		
Notes payable	305,000	235,000
Stockholders' equity:		
Common stock	400,000	400,000
Retained earnings	207,000	133,000
Total liabilities and stockholders' equity	$1,010,000	$886,000

(concluded)

> **Additional Information for 2024:**
> 1. Purchased investment in bonds for $115,000.
> 2. Sold land for $31,000. The land originally was purchased for $40,000, resulting in a $9,000 loss being recorded at the time of the sale.
> 3. Purchased $70,000 in equipment by issuing a $70,000 long-term note payable to the seller. No cash was exchanged in the transaction.
> 4. Declared and paid a cash dividend of $30,000.

Required:

Prepare the statement of cash flows using the *indirect* method. Disclose any noncash transactions in an accompanying note.

Calculate and analyze ratios (LO11–6)

P11–5A Cyberdyne Systems and Virtucon are competitors focusing on the latest technologies. Selected financial data is provided below.

($ in millions)	Cyberdyne	Virtucon
Net sales	$37,905	$ 4,984
Net income	9,737	1,049
Operating cash flows	14,565	1,324
Total assets, beginning	57,851	14,928
Total assets, ending	72,574	14,783

Required:
1. Calculate the return on assets for both companies.
2. Calculate the cash return on assets for both companies.
3. Calculate the cash flow to sales ratio and the asset turnover ratio for both companies.
4. Which company has the more favorable ratios?

Calculate operating activities—direct method (LO11–7)

P11–6A Refer to the information provided in P11–3A for Alliance Technologies.

Required:

Prepare the operating activities section of the statement of cash flows for Alliance Technologies using the *direct* method.

Calculate operating activities—direct method (LO11–7)

P11–7A Data for Video Phones, Inc., are provided in P11–4A.

Required:

Prepare the statement of cash flows for Video Phones, Inc., using the *direct* method. Disclose any noncash transactions in an accompanying note.

Prepare an income statement using operating cash flow information—indirect and direct methods (LO11–3, 11–7)

P11–8A Cash flows from operating activities for both the indirect and direct methods are presented for Reverse Logic. All amounts are in thousands (000s).

Cash Flows from Operating Activities (Indirect method)

Net income	$174	
Adjustments to reconcile net income to net cash flows from operating activities:		
Depreciation expense	62	
Increase in accounts receivable	(38)	
Decrease in inventory	50	
Increase in prepaid rent	(5)	
Decrease in accounts payable	(11)	
Decrease in income tax payable	(9)	
Net cash flows from operating activities		$223

Cash Flows from Operating Activities (Direct method)

Cash received from customers	$ 4,070	
Cash paid to suppliers	(2,585)	
Cash paid for operating expenses	(1,163)	
Cash paid for income taxes	(99)	
Net cash flows from operating activities		$223

Required:

Complete the following income statement for Reverse Logic. Assume all accounts payable are to suppliers.

REVERSE LOGIC
Income Statement
For the year ended December 31, 2024

Net sales		$?
Expenses:		
Cost of goods sold	$?	
Operating expenses	?	
Depreciation expense	62	
Income tax expense	?	
Total expenses		?
Net income		$174

[*Hint:* Use the following calculations and work backwards from bottom (in red) to top for each item.]

Net sales	
± Change in accounts receivable	_____
= Cash received from customers	_____
Cost of goods sold	
± Change in inventory	_____
= Purchases	
± Change in accounts payable	_____
= Cash paid to suppliers	_____
Operating expenses	
± Change in prepaid rent	_____
= Cash paid for operating expenses	_____
Income tax expense	
± Change in income tax payable	_____
= Cash paid for income taxes	_____

Mc Graw Hill connect

Determine proper classification (LO11–1)

P11–1B Listed below are several transactions. For each transaction, indicate by letter whether the cash effect of each transaction is reported in a statement of cash flows as an operating (O), investing (I), financing (F), or noncash (NC) activity. Also, indicate whether the transaction is a cash inflow (CI) or cash outflow (CO), or has no effect on cash (NE). The first answer is provided as an example.

Transaction	Type of Activity	Cash Inflow or Outflow
1. *Issuance of common stock.*	*F*	*CI*
2. Sale of land for cash.		
3. Purchase of treasury stock.		
4. Collection of an account receivable.		
5. Issuance of a note payable.		
6. Purchase of inventory.		
7. Repayment of a note payable.		
8. Payment of employee salaries.		
9. Sale of equipment for a note receivable.		
10. Issuance of bonds.		
11. Investment in bonds.		
12. Payment of interest on bonds payable.		
13. Payment of a cash dividend.		
14. Purchase of a building.		
15. Collection of a note receivable.		

Classify items and prepare the statement of cash flows (LO11–1, 11–3, 11–4, 11–5)

P11–2B Natalie King has completed the basic format to be used in preparing the statement of cash flows (indirect method) for CPU Hardware Designers. All amounts are in thousands (000s).

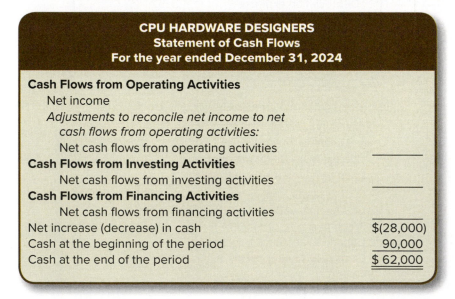

CPU HARDWARE DESIGNERS
Statement of Cash Flows
For the year ended December 31, 2024

Cash Flows from Operating Activities	
Net income	
Adjustments to reconcile net income to net cash flows from operating activities:	
Net cash flows from operating activities	_____
Cash Flows from Investing Activities	
Net cash flows from investing activities	_____
Cash Flows from Financing Activities	
Net cash flows from financing activities	_____
Net increase (decrease) in cash	$(28,000)
Cash at the beginning of the period	90,000
Cash at the end of the period	$ 62,000

Below, in random order, are line items to be included in the statement of cash flows.

Cash received from the sale of land (no gain or loss)	$ 4,000
Issuance of common stock	300,000
Depreciation expense	30,000
Increase in accounts receivable	70,000
Increase in accounts payable	11,000
Loss on sale of land	8,000
Purchase of equipment	230,000
Increase in inventory	40,000
Increase in prepaid rent	11,000
Payment of dividends	50,000
Net income	80,000
Repayment of notes payable	60,000

Required:

Prepare the statement of cash flows for CPU Hardware Designers using the *indirect* method.

P11–3B Portions of the financial statements for Software Associates are provided below.

Calculate operating activities—indirect method **(LO11–3)**

SOFTWARE ASSOCIATES
Income Statement
For the year ended December 31, 2024

Net sales		$710,000
Expenses:		
Cost of goods sold	$420,000	
Operating expenses	130,000	
Depreciation expense	33,000	
Income tax expense	49,000	
Total expenses		632,000
Net income		$ 78,000

SOFTWARE ASSOCIATES
Selected Balance Sheet Data
December 31, 2024, compared to December 31, 2023

Decrease in accounts receivable	$10,000
Decrease in inventory	13,000
Increase in prepaid rent	3,000
Decrease in salaries payable	4,000
Increase in accounts payable	7,000
Increase in income tax payable	8,000

Required:

Prepare the operating activities section of the statement of cash flows for Software Associates using the *indirect* method.

P11–4B The income statement, balance sheets, and additional information for Virtual Gaming Systems are provided.

Prepare a statement of cash flows—indirect method **(LO11–2, 11–3, 11–4, 11–5)**

VIRTUAL GAMING SYSTEMS
Income Statement
For the year ended December 31, 2024

Net sales		$2,600,000
Gain on sale of land		7,000
Total revenues		2,607,000
Expenses:		
Cost of goods sold	$1,650,000	
Operating expenses	615,000	
Depreciation expense	33,000	
Interest expense	34,000	
Income tax expense	80,000	
Total expenses		2,412,000
Net income		$ 195,000

VIRTUAL GAMING SYSTEMS
Balance Sheets
December 31

	2024	2023
Assets		
Current assets:		
Cash	$ 409,500	$ 343,800
Accounts receivable	64,000	80,000
Inventory	160,000	145,000
Prepaid rent	4,600	7,200
Long-term assets:		
Investments	205,000	110,000
Land	215,000	270,000
Equipment	250,000	220,000
Accumulated depreciation	(143,000)	(110,000)
Total assets	$1,165,100	$1,066,000
Liabilities and Stockholders' Equity		
Current liabilities:		
Accounts payable	$ 35,000	$ 98,000
Interest payable	5,100	4,000
Income tax payable	25,000	29,000
Long-term liabilities:		
Notes payable	265,000	235,000
Stockholders' equity:		
Common stock	460,000	400,000
Retained earnings	375,000	300,000
Total liabilities and stockholders' equity	$1,165,100	$1,066,000

Additional Information for 2024:
1. Purchased additional investment in stocks for $95,000.
2. Sold land for $62,000. The land originally was purchased for $55,000, resulting in a $7,000 gain being recorded at the time of the sale.
3. Purchased $30,000 in equipment by issuing a $30,000 long-term note payable to the seller. No cash was exchanged in the transaction.
4. Declared and paid a cash dividend of $120,000.
5. Issued common stock for $60,000.

Required:

Prepare the statement of cash flows using the *indirect* method. Disclose any noncash transactions in an accompanying note.

P11–5B International Genetic Technologies (InGen) and The Resources Development Association (RDA) are companies involved in cutting-edge genetics research. Selected financial data are provided below:

Calculate and analyze ratios (LO11–6)

($ in millions)	InGen	RDA
Net sales	$127,245	$106,916
Net income	7,074	15,855
Operating cash flows	12,639	19,846
Total assets, beginning	124,503	113,452
Total assets, ending	129,517	116,433

Required:

1. Calculate the return on assets for both companies.
2. Calculate the cash return on assets for both companies.
3. Calculate the cash flow to sales ratio and the asset turnover ratio for both companies.
4. Which company has the more favorable ratios?

P11–6B Refer to the information provided in P11–3B for Software Associates.

Calculate operating activities—direct method (LO11–7)

Required:

Prepare the operating activities section of the statement of cash flows for Software Associates using the *direct* method.

P11–7B Data for Virtual Gaming Systems are provided in P11–4B.

Calculate operating activities—direct method (LO11–7)

Required:

Prepare the statement of cash flows for Virtual Gaming Systems using the *direct* method. Disclose any noncash transactions in an accompanying note.

P11–8B Cash flows from operating activities for both the indirect and direct methods are presented for Electronic Transformations.

Prepare an income statement using operating cash flow information—indirect and direct methods (LO11–3, 11–7)

Cash Flows from Operating Activities (Indirect method)

Net income	$36,000	
Adjustments to reconcile net income to net cash flows from operating activities:		
Depreciation expense	9,000	
Increase in accounts receivable	(13,000)	
Increase in accounts payable	8,000	
Increase in income tax payable	6,000	
Net cash flows from operating activities		$46,000

Cash Flows from Operating Activities (Direct method)

Cash received from customers	$ 83,000	
Cash paid for operating expenses	(26,000)	
Cash paid for income taxes	(11,000)	
Net cash flows from operating activities		$46,000

Required:

Complete the following income statement for Electronic Transformations. Assume all accounts payable are to suppliers.

ELECTRONIC TRANSFORMATIONS **Income Statement** **For the year ended December 31, 2024**		
Net sales		$?
Expenses:		
Operating expenses	$?	
Depreciation expense	9,000	
Income tax expense	?	
Total expenses		?
Net income		$36,000

[*Hint:* Use the following calculations and work backwards from bottom (in red) to top for each item.]

Net sales	
± Change in accounts receivable	_____
= Cash received from customers	=========
Operating expenses	
± Change in accounts payable	_____
= Cash paid for operating expenses	=========
Income tax expense	
± Change in income tax payable	_____
= Cash paid for income taxes	=========

REAL-WORLD PERSPECTIVES

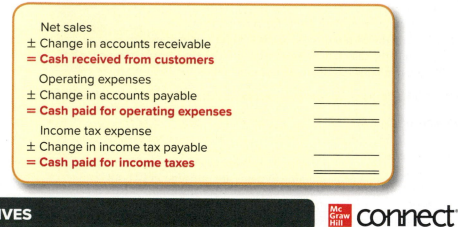

Data Analytics & Excel

Visit Connect to find a variety of Data Analytics questions that help build Excel, Tableau, and data visualization skills. Assignable materials include Integrated Excel, Applying Excel, Data Visualizations, Tableau Dashboard Activities, and Applying Tableau cases.

General Ledger Continuing Case

Great Adventures

(This is a continuation of the Great Adventures problem from earlier chapters.)

RWP11–1 The income statement, balance sheets, and additional information for Great Adventures, Inc., are provided below.

GREAT ADVENTURES, INC. **Income Statement** **For the year ended December 31, 2025**		
Net revenues:		$164,270
Expenses:		
Cost of goods sold	$38,500	
Operating expenses	51,400	
Depreciation expense	17,250	
Interest expense	6,785	
Income tax expense	14,500	
Total expenses		128,435
Net income		$ 35,835

GREAT ADVENTURES, INC.
Balance Sheets
December 31, 2025 and 2024

	2025	2024	Increase (I) or Decrease (D)
Assets			
Current assets:			
Cash	$ 180,568	$ 64,500	$ 116,068 (I)
Accounts receivable	47,600	0	47,600 (I)
Inventory	7,000	0	7,000 (I)
Other current assets	900	4,500	3,600 (D)
Long-term assets:			
Land	500,000	0	500,000 (I)
Buildings	800,000	0	800,000 (I)
Equipment	62,000	40,000	22,000 (I)
Accumulated depreciation	(25,250)	(8,000)	17,250 (I)
Total assets	$1,572,818	$101,000	
Liabilities and Stockholders' Equity			
Current liabilities:			
Accounts payable	$ 20,800	$ 2,800	$ 18,000 (I)
Interest payable	750	750	
Income tax payable	14,500	14,000	500 (I)
Other current liabilities	21,000	0	21,000 (I)
Notes payable (current and long-term)	523,883	30,000	493,883 (I)
Stockholders' equity:			
Common stock	120,000	20,000	100,000 (I)
Paid-in capital	904,000	0	904,000 (I)
Retained earnings	57,885	33,450	24,435 (I)
Treasury stock	(90,000)	0	(90,000) (I)
Total liabilities and stockholders' equity	$1,572,818	$101,000	

Additional Information for 2025:
1. Land of $500,000 was obtained by issuing a note payable to the seller.
2. Buildings of $800,000 and equipment of $22,000 were purchased using cash.
3. Monthly payments during the year reduced notes payable by $6,117.
4. Issued common stock for $1,000,000.
5. Purchased 10,000 shares of treasury stock for $15 per share.
6. Sold 4,000 shares of treasury stock at $16 per share.
7. Declared and paid a cash dividend of $11,400.

Required:
Prepare the statement of cash flows for the year ended December 31, 2025, using the *indirect* method.

American Eagle Outfitters, Inc.

Financial Analysis
Continuing Case

RWP11–2 Financial information for **American Eagle** is presented in **Appendix A** at the end of the book.

Required:
1. What was the amount of increase or decrease in cash and cash equivalents for the most recent year?

2. What was net cash from operating activities for the most recent year? Is net cash from operating activities increasing in the most recent year? What is the largest reconciling item between net income and net operating cash flows during the most recent year?
3. What was net cash from investing activities for the most recent year? What is the largest investing activity during the most recent year?
4. What was net cash from financing activities for the most recent year? What is the largest financing activity during the most recent year?

Financial Analysis Continuing Case

The Buckle, Inc.

RWP11–3 Financial information for **Buckle** is presented in **Appendix B** at the end of the book.

Required:

1. What was the amount of increase or decrease in cash and cash equivalents for the most recent year?
2. What was net cash from operating activities for the most recent year? Is net cash from operating activities increasing in the most recent year? What is the largest reconciling item between net income and net operating cash flows during the most recent year?
3. What was net cash from investing activities for the most recent year? What is the largest investing activity during the most recent year?
4. What was net cash from financing activities for the most recent year? What is the largest financing activity during the most recent year?

Comparative Analysis Continuing Case

American Eagle Outfitters, Inc. vs. The Buckle, Inc.

RWP11–4 Financial information for **American Eagle** is presented in **Appendix A** at the end of the book, and financial information for **Buckle** is presented in **Appendix B** at the end of the book.

Required:

1. Calculate American Eagle's cash return on assets, cash flow to sales, and asset turnover ratio.
2. Calculate Buckle's cash return on assets, cash flow to sales, and asset turnover ratio.
3. Which company is doing better based on cash return on assets? Which company has the higher cash flow to sales? Which company has the higher asset turnover?

EDGAR Research

RWP11–5 Using EDGAR (Electronic Data Gathering, Analysis, and Retrieval system), find the annual report (10-K) for **Alphabet Inc.** for the year ended **December 31, 2019.** Locate the "Consolidated Statements of Cash Flows" and the "Consolidated Balance Sheets." You may also find the annual report at the company's website.

Required:

1. The following items were reported in the most recent year. Determine whether each item is reported in the operating, investing or financing activities section of the statement of cash flows:
   a. Changes in accounts receivable
   b. Repayments of debt
   c. Purchase of property and equipment
   d. Maturities and sales of marketable securities
   e. Depreciation
2. Which is greater—net income or operating cash flows? By how much?
3. What is the company's largest cash *outflow* from investing activities in the most recent year?
4. What is the company's largest cash *outflow* from financing activities in the most recent year?
5. What is the total change in cash from operating, investing and financing activities? Identify the amount of cash reported in the balance sheet for the most recent year and the previous year. Does the change in the cash balance equal the change in cash reported in the statement of cash flows?

Ethics

RWP11–6 Aggressive Corporation approaches Matt Taylor, a loan officer for Oklahoma State Bank, seeking to increase the company's borrowings with the bank from $100,000 to $200,000. Matt has an uneasy feeling as he examines the loan application from Aggressive Corporation, which just completed its first year of operations. The application included the following financial statements.

AGGRESSIVE CORPORATION
Income Statement
For the year ended December 31, 2024

Net sales		$275,000
Expenses:		
Cost of goods sold	$150,000	
Operating expenses	50,000	
Depreciation expense	10,000	
Total expenses		210,000
Net income		$ 65,000

AGGRESSIVE CORPORATION
Balance Sheets
December 31, 2024

	2024	2023
Assets		
Current assets:		
Cash	$150,000	$0
Accounts receivable	0	0
Inventory	0	0
Long-term assets:		
Equipment	160,000	0
Accumulated depreciation	(10,000)	0
Total assets	$300,000	$0
Liabilities and Stockholders' Equity		
Current liabilities:		
Accounts payable	$ 25,000	$0
Interest payable	10,000	0
Long-term liabilities:		
Note payable	100,000	0
Stockholders' equity:		
Common stock	100,000	0
Retained earnings	65,000	0
Total liabilities and stockholders' equity	$300,000	$0

Matt notices that the company has no ending accounts receivable and no ending inventory, which seems suspicious. Matt is also wondering why a company with $150,000 in cash is seeking an additional $100,000 in borrowing.

Seeing Matt's hesitation, Larry Bling, the CEO of Aggressive Corporation, closes the conference room door. He shares with Matt the following additional information:

- The ending accounts receivable balance is actually $60,000, but because those accounts are expected to be collected very soon, I assumed a balance of $0 and counted those receivables as cash collected.

- The ending inventory balance is actually $40,000, but I believe that inventory can easily be sold for $75,000 in the near future. So, I included sales revenue of $75,000 (and cost of goods of $40,000) in the income statement and cash collected of $75,000 (and no inventory) in the balance sheet.

Plus, Larry tells Matt that he'll be looking for a new CFO in another year to run Aggressive Corporation, along with his other businesses, and Matt is just the kind of guy he is looking for. Larry mentions that as CFO, Matt would receive a significant salary. Matt is flattered and says he will look over the loan application and get back to Larry concerning the additional $100,000 loan by the end of the week.

Required:

1. Understand the reporting effect: Calculate operating cash flows using the financial statements provided by Larry.
2. Specify the options: Calculate operating cash flows without the two assumptions made by Larry.
3. Identify the impact: Could Larry's assumptions affect Matt's decision for the bank to lend an additional $100,000 to Larry?
4. Make a decision: Should Matt use Larry's assumption in analyzing the loan for Aggressive Corporation?

Written Communication

RWP11–7 "Why can't we pay our shareholders a dividend?" shouts your new boss at Polar Opposites. "This income statement you prepared for me says we earned $5 million in our first year!" You recently prepared the financial statements below.

POLAR OPPOSITES
Income Statement
For the year ended December 31, 2024

	($ in millions)
Net sales	$65
Cost of goods sold	(35)
Depreciation expense	(4)
Operating expenses	(21)
Net income	$ 5

POLAR OPPOSITES
Balance Sheet
December 31, 2024

	($ in millions)
Cash	$ 1
Accounts receivable (net)	16
Merchandise inventory	14
Machinery (net)	44
Total assets	$75
Accounts payable	$ 7
Accrued expenses payable	9
Notes payable	29
Common stock	25
Retained earnings	5
Total liabilities and stockholders' equity	$75

Although net income was $5 million, cash flow from operating activities was a negative $5 million. This just didn't make any sense to your boss.

Required:

Prepare a memo explaining how net income could be positive and operating cash flows negative. Include in your report a determination of operating cash flows of negative $5 million using the *indirect* method.

Earnings Management

RWP11–8 Bryan Eubank began his accounting career as an auditor for a Big 4 CPA firm. He focused on clients in the high-technology sector, becoming an expert on topics such as inventory write-downs, stock options, and business acquisitions. Impressed with his technical skills and experience, General Electronics, a large consumer electronics chain, hired Bryan as the company controller responsible for all of the accounting functions within the corporation. Bryan was excited about his new position. To better understand the company's financial position, he began by making the following comparison over time ($ in millions):

	2024	2023	2022	2021
Operating income	$1,400	$1,320	$1,275	$1,270
Net income	385	350	345	295
Cash flows from operations	16	110	120	155

Bryan also noticed a couple of other items:

a. The company's credit policy has been loosened, credit terms relaxed, and payment periods lengthened. This has resulted in a large increase in accounts receivable.

b. Several of the company's salary arrangements, including that of the CEO and CFO, are based on reported net income.

Required:

1. What effect does relaxing credit terms and lengthening payment periods likely have on the balance of accounts receivable? Does the change in accounts receivable affect net income differently than operating cash flows?

2. Do salary arrangements for officers, such as the CEO and CFO, increase the risk of earnings management?

3. What trend in the information could be a source of concern for Bryan?

Answers to Chapter Framework Questions

1. a   2. b   3. b   4. c   5. a

Answers to Self-Study Questions

1. b   2. c   3. c   4. b   5. d   6. a   7. c   8. b   9. d   10. c   11. a   12. b   13. d   14. c   15. b

Financial Statement Analysis

PART A: COMPARISON OF FINANCIAL ACCOUNTING INFORMATION

- **LO12–1** Perform vertical analysis.
- **LO12–2** Perform horizontal analysis.

PART B: USING RATIOS TO ASSESS RISK AND PROFITABILITY

- **LO12–3** Use ratios to analyze a company's risk.
- **LO12–4** Use ratios to analyze a company's profitability.

PART C: EARNINGS PERSISTENCE AND EARNINGS QUALITY

- **LO12–5** Distinguish persistent earnings from one-time items.
- **LO12–6** Distinguish between conservative and aggressive accounting practices.

SELF-STUDY MATERIALS

- Let's Review—Horizontal analysis (p. 606).
- Let's Review—Risk ratios (p. 613).
- Let's Review—Profitability ratios (p. 618).
- Let's Review—Conservative or aggressive accounting practices (p. 626).
- Chapter Framework with questions and answers available (p. 627).
- Key Points by Learning Objective (p. 628).
- Glossary of Key Terms (p. 628).
- Self-Study Questions with answers available (p. 629).
- Videos including Concept Overview, Applying Excel, Let's Review, and Interactive Illustrations to demonstrate key topics (in Connect).

VF CORPORATION: MAKING THE COMPETITION SWEAT

VF Corporation's (simply VF hereafter) desire is to outfit the world. The company was founded in 1899 as the Reading Glove and Mitten Manufacturing Company. It was rebranded to Vanity Fair in 1910, and has since grown into a massive conglomerate of some of the world's most recognizable brands, including Vans, The North Face, and Timberland.

VF's first major acquisition occurred in the 1960s when it acquired Lee Brands in an effort to diversify its product line. This acquisition prompted another name change to VF Corporation. Additional acquisitions were made over the next 50 years. The company's most recent acquisition was Altra, which designs and manufactures high-performance running shoes. In total, VF boasts 19 distinct brands in its portfolio.

Feature Story

VF's growth strategy over the years has relied on acquisitions. This is a common feature in the shoe and apparel industry. One of VF's primary competitors, **Nike**, has also acquired a few brands over the years (such as Converse and Hurley), but not nearly to the same extent as VF. Nike is almost four times the size of VF, and, for the most part, Nike has largely relied on organic growth to grow its business. Given the differences in size of these two companies, how do we compare their financial performance?

In this chapter, we'll use financial analysis tools to analyze financial statements—the same statements you've learned to prepare in the preceding chapters. The techniques we introduce here—such as vertical analysis, horizontal analysis, and ratio analysis—help in evaluating the growth and performance of companies such as VF and comparing them to competitors like Nike.

At the end of the chapter, we provide examples of conservative and aggressive accounting practices. Accounting is not black and white. Many accounting decisions fall into a gray area subject to potential earnings manipulation and biases of managers.

Top left: Soundaholic studio/Shutterstock; Top right: Andrew Resek/McGraw Hill; Middle: Pegasus Pics/Shutterstock

Tetra Images/Alamy Stock Photo

COMPARISON OF FINANCIAL ACCOUNTING INFORMATION

We use ratios to make comparisons every day. Consider major sports. Batting averages provide feedback in baseball about how well a player is hitting. Basketball and football use points per game to compare teams' offensive and defensive performance. In each case, the ratio is more meaningful than a single number by itself. For example, are 100 hits in baseball a good number? It depends on the number of at-bats.

Likewise, we can use ratios to help evaluate a firm's performance and financial position. Is net income of $10 million a cause for shareholders to celebrate? Probably not, because if shareholders' equity is $1 billion, $10 million is then only a 1% return on equity. But if shareholders' equity is $20 million, net income of $10 million is a 50% return on equity and definitely something to celebrate. Ratios are most useful when compared to some standard. That standard of comparison may be the performance of another company, last year's performance by the same company, or the average performance of companies in the same industry. Illustration 12–1 provides a summary of these three different types of comparisons.

ILLUSTRATION 12–1   Three Types of Comparisons

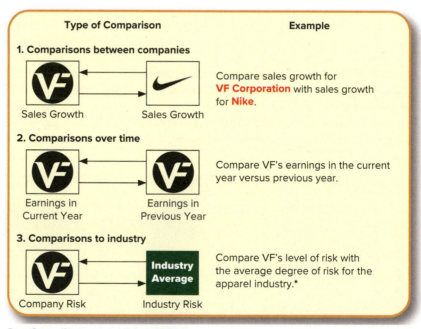

Rose Carson/Shutterstock; VF Corporation

*Industry averages can be obtained from websites such as Yahoo! Finance or from financial ratings agencies such as Dun & Bradstreet, Moody's, and Standard & Poor's.

When doing financial statement analysis, it's always important to learn about the company and its history and to let ratios guide further questioning about items. This will typically lead to further research before making final decisions about a company. In this chapter, we'll calculate ratios commonly used as bases for exploring financial statements and understanding company strategies.

Vertical Analysis

■ **LO12–1**
Perform vertical analysis.

Common Terms Vertical analysis is also known as *common-size analysis.*

In performing **vertical analysis**, we express each item in a financial statement as a percentage of the same base amount measured in the same period. For instance, we can express each line item in an income statement as a percentage of sales. In a balance sheet, we can express each item as a percentage of total assets. Let's look at an example to see the benefits of vertical analysis.

VF AND NIKE Common-Size Income Statements For the years ended March 31, 2020, and May 31, 2020 ($ in millions)				
	VF		**NIKE**	
	Amount	**%**	**Amount**	**%**
Net sales	$10,489	**100.0**	$37,403	**100.0**
Cost of goods sold	4,691	**44.7**	21,162	**56.6**
Gross profit	5,798	**55.3**	16,241	**43.4**
Operating expenses	4,870	**46.4**	13,126	**35.1**
Operating income	928	**8.8**	3,115	**8.3**
Other income (expenses)	(201)	**(1.9)**	(228)	**(0.6)**
Income before tax	727	**6.9**	2,887	**7.7**
Income tax expense	98	**0.9**	348	**0.9**
Net income	$ 629	**6.0**	$ 2,539	**6.8**

ILLUSTRATION 12–2

Common-Size Income Statements

The red arrow indicates the direction in which to read this statement.

VERTICAL ANALYSIS OF THE INCOME STATEMENT

Illustration 12–2 provides common-size income statements for VF and Nike. Notice that the two companies end their fiscal years on different dates. VF's year-end is March 31 while Nike's is May 31. Even though the year-ends do not exactly match, we can still make meaningful comparisons between the two companies.

What do we learn from this comparison? Nike reports much higher net income. Does this mean Nike's operations are much more profitable than VF's? Not necessarily. Nike is a much larger company, reporting sales of almost four times that of VF. Because of its greater size, we expect Nike to report a greater *amount* of net income. To better compare the performance of the two companies, we use vertical analysis to express each income statement item as a *percentage of sales.*

VF's gross profit equals 55.3% of sales ($5,798 ÷ $10,489) compared to Nike's 43.4%. This means that VF earns a higher gross profit for each dollar of sales, consistent with its business strategy of focusing on high-quality performance apparel. However, VF's higher gross profit is offset by its proportionately higher operating expenses, 46.4% of sales compared to 35.1% for Nike. The net result is that operating income, as a percentage of sales, is about the same for the two companies. Finally, Nike's net income, as a percentage of sales, slightly exceeds VF's.

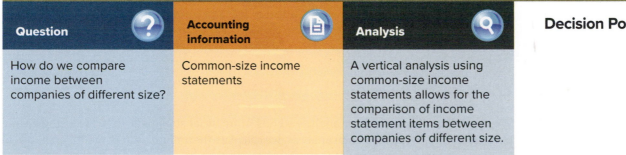

Decision Point

Question	Accounting information	Analysis
How do we compare income between companies of different size?	Common-size income statements	A vertical analysis using common-size income statements allows for the comparison of income statement items between companies of different size.

VERTICAL ANALYSIS OF THE BALANCE SHEET

Vertical analysis of the balance sheet is useful, too. For this, we divide each balance sheet item by total assets to get an idea of its relative significance. Illustration 12–3 provides common-size balance sheets for VF and Nike.

ILLUSTRATION 12–3

Common-Size Balance Sheets

The red arrow indicates the direction in which to read this statement.

	VF		NIKE	
	Amount	**%**	**Amount**	**%**
Assets				
Current assets	$ 5,027	45.2	$20,556	65.6
Property and equipment	954	8.6	4,866	15.5
Intangible assets	3,011	27.0	497	1.6
Other assets	2,141	19.2	5,423	17.3
Total assets	$11,133	100.0	$31,342	100.0
Liabilities and Stockholders' Equity				
Current liabilities	$ 3,024	27.2	$ 8,284	26.4
Long-term liabilities	4,752	42.7	15,003	47.9
Stockholders' equity	3,357	30.2	8,055	25.7
Total liabilities and equities	$11,133	100.0	$31,342	100.0

VF AND NIKE
Common-Size Balance Sheets
March 31, 2020, and May 31, 2020
($ in millions)

What can we learn by analyzing the common-size balance sheets? Focusing on the asset portion of the balance sheet, we discover that VF has a lower percentage of current assets and property, plant, and equipment, and a higher percentage of intangible assets than does Nike. These differences are consistent with the differences in the companies' growth strategies. VF is a conglomerate of companies that have been acquired over the years. As we discussed in Chapter 7, acquisitions often result in the recording of Goodwill, and intangible assets.

Looking at liabilities and stockholders' equity, we see little difference between the two companies. Later in Part B, we'll examine the current ratio and acid-test ratio to better understand the companies' ability to pay current liabilities with current assets. Both companies maintain similar proportions of liabilities and are financed approximately equally by equity and debt, suggesting they have a similar **capital structure**, although Nike is slightly more debt-financed.

KEY POINT

For vertical analysis, we express each item as a percentage of the same base amount, such as a percentage of sales in the income statement or as a percentage of total assets in the balance sheet.

Horizontal Analysis

■ **LO12–2**
Perform horizontal analysis.

Common Terms
Horizontal analysis is also known as *trend analysis* or *time-series analysis.*

We use **horizontal analysis** to analyze trends in financial statement data for a single company over time. With horizontal analysis, we calculate the amount and percentage change in an account from last year to this year. This data can then be used to compare rates of change across accounts. Are sales growing faster than cost of goods sold? Are operating expenses growing faster than sales? Are any specific expenses increasing at a greater rate than others? Questions such as these can help identify areas of concern or, perhaps, indications of better things to come.

HORIZONTAL ANALYSIS OF THE INCOME STATEMENT

Illustration 12–4 provides income statements over two years for VF. The final two columns show the dollar amount and percentage changes.

VF Income Statements For the years ended March 31 ($ in millions)				
	Year		**Increase (Decrease)**	
	2020	**2019**	**Amount**	**%**
Net sales	$10,489	$10,267	$ 222	2.2
Cost of goods sold	4,691	4,656	35	0.8
Gross profit	5,798	5,611	187	3.3
Operating expenses	4,870	4,421	449	10.2
Operating income	928	1,190	(262)	(22.0)
Other income (expenses)	(201)	(152)	49	(32.2)
Income before tax	727	1,038	(311)	(30.0)
Income tax expense	98	168	(70)	(41.7)
Net income	$ 629	$ 870	$ (241)	(27.7)

ILLUSTRATION 12–4

Horizontal Analysis of VF's Income Statements

The red arrow indicates the direction in which to read this statement.

We calculate the *amount* of the increases or decreases by simply subtracting the 2019 balance from the 2020 balance. A positive difference indicates the amount increased in 2020. A negative amount represents a decrease. We calculate the *percentage* increase or decrease based on the following formula:

$$\% \text{ Increase (Decrease)} = \frac{\text{Current-year amount} - \text{Prior-year amount}}{\text{Prior-year amount}}$$

In our example, the calculation would be

$$\% \text{ Increase (Decrease)} = \frac{\text{2020 amount} - \text{2019 amount}}{\text{2019 amount}}$$

For example, the *amount* of sales increased $222 million—equal to sales of $10,489 million in 2020 minus sales of $10,267 million in 2019. We calculate the percentage increase of 2.2% by dividing the $222 million increase in sales by 2019 sales of $10,267 million. If the base-year amount (2019 in our example) is ever zero, we can't calculate a percentage for that item.

The horizontal analysis demonstrates that while sales increased slightly, there was a decrease in profitability overall. You can see that the decrease is the result of an increase in operating expenses. Most of this was a goodwill impairment charge related to VF's Timberland operations.

HORIZONTAL ANALYSIS OF THE BALANCE SHEET

Illustration 12–5 provides balance sheet information for VF. The horizontal analysis of VF's balance sheet further reflects its growth in operations during the year. Total assets grew by 7.5%. Much of that growth was funded through additional liabilities. The decline in total stockholders' equity is attributable to a decrease in retained earnings. The decline in retained earnings occurred because the amount of dividends and repurchased stock far exceeded the amount of net income.

ILLUSTRATION 12–5

Horizontal Analysis of
VF's Balance Sheets

The red arrow indicates
the direction in which to
read this statement.

	VF **Balance Sheets** **March 31** **($ in millions)**			
	Year		**Increase (Decrease)**	
	2020	**2019**	**Amount**	**%**
Assets				
Current assets	$ 5,027	$ 4,673	$ 354	7.6
Property and equipment	954	876	78	8.9
Intangible assets	3,011	3,399	(388)	(11.4)
Other assets	2,141	1,409	732	52.0
Total assets	$11,133	$10,357	$ 776	7.5
Liabilities and Stockholders' Equity				
Current liabilities	$ 3,024	$ 2,662	$ 362	13.6
Long-term liabilities	4,752	3,396	1,356	39.9
Stockholders' equity	3,357	4,299	(942)	(21.9)
Total liabilities and equities	$11,133	$10,357	$ 776	7.5

KEY POINT

We use horizontal analysis to analyze trends in financial statement data, such as the amount
of change and the percentage change, for one company over time.

Let's Review

The income statements for **Nike** for the years ending May 31, 2020 and 2019, are as follows:

	NIKE **Income Statements** **For the years ended May 31** **($ in millions)**			
			Increase (Decrease)	
	2020	**2019**	**Amount**	**%**
Net sales	$37,403	$39,117		
Cost of goods sold	21,162	21,643		
Gross profit	16,241	17,474		
Operating expenses	13,126	12,702		
Operating income	3,115	4,772		
Other income	(228)	29		
Income before tax	2,887	4,801		
Income tax expense	348	772		
Net income	$ 2,539	$ 4,029		

Required:

Complete the "Amount" and "%" columns in a horizontal analysis of Nike's income statements. Discuss the meaning of the major fluctuations during the year.

Solution:

NIKE Income Statements For the years ended May 31 ($ in millions)			Increase (Decrease)	
	2020	**2019**	**Amount**	**%**
Net sales	$37,403	$39,117	(1,714)	(4.4)
Cost of goods sold	21,162	21,643	(481)	(2.2)
Gross profit	16,241	17,474	(1,233)	(7.1)
Operating expenses	13,126	12,702	424	3.3
Operating income	3,115	4,772	(1,657)	(34.7)
Other income (expenses)	(228)	29	(257)	(886.2)
Income before tax	2,887	4,801	(1,914)	(39.9)
Income tax expense	348	772	(424)	(54.9)
Net income	$ 2,539	$ 4,029	(1,490)	(37.0)

All amounts for Nike declined in 2020 except for operating expenses. Nike's year end was May 31, 2020, approximately three months after the outbreak of COVID-19 in the United States. These three months were severely impacted, as most individuals sheltered in place and businesses shut down. Thus, the decrease in operations and profitability was normal for many companies at this time.

Suggested Homework:
**BE12–1, BE12–2;
E12–2, E12–3;
P12–2A&B, P12–3A&B**

USING RATIOS TO ASSESS RISK AND PROFITABILITY

PART B

Beginning in Chapter 4, we provided an example of ratio analysis between two competing companies at the end of each chapter. Let's now apply what we learned in those separate ratio analyses in a detailed examination of **VF**, comparing the results to the sports apparel industry leader—**Nike**. The income statement and balance sheet for VF are presented in Illustration 12–6.

We'll review ratios classified into two categories: risk ratios and profitability ratios. When calculating ratios, remember how income statement accounts differ from balance sheet accounts: We measure income statement accounts over a *period* of time (like a video).

⊗ COMMON MISTAKE

In comparing an income statement account with a balance sheet account, some students incorrectly use the balance sheet account's ending balance, rather than the *average* of its beginning and ending balances. Since income statement accounts are measured over a period of time, comparisons to related balance sheet accounts also need to be over time by taking the average of the beginning and ending balances.

ILLUSTRATION 12–6

VF's Financial
Statements

VF
Income Statement
For the year ended March 31, 2020
($ in millions)

	2020
Net sales	$10,489
Cost of goods sold	4,691
Gross profit	5,798
Operating expenses	4,870
Operating income	928
Other expense	$ (201)
Income before tax	727
Income tax expense	98
Net income	$ 629

*Other expense includes interest expense of $92 million

VF
Balance Sheets
March 31
($ in millions)

	2020	2019
Assets		
Current assets:		
Cash	$ 1,369	$ 402
Net receivables	1,308	1,373
Inventory	1,294	1,173
Other current assets	1,056	1,725
Total current assets	5,027	4,673
Property and equipment	954	876
Intangible assets	3,011	3,399
Other assets	2,141	1,409
Total assets	$11,133	$10,357
Liabilities and Stockholders' Equity		
Current liabilities	$ 3,024	$ 2,662
Long-term liabilities	4,752	3,396
Stockholders' equity	3,357	4,299
Total liabilities and stockholders' equity	$11,133	$10,357

We measure balance sheet accounts at a *point* in time (like a photograph). Therefore, ratios that compare an income statement account with a balance sheet account should express the balance sheet account as an *average* of the beginning and ending balances.

Risk Analysis

■ **LO12–3**

Use ratios to analyze a company's risk.

Illustration 12–7 summarizes eight risk ratios, the chapters in which we discussed them, and how they're calculated. We divide the eight risk ratios into six liquidity ratios and two solvency ratios. **Liquidity** refers to having sufficient cash (or other assets readily convertible into cash) to pay its *current* liabilities. The accounts used to calculate liquidity ratios are located in the current assets and current liabilities sections of the balance sheet. **Solvency** refers to a company's ability to pay all its liabilities, which includes *long-term* liabilities as well.

Let's calculate each of the eight risk ratios for VF and then compare the results with Nike's. **We show the detailed calculations for Nike in a review problem at the end of this section.**

RECEIVABLES TURNOVER RATIO

The **receivables turnover ratio** measures how many times, on average, a company collects its receivables during the year. A low receivables turnover ratio may indicate that the company is having trouble collecting its accounts receivable. This often occurs when a company loosens its credit terms to generate additional sales. A high receivables turnover ratio is a positive sign that a company can quickly turn its receivables into cash. Illustration 12–8 shows the calculation of the receivables turnover ratio for VF and compares it to Nike's.

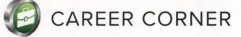

CAREER CORNER

Investors and creditors, as well as suppliers, customers, employees, and the government, among others, rely heavily on financial accounting information. Who checks big companies like VF and Nike to make sure they are reporting accurately? Auditors. Many accounting majors begin their careers in auditing. They then use the experience they gain in auditing to obtain management and accounting positions in private industry, sometimes even with a company they previously audited.

However, auditing is not just for accounting majors. Finance majors are hired as auditors in the banking and insurance industries. Management information systems (MIS) majors are hired to audit computer systems. Management majors are hired to audit the effectiveness and efficiency of management operations. There even are marketing auditors who identify strengths and weaknesses in marketing strategy and overall marketing structures.[1] Analysis skills, like those covered in this chapter, are the types of skills necessary for a successful career in auditing, and for that matter, in almost any career in business.

ridvan celik/Getty Images

ILLUSTRATION 12–7   Risk Ratios

Risk Ratios	Chapter	Calculations
Liquidity		
Receivables turnover ratio	5	$\dfrac{\text{Net credit sales}}{\text{Average accounts receivable}}$
Average collection period	5	$\dfrac{\text{365 days}}{\text{Receivables turnover ratio}}$
Inventory turnover ratio	6	$\dfrac{\text{Cost of goods sold}}{\text{Average inventory}}$
Average days in inventory	6	$\dfrac{\text{365 days}}{\text{Inventory turnover ratio}}$
Current ratio	8	$\dfrac{\text{Current assets}}{\text{Current liabilities}}$
Acid-test ratio	8	$\dfrac{\text{Cash + Current investments + Accounts receivable}}{\text{Current liabilities}}$
Solvency		
Debt to equity ratio	9	$\dfrac{\text{Total liabilities}}{\text{Stockholders' equity}}$
Times interest earned ratio	9	$\dfrac{\text{Net income + Interest expense + Income tax expense}}{\text{Interest expense}}$

---

[1]J. Mylonakis. 2003. "Functions and Responsibilities of Marketing Auditors in Measuring Organizational Performance." *International Journal of Technology Management 25,* no. 8, pp. 814–25.

ILLUSTRATION 12–8

Receivables Turnover Ratio

Receivables Turnover Ratio	VF	Nike
$\dfrac{\text{Net credit sales}}{\text{Average accounts receivable}}$	$\dfrac{\$10,489}{(\$1,308 + \$1,373)/2} = 7.8 \text{ times}$	10.7 times

In calculating the receivables turnover ratio, we have assumed that VF's sales are all credit sales. (VF does not usually sell directly to customers, but to retailers such as **Dick's Sporting Goods**.) Most companies don't separately report their credit sales. The bottom half of the fraction is the *average* accounts receivable during the year, calculated as beginning receivables plus ending receivables divided by two. VF's receivables turnover ratio is 7.8, indicating that receivables turn over (are collected) 7.8 times per year. This is lower than Nike's receivables turnover ratio of 10.7.

AVERAGE COLLECTION PERIOD

We often convert the receivables turnover ratio into days and call it the **average collection period**. The shorter the average collection period, the better. Illustration 12–9 displays the average collection period for VF and Nike.

ILLUSTRATION 12–9

Average Collection Period

Average Collection Period	VF	Nike
$\dfrac{365 \text{ days}}{\text{Receivables turnover ratio}}$	$\dfrac{365}{7.8} = 46.8 \text{ days}$	34.1 days

VF's average collection period of 46.8 days is 365 days divided by the receivables turn-over ratio of 7.8. It takes VF an average of over one month (46.8 days) to collect its accounts receivable. Nike's average collection period, at 34.1 days, indicates that it receives cash more quickly from customers.

INVENTORY TURNOVER RATIO

The **inventory turnover ratio** measures how many times, on average, a company sells its entire inventory during the year. A high inventory turnover ratio usually is a positive sign. It indicates that inventory is selling quickly, less cash is tied up in inventory, and the risk of outdated inventory is lower. However, an extremely high inventory turnover ratio might be a signal that the company is losing sales due to inventory shortages. Illustration 12–10 provides the inventory turnover ratios for VF and Nike.

ILLUSTRATION 12–10

Inventory Turnover Ratio

Inventory Turnover Ratio	VF	Nike
$\dfrac{\text{Cost of goods sold}}{\text{Average inventory}}$	$\dfrac{\$4,691}{(\$1,294 + \$1,173)/2} = 3.8 \text{ times}$	3.3 times

Inventory at VF turns over, on average, 3.8 times per year compared to 3.3 times per year at Nike. The slower inventory turnover at Nike is a negative sign, indicating a greater risk of slow-moving inventory items, although the two ratios do not differ much.

AVERAGE DAYS IN INVENTORY

We can convert the inventory turnover ratio into days and call it the **average days in inventory**. As you can imagine, companies try to minimize the number of days they hold inventory. We calculate the average days in inventory in Illustration 12–11.

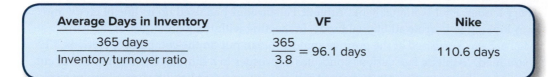

Average Days in Inventory	VF	Nike
$\dfrac{365 \text{ days}}{\text{Inventory turnover ratio}}$	$\dfrac{365}{3.8} = 96.1 \text{ days}$	110.6 days

ILLUSTRATION 12–11

Average Days in Inventory

VF's average days in inventory is 96.1 days, calculated as 365 days divided by the inventory turnover ratio of 3.8. In comparison, Nike's average days in inventory is higher at 110.6 days.

Inventory turnover ratios and the resulting average days in inventory vary significantly by industry. For example, compared with the sporting goods apparel industry, the dairy industry with its perishable products has a much higher inventory turnover, and car dealerships have a lower inventory turnover. Inventory turnover might even vary by product within the same industry. For instance, within the dairy industry, the inventory turnover for milk is much higher than that for aged cheddar cheese. Similarly, within the auto industry, the inventory turnover for cars like the Toyota Corolla is much higher than for the higher-priced Toyota Land Cruiser.

CURRENT RATIO

The current ratio compares current assets to current liabilities. It's probably the most widely used of all liquidity ratios. A high current ratio indicates that a company has sufficient current assets to pay current liabilities as they become due. Illustration 12–12 presents the current ratios for VF and Nike.

Current Ratio	VF	Nike
$\dfrac{\text{Current assets}}{\text{Current liabilities}}$	$\dfrac{\$5,027}{\$3,024} = 1.7 \text{ to } 1$	2.5 to 1

ILLUSTRATION 12–12

Current Ratio

VF's current ratio of 1.7 means the firm has $1.70 in current assets for each $1 in current liabilities. Nike has a much higher current ratio. A company needs to maintain sufficient current assets to pay current liabilities as they become due. Thus, a higher current ratio usually indicates less risk.

However, a high current ratio is not always a good signal. A high current ratio might occur when a company has difficulty collecting receivables or carries too much inventory. Analysts become concerned if a company reports an increasing current ratio combined with either a lower receivables turnover ratio or a lower inventory turnover ratio.

ETHICAL DILEMMA

fizkes/Shutterstock

Michael Hechtner was recently hired as an assistant controller for Athletic Persuasions, a recognized leader in the promotion of athletic events. However, the past year has been a difficult one for the company's operations. In order to help with slowing sales, the company has extended credit to more customers and accepted payment over longer time periods, resulting in a significant increase in accounts receivable. Similarly, with slowing sales, its inventory of promotional supplies has increased dramatically.

One afternoon, Michael joined the controller, J.P. Sloan, for a visit with their primary lender, First National Bank. Athletic Persuasions had used up its line of credit and was looking to borrow additional funds. In meeting with the loan officer at the bank, Michael was surprised at the positive spin J.P. Sloan put on the company operations. J.P. exclaimed, "Athletic Persuasions continues to prosper in a difficult environment. Our current assets have significantly increased in relation to current liabilities, resulting in a much improved current ratio over the prior year. It seems wherever I look, the company has been successful."

Is there anything unethical in the controller's statement to the banker? What should Michael do in this situation? Is it acceptable for Michael just to keep quiet?

ACID-TEST RATIO

The **acid-test ratio** is similar to the current ratio but is a more conservative measure of current assets available to pay current liabilities. Specifically, the top part of the fraction includes only cash, current investments, and accounts receivable. Because it eliminates current assets such as inventories and prepaid expenses that are less readily convertible into cash, the acid-test ratio often provides a better indication of a company's liquidity than does the current ratio. We calculate the acid-test ratio in Illustration 12–13.

ILLUSTRATION 12–13

Acid-Test Ratio

Acid-Test Ratio	VF	Nike
$\dfrac{\text{Cash + Current investments + Accounts receivable}}{\text{Current liabilities}}$	$\dfrac{\$1{,}369 + \$0 + \$1{,}308}{\$3{,}024} = 0.9 \text{ to } 1$	1.4 to 1

VF did not report any current investments, so a $0 is recorded for current investments in the top part of the fraction. VF's acid-test ratio is 0.9 and does not compare favorably with Nike's ratio of 1.4.

DEBT TO EQUITY RATIO

The first six ratios we covered relate to liquidity, or a company's ability to pay its current liabilities. The final two ratios we cover (debt to equity and times interest earned) relate to solvency, or a company's ability to pay its long-term liabilities as well.

Other things being equal, the higher the **debt to equity ratio**, the higher the risk of bankruptcy. The reason is that, unlike shareholders, debt holders have the ability to force a company into bankruptcy for failing to pay interest or repay the debt in a timely manner. Illustration 12–14 shows the calculation of the debt to equity ratio for VF and Nike.

ILLUSTRATION 12–14

Debt to Equity Ratio

Debt to Equity Ratio	VF	Nike
$\dfrac{\text{Total liabilities}}{\text{Stockholders' equity}}$	$\dfrac{\$3{,}024 + \$4{,}752}{\$3{,}357} = 231.6\%$	289.1%

VF has a debt to equity ratio of 231.6%, or about $2.32 in liabilities for each $1 in stockholders' equity. Nike's debt to equity ratio is higher, at 289.1%.

Additional debt can be good for investors, as long as a company earns a return on borrowed funds in excess of interest costs. However, taking on additional debt can also be bad for investors, if interest costs exceed a company's return on borrowed funds. This highlights the risk-return trade-off of debt. More debt increases the risk of bankruptcy, but it also increases the potential returns investors can enjoy.

TIMES INTEREST EARNED RATIO

We use the **times interest earned ratio** to compare interest payments with a company's income available to pay those charges. Interest payments are more often associated with long-term liabilities than with current liabilities such as wages, taxes, and utilities. That's why we classify this ratio as a solvency ratio rather than a liquidity ratio.

We calculate the times interest earned ratio by dividing net income *before* interest expense and income taxes by interest expense. To get to this amount, we just add interest expense and income tax expense back to net income. We use net income before interest expense and income taxes as a reliable indicator of the amount available to pay the interest. Illustration 12–15 shows how the ratio is calculated.

ILLUSTRATION 12–15

Times Interest Earned Ratio

Times Interest Earned Ratio	VF	Nike
$\dfrac{\text{Net income} + \text{Interest expense} + \text{Income tax expense}}{\text{Interest expense}}$	$\dfrac{\$629 + \$92 + \$98}{\$92} = 8.9$ times	20.1 times

The times interest earned ratio for VF is 8.9. That means VF's net income before interest and taxes was 8.9 times the amount it needed for interest expense alone. In comparison, Nike has an even better times interest earned ratio of 20.1. Both VF and Nike generate more than enough income to cover their interest payments.

 KEY POINT

We categorize risk ratios into liquidity ratios and solvency ratios. Liquidity ratios focus on the company's ability to pay *current* liabilities, whereas solvency ratios include *long-term* liabilities as well.

The income statement and balance sheets for **Nike** are shown below.

Let's Review

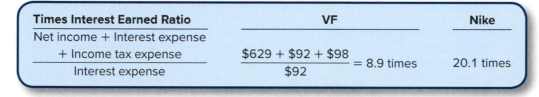

NIKE Income Statement For the year ended May 31, 2020 ($ in millions)	
Net sales	$37,403
Cost of goods sold	21,162
Gross profit	16,241
Operating expenses	13,126
Operating income	3,115
Other income	$ (228)
Income before tax	2,887
Income tax expense	348
Net income	$ 2,539

*Includes interest expense of $151 million

NIKE Balance Sheets May 31 ($ in millions)	2020	2019
Assets		
Current assets:		
Cash	$ 8,348	$ 4,466
Current investments	439	197
Net receivables	2,749	4,272
Inventory	7,367	5,622
Other current assets	1,653	1,968
Total current assets	20,556	16,525
Property and equipment	4,866	4,744
Intangible assets	497	437
Other assets	5,423	2,011
Total assets	$31,342	$23,717
Liabilities and Stockholders' Equity		
Current liabilities	$ 8,284	$ 7,866
Long-term liabilities	15,003	6,811
Stockholders' equity	8,055	9,040
Total liabilities and stockholders' equity	$31,342	$23,717

Required:

Calculate the eight risk ratios we've discussed for Nike for the year ended May 31, 2020.

Solution:

Risk Ratios	Calculations	
Liquidity		
Receivables turnover ratio	$\dfrac{\$37,403}{(\$2,749 + \$4,272)/2}$	= 10.7 times
Average collection period	$\dfrac{365}{10.7}$	= 34.1 days
Inventory turnover ratio	$\dfrac{\$21,162}{(\$7,367 + \$5,622)/2}$	= 3.3 times
Average days in inventory	$\dfrac{365}{3.3}$	= 110.6 days
Current ratio	$\dfrac{\$20,556}{\$8,284}$	= 2.5 to 1
Acid-test ratio	$\dfrac{\$8,348 + \$439 + \$2,749}{\$8,284}$	= 1.4 to 1
Solvency		
Debt to equity ratio	$\dfrac{\$8,284 + \$15,003}{\$8,055}$	= 289.1%
Times interest earned ratio	$\dfrac{\$2,539 + \$151 + \$348}{\$151}$	= 20.1 times

Suggested Homework:
BE12–6, BE12–7;
E12–5, E12–7;
P12–4A&B, P12–6A&B

Profitability Analysis

Our next six ratios focus on profitability, the primary measure of company success. **Profitability ratios** measure the earnings or operating effectiveness of a company. Not only is profitability necessary just to survive as a company, it's the primary indicator used by investors and creditors in making financial decisions. Illustration 12–16 summarizes the six profitability ratios we have examined (plus earnings per share), the chapters in which we discussed them, and how we calculate them.

 LO12–4
Use ratios to analyze a company's profitability.

ILLUSTRATION 12–16
Profitability Ratios

Profitability Ratios	Chapter	Calculations
Gross profit ratio	6	$\dfrac{\text{Gross profit}}{\text{Net sales}}$
Return on assets	7	$\dfrac{\text{Net income}}{\text{Average total assets}}$
Profit margin	7	$\dfrac{\text{Net income}}{\text{Net sales}}$
Asset turnover	7	$\dfrac{\text{Net sales}}{\text{Average total assets}}$
Return on equity	10	$\dfrac{\text{Net income}}{\text{Average stockholders' equity}}$
Earnings per share	10	$\dfrac{\text{Net income} - \text{Dividends on preferred stock}}{\text{Average shares of common stock outstanding}}$
Price-earnings ratio	10	$\dfrac{\text{Stock price}}{\text{Earnings per share}}$

GROSS PROFIT RATIO

The **gross profit ratio** indicates the portion of each dollar of sales above its cost of goods sold. We calculate this ratio as gross profit (net sales minus cost of goods sold) divided by net sales. Gross profit ratios vary considerably by industry. For example, consider the average gross profit ratio for the following major industries: retail grocery stores (25%), apparel stores (47%), major drug manufacturers (68%), and software (77%). Illustration 12–17 presents the calculation of the gross profit ratio for VF and a comparison with Nike. **We'll calculate Nike's profitability ratios in a review problem at the end of this section.**

Common Terms Gross profit is also called *gross margin* or *gross profit margin.*

ILLUSTRATION 12–17
Gross Profit Ratio

Gross Profit Ratio	VF	Nike
$\dfrac{\text{Gross profit}}{\text{Net sales}}$	$\dfrac{\$5,798}{\$10,489} = 55.3\%$	43.4%

With a gross profit ratio of 55.3%, VF sells its merchandise for about twice what it costs to produce. In comparison, Nike has a gross profit ratio of 43.4%. Nike's gross profit is still quite high, but not as high as VF's. Regardless of the difference between the two companies, they both are in the range of the apparel industry gross profit ratio (47%).

Gross profit ratios normally decline as competition increases. For example, a patented drug can sell for many times its production cost. However, when the patent expires, competition from generic drug companies drives down selling prices, resulting in lower gross profit ratios.

Decision Maker's Perspective

How Warren Buffett Interprets Financial Statements

Warren Buffett is one of the world's wealthiest individuals, with investments in the billions. As founder and CEO of **Berkshire Hathaway**, an investment company located in Omaha, Nebraska, he is also highly regarded as one of the world's top investment advisors. So, what's the secret to his success? Warren Buffett is best known for his attention to details, carefully examining each line in the financial statements.

Warren Buffett seeks to invest in companies with a "durable competitive advantage." That means he is looking for profitable companies that can maintain their profitability over time. To find these companies, he carefully studies their income statements for evidence of above-average profits that can be sustained despite actions taken by competing companies. He also studies their balance sheets looking for financially healthy companies. Some of his major investments include **GEICO**, **Burlington Northern**, **Coca-Cola**, **Dairy Queen**, **Duracell**, **Heinz**, **See's Candies**, and **Fruit of the Loom**. Warren Buffett uses ratios just like the ones covered in this chapter, but it's his ability to interpret those ratios in selecting the best possible investments that sets him apart.

RETURN ON ASSETS

Common Terms Return on assets is referred to as *ROA*.

Return on assets measures the income the company earns on each dollar invested in assets. We calculate it as net income divided by *average* (not *ending*) total assets. Average total assets are calculated as beginning total assets plus ending total assets divided by 2. Illustration 12–18 provides the calculation of return on assets for VF and a comparison to Nike.

ILLUSTRATION 12–18

Return on Assets

Return on Assets	VF	Nike
$\dfrac{\text{Net income}}{\text{Average total assets}}$	$\dfrac{\$629}{(\$11{,}133 + \$10{,}357)/2} = 5.9\%$	9.2%

VF earned a return on assets lower than Nike's return on assets. As we learned in Chapter 7, we can further separate return on assets into two ratios: profit margin and asset turnover. Illustration 12–19 shows the calculations.

ILLUSTRATION 12–19

Components of Return on Assets

Return on Assets	=	Profit margin	×	Asset turnover
$\dfrac{\text{Net income}}{\text{Average total assets}}$	=	$\dfrac{\text{Net income}}{\text{Net sales}}$	×	$\dfrac{\text{Net sales}}{\text{Average total assets}}$

Some companies, like **Saks Fifth Avenue**, rely more on high profit margins, while other companies, like **Dollar General**, rely more on asset turnover. Investors are especially intrigued by companies that can obtain both—high profit margins and high asset turnover. For example, **Apple Inc.** introduced several extremely popular products such as the iPhone and the Apple watch that generate both high profit margin and high asset turnover for the company.

PROFIT MARGIN

Profit margin measures the income earned on each dollar of sales. We calculate it by dividing net income by net sales. Illustration 12–20 provides the calculation of profit margin for VF and Nike.

Profit Margin	VF	Nike
$\dfrac{\text{Net income}}{\text{Net sales}}$	$\dfrac{\$629}{\$10,489} = 6.0\%$	6.8%

ILLUSTRATION 12–20
Profit Margin

VF has a profit margin of 6.0%, meaning that for every dollar of sales, 6 cents goes toward net income. Nike has a higher profit margin of 6.8%. Now let's look at asset turnover, the second factor influencing return on assets. Companies in more competitive industries, like sports apparel, typically have lower profit margins.

ASSET TURNOVER

Asset turnover measures sales volume in relation to the investment in assets. We calculate asset turnover as sales divided by *average* (not *ending*) total assets. Illustration 12–21 presents the calculation of asset turnover.

Asset Turnover	VF	Nike
$\dfrac{\text{Net sales}}{\text{Average total assets}}$	$\dfrac{\$10,489}{(\$11,133 + \$10,357)/2} = 1.0 \text{ times}$	1.4 times

ILLUSTRATION 12–21
Asset Turnover

VF's asset turnover is 1.0. VF generates $1.00 in annual sales for every dollar it invests in assets. Nike's asset turnover is higher at 1.4.

RETURN ON EQUITY

Return on equity measures the income earned for each dollar in stockholders' equity. Return on equity relates net income to the investment made by owners of the business. The ratio is calculated by dividing net income by *average* stockholders' equity. Average stockholders' equity is calculated as beginning stockholders' equity plus ending stockholders' equity divided by 2. Illustration 12–22 shows the calculation of return on equity.

Common Terms Return on equity is referred to as *ROE.*

Return on Equity	VF	Nike
$\dfrac{\text{Net income}}{\text{Average stockholders' equity}}$	$\dfrac{\$629}{(\$3,357 + \$4,299)/2} = 16.4\%$	29.7%

ILLUSTRATION 12–22
Return on Equity

VF has a return on equity of 16.4%. Its net income is 16.4 cents for every dollar invested in equity. Nike has a much higher return on equity of 29.7%.

Why is Nike's return on assets 3.3 percentage points higher than VF's, while its return on equity is 13.3 percentage points higher than VF's? The answer relates to *financial leverage*—the amount of debt each company carries. Recall that Nike has a higher debt to equity ratio. Remember, too, that debt can be good for the company as long as the return on investment exceeds the interest cost of borrowing. Both VF and Nike enjoy returns well in excess of the interest cost on borrowed funds. By carrying greater debt, Nike is able to provide a higher return on equity in relationship to its return on assets, further benefiting the investors in the company.

PRICE-EARNINGS RATIO

The **price-earnings (PE) ratio** compares a company's share price with its earnings per share. Share price reflects the value of owning one share of the company's stock. This value ties closely to investors' assessment of a company's *future* profitability. In comparison,

earnings per share (EPS) measures a company's *current* profitability per share. Therefore, one way to think about the PE ratio is that the ratio represents investors' expectations of earnings growth. Illustration 12–23 presents the PE ratios for VF and Nike.

ILLUSTRATION 12–23

Price-Earnings Ratio

Price-Earnings Ratio	VF	Nike
$\dfrac{\text{Stock price}}{\text{Earnings per share}}$	$\dfrac{\$54.08}{\$1.59} = 34.0$	60.5

At its 2020 year-end, VF's closing stock price was $54.08, and the company reported earnings per share for 2020 of $1.59. This represents a PE ratio of 34.0. The stock price is trading at 34 times earnings. In contrast, the PE ratio for Nike is 60.5. In recent years, PE ratio averages were somewhere between 20 and 25. Both companies have high ratios, especially Nike. Nike had a decline in earnings per share in 2020 due to the impact of COVID-19 on its business. The market appears to view these lower earnings as temporary and for Nike's longer-term earnings to be much higher.

As we discussed in Chapter 10, investors pursue two basic types of stock investments: growth stocks and value stocks. **Growth stocks** have high expectations of future earnings growth and, therefore, usually trade at higher PE ratios. Growth stocks are said to be *great* stocks at a *good* price. **Value stocks** have lower share prices in relationship to their fundamental ratios and therefore trade at lower (bargain) PE ratios. Value stocks are said to be *good* stocks at a *great* price. Some investors take the strategy of picking the stocks with the best future potential (growth stocks); other investors shop for the best bargains (value stocks). Most investors take a combined approach, searching for stocks based on both future potential and current stock price.

KEY POINT

Profitability ratios measure the earnings or operating effectiveness of a company over a period of time, such as a year. Investors view profitability as the number one measure of company success.

Let's Review

The income statement and balance sheets for **Nike** follow. In addition, Nike reported earnings per share for the year ended May 31, 2020, of $1.63, and the closing stock price on May 31, 2020, was $98.58.

Required:

Calculate the six profitability ratios we've discussed for Nike.

NIKE
Income Statement
For the year ended May 31, 2020
($ in millions)

Net sales	$37,403
Cost of goods sold	21,162
Gross profit	16,241
Operating expenses	13,126
Operating income	3,115
Other income	−228*
Income before tax	2,887
Income tax expense	348
Net income	$ 2,539

*Includes interest expense of $151 million.

NIKE
Balance Sheets
May 31
($ in millions)

	2020	2019
Assets		
Current assets:		
Cash	$ 8,348	$ 4,466
Current investments	439	197
Net receivables	2,749	4,272
Inventory	7,367	5,622
Other current assets	1,653	1,968
Total current assets	20,556	16,525
Property and equipment	4,866	4,744
Intangible assets	497	437
Other assets	5,423	2,011
Total assets	$31,342	$23,717
Liabilities and Stockholders' Equity		
Current liabilities	$ 8,284	$ 7,866
Long-term liabilities	15,003	6,811
Stockholders' equity	8,055	9,040
Total liabilities and stockholders' equity	$31,342	$23,717

Solution:

Profitability Ratios	Calculations	
Gross profit ratio	$\dfrac{\$16,241}{\$37,403}$	= 43.4%
Return on assets	$\dfrac{\$2,539}{(\$31,342 + \$23,717)/2}$	= 9.2%
Profit margin	$\dfrac{\$2,539}{\$37,403}$	= 6.8%
Asset turnover	$\dfrac{\$37,403}{(\$31,342 + \$23,717)/2}$	= 1.4 times
Return on equity	$\dfrac{\$2,539}{(\$8,055 + \$9,040)/2}$	= 29.7%
Price-earnings ratio	$\dfrac{\$98.58}{\$1.63}$	= 60.5

Suggested Homework:
BE12–10, BE12–11;
E12–6, E12–8;
P12–5A&B, P12–6A&B

EARNINGS PERSISTENCE AND EARNINGS QUALITY   **PART C**

As we just saw when analyzing the PE ratio, investors expect **Nike**'s earnings will grow at a faster rate than **VF**'s. That's why Nike's stock price is higher relative to its current earnings. If, for some reason, investors see Nike's growth in earnings begin to slow, the stock price will fall. Investors are interested in whether earnings will remain strong and in the quality of those earnings. We look at those topics in this section.

Earnings Persistence and One-Time Income Items

Leonard Zhukovsky/Shutterstock

To make predictions of future earnings, investors look for current earnings that will continue or *persist* into future years. Some items that are part of net income in the current year are not expected to persist. We refer to these as *one-time income items*. Discontinued operations, discussed below, is a prime example.

DISCONTINUED OPERATIONS

A **discontinued operation** is a business, or a component of a business, that the organization has already discontinued or plans to discontinue. **Income from discontinued operations in the current year is reported separately from income on continuing operations.** This allows investors the opportunity to exclude discontinued operations in their estimate of income that will persist into future years.

Only disposals of businesses representing strategic shifts that have a major effect on an organization's operations and financial results are reported in discontinued operations. Examples include a disposal of a major geographical area, a major line of business, or a major investment in which the company has significant influence.

As an example, let's consider Federer Sports Apparel, which has two business activities: a very profitable line of tennis apparel and a less profitable line of tennis shoes. Let's say that during 2024, the company decides to sell the tennis shoe business to a competitor. The tennis shoe business has income for the year, including a gain on disposal of its assets, of $1.5 million. We report the income from the discontinued segment "net of tax." This means the $1.5 million income (before tax), less $500,000 in related taxes, is reported in the income statement as $1 million of income from discontinued operations. Illustration 12–24 shows the income statement presentation of discontinued operations for Federer Sports Apparel.

ILLUSTRATION 12–24

Presentation of a Discontinued Operation

FEDERER SPORTS APPAREL Income Statement For the year ended December 31, 2024	
Net sales	$15,500,000
Cost of goods sold	7,000,000
Gross profit	8,500,000
Operating expenses	1,200,000
Depreciation expense	1,000,000
Other revenues and expenses	300,000
Income before tax	6,000,000
Income tax expense	2,000,000
Income from continuing operations	4,000,000
Discontinued operation:	
Income from tennis shoe segment, net of tax	**1,000,000**
Net income	$ 5,000,000

With discontinued operations reported separately in the income statement, investors can clearly see the reported net income, *excluding* the effects of the discontinued tennis shoe segment, $4.0 million in this situation. Investors then can use the income from continuing operations, $4.0 million, to estimate income that persists into future periods.

Question	Accounting information	Analysis
Are any parts of the company's earnings not expected to persist into the future?	Discontinued operations reported near the bottom of the income statement	Investors should normally exclude discontinued operations in estimating future earnings performance.

OTHER REVENUES AND EXPENSES

As we just discussed, the income related to the sale or disposal of a significant component of a company's operations is reported separately as discontinued operations. What if instead a company sells assets that are not classified as discontinued operations? For example, suppose Federer Sports Apparel decides to sell the land, building, and equipment of a single store (rather than sell the entire tennis shoe division). The income from that store and any gain or loss on the sale of those assets would be reported as part of continuing operations, even though they are not expected to recur.

There are many other revenue and expense activities that are not expected to recur. However, no matter how unusual or infrequent these activities are, they are not allowed to be reported as part of discontinued operations. They must be reported as part of continuing operations. Illustration 12–25 lists several common examples.

ILLUSTRATION 12–25

Other Revenues and Expenses

Other Revenues and Expenses

Examples
1. Losses due to the write-down of receivables, inventory, or long-term assets.
2. Gains or losses on the sale of long-term assets.
3. Losses due to an employee strike.
4. Losses due to business restructuring.
5. Uninsured losses from a natural disaster such as a flood, earthquake, or hurricane.

Decision Maker's Perspective

Does Location in the Income Statement Matter?

As manager of a company, would you prefer to show an expense as part of continuing operations or as a part of discontinued operations? Your first response might be that it really doesn't matter, since the choice affects only the location in the income statement and has no effect on the final net income number. True, but investors often use the location of items reported in the income statement as a signal of future profitability. Expenses and losses that are listed as part of discontinued operations are, by their classification, not expected to recur in the following year(s). For this reason, managers might prefer to report certain expenses and losses as part of discontinued operations to provide the appearance of more profitable, continuing operations.

However, managers do not have the choice of where to report expenses and losses in the income statement. Expenses and losses, no matter how unusual or infrequent, must be reported as part of income from continuing operations. Only those expenses and losses associated with the sale or disposal of a significant component of the business can be reported as part of discontinued operations.

KEY POINT

When using a company's current earnings to estimate future earnings performance, investors normally should exclude discontinued operations.

Quality of Earnings

■ **LO12–6**
Distinguish between conservative and aggressive accounting practices.

Quality of earnings refers to the ability of reported earnings to reflect the company's true earnings, as well as the usefulness of reported earnings to predict future earnings. To illustrate the concept, we continue our example of Federer Sports Apparel.

Let's move one year forward to 2025 for our example company, Federer Sports Apparel. Mr. Nadal, as chief financial officer (CFO), is responsible for all the accounting, finance, and MIS operations of the business. He has developed a reputation for his conservative yet powerful management style. Illustration 12–26 presents the preliminary financial statements for 2025, prepared under the supervision of Mr. Nadal.

ILLUSTRATION 12–26

Financial Statements Prepared by Mr. Nadal

FEDERER SPORTS APPAREL
Income Statement
For the year ended December 31, 2025

Net sales	$18,800,000
Cost of goods sold	13,400,000
Gross profit	5,400,000
Operating expenses	1,600,000
Depreciation expense	1,000,000
Loss (litigation)	1,500,000
Income before tax	1,300,000
Income tax expense	450,000
Net income	$ 850,000

FEDERER SPORTS APPAREL
Balance Sheets
December 31

	2025	2024
Cash	$ 2,300,000	$ 800,000
Accounts receivable	1,500,000	1,200,000
Inventory	2,800,000	1,700,000
Buildings	11,000,000	11,000,000
Less: Accumulated depreciation	(2,000,000)	(1,000,000)
Total assets	$15,600,000	$13,700,000
Accounts payable	$ 1,450,000	$ 1,700,000
Contingent liability	1,500,000	0
Common stock	8,000,000	8,000,000
Retained earnings	4,650,000	4,000,000
Total liabilities and stockholders' equity	$15,600,000	$13,700,000

(continued)

ILLUSTRATION 12–26
(concluded)

FEDERER SPORTS APPAREL
Statement of Cash Flows
For the year ended December 31, 2025

Cash Flows from Operating Activities

Net income	$ 850,000	
Adjustments to reconcile net income to net cash flows from operating activities:		
Depreciation expense	1,000,000	
Increase in accounts receivable	(300,000)	
Increase in inventory	(1,100,000)	
Decrease in accounts payable	(250,000)	
Increase in contingent liability	1,500,000	
Net cash flows from operating activities		$1,700,000

Cash Flows from Investing Activities

Net cash flows from investing activities		0

Cash Flows from Financing Activities

Payment of cash dividends	(200,000)	
Net cash flows from financing activities		(200,000)
Net increase (decrease) in cash		1,500,000
Cash at the beginning of the period		800,000
Cash at the end of the period		$2,300,000

NADAL RETIRES AND DJOKOVIC IS HIRED

After completing the preliminary financial statements for 2025, Mr. Nadal retires, and the company hires a new CFO, Mr. Djokovic. In contrast to Mr. Nadal, Mr. Djokovic has a more aggressive, quick-hitting management style. Mr. Djokovic has made it clear that he is now in charge and changes will be made. Illustration 12–27 outlines four accounting changes Mr. Djokovic proposes. They are based on accounting topics we discussed in Chapters 5, 6, 7, and 8.

ILLUSTRATION 12–27
Mr. Djokovic's Proposed
Changes

Mr. Djokovic's Proposed Changes

1. **Estimate of bad debts.** At the end of 2025, Mr. Nadal estimated that future bad debts will be 6% to 10% of current accounts receivable. He decided to play it safe and recorded an allowance equal to 10% of accounts receivable, or $150,000. Mr. Djokovic proposes changing the estimate to be 6% of accounts receivable, or $90,000. This change would increase net accounts receivable and decrease bad debt expense by $60,000.

2. **Write-down of inventory.** Mr. Nadal recorded a $200,000 write-down of inventory as follows:

December 31, 2025	Debit	Credit
Cost of Goods Sold	200,000	
Inventory		200,000
(Write-down inventory)		

Mr. Djokovic insists the write-down was not necessary because the decline in inventory value was only temporary. Therefore, he proposes eliminating this entry, which would increase inventory and decrease cost of goods sold by $200,000.

3. **Change in depreciation estimate.** For the building purchased for $11 million at the beginning of 2024, Mr. Nadal recorded depreciation expense of $1 million in 2024 and 2025, using the straight-line method over 10 years with an estimated

(continued)

ILLUSTRATION 12–27

(concluded)

salvage value of $1 million. Beginning in 2025, Mr. Djokovic proposes calculating depreciation over a total of 20 years instead of 10 and using an estimated salvage value of $500,000. That change decreases accumulated depreciation and depreciation expense in 2025 by $500,000.

4. **Loss contingency.** At the end of 2025, the company's lawyer advised Mr. Nadal that there was a 70% chance of losing a litigation suit of $1,500,000 filed against the company. Mr. Nadal recorded the possible loss as follows:

December 31, 2025	Debit	Credit
Loss	1,500,000	
Contingent Liability		1,500,000
(Record litigation against the company)		

Mr. Djokovic argues that the likelihood of losing the litigation is reasonably possible, but not probable. Therefore, he proposes removing the litigation entry from the accounting records. The change would remove the loss and decrease liabilities by $1,500,000.

How will the proposed accounting changes affect net income? Illustration 12–28 presents the preliminary income statement prepared by Mr. Nadal, the effect of the accounting changes, and the updated income statement prepared by Mr. Djokovic.

ILLUSTRATION 12–28

Income Statement
Revised by Mr. Djokovic

FEDERER SPORTS APPAREL
Income Statement
For the year ended December 31, 2025

	Nadal	Changes	Djokovic
Net sales	$18,800,000		$18,800,000
Cost of goods sold	13,400,000	$ (200,000)	13,200,000
Gross profit	5,400,000		5,600,000
Operating expenses	1,600,000	$ (60,000)	1,540,000
Depreciation expense	1,000,000	(500,000)	500,000
Loss (litigation)	1,500,000	(1,500,000)	0
Income before tax	1,300,000	2,260,000	3,560,000
Income tax expense	450,000		450,000
Net income	$ 850,000	$ 2,260,000	$ 3,110,000

The four proposed accounting changes cause net income to more than triple, from $850,000 to $3,110,000. Notice that all four changes proposed by Mr. Djokovic increase net income: The reduction in the estimated allowance for uncollectible accounts increases net income $60,000, the elimination of the inventory write-down increases net income $200,000, the reduction in depreciation estimate increases net income $500,000, and the elimination of the contingent litigation liability increases net income $1,500,000. **Note that income tax expense did not change because all of these changes affect financial income but not taxable income.**

How do positive changes to net income affect the balance sheet? Illustration 12–29 presents the balance sheet originally prepared by Mr. Nadal, the effect of the four accounting changes, and the updated balance sheet prepared by Mr. Djokovic.

The balance sheet also improves from the proposed adjustments. Total assets increase due to increases in receivables and inventory plus a decrease in accumulated depreciation. Total liabilities decrease due to the elimination of the $1.5 million litigation liability. Stockholders' equity also goes up due to the increase in retained earnings caused by the increase in reported net income for the year.

ILLUSTRATION 12–29
Balance Sheet Revised
by Mr. Djokovic

FEDERER SPORTS APPAREL
Balance Sheet
December 31, 2025

	Nadal	Changes	Djokovic
Assets			
Cash	$ 2,300,000		$ 2,300,000
Accounts receivable	1,500,000	$ 60,000	1,560,000
Inventory	2,800,000	200,000	3,000,000
Buildings	11,000,000		11,000,000
Less: Accumulated depreciation	(2,000,000)	500,000	(1,500,000)
Total assets	$15,600,000	$ 760,000	$16,360,000
Liabilities and Stockholders' Equity			
Accounts payable	$ 1,450,000		$ 1,450,000
Contingent liability	1,500,000	$(1,500,000)	0
Common stock	8,000,000		8,000,000
Retained earnings	4,650,000	2,260,000	6,910,000
Total liabilities and stockholders' equity	$15,600,000	$ 760,000	$16,360,000

Decision Maker's Perspective

Look Out for Earnings Management at Year-End

Let's assume you're an auditor, and all four of the final changes to the accounting records near year-end increase income. Wouldn't you be just a little concerned? It may be that all four adjustments are perfectly legitimate, but it also may be an indication management is inflating earnings. Year-end adjustments, especially those with an increasing or decreasing pattern, should be investigated with greater skepticism.

What about the effects of the proposed adjustments on the statement of cash flows? Illustration 12–30 provides the statement of cash flows as revised by Mr. Djokovic.

Interestingly, the proposed changes have **no effect at all on total operating cash flows or on the overall change in cash.** Net cash flows from operating activities remain at $1,700,000 after the four proposed transactions. The net increase in cash remains at $1,500,000. None of the proposed changes affects the underlying cash flows of the company. **Rather, each proposed change improves the** *appearance* **of amounts reported in the income statement and the balance sheet.**

CONSERVATIVE VERSUS AGGRESSIVE ACCOUNTING

In our previous example, Mr. Nadal represents conservative accounting practices. Conservative accounting practices are those that result in reporting lower income, lower assets, and higher liabilities. The larger estimation of the allowance for uncollectible accounts, the write-down of overvalued inventory, the use of a shorter useful life for depreciation, and the reporting of a contingent litigation loss are all examples of conservative accounting.

In contrast, Mr. Djokovic represents aggressive accounting practices. Aggressive accounting practices result in reporting higher income, higher assets, and lower liabilities. Mr. Djokovic's lower estimation of the allowance for uncollectible accounts, waiting to report an inventory write-down, choosing a longer useful life for depreciation, and waiting to report a litigation loss all are examples of more aggressive accounting. Being able to distinguish between conservative and aggressive accounting practices is important. Everyone

ILLUSTRATION 12–30

Statement of Cash Flows Revised by Mr. Djokovic

FEDERER SPORTS APPAREL Statement of Cash Flows For the year ended December 31, 2025			
	Nadal	Changes	Djokovic
Operating Activities			
Net income	$ 850,000	$2,260,000	$3,110,000
Adjustments to reconcile net income to net cash flows from operating activities:			
Depreciation expense	1,000,000	(500,000)	500,000
Increase in accounts receivable	(300,000)	(60,000)	(360,000)
Increase in inventory	(1,100,000)	(200,000)	(1,300,000)
Decrease in accounts payable	(250,000)		(250,000)
Increase in contingent liability	1,500,000	(1,500,000)	0
Net cash flows from operating activities	1,700,000	0	1,700,000
Investing Activities	0		0
Financing Activities			
Payment of cash dividends	(200,000)		(200,000)
Net cash flows from financing activities	(200,000)		(200,000)
Net increase (decrease) in cash	**1,500,000**		**1,500,000**
Cash at the beginning of the period	800,000		800,000
Cash at the end of the period	$2,300,000		$2,300,000

involved in business, not just accountants, needs to recognize that accounting is not just black and white. There are actually many gray areas in accounting, requiring management judgment in the application of accounting principles.

 KEY POINT

Changes in accounting estimates and practices alter the appearance of amounts reported in the income statement and the balance sheet. However, changes in accounting estimates and practices usually have no effect on a company's underlying cash flows.

Let's Review

Classify each of the following accounting practices as conservative or aggressive.

1. Increase the allowance for uncollectible accounts.
2. When costs are going up, change from LIFO to FIFO.
3. Increase the useful life for calculating depreciation.
4. Record a larger expense for warranties.
5. Wait to record revenue until the cash is collected.

Solution:

1. Conservative.
2. Aggressive.
3. Aggressive.
4. Conservative.
5. Conservative.

Suggested Homework:
BE12–14, BE12–15;
E12–14, E12–15

CHAPTER FRAMEWORK

This chapter discusses some of the techniques used by investors, creditors, managers and others that help compare one company to another company or help evaluate a single company's performance over time. Comparisons are made easier by transforming financial statement items into ratios and understanding how managers' conservative and aggressive choices in accounting practices can affect reported amounts.

	Vertical Analysis	Horizontal Analysis
Comparative Analysis	Express all income statement items as a percentage of sales or all balance sheet items as a percentage of total assets.	Determine the amount of change and the percentage change for each financial statement item over time.
	Risk Ratios	**Profitability Ratios**
Ratio Analysis	Understand a company's ability to pay current liabilities (liquidity risk), as well as long-term liabilities (solvency risk). See Illustration 12–7 for a list of risk ratios.	Understand a company's ability to make profits from its assets, sales to customers, and equity of owners. See Illustration 12–16 for a list of profitability ratios.
	Conservative	**Aggressive**
Accounting Practices	Managers' choices of accounting practices that lead to the appearance of a company having higher risk or lower profitability in the current year.	Managers' choices of accounting practices that lead to the appearance of a company having lower risk or higher profitability in the current year.

Chapter Framework Questions

1. **Comparative Analysis.** When using vertical analysis, we express balance sheet accounts as a percentage of
   a. Net income.
   b. Last year's amount.
   c. Sales.
   d. Total assets.

2. **Comparative Analysis.** To better compare one company's growth in sales to another company's growth in sales, we could use
   a. Vertical analysis.
   b. Risk ratio analysis.
   c. Horizontal analysis.
   d. Profitability ratio analysis.

3. **Ratio Analysis.** Which of the following ratios best represents a company's risk of not being able to pay current obligations using current resources?
   a. Profit margin.
   b. Return on assets.
   c. Current ratio.

4. **Ratio Analysis.** Which of the following profitability ratios uses information only from the income statement to measure a company's ability to generate profits from sales?
   a. Return on assets.
   b. Profit margin.
   c. Return on equity.

5. **Accounting Practices.** A manager decides to overestimate the company's future uncollectible accounts receivable, which lowers reported net income for the current year. This would be an example of
   a. Conservative accounting practices.
   b. Aggressive accounting practices.

Note: For answers, see the last page of the chapter.

KEY POINTS BY LEARNING OBJECTIVE

LO12–1 Perform vertical analysis.

For vertical analysis, we express each item as a percentage of the same base amount, such as a percentage of sales in the income statement or as a percentage of total assets in the balance sheet.

LO12–2 Perform horizontal analysis.

We use horizontal analysis to analyze trends in financial statement data, such as the amount of change and the percentage change, for one company over time.

LO12–3 Use ratios to analyze a company's risk.

We categorize risk ratios into liquidity ratios and solvency ratios. Liquidity ratios focus on the company's ability to pay *current* liabilities, whereas solvency ratios include *long-term* liabilities as well.

LO12–4 Use ratios to analyze a company's profitability.

Profitability ratios measure the earnings or operating effectiveness of a company over a period of time, such as a year. Investors view

profitability as the number one measure of company success.

LO12–5 Distinguish persistent earnings from one-time items.

When using a company's current earnings to estimate future earnings performance, investors normally should exclude discontinued operations.

LO12–6 Distinguish between conservative and aggressive accounting practices.

Changes in accounting estimates and practices alter the appearance of amounts reported in the income statement and the balance sheet. However, changes in accounting estimates and practices usually have no effect on a company's underlying cash flows.

GLOSSARY

Acid-test ratio: Cash, current investments, and accounts receivable divided by current liabilities; measures the availability of liquid current assets to pay current liabilities. **p. 612**

Aggressive accounting practices: Practices that result in reporting higher income, higher assets, and lower liabilities. **p. 625**

Asset turnover: Net sales divided by average total assets, which measures the sales per dollar of assets invested. **p. 617**

Average collection period: Approximate number of days the average accounts receivable balance is outstanding. It equals 365 days divided by the receivables turnover ratio. **p. 610**

Average days in inventory: Approximate number of days the average inventory is held. It equals 365 days divided by the inventory turnover ratio. **p. 610**

Capital structure: The mixture of liabilities and stockholders' equity in a business. **p. 604**

Conservative accounting practices: Practices that result in reporting lower income, lower assets, and higher liabilities. **p. 625**

Current ratio: Current assets divided by current liabilities; measures the availability of current assets to pay current liabilities. **p. 611**

Debt to equity ratio: Total liabilities divided by stockholders' equity; measures a company's risk. **p. 612**

Discontinued operation: The sale or disposal of a significant component of a company's operations. **p. 620**

Earnings per share (EPS): Net income available to common shareholders divided by average shares of common stock outstanding. **p. 618**

Gross profit ratio: Measure of the amount by which the sale of inventory exceeds its cost per dollar of sales. It equals gross profit divided by net sales. **p. 615**

Growth stocks: Stocks that tend to have higher price-earnings ratios and are expected to have higher future earnings. **p. 618**

Horizontal analysis: Analyzes trends in financial statement data for a single company over time. **p. 604**

Inventory turnover ratio: The number of times a firm sells its average inventory balance during a reporting period. It equals cost of goods sold divided by average inventory. **p. 610**

Liquidity: Having sufficient cash (or other assets convertible to cash in a relatively short time) to pay currently maturing debts. **p. 608**

Price-earnings (PE) ratio: Compares a company's share price with its earnings per share. **p. 617**

Profit margin: Net income divided by net sales; indicates the earnings per dollar of sales. **p. 616**

Profitability ratios: Measure the earnings or operating effectiveness of a company. **p. 615**

Quality of earnings: Refers to the ability of reported earnings to reflect the company's true earnings, as well as the usefulness of reported earnings to predict future earnings. **p. 622**

Receivables turnover ratio: Number of times during a year that the average accounts receivable balance is collected (or "turns over"). It equals net credit sales divided by average accounts receivable. **p. 609**

Return on assets: Net income divided by average total assets; measures the amount of net income generated for each dollar invested in assets. **p. 616**

Return on equity: Net income divided by average stockholders' equity; measures the income generated per dollar of stockholders' equity. **p. 617**

Solvency: Refers to a company's ability to pay its current and long-term liabilities. **p. 609**

Times interest earned ratio: Ratio that compares interest expense with income available to pay those charges. **p. 613**

Value stocks: Stocks that tend to have lower price-earnings ratios and are priced low in relation to current earnings. **p. 618**

Vertical analysis: Expresses each item in a financial statement as a percentage of the same base amount measured in the same period. **p. 602**

SELF-STUDY QUESTIONS

1. When using vertical analysis, we express income statement accounts as a percentage of **(LO12–1)**
   a. Net income.
   b. Sales.
   c. Gross profit.
   d. Total assets.

2. When using vertical analysis, we express balance sheet accounts as a percentage of **(LO12–1)**
   a. Total assets.
   b. Total liabilities.
   c. Total stockholders' equity.
   d. Sales.

3. Horizontal analysis examines trends in a company **(LO12–2)**
   a. Between income statement accounts in the same year.
   b. Between balance sheet accounts in the same year.
   c. Between income statement and balance sheet accounts in the same year.
   d. Over time.

4. Which of the following is an example of horizontal analysis? **(LO12–2)**
   a. Comparing operating expenses with sales.
   b. Comparing the growth in sales with the growth in cost of goods sold.
   c. Comparing property, plant, and equipment with total assets.
   d. Comparing gross profit across companies.

5. Which of the following ratios is most useful in evaluating solvency? **(LO12–3)**
   a. Receivables turnover ratio.
   b. Inventory turnover ratio.
   c. Debt to equity ratio.
   d. Current ratio.

6. The current ratio measures **(LO12–3)**
   a. The ability of a company to quickly collect cash from customers.
   b. The ability of a company to quickly sell its inventory to customers.
   c. The ability of a company to report profits in the current year.
   d. The ability of a company to pay its current obligations.

7. Which of the following is a positive sign that a company can quickly turn its receivables into cash? **(LO12–3)**
   a. A low receivables turnover ratio.
   b. A high receivables turnover ratio.
   c. A low average collection period.
   d. Both a high receivables turnover ratio and a low average collection period.

8. The Sports Shack reports net income of $120,000, sales of $1,200,000, and average assets of $960,000. The profit margin is **(LO12–4)**
   a. 10%.
   b. 12.5%.
   c. 80%.
   d. 125%.

9. The Sports Shack reports net income of $120,000, sales of $1,200,000, and average assets of $960,000. The asset turnover is **(LO12–4)**
   a. 0.10 times.
   b. 0.80 times.
   c. 8 times.
   d. 1.25 times.

10. Which of the following typically is true for profitability ratios? **(LO12–4)**
    a. Growth stocks have lower price to earnings ratios.
    b. Companies in more competitive industries have higher profit margins.

c. The gross profit ratio declines as competition increases.

d. When a company has debt, its return on equity will be lower than its return on assets.

11. Company 1 has return on assets of 8.2% and a debt to equity ratio of 67.2%. Company 2 has return on assets of 6.3% and a debt to equity ratio of 53.4%. Based on these ratios, what is generally true about these two companies? **(LO12–3, LO12–4)**

a. Company 1 has lower profitability and higher risk.

b. Company 1 has higher profitability and higher risk.

c. Company 1 has lower profitability and lower risk.

d. Company 1 has higher profitability and lower risk.

12. Which of the following items would we report in the income statement just before net income? **(LO12–5)**

a. Losses due to the write-down of inventory.

b. Gain on the sale of long-term assets.

c. Discontinued operations.

d. Losses due to restructuring.

13. A company suffers an inventory loss from water damage due to a broken pipe. The company has never incurred a loss of this type and does not expect this type of damage to occur again. The loss would be reported as **(LO12–5)**

a. A reduction of sales revenue.

b. Part of income from continuing operations.

c. Part of income from discontinued operations.

d. Not reported.

14. Which of the following is an example of a conservative accounting practice? **(LO12–6)**

a. Estimate the allowance for uncollectible accounts to be a larger amount.

b. Do not write down inventory for declines in net realizable value (estimated selling price).

c. Record a lower amount of depreciation expense in the earlier years of an asset's life.

d. Record sales revenue before it is actually earned.

15. Which of the following would be an example of conservative accounting? **(LO12–6)**

a. Recording an increase in fair value of certain assets as a gain in net income but not recording a decrease in fair value as a loss.

b. Estimating the percentage of bad debts as 6% of accounts receivable instead of 10% of accounts receivable.

c. Estimating warranty costs to be 4% of sales instead of 9% of sales.

d. Assessing the probability of a contingent liability as probable instead of reasonably likely.

Note: For answers, see the last page of the chapter.

DATA ANALYTICS & EXCEL

Mc Graw Hill **connect**

Visit Connect to find a variety of Data Analytics questions that help build Excel, Tableau, and data visualization skills. Assignable materials include **Integrated Excel, Applying Excel, Data Visualizations, Tableau Dashboard Activities,** and **Applying Tableau cases.**

REVIEW QUESTIONS

■ **LO12–1, 12–2**	1. Identify the three types of comparisons commonly used in financial statement analysis.
■ **LO12–1, 12–2**	2. Explain the difference between vertical and horizontal analysis.
■ **LO12–1**	3. In performing vertical analysis, we express each item in a financial statement as a percentage of a base amount. What base amount is commonly used for income statement accounts? For balance sheet accounts?
■ **LO12–1**	4. Two profitable companies in the same industry have similar total stockholders' equity. However, one company has most of its equity balance in common stock, while the other company has most of its equity balance in retained earnings. Neither company has ever paid a dividend. Which one is more likely to be an older and more established company? Why?
■ **LO12–2**	5. In performing horizontal analysis, why is it important to look at both the amount and the percentage change?
■ **LO12–3**	6. Explain why ratios that compare an income statement account with a balance sheet account should express the balance sheet account as an average of the beginning and ending balances.
■ **LO12–3**	7. What is the difference between liquidity and solvency?

8. Which risk ratios best answer each of the following financial questions?   ■ LO12–3
   a. How quickly is a company able to collect its receivables?
   b. How quickly is a company able to sell its inventory?
   c. Is the company able to make interest payments as they become due?

9. Determine whether each of the following changes in risk ratios is good news or bad news   ■ LO12–3
   about a company.
   a. Increase in receivables turnover.
   b. Decrease in inventory turnover.
   c. Increase in the current ratio.
   d. Increase in the debt to equity ratio.

10. Pro Leather, a supplier to sporting goods manufacturers, has a current ratio of 0.90, based   ■ LO12–3
    on current assets of $450,000 and current liabilities of $500,000. How, if at all, will a
    $100,000 purchase of inventory on account affect the current ratio?

11. Which profitability ratios best answer each of the following financial questions?   ■ LO12–4
    a. What is the income earned for each dollar invested in assets?
    b. What is the income earned for each dollar of sales?
    c. What is the amount of sales for each dollar invested in assets?

12. Determine whether each of the following changes in profitability ratios normally is good   ■ LO12–4
    news or bad news about a company.
    a. Increase in profit margin.
    b. Decrease in asset turnover.
    c. Decrease in return on equity.
    d. Increase in the price-earnings ratio.

13. Hash Mark, Inc., reports a return on assets of 8% and a return on equity of 12%. Why do   ■ LO12–4
    the two rates differ?

14. Define earnings persistence. How does earnings persistence relate to the reporting of   ■ LO12–5
    discontinued operations?

15. Shifting Formations, Inc., reports earnings per share of $1.30. In the following year,   ■ LO12–5
    it reports bottom-line earnings per share of $1.25 but earnings per share on income
    before discontinued operations of $1.50. Is this trend in earnings per share favorable or
    unfavorable? Explain why.

16. Explain the difference between conservative and aggressive accounting practices.   ■ LO12–6

17. Provide an example of a conservative accounting practice. Why is this practice   ■ LO12–6
    conservative?

18. Provide an example of an aggressive accounting practice. Why is this practice aggressive?   ■ LO12–6

19. Goal Line Products makes several year-end adjustments, including an increase in the   ■ LO12–6
    allowance for uncollectible accounts, a write-down of inventory, a decrease in the estimated
    useful life for depreciation, and an increase in the liability reported for litigation. What, if
    anything, do all these adjustments have in common?

20. Provide an example of an adjustment that improves the income statement and the balance   ■ LO12–6
    sheet, but has no effect on cash flows.

BRIEF EXERCISES

BE12–1 Perform a vertical analysis on the following information.

Prepare vertical
analysis (LO12–1)

	2024	2023
Cash	$ 420,000	$1,050,000
Accounts receivable	660,000	300,000
Inventory	1,020,000	925,000
Long-term assets	3,900,000	2,725,000
Total assets	$6,000,000	$5,000,000

Prepare horizontal analysis (LO12–2)

BE12–2 Using the information presented in BE12–1, perform a horizontal analysis providing both the amount and percentage change.

Understand vertical analysis (LO12–1)

BE12–3 Athletic World reports the following vertical analysis percentages.

	2024	2023
Sales	100%	100%
Cost of goods sold	48%	56%
Operating expenses	35%	30%

Did Athletic World's income before tax as a percentage of sales increase, decrease, or stay the same? If net income as a percentage of sales increases, does that mean net income also increases? Explain.

Understand horizontal analysis (LO12–2)

BE12–4 Sales are $2.6 million in 2023, $2.7 million in 2024, and $2.5 million in 2025. What is the percentage change from 2023 to 2024? What is the percentage change from 2024 to 2025? Be sure to indicate whether the percentage change is an increase or a decrease.

Understand percentage change (LO12–2)

BE12–5 If sales are $1,150,000 in 2025 and this represents a 15% increase over sales in 2024, what were sales in 2024?

Calculate receivables turnover (LO12–3)

BE12–6 Universal Sports Supply began the year with an accounts receivable balance of $200,000 and a year-end balance of $220,000. Credit sales of $750,000 generate a gross profit of $250,000. Calculate the receivables turnover ratio for the year.

Calculate inventory turnover (LO12–3)

BE12–7 Universal Sports Supply began the year with an inventory balance of $65,000 and a year-end balance of $75,000. Sales of $750,000 generate a gross profit of $250,000. Calculate the inventory turnover ratio for the year.

Understand inventory turnover (LO12–3)

BE12–8 The Intramural Sports Club reports sales revenue of $1,140,000. Inventory at both the beginning and end of the year totals $200,000. The inventory turnover ratio for the year is 4.9. What amount of gross profit does the company report in its income statement?

Understand the current ratio (LO12–3)

BE12–9 Dungy Training Company has a current ratio of 0.70 to 1, based on current assets of $3.43 million and current liabilities of $4.90 million. How, if at all, will a $900,000 cash purchase of inventory affect the current ratio? How, if at all, will a $900,000 purchase of inventory on account affect the current ratio?

Calculate profitability ratios (LO12–4)

BE12–10 Peyton's Palace has net income of $15 million on sales revenue of $130 million. Total assets were $96 million at the beginning of the year and $104 million at the end of the year. Calculate Peyton's return on assets, profit margin, and asset turnover ratios.

Calculate profitability ratios (LO12–4)

BE12–11 LaDanion's Limos reports net income of $130,000, average total assets of $700,000, and average total liabilities of $340,000. Calculate LaDanion's return on assets and return on equity ratios.

Report discontinued operations (LO12–5)

BE12–12 Kobe's Clinics provides health services and career counseling. Net income from the health services business this year is $32 million after tax. During the year, Kobe's Clinics sold the career counseling side of the business at a loss after tax of $7.5 million. Show how Kobe's Clinics would report this loss in the income statement, beginning with income from continuing operations of $32 million.

Classify income statement items (LO12–5)

BE12–13 Game Time Sports owns a recreational facility with basketball courts, pitching machines, and athletic fields. Determine whether the firm should report each of the following items as discontinued operations, other revenues, or other expenses.

1. Due to insurance concerns, Game Time sells a trampoline basketball game for a loss of $1,500.
2. Game Time experiences water damage due to a flood from a recent heavy storm. The company replaces the basketball floors at a cost of $75,000. Unfortunately, Game Time does not carry flood insurance.
3. Game Time has revenues from three sources: basketball, baseball, and football. It sells the baseball operations for a loss of $55,000 to focus on the more profitable basketball and football operations.
4. Game Time sells one of the buildings used for basketball operations at a gain of $250,000. The company has two other buildings for basketball and plans to build a new facility for basketball in another year or two.

BE12–14 Classify each of the following accounting practices as conservative or aggressive.
1. Increase the allowance for uncollectible accounts.
2. When costs are rising, change from LIFO to FIFO.
3. Change from declining-balance to straight-line depreciation in the second year of an asset depreciated over 20 years.

Distinguish between conservative and aggressive accounting practices (LO12–6)

BE12–15 Classify each of the following accepted accounting practices as conservative or aggressive.
1. Use lower-of-cost-or-market to value inventory.
2. Expense all research and development costs rather than recording some research and development costs as an asset.
3. Record loss contingencies when they are probable and can be reasonably estimated, but do not record gain contingencies until they are certain.

Distinguish between conservative and aggressive accounting practices (LO12–6)

EXERCISES

E12–1 Match (by letter) the following items with the description or example that best fits. Each letter is used only once.

Match terms with their definitions (LO12–1, 12–2, 12–3, 12–4, 12–5, 12–6)

Terms

_____ 1. Vertical analysis
_____ 2. Horizontal analysis
_____ 3. Liquidity
_____ 4. Solvency
_____ 5. Discontinued operations
_____ 6. Quality of earnings
_____ 7. Conservative accounting practices
_____ 8. Aggressive accounting practices

Descriptions

a. A company's ability to pay its current liabilities.
b. Accounting choices that result in reporting lower income, lower assets, and higher liabilities.
c. Accounting choices that result in reporting higher income, higher assets, and lower liabilities.
d. The ability of reported earnings to reflect the company's true earnings as well as the usefulness of reported earnings to help investors predict future earnings.
e. A tool to analyze trends in financial statement data for a single company over time.
f. The sale or disposal of a significant component of a company's operations.
g. A means to express each item in a financial statement as a percentage of a base amount.
h. A company's ability to pay its current and long-term liabilities.

Prepare vertical
analysis (LO12–1)

E12–2 The income statements for Federer Sports Apparel for 2025 and 2024 are presented below.

FEDERER SPORTS APPAREL Income Statements For the years ended December 31		
	2025	**2024**
Net sales	$18,800,000	$15,500,000
Cost of goods sold	13,200,000	7,000,000
Gross profit	5,600,000	8,500,000
Operating expenses	1,600,000	1,200,000
Depreciation expense	1,000,000	1,000,000
Inventory write-down	200,000	
Loss (litigation)	1,500,000	300,000
Income before tax	1,300,000	6,000,000
Income tax expense	450,000	2,000,000
Net income	$ 850,000	$ 4,000,000

Required:

Prepare a vertical analysis of the data for 2025 and 2024.

Prepare horizontal
analysis (LO12–2)

E12–3 Refer to the information provided in E12–2.

Required:

Prepare a horizontal analysis for 2025 using 2024 as the base year.

Prepare vertical
and horizontal
analyses (LO12–1, 12–2)

E12–4 The balance sheets for Federer Sports Apparel for 2025 and 2024 are presented below.

FEDERER SPORTS APPAREL Balance Sheets DECEMBER 31		
	2025	**2024**
Assets		
Cash	$ 2,300,000	$ 800,000
Accounts receivable	1,500,000	2,200,000
Inventory	2,800,000	1,700,000
Buildings	11,000,000	11,000,000
Less: Accumulated depreciation	(2,000,000)	(1,000,000)
Total assets	$15,600,000	$14,700,000
Liabilities and Stockholders' Equity		
Accounts payable	$ 1,450,000	$ 1,700,000
Contingent liability	1,500,000	1,000,000
Common stock	8,000,000	8,000,000
Retained earnings	4,650,000	4,000,000
Total liabilities and stockholders' equity	$15,600,000	$14,700,000

Required:

1. Prepare a vertical analysis of the balance sheet data for 2025 and 2024. Express each amount as a percentage of total assets.
2. Prepare a horizontal analysis for 2025 using 2024 as the base year.

E12–5 The 2024 income statement of Adrian Express reports sales of $19,310,000, cost of goods sold of $12,250,000, and net income of $1,700,000. Balance sheet information is provided in the following table.

Evaluate risk ratios (LO12–3)

ADRIAN EXPRESS Balance Sheets December 31, 2024 and 2023		
	2024	**2023**
Assets		
Current assets:		
Cash	$ 700,000	$ 860,000
Accounts receivable	1,600,000	1,100,000
Inventory	2,000,000	1,500,000
Long-term assets	4,900,000	4,340,000
Total assets	$9,200,000	$7,800,000
Liabilities and Stockholders' Equity		
Current liabilities	$1,920,000	$1,760,000
Long-term liabilities	2,400,000	2,500,000
Common stock	1,900,000	1,900,000
Retained earnings	2,980,000	1,640,000
Total liabilities and stockholders' equity	$9,200,000	$7,800,000

Industry averages for the following four risk ratios are as follows:

Average collection period	25 days
Average days in inventory	60 days
Current ratio	2 to 1
Debt to equity ratio	50%

Required:
1. Calculate the four risk ratios listed above for Adrian Express in 2024.
2. Do you think the company is more risky or less risky than the industry average? Explain your answer.

E12–6 Refer to the information for Adrian Express in E12–5. Industry averages for the following profitability ratios are as follows:

Evaluate profitability ratios (LO12–4)

Gross profit ratio	45%
Return on assets	25%
Profit margin	15%
Asset turnover	2.5 times
Return on equity	35%

Required:
1. Calculate the five profitability ratios listed above for Adrian Express.
2. Do you think the company is more profitable or less profitable than the industry average? Explain your answer.

Calculate risk
ratios (LO12–3)

E12–7 The balance sheets for Plasma Screens Corporation and additional information are provided below.

PLASMA SCREENS CORPORATION
Balance Sheets
December 31, 2024 and 2023

	2024	2023
Assets		
Current assets:		
Cash	$ 242,000	$ 130,000
Accounts receivable	98,000	102,000
Inventory	105,000	90,000
Investments	5,000	3,000
Long-term assets:		
Land	580,000	580,000
Equipment	890,000	770,000
Less: Accumulated depreciation	(528,000)	(368,000)
Total assets	$1,392,000	$1,307,000
Liabilities and Stockholders' Equity		
Current liabilities:		
Accounts payable	$ 109,000	$ 95,000
Interest payable	7,000	13,000
Income tax payable	9,000	6,000
Long-term liabilities:		
Notes payable	110,000	220,000
Stockholders' equity:		
Common stock	800,000	800,000
Retained earnings	357,000	173,000
Total liabilities and stockholders' equity	$1,392,000	$1,307,000

Additional Information for 2024:
1. Net income is $184,000.
2. Sales on account are $1,890,000.
3. Cost of goods sold is $1,394,250.

Required:
1. Calculate the following risk ratios for 2024:
   a. Receivables turnover ratio.
   b. Inventory turnover ratio.
   c. Current ratio.
   d. Acid-test ratio.
   e. Debt to equity ratio.
2. When we compare two companies, can one have a higher current ratio while the other has a higher acid-test ratio? Explain your answer.

Calculate profitability
ratios (LO12–4)

E12–8 Refer to the information provided for Plasma Screens Corporation in E12–7.

Required:
1. Calculate the following profitability ratios for 2024:
   a. Gross profit ratio.
   b. Return on assets.
   c. Profit margin.
   d. Asset turnover.
   e. Return on equity.

2. When we compare two companies, can one have a higher return on assets while the other has a higher return on equity? Explain your answer.

E12–9 The following condensed information is reported by Sporting Collectibles.

Calculate profitability ratios (LO12–4)

	2024	2023
Income Statement Information		
Sales revenue	$14,820,000	$9,400,000
Cost of goods sold	9,544,080	6,900,000
Net income	418,000	348,000
Balance Sheet Information		
Current assets	$ 1,700,000	$1,600,000
Long-term assets	2,300,000	2,000,000
Total assets	$ 4,000,000	$3,600,000
Current liabilities	$ 1,300,000	$1,000,000
Long-term liabilities	1,400,000	1,400,000
Common stock	900,000	900,000
Retained earnings	400,000	300,000
Total liabilities and stockholders' equity	$ 4,000,000	$3,600,000

Required:
1. Calculate the following profitability ratios for 2024:
   a. Gross profit ratio.
   b. Return on assets.
   c. Profit margin.
   d. Asset turnover.
   e. Return on equity.
2. Determine the amount of dividends paid to shareholders in 2024.

E12–10 The income statement for Stretch-Tape Corporation reports net sales of $540,000 and net income of $65,700. Average total assets for the year are $900,000. Stockholders' equity at the beginning of the year was $600,000, and $30,000 was paid to stockholders as dividends during the year. There were no other stockholders' equity transactions that occurred during the year.

Calculate profitability ratios (LO12–4)

Required:
Calculate the return on assets, profit margin, asset turnover, and return on equity ratios.

E12–11 As an auditor for Bernard and Thomas, you are responsible for determining the proper classification of income statement items in the audit of California Sports Grill.

Classify income statement items (LO12–5)

a. One of the company's restaurants was destroyed in a forest fire that raged through Southern California. Uninsured losses from the fire are estimated to be $450,000.
b. California Sports Grill has three operating divisions: restaurants, catering, and frozen retail foods. The company sells the frozen retail foods division of the business for a profit of $2.4 million in order to focus more on the restaurant and catering business.
c. An employee strike to increase wages and benefits shut down operations for several days at an estimated cost of $200,000.
d. A restaurant waiter slipped on a wet floor and sued the company. The employee won a settlement for $100,000, but California Sports Grill has not yet paid the settlement.
e. The company owns and operates over 40 restaurants but sold one restaurant this year at a gain of $650,000.

Required:
Indicate whether each item should be classified as discontinued operations, other revenues, or other expenses.

Report discontinued operations (LO12–5)

E12–12 LeBron's Bookstores has two divisions: books and electronics. The electronics division had another great year in 2024 with net sales of $11 million, cost of goods sold of $6.5 million, operating expenses of $3 million, and income tax expense of $375,000. The book division did not do as well and was sold during the year. The loss from operations and sale of the book division was $900,000 before taxes and $675,000 after taxes.

Required:
Prepare the multiple-step income statement for LeBron's Bookstores, including the proper reporting for the discontinued book division.

Report discontinued operations and other expenses (LO12–5)

E12–13 Shaquille Corporation has operating income of $1.7 million, a loss on sale of investments of $200,000, and income tax expense of $425,000 for the year ended December 31, 2024, before considering the following item: a $275,000 gain, after tax, from the disposal of an operating segment.

Required:
Prepare the 2024 multiple step income statement for Shaquille Corporation beginning with operating income.

Distinguish between conservative and aggressive accounting practices (LO12–6)

E12–14 Dwight's Trophy Shop is considering the following accounting changes:
a. Increase the allowance for uncollectible accounts.
b. When costs are going up, change from LIFO to FIFO.
c. Change from the straight-line method of depreciation to declining-balance in the second year of equipment with a 10-year life.
d. Record a smaller expense for warranties.

Required:
Classify each accounting change as either conservative or aggressive.

Distinguish between conservative and aggressive accounting practices (LO12–6)

E12–15 Attached is a schedule of five proposed changes at the end of the year.

($ in 000s)	Before the Change	Proposed Change	After the Change
Net sales	$18,800,000	(a) $200,000	$19,000,000
Cost of goods sold	13,200,000	(b) 400,000	13,600,000
Operating expenses	1,600,000	(c) (100,000)	1,500,000
Other revenue	500,000	(d) 50,000	550,000
Other expense	450,000	(e) (50,000)	400,000
Net income	$ 4,050,000		$ 4,050,000

Required:
1. Indicate whether each of the proposed changes is conservative, aggressive, or neutral.
2. Indicate whether the total effect of all the changes is conservative, aggressive, or neutral.

PROBLEMS: SET A

P12–1A Sports Emporium has two operating segments: sporting goods and sports apparel. The income statement for each operating segment is presented below.

Perform vertical analysis **(LO12–1)**

SPORTS EMPORIUM
Income Statement
For the year ended December 31, 2024

	Sporting Goods		Sports Apparel	
	Amount	%	Amount	%
Net sales	$1,800,000		$970,000	
Cost of goods sold	1,040,000		440,000	
Gross profit	760,000		530,000	
Operating expenses	450,000		340,000	
Operating income	310,000		190,000	
Other income (expense)	20,000		(15,000)	
Income before tax	330,000		175,000	
Income tax expense	80,000		70,000	
Net income	$ 250,000		$105,000	

Required:
1. Complete the "%" columns to be used in a vertical analysis of Sports Emporium's two operating segments. Express each amount as a percentage of sales.
2. Use vertical analysis to compare the profitability of the two operating segments. Which segment is more profitable?

P12–2A The income statements for Anything Tennis for the years ending December 31, 2024 and 2023, are provided below.

Perform horizontal analysis **(LO12–2)**

ANYTHING TENNIS
Income Statements
For the years ended December 31

	2024	2023	Increase (Decrease)	
			Amount	%
Net sales	$3,500,000	$2,620,000		
Cost of goods sold	2,150,000	1,380,000		
Gross profit	1,350,000	1,240,000		
Operating expenses	810,000	630,000		
Operating income	540,000	610,000		
Other income (expense)	10,000	6,000		
Income before tax	550,000	616,000		
Income tax expense	100,000	140,000		
Net income	$ 450,000	$ 476,000		

Required:
1. Complete the "Amount" and "%" columns to be used in a horizontal analysis of the income statements for Anything Tennis.
2. Discuss the major fluctuations in income statement items during the year.

Perform vertical and horizontal analysis (LO12–1, 12–2)

P12–3A The balance sheets for Sports Unlimited for 2024 and 2023 are provided below.

SPORTS UNLIMITED Balance Sheets For the years ended December 31	2024	2023
Assets		
Current assets:		
Cash	$103,500	$ 70,400
Accounts receivable	46,800	32,000
Inventory	44,550	71,200
Prepaid rent	7,200	3,600
Long-term assets:		
Investment in bonds	54,900	15,100
Land	117,450	126,500
Equipment	106,200	102,000
Less: Accumulated depreciation	(30,600)	(20,800)
Total assets	$450,000	$400,000
Liabilities and Stockholders' Equity		
Current liabilities:		
Accounts payable	$ 30,150	$ 46,800
Interest payable	7,200	3,600
Income tax payable	12,150	10,000
Long-term liabilities:		
Notes payable	138,150	127,600
Stockholders' equity:		
Common stock	144,000	144,000
Retained earnings	118,350	68,000
Total liabilities and stockholders' equity	$450,000	$400,000

Required:

1. Prepare a vertical analysis of Sports Unlimited's 2024 and 2023 balance sheets. Express each amount as a percentage of total assets for that year.
2. Prepare a horizontal analysis of Sports Unlimited's 2024 balance sheet using 2023 as the base year.

Calculate risk ratios (LO12–3)

P12–4A The following income statement and balance sheets for Virtual Gaming Systems are provided.

VIRTUAL GAMING SYSTEMS Income Statement For the year ended December 31, 2024		
Net sales		$ 3,086,000
Cost of goods sold		1,960,000
Gross profit		1,126,000
Expenses:		
Operating expenses	$868,000	
Depreciation expense	32,000	
Loss on sale of land	9,000	
Interest expense	20,000	
Income tax expense	58,000	
Total expenses		987,000
Net income		$ 139,000

VIRTUAL GAMING SYSTEMS
Balance Sheets
December 31

	2024	2023
Assets		
Current assets:		
Cash	$196,000	$154,000
Accounts receivable	91,000	70,000
Inventory	115,000	145,000
Prepaid rent	13,000	7,200
Long-term assets:		
Investment in bonds	115,000	0
Land	220,000	250,000
Equipment	280,000	220,000
Less: Accumulated depreciation	(84,000)	(52,000)
Total assets	$946,000	$794,200
Liabilities and Stockholders' Equity		
Current liabilities:		
Accounts payable	$ 76,000	$ 91,000
Interest payable	8,000	4,000
Income tax payable	20,000	15,000
Long-term liabilities:		
Notes payable	295,000	235,000
Stockholders' equity:		
Common stock	310,000	310,000
Retained earnings	237,000	139,200
Total liabilities and stockholders' equity	$946,000	$794,200

Required:

Assuming that all sales were on account, calculate the following risk ratios for 2024.

1. Receivables turnover ratio.
2. Average collection period.
3. Inventory turnover ratio.
4. Average days in inventory.
5. Current ratio.
6. Acid-test ratio.
7. Debt to equity ratio.
8. Times interest earned ratio.

P12–5A Data for Virtual Gaming Systems are provided in P12–4A. Earnings per share for the year ended December 31, 2024, are $1.40. The closing stock price on December 31, 2024, is $28.30.

Calculate profitability ratios **(LO12–4)**

Required:

Calculate the following profitability ratios for 2024.

1. Gross profit ratio.
2. Return on assets.
3. Profit margin.
4. Asset turnover.
5. Return on equity.
6. Price-earnings ratio.

Use ratios to analyze risk
and profitability
(LO12–3, 12–4)

P12–6A Income statement and balance sheet data for Virtual Gaming Systems are provided below.

VIRTUAL GAMING SYSTEMS
Income Statements
For the years ended December 31

	2025	2024
Net sales	$3,560,000	$3,086,000
Cost of goods sold	2,490,000	1,960,000
Gross profit	1,070,000	1,126,000
Expenses:		
Operating expenses	965,000	868,000
Depreciation expense	40,000	32,000
Loss on sale of land	0	9,000
Interest expense	23,000	20,000
Income tax expense	9,000	58,000
Total expenses	1,037,000	987,000
Net income	$ 33,000	$ 139,000

VIRTUAL GAMING SYSTEMS
Balance Sheets
December 31

	2025	2024	2023
Assets			
Current assets:			
Cash	$ 216,000	$196,000	$154,000
Accounts receivable	90,000	91,000	70,000
Inventory	140,000	115,000	145,000
Prepaid rent	15,000	13,000	7,200
Long-term assets:			
Investment in bonds	115,000	115,000	0
Land	310,000	220,000	250,000
Equipment	310,000	280,000	220,000
Less: Accumulated depreciation	(124,000)	(84,000)	(52,000)
Total assets	$1,072,000	$946,000	$794,200
Liabilities and Stockholders' Equity			
Current liabilities:			
Accounts payable	$ 161,000	$ 76,000	$ 91,000
Interest payable	12,000	8,000	4,000
Income tax payable	13,000	20,000	15,000
Long-term liabilities:			
Notes payable	450,000	295,000	235,000
Stockholders' equity:			
Common stock	310,000	310,000	310,000
Retained earnings	126,000	237,000	139,200
Total liabilities and stockholders' equity	$1,072,000	$946,000	$794,200

Required:
1. Calculate the following risk ratios for 2024 and 2025:
    a. Receivables turnover ratio.   c. Current ratio.
    b. Inventory turnover ratio.   d. Debt to equity ratio.
2. Calculate the following profitability ratios for 2024 and 2025:
    a. Gross profit ratio.   c. Profit margin.
    b. Return on assets.   d. Asset turnover.
3. Based on the ratios calculated, determine whether overall risk and profitability improved
    from 2024 to 2025.

PROBLEMS: SET B

P12–1B Game-On Sports operates in two distinct segments: athletic equipment and accessories. The income statement for each operating segment is presented below.

Perform vertical analysis (LO12–1)

GAME-ON SPORTS
Income Statement
For the year ended December 31, 2024

	Athletic Equipment		Accessories	
	Amount	%	Amount	%
Net sales	$3,050,000		$3,500,000	
Cost of goods sold	1,350,000		1,670,000	
Gross profit	1,700,000		1,830,000	
Operating expenses	750,000		800,000	
Operating income	950,000		1,030,000	
Other income (expense)	80,000		(15,000)	
Income before tax	1,030,000		1,015,000	
Income tax expense	235,000		210,000	
Net income	$ 795,000		$ 805,000	

Required:

1. Complete the "%" columns to be used in a vertical analysis of Game-On Sports' two operating segments. Express each amount as a percentage of sales.
2. Use vertical analysis to compare the profitability of the two operating segments. Which segment is more profitable?

P12–2B The income statements for Galaxy Tennis for the years ending December 31, 2024 and 2023, are provided below.

Perform horizontal analysis (LO12–2)

GALAXY TENNIS
Income Statements
For the years ended December 31

	2024	2023	Increase (Decrease)	
			Amount	%
Net sales	$6,150,000	$6,250,000		
Cost of goods sold	2,850,000	2,920,000		
Gross profit	3,300,000	3,330,000		
Operating expenses	1,510,000	1,390,000		
Operating income	1,790,000	1,940,000		
Other income (expense)	60,000	85,000		
Income before tax	1,850,000	2,025,000		
Income tax expense	390,000	435,000		
Net income	$1,460,000	$1,590,000		

Required:

1. Complete the "Amount" and "%" columns to be used in a horizontal analysis of Galaxy Tennis income statement.
2. Discuss the major fluctuations in income statement items during the year.

Perform vertical and
horizontal analysis
(LO12–1, 12–2)

P12–3B The balance sheets for Fantasy Football for 2024 and 2023 are provided below.

FANTASY FOOTBALL Balance Sheets December 31	2024	2023
Assets		
Current assets:		
Cash	$ 208,000	$ 262,200
Accounts receivable	856,000	999,400
Inventory	1,900,000	1,349,000
Supplies	124,000	87,400
Long-term assets:		
Equipment	1,292,000	1,292,000
Less: Accumulated depreciation	(380,000)	(190,000)
Total assets	$4,000,000	$3,800,000
Liabilities and Stockholders' Equity		
Current liabilities:		
Accounts payable	$ 168,000	$ 129,200
Interest payable	0	3,800
Income tax payable	76,000	76,000
Long-term liabilities:		
Notes payable	760,000	760,000
Stockholders' equity:		
Common stock	786,600	786,600
Retained earnings	2,209,400	2,044,400
Total liabilities and stockholders' equity	$4,000,000	$3,800,000

Required:

1. Prepare a vertical analysis of Fantasy Football's 2024 and 2023 balance sheets. Express each amount as a percentage of total assets for that year.
2. Prepare a horizontal analysis of Fantasy Football's 2024 balance sheet using 2023 as the base year.

Calculate risk
ratios **(LO12–3)**

P12–4B The following income statement and balance sheets for The Athletic Attic are provided.

THE ATHLETIC ATTIC Income Statement For the year ended December 31, 2024		
Net sales		$8,900,000
Cost of goods sold		5,450,000
Gross profit		3,450,000
Expenses:		
Operating expenses	$1,600,000	
Depreciation expense	210,000	
Interest expense	50,000	
Income tax expense	360,000	
Total expenses		2,220,000
Net income		$1,230,000

THE ATHLETIC ATTIC
Balance Sheets
December 31

	2024	2023
Assets		
Current assets:		
Cash	$ 164,000	$ 214,000
Accounts receivable	790,000	810,000
Inventory	1,405,000	1,075,000
Supplies	110,000	85,000
Long-term assets:		
Equipment	1,150,000	1,150,000
Less: Accumulated depreciation	(420,000)	(210,000)
Total assets	$3,199,000	$3,124,000
Liabilities and Stockholders' Equity		
Current liabilities:		
Accounts payable	$ 115,000	$ 91,000
Interest payable	0	5,000
Income tax payable	40,000	31,000
Long-term liabilities:		
Notes payable	600,000	600,000
Stockholders' equity:		
Common stock	700,000	700,000
Retained earnings	1,744,000	1,697,000
Total liabilities and stockholders' equity	$3,199,000	$3,124,000

Required:

Assuming that all sales were on account, calculate the following risk ratios for 2024:

1. Receivables turnover ratio.
2. Average collection period.
3. Inventory turnover ratio.
4. Average days in inventory.
5. Current ratio.
6. Acid-test ratio.
7. Debt to equity ratio.
8. Times interest earned ratio.

P12–5B Data for The Athletic Attic are provided in P12–4B. Earnings per share for the year ended December 31, 2024, are $1.36. The closing stock price on December 31, 2024, is $22.42.

Calculate profitability ratios (LO12–4)

Required:

Calculate the following profitability ratios for 2024:

1. Gross profit ratio.
2. Return on assets.
3. Profit margin.
4. Asset turnover.
5. Return on equity.
6. Price-earnings ratio.

Use ratios to analyze risk
and profitability
(LO12–3, 12–4)

P12–6B Income statement and balance sheet data for The Athletic Attic are provided below.

THE ATHLETIC ATTIC Income Statements For the years ended December 31		
	2025	**2024**
Net sales	$10,400,000	$8,900,000
Cost of goods sold	6,800,000	5,450,000
Gross profit	3,600,000	3,450,000
Expenses:		
Operating expenses	1,600,000	1,600,000
Depreciation expense	200,000	210,000
Interest expense	40,000	50,000
Income tax expense	400,000	360,000
Total expenses	2,240,000	2,220,000
Net income	$ 1,360,000	$1,230,000

THE ATHLETIC ATTIC Balance Sheets December 31			
	2025	**2024**	**2023**
Assets			
Current assets:			
Cash	$ 225,000	$ 164,000	$ 214,000
Accounts receivable	990,000	790,000	810,000
Inventory	1,725,000	1,405,000	1,075,000
Supplies	130,000	110,000	85,000
Long-term assets:			
Equipment	1,100,000	1,150,000	1,150,000
Less: Accumulated depreciation	(600,000)	(420,000)	(210,000)
Total assets	$3,570,000	$3,199,000	$3,124,000
Liabilities and Stockholders' Equity			
Current liabilities:			
Accounts payable	$ 175,000	$ 115,000	$ 91,000
Interest payable	4,000	0	5,000
Income tax payable	40,000	40,000	31,000
Long-term liabilities:			
Notes payable	500,000	600,000	600,000
Stockholders' equity:			
Common stock	600,000	700,000	700,000
Retained earnings	2,251,000	1,744,000	1,697,000
Total liabilities and stockholders' equity	$3,570,000	$3,199,000	$3,124,000

Required:

1. Calculate the following risk ratios for 2024 and 2025:
   a. Receivables turnover ratio.   c. Current ratio.
   b. Inventory turnover ratio.   d. Debt to equity ratio.
2. Calculate the following profitability ratios for 2024 and 2025:
   a. Gross profit ratio.   c. Profit margin.
   b. Return on assets.   d. Asset turnover.
3. Based on the ratios calculated, determine whether overall risk and profitability improved
   from 2024 to 2025.

REAL-WORLD PERSPECTIVES

Data Analytics & Excel

Visit Connect to find a variety of Data Analytics questions that help build Excel, Tableau, and data visualization skills. Assignable materials include Integrated Excel, Applying Excel, Data Visualizations, Tableau Dashboard Activities, and Applying Tableau cases.

Great Adventures

General Ledger Continuing Case

(This is the conclusion of the Great Adventures problem from earlier chapters.)

RWP12–1 Income statement and balance sheet data for Great Adventures, Inc., are provided below.

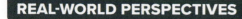

GREAT ADVENTURES, INC.
Income Statement
For the year ended December 31, 2025

Net sales revenues		$164,150
Interest revenue		120
Expenses:		
Cost of goods sold	$38,500	
Operating expenses	51,400	
Depreciation expense	17,250	
Interest expense	6,785	
Income tax expense	14,500	
Total expenses		128,435
Net income		$ 35,835

GREAT ADVENTURES, INC.
Balance Sheets
December 31, 2025 and 2024

	2025	2024
Assets		
Current assets:		
Cash	$ 180,568	$ 64,500
Accounts receivable	47,600	0
Inventory	7,000	0
Other current assets	900	4,500
Long-term assets:		
Land	500,000	0
Buildings	800,000	0
Equipment	62,000	40,000
Accumulated depreciation	(25,250)	(8,000)
Total assets	$1,572,818	$101,000
Liabilities and Stockholders' Equity		
Current liabilities:		
Accounts payable	$ 20,800	$ 2,800
Interest payable	750	750
Income tax payable	14,500	14,000
Other current liabilities	21,000	0
Notes payable (current)	48,014	0
Notes payable (long-term)	475,869	30,000
Stockholders' equity:		
Common stock	120,000	20,000
Paid-in capital	904,000	0
Retained earnings	57,885	33,450
Treasury stock	(90,000)	0
Total liabilities and stockholders' equity	$1,572,818	$101,000

As you can tell from the financial statements, 2025 was an especially busy year. Tony and Suzie were able to use the money received from borrowing and the issuance of stock to buy land and begin construction of cabins, dining facilities, ropes course, and the outdoor swimming pool. They even put in a baby pool to celebrate the birth of their first child.

Required:
1. Calculate the following risk ratios for 2025.
   a. Receivables turnover ratio. (*Hint:* Use net sales revenues for net credit sales.)
   b. Average collection period.
   c. Inventory turnover ratio.
   d. Average days in inventory.
   e. Current ratio.
   f. Acid-test ratio. (*Hint:* There are no current investments.)
   g. Debt to equity ratio.
   h. Times interest earned ratio.
2. Calculate the following profitability ratios for 2025.
   a. Gross profit ratio. (*Hint:* Use net sales revenues.)
   b. Return on assets.
   c. Profit margin. (*Hint:* Use net sales revenues.)
   d. Asset turnover. (*Hint:* Use net sales revenues.)
   e. Return on equity.

Financial Analysis Continuing Case

American Eagle Outfitters, Inc.

RWP12–2 Financial information for **American Eagle** is presented in **Appendix A** at the end of the book.

Required:
1. Calculate the following risk ratios for the most recent year:
   a. Receivables turnover ratio.
   b. Average collection period.
   c. Inventory turnover ratio.
   d. Average days in inventory.
   e. Current ratio.
   f. Acid-test ratio.
   g. Debt to equity ratio.
2. Calculate the following profitability ratios for the most recent year:
   a. Gross profit ratio.
   b. Return on assets.
   c. Profit margin.
   d. Asset turnover.
   e. Return on equity.

The Buckle, Inc.

Financial Analysis Continuing Case

RWP12–3 Financial information for **Buckle** is presented in **Appendix B** at the end of the book.

Required:
1. Calculate the following risk ratios for the most recent year:
   a. Receivables turnover ratio.
   b. Average collection period.
   c. Inventory turnover ratio.
   d. Average days in inventory.
   e. Current ratio.
   f. Acid-test ratio.
   g. Debt to equity ratio.

2. Calculate the following profitability ratios for the most recent year:
   a. Gross profit ratio.
   b. Return on assets.
   c. Profit margin.
   d. Asset turnover.
   e. Return on equity.

American Eagle Outfitters, Inc., vs. The Buckle, Inc.

Comparative Analysis
Continuing Case

RWP12–4 Financial information for **American Eagle** is presented in **Appendix A** at the end of the book, and financial information for **Buckle** is presented in **Appendix B** at the end of the book.

Required:

1. Calculate the following risk ratios for both companies for the most recent year. Based on these calculations, which company appears to be more risky?
   a. Receivables turnover ratio.
   b. Average collection period.
   c. Inventory turnover ratio.
   d. Average days in inventory.
   e. Current ratio.
   f. Acid-test ratio.
   g. Debt to equity ratio.
2. Calculate the following profitability ratios for both companies for the most recent year. Based on these calculations, which company appears to be more profitable?
   a. Gross profit ratio.
   b. Return on assets.
   c. Profit margin.
   d. Asset turnover.
   e. Return on equity.

EDGAR Research

RWP12–5 Using EDGAR (Electronic Data Gathering, Analysis, and Retrieval system), find the annual report (10-K) for **Dick's Sporting Goods** for the year ended **February 1, 2020.** Locate the "Consolidated Statements of Income" (income statement) and "Consolidated Balance Sheets." You may also find the annual report at the company's website.

Required:

1. Calculate the following risk ratios. In parentheses are the corresponding ratios for the industry. Determine for each ratio whether Dick's Sporting Goods would generally be considered to have lower or higher risk relative to the industry under normal conditions.
   a. Receivables turnover ratio. (Industry = 85.9)
   b. Inventory turnover ratio. (Industry = 7.48)
   c. Current ratio. (Industry = 1.45)
   d. Acid-test ratio. (Industry = 0.6)
   e. Debt to equity ratio. (Industry = 68.0%)
2. Calculate the following profitability ratios. In parentheses are the corresponding ratios for the industry. Determine for each ratio whether Dick's Sporting Goods would generally be considered to have lower or higher profitability relative to the industry under normal conditions.
   a. Gross profit ratio. (Industry = 30.3%)
   b. Return on assets. (Industry = 6.7%)
   c. Profit margin. (Industry = 3.8%)
   d. Asset turnover. (Industry = 1.9 times)
   e. Return on equity. (Industry = 20.1%)

Ethics

RWP12–6 After years of steady growth in net income, Performance Drug Company reported a preliminary net loss in 2024. The CEO, Joe Mammoth, notices the following estimates are included in reported performance:

1. Warranty expense and liability for estimated future warranty costs associated with sales in the current year.
2. Loss due to ending inventory's net realizable value (estimated selling price) falling below its cost. This type of inventory write down occurs most years.
3. Depreciation of major equipment purchased this year, which is estimated to have a 10-year service life.

Joe is worried that the company's poor performance will have a negative impact on the company's risk and profitability ratios. This will cause the stock price to decline and hurt the company's ability to obtain needed loans in the following year. Before releasing the financial statements to the public, Joe asks his CFO to reconsider these estimates. He argues that (1) warranty work won't happen until next year, so that estimate can be eliminated; (2) there's always a chance we'll find the right customer and sell inventory above cost, so the estimated loss on inventory write-down can be eliminated; and (3) we may use the equipment for 20 years (even though equipment of this type has little chance of being used for more than 10 years). Joe explains that all of his suggestions make good business sense and reflect his optimism about the company's future. Joe further notes that executive bonuses (including his and the CFO's) are tied to net income, and if we don't show a profit this year, there will be no bonuses.

Required:

1. Understand the reporting effect: How would excluding the warranty adjustment affect the debt to equity ratio? How would excluding the inventory adjustment affect the gross profit ratio? How would extending the depreciable life to 20 years affect the profit margin?
2. Specify the options: If the adjustments are kept, what will they indicate about the company's overall risk and profitability?
3. Identify the impact: Could these adjustments affect stockholders, lenders, and management?
4. Make a decision: Should the CFO follow Joe's suggestions of not including these adjustments?

Written Communication

RWP12–7 Roseburg Corporation manufactures cardboard containers. In 2017, the company purchased several large tracts of timber for $20 million with the intention of harvesting its own timber rather than buying timber from outside suppliers. However, in 2024, Roseburg abandoned the idea, and sold all of the timber tracts for $30 million. Net income for 2024, before considering this event, was $12 million.

Required:

Write a memo providing your recommended income statement presentation of the gain on the sale of the timber tracts. Be sure to include a discussion of the alternatives that might be considered.

Earnings Management

RWP12–8 Major League Products provides merchandise carrying the logos of each fan's favorite major league team. In recent years, the company has struggled to compete against new Internet-based companies selling products at much lower prices. Andrew Ransom, in his second year out of college, was assigned to audit the financial statements of Major League Products. One of the steps in the auditing process is to examine the nature of year-end adjustments. Andrew's investigation reveals that the company has made several year-end adjustments, including (a) a decrease in the allowance for uncollectible accounts, (b) a reversal in the previous write-down of inventory, (c) an increase in the estimated useful life used to calculate depreciation expense, and (d) a decrease in the liability reported for litigation.

Required:

1. Classify each adjustment as conservative or aggressive.
2. What effect do these adjustments have on expenses in the current year?
3. What effect do these adjustments have on the company's cash balance in the current year?
4. Do these year-end adjustments, taken together, raise concerns about earnings management?

Answers to Chapter Framework Questions

1. d   2. c   3. c   4. b   5. a

Answers to Self-Study Questions

1. b   2. a   3. d   4. b   5. c   6. d   7. d   8. a   9. d   10. c   11. b   12. c   13. b   14. a   15. d

American Eagle Outfitters, Inc., 2020 Annual Report

Appendix A

UNITED STATES
SECURITIES AND EXCHANGE COMMISSION
WASHINGTON, D.C. 20549

FORM 10-K

☒   ANNUAL REPORT PURSUANT TO SECTION 13 OR 15(d) OF THE SECURITIES EXCHANGE ACT OF 1934

For the fiscal year ended February 1, 2020

OR

☐   TRANSITION REPORT PURSUANT TO SECTION 13 OR 15(d) OF THE SECURITIES EXCHANGE ACT OF 1934

Commission file number: **1-33338**

AMERICAN EAGLE OUTFITTERS, INC.

(Exact name of registrant as specified in its charter)

Delaware	**13-2721761**
(State or other jurisdiction of incorporation or organization)	(I.R.S. Employer Identification No.)
77 Hot Metal Street, Pittsburgh, PA	**15203-2329**
(Address of principal executive offices)	(Zip Code)

Registrant's telephone number, including area code: **(412) 432-3300**

Securities registered pursuant to Section 12(b) of the Act:

Title of each class	Trading Symbol(s)	Name of each exchange on which registered
Common Stock, $0.01 par value	**AEO**	**New York Stock Exchange**

Securities registered pursuant to Section 12(g) of the Act: **None**

Indicate by check mark if the registrant is a well-known seasoned issuer, as defined in Rule 405 of the Securities Act.   YES ☒   NO ☐

Indicate by check mark if the registrant is not required to file reports pursuant to Section 13 or Sections 15(d) of the Act.   YES ☐   NO ☒

Indicate by check mark whether the registrant (1) has filed all reports required to be filed by Section 13 or 15(d) of the Securities Exchange Act of 1934 during the preceding 12 months (or for such shorter period that the registrant was required to file such reports), and (2) has been subject to the filing requirements for at the past 90 days.   YES ☒   NO ☐

Indicate by check mark whether the registrant has submitted electronically every Interactive Data File required to be submitted pursuant to Rule 405 of Regulation S-T (§232.405 of this chapter) during the preceding 12 months (or for such shorter period that the registrant was required to submit such files).   YES ☒   NO ☐

Indicate by check mark whether the registrant is a large accelerated filer, an accelerated filer, a non-accelerated filer, a smaller reporting company, or an emerging growth company. See the definitions of "large accelerated filer," "accelerated filer," "smaller reporting company," and "emerging growth company" in Rule 12b-2 of the Exchange Act.

Large accelerated filer	☒	Accelerated filer	☐
Non-accelerated filer	☐	Smaller reporting company	☐
		Emerging growth company	☐

If an emerging growth company, indicate by check mark if the registrant has elected not to use the extended transition period for complying with any new or revised financial accounting standards provided pursuant to Section 13(a) of the Exchange Act. ☐

Indicate by check mark whether the registrant is a shell company (as defined in Rule 12b-2 of the Act).   YES ☐   NO ☒

The aggregate market value of voting and non-voting common equity held by non-affiliates of the registrant as of August 3, 2019 was $2,507,621,307.

Indicate the number of shares outstanding of each of the registrant's classes of common stock, as of the latest practicable date: 167,203,263 Common Shares were outstanding at March 9, 2020.

DOCUMENTS INCORPORATED BY REFERENCE

Portions of the Company's Proxy Statement for the 2020 Annual Meeting of Stockholders are incorporated into Part III herein.

Report of Independent Registered Public Accounting Firm (in part)

To the Stockholders and the Board of Directors of American Eagle Outfitters, Inc.

Opinion on the Financial Statements

We have audited the accompanying consolidated balance sheets of American Eagle Outfitters, Inc. (the Company) as of February 1, 2020 and February 2, 2019, the related consolidated statements of operations, comprehensive income, stockholders' equity and cash flows for each of the three years in the period ended February 1, 2020, and the related notes (collectively referred to as the "consolidated financial statements"). In our opinion, the consolidated financial statements present fairly, in all material respects, the financial position of the Company at February 1, 2020 and February 2, 2019, and the results of its operations and its cash flows for each of the three years in the period ended February 1, 2020, in conformity with U.S. generally accepted accounting principles.

We also have audited, in accordance with the standards of the Public Company Accounting Oversight Board (United States) (PCAOB), the Company's internal control over financial reporting as of February 1, 2020, based on criteria established in Internal Control-Integrated Framework issued by the Committee of Sponsoring Organizations of the Treadway Commission (2013 Framework), and our report dated March 12, 2020 expressed an unqualified opinion thereon.

Adoption of ASU No. 2016-02

As discussed in the paragraph under the caption "Recent Accounting Pronouncements" described in Note 2 to the consolidated financial statements, effective February 3, 2019, the Company changed its method of accounting for leases due to the adoption of Accounting Standards Update No. 2016-02, *Leases* (Topic 842).

Basis for Opinion

These financial statements are the responsibility of the Company's management. Our responsibility is to express an opinion on the Company's financial statements based on our audits. We are a public accounting firm registered with the PCAOB and are required to be independent with respect to the Company in accordance with the U.S. federal securities laws and the applicable rules and regulations of the Securities and Exchange Commission and the PCAOB.

We conducted our audits in accordance with the standards of the PCAOB. Those standards require that we plan and perform the audit to obtain reasonable assurance about whether the financial statements are free of material misstatement, whether due to error or fraud. Our audits included performing procedures to assess the risks of material misstatement of the financial statements, whether due to error or fraud, and performing procedures that respond to those risks. Such procedures included examining, on a test basis, evidence regarding the amounts and disclosures in the financial statements. Our audits also included evaluating the accounting principles used and significant estimates made by management, as well as evaluating the overall presentation of the financial statements. We believe that our audits provide a reasonable basis for our opinion.

/s/ Ernst & Young LLP

We have served as the Company's auditor since 1993.
Pittsburgh, Pennsylvania
March 12, 2020

AMERICAN EAGLE OUTFITTERS, INC.
Consolidated Balance Sheets

(In thousands, except per share amounts)	February 1, 2020	February 2, 2019
Assets		
Current assets:		
Cash and cash equivalents	$ 361,930	$ 333,330
Short-term investments (available for sale)	55,000	92,135
Merchandise inventory	446,278	424,404
Accounts receivable, net	119,064	93,477
Prepaid expenses and other	65,658	102,907
Total current assets	1,047,930	1,046,253
Property and equipment, at cost, net of accumulated depreciation	735,120	742,149
Operating lease right-of-use assets	1,418,916	-
Intangible assets, net, including goodwill	53,004	58,167
Non-current deferred income taxes	22,724	14,062
Other assets	50,985	42,747
Total assets	$ 3,328,679	$ 1,903,378
Liabilities and Stockholders' Equity		
Current liabilities:		
Accounts payable	$ 285,746	$ 240,671
Current portion of operating lease liabilities	299,161	-
Accrued income and other taxes	9,514	20,064
Accrued compensation and payroll taxes	43,537	82,173
Unredeemed gift cards and gift certificates	56,974	53,997
Other current liabilities and accrued expenses	56,824	145,740
Total current liabilities	751,756	542,645
Non-current liabilities:		
Non-current operating lease liabilities	1,301,735	-
Other non-current liabilities	27,335	73,178
Total non-current liabilities	1,329,070	73,178
Commitments and contingencies	—	—
Stockholders' equity:		
Preferred stock, $0.01 par value; 5,000 shares authorized; none issued and outstanding	—	—
Common stock, $0.01 par value; 600,000 shares authorized; 249,566 shares issued; 166,993 and 172,436 shares outstanding, respectively	2,496	2,496
Contributed capital	577,856	574,929
Accumulated other comprehensive loss, net of tax	(33,168)	(34,832)
Retained earnings	2,108,292	2,054,654
Treasury stock, 82,573 and 77,130 shares, respectively, at cost	(1,407,623)	(1,309,692)
Total stockholders' equity	1,247,853	1,287,555
Total liabilities and stockholders' equity	$ 3,328,679	$ 1,903,378

Refer to Notes to Consolidated Financial Statements

AMERICAN EAGLE OUTFITTERS, INC.
Consolidated Statements of Operations

	For the Years Ended		
(In thousands, except per share amounts)	February 1, 2020	February 2, 2019	February 3, 2018
Total net revenue	$ 4,308,212	$ 4,035,720	$ 3,795,549
Cost of sales, including certain buying, occupancy and warehousing expenses	2,785,911	2,548,082	2,425,044
Gross profit	1,522,301	1,487,638	1,370,505
Selling, general and administrative expenses	1,029,412	980,610	879,685
Impairment and restructuring charges	80,494	1,568	20,611
Depreciation and amortization expense	179,050	168,331	167,421
Operating income	233,345	337,129	302,788
Other income (expense), net	11,933	7,971	(15,615)
Income before income taxes	245,278	345,100	287,173
Provision for income taxes	54,021	83,198	83,010
Net income	$ 191,257	$ 261,902	$ 204,163
Basic net income per common share	$ 1.13	$ 1.48	$ 1.15
Diluted net income per common share	$ 1.12	$ 1.47	$ 1.13
Weighted average common shares outstanding - basic	169,711	176,476	177,938
Weighted average common shares outstanding - diluted	170,867	178,035	180,156

Refer to Notes to Consolidated Financial Statements

AMERICAN EAGLE OUTFITTERS, INC.
Consolidated Statements of Comprehensive Income

| | | For the Years Ended | | | | |
| | February 1, 2020 | | February 2, 2019 | | February 3, 2018 | |
(In thousands)						
Net income	$	191,257	$	261,902	$	204,163
Other comprehensive gain (loss):						
Foreign currency translation gain (loss)		1,664		(4,037)		5,667
Other comprehensive gain (loss)		1,664		(4,037)		5,667
Comprehensive income	$	192,921	$	257,865	$	209,830

Refer to Notes to Consolidated Financial Statements

AMERICAN EAGLE OUTFITTERS, INC.
Consolidated Statements of Stockholders' Equity

(In thousands, except per share amounts)	Shares Outstanding (1)	Common Stock	Contributed Capital	Retained Earnings	Treasury Stock (2)	Accumulated Other Comprehensive Income (Loss)	Stockholders' Equity
Balance at January 28, 2017	181,886	$ 2,496	$ 603,890	$ 1,775,775	$ (1,141,130)	$ (36,462)	$ 1,204,569
Stock awards	—	—	17,202	—	—	—	17,202
Repurchase of common stock as part of publicly announced programs	(6,000)	—	—	—	(87,672)	—	(87,672)
Repurchase of common stock from employees	(871)	—	—	—	(12,513)	—	(12,513)
Reissuance of treasury stock	2,301	—	(29,632)	(5,488)	39,043	—	3,923
Net income	—	—	—	204,163	—	—	204,163
Other comprehensive loss	—	—	—	—	—	5,667	5,667
Cash dividends and dividend equivalents ($0.50 per share)	—	—	2,310	(90,858)	—	—	(88,548)
Balance at February 3, 2018	177,316	$ 2,496	$ 593,770	$ 1,883,592	$ (1,202,272)	$ (30,795)	$ 1,246,791
Stock awards	—	—	27,057	—	—	—	27,057
Repurchase of common stock as part of publicly announced programs	(7,300)	—	—	—	(144,405)	—	(144,405)
Repurchase of common stock from employees	(943)	—	—	—	(19,668)	—	(19,668)
Reissuance of treasury stock	3,363	—	(48,022)	8,407	56,653	—	17,038
Net income	—	—	—	261,902	—	—	261,902
Other comprehensive loss	—	—	—	—	—	(4,037)	(4,037)
Cash dividends and dividend equivalents ($0.55 per share)	—	—	2,124	(99,247)	—	—	(97,123)
Balance at February 2, 2019	172,436	$ 2,496	$ 574,929	$ 2,054,654	$ (1,309,692)	$ (34,832)	$ 1,287,555
Stock awards	—	—	22,742	—	—	—	22,742
Repurchase of common stock as part of publicly announced programs	(6,336)	—	—	—	(112,381)	—	(112,381)
Repurchase of common stock from employees	(431)	—	—	—	(8,087)	—	(8,087)
Adoption of ASC 842, net of tax	—	—	—	(44,435)	—	—	(44,435)
Reissuance of treasury stock	1,324	—	(22,175)	1,959	22,537	—	2,321
Net income	—	—	—	191,257	—	—	191,257
Other comprehensive loss	—	—	—	—	—	1,664	1,664
Cash dividends and dividend equivalents ($0.55 per share)	—	—	2,360	(95,143)	—	—	(92,783)
Balance at February 1, 2020	166,993	$ 2,496	$ 577,856	$ 2,108,292	$ (1,407,623)	$ (33,168)	$ 1,247,853

(1)   600,000 authorized, 249,566 issued and 166,993 outstanding, $0.01 par value common stock at February 1, 2020; 600,000 authorized, 249,566 issued and 172,436 outstanding, $0.01 par value common stock at February 2, 2019; 600,000 authorized, 249,566 issued and 177,316 outstanding, $0.01 par value common stock at February 3, 2018; 600,000 authorized, 249,566 issued and 181,886 outstanding, $0.01 par value common stock at January 28, 2017. The Company has 5,000 authorized, with none issued or outstanding, $0.01 par value preferred stock for all periods presented.

(2)   82,573 shares, 77,130 shares and 72,250 shares at February 1, 2020, February 2, 2019 and February 3, 2018 respectively. During Fiscal 2019, Fiscal 2018, and Fiscal 2017, 1,324 shares, 3,363 shares, and 2,301 shares, respectively, were reissued from treasury stock for the issuance of share-based payments.

Refer to Notes to Consolidated Financial Statements

AMERICAN EAGLE OUTFITTERS, INC.
Consolidated Statements of Cash Flows

	For the Years Ended		
(In thousands)	February 1, 2020	February 2, 2019	February 3, 2018
Operating activities:			
Net income	$ 191,257	$ 261,902	$ 204,163
Adjustments to reconcile net income to net cash provided by operating activities			
Depreciation and amortization	181,379	170,504	169,473
Share-based compensation	23,038	27,506	16,890
Deferred income taxes	6,541	(4,391)	44,312
Loss on impairment of assets	66,252	546	—
Changes in assets and liabilities:			
Merchandise inventory	(21,615)	(28,496)	(35,912)
Operating lease assets	261,303	—	—
Operating lease liabilities	(271,519)	—	—
Other assets	(32,845)	(22,206)	13,755
Accounts payable	44,949	4,329	(16,663)
Accrued compensation and payroll taxes	(38,603)	28,043	1,289
Accrued and other liabilities	5,279	18,908	(2,881)
Net cash provided by operating activities	**415,416**	**456,645**	**394,426**
Investing activities:			
Capital expenditures for property and equipment	(210,360)	(189,021)	(169,469)
Purchase of available-for-sale investments	(85,000)	(202,912)	—
Sale of available-for-sale investments	122,135	109,776	—
Other investing activities	(1,669)	(672)	(2,681)
Net cash used for investing activities	**(174,894)**	**(282,829)**	**(172,150)**
Financing activities:			
Repurchase of common stock as part of publicly announced programs	(112,381)	(144,405)	(87,682)
Repurchase of common stock from employees	(8,087)	(19,668)	(12,513)
Net proceeds from stock options exercised	2,119	15,495	3,355
Cash dividends paid	(92,783)	(97,123)	(88,548)
Other financing activities	(94)	(6,802)	(3,384)
Net cash used for financing activities	**(211,226)**	**(252,503)**	**(188,772)**
Effect of exchange rates on cash	(696)	(1,596)	1,496
Net change in cash and cash equivalents	**28,600**	**(80,283)**	**35,000**
Cash and cash equivalents - beginning of period	$ 333,330	$ 413,613	$ 378,613
Cash and cash equivalents - end of period	361,930	333,330	413,613

Refer to Notes to Consolidated Financial Statements

AMERICAN EAGLE OUTFITTERS, INC.

Notes to Consolidated Financial Statements
For the Year Ended February 1, 2020

1. Business Operations

American Eagle Outfitters, Inc. (the "Company," "we" and "our"), a Delaware corporation, operates under the American Eagle® ("AE") and Aerie® brands. We also operate Tailgate, a vintage, sports-inspired apparel brand with a college town store concept, and Todd Snyder New York, a premium menswear brand.

Founded in 1977, the Company is a leading multi-brand specialty retailer that operates more than 1,000 retail stores in the U.S. and internationally, online at www.ae.com and www.aerie.com, www.toddsnyder.com and more than 200 international store locations managed by third-party operators. Through its portfolio of brands, the Company offers high quality, on-trend clothing, accessories, and personal care products at affordable prices. The Company's online business, AEO Direct, ships to 81 countries worldwide.

Merchandise Mix

The following table sets forth the approximate consolidated percentage of total net revenue from operations attributable to each merchandise group for each of the periods indicated:

	For the Years Ended		
	February 1, 2020	February 2, 2019	February 3, 2018
Men's apparel and accessories	29%	32%	34%
Women's apparel and accessories (excluding Aerie)	52%	52%	53%
Aerie	19%	16%	13%
Total	100%	100%	100%

2. Summary of Significant Accounting Policies

Principles of Consolidation

The Consolidated Financial Statements include the accounts of the Company and its wholly owned subsidiaries. All intercompany transactions and balances have been eliminated in consolidation. At February 1, 2020, the Company operated in one reportable segment.

Fiscal Year

Our fiscal year is a 52- or 53-week year that ends on the Saturday nearest to January 31. As used herein, "Fiscal 2020" refers to the 52-week period that will end on January 30, 2021. "Fiscal 2019" refers to the 52-week period ended February 1, 2020. "Fiscal 2018" refers to the 52-week period ended February 2, 2019. "Fiscal 2017" refers to the 53-week period ended February 3, 2018.

Estimates

The preparation of financial statements in conformity with accounting principles generally accepted in the United States of America ("GAAP") requires the Company's management to make estimates and assumptions that affect the reported amounts of assets and liabilities and disclosure of contingent assets and liabilities at the date of the financial statements and the reported amounts of revenues and expenses during the reporting period. Actual results could differ from those estimates. On an ongoing basis, our management reviews its estimates based on currently available information. Changes in facts and circumstances may result in revised estimates.

Cash, Cash Equivalents, and Short-term Investments

The Company considers all highly liquid investments purchased with a remaining maturity of three months or less to be cash equivalents.

Short-term investments classified as available-for-sale included certificates of deposit as of February 1, 2020, and they included certificates of deposit and commercial paper with a maturity of greater than three months, but less than one year as of February 2, 2019.

Refer to Note 3 to the Consolidated Financial Statements for information regarding cash, cash equivalents, and short-term investments.

Merchandise Inventory

Merchandise inventory is valued at the lower of average cost or net realizable value, utilizing the retail method. Average cost includes merchandise design and sourcing costs and related expenses. The Company records merchandise receipts when control of the merchandise has transferred to the Company.

The Company reviews its inventory levels to identify slow-moving merchandise and generally uses markdowns to clear merchandise. Additionally, the Company estimates a markdown reserve for future planned permanent markdowns related to current inventory. Markdowns may occur when inventory exceeds customer demand for reasons of style, seasonal adaptation, changes in customer preference, lack of consumer acceptance of fashion items, competition, or if it is determined that the inventory in stock will not sell at its currently ticketed price. Such markdowns may have a material adverse impact on earnings, depending on the extent and amount of inventory affected.

The Company also estimates a shrinkage reserve for the period between the last physical count and the balance sheet date. The estimate for the shrinkage reserve, based on historical results, can be affected by changes in merchandise mix and changes in actual shrinkage trends.

Property and Equipment

Property and equipment is recorded on the basis of cost with depreciation computed utilizing the straight-line method over the assets' estimated useful lives. The useful lives of our major classes of assets are as follows:

Buildings	25 years
Leasehold improvements	Lesser of 10 years or the term of the lease
Fixtures and equipment	Five years
Information technology	Three - five years

As of February 1, 2020, the weighted average remaining useful life of our assets was approximately 7.5 years.

In accordance with ASC 360, *Property, Plant, and Equipment* ("ASC 360"), the Company's management evaluates the value of leasehold improvements, store fixtures, and operating lease ROU assets associated with retail stores, which have been open for a period sufficient to reach maturity. The Company evaluates long-lived assets for impairment at the individual store level, which is the lowest level at which individual cash flows can be identified. Impairment losses are recorded on long-lived assets used in operations when events and circumstances indicate that the assets might be impaired and the projected undiscounted cash flows estimated to be generated by those assets are less than the carrying amounts. When events such as these occur, the impaired assets are adjusted to their estimated fair value and an impairment loss is recorded separately as a component of operating income under impairment and restructuring charges.

During Fiscal 2019, the Company recorded asset impairment charges of $64.5 million on the assets of 20 retail stores. Of the total, $39.5 million related to the impairment of leasehold improvements and store fixtures, and $25.0 million related to the impairment of operating lease ROU assets. The impairments were recorded as a result of store performance up to and including the holiday selling season and a significant portfolio review in the fourth quarter of Fiscal 2019 that considered current and future performance projections and strategic real estate initiatives. The Company determined that these stores would not be able to generate sufficient cash flows over the expected remaining lease term to recover the carrying value of the respective stores' assets.

During Fiscal 2018, the Company recorded no significant asset impairment charges.

When the Company closes, remodels, or relocates a store prior to the end of its lease term, the remaining net book value of the assets related to the store is recorded as a write-off of assets within depreciation and amortization expense.

Refer to Note 7 to the Consolidated Financial Statements for additional information regarding property and equipment, and refer to Note 15 for additional information regarding impairment charges.

Intangible Assets, including Goodwill

The Company's goodwill is primarily related to the acquisition of its importing operations, Canada business, and Tailgate and Todd Snyder brands. In accordance with ASC 350, *Intangibles – Goodwill and Other* ("ASC 350"), the Company evaluates goodwill for possible impairment on at least an annual basis and last performed an annual impairment test as of February 1, 2020. As a result, the Company concluded that certain goodwill was impaired resulting in a $1.7 million charge included within impairment and restructuring charges in the Consolidated Statements of Operations. There were no goodwill impairment charges recorded during Fiscal 2018.

Definite-lived intangible assets are recorded on the basis of cost with amortization computed utilizing the straight-line method over the assets' estimated useful lives. The Company's definite-lived intangible assets, which consist primarily of trademark assets, are generally amortized over 15 to 25 years.

The Company evaluates definite-lived intangible assets for impairment in accordance with ASC 360 when events or circumstances indicate that the carrying value of the asset may not be recoverable. Such an evaluation includes the estimation of undiscounted future cash flows to be generated by those assets. If the sum of the estimated future undiscounted cash flows is less than the carrying amounts of the assets, then the assets are impaired and are adjusted to their estimated fair value. No definite-lived intangible asset impairment charges were recorded for all periods presented.

Refer to Note 8 to the Consolidated Financial Statements for additional information regarding intangible assets, including goodwill.

Gift Cards

Revenue is not recorded on the issuance of gift cards. The value of a gift card is recorded as a current liability upon issuance and revenue is recognized when the gift card is redeemed for merchandise. The Company estimates gift card breakage and recognizes revenue in proportion to actual gift card redemptions as a component of total net revenue.

The Company determines an estimated gift card breakage rate by continuously evaluating historical redemption data and the time when there is a remote likelihood that a gift card will be redeemed. The Company recorded $9.5 million, $8.9 million, and $10.1 million during Fiscal 2019, Fiscal 2018, and Fiscal 2017, respectively, of revenue related to gift card breakage.

Customer Loyalty Program

In 2017, the Company launched a highly digitized loyalty program called AEO Connected™ (the "Program"). This Program integrates the credit card rewards program and the AEREWARDS® loyalty program into one combined customer offering. Under the Program, customers accumulate points based on purchase activity and earn rewards by reaching certain point thresholds. Customers earn rewards in the form of discount savings certificates. Rewards earned are valid through the stated expiration date, which is 45 days from the issuance date of the reward. Rewards not redeemed during the 45-day redemption period are forfeited. Additional rewards are also given for key items such as jeans and bras.

Points earned under the Program on purchases at American Eagle and Aerie are accounted for in accordance with ASC 606. The portion of the sales revenue attributed to the award points is deferred and recognized when the award is redeemed or when the points expire, using the relative stand-alone selling price method. Additionally, reward points earned using the co-branded credit card on non-AE or Aerie purchases are accounted for in accordance with ASC 606. As the points are earned, a current liability is recorded for the estimated cost of the award, and the impact of the adjustments are recorded in revenue.

Sales Return Reserve

Revenue is recorded net of estimated and actual sales returns and deductions for coupon redemptions and other promotions. The Company records the impact of adjustments to its sales return reserve quarterly within total net revenue and cost of sales. The sales return reserve reflects an estimate of sales returns based on projected merchandise returns determined using historical average return percentages.

	For the Years Ended		
(In thousands)	February 1, 2020	February 2, 2019	February 3, 2018
Beginning balance	$ 4,620	$ 4,717	$ 3,639
Returns	(121,513)	(113,805)	(103,393)
Provisions	122,718	113,708	104,471
Ending balance	$ 5,825	$ 4,620	$ 4,717

The presentation on a gross basis consists of a separate right of return asset and liability. These amounts are recorded within (i) prepaid expenses and other and (ii) other current liabilities and accrued expenses, respectively, on the Consolidated Balance Sheets.

Income Taxes

The Company calculates income taxes in accordance with ASC 740, *Income Taxes* ("ASC 740"), which requires the use of the asset and liability method. Under this method, deferred tax assets and liabilities are recognized based on the difference between the Consolidated Financial Statement carrying amounts of existing assets and liabilities and their respective tax bases as computed pursuant to ASC 740. Deferred tax assets and liabilities are measured using the tax rates, based on certain judgments regarding enacted tax laws and published guidance, in effect in the years when those temporary differences are expected to reverse. A valuation allowance is established against the deferred tax assets when it is more likely than not that some portion or all of the deferred taxes may not be realized. Changes in the Company's level and composition of earnings, tax laws or the deferred tax valuation allowance, as well as the results of tax audits, may materially affect the Company's effective income tax rate.

The Company evaluates its income tax positions in accordance with ASC 740, which prescribes a comprehensive model for recognizing, measuring, presenting, and disclosing in the financial statements tax positions taken or expected to be taken on a tax return, including a decision whether to file or not to file in a particular jurisdiction. Under ASC 740, a tax benefit from an uncertain position may be recognized only if it is more likely than not that the position is sustainable based on its technical merits.

The calculation of the deferred tax assets and liabilities, as well as the decision to recognize a tax benefit from an uncertain position and to establish a valuation allowance require management to make estimates and assumptions. The Company believes that its assumptions and estimates are reasonable, although actual results may have a positive or negative material impact on the balances of deferred tax assets and liabilities, valuation allowances or net income.

Refer to Note 14 to the Consolidated Financial Statements for additional information.

Revenue Recognition

In May 2014, the FASB issued ASC 606, a comprehensive revenue recognition model that expands disclosure requirements and requires a company to recognize revenue to depict the transfer of goods or services to a customer at an amount that reflects the consideration it expects to receive in exchange for those goods or services. The Company adopted ASC 606 on February 4, 2018. Results for reporting periods beginning on or after February 4, 2018 are presented under ASC 606, while prior period amounts are not adjusted and continue to be reported in accordance with our historic accounting. The Company recorded a net increase to opening retained earnings of $0.2 million as of February 4, 2018 due to the cumulative impact of adoption. The impact was the result of accounting for customer loyalty programs using a relative stand-alone selling price method vs. incremental cost method. The Company defers a portion of the sales revenue attributed to the loyalty points and recognizes revenue when the points are redeemed or expire, consistent with the requirements of ASC 606. Refer to the Customer Loyalty Program caption above for additional information.

Revenue is recorded for store sales upon the purchase of merchandise by customers. The Company's e-commerce operation records revenue upon the estimated customer receipt date of the merchandise. Shipping and handling revenues are included in total net revenue on the Company's Consolidated Statements of Operations. Sales tax collected from customers is excluded from revenue and is included as part of accrued income and other taxes on the Company's Consolidated Balance Sheets.

Revenue is recorded net of estimated and actual sales returns and promotional price reductions. The Company records the impact of adjustments to its sales return reserve quarterly within total net revenue and cost of sales. The sales return reserve reflects an estimate of sales returns based on projected merchandise returns determined using historical average return percentages.

Revenue is not recorded on the issuance of gift cards. A current liability is recorded upon issuance, and revenue is recognized when the gift card is redeemed for merchandise. Additionally, the Company recognizes revenue on unredeemed gift cards based on an estimate of the amounts that will not be redeemed ("gift card breakage"), determined through historical redemption trends. Gift card breakage revenue is recognized in proportion to actual gift card redemptions as a component of total net revenue. For further information on the Company's gift card program, refer to the Gift Cards caption above.

The Company recognizes royalty revenue generated from its license or franchise agreements based upon a percentage of merchandise sales by the licensee/franchisee. This revenue is recorded as a component of total net revenue when earned and collection is probable.

Cost of Sales, Including Certain Buying, Occupancy, and Warehousing Expenses

Cost of sales consists of merchandise costs, including design, sourcing, importing, and inbound freight costs, as well as markdowns, shrinkage and certain promotional costs (collectively "merchandise costs") and buying, occupancy and warehousing costs.

Design costs are related to the Company's Design Center operations and include compensation, travel and entertainment, supplies and samples for our design teams, as well as rent and depreciation for our Design Center. These costs are included in cost of sales as the respective inventory is sold.

Buying, occupancy and warehousing costs consist of: compensation, employee benefit expenses and travel and entertainment for our buyers and certain senior merchandising executives; rent and utilities related to our stores, corporate headquarters, distribution centers and other office space; freight from our distribution centers to the stores; compensation and supplies for our distribution centers, including purchasing, receiving and inspection costs; and shipping and handling costs related to our e-commerce operation. Gross profit is the difference between total net revenue and cost of sales.

Selling, General, and Administrative Expenses

Selling, general, and administrative expenses consist of compensation and employee benefit expenses, including salaries, incentives, and related benefits associated with our stores and corporate headquarters. Selling, general, and administrative expenses also include advertising costs, supplies for our stores and home office, communication costs, travel, and entertainment, leasing costs and services purchased. Selling, general, and administrative expenses do not include compensation, employee benefit expenses and travel for our design, sourcing and importing teams, our buyers and our distribution centers as these amounts are recorded in cost of sales. Additionally, selling, general, and administrative expenses do not include rent and utilities related to our stores, operating costs of our distribution centers, and shipping and handling costs related to our e-commerce operations.

Advertising Costs

Certain advertising costs, including direct mail, in-store photographs, and other promotional costs are expensed when the marketing campaign commences. As of February 1, 2020 and February 2, 2019, the Company had prepaid advertising expense of $14.5 million and $12.6 million, respectively. All other advertising costs are expensed as incurred. The Company recognized $151.5 million, $143.2 million, and $129.8 million in advertising expense during Fiscal 2019, Fiscal 2018, and Fiscal 2017, respectively.

Store Pre-Opening Costs

Store pre-opening costs consist primarily of rent, advertising, supplies, and payroll expenses. These costs are expensed as incurred.

Other Income (Expense), Net

Other income (expense), net consists primarily of foreign currency transaction gains (losses), interest income (expense), and realized investment gains (losses).

Legal Proceedings and Claims

The Company is subject to certain legal proceedings and claims arising out of the conduct of its business. In accordance with ASC 450, *Contingencies* ("ASC 450"), the Company records a reserve for estimated losses when the loss is probable and the amount can be reasonably estimated. If a range of possible loss exists and no anticipated loss within the range is more likely than any other anticipated loss, the Company records the accrual at the low end of the range, in accordance with ASC 450. As the Company believes that it has provided adequate reserves, it anticipates that the ultimate outcome of any matter currently pending against the Company will not materially affect the consolidated financial position, results of operations or cash flows of the Company. However, our assessment of any litigation or other legal claims could potentially change in light of the discovery of facts not presently known or determinations by judges, juries, or other finders of fact that are not in accord with management's evaluation of the possible liability or outcome of such litigation or claims.

Supplemental Disclosures of Cash Flow Information

The table below shows supplemental cash flow information for cash amounts paid during the respective periods:

	For the Years Ended		
(In thousands)	February 1, 2020	February 2, 2019	February 3, 2018
Cash paid during the periods for:			
Income taxes	$ 69,689	$ 81,248	$ 47,094
Interest	$ 828	$ 1,207	$ 1,098

3. Cash, Cash Equivalents, and Short-term Investments

The following table summarizes the fair market value of our cash and short-term investments, which are recorded on the Consolidated Balance Sheets:

(In thousands)	February 1, 2020	February 2, 2019
Cash and cash equivalents:		
Cash	$ 126,087	$ 108,216
Interest bearing deposits	235,843	165,274
Commercial paper	—	59,840
Total cash and cash equivalents	$ 361,930	$ 333,330
Short-term investments:		
Certificates of deposits	55,000	70,000
Commercial paper	—	22,135
Total short-term investments	55,000	92,135
Total cash and short-term investments	$ 416,930	$ 425,465

4. Fair Value Measurements

ASC 820, *Fair Value Measurement Disclosures* ("ASC 820"), defines fair value, establishes a framework for measuring fair value in accordance with GAAP, and expands disclosures about fair value measurements. Fair value is defined under ASC 820 as the exit price associated with the sale of an asset or transfer of a liability in an orderly transaction between market participants at the measurement date.

Financial Instruments

Valuation techniques used to measure fair value under ASC 820 must maximize the use of observable inputs and minimize the use of unobservable inputs. In addition, ASC 820 establishes a three-tier fair value hierarchy, which prioritizes the inputs used in measuring fair value. These tiers include:

- *Level 1* — Quoted prices in active markets.

- *Level 2* — Inputs other than Level 1 that are observable, either directly or indirectly.

- *Level 3* — Unobservable inputs that are supported by little or no market activity and that are significant to the fair value of the assets or liabilities.

The Company's cash equivalents and short-term investments are Level 1 financial assets and are measured at fair value on a recurring basis, for all periods presented. Refer to Note 3 to the Consolidated Financial Statements for additional information regarding cash equivalents and short-term investments.

The Company had no other financial instruments that required fair value measurement for any of the periods presented.

Non-Financial Assets

The Company's non-financial assets, which include intangible assets and property and equipment, are not required to be measured at fair value on a recurring basis. However, if certain triggering events occur and the Company is required to evaluate the non-financial asset for impairment, a resulting impairment would require that the non-financial asset be recorded at the estimated fair value. During Fiscal 2019, the Company concluded that certain goodwill was impaired resulting in a $1.7 million charge included within impairment and restructuring charges in the Consolidated Statements of Operations. The measurement of the goodwill impairment included Level 3 measurements.

Certain long-lived assets were measured at fair value on a nonrecurring basis using Level 3 inputs as defined in ASC 820. During Fiscal 2019, the Company recorded asset impairment charges of $64.5 million on the assets of 20 retail stores. Of the total, $39.5 million related to the impairment of leasehold improvements and store fixtures and $25.0 million related to the impairment of operating lease ROU assets. The assets were adjusted to their fair value and the loss on impairment was recorded within impairment and restructuring charges in the Consolidated Statements of Operations. The fair value of the impaired assets on these stores, after the recorded loss, is approximately $145.2 million including $3.9 million of leasehold improvements and store fixtures and $141.3 million of operating lease ROU assets.

The fair value of the Company's stores was determined by estimating the amount and timing of net future cash flows and discounting them using a risk-adjusted rate of interest. The Company estimates future cash flows based on its experience and knowledge of the market in which the store is located.

5. Earnings per Share

The following is a reconciliation between basic and diluted weighted average shares outstanding:

| | For the Years Ended | | |
	February 1, 2020	February 2, 2019	February 3, 2018
(In thousands, except per share amounts)			
Weighted average common shares outstanding:			
Basic number of common shares outstanding	169,711	176,476	177,938
Dilutive effect of stock options and non-vested restricted stock	1,156	1,559	2,218
Diluted number of common shares outstanding	170,867	178,035	180,156
Potentially issuable common shares excluded due to anti-dilutive effect	700	393	3,082

Dilutive and anti-dilutive shares relate to share-based compensation.

Refer to Note 12 to the Consolidated Financial Statements for additional information regarding share-based compensation.

6. Accounts Receivable, net

Accounts receivable, net is comprised of the following:

(In thousands)	February 1, 2020	February 2, 2019
Franchise and license receivable	$ 36,060	$ 31,474
Merchandise sell-offs and vendor receivables	24,474	12,943
Credit card program receivable	30,578	21,129
Tax refunds	4,868	7,483
Landlord construction allowances	12,038	9,001
Gift card receivable	1,794	3,514
Other items	9,252	7,933
Total	$ 119,064	$ 93,477

7. Property and Equipment, net

Property and equipment, net consists of the following:

(In thousands)	February 1, 2020	February 2, 2019
Land	$ 17,910	$ 17,910
Buildings	211,814	209,487
Leasehold improvements	721,514	698,029
Fixtures and equipment	1,316,198	1,221,203
Construction in progress	46,992	34,221
Property and equipment, at cost	$ 2,314,428	$ 2,180,850
Less: Accumulated depreciation	(1,579,308)	(1,438,701)
Property and equipment, net	$ 735,120	$ 742,149

Depreciation expense is as follows:

| | For the Years Ended | | |
(In thousands)	February 1, 2020	February 2, 2019	February 3, 2018
Depreciation expense	$ 178,038	$ 164,265	$ 158,969

Additionally, during Fiscal 2019, Fiscal 2018, and Fiscal 2017, the Company recorded $4.3 million, $2.0 million and $6.0 million, respectively, related to asset write-offs within depreciation and amortization expense.

8. Intangible Assets, net, including Goodwill

Intangible assets, net, including goodwill, consists of the following:

(In thousands)	February 1, 2020	February 2, 2019
Goodwill, gross	$ 17,353	$ 17,383
Accumulated impairment (1)	(4,196)	(2,484)
Goodwill, net	$ 13,157	$ 14,899
Trademarks, at cost	71,685	70,994
Accumulated amortization	(31,838)	(27,726)
Trademarks, net	$ 39,847	$ 43,268
Intangibles, net, including goodwill	$ 53,004	$ 58,167

(1)   Accumulated impairment includes $2.5 million recorded in Fiscal 2016 and $1.7 million recorded in Fiscal 2019

Amortization expense is as follows:

| | For the Years Ended | | |
(In thousands)	February 1, 2020	February 2, 2019	February 3, 2018
Amortization expense	$ 4,184	$ 4,225	$ 4,551

The table below summarizes the estimated future amortization expense for intangible assets existing as of February 1, 2020 for the next five Fiscal Years:

(In thousands)		Future Amortization
2020	$	3,493
2021	$	3,166
2022	$	3,164
2023	$	3,110
2024	$	2,902

9. Other Credit Arrangements

In January 2019, the Company entered into an amended and restated Credit Agreement ("Credit Agreement") for five-year, syndicated, asset-based revolving credit facilities (the "Credit Facilities"). The Credit Agreement provides senior secured revolving credit for loans and letters of credit up to $400 million, subject to customary borrowing base limitations. The Credit Facilities provide increased financial flexibility and take advantage of a favorable credit environment.

All obligations under the Credit Facilities are unconditionally guaranteed by certain subsidiaries. The obligations under the Credit Agreement are secured by a first-priority security interest in certain working capital assets of the borrowers and guarantors, consisting primarily of cash, receivables, inventory and certain other assets, and will be further secured by first-priority mortgages on certain real property.

As of February 1, 2020, the Company was in compliance with the terms of the Credit Agreement and had $7.9 million outstanding in stand-by letters of credit. No loans were outstanding under the Credit Agreement as of February 1, 2020 or at any time throughout Fiscal 2019.

10. Leases

The Company leases all store premises, some of its office space and certain information technology and office equipment. These leases are generally classified as operating leases.

Store leases generally provide for a combination of base rentals and contingent rent based on store sales. Additionally, most leases include lessor incentives such as construction allowances and rent holidays. The Company is typically responsible for tenant occupancy costs including maintenance costs, common area charges, real estate taxes, and certain other expenses.

Most leases include one or more options to renew. The exercise of lease renewal options is at the Company's discretion and is not reasonably certain at lease commencement. When measuring operating lease ROU assets and operating lease liabilities after the date of adoption of ASC 842 (February 3, 2019), the Company only includes cash flows related to options to extend or terminate leases once those options are executed.

Some leases have variable payments. However, because they are not based on an index or rate, they are not included in the measurement of operating lease ROU assets and operating lease liabilities.

When determining the present value of future payments for an operating lease that does not have a readily determinable implicit rate, the Company uses its incremental borrowing rate as of the date of initial possession of the leased asset.

For leases that qualify for the short-term lease exemption, the Company does not record an operating lease liability or operating lease ROU asset. Short-term lease payments are recognized on a straight-line basis over the lease term of 12 months or less.

The following table summarizes expense categories and cash payments for operating leases during the period. It also includes the total non-cash transaction activity for new operating lease ROU assets and related operating lease liabilities entered into during the period.

(In thousands)		For the Year Ended February 1, 2020
Lease costs		
Operating lease costs	$	349,429
Variable lease costs		102,797
Short-term leases and other lease costs		37,293
Total lease costs	$	489,519
Other information		
Cash paid for operating lease liability	$	(328,925)
New operating lease ROU asset entered into during the period	$	277,562

The following table contains the average remaining lease term and discount rate, weighted by outstanding operating lease liability as of the end of the period:

Lease term and discount rate	February 1, 2020
Weighted-average remaining lease term - operating leases	6.2 years
Weighted-average discount rate - operating leases	5.1%

The table below is a maturity analysis of the operating leases in effect as of the end of the period. Undiscounted cash flows for finance leases and short-term leases are not material for the periods reported and are excluded from the table below:

(In thousands)		Undiscounted cash flows February 1, 2020
Fiscal years:		
2020	$	374,819
2021		331,578
2022		277,954
2023		255,695
2024		184,591
Thereafter		471,160
Total undiscounted cash flows	$	1,895,797
Less: discount on lease liability		(294,901)
Total lease liability	$	1,600,896

The Company adopted ASC 842 as of February 3, 2019 through the modified retrospective method. Prior period amounts have not been adjusted and continue to be reported in accordance with our historical accounting treatment. In accordance with the transition guidance within ASC 842, the following table provides the disclosures related to Fiscal Years 2018 and 2017 as required under ASC 840, *Leases*. Refer to Note 2 for further information about the Company's adoption of ASC 842.

(In thousands)	For the Years Ended	
	February 2, 2019	February 3, 2018
Store rent:		
Fixed minimum	$ 303,123	$ 298,458
Contingent	13,883	9,566
Total store rent, excluding common area maintenance charges, real estate taxes and certain other expenses	$ 317,006	$ 308,025
Offices, distribution facilities, equipment and other	18,636	26,960
Total rent expense	$ 335,642	$ 334,985

14. Income Taxes

On December 22, 2017, the U.S. government enacted comprehensive tax legislation in the form of the Tax Act. The Tax Act made broad and complex changes to the U.S. tax code including reducing the U.S. federal corporate tax rate from 35% to 21% effective January 1, 2018, and implementing a one-time transition tax on undistributed earnings of foreign subsidiaries. During the fourth quarter of Fiscal 2018, the Company completed its accounting for the tax effects of the Tax Act with no material net changes to the provisional amounts recorded for the one-time transition tax and the re-measurement of deferred tax assets and liabilities.

Additionally, the Tax Act included a provision designed to currently tax global intangible low-taxed income ("GILTI") earned by non-U.S. corporate subsidiaries of large U.S. shareholders starting in 2018. The Company has elected, as permitted in FASB Staff Q&A - Topic 740 - No. 5, to treat any future GILTI tax liabilities as period costs and will expense those liabilities in the period incurred. The Company therefore will not record deferred taxes associated with the GILTI provision of the Tax Act. The Company has no changes to this election for Fiscal 2019.

The components of income before income taxes from continuing operations were:

(In thousands)	For the Years Ended		
	February 1, 2020	February 2, 2019	February 3, 2018
U.S.	$ 229,906	$ 308,424	$ 255,621
Foreign	15,372	36,676	31,552
Total	$ 245,278	$ 345,100	$ 287,173

15. Impairment and Restructuring Charges

The following table represents impairment and restructuring charges. All amounts were recorded within impairment and restructuring charges on the Consolidated Statements of Operations, unless otherwise noted.

(In thousands)	For the years ended		
	February 1, 2020	February 2, 2019	February 3, 2018
Asset impairment charges (1)	$ 66,252	$ —	$ —
Severance and related employee costs	6,691	1,568	10,660
Joint business venture exit charges (2)	4,194	—	7,964
Japan market transition costs	1,814	—	—
China restructuring (3)	1,543	—	—
Lease termination and store closure costs	—	—	9,951
Inventory charges (4)	—	—	1,669
Total impairment and restructuring charges	$ 80,494	$ 1,568	$ 30,244

(1) Fiscal 2019 asset impairment charges of $64.5 million on the assets of 20 retail stores. Of the total, $39.5 million related to the impairment of leasehold improvements and store fixtures, and $25.0 million related to the impairment of operating lease ROU assets. The Company also concluded that certain goodwill was impaired resulting in a $1.7 million charge in Fiscal 2019.
(2) Fiscal 2017 joint business venture exit charges were recorded within other (expense) income, net on the Consolidated Statements of Operations
(3) Pre-tax corporate restructuring charges of $1.5 million, primarily consisting of severance and closure costs for our company-owned and operated stores in China recorded in the first quarter of Fiscal 2019
(4) Fiscal 2017 inventory charges were recorded within cost of sales, including certain buying, occupancy, and warehousing expenses on the Consolidated Statements of Operations

A rollforward of the restructuring liabilities recognized in the Consolidated Balance Sheet is as follows:

(In thousands)	February 1, 2020
Accrued liability as of February 2, 2019	$ 6,629
Add: Costs incurred, excluding non-cash charges	10,686
Less: Cash payments and adjustments	(13,128)
Accrued liability as of February 1, 2020	$ 4,187

The accrued liability as of February 2, 2019 relates to previous restructuring activities disclosed in the Company's Fiscal 2018 Form 10-K, which remained unpaid at the beginning of Fiscal 2019.

Item 9. Changes in and Disagreements with Accountants on Accounting and Financial Disclosure.

None.

Item 9A. Controls and Procedures.

Disclosure Controls and Procedures

We maintain disclosure controls and procedures that are designed to provide reasonable assurance that information required to be disclosed in our reports under the Securities Exchange Act of 1934, as amended (the "Exchange Act"), is recorded, processed, summarized and reported within the time periods specified in the SEC's rules and forms, and that such information is accumulated and communicated to the management of American Eagle Outfitters, Inc. (the "Management"), including our principal executive officer and our principal financial officer, as appropriate, to allow timely decisions regarding required disclosure. In designing and evaluating the disclosure controls and procedures, Management recognized that any controls and procedures, no matter how well designed and operated, can provide only reasonable assurance of achieving the desired control objectives.

As of the end of the period covered by this Annual Report on Form 10-K, the Company performed an evaluation under the supervision and with the participation of Management, including our principal executive officer and principal financial officer, of the design and effectiveness of our disclosure controls and procedures (as defined in Rules 13a-15(e) or 15d-15(e) under the Exchange Act). Based upon that evaluation, our principal executive officer and principal financial officer concluded that, as of the end of the period covered by this Annual Report, our disclosure controls and procedures were effective in the timely and accurate recording, processing, summarizing, and reporting of material financial and non-financial information within the periods specified within the SEC's rules and forms. Our principal executive officer and principal financial officer also concluded that our disclosure controls and procedures were effective to ensure that information required to be disclosed in the reports that we file or submit under the Exchange Act is accumulated and communicated to our Management, including our principal executive officer and principal financial officer, to allow timely decisions regarding required disclosure.

Management's Annual Report on Internal Control over Financial Reporting

Our Management is responsible for establishing and maintaining adequate internal control over financial reporting (as defined in Rule 13a-15(f) or Rule 15(d)-15(f) under the Exchange Act). Our internal control over financial reporting is designed to provide a reasonable assurance to our Management and our Board that the reported financial information is presented fairly, that disclosures are adequate, and that the judgments inherent in the preparation of financial statements are reasonable.

All internal control systems, no matter how well designed, have inherent limitations, including the possibility of human error and the overriding of controls. Therefore, even those systems determined to be effective can provide only reasonable, not absolute, assurance with respect to financial statement preparation and presentation.

Our Management assessed the effectiveness of our internal control over financial reporting as of February 1, 2020. In making this assessment, our Management used the framework and criteria set forth in *Internal Control – Integrated Framework (2013),* issued by the Committee of Sponsoring Organizations of the Treadway Commission (COSO). Based on this assessment, our Management concluded that the Company's internal control over financial reporting was effective as of February 1, 2020.

Our independent registered public accounting firm, Ernst & Young LLP, was retained to audit the Company's consolidated financial statements included in this Annual Report on Form 10-K and the effectiveness of the Company's internal control over financial reporting. Ernst & Young LLP has issued an attestation report on our internal control over financial reporting as of February 1, 2020, which is included herein.

Changes in Internal Control over Financial Reporting

There were no changes in our internal control over financial reporting (as defined in Rules 13a-15(f) or 15d-15(f) of the Exchange Act) during our most recently-completed fiscal quarter that have materially affected, or are reasonably likely to materially affect, our internal control over financial reporting.

Report of Independent Registered Public Accounting Firm

To the Stockholders and the Board of Directors of American Eagle Outfitters, Inc.

Opinion on Internal Control over Financial Reporting

We have audited American Eagle Outfitters, Inc.'s internal control over financial reporting as of February 1, 2020, based on criteria established in Internal Control—Integrated Framework issued by the Committee of Sponsoring Organizations of the Treadway Commission (2013 framework) (the COSO criteria). In our opinion, American Eagle Outfitters, Inc. (the Company) maintained, in all material respects, effective internal control over financial reporting as of February 1, 2020, based on the COSO criteria.

We also have audited, in accordance with the standards of the Public Company Accounting Oversight Board (United States) (PCAOB), the consolidated balance sheets of the Company as of February 1, 2020 and February 2, 2019, the related consolidated statements of operations, comprehensive income, stockholders' equity and cash flows for each of the three years in the period ended February 1, 2020, and the related notes and our report dated March 12, 2020 expressed an unqualified opinion thereon.

Basis for Opinion

The Company's management is responsible for maintaining effective internal control over financial reporting and for its assessment of the effectiveness of internal control over financial reporting included in the accompanying Management's Annual Report on Internal Control over Financial Reporting. Our responsibility is to express an opinion on the Company's internal control over financial reporting based on our audit. We are a public accounting firm registered with the PCAOB and are required to be independent with respect to the Company in accordance with the U.S. federal securities laws and the applicable rules and regulations of the Securities and Exchange Commission and the PCAOB.

We conducted our audit in accordance with the standards of the PCAOB. Those standards require that we plan and perform the audit to obtain reasonable assurance about whether effective internal control over financial reporting was maintained in all material respects.

Our audit included obtaining an understanding of internal control over financial reporting, assessing the risk that a material weakness exists, testing and evaluating the design and operating effectiveness of internal control based on the assessed risk, and performing such other procedures as we considered necessary in the circumstances. We believe that our audit provides a reasonable basis for our opinion.

Definition and Limitations of Internal Control Over Financial Reporting

A company's internal control over financial reporting is a process designed to provide reasonable assurance regarding the reliability of financial reporting and the preparation of financial statements for external purposes in accordance with generally accepted accounting principles. A company's internal control over financial reporting includes those policies and procedures that (1) pertain to the maintenance of records that, in reasonable detail, accurately and fairly reflect the transactions and dispositions of the assets of the company; (2) provide reasonable assurance that transactions are recorded as necessary to permit preparation of financial statements in accordance with generally accepted accounting principles, and that receipts and expenditures of the company are being made only in accordance with authorizations of management and directors of the company; and (3) provide reasonable assurance regarding prevention or timely detection of unauthorized acquisition, use, or disposition of the company's assets that could have a material effect on the financial statements.

Because of its inherent limitations, internal control over financial reporting may not prevent or detect misstatements. Also, projections of any evaluation of effectiveness to future periods are subject to the risk that controls may become inadequate because of changes in conditions, or that the degree of compliance with the policies or procedures may deteriorate.

/s/ Ernst & Young LLP

Pittsburgh, Pennsylvania

March 12, 2020

For the complete annual report, go online to corporate.buckle.com/investors/annual-reports.

UNITED STATES
SECURITIES AND EXCHANGE COMMISSION
WASHINGTON, D.C. 20549

FORM 10-K

☒ **ANNUAL REPORT PURSUANT TO SECTION 13 OR 15(d) OF THE SECURITIES EXCHANGE ACT OF 1934**

For the Fiscal Year Ended **February 1, 2020**

☐ **TRANSITION REPORT PURSUANT TO SECTION 13 OR 15(d) OF THE SECURITIES EXCHANGE ACT OF 1934**

For the Transition Period from _____ to _____

Commission File Number: 001-12951

THE BUCKLE, INC.
(Exact name of Registrant as specified in its charter)

Nebraska	**47-0366193**
(State or other jurisdiction of incorporation or organization)	(I.R.S. Employer Identification No.)

2407 West 24th Street, Kearney, Nebraska 68845-4915
(Address of principal executive offices)   (Zip Code)

Registrant's telephone number, including area code: **(308) 236-8491**

Securities registered pursuant to Section 12(b) of the Act:

<u>Title of each class</u>	<u>Trading Symbol(s)</u>	<u>Name of Each Exchange on Which Registered</u>
Common Stock, $.01 par value	BKE	New York Stock Exchange

Securities registered pursuant to Section 12(g) of the Act: None

Indicate by check mark if the registrant is a well-known seasoned issuer, as defined in Rule 405 of the Securities Act. Yes ☑   No ☐

Indicate by check mark if the registrant is not required to file reports pursuant to Section 13 or 15(d) of the Act. Yes ☐   No ☑

Indicate by check mark whether the registrant (1) has filed all reports required to be filed by Section 13 or 15(d) of the Securities Exchange Act of 1934 during the preceding 12 months (or for such shorter period that the Registrant was required to file such reports) and (2) has been subject to such filing requirements for the past 90 days. Yes ☑ No ☐

Indicate by check mark whether the registrant has submitted electronically every Interactive Data File required to be submitted pursuant to Rule 405 of Regulation S-T during the preceding 12 months (or for a shorter period that the registrant was required to submit such files). Yes ☑ No ☐

Indicate by check mark whether the registrant is a large accelerated filer, an accelerated filer, a non-accelerated filer, a smaller reporting company, or an emerging growth company. (See definition of "large accelerated filer," "accelerated filer," "smaller reporting company, " and "emerging growth company" in Rule 12b-2 of the Exchange Act). Check one.
☐   Large accelerated filer; ☑ Accelerated filer; ☐ Non-accelerated filer; ☐ Smaller Reporting Company; ☐ Emerging Growth Company

If an emerging growth company, indicate by check mark if the registrant has elected not to use the extended transition period for complying with any new or revised financial accounting standards provided pursuant to Section 13(a) of the Exchange Act. ☐

Indicate by check mark whether the registrant is a shell company (as defined in Rule 12b-2 of the Act). Yes ☐   No ☑

The aggregate market value (based on the closing price of the New York Stock Exchange) of the common stock of the registrant held by non-affiliates of the registrant was $554,715,851 on August 3, 2019. For purposes of this response, executive officers and directors are deemed to be the affiliates of the Registrant and the holdings by non-affiliates was computed as 28,229,814 shares.

The number of shares outstanding of the Registrant's Common Stock, as of March 27, 2020, was 49,408,181.

DOCUMENTS INCORPORATED BY REFERENCE

Portions of the definitive Proxy Statement for the registrant's 2020 Annual Meeting of Shareholders are incorporated by reference in Part III.

ITEM 8 - FINANCIAL STATEMENTS AND SUPPLEMENTARY DATA

REPORT OF INDEPENDENT REGISTERED PUBLIC ACCOUNTING FIRM

To the stockholders and the Board of Directors of The Buckle, Inc.

Opinion on the Financial Statements

We have audited the accompanying consolidated balance sheets of The Buckle, Inc. and subsidiary (the "Company") as of February 1, 2020 and February 2, 2019, the related consolidated statements of income, comprehensive income, stockholders' equity, and cash flows, for each of the three fiscal years in the period ended February 1, 2020, and the related notes and the schedule listed in the Index at Item 15 (collectively referred to as the "financial statements"). In our opinion, the financial statements present fairly, in all material respects, the financial position of the Company as of February 1, 2020 and February 2, 2019, and the results of its operations and its cash flows for each of the three fiscal years in the period ended February 1, 2020, in conformity with accounting principles generally accepted in the United States of America.

We have also audited, in accordance with the standards of the Public Company Accounting Oversight Board (United States) (PCAOB), the Company's internal control over financial reporting as of February 1, 2020 based on criteria established in *Internal Control - Integrated Framework (2013)* issued by the Committee of Sponsoring Organizations of the Treadway Commission and our report dated April 1, 2020, expressed an unqualified opinion on the Company's internal control over financial reporting.

Change in Accounting Principle

As discussed in Note A to the financial statements, effective February 3, 2019, the Company adopted Financial Accounting Standards Board Accounting Standards Update No. 2016-02, *Leases (Topic 842)*.

Basis for Opinion

These financial statements are the responsibility of the Company's management. Our responsibility is to express an opinion on the Company's financial statements based on our audits. We are a public accounting firm registered with the PCAOB and are required to be independent with respect to the Company in accordance with the U.S. federal securities laws and the applicable rules and regulations of the Securities and Exchange Commission and the PCAOB.

We conducted our audits in accordance with the standards of the PCAOB. Those standards require that we plan and perform the audit to obtain reasonable assurance about whether the financial statements are free of material misstatement, whether due to error or fraud. Our audits included performing procedures to assess the risks of material misstatement of the financial statements, whether due to error or fraud, and performing procedures that respond to those risks. Such procedures included examining, on a test basis, evidence regarding the amounts and disclosures in the financial statements. Our audits also included evaluating the accounting principles used and significant estimates made by management, as well as evaluating the overall presentation of the financial statements. We believe that our audits provide a reasonable basis for our opinion.

/s/ Deloitte & Touche LLP

Omaha, Nebraska
April 1, 2020

We have served as the Company's auditor since 1990.

THE BUCKLE, INC.

CONSOLIDATED BALANCE SHEETS
(Amounts in Thousands Except Share and Per Share Amounts)

ASSETS	February 1, 2020	February 2, 2019
CURRENT ASSETS:		
Cash and cash equivalents	$ 220,969	$ 168,471
Short-term investments (Notes B and C)	12,532	51,546
Receivables	3,136	7,089
Inventory	121,258	125,190
Prepaid expenses and other assets	20,935	18,136
Total current assets	378,830	370,432
PROPERTY AND EQUIPMENT (Note E)	452,205	452,187
Less accumulated depreciation and amortization	(338,357)	(321,505)
	113,848	130,682
OPERATING LEASE RIGHT-OF-USE ASSETS (Note D)	350,088	—
LONG-TERM INVESTMENTS (Notes B and C)	15,863	18,745
OTHER ASSETS (Notes G and H)	9,261	7,443
Total assets	$ 867,890	$ 527,302

LIABILITIES AND STOCKHOLDERS' EQUITY

	February 1, 2020	February 2, 2019
CURRENT LIABILITIES:		
Accounts payable	$ 26,491	$ 29,008
Accrued employee compensation	22,929	21,452
Accrued store operating expenses	17,837	17,982
Gift certificates redeemable	15,319	16,634
Current portion of operating lease liabilities (Note D)	87,314	—
Income taxes payable (Note G)	2,751	5,142
Total current liabilities	172,641	90,218
DEFERRED COMPENSATION (Note J)	15,863	13,978
NON-CURRENT OPERATING LEASE LIABILITIES (Note D)	290,238	—
DEFERRED RENT LIABILITY	—	29,229
Total liabilities	478,742	133,425
COMMITMENTS (Notes F and I)		
STOCKHOLDERS' EQUITY (Note K):		
Common stock, authorized 100,000,000 shares of $.01 par value; 49,205,681 and 49,017,395 shares issued and outstanding at February 1, 2020 and February 2, 2019, respectively	492	490
Additional paid-in capital	152,258	148,564
Retained earnings	236,398	244,823
Total stockholders' equity	389,148	393,877
Total liabilities and stockholders' equity	$ 867,890	$ 527,302

See notes to consolidated financial statements.

THE BUCKLE, INC.

CONSOLIDATED STATEMENTS OF INCOME
(Amounts in Thousands Except Per Share Amounts)

	Fiscal Years Ended		
	February 1, 2020	February 2, 2019	February 3, 2018
SALES, Net of returns and allowances	$ 900,254	$ 885,496	$ 913,380
COST OF SALES (Including buying, distribution, and occupancy costs)	522,780	519,423	533,357
Gross profit	377,474	366,073	380,023
OPERATING EXPENSES:			
Selling	204,480	202,032	206,068
General and administrative	41,497	43,113	39,877
	245,977	245,145	245,945
INCOME FROM OPERATIONS	131,497	120,928	134,078
OTHER INCOME, Net	6,210	5,716	5,407
INCOME BEFORE INCOME TAXES	137,707	126,644	139,485
PROVISION FOR INCOME TAXES (Note G)	33,278	31,036	49,778
NET INCOME	$ 104,429	$ 95,608	$ 89,707
EARNINGS PER SHARE (Note L):			
Basic	$ 2.15	$ 1.97	$ 1.86
Diluted	$ 2.14	$ 1.97	$ 1.85

See notes to consolidated financial statements.

THE BUCKLE, INC.

CONSOLIDATED STATEMENTS OF COMPREHENSIVE INCOME
(Amounts in Thousands)

	Fiscal Years Ended		
	February 1, 2020	February 2, 2019	February 3, 2018
NET INCOME	$ 104,429	$ 95,608	$ 89,707
OTHER COMPREHENSIVE INCOME, NET OF TAX:			
Change in unrealized loss on investments, net of tax of $0, $31, and $17, respectively	—	89	(7)
Other comprehensive income	—	89	(7)
COMPREHENSIVE INCOME	$ 104,429	$ 95,697	$ 89,700

See notes to consolidated financial statements.

THE BUCKLE, INC.

CONSOLIDATED STATEMENTS OF STOCKHOLDERS' EQUITY
(Amounts in Thousands Except Share and Per Share Amounts)

	Number of Shares	Common Stock	Additional Paid-in Capital	Retained Earnings	Accumulated Other Comprehensive Loss	Total
BALANCE, January 28, 2017	48,622,780	$ 486	$ 139,398	$ 290,737	$ (82)	$ 430,539
Net income	—	—	—	89,707	—	89,707
Dividends paid on common stock, ($2.75 per share)	—	—	—	(133,874)	—	(133,874)
Issuance of non-vested stock, net of forfeitures	193,390	2	(2)	—	—	—
Amortization of non-vested stock grants, net of forfeitures	—	—	4,883	—	—	4,883
Change in unrealized loss on investments, net of tax	—	—	—	—	(7)	(7)
BALANCE, February 3, 2018	48,816,170	$ 488	$ 144,279	$ 246,570	$ (89)	$ 391,248
Net income	—	—	—	95,608	—	95,608
Dividends paid on common stock, ($2.00 per share)	—	—	—	(97,744)	—	(97,744)
Issuance of non-vested stock, net of forfeitures	201,225	2	(2)	—	—	—
Amortization of non-vested stock grants, net of forfeitures	—	—	4,287	—	—	4,287
Change in unrealized loss on investments, net of tax	—	—	—	—	89	89
Cumulative effect of change in accounting upon adoption of ASC Topic 606	—	—	—	389	—	389
BALANCE, February 2, 2019	49,017,395	$ 490	$ 148,564	$ 244,823	$ —	$ 393,877
Net income	—	—	—	104,429	—	104,429
Dividends paid on common stock, ($2.30 per share)	—	—	—	(112,854)	—	(112,854)
Issuance of non-vested stock, net of forfeitures	192,838	2	(2)	—	—	—
Amortization of non-vested stock grants, net of forfeitures	—	—	3,764	—	—	3,764
Common stock purchased and retired	(4,552)	—	(68)	—	—	(68)
BALANCE, February 1, 2020	49,205,681	$ 492	$ 152,258	$ 236,398	$ —	$ 389,148

See notes to consolidated financial statements.

THE BUCKLE, INC.

CONSOLIDATED STATEMENTS OF CASH FLOWS
(Amounts in Thousands)

	Fiscal Years Ended		
	February 1, 2020	February 2, 2019	February 3, 2018
CASH FLOWS FROM OPERATING ACTIVITIES:			
Net income	$ 104,429	$ 95,608	$ 89,707
Adjustments to reconcile net income to net cash flows from operating activities:			
Depreciation and amortization	23,789	26,848	30,745
Amortization of non-vested stock grants, net of forfeitures	3,764	4,287	4,883
Deferred income taxes	(1,986)	(1,099)	(340)
Other	504	1,925	1,628
Changes in operating assets and liabilities:			
Receivables	815	(550)	(413)
Inventory	3,932	(7,487)	7,687
Prepaid expenses and other assets	(2,799)	(66)	(12,047)
Accounts payable	(2,667)	276	4,584
Accrued employee compensation	1,477	(855)	(4,599)
Accrued store operating expenses	(1,108)	2,336	951
Gift certificates redeemable	(1,315)	(1,568)	(2,997)
Income taxes payable	747	(5,173)	1,662
Other assets and liabilities	1,083	(5,755)	(1,730)
Net cash flows from operating activities	130,665	108,727	119,721
CASH FLOWS FROM INVESTING ACTIVITIES:			
Purchases of property and equipment	(7,322)	(10,021)	(13,462)
Proceeds from sale of property and equipment	13	150	263
Change in other assets	168	158	92
Purchases of investments	(25,629)	(74,215)	(56,631)
Proceeds from sales/maturities of investments	67,525	76,330	52,441
Net cash flows from investing activities	34,755	(7,598)	(17,297)
CASH FLOWS FROM FINANCING ACTIVITIES:			
Purchases of common stock	(68)	—	—
Payment of dividends	(112,854)	(97,744)	(133,874)
Net cash flows from financing activities	(112,922)	(97,744)	(133,874)
NET INCREASE (DECREASE) IN CASH AND CASH EQUIVALENTS	52,498	3,385	(31,450)
CASH AND CASH EQUIVALENTS, Beginning of year	168,471	165,086	196,536
CASH AND CASH EQUIVALENTS, End of year	$ 220,969	$ 168,471	$ 165,086

See notes to consolidated financial statements.

THE BUCKLE, INC.
NOTES TO CONSOLIDATED FINANCIAL STATEMENTS
(Dollar Amounts in Thousands Except Share and Per Share Amounts)

A. SUMMARY OF SIGNIFICANT ACCOUNTING POLICIES

Fiscal Year - The Buckle, Inc. (the "Company") has its fiscal year end on the Saturday nearest January 31. All references in these consolidated financial statements to fiscal years are to the calendar year in which the fiscal year begins. Fiscal 2019 represents the 52-week period ended February 1, 2020, fiscal 2018 represents the 52-week period ended February 2, 2019, and fiscal 2017 represents the 53-week period ended February 3, 2018.

Nature of Operations - The Company is a retailer of medium to better-priced casual apparel, footwear, and accessories for fashion-conscious young men and women. The Company operates its business as one reportable segment and sells its merchandise through its retail stores and e-Commerce platform. The Company operated 448 stores located in 42 states throughout the United States as of February 1, 2020.

During fiscal 2019, the Company opened 2 new stores, substantially remodeled 5 stores, and closed 4 stores. During fiscal 2018, the Company did not open any new stores, substantially remodeled 6 stores, and closed 7 stores. During fiscal 2017, the Company opened 2 new stores, substantially remodeled 8 stores, and closed 12 stores.

Principles of Consolidation - The consolidated financial statements include the accounts of The Buckle, Inc. and its wholly-owned subsidiary. All intercompany accounts and transactions have been eliminated in consolidation.

Revenue Recognition - Retail store sales are recorded, net of expected returns, upon the purchase of merchandise by customers. Online sales are recorded, net of expected returns, when the merchandise is tendered for delivery to the common carrier. Shipping fees charged to customers are included in revenue and shipping costs are included in selling expenses. The Company recognizes revenue from sales made under its layaway program upon delivery of the merchandise to the customer. Revenue is not recorded when gift cards and gift certificates are sold, but rather when a card or certificate is redeemed for merchandise. A current liability for unredeemed gift cards and certificates is recorded at the time the card or certificate is purchased. The liability recorded for unredeemed gift certificates and gift cards was $15,319 and $16,634 as of February 1, 2020 and February 2, 2019, respectively. Gift card and gift certificate breakage is recognized as revenue in proportion to the redemption pattern of customers by applying an estimated breakage rate. The estimated breakage rate is based on historical issuance and redemption patterns and is re-assessed by the Company on a regular basis. Sales tax collected from customers is excluded from revenue and is included as part of "accrued store operating expenses" on the Company's consolidated balance sheets.

The Company establishes a liability for estimated merchandise returns, based upon the historical average sales return percentage, that is recognized at the transaction value. The Company also recognizes a return asset and a corresponding adjustment to cost of sales for the Company's right to recover returned merchandise, which is measured at the estimated carrying value, less any expected recovery costs. The accrued liability for reserve for sales returns was $2,257 as of February 1, 2020 and $2,182 as of February 2, 2019.

The Company's Guest Loyalty program allows participating guests to earn points for every qualifying purchase, which (after achievement of certain point thresholds) are redeemable as a discount off a future purchase. Reported revenue is net of both current period reward redemptions and accruals for estimated future rewards earned under the Guest Loyalty program. A liability has been recorded for future rewards based on the Company's estimate of how many earned points will turn into rewards and ultimately be redeemed prior to expiration. As of February 1, 2020 and February 2, 2019, $9,615 and $10,910 was included in "accrued store operating expenses" as a liability for estimated future rewards.

Through partnership with Comenity Bank, the Company offers a private label credit card ("PLCC"). Customers with a PLCC are enrolled in our B-Rewards incentive program and earn points for every qualifying purchase on their card. At the end of each rewards period, customers who have exceeded a minimum point threshold receive a reward to be redeemed on a future purchase. The B-Rewards program also provides other discount and promotional opportunities to cardholders on a routine basis. Reported revenue is net of both current period reward redemptions, current period discounts and promotions, and accruals for estimated future rewards earned under the B-Rewards program. A liability has been recorded for future rewards based on the Company's estimate of how many earned points will turn into rewards and ultimately be redeemed prior to expiration, which is included in "gift certificates redeemable" on the Company's consolidated balance sheets.

Cash and Cash Equivalents - The Company considers all debt instruments with an original maturity of three months or less when purchased to be cash equivalents.

Investments - Investments classified as short-term investments include securities with a maturity of greater than three months and less than one year. Available-for-sale securities are reported at fair value, with unrealized gains and losses excluded from earnings and reported as a separate component of stockholders' equity (net of the effect of income taxes), using the specific identification method, until they are sold. Held-to-maturity securities are carried at amortized cost. Trading securities are reported at fair value, with unrealized gains and losses included in earnings, using the specific identification method.

Inventory - Inventory is valued at the lower of cost or net realizable value. Cost is determined using an average cost method that approximates the first-in, first-out (FIFO) method. Management makes adjustments to inventory and cost of goods sold, based upon estimates, to account for merchandise obsolescence and markdowns that could affect net realizable value, based on assumptions using calculations applied to current inventory levels within each different markdown level. Management also reviews the levels of inventory in each markdown group and the overall aging of the inventory versus the estimated future demand for such product and the current market conditions. The adjustment to inventory for markdowns and/or obsolescence reduced the Company's inventory valuation by $12,178 and $10,586 as of February 1, 2020 and February 2, 2019, respectively.

Property and Equipment - Property and equipment are stated on the basis of historical cost. Depreciation is provided using a combination of accelerated and straight-line methods based upon the estimated useful lives of the assets. The majority of property and equipment have useful lives of five to ten years with the exception of buildings, which have estimated useful lives of 31.5 to 39 years. Leasehold improvements are stated on the basis of historical cost and are amortized over the shorter of the life of the lease or the estimated economic life of the assets. When circumstances indicate the carrying values of long-lived assets may be impaired, an evaluation is performed on current net book value amounts. Judgments made by the Company related to the expected useful lives of property and equipment and the ability to realize cash flows in excess of carrying amounts of such assets are affected by factors such as changes in economic conditions and changes in operating performance. As the Company assesses the expected cash flows and carrying amounts of long-lived assets, adjustments are made to such carrying values.

Pre-Opening Expenses - Costs related to opening new stores are expensed as incurred.

Advertising Costs - Advertising costs are expensed as incurred and were $11,406, $10,661, and $18,075 for fiscal years 2019, 2018, and 2017, respectively.

Health Care Costs - The Company is self-funded for health and dental claims up to $200 per individual per plan year. The Company's plan covers eligible employees, and management makes estimates at period end to record a reserve for unpaid claims based upon historical claims information. The accrued liability as a reserve for unpaid health care claims was $685 and $890 as of February 1, 2020 and February 2, 2019, respectively.

Leases - The Company adopted Financial Accounting Standards Board ("FASB") Accounting Standards Update ("ASU") 2016-02, Leases (Topic 842) effective February 3, 2019. For fiscal years ending prior to this date, the Company followed the guidance for leases under FASB Accounting Standards Codification ("ASC") Topic 840, Leases. See Recently Issued Accounting Pronouncements below and Footnote D, Leases, for further details.

Other Income - The Company's other income is derived primarily from interest and dividends received on cash and investments.

Use of Estimates - The preparation of consolidated financial statements in conformity with accounting principles generally accepted in the United States of America requires management to make estimates and assumptions that affect the reported amounts of certain assets and liabilities, the disclosure of contingent assets and liabilities at the date of the financial statements, and the reported amounts of revenues and expenses during the reporting period. Actual results could differ from these estimates.

D. LEASES

The Company's lease portfolio is primarily comprised of leases for retail store locations. The Company also leases certain equipment and corporate office space. Store leases for new stores typically have an initial term of 10 years, with options to renew for an additional 1 to 5 years. The exercise of lease renewal options is at the Company's sole discretion and is included in the lease term for calculations of its right-of-use assets and liabilities when it is reasonably certain that the Company plans to renew these leases. Certain store lease agreements include rental payments based on a percentage of retail sales over contractual levels and others include rental payments adjusted periodically for inflation. Lease agreements do not contain any residual value guarantees, material restrictive covenants, or options to purchase the leased property.

The table below reconciles undiscounted future lease payments (e.g. fixed payments for rent, insurance, real estate taxes, and common area maintenance) for each of the next five fiscal years and the total of the remaining years to the operating lease liabilities recorded on the consolidated balance sheet as of February 1, 2020:

Fiscal Year	Operating Leases [(a)]
2020	$ 100,016
2021	85,436
2022	72,503
2023	59,436
2024	44,677
Thereafter	55,391
Total lease payments	417,459
Less: Imputed interest	39,907
Total operating lease liability	$ 377,552

[(a)]   Operating lease payments exclude $1,355 of legally binding minimum lease payments for leases signed, but not yet commenced.

E. PROPERTY AND EQUIPMENT

	February 1, 2020	February 2, 2019
Land	$ 2,491	$ 2,491
Building and improvements	43,267	43,243
Office equipment	12,494	12,388
Transportation equipment	21,010	20,993
Leasehold improvements	166,539	167,023
Furniture and fixtures	176,150	176,389
Shipping/receiving equipment	29,325	29,266
Construction-in-progress	929	394
Total	$ 452,205	$ 452,187

F. FINANCING ARRANGEMENTS

The Company has available an unsecured line of credit of $25,000 with Wells Fargo Bank, N.A. for operating needs and letters of credit. The line of credit agreement has an expiration date of July 31, 2021 and provides that $10,000 of the $25,000 line is available for letters of credit. Borrowings under the line of credit provide for interest to be paid at a rate based on LIBOR. The Company has, from time to time, borrowed against these lines of credit. There were no bank borrowings as of February 1, 2020 and February 2, 2019. There were no bank borrowings during fiscal 2019, 2018, and 2017. The Company had outstanding letters of credit totaling $1,523 and $1,986 as of February 1, 2020 and February 2, 2019, respectively.

G. INCOME TAXES

On December 22, 2017, the U.S. government enacted comprehensive tax legislation commonly referred to as the Tax Cuts and Jobs Act (the "Tax Act"). The Tax Act included many changes to the U.S. tax code including reducing the U.S. federal corporate tax rate from 35.0% to 21.0% effective January 1, 2018. This change reduced the Company's effective tax rate for the fiscal year ended February 3, 2018, based on the 21.0% rate being in effect for one month of the fiscal year, and then further reduced the Company's effective tax rate for the full fiscal years ended February 2, 2019 and February 1, 2020.

The provision for income taxes consists of:

	Fiscal Years Ended		
	February 1, 2020	February 2, 2019	February 3, 2018
Current income tax expense:			
Federal	$ 29,660	$ 27,278	$ 46,158
State	5,604	4,857	3,960
Deferred income tax expense (benefit)	(1,986)	(1,099)	(340)
Total	$ 33,278	$ 31,036	$ 49,778

I. COMMITMENTS AND CONTINGENCIES

Litigation - From time to time, the Company is involved in litigation relating to claims arising out of its operations in the normal course of business. As of the date of these consolidated financial statements, the Company was not engaged in any legal proceedings that are expected, individually or in the aggregate, to have a material effect on the Company's consolidated results of operations and financial position.

L. EARNINGS PER SHARE

The following table provides a reconciliation between basic and diluted earnings per share:

	Fiscal Years Ended								
	February 1, 2020			February 2, 2019			February 3, 2018		
	Income	Weighted Average Shares (a)	Per Share Amount	Income	Weighted Average Shares (a)	Per Share Amount	Income	Weighted Average Shares (a)	Per Share Amount
Basic EPS	$ 104,429	48,587	$ 2.15	$ 95,608	48,413	$ 1.97	$ 89,707	48,250	$ 1.86
Effect of Dilutive Securities:									
Non-vested shares	—	226	(0.01)	—	201	—	—	123	(0.01)
Diluted EPS	$ 104,429	48,813	$ 2.14	$ 95,608	48,614	$ 1.97	$ 89,707	48,373	$ 1.85

(a) Shares in thousands.

M. REVENUES

The Company is a retailer of medium to better priced casual apparel, footwear, and accessories for fashion conscious young men and women. The Company operates its business as one reportable segment. The Company sells its merchandise through its retail stores and e-Commerce platform. The Company operated 448 stores located in 42 states throughout the United States as of February 1, 2020.

During fiscal years 2019, 2018, and 2017, online revenues accounted for 12.3%, 11.7%, and 10.7%, respectively, of the Company's net sales. No sales to an individual customer or country, other than the United States, accounted for more than 10.0% of net sales.

The following is information regarding the Company's major product lines, stated as a percentage of the Company's net sales:

Merchandise Group	Fiscal Years Ended		
	February 1, 2020	February 2, 2019	February 3, 2018
Denims	40.7%	41.0%	41.5%
Tops (including sweaters)	32.2	32.8	32.3
Accessories	8.9	8.8	9.1
Footwear	8.0	6.7	6.1
Sportswear/Fashions	5.5	6.0	6.2
Outerwear	2.0	2.1	2.0
Casual bottoms	1.1	1.2	1.3
Other	1.6	1.4	1.5
Total	100.0%	100.0%	100.0%

ITEM 9 - CHANGES IN AND DISAGREEMENTS WITH ACCOUNTANTS ON ACCOUNTING AND FINANCIAL DISCLOSURE

None.

ITEM 9A – CONTROLS AND PROCEDURES

The Company maintains a system of disclosure controls and procedures that are designed to provide reasonable assurance that material information, which is required to be timely disclosed, is accumulated and communicated to management in a timely manner. An evaluation of the effectiveness of the design and operation of the Company's disclosure controls and procedures (as defined in Rules 13a-15(e) of the Securities Exchange Act of 1934 (the "Exchange Act")) was performed as of the end of the period covered by this report. This evaluation was performed under the supervision and with the participation of the Company's Chief Executive Officer and Chief Financial Officer. Based upon that evaluation, the Chief Executive Officer and Chief Financial Officer concluded that the Company's disclosure controls and procedures as of the end of the period covered by this report were effective to provide reasonable assurance that information required to be disclosed by the Company in the Company's reports that it files or submits under the Exchange Act is accumulated and communicated to management, including its Chief Executive Officer and Chief Financial Officer, as appropriate, to allow timely decisions regarding required disclosure and are effective to provide reasonable assurance that such information is recorded, processed, summarized, and reported within the time periods specified by the SEC's rules and forms.

Change in Internal Control Over Financial Reporting - There were no changes in the Company's internal control over financial reporting that occurred during the Company's last fiscal quarter that have materially affected, or are reasonably likely to materially affect, the Company's internal control over financial reporting.

Management's Report on Internal Control Over Financial Reporting - Management of the Company is responsible for establishing and maintaining adequate internal control over financial reporting as defined in Rules 13a-15(f) and 15d-15(f) under the Securities Exchange Act of 1934. The Company's internal control over financial reporting is designed to provide reasonable assurance regarding the reliability of financial reporting and the preparation of financial statements for external purposes in accordance with accounting principles generally accepted in the United State of America ("GAAP").

All internal control systems, no matter how well designed, have inherent limitations. Therefore, even those systems determined to be effective can provide only reasonable assurance with respect to financial statement preparation and presentation. Because of its inherent limitations, internal control over financial reporting may not prevent or detect misstatements.

Management has assessed the effectiveness of the Company's internal control over financial reporting as of February 1, 2020, based on the criteria set forth by the Committee of Sponsoring Organizations ("COSO") of the Treadway Commission in their *Internal Control-Integrated Framework (2013)*. In making its assessment of internal control over financial reporting, management has concluded that the Company's internal control over financial reporting was effective as of February 1, 2020.

The Company's independent registered public accounting firm, Deloitte & Touche LLP, has audited the effectiveness of the Company's internal control over financial reporting. Their report appears herein.

REPORT OF INDEPENDENT REGISTERED PUBLIC ACCOUNTING FIRM

To the stockholders and the Board of Directors of The Buckle, Inc.

Opinion on Internal Control over Financial Reporting

We have audited the internal control over financial reporting of The Buckle, Inc. and subsidiary (the "Company") as of February 1, 2020, based on criteria established in *Internal Control - Integrated Framework (2013)* issued by the Committee of Sponsoring Organizations of the Treadway Commission (COSO). In our opinion, the Company maintained, in all material respects, effective internal control over financial reporting as of February 1, 2020, based on criteria established in *Internal Control - Integrated Framework (2013)* issued by COSO.

We have also audited, in accordance with the standards of the Public Company Accounting Oversight Board (United States) (PCAOB), the consolidated financial statements as of and for the fiscal year ended February 1, 2020, of the Company and our report dated April 1, 2020, expressed an unqualified opinion on those financial statements and included an explanatory paragraph regarding the Company's adoption of Financial Accounting Standards Board Accounting Standards Update No. 2016-02, *Leases (Topic 842)*.

Basis for Opinion

The Company's management is responsible for maintaining effective internal control over financial reporting and for its assessment of the effectiveness of internal control over financial reporting, included in the accompanying *Management's Report on Internal Control Over Financial Reporting*. Our responsibility is to express an opinion on the Company's internal control over financial reporting based on our audit. We are a public accounting firm registered with the PCAOB and are required to be independent with respect to the Company in accordance with the U.S. federal securities laws and the applicable rules and regulations of the Securities and Exchange Commission and the PCAOB.

We conducted our audit in accordance with the standards of the PCAOB. Those standards require that we plan and perform the audit to obtain reasonable assurance about whether effective internal control over financial reporting was maintained in all material respects. Our audit included obtaining an understanding of internal control over financial reporting, assessing the risk that a material weakness exists, testing and evaluating the design and operating effectiveness of internal control based on the assessed risk, and performing such other procedures as we considered necessary in the circumstances. We believe that our audit provides a reasonable basis for our opinion.

Definition and Limitations of Internal Control over Financial Reporting

A company's internal control over financial reporting is a process designed to provide reasonable assurance regarding the reliability of financial reporting and the preparation of financial statements for external purposes in accordance with generally accepted accounting principles. A company's internal control over financial reporting includes those policies and procedures that (1) pertain to the maintenance of records that, in reasonable detail, accurately and fairly reflect the transactions and dispositions of the assets of the company; (2) provide reasonable assurance that transactions are recorded as necessary to permit preparation of financial statements in accordance with generally accepted accounting principles, and that receipts and expenditures of the company are being made only in accordance with authorizations of management and directors of the company; and (3) provide reasonable assurance regarding prevention or timely detection of unauthorized acquisition, use, or disposition of the company's assets that could have a material effect on the financial statements.

Because of its inherent limitations, internal control over financial reporting may not prevent or detect misstatements. Also, projections of any evaluation of effectiveness to future periods are subject to the risk that controls may become inadequate because of changes in conditions, or that the degree of compliance with the policies or procedures may deteriorate.

/s/ Deloitte & Touche LLP

Omaha, Nebraska
April 1, 2020

REPORT OF INDEPENDENT REGISTERED PUBLIC ACCOUNTING FIRM

To the Stockholders and the Board of Directors of The Buckle, Inc.

Opinion on Internal Control over Financial Reporting

Time Value of Money

Learning Objectives

- **LO C–1** Contrast simple and compound interest.
- **LO C–2** Calculate the future value of a single amount.
- **LO C–3** Calculate the present value of a single amount.
- **LO C–4** Calculate the future value of an annuity.
- **LO C–5** Calculate the present value of an annuity.

SELF-STUDY MATERIALS

- Let's Review—Future value and present value of a single amount (p. C-8).
- Let's Review—Future value and present value of an annuity (p. C-12).
- Key Points by Learning Objective (p. C-13).
- Glossary of Key Terms (p. C-13).
- Self-Study Questions with answers available (p. C-13).

Congratulations! While at a local convenience store, you bought a lottery ticket and won $1,000. The ticket gives you the option of receiving (a) $1,000 today or (b) $1,000 one year from now. Which do you choose?

Probably, all of us would choose $1,000 today. Choosing to take the money today instead of one year from now just makes common sense. It also makes good economic sense. You could take your $1,000 winnings today, put it in a savings account, earn interest on it for one year, and have an amount greater than $1,000 a year from now. So, $1,000 today is not equal to $1,000 a year from now. This simple example demonstrates the **time value of money**, which means that interest causes the value of money received today to be greater than the value of that same amount of money received in the future.

Time value of money concepts are useful—in fact, essential—in solving many business decisions. These decisions include valuing assets and liabilities, making investment decisions, paying off debts, and establishing a retirement plan, to name just a few. We'll discuss some of these next.

Simple versus Compound Interest

Interest is the cost of borrowing money. If you borrow $1,000 today and agree to pay 10% interest, you will pay back $1,100 a year from now. It is this interest that gives money its time value.

Simple interest is interest you earn on the initial investment only. Calculate it as the initial investment times the applicable interest rate times the period of the investment or loan.

Simple interest = Initial investment × Interest rate × Time

For example, suppose you put $1,000 into a savings account that pays simple interest of 10% and then withdraw the money at the end of three years. Illustration C–1 demonstrates that the amount of simple interest you earned on your $1,000 in each of the three years is $100 (= $1,000 × 10%).

■ LO C–1
Contrast simple and compound interest.

ILLUSTRATION C–1

Calculation of Simple Interest

Time	Simple Interest (= Initial investment × Interest rate)	Outstanding Balance
Initial investment		$1,000
End of year 1	$1,000 × 10% = $100	$1,100
End of year 2	$1,000 × 10% = $100	$1,200
End of year 3	$1,000 × 10% = $100	**$1,300**

With simple interest at 10% annually, the $1,000 initial investment generates $100 of interest each year and grows to **$1,300** by the end of the third year.

Compound interest works differently. **Compound interest** is interest you earn on the initial investment *and on previous interest.* Because you are earning "interest on interest" each period, compound interest yields increasingly larger amounts of interest earnings for each period of the investment (unlike simple interest, which yielded the same $100 in each year of our example above). Illustration C–2 shows calculations of compound interest for a $1,000, three-year investment that earns 10%.

ILLUSTRATION C–2

Calculation of Compound Interest

Time	Compound Interest (= Outstanding balance × Interest rate)	Outstanding Balance
Initial investment		$1,000
End of year 1	$1,000 × 10% = $100	$1,100
End of year 2	$1,100 × 10% = $110	$1,210
End of year 3	$1,210 × 10% = $121	**$1,331**

With compound interest at 10% annually, the $1,000 initial investment grows to **$1,331** at the end of three years. This compares to only **$1,300** for simple interest. The extra $31 represents *compounding,* or interest earned on interest. Nearly all business applications use compound interest, and compound interest is what we use in calculating the time value of money.

KEY POINT

Simple interest is interest we earn on the initial investment only. Compound interest is the interest we earn on the initial investment plus previous interest. We use compound interest in calculating the time value of money.

Time Value of a Single Amount

To better understand how compound interest affects the time value of money, we'll examine this topic from two perspectives. First, we'll calculate how much an amount today will grow to be at some point in the future (*future value*), and then we'll take the opposite perspective and examine how much an amount in the future is worth today (*present value*).

FUTURE VALUE

■ **LO C–2**

Calculate the future value of a single amount.

In the example above, in which we invested $1,000 for three years at 10% compounded annually, we call $1,331 the future value. **Future value** is how much an amount today will grow to be in the future. The timeline in Illustration C–3 provides a useful way to visualize future values. Time $n = 0$ indicates today, the date of the initial investment.

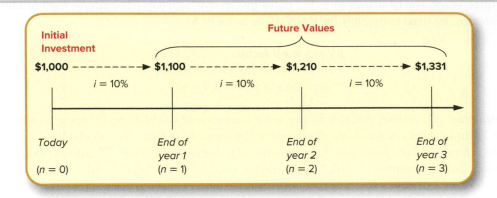

ILLUSTRATION C–3

Future Value of a Single Amount

Notice that at the end of each year, the investment grows by 10%. The future value at the end of the first year is **$1,100** (= $1,000 × 1.10). After three years, the investment has a future value of **$1,331** (= $1,000 × 1.10 × 1.10 × 1.10), representing 10% growth of a growing base amount each year.

To calculate future value, we can use a mathematical formula, time value of money tables, a calculator, or a computer spreadsheet. We show all four methods below.

Formula.   We can determine the future value of any amount with a formula, as follows:

$$FV = I\,(1 + i)^n$$

where:

FV = future value of the invested amount
I = initial investment
i = interest rate
n = number of compounding periods

Table 1.   Instead of using a formula, we can also determine future value by using time value of money tables. Table 1, Future Value of $1, located at the end of this book, contains the future value of $1 invested for various periods of time, n, and various interest rates, i. With this table, it's easy to determine the future value of any invested amount. To do so, simply multiply the invested amount by the table value you find at the intersection of the *column* for the desired interest rate and the *row* for the number of periods. Illustration C–4 contains an excerpt from Table 1.

ILLUSTRATION C–4

Future Value of $1 (excerpt from Table 1)

| | | Interest Rates (i) | | | | |
Periods (n)	7%	8%	9%	10%	11%	12%
1	1.07000	1.08000	1.09000	1.10000	1.11000	1.12000
2	1.14490	1.16640	1.18810	1.21000	1.23210	1.25440
3	1.22504	1.25971	1.29503	1.33100	1.36763	1.40493
4	1.31080	1.36049	1.41158	1.46410	1.51807	1.57352
5	1.40255	1.46933	1.53862	1.61051	1.68506	1.76234
6	1.50073	1.58687	1.67710	1.77156	1.87041	1.97382
7	1.60578	1.71382	1.82804	1.94872	2.07616	2.21068
8	1.71819	1.85093	1.99256	2.14359	2.30454	2.47596

The table shows various values of $(1 + i)^n$ for different combinations of i and n. From the table you can find the future value factor for three periods ($n = 3$) at 10% interest to be 1.33100. This means that $1 invested at 10% compounded annually will grow to $1.331 (= $1 × 1.331) in three years. The table uses $1 as the initial investment, whereas our example used $1,000. Therefore, we need to multiply the future value factor by $1,000.

$$FV = I \times FV \text{ factor}$$
$$FV = \$1,000 \times 1.33100^* = \$1,331$$
*Future value of $1; $n = 3$, $i = 10\%$

Calculator. Of course, you can do the same future value calculations by using a calculator. Future values are automatically stored in the memory of financial calculators. To compute a future value, you input three amounts: (1) initial investment, (2) interest rate per period, and (3) number of periods. Illustration C–5 shows the inputs and output using a financial calculator.

ILLUSTRATION C–5

Calculate the Future Value of a Single Amount Using a Financial Calculator

The key symbols used to input the interest rate and number of periods differ across calculators, so be sure to check which key is appropriate for your calculator.

CALCULATOR INPUTS

Inputs	Key	Amount
1. Present value (initial investment)	PV	$1,000
2. Interest rate per period	i	10%
3. Number of periods	n	3

CALCULATOR OUTPUT

Future value	FV	$1,331

Excel. Another option is to use an Excel spreadsheet, which has automatically stored the time value factors. To see how this is performed, see Illustration C–6.

ILLUSTRATION C–6

Calculate the Future Value of a Single Amount Using Excel

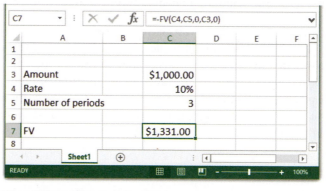

Microsoft Corporation

Interest Compounding More Than Annually. In our example, interest was compounded annually (once per year). Remember that the n in the future value formula refers to the number of compounding *periods*—which is not necessarily the number of years. For example, suppose the three-year, $1,000 investment earns 10% compounded *semiannually,* or twice per year. The number of periods over three years is now six (= 3 years × 2 semiannual periods per year). The interest rate per period is 5% (= 10% annual rate ÷ 2).[1] The future value of the three-year, $1,000 investment that earns 10% compounded semiannually is calculated below.

$$FV = I \times FV \text{ factor}$$
$$FV = \$1,000 \times 1.34010^* = \$1,340$$
*Future value of $1; $n = 6$, $i = 5\%$

---

[1]The rate of compounding can be broken into any number of periods. For example, if we instead assume *quarterly* compounding (four times per year), the number of periods over three years would be 12 (= 3 years × 4 quarters) and the interest rate per period would be 2.5% (= 10% ÷ 4 quarters).

Notice that the future amount is slightly higher for semiannual compounding ($1,340) compared to annual compounding ($1,331). **The more frequent the rate of compounding, the more interest we earn on previous interest, resulting in a higher future value.**

To confirm your understanding, let's look at a couple of examples of how to calculate the future value of a single amount.

Example 1.   Suppose a company's top executive, Shirley McDaniel, currently owns stock in the company worth $800,000. Shirley is ready to retire but will not do so until her stock is worth at least $1,000,000. Over the next three years, the company's stock is expected to grow 8% annually. Will Shirley be ready to retire in three years?

The future value of $800,000 in three years with an annual interest rate of 8% equals $1,007,768 (= $800,000 × 1.25971, time value factor from Table 1, Future Value of $1, with $n = 3$ and $i = 8\%$). With 8% growth, Shirley *will* be ready to retire in three years.

Example 2.   Now suppose you are 20 years old and would like to retire by age 60. A goal of yours has always been to retire as a millionaire. You don't have any money to invest, but you do have a pretty nice car. If you sold your car for $28,000, bought a six-year-old car for $5,000, and invested the difference of $23,000 earning a 10% annual return, how much would you have at retirement?

The future value of $23,000 in 40 years (your proposed retirement age minus your present age) with an annual interest rate of 10% equals $1,040,963 (= $23,000 × 45.25926, time value factor from Table 1, Future Value of $1, with $n = 40$ and $i = 10\%$). With a 10% annual return, just $23,000 today will grow to over one million dollars in 40 years. If you swap your expensive wheels, you'll have that million-dollar nest egg.

 KEY POINT

> The future value of a single amount is how much that amount today will grow to be in the future.

PRESENT VALUE

Present value is precisely the opposite of future value. Instead of telling us how much some amount today will grow to be in the future, **present value** tells us the value today of receiving some larger amount in the future. What is it worth today to receive $1,331 in three years? To answer this, we need to determine the discount rate. The **discount rate** is the rate at which we would be willing to give up current dollars for future dollars. If you would be willing to give up $100 today to receive $108 in one year, then your discount rate, or time value of money, equals 8%.

■ **LO C–3**

Calculate the present value of a single amount.

Continuing with our example, let's assume that your discount rate is 10%. In this case, the present value of receiving $1,331 in three years is $1,000. We could have figured this from Illustration C–3 by working backwards from the future value. The timeline in Illustration C–7 depicts this relationship between present value and future value.

ILLUSTRATION C–7

Present Value of a Single Amount

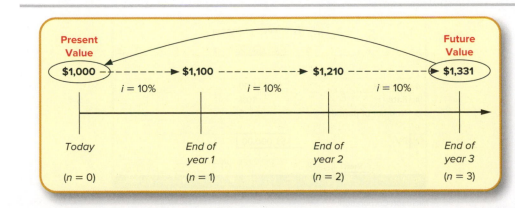

To calculate present value, we can use a formula, time value of money tables, a calculator, or a computer spreadsheet. We show all four methods below.

Formula.   We can calculate present values with the following formula:

$$PV = \frac{FV}{(1 + i)^n}$$

Table 2.   Alternatively, we can use Table 2, Present Value of $1, located at the end of this book. Illustration C–8 shows an excerpt of Table 2.

ILLUSTRATION C–8

Present Value of $1 (excerpt from Table 2)

	Interest Rates (*i*)					
Periods (*n*)	**7%**	**8%**	**9%**	**10%**	**11%**	**12%**
1	0.93458	0.92593	0.91743	0.90909	0.90090	0.89286
2	0.87344	0.85734	0.84168	0.82645	0.81162	0.79719
3	0.81630	0.79383	0.77218	0.75131	0.73119	0.71178
4	0.76290	0.73503	0.70843	0.68301	0.65873	0.63552
5	0.71299	0.68058	0.64993	0.62092	0.59345	0.56743
6	0.66634	0.63017	0.59627	0.56447	0.53464	0.50663
7	0.62275	0.58349	0.54703	0.51316	0.48166	0.45235
8	0.58201	0.54027	0.50187	0.46651	0.43393	0.40388

From the table you can find the present value factor for three periods ($n = 3$) at 10% is 0.75131. This means that $1 received in three years where there is interest of 10% compounded annually is worth about $0.75 today. So, the present value of $1,331 is approximately $1,000.

PV = FV × PV factor
PV = $1,331 × 0.75131 = $1,000*
*Rounded to the nearest whole dollar

Calculator.   Illustration C–9 shows the same example worked out with a financial calculator.

ILLUSTRATION C–9

Calculate the Present Value of a Single Amount Using a Financial Calculator

CALCULATOR INPUTS

Inputs	Key	Amount
1. Future value	FV	$1,331
2. Interest rate per period	*i*	10%
3. Number of periods	*n*	3

CALCULATOR OUTPUT

Present value	PV	$1,000

Excel.   In Illustration C–10, we see the same example worked out using an Excel spreadsheet.

ILLUSTRATION C–10

Calculate the Present Value of a Single Amount Using Excel

Microsoft Corporation

To confirm your understanding, let's look at a couple of examples of how to calculate the present value of a single amount.

Example 1.   Suppose Fisher Realtors lists for sale a 2,500-square-foot business building for $500,000. Someone offers to purchase the building, taking occupancy today, and then pay $575,000 in two years. If Fisher's discount rate is 7% compounded annually, should it accept the customer's offer?

The present value of receiving $575,000 in two years with an annual interest rate of 7% equals $502,228 (= $575,000 × 0.87344, time value factor from Table 2, Present Value of $1, with $n = 2$ and $i = 7\%$). Because the present value ($502,228) of the future payment is greater than the $500,000 listed selling price, Fisher should accept the offer.

Example 2.   Let's assume you would like to be a millionaire in 40 years. Investing aggressively in higher-risk securities, you are pretty confident you can earn an average return of 12% a year. How much do you need to invest today to have $1,000,000 in 40 years?

The present value of $1,000,000 in 40 years with an annual interest rate of 12% equals $10,750 (= $1,000,000 × 0.01075, time value factor from Table 2, Present Value of $1, with $n = 40$ and $i = 12\%$). An investment of only $10,750 today would grow to $1,000,000 in 40 years, assuming a 12% annual interest rate.

If you could earn only 6% annually rather than 12%, you would have to invest quite a bit more. The present value of $1,000,000 in 40 years with an interest rate of 6% equals $97,220 (= $1,000,000 × 0.09722, time value factor from Table 2, Present Value of $1, with $n = 40$ and $i = 6\%$). Over longer periods, the investment return you can achieve really makes a difference in the wealth you can accumulate.

Discount Rates.   As shown in Illustration C–11, as the interest rate increases, the more the present value of $1,000 grows in the future. For each of the four interest rates, the present value is the same ($1,000), but the future values are very different. Another way to look at this is by noticing that future values are discounted by a greater amount as the interest rate increases. For example, the present value of both (1) $1,728 discounted at 20% and (2) $1,061 discounted at 2% is $1,000. This illustration demonstrates the importance of understanding interest rates and the time value of money when making decisions over time.

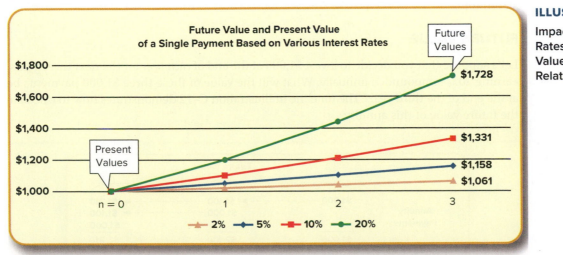

ILLUSTRATION C–11

Impact of Interest Rates on Present Value/Future Value Relationship

---

KEY POINT

The *present value* of a single amount is the value today of receiving that amount in the future.

Let's Review

Below are four scenarios related to the future value and present value of a single amount.

1. Manuel is saving for a new car. He puts $10,000 into an investment account today. He expects the account to earn 12% annually. How much will Manuel have in five years?

2. Ingrid would like to take her family to Disney World in three years. She expects the trip to cost $4,500 at that time. If she can earn 9% annually, how much should she set aside today so that she can pay for the trip in three years?

3. John puts $6,000 in a savings account today that earns 8% interest compounded semiannually. How much will John have in six years?

4. Anna purchases a ring with a selling price of $4,000 today but doesn't have to pay cash until one year from the purchase date. Assuming a discount rate of 16% compounded quarterly, what is Anna's actual cost of the ring today?

Required:

Calculate the time value of money for each scenario.

Solution:

(Rounded to the nearest whole dollar)

1. $10,000 × 1.76234 (FV of $1, $n = 5$, $i = 12\%$) = $17,623
2. $4,500 × 0.77218 (PV of $1, $n = 3$, $i = 9\%$) = $3,475
3. $6,000 × 1.60103 (FV of $1, $n = 12$, $i = 4\%$) = $9,606
4. $4,000 × 0.85480 (PV of $1, $n = 4$, $i = 4\%$) = $3,419

Suggested Homework:
BEC–2, BEC–4;
EC–1, EC–3;
PC–1A&B

Time Value of an Annuity

Up to now, we've focused on calculating the future value and present value of a *single* amount. However, many business transactions are structured as a series of receipts and payments of cash rather than a single amount. If we are to receive or pay the same amount each period, we refer to the cash flows as an **annuity**. Familiar examples of annuities are monthly payments for a car loan, house loan, or apartment rent. Of course, payments need not be monthly. They could be quarterly, semiannually, annually, or any interval. **An annuity includes cash payments of equal amounts over time periods of equal length.**

As with single amounts, we can calculate both the future value and the present value of an annuity.

FUTURE VALUE

■ **LO C–4**
Calculate the future value of an annuity.

Let's suppose that you decide to invest $1,000 at the end of *each year* for the next three years, earning 10% compounded annually. What will the value of these three $1,000 payments be at the end of the third year? The timeline in Illustration C–12 demonstrates how to calculate the future value of this annuity.

ILLUSTRATION C–12

Future Value of an Annuity

By the end of year 1, the investment's future value equals the **$1,000** annuity payment. No interest has been earned because you invest the $1,000 at the *end* of the year. By the end of year 2, though, the first annuity payment has grown by 10% ($1,100 = $1,000 × 1.10), and you make the second **$1,000** annuity payment. Adding these together, your total investment has grown to **$2,100**. By the end of the third year, the first annuity payment has grown by another 10% ($1,210 = $1,100 × 1.10), the second annuity payment has grown by 10% ($1,100 = $1,000 × 1.10), and you make the final **$1,000** annuity payment. Add these together to find that the total investment has grown to **$3,310**. This is the future value of a $1,000 annuity for three years at 10% interest compounded annually.

Table 3. Since annuities consist of multiple payments, calculating the future value of an annuity can be time-consuming, especially as the length of the annuity increases. To make this task more efficient, we can calculate the future value of an annuity using the time value of money tables located at the end of this book, a financial calculator, or a computer spreadsheet.[2]

Illustration C–13 shows an excerpt of Table 3, Future Value of an Annuity of $1.

Periods (*n*)	Interest Rates (*i*)					
	7%	**8%**	**9%**	**10%**	**11%**	**12%**
1	1.0000	1.0000	1.0000	1.0000	1.0000	1.0000
2	2.0700	2.0800	2.0900	2.1000	2.1100	2.1200
3	3.2149	3.2464	3.2781	3.3100	3.3421	3.3744
4	4.4399	4.5061	4.5731	4.6410	4.7097	4.7793
5	5.7507	5.8666	5.9847	6.1051	6.2278	6.3528
6	7.1533	7.3359	7.5233	7.7156	7.9129	8.1152
7	8.6540	8.9228	9.2004	9.4872	9.7833	10.0890
8	10.2598	10.6366	11.0285	11.4359	11.8594	12.2997

ILLUSTRATION C–13

Future Value of an Annuity of $1 (excerpt from Table 3)

We calculate the future value of an annuity (FVA) by multiplying the annuity payment by the factor corresponding to three periods and 10% interest:

$$\text{FVA} = \$1,000 \times 3.3100 = \$3,310$$

Calculator. You can also calculate the future value of an annuity using a financial calculator. To compute the future value of an annuity, you simply input three amounts: (1) payment amount, (2) interest rate per period, and (3) number of periods. Make sure the present value (PV) is set equal to zero. Illustration C–14 presents the inputs and output using a financial calculator.

CALCULATOR INPUTS		
Inputs	**Key**	**Amount**
1. Payment amount	PMT	$1,000
2. Interest rate per period	*i*	10%
3. Number of periods	*n*	3
CALCULATOR OUTPUT		
Future value	FV	$3,310

ILLUSTRATION C–14

Calculate the Future Value of an Annuity Using a Financial Calculator

---

[2]The mathematical formula for calculating the future value of an annuity is a bit more complicated than are these other methods, so we'll focus on those.

Excel.   Illustration C–15 shows the Excel method for calculating the future value of an annuity.

ILLUSTRATION C–15

Calculate the Future
Value of an Annuity
Using Excel

C7		f_x	=-FV(C4,C5,C3,0,0)		
	A	B	C	D	E	F
1					
2					
3	Amount		$1,000.00		
4	Rate		10%		
5	Number of periods		3		
6					
7	FV		$3,310.00		
8					

Microsoft Corporation

Again, let's look at two examples.

Example 1.   Suppose **Warner Bros.** borrows $300 million to produce another *Batman* movie and is required to pay back this amount in five years. If, at the end of each of the next five years, Warner Bros. puts $50 million in an account that is expected to earn 12% interest compounded annually, will the company have enough cash set aside to pay its debt?

The future value of a $50 million annuity over five years that earns 12% annually equals $317,640,000 (= $50,000,000 × 6.3528, time value factor from Table 3, Future Value of an Annuity of $1, with $n = 5$ and $i = 12\%$). Warner Bros. will have enough cash to pay its $300 million debt.

Example 2.   You still have aspirations of being a millionaire in 40 years, but you do not have much money to invest right now. If you set aside just $2,500 at the end of each year with an average annual return of 10%, how much will you have at the end of 40 years?

The future value of a $2,500 annuity over 40 years that earns 10% annually equals $1,106,482 (= $2,500 × 442.5926, time value factor from Table 3, Future Value of an Annuity of $1, with $n = 40$ and $i = 10\%$). You will have quite a bit less assuming an average annual return of 8% ($647,641) and quite a bit more if you can achieve an average annual return of 12% ($1,917,729). Interest rates matter!

 KEY POINT

Cash payments of equal amounts over time periods of equal length are called an annuity. The future value of an annuity is the sum of the future values of a series of cash payments.

PRESENT VALUE

■ **LO C–5**

Calculate the present
value of an annuity.

One application of the present value of an annuity relates back to Chapter 9. There, you learned that we report certain liabilities in financial statements at their present values (leases and bonds). Most of these liabilities specify that the borrower must pay the lender periodic payments (or an annuity) over the life of the loan. As a result, we use the present value of an annuity to determine what portion of these future payments the borrower must report as a liability today.

To understand the idea behind the present value of an annuity, you need to realize that each annuity payment represents a single future amount. We calculate the present value of *each* of these future amounts and then add them together to determine the present value of an annuity. This idea is depicted in the timeline in Illustration C–16.

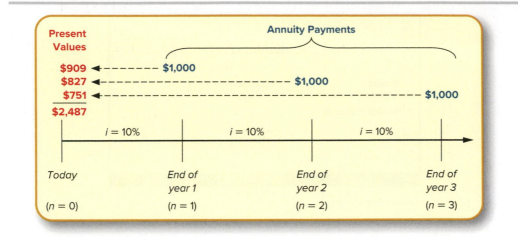

ILLUSTRATION C–16

Present Value of an Annuity

The present value of three **$1,000** annual payments discounted at 10% equals the present value of the first payment (**$909**), plus the present value of the second payment (**$827**), plus the present value of the third payment (**$751**). You can verify these amounts by looking at the present value factors in Table 2, Present Value of $1, with $n = 1, 2,$ and 3 and $i = 10\%$. The total present value of the annuity is **$2,487**.

Table 4.   Instead of calculating the present value of each annuity payment, a more efficient method is to use time value of money tables. An excerpt of Table 4, Present Value of an Annuity of $1, located at the end of this book, is shown in Illustration C–17.

ILLUSTRATION C–17

Present Value of an Annuity of $1 (excerpt from Table 4)

	Interest Rates (i)					
Periods (n)	**7%**	**8%**	**9%**	**10%**	**11%**	**12%**
1	0.93458	0.92593	0.91743	0.90909	0.90090	0.89286
2	1.80802	1.78326	1.75911	1.73554	1.71252	1.69005
3	2.62432	2.57710	2.53129	2.48685	2.44371	2.40183
4	3.38721	3.31213	3.23972	3.16987	3.10245	3.03735
5	4.10020	3.99271	3.88965	3.79079	3.69590	3.60478
6	4.76654	4.62288	4.48592	4.35526	4.23054	4.11141
7	5.38929	5.20637	5.03295	4.86842	4.71220	4.56376
8	5.97130	5.74664	5.53482	5.33493	5.14612	4.96764

We calculate the present value of an annuity (PVA) by multiplying the annuity payment by the factor corresponding to three periods and 10% interest:

$$PVA = \$1,000 \times 2.48685 = \$2,487$$

Calculator.   Illustration C–18 shows the calculator solution.

ILLUSTRATION C–18

Calculate the Present Value of an Annuity Using a Financial Calculator

CALCULATOR INPUTS

Inputs	Key	Amount
1. Payment amount	PMT	$1,000
2. Interest rate per period	i	10%
3. Number of periods	n	3

CALCULATOR OUTPUT

Present value	PV	$2,487

Excel.   Illustration C–19 shows the Excel solution.

ILLUSTRATION C–19

Calculate the Present
Value of an Annuity
Using Excel

C7	▾	:	✗ ✓ f_x	=-PV(C4,C5,C3,0,0)			▾
◢	A	B	C	D	E	F
1						
2						
3	Amount		$1,000.00			
4	Rate		10%			
5	Number of periods		3			
6						
7	PV		$2,486.85			
8						

Sheet1   ⊕

READY   100%

Microsoft Corporation

Again, let's look at some examples.

Example 1.   A movie theatre considers upgrading its concessions area at a cost of $10,000. The upgrades are expected to produce additional cash flows from concession sales of $2,000 per year over the next six years. Should the movie theatre upgrade its concessions area if its discount rate is 8% annually?

The present value of a $2,000 annuity over six years at 8% interest is $9,245.76 (= $2,000 × 4.62288, time value factor from Table 4, Present Value of an Annuity of $1, with $n = 6$ and $i = 8\%$). The $10,000 cost of the upgrade is greater than the present value of the future cash flows of $9,245.76 generated. The theatre will be better off *not* making the investment.

Example 2.   Each year you play the Monopoly game at **McDonald's**. This is your year: As you peel back the sticker, you realize you have both Park Place and Boardwalk. You have just won a million dollars payable in $50,000 installments over the next 20 years. Assuming a discount rate of 10%, how much did you really win?

The present value of a $50,000 annuity over 20 periods at 10% is $425,678 (= $50,000 × 8.51356, time value factor from Table 4, Present Value of an Annuity of $1, with $n = 20$ and $i = 10\%$). The value today of $50,000 per year for the next 20 years is actually less than half a million dollars, though you'd probably not be too disappointed with these winnings.

 **KEY POINT**

The *present* value of an annuity is the sum of the present values of a series of cash payments.

Let's Review

Below are four scenarios related to the future value and present value of an annuity.

1. Manuel is saving for a new car. He puts $2,000 into an investment account at the end of each year for the next five years. He expects the account to earn 12% annually. How much will Manuel have in five years?

2. Ingrid would like to take her family to Disney World in three years. She decides to purchase a vacation package that requires her to make three annual payments of $1,500 at the end of each year for the next three years. If she can earn 9% annually, how much should she set aside today so that the three annual payments can be made?

3. John puts $500 in a savings account at the end of each six months for the next six years that earns 8% interest compounded semiannually. How much will John have in six years?

4. Anna purchases a ring with a selling price of $4,000 and will make four payments of $1,000 at the end of each quarter for the next four quarters. Assuming a discount rate of 16% compounded quarterly, what is Anna's actual cost of the ring today?

Required:

Calculate the time value of money for each scenario.

Solution:

(Rounded to the nearest whole dollar)
1. $2,000 × 6.3528 (FV of Annuity of $1, $n = 5$, $i = 12\%$) = $12,706
2. $1,500 × 2.53129 (PV of Annuity of $1, $n = 3$, $i = 9\%$) = $3,797
3. $500 × 15.0258 (FV of Annuity of $1, $n = 12$, $i = 4\%$) = $7,513
4. $1,000 × 3.62990 (PV of Annuity of $1, $n = 4$, $i = 4\%$) = $3,630

Suggested Homework:
BEC–8, BEC–11;
EC–6, EC–8;
PC–3A&B

KEY POINTS BY LEARNING OBJECTIVE

LO C–1   Contrast simple and compound interest.
Simple interest is interest we earn on the initial investment only. Compound interest is the interest we earn on the initial investment plus previous interest. We use compound interest in calculating the time value of money.

LO C–2   Calculate the future value of a single amount.
The future value of a single amount is how much that amount today will grow to be in the future.

LO C–3   Calculate the present value of a single amount.
The present value of a single amount is the value today of receiving that amount in the future.

LO C–4   Calculate the future value of an annuity.
Cash payments of equal amounts over time periods of equal length are called an annuity. The future value of an annuity is the sum of the future values of a series of cash payments.

LO C–5   Calculate the present value of an annuity.
The present value of an annuity is the sum of the present values of a series of cash payments.

GLOSSARY

Annuity: Cash payments of equal amounts over time periods of equal length. **p. C–8**

Compound interest: Interest earned on the initial investment and on previous interest. **p. C–2**

Discount rate: The rate at which someone would be willing to give up current dollars for future dollars. **p. C–5**

Future value: How much an amount today will grow to be in the future. **p. C–2**

Present value: The value today of receiving some amount in the future. **p. C–5**

Simple interest: Interest earned on the initial investment only. **p. C–1**

Time value of money: The value of money today is greater than the value of that same amount of money in the future. **p. C–1**

SELF-STUDY QUESTIONS

1. How does simple interest differ from compound interest? **(LO C–1)**
   a. Simple interest includes interest earned on the initial investment plus interest earned on previous interest.
   b. Simple interest includes interest earned on the initial investment only.
   c. Simple interest is for a shorter time interval.
   d. Simple interest is for a longer time interval.

2. What is the future value of $100 invested in an account for eight years that earns 10% annual interest, compounded semiannually (rounded to the nearest whole dollar)? **(LO C–2)**

   a. $214.
   b. $216.
   c. $218.
   d. $220.

3. Present value represents **(LO C–3)**
   a. The value today of receiving money in the future.
   b. The amount that an investment today will grow to be in the future.
   c. The difference between the initial investment and the growth of that investment over time.
   d. A series of equal payments.

4. Cooper wants to save for college. Assuming he puts $5,000 into an account at the end of each year for five years and earns 12% compounded annually, how much will he have saved by the end of the fifth year (rounded to the nearest whole dollar)? **(LO C–4)**
   a. $25,000.
   b. $31,764.
   c. $18,024.
   d. $14,096.

5. A company agrees to pay $100,000 each year for five years for an exclusive franchise agreement. Assuming a discount rate of 8%, what is the cost today of the agreement (rounded to the nearest whole dollar)? **(LO C–5)**
   a. $500,000.
   b. $586,660.
   c. $399,271.
   d. $146,933.

Note: For answers, see the last page of the appendix.

REVIEW QUESTIONS

■ **LO C–1**   1. Define interest. Explain the difference between simple interest and compound interest.

■ **LO C–2**   2. Identify the three items of information necessary to calculate the future value of a single amount.

■ **LO C–3**   3. Define the present value of a single amount. What is the discount rate?

■ **LO C–4**   4. What is the relationship between the future value of a single amount and the future value of an annuity?

■ **LO C–5**   5. What is the relationship between the present value of a single amount and the present value of an annuity?

BRIEF EXERCISES

Mc Graw Hill **connect®**

Understand simple versus compound interest (LO C–1)

BEC–1 Oprah is deciding between investment options. Both investments earn an interest rate of 7%, but interest on the first investment is compounded annually, while interest on the second investment is compounded semiannually. Which investment would you advise Oprah to choose? Why?

Understand simple versus compound interest for future value (LO C–1, C–2)

BEC–2 An investments account offers a 12% annual return. If $50,000 is placed in the account for two years, by how much will the investment grow if interest is compounded (a) annually, (b) semiannually, (c) quarterly, or (d) monthly?

Calculate the future value of a single amount (LO C–2)

BEC–3 Dusty would like to buy a new car in six years. He currently has $15,000 saved. He's considering buying a car for around $19,000 but would like to add a Turbo engine to increase the car's performance. This would increase the price of the car to $23,000. If Dusty can earn 9% interest, compounded annually, will he be able to get a car with a Turbo engine in six years?

Calculate the future value of a single amount (LO C–2)

BEC–4 Arnold and Helene would like to visit Austria in two years to celebrate their 25th wedding anniversary. Currently, the couple has saved $27,000, but they expect the trip to cost $31,000. If they put $27,000 in an account that earns 7% interest, compounded annually, will they be able to pay for the trip in two years?

Calculate the future value of a single amount (LO C–2)

BEC–5 Calculate the future value of the following single amounts.

	Initial Investment	Annual Rate	Interest Compounded	Period Invested
1.	$8,000	10%	Annually	7 years
2.	6,000	12	Semiannually	4 years
3.	9,000	8	Quarterly	3 years

BEC–6 Maddy works at Burgers R Us. Her boss tells her that if she stays with the company for five years, she will receive a bonus of $6,000. With an annual discount rate of 8%, calculate the value today of receiving $6,000 in five years.

Calculate the present value of a single amount (LO C–3)

BEC–7 Ronald has an investment opportunity that promises to pay him $55,000 in three years. He could earn a 6% annual return investing his money elsewhere. What is the most he would be willing to invest today in this opportunity?

Calculate the present value of a single amount (LO C–3)

BEC–8 Calculate the present value of the following single amounts.

Calculate the present value of a single amount (LO C–3)

	Future Value	Annual Rate	Interest Compounded	Period Invested
1.	$10,000	6%	Annually	5 years
2.	7,000	8	Semiannually	8 years
3.	6,000	12	Quarterly	4 years

BEC–9 Tom and Suri decide to take a worldwide cruise. To do so, they need to save $30,000. They plan to invest $4,000 at the end of each year for the next seven years to earn 8% compounded annually. Determine whether Tom and Suri will reach their goal of $30,000 in seven years.

Calculate the future value of an annuity (LO C–4)

BEC–10 Matt plans to start his own business once he graduates from college. He plans to save $3,000 every six months for the next five years. If his savings earn 10% annually (or 5% every six months), determine how much he will save by the end of the fifth year.

Calculate the future value of an annuity (LO C–4)

BEC–11 Calculate the future value of the following annuities, assuming each annuity payment is made at the end of each compounding period.

Calculate the future value of an annuity (LO C–4)

	Annuity Payment	Annual Rate	Interest Compounded	Period Invested
1.	$3,000	7%	Annually	6 years
2.	6,000	8	Semiannually	9 years
3.	5,000	12	Quarterly	5 years

BEC–12 Tatsuo has just been awarded a four-year scholarship to attend the university of his choice. The scholarship will pay $8,000 each year for the next four years to reimburse normal school-related expenditures. Each $8,000 payment will be made at the end of the year, contingent on Tatsuo maintaining good grades in his classes for that year. Assuming an annual interest rate of 6%, determine the value today of receiving this scholarship if Tatsuo maintains good grades.

Calculate the present value of an annuity (LO C–5)

BEC–13 Monroe Corporation is considering the purchase of new equipment. The equipment will cost $35,000 today. However, due to its greater operating capacity, Monroe expects the new equipment to earn additional revenues of $5,000 by the end of each year for the next 10 years. Assuming a discount rate of 10% compounded annually, determine whether Monroe should make the purchase.

Calculate the present value of an annuity (LO C–5)

BEC–14 Calculate the present value of the following annuities, assuming each annuity payment is made at the end of each compounding period.

Calculate the present value of an annuity (LO C–5)

	Annuity Payment	Annual Rate	Interest Compounded	Period Invested
1.	$4,000	7%	Annually	5 years
2.	9,000	8	Semiannually	3 years
3.	3,000	8	Quarterly	2 years

EXERCISES

McGraw Hill **connect**

Calculate the future value of a single amount (LO C–2)

EC–1 The four people below have the following investments.

	Invested Amount	Interest Rate	Compounding
Jerry	$13,000	12%	Quarterly
Elaine	16,000	6	Semiannually
George	23,000	8	Annually
Kramer	19,000	10	Annually

Required:

Determine which of the four people will have the greatest investment accumulation in six years.

Calculate the future value of a single amount (LO C–2)

EC–2 You want to save for retirement. Assuming you are now 25 years old and you want to retire at age 55, you have 30 years to watch your investment grow. You decide to invest in the stock market, which has earned about 13% per year over the past 80 years and is expected to continue at this rate. You decide to invest $2,000 today.

Required:

How much do you expect to have in 40 years?

Calculate the future value of a single amount (LO C–2)

EC–3 You are saving for a new car. You place $10,000 into an investment account today. How much will you have after four years if the account earns (a) 4%, (b) 6%, or (c) 8% compounded annually?

Calculate the future value of a single amount (LO C–2)

EC–4 You are saving for a new boat. You place $25,000 in an investment account today that earns 6% compounded annually. How much will be in the account after (a) three years, (b) four years, or (c) five years?

Calculate the present value of a single amount (LO C–3)

EC–5 The four actors below have just signed a contract to star in a dramatic movie about relationships among hospital doctors. Each person signs independent contracts with the following terms:

	Contract Terms	
	Contract Amount	**Payment Date**
Derek	$600,000	2 years
Isabel	640,000	3 years
Meredith	500,000	Today
George	500,000	1 year

Required:

Assuming an annual discount rate of 9%, which of the four actors is actually being paid the most?

Calculate the present value of a single amount (LO C–3)

EC–6 Ray and Rachel are considering the purchase of two deluxe kitchen ovens. The first store offers the two ovens for $3,500 with payment due today. The second store offers the two ovens for $3,700 due in one year.

Required:

Assuming an annual discount rate of 9%, from which store should Ray and Rachel buy their ovens?

Calculate the present value of a single amount (LO C–3)

EC–7 You have entered into an agreement for the purchase of land. The agreement specifies that you will take ownership of the land immediately. You have agreed to pay $50,000 today and another $50,000 in three years. Calculate the total cost of the land today, assuming a discount rate of (a) 5%, (b) 7%, or (c) 9%.

EC–8 You believe you have discovered a new medical device. You anticipate it will take additional time to get the device fully operational, run clinical trials, obtain FDA approval, and sell to a buyer for $250,000. Assume a discount rate of 7% compounded annually. What is the value today of discovering the medical device, assuming you sell it for $250,000 in (a) two years, (b) three years, or (c) four years?

Calculate the present value of a single amount (LO C–3)

EC–9 Lights, Camera, and More sells filmmaking equipment. The company offers three purchase options: (1) pay full cash today, (2) pay one-half down and the remaining one-half plus 10% in one year, or (3) pay nothing down and the full amount plus 15% in one year. George is considering buying equipment from Lights, Camera, and More for $150,000 and therefore has the following payment options:

Calculate the present value of a single amount (LO C–3)

	Payment Today	Payment in One Year	Total Payment
Option 1	$150,000	$ 0	$150,000
Option 2	75,000	82,500	157,500
Option 3	0	172,500	172,500

Required:
Assuming an annual discount rate of 11%, calculate which option's cost has the lowest present value.

EC–10 GMG Studios plans to invest $60,000 at the end of each year for the next three years. There are three investment options available.

Calculate the future value of an annuity (LO C–4)

	Annual Rate	Interest Compounded	Period Invested
Option 1	7%	Annually	3 years
Option 2	9	Annually	3 years
Option 3	11	Annually	3 years

Required:
Determine the accumulated investment amount by the end of the third year for each of the options.

EC–11 You would like to start saving for retirement. Assuming you are now 25 years old and you want to retire at age 55, you have 30 years to watch your investment grow. You decide to invest in the stock market, which has earned about 13% per year over the past 80 years and is expected to continue at this rate. You decide to invest $2,000 at the end of each year for the next 30 years.

Calculate the future value of an annuity (LO C–4)

Required:
Calculate how much your accumulated investment is expected to be in 30 years.

EC–12 You are saving for a new house. You place $40,000 into an investment account each year for five years. How much will you have after five years if the account earns (a) 3%, (b) 6%, or (c) 9% compounded annually?

Calculate the future value of an annuity (LO C–4)

EC–13 You want to buy a nice road bike. You place $3,000 each year in an investment account that earns 8% compounded annually. How much will be in the account after (a) two years, (b) three years, or (c) four years?

Calculate the future value of an annuity (LO C–4)

EC–14 Denzel needs a new car. At the dealership, he finds the car he likes. The dealership gives him two payment options:
1. Pay $35,000 for the car today.
2. Pay $4,000 at the end of each quarter for three years.

Calculate the present value of an annuity (LO C–5)

Required:
Assuming Denzel uses a discount rate of 12% (or 3% quarterly), determine which option gives him the lower cost.

Calculate the present
value of an annuity
(LO C–5)

EC–15 You have entered into an agreement to purchase a local accounting firm. The agreement specifies you will pay the seller $150,000 each year for six years. What is the cost today of the purchase, assuming a discount rate of (a) 8%, (b) 10%, or (c) 12%.

Calculate the present
value of an annuity (LO
C–5)

EC–16 You have been issued a patent giving you exclusive rights to sell a new type of software. You believe the patent will produce sales of $200,000 each year as long as the software remains in demand. Assume a discount rate of 7% compounded annually. What is the value today of having the patent, assuming sales last for (a) three years, (b) four years, or (c) five years?

PROBLEMS: SET A

Calculate the future value
of a single amount
(LO C–2)

PC–1A Alec, Daniel, William, and Stephen decide today to save for retirement. Each person wants to retire by age 65 and puts $11,000 into an account earning 10% compounded annually.

Person	Age	Initial Investment	Accumulated Investment by Retirement (age 65)
Alec	55	$11,000	$_____
Daniel	45	11,000	$_____
William	35	11,000	$_____
Stephen	25	11,000	$_____

Required:
Calculate how much each person will have accumulated by the age of 65.

Consider present
value (LO C–3, LO C–5)

PC–2A Bruce is considering the purchase of a restaurant named Hard Rock Hollywood. The restaurant is listed for sale at $1,000,000. With the help of his accountant, Bruce projects the net cash flows (cash inflows less cash outflows) from the restaurant to be the following amounts over the next 10 years:

Years	Amount
1–6	$100,000 (each year)
7	110,000
8	120,000
9	130,000
10	140,000

Bruce expects to sell the restaurant after 10 years for an estimated $1,300,000.

Required:
If Bruce wants to make at least 11% annually on his investment, should he purchase the restaurant? (Assume all cash flows occur at the end of each year.)

Determine present value
alternatives (LO C–3, C–5)

PC–3A Hollywood Tabloid needs a new state-of-the-art camera to produce its monthly magazine. The company is looking at two cameras that are both capable of doing the job and has determined the following:

Camera 1 costs $6,000. It should last for eight years and have annual maintenance costs of $300 per year. After eight years, the magazine can sell the camera for $300.
Camera 2 costs $5,500. It will also last for eight years and have maintenance costs of $900 in year three, $900 in year five, and $1,000 in year seven. After eight years, the camera will have no resale value.

Required:

Determine which camera Hollywood Tabloid should purchase. Assume that an interest rate of 9% properly reflects the discount rate in this situation and that maintenance costs are paid at the end of each year.

PROBLEMS: SET B

PC–1B Mary Kate, Ashley, Dakota, and Elle each want to buy a new home. Each needs to save enough to make a 25% down payment. For example, to buy a $100,000 home, a person would need to save $25,000. At the end of each year for four years, the women make the following investments:

Calculate the future value of an annuity (LO C–4)

Person	Annuity Payment	Type of Account	Expected Annual Return	Four-Year Accumulated Investment	Maximum Home Purchase
Mary Kate	$4,000	Savings	2%	$_____	$_____
Ashley	5,000	CDs	4	$_____	$_____
Dakota	6,000	Bonds	7	$_____	$_____
Elle	6,000	Stocks	11	$_____	$_____

Required:

1. Calculate how much each woman is expected to accumulate in the investment account by the end of the fourth year.
2. What is the maximum amount each woman can spend on a home, assuming she uses her accumulated investment account to make a 25% down payment?

PC–2B Woody Lightyear is considering the purchase of a toy store from Andy Enterprises. Woody expects the store will generate net cash flows (cash inflows less cash outflows) of $60,000 per year for 20 years. At the end of the 20 years, he intends to sell the store for $600,000. To finance the purchase, Woody will borrow using a 20-year note that requires 9% interest.

Consider the present value of investments (LO C–3, LO C–5)

Required:

What is the maximum amount Woody should offer Andy for the toy store? (Assume all cash flows occur at the end of each year.)

PC–3B Star Studios is looking to purchase a new building for its upcoming film productions. The company finds a suitable location that has a list price of $1,600,000. The seller gives Star Studios the following purchase options:

Determine present value alternatives (LO C–3, LO C–5)

1. Pay $1,600,000 immediately.
2. Pay $600,000 immediately and then pay $150,000 each year over the next 10 years, with the first payment due in one year.
3. Make 10 annual installments of $250,000, with the first payment due in one year.
4. Make a single payment of $2,300,000 at the end of five years.

Required:

Determine the lowest-cost alternative for Star Studios, assuming that the company can borrow funds to finance the purchase at 8%.

Answers to Self-Study Questions

1. b   2. c   3. a   4. b   5. c

Learning Objectives

- ■ **LO D–1** Explain why companies invest in other companies.
- ■ **LO D–2** Account for investments in equity securities when the investor has *insignificant* influence.
- ■ **LO D–3** Account for investments in equity securities when the investor has *significant* influence.
- ■ **LO D–4** Account for investments in equity securities when the investor has *controlling* influence.
- ■ **LO D–5** Account for investments in debt securities.

SELF-STUDY MATERIALS

- ■ Let's Review—Equity investment with insignificant influence (p. D-6).
- ■ Let's Review—Equity investment with significant influence (p. D-9).
- ■ Let's Review—Debt investment at face amount (p. D-14).
- ■ Let's Review—Debt investment at discount and premium (p. D-16).
- ■ Key Points by Learning Objective (p. D-17).
- ■ Glossary of Key Terms (p. D-17).
- ■ Self-Study Questions with answers available (p. D-18).

Why Companies Invest in Other Companies

To finance growing operations, a company raises additional funds either by issuing *equity securities,* such as the common and preferred stock we discussed in Chapter 10, or by issuing *debt securities,* such as the bonds we discussed in Chapter 9. These equity and debt securities are purchased by individual investors, by mutual funds, and also by other companies. In this appendix, we focus on investments by companies in equity and debt securities issued by other companies. Companies invest in other companies for a variety of reasons, primarily those indicated in Illustration D–1.

■ **LO D–1**
Explain why companies invest in other companies.

 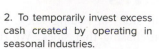 

ILLUSTRATION D–1

Why Companies Invest in Other Companies

1. To receive dividends, earn interest, and gain from the increase in the value of their investment.

2. To temporarily invest excess cash created by operating in seasonal industries.

3. To build strategic alliances, increase market share, or enter new industries.

Companies purchase *equity securities* for dividend income and for appreciation in the value of the stock. Many companies pay a stable dividend stream to their investors. Historically, **General Electric** has been one of the most reliable, highest-dividend-paying stocks on the New York Stock Exchange. In contrast, some companies pay little or no dividends. Companies with large expansion plans, called *growth companies,* prefer to reinvest earnings in the growth of the company rather than distribute earnings to investors in the form of cash dividends. For example, Starbucks, founded in 1987, did not pay a cash dividend until March 2010. Even without receiving dividends, investors still benefit when companies reinvest earnings, leading to even more profits in the future and eventually higher stock prices.

Companies purchase *debt securities* primarily for the interest revenue they provide, although investment returns also are affected when the values of debt securities change over time. As we discussed in Chapter 9, the value of a debt security with fixed interest payments changes in the opposite direction of interest rates. For example, when general market interest rates decrease, the market value of a bond with fixed interest payments goes up because the fixed interest payments are now more attractive to investors.

The seasonal nature of some companies' operations also influences their investment balances. *Seasonal* refers to the revenue activities of a company varying based on the time (or season) of the year. For instance, agricultural and construction companies enjoy more revenues in the summer, and ski resorts earn most of their revenues in the winter. Most retail companies see their sales revenues increase dramatically during the holiday season. As a result of having seasonal operations, companies save excess cash generated during the busy part of the year to maintain operations during the slower time of the year. With this excess cash, companies tend to purchase low-risk investments such as money market funds (savings accounts), government bonds, or highly rated corporate bonds. These low-risk investments enable companies to earn some interest, while ensuring the funds will be available when needed during the slow season. Investing excess cash in stocks is more risky because the value of stocks varies more than the value of bonds. Stocks typically have greater upside potential, providing a higher average return to their investors than do bonds over the long run. However, stocks can lose value in the short run, making them a better choice for investments that are more long-term in nature.

Companies also can make sizable long-run stock investments in other companies for strategic purposes. For instance, AT&T acquired Cingular Wireless to gain a stronger presence in the market for cell phones. Coca-Cola acquired Minute Maid, and PepsiCo purchased Tropicana, in order to diversify beyond soft drinks. Sometimes, a company will remove competition and increase market share by purchasing a controlling interest (more than 50% of its voting stock) in a competing company. Companies also might purchase a controlling interest in an established company in a *different* industry to expand into that industry and avoid many of the start-up costs associated with beginning a new business from scratch.

 KEY POINT

Companies invest in other companies primarily to receive dividends, earn interest, and gain from the increase in the value of their investment. Companies in seasonal industries often invest excess funds generated during the busy season and draw on these funds in the slow season. Many companies also make investments for strategic purposes to develop closer business ties, increase market share, or expand into new industries.

PART A

EQUITY INVESTMENTS

Equity investments are the "flip side" of issuing stock. One company issues stock, and another company invests by purchasing that stock. We discussed the issuance of stock in Chapter 10. Here, we discuss how companies that purchase stock account for their investment.

The way we account for equity investments is determined by the *degree of influence* an investor has over the company in which it invests. **A guideline for determining the degree of influence is the percentage of stock held by the investor.** Illustration D–2 summarizes the reporting methods for equity investments.

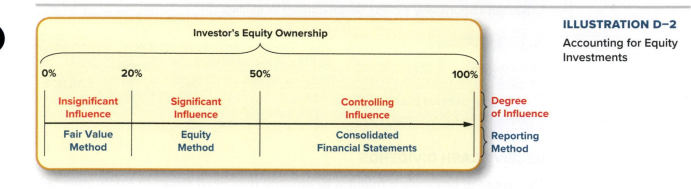

ILLUSTRATION D–2

Accounting for Equity Investments

The **fair value method** is used when a company (investor) purchases less than 20% of the voting shares of another company's stock (investee). In this case, the investor typically is presumed to have *insignificant* influence over the investee. Under the fair value method:

1. Equity securities are reported in the balance sheet at their fair value.
2. Changes in fair value from one period to the next are reported as gains and losses in the income statement.

Fair value is the amount an investment could be bought or sold for in a current transaction between willing parties. For example, when you purchased your car, you and the car dealership (or whomever you bought the car from) came to an agreement on the purchase price, or fair value, of the car. What could you sell that car for today? That's the car's current fair value.

The **equity method** is used when an investor purchases between 20% and 50% of the voting stock of a company. In this case, the investor typically is presumed to have *significant influence* over the investee. By voting all those shares with a single intent, the investor can influence decisions in the direction it desires.

Consolidated financial statements are prepared when an investor purchases more than 50% of the voting stock of a company. In this case, the investor typically is presumed to have *controlling influence;* by voting those shares, the investor (referred to as the parent) actually can control the operations of the investee (referred to as the subsidiary). Both companies continue to operate as separate legal entities, but the parent company reports as if the two companies were operating as a single combined company.

Equity Investments with Insignificant Influence

The critical events over the life of an equity investment in another company, such as shares of common stock, include the following:

■ **LO D–2**

Account for investments in equity securities when the investor has *insignificant* influence.

1. Purchasing the equity security.
2. Receiving dividends (for some equity securities).
3. Holding the investment during periods in which the investment's fair value changes (*unrealized* holding gains and losses).
4. Selling the investment (*realized* gains and losses).

Let's go through each of these events.

PURCHASE EQUITY INVESTMENTS

To see how a company accounts for the purchase of an equity investment, let's assume Nathan's Sportswear purchases 1,000 shares of Canadian Falcon common stock for $30 per share on December 6, 2024. Canadian Falcon's total number of shares outstanding is 20,000, so Nathan's Sportswear owns 5% of the shares, requiring it to account for the investment using the fair value method.

Nathan's Sportswear records the investment as follows:

Income Statement
R − E = NI
No Effect

Balance Sheet
A = L + SE
+30,000
Investments
−30,000
Cash

December 6, 2024	Debit	Credit
Investments	**30,000**	
Cash		**30,000**
(Purchase common stock)		
($30,000 = 1,000 shares × $30)		

RECEIVE CASH DIVIDENDS

The receipt of dividends is recorded as dividend revenue. If Canadian Falcon pays cash dividends of $0.50 per share on December 15, 2024, Nathan's Sportswear records the cash received on its 1,000 shares of stock as follows:

Income Statement
R − E = NI
+500   +500
Dividend Rev.

Balance Sheet
A = L + SE
+500   +500
Cash

December 15, 2024	Debit	Credit
Cash	**500**	
Dividend Revenue		**500**
(Receive cash dividends)		
($500 = 1,000 shares × $0.50)		

ADJUST TO FAIR VALUE

At the end of each period, we report these investment assets at their *fair value*. We do this with an adjusting entry. If Canadian Falcon's stock at the end of 2024 has a current price of $28 per share, then Nathan's Sportswear needs to decrease the recorded amount of the investment ($30 per share) to its current fair value ($28 per share). This requires a downward adjustment to the Investments account of $2 for each of the 1,000 shares.[1]

Income Statement
R − E = NI
+2,000 −2,000
Loss

Balance Sheet
A = L + SE
−2,000   −2,000
Investments

December 31, 2024	Debit	Credit
Unrealized Holding Loss—Net Income	**2,000**	
Investments		**2,000**
(Decrease investments to fair value)		
($2,000 = 1,000 shares × $2)		

The downward adjustment to fair value also involves an account we've not yet discussed called *Unrealized Holding Loss—Net Income*. The term *unrealized* means the loss has not been realized (has not been obtained) in the form of less cash received (or the right to receive less cash). The loss is *realized* when the investment has been sold, and the loss is "locked in." **The unrealized holding loss is reported in the current year's income statement when calculating net income.** Even though the loss is unrealized, reporting it as part of current net income helps to reflect that most equity investments could be sold immediately, and any fair value changes would be realized in cash.

Unrealized holding gains and losses are reported as part of nonoperating revenues and expenses. Illustration D–3 shows an example of the income statement for Nathan's Sportswear. To complete the income statement, we assume sales revenue totals $100,000 and operating expenses are $60,000 for the year ended December 31, 2024. From the transactions recorded above, the income statement also reports as nonoperating items:

- **$500** in dividend revenue from December 15.
- **$2,000** unrealized holding loss resulting from the downward fair value adjustment at the end of the year.

---

[1]Many companies decrease the investment indirectly with a credit to a Fair Value Adjustment allowance rather than to the Investments account itself. We record the fair value adjustment directly to the Investments account, but both methods are acceptable.

NATHAN'S SPORTSWEAR
Income Statement
For the year ended December 31, 2024

Sales revenue	$100,000
Operating expenses	60,000
Operating income	40,000
Dividend revenue	**500**
Unrealized holding loss	**(2,000)**
Net income	$ 38,500

ILLUSTRATION D–3
Income Statement

If the fair value of Canadian Falcon's stock had *increased* by $2 per share by the end of the year, Nathan's Sportswear would have reported a $2,000 *Unrealized Holding Gain—Net Income.*

SELL EQUITY INVESTMENTS

We record the sale of equity investments similar to the sale of many other assets, such as land (discussed in Chapter 7).

- If the investment sells for *more* than its recorded amount, we realize a *gain* on the sale of investments.
- If the investment sells for *less* than its recorded amount, we realize a *loss* on the sale of investments.

Gains and losses on the sale of investments are reported as nonoperating revenues and expenses in the income statement.

Suppose Nathan's Sportswear sells 100 shares of Canadian Falcon for $24 per share on January 18, 2025. How much is the gain or loss on the sale? Let's first remember that at the end of 2024 (prior year), Nathan's Sportswear adjusted the Investments account by decreasing it $2,000. Since the investment was originally recorded for $30,000, the investment is now in the accounting records at $28,000, or $28 per share for 1,000 shares. By selling shares at $24 per share, there is a $4 loss per share on each of the 100 shares sold. Nathan's Sportswear would record the following:

January 18, 2025	Debit	Credit
Cash (100 *shares* × $24)	2,400	
Loss (difference)	400	
Investments (100 *shares* × $28)		2,800
(Sell investments below recorded amount)		

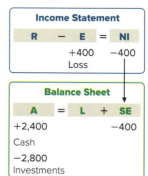

Now suppose the price of the stock has risen to $32 per share by February 26, 2025, and Nathan's Sportswear decides to sell another 100 shares. Since these shares are carried at $28 per share, there is a $4 gain per share on each of the 100 shares sold. At the date of selling these shares, we record the following:

February 26, 2025	Debit	Credit
Cash (100 *shares* × $32)	3,200	
Investments (100 *shares* × $28)		2,800
Gain (difference)		400
(Sell investments above recorded amount)		

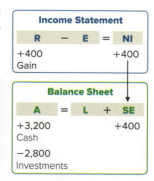

KEY POINT

We report investments at fair value when a company has an insignificant influence over another company in which it invests, often indicated by an ownership interest of less than 20%. Unrealized holding gains and losses are included in net income.

Let's Review

Sheer Designs, a custom clothing designer, has heard great things about Slacks 5th Avenue and has decided to make a small investment (insignificant influence) in the corporation's common stock. Sheer Designs has the following transactions relating to its investment in Slacks 5th Avenue.

January	15	Purchase 500 shares of common stock for $20 per share.
June	30	Receive a cash dividend of $2 per share.
October	1	Sell 100 shares of common stock for $25 per share.
December	31	The fair value of Slacks 5th Avenue's stock equals $23 per share.

Required:

1. Record each of these transactions, including the fair value adjusting entry on December 31.

2. Calculate the balance in the Investments account on December 31.

Solution:

1. Record transactions:

January 15	Debit	Credit
Investments	**10,000**	
Cash		**10,000**
(Purchase common stock)		
($10,000 = 500 shares × $20)		
June 30		
Cash	**1,000**	
Dividend Revenue		**1,000**
(Receive cash dividends)		
($1,000 = 500 shares × $2)		
October 1		
Cash (100 *shares* × $25)	**2,500**	
Investments (100 *shares* × $20)		**2,000**
Gain (difference)		**500**
(Sell investments above recorded amount)		
December 31		
Investments	**1,200**	
Unrealized Holding Gain—Net Income		**1,200**
(Adjust investments to fair value)		
($1,200 = 400 shares × $3)		

2. The balance in the Investments account on December 31 is $9,200, which equals the 400 remaining shares times $23 per share fair value. The balance in the Investments account can be verified by posting all transactions to a T-account, as follows.

Investments	
10,000	
	2,000
1,200	
Bal. 9,200	

Suggested Homework:
BED–3, BED–4;
ED–2, ED–3;
PD–1A& B

Equity Investments with Significant Influence

When a company owns between 20% and 50% of the common stock in another company, it is presumed that the investing company exercises significant influence over the investee. Share ownership provides voting rights, and by voting these shares, the investing company can sway decisions in the direction it desires, such as the selection of members of the board of directors or the payment of dividends. This significant influence changes the accounting for the investment. When a company has significant influence over an investee, the company is required to use the equity method.

Under the equity method, the investment is initially recorded at cost. After that, the investment balance is

1. Increased by the investor's percentage share of the investee's net income (or decreased by its share of a loss).
2. Decreased by the investor's percentage share of the investee's dividends paid.
3. Not adjusted for changes in fair value while held.

The rationale for this approach is the presumption that the fortunes of the investor and investee are so intertwined that, as the investee prospers, the investor prospers proportionately. Stated differently, as the investee earns additional net assets (income), the investor's share of those net assets increases. When the investee pays out assets (dividends), the investor's share of the remaining net assets decreases. **It's also important to recognize that the equity method ignores fair value changes in the investment.** Let's now walk through an example of the equity method.

■ **LO D–3**
Account for investments in equity securities when the investor has *significant* influence.

PURCHASE EQUITY INVESTMENTS

On January 2, 2025, Nathan's Sportswear purchases 5,000 shares of International Outfitter's common stock for $30 per share. International Outfitter's total number of shares outstanding is 20,000, so Nathan's owns 25% of the common stock (= 5,000/20,000 shares). By holding 25% of the stock, Nathan's Sportswear can exert significant influence over the operations of International Outfitter and is required to account for its investment using the equity method.

Nathan's Sportswear records this equity investment as follows:

January 2, 2025	Debit	Credit
Investments	150,000	
Cash		150,000
(Purchase common stock)		
($150,000 = 5,000 shares × $30)		

Income Statement

R	–	E	=	NI
		No Effect		

Balance Sheet

A	=	L	+	SE
+150,000				
Investments				
–150,000				
Cash				

RECOGNIZE EQUITY INCOME

Under the equity method, the investor (Nathan's Sportswear) includes in net income its portion of the investee's (International Outfitter's) net income. Assume that on

December 31, 2025, International Outfitter reports net income of $30,000 for the year. Nathan's Sportswear records $7,500 of equity income, which represents its 25% ownership share of International Outfitter's net income of $30,000.

Income Statement

R	–	E	=	NI
+7,500				+7,500
Equity Inc.				

Balance Sheet

A	=	L	+	SE
+7,500				+7,500
Investment				

December 31, 2025	Debit	Credit
Investments	**7,500**	
Equity Income		**7,500**
(Earn equity income)		
($7,500 = $30,000 × 25% ownership)		

The investee's net income increases the investor's Investments account and Equity Income account. Equity Income is a revenue account included as a nonoperating revenue in the income statement. The reason Nathan's Sportswear can record a portion of International Outfitter's net income as its own is that significant ownership essentially eliminates the independent operations of the two companies. Nathan's Sportswear can significantly influence the operations of International Outfitter. **Therefore, the success (or failure) of International Outfitter's operations should partially be assigned to Nathan's Sportswear and recognized as income (or loss) in its income statement, based on its portion of ownership.**

RECEIVE CASH DIVIDENDS

Because we record equity income when the investee reports net income (as in the entry above), it would be inappropriate to record equity income again when the investee distributes that same net income as dividends to the investor. To do so would be to double-count equity income. Instead, the investor records dividend payments received from the investee as a *reduction* in the Investments account. Assuming International Outfitter pays total dividends of $10,000 to all shareholders on December 31, 2025, Nathan's Sportswear receives its share of $2,500 (= $10,000 × 25% ownership) and records the following:

Income Statement

R	–	E	=	NI
		No Effect		

Balance Sheet

A	=	L	+	SE
+2,500				
Cash				
–2,500				
Investments				

December 31, 2025	Debit	Credit
Cash	**2,500**	
Investments		**2,500**
(Receive cash dividends)		
($2,500 = $10,000 × 25% ownership)		

The rationale for this accounting is that the investee is distributing cash in the form of dividends. This distribution of assets by the investee reduces that company's equity. To account for the investee's decrease in equity, the investor decreases its Investments account based on its portion of ownership.

We can see the balances in the Investments and Equity Income accounts for Nathan's Sportswear after posting the three transactions above.

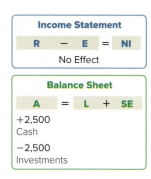

	Investments	
Initial investment	150,000	
25% of net income	7,500	2,500 25% of dividends
Bal. 155,000		

	Equity Income	
		7,500 25% of net income
		Bal. 7,500

The Investments account increases by the initial investment and the investor's share of the investee's net income, and it decreases by the investor's share of the investee's dividends. The Equity Income account reflects the investor's share of net income rather than its share of dividends.

KEY POINT

We initially record equity investments at cost. Under the equity method, the balance of the Investments account increases for the investor's share of the investee's net income and decreases for the investor's share of the investee's cash dividends. Equity Income reflects the investor's share of the investee's net income.

The equity method can differ significantly from recording investments under the fair value method. Under the fair value method, the investment by Nathan's Sportswear would be recorded at the purchase price of $150,000 and then be adjusted to fair value at the end of each period. Under the equity method, no adjustment is made to fair value.[2] In addition, Nathan's Sportswear would record only $2,500 of dividend revenue under the fair value method, rather than the $7,500 of equity income recorded using the equity method.

Let's Review

To help ensure control over availability and delivery of its inventory, Designer Dresses purchases a 40% investment (significant influence) in Anderson Textile's common stock. Designer Dresses has the following transactions relating to its investment in Anderson Textile.

January	1	Purchase 500 shares of common stock for $20 per share.
June	30	Receive a cash dividend of $500 (or $1 per share), representing its 40% share of Anderson Textile's total dividend distribution of $1,250.
December 31		Anderson Textile reports total net income of $5,000 for the year.
December 31		The fair value of Anderson Textile's stock equals $23 per share.

Required:

1. Record each of these transactions.
2. Calculate the balance of the Investments account on December 31.

Solution:

1. Record transactions:

January 1	Debit	Credit
Investments	10,000	
Cash		10,000
(Purchase common stock)		
June 30		
Cash	500	
Investments		500
(Receive cash dividends)		
($500 = 500 shares × $1)		
December 31		
Investments	2,000	
Equity Income		2,000
(Earn equity income)		
($2,000 = $5,000 × 40%)		
December 31		
No adjustments are recorded for fair value changes when using the equity method.		

[2]Adjustment to fair value is an allowable alternative under the equity method but is not common in practice.

2. The balance of the Investments account on December 31 is $11,500. The balance of the Investments account can be verified by posting all transactions to a T-account.

Investments	
10,000	
	500
2,000	
Bal. 11,500	

Suggested Homework:
BED–7, BED–8;
ED–6, ED–7;
PD–2A&B

Equity Investments with Controlling Influence

■ **LO D–4**

Account for investments in equity securities when the investor has *controlling* influence.

If a company purchases more than 50% of the voting stock of another company, it's said to have a *controlling influence.* By voting these shares, the investor actually can control the acquired company. The investor is referred to as the *parent;* the investee is the *subsidiary.*

Investments involving the purchase of more than 50% of the voting stock require the parent company to prepare **consolidated financial statements**. These statements combine the parent's and subsidiary's financial statements as if the two companies were a *single* reporting company, even though both companies continue to operate as separate legal entities. Illustration D–4 demonstrates the concept of consolidation.

ILLUSTRATION D–4

Consolidation Method

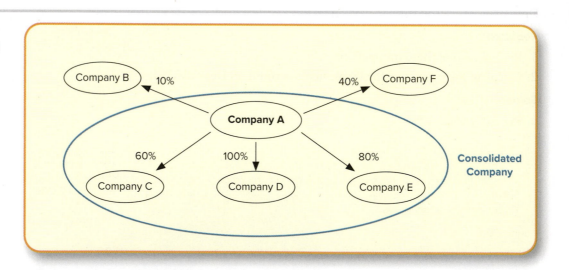

Suppose Company A owns common stock in five other companies. When preparing financial statements, Company A combines its financial statement results with all companies in which it has greater than 50% ownership (in this instance, Companies C, D, and E). For example, if Company A has $10 million cash and Companies C, D, and E have $2 million, $4 million, and $6 million, respectively, the consolidated balance sheet would report cash of $22 million.[3] The cash balances for Companies B and F are not included in the consolidated financial statements of Company A. The 10% ownership (insignificant influence)

---

[3]Any transactions between Companies A, C, D, and E are eliminated from consolidated reporting because these transactions are not with external parties. This avoids "double-counting" those amounts in the consolidated statements. For example, we report amounts owed by Company C to Company D as accounts payable in Company C's balance sheet and as accounts receivable in Company D's balance sheet. However, these amounts are not included in the consolidated balance sheet because a company can't owe money to itself, and the consolidated company is treated as a single company for financial reporting purposes.

in Company B is accounted for using the fair value method, while the 40% ownership (significant influence) in Company F is accounted for using the equity method. The process of consolidating financial statements is beyond the scope of this introductory book and is covered in advanced accounting books.

KEY POINT

Investments involving one company (parent) purchasing more than 50% of the voting stock of another company (subsidiary) require the parent company to prepare consolidated financial statements. These statements combine the parent's and subsidiary's financial statements as if the two companies were a single reporting company.

DEBT INVESTMENTS

PART B

Debt investments are the "flip side" of long-term debt: One party *borrows* by issuing a debt instrument, while another party *lends* by investing in the debt instrument. In Chapter 9, we discussed how to report the issuance of bonds (a specific type of debt instrument recorded as bonds payable). While bonds payable incur interest expense, investment in bonds earns interest revenue. Here, we discuss how to report an investment in bonds and the interest revenue.

■ **LO D–5**
Account for investments in debt securities.

The critical events over the life of a debt investment in another company, such as a bond, include the following:

1. Purchasing the debt security.
2. Receiving interest (for some debt securities).
3. Holding the investment during periods in which the investment's fair value changes (*unrealized* holding gains and losses).
4. Either selling the investment before maturity (*realized* gains and losses) or receiving principal payment at maturity.

Flip Side

Let's go through each of these events.

PURCHASE DEBT INVESTMENTS

Assume that on January 1, 2024, Nathan's Sportswear purchases $100,000 of 7%, 10-year bonds issued by California Coasters, with interest receivable semiannually on June 30 and December 31 each year. The bonds were issued "at par" which means they were purchased at face amount. Nathan's Sportswear records this bond investment as follows:

January 1, 2024	Debit	Credit
Investments	$100,000	
Cash		$100,000
(Purchase bonds)		

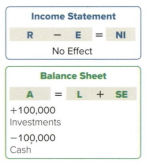

EARN INTEREST REVENUE

On June 30, 2024, six months after the initial bond investment, Nathan's Sportswear will receive cash from California Coasters equal to the investment's face amount ($100,000) times the stated rate (7% annually, or 3.5% semiannually). These amounts are recorded as:

June 30, 2024	Debit	Credit
Cash (= $100,000 × 7% × ½)	3,500	
Interest Revenue		3,500
(Receive semiannual interest revenue)		

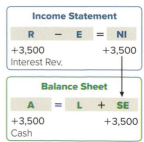

This same amount of interest is received and recorded on December 31, 2024, and every six-month period until the investment matures at the end of its 10-year life.

 KEY POINT

Bond investments are the "flip side" of bonds payable. Bond investments are long-term assets that earn interest revenue, while bonds payable are long-term liabilities that incur interest expense.

THREE CLASSIFICATIONS OF DEBT INVESTMENTS

The bonds issued by California Coasters had a 7% rate of interest and a fair value (or issue price) of $100,000 on January 1, 2024. This fair value reflected the price investors were willing to pay at the time of the issuance for the future cash flows of the bonds—principal at maturity and periodic interest payments. However, market conditions may change over time, causing investors to apply a different discount rate to the future cash flows of the bonds.

Rising interest rates cause unrealized holding losses.

If market conditions cause investors' discount rate to increase, the fair value of the bonds will decrease. In that case, the investors holding the bonds suffer an *unrealized* holding loss. The loss hasn't been realized because the investment hasn't been sold. Alternatively, market conditions could lower investors' discount rate applied to future cash flows of the bonds. In this case, the fair value of the bonds will increase, and investors will enjoy an unrealized holding gain.

Falling interest rates cause unrealized holding gains.

Accounting for these changes in fair value depends on the classification of the debt investment. There are three types:

Do not report fair value changes.

- **Held-to-maturity securities** are debt securities that a company expects to hold until they *mature,* which means until the issuer is required to repay the full amount of the bonds to the investors. Companies are not required to adjust held-to-maturity securities to fair value because there is not an expectation of selling these securities in the bond market before they mature. Instead, these securities are carried at historical cost (or at amortized cost if the bonds were issued at a discount or premium).[4]

Report fair value changes in net income.

- **Trading securities** are debt investments that the investor expects to sell (trade) in the near future. These securities are reported the same way we report equity investments with insignificant influence; we report trading securities as current assets at their fair value, and any unrealized gains or losses are recognized in the income statement as part of net income.

Report fair value changes in other comprehensive income.

- **Available-for-sale securities** are debt investments held for reasons other than attempting to profit from trading in the near future and can be classified as either current or long-term assets. Like trading securities, these securities are reported at their fair value. However, unlike trading securities, unrealized gains and losses are reported as *other comprehensive income,* which we discuss next.

ADJUST TO FAIR VALUE: AVAILABLE-FOR-SALE SECURITIES

As discussed in the section above, we don't adjust held-to-maturity securities for changes in fair value, because we don't plan to sell them. We do adjust trading securities to fair value, and the accounting is the same as we saw in Part A of this appendix for equity investments with insignificant influence. Here, we discuss how to adjust available-for-sale securities for changes in fair value.

Continuing our previous example, assume Nathan's Sportswear accounts for its investment in California Coaster's bond as an available-for-sale security. Suppose interest rates fall during the year, and the bond's fair value increases to $101,035. This means the Investments account needs a fair value adjustment of $1,035 (= $101,035 − $100,000).

---

[4] However, U.S. GAAP does allow companies to elect a fair value option. Under this option, companies may report held-to-maturity securities at fair value, with unrealized gains and losses recognized in income in the period in which they occur—the same approach we use to account for trading securities.

December 31, 2024	Debit	Credit
Investments	1,035	
Unrealized Holding Gain—Other Comprehensive Income		1,035
(Increase debt investment to fair value)		
($1,035 = $101,035 − $100,000)		

Because this investment is classified as available-for-sale, the unrealized holding gain associated with the increase in the fair value of the bond investment will be reported in "Other Comprehensive Income."

Comprehensive income consists of two components. You already have been introduced to the first component—**net income**. Net income consists of *all* revenues and expenses and *most* gains and losses. These items are reported in the income statement. However, there are a *few* gains and losses from nonowner transactions that we don't report in the income statement; instead, we report these gains and losses separately as the second component of comprehensive income known as **other comprehensive income**. Together, net income and other comprehensive income embody comprehensive income.

$$\text{Net income} + \text{Other comprehensive income} = \text{Comprehensive income}$$

Other comprehensive income (OCI) items are reported as a component of stockholders' equity, separate from other components such as common stock, retained earnings, and treasury stock. This means any balance at the end of the year carries forward into the next year.

Illustration D–5 shows an example of the income statement and the statement of comprehensive income for Nathan's Sportswear. Recall the income statement for Nathan's Sportswear in Illustration D–3 included **$500** dividend revenue from the equity investment in Canadian Falcon, as well as the unrealized holding loss of **$2,000** for the change in that investment's fair value. For the investment in California Coaster's available-for-sale debt security, we also need to report:

- **$7,000** as interest revenue during 2024 ($3,500 on June 30 plus $3,500 on December 31)
- **$1,035** unrealized holding gain for the increase in fair value as of December 31, 2024.

Nathan's Sportswear would report the available-for-sale security as an asset in the balance sheet for its fair value of $101,035.

ILLUSTRATION D–5

Income Statement and Statement of Comprehensive Income

Nathan's Sportswear Income Statement and Statement of Comprehensive Income For the year ended December 31, 2024	
Sales revenue	$100,000
Operating expenses	60,000
Operating income	40,000
Dividend revenue	500
Interest revenue	**7,000**
Unrealized holding loss (equity investment)	**(2,000)**
Net income	45,500
Unrealized holding gain (AFS debt investment)	**1,035**
Comprehensive income	$ 46,535

SELL DEBT INVESTMENTS

Prior to Maturity.   Let's assume in the following year on July 1, 2025, Nathan's Sportswear sells the bonds for $102,000. When an actual sale occurs, the first thing we do is to remove the effects of any unrealized holding gains or losses that have previously been recorded. In this case, we would remove the $1,035 unrealized holding gain, which would bring the investment balance back to its original value of $100,000. We then record any realized gain or loss on the sale in net income equal to the difference between the carrying value of the investment ($100,000) and the amount of cash received on the sale ($102,000). In this case, a gain of $2,000 is realized.

Income Statement

R	−	E	=	NI
+2,000 Gain				+2,000

Balance Sheet

A	=	L	+	SE
+102,000 Cash				+2,000
−101,135 Investments				−1,035 Gain-OCI

July 1, 2025	Debit	Credit
Cash	102,000	
Unrealized Holding Gain—Other Comprehensive Income (from 2024)	1,035	
Investments (see calculation above)		101,035
Gain (difference)		2,000
(Sell bonds before maturity)		

 KEY POINT

For debt investments, trading securities and available-for-sale securities are reported at fair value, while held-to-maturity securities are carried at historical cost (or at amortized cost if the bonds were issued at a discount or premium). Unrealized holding gains and losses from fair value changes are reported as part of net income for trading securities and as part of other comprehensive income for available-for-sale securities.

Income Statement

R	−	E	=	NI
		No Effect		

Balance Sheet

A	=	L	+	SE
+100,000 Cash				
−100,000 Investments				

Held to Maturity.   If Nathan's Sportswear decides to hold the bonds for 10 years until maturity, then they will receive the principal payment equal to the face value of the bond of $100,000.

December 30, 2033	Debit	Credit
Cash	100,000	
Investments		100,000
(Receive cash at bond's maturity)		

Let's Review

Assume that on January 1, 2024, Wally World issues $200,000 of 9% bonds, due in 10 years, with interest payable semiannually on June 30 and December 31 each year. American Life Insurance Company (ALICO) purchases all of the bonds.

Required:

Assume the bonds sell for $200,000. Record the investment in bonds by ALICO on January 1, 2024, and receipt of the first semiannual interest payment on June 30, 2024.

Solution:

January 1, 2024	Debit	Credit
Investments	200,000	
Cash		200,000
(Purchase bonds)		

June 30, 2024		
Cash	9,000	
Interest Revenue		9,000
(Receive semiannual interest revenue)		
($9,000 = $200,000 × 9% × ½)		

Debt Investments Purchased at a Discount or Premium. Let's return to our example of Nathan's Sportswear, but now assume the market rate of interest is 8%. This rate is higher than the bond's stated rate of 7%, and Nathan's Sportswear will purchase the bonds at a discount, paying only $93,205 for the $100,000 bonds.[5] Nathan's Sportswear will record the investment according to the amortization schedule shown in Illustration D–6.

(1) Date	(2) Cash Received	(3) Interest Revenue	(4) Amortization of Discount	(5) Amortized Cost
	Face Amount × Stated Rate	Amortized Cost × Market Rate	(3) − (2)	Prior Amortized Cost + (4)
1/1/2024				$ 93,205
6/30/2024	$3,500	$3,728	$228	93,433
12/31/2024	3,500	3,737	237	93,670
6/30/2025	3,500	3,747	247	93,917
*	*	*	*	*
*	*	*	*	99,057
6/30/2033	3,500	3,962	462	99,519
12/31/2033	3,500	3,981	481	100,000

ILLUSTRATION D–6
Amortization Schedule for Bonds Issued at a Discount

The initial investment on January 1, 2024, is recorded for $93,205.

January 1, 2024	Debit	Credit
Investments	93,205	
Cash		93,205
(Purchase bonds)		

Income Statement

R	−	E	=	NI
		No Effect		

Balance Sheet

A	=	L	+	SE
+93,205 Investments				
−93,205 Cash				

The amount of cash interest received every six months continues to be $3,500, but the amount of interest revenue to record is greater, as shown in column (3) of Illustration D–6. The interest revenue equals current amortized cost (column 5) times the six-month market rate (8% × ½ in this example). For June, the investment earned interest revenue of $3,728 (= $93,205 × 8% × ½). The additional $228 of revenue represents a piece of the cost savings from purchasing the investment at a discount. This piece of the cost savings increases the 7% rate that the bond pays to the higher 8% rate that Nathan's Sportswear required to invest in the bonds. After recording the first interest payment, the investment's amortized cost has increased to $93,433 (= $93,205 original cost + $228 amortization of the discount).

June 30, 2024	Debit	Credit
Cash (= $100,000 × 7% × ½)	3,500	
Investments (difference)	228	
Interest Revenue (= $93,205 × 8% × ½)		3,728
(Receive semiannual interest revenue)		

Income Statement

R	−	E	=	NI
+3,728 Interest Rev.				+3,728

Balance Sheet

A	=	L	+	SE
+3,500 Cash				+3,728
+228 Investments				

At the time of the second semiannual interest payment in December, cash received once again equals $3,500, but the amount of interest revenue changes. Interest revenue equals the investment's current amortized cost of $93,433 times the semiannual market rate of 4%. The difference of $237 represents another piece of the investment's initial discount being amortized and recorded as additional revenue.

---

[5] The bond price of $93,205 is calculated in Illustration 9–12, 9–13, or 9–14.

Income Statement

R	−	E	=	NI
+3,737				+3,737
Interest Rev.				

Balance Sheet

A	=	L	+	SE
+3,500				+3,737
Cash				
+237				
Investments				

December 31, 2024	Debit	Credit
Cash (= $100,000 × 7% × ½)	3,500	
Investments (difference)	237	
Interest Revenue (= [$93,205 + 228] × 8% × ½)		3,737
(Receive semiannual interest revenue)		

The amortization of the discount slowly raises the investment's amortized cost to its face amount of $100,000 by the time of maturity. If the bonds had originally been issued for a premium (greater than $100,000 in our example), then amortization of the premium would have resulted in (1) interest revenue being less than cash received and (2) a decreasing amortized cost of the investment over time.

Let's Review

Assume that on January 1, 2024, Wally World issues $200,000 of 9% bonds, due in 10 years, with interest payable semiannually on June 30 and December 31 each year. American Life Insurance Company (ALICO) purchases all of the bonds.

Required:

1. If the market rate is 10%, the bonds will sell for $187,538. Record the investment in bonds by ALICO on January 1, 2024, and receipt of the first semiannual interest payment on June 30, 2024.

2. If the market rate is 8%, the bonds will sell at $213,590. Record the investment in bonds by ALICO on January 1, 2024, and receipt of the first semiannual interest payment on June 30, 2024.

Solution:

1. Market rate of 10%:

January 1, 2024	Debit	Credit
Investments	187,538	
Cash		187,538
(Purchase bonds)		
June 30, 2024		
Cash (= $200,000 × 9% × ½)	9,000	
Investments (difference)	377	
Interest Revenue (= $187,538 × 10% × ½)		9,377
(Receive semiannual interest revenue)		

2. Market rate of 8%:

January 1, 2024	Debit	Credit
Investments	213,590	
Cash		213,590
(Purchase bonds)		
June 30, 2024		
Cash (= $200,000 × 9% × ½)	9,000	
Investments (difference)		456
Interest Revenue (= $213,590 × 8% × ½)		8,544
(Receive semiannual interest revenue)		

KEY POINTS BY LEARNING OBJECTIVE

LO D–1 Explain why companies invest in other companies.

Companies invest in other companies primarily to receive dividends, earn interest, and gain from the increase in the value of their investment. Companies in seasonal industries often invest excess funds generated during the busy season and draw on these funds in the slow season. Many companies also make investments for strategic purposes to develop closer business ties, increase market share, or expand into new industries.

LO D–2 Account for investments in equity securities when the investor has *insignificant* influence.

We report investments at fair value when a company has an insignificant influence over another company in which it invests, often indicated by an ownership interest of less than 20%. Unrealized holding gains and losses are included in net income.

LO D–3 Account for investments in equity securities when the investor has *significant* influence.

We initially record equity investments at cost. Under the equity method, the balance of the Investments account increases for the investor's share of the investee's net income and decreases for the investor's share of the investee's cash

dividends. Equity Income reflects the investor's share of the investee's net income.

LO D–4 Account for investments in equity securities when the investor has *controlling* influence.

Investments involving one company (parent) purchasing more than 50% of the voting stock of another company (subsidiary) require the parent company to prepare consolidated financial statements. These statements combine the parent's and subsidiary's financial statements as if the two companies were a single reporting company.

LO D–5 Account for investments in debt securities.

Bond investments are the "flip side" of bonds payable. Bond investments are long-term assets that earn interest revenue, while bonds payable are long-term liabilities that incur interest expense.

For debt investments, trading securities and available-for-sale securities are reported at fair value, while held-to-maturity securities are carried at historical cost (or at amortized cost if the bonds were issued at a discount or premium). Unrealized holding gains and losses from fair value changes are reported as part of net income for trading securities and as part of other comprehensive income for available-for-sale securities.

GLOSSARY

Available-for-sale securities: Debt securities held for reasons other than attempting to profit from trading in the near future. **p. D–13**

Comprehensive income: A broader definition of income that includes *all* revenues, expenses, gains, and losses; it's all changes in stockholders' equity other than investments by stockholders and distributions to stockholders. **p. D–14**

Consolidated financial statements: Combination of the separate financial statements of the parent (purchasing company) and the subsidiary (acquired company) into a single set of financial statements. **pp. D–3, D–10**

Debt investments: Investments made in the debt issued by another party. **p. D–11**

Equity investments: Investments made in the equity (or stock) issued by another party. **p. D–2**

Equity method: Method of recording equity investments when an investor has significant influence over, yet does not control, the operations of the investee, often indicated by ownership of between 20% and 50% of the voting shares. Under this method, the investor company records the investment as if the investee is a part of the company. **pp. D–3, D–7**

Fair value: The amount for which the investment could be bought or sold in a current transaction between willing parties. **p. D–3**

Fair value method: Method of recording equity investments when an investor has insignificant influence, often indicated by ownership of less than 20% of the voting shares. Under this method, equity securities are reported in the balance sheet at their fair value, with changes in fair value from one period to the next being reported as gains and losses in the income statement. **p. D–3**

Held-to-maturity securities: Debt securities that are expected to be held until they *mature,* which means until the issuer is required to repay the full amount of the bonds to the investors. **p. D–13**

Net income: Profitability reported in the income statement, consisting of all revenues and expenses and most gains and losses **p. D–13**

Other comprehensive income: Gains and losses from non-owner transactions that are not reported in the income statement. **p. D–13**

Trading securities: Debt securities that the investor expects to sell in the near future. **p. D–13**

SELF-STUDY QUESTIONS

1. One of the primary reasons for investing in equity securities includes **(LO D–1)**
   a. Receiving dividend payments.
   b. Acquiring debt of competing companies.
   c. Earning interest revenue.
   d. Deducting dividend payments for tax purposes.

2. One of the primary reasons for investing in debt securities includes **(LO D–1)**
   a. Deducting interest payments for tax purposes.
   b. Receiving dividend payments.
   c. Earning interest revenue.
   d. Acquiring ownership control in other companies.

3. On November 17, Tasty Foods purchased 1,000 shares (10%) of Eco-Safe Packaging's voting stock for $12 per share. By the end of the year, Eco-Safe Packaging's stock price has dropped to $10 per share. How would the drop in stock price affect Tasty Foods' net income for the year? **(LO D–2)**
   a. Decrease net income by $12,000.
   b. Decrease net income by $10,000.
   c. Decrease net income by $2,000.
   d. No effect.

4. On November 17, Tasty Foods purchased 1,000 shares (10%) of Eco-Safe Packaging's voting stock for $12 per share. By the end of the year, Eco-Safe Packaging's stock price has increased to $14 per share. How would the increase in stock price affect Tasty Foods' net income for the year? **(LO D–2)**
   a. Increase net income by $12,000.
   b. Increase net income by $10,000.
   c. Increase net income by $2,000.
   d. No effect.

5. On January 1, Tasty Foods purchased 3,000 shares (30%) of Eco-Safe Packaging's voting stock for $12 per share. On December 31, Eco-Safe Packaging reports net income $10,000 and a total dividend payment of $2,000, and the stock price has dropped to $10 per share. For how much would Tasty Foods report its investment in Eco-Safe Packaging at the end of the year? **(LO D–3)**
   a. $30,000.
   b. $38,400.
   c. $36,000.
   d. $39,000.

6. On January 1, Tasty Foods purchased 10,000 shares (100%) of Eco-Safe Packaging's voting stock for $12 per share. Throughout the year, both companies continue to operate as separate legal entities. By December 31, Eco-Safe Packaging's cash balance is $2,000, and Tasty Foods' cash balance is $5,000. In preparing its year-end financial statements, for how much would Tasty Foods report its cash balance? **(LO D–4)**
   a. $7,000.
   b. $5,000.
   c. $3,000.
   d. $2,000.

7. On January 1, Eco-Safe Packaging issues $100,000 of 8%, 5-year bonds with interest payable semiannually on June 30 and December 31. Tasty Foods purchases all of the bonds for $100,000 and plans to hold them to maturity. For how much would Tasty Foods report its investment in Eco-Safe Packaging's bonds at the end of the year? **(LO D–5)**
   a. $108,000.
   b. $100,000.
   c. $96,000.
   d. $92,000.

8. Refer to *Question 7*. How much interest revenue would Tasty Foods record at the time it receives the first semiannual payment on June 30? **(LO D–5)**
   a. $800.
   b. $8,000.
   c. $1,600.
   d. $4,000.

Note: For answers, see the last page of the appendix.

REVIEW QUESTIONS

■ **LO D–1**   1. Explain why a company might invest in another company.

■ **LO D–1**   2. How can an investor benefit from an equity investment that does not pay dividends?

■ **LO D–1**   3. How might the investing activity for a company that operates a ski resort vary throughout the year?

4. Provide an example of an equity investment in another company undertaken for strategic purposes.   ■ LO D–1

5. What is the "flip side" of an investment in equity securities?   ■ LO D–1

6. How does a company determine whether to account for an equity investment using the fair value method or equity method or to prepare consolidated financial statements?   ■ LO D–1

7. Investments in *equity* securities for which the investor has insignificant influence over the investee are classified for reporting purposes under the fair value method. What is fair value?   ■ LO D–2

8. Explain how we report dividends received from an investment under the fair value method.   ■ LO D–2

9. Discuss the difference between an unrealized holding gain and a realized gain.   ■ LO D–2

10. When using the fair value method, we adjust the reported amount of the investment for changes in fair value after its acquisition. How is the change in fair value reflected in the income statement?   ■ LO D–2

11. When using the fair value method, we adjust the reported amount of the investment for changes in fair value after its acquisition. How is the change in fair value reflected in the balance sheet?   ■ LO D–2

12. Under what circumstances do we use the equity method to account for an investment in stock?   ■ LO D–3

13. Explain how we report dividends received from an investment under the equity method.   ■ LO D–3

14. Discuss the meaning of consolidated financial statements.   ■ LO D–4

15. When is it appropriate to consolidate financial statements of two companies? Discuss your answer in terms of the relation between the parent and the subsidiary.   ■ LO D–4

16. What is the "flip side" of an investment in debt securities?   ■ LO D–5

17. If bonds are purchased at a *discount,* what will happen to the carrying value of the investment in bonds and the amount recorded for interest revenue over time?   ■ LO D–5

18. If bonds are purchased at a *premium,* what will happen to the carrying value of the investment in bonds and the amount recorded for interest revenue over time?   ■ LO D–5

19. When interest rates go down, what happens to the value of an investment in bonds that pay a fixed interest rate?   ■ LO D–5

20. Investments in *debt* securities are classified for reporting purposes in one of three categories. Explain each of these three categories.   ■ LO D–5

BRIEF EXERCISES

BED–1 Indicate with an "X" any of the following that represent a common reason why companies invest in other companies.

_____ 1. To invest excess cash created by operating in seasonal industries.
_____ 2. To increase employees' morale.
_____ 3. To build strategic alliances.
_____ 4. To reduce government regulation.
_____ 5. To receive interest and dividends.

Identify reasons companies invest (LO D–1)

BED–2 On September 1, Leather Suppliers, Inc., purchases 150 shares of Western Wear Clothing for $13 per share. On November 1, Leather Suppliers sells the investment for $17 per share. Record the transactions made by Leather Suppliers for the purchase and sale of the investment in Western Wear Clothing.

Record equity investments using the fair value method (LO D–2)

BED–3 On December 28, Summit purchased Microsoft common shares for $485,000. On December 31, the shares had a fair value of $483,000. Record the initial investment by Summit and, if appropriate, an adjusting entry to record the investment at fair value.

Record equity investments using the fair value method (LO D–2)

Record equity investments using the fair value method (LO D–2)

BED–4 On December 28, Summit purchased **Microsoft** common shares for $485,000. On December 31, the shares had a fair value of $487,000. Record the initial investment by Summit and, if appropriate, an adjusting entry to record the investment at fair value.

Record equity investments using the fair value method (LO D–2)

BED–5 On December 29, 2024, Adams Apples purchased 1,000 shares of **General Electric** common stock for $19 per share. On December 31, the market value of the stock increased to $20 per share. On January 24, 2025, all of the shares are sold for $22 per share. Record the initial investment, any fair value adjusting entry at the end of 2024, and the sale in 2025.

Record equity investments using the fair value method (LO D–2)

BED–6 On December 29, 2024, Adams Apples purchased 1,000 shares of **General Electric** common stock for $19 per share. On December 31, the market value of the stock increased to $20 per share. On January 24, 2025, all of the shares are sold for $16 per share. Record the initial investment, any fair value adjusting entry at the end of 2024, and the sale in 2025.

Determine the effect of net income by the investee in an equity method investment (LO D–3)

BED–7 Wendy Day Kite Company owns 40% of the outstanding stock of Strong String Company. During the current year, Strong String reported net income of $15 million. What effect does Strong String's reported net income have on Wendy Day's financial statements?

Determine the effect of dividends by the investee in an equity method investment (LO D–3)

BED–8 Wendy Day Kite Company owns 40% of the outstanding stock of Strong String Company. During the current year, Strong String paid a $10 million cash dividend on its common shares. What effect does Strong String's dividend have on Wendy Day's financial statements?

Calculate consolidated amounts (LO D–4)

BED–9 Wendy Day Kite Company owns 100% of the outstanding stock of Strong String Company. At the end of the year, Wendy Day has total inventory of $14,000 and Strong String has total inventory of $8,000. Determine the amount of inventory that would be reported in Wendy Day's consolidated financial statements (assuming no transactions involving inventory occurred between the two companies).

Record investment in bonds at face value (LO D–5)

BED–10 Salt Foods purchases forty $1,000, 7%, 10-year bonds issued by Pretzelmania, Inc., for $40,000 on January 1. The market interest rate for bonds of similar risk and maturity is 7%. Salt Foods receives interest semiannually on June 30 and December 31.
1. Record the investment in bonds.
2. Record receipt of the first interest payment on June 30.

Record investment in bonds at a discount (LO D–5)

BED–11 Salt Foods purchases forty $1,000, 7%, 10-year bonds issued by Pretzelmania, Inc., for $37,282 on January 1. The market interest rate for bonds of similar risk and maturity is 8%. Salt Foods receives interest semiannually on June 30 and December 31.
1. Record the investment in bonds.
2. Record receipt of the first interest payment on June 30.

Record investment in bonds at a premium (LO D–5)

BED–12 Salt Foods purchases forty $1,000, 7%, 10-year bonds issued by Pretzelmania, Inc., for $42,975 on January 1. The market interest rate for bonds of similar risk and maturity is 6%. Salt Foods receives interest semiannually on June 30 and December 31.
1. Record the investment in bonds.
2. Record receipt of the first interest payment on June 30.

EXERCISES

Identify reasons companies invest (LO D–1)

ED–1 Consider the following statements.

_____ 1. A reason companies invest in other companies is to build strategic alliances.
_____ 2. All companies are required to pay dividends to their investors.
_____ 3. When market interest rates increase, the market value of a bond increases as well.
_____ 4. One way for a company to expand operations into a new industry is to acquire the majority of common stock in another company that already operates in that industry.
_____ 5. Stocks typically have greater upside potential, providing a higher average return to their investors over the long run than do bonds.
_____ 6. Companies purchase debt securities primarily for the dividend revenue they provide.

Required:
Indicate whether each statement is true (T) or false (F).

ED–2 First National Bank buys and sells securities. The company's fiscal year ends on December 31. The following selected transactions relating to First National's trading account occurred during the year.

Record equity investments using the fair value method **(LO D–2)**

December 20   Purchases 300,000 shares in Classic Computers common stock for $1,500,000 ($5 per share).
December 28   Receives cash dividends of $6,000 from the Classic Computers shares.
December 31   The fair value of Classic Computers' stock is $4.80 per share.

Required:
1. Record each of these transactions, including an adjusting entry on December 31 for the investment's fair value, if appropriate.
2. Calculate the balance of the Investments account on December 31.

ED–3 Mr. T's Fashions, once a direct competitor to Italian Stallion's clothing line, has formed a friendship in recent years leading to a small investment (less than 5%) by Mr. T in the common stock of Italian Stallion. Mr. T's engages in the following transactions relating to its investment.

Record equity investments using the fair value method **(LO D–2)**

February   1   Purchases 150 shares of Italian Stallion common stock for $16 per share.
June   15   Sells 50 shares of Italian Stallion stock for $14 per share.
October   31   Receives a cash dividend of $0.50 per share.
December 31   The fair value of Italian Stallion's stock is $12 per share.

Required:
1. Record each of these transactions, including an adjusting entry on December 31 for the investment's fair value, if appropriate.
2. Calculate the balance of the Investments account on December 31.

ED–4 Gator Shoes, Inc., manufactures a line of stylish waterproof footwear. The following transactions relate to investments in common stock during 2024.

Record equity investments using the fair value method **(LO D–2)**

March   1   Purchases 3,000 shares (10%) of Power Drive Corporation's common stock for $62 per share.
July   1   Receives a cash dividend of $1.25 per share.
December 31   The fair value of Power Drive Corporation's common stock is $75 per share.

On February 1, 2025 (the following year), Gator Shoes sells 1,000 shares of Power Drive Corporation's common stock for $70 per share.

Required:
1. Record each of these transactions in 2024, including an adjusting entry on December 31 for the investment's fair value, if appropriate.
2. Record the sale on February 1, 2025.

ED–5 Refer to the transactions in ED–4, but now assume the 1,000 shares are sold on February 1, 2025, for $80 per share.

Record equity investments using the fair value method **(LO D–2)**

Required:
1. Record each of these transactions in 2024, including an adjusting entry on December 31 for the investment's fair value, if appropriate.
2. Record the sale on February 1, 2025.

ED–6 On January 1, Lifestyle Pools purchased 25% of Marshall Fence's common stock for $700,000 cash. By the end of the year, Marshall Fence reported net income of $160,000 and paid dividends of $60,000 to all shareholders.

Record transactions using the equity method **(LO D–3)**

Required:
For Lifestyle Pools, record the initial purchase and its share of Marshall Fence's net income and dividends for the year.

ED–7 On January 1, Marcum's Landscape purchased 10,000 shares (35%) of the common stock of Atlantic Irrigation for $600,000. Below are amounts reported by both companies for the year.

Record transactions using the equity method **(LO D–3)**

	Marcum's Landscape	Atlantic Irrigation
Stock price on January 1	$85	$60
Net income for the year	$500,000	$130,000
Dividends paid for the year	$60,000	$40,000
Stock price on December 31	$94	$68

Required:

For Marcum's Landscape, record the initial purchase, its share of Atlantic's net income and dividends, and the adjusting entry for Atlantic's fair value at the end of the year, if appropriate.

Compare the fair value method to the equity method (LO D–2, LO D–3)

ED–8 As a long-term investment, Fair Company purchased 20% of Midlin Company's 300,000 shares for $360,000 at the beginning of the reporting year of both companies. During the year, Midlin earned net income of $135,000 and distributed cash dividends of $0.25 per share. At year-end, the fair value of the shares is $375,000.

Required:

1. Assume no significant influence was acquired. Record the transactions from the purchase through the end of the year, including any adjusting entry for the investment's fair value, if appropriate.
2. Assume significant influence was acquired. Record the transactions from the purchase through the end of the year, including any adjusting entry for the investment's fair value, if appropriate.

Determine which companies to consolidate (LO D–4)

ED–9 Alpha has made the following investments.

_____ 1. 10% of the common stock of Beta.
_____ 2. 40% of the bonds of Gamma.
_____ 3. 75% of the common stock of Delta.
_____ 4. 15% of the bonds of Epsilon.
_____ 5. 25% of the common stock of Zeta.
_____ 6. 60% of the bonds of Eta.
_____ 7. 100% of the common stock of Theta.

Required:

Indicate with an "X" which of the companies above would be accounted for using the consolidation method.

Record investment in bonds at face amount (LO D–5)

ED-10 On January 1, Neddar purchases $800,000 of 6% bonds, due in 10 years, with interest receivable semiannually on June 30 and December 31 each year. The bonds were purchased at face amount.

Required:

1. Record the purchase of the bonds by Neddar on January 1.
2. Record the receipt of the first two semiannual interest payments on June 30 and December 31.

Record investment in bonds at a discount (LO D–5)

ED–11 On January 1, Dora purchases 175 of the $1,000, 7%, 15-year bonds issued by Splash City, with interest receivable semiannually on June 30 and December 31 each year.

Required:

Assuming the market interest rate on the issue date is 8%, Dora will purchase the bonds for $159,869.
1. Complete the first three rows of an amortization table for Dora.
2. Record the purchase of the bonds by Dora on January 1 and the receipt of the first two semiannual interest payments on June 30 and December 31.

Record investment in bonds at a premium (LO D–5)

ED–12 On January 1, Splash City issues $500,000 of 7% bonds, due in 15 years, with interest payable semiannually on June 30 and December 31 each year. T. Bone Investment Company (TBIC) purchases all of the bonds in a private placement.

Required:

Assuming the market interest rate on the issue date is 6%, TBIC will purchase the bonds for $549,001.

1. Complete the first three rows of an amortization table for TBIC.
2. Record the purchase of the bonds by TBIC on January 1 and the receipt of the first two semiannual interest payments on June 30 and December 31.

ED–13 On January 1, Ralston Corp. issues $800,000 of 8% bonds, due in 10 years, with interest payable semiannually on June 30 and December 31 each year. Price Investment Company purchases all of the bonds and classifies them as available-for-sale.

Record transactions for a debt investment and calculate comprehensive income (LO D–5)

Required:

Assuming the market interest rate on the issue date is 9%, Price will purchase the bonds for $747,968.

1. Complete the first three rows of an amortization table for Price.
2. Record the purchase of the bonds by Price on January 1 and the receipt of the first two semiannual interest payments on June 30 and December 31.
3. Assume the fair value of the bonds equals $750,000 on December 31. Record any necessary fair value adjusting entry.
4. Calculate net income and comprehensive income. Assume the company has sales revenue of $2,600,000 and operating expenses of $1,400,000.

PROBLEMS: SET A

PD–1A Barry, Hank, and Babe form a company named Long Ball Investments, hoping to find that elusive home run stock. A new clothing company by the name of Major League Apparel has caught their eye. Major League Apparel has two classes of stock authorized: 5%, $10 par preferred and $1 par value common. Long Ball Investments has the following transactions during the year. None of the investments are large enough to exert a significant influence.

Account for investments using the fair value method (LO D–2)

January	2	Purchase 1,500 shares of Major League common stock for $70 per share.
February	14	Purchase 600 shares of Major League preferred stock for $12 per share.
May	15	Sell 300 shares of Major League's common stock for $62 per share.
December	30	Receive a cash dividend on Major League's common stock of $0.50 per share and preferred stock of $0.50 per share.
December	31	The fair values of the common and preferred shares are $73 and $14, respectively.

Required:

1. Record each of these investment transactions. (*Hint:* Preferred stock transactions are recorded like common stock transactions, but preferred stock has no voting rights and therefore ownership provides no influence.)
2. Calculate the balance in the Investments account as of December 31.

PD–2A As a long-term investment at the beginning of the year, Willie Winn Track Shoes purchased 25% of Betty Will Company's 34 million shares outstanding for $178 million. During the year, Betty Will earned net income of $130 million and distributed cash dividends of $1.10 per share.

Account for investments using the equity method (LO D–3)

Required:

Record for Willie Winn Track Shoes the purchase of the investment and its share of Betty Will's net income and dividends using the equity method.

PD–3A On January 1, Twister Enterprises issues $600,000 of 6% bonds, due in 20 years, with interest payable semiannually on June 30 and December 31 each year. The market interest rate on the issue date is 7%. National Hydraulics, a supplier of mechanical parts to Twister Enterprises, purchases 25% of the bond issue ($150,000 face amount) at a discount for $133,984.

Account for investments in debt securities (LO D–5)

Required:

1. Complete the first three rows of an amortization table for National Hydraulics.
2. Record the purchase of the bonds by National Hydraulics and the receipt of the first two semiannual interest payments on June 30 and December 31.
3. Record the sale of the bonds by National Hydraulics on December 31, for $145,000.
4. What happened to market interest rates between the beginning and end of the year?

Account for investments in debt securities (LO D–5)

PD–4A Justin Investor, Inc., purchases $180,000 of 8% bonds from M.R. Bonds Company on January 1. Management intends to hold the debt securities to maturity. For bonds of similar risk and maturity, the market yield is 10%. Justin paid $152,000 for the bonds. It receives interest semiannually on June 30 and December 31. Due to changing market conditions, the fair value of the bonds at December 31 is $160,000.

Required:

1. Record Justin Investor's investment on January 1.
2. Record the interest revenue earned by Justin Investor for the first six months ended June 30.
3. Record the interest revenue earned by Justin Investor for the next six months ended December 31.
4. At what amount will Justin Investor report its investment in the December 31 balance sheet? Why?
5. Suppose Justin Investor decides on December 31 that it no longer intends to hold the debt securities until maturity but also has no intention to sell them any time soon. Record any necessary fair value adjusting entry.

PROBLEMS: SET B

Account for investments using the fair value method (LO D–2)

PD–1B Emmitt, Walter, and Barry form a company named Long Run Investments, with the intention of investing in stocks with great long-run potential. A clothing company named National League Gear looks like a great investment prospect. National League Gear has two classes of stock authorized: 6%, $30 par preferred and $5 par value common. Long Run Investments has the following transactions during the year. None of the investments are large enough to exert a significant influence.

February	2	Purchases 1,500 shares of National League Gear's common stock for $35 per share.
February	4	Purchases 600 shares of National League Gear's preferred stock for $32 per share.
July	15	Sells 400 shares of National League Gear's common stock for $40 per share.
November	30	Receives a cash dividend on National League Gear's common stock of $1.10 per share and preferred stock of $1.80 per share.
December	31	The fair value of the common and preferred shares equal $31 and $30, respectively.

Required:

1. Record each of these investment transactions. (*Hint:* Preferred stock transactions are recorded like common stock transactions, but preferred stock has no voting rights and therefore ownership provides no influence.)
2. Calculate the balance in the Investments account as of December 31.

Account for investments using the equity method (LO D–3)

PD–2B As a long-term investment at the beginning of the year, Acquisitions, Inc., purchased 3 million shares (30%) of Takeover Target's 10 million shares outstanding for $52 million. During the year, Takeover Target earned net income of $9 million and distributed cash dividends of $0.50 per share.

Required:

Record for Acquisitions, Inc., the purchase of the investment and its share of Takeover Target's net income and dividends using the equity method.

Account for investments in debt securities (LO D–5)

PD–3B Viking Voyager specializes in the design and production of replica Viking boats. On January 1, the company issues $3,000,000 of 7% bonds, due in 10 years, with interest payable semiannually on June 30 and December 31 each year. The market interest rate on the issue date is 8%. Antique Boat World, one of Viking Voyager's best customers, purchases 15% of the bond issue ($450,000 face amount) at a discount for $419,422.

Required:

1. Complete the first three rows of an amortization table for Antique Boat World.
2. Record the purchase of the bonds by Antique Boat World and the receipt of the first two semiannual interest payments on June 30 and December 31.
3. Record the sale of the bonds by Antique Boat World on December 31 for $415,000.
4. What happened to market interest rates between the beginning and end of the year?

PD–4B Tsunami Sushi purchases $130,000 of 5-year, 7% bonds from Deep Sea Explorers on January 1. Management intends to hold the debt securities to maturity. For bonds of similar risk and maturity, the market rate is 8%. Tsunami paid $124,728 for the bonds. It receives interest semiannually on June 30 and December 31. Due to changing market conditions, the fair value of the bonds at December 31 is $124,000.

Account for investments in debt securities (LO D–5)

Required:

1. Record Tsunami Sushi's investment on January 1.
2. Record the interest revenue earned by Tsunami Sushi for the first six months ended June 30.
3. Record the interest revenue earned by Tsunami Sushi for the next six months ended December 31.
4. At what amount will Tsunami Sushi report its investment in the December 31 balance sheet? Why?
5. Suppose Tsunami Sushi decides on December 31 that it no longer intends to hold the debt securities until maturity and will likely sell them early next year. Record any necessary fair value adjusting entry.

Answers to the Self-Study Questions
1. a   2. c   3. c   4. c   5. b   6. a   7. b   8. d

Subject Index

Note: Page numbers followed by *n* indicate footnotes

Company Index

Future Value and Present Value Tables

This table shows the future value of $1 at various interest rates (*i*) and time periods (*n*). It is used to calculate the future value of any single amount.

TABLE 1 Future Value of $1

$$FV = \$1\,(1 + i)^n$$

n/i	1.0%	1.5%	2.0%	2.5%	3.0%	3.5%	4.0%	4.5%	5.0%	5.5%	6.0%	7.0%	8.0%	9.0%	10.0%	11.0%	12.0%	13.0%
1	1.01000	1.01500	1.02000	1.02500	1.03000	1.03500	1.04000	1.04500	1.05000	1.05500	1.06000	1.07000	1.08000	1.09000	1.10000	1.11000	1.12000	1.13000
2	1.02010	1.03022	1.04040	1.05063	1.06090	1.07123	1.08160	1.09203	1.10250	1.11303	1.12360	1.14490	1.16640	1.18810	1.21000	1.23210	1.25440	1.27690
3	1.03030	1.04568	1.06121	1.07689	1.09273	1.10872	1.12486	1.14117	1.15763	1.17424	1.19102	1.22504	1.25971	1.29503	1.33100	1.36763	1.40493	1.44290
4	1.04060	1.06136	1.08243	1.10381	1.12551	1.14752	1.16986	1.19252	1.21551	1.23882	1.26248	1.31080	1.36049	1.41158	1.46410	1.51807	1.57352	1.63047
5	1.05101	1.07728	1.10408	1.13141	1.15927	1.18769	1.21665	1.24618	1.27628	1.30696	1.33823	1.40255	1.46933	1.53862	1.61051	1.68506	1.76234	1.84244
6	1.06152	1.09344	1.12616	1.15969	1.19405	1.22926	1.26532	1.30226	1.34010	1.37884	1.41852	1.50073	1.58687	1.67710	1.77156	1.87041	1.97382	2.08195
7	1.07214	1.10984	1.14869	1.18869	1.22987	1.27228	1.31593	1.36086	1.40710	1.45468	1.50363	1.60578	1.71382	1.82804	1.94872	2.07616	2.21068	2.35261
8	1.08286	1.12649	1.17166	1.21840	1.26677	1.31681	1.36857	1.42210	1.47746	1.53469	1.59385	1.71819	1.85093	1.99256	2.14359	2.30454	2.47596	2.65844
9	1.09369	1.14339	1.19509	1.24886	1.30477	1.36290	1.42331	1.48610	1.55133	1.61909	1.68948	1.83846	1.99900	2.17189	2.35795	2.55804	2.77308	3.00404
10	1.10462	1.16054	1.21899	1.28008	1.34392	1.41060	1.48024	1.55297	1.62889	1.70814	1.79085	1.96715	2.15892	2.36736	2.59374	2.83942	3.10585	3.39457
11	1.11567	1.17795	1.24337	1.31209	1.38423	1.45997	1.53945	1.62285	1.71034	1.80209	1.89830	2.10485	2.33164	2.58043	2.85312	3.15176	3.47855	3.83586
12	1.12683	1.19562	1.26824	1.34489	1.42576	1.51107	1.60103	1.69588	1.79586	1.90121	2.01220	2.25219	2.51817	2.81266	3.13843	3.49845	3.89598	4.33452
13	1.13809	1.21355	1.29361	1.37851	1.46853	1.56396	1.66507	1.77220	1.88565	2.00577	2.13293	2.40985	2.71962	3.06580	3.45227	3.88328	4.36349	4.89801
14	1.14947	1.23176	1.31948	1.41297	1.51259	1.61869	1.73168	1.85194	1.97993	2.11609	2.26090	2.57853	2.93719	3.34173	3.79750	4.31044	4.88711	5.53475
15	1.16097	1.25023	1.34587	1.44830	1.55797	1.67535	1.80094	1.93528	2.07893	2.23248	2.39656	2.75903	3.17217	3.64248	4.17725	4.78459	5.47357	6.25427
16	1.17258	1.26899	1.37279	1.48451	1.60471	1.73399	1.87298	2.02237	2.18287	2.35526	2.54035	2.95216	3.42594	3.97031	4.59497	5.31089	6.13039	7.06733
17	1.18430	1.28802	1.40024	1.52162	1.65285	1.79468	1.94790	2.11338	2.29202	2.48480	2.69277	3.15882	3.70002	4.32763	5.05447	5.89509	6.86604	7.98608
18	1.19615	1.30734	1.42825	1.55966	1.70243	1.85749	2.02582	2.20848	2.40662	2.62147	2.85434	3.37993	3.99602	4.71712	5.55992	6.54355	7.68997	9.02427
19	1.20811	1.32695	1.45681	1.59865	1.75351	1.92250	2.10685	2.30786	2.52695	2.76565	3.02560	3.61653	4.31570	5.14166	6.11591	7.26334	8.61276	10.19742
20	1.22019	1.34686	1.48595	1.63862	1.80611	1.98979	2.19112	2.41171	2.65330	2.91776	3.20714	3.86968	4.66096	5.60441	6.72750	8.06231	9.64629	11.52309
21	1.23239	1.36706	1.51567	1.67958	1.86029	2.05943	2.27877	2.52024	2.78596	3.07823	3.39956	4.14056	5.03383	6.10881	7.40025	8.94917	10.80385	13.02109
22	1.24472	1.38756	1.54598	1.72157	1.91610	2.13151	2.36992	2.63365	2.92526	3.24754	3.60354	4.43040	5.43654	6.65860	8.14027	9.93357	12.10031	14.71383
23	1.25716	1.40838	1.57690	1.76461	1.97359	2.20611	2.46472	2.75217	3.07152	3.42615	3.81975	4.74053	5.87146	7.25787	8.95430	11.02627	13.55235	16.62663
24	1.26973	1.42950	1.60844	1.80873	2.03279	2.28333	2.56330	2.87601	3.22510	3.61459	4.04893	5.07237	6.34118	7.91108	9.84973	12.23916	15.17863	18.78809
25	1.28243	1.45095	1.64061	1.85394	2.09378	2.36324	2.66584	3.00543	3.38635	3.81339	4.29187	5.42743	6.84848	8.62308	10.83471	13.58546	17.00006	21.23054
30	1.34785	1.56308	1.81136	2.09757	2.42726	2.80679	3.24340	3.74532	4.32194	4.98395	5.74349	7.61226	10.06266	13.26768	17.44940	22.89230	29.95992	39.11590
35	1.41660	1.68388	1.99989	2.37321	2.81386	3.33359	3.94609	4.66735	5.51602	6.51383	7.68609	10.67658	14.78534	20.41397	28.10244	38.57485	52.79962	72.06851
40	1.48886	1.81402	2.20804	2.68506	3.26204	3.95926	4.80102	5.81636	7.03999	8.51331	10.28572	14.97446	21.72452	31.40942	45.25926	65.00087	93.05097	132.78155
45	1.56481	1.95421	2.43785	3.03790	3.78160	4.70236	5.84118	7.24825	8.98501	11.12655	13.76461	21.00245	31.92045	48.32729	72.89048	109.53024	163.98760	244.64140
50	1.64463	2.10524	2.69159	3.43711	4.38391	5.58493	7.10668	9.03264	11.46740	14.54196	18.42015	29.45703	46.90161	74.35752	117.39085	184.56483	289.00219	450.73593

This table shows the present value of $1 at various interest rates (*i*) and time periods (*n*). It is used to calculate the present value of any single amount.

TABLE 2 Present Value of $1

$$PV = \frac{\$1}{(1+i)^n}$$

n/i	1.0%	1.5%	2.0%	2.5%	3.0%	3.5%	4.0%	4.5%	5.0%	5.5%	6.0%	7.0%	8.0%	9.0%	10.0%	11.0%	12.0%	13.0%
1	0.99010	0.98522	0.98039	0.97561	0.97087	0.96618	0.96154	0.95694	0.95238	0.94787	0.94340	0.93458	0.92593	0.91743	0.90909	0.90090	0.89286	0.88496
2	0.98030	0.97066	0.96117	0.95181	0.94260	0.93351	0.92456	0.91573	0.90703	0.89845	0.89000	0.87344	0.85734	0.84168	0.82645	0.81162	0.79719	0.78315
3	0.97059	0.95632	0.94232	0.92860	0.91514	0.90194	0.88900	0.87630	0.86384	0.85161	0.83962	0.81630	0.79383	0.77218	0.75131	0.73119	0.71178	0.69305
4	0.96098	0.94218	0.92385	0.90595	0.88849	0.87144	0.85480	0.83856	0.82270	0.80722	0.79209	0.76290	0.73503	0.70843	0.68301	0.65873	0.63552	0.61332
5	0.95147	0.92826	0.90573	0.88385	0.86261	0.84197	0.82193	0.80245	0.78353	0.76513	0.74726	0.71299	0.68058	0.64993	0.62092	0.59345	0.56743	0.54276
6	0.94205	0.91454	0.88797	0.86230	0.83748	0.81350	0.79031	0.76790	0.74622	0.72525	0.70496	0.66634	0.63017	0.59627	0.56447	0.53464	0.50663	0.48032
7	0.93272	0.90103	0.87056	0.84127	0.81309	0.78599	0.75992	0.73483	0.71068	0.68744	0.66506	0.62275	0.58349	0.54703	0.51316	0.48166	0.45235	0.42506
8	0.92348	0.88771	0.85349	0.82075	0.78941	0.75941	0.73069	0.70319	0.67684	0.65160	0.62741	0.58201	0.54027	0.50187	0.46651	0.43393	0.40388	0.37616
9	0.91434	0.87459	0.83676	0.80073	0.76642	0.73373	0.70259	0.67290	0.64461	0.61763	0.59190	0.54393	0.50025	0.46043	0.42410	0.39092	0.36061	0.33288
10	0.90529	0.86167	0.82035	0.78120	0.74409	0.70892	0.67556	0.64393	0.61391	0.58543	0.55839	0.50835	0.46319	0.42241	0.38554	0.35218	0.32197	0.29459
11	0.89632	0.84893	0.80426	0.76214	0.72242	0.68495	0.64958	0.61620	0.58468	0.55491	0.52679	0.47509	0.42888	0.38753	0.35049	0.31728	0.28748	0.26070
12	0.88745	0.83639	0.78849	0.74356	0.70138	0.66178	0.62460	0.58966	0.55684	0.52598	0.49697	0.44401	0.39711	0.35553	0.31863	0.28584	0.25668	0.23071
13	0.87866	0.82403	0.77303	0.72542	0.68095	0.63940	0.60057	0.56427	0.53032	0.49856	0.46884	0.41496	0.36770	0.32618	0.28966	0.25751	0.22917	0.20416
14	0.86996	0.81185	0.75788	0.70773	0.66112	0.61778	0.57748	0.53997	0.50507	0.47257	0.44230	0.38782	0.34046	0.29925	0.26333	0.23199	0.20462	0.18068
15	0.86135	0.79985	0.74301	0.69047	0.64186	0.59689	0.55526	0.51672	0.48102	0.44793	0.41727	0.36245	0.31524	0.27454	0.23939	0.20900	0.18270	0.15989
16	0.85282	0.78803	0.72845	0.67362	0.62317	0.57671	0.53391	0.49447	0.45811	0.42458	0.39365	0.33873	0.29189	0.25187	0.21763	0.18829	0.16312	0.14150
17	0.84438	0.77639	0.71416	0.65720	0.60502	0.55720	0.51337	0.47318	0.43630	0.40245	0.37136	0.31657	0.27027	0.23107	0.19784	0.16963	0.14564	0.12522
18	0.83602	0.76491	0.70016	0.64117	0.58739	0.53836	0.49363	0.45280	0.41552	0.38147	0.35034	0.29586	0.25025	0.21199	0.17986	0.15282	0.13004	0.11081
19	0.82774	0.75361	0.68643	0.62553	0.57029	0.52016	0.47464	0.43330	0.39573	0.36158	0.33051	0.27651	0.23171	0.19449	0.16351	0.13768	0.11611	0.09806
20	0.81954	0.74247	0.67297	0.61027	0.55368	0.50257	0.45639	0.41464	0.37689	0.34273	0.31180	0.25842	0.21455	0.17843	0.14864	0.12403	0.10367	0.08678
21	0.81143	0.73150	0.65978	0.59539	0.53755	0.48557	0.43883	0.39679	0.35894	0.32486	0.29416	0.24151	0.19866	0.16370	0.13513	0.11174	0.09256	0.07680
22	0.80340	0.72069	0.64684	0.58086	0.52189	0.46915	0.42196	0.37970	0.34185	0.30793	0.27751	0.22571	0.18394	0.15018	0.12285	0.10067	0.08264	0.06796
23	0.79544	0.71004	0.63416	0.56670	0.50669	0.45329	0.40573	0.36335	0.32557	0.29187	0.26180	0.21095	0.17032	0.13778	0.11168	0.09069	0.07379	0.06014
24	0.78757	0.69954	0.62172	0.55288	0.49193	0.43796	0.39012	0.34770	0.31007	0.27666	0.24698	0.19715	0.15770	0.12640	0.10153	0.08170	0.06588	0.05323
25	0.77977	0.68921	0.60953	0.53939	0.47761	0.42315	0.37512	0.33273	0.29530	0.26223	0.23300	0.18425	0.14602	0.11597	0.09230	0.07361	0.05882	0.04710
30	0.74192	0.63976	0.55207	0.47674	0.41199	0.35628	0.30832	0.26700	0.23138	0.20064	0.17411	0.13137	0.09938	0.07537	0.05731	0.04368	0.03338	0.02557
35	0.70591	0.59387	0.50003	0.42137	0.35538	0.29998	0.25342	0.21425	0.18129	0.15352	0.13011	0.09366	0.06763	0.04899	0.03558	0.02592	0.01894	0.01388
40	0.67165	0.55126	0.45289	0.37243	0.30656	0.25257	0.20829	0.17193	0.14205	0.11746	0.09722	0.06678	0.04603	0.03184	0.02209	0.01538	0.01075	0.00753
45	0.63905	0.51171	0.41020	0.32917	0.26444	0.21266	0.17120	0.13796	0.11130	0.08988	0.07265	0.04761	0.03133	0.02069	0.01372	0.00913	0.00610	0.00409
50	0.60804	0.47500	0.37153	0.29094	0.22811	0.17905	0.14071	0.11071	0.08720	0.06877	0.05429	0.03395	0.02132	0.01345	0.00852	0.00542	0.00346	0.00222

This table shows the future value of an ordinary annuity of $1 at various interest rates (*i*) and time periods (*n*). It is used to calculate the future value of any series of equal payments made at the end of each compounding period.

TABLE 3 Future Value of an Ordinary Annuity of $1

$$FVA = \frac{(1+i)^n - 1}{i}$$

n/i	1.0%	1.5%	2.0%	2.5%	3.0%	3.5%	4.0%	4.5%	5.0%	5.5%	6.0%	7.0%	8.0%	9.0%	10.0%	11.0%	12.0%	13.0%
1	1.0000	1.0000	1.0000	1.0000	1.0000	1.0000	1.0000	1.0000	1.0000	1.0000	1.0000	1.0000	1.0000	1.0000	1.0000	1.0000	1.0000	1.0000
2	2.0100	2.0150	2.0200	2.0250	2.0300	2.0350	2.0400	2.0450	2.0500	2.0550	2.0600	2.0700	2.0800	2.0900	2.1000	2.1100	2.1200	2.1300
3	3.0301	3.0452	3.0604	3.0756	3.0909	3.1062	3.1216	3.1370	3.1525	3.1680	3.1836	3.2149	3.2464	3.2781	3.3100	3.3421	3.3744	3.4069
4	4.0604	4.0909	4.1216	4.1525	4.1836	4.2149	4.2465	4.2782	4.3101	4.3423	4.3746	4.4399	4.5061	4.5731	4.6410	4.7097	4.7793	4.8498
5	5.1010	5.1523	5.2040	5.2563	5.3091	5.3625	5.4163	5.4707	5.5256	5.5811	5.6371	5.7507	5.8666	5.9847	6.1051	6.2278	6.3528	6.4803
6	6.1520	6.2296	6.3081	6.3877	6.4684	6.5502	6.6330	6.7169	6.8019	6.8881	6.9753	7.1533	7.3359	7.5233	7.7156	7.9129	8.1152	8.3227
7	7.2135	7.3230	7.4343	7.5474	7.6625	7.7794	7.8983	8.0192	8.1420	8.2669	8.3938	8.6540	8.9228	9.2004	9.4872	9.7833	10.0890	10.4047
8	8.2857	8.4328	8.5830	8.7361	8.8923	9.0517	9.2142	9.3800	9.5491	9.7216	9.8975	10.2598	10.6366	11.0285	11.4359	11.8594	12.2997	12.7573
9	9.3685	9.5593	9.7546	9.9545	10.1591	10.3685	10.5828	10.8021	11.0266	11.2563	11.4913	11.9780	12.4876	13.0210	13.5795	14.1640	14.7757	15.4157
10	10.4622	10.7027	10.9497	11.2034	11.4639	11.7314	12.0061	12.2882	12.5779	12.8754	13.1808	13.8164	14.4866	15.1929	15.9374	16.7220	17.5487	18.4197
11	11.5668	11.8633	12.1687	12.4835	12.8078	13.1420	13.4864	13.8412	14.2068	14.5835	14.9716	15.7836	16.6455	17.5603	18.5312	19.5614	20.6546	21.8143
12	12.6825	13.0412	13.4121	13.7956	14.1920	14.6020	15.0258	15.4640	15.9171	16.3856	16.8699	17.8885	18.9771	20.1407	21.3843	22.7132	24.1331	25.6502
13	13.8093	14.2368	14.6803	15.1404	15.6178	16.1130	16.6268	17.1599	17.7130	18.2868	18.8821	20.1406	21.4953	22.9534	24.5227	26.2116	28.0291	29.9847
14	14.9474	15.4504	15.9739	16.5190	17.0863	17.6770	18.2919	18.9321	19.5986	20.2926	21.0151	22.5505	24.2149	26.0192	27.9750	30.0949	32.3926	34.8827
15	16.0969	16.6821	17.2934	17.9319	18.5989	19.2957	20.0236	20.7841	21.5786	22.4087	23.2760	25.1290	27.1521	29.3609	31.7725	34.4054	37.2797	40.4175
16	17.2579	17.9324	18.6393	19.3802	20.1569	20.9710	21.8245	22.7193	23.6575	24.6411	25.6725	27.8881	30.3243	33.0034	35.9497	39.1899	42.7533	46.6717
17	18.4304	19.2014	20.0121	20.8647	21.7616	22.7050	23.6975	24.7417	25.8404	26.9964	28.2129	30.8402	33.7502	36.9737	40.5447	44.5008	48.8837	53.7391
18	19.6147	20.4894	21.4123	22.3863	23.4144	24.4997	25.6454	26.8551	28.1324	29.4812	30.9057	33.9990	37.4502	41.3013	45.5992	50.3959	55.7497	61.7251
19	20.8109	21.7967	22.8406	23.9460	25.1169	26.3572	27.6712	29.0636	30.5390	32.1027	33.7600	37.3790	41.4463	46.0185	51.1591	56.9395	63.4397	70.7494
20	22.0190	23.1237	24.2974	25.5447	26.8704	28.2797	29.7781	31.3714	33.0660	34.8683	36.7856	40.9955	45.7620	51.1601	57.2750	64.2028	72.0524	80.9468
21	23.2392	24.4705	25.7833	27.1833	28.6765	30.2695	31.9692	33.7831	35.7193	37.7861	39.9927	44.8652	50.4229	56.7645	64.0025	72.2651	81.6987	92.4699
22	24.4716	25.8376	27.2990	28.8629	30.5368	32.3289	34.2480	36.3034	38.5052	40.8643	43.3923	49.0057	55.4568	62.8733	71.4027	81.2143	92.5026	105.4910
23	25.7163	27.2251	28.8450	30.5844	32.4529	34.4604	36.6179	38.9370	41.4305	44.1118	46.9958	53.4361	60.8933	69.5319	79.5430	91.1479	104.6029	120.2048
24	26.9735	28.6335	30.4219	32.3490	34.4265	36.6665	39.0826	41.6892	44.5020	47.5380	50.8156	58.1767	66.7648	76.7898	88.4973	102.1742	118.1552	136.8315
25	28.2432	30.0630	32.0303	34.1578	36.4593	38.9499	41.6459	44.5652	47.7271	51.1526	54.8645	63.2490	73.1059	84.7009	98.3471	114.4133	133.3339	155.6196
30	34.7849	37.5387	40.5681	43.9027	47.5754	51.6227	56.0849	61.0071	66.4388	72.4355	79.0582	94.4608	113.2832	136.3075	164.4940	199.0209	241.3327	293.1992
35	41.6603	45.5921	49.9945	54.9282	60.4621	66.6740	73.6522	81.4966	90.3203	100.2514	111.4348	138.2369	172.3168	215.7108	271.0244	341.5896	431.6635	546.6808
40	48.8864	54.2679	60.4020	67.4026	75.4013	84.5503	95.0255	107.0303	120.7998	136.6056	154.7620	199.6351	259.0565	337.8824	442.5926	581.8261	767.0914	1013.7042
45	56.4811	63.6142	71.8927	81.5161	92.7199	105.7817	121.0294	138.8500	159.7002	184.1192	212.7435	285.7493	386.5056	525.8587	718.9048	986.6386	1358.2300	1874.1646
50	64.4632	73.6828	84.5794	97.4843	112.7969	130.9979	152.6671	178.5030	209.3480	246.2175	290.3359	406.5289	573.7702	815.0836	1163.9085	1668.7712	2400.0182	3459.5071

This table shows the present value of an ordinary annuity of $1 at various interest rates (i) and time periods (n). It is used to calculate the present value of any series of equal payments made at the end of each compounding period.

TABLE 4 Present Value of an Ordinary Annuity of $1

$$PVA = \frac{1 - \frac{1}{(1+i)^n}}{i}$$

n/i	1.0%	1.5%	2.0%	2.5%	3.0%	3.5%	4.0%	4.5%	5.0%	5.5%	6.0%	7.0%	8.0%	9.0%	10.0%	11.0%	12.0%	13.0%
1	0.99010	0.98522	0.98039	0.97561	0.97087	0.96618	0.96154	0.95694	0.95238	0.94787	0.94340	0.93458	0.92593	0.91743	0.90909	0.90090	0.89286	0.88496
2	1.97040	1.95588	1.94156	1.92742	1.91347	1.89969	1.88609	1.87267	1.85941	1.84632	1.83339	1.80802	1.78326	1.75911	1.73554	1.71252	1.69005	1.66810
3	2.94099	2.91220	2.88388	2.85602	2.82861	2.80164	2.77509	2.74896	2.72325	2.69793	2.67301	2.62432	2.57710	2.53129	2.48685	2.44371	2.40183	2.36115
4	3.90197	3.85438	3.80773	3.76197	3.71710	3.67308	3.62990	3.58753	3.54595	3.50515	3.46511	3.38721	3.31213	3.23972	3.16987	3.10245	3.03735	2.97447
5	4.85343	4.78264	4.71346	4.64583	4.57971	4.51505	4.45182	4.38998	4.32948	4.27028	4.21236	4.10020	3.99271	3.88965	3.79079	3.69590	3.60478	3.51723
6	5.79548	5.69719	5.60143	5.50813	5.41719	5.32855	5.24214	5.15787	5.07569	4.99553	4.91732	4.76654	4.62288	4.48592	4.35526	4.23054	4.11141	3.99755
7	6.72819	6.59821	6.47199	6.34939	6.23028	6.11454	6.00205	5.89270	5.78637	5.68297	5.58238	5.38929	5.20637	5.03295	4.86842	4.71220	4.56376	4.42261
8	7.65168	7.48593	7.32548	7.17014	7.01969	6.87396	6.73274	6.59589	6.46321	6.33457	6.20979	5.97130	5.74664	5.53482	5.33493	5.14612	4.96764	4.79877
9	8.56602	8.36052	8.16224	7.97087	7.78611	7.60769	7.43533	7.26879	7.10782	6.95220	6.80169	6.51523	6.24689	5.99525	5.75902	5.53705	5.32825	5.13166
10	9.47130	9.22218	8.98259	8.75206	8.53020	8.31661	8.11090	7.91272	7.72173	7.53763	7.36009	7.02358	6.71008	6.41766	6.14457	5.88923	5.65022	5.42624
11	10.36763	10.07112	9.78685	9.51421	9.25262	9.00155	8.76048	8.52892	8.30641	8.09254	7.88687	7.49867	7.13896	6.80519	6.49506	6.20652	5.93770	5.68694
12	11.25508	10.90751	10.57534	10.25776	9.95400	9.66333	9.38507	9.11858	8.86325	8.61852	8.38384	7.94269	7.53608	7.16073	6.81369	6.49236	6.19437	5.91765
13	12.13374	11.73153	11.34837	10.98319	10.63496	10.30274	9.98565	9.68285	9.39357	9.11708	8.85268	8.35765	7.90378	7.48690	7.10336	6.74987	6.42355	6.12181
14	13.00370	12.54338	12.10625	11.69091	11.29607	10.92052	10.56312	10.22283	9.89864	9.58965	9.29498	8.74547	8.24424	7.78615	7.36669	6.98187	6.62817	6.30249
15	13.86505	13.34323	12.84926	12.38138	11.93794	11.51741	11.11839	10.73955	10.37966	10.03758	9.71225	9.10791	8.55948	8.06069	7.60608	7.19087	6.81086	6.46238
16	14.71787	14.13126	13.57771	13.05500	12.56110	12.09412	11.65230	11.23402	10.83777	10.46216	10.10590	9.44665	8.85137	8.31256	7.82371	7.37916	6.97399	6.60388
17	15.56225	14.90765	14.29187	13.71220	13.16612	12.65132	12.16567	11.70719	11.27407	10.86461	10.47726	9.76322	9.12164	8.54363	8.02155	7.54879	7.11963	6.72909
18	16.39827	15.67256	14.99203	14.35336	13.75351	13.18968	12.65930	12.15999	11.68959	11.24607	10.82760	10.05909	9.37189	8.75563	8.20141	7.70162	7.24967	6.83991
19	17.22601	16.42617	15.67846	14.97889	14.32380	13.70984	13.13394	12.59329	12.08532	11.60765	11.15812	10.33560	9.60360	8.95011	8.36492	7.83929	7.36578	6.93797
20	18.04555	17.16864	16.35143	15.58916	14.87747	14.21240	13.59033	13.00794	12.46221	11.95038	11.46992	10.59401	9.81815	9.12855	8.51356	7.96333	7.46944	7.02475
21	18.85698	17.90014	17.01121	16.18455	15.41502	14.69797	14.02916	13.40472	12.82115	12.27524	11.76408	10.83553	10.01680	9.29224	8.64869	8.07507	7.56200	7.10155
22	19.66038	18.62082	17.65805	16.76541	15.93692	15.16712	14.45112	13.78442	13.16300	12.58317	12.04158	11.06124	10.20074	9.44243	8.77154	8.17574	7.64465	7.16951
23	20.45582	19.33086	18.29220	17.33211	16.44361	15.62041	14.85684	14.14777	13.48857	12.87504	12.30338	11.27219	10.37106	9.58021	8.88322	8.26643	7.71843	7.22966
24	21.24339	20.03041	18.91393	17.88499	16.93554	16.05837	15.24696	14.49548	13.79864	13.15170	12.55036	11.46933	10.52876	9.70661	8.98474	8.34814	7.78432	7.28288
25	22.02316	20.71961	19.52346	18.42438	17.41315	16.48151	15.62208	14.82821	14.09394	13.41393	12.78336	11.65358	10.67478	9.82258	9.07704	8.42174	7.84314	7.32998
30	25.80771	24.01584	22.39646	20.93029	19.60044	18.39205	17.29203	16.28889	15.37245	14.53375	13.76483	12.40904	11.25778	10.27365	9.42691	8.69379	8.05518	7.49565
35	29.40858	27.07559	24.99862	23.14516	21.48722	20.00066	18.66461	17.46101	16.37419	15.39055	14.49825	12.94767	11.65457	10.56682	9.64416	8.85524	8.17550	7.58557
40	32.83469	29.91585	27.35548	25.10278	23.11477	21.35507	19.79277	18.40158	17.15909	16.04612	15.04630	13.33171	11.92461	10.75736	9.77905	8.95105	8.24378	7.63438
45	36.09451	32.55234	29.49016	26.83302	24.51871	22.49545	20.72004	19.15635	17.77407	16.54773	15.45583	13.60552	12.10840	10.88120	9.86281	9.00791	8.28252	7.66086
50	39.19612	34.99969	31.42361	28.36231	25.72976	23.45562	21.48218	19.76201	18.25593	16.93152	15.76186	13.80075	12.23348	10.96168	9.91481	9.04165	8.30450	7.67524

Summary of Ratios Used in This Book

	Chapter	Calculations
RISK RATIOS		
Liquidity		
Receivables turnover ratio	5	$\dfrac{\text{Net credit sales}}{\text{Average accounts receivables}}$
Average collection period	5	$\dfrac{365 \text{ days}}{\text{Receivables turnover ratio}}$
Inventory turnover ratio	6	$\dfrac{\text{Cost of goods sold}}{\text{Average inventory}}$
Average days in inventory	6	$\dfrac{365 \text{ days}}{\text{Inventory turnover ratio}}$
Current ratio	8	$\dfrac{\text{Current assets}}{\text{Current liabilities}}$
Acid-test ratio	8	$\dfrac{\text{Cash} + \text{Current investments} + \text{Accounts receivable}}{\text{Current liabilities}}$
Solvency		
Debt to equity ratio	9	$\dfrac{\text{Total liabilities}}{\text{Stockholders' equity}}$
Times interest earned ratio	9	$\dfrac{\text{Net income} + \text{Interest expense} + \text{Income Tax expense}}{\text{Interest expense}}$
PROFITABILITY RATIOS		
Gross profit ratio	6	$\dfrac{\text{Gross profit}}{\text{Net sales}}$
Return on assets	7	$\dfrac{\text{Net income}}{\text{Average total assets}}$
Profit margin	7	$\dfrac{\text{Net income}}{\text{Net sales}}$
Asset turnover	7	$\dfrac{\text{Net sales}}{\text{Average total assets}}$
Return on equity	10	$\dfrac{\text{Net income}}{\text{Average stockholders' equity}}$
Dividend Yield	10	$\dfrac{\text{Dividends per share}}{\text{Stock price}}$
Earnings per share	10	$\dfrac{\text{Net income} - \text{Dividends on preferred stock}}{\text{Average shares of common stock outstanding}}$
Price-earnings ratio	10	$\dfrac{\text{Stock price}}{\text{Earnings per share}}$

Framework for Financial Accounting

...ary functions of financial accounting are to **measure** activities of a company and **communicate** those mea-
...nts to investors and other people for making decisions. The measurement process involves recording transac-
...into accounts. The balances of these accounts are used to communicate information in the four primary financial
...ements, which are linked. For more detailed illustrations of financial statements, see the corresponding illustrations
... Chapter 1. A comprehensive list of accounts used to measure activities in this textbook is provided on the next page.

Financial Statements (in order)

Income Statement
(Illustration 1–5, p. 10)

Revenues
− Expenses
= Net income

Statement of Stockholders' Equity
(Illustration 1–6, p. 11)

Common Stock	+	Retained Earnings	=	Stockholders' Equity
Beginning balance		Beginning balance		Beginning total
+ New issuances				+ New issuances
		+ Net income		+ Net income
		− Dividends		− Dividends
Ending balance	+	Ending balance	=	Ending total

Balance Sheet
(Illustration 1–7, p. 13)

Assets = Liabilities + Stockholders' Equity
(including Cash)

Statement of Cash Flows
(Illustration 1–8, p. 15)

Cash flows from operating activities
+ Cash flows from investing activities
+ Cash flows from financing activities
= Change in Cash

Accounts Used to Measure Activities

1. **Assets** – Resources of a company
2. **Liabilities** – Amounts owed by the company
3. **Stockholders' Equity** – Owners' claims
4. **Dividends** – Distributions to owners
5. **Revenues** – Sales of products or services
6. **Expenses** – Costs of providing sales

Effect of Debit and Credit on Account Balances

Assets	Liabilities
Dividends	Stockholders' Equity
Expenses	Revenues
Debit = ↑	Credit = ↑
Credit = ↓	Debit = ↓

Recording Business Transactions

Date		Debit	Credit
Account Title		Amount	
Account Title			Amount
(Description of transaction)			

Representative Chart of Accounts*

BALANCE SHEET

ASSETS

Cash

Petty Cash

Accounts Receivable

   Less: Allow. for Uncollectible Accts.

Notes Receivable

Interest Receivable

Supplies

Inventory

Prepaid Advertising

Prepaid Insurance

Prepaid Rent

Investments

Land

Land Improvements

Buildings

Equipment

   Less: Accumulated Depreciation

Lease Asset

Natural Resources

Patents

Copyrights

Trademarks

Franchises

Goodwill

LIABILITIES

Accounts Payable

Notes Payable

Deferred Revenue

Salaries Payable

Interest Payable

Utilities Payable

Dividends Payable

Income Tax Payable

Employee Income Tax Payable

FICA Tax Payable

Fringe Benefits Payable

Unemployment Tax Payable

Sales Tax Payable

Contingent Liability

Warranty Liability

Lease Payable

Bonds Payable

STOCKHOLDERS' EQUITY

Common Stock

Preferred Stock

Additional Paid-in Capital

Retained Earnings

   Less: Treasury Stock

Unrealized Holding Gain—
Other Comprehensive Income

Unrealized Holding Loss—
Other Comprehensive Income

INCOME STATEMENT

REVENUES

Service Revenue

Sales Revenue

   Less: Sales Discounts

   Less: Sales Returns

   Less: Sales Allowances

Interest Revenue

Dividend Revenue

Equity Income

Gain

Unrealized Holding Gain—Net Income

EXPENSES

Advertising Expense

Amortization Expense

Bad Debt Expense

Cost of Goods Sold

Delivery Expense

Depreciation Expense

Entertainment Expense

Income Tax Expense

Insurance Expense

Interest Expense

Legal Fees Expense

Payroll Tax Expense

Postage Expense

Property Tax Expense

Rent Expense

Repairs and Maintenance Expense

Research and Development Expense

Salaries Expense

Service Fee Expense

Supplies Expense

Utilities Expense

Warranty Expense

Loss

Unrealized Holding Loss—Net Income

You will see these account titles used in this book and in your homework. In practice, companies often use variations of these account titles, many of which are specific to particular industries or businesses.

DIVIDENDS**

Dividends (Cash)

Stock Dividends

**Reported in the statement of stockholders' equity.